E S S E N T I A L S   O F
PSYCHOLOGY

E S S E N T I A L S   O F

PSYCHOLOGY

Benjamin B. Lahey

University of Chicago

Boston   Burr Ridge, IL   Dubuque, IA   Madison, WI   New York   San Francisco   St. Louis
Bangkok   Bogotá   Caracas   Kuala Lumpur   Lisbon   London   Madrid   Mexico City
Milan   Montreal   New Delhi   Santiago   Seoul   Singapore   Sydney   Taipei   Toronto

McGraw-Hill Higher Education ✧

A Division of The McGraw-Hill Companies

ESSENTIALS OF PSYCHOLOGY

Published by McGraw-Hill, a business unit of The McGraw-Hill Companies, Inc., 1221 Avenue of the Americas, New York, NY 10020. Copyright © 2002 by The McGraw-Hill Companies, Inc. All rights reserved. No part of this publication may be reproduced or distributed in any form or by any means, or stored in a database or retrieval system, without the prior written consent of The McGraw-Hill Companies, Inc., including, but not limited to, in any network or other electronic storage or transmission, or broadcast for distance learning.

Some ancillaries, including electronic and print components, may not be available to customers outside the United States.

✪ This book is printed on recycled, acid-free paper containing 10% postconsumer waste.

1 2 3 4 5 6 7 8 9 0 QPD/QPD 0 9 8 7 6 5 4 3 2 1 0

ISBN 0–07–243404–X
ISBN 0–07–112119–6 (ISE)

Editorial director: *Jane E. Karpacz*
Senior sponsoring editor: *Melissa Mashburn*
Developmental editor: *Mindy De Palma*
Senior marketing manager: *Chris Hall*
Senior project manager: *Marilyn Rothenberger*
Senior production supervisor: *Sandy Ludovissy*
Designer: *K. Wayne Harms*
Cover designer: *Christopher Reese*
Cover image: *EyeWire*
Photo research coordinator: *John C. Leland*
Photo research: *Feldman & Associates, Inc.*
Supplement producer: *Tammy Juran*
Media technology senior producer: *Sean Crowley*
Compositor: *GAC—Indianapolis*
Typeface: *10/12 Times Roman*
Printer: *Quebecor World Dubuque, IA*

The credits section for this book begins on page C-1 and is considered an extension of the copyright page.

Library of Congress Cataloging-in-Publication Data

Lahey, Benjamin B.
     Essentials of psychology / Benjamin B. Lahey. — 1st ed.
          p.   cm.
     Includes bibliographical references and indexes.
     ISBN 0–07–243404–X — ISBN 0–07–112119–6 (ISE)
     1. Psychology. I. Title.

BF121 .L213   2002
150—dc21   2001030692
                                                                                    CIP

INTERNATIONAL EDITION ISBN 0–07–112119–6
Copyright © 2002. Exclusive rights by The McGraw-Hill Companies, Inc., for manufacture and export. This book cannot be re-exported from the country to which it is sold by McGraw-Hill. The International Edition is not available in North America.

www.mhhe.com

For Megan, Ted, Erin,
Clare, Eamonn, and Kate

CONTENTS IN BRIEF

CONTENTS

PREFACE

In 1983, I published a textbook for the introductory course in psychology, titled *Psychology: An Introduction,* which recently appeared in its seventh edition. That text is designed to teach the greatest number of students the greatest amount of information about psychology. Because I deeply believe that the concepts and facts of psychology are important and useful to everyone, my goal is not to educate only the small percentage of students who will major in psychology, but to teach psychology to every student who takes the introductory course. Over the years, the book has been a gratifying sucess, giving me the opportunity to help teach psychology to hundreds of thousands of students.

Based on the 17-chapter *Psychology: An Introduction,* I have now created a brief, more concise version in *Essentials of Psychology.* This 15-chapter text encompasses all of the highlights of the seventh edition, yet it is tailored to facilitate teaching introductory psychology in the standard 15-week semester with a balanced combination of breadth and depth.

Based on feedback from instructors, I have written *Essentials of Psychology* to differ from *Psychology: An Introduction* in the following ways:

1. One full chapter, "Applications of Psychology," was eliminated from *Psychology: An Introduction.* The "applications" sections at the end of each chapter, which give students a look at some of the applied significance of the material that they have just covered, are retained, however.

2. The chapter on research methods was combined with the introductory chapter, covering the basic concepts of research. Other key concepts about research methods are in the appendix on statistics.

3. Edits were made to the chapter on consciousness, but the essential material on waking consciousness, sleep and dreams, and the effect of psychoactive drugs on consciousness are retained.

4. Finally, although the fundamentally important chapter on gender remains in *Essentials of Psychology,* the extensive coverage of sexuality that is in the full text is not in this briefer version.

Thus, I am presenting to students and instructors a book that is leaner than *Psychology: An Introduction,* but very student-friendly by being more tightly focused on basic concepts and facts.

As important as the differences between this brief text and the longer text on which it is based are, however, three key *similarities* are equally important:

1. *Essentials of Psychology* retains all of the pedagogical features of the longer text. These pedagogical features are used in *Essentials of Psychology* for two fundamentally important reasons. First, they are the subtle characteristics of written text that researchers have found to greatly improve learning and memory of concepts and facts. Second, they are the features that students and instructors consistently tell me they find useful. The frequent use of real world examples to explain each basic concept of psychology remains an important feature throughout this book. These pedagogical features are described in detail in the following sections entitled "To the Instructor" and "To the Student."

2. The illustrations used in *Essentials of Psychology* are the same illustrations that have evolved over 20 years of writing and revising the longer book. No illustration is included to decorate the text! Every illustration is designed to *teach* a key concept to the student. Every line and color was chosen to be visual pedagogy.

3. *Essentials of Psychology* is written in the same style that students and instructors have graciously described as "clear" and "friendly."

4. The successful section on 'Study Skills' that is in the longer version of the text is also placed at the front of *Essentials of Psychology.* This provides students with empirically-based strategies for improving their learning and memory for the information in this and all other college courses.

▶ WHAT'S NEW

Concept Web Links This first edition of *Essentials of Psychology* includes a brand new feature, "Concept Web Links," in the margins of the text. This feature specifically targets the two to three most difficult concepts for students in each chapter by providing the most useful Web links available as additional study aids. Icons denote the concepts location in the text. The name of the concept and the book's URL, which houses the Web links, are placed below the icons for clarity. **www.mhhe.com/laheye1**. Supplemental Audio Lectures pertaining to these concepts are also available on the book's online learning center.

Interactive Visual Reviews The popular feature called "Visual Reviews," has been retained from the seventh edition text. In a marvelous use of internet technology, these Visual Reviews have also been made into interactive exercises that can be found on the book's online learning center. These visual reviews are designed to facilitate student learning and can be found at the end of chapters, such as *Biological Foundations of Behavior* and *Sensation and Perception*. An icon is placed next to those figures that are interactive.

▶ ACKNOWLEDGEMENTS

I am most appreciative of the combined efforts of the many studens, instructors, editors, and illustrators who have contributed in profoundly important ways to this book. I invite you to use this book's Web site to provide me with feedback that will help us do an even better job in the next edition.

Cheryl Bluestone
Queensborough Community College

Barnie Carducci
Indiana University Southeast

Lilli Downes
Hartford Community College

David Federhar
Pima Community College

Dan Grangaard
Austin Community College

Roland Haris
William and Mary

Susan Horton
Maricopa Community College

Gene Indenbaum
SUNY Farmingdale

Steve Link
Brookhaven College

Maria Lopez
Mt. San Jacinto College

Judith Muller
Southwestern Community College

Jane Smith
Concordia University

Tim Tomczak
Genesee Community College

Richard Torquato
Los Angeles Valley College

TO THE INSTRUCTOR

Essentials of Psychology offers thorough topic coverage and standard organization designed to fit briefer college courses as they are most commonly taught. It differs significantly from other textbooks in two main ways, however. First, every effort has been made to create a writing style that is—as one former student kindly described it—"friendly." This book does not attempt to impress students with the arcane complexities of the science of psychology. It was written to provide a clear, informative, challenging, exciting, and personal introduction to psychology. All of the necessary complexities are taught, but in the clearest manner possible.

Second, *Essentials of Psychology* differs from other textbooks in its emphasis on *meaningful* learning. This book contains many elements designed to enhance learning and remembering based on an organizational model of semantic memory. The content of the first course in psychology can be thought of as a *hierarchical organization* of concepts and facts. Quite simply, this means that information about psychology is not a disorganized jumble of new facts. Some information "goes with" other information, some concepts are detailed elaborations of more general concepts, and so on. To improve learning and memory, it is as important for students to understand the overall organization of new information as it is for them to understand the individual concepts and facts themselves.

Based on what is well known about learning from textbooks, this book helps the student understand how new information about psychology is organized and to process that information more deeply in five primary ways:

1. *Advance organizers.* Considerable research indicates that students learn and retain information better when they have an advance understanding of the hierarchical organization of the information being learned. To accomplish this, the student is given two kinds of advance organizers before reading the main body of the text. The student is first presented with a **chapter outline** of the major topics covered within the chapter, a device common to many textbooks. But to add to the effectiveness of this bare-bones overview, a prose organizer, called the **prologue,** both piques the student's interest with exciting information and highlights the major concepts in the forthcoming chapter. Thus, the student is provided with two forward looks at the chapter to create a cognitive organization on which to "hang" new facts and concepts.

2. *Questions to stimulate critical thinking.* An important feature of the book is the set of questions designed to stimulate critical thinking (Baron & Sternberg, 1987). These critical thinking questions appear at the end of each section. They are designed to catch the student's attention and stimulate thought for two reasons. First, it is important that students not passively absorb new information but, rather, critically evaluate and ponder what they are learning. Moreover, it may be more effective to teach critical thinking skills through the content of a specific course than in the abstract. And what course is more appropriate than psychology—in which human beings ponder themselves? Second, current research suggests that thinking about what you have just learned leads to deeper semantic processing and better retention. Thus, both as an aid to student reading and as a stimulus for classroom discussion, these high-interest questions at the end of each section are important pedagogical tools. To help students prepare to use these critical thinking questions, a section on critical thinking appears in the "To the Student" section. In addition, the *Instructor's Course Planner* includes pertinent information to help the instructor.

3. *Nested hierarchical reviews.* The interrelationships among new concepts are highlighted further in **review** and **summary** sections. Following each major section within each chapter, the content of that section is briefly reviewed in prose. In addition, the student can test his or her knowledge of each section in the **check your learning** sections. At the end of each chapter, the main content of the chapter is again summarized, but this time in a hierarchical outline that visually highlights the organization of the material.

4. *Visual organizational cues.* Using hierarchical outlines in the end-of-chapter summaries is only one way in which the student is actually shown the organization of the new material. Close attention has been paid to the use of visual cues—such as typeface, type size, color of type, and indentations—to indicate the organization of the text. The difference between this book and others is intentionally subtle in this respect, but students should have little trouble distinguishing the superordinate-subordinate structure of A, B, and C levels of headings. In diagrams and figures, colors were chosen not to be decorative but to show students which elements are related and which are different. In addition, lists—like the one you are reading now—have been frequently (but not excessively) used to show that each element in the list is at the same level of organization and subordinate to the title of the list ("five ways to help students understand organizational structure," in the case of the list you are reading now).

5. *Verbal cues to organization.* Another important way to help readers see how concepts and facts are related is simply to tell them in words. Therefore, this textbook makes many references to the organization of the new information. This is done in two main ways. First, when a newly introduced concept is related to another concept that was discussed in an earlier section, this fact is specifically pointed out. Second, information that is subordinate to a concept is frequently introduced in a way that makes that relationship very clear (e.g., "The two factors that cause forgetting in short-term memory are . . ."). Although these cues are subtle so as not to interrupt the flow of the discussion, they have been added to help improve the student's comprehension and memory.

The use of these pedagogical devices was chosen over two other pedagogical approaches after much consideration. I chose not to use the SQ3R (survey, question, read, recite, review) method of organizing the text because the author, not the student, must ask the questions, which reduces student involvement and discourages the student from critically evaluating and deeply processing the new information. It is much better for the *student* to use SQ3R than for the *author* to use it. Therefore, instructions to the student on the use of SQ3R are included in the **study skills** section, which follows the preface. For those instructors who wish to use instructional objectives, we have included them in the *Student Study Guide* and the *Instructor's Course Planner* that accompany this book.

SUPPLEMENTARY MATERIALS

Essentials of Psychology is accompanied by an integrated ancillary package designed to meet the unique needs of instructors and students. The goal has been to create a teaching package that is as enjoyable to teach with as it is to study from. Each element of the ancillary package has been created by talented individuals with many years of experience in teaching psychology.

Supplements

The *Instructor's Course Planner* is a flexible planner that provides many useful tools to enhance your teaching. For each chapter, learning objectives, an extended chapter outline, suggestions for teaching, lecture/discussion suggestions, video and film suggestions, classroom activities, and handout forms are provided.

A *Test Item File* with questions for all fifteen chapters will be available to instructors who adopt *Essentials of Psychology.* The questions in the *Test Item File* are also available on **Diploma Testing Software,** a powerful but easy-to-use test-generating program by Brownstone Research Group. Diploma is available for your use in a cross-platform CD-ROM. With its Test Generator, On-Line Testing Program, Internet Testing, and Grade Management Systems, Diploma is instructor-friendly software.

The *Student Study Guide* was created by author Steven A. Schneider. For each chapter of the text, the student is provided with

learning objectives, a detailed chapter outline, a guided review of terms and concepts, a section that promotes student's awareness of human/cultural diversity, and a practice quiz that tests students' mastery of the chapters' main ideas and important material.

MULTIMEDIA

 McGraw-Hill's Psycafe & the Lahey Online Learning Center, the virtual coffeehouse for introductory psychology on the World Wide Web, is a treasure trove of resources for teaching and learning. Inside you will find images, links, newsletters, discussion groups, PowerPoint® slide shows, crossword puzzles, and interactive exercises structured within a robust textbook Web site designed to facilitate learning.
www.mhhe.com/psycafe and www.mhhe.com/laheye1

 The state-of-the-art *PRISM II CD-ROM* combines 60 interactive simulations and exercises with text-specific study materials, including learning objectives, review exercises, key terms, and practice quizzes to create a truly interactive learning experience. In addition to all of this, standard features include "Psychology Around the Globe" interactive articles, Web links, "Frequently Asked Questions," "Internet Primer," "Statistics Primer," "Study Skills and Time Management Primer," and a "Psychology Careers Appendix."

Packaged for FREE, this new user-friendly Making the Grade Student CD-ROM gives students an opportunity to test their comprehension of the course material in the manner most comfortable and beneficial to them. The CD-ROM opens with a "Learning Style/Study Skills" questionnaire that the student can complete to help them identify how they best study. Also included are practice tests that cover topics in the introductory psychology course, an Internet primer, a statistics primer, a careers appendix, and more!

Build your own course Web site in less than an hour with PageOut™. With PageOut™ even the most inexperienced computer user can quickly and easily create a professional-looking course Web site. Fill in our templates with your information and with excellent content provided by McGraw-Hill, choose a design, and you've got a bang-up Web site specifically designed for your course! Best of all, it's FREE! Visit us at www.pageout.net to find out more.

Annual Editions®

Magazines, newspapers, and journals can provide current, first-rate, relevant educational information. *Annual Editions* provides convenient, inexpensive access to a wide range of current, carefully selected articles from magazines, newspapers, and journals. Written by psychologists, researchers, and educators, *Annual Editions: Psychology* provides useful perspectives on important and timely topics. *Annual Editions* is updated yearly and contains a number of features designed to make it particularly useful, including a topic guide, an annotated table of contents, and unit overviews. For the professor using *Annual Editions* in the classroom, an *Instructor's Resource Guide* with test questions is available.

Taking Sides® and Sources

Are you interested in generating classroom discussion or in finding a tool to fully involve your students in their experience of your course? Would you like to encourage your students to become more active learners and critical thinkers? *Taking Sides: Clashing Views on Psychological Issues* is a debate-style reader designed to introduce students to controversies in psychology. By requiring students to analyze opposing viewpoints and reach considered judgments, *Taking Sides* actively develops students' critical thinking skills.

Sources: Notable Selections in Psychology, second edition, brings together over 40 selections including classic articles, book excerpts, and research studies that have shaped the study of psychology. New to the 2nd edition are 21 selections from some of the most distinguished researchers, theorists, writers, and practitioners of psychology. If you want your students to gain greater background knowledge in reading and interpreting first-hand from source material, *Sources* collects a diverse array of accessible but significant readings in one place.

TO THE STUDENT

HOW THE BOOK WORKS

This book contains several learning devices, each of which is designed to accomplish five goals:

1. To focus your attention on the subject of the chapter
2. To give you an advance overall view of what you are about to learn
3. To show you how each fact and concept is related to the overall theme of the chapter
4. To help you review what you have just learned to be sure that you have gotten it all and to strengthen the newly formed memories
5. To help you think critically about the new information that you have learned and relate it to your own life

These five goals must be reached if you are going to learn about psychology in a meaningful way, rather than just blindly memorizing facts and definitions. Let me show you how each feature of the book contributes to these five goals.

◆1 Chapter Outline Each chapter begins with an outline that organizes the key ideas of the chapter. Examine the outline carefully to see which topics will be studied, but notice also how the topics are arranged. Headings that show the major topics are called A heads (printed in capital letters); they define the breadth of coverage in each chapter. Under each A head are B heads (indented); they reveal the more specific topics related to the broader topic of each A head. Studying the outline for a few minutes will give you an advance look at the content of the chapter and show you how topics relate to one another. When you read a chapter, you may wish to refer to the outline from time to time. It will reinforce the relationships among topics and help you understand the structure of the chapter.

◆2 Prologue Each chapter begins with a short section designed to focus your attention on the theme of the chapter. It is a high-interest essay that introduces a bit of research or history to prepare you for the content of the chapter. The prologue also highlights the most important concepts that will be covered in the

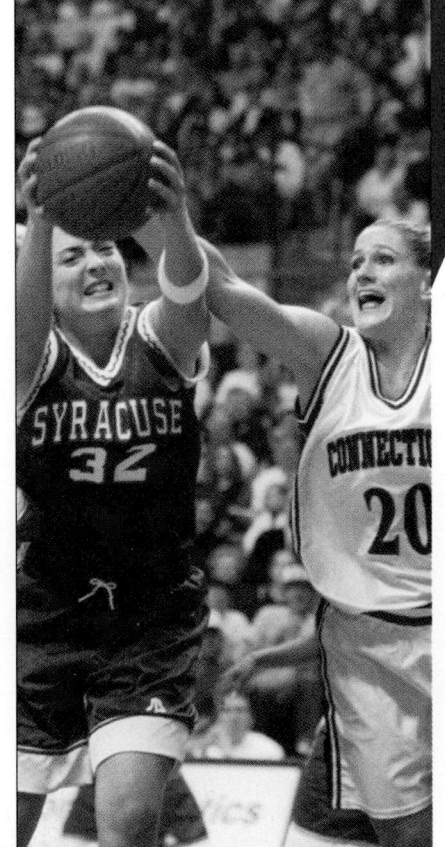

Sensation and Perception

CHAPTER

3

◆2 PROLOGUE

L ast night I "saw" the University of North Carolina play Notre Dame in basketball—by listening to the radio. The play-by-play announcer watched the game, and he translated what he saw into a kind of information (words) that could be transmitted over the radio. Then I used that information to form a mental picture of the game. I did not see with my eyes, yet I was able to "watch" the game in my head.

I realized this morning that my way of seeing the game last night was not very different from how I see games in person. We never really "see" with our eyes alone. We use our eyes to gather information and translate it into a form that can be transmitted to the brain. It's in the brain that visual perception is created out of the incoming sensory information.

We usually assume that we really "see" what is "out there." The processes of seeing, smelling, or touching seem so straightforward. In reality, however, perception is based on a complex chain of receiving, transmitting, and interpreting sensory information. Each step of this process actively changes the information in significant ways. Because we know "reality" only through our sensations and perceptions, we must understand the sense organs and the ways in which the processes of sensation and perception change sensory information.

In this chapter, we will study the four major senses: vision, hearing, the body senses, and the chemical senses. In vision, the eye collects, translates, and transmits energy from light to the brain. The ear—the sense organ for hearing—accomplishes the same for the energy in vibrating molecules of air. The body senses provide the brain with information from the skin about temperature, touch, and pain; and information from receptors in the inner ear, joints, and muscles tells us about the position and movement of the body—where we are and where we are going. The chemical senses use receptor cells in the nose and on the tongue to provide information to the brain about the chemicals in the air we breathe and in the things we drink and eat.

Raw sensations have little meaning until they are organized and interpreted in the process of perception. Perception is an active process that changes sensory information. As we discussed in chapter 1, we perceive actors as moving when we watch a motion picture. In reality, however, the sensory information is just a series of rapidly changing *still photographs*. The people on the movie screen don't actually move at all. We perceive them as moving only because the process of perception often goes well beyond the immediate sensory information. The brain creates the perception of motion in a movie that the sensory information only hints at.

In most cases, the ways in which the brain interprets information in the process of perception appear to be inborn. Our perceptions of reality are also colored by individual expectations, cultural learning experiences, and needs, however. As a result, different people sometimes have rather different views of the same world.

Human life would be very different without our ability to sense and perceive. Take friendships as an example. How could we have friends if we could not distinguish one person from another by sensing their differences? How could we communicate with our friends if we could not hear their words properly or read their notes accurately or notice the expressions on their faces? How could we let them know that we cared if they could not feel a pat on the back?

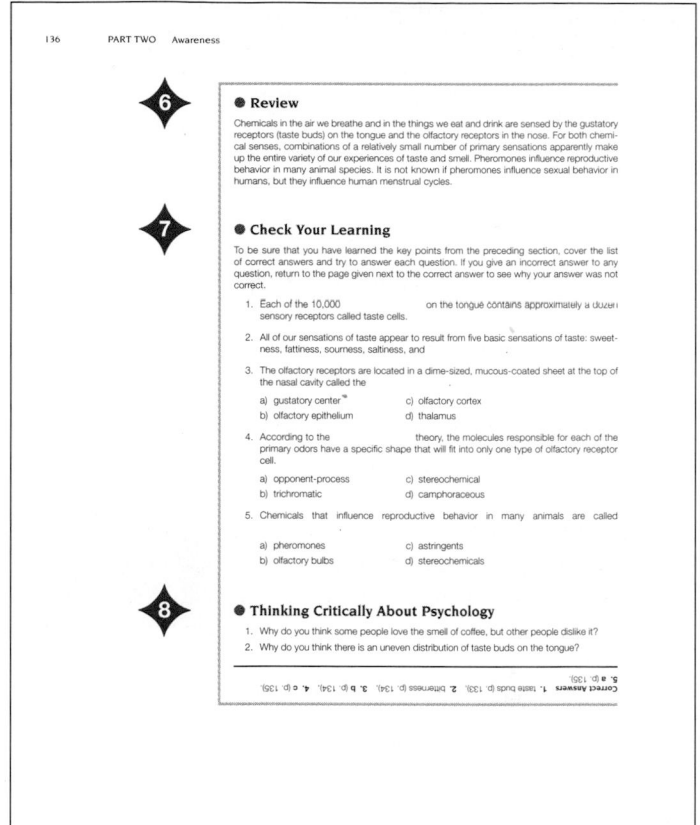

chapter. Along with the chapter outline, it allows you to see what the chapter is going to be about before you read and start to grasp the details. A great deal of research suggests that having a general understanding of what is going to be learned will improve learning and memory of the new material. The prologue will help you *understand* what you are learning, which is far better than rote memorization of details.

3 Key Terms A list of the key terms you will encounter in the chapter is presented at the beginning of each chapter. You can use these terms to focus your learning. Because learning new vocabulary is half the battle in psychology, be sure you understand the meaning of each of these terms by the time you have finished studying each chapter. This will help you make sure that you have learned the most important terms when you are reviewing for a test.

4 Margin Glossary A running glossary with pronunciation guidelines defines new terms and shows you how to pronounce those that may be difficult. You will find these definitions and pronunciations in the outside margin of the text near the new terms that appear in boldface type within the text. These entries provide a convenient way of learning definitions without disrupting your reading.

5 Concept Web Links This feature targets the two to three most difficult concepts for students in each chapter by providing useful web links as additional study aids.

6 Section Reviews Within each chapter are three to seven major sections. These are self-contained in the sense that they can be understood without an extensive understanding of the sections that precede or follow them. This flexibility will allow your instructor to assign sections to be read when the need arises instead of an entire chapter.

Following each major section is a brief review that summarizes the main ideas introduced in that section. This device will help you keep the overall organization of the new material in mind as you study and master the details.

7 Check Your Learning Questions At the end of each section, you will also find "Check Your Learning" questions. These multiple-choice questions give you a chance to see if you have mastered the material in that section before moving on. The answers are provided to give you immediate feedback on the correctness of your own answers. If you give an incorrect answer, use the page number provided with each answer to guide you to the page or pages you should review.

8 Critical Thinking Questions Questions designed to stimulate critical thinking appear at the end of each section. These questions will further your critical thinking if you let them involve you actively in the process of learning. The few minutes of thought that each question provokes should help you personalize your new knowledge of psychology, making it "your own" to keep and use over your lifetime. Later in this preface is a short

Left column — facsimile textbook pages

CHAPTER 4   Sensation and Perception   131

HUMAN DIVERSITY   9

CULTURE AND PAIN

In this section, we examine the ways in which neural impulses from the sense organs are experienced as sensations and perceptions. Although much of this process is determined by the biological nature of the sense organs and neurons, learning experiences in our cultures apparently can influence even basic sensations such as pain.

Let's consider an example of the impact of culture on the perception of pain. Members of the Bariba society in Benin, West Africa, appear to be able to tolerate pain more easily than members of most cultures. Bariba folklore includes many examples of honored people who showed strength in the face of pain, and this calm response to pain is seen as an integral part of Bariba pride (Sargent, 1984). For example, pregnant women are expected not to let the fact that they are experiencing labor pains show to others. When labor becomes advanced, they leave the company of others to go through labor and childbirth alone, only calling for help with cutting the umbilical cord.

To the Bariba, letting other people see that they are in pain is cause for great shame. When discussing pain, many Bariba quote a Bariba proverb that translates to "Between death and shame, death has the greater beauty." According to a Bariba physician, an individual who displays pain lacks courage, and cowardice is the essence of shame. Rather than live in shame, a Bariba would rather die (Sargent, 1984). In this cultural context, one would do everything possible to avoid displaying signs of pain.

Do Bariba women who are in labor actually experience less pain than women in other cultures, or have they simply learned not to let the pain show? It is difficult to answer such questions, partly because of the difficulties involved in describing pain to another person. Because pain is a private experience, language must be used to communicate the experience to others, and language is shaped by culture. It is not surprising that there is a more limited vocabulary for describing pain in the Bariba language than in most other languages. When the Bariba discuss the experience of pain, therefore, it is difficult to know how much their description is influenced by their language.

But there is some reason to believe that the cultural emphasis on not showing reactions to pain might actually reduce the amount of pain that the Bariba experience. As noted on page 390 of chapter 10, there is evidence that facial expressions are an important part of the experience of pain (Izard, 1977). Apparently, sensory feedback to the brain from facial muscles supplies part of the neural input for the perception of pain (along with input from the part of the body that is cramped or injured). Indeed, persons who were given electrical shocks reported less pain when they were told to make no facial reactions than when they let their emotions show in their faces (Colby, Lanzetta, & Kleck, 1977). Maybe the calm face of a Bariba woman in labor results in the experience of less pain than does the agonized grimace of women in other cultures.

According to Linda Garro (1990), it is important for medical professionals who work with people in pain to understand the impact of culture on the expression of pain. If culture is not taken into account, the physician may overestimate or underestimate the amount of pain experienced by the patient. On the other hand, it is important to remember that not all members of a culture are the same. As in all other aspects of human diversity, it is important to be aware of variation within cultures.

What did you learn about pain in your own culture? Were you taught to minimize pain because it is important to be tough? Did you learn that no one will pay attention to your pain unless you exaggerate it? How do you respond when your parent or friends are in pain? Such questions will help you think about cultural influences on perception.

mine recently wrote to say, "My mother, who lost her left leg to polio in her early 20s, is now 73, and sometimes when I ask how her arthritis is, she often responds, 'The foot I don't have aches as much as my good one.'" Amputees are not the only persons who experience such sensations. Persons with spinal cord injuries can experience no true sensations from the parts of their body below the break in the neural pathways in the spinal cord, but they sometimes experience phantom sensations in their limbs or genitals. Similarly, persons born without arms or legs often experience phantom sensations in the missing limb (Melzack, 1992).

How is it possible to "feel" sensations from a limb that does not exist and, therefore, cannot be transmitting sensations to the brain? A team of researchers from Germany and the United States appears to have provided the answer (Flor & others, 1995). Using brain-imaging techniques, they found that, when sensory and pain neurons from one part of the body have been cut, the area of the somatosensory cortex that served that part of the body becomes sensitive to input from parts of the body that activate *nearby* portions of the

---

10   Application *of* Psychology

VISUAL PERCEPTION, ILLUSION, AND ART

During the winter of 1993, I went to New York with my best friend to see an amazing collection of paintings, drawings, and sculpture by Henri Matisse at the Museum of Modern Art. The works were arranged in chronological order, showing the progression in his art from his first paintings to the collages that he assembled on his death bed. The sheer beauty and emotional impact of these works was amazing. But, ever being the psychologist, I sometimes found myself thinking about his paintings in terms of the monocular cues to depth perception.

Now, I have never said, and will I ever say, that the study of depth perception is more than just barely interesting. I know that depth perception is important to understand, but it is just not very interesting. On the other hand, the paintings of Matisse and other great artists are extremely interesting. And, as I thought about it, I found that the way Matisse used monocular cues of depth perception in his art was pretty interesting, too. Maybe looking at some paintings from this perspective will add to our appreciation of the visual arts and teach us something about depth perception.

Painting and Depth Cues: Art Appreciation

The artist who paints a landscape, a still life, or a portrait of a person is creating a visual illusion. He or she uses what is known about the monocular cues of depth perception to create the *illusion* of a three-dimensional object (one with height, width, and depth) on a two-dimensional canvas (one with height and width only). No part of the flat canvas is farther away from the viewer than any other part, but the artist creates the illusion of depth—the impression that some parts of the painting are farther away from others—mostly by using the cues of texture gradient, linear perspective, superposition, shadowing, and aerial perspective. Cues based on the way in which the eyes focus on objects that are at different distances from the eye and the binocular cues that are based on differences in the

alignment of the two eyes cannot be used by the artist, but artists often achieve striking illusions of depth with the few cues at their disposal.

Look at the striking illusions of depth created in two paintings. The painting in figure 4.43 by the Spanish painter Diego Velazquez (*Las Meninas*, 1656) uses four depth perception cues to suggest depth very effectively. Notice that the man standing in the doorway is smaller than the man standing on the left (a self-portrait of the artist) and even smaller than the young blonde child who appears to be standing in the front of the painting. Note also that the wall on the right is painted on the canvas as if it is shorter at the rear of

FIGURE 4.43
Las Meninas (1656) by Diego Velazquez.
Erich Lessing/Art Resource, NY

the room than in the front of the room. These are uses of the monocular cue of *linear perspective*, and they give a powerful illusion of depth to the room. Notice also that the persons that Velazquez wishes us to perceive as being in the front of the room partially cover the persons portrayed as being at the rear of the room (the cue of *superposition*). The detailed texture of the clothing of the persons in the front of the room is also clearer than that of persons at the rear of the room (the cue of *texture gradient*). Velazquez also uses shadowing effectively to create an illusion of depth, but let's study this cue in the even more subtle example by Artemisia Gentileschi (fig. 4.44).

A more subtle, but wonderfully effective illusion of depth has been created in this extraordinary self-portrait. Gentileschi gives us an amazingly three-dimensional view of herself by using linear perspective. Notice, for example, that her right

hand appears to be farther away from us partly because it is smaller on the canvas than her left hand, which seems to be very close to us. In addition, her face partially hides the right shoulder, which seems farther away from us (superposition). But, it is Gentileschi's exceptional mastery of shadowing that brings the illusion of subtle depth to life. Her face is painted on a flat canvas, but it seems as rounded as an apple. As a result, her left cheek seems inches closer to us than does her nose.

Sometimes, Matisse was interested in creating a sense of depth, but sometimes he intentionally ignored depth. The reclining nude in figure 4.45 (*L'Atelier du Quai Saint-Michel*), for example, is positioned in a scene painted with powerful depth cues. Notice that the building seen outside the window is shorter on the canvas than the delicate table standing in front of the window. Compare that painting with a later painting in which he has portrayed exactly

148

Right column — To the Student (main text)

section titled "Critical Thinking." Taking the time to read it now can help you get more out of the critical thinking questions in the rest of the book.

9 Human Diversity Features   Human diversity sections give special emphasis to major themes of this book, the importance of understanding and respecting the differences among people and learning about the sociocultural factors that can contribute to the variety among individuals. You'll find a human diversity section in most chapters.

10 Applications of Psychology   An application of psychology is discussed near the end of every chapter. This section ties together the information in the chapter and helps you understand how your new knowledge of psychology can be used in your own life.

11 Chapter Summaries   At the end of each chapter, the content of the chapter is summarized in outline form. This outline format is designed to give you one last look at the content of the chapter to see how all the pieces of new information fit together.

12 Resources   A list of suggested readings and Web sites is presented at the end of each chapter. This information will help you learn more about a specific topic covered in the chapter.

13 Visual Reviews   In many chapters, you'll find key illustrations from the chapter reprinted at the end of the chapter, only this time *without* the labels. Fill in the labels yourself to test your

---

Right column — facsimile textbook pages

Kicking Legal Drug Habits

What about people who want to stop using these legal consciousness-altering drugs? How can they stop? Some people just stop, of course. But, for those who find stopping difficult, psychologists have designed a number of programs to help individuals stop smoking and reduce caffeine consumption. Because most heavy smokers are physically addicted to the nicotine in cigarettes, one of the best, time-tested methods is to gradually reduce the individual's dependence on nicotine before asking him or her to stop smoking altogether (Foxx & Brown, 1979). In an experimental evaluation of this method, smokers were given a list of cigarettes that stated the nicotine content of each brand.

During the first week, the smokers were allowed to smoke their accustomed number per day of their own high-nicotine brand. During the second week, they were asked to smoke the same number of a brand of cigarettes that contained 30 percent less nicotine. During the third week, they were instructed to smoke the same number of a brand containing 60 percent less nicotine, and the fourth week brought a change to a brand containing 90 percent less nicotine. At that time, 40 percent of the smokers were able to stop smoking permanently, and another 30 percent were able to smoke at reduced rates of nicotine and tar intake. Similar methods have also been developed to help people reduce caffeine consumption by gradually switching to

decaffeinated coffee (Foxx & Rubinoff, 1981). There is also computer software to allow individuals to enter information about their progress in quitting smoking. The individuals receive feedback from the computer, telling them when it is time either to switch to the next lower level of nicotine cigarette or to quit altogether (Burling & others, 1989).

Because dependence on alcohol is a more complicated issue, the individual who cannot reduce drinking to a controlled and healthy level or quit altogether should, by all means, seek professional assistance. The same advice holds for any consciousness-altering drug from which anyone cannot walk away.

---

11 ● Summary

Chapter 5 explores human awareness, normal waking consciousness, sleeping and dreaming, and altered states of consciousness.

I. Consciousness is defined as "a state of awareness" and is experienced in a variety of states.
   A. Directed consciousness occurs when awareness is directed toward a single focus.
   B. In the state of flowing consciousness, awareness drifts from one thought to another.
   C. Daydreams combine the features of directed consciousness and dreamlike fantasies.
   D. At times, consciousness appears to become divided, with different conscious activities occurring simultaneously.
   E. Psychologists have conducted studies that suggest that it makes sense to say that unconscious mental processes operate in our lives.

II. Approximately one-third of our lives is spent in sleep, but not all of sleep is unconscious.
   A. Sleep begins with a semiwakeful, hypnagogic state and moves through stages of progressively deeper sleep.
   B. Dreams occur mostly during the phase of sleep known as REM sleep, but a different type of dream is common in non-REM sleep as well.
   C. Sleeping and dreaming seem important to health, but even extended periods of sleep deprivation have been shown to cause only fatigue, inefficiency, and irritability.
   D. Nightmares, night terrors, sleepwalking, and sleeptalking are fairly common sleep phenomena.
   E. Some persons suffer from the sleep disorders of insomnia (inability to get sufficient sleep), narcolepsy (falling asleep during daily activities), and sleep apnea (breathing stops briefly during sleep).

III. We sometimes experience more unusual altered states of consciousness.
   A. Many individuals practice meditation to achieve a highly relaxed state.
   B. Hypnosis is sometimes used to alter consciousness and to relieve pain.
   C. Altered consciousness is sometimes experienced in the form of depersonalization.

190

CHAPTER 5   States of Consciousness   191

IV. Consciousness can also be altered through the use of various psychotropic drugs.
   A. Psychotropic drugs can be classified as stimulants, depressants, hallucinogens, and inhalants; the drug marijuana does not fit easily into this classification.
   B. Though risks differ from drug to drug, drug use can lead to abuse, dependence, or addiction.
   C. Even the more common legal drugs (caffeine, nicotine, alcohol) produce definite physical and psychological effects and can be quite harmful if used in excess.
   D. The more powerful drugs cause radical changes in consciousness, they can lead to serious physical and psychological problems, and many are illegal.
      1. Stimulants are not physically addictive but produce psychological dependence; they can be dangerous, particularly in their effects on the heart.
      2. Sedatives and tranquilizers are highly addictive and can be highly dangerous, particularly when taken in large doses or with alcohol.
      3. Narcotics are powerful and dangerous depressants; physiological addiction occurs rapidly, and prolonged use has profoundly damaging effects on the body.
      4. Inhalants are usually toxic and often cause permanent brain damage.
      5. Hallucinogens radically alter perception, cause hallucinations, and are often associated with bizarre or even violent behavior. Although hallucinogens are not physiologically addictive, psychological dependence is common.
      6. Marijuana is a drug that produces a sense of well-being in most people and sometimes alters perception.

● Resources

1. For a readable discussion of meditation without its metaphysical or religious trimmings, read Benson, H. (1975). The relaxation response. New York: Morrow. For an intelligent discussion of Zen meditation, see Austin, J. H. (1998). Zen and the brain toward an understanding of meditation and consciousness. Cambridge, MA: MIT Press.
2. For a fascinating and sensible look at hypnosis, see Bowers, K. S. (1976). Hypnosis for the seriously curious. Monterey, CA: Brooks/Cole.
3. For more on the contents of dreams, written by Freudian psychologist, see Hall, C. S. (1951). What people dream about. Scientific American, 84: 60–63. For additional information on the study of sleeping and dreaming, see Webb, W. B., & Agnew, H. W. (1973). Sleep and dreams. Dubuque, IA: Wm. C. Brown; Horne, J. (1988). Why we sleep. New York: Oxford University Press; Hobson, J. A. (1989). Sleep. New York: Scientific American Library; and Stauch, I., & Meier, B. (1996). In search of dreams: Experimental dream research. Albany: State University of New York Press.
4. A fascinating and in-depth analysis of the hypnogogic state is Mavromatis, A. (1987). Hypnogogia. London: Routledge.
5. For thorough summaries of mind-altering drugs, see Carroll, C. R. (2000). Drugs in modern society (5th ed.). Boston: McGraw-Hill; and Julien, R. M. (1992). A primer of drug addiction (6th ed.). San Francisco: Freeman.
6. Broad overviews of the topic of consciousness are provided by Wallace, B., & Fisher, L. E. (1991). Consciousness and behavior, (3rd ed.). Boston: Allyn & Bacon; Ornstein, R. (1991). The evolution of consciousness. New York: Prentice-Hall; and Rychlak, J. F. (1997). In defense of human consciousness. Washington, DC: American Psychological Association.
7. If you smoke or use smokeless tobacco and are thinking about quitting, this Web site offers useful information and links to other sites: http://unr.edu/homepage/shubinsk/smoke.html

CHAPTER 4   Sensation and Perception   153

Outer ear   Middle ear   Inner ear

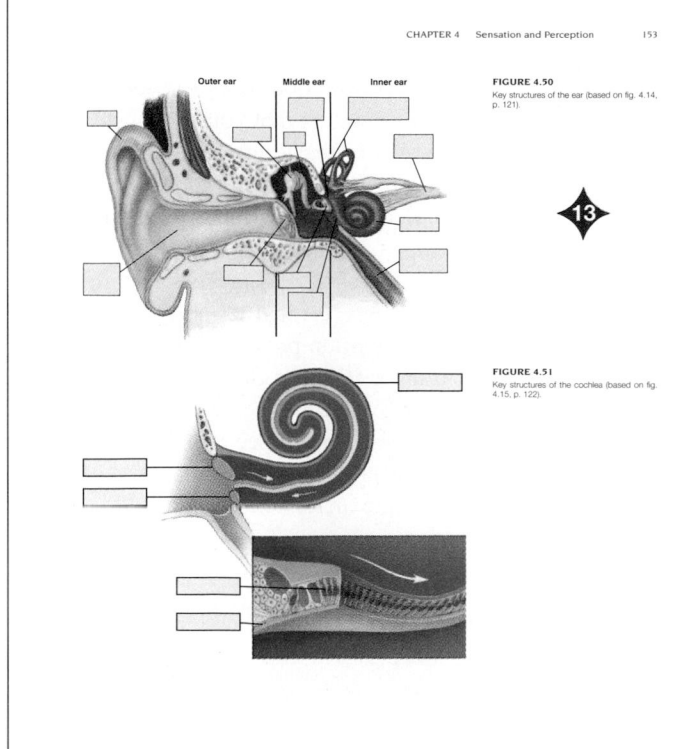

FIGURE 4.50
Key structures of the ear (based on fig. 4.14, p. 121).

FIGURE 4.51
Key structures of the cochlea (based on fig. 4.15, p. 122).

learning of the information. The original figure number, title, and page reference are given. Return to the original figure and description to check your answers and review if necessary.

CRITICAL THINKING

Like most college courses, the goal of this course is to teach you a great deal of new information. But there is a second goal even more important than the first—to teach you to *think critically about human beings.* You are enrolled in a college or university to become well educated. That means, of course, that you want to learn more information, but it also means that you want to be better prepared to make decisions, plan for the future, and realize your goals. If we human beings are to be able to continue to inhabit this fragile planet, and if we are to make the most of our time here, we must all try to hone our intellectual skills.

Psychology provides an excellent vehicle for teaching critical thinking skills. By its very nature—as a *science* of human behavior—we will be looking critically at ourselves. As we discuss the many new facts and concepts that make up this course, we will describe many of the experiments that have helped psychologists reach tentative conclusions about the nature of our behavior and experience. *Psychological research is critical thinking in practice.* As you read about each experiment, take a moment to consider the logic that went into its design. Think for a moment about the thinking that helped the researcher decide between rival explanations for that facet of human life.

But, more important than seeing how scientists use their critical thinking skills, a major goal of this course is to encourage *you* to improve your own critical thinking skills. Success in every walk of life and meaningful participation in democratic society require more than the simple knowledge of facts—they require using facts intelligently.

What, then, is critical thinking? There are many aspects of critical thinking, but the steps that I will describe are a good start. As you read this textbook or approach any other source of new information—from political speeches to newspaper articles—try the following steps:

1. *What is the evidence?* I will present you with many statements in this textbook, and I expect you to demand that I back up my statements with evidence. When I tell you that, unlike 20 years ago, women and men place the same importance on love in marriage, you should look to see if I present evidence to support that conclusion. If I make a statement without supporting evidence, you should strongly question my statement.

2. *How good is the evidence?* Suppose I tell you that the reason that I believe that women and men place the same value on romance today is because my wife and my daughters say so. My wife and daughters happen to be very smart people, but would you believe the opinions of just three people? Would you be more convinced if I cite a study of 20,000 men and women? Not only should we demand evidence to support statements of fact, we also should examine the quality of that evidence. In this book, I can tell you

that I have thought carefully about the quality of evidence that supports every statement. But you should completely disregard my reassurances and think critically about the evidence yourself. You might very well decide that I am wrong on some key issues, but, at the very least, you will sharpen your critical thinking skills.

3. *What are the alternative interpretations of the evidence?* Even if I do provide you with solid evidence to support every conclusion, critical thinking cannot stop there. Facts are meaningless until they are *interpreted,* and there is almost always more than one interpretation of every set of facts in psychology.

   Let's think about an example. There is strong evidence that, other things being equal, women tend to be attracted to men as marriage partners if they are more intelligent, hardworking, and successful. Those are the "facts," but what do they mean? One group of scholars believe that women have an *innate* need (part of every female in the human species) to guarantee the well-being of their children that leads them to prefer successful husbands who can help them provide for their children. Do you agree? Even if you agree, are there alternative explanations of these facts that would make just as much sense? Take a moment now to think about alternative explanations for these facts (really—I hope you will stop reading and try to think of alternative interpretations of these facts for a moment). Did you come up with any alternative explanations? It doesn't matter if you didn't come up with a brilliant explanation, but it is important that you see that alternative explanations of almost any set of facts are possible.

   So what do we do with facts that can be interpreted in several different ways? Critical thinking requires two approaches to this situation. The first and most important step is to look for *more facts* that will help you choose between the alternative explanations. For example, do women in *all* cultures find successful men to be attractive? Do highly successful women in our culture find the man's success to be unimportant? Do women who do not want to have children still find successful men to be attractive? If the answers to these questions are not all yes, you might be less likely to believe that the preference for successful men reflects an innate need shared by all women. There are many ways in which new facts can be sought that might allow you to decide between alternative explanations for facts. Indeed, that is what science is all about.

   The other way in which the critical thinker deals with alternative explanations of facts, however, is to learn to live with alternative explanations. At this point in the history of the science of psychology, there are many alternative explanations of facts that we cannot yet choose among. Indeed, one of the things that makes psychology exciting is that there is so much yet to learn. Many of the current disagreements among psychologists will be resolved ultimately through better experiments—the use of critical thinking to plan the logic of scientific studies. But, in other cases, the different ways of viewing the same phenomena will prove to be equally valid conceptions. Therefore, the ability to consider more than one perspective on issues in psychology—as in all walks of life—is important. Moreover, the discussion of these differing views will help refine your critical thinking about yourself and the human race in general.

4. *Go beyond the book.* This book only scratches the surface of psychology, and it provides only a few examples of how the facts and concepts of psychology might apply to your life. The final step in critical thinking is to ask questions about the information given in the textbook to expand its application to your experience. Each section of a chapter ends with critical thinking questions. These questions have no right or wrong answers but are designed to stimulate and challenge you as you read the book. (The *Student Study Guide* contains more of these kinds of questions in the sections titled "Encouraging Critical Thinking: Beyond the Text.") But these questions are just a start. The most important critical thinking questions that you ask will be your own.

   Critical thinking is not only an academic exercise—it is a part of living. The thinking and evaluative skills that you develop in this and other courses will also serve you well as you solve problems and confront the challenges of daily life.

   If you are concerned that critical thinking takes time and might detract from your ability to memorize information that will be on tests, I have good news for you. Thinking critically about the information that you have just read will improve your memory for that information. In chapter 6, we will discuss the "deep processing" of information and present evidence that the more you think about information the more information you will remember. So, although you will still need to use the strategies presented in the **study skills** section that follows, critical thinking will improve your memory for information presented in this book. But don't take my word for it! Read the section on levels of processing in chapter 6 and think about it critically. Better yet, try your own experiment to see if thinking critically about the information presented in this book makes this course a better learning experience.

BEFORE YOU BEGIN: A Primer on Study Skills

You are about to begin your introduction to the science of psychology. Before you do, I would like to offer you some suggestions that are based on psychological principles. Psychology is a science that addresses a great many topics, most of which have some direct relevance to our lives. One topic that has long been of interest to psychologists is human learning—the ways in which we learn and remember new information, such as the new information that you are learning about the field of psychology. Much has been discovered about learning and memory that can be translated into suggestions for more efficient learning in this course and all of your other courses.

People do not absorb information as a sponge absorbs water; we have to *work* at learning new information in college courses. Human beings are highly effective learners, but we learn better in some ways than we do in others. If we understand the characteristics and quirks of the human learner, we can make better use of our study time. These characteristics will be discussed in some detail in chapters 5 and 6 on learning and memory, but, before you begin to study the science of psychology, it may be useful to summarize some of the more helpful hints provided by psychologists for more effective learning and recall.

I have kept this section brief because I know how busy the beginning of the term can be, but the information contained in this section is worth your attention. From my own experience as a student, and from working with many students since that time, I know that learning better ways to study can make the learning process more enjoyable, can increase the amount of information that you learn and retain, and can improve your grades. I hope that the following suggestions will help you.

The SQ3R Method

Francis Robinson of Ohio State University suggested a method for studying textbooks known as the SQ3R method. These initials stand for the five steps in effective textbook study outlined by Robinson:

S: Survey. Look ahead at the content of the text before you begin to read.

Q: Question. Ask yourself questions about the material you are reading before and as you read.

R: Read. Read through the material in the normal way.

R: Recite. Recite the new information that you are learning out loud or silently.

R: Review. Go over the material that you have learned several times before you are tested on it.

Let's go through these steps in more detail to better understand them.

Survey

Most of us think there is just one way to read—you start at the beginning and read to the end. That is the best way to read a novel because you don't want to know about the next plot twist or the surprise ending until you get there. But a very different strategy is needed when reading a textbook. It's important to survey, or look ahead, at what you are going to read. In fact, you should try to find out as much as possible about the text material you are going to read *before* you read it.

The reason behind this strategy of surveying before reading is based on the way humans learn and store new information in memory. Speaking loosely, we "hang" new information on what we already know. If we learn a new fact about marijuana, we hang that information on what we already know about mind-altering drugs; and, the more organized knowledge we have of a topic, the better we are able to learn and remember new information about it. In particular, the more general information we possess about a topic, the easier it is to learn and remember new specific information about the topic (Ausubel, 1960; Deese & Deese, 1979).

There are several effective ways to survey this textbook. As in studying any text, you should look at the general content

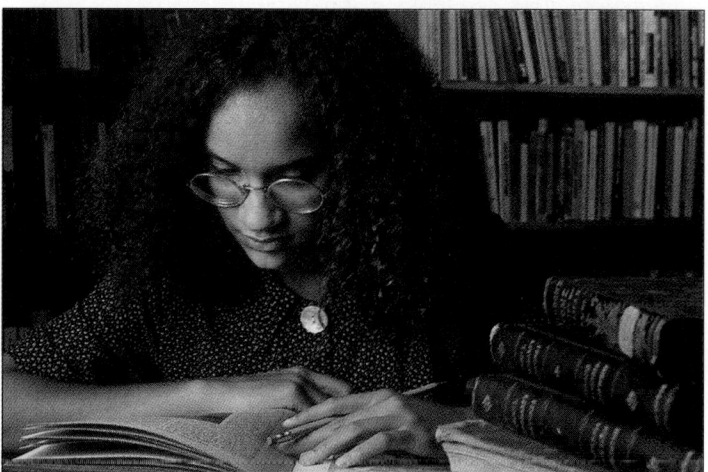

Human beings are highly effective learners, but we learn better in some ways than we do in others. If we understand the characteristics and quirks of the human learner, we can make better use of our study time.

Where is the thyroid gland located? What role does the thyroid gland play in Metabolism? What are the effects of thyroxin?

The **thyroid gland,** located just below the larynx, or voice box, plays an important role in the regulation of **metabolism.** It does so by secreting a hormone called **thyroxin.** The level of thyroxin in a person's bloodstream and the resulting metabolic rate are important in many ways. In children, proper functioning of the thyroid is necessary for proper mental development. A serious thyroid deficiency in childhood will produce sluggishness, poor muscle tone, and a type of mental retardation called **cretinism.**

of each chapter by reading the headings within it. For your convenience, the headings within each chapter of this text are placed in an outline on the chapter opening page. Novels do not have headings because there is no reason to survey their content in advance; textbooks have them because they greatly aid surveying and reviewing. For example, did you look ahead at the headings in this section before beginning to read it? If you did, you developed an overall view of its content.

Next look at the prologue section at the beginning of each chapter. It gives you an advance look at the main points of the content you will be reading. Study this section carefully before going on, and it will increase the amount of information you learn as you read. When surveying some textbooks, you may need to add to what you learn from the headings by briefly skimming sections and looking at illustrations, but, in this text, the chapter outlines and prologues provide the best sources of advance information. Is it really worth the time and effort to read the prologue section of each chapter to get an overview of what is ahead? Actually, I spent a considerable amount of time researching this question before I started writing this book. I didn't want to waste my time in writing the prologues—and your time in reading them— unless they would actually increase what you learn. The value of prologues was tested by David Ausubel (1960) in a classic experiment conducted at the University of Illinois. One hundred twenty students were divided into two groups that read a long passage with and without a prologue section preceding it. The passage covered the properties of carbon steel and contained many facts that were new to the students. After both groups had read the passage on carbon steel, they took a brief

multiple-choice test covering the facts presented in the passage. As predicted, the group that read the prologue first correctly answered approximately 20 percent more of the questions (the difference between an *F* and a *B* in most courses). That is why a prologue was written to precede each chapter in this text—and that is why giving them your close attention is worth the effort.

Question

After you have surveyed the material you will be reading by reading the prologue and looking over the headings, Robinson suggests that you ask questions. Do this before and as you are reading. These questions should be those raised during your survey and first reading. They should reflect your own personal struggle to understand and digest the contents of this book. For example, included here are sample questions that you might ask while studying the thyroid gland in chapter 2. Asking such questions will help you become actively involved in the learning process and will focus your attention on relevant information. As you locate the information that answers your questions, you may find it helpful to underline or highlight such information with a felt-tip pen.

Read

After the *S* and *Q* steps, you are ready to begin reading in the usual way. Although you have put in a lot of time preparing for this step, your reading probably will be so much more efficient that it's worth the extra time. In fact, if you have the time to invest, you could improve the efficiency of your reading even more by skimming the material quickly before reading it more closely.

Recite

When studying, is it more beneficial to spend your time reading the material over and over again, or to read it and then practice reciting it (repeating it to yourself)? Reciting is definitely the most useful part of the study process. If nothing else, it alerts you to those things you do not really know yet (the things you cannot recite), and it may actually make learning more efficient. Regardless of how recitation works, it works. A. I. Gates (1917) found that individuals who spent 80 percent of their time reciting lists and only 20 percent reading them recalled twice as much as those who spent all of their time reading. This seems to be especially true of students who take the time to understand the meaning of what they are learning rather than memorizing it in rote fashion (Honeck, 1973). The "Check Your Learning" questions at the end of each section will help you "recite" what you have learned. In addition, the list of key terms at the beginning of each chapter and the marginal glossary can help you with this recitation. If you can recite the basic definitions of these terms, you will have learned the most important material.

Review

After you have learned the new information in the text by reading and reciting, you will need to add one final step that most students neglect: Review what you have learned several times before you are tested on it. The goal of the review process is to overlearn the material, which means to continue studying material after you have first mastered it. The learning process is not over when you can first recite the new information to yourself without error. Your ability to recall this information can be significantly strengthened later by reciting it several more times before you are tested (Krueger, 1929). To aid you with the review step, this text provides you with a review section following each major heading within the chapter and a sentence outline summary at the end of each chapter.

Strategies for Studying

The SQ3R method can improve your ability to learn information from textbooks. Several other study strategies may help you make even more efficient use of your study time.

Be Sure That You Are Actually Learning

The most common reason students "forget" information when taking tests is that they did not actually learn it in the first place. Because studying is an effort, even when you are efficient at it, it's far too easy to act as if you are studying when, in fact, you are really listening to the radio, thinking about your sweetheart, or clipping your nails. If you are good at acting as if you were studying—I was a master of it during my first two years of college— you can easily fool your roommate, your best friend, and even yourself. Fooling yourself is the most dangerous possibility; do not fool yourself into thinking that you are studying when you are not really exerting the effort to become absorbed in the material. When you study, really study.

Find a Good Place to Study and Only Study There

One way to help you really study during your study periods is to find a good place to study, and only study in that place. The goal is to associate that place only with effective studying. Begin by choosing a

spot that is free from distractions. Some places in libraries are ideal for studying, but other places in libraries are great for talking and making new friends. Avoid the latter when you are studying, but feel free to visit these places when you are taking breaks. After you find a good place to study, never do anything there except study. If a friend comes over for conversation, get up and move to another area to talk. Return only when you are ready to study. Similarly, if you are in your study place and find that your mind is wandering, leave it until you are ready to study again. If you do this consistently—if you only study when you are in your study place—this spot will "feel" like a place to study, and you will be more apt to study efficiently while you are there. This doesn't mean that you cannot also study in other places—such as on the bus when you have a 20-minute ride—but having a good place to study that becomes associated only with studying will help you study efficiently when you are there.

Space Out Your Study Time

As long ago as 1885, Hermann Ebbinghaus found that studying a list of new information once a day for several days resulted in better recall of that information than studying the list several times in one day.

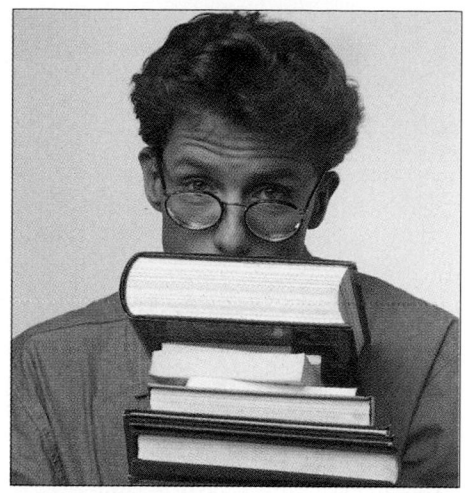

Spaced practice or study is much more efficient than massed practice (cramming).

Since then, a great deal of research has shown that spaced practice often results in better learning and memory than massed practice (Bahrick, Bahrick, Bahrick, & Bahrick, 1993). This is especially true in learning motor skills (such as learning to play a musical instrument or learning large amounts of unfamiliar verbal material, such as studying for a psychology test). This is why cramming (massing all your study time into one long session) is terribly inefficient. You can get much better grades by spacing the same amount of study time over a longer period.

Use Mnemonic Devices

The suggestions given thus far concern how to study. The following suggestions are about how to memorize information when you are studying. Mnemonic devices are methods for storing memories so that they will be easier to recall. In each mnemonic device, an additional indexing cue is memorized along with the material to be learned. More is less with mnemonics; memorizing something more will result in less forgetting.

1. *Method of loci. Loci* is the Latin word for "places." In this method, the items in a list are mentally placed in a series of logically connected places. For example, if you are trying to remember a grocery list, you might think of a bag of sugar hanging on your garage door, a gallon of milk sitting in the front seat of your

When you study, really study. Don't just go through the motions.

car, a carton of eggs perched on your steering wheel, and a box of donuts sitting in front of the grocery store door. Stanford University psychologist Gordon Bower (1973) found that persons who used the method of loci were able to recall almost three times as many words from lists as those who did not.

2. *Acronym method.* My favorite mnemonic device is the method of acronyms. Nearly every list of facts in psychology that I successfully memorized in college was memorized in terms of acronyms. In this simple method, the first letters of each word in a list are combined to form an acronym. For example, the four stages of alcoholism, which are prealcoholic, prodromal, crucial, and chronic, can be memorized using the acronym PPCC. Acronyms are even more useful if they form a real word. For most people, the word *ape* means an animal in a zoo, but the acronym APE helps me remember the names of the three subscales of the psychological test called the Semantic Differential Scale: activity, potency, and evaluation.

A system closely related to acronyms takes the first letter of each word in an ordered series but uses them in a new sentence. My high school biology teacher taught me to remember the hierarchy of biological classification using the sentence "Kathy pulls candy on Friday, good stuff." Notice that the first letter in each word of this sentence is the same as in kingdom, phylum, class, order, family, genus, species. As with acronyms, memory of a phrase or sentence is likely to spark recall of an entire list.

3. *Keyword method.* We will see later in chapter 6 when we look at the psychology of memory that it is easier to memorize information that you understand than information that you do not. Some of the things that you need to memorize for college courses will be meaningful to you if you take the time to think about them before you try to memorize them, but sometimes you will have to give additional meaning to the things you are memorizing. Raugh and Atkinson (1975) demonstrated the value of teaching students to do this in memorizing Spanish vocabulary words, using what they called the *keyword* method. They asked one group of students to memorize English translations in the standard way of rotely associating the English word with the unknown Spanish word. Another group was taught to increase the meaningfulness of the association between the English and Spanish word pairs. As shown in figure 1, they were told to think of an English word that sounded like the Spanish word (such as *charcoal* for the Spanish word for puddle, *charco*) and to form a mental image of the English sound-alike word and the actual English translation (charcoal grill sitting in a puddle). Students who learned the Spanish vocabulary in this more meaningful fashion were able to recall an average of 88 percent of the words, whereas the students who used rote memorization were able to recall an average of only 28 percent when tested later. By actively enhancing the meaningfulness of what was learned using the keyword method, the students were able to greatly improve its storage in memory.

Try some of these prescriptions for better learning and memory; they could make a big difference.

Additional Information on Study Skills

If you are interested in learning more about study skills, you might want to consult five books that deal with the topic in more depth:

Ellis, D. B. (1994). *Becoming a master student* (7th ed.). Rapid City, SD: College Survival, Inc.

Hettich, P. I. (1992). *Learning skills for college and career.* Pacific Grove, CA: Brooks/Cole.

Higgins, R. D. (Ed.). (1993). *The black student's guide to college success.* Westport, CT: Greenwood Press.

Parrott, L. (1994). *How to write psychology papers.* New York: HarperCollins.

Weinstein, C. E., & Hume, L. M. (1998). *Strategies for lifelong learning.* Washington, DC: APA Books.

FIGURE 1

In the "keyword" method of learning Spanish vocabulary, the student visualizes the Spanish noun with a noun that sounds like it in English. For example, the Spanish words for *puddle, lizard,* and *clown* sound similar to the English words for *charcoal, log,* and *pie.*

ESSENTIALS OF
PSYCHOLOGY

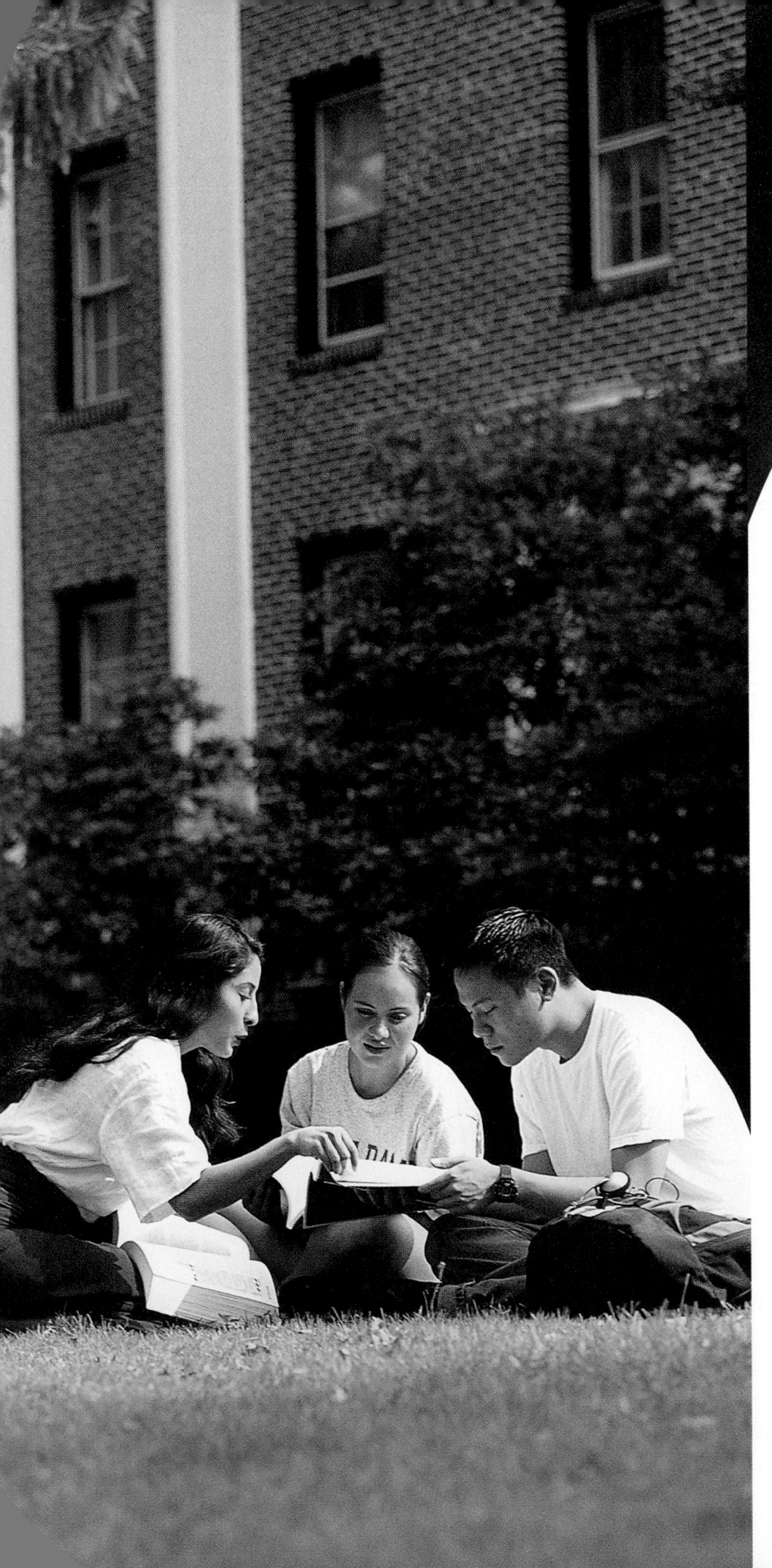

CHAPTER

1

CHAPTER OUTLINE

What Is Psychology?

PROLOGUE

W hat will this course in psychology be about? You may have already glanced through the book and noticed the illustrations of nerve cells, the discussion of color vision, and the story of the dogs that were taught to salivate to the sound of a bell. This is psychology?! Are you getting worried that you signed up for the wrong course? If you're like me when I opened my first psychology textbook, you were surprised to see such topics in a book about psychology. I had expected to read tales of madness, love, and social ills, but instead I saw illustrations of brain structures, salivating dogs, and odor receptors.

I hope you looked through the book long enough to see that love, violence, and mental disorders, are in here, too. Almost everything that you expected is in this course, but a lot of topics that you probably didn't expect also will be covered. If I hadn't had an instructor who explained how all of these topics related to people, I think I would have changed majors. Why on earth would I want to know how to teach dogs to salivate on command? Why did I need to know how a taste bud works? Because I remember very clearly what it was like to take my first psychology course, I wrote this book to help your instructor explain to you how all of these topics fit together to make up the field of psychology.

This text surveys the basic principles of psychology and shows you how these principles can be applied to solve some significant human problems. Because this is a first course in psychology, we cover more basic facts and principles than applications. But to help you make better sense of the fundamental concepts, this book describes applications throughout the course to illustrate the abstract principles in a concrete way. All of the material in this book, even the most basic material, is relevant to human lives. And many topics relate directly to everyone's personal efforts to make sense out of life.

In this first chapter, you will begin your study of psychology by exploring the things psychologists study and how they study them. You will be struck by the fact that psychology is a very broad field. Psychologists use the methods of science to study these things. They learn about behavior, thoughts, and feelings by systematically *observing* them. Certainly, psychologists *think* about human behavior, but, as scientists, they believe that people always learn more by actually observing people behave than from speculating about it.

Observation is the heart of the scientific method of all the sciences, including psychology. Psychologists use a variety of methods of scientific observation, ranging from surveys to laboratory experiments. Each method of observation is valuable in helping us fit new pieces into the puzzle of human behavior and mental processes. The goal of all of this scientific observation is to describe behavior with enough precision that we can predict it better, understand it more fully, and learn how to influence human behavior in positive ways.

Although the first systematic writings about human behavior date back to the time of Aristotle, psychology did not become an independent science until 1879, when Wilhelm Wundt founded the first laboratory of psychology in Germany. Psychology actually had many "beginnings" in the late 1800s, led by a number of scientists who were interested in very different aspects of human behavior and mental processes. These were exciting times for the early psychologists, filled with intense disagreements, sharp remarks, and occasional scandals. As you will soon see, psychology is still a very broad field today in which different theories abound and many facets of the human condition are studied. But we are making good progress toward our goal of using observation to describe, predict, and understand human behavior.

KEY TERMS

▶ PSYCHE AND SCIENCE = PSYCHOLOGY

Welcome to psychology! You are invited to learn about one of life's most interesting subjects—yourself. You enrolled in this course knowing that it had something to do with people. But what exactly is psychology?

The earliest origins of psychology are in the writings of the ancient Greek philosophers about the nature of *life,* particularly the writings of Aristotle. Aristotle, who was born in 384 B.C., was interested in learning everything he could about the nature of life itself. He collected and dissected plants and animals in an attempt to see how their organs sustained life. He studied reproduction to see how life was re-created in each generation, and he studied the everyday actions of living people as they reasoned, remembered, and learned.

It was Aristotle's habit in his later years to discuss philosophy with his students as they strolled the covered walks of his school, the Lyceum. Imagine what he might have said to them about the nature of life:

> You'll understand what life is if you think about the act of dying. When I die, how will I be different from the way I am right now? In the first moments after death, my body will be scarcely different in physical terms than it was in the last seconds of life, but I will no longer move, no longer sense, nor speak, nor feel, nor care. It's these things that are life.

Aristotle used the term *psyche* to refer to the essence of life. This term is translated from Greek to mean "mind," but it is closely linked in meaning to the word *breath.* Aristotle believed that psyche escaped in the last dying breath that was exhaled. Modern psychologists are interested in the same actions, thoughts, and feelings of human beings as Aristotle. Indeed, the term *psychology* comes from Aristotle's word *psyche* plus the Greek word *logos,* which means "the study of."

Aristotle received his training in philosophical methods from famous philosopher Plato, but he disagreed with Plato's belief that one could achieve a full understanding of anything simply by *thinking* about it. Aristotle felt that one must also *observe* the thing being studied—look at it, listen to it, touch it. Although he was not a scientist in the modern sense of the word, Aristotle's emphasis on observation is the basis for the methods of contemporary science. Progress in scientific methods from Aristotle to the present has involved no basic changes in this idea; scientists have only developed more precise and efficient ways of observing. Thus, Aristotle launched the study of life that eventually evolved into the modern science of psychology.

Philosopher and early scientist Aristotle.

Definition of Psychology

In some ways, it would be correct to say that psychologists still define psychology as the "study of life." The only thing that would be incorrect about this definition is that it is not specific enough to distinguish the modern discipline of psychology from other sciences, such as biology, that also study life. Today, therefore, **psychology** is defined as the *science of behavior and mental processes.*

Notice that this definition contains three key terms—*science, behavior,* and *mental processes.* Let's look at each of these terms separately. Psychology is considered to be a **science** because psychologists attempt to understand people through careful, controlled observation. This reliance on rigorous scientific methods of observation is the basis of all sciences, including psychology. The term **behavior** refers to all of a person's overt actions that others can directly observe. When you walk, speak, throw a Frisbee, or show a facial expression, you are behaving in this sense. The term **mental processes** refers to the private thoughts, emotions, feelings, and

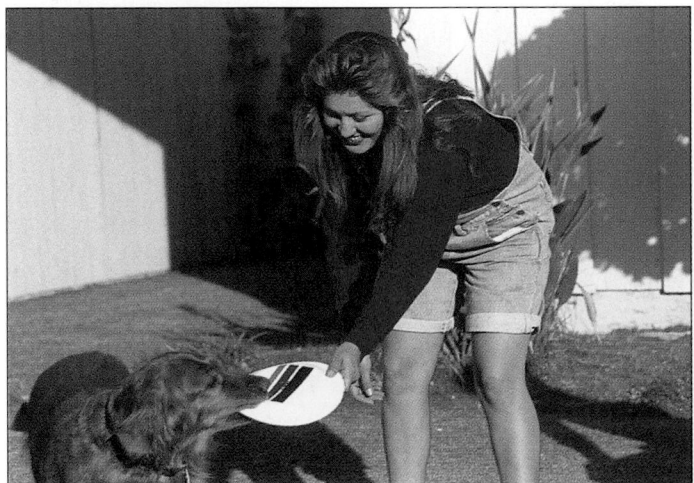

The term *behavior* refers to all of a person's overt actions that others can directly observe. When you walk, speak, throw a Frisbee, or show facial expression, you are behaving in this sense.

motives that others cannot directly observe. Your private thoughts and feelings about your dog catching a Frisbee in midair are examples of mental processes.

Goals of Psychology

What are the goals of the science of psychology? What are psychologists trying to accomplish? Psychologists study people by using scientific methods. The goals of this scientific enterprise are to describe, predict, understand, and influence behavior and mental processes:

1. *Describe.* The information gathered through scientific research helps psychologists describe psychological phenomena more accurately and completely. For example, information gathered in a survey on the frequency of sexual behavior among college students without the protection of a condom would reveal how many are at high risk for the spread of sexually transmitted diseases such as AIDS.

2. *Predict.* In some cases, psychologists are able to predict future behavior. For example, psychologists have developed tests that enable employers to improve their prediction of which job applicants will perform well.

The goals of psychology are to describe, predict, understand, and influence human behavior.

3. *Understand.* We understand behavior and mental processes when we can explain why they happen. Because there is still much more to learn, however, our current explanations are always tentative. In other words, our explanations are **theories,** not truths. Theories are tentative explanations of facts and relationships in sciences. It's essential that you understand this basic fact about science as you read this textbook. The knowledge that we can offer you is always tentative. As the science of psychology progresses through research, our theories are always subject to revision.

4. *Influence.* Finally, psychologists hope to go beyond description, understanding, and prediction to influence behavior in beneficial ways. What can we do to help a teenage boy climb out of a period of severe depression? How can we help parents raise their rambunctious children better? What is the best way to help college students select a career? It's not until we can intentionally influence behavior that psychology completely fulfills its promise.

psychology
The science of behavior and mental processes.

science
Approach to knowledge based on systematic observation.

behavior
Directly observable and measurable human actions.

mental processes
Private psychological activities that include thinking, perceiving, and feeling.

theories
Tentative explanations of facts and relationships in sciences.

▶ THE MANY VIEWPOINTS IN PSYCHOLOGY AND THEIR ORIGINS

There was no formal discipline of psychology during the time of Aristotle and for 2,200 years after he lived. Like the other sciences, psychology was a part of philosophy. It wasn't until modern times that the sciences emerged from the general field of philosophy. In the seventeenth and eighteenth centuries, physics, biology, medicine, and other disciplines

● Review

We have defined psychology as the science of behavior and mental processes. Behavior refers to all of your actions that other people can directly observe. Mental processes, in contrast, are private events, such as thinking and feeling. The goals of psychology are to describe, predict, understand, and influence behavior and mental processes. Using the methods of science, we gather information through systematic observation, which enables us to accurately describe psychological facts and relationships. When adequate descriptive information has been acquired, reasonably accurate predictions can be made and explanations proposed to help us understand these facts and relationships. Finally, when enough understanding and ability to predict has been acquired, we can sometimes intentionally influence people in ways that improve and enrich their lives.

● Check Your Learning

One efficient way to learn information from textbooks is to be sure that you have mastered the key points in each major section before moving on to the next one. You can do this by asking yourself questions about the material you have just read. If you cannot answer some of the questions, you can easily go back to that part of the section and reread it. Then, when you can answer all of your questions, it will be time to move on to the next part of the chapter. This step of asking and answering questions will take a little time, but you will learn and remember much more information.

To make it easier for you to check your learning in this way, I have written some questions at the end of each section. If you give an incorrect answer to any question, return to the page number given next to the correct answer to see why your answer was not correct. When you have mastered the information in this section, you will be ready to move on to the next section.

It is important for you also to ask *your own* questions, however, for two reasons. First, asking your own questions will help you personalize the course and make it a more worthwhile learning experience for you. Second, I have asked you questions only about some of the key points in each section. If you learn only what is emphasized in these few questions, you will miss a great deal of information. Therefore, it is best to use these questions only as a starting point in checking your learning.

1. The ancient Greek philosopher who wrote about "psyche" and first broadly defined the subject matter of psychology was

   a) Plato.   b) Aristotle.   c) Hippocrates.   d) Epicurus.

2. The modern definition of psychology is "the science of _____ and _____."

3. Mental processes are

   a) directly observable.   b) private.

4. The four goals of the science of psychology are to _____ behavior.

   a) _____

   b) _____

   c) _____

   d) _____

● Thinking Critically About Psychology

1. What do you personally want to learn in this course?
2. How do your personal goals as a student of psychology relate to the four goals of the science of psychology?

Correct Answers 1. b (p. 4),   **2.** behavior and mental processes (p. 4),   **3. b** (p. 4),   **4. a.** describe, **b.** predict, **c.** understand, **d.** influence (p. 5).

began to accumulate knowledge that set each somewhat apart from the others. Also, each science developed distinct ways of viewing nature. Eventually, psychology also developed its own distinct subject matter and scientific methods.

The launching of the separate field of psychology is usually credited to Wilhelm Wundt for establishing the first Laboratory of Psychology in Leipzig, Germany, in 1879. Some historians feel that William James deserves the honor for a less-publicized laboratory at Harvard University, however, which opened in 1875. Actually, many people "founded" psychology. Their varied interests and talents laid the foundations for the diverse field surveyed in this text. As you read about some of the most influential early psychologists, imagine how different their answers would be if you asked each of them, "What is the most important question for psychology?"

Nature of Conscious Experience

The first topic studied by psychologists was private conscious experience. What are you thinking and feeling right now? Everything that you are aware of right now is part of your conscious experience. The first psychologists wanted to understand the basic elements of consciousness and how they worked together to create the experience of being alive.

Wundt, Titchener, and the Structuralists

Wilhelm Wundt was a professor of biology in Germany who was fascinated by human consciousness. His work was expanded by his student Edward Titchener, who later taught in the United States at Cornell University. Just as chemists seek to discover the basic elements that make up physical substances, Wundt and Titchener wanted to identify the basic elements of conscious experience. Indeed, sometimes their work is referred to as "mental chemistry." Wundt and Titchener studied the elements of consciousness using a method of looking inward at one's own conscious experiences, called **introspection.** Wundt and Titchener trained themselves to observe the contents of their own minds as accurately and unemotionally as possible in an attempt to isolate the basic elements of the mind. What does that mean exactly?

Suppose that I visit your school some day and your instructor asks me to give a guest lecture on the history of psychology. Suppose also that I am in a particularly dramatic mood and decide to give the lecture playing the role of Edward Titchener. I arrive wearing a fake beard and the flowing black academic robes that he always wore and I choose you to be the subject of a demonstration of introspection. I ask you to close your eyes and I place a bit of apple in your mouth that you have not seen. Then I ask you to describe to me the raw *sensations* that this physical stimulus creates in your mind.

You hesitate a moment, then announce with a smile, "It's an apple!"

"Nein! Nein! Nein!" I shout, using the only word I can remember from German 101. "I asked you to tell me what you *sense,* not what the stimulus is. Don't tell me what the thing is on your tongue. Describe the sensations that you experience!"

You hesitate again, regain your composure, and hesitatingly say, "Sweet?"

"Yes! Yes!" I cry. "What else do you sense?"

"A little bit of sourness, a grainy texture, and a wetness."

"Wonderful!" I shout, leading you to break into a grin. "Now you're introspecting. Now you're describing the elemental contents of your mind. Sweet, sour, grainy . . . those are a few of the building blocks from which consciousness is structured. Everything that you experience in life is based on a small number of these basic elements."

Because Wundt and Titchener were interested in the basic elements of the conscious experience and how those elements are organized, their viewpoint is known as **structuralism.** That is, they sought to determine the *structure* of the mind through controlled introspection.

J. Henry Alston

Although Wundt and Titchener were the first psychologists to study conscious experience, other scientists soon joined the effort. One notable early structuralist was J. Henry Alston. Alston is best known for his studies of the sensations of heat and cold. Alston discovered that we feel cold when one kind of nerve ending in the skin is stimulated, and we feel warm when a different kind of nerve ending is stimulated. Most interestingly, he found that we feel intense heat only when *both* the warmth and cold receptors in the skin are stimulated at the same time. Very hot objects—such as a hot iron—not only stimulate the warmth receptors, but they also stimulate the nerve endings that ordinarily respond only when it is cold.

Wilhelm Wundt (1832–1920).

Edward Titchener (1867–1927).

introspection
(in´tro-spek´shun)   The process of looking inward at one's own consciousness.

structuralism
(struk´tūr-al-izm)   The nineteenth-century school of psychology that sought to determine the structure of the mind through controlled introspection.

Structuralism

www.mhhe.com/laheye1

J. Henry Alston.

Warm Cold
water water

FIGURE 1.1

When you grasp a coil made up of two twisted pipes, one carrying cold water and the other carrying moderately warm water, the sensation is one of extreme heat because the receptors for both cold and heat are stimulated.

Gestalt psychology
The school of thought based on the belief that human consciousness cannot be broken down into its elements.

gestalt
(ges-tawlt´) An organized or unified whole.

phi phenomenon
(fī fe-nom´ĕ-non) The perception of apparent movement between two stationary stimuli.

functionalism
(funk´shun-al-izm) The nineteenth-century school of psychology that emphasized the useful functions of consciousness.

Alston demonstrated this fact in a simple but elegant experiment in 1920. He constructed the apparatus shown in figure 1.1 by wrapping two water pipes together, one carrying moderately warm water and the other carrying cold water. When people grasped these pipes, they felt the sensation of intense heat! Because both the warmth and the cold receptors in the skin were stimulated by the twisted pipes, the individual in the experiment felt the sensation of intense heat.

J. Henry Alston is a notable figure in the history of psychology for another reason as well. The first research article published by an African American psychologist in a journal of the American Psychological Association was written by J. Henry Alston.

Max Wertheimer and the Gestalt Psychologists

Max Wertheimer, a professor of psychology at the University of Frankfurt in the early 1900s, also was interested in the nature of conscious experience. His ideas about consciousness were quite different from those of the structuralists, however. Wertheimer led a group of psychologists known as **Gestalt psychologists.** Their approach to psychology was founded on the concept of the **gestalt,** or *whole.* The Gestalt psychologists felt that human consciousness could not be meaningfully broken down into raw elements, as the structuralists tried to do. As they were fond of saying, "The whole is different from the sum of its parts." To illustrate, the two examples in figure 1.2 are drawn from exactly the same angled lines, but their organization greatly changes our perception of them. Although the parts are the same in each example, the whole is seen as a triangle in one example and arrows in the other. Similarly, the second element in the two rows in figure 1.2 is exactly the same each time, but it is perceived as a "13" in the first row and as a "B" in the second.

Gestalt psychologists also used the **phi phenomenon** to demonstrate that the whole is different from the sum of its parts (see fig. 1.3). When two lights are presented in rapid sequence, the viewer sees an apparent movement in the stimuli. That is, rather than perceiving two stationary lights, the viewer sees one light moving from one position to another. This is a highly important phenomenon to Gestalt psychologists, because what is seen—a moving light—is not present in the two parts of the stimulus at all. Movement is a property of the whole perception—the gestalt—but movement is not part of the stimulus. Motion pictures are based on the phi phenomenon. A series of still images that change slightly in each frame is projected on the screen so quickly that the image appears to be moving. The Gestalt psychologists used such examples to make their point that perception has meaning only when it's seen as a whole, rather than as a simple collection of elements, as the structuralists implied.

Functions of the Conscious Mind

While many of the early psychologists were studying the nature of conscious experience, another group was trying to understand the *value* of consciousness to us as a species. What useful *functions* does consciousness serve?

William James and the Functionalists

In 1875, a young professor of biology and philosophy at Harvard University named William James taught the first course on "psychology," and in 1890 he published an influential early textbook of psychology. James was impressed with the work of biologist Charles Darwin, who suggested in his theory of evolution that every physical characteristic evolved in a species because it served a purpose. James suspected that the same thing could be said about the human mind. He speculated that thinking, feeling, learning, remembering, and other processes of human consciousness existed only because they helped us survive as a species. Because we can think, for example, we are better able to find food, avoid danger, and care for our children—all of which help the human species survive. Because of its emphasis on the *functions* of consciousness, the school of thought known as **functionalism** emerged from the work of William James.

FIGURE 1.2
The organization of the lines in these two illustrations shows that only "whole" perceptions have meaning. The lines do not change, but their meaning does.

James was particularly interested in topics he considered to be evolutionarily important: conscious awareness, voluntary action (free will), habits, and emotions. Because James was concerned with what the mind could do rather than its structure, he criticized the structuralists for creating a barren approach to psychology. He compared human consciousness to a flowing stream: We could study that stream by isolating single molecules of water like the structuralists, but by doing so we would miss the nature and beauty of the whole stream. Moreover, studying the water molecules in a stream would tell us nothing about what the stream *does*—that it erodes riverbanks, provides a home for fish, carries barges, and so on. Similarly, studying the elements of the mind tells us nothing about how it helps us adapt to the demands of life. The functions of the mind, not its raw elements, were the subject matter of psychology to the functionalists.

Functionalism continues to have a strong influence on contemporary psychology, but the terminology has changed. Rather than speaking about the functions of human consciousness, psychologists now use the term *cognitive processes*. **Cognition** is a broad term that refers to all intellectual processes—perceiving, believing, thinking, remembering, knowing, deciding, and so on. Contemporary **cognitive psychology** can be thought of as a modern version of functionalism, but with some key ideas from Gestalt psychology and structuralism thrown in for good measure. A recent analysis of trends in the content of leading psychology journals and dissertation research in psychology found that cognitive psychology is by far the dominant perspective in North American psychology and probably in most of the world (Robins, Goslin, & Clark, 1999).

Behaviorism and Social Learning Theory

While Wundt and his followers studied the nature of conscious experience and James, Binet, and others examined the usefulness of the conscious mental processes, another group of founders of the science of psychology was getting started in Russia. Like James, this group was influenced by Darwin to study psychological processes that are useful in the struggle to survive. In this case, their emphasis was on *learning* from experience.

Ivan Pavlov

In the 1890s, Russian psychologist Ivan Pavlov and his coworkers were conducting research on digestion in dogs when they noticed a curious thing. They had surgically implanted tubes in the cheeks of the dogs to study the reflexive secretion of saliva during eating. Pavlov noticed that after several feedings the dogs started salivating when they saw food being brought to them rather than when the food was placed in their mouths. He recognized that the dogs had learned to associate the sight of the food being brought with the

Max Wertheimer (1880–1943).

William James (1842–1910).

 Functionalism

www.mmhe.com/laheye1

cognition
(kog-nish´un)   Mental processes of perceiving, believing, thinking, remembering, knowing, deciding, and so on.

cognitive psychology
The viewpoint in psychology that emphasizes the importance of cognitive processes, such as perception, memory, and thinking.

FIGURE 1.3
Although these lights are stationary, the rapid, consecutive lighting of them creates an illusion of motion.

Ivan Pavlov (1849–1936).

John B. Watson (1878–1958).

Margaret Floy Washburn (1871–1939).

food itself. Because the sight had immediately preceded the food on many occasions, the dogs came to respond to the sight of food by salivating. He demonstrated that this interpretation was correct by conducting careful experiments using a clicking metronome instead of the sight of food and small quantities of powdered meat. When the metronome and the meat powder were presented together, the dogs quickly learned to salivate to the metronome alone.

Although teaching dogs to salivate to the sound of the metronome certainly is not important in its own right, Pavlov's accidental discovery was of tremendous importance to the new field of psychology. He had identified a simple form of learning—or *conditioning,* to use his term—in which an inherited reflex (salivating) comes to be triggered by a stimulus that has nothing to do with that reflex (the metronome). Pavlov had shown that even inherited reflexes could be influenced dramatically by learning experiences. Pavlov felt that the study of conditioning was such an important breakthrough that he abandoned his research on digestion, for which he would later win the Nobel Prize, and spent the rest of his career studying his new discovery.

John B. Watson and Margaret Floy Washburn

Pavlov's research and theories were not immediately accepted in the United States, but in the 1920s the concepts were taken up in the writings of John B. Watson. He was deeply impressed by Pavlov's work on conditioning because of its scientific precision. Watson agreed with Pavlov that the importance of conditioning went far beyond salivating dogs and that most human behavior was learned through classical conditioning. Watson felt that it was impossible to study private mental processes because only outward behavior could be measured and scientifically understood. Because he felt that psychologists should study only overt behavior, Watson called the school of thought that was founded on Pavlov's work **behaviorism.**

Margaret Floy Washburn was another influential early behaviorist. She was the first woman to receive a Ph.D. in psychology, obtaining her degree in 1908 from Cornell University (Furomoto, 1992). During her many years of teaching at Vassar College, Washburn published 90 scientific articles and books on learning and perception in animals.

Contemporary Behaviorism and Social Learning Theory

To some extent, behaviorism has survived as a distinct school of thought in contemporary psychology. Some psychologists are strict adherents of behaviorism and rule out the study of mental processes, as did John B. Watson. Until his death in 1990, B. F. Skinner of Harvard University was the leading exponent of this strict form of behaviorism. Most contemporary behavioral psychologists endorse a broader version of behaviorism, which integrates the study of behavior with the study of cognition. Albert Bandura of Stanford University is the leading spokesperson for this broader viewpoint, which is often referred to as **social learning theory.** This viewpoint states that the most important aspects of our behavior are learned from other persons in society—we learn to be who we are from our family, friends, and culture. As judged by the number of publications in recent years, the influence of the strict behavioral approach has declined considerably (Robins & others, 1999), but the broader social learning viewpoint, which integrates aspects of behaviorism and the cognitive perspective, is an important theoretical perspective today.

The Nature of the "Unconscious Mind"

While most of the founders of psychology were focusing on either conscious mental processes or overt behavior, others were moving in a very different direction. They believed that the most important aspect of human psychology was neither the mental processes nor the behavior that we are aware of but, rather, the mental processes that we are *unaware* of. Thus, this group of pioneers in psychology focused on the so-called unconscious mind.

Sigmund Freud and Psychoanalysis

Sigmund Freud was an Austrian physician who practiced neurology, the treatment of diseases of the nervous system. Unlike the other founders of psychology, he was responsible for the day-to-day care of a large number of patients, many of whom had serious psychological problems. This fact, perhaps more than anything else, explains the enormous differences between his view of psychology and those of the other founders.

Freud believed conscious mental processes were of trivial importance compared with the workings of the **unconscious mind.** Sensation, learning, memory, and other cognitive processes so important to the other founding psychologists were of little interest to Freud. Freud felt that the roots of the psychological problems that he tried to treat were innate **motives,** particularly sexual and aggressive ones, that reside in an unconscious part of the mind. He believed that these unconscious motives and the conflicts that surround them influenced our behavior, even though we do not know they exist.

Freud's theory of **psychoanalysis** has been subjected to a number of revisions since his death. Modern psychoanalysts still adhere to Freud's view that conflicts in the unconscious mind are the chief source of psychological problems. However, there are few "orthodox" psychoanalysts today. Most feel that Freud made an important contribution in calling our attention to the role often played by unconscious sexual and aggressive motives in our emotional conflicts but feel that other motives, such as the need to feel adequate in social relationships, are of even greater importance (Westen, 1998). In terms of publications in core journals and dissertation research, the psychoanalytic perspective is not a dominant force in mainstream North American psychology today (Robins & others, 1999).

Humanistic Psychology and the Unconscious Mind

During the 1950s, another movement that focused on the role of the unconscious in psychological problems emerged, known as **humanistic psychology.** Leading humanists such as Carl Rogers did not agree with Freud that conscious processes were unimportant, however. Indeed, the humanists believe that human beings determine their own fates through the conscious decisions they make. Like Freud, however, the humanists believe that the unconscious mind often defeats efforts to make good decisions.

To the humanists, the most important aspect of people is our view of what we are like—our *self-concept.* Society often makes it difficult to have an *accurate* self-concept, however. For example, we are constantly bombarded with information that says that only witty, athletic, and attractive people are worth loving. So what if you are like most of us and are a little dull, slightly clumsy, and not so attractive? The humanists believe that we often push such upsetting information about ourselves into the unconscious. This causes two kinds of problems. First, it means that most of us have an inaccurate self-concept—because we push out of consciousness information about ourselves that doesn't match what society values. Second, the negative unconscious information sometimes threatens our self-concept and makes us anxious. Thus, although the psychoanalysts and humanists view the unconscious mind in very different ways, they both see it as the most important cause of human problems. Like the psychoanalytic perspective, few current dissertations and papers in core journals are on humanistic themes (Robins & others, 1999).

B. F. Skinner (1904–1990).

Sigmund Freud (1856–1939).

behaviorism
(be-hāv´yor-izm)   The school of psychology that emphasizes the process of learning and the measurement of overt behavior.

social learning theory
The viewpoint that the most important aspects of our behavior are learned from other persons in society—family, friends, and culture.

unconscious mind
All mental activity of which we are unaware.

motives
Internal states or conditions that activate behavior and give it direction.

psychoanalysis
(sī´´kō-ah-nal´i-sis)   The technique of helping persons with emotional problems based on Sigmund Freud's theory of the unconscious mind.

humanistic psychology
The psychological view that human beings possess an innate tendency to improve and determine their lives by the decisions they make.

● Review

There was no formal science of psychology for 2,200 years after the time of Aristotle. Then, in the late nineteenth century, a number of events led to the emergence of an independent discipline. Wilhelm Wundt founded his psychology laboratory in 1879. Wundt and his followers Edward Titchener and J. Henry Alston engaged in controlled introspective studies of human consciousness. Max Wertheimer and his associates in Germany developed Gestalt psychology, which emphasized the need to study consciousness in whole, meaningful units rather than the artificial elements studied by the structuralists. William James taught the first psychology course and published an influential early textbook stressing the evolutionary significance of

Carl Rogers (1902–1987).

consciousness. John B. Watson and Margaret Floy Washburn introduced the United States to the research on classical conditioning conducted by Russian biologist Ivan Pavlov. Based on Pavlov's work, Watson advocated a science of psychology that included only overt behavior and made no attempt to study mental processes. Physician Sigmund Freud published his observations on psychoanalysis and the unconscious, which were followed half a century later by the different perspective on the unconscious of the humanists. Together these many founders of psychology launched a diverse science amid a storm of energetic controversy.

● Check Your Learning

To be sure that you have learned the key points from the preceding section, cover the list of correct answers and try to answer each question. If you give an incorrect answer to any question, return to the page given next to the correct answer to see why your answer was not correct.

1. The early psychologist who first pioneered the introspective study of human consciousness and who is generally credited with founding the first laboratory of psychology in 1879 was

   a) Ivan Pavlov.   c) Hermann Ebbinghaus.
   b) William James.   d) Wilhelm Wundt.

2. The early American psychologist who founded the school of "functionalism," which emphasized the evolutionary importance of human consciousness, and who taught the first psychology course in a college was

   a) Sigmund Freud.   c) Alfred Binet.
   b) William James.   d) Wilhelm Wundt.

3. The physician who founded psychoanalysis and its study of the unconscious mind and abnormal behavior was

   a) Sigmund Freud.   c) Alfred Binet.
   b) William James.   d) Max Wertheimer.

● Thinking Critically About Psychology

1. Each founder of psychology focused on a different aspect of behavior and mental processes. If you had been one of the founders, on what topic do you think you would have focused?
2. Can you think of barriers that exist today to the success of women and minorities in scientific and professional fields that psychologists could study and help eliminate?

Correct Answers 1. **d** (p. 7), 2. **b** (p. 8), 3. **a** (p. 11).

▶ CONTEMPORARY PERSPECTIVES IN PSYCHOLOGY

We have just looked at several viewpoints in psychology that emerged in the work of a number of turn-of-the-century scientists. Each perspective had different interests and assumptions about human nature, so each defined the methods and subject matter of psychology in a different way. As you can imagine, the debates between adherents of these different points of view were often very heated in the early days of psychology.

Where are we today in psychology? No single point of view from the early days has emerged as the correct way of viewing human behavior and mental processes. Contemporary psychology could be said to combine the best ideas from all of its founders. In some ways, the impact of their intermingled ideas is even more important than the original schools of thought.

Before we begin studying the methods and findings of psychology, it is important for us to look at two other perspectives that strongly influence contemporary psychology, the neuroscience perspective and sociocultural perspective.

Neuroscience Perspective

Psychologists have long been interested in the relationship between our psychological nature and our biological nature, particularly our brains. Spanish scientist Santiago Ramón y Cajal first identified *neurons*—the cells that make up the brain and nervous system—in the early 1900s. His view that the brain was made up of a network of interacting neural cells laid the foundation for our modern understanding of the role of the brain in psychology.

Psychologists who approach the science from the **neuroscience perspective** are interested in the structures of the brain that play roles in emotion, reasoning, speaking, and other psychological processes. They seek to determine the extent to which our psychological characteristics, such as intelligence and emotional stability, are influenced by heredity. Neuroscientists study the chemical substances that carry messages in the nervous system from one neuron to another, and they examine how some drugs, such as cocaine and marijuana, alter the action of these important brain chemicals. Similarly, neuroscientists conduct experiments on the role of hormones in the regulation of behavior.

Sociocultural Perspective

An important perspective that has emerged in psychology in recent years is termed the **sociocultural perspective.** Like social learning theory, the sociocultural approach is based on the assumption that our personalities, beliefs, attitudes, and skills are learned from others. The sociocultural approach goes further, however, in stating that it is impossible to fully understand a person without understanding his or her culture, ethnic identity, gender identity, and other important sociocultural factors (Miller, 1999; Phinney, 1996a).

For example, we are all shaped by our culture and must be understood in that context. **Culture** is defined as the patterns of behavior, beliefs, and values that are shared by a group of people. Culture includes everything—from language and superstitions to moral beliefs and food preferences—that we learn from the people with whom we live. When I worked in Miami for 3 years, I met many persons who were born in Cuba and had moved to the United States. They brought with them all of the beliefs, attitudes, and ways of Cuban culture, but they are now part of the culture of the United States. To fully understand my Miami friends, you would need to understand the ways in which Cuban and U.S. cultures are similar and different and how each has influenced their lives.

In addition, we must all be understood in terms of our ethnic group and ethnic identity. An **ethnic group** is a group of persons who are descendants of a common group of ancestors, usually from a particular country or area. **Ethnic identity** refers to each person's sense of belonging to a particular ethnic group and of sharing that group's beliefs, attitudes, skills, music, ceremonies, and the like. Members of less powerful ethnic groups in a country also often share a history of discrimination and repression by more powerful ethnic groups.

Members of an ethnic group often share similar racial characteristics. Knowing a person's race is often less informative than knowing his or her ethnic identity, however. For example, my friend Maria is an immigrant to the United States from San Salvador. She grew up speaking Spanish and learned English only after moving to the United States as a teenager. She sees herself as a Hispanic, but she is of African descent and also identifies strongly with her fellow African Americans. Her racial heritage, then, reveals only part of her sense of ethnic identity. To take another example, my friend Barbara says that three of her grandparents are white and one is African American. In racial terms, she is not mostly of African descent, but she was raised by her parents in a mostly African American neighborhood in Los Angeles and proudly considers herself to be an African American. In the case of both of these women, understanding their ethnic identity will lead to more understanding of them as persons than just knowing their race.

Santiago Ramón y Cajal (1852–1934).

neuroscience perspective
The viewpoint in psychology that focuses on the nervous system in explaining behavior and mental processes.

sociocultural perspective
The theory of psychology that states that it is necessary to understand one's culture, ethnic identity, and other sociocultural factors to fully understand a person.

culture
The patterns of behavior, beliefs, and values shared by a group of people.

ethnic group
A group of persons who are descendants of a common group of ancestors.

ethnic identity
Each person's sense of belonging to a particular ethnic group.

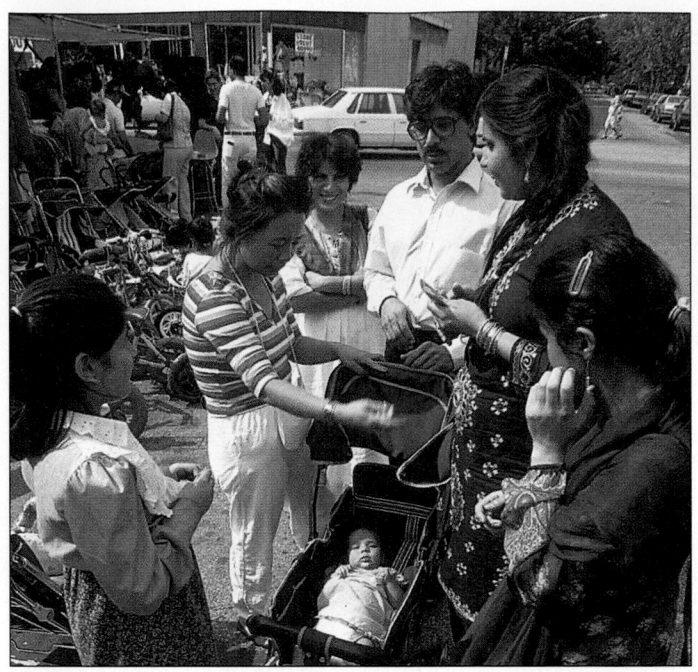

Ethnic identity refers to each person's sense of belonging to a particular ethnic group and of sharing that group's beliefs, attitudes, skills, music, ceremonies, and the like.

gender identity
One's view of oneself as male or female.

cultural relativity
The perspective that promotes thinking of different cultures in relative terms rather than judgmental terms.

A third term that is important to the sociocultural perspective is **gender identity.** This term refers to one's view of oneself as male or female. As boys and girls interact with their parents, siblings, teachers, and friends, they learn what it means to be a male or female in their society. In the United States, for example, males traditionally have been taught to be strong and assertive, whereas females have been taught to be nurturing and gentle. And, although strides have been made in recent years to reduce the shaping of the two genders into narrow sex roles, the impact of socialization of this sort has had an impact on each of our gender identities.

According to the sociocultural perspective, all of us can be fully understood only if our culture, ethnic identity, and gender identity are taken into consideration. Other sociocultural factors must be considered as well. For example, gay men and lesbian women have identities as homosexuals that shape their lives. Similarly, women and men who have integrated a feminist perspective into their lives must be understood partly in that context. Any social or cultural force that influences human lives is important to the sociocultural perspective.

The sociocultural perspective not only encourages us to consider cultural and social factors when attempting to understand a neighbor or coworker but also requires that we not *misuse* that information. Two aspects of this perspective are particularly relevant to our discussion. First, the sociocultural perspective promotes **cultural relativity.** Although virtually every culture in the world views other cultures as inferior to itself (Triandis, 1991), the sociocultural perspective encourages us to think of different cultures in *relative* terms rather than judgmental terms. That is, the sociocultural perspective promotes the view that different cultures, ethnic groups, genders, and sexual orientations are simply *different* from, rather than inferior to, another. Indeed, the sociocultural perspective encourages us to view differences among persons in our diverse world as rich sources of new ideas and ways of coping with the demands of human life.

Second, the sociocultural perspective reminds us that not all members of a given culture, ethnic group, or gender are *alike.* Some Asian men, for example, are tall and some are short; some are good at mathematics and some are not. The same is true of any sociocultural group. On most characteristics (moral beliefs, interest in music, willingness to work hard in school, sports ability, etc.), there are usually more differences among persons *within* each group than *between* different groups.

The United States is rapidly becoming a multicultural and multiethnic country. In 1989, 20 percent of all youth (up to 17 years of age) were members of minority ethnic groups. By the year 2000, that proportion grew to over 33 percent. If the United States is to continue to succeed and prosper, we must all learn to understand one another better and to extend more opportunity to groups that have been held at the bottom of the economic ladder by the kind of prejudice and discrimination that comes from lack of understanding.

▶ SPECIALTY AREAS OF MODERN PSYCHOLOGY

Psychology is, as we have seen, an unusually broad and diverse field. From the very beginnings of psychology, different founders studied different aspects of human behavior and declared their own theories and methods to be the correct way to look at psychology. Theoretical divisions still exist today, but the greatest diversity in modern psychology is in terms of subject-matter specialties. Even though a basic core of knowledge is shared by all psychologists, the interests and expertise of a psychologist who studies the sense of taste, for example, are distinct from those of one who evaluates employees in a large company

HUMAN DIVERSITY

DIFFERENT YET THE SAME

It could be said that the theme of this book involves two opposite concepts. As will be said often throughout this book, all people are the same in some fundamentally important ways and yet different in other equally important ways. We are the same in the sense that the principles of psychology apply equally to all of us. Your brain has the same working parts whether you are a woman of Chinese descent who was raised in Holland or a man of Swedish descent raised in Minneapolis. In the same sense, the principles of perception, motivation, learning, and personality also apply to all human beings. But people are also different from one another. Their gender, cultural heritage, genes, age, sexual orientation, and unique experiences all contribute to these differences. What is your age, gender, and ethnic heritage? How well educated are the members of your family? What is your political philosophy and your sexual orientation? If all of these things about you were different, would you be a different person in any important ways? I am not asking if you would be a better or a worse person, because we are not talking of value judgments here. I am only asking if you would be psychologically *different*.

What are the sociocultural factors that must be understood to understand people? We will look at many such factors throughout this text, but one sociocultural factor that will be discussed in many contexts is the differences between persons raised in individualistic and collectivistic cultures (Kitayama & others, 1997; Miller, 1999). As the name implies, individualistic cultures (such as the mainstream U.S. culture) emphasize the importance of individual rights, goals, and accomplishments. Persons in such cultures tend to feel good about themselves if they believe that they are smarter, stronger, richer, funnier, better looking, and more successful than other people. They believe that it is perfectly acceptable to make a profit by selling something to another person for more than they paid for it (free enterprise).

People raised in collectivistic cultures such as Japan, China, and India, however, place much greater emphasis on performing the expected role in the family, company, and broader society. The focus is not on individual accomplishment but on the individual's contributions and obligations to the group. Equal sharing of resources seems more appropriate

than making a profit off a fellow citizen in collectivistic countries. While North Americans are likely to compliment themselves on a job well done, the Japanese are likely to criticize themselves after the same good performance to help themselves better play the role expected by the group in the future (Kitayama & others, 1997; Miller, 1999). Although not everyone holds the same views in individualistic and collectivistic nations, it is not possible to understand people of different cultures without understanding these marked differences.

During the past decade, many psychologists have come to believe that the basic course in psychology overemphasizes the ways in which people are the same and neglects the important message that the human race comes in a rainbow of sociocultural varieties. Therefore, a boxed feature termed *Human Diversity* appears in every chapter in this text to further counteract the false impression that all human beings are the same in the eyes of psychology. These boxed statements will explore differences related to gender, ethnicity, age, physical disability, and other factors.

Therefore, it would be fair to say that this text takes a "sociocultural" approach, as described in this chapter. As you read this text, please keep in mind that human diversity is discussed in every chapter to help us understand the broad natural range of differences among human beings. Those differences are never discussed in evaluative terms, but simply as elements of the human condition. While it will be said, for example, that males and females are different in some ways, those differences will never be taken to mean that one gender is superior to the other. The same holds for differences associated with ethnic groups and all other sociocultural factors.

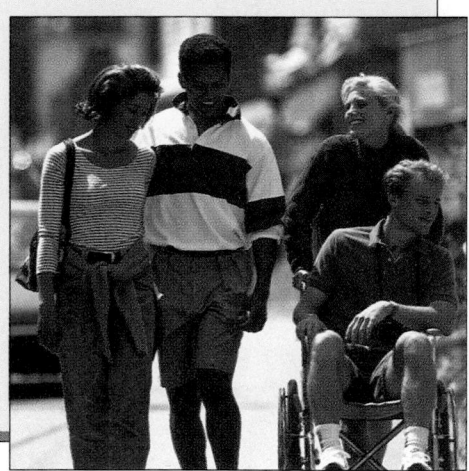

for possible promotion to management positions, or those of one who works in a mental health clinic. Contemporary psychologists can be roughly divided into two groups: those who work in basic areas and those who work in applied areas of psychology (see fig. 1.4). Psychologists in the basic areas conduct research on psychological processes such as emotion, thinking, learning, prejudice, and gender identity by using the scientific methods described in the next section of this chapter. **Applied psychologists** use knowledge acquired by psychologists in the basic areas, and by their own applied research studies, to solve and prevent significant human problems, such as emotional instability, marital difficulties, underachievement in school, and job dissatisfaction.

applied psychologists
Psychologists who use knowledge of psychology to solve and prevent human problems.

FIGURE 1.4

The percentage of psychologists engaged in each of the major basic and applied fields within psychology.

Source: Based on data from J. Stapp, et al., "Census of Psychological Personnel: 1983," in *American Psychologist,* 12:1317–1351. Copyright ©1985 by the American Psychological Association.

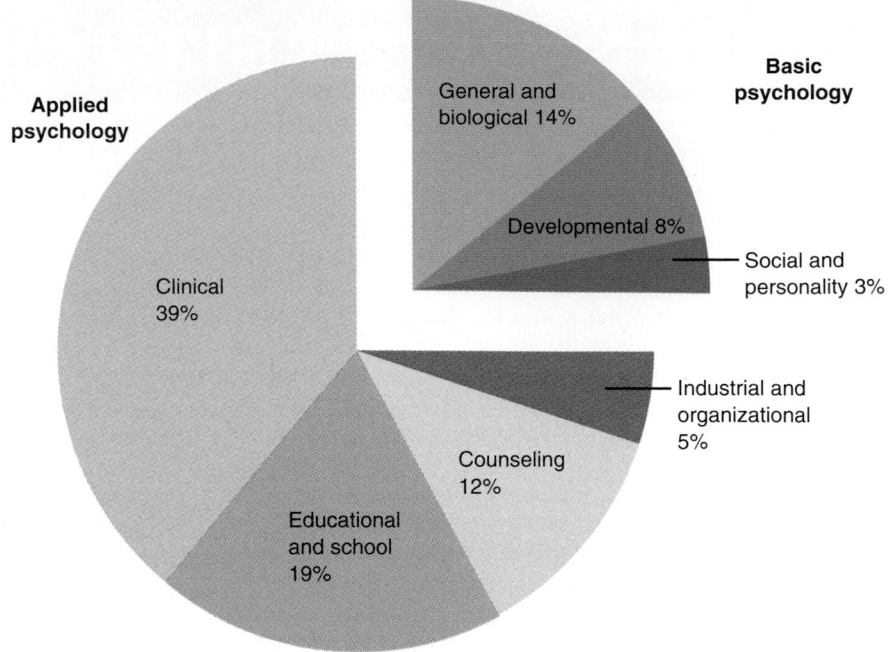

Basic Areas of Modern Psychology

About one-fourth of all psychologists work in basic experimental areas of psychology (Stapp, Tucker, & VandenBos, 1985). They are broadly trained, but they tend to specialize in the study of a single psychological process. Most psychologists in the basic areas work in colleges and universities, where they teach and conduct research, but some work in research institutions, government agencies, or other settings. Their domain is the basic knowledge of psychology on which all applications are built. The largest specialties within the basic experimental areas of psychology are as follows:

1. *Biological psychology.* Psychologists in this specialty field study the ways in which the nervous system and other organs provide the basis for behavior. Biological psychologists also study animal behavior, both to compare it with human behavior and to gain a better understanding of other species.

2. *Sensation and perception.* This specialty is concerned with how the sense organs operate and how we interpret incoming sensory information in the process of perception.

3. *Learning and memory.* The ways in which we learn and remember new information, new skills, new habits, and new ways of relating to other people are studied in this specialty.

4. *Cognition.* Psychologists in this area are concerned with intelligent action: thinking, perceiving, planning, imagining, creating, dreaming, speaking, listening, and problem solving.

5. *Developmental psychology.* This field of psychology is concerned with changes that take place in people during their life span, as they grow from birth to old age.

6. *Motivation and emotion.* In this specialty, psychologists study the needs and states that activate and guide behavior, such as hunger, thirst, sex, the need for achievement, and the need to have relationships with others. The nature of the feelings and moods that color human experience is also a topic of this specialty.

7. *Personality.* The field of personality focuses on the more or less consistent ways of behaving that characterize our personalities.

8. *Social psychology.* This specialty area studies the influence of other people on our behavior: the behavior of people in groups, mobs, or organizations; interpersonal attraction and intimate relationships; and attitudes and prejudice toward others.

9. *Sociocultural psychology.* Psychologists in this area focus on ethnic and cultural factors, gender identity, sexual orientation, and related issues. Scholars in African American psychology, Hispanic psychology, and Asian psychology have a long tradition of work in this area, but great advances in interest in other ethnic groups have been made in recent years. Feminist psychology and gay and lesbian psychology are other key areas of sociocultural scholarship.

Applied Areas of Modern Psychology

The other three-fourths of psychologists use basic psychological knowledge to solve human problems (see fig. 1.4). Some applied psychologists teach and do research, but most work in mental health centers, industries, school systems, medical centers, and other applied settings. The following are the major specialties within applied psychology:

1. *Clinical psychology.* Clinical psychologists try to understand and treat emotional problems and correct abnormal behavior.

2. *Counseling psychology.* Specialists in this field help people with personal or school problems and with career choices.

3. *Industrial and organizational psychology.* This field focuses on ways to match employees to jobs, to train and motivate workers, and to promote job satisfaction and good relationships among workers.

4. *Educational and school psychology.* Educational psychology is concerned with the ways children learn in the classroom and with the construction of psychological and educational tests. School psychologists consult with teachers about children who are experiencing learning or behavioral problems, and they test children to see whether they could benefit from special educational programs.

5. *Health psychology.* Specialists in this field focus on the ways in which pressures, conflicts, hardships, and other factors contribute to poor health. They seek to prevent health problems such as heart disease by teaching people to relax, exercise, control their diets, and stop high-risk behaviors, such as smoking.

The distinction between the basic and applied fields is not hard and fast. Often psychologists in the experimental fields work on important applied topics. There is something in psychology to interest or help just about everyone. If you glance ahead, you will see that the chapters of this book are organized to cover these experimental and applied facets of psychology.

Relationship Between Psychology and Psychiatry

Perhaps the question most often asked of a psychology instructor is, "What is the difference between a psychologist and a psychiatrist?" Although there are many similarities, there are numerous differences as well. A psychiatrist has completed medical school and has obtained the M.D. (doctor of medicine) degree, and has completed residency training in psychiatry. Although some psychiatrists work as researchers, most are practitioners in clinics who see patients with emotional or behavioral problems. Because of their medical training, psychiatrists are licensed to prescribe drugs and use other medical treatments.

A psychologist has been trained in psychology but has not attended medical school. Psychology is a much broader field than psychiatry and contains many different specialty areas. The specialty within psychology that is most similar to psychiatry is clinical psychology. Clinical psychologists have attended graduate school in psychology, have obtained the degree of Ph.D. (doctor of philosophy) or Psy.D. (doctor of psychology), and have completed an internship in clinical psychology. Because they do not have medical training, they do not prescribe drugs or other medical treatments.

In addition to these professions, people with psychological problems often also seek help from clinical social workers, counselors, and other individuals. It is worth noting, however, that, although nearly every state regulates the practice of clinical psychology, psychiatry, and clinical social work, most states do not regulate other helping professions. That means that persons with no training in psychology or any related field can advertise themselves as a "counselor" or "therapist" in many states. It's good advice, then, to ask about the training and professional background of anyone who is not licensed in her or his profession by the state.

● Review

The sociocultural perspective emphasizes the need to understand persons in the context of the cultural, ethnic, and gender identities that shape their lives. In recent years a growth in the importance of the neuroscience perspective has helped us better understand the relationship between the biological functioning of the brain and other parts of the body and our behavior and mental processes.

Generally, contemporary psychologists do not align themselves with a single theoretical position. Rather, they integrate the best contributions of each perspective into their own eclectic view. Although it is useful to study the different theoretical perspectives within psychology, it is also important to look at how psychologists divide the subject matter of psychology. Psychology can be divided into its basic areas, which use a variety of scientific methods to study psychological processes, and applied areas, which apply psychological knowledge to the solution of human problems. Each of these two major divisions of psychology can be further subdivided in terms of the specific subject matter studied or the kind of human problems to which the application is addressed.

● Check Your Learning

To be sure that you have learned the key points from the preceding section, cover the list of correct answers and try to answer each question. If you give an incorrect answer to any question, return to the page given next to the correct answer to see why your answer was not correct.

1. The approach that states that a person can be understood only in terms of her or his experiences related to culture, ethnicity, and gender that shape human lives is termed the

   a) psychodynamic perspective.   c) humanistic perspective.

   b) cognitive perspective.   d) sociocultural perspective.

2. The scientist who first discovered neurons (individual nerve cells) in the brain was

   a) B. F. Skinner.   c) Santiago Ramón y Cajal.

   b) Ivan Pavlov.   d) Margaret Floy Washburn.

3. The basic area of psychology that studies intimate relationships and prejudice is

   a) neuroscience.   c) counseling psychology.

   b) health psychology.   d) social psychology.

● Thinking Critically About Psychology

1. Which of the contemporary perspectives in psychology makes the most sense to you? Do any of these perspectives seem to have no value whatsoever?
2. Do you think that the ethnic identity or gender identity of a psychologist would influence the way in which she or he does research or counsels others? Should it?
3. In terms of helping solve an important social problem, such as crime, which basic or applied area of psychology do you think is most important?

▶ SCIENTIFIC METHODS: HOW WE LEARN ABOUT BEHAVIOR AND MENTAL PROCESSES

As we mentioned earlier, psychologists use scientific methods to describe, predict, understand, and influence behavior. But although it is easy to see how we might use the methods of science to study chemicals in a test tube, it is sometimes difficult to see how something as varied, complex, and apparently unpredictable as human behavior can be the subject matter of science. How can this be?

First, all scientists must believe that their subject matter is orderly and lawful before they begin their research. For example, if astronomers felt that the planets wandered aimlessly and randomly through space, they would have little reason to study their paths. The same is true of people. To have a science of psychology, we must believe that human behavior is at least somewhat predictable. Often, though, we see ourselves as capable of doing whatever we choose without being subject to the laws of nature. Although there may be some truth to that, psychologists believe that our behavior is much more orderly and predictable than most of us think.

I regularly begin teaching my own course in psychology with a disguised demonstration that human behavior is actually fairly predictable under some circumstances. It's a little corny, but it makes the point. After telling the students that I'm a very democratic fellow, I ask the class to decide how they want to be evaluated in the course. I tell them that I have to require a cumulative final examination, but that everything else is open to a vote! I give them the option of doing a term paper (to give them a way of being evaluated that is free from the pressure of classroom testing), and I also give them the options of having one, two, or three tests plus the final, or no tests plus the final. Then I take a vote.

In every class, a couple of students vote for the term paper (one student who writes well and one who thinks I'm too lazy to read the papers), but that option is always soundly defeated. A few students vote for no test or one test, and about 20 percent vote for two tests, but about three-quarters always choose three tests plus the final.

When the voting is over, I thank the students for their judicious decision and hand out the course syllabus. Then I point out that I correctly predicted their behavior—that 250 copies of the syllabus have already been printed that include no requirement of a term paper and give the dates of three tests plus the final examination. After the laughing, booing, and hissing have subsided, I say something like, "The science of psychology rests on the assumption that your behavior is a good deal more predictable than you might think. That's not to take anything away from the mysteries and complexities of human existence; it's just to say that we aren't immune to the laws of nature. We're predictable enough to study scientifically."

In the sections that follow, we will briefly examine three general types of **scientific methods** used by psychologists—descriptive methods, correlational methods, and formal experiments. We will also examine some of the more specific strategies that psychologists employ in attempting to reach the goals of the science of psychology.

scientific methods
Methods of gathering information based on systematic observation.

Descriptive Methods

As mentioned earlier, a number of rather different scientific methods are used in psychology, each with its own advantages and disadvantages. The different methods are best suited for answering different kinds of questions, so they tend to be relied upon to varying extent by individual specialties within psychology. The simplest methods of scientific inquiry involve description. Three descriptive methods are used in psychology: surveys, naturalistic observation, and the clinical method.

Survey Method

One of the most direct ways to answer a question about people is simply to ask the question of many people, called the **survey method.** Surveys are perhaps most widely used

survey method
A research method that utilizes interviews and questionnaires with individuals in the community.

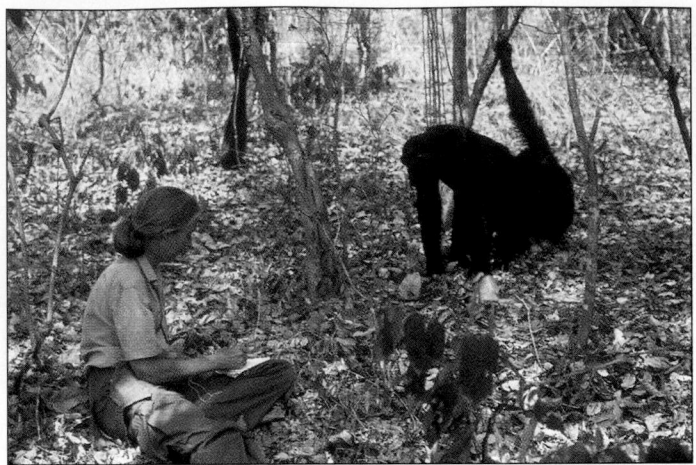

Jane Goodall

today by psychologists interested in consumer opinions about television programs, soft drinks, political candidates, and similar subjects. Surveys are frequently used for other purposes as well. For example, the myth-shattering surveys of sex researcher Alfred Kinsey (Kinsey, Pomeroy, & Martin, 1948) revealed that the number of people who engage in masturbation and extramarital intercourse was much higher in the general population than expected at the time.

Naturalistic Observation

Another straightforward way to learn about behavior is simply to watch and describe it as it naturally occurs. The careful observation and recording of behavior in real-life settings is called **naturalistic observation.** When internationally known scientist Jane Goodall goes to Africa, sits down in the jungle, and watches a troop of apes, she is using the method of naturalistic observation. She watches the apes in their natural habitat over long periods of time, taking careful notes of what she sees until specific patterns of behavior become evident. Using this method, she and her coworkers have learned that the social behavior and use of some tools by apes is often strikingly similar to that of humans. Sadly, she has discovered that apes are also capable of murder—ambushing and killing other apes over relatively minor incidents in a way that looks "intentional."

The method of naturalistic observation is not restricted to the study of animal behavior. It's a method also used to study such topics as the play and friendship patterns of young children, the leadership tactics of effective business managers, and the ways in which juvenile delinquents encourage antisocial behavior in one another.

"Don't shush me—and I don't care if she IS writing in her little notebook; just tell me where you were last night!"

THE FAR SIDE cartoon by Gary Larson is reprinted by permission of Chronicle Features, San Francisco, CA. All rights reserved.

naturalistic observation
A research method based on recording behavior as it occurs in natural life settings.

clinical method
The method of studying people while they are receiving psychological help from a psychologist.

Clinical Method

An important variation on naturalistic observation is the **clinical method,** which simply involves observing people while they receive help from a psychologist for their psychological problems. Although clinical observation is not as useful as observing people in the natural situations where they encounter problems—at home, school, or work—it does provide useful information. Sigmund Freud, for example, developed his theories of abnormal behavior from years of intensive work with patients in his "consulting room." He was able to observe their behavior in this one situation over long periods of time until he felt he saw consistent patterns in what they did, thought, and felt. The clinical method is also often used today for the preliminary evaluation of clinical treatment methods. For example, daily measures of anxiety might be taken on an individual before, during, and after treatment to evaluate a new method of treating excessive anxiety.

Correlational Method

Suppose that a few years after graduation, you are asked to be the vice-president in charge of sales for a major toothbrush manufacturer. Your first assignment is to hire a group of new sales representatives to do something that has never been tried—to sell toothbrushes in little booths in shopping malls. You want to choose the best sales personnel, but you are not sure what characteristics they should have. For example, should they be intelligent? Intelligent salespeople might be able to think of clever ways to interest customers in your toothbrushes, but on the other hand, they might get bored spending every day selling such a commonplace product in shopping malls. In other words, it would not be possible to predict whether highly intelligent salespeople would be effective or ineffective based on commonsense reasoning. What should you do? You need to conduct a correlational study to see whether you can predict good sales performance on the basis of intelligence.

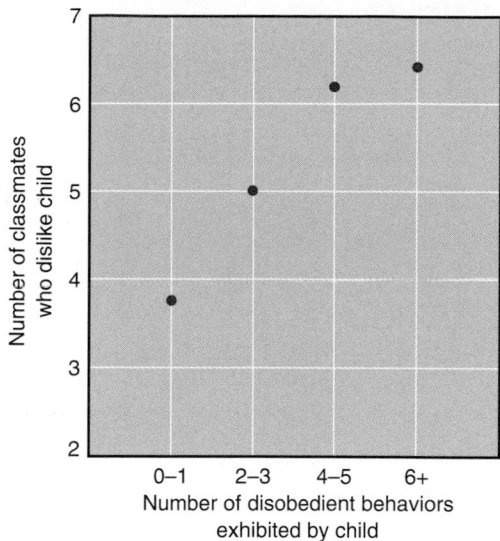

FIGURE 1.5

Example of a correlational study. Children who engage in more disobedient behaviors (fighting, lying, stealing, etc.) tend to be disliked by more of their classmates.

Being able to predict behavior and mental processes is the goal of psychological studies using the **correlational method.** This research method requires a knowledge of the relationship between two or more psychological variables. A **variable** is anything that can be measured and whose numerical value can vary. For example, intelligence is a variable because it can be measured (using an intelligence test) and because people vary in intelligence. Similarly, sales effectiveness can be measured, in this case, in terms of the number of toothbrushes sold. You would conduct your correlational study simply by measuring the intelligence of a number of salespeople and by measuring the number of toothbrushes each sold. You might find that salespeople with higher intelligence scores would be found to sell more toothbrushes. Because many other factors probably also influence sales performance (e.g., attractiveness, sense of humor, and emotional stability), its relationship to intelligence would not be a perfect one, but it might be strong enough to be useful. If so, you would want to hire mostly highly intelligent salespeople.

Let's look at an actual example of the use of the correlational method from my own research. As part of a larger study of the origins of juvenile delinquency, we wanted to test the commonsense notion that elementary schoolchildren who are disobedient are disliked by their classmates. The correlation between these two variables is shown in figure 1.5. As you can see, children who have more serious behavior problems (fighting, lying, stealing, etc.) tend to be disliked by more of their classmates. So, not surprisingly, having behavior problems is correlated to a considerable extent with being disliked by your peers.

When interpreting correlational data, we must remember that a relationship between two variables does not mean that one causes the other. The correlation between behavior problems and unpopularity may mean that having behavior problems leads other children to dislike the disobedient child, but it could also mean that being unpopular is so upsetting to some children that it leads them to develop behavior problems. Correlations tell us very little about which variable is the cause in cause-and-effect relationships. In fact, correlations often exist between two variables that are not causally related at all. For example, it could be that having abusive parents causes children to be both disobedient and unpopular, but that disobedience and unpopularity are not causally related to each other. We must be very careful about drawing conclusions from correlational evidence.

Formal Experiments

The most useful scientific method of observation is the **formal experiment.** Experiments are particularly helpful in reaching the goals of understanding and influencing behavior.

 Correlational Method

www.mmhe.com/laheye1

correlational method
kor″ēlā′shun-al)
A research method that measures the strength of the relation between variables.

variable
A factor whose numerical value can change.

formal experiment
Research method that allows the researcher to manipulate the independent variable to study its effect on the dependent variable.

FIGURE 1.6

Example of a formal experiment. The percentage of pedestrians who stopped to help a man with an arm cast who had dropped his books is compared under conditions of low and high noise.

Source: Data for graph from K. E. Mathews and L. K. Cannon, in *Journal of Personality and Social Psychology,* 32:571–577, 1975.

quantitative measures
(kwon´ti-tā-tiv)   Capable of being measured in numerical terms.

Like the correlational method, experiments are designed to tell us about the relationship between two or more variables. Unlike other methods, however, the experiment involves deliberate arrangement of the variables involved. And unlike correlational methods, a carefully conducted experiment allows the researcher to draw conclusions about cause-and-effect relationships with more confidence.

The heart of an experiment is the comparison of **quantitative measures** of behavior under different conditions. For example, we have all heard about the supposedly damaging effects of "noise pollution." Do high levels of noise have a negative effect on our behavior and mental processes? Two psychologists (Mathews & Canon, 1975) conducted a simple, but very informative, study to shed experimental light on this question. They examined the effects of high levels of noise on one of the more admirable aspects of human behavior—our tendency to help others when they are in need. In this experiment, a person wearing a cast on his arm emerged from a car and dropped a large pile of books in front of a pedestrian. If you were the pedestrian, would you have stopped to help him pick up his books? You might not have if there had been a lot of noise in the background. Remember, the purpose of an experiment is to compare measures of helping behavior under different levels of noise. In this case, the number of people who stopped to help was compared under conditions of high noise (when a lawn mower without a muffler was running) or low noise (when no lawn mower was running). Figure 1.6 illustrates the results of this study. When there was little noise in the background, over five times as many pedestrians stopped to help the fellow with the broken arm than when there was a high noise level.

An important advantage of formal experiments is that they allow us to control the influence of variables other than those on which the experiment focuses. The goal is to eliminate all explanations for differences between the groups except the relevant one. This was accomplished in the study of noise levels by not changing anything in the two conditions except the amount of noise that the two groups received.

The number of people who stopped to help in the experiment on noise is termed the **dependent variable** because its value depends on the effects of the noise. The amount of noise is the **independent variable,** because the experimenter can independently control it. All formal experiments have at least one independent and one dependent variable. In the simplest experiments, one group receives none of the independent variable and is called the **control group.** The group that receives the independent variable is called the **experimental group.** Often there is more than one experimental group (the researchers could have exposed three experimental groups to different levels of noise), and sometimes there is more than one control group designed to rule out different alternative explanations for the results of the study.

Dependent Variable

www.mmhe.com/laheye1

Independent Variable

www.mmhe.com/laheye1

Through the logic and control of experiments, it's possible to test hypotheses about causal relationships. That is the primary advantage of formal experiments over other scientific methods. For all their utility, however, experiments also have their drawbacks. First and foremost, all experiments require some degree of artificiality. Remember that experiments allow the researcher to create and control conditions. In doing so, scientists risk creating experiments that are so artificial that the findings are difficult to apply to the real world, or they may even be entirely inapplicable. For example, the results of studies of crowding due to overpopulation in which college students are crowded into small rooms for an hour may not have much relevance to the long-term effects of crowded urban living conditions.

Second, experiments can also lead us to believe that because a scientist conducted them, the conclusions are necessarily valid. Experiments are complicated affairs and even the best experimenters make errors. We should be careful when evaluating experimental conclusions to question the logic, control, and relevance of the experiment. Finally, the power of formal experiments often leads us to reject the other scientific methods. Each method is valid within its restrictions and weaknesses. Psychology, like all sciences, depends on a blend of scientific methods and a healthy skepticism about their results.

Ethical Principles of Research

Psychological research is conducted to advance knowledge and improve the lives of all living things. It is a noble goal, but not so noble that any method of conducting research would be justifiable. To be considered ethical, research conducted on humans and animals must follow the ethical principles described in the next two sections.

Ethics of Research with Human Participants

Psychology depends heavily on research conducted with human participants for its database. But while researchers have an obligation to collect meaningful information through research, they also have an ethical responsibility to protect the welfare of their participants. Often the ethics of research with humans pose complicated issues for the researcher—issues that do not have simple solutions. As a human being, and especially as one who may be asked to serve as a participant in psychological research, you may wish to review some of the key ethical issues involved in psychological research with humans. A more complete discussion of these issues can be found in the American Psychological Association's Ethics in Research with Human Participants (Sales & Folkman, 2000).

1. *Freedom from Coercion.* It's not ethical to coerce or pressure an individual into participating in an experiment. Students in college courses, for example, cannot be required to participate. They must be given an alternative way to meet any course requirement. Similarly, it would be considered unethical to offer special consideration in parole hearings to prisoners who volunteer to participate in psychological studies, since the promise of special considerations might constitute undue coercion.

2. *Informed Consent.* The experimenter must, under most circumstances, give potential participants a full description of the experiment in language they can understand before they are asked to participate. It's not ethical to allow individuals to participate in an experiment without knowing what they are getting into. Furthermore, once the experiment has begun, it must be made clear to participants that they are fully free to change their minds and withdraw from the experiment without penalty, such as embarrassment, loss of course credit, and so on.

3. *Limited Deception.* Sometimes it's necessary to conduct experiments without the participant's knowing the true purpose of the study. Current ethical guidelines state that deceptions can be used only if two conditions are met. First, the potential participants must be told everything they could reasonably be expected to need to know to make an informed decision about participation. That is, the deception can only involve aspects of the study that do not influence the decision to participate. Second, the nature

dependent variable
The variable whose quantitative value depends on the effects of the independent variable.

independent variable
The variable whose quantitative value can be independently controlled by the researcher.

control group
The group in simple experiments that receives none of the independent variable and is used for comparisons with the treatment group.

experimental group
The group in an experiment that receives some value of the independent variable.

of the deception must be fully revealed to individuals immediately after their participation in the experiment. Only under these conditions is it considered ethical to deceive research participants.

4. *Adequate Debriefing.* Research participants have a right to know the results of the study. Current practice dictates that all persons be provided with a summary of the study in language they can understand. If the results are not immediately available, the participants have a right to receive it when it is available.

5. *Confidentiality.* Researchers have an obligation to keep everything that they learn about the research participant absolutely confidential. This means that data from the study must be published in a way that protects the anonymity of the participants (no names or detailed descriptions of individuals). In addition, data must be stored without names attached in most cases to protect against future abuses of the information.

These are not all of the ethical issues raised by psychological research with humans, but they are some of the major ones. All institutions where research is conducted now require that proposals for human experimentation be approved by a board of other scientists to protect individuals from potential abuses.

Ethics of Research with Non-human Animal Subjects

A great deal of research is also carried out using nonhuman animals as subjects. Why would some psychologists study animals when they could be studying people? There are a number of important reasons why psychologists study animal behavior.

Some kinds of studies are conducted using animals because it would be unethical to do the research to humans. Studies of the brain, for example, sometimes require surgically removing a part of the brain to discover its precise role in behavior. For similar reasons, studies in which infants are isolated from all social contact to study the absence of parental and peer relationships on development must be conducted with animals rather than humans. Although we must be very careful not to assume automatically that what is learned about animal behavior will apply to human behavior, much useful information has been learned from animal research.

In addition, it's possible to conduct experiments that are far more precisely controlled if we use animals rather than humans. A researcher can know and control almost every detail of a laboratory animal's life from birth: its environment, diet, and social experiences. This makes it possible to control a multiplicity of factors that must be left uncontrolled when using humans.

A great deal can be learned also by comparing the behavior of animals of different species. For example, a number of insights about human aggression have come from studies of aggression in other animal species. Similarly, much has been learned about the brain structures involved in sleep by identifying animals who have differing sleep patterns and comparing the evolutionary development of the sleep centers in these different species. Furthermore, many psychologists study animal behavior not to learn about humans but to learn more about other animal species. If we are going to protect endangered species, we must understand their patterns of behavior. We must know, for example, how an endangered species hunts, mates, and raises its young before we can protect its ability to survive.

As with human participants, a number of principles govern the ethical conduct of research with animal subjects in psychology. Research with animals is considered ethical by the American Psychological Association only when all of the following conditions are met:

1. *Necessity.* Studies of animals are considered to be ethical only when they are necessary to significantly advance the understanding of human or animal behavior and mental processes.

2. *Health.* All animal subjects must be cared for in a manner that ensures good health.

3. *Humane treatment.* Every effort must be made to minimize the discomfort of the animal subject. Necessary surgery must be performed under anesthesia, and the

The use of animals in research has received a great deal of public attention in recent years due to the activities of animal rights groups.

animal's death must be as painless as possible. Studies that inflict pain or stress are considered ethical only when they are considered essential to worthwhile scientific aims.

The use of animals in research has received a great deal of public attention in recent years due to the activities of animal rights groups. Humans have long been concerned with the protection of their fellow animals, however. The Society for the Prevention of Cruelty to Animals was founded in 1824 in London, for example, and the American Psychological Association formed its Committee on Precautions in Animal Experimentation in 1925 (Dewsbury, 1990). Today, oversight committees at all research universities closely monitor all uses of laboratory animals.

● Review

Psychology is a science, which means that it uses scientific methods to gather information and test ideas. Psychologists acquire new information through carefully controlled methods of observation. Although they are many and varied, scientific methods are all based on the assumption that behavior is lawful and orderly and capable of being understood in scientific terms. Each scientific method has different advantages and disadvantages and is best suited to answering different types of questions. The simplest scientific methods are descriptive methods. Information that allows us to describe a psychological phenomenon can be gathered by asking questions about it in surveys, by observing it in natural settings, or through extensive experience with it in clinical cases. When the scientific question concerns the relationship between two variables, correlational methods are often used. Both variables are measured quantitatively and the relationship between the two is noted; however, it's not possible to determine from such information whether one variable causes the other to change. To determine whether cause-and-effect relationships exist, formal experiments must be conducted.

In formal experiments, scientists rigorously control the conditions of the experiment so that only one explanation for the results is likely. In the simplest experiments, one factor—the independent variable—is artificially manipulated by the experimenter to see what effect it has on another variable—the dependent variable. Often one group of participants—the control group—receives none of the independent variable, whereas the independent variable is present in another group—the experimental group. In a study of the effects of alcohol on the memory of a list of words, for example, the alcohol is the independent variable. Alcohol is given to participants in the experimental group and not given to those in the control group, so its effects on the dependent variable, memory of the list, can be determined.

While it's important to conduct psychological research using humans, it's essential that we protect the rights of participants. Individuals must not be coerced in any way into participating and must be informed about the nature of the study before they are asked for their consent to participate. Research participants may be deceived about a study only if (1) the information withheld is not relevant to their decision to participate, and (2) they are informed about the true nature of the study immediately after it's over. Furthermore, the experimenter has an obligation to keep all information learned about the participant in an experiment confidential. Research with animal subjects is similarly considered to be ethical only when (1) the research is necessary, (2) the health of the animal is protected, and (3) pain and suffering are minimized.

● Check Your Learning

To be sure that you have learned the key points from the preceding section, cover the answers below and try to answer each question. If you give an incorrect answer to any question, return to the page given next to the correct answer to see why your answer was not correct.

1. The basis of all scientific methods is systematic _____ .

2. A study of the relationship between intelligence scores and the number of illegal acts committed by teenagers would use which method?

a) naturalistic
c) correlational

b) clinical
d) formal experimental

3. The scientific method that allows the researcher to reach the strongest conclusions about cause and effect is

a) naturalistic.
c) correlational.

b) clinical.
d) formal experimental.

4. Research on humans is considered to be ethical only when the following five conditions are met:

1. _____

2. _____

3. _____

4. _____

5. _____

● Thinking Critically About Psychology

1. In what ways is conducting research in psychology similar to conducting research in other scientific fields, such as biology and chemistry? How is it different?
2. Even though research using animals has produced many beneficial results, not everyone agrees that it should be allowed. How do you think we should balance the rights of animals against the benefits to human society?

Correct Answers 1. observation (p. 19), **2. c** (p. 20), **3. d** (p. 22). **4. absence of coercion, informed consent, limited deception, adequate debriefing, and confidentiality** (p. 23).

● Summary

Chapter 1 defines psychology and previews what psychologists have learned about human behavior.

I. Psychology is defined as "the science of behavior and mental processes."

　A. Psychology is considered to be a science because—like all sciences—knowledge is acquired through systematic observation.

　B. The goals of psychology are to

　　1. describe,

　　2. predict,

　　3. understand,

　　4. and influence behavior and mental processes.

II. Modern psychology developed from the pioneering work of many individuals during the late nineteenth and early twentieth centuries.

　A. Early psychologists who studied the nature of conscious experience included

　　1. Wilhelm Wundt (structuralism)

　　2. Edward Titchener (structuralism)

　　3. J. Henry Alston (structuralism)

　　4. Max Wertheimer (Gestalt psychology)

B. The founder of psychology who focused on the useful functions of conscious mental processes (functionalism) was William James.

C. Early psychologists who focused on observable behavior and the importance of learning (behaviorism) were
  1. Ivan Pavlov
  2. John B. Watson
  3. Margaret Floy Washburn

D. Pioneers of psychology who examined the "unconscious mind" were
  1. Sigmund Freud (psychoanalysis)
  2. Carl Rogers (humanistic psychology)

E. Two modern perspectives that strongly influence contemporary psychology are
  1. The sociocultural perspective, which states that people can be understood only in terms of their culture, gender, and other sociocultural factors.
  2. The neuroscience perspective, which states that we must understand the nature of the nervous system and other biological systems to understand our psychological nature.

F. Modern psychology can be divided into basic and applied areas.
  1. Psychologists working in the basic areas teach and conduct research on the biological basis of behavior, the processes of sensation and perception, learning and memory, cognition, human development, emotion, personality, social behavior, ethnic and gender identity, and sexual orientation.
  2. Applied psychologists put the basic knowledge of psychology to work in helping people. Then they specialize in applied fields, such as clinical treatment, personal or marital counseling, industrial or educational applications, or health psychology.

III. The general scientific method involves careful observation, forming hypotheses, and testing hypotheses against empirical facts.

A. Psychologists use three major scientific methods: descriptive methods, correlational methods, and formal experiments.
  1. Descriptive methods include the use of surveys, naturalistic observation, and clinical methods to describe behavior and mental processes; these help us reach the goal of description.
  2. Correlational methods are used to study the relationships between variables; these help us reach the goal of prediction.
  3. Formal experiments can be used to reach conclusions about cause-and-effect relationships between variables; these help us to reach the goals of understanding and influencing behavior.

B. Experiments usually involve at least one experimental group, which receives the independent variable, and a control group. Differences between the groups in the dependent variable can be said to be caused by the independent variable.

C. Ethical research carefully protects the rights of participants. Research using humans is considered to be ethical when the following conditions are met.
  1. Individuals are asked to participate without coercion.
  2. Individuals are informed about the nature of the experiment before giving consent to participate.
  3. Unnecessary deception of participants is avoided and carefully regulated when required.
  4. The nature of the study is fully explained to the participant after the study is over.
  5. All information learned about the participant is kept confidential.

D. Research involving animals is considered ethical when the following conditions are met.
  1. The study is necessary to understand an important issue concerning behavior and mental processes.
  2. The health of the animal subjects is protected.
  3. The animal subjects are treated humanely.

● Resources

1. The head of Information Technologies at the University of Maryland has prepared a reference guide to Web sites relevant to students of psychology: Wallace, P. M. (1999). *Psychology online* (2nd ed.). Boston: McGraw-Hill. Use any Web site with caution, as there is a lot of misinformation on the Web about psychology.

2. The following three books provide more on the people who founded psychology and their ideas. Kimble, G. A., Wertheimer, M., & White, C. L. (Eds.). (1991). *Portraits of pioneers in psychology.* Washington, DC: American Psychological Association. Benjamin, L. (1997). *A history of psychology* (2nd ed.). Boston: McGraw-Hill. Marks, R. W. (1966). *Great ideas in psychology.* New York: Bantam.

3. Although there are fewer intense debates among psychologists today than in the past, there are still many controversial issues. A fascinating guide to these debates that is designed to encourage critical thinking in students is Slife, B. (1998). *Taking sides: Clashing views on controversial psychological issues* (10th ed.). Boston: McGraw-Hill.

4. For more on the psychological importance of gender, race, and ethnicity, see Garcia, J., & Keough, K. (2000). *Social psychology of gender, race, and ethnicity.* Boston: McGraw-Hill.

5. For an excellent discussion of the psychology of women, along with brief biographies of many women who are prominent in contemporary psychology, see Paludi, M. (1992). *The psychology of women.* Dubuque, IA: Brown & Benchmark.

6. The following are two readable and thought-provoking sources on the psychological forces that influence men in U.S. culture. Graham, S. R. (1992). What does a man want? *American Psychologist, 47,* 837–841. Kilmartin, C. (2000). *The masculine self* (2nd ed.). Boston: McGraw-Hill.

7. For more on international aspects of the sociocultural perspective, see Triandis, H. C. (1994). *Culture and social behavior.* Boston: McGraw-Hill. Betancourt, H., & Lopez, S. R. (1993). The study of culture, ethnicity, and race in American psychology. *American Psychologist, 48,* 629–637. Kitayama, S., Markus, H. R., Masumoto, H., & Norasakkunkit, V. (1997). Individual and collective processes in the construction of the self: Self-enhancement in the United States and self-criticism in Japan. *Journal of Personality and Social Psychology, 72,* 1245–1267.

8. For information on career opportunities in psychology, see American Psychological Association. *A career in psychology.* This can be obtained free from the American Psychological Association, 750 First Street, N.E., Washington, DC 20002–4242, www.apa.org. More detailed information is found in Sternberg, R. J. (1997). *Career paths in psychology: Where your degree can take you.* Washington, DC: APA Books.

9. An extremely readable introduction to scientific research in psychology for students is provided by Meltzoff, J. (1998). *Critical thinking about research: Psychology and related fields.* Washington, DC: American Psychological Association.

10. For more on the protection of animal subjects in research, see Dewsbury, D. A. (1990). Early interactions between animal psychologists and animal activists and the founding of the APA Committee on Precautions in Animal Experimentation. *American Psychologist, 45,* 315–327. Also see Thomas, G. V., & Blackman, D. (1992). The future of animal studies in psychology. *American Psychologist, 47,* 16–79. The position of medical researchers is described in *Science, Medicine, and Animals* by the National Academy of Sciences in 1991, published by National Academy Press in Washington, DC.

11. For a terrific discussion of the validity of psychological experiments, see Anderson, C. A., Lindsay, J. J., & Bushman, B. J. (1999). Research in the psychological laboratory: Truth or triviality? *Current Directions in Psychological Science, 8,* 3–9.

12. For more on the ethics of research using both human and nonhuman animal participants, contact the Web site of the American Psychological Association at www.apa.org/ethics.code.html. This site includes the full text of the latest version of the *Ethical*

Principles of Psychologists and Code of Conduct of the American Psychological Association.

13. For more information on the rights of human research participants that is relevant to college students, see Chastain, G., & Landrum, R. E. (1999). *Protecting human subjects: Departmental subject pools and institutional review boards.* Washington, DC: American Psychological Association.

CHAPTER

2

Biological Foundations of Behavior

PROLOGUE

W here do you live? You probably don't think about it much, but the thinking, feeling, and acting part of you has to have a body to live in. Psychological life depends on biological life for its very existence. This means that the way we behave is influenced to a great extent by the nature of the body. If humans did not have hands that grasp, we might never have learned to write, paint, or play racquetball.

The brain is the part of the body that is most intimately linked to psychological life. A simple experiment conducted by Canadian brain surgeon Wilder Penfield in the 1930s dramatically illustrates the key role played by the brain. Dr. Penfield was conducting surgery on the surface layer of the brain known as the cerebral cortex while the patient was awake during local anesthesia. When Penfield placed a small rod that carried a mild electric current against the brain, there were astonishing results. The patient began to recall in vivid detail an incident from years before. She was in her kitchen, listening to the voice of her little boy playing in the yard. In the background, she could hear the noises of the neighborhood, the cars passing in the street. Penfield was amazed to discover that stimulation of particular spots on the brain could produce memories recalled by the patient in cinematic detail. Another patient recalled a small-town baseball game that included a boy trying to crawl under a fence. Another woman recalled a melody each time a certain point on the cortex was stimulated. The lesson of Penfield's experiments is clear—the brain and our psychological lives are intimately connected.

This chapter is about topics that you would expect to find in a biology course, but it was written to help you understand psychology better. We will discuss only those aspects of human biology that are directly relevant to understanding behavior: the brain and nervous system, endocrine glands, and genetic mechanisms. Without these biological systems, psychological life could not exist.

When we look at ourselves in this way, we see that we are psychological beings living in biological "machines." Just as electronic machines are built from wires, transistors, and other components, the nervous system is built from specialized cells called neurons. Billions of neurons in your nervous system transmit messages to one another in complex ways that make the nervous system both the computer and communication system of the body. The biological control center of the nervous system is the brain. It has many parts that carry out different functions, but the many parts of the brain operate together in an integrated way.

The nervous system can be thought of as consisting of two large parts. One part consists of the brain and the bundle of nerves that run through the spinal column. Because it is located within the skull and spine, this part is called the central nervous system. The many nerves that lie outside of the skull and spine comprise the second part of the nervous system. Because it reaches the periphery of the body, this part is called the peripheral nervous system.

The brain communicates with the body through an intricate network of neurons that fan out to every part of the body. But the brain also uses the endocrine glands to communicate with the body. These glands secrete chemical messengers, called hormones, that travel to the body through the bloodstream. Hormones regulate the functions of many parts of the body and influence our behavior and experience. Hormones are powerful tools of the brain, but they influence us in diffuse rather than precise ways.

The fact that the nature of the nervous and endocrine systems influences our psychological functioning means that heredity can influence our behavior by shaping our nervous and endocrine systems. Heredity operates through genes in the nucleus of the body's cells. These genes contain codes that allow heredity to influence the development of our bodies. We do not inherit specific behaviors in the same way that we inherit eye color, though. Instead, genes influence the development of the brain, endocrine glands, and other body structures in ways that influence our behavior in very *broad* ways. For example, we do not inherit the ability to read, but it appears that heredity is one of the factors that influences how quickly a child learns to read. This is because heredity seems to be one of the factors that determines our intelligence. Similarly, it appears that heredity influences broad aspects of personality.

◣ NERVOUS SYSTEM: BIOLOGICAL CONTROL CENTER

The nervous system is both a powerful computer and a complex communication system. But unlike any computer, the complex mass of nerve cells called the **brain** not only thinks and calculates but also feels and controls motivation. The brain is connected to a thick bundle of long nerves running through the spine, called the **spinal cord.** Individual nerves exit or enter the spinal cord and brain, linking every part of the body to the brain. Some of these nerves carry messages from the body to the brain to keep the brain informed about what is going on in the body. Other nerves carry messages from the brain to the body to regulate the body's functions and the person's behavior. Without the nervous system, the body would be no more than a mass of uncoordinated parts that could not act, reason, or experience emotions. In other words, without a nervous system, there would be no psychological life.

Neurons: The Units of the Nervous System

Computers, telephone systems, and other electronic systems are made of individual wires, transistors, microchips, and other components that transmit and regulate electricity. These components are arranged in complex patterns to create functioning systems. The nervous system is similarly made up of components. The most important unit of the nervous system is the individual nerve cell, or **neuron.** We will begin our discussion of the nervous system with the neuron and then progress to a discussion of the larger parts of the nervous system. As we discuss the neuron in technical, biological terms, try not to forget its importance to consciousness and behavior.

Parts of Neurons

Neurons range in length from less than a millimeter to more than a meter in length, yet all neurons are made up of essentially the same parts (see fig. 2.1). The **cell body** is the central part of the nerve cell. It contains the cell's control center, or *nucleus*, and other components of the cell necessary for the cell's preservation and nourishment. **Dendrites** are small branches that extend out from the cell body and receive messages from other neurons.

The **axons** are small branches at the other end of the neuron that perform a function opposite that of the dendrites. They carry messages away from the cell body and transmit these messages to the next neuron. (It's easy to remember the difference between the functions of the dendrites and axons by remembering that the axon "acts on" the next cell.) The message transmitted along the axon may be picked up by the dendrites of one or more other neurons. Neurons, then, have a cell body, dendrites, and an axon. The shape and size of these parts can vary greatly, depending on what function the neuron serves.

Neurons are grouped in complex networks that make the largest computer seem like a child's toy. The nervous system is composed of 100 billion neurons (Kandel, Schwartz,

brain
The complex mass of neural cells and related cells encased in the skull.

spinal cord
The nerve fibers in the spinal column.

neuron
(nu´ron)   An individual nerve cell.

cell body
The central part of the neuron that includes the nucleus.

dendrites
(den´ drīts)   Extensions of the cell body that receive messages from other neurons.

axons
(ak´sonz)   Neuron branches that transmit messages to other neurons.

The knoblike tips of the axons transmit messages to the next nerve cell.

Dendrites

Direction of impulse

Nucleus

Axon

Direction of impulse

To next neuron

To next neuron

FIGURE 2.1

Neurons are typically composed of a cell body, which contains the nucleus of the cell, dendrites that receive impulses from other neurons, and an axon that passes the neural impulse on to the next neuron.

& Jessel, 1995), about as many as the number of stars in our galaxy. Each neuron can receive messages from or transmit messages to 1,000 to 10,000 other neural cells. All told, your body contains trillions of neural connections, most of them in the brain. These numbers are not important in their own right, but they may help us understand the incredibly rich network of neural interconnections that makes us humans. Incidentally, be careful not to confuse the term *neuron* with the term **nerve;** they are not synonyms. A nerve is a bundle of many long neurons—sometimes thousands of them—outside the brain and spinal cord.

As described in the next two sections, neurons transmit messages in the nervous system in two steps: the transmission of the message from one end of the neuron to the other end (neural transmission) and transmission from one neuron to the next neuron (synaptic transmission).

Neural Transmission

Neurons are the "wires" of the nervous system—messages are transmitted over the neuron much like your voice is transmitted over a telephone line. But neurons are living wires, with their own built-in supplies of electrical power—they are the "batteries" of the nervous system, too.

Neurons can take on the functions of wires and batteries because, like all living cells, they are wet. Neurons are sacs filled with one type of fluid on the inside and bathed in a different type of fluid on the outside. This is an important fact. Both types of fluid are thick "soups" of dissolved chemicals, including **ions,** which are particles that carry either a positive or negative electrical charge. More of the ions inside neurons are negatively than positively charged, making the overall charge of the cell a negative one. This negative charge attracts positively charged ions, just as the negative pole of a magnet attracts the positive pole of another magnet. Thus, the outside of the cell membrane becomes cloaked in positive ions, particularly sodium (Na^+). In the resting state, there are 10 times as many positively charged sodium ions outside the membrane of the neuron than inside. This is the source of the neuron's electrical energy—it is electrically positive on one side of the membrane and negative on the other.

If you have trouble remembering which side of the membrane has most of the positive sodium ions, keep in mind that there is a lot of sodium in salty seawater. The fluid on the *outside* of neurons is

nerve
A bundle of long neurons outside the brain and spinal cord.

ions
(i'ons)   Electrically charged particles.

A neuron in the human brain, showing the cell body and dendrites.

FIGURE 2.2

Short sections of an axon illustrating neural transmission (an action potential). (a) When an axon is in its resting state, there is a balance between the number of positively and negatively charged ions along the membrane. (b) When the axon is sufficiently stimulated, the membrane allows positively charged sodium ions to pass into the cell, depolarizing that spot on the membrane. (c) This depolarization disturbs the adjacent section of the membrane, allowing sodium ions to flow in again while sodium ions are being pumped back out of the first section. (d) This process continues as the swirling storm of depolarization continues to the end of the axon.

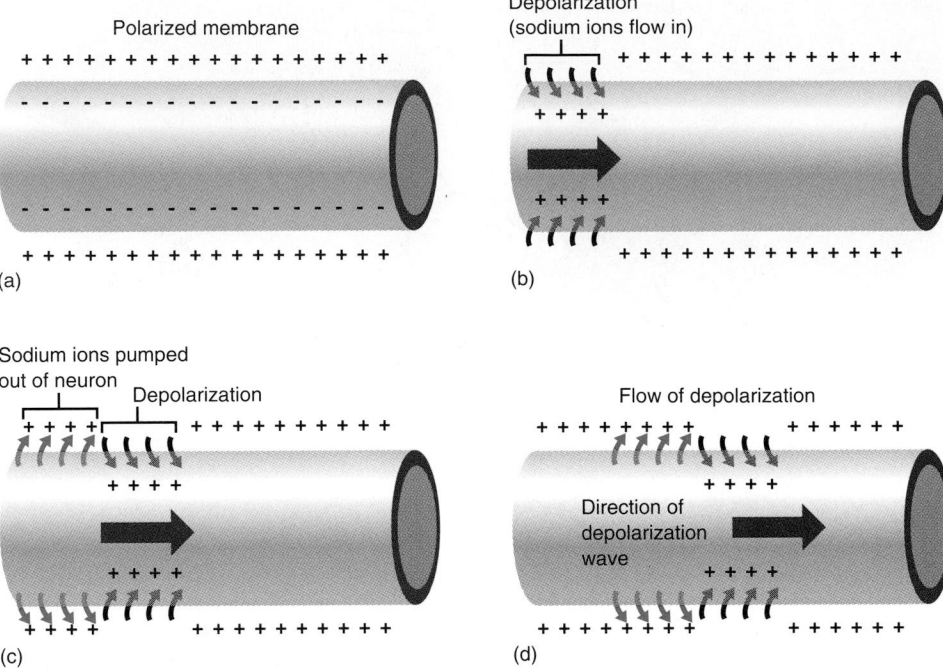

cell membrane
The covering of a neuron or another cell.

semipermeable
sem´´e-per´-mē-ah-b´l)   A surface that allows some, but not all, particles to pass through.

polarized
(pō´lar-īz´d)   The resting state of a neuron, when mostly negative ions are inside and mostly positive ions are outside the cell membrane.

depolarization
The process during which positively charged ions flow into the axon, making it less negatively charged inside.

all-or-none principle
The law that states that, once a neural action potential is produced, its magnitude is always the same.

action potential
A brief electrical signal that travels the length of the axon.

almost identical to seawater in its chemical contents, including the high amounts of sodium. Why is this so? According to the theory of evolution, as animals evolved and moved from the oceans onto the land, they brought seawater with them *in their bodies.* This seawater-like liquid fills the space between the body's cells. Therefore, it makes sense that the fluid bathing the neural cells is rich in sodium ions.

Many ions are able to move freely through the **cell membrane** of the neuron, but other ions cannot, including the sodium ions. For this reason, the membrane is said to be **semipermeable**—only some chemicals can permeate, or pass through, "holes" in the membrane. When the neuron is in its normal resting state, the membrane is semipermeable and does not let positive ions into the cell. Therefore, a balance exists between the mostly negative ions on the inside and the mostly positive ions on the outside. In this condition, the neuron is said to be electrically **polarized** (see fig. 2.2).

When the membrane is stimulated by an adjacent neuron, however, the semipermeability of the membrane is changed. Positively charged ions, including the important sodium ions, are then allowed to enter the neuron, making the inside less negative. This process is called **depolarization.**

Neural transmission operates according to the **all-or-none principle.** This means that a small amount of depolarization will not affect the neuron. A larger depolarization, however, will trigger a dramatic chain of events known as the **action potential.** It is the action potential that transmits the neural message. The depolarization must be strong enough to trigger an action potential, but the strength of the action potential does not depend on the strength of the depolarization. They are all the same once they get started. In a sense, then, our nervous systems are more like digital electronic systems (that transmit either 1s or 0s) than analog systems (that transmit signals of different strengths). If the depolarization is strong enough to fire the neuron, it is a "1." If not, no transmission occurs at all (it is a "0").

During an action potential, a small section of the axon adjacent to the cell body becomes more permeable to the positive sodium ions. The sodium ions rush in, producing a dramatic depolarization in that part of the axon. Very quickly, however, the membrane regains its semipermeability and "pumps" the positive sodium ions back out, reestablishing the neuron's polarization. This tiny electrical storm of sodium ions flowing in and out of

FIGURE 2.3
Many neurons are wrapped like a jelly roll in a white, fatty substance called myelin. The myelin sheath insulates the axon and speeds neural transmission.

the neuron—which lasts approximately one-thousandth of a second—does not stop there, however. It disturbs the adjacent section of the membrane of the axon, so that it depolarizes, which in turn disturbs the next section of the membrane, and so on. Thus, the action potential—the flowing storm of ions rushing in and out—travels the length of the axon. Local anesthetics, such as the Novocain that your dentist injects, stop pain by chemically interrupting this flowing process of depolarization in the axons of nerves that carry pain messages to the brain.

Many axons are encased in a white, fatty coating called the **myelin sheath.** This sheath, which is wrapped around the axon like the layers of a jelly roll, insulates the axon and greatly improves its capacity to conduct neural impulses (see fig. 2.3).

The myelin sheath continues to grow in thickness into late adulthood. Interestingly, from early childhood to late adulthood, the average thickness of myelin is greater in females than males in some areas of the brain (Benes, 1998). This may indicate more efficient neural processing of some kinds of information by females. Sadly, the importance of the myelin sheath in neural transmission can be seen in victims of multiple sclerosis. This disease destroys the myelin sheath of many neurons, leaving them unable to operate at normal efficiency. As a result, individuals with multiple sclerosis have severe difficulties controlling their muscles, and they suffer serious vision problems (Morell & Norton, 1980).

Synaptic Transmission

Neurons are linked together in complex chains, but they are not directly connected to each other. The junction between one neuron and another is called the **synapse.** The small space between two neurons is known as the **synaptic gap.** The electrical action potential cannot jump across this gap, however. Instead, the neural message is carried across the gap by chemical substances called **neurotransmitters.** Neurotransmitters are stored in tiny packets called **synaptic vesicles** located in the knoblike ends of the axons—called **synaptic knobs.** When an action potential reaches the axon knob, it stimulates the vesicles to release the neurotransmitter into the gap. The neurotransmitter floats across the gap and "fits" into **receptor sites** on the adjacent dendrite membrane like keys fitting into locks. This depolarizes the receiving neuron, causing an action potential that continues the neural message on its way (see fig. 2.4).

Many different neurotransmitter substances operate in different parts of the brain, carrying out different functions—probably as many as 50 different neurotransmitters (Kandel & others, 1995). Because of this fact, the process of synaptic transmission in a particular portion of the brain can be altered through the use of drugs that chemically alter the function of one of these neurotransmitters. Thus, emerging knowledge about neurotransmitters has made possible the use of psychiatric drugs to help control anxiety, depression, and other psychological problems. These drugs operate by increasing or decreasing the

myelin sheath
(mī´ e-lin)   The insulating fatty covering wrapped around part of the neuron.

synapse
(sin-aps´)   The space between the axon of one neuron and the dendrite of another.

synaptic gap
The small space between two neurons at a synapse.

neurotransmitters
(nu˝rō-tranz´-mit-erz)   Chemical substances, produced by axons, that transmit messages across the synapse.

synaptic vesicles
Tiny vessels containing stored quantities of the neurotransmitter substance held in the synaptic knobs of the axon.

synaptic knobs
(si-nap´tik)   The knoblike tips of axons.

receptor sites
Sites on the dendrite that receive the neurotransmitter substance.

Synaptic Transmission

www.mmhe.com/laheye1

FIGURE 2.4

Neural messages are transmitted chemically from the axon of the sending neuron to the dendrite of the receiving neuron. The neurotransmitter substance contained in the synaptic vesicles is secreted across the synaptic gap. The neurotransmitter is able to stimulate the receiving neuron because its chemical "shape" matches that of receptor sites on the dendrite of the receiving neuron.

effectiveness of a specific neurotransmitter. Most drugs that have psychological effects influence neural transmission at the synapse. Some drugs have a chemical structure that is similar enough to a neurotransmitter to fit the receptor sites of the dendrite. This increases the neurotransmitter's effect on that neuron and increases the likelihood of an action potential. Other drugs are similar in chemical structure to a neurotransmitter, but they block the receptor site and reduce the likelihood of neural transmission. Still another class of drugs reduces the amount of neurotransmitter that is reabsorbed by the axon, keeping it active in the synapse longer and increasing the likelihood of neural transmission. The drug Prozac, which is widely used for depression, operates by reducing the reabsorption of a neurotransmitter.

The capacity of the brain to process information is multiplied many times by the fact that not all neurotransmitters are *excitatory*. Some axons transmit *inhibitory* substances across synapses, which makes it more difficult for the next neuron to fire. Thus, the brain is composed of a staggering network of "yes" and "no" circuits that process and create our experiences (Kandel & others, 1995).

TABLE 2.1   Selected Neurotransmitters

The neurons of the brain and nervous system use a large number of different neurons to intricately manage its complex functions. Each year, new neurotransmitters are discovered and more is learned about their biological and psychological functions. A few of the many neurotransmitters are described here to provide examples of their diversity and to lay a foundation for more detailed discussions in later chapters (Cooper, Blum, & Roth, 1996).

Acetylcholine

Acetylcholine is used by the somatic neurons that contract the body's large muscles. Some poisonous snakes and spiders secrete venoms that disrupt the action of acetylcholine in the synapse, suffocating their prey by interfering with the muscular control of breathing. Similarly, some native peoples of South America put *curare* on the tips of blowgun darts to paralyze animals by blocking the action of acetylcholine. Acetylcholine also plays a role in regulating wakefulness in the brain and is one of the neurotransmitters believed to play a role in controlling dreaming.

Dopamine

One large group of neurons in the brain that uses **dopamine** as the neurotransmitter is involved in the control of large muscle movements. Persons with Parkinson's disease experience uncontrollable muscle tremors and other movement problems because of the depletion of dopamine in these neural circuits. A second group of dopamine neurons appears to play a central role in pleasure and reward systems in the brain and may be involved in the mental disorders of schizophrenia and attention-deficit hyperactivity disorder.

Serotonin

Serotonin plays an important role in a number of seemingly unrelated psychological processes. Serotonin is one of the brain neurotransmitters that is believed to regulate sleep cycles and dreaming, appetite, anxiety, depression, and the inhibition of violence. The widely discussed drug Prozac increases the action of serotonin by keeping it active in the synapse longer.

Norepinephrine

Systems of neurons in the brain that use **norepinephrine** (also known as *noradrenaline*) as the neurotransmitter are believed to play a role in vigilance and attention to important events, such as the presence of rewards or dangers in the environment. It is also thought to be one of the neurotransmitters involved in anxiety and depression. Norepinephrine is also the neurotransmitter in many neurons of the sympathetic division of the autonomic nervous system and is released by the adrenal glands.

acetylcholine
(a″suh-teel′ koh″leen)   A neurotransmitter used by somatic neurons that contract the body's large muscles and by neurons in the brain that apparently regulate wakefulness and dream sleep.

dopamine
(do″pah′meen)   A neurotransmitter substance used by neurons in the brain that control large muscle movements and by neurons in pleasure and reward systems in the brain.

serotonin
(ser′uh-to″nin)   A neurotransmitter used by systems of neurons believed to regulate sleep, dreaming, appetite, anxiety, depression, and the inhibition of violence.

norepinephrine
(nor′ep-i-nef′rin)   A neurotransmitter believed to be involved in vigilance and attention and released by sympathetic autonomic neurons and the adrenal glands.

● Review

The nervous system is a highly effective living computer and communication system built of neurons. These specialized cells transmit neural messages from their dendrites to their axons in a flowing swirl of electrically charged molecules produced by the changing semipermeability of their membranes. When the neural message reaches the tip of the axon, it is transmitted across the synaptic gap to the next neuron by a neurotransmitter substance. Many of the longer neurons are wrapped in an insulating layer called the myelin sheath, which increases the speed of transmission of neural messages.

● Check Your Learning

To be sure that you have learned the key points from the preceding section, cover the list of correct answers and try to answer each question. If you give an incorrect answer to any question, return to the page given next to the correct answer to see why your answer was not correct. Remember that these questions cover only some of the important information in this section; it is important that you make up your own questions to check your learning of other facts and concepts.

1. The part of the neuron that receives messages from other neurons is called the

   a) axon.   c) dendrite.

   b) cell body.   d) myelin sheath.

2. The part of the neuron that transmits the neural message to the next neuron by releasing a neurotransmitter across the synaptic gap is called the

   a) axon.   c) dendrite.

   b) cell body.   d) myelin sheath.

3. During the process of neural transmission (action potential), the balance of positive ions on the outside of the neuron and negative ions on the inside is disturbed for a moment (called "depolarization") when the _____ are allowed to rush into the neuron through the semipermeable membrane of the cell.

   a) sodium ions   c) LSD

   b) neurotransmitters   d) negative ions

4. The fatty covering of some long neurons that insulates them and allows them to carry messages more rapidly is called the _____.

● Thinking Critically About Psychology

1. The neurons in the nervous system are not directly connected to one another, and messages must be transmitted across the synaptic gap using neurotransmitters. How would we be different if the neurons were simply connected like wires?

2. Some drugs that affect the nervous system are thought of as useful medications, whereas others are illegal because they are thought to be harmful. Why do such drugs have the potential to harm or help?

Correct Answers 1. c (p. 32), **2. a** (p. 32), **3. a** (p. 34), **4.** myelin sheath (p. 35).

▶ DIVISIONS OF THE NERVOUS SYSTEM

central nervous system
The brain and the nerve fibers that make up the spinal cord.

peripheral nervous system
(pĕ-rif´er-al) The network of nerves that branches from the brain and spinal cord to all parts of the body.

afferent neurons
(af´er-ent) Neurons that transmit messages from sense organs to the central nervous system.

efferent neurons
(ef´er-ent) Neurons that transmit messages from the central nervous system to organs and muscles.

Neurons are the building blocks of the nervous system. But they do not fit together to create a single, simple nervous system that serves only one function. Ours is a nervous system with many different parts, or divisions. The major divisions of the nervous system are the central nervous system and the peripheral nervous system. The **central nervous system** consists of the brain and the spinal cord. The **peripheral nervous system** is composed of the nerves that branch from the brain and the spinal cord to all parts of the body (see fig. 2.5). Nerves of the peripheral nervous system transmit messages from the body to the central nervous system. They also transmit messages from the central nervous system to the muscles, glands, and organs that put the messages into action.

Messages can travel across the synapse in only one direction. So messages coming from the body into the central nervous system are carried by one set of neurons, the **afferent neurons.** Messages going out from the central nervous system to the organs and muscles are carried by another set, the **efferent neurons.**

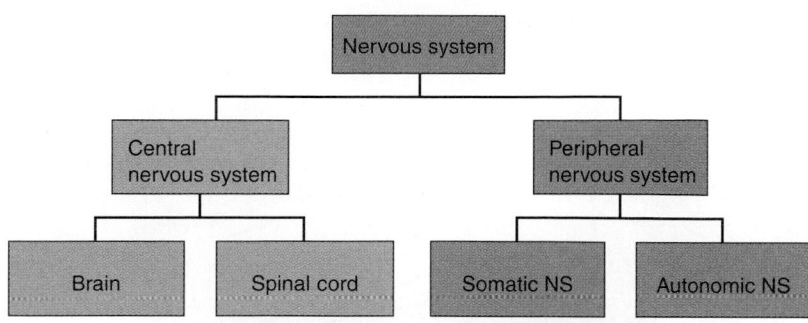

FIGURE 2.5
Organization of the human nervous system.

The spinal cord's primary function is to relay messages between the brain and the body, but it also does some rudimentary processing of information on its own. A simple reflex, such as the reflexive withdrawal from a hot object, is a good example. The impulse caused by the hot object travels up an afferent nerve to the spinal cord. Here a neuron, called an **interneuron,** transmits the message to an efferent neuron that, in turn, stimulates the muscles of the limb to contract (see fig. 2.6). Any behavior more complicated than a simple reflex, however, usually requires processing within the mass of interneurons that makes up the brain.

Divisions of the Peripheral Nervous System

The peripheral nervous system is further divided into the somatic and autonomic nervous systems. The **somatic nervous system** carries messages from the central nervous system

interneuron
Neurons in the central nervous system that connect other neurons.

somatic nervous system
(sō-mat′ik)   The division of the peripheral nervous system that carries messages from the sense organs, muscles, joints, and skin to the central nervous system and from the central nervous system to the skeletal muscles.

FIGURE 2.6

Some simple reflexes, such as the reflexive withdrawal of the hand from a hot object, are a result of a message's traveling along an afferent neuron from the hot spot on the hand to the spinal cord. In the spinal cord, the message travels across a short interneuron to an efferent neuron, which causes the muscles in the limb to contract.

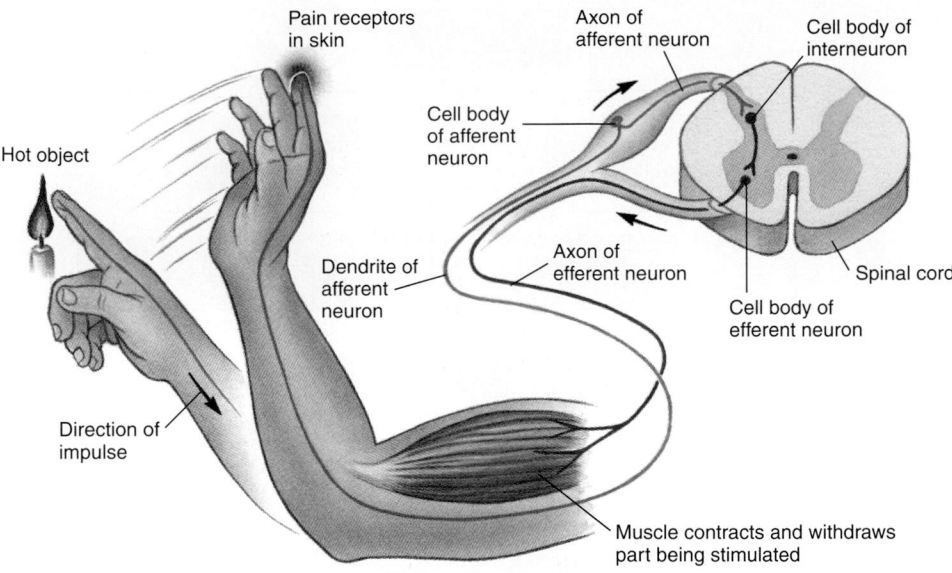

Pain receptors in skin

Axon of afferent neuron

Cell body of interneuron

Cell body of afferent neuron

Hot object

Dendrite of afferent neuron

Axon of efferent neuron

Spinal cord

Cell body of efferent neuron

Direction of impulse

Muscle contracts and withdraws part being stimulated

to the skeletal muscles that control movements of the body. These include voluntary movements, as when I type the words on a manuscript page, and involuntary movements, as when my eyes maintain fixation on the screen of my word processor in spite of small but frequent changes in the position of my head as I type. The somatic nervous system also receives incoming messages from the sense organs, muscles, joints, and skin and transmits them to the central nervous system.

The **autonomic nervous system** is composed of nerves that carry messages to the glands and visceral organs (heart, stomach, intestines, etc.). The autonomic nervous system only affects the skeletal muscles by influencing general muscle tension during stress. The autonomic nervous system plays a role in two primary functions:

1. *Essential body functions.* The autonomic nervous system automatically controls many essential functions of the body. Heartbeat, breathing, digestion, sweating, and sexual arousal operate through the autonomic nervous system.

2. *Emotion.* The autonomic nervous system also plays a role in emotion. Have you ever wondered why you sometimes get a stomachache, diarrhea, a pounding heart, or a headache when you feel anxious? It's because the autonomic nervous system is activated during emotional states. When a person becomes very emotional, the autonomic system throws the internal organs out of balance in minor, but uncomfortable, ways. As we will see in chapter 12, prolonged emotional arousal can adversely affect the health of the organs controlled by the autonomic nervous system.

autonomic nervous system
(aw″to-nom′ik)   The division of the peripheral nervous system that controls the involuntary actions of internal body organs, such as heartbeat and breathing, and is important in the experience of emotion.

Divisions of the Autonomic Nervous System

The autonomic nervous system can be divided into two parts. In general, the **sympathetic division** of the autonomic nervous system tends to activate the visceral organs during emotional arousal or when physical demands are made on the body. The **parasympathetic division** tends to "calm" the visceral organs after arousal (see fig. 2.7). For example, the sympathetic division increases the rate of heartbeat, whereas the parasympathetic division decreases heartbeat. In tandem, therefore, these two divisions of the autonomic nervous system control and balance the functioning of the visceral organs. Not all of the functions of the two autonomic divisions are in opposition to one another, however. For example, the parasympathetic division is responsible for vaginal lubrication and erection of the penis during sexual arousal, whereas the sympathetic division controls sexual orgasm.

sympathetic division
(sim″pah-thet′ik)   The division of the autonomic nervous system that generally activates internal organs during emotional arousal or when physical demands are placed on the body.

parasympathetic division
(par″ah-sim″pah-thet′ik)   The division of the autonomic nervous system that generally "calms" internal organs.

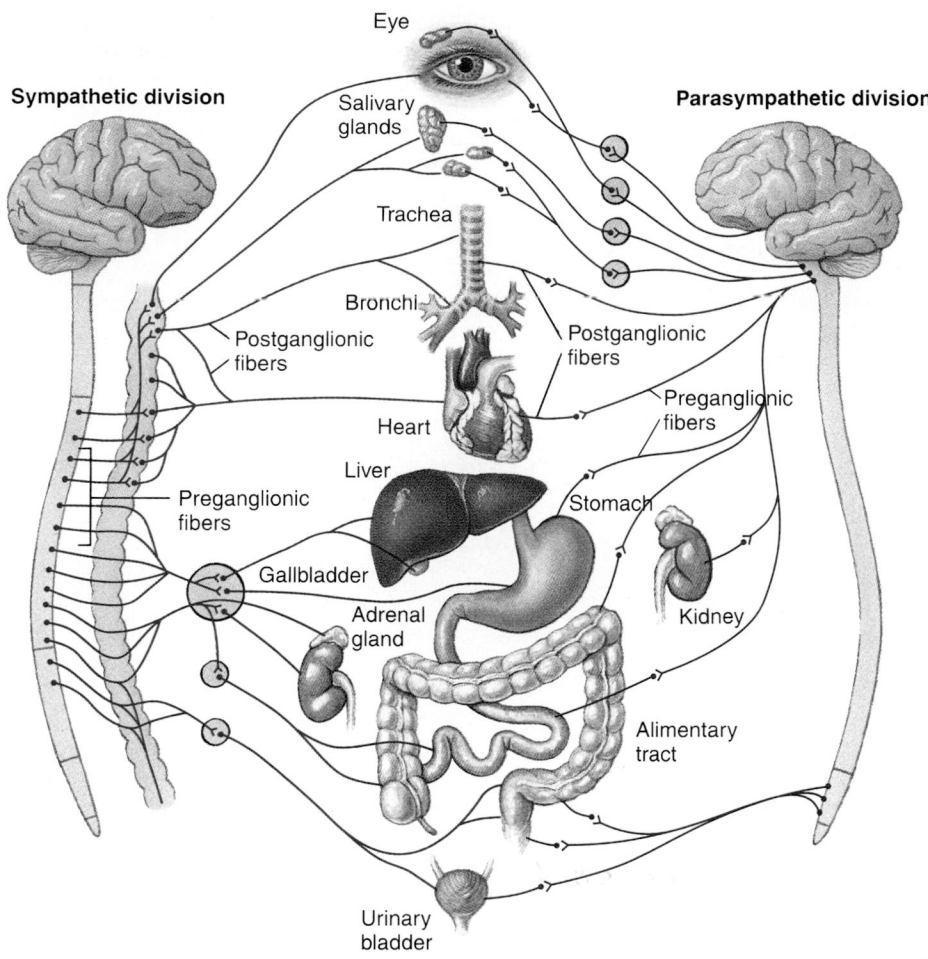

Eye

Salivary glands

Sympathetic division

Trachea

Bronchi

Postganglionic fibers

Heart

Liver

Preganglionic fibers

Gallbladder

Adrenal gland

Parasympathetic division

Postganglionic fibers

Preganglionic fibers

Stomach

Kidney

Alimentary tract

Urinary bladder

FIGURE 2.7

The sympathetic and parasympathetic divisions of the autonomic nervous system regulate many of the body's organs and play key roles in emotion and motivation.

The structure and functions of these two divisions of the autonomic nervous system can be seen more clearly by referring to figure 2.7. Essentially, all organs that are served by the sympathetic division are also served by the parasympathetic division. Note also that the clusters of cell bodies of neurons—called **ganglia**—are organized in different ways in the two divisions of the autonomic nervous system. The ganglia of the sympathetic division are all connected in a chain near the spinal column. This arrangement results in the sympathetic division's operating in a diffuse manner. That is, when the sympathetic division is aroused, it tends to stimulate all of the organs it serves to some extent—because all of its parts are chained together through the ganglia. The ganglia of the parasympathetic division, in contrast, are separate and located near the individual organs. This allows the parasympathetic division to operate more selectively, which is particularly fortunate in some instances. For example, the parasympathetic division stimulates the flow of saliva and the flow of urine. If the parasympathetic ganglia that control the salivary glands and the urinary system were not separate, we would wet our pants every time we salivated.

We generally are not conscious of the actions of the autonomic nervous system. It carries out its regulation of the heart, lungs, intestines, sweat glands, and so on in an automatic way that does not require our awareness or intentional control. It plays its role in emotion in an equally automatic way.

ganglia
(gang′glē-ah)   Clusters of cell bodies of neurons outside of the central nervous system.

● Review

The nervous system can be divided into a central nervous system, composed of the brain and spinal cord, and a peripheral nervous system, composed of nerves that carry messages to and from the body. The peripheral nervous system is further divided into the somatic and autonomic nervous systems. The somatic nervous system carries messages from the sense organs, muscles, and joints to the central nervous system and from the central nervous system to the skeletal muscles. The autonomic nervous system is responsible for the regulation of the internal organs and plays a role in emotion. The autonomic nervous system can be divided into two working parts: the sympathetic division, which primarily activates visceral organs, and the parasympathetic division, which primarily calms these organs.

● Check Your Learning

To be sure that you have learned the key points from the preceding section, cover the list of correct answers and try to answer each question. If you give an incorrect answer to any question, return to the page given next to the correct answer to see why your answer was not correct.

1. The nervous system can be divided into two major parts, the peripheral and the _____ nervous system.

   a) autonomic   c) somatic
   b) afferent   d) central

2. The neurons in the somatic division of the peripheral nervous system that transmit messages from the sense organs to the central nervous system are called _____ neurons.

   a) efferent   c) sympathetic
   b) afferent   d) parasympathetic

3. The division of the peripheral nervous system that controls essential body functions and plays a role in emotion is called the _____ nervous system.

   a) autonomic   c) automatic
   b) somatic   d) central

4. During stress, the division of the autonomic nervous system that arouses the heart and prepares the body for exertion or danger is called the _____ division.

   a) visceral   c) parasympathetic
   b) sympathetic   d) central

● Thinking Critically About Psychology

1. What are the advantages and disadvantages to human beings of an autonomic nervous system that operates largely automatically (that we do not voluntarily control)?

2. Why do you think the autonomic nervous system controls such different functions as fear and heart rate?

Correct Answers 1. d (p. 38), **2. b** (p. 38), **3. a** (p. 40), **4. b** (p. 40).

▶ STRUCTURES AND FUNCTIONS OF THE BRAIN

The brain is the fundamental basis for psychological life. We will begin our discussion of the brain with a brief description of the brain-imaging techniques that have revolutionized the study of the brain. We will then turn to the structures of the brain and their functions.

FIGURE 2.8
Image of the brain at work created by a computer from electrical recordings (EEG) of the activity of the brain. The image shows the activation of areas of the cerebral cortex of Dr. Monte Buchsbaum immediately after he administered a mild electric shock to his own arm.

Images of the Brain at Work

Scientists have long studied the brain, but during the past 30 years, a number of exciting scientific tools have made the study of brain functions much easier. These techniques create images of the activities of the *living* brain by using computers to compile and interpret huge amounts of information from electrical activity, magnetic waves, and other forms of radiation. These computer-enhanced images of the brain are far more accurate and revealing than conventional X rays. In a very real sense, the advent of modern brain-imaging techniques is as important to the development of psychology and medicine's understanding of the brain as the invention of the telescope was to astronomy.

A traditional method of studying the brain's activity is the **electroencephalogram,** or **EEG.** Electrodes are placed on the surface of the person's scalp, and electrical activity from the brain is recorded. The EEG is commonly used to study the sleep cycle and to diagnose medical conditions, such as seizure disorder. One brain-imaging technique converts EEG recordings into computer-generated "maps" of brain activity. The head is covered with closely spaced electrodes to record brain activity. The computer converts these recordings into color images of the brain. The image in figure 2.8 shows the pattern of activity in the brain of psychiatric researcher Monte Buchsbaum moments after he administered a mild electrical shock to his own arm. The area of greatest neural activity (red and orange) is at the top of the brain. We will see later in this section that this is the area of the brain that receives skin sensations (Buchsbaum, 1983).

Magnetic resonance imaging, or **MRI** is a painless technique that detects magnetic activity from the nuclei of atoms in living cells and creates visual images of the anatomy of the brain. Figure 2.9 shows an MRI of a living brain. Notice the amazingly accurate picture of the anatomy of the brain provided by MRI. More recently, a type of MRI has been developed that allows researchers not only to image the anatomy of the brain but also to measure the *activity* of specific parts of the brain. **Functional MRI** measures changes in the use of oxygen by neurons that reflect their levels of activity.

electroencephalogram (EEG)
(e-lek´´trō-en-sef´ah-lo-gram) A recording of the electrical activity of the brain obtained through electrodes placed on the scalp.

magnetic resonance imaging (MRI)
An imaging technique using magnetic resonance to obtain detailed views of brain structure and function.

functional MRI
A type of MRI that measures the activity of parts of the brain by measuring the use of oxygen by groups of neurons.

Hindbrain and Midbrain: Housekeeping Chores and Reflexes

All mental functions require the integrated functioning of many parts of the brain; no function of the brain is carried out solely in one part. Still, the brain does have many specialized parts, each bearing primary responsibility for certain activities. The brain's many and

FIGURE 2.9
Three-dimensional image of the living brain based on computer-enhanced MRI.

complex structures can be classified in various ways. The most convenient classification divides the brain into three major parts: the hindbrain, the midbrain, and the forebrain. The major structures and functions of each part are described on the following pages. As we look at the brain, we will start at the bottom and work our way up.

The **hindbrain** is the lowest part of the brain, located at the rear base of the skull. Its primary responsibility is to perform routine "housekeeping" functions that keep the body working properly. The hindbrain has three principal parts: the medulla, the pons, and the cerebellum (see fig. 2.10). The **medulla** is a swelling at the top of the spinal cord, where the cord enters the brain. It controls breathing and a variety of reflexes, including those that enable you to maintain an upright posture. The **pons** is concerned with balance, hearing, and some parasympathetic functions. It is located just above the medulla. The **cerebellum** consists of two rounded structures with a complex architecture located to the rear of the pons. It has long been known that the cerebellum plays a key role in the coordination of complex muscle movements, but it has become clear in recent years that it also plays an important role in types of learning and memory that involve coordinated sequences of information (Andreason, 1999; Woodruff-Pak, 1999).

The **midbrain** is a small area at the top of the hindbrain that serves primarily as a center for several postural reflexes, particularly those associated with the senses. For example, the automatic movement of the eyes to keep them fixed on an object as the head moves and the reflexive movement of the head to better orient the ears to a sound are both controlled in the midbrain.

Forebrain: Cognition, Motivation, Emotion, and Action

By far the most interesting part of the brain to psychologists is the **forebrain.** Structurally, the forebrain consists of two distinct areas. One area, which contains the thalamus, hypothalamus, and most of the limbic system rests at the top of the hindbrain and midbrain (see fig. 2.11). The other area, made up primarily of the cerebral cortex, sits over the lower parts of the brain like the fat cap of an acorn covering its kernel. Not only are these two areas distinctly different in terms of structure, but they control very different functions as well.

hindbrain
The lowest part of the brain, located at the base of the skull.

medulla
(mĕ-dul′ah)   The swelling at the top of the spinal cord responsible for controlling breathing and a variety of reflexes.

pons
(ponz)   The part of the hindbrain that is involved in balance, hearing, and some parasympathetic functions.

cerebellum
(ser″e-bel′um)   Two rounded structures behind the pons involved in the coordination of muscle movements, learning, and memory.

midbrain
The small area at the top of the hindbrain that serves primarily as a reflex center for orienting the eyes and ears.

forebrain
The parts of the brain, including the thalamus, hypothalamus, and cerebral cortex, that cover the hindbrain and midbrain and fill much of the skull.

Midbrain
Hindbrain
Pons
Cerebellum
Medulla

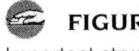 **FIGURE 2.10**
Important structures of the hindbrain and midbrain.

Cerebral cortex
Corpus callosum
Thalamus
Hypothalamus

 FIGURE 2.11
Key structures of the forebrain.

Thalamus, Hypothalamus, and Limbic System

The **thalamus** is a switching station for messages going to and from the brain. It routes incoming stimuli from the sense organs to the appropriate parts of the brain and links the upper and lower centers of the brain. It also plays an important role in the filtering and preliminary processing of sensory information.

The **hypothalamus** is a small, but vitally important, part of the brain. It lies underneath the thalamus, just in front of the midbrain. The hypothalamus is intimately involved in our motives and emotions: eating, drinking, sexual motivation, pleasure, anger, and fear. It also plays a key role in regulating body temperature, sleep, endocrine gland activity, and resistance to disease; controlling glandular secretions of the stomach and intestines; and maintaining the normal pace and rhythm of such body functions as blood pressure and heartbeat (Brooks, 1988). Thus, the hypothalamus is the brain center most directly linked to the functions of the autonomic nervous system.

The hypothalamus plays a role in emotional arousal by working in close harmony with the **limbic system.** This complex neural system is composed of the parts shown in figure 2.12. The **amygdala,** a close neighbor to the hypothalamus, appears to play a part in the emotions of fear and rage. Damage to the amygdala typically results in a complete absence of anger and rage, but sometimes results in uncontrollable rage. Electrical stimulation of the amygdala similarly results in either intense fearfulness or the opposite, apparently fearless rage. Because the amygdala is involved in the emotions, it plays a key role in the formation of memories about emotionally charged events (Adolphs, Tranel, & Denburg, 2000; Kandel, 1999).

Other structures of the limbic system play different but equally important roles. The **hippocampus** is not only important in the regulation of emotion, but it also is involved in the formation of new memories. The hippocampus is believed to "tie together" the elements of memories (their sights, sounds, meaning, etc.) that are stored in various parts

thalamus
(thal′-ah-mus)   The part of the forebrain that primarily routes sensory messages to appropriate parts of the brain.

hypothalamus
(hī″po-thal′ah-mus)   The small part of the forebrain involved with motives, emotions, and the functions of the autonomic nervous system.

limbic system
A complex brain system, composed of the amygdala, hippocampus, septal area, and cingulate cortex, that works with the hypothalamus in emotional arousal.

amygdala
(ah-mig′dah-lah)   A part of the limbic system that plays a role in emotional arousal.

hippocampus
(hip″o-kam′pus)   A part of the limbic system that plays a role in emotional arousal and memory.

 FIGURE 2.12

The structures of the limbic system, which play an important role in emotional arousal.

Cingulate cortex

Septal area

Hypothalamus

Hippocampus

Amygdala

septal area
A part of the limbic system that processes cognitive information in emotion.

cingulate cortex
A part of the limbic system lying in the cerebral cortex that processes cognitive information in emotion.

cerebral cortex
(ser'ĕ-bral) The largest structure in the forebrain, controlling conscious experience and intelligence and being involved with the somatic nervous system.

Cerebral Cortex

www.mmhe.com/laheye1

frontal lobes
The part of the cerebral cortex in the front of the skull involved in planning, organization, voluntary motor movements, and speech.

Broca's area
An area of the frontal lobe of the left cerebral hemisphere that plays a role in speaking language.

stroke
A rupture of a blood vessel in the brain that often results in the destruction of a part of the brain.

aphasia
(ah-fā'ze-ah) An impairment of the ability to understand or use language.

of the cerebral cortex (Nadel & Jacobs, 1998). The memory loss experienced by patients suffering from Alzheimer's disease results in part from damage to the hippocampus.

Along with the **septal area** and the **cingulate cortex**, the hippocampus also brings important cognitive elements into emotion. Compared to the amygdala, which could be thought of as the "raging bull" of emotion, the hippocampus, septal area, and cingulate cortex are the "accountants" of emotion. They watch carefully for signs of possible danger and compare current information with information stored in memory.

Cerebral Cortex: Sensory, Cognitive, and Motor Functions

The largest structure in the forebrain is called the **cerebral cortex.** It is involved in conscious experience, voluntary actions, language, and intelligence—many of the things that make us human (Gazzaniga, 2000). As such, it is the primary brain structure related to the somatic nervous system. The word *cortex* means "bark," referring to the fact that the thin outer surface of the cerebrum is a densely packed mass of billions of neurons. The cortex has a gray appearance due to the presence of the cell bodies of the neurons and is often called the gray matter of the brain. The area of the cerebrum beneath the quarter inch of cortex is often referred to as the white matter, as it is composed primarily of the axons of the cortical neurons. The fatty myelin coating of these neurons gives them their white appearance. The gray and white areas of the cerebrum work together, but, because of its rich interconnections, it is often said that the "business" of the cerebrum is mostly conducted in the cortex. Hence, we often say that an intelligent person "has a lot of gray matter."

Lobes of the Cerebral Cortex

Because of the importance of the cerebral cortex to our psychological functioning, let's look at it in more detail. The cerebral cortex can be thought of as being composed of four sections, or *lobes* (see fig. 2.13). Learning the names and locations of these lobes will help us discuss the major functions of the cerebral cortex.

1. **Frontal lobes.** The frontal lobes occupy the part of the skull behind your forehead and extend back to the middle of the top of your head. The frontal cortex has a wide variety of functions, not all of which are understood. The frontal lobes play an important role in thinking, memory, and organizing our behavior, and predicting the consequences of our actions (Kimberg, Esposito, & Farah, 1998; Schachter, 1999).

   The frontal lobe of the left cerebral hemisphere also contains **Broca's area,** which plays a very specific role in our ability to speak language. This area is named for French neurologist Paul Broca, who discovered its function in the late 1800s. He performed autopsies on persons who had earlier had a nonfatal **stroke,** which had left them with a form of the language disorder termed **aphasia,** in which affected persons are unable to understand language or to speak. He found that the strokes these patients had suffered had occurred in what is now known as Broca's area. He concluded from his early studies that Broca's area was involved only in speaking language and that another area of the brain must have been involved in understanding language.

   The frontal lobes also are the major center for the control of voluntary movements of the limbs and the body. Near the middle of the top of the head, a strip, called the motor area, runs across the back portion of the frontal lobes. Damage to this area of the cortex from strokes and other causes can result in paralysis and loss of motor control. Not surprisingly, the part of the motor area that serves the mouth, throat, and tongue is located near Broca's area and controls the motor movements required by speech.

   In addition, the frontal lobes are believed to play a role in the inhibition of socially inappropriate behavior. This function of the frontal lobes is revealed by the dramatic case of Phineas Gage. In 1848, Gage was excavating rock to make way for a new section of track for the Rutland and Burlington Railroad in Vermont. Gage,

FIGURE 2.13

The four lobes of the cerebral cortex and the functions of key areas of the cerebral cortex.

known as a reasonable, polite, and hardworking man, had been made a foreman by the railroad. On one particular afternoon, he was hard at work preparing to blast a section of rock when an accident happened. Gage was packing blasting powder into a hole with a long tamping rod when a spark ignited the powder. The explosion shot the rod up through his upper left jaw and completely through his skull. As you can see in figure 2.14, the damage from the rod was to the frontal lobes on his left side (close enough to the front to miss the Broca language area). When Gage's coworkers reached him, he was conscious and able to tell them what had happened. He was rushed to a physician, who was able to stop the bleeding and save his life, but the destruction of such a large amount of his left frontal lobe took a terrific toll on him. Gage became irritable, publicly profane, and impossible to reason with. He also seemed to lose much of his ability to think rationally and plan. As a result, he had trouble holding a job and was regarded as a "totally changed" man by his former friends (Bigelow, 1850).

Nearly 150 years later, psychologist Christina Meyers and her colleagues (1992) at the University of Texas Medical Center described a case that is strikingly similar to Phineas Gage. A 33-year-old man, known to us as J.Z., had surgery to remove a tumor from the same area of the left frontal lobe that was destroyed in Phineas Gage. The lesion is shown clearly in an MRI image of his brain (fig. 2.15). Before the surgery, J.Z., was an "honest, stable and reliable worker and husband" (p. 122). His personalty changed dramatically after the surgery, however. Like Phineas Gage, he became irritable, dishonest, irresponsible, and grandiose. In spite of no apparent changes in his intellectual skills, he was no longer employable, and he created serious legal and financial problems for his family. The dramatic changes in the behavior of Phineas Gage and J.Z. tell us that the frontal lobes play an important role in the control of complex aspects of our behavior.

FIGURE 2.14

A drawing of Phineas Gage's skull and the tamping rod that passed through his brain.

FIGURE 2.15
An MRI image of the brain of J.Z. (viewed from the front) shows the damage to the frontal lobe created when a tumor was removed.

Right   Left

Area of damage to
left frontal lobe

parietal lobes
(pah-rī´e-tal)   The part of the cerebral cortex that is located behind the frontal lobes at the top of the skull and that contains the somatosensory area.

somatosensory area
The strip of parietal cortex running parallel to the motor area of the frontal lobes that plays a role in body senses.

temporal lobes
The part of the cerebral cortex that extends back from the area of the temples beneath the frontal and parietal lobes and that contains areas involved in the sense of hearing and understanding language.

Wernicke's area
The language area of the cortex that plays an essential role in understanding spoken language.

Wernicke's aphasia
A form of aphasia in which persons can speak normally but cannot make sense out of language spoken to them by others.

occipital lobes
(ok-sip´ĭ-tal)   The part of the cerebral cortex, located at the base of the back of the head, that plays an essential role in the processing of sensory information from the eyes.

2. **Parietal lobes.** The parietal lobes are located just behind the frontal lobes at the top of the skull. The strip of parietal cortex running parallel to the motor area of the frontal lobes is termed the **somatosensory area.** This area is important in the sense of touch and the other body senses that tell us, among other things, where our hands and feet are and what they are doing. It is not surprising, then, that the somatosensory area is located next to the motor area, as their functions clearly go hand in hand. As noted earlier when we discussed brain imaging, the area that was activated when Monte Buchsbaum received a mild shock to his arm was the somatosensory area of the cerebral cortex (see fig. 2.8).

Different areas of the somatosensory and motor areas serve different parts of the body. The amount of area of the cortex devoted to a particular part of the body is not in proportion to the size of that body part, however. Rather, it is proportional to the number of sensory and motor neurons going to and from that part of the body. Brain scientists have drawn amusing, yet informative, drawings of people with body features proportional to the space allocated to them in the somatosensory and motor areas (see fig. 2.16).

3. **Temporal lobes.** As suggested by their name, the temporal lobes extend backward from the area of the temples, occupying the middle area at the base of the brain beneath the frontal and parietal lobes. In both hemispheres, the temporal lobes contain the auditory areas. These areas are located just inside the skull near the ears, immediately below the somatosensory area of the parietal lobes, and are involved in the sense of hearing.

Wernicke's area is located just behind the auditory area in the left hemisphere. This is the other language area of the cortex, the one that plays an essential role in the understanding of spoken language. In this sense, Wernicke's area further processes the messages arriving from the ears, which are first processed in its next door neighbor, the auditory area. Damage from strokes and other sources of injury to this area of the cortex result in **Wernicke's aphasia.** Although persons with this form of aphasia can speak normally, they cannot make sense out of language that is spoken to them by others.

4. **Occipital lobes.** The occipital lobes are located at the base of the back of the head. Although it is the part of the brain that is located farthest from the eyes, the most important part of the occipital lobes is the visual area. The visual area plays an essential role in the processing of sensory information from the eyes. Damage to the visual area of the occipital lobes can result in partial or complete blindness, even though the eyes are able to function normally.

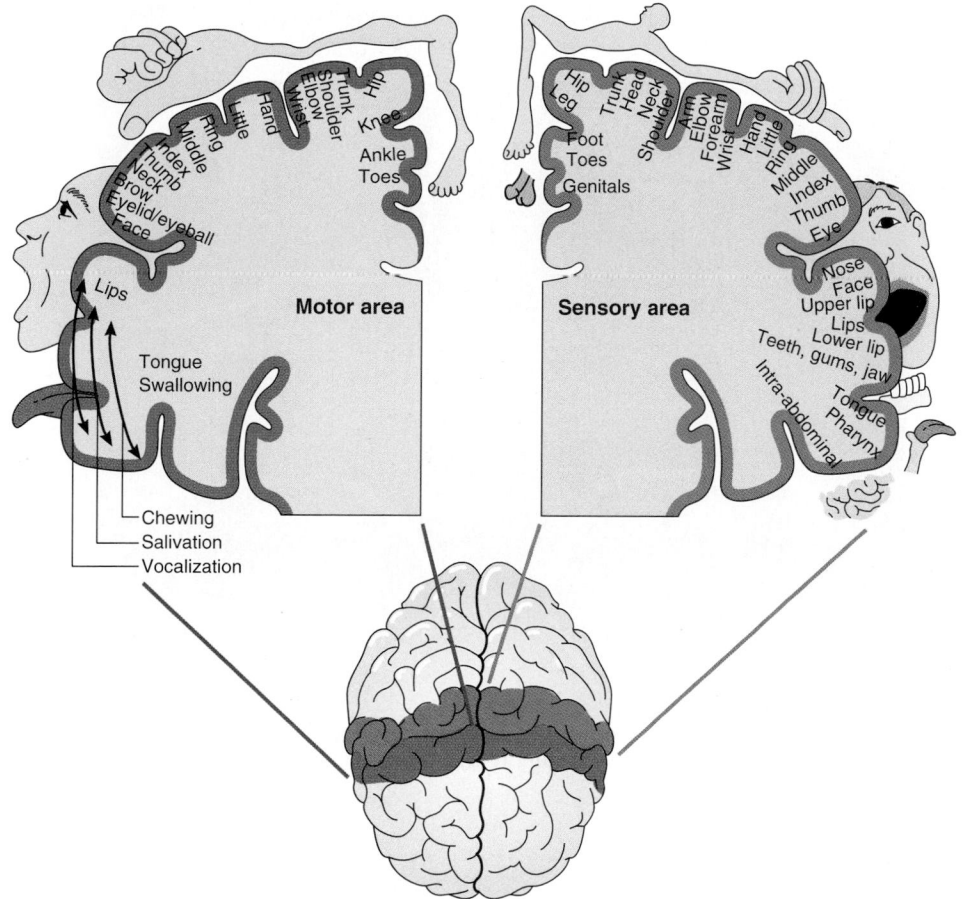

Top view of cerebral cortex

FIGURE 2.16

A cross section of the cerebral cortex in the motor control area and the skin sense area showing the areas in the cortex serving each part of the body. The size of the body feature in the drawing is proportional to the size of the related brain area.

Source: Data from W. Penfield and T. Rasmussen, *The Cerebral Cortex of Man.* Copyright © 1950 Macmillan Publishing Co., New York.

Notice in figure 2.13 that the specific functions of some areas of each of the four lobes of the cerebral hemispheres have been labeled, but many areas of each lobe have been left unlabeled. These unlabeled parts of the cerebral cortex are known as the **association areas.** The association areas play more general roles in cerebral activities, but they often work in close coordination with one of the nearby specific ability areas. This can be seen in the series of images presented in figure 2.17. The areas of the cerebral cortex that are yellow and red have the greatest amount of neural activity. Notice that, when the person is hearing words, there is activity in and around Wernicke's area and in the association areas just behind it. When the person is seeing words, the visual area in the occipital lobe is activated, along with part of the nearby association area. In contrast, when the person is speaking words, activation is found only in Broca's area and the motor area of the frontal lobes that controls speech movements; when the person is thinking, the frontal lobes are active.

Neurologists sometimes call the association areas the "silent areas" of the cortex because strokes and other damage to them produce no permanent loss of motor control, language, or other specific abilities. They apparently serve the areas of the cortex that control specific abilities, but we can function quite well after the loss of considerable amounts of the association areas.

Hemispheres of the Cerebral Cortex

We just saw that the cerebral cortex is composed of four lobes—each of which is involved in different psychological functions. If we look down at the cerebral cortex from the top, however, we can see that it also is made up of two halves called the **cerebral hemispheres.**

association areas
Areas within each lobe of the cerebral cortex believed to play general rather than specific roles.

cerebral hemispheres
The two main parts of the cerebral cortex, divided into left and right hemispheres.

FIGURE 2.17
Images of the brain at work on four different tasks.

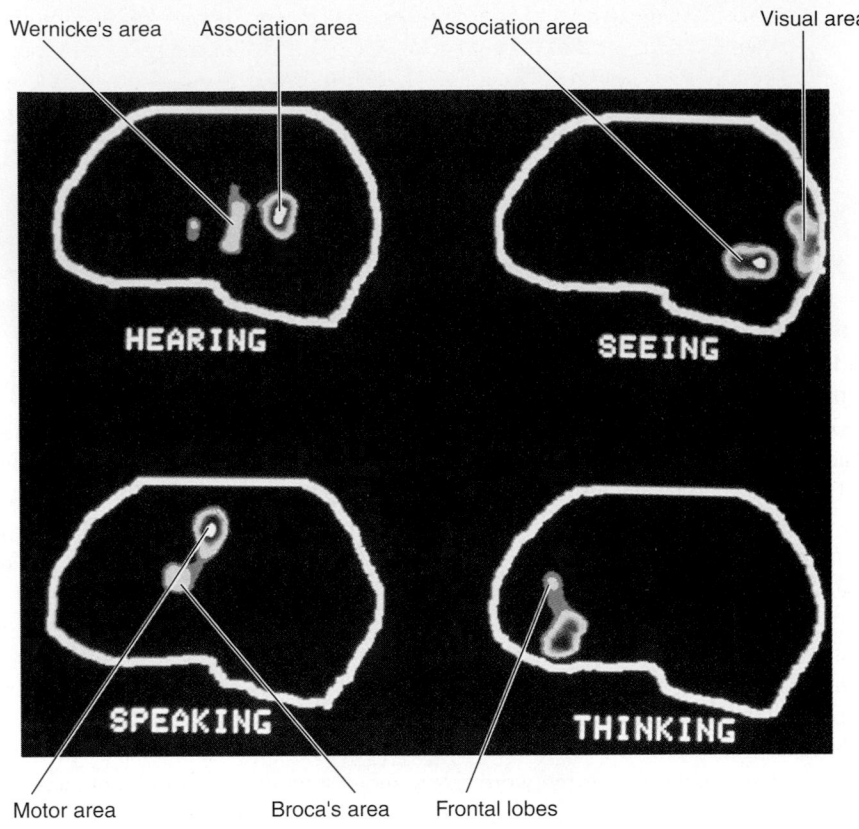

Wernicke's area · Association area · Association area · Visual area

HEARING · SEEING

SPEAKING · THINKING

Motor area · Broca's area · Frontal lobes

corpus callosum
(kor´pus kah-lo´-sum)   The link between the cerebral hemispheres.

These two separate hemispheres are linked by the **corpus callosum,** allowing communication between the two halves of the cortex (see fig. 2.11). Many of the functions of the cerebral cortex are shared by both hemispheres. However, the two hemispheres work together in a way that is different from what we might think. Input from the senses of vision and touch, for example, goes to the opposite hemisphere. Stimulation of the skin on the left hand goes to the right cerebral hemisphere, visual stimulation falling on the right visual field of each eye goes to the left hemisphere, and wiggling the toes on your left foot is controlled by the right hemisphere. To accomplish this, the major sensory and motor nerves entering and leaving the brain twist and cross over each other.

The left and right cerebral hemispheres also play different but complementary roles in processing information. For example, strong evidence suggests that the areas that exercise the greatest control over language are located in the left cerebral hemisphere in over 90 percent of the population (Banich & Heller, 1998; Milner, 1974). The right hemisphere plays a role in processing language, but the left hemisphere is better suited to analyzing logical verbal information (Beeman & Chiarello, 1998). The right cerebral hemisphere, in contrast, appears to play a greater role in processing information about the shapes and locations of things in space. For example, when you study a list of verbal items—such as memorizing the names of the four lobes of the cerebrum—there will be more activity in your left frontal lobe than in your right frontal lobe. On the other hand, if you study a drawing to memorize the shapes and locations of the lobes of the cerebrum, the right side of your frontal lobes will be more active (Craik & others, 1999; Wheeler, Stuss, & Tulving, 1997). The left side of the cerebral cortex tends to handle verbal information, and the right side tends to handle visual and spatial information.

"Split Brains"

Coordination of the shared functions of the two cerebral hemispheres is possible, in large part, because they communicate through the corpus callosum. It is sometimes necessary, however, to control the neurological disease of epilepsy by surgically cutting the corpus callosum to prevent seizures from spreading from one cerebral hemisphere to the other. When this is done, the right and left hemispheres have no way of exchanging information; the left brain literally does not know what the right brain is doing and vice versa. A number of experiments performed on these patients (referred to as "split-brain" patients) provide a major source of our knowledge about the different functions of the two cerebral hemispheres (Franz and others, 2000; Gazzaniga, 1967, 1998, 2000).

What would be the result of cutting the only line of communication between the two cerebral hemispheres? Surprisingly, a patient with a severed corpus callosum changes very little at first glance. But, although it would be difficult for you—or even for the patient— to notice any difference in daily living, clever psychological experiments have revealed the effects of cutting the connection between the cerebral hemispheres. In one experiment, the split-brain patient was seated in front of a screen and asked to stare at a spot in the middle. A slide projector briefly flashed a word on one side of the screen, so that it was seen by only the left or only the right visual field of the eye. This was done because the left visual field sends information only to the right cerebral hemisphere, and the right visual field sends information only to the left cerebral hemisphere. The nerves from the eyes cross at the optic chiasm (see fig. 2.18), which is left uncut.

If the word *pencil* is presented in the right visual field of each eye, the information travels to the language control areas in the left hemisphere. In this situation, the patient has no difficulty reading aloud the word *pencil*. But, if the same word is presented to the left visual field of each eye, the split-brain patient would typically not be able to respond when asked what word had been presented. This does not mean that the right side of the brain does not receive or understand the word *pencil*. Rather, it means that the patient cannot verbalize what she sees. Using the sense of touch, the split-brain patient can easily pick out a pencil as the object that matches the word from among a number of unseen objects—but only if she uses her left hand, which has received the message from the right cerebral cortex.

However, if the split-brain patient holds an unseen pencil in her left hand, she cannot tell you what she is holding. It's not that the right cortex does not know, but, because it has no area controlling verbal expression, it cannot tell you what it knows. The left cortex that is "talking" to you cannot tell you either, because information in the right cortex cannot reach it in the split-brain patient. Such studies with split-brain patients clearly reveal the localization of language expression abilities in the left cerebral hemisphere (Gazzaniga, 1967, 1998).

Hemispheres of the Cerebral Cortex and Emotion

Although the cerebral cortex is primarily involved in sensory, motor, and cognitive processes, it also plays a key role in the processing of emotional information. As we have seen, there are marked differences in the cognitive functions of the two cerebral hemispheres. It is of great interest to psychologists, therefore, that the cerebral hemispheres also appear to play different roles in emotion (Davidson, 1992).

In general, the right hemisphere plays a greater role in both the expression and perception of emotions. The left side of the face, which is primarily controlled by the right cerebral hemisphere, makes stronger expressions of emotion (Moscovitch & Olds, 1982). In other words, the left side of our mouth "smiles" and "frowns" more dramatically than the right side. The right hemisphere is also essential for understanding the emotions expressed by others (Adolphs and others, 2000; Blonder and others, 1991). For example, Beatty (1995) described how patients with right-hemisphere damage failed to match emotional tones of voice to pictures of people expressing anger, happiness, sadness, and indifference. Patients with left-hemisphere damage, although they had difficulty understanding the meaning of what was said, had no problems identifying the emotions.

Does this mean that there is no role for the left hemisphere in emotion? Not at all. Think about the implications of the following observation. As long ago as 1861, physician Paul Broca noticed that patients who had suffered strokes in the left cerebral hemisphere often became depressed, whereas patients with right hemisphere strokes were much less likely to do so. Since Broca's time, his observation has been repeated many times

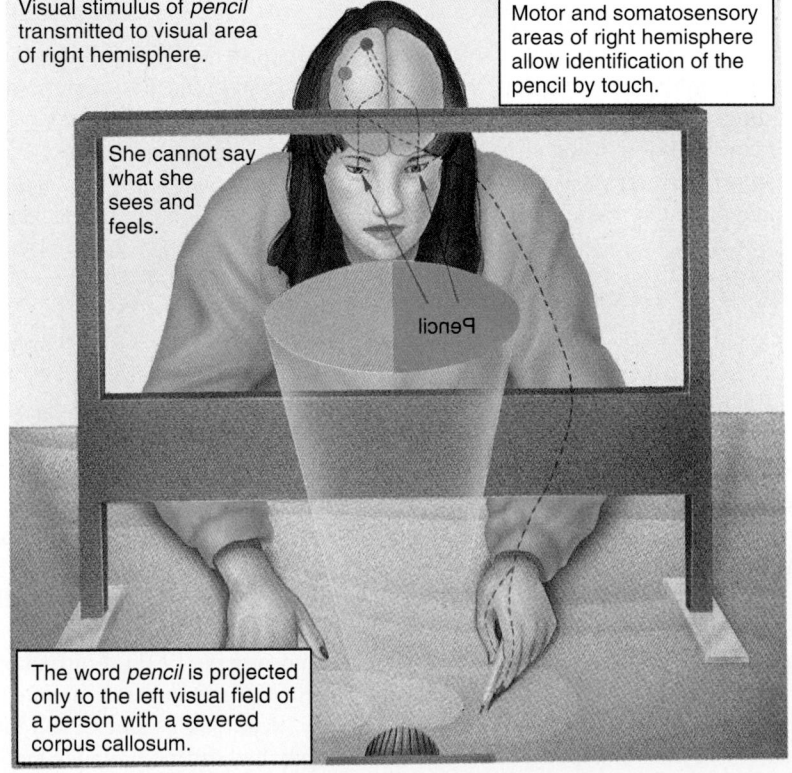

FIGURE 2.18

Studies of persons whose corpus callosum has been surgically cut to treat epilepsy tell us much about the different functions of the cerebral hemispheres and the important role that the corpus callosum normally plays in allowing communication between the hemispheres. When the word **pencil** is shown only to the right visual field, the information is sent only to the left cerebral hemisphere. The language areas in the left hemisphere allow the person to say that the word **pencil** has been seen. But, when the stimulus is shown only to the left visual field, the information is sent only to the right hemisphere, which does not have language areas. In this case, the person cannot confirm verbally that the word has been seen but can identify the pencil as the correct stimulus by the sense of touch.

(Kinsbourne, 1988; Robinson & Starkstein, 1990; Starkstein, Robinson, & Price, 1988). In striking contrast, many patients with right-hemisphere damage are cheerful, happy, and not at all depressed by their disability (Kinsbourne, 1988). It appears that the reason left-hemisphere strokes cause depression has to do with the way in which the two hemispheres process emotional information. The right hemisphere appears to be more involved with the processing of negative emotions, whereas the left hemisphere plays a greater role in the processing of positive emotions. Some theorists believe that, when the left hemisphere is damaged by a stroke, the negative emotions processed in the right hemisphere become dominant and cause depression (Starkstein & Robinson, 1988). This theory is strongly supported by studies in which a sedative injected directly into the artery supplying only the left side of the brain results in a sudden and unexplained sadness. The left side of the brain is sedated, but the "gloomy" right side still functions (Kinsbourne, 1988).

The theory that the left cerebral hemisphere plays a greater role in processing positive emotions, whereas the right cerebral hemisphere is more involved with negative emotions, has been strengthened by findings reported by Richard Davidson of the University of Wisconsin (Davidson, Ekman, Saron, Senulis, & Friesen, 1990). In this study, several short films were shown to college students—some entertaining films of playful animals and some "quite gruesome" films of amputations and burn victims. As the students watched the films, their facial expressions were monitored. When they were smiling, EEG recordings indicated more activity in the left cerebral hemisphere, but, when they showed disgust, their right hemisphere was more active. Apparently, positive emotions are processed more in the left hemisphere and negative emotions in the right hemisphere (Heller, Nitscke, & Miller, 1998).

● Review

The brain is a complex system composed of many parts that carry out different functions but work together in an integrated fashion. The hindbrain and midbrain mostly handle the housekeeping responsibilities of the body, such as breathing, posture, reflexes, and other basic processes. The larger forebrain area carries out the more "psychological" functions of the brain: The thalamus integrates sensory input, and the hypothalamus controls motivation, emotion, and other basic bodily processes. Both the thalamus and the hypothalamus lie beneath the cap of the cerebral cortex. Most of the limbic system, which plays an important role in emotional arousal, is located below the cortex, but lower cortical structures are involved as well. The cerebral cortex provides the neural basis for thinking, language, control of motor movements, perception, and other cognitive processes, but it also processes emotional information. The cortex is composed of two halves, the cerebral hemispheres, which are connected to each other by the corpus callosum. The two cerebral hemispheres are involved in somewhat different aspects of these cognitive processes. The right hemisphere plays a role in spatial and artistic cognitive processes and some aspects of language, whereas the left hemisphere is more involved in logical, mathematical, and language-based processes. The two cerebral hemispheres also appear to process different aspects of emotion, with the left hemisphere being more involved in positive emotion and the right hemisphere playing a greater role in negative emotion.

● Check Your Learning

To be sure that you have learned the key points from the preceding section, cover the list of correct answers and try to answer each question. If you give an incorrect answer to any question, return to the page given next to the correct answer to see why your answer was not correct.

1. The midbrain and hindbrain play the greatest role in which functions?

   a) motivation and emotion   c) planning for the future

   b) learning and thinking   d) bodily housekeeping and reflexes

2. The small but vitally important part of the forebrain that plays a key role in the control of emotion, endocrine gland activity, blood pressure, and heartbeat (because it is the brain center most linked to the autonomic nervous system) is the

   a) cerebrum.   c) hypothalamus.
   b) cerebellum.   d) thalamus.

3. Broca's area, which controls speaking, is located in the _____ lobe of the left cerebral hemisphere.

   a) frontal   c) parietal
   b) temporal   d) occipital

4. Vision involves areas in the _____ lobe.

   a) frontal   c) parietal
   b) temporal   d) occipital

5. Positive emotions are processed more by the _____ cerebral hemisphere.

● Thinking Critically About Psychology

1. Imagine that you have put down this book and are taking a huge bite of your favorite kind of pizza. Think of the role that each part of the brain plays in this simple act.

2. Does what you have learned about the two cerebral hemispheres suggest that we should think of ourselves as having "two brains" or one? How about the autonomic nervous system—is that "another brain with a mind of its own"?

Correct Answers: **1. d** (p. 45) **2. c** (p. 45) **3. a** (p. 46) **4. d** (p. 48) **5. left** (p. 53).

▶ ENDOCRINE SYSTEM: CHEMICAL MESSENGERS OF THE BODY

As we have just seen, the nervous system is the vital computer and communication system that forms the biological basis for behavior and conscious experience. Another biological system also plays an important role in communication and the regulation of bodily processes—the **endocrine system.** This system consists of a number of **glands** that secrete **hormones** into the bloodstream, where they are carried throughout the body. Hormones influence a wide variety of organ systems and sometimes others glands. The action of hormones is closely related to that of the nervous system in three ways. First, the hormones are directly regulated by the brain, particularly the hypothalamus. Second, some of the hormones are chemically identical to some of the neurotransmitters. Third, the hormones aid the nervous system's ability to control the body by activating many organs during physical stress or emotional arousal and by influencing such things as metabolism, blood-sugar level, and sexual functioning. Hormones affect target organs by passing into the body of cells and influencing the way in which genetic codes in their nuclei are translated. Let's look briefly at the seven endocrine glands that are most important to our psychological lives (see fig. 2.19).

Pituitary Gland

The **pituitary gland** is located near the bottom of the brain, connected to and largely controlled by the hypothalamus. It is sometimes thought of as the body's master gland because its secretions help regulate the activity of the other glands in the endocrine system. Perhaps

endocrine system
(en´dō-krin)   The system of glands that secretes hormones.

glands
Structures in the body that secrete substances.

hormones
(hor´mōnz)   Chemical substances, produced by endocrine glands, that influence internal organs.

pituitary gland
(pĭ-tu´ĭ-tār˝ē)   The body's master gland, located near the bottom of the brain, whose secretions help regulate the activity of the other glands in the endocrine system.

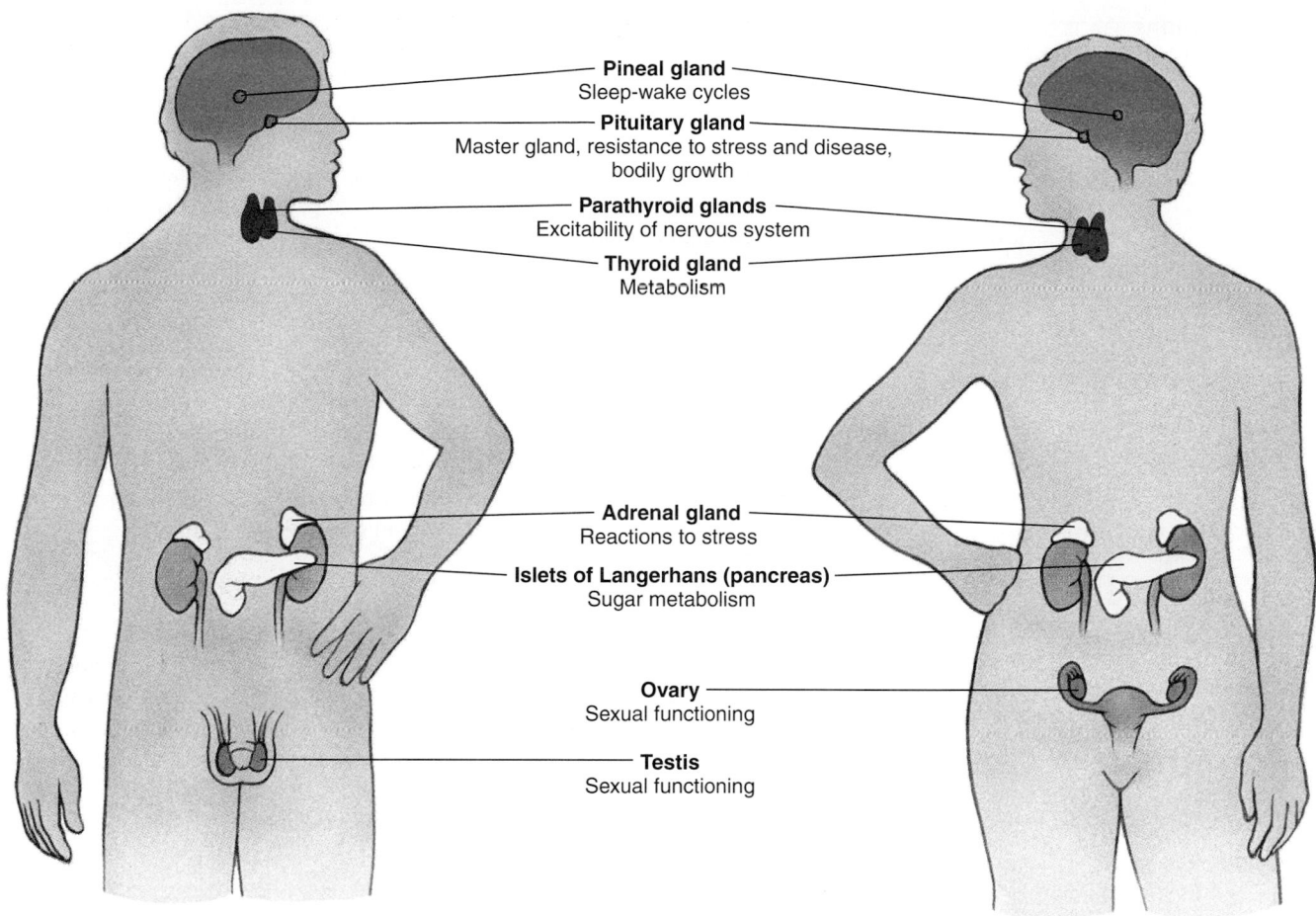

FIGURE 2.19

Locations of major endocrine glands and their principal functions.

Within the figure:

Pineal gland
Sleep-wake cycles

Pituitary gland
Master gland, resistance to stress and disease,
bodily growth

Parathyroid glands
Excitability of nervous system

Thyroid gland
Metabolism

Adrenal gland
Reactions to stress

Islets of Langerhans (pancreas)
Sugar metabolism

Ovary
Sexual functioning

Testis
Sexual functioning

its most important function is regulating the body's reactions to stress and resistance to disease (Muller & Nistico, 1989).

Adrenal Glands

The **adrenal glands** are a pair of glands that sit atop the two kidneys. They play an important role in emotional arousal and secrete a variety of hormones important to metabolism. When stimulated either by a hormone from the pituitary gland or by the sympathetic division of the autonomic nervous system, the adrenal glands secrete three hormones involved in reactions to stress. **Epinephrine** and **norepinephrine** (which are also neurotransmitters) stimulate changes to prepare the body to deal with physical demands that require intense body activity, including psychological threats or danger (even when the danger cannot be dealt with physically). The effects of these two adrenal hormones are quite similar, but they can be distinguished in terms of their most potent effects. Epinephrine increases blood pressure by increasing heart rate and blood flow, causes the liver to convert and release some of its supply of stored sugar into the bloodstream, and increases the rate at which the body uses energy (i.e., metabolism), sometimes by as much as 100 percent over normal. Norepinephrine also increases blood pressure, but it does this by constricting the diameter of blood vessels in the body's muscles and by reducing the activity of the digestive system (Groves & Rebec, 1988; Hole, 1990). The adrenal glands also secrete the hormone **cortisol,** which also activates the body at times of stress (Bandelow & others, 2000) and plays a particularly important role in the regulation of immunity to disease.

adrenal glands
(ah-drḗnal)   Two glands on the kidneys, which are involved in physical and emotional arousal.

epinephrine
(ep″ĭ-nefʹrin)   A hormone produced by the adrenal glands.

norepinephrine
(nor″ep-i-nefʹrin)   A hormone produced by the adrenal glands.

cortisol
A hormone produced by the adrenal glands.

islets of Langerhans
(i′lets of lahng′er-hanz)   Endocrine cells in the pancreas that regulate the level of sugar in the blood.

pancreas
(pan′krē-as)   The organ near the stomach that contains the islets of Langerhans.

glucagon
(gloo′kah-gon)   A hormone produced by the islets of Langerhans that causes the liver to release sugar into the bloodstream.

insulin
(in′su-lin)   A hormone produced by the islets of Langerhans that reduces the amount of sugar in the bloodstream.

ovaries
(o′vah-rēz)   Female endocrine glands that secrete sex-related hormones and produce ova, or eggs.

testes
(tes′tēz)   Male endocrine glands that secrete sex-related hormones and produce sperm cells.

gonads
(gō′nadz)   The glands that produce sex cells and hormones important in sexual arousal and that contribute to the development of secondary sex characteristics.

estrogen
(es′tro-jen)   A female sex hormone.

testosterone
(tes-tos′ter-ōn)   A male sex hormone.

thyroid gland
(thī′roid)   The gland below the voice box that regulates metabolism.

metabolism
(me-tab′o-lizm)   The process through which the body uses energy.

thyroxin
(thī-rok′sin)   A hormone produced by the thyroid that is necessary for proper mental development in children and helps determine metabolism and level of activity in adults.

cretinism
(krē′tin-izm)   A type of mental retardation in children caused by a deficiency of thyroxin.

parathyroid glands
(par′′ah-thī′roid)   Four glands embedded in the thyroid that produce parathormone.

parathormone
(par′′ah-thor′mōn)   A hormone that regulates ion levels in neurons and controls excitability of the nervous system.

pineal gland
(pin′e-al)   The endocrine gland that is largely responsible for the regulation of biological rhythms.

Islets of Langerhans

The **islets of Langerhans,** which are embedded in the **pancreas,** regulate the level of sugar in the blood by secreting two hormones that have opposing actions. **Glucagon** causes the liver to convert its stored sugar into blood sugar and to dump it into the bloodstream. **Insulin,** in contrast, reduces the amount of blood sugar by helping the body's cells absorb sugar in the form of fat. Blood sugar level is important psychologically because it's one of the factors in the hunger motive, and it helps determine how energetic a person feels.

Gonads

There are two sex glands—the **ovaries** in females, the **testes** in males. The **gonads** produce the sex cells—ova in females, sperm in males. They also secrete hormones that are important in sexual arousal and contribute to the development of so-called secondary sex characteristics (e.g., breast development in women, growth of chest hair in men, deepening of the voice in males at adolescence, and growth of pubic hair in both sexes). The most important sex hormones are **estrogen** in females and **testosterone** in males.

Thyroid Gland

The **thyroid gland,** located just below the larynx, or voice box, plays an important role in the regulation of **metabolism.** It does so by secreting a hormone called **thyroxin.** The level of thyroxin in a person's bloodstream and the resulting metabolic rate are important in many ways. In children, proper functioning of the thyroid is necessary for proper mental development. A serious thyroid deficiency in childhood produces sluggishness, poor muscle tone, and a rare type of mental retardation called **cretinism.**

Parathyroid Glands

The four small glands embedded in the thyroid gland are the **parathyroid glands.** They secrete **parathormone,** which is important in the functioning of the nervous system. Parathormone controls the excitability of the nervous system by regulating ion levels in the neurons. Too much parathormone inhibits nervous activity and leads to lethargy; too little of it may lead to excessive nervous activity and tension.

Pineal Gland

The **pineal gland** is located between the cerebral hemispheres, attached to the top of the thalamus. Its primary secretion is *melatonin*. Melatonin is important in the regulation of biological rhythms, including the menstrual cycles in females and the daily regulation of sleep and wakefulness. Melatonin levels seem to be affected by the amount of exposure to sunlight and, hence, "clock" the time of day partly in that fashion.

● Review

The hormones of the endocrine glands supplement the brain's ability to coordinate the body's reactions and activities. These chemical messengers are involved in the regulation of metabolism, blood-sugar level, sexual functioning, and other body functions. Most important from the viewpoint of psychology is the role of epinephrine and norepinephrine in emotional arousal. These hormones, secreted by the adrenal glands, activate body organs in a diffuse and long-lasting way that is partially responsible for the length of time necessary for us to feel calm following a stressful event.

● Check Your Learning

To be sure that you have learned the key points from the preceding section, cover the list of correct answers and try to answer each question. If you give an incorrect answer to any question, return to the page given next to the correct answer to see why your answer was not correct.

1. The _____ secretes epinephrine, norepinephrine, and cortisol, which activate the body during stress (such as by increasing heart rate and blood pressure).

   a) adrenal gland   c) thyroid gland

   b) parathyroid gland   d) pituitary gland

2. Sugar metabolism and hunger are influenced by the _____ in the pancreas.

3. The _____ gland is called the "master gland" because its secretions influence many other glands.

   a) adrenal   c) thyroid

   b) parathyroid   d) pituitary

4. The excitability of the nervous system is regulated by parathormone, which is secreted by the

   a) adrenal gland.   c) thyroid gland.

   b) parathyroid gland.   d) pituitary gland.

● Thinking Critically About Psychology

1. In what ways does epinephrine resemble a drug like alcohol?

2. When doing something stressful, such as speaking in public, how do the effects of hormones secreted by the adrenal glands help us—how are they adaptive? Or are they only maladaptive?

Correct Answers **1. a** (p. 55), **2.** islets of Langerhans (p. 56), **3. d** (p. 54), **4. b** (p. 56).

▶ GENETIC INFLUENCES ON BEHAVIOR: BIOLOGICAL BLUEPRINTS?

If you speak loudly like your father, is it because you inherited a loud voice from him or because you learned to talk that way by living with him? If you are good in math like your mother, was that inherited or learned? In general, what is the role of heredity in human behavior?

What Is Inherited?

It's obvious that children inherit many of their physical characteristics from their parents. Light or dark skin, blue or brown eyes, tall or short stature—these are all traits we routinely expect to be passed from parents to children. Many aspects of human behavior are also influenced by inheritance.

   Research on the inheritance of behavior in animals has provided some valuable insights. For example, considerable research has been done on the nest-building behavior of a seabird called the tern. How does every female tern know how to build a nest? Is it a learned skill, or are the instructions for this behavior biologically programmed into the bird from birth? Experiments have made it clear that the latter is the case. If you raise a female tern alone in a laboratory, depriving it of the opportunity to see any tern nests from the time it hatches, it will still build precisely the same kind of nest its mother built.

Inheritance does not play such a direct and complete role in governing the behavior of humans, however. Humans do not inherit specific patterns of behavior, like nest building in terns; rather, inheritance seems to influence broad dimensions of our behavior, such as sociability, anxiousness, and intelligence (Plomin, 1989; 1999). Psychologists are not yet sure *how much* heredity influences these dimensions of behavior. It's never the sole cause, however, but always operates in conjunction with the effects of the environment.

Biological Mechanisms of Inheritance: Genetic Codes

People long wondered how inherited characteristics are passed on. For many years, it was thought that they were transmitted through the blood—hence old sayings such as, "He has his family's bad blood." We now know that inheritance operates through genetic material, called **genes,** found in the nuclei of all human cells. The existence of genes was guessed more than a century ago by Gregor Mendel, an Austrian monk who helped found the science of genetics. It has been only during the last half of this century, however, that genes have actually been seen with the aid of electron microscopes.

Mendel's theory that there are genes for a wide variety of traits, or characteristics, was based on a study of pea plants. If a pea was wrinkled, it was because it had a gene for wrinkled skin. If a pea plant (or, by extension, a person) was tall, it was because it (or he or she) had a gene for tallness. The genes, Mendel reasoned, were passed on from parents to children. If both parents were to pass on a gene for a particular trait, clearly that trait would be perpetuated. If the parents were to pass on conflicting genes, however, only one of the genes would dominate, and the child would show the trait reflecting the dominant gene. Although Mendel's theory attracted little notice in the nineteenth century, it gained a widespread following in the twentieth century, and research has largely borne it out.

Genes and Chromosomes

Genes provide their instructions to the organism through a complex substance called **DNA,** short for **deoxyribonucleic acid.** Not until the early 1950s did scientists begin to unravel the structure of DNA and begin to understand the way in which strands of DNA form a code that, in effect, instructs an organism how to develop and function. Research on DNA and its role in the genetic process is continuing at an intense pace today.

The genes are arrayed on strips called **chromosomes,** which are found within the nucleus of each body cell (see fig. 2.20). Each of the 46 chromosomes of a normal human cell contains thousands of genes. The chromosomes are arranged in 23 pairs. When cells divide in the normal process of tissue growth and repair, they create exact copies of themselves. However, when sex cells (sperm or ova) are formed, the chromosome pairs split, so that the resulting sex cell has only 23 unpaired chromosomes. These sex cells, or **gametes,** are short-lived, but, when a sperm unites successfully with an ovum in the act of **fertilization,** a stable cell, capable of life, is formed. The new cell, called a **zygote,** has a full complement of 23 pairs of chromosomes, 23 from the mother (ovum) and 23 from the father (sperm). If conditions are right, the zygote becomes implanted in the lining of the mother's uterus, and the embryo develops.

The chromosomes you receive from each parent are a matter of chance. That is why sisters and brothers can have substantially different genes and substantially different inherited traits. Think of each of your parents' 23 pairs of chromosomes for a moment as if they were labeled A and B. Let's say, for the sake of speculation, that the gene for blue eyes is found on chromosome pair 18. You might inherit chromosome 18A from your mother and chromosome 18B from your father. Your sister might inherit 18B from your mother and 18A from your father. In regard to this trait, you and your sister would have no genetic inheritance in common. On the average, brothers and sisters have about 50 percent of their genes in common. The exception is identical (monozygotic) twins. Because they are formed from a single zygote, they share all their genes.

genes
(jēnz)   The hereditary units made up of deoxyribonucleic acid (DNA).

deoxyribonucleic acid (DNA)
(dē-ok″sē-rī″bō-nu-klā′ik)   The complex molecule containing the genetic code.

chromosomes
(krō′mo-sōmz)   The strips in cell nuclei that contain genes.

gamete
(gam′ēt)   A sex cell, which contains 23 chromosomes instead of the normal 46.

fertilization
(fer′tī-li-zā′shun)   The uniting of sperm and ovum, which produces a zygote.

zygote
(zī′gōt)   The stable cell resulting from fertilization; in humans, it has 46 chromosomes—23 from the sperm and 23 from the ovum.

FIGURE 2.20
The nucleus of each human cell (except sex cells) contains 46 chromosomes united in pairs, 23 from the sperm and 23 from the ovum. In this photograph, the 23rd pair is labeled X and Y.

A human egg cell.

dominant gene
The gene that produces a trait in an individual even when paired with a recessive gene.

recessive gene
The gene that produces a trait in an individual only when the same recessive gene has been inherited from both parents.

Dominant and Recessive Traits

As we have seen, the 23 chromosomes you get from your mother are matched to the 23 you get from your father. Each pair of chromosomes carries a gene from each of the two parents for the same characteristic. But what if they conflict? What if the gene from father carries the code for "blue eyes" and the gene from mother carries the code for "brown eyes"? The answer depends on which is the **dominant gene.** In the case of eye color, a gene for brown eyes is typically dominant over one for blue eyes. The gene for blue eyes is said to be **recessive.** A dominant gene normally reveals its trait whenever the gene is present. A recessive gene reveals a trait only when the same recessive gene has been inherited from both parents and there is no dominant gene giving instructions to the contrary. Brown eyes, dark hair, curly hair, farsightedness, and dimples are common examples of dominant traits. On the other hand, blue eyes, light hair, normal vision, and freckles are recessive traits.

This description of genetic inheritance is a simplified one. For example, many physical and behavioral traits appear to be controlled not simply by one gene but by the interaction of several

Human sperm, the tiny cells with the long tails.

genes. A person's height is controlled by four genes, for example. Still, the basic principles described here are the same in all aspects of genetic inheritance.

Research on Inheritance in Humans

When Mendel wanted to study genetic influences on the physical characteristics of pea plants, he was able to breed selectively those plants with a particular characteristic, such as smooth skin, to see what that characteristic would be like in the next generation. That research strategy has been used successfully with animals, showing, for example, that aggressiveness and learning ability in rats and emotionality in monkeys are partially determined by heredity (Ebert & Hyde, 1976; Petitto & others, 1999; Suomi, 1988). Selective breeding experiments cannot be carried out with humans for ethical reasons, of course, so it's much harder to untangle the strands of nature and nurture in human behavior.

Instead, researchers interested in hereditary influences have had to use two descriptive methods of research. These are based on unusual situations that are not contrived by the experimenter but nevertheless allow some conclusions to be reached about the role of the variable being studied. Because these studies do not allow for the same degree of experimental control as do formal experiments, conclusions drawn from them must be viewed cautiously. Still, they are of great importance in research on heredity. The two most common types of naturally occurring experiments in this area involve the study of twins and the study of adopted children (Plomin, 1994; 1999).

Studies of Twins

There are two kinds of twins formed in two very different ways. In the case of *identical,* or **monozygotic twins,** a single fertilized egg begins to grow in the normal way through cell division in the mother's womb. Ordinarily, this cluster of cells grows over the course of about 9 months until it emerges as a baby. Monozygotic twins are formed, however, when that cluster of cells breaks apart into two clusters early in the growth process. If conditions are right, each of these clusters grows into a baby. These infants are "identical" not only in appearance but also identical in genetic structure, since they came from the same fertilized egg.

Dizygotic twins, in contrast, are formed when the female produces two separate eggs, which are fertilized by two different sperm cells. These two fertilized eggs grow into two babies that are born at about the same time, but they are not genetically identical. Dizygotic twins are no more alike genetically than are siblings born at different times. Like other siblings, dizygotic twins share 50 percent of their genes on average.

The natural experiment comes from the fact that both types of twins provide us with pairs of children who grow up in essentially the same home environment. They have the same parents, they are reared during the same time period, and they have the same sisters and brothers. On the other hand, the two kinds of twins differ genetically. If a characteristic of behavior is influenced to some degree by heredity, therefore, monozygotic twin pairs will be more similar to one another than would dizygotic twin pairs.

The many experiments conducted using twins have revealed the influence of heredity on behavior (Angoff, 1988). For example, studies of twins have suggested that intelligence, or IQ, is partly determined by heredity (Plomin, 1999; Plomin & Petrill, 1997). Figure 2.21 summarizes the findings of a number of studies indicating the degree of similarity in the intelligence test scores among various types of twins and siblings (Bouchard & McGue, 1981). Monozygotic twins who share both identical genetic structure and common environments have almost identical IQ scores. Dizygotic twins, on the other hand, are only slightly more similar in their IQ scores than are other pairs of siblings who are not twins.

monozygotic twins
(mon″ō-zī-got′ik)   Twins formed from a single ovum; they are identical in appearance because they have the same genetic structure.

dizygotic twins
(dī″zī-got′ik)   Twins formed from the fertilization of two ova by two sperm.

Identical, or monozygotic, twins are formed when a single fertilized egg breaks apart into two clusters of cells, each growing into a separate person.

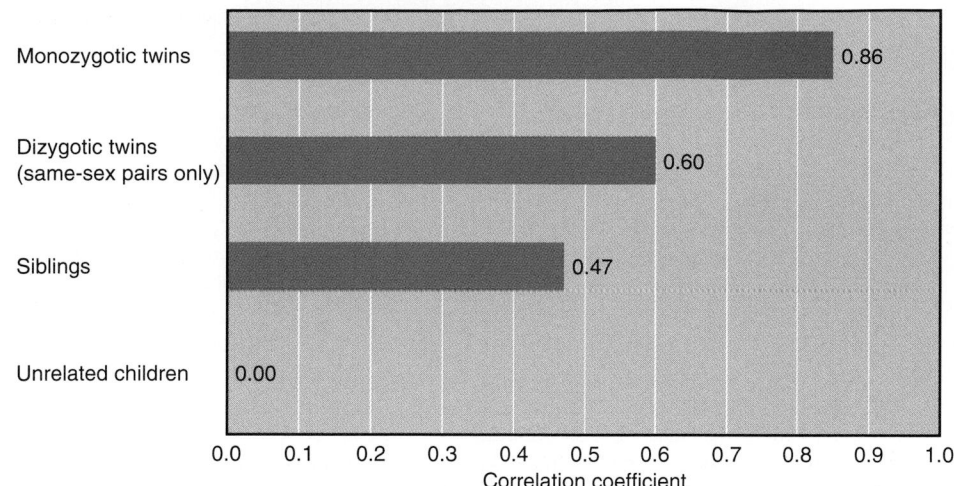

FIGURE 2.21

The degree of similarity among monozygotic twins, dizygotic twins, and other siblings on measures of intelligence.

Studies of Adopted Children

Studies of adopted children have also shown that inheritance influences behavior (Angoff, 1988; Plomin, 1994). Take the case of IQ again. It's well known that the IQs of children are pretty similar to those of their parents. But why is this so? Is it because bright parents provide a stimulating intellectual environment that makes their children bright like them, whereas unintelligent parents do just the opposite? Or is it because the children inherit their intellectual potential from their parents? As it turns out, *both* heredity and environment work together to influence IQ, but studies of adopted children have helped show us that the role played by heredity is a strong one. These studies have shown that the IQs of adopted children are more similar to those of their biological parents than to those of the adoptive parents who raised them since infancy (Plomin, 1994). Because they spent no time living with their biological parents, the only explanation for the similarity in IQs is the link of inheritance.

Genetic Influences on Complex Human Behavior

I have a friend who has an outgoing, dominant personality that makes her the "leader" of almost any group she is in. And her mother is just like her. Does this dominant young woman resemble her mother because she imitated her mother and learned to deal with others in the same dominant way, or did she inherit this personality characteristic in the same way that she inherited her mother's green eyes? Since the time of Plato, it has been suspected that positive and negative characteristics of our personalities—and even psychological disorders—might be influenced by genetic factors. Until recently, however, little solid evidence has been available to test this genetic hypothesis. In recent years, strong evidence from a number of studies from several countries suggests that *both* heredity and experience work together to influence normal and abnormal aspects of personality, including sociability, aggressiveness, kindness, and anxiousness (Plomin, 1989, 1995).

But the fact that an aspect of our physical or psychological selves is influenced to some extent by heredity does not mean that it is etched in stone. Even highly heritable characteristics can be influenced by environment factors. William Angoff (1988) reminds us that, even though height is strongly influenced by heredity, the average height in some countries has increased by over 3 inches since World War II. He believes that the characteristic of intelligence, in the right circumstances, has the same potential for change over time. Notice, too, that even the strongest estimate of the role of genetics in the formation of our personalities leaves a major role to be played by our child rearing, the stresses and strains of our lives, our social relationships, and other psychological factors. Heredity and experience always work together to influence our psychological characteristics.

● Review

Specific patterns of behavior are not inherited by humans, but heredity does influence broad dimensions of behavior. Among the characteristics that appear to be influenced to some degree by inheritance are intelligence, several aspects of personality, and some aspects of abnormal behavior. The hereditary blueprints that exert this influence are coded in thousands of genes arranged on pairs of chromosome strips in the nuclei of cells. One member of each chromosome pair comes from each parent, giving each individual two sets of genes. Sometimes these genes are in conflict, as when a person inherits a gene for blue eyes from her mother and brown eyes from her father. When this happens, some genes are dominant because they suppress the influence of the other conflicting gene for the same trait; other genes are recessive and have an effect only when the same recessive gene is inherited from both parents.

The effects of heredity on human behavior have been examined in studies using twins and adopted children. For example, the fact that monozygotic (identical) twins have exactly the same genes, whereas dizygotic twins share only about 50 percent of their genes, can be used to study the role of heredity. Even though both kinds of twins grow up in comparably similar environments, monozygotic twins are more similar than dizygotic twins on several dimensions of behavior, suggesting that genetics plays some role in behavior. In addition, studies showing that adopted children resemble their biological parents in some ways more than they resemble the adoptive parents who reared them indicate the role of inheritance. Although the influence of heredity on behavior is significant, many other factors influence behavior as well. We are far from being as rigidly programmed by our inheritance as some species of animals are.

● Check Your Learning

To be sure that you have learned the key points from the preceding section, cover the list of correct answers and try to answer each question. If you give an incorrect answer to any question, return to the page given next to the correct answer to see why your answer was not correct.

1. The genetic code is contained in structures, called genes, that are arranged on structures called _____.

   a) chromosomes.   c) neurons.

   b) DNA.   d) hormones.

2. A trait that will be found in a child only when the child receives the same gene for the same trait from both parents is a _____ trait.

   a) recessive   c) Mendelian

   b) dominant   d) dizygotic

3. To study inheritance in humans, scientists often study twins because one type of twins is genetically identical, whereas the other type shares only about 50 percent of the same genes; the type of twin that is genetically identical is called

   a) Mendelian.   c) monozygotic.

   b) adopted.   d) dizygotic.

4. The results of a study of adopted children would indicate that a characteristic was influenced by inheritance if the children resembled more their _____ parents.

   a) adoptive   c) nonparous

   b) biological   d) dizygotic

● Thinking Critically About Psychology

1. What are the social implications of research suggesting that intelligence and some personality traits are, to a considerable extent, inherited?

2. What are the advantages of studying twins who have been raised apart? Can such studies give us a complete answer about the influence of heredity on human behavior?

Correct Answers: **1. a** (p. 58), **2. a** (p. 59), **3. c** (p. 60), **4. b** (p. 61).

Application *of Psychology*

MADNESS AND THE BRAIN

We began this chapter by stating the obvious fact that the brain is the most important biological organ to psychology. We will end the chapter by looking at a striking and sad example in which the psychological lives of some people are seriously disturbed because the brain does not function normally—schizophrenia.

Schizophrenia and the Brain

Schizophrenia is an uncommon disorder that affects a little less than 1 percent of the general population. However, it's a severe psychological disorder that, unless successfully treated, renders normal patterns of living impossible. The central feature of schizophrenia is a marked abnormality in thought processes that leaves the schizophrenic "out of touch with reality." Persons with schizophrenia often hold strange and disturbing beliefs (such as believing that they receive telepathic messages from devils in another universe). They also often have strangely distorted perceptual experiences (such as hearing voices that are not really there that tell them to do dangerous things) and think in fragmented and illogical ways. At the same time, the emotions and social relationships of the person with schizophrenia are often severely disturbed.

Because schizophrenia is such a serious disorder, it has been the major focus of federal research funding from the National Institute of Mental Health for the past 30 years. As a result, great strides have been made recently in understanding the link between schizophrenia and the brain. Although this evidence is strong and impressive, a few words of caution might be wise before we look at this topic. First, researchers tend to study very severe cases of any disorder, including schizophrenia, to make the difficult task of finding the cause of the disorder a little easier. Therefore, when we look at the striking images in this section of the very abnormal brains of persons with schizophrenia, keep in mind that these are the brains of severe cases. Individuals with milder schizophrenia may have more normal brains or may not have any abnormalities of the structure of the brain at all.

Second, although schizophrenia is uncommon, most of us know a relative, neighbor, or loved one who has been diagnosed as having schizophrenia. I hope that you will not think that you are looking at photographs of the brain of that person when you look at the images in this section. Not only might that person have a very mild form of the disorder and not have the kind of brain abnormalities described in this section, the person you know may not have been diagnosed correctly as having schizophrenia in the first place. Schizophrenia is a difficult diagnosis that should be made by an experienced specialist, but the term is often used loosely by less-trained physicians. Therefore, the discussion of the brain in this section may not apply to that person at all.

With that caution in mind, let's look at what is known about schizophrenia and the brain. First, remember that there is strong evidence that a predisposition to schizophrenia is inherited. As discussed earlier in this chapter (p. 60), the role of genetics can be examined in studies comparing identical twins (who have identical genes) with fraternal twins (who share only about half of their genes). The fact that about 50 percent of identical twins both have schizophrenia if one has schizophrenia, compared with only about 10 percent of fraternal twins, is strong evidence for a genetic factor in the disorder. However, the fact that not *all* of the identical twins of persons with schizophrenia also have the disorder clearly shows that more than just heredity is involved. Some other factor or factors must play key roles in the cause of schizophrenia (Fowles, 1992).

Images of the Brains of Persons with Schizophrenia

Whatever those factors are that work along with heredity to cause schizophrenia, they produce marked changes in the brains of severe schizophrenics. An impressive number of studies using magnetic resonance imaging (MRI) and other brain-imaging techniques show that the cerebral cortex and key structures of the limbic system are literally "shrunken" in persons with schizophrenia (Andreason, 1999; Cannon & others, 1998; Kelsoe, Cadet, Pickar, & Weinberger, 1988; McCarley & others, 1989; Nopoulos & others, 1995; Pearlson & others, 1989). The easiest way to see the reduced size of the brain in schizophrenics using MRI is to measure the size of structures called the *ventricles*. The ventricles are hollow pathways inside the cortex and midbrain that bathe the brain in fluid. If the underside of the cortex and nearby structures are shrunken, the ventricles are enlarged.

The enlargement of the ventricles in schizophrenics is shown clearly in the two striking brain images in figure 2.22. These are MRI images of the brains of two identical twins, only one of whom has schizophrenia (Horgan, 1993). These images were made looking at the *back* of the head. The two lobes of the cerebral cortex can be seen at the top of the head, with the slightly darker cerebellum clearly visible at the base of the skull. The ventricles are two dark spots toward the bottom of the two hemispheres of the cerebral cortex. Which identical twin has schizophrenia—can you tell? The brain of the twin with schizophrenia is shown on the right. Notice that the ventricles are greatly enlarged because the interior portions of the cerebral cortex and limbic system are reduced in size.

An even more dramatic set of images is shown in figure 2.23 on page 64. These three-dimensional color photographs were constructed from computer-enhanced MRI images in the laboratory of Nancy Andreason at the University of Iowa School of Medicine (from Gershon & Rieder, 1992). In these images, the brain is seen from an angle, looking at the head from the front on the left side. In these images, the computer program has colored the ventricle closer to us in silver and the ventricle in the cerebral hemisphere that is farther away from us in white. Both the cerebral cortex and the cerebellum are colored in red. The image at the right is of a person with schizophrenia, whereas the image at the left is of a normal person. Notice that the ventricles of the schizophrenic are enlarged in the middle and rear portions of the brain, showing reductions in size of the interior portions of the brain in these areas. Perhaps more interestingly, these color images also allow us to directly measure a key structure in the limbic system, the hippocampus, which is color coded in yellow. Recall that the hippocampus plays a key role in the regulation of both emotion and memory (see p. 45). In this image, the person with schizophrenia has a markedly smaller hippocampus.

The parts of the brain surrounding the ventricles are important in their own right, but they also are the source of neurons that activate the frontal lobes of the cerebral cortex (p. 46). The frontal lobes play important roles in emotional control and logical planning—two qualities that are quite disturbed in schizophrenia. Look at

the two images of the cerebral cortex shown in figure 2.24 that reveal more about the level of brain activity than the size of the structures. We are looking at the brain from the top, with the frontal lobes shown at the top of these images. High levels of activity in an area of the brain are shown in yellow and red, whereas cool greens indicate low levels of brain activity. Notice that the level of activity in the frontal lobes of the normal person (the right image) is high during a task that requires close attention. In contrast, the person with schizophrenia in the left-hand image shows little activity in the frontal lobes—they appear to be "turned off."

More recent findings indicate that the thalamus may not function normally in individuals with schizophrenia (Hazlett & others, 1999). This is important because, as mentioned earlier in this chapter, the thalamus routes incoming sensory information. Perhaps the hallucinations experienced by schizophrenics result in part because the thalamus does not function normally.

Causes of Schizophrenia

A great deal of evidence suggests that the brains of persons with schizophrenia are abnormal in structure and function. There is also evidence that a predisposition to schizophrenia is inherited, but it is also clear that some other factor or factors must play a role in causing schizophrenia because not even all identical twins both exhibit schizophrenia. What might be the other factor or factors that can cause schizophrenia in genetically predisposed

Ventricles

Ventricles

FIGURE 2.22

These are MRI images of the brains of two identical twins. The twin on the right has schizophrenia, but the twin on the left does not. Notice that the open spaces inside the brain, called the ventricles, are enlarged in the schizophrenic because the interior regions of the brain are reduced in size.

FIGURE 2.23

The brain of a person with schizophrenia (left) shows a shrunken hippocampus (in yellow) and enlarged, fluid-filled ventricles (gray) in comparison with the brain of a person without schizophrenia (right).

FIGURE 2.24

These images demonstrate how functioning of the cerebral cortex can be affected in schizophrenia. The level of activity in the brain is indicated by the colors on the scan. Yellow and red indicate high levels, whereas green signifies a low activity level. During a task that requires close attention, the frontal lobes of the cerebral cortex (at the top of each scan) are highly active in a person without schizophrenia (left). In contrast, a person with schizophrenia, shown on the right, has little activity in the same area during the same task.

persons? For one thing, there is evidence that *stress* causes persons who are genetically predisposed to have episodes of schizophrenia (Ventura, Neuchterlein, Lukoff, & Hardesty, 1989). However, because this is the chapter on the biological foundations of behavior, we focus on evidence that the genetic predisposition is most likely to lead to schizophrenia if the predisposed person suffered some disturbance of the development of the *brain* before birth or during birth (McNeil, Cantor-Graae, & Weinberger, 2000; Mednick, Machon, Huttunen, & Bonett, 1988; Wyatt, 1996).

Studies by Sarnoff Mednick and his associates at the University of Southern California and the Institute of Psychiatric Demography in Denmark (Barr, Mednick, & Munk-Jorgensen, 1990; Cannon, Mednick & others, 1993; Mednick & others, 1988) support the so-called double strike theory of schizophrenia. Mednick hypothesizes that schizophrenia is most likely in persons with (a) a genetic predisposition to schizophrenia and (b) some form of complication during pregnancy that alters the brains of individuals who are genetically predisposed to schizophrenia. According to this theory, a genetically

predisposed individual who has no complications during pregnancy or birth would be unlikely to develop schizophrenia. Similarly, pregnancy complications would be unlikely to cause schizophrenia in individuals who are not genetically predisposed to it.

Emerging evidence suggests that brain development in genetically predisposed infants can be damaged by dehydration of the mother when she contracts influenza during pregnancy, by severe malnutrition of the mother during pregnancy, by an uncommon Rh incompatibility between the blood of the mother and the fetus, and by birth complications that deprive the newborn of oxygen during birth (Kunugi & others, 1995; Susser & others, 1996; Wyatt, 1996).

For example, studies of large samples suggest that schizophrenia is more common in children whose mothers were pregnant during periods of influenza epidemics. Other studies show that severe malnutrition of the mother during pregnancy and other pregnancy complications can also cause the same damage to the developing brain as influenza (Bracha, Torrey, Gottesman, Bigelow, & Cunniff, 1992; Susser & Lin, 1992). Mednick's double strike hypothesis of the origins of schizophrenia has been confirmed by a number of independent studies (Dalman & others, 1999; Kinney & others, 1998; Kirkpatrick & others, 1998). Thus, these studies provide strong support for the idea that both genetic predisposition and pregnancy and birth complications operate together to cause schizophrenia.

● Summary

Chapter 2 describes people as psychological beings who live in biological bodies; it looks at the role played by the nervous system, the endocrine system, and genetic mechanisms in our behavior and mental processes.

I. The nervous system is a complex network of neural cells that carry messages and regulate body functions and personal behavior.

    A. The individual cells of the nervous system (neurons) transmit electrical signals along their length.

    B. Chemical substances called neurotransmitters transmit neural messages across the gap (synapse) between the axon of one neuron and the dendrite of the next.

    C. The central nervous system is composed of the brain and spinal cord. The peripheral nervous system carries messages to and from the rest of the body. It consists of the somatic and autonomic nervous systems.

      1. The somatic nervous system carries messages from the sense organs, skeletal muscles, and joints to the central nervous system, and it carries messages from the central nervous system to the skeletal muscles.

      2. The autonomic nervous system regulates the visceral organs and other body functions, and plays a role in emotional activity.

II. The brain has three basic parts: the hindbrain, the midbrain, and the forebrain.

    A. The hindbrain consists of the medulla, the pons, and the cerebellum.

      1. The medulla controls breathing and a variety of reflexes.

      2. The pons is concerned with balance, hearing, and several parasympathetic functions.

      3. The cerebellum is chiefly responsible for maintaining muscle tone and coordination of muscular movements, but also plays a role in learning and memory involving sequenced events.

    B. The midbrain is a center for reflexes related to vision and hearing.

    C. Most cognitive, motivational, and emotional activity is controlled by the forebrain, which includes the thalamus, hypothalamus, limbic system, and cerebral cortex.

      1. The thalamus is a switching station for routing sensory information to appropriate areas of the brain.

      2. The hypothalamus and limbic system are involved with motives and emotions.

      3. The largest part of the brain is the cerebral cortex, made up of two cerebral hemispheres connected by the corpus callosum. The cortex controls conscious experience, intellectual activities, the senses, and voluntary functions.

    D. Each part of the brain interacts with the entire nervous system, and the parts work together in intellectual, physical, and emotional functions.

III. Whereas the nervous system forms the primary biological basis for behavior and mental processes, the endocrine system of hormone-secreting glands influences emotional arousal, metabolism, sexual functioning, and other body processes.

    A. Adrenal glands secrete epinephrine and norepinephrine, which are involved in emotional arousal, heart rate, and metabolism.

    B. Islets of Langerhans secrete glucagon and insulin, which control blood-sugar and energy levels.

    C. Gonads produce sex cells (ova and sperm) for human reproduction and estrogen and testosterone, which are hormones important to sexual functioning and the development of secondary sex characteristics.

    D. The thyroid gland secretes thyroxin, which controls the rate of metabolism.

    E. Parathyroid glands secrete parathormone, which controls the level of nervous activity.

    F. The pituitary gland secretes various hormones that control the activities of other endocrine glands.

IV. Some human characteristics and behaviors are influenced by genetic inheritance.

    A. Inherited characteristics are passed on through genes (containing DNA found in chromosome strips).

    B. Most normal human cells contain 46 chromosomes (23 pairs).

    C. The sex cells contain only 23 chromosomes each and are capable of combining into a new zygote with a unique set of chromosomes.

    D. Research has shown that inheritance plays a significant role in influencing behavior—including intelligence, some aspects of personality, and some aspects of abnormal behavior—but environmental and other personal factors are very important as well. Genetic and environmental factors always operate together to influence psychological characteristics.

Visual Review of Brain Structures

Because so much information was covered in chapter 2 on the structures of the brain and endocrine system, a set of unlabeled illustrations has been prepared to help you check your learning of these structures. These reviews will be most helpful if you glance at the first one and then refer back to the illustration or illustrations on which they are based to memorize the names of the structures. Then, return to the illustration in this review section and try to write in the names of the brain structures. Check your labels by looking at the original figures once again. When you can label all of the structures in one of the illustrations, you can move on to the next one.

This review section should help you learn the names of the structures of the many parts of the brain. Don't forget, however, to learn what the structures *do* (their functions). After you have gotten the names and locations of the structures straight, it should be easier for you to remember their functions.

 FIGURE 2.25
Key structures of the hindbrain and midbrain (based on fig. 2.10, p. 44).

FIGURE 2.26

Key structures of the forebrain (based on fig. 2.11, p. 44).

 FIGURE 2.27

Key structures of the limbic system (based on fig. 2.12, p. 45).

FIGURE 2.28
The four lobes of the cerebral cortex and areas with specific functions in the cerebral cortex (based on fig. 2.13, p. 47).

 FIGURE 2.29
Endocrine glands (based on fig. 2.19, p. 55).

● Resources

1. For a very readable discussion of the relationship between brain and behavior written for the intelligent public, see LeDoux, J. *The emotional brain.* New York: Touchstone. A more sophisticated summary for college students is provided by Beatty, J. (1995). *Principles of behavioral neuroscience.* Boston: McGraw-Hill.

2. The classic studies of patients with "split brains" are described in readable detail in Gazzaniga, M. S. (1992). *Nature's mind: The biological roots of thinking, emotion, sexuality, language, and intelligence.* Boston: Houghton Mifflin. A great collection of papers on the relationship between brain and cognition is found in Gazzaniga, M.S. (2000). *Cognitive neuroscience: A reader.* Malden, MA: Blackwell.

3. A fascinating look at the possible role played by neural factors in mental disorders is provided by Andreason, N. C. (1983). *The broken brain: The biological revolution in psychiatry.* New York: Harper & Row. She has also published an updated report of such research in Andreason, N. C. (1999). A unitary model of schizophrenia: Bleuler's "fragmented phrene" as schizoencephaly. *Archives of General Psychiatry, 56,* 781–787.

4. For more on the interplay of genetic and environmental influences on behavior and mental processes, see Plomin, R. (1994). *Genetics and experience.* Thousand Oaks, CA: Sage.

5. For an easy-to-understand discussion of genetic influences on intelligence and learning problems, see Plomin, R., & DeFries, J.C. (1998, May). The genetics of cognitive abilities and disabilities. *Scientific American,* pp. 62–69.

CHAPTER

3

CHAPTER OUTLINE

Sensation and Perception

PROLOGUE

L ast night I "saw" the University of North Carolina play Notre Dame in basketball—by listening to the radio. The play-by-play announcer watched the game, and he translated what he saw into a kind of information (words) that could be transmitted over the radio. Then I used that information to form a mental picture of the game. I did not see with my eyes, yet I was able to "watch" the game in my head.

I realized this morning that my way of seeing the game last night was not very different from how I see games in person. We never really "see" with our eyes alone. We use our eyes to gather information and translate it into a form that can be transmitted to the brain. It's in the brain that visual perception is created out of the incoming sensory information.

We usually assume that we simply "see" what is "out there." The processes of seeing, smelling, or touching seem so straightforward. In reality, however, perception is based on a complex chain of receiving, transmitting, and interpreting sensory information. Each step of this process actively changes the information in significant ways. Because we know "reality" only through our sensations and perceptions, we must understand the sense organs and the ways in which the processes of sensation and perception change sensory information.

In this chapter, we will study the four major senses: vision, hearing, the body senses, and the chemical senses. In vision, the eye collects, translates, and transmits energy from light to the brain. The ear—the sense organ for hearing—accomplishes the same for the energy in vibrating molecules of air. The body senses provide the brain with information from the skin about temperature, touch, and pain; and information from receptors in the inner ear, joints, and muscles tells us about the position and movement of the body—where we are and where we are going. The chemical senses use receptor cells in the nose and on the tongue to provide information to the brain about the chemicals in the air we breathe and in the things we drink and eat.

Raw sensations have little meaning until they are organized and interpreted in the process of perception. Perception is an active process that changes sensory information. As we discussed in chapter 1, we perceive actors as moving when we watch a motion picture. In reality, however, the sensory information is just a series of rapidly changing *still photographs*. The people on the movie screen don't actually move at all. We perceive them as moving only because the process of perception often goes well beyond the immediate sensory information. The brain creates the perception of motion in a movie that the sensory information only hints at.

In most cases, the ways in which the brain interprets information in the process of perception appear to be inborn. Our perceptions of reality are also colored by individual expectations, cultural learning experiences, and needs, however. As a result, different people sometimes have rather different views of the same world.

Human life would be very different without our ability to sense and perceive. Take friendships as an example. How could we have friends if we could not distinguish one person from another by sensing their differences? How could we communicate with our friends if we could not hear their words properly or read their notes accurately or notice the expressions on their faces? How could we let them know that we cared if they could not feel a pat on the back?

KEY TERMS

sense organs 74
sensory receptor cells 74
sensation 74
perception 74
stimulus 74
transduction 74
absolute threshold 75
difference threshold 75
sensory adaptation 75
psychophysics 76
Weber's law 76
retina 79
rods 79
cones 79
fovea 79
optic nerve 80
blind spot 80
dark adaptation 80
light adaptation 81
trichromatic theory 82
opponent-process theory 83
audition 86
eardrum 87
hammer, anvil, stirrup 87
cochlea 87
basilar membrane 88
organ of Corti 88
vestibular organ 91
kinesthetic receptors 91
semicircular canals 91
gustation 99
olfaction 99
stereochemical theory 100
perceptual constancy 103
monocular and binocular cues 104

sense organs
Organs that receive stimuli.

sensory receptor cells
Cells in sense organs that translate messages into neural impulses that are sent to the brain.

sensation
(sen-sā´-shun)   The process of receiving, translating, and transmitting messages from the outside world to the brain.

perception
(per-sep´-shun)   The process of organizing and interpreting information received from the outside world.

stimulus
(stim´ū-lus)   Any aspect of the outside world that directly influences our behavior or conscious experience.

Transduction

www.mmhe.com/laheye1

transduction
(trans-duk´shun)   The translation of energy from one form to another.

▶ SENSATION: RECEIVING MESSAGES ABOUT THE WORLD

We are aware of an outside world and the internal world of our own bodies only because we have a number of **sense organs** able to receive messages. These organs enable us to see, hear, taste, smell, touch, balance, and experience such feelings as body stiffness, soreness, fullness, warmth, pleasure, pain, and movement. Sense organs operate through **sensory receptor cells,** which *receive* outside forms of energy (light, vibrations, heat) and *translate* them into *neural impulses* that can be *transmitted* to the brain for interpretation. Sense organs do the job of the basketball announcer who translates what he or she sees into words that can be transmitted on the radio. The process of receiving information from the outside world, translating it, and transmitting it to the brain is called **sensation.** The process of interpreting that information and forming images of the world is called **perception.**

Stimuli: What Messages Can Be Received?

A key concept you will run into frequently throughout this text is **stimulus,** which refers to any aspect of the outside world that directly influences our behavior or conscious experience. The term *stimulus* comes from the action of *stimulating* sensory receptor cells.

Virtually anything that can excite receptor cells can be a stimulus. When you take a seat at a dinner party, the chair is a stimulus through your senses of sight and touch. When you begin to eat, the food becomes a stimulus through your senses of taste, smell, and sight. If the room is too hot, the temperature acts as a stimulus through the sensory receptors in your skin. The compliments you lavish on your hosts are also stimuli, which increase your chances of being invited for dinner again. Whenever a person is aware of, or in some other way responds to, a part of the outside world, she or he receives a stimulus.

When I say that any part of the outside world can be a stimulus, I am using the term *outside* broadly. Even parts of the internal world of the body can be stimuli. If you eat too much at the dinner party, the bloated stretching of your stomach is a very noticeable stimulus.

Transduction: Translating Messages for the Brain

Energy from stimuli cannot go directly to the brain. Light, sound, and other kinds of energy from the outside world are not able to travel through the nerves, and the brain cannot "understand" what they mean. To be useful to the brain, sensory messages must be translated into neural impulses that the neurons carry and the brain understands. The translation of one form of energy into another is called **transduction.**

Sense organs transduce sensory energy into neural energy. This is accomplished in the sense organ by the sensory receptor cells, which are specialized neurons that are excited by specific kinds of sensory energy and give off neural impulses from their axons. Some sensory receptor cells are sensitive to sound, some to light, some to chemicals, and so on. But, in every case, the receptor cells give off coded neural impulses that carry the transduced sensory message to one of the sensory areas of the brain. The sense organs themselves (such as the ear, eye, and nose) are constructed in special ways that expose the receptor cells to sensory energy and help them transduce it into neural impulses. At the center of every sense organ are receptor cells that do the transducing.

Sensory Limits: How Strong Must Messages Be?

Even when we have receptor cells that can transduce a kind of sensory message, not every message will be strong enough to be detected. The term *threshold* refers to the lower limits of sensory experience. The two primary kinds of thresholds are (a) the smallest *magnitude* of a stimulus that can be detected and (b) the smallest *difference* between two stimuli that can be detected.

Sense	Weakest detectable stimulus
Vision	A candle flame seen at 30 miles on a clear, dark night

Sense	Weakest detectable stimulus
Smell	One drop of perfume diffused into the entire volume of a 3-room apartment

Hearing	The tick of a watch under quiet conditions at 20 feet

Touch	The wing of a bee falling on your cheek from a height of 1 centimeter

Taste	One teaspoon of sugar in 2 gallons of water

FIGURE 3.1

The human senses are remarkably sensitive systems. Psychologist Eugene Galanter (1962) has offered these illustrative estimates of the weakest stimuli that we are capable of sensing.

The **absolute threshold** is the smallest magnitude of a stimulus that can be detected. Look at the absolute thresholds for a number of common stimuli shown in figure 3.1 to gain a fuller appreciation of your remarkably sensitive receptor cells. Measuring such thresholds is no simple matter. People differ considerably in their sensitivity to weak stimuli, and the sensitivity of each of us differs from time to time. For this reason, absolute thresholds are defined as the magnitude of a stimulus that subjects can detect *half the time*. The smallest difference between two stimuli that can be detected half the time is called the **difference threshold.** For example, the smallest change in intensity of your stereo that you can distinguish as "louder" 50 percent of the time is your difference threshold for that stimulus. Detailed knowledge of absolute and difference thresholds has, in fact, been used by the electronics industry to design better stereo systems.

Sensory Adaptation

Recall that an individual's sensitivity to a stimulus differs from time to time. There are many reasons why this happens, such as fatigue or inattention, but **sensory adaptation** is

Absolute Threshold

www.mmhe.com/laheye1

absolute threshold
The smallest magnitude of a stimulus that can be detected half the time.

difference threshold
The smallest difference between two stimuli that can be detected half the time.

sensory adaptation
Weakened magnitude of a sensation resulting from prolonged presentation of the stimulus.

At first, cold water bombards us with sensations. After being in cold water for a while, receptors in the skin adapt to changes in temperature and lessen the sensation of coldness.

psychophysics
(sī″kō-fiz′iks)   A specialty area of psychology that studies sensory limits, sensory adaptation, and related topics.

Weber's law
A law stating that the amount of change in a stimulus needed to detect a difference is in direct proportion to the intensity of the original stimulus.

one of the major causes. When a stimulus is continuously present or repeated at short intervals, the sensation that the same amount of sensory energy causes becomes gradually weaker, largely because the receptor cells become fatigued. When I was a teenager, I frequently went skin diving in an extremely cold spring in central Florida. At first the water was almost unbearably cold; when I jumped in from the dock, the intensity of the cold grabbed my attention so totally that for a moment I felt like only the cold skin of a person rather than a whole person. But after a few minutes the water felt comfortably cool. The water did not change in temperature, of course, but the sensation changed considerably because the temperature receptors in the skin adapted to the temperature of the water. This is sensory adaptation. It happens to some extent in all the senses; loud sounds and offensive odors, fortunately, also seem less intense as time goes by.

Psychophysics

The specialty area within the field of psychology that studies sensory limits, sensory adaptation, and related topics is called **psychophysics.** The subject matter of this field is the relationship between the *physical* properties of stimuli and the *psychological* sensations they produce. Psychophysics is an important field because frequently there is *not* a direct or simple relationship between stimuli and sensations. Because our knowledge of the outside world is limited to what our sensations tell us, we need to understand under what conditions our sensations do not directly reflect the physical nature of the stimulus. Sensory adaptation is a process that alters the relationship between stimuli and sensations, but numerous other circumstances provide examples of this lack of a one-to-one relationship. The concept of the difference threshold provides another good example.

A fact about difference thresholds that has captured the attention of psychophysicists since the nineteenth century is that the size of the difference threshold increases as the strength of the stimulus increases. When a stimulus is strong, changes in it must be bigger to be noticed than when the stimulus is weak. You can see this for yourself the next time you turn on a three-way light in a dark room. Most three-way bulbs provide light energy in three approximately equal steps (such as a 50-, 100-, and 150-watt bulb), but the greatest difference in brightness in the room is noticeable after the first click of the switch—the sofa that you just tripped over in the darkness is now plainly visible. Turning up the light to the next level adds a less noticeable increase in perceived brightness, and the third level adds even less in apparent brightness. At each level of increasing illumination, the difference threshold is greater, so the perceived increase in brightness is less. If you were to turn on another 50-watt bulb at this point—with the three-way bulb at its highest illumination—you might not see any increase in apparent brightness because your difference threshold is so high.

The ability to detect small changes in the intensity of weak stimuli, but only large changes in the intensity of strong stimuli, was first formally noted by German psychophysicist Ernst Weber. Today this phenomenon is known as **Weber's law.** Interestingly, the amount of the change needed to be detected half the time (the difference threshold) is almost always in direct proportion to the intensity of the original stimulus. Thus, if a waiter holding a tray on which four glasses had been placed is just able to detect the added weight of one glass, he would just be able to feel the added weight from *two* more glasses if the tray were already holding eight glasses. The amount of detectable added weight would always be in the same proportion, in this case 1/4.

What is the relevance of this bit of information? Weber's law tells us that what we sense is not always the same as the energy that enters the sense organ. The same magnitude of physical change in intensity can be obvious one time, yet would go undetected under different circumstances. This fact has important practical implications. Suppose, for example, that you are chosen to help design the instruments for a new airplane. The pilot wants an easier way to monitor the plane's altitude, so you put in a light that increases in intensity as the plane nears the earth—the lower the altitude, the more intense the light. That way, you assume, the pilot can easily monitor changes in altitude by seeing changes in brightness. Right? According to Weber's law, this would be a dangerous way to monitor altitude. At high altitudes, the intensity of the light would be low, so small changes could be detected easily; at low altitudes, however, the intensity would be so great that large changes in altitude—even fatal ones—might not be noticed. That is why the people who design instruments for airplanes, cars, and the like need to know about psychophysics.

● Review

The world is known to us only indirectly because our brains are not in direct contact with the outside world. But sensory receptor cells have the ability to transduce physical energy into coded neural messages (sensation) that are sent to the brain, where they are interpreted (perception). Not all forms of physical energy can become part of our perception of the world: We must have sensory receptor cells that can transduce that form of energy and the stimulation must be strong enough to exceed the sensory threshold. Our perception of external reality is complicated because there is no simple and direct relationship between the properties of physical stimuli and our conscious sensations. For example, a small change in the intensity of sound from a stereo is noticeable when the stereo is being played softly, but the same size change would go unnoticed if the stereo were at high volume. The complicated relationship between physical stimuli and conscious sensations is the subject matter of psychophysics.

● Check Your Learning

To be sure that you have learned the key points from the preceding section, cover the list of correct answers and try to answer each question. If you give an incorrect answer to any question, return to the page given next to the correct answer to see why your answer was not correct. Remember that these questions cover only some of the important information in this section; it is important that you make up your own questions to check your learning of other facts and concepts.

1. The _____ is the smallest magnitude of a stimulus that can be detected half the time.

   a) absolute threshold   c) difference threshold

   b) visual threshold   d) relative threshold

2. When a stimulus is continuously present or repeated at short intervals, the sensation gradually becomes weaker. This is termed

   a) sensory adaptation.   c) desensitization.

   b) psychophysics.

3. According to _____, the amount of the change in a stimulus needed to be detected half the time is almost always in direct proportion to the intensity of the original stimulus.

   a) psychophysical dualism   c) Weber's law

   b) McGurty's law   d) threshold variation

4. The specialty area within the field of psychology that studies sensory limits, sensory adaptation, and related topics is called _____.

● Thinking Critically About Psychology

1. How would life be different if human beings had a lower absolute threshold for the sense of sound? How about a higher absolute threshold for taste?

2. What is the difference between sensation and perception? Can you have a perception without a sensation?

Correct Answers 1. a (p. 75), **2.** a (p. 75), **3.** c (p. 76), **4.** psychophysics (p. 76).

VISION: YOUR HUMAN CAMERA

In 1950, psychologist George Wald wrote an important paper comparing the eye to a camera. This is still a good analogy today. Both the eye and a camera are instruments that use a lens to focus light onto a light-sensitive surface on which the visual image is registered. The gross anatomy of the human eye shown in figure 3.2 makes the resemblance to a camera very apparent. This intricate and efficient instrument transduces the physical properties of light into elaborately coded neural messages.

Light: What Is It?

We need to have some knowledge of the nature of light to understand vision. Light is one small part of the form of energy known as **electromagnetic radiation,** which also includes radio waves and X rays. Only a small portion of this radiation is visible—that is, our senses can transduce only a small part of it. We can best think of light as being composed of *waves* that vary in *frequency* and *intensity.* These two properties of light waves provide us with most of our information about vision.

The *intensity* of the light wave largely determines the *brightness* of the visual sensation. The light reflected by an apple that is lighted by a single candle is low in intensity, so we see the red of the apple as a dim rather than a bright sensation. The **wavelength** of the light largely determines the *color,* or *hue,* that we see—that is, light waves of different wavelengths are seen as different colors. But most light waves are not made up of a single wavelength and are therefore not seen as a pure color. Rather, they are made up of light waves of more than one wavelength. The more a color is composed of multiple wavelengths, the less *saturated* (or pure) the color is said to be. The relationship between the physical properties of light and what is seen is not always simple and direct, however.

electromagnetic radiation
(e-lek″trō-mag-net′ik)   A form of energy including electricity, radio waves, and X rays, of which visible light is a part.

wavelength
The frequency of light waves, which determines the color we see.

FIGURE 3.2

Optical similarities between an eye and a camera are apparent in their cross sections. Both use a lens to focus an inverted image onto a light-sensitive surface. Both possess an iris to adjust to various intensities of light.

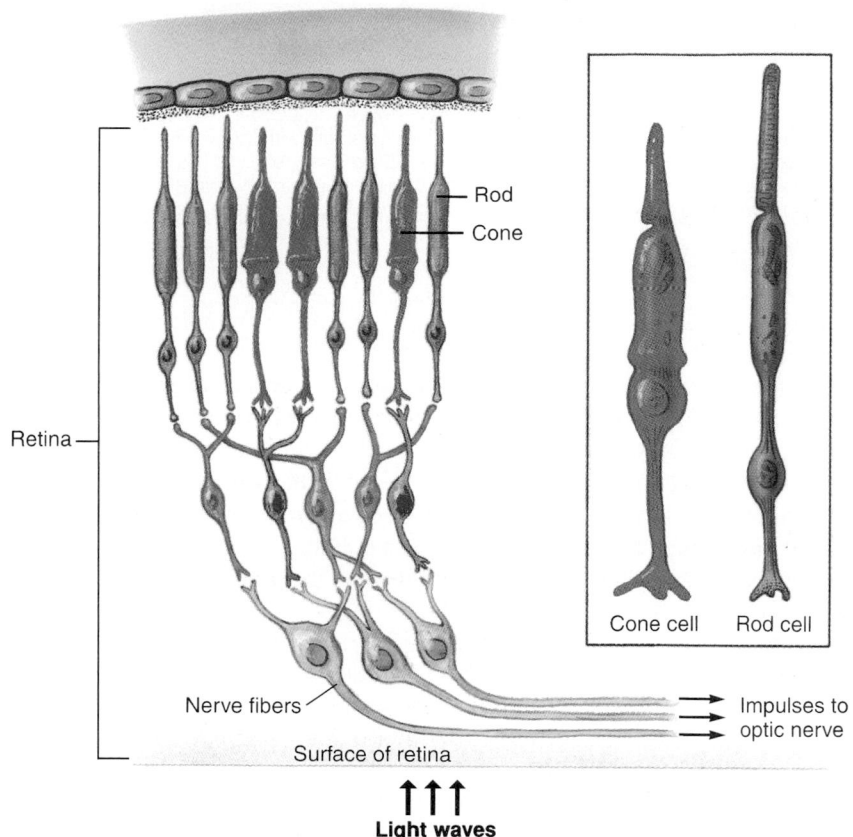

Rod

Cone

Retina

Cone cell   Rod cell

Nerve fibers

Surface of retina

Impulses to optic nerve

Light waves

FIGURE 3.3
Diagram of the microscopic structure of a section of the retina showing the rods and cones and their principal neural interconnections. The blowup shows individual rod and cone cells.

The Eye: How Does It Work?

The eye is an almost perfect sphere composed of two fluid-filled chambers. Light passes through the clear **cornea** into the first chamber. At the back of this chamber, the colored **iris** opens and closes to regulate how much light passes through the **pupil** into the **lens.** The lens is held in place by ligaments attached to the **ciliary muscle.** This muscle focuses images by controlling the thickness of the lens, so that a clear image falls onto the light-sensitive **retina** at the back of the second chamber (see fig. 3.2). When the ciliary muscle is uncontracted, the tension of the ligaments stretches the lens relatively flat. When the ciliary muscle contracts, it lessens the tension of the ligaments and the lens thickens. The lens must be thickened to focus on close objects; that is why reading for long periods—which involves prolonged contraction of the ciliary muscle—makes your eyes feel tired.

The real business of transducing light waves is carried out in the retina by two types of receptor cells named the **rods** and the **cones** because of their shape (see fig. 3.3). The cones are far less numerous than the rods—about 6 million cones compared with 125 million rods in each eye (Pugh, 1988). Cones are concentrated in the center of the retina, with the greatest concentration at a central spot called the **fovea.** In good light, **visual acuity** (the clearness and sharpness of vision) is best for images that are focused directly on the fovea, largely because of the high concentration of cones.

The rods are located throughout the retina, except in the center (the fovea). Their role in vision differs from that of the cones in four main ways. First, because of their location, they are largely responsible for peripheral vision—vision at the top, bottom, and sides of the visual field—whereas the cones play little role in this aspect of seeing. Second, the rods are hundreds of times more sensitive to light than the cones. This means that they play a far more important role in vision in dim light than do the cones. Third, the rods produce images that are perceived with less visual acuity than do cones. This is largely because neurons leading from several rods often converge, so that their impulses are sent to the brain on a single nerve fiber (shown in fig. 3.3). In contrast, cones more commonly send their

cornea
(kor′nē-ah) The protective coating on the surface of the eye through which light passes.

iris
(ī′ris) The colored part of the eye behind the cornea that regulates the amount of light that enters.

pupil
(pyoo′pil) The opening of the iris.

lens
The transparent portion of the eye that focuses light on the retina.

ciliary muscle
(sil′ē-ar″e) The muscle in the eye that controls the shape of the lens.

retina
(ret′i-nah) The area at the back of the eye on which images are formed and that contains the rods and cones.

rods
The 125 million cells located outside the center of the retina that transduce light waves into neural impulses, thereby coding information about light and dark.

cones
The 6 million receptor cells located mostly in the center of the retina that transduce light waves into neural impulses, thereby coding information about light, dark, and color.

fovea
(fō′vē-ah) The central spot of the retina, which contains the greatest concentration of cones.

visual acuity
(vizh′u-al ah-ku′i-tē) Clearness and sharpness of vision.

FIGURE 3.4

You can demonstrate to yourself the existence of the "blind spot" in the following way. Hold your book at about arm's length with the word *Spot* in front of your eyes. Close your right eye and stare at the word *Spot*. Move the book in slowly until the word *Blind* disappears. At this point, its image is falling on the spot in the retina where the optic nerve is attached and there are no receptors. We are not normally aware of the existence of this blind spot because we "fill in" our perceptions to compensate for the missing information. In this case, we see the dotted line as continuous after the word *Blind* disappears.

optic nerve
The nerve that carries neural messages about vision to the brain.

blind spot
The spot where the optic nerve attaches to the retina, which contains no rods or cones.

optic chiasm
The area in the brain where the optic nerves cross.

dark adaptation
Increased sensitivity of the eye in semidarkness following an abrupt reduction in overall illumination.

messages to the brain along separate nerve fibers, giving the brain more precise information about the location of the stimulation on the retina.

The fourth difference between the rods and cones concerns color vision. Both types of receptors respond to variations in light and dark (in terms of the number of receptors that fire and the frequency with which they fire), but only the cones can code information about color. Because the rods do not detect color, and because the cones can respond only in bright light, we can see only indistinct forms of black and gray in an almost dark room. Although light of different wavelengths is still present in the room during near darkness, the rods have no way of sending messages about them to the brain, so colors "disappear" from view.

Would you be surprised to learn that you are partially blind in each eye? The spot near the center of the retina where the **optic nerve** is attached contains no rods or cones. Because there is no visual reception at this point, it is known as the **blind spot.** We are not normally aware of this blind spot because we "fill in" the missing information during the process of seeing by using information coming in from the other parts of the retina. However, look at figure 3.4 for a demonstration of its existence.

Coded messages from the rods and cones are processed in a preliminary way in the neurons of the retina and are then sent to the visual areas of the left and right occipital lobe of the cerebral cortex for interpretation. Recall from chapter 2 that the information from the eyes is transmitted to the visual areas in a complicated fashion. As shown in figure 3.5, stimuli that are on your right fall on the left side of each eye. Information from the right visual field of both eyes is sent to the visual area in the occipital lobe of the left visual hemisphere after the optic nerves cross over at the **optic chiasm** in the brain. Information from stimuli on your left falls on the right side of each eye and is sent to the visual area in the right cerebral hemisphere. It's a bit confusing when you read about it for the first time, but the brain manages to keep it all straight.

Dark and Light Adaptation

When you walk into a dark movie theater from the daylight, you are "blind" at first; your eyes can pick up very little visual information. Within about 5 minutes, however, your vision in the darkened room has improved considerably, and very slowly it improves over the next 25 minutes until you can see fairly well. When you exit the theater from the matinee performance, you have the opposite experience. At first the intense light "blinds" you. You squint and block out the painful light, but in a little while you can see normally again. What is going on? How can you be sighted one moment and blind the next just because the intensity of light has suddenly changed?

The phenomena are called *dark adaptation* and *light adaptation.* Here is what happens in the retina during **dark adaptation.** In a lighted room, the rods and cones are being used frequently, so they are not very sensitive. When we enter darkness, the rods and cones are not sensitive enough to be stimulated by the low-intensity light and they stop firing almost completely. This gives the receptors a "rest," so they begin to gain sensitivity by making a fresh supply of the chemicals used in light reception, which have been literally "bleached out" by the intense light.

At first, both the rods and the cones are recovering their sensitivity, so improvement is fairly rapid. But the cones become fully sensitive (remember, they are not very sensitive

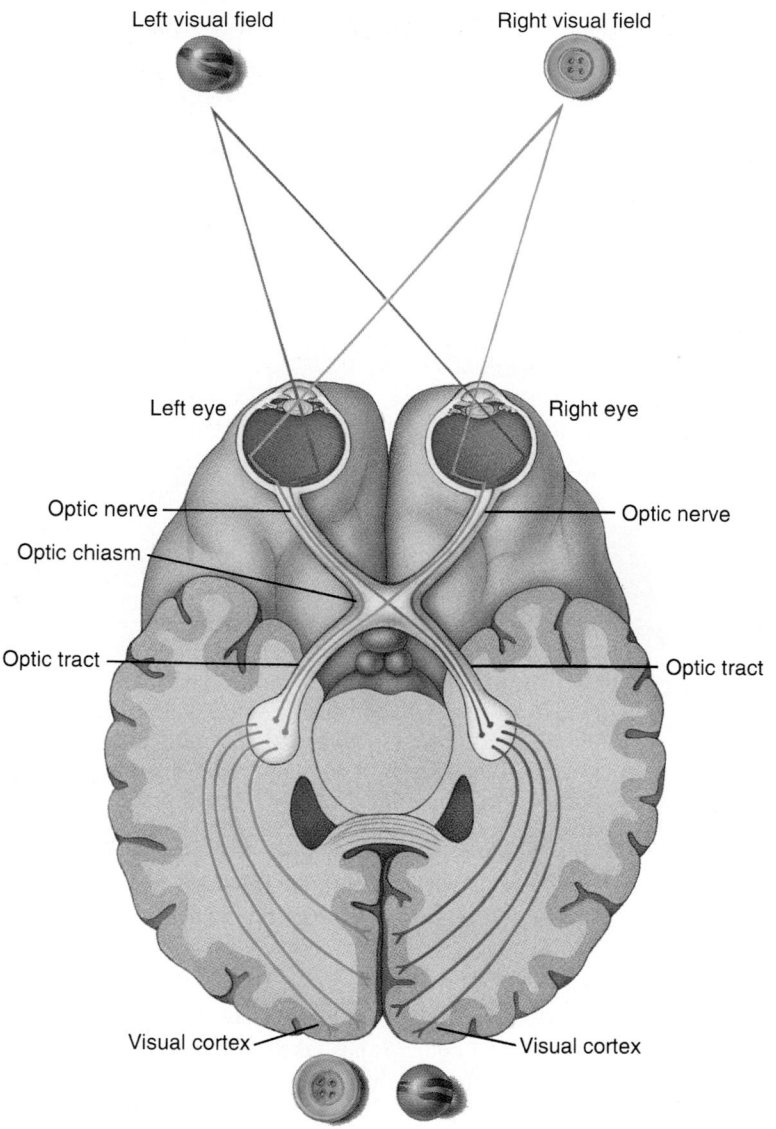

Left visual field

Right visual field

Left eye

Right eye

Optic nerve

Optic nerve

Optic chiasm

Optic tract

Optic tract

Visual cortex

Visual cortex

FIGURE 3.5
Images of objects in the right visual field are focused on the left side of each retina, and images of objects in the left visual field are focused on the right side of each retina. This information is conveyed along the optic nerves to the optic chiasm and the thalamus. The thalamus then relays the information to the visual cortex of the occipital lobes. Note that images of objects in the right visual field are processed by the left occipital lobe and images of objects in the left visual field are processed by the right occipital lobe.

in weak light) within about 5 minutes, so the rate of improvement slows after that. The rods continue to improve in sensitivity slowly, reaching a level of sensitivity to light that is an amazing *100,000 times greater* than in bright illumination after about 30 minutes in the dark.

In **light adaptation,** eyes that have been in the dark for a while have built up a full supply of the chemicals used in light reception and are very responsive to light. When we are suddenly exposed to intense light, a barrage of rods and cones fires almost at once and, in essence, "overloads" the visual circuits. It's not until the intense light has had a chance to bleach out some of the receptor chemicals and reduce the sensitivity of the receptors to a normal level that we can see comfortably again. Fortunately, this process takes place in about a minute.

By the way, your parents were right about carrots and good vision. The chemical involved in light reception in the rods is largely made up of vitamin A. This is why a deficiency of vitamin A can lead to "night blindness." And, yes, there is a lot of vitamin A in carrots.

Color Vision

Energy of any wavelength within the spectrum of visible light evokes a sensation of color when it stimulates the human visual system. But light energy is just that—energy; it has no

light adaptation
Regaining sensitivity of the eye to bright light following an abrupt increase in overall illumination.

In dim light, the color of this red apple hasn't changed, but its color appears to fade. Cones in the eye pick up color, but they work well only in bright light.

FIGURE 3.6

The trichromatic theory of color vision is based on the observation that all colors can be produced by various combinations of red, blue, and green light (and that all three lights together create white).

color of its own. Color is the conscious experience that results from the processing of light energy by the eye and nervous system.

It's obviously useful to be able to discriminate among lights of different wavelengths: "Blue" berries are ready to be eaten; "green" berries are not. But how does the human visual system produce the sensation of color? It has taken psychologists and other scientists more than a hundred years to reach the current understanding of the complex mechanisms of color vision.

In the early 1800s, Thomas Young and Hermann von Helmholz made the observation that any color can be created by shining different combinations of the wavelengths of light for red, blue, and green on a single spot. For example, as illustrated in figure 3.6, the combination of red and green light produces yellow. Based on this observation, Young and Helmholz guessed that there are three kinds of cones in the retina that respond mostly to light in either the red, green, or blue range of wavelengths. Their theory is referred to as the **trichromatic theory** of color vision. According to this theory, all sensations of colors result from different levels of stimulation of the red, green, and blue receptors.

Over the years, many types of studies have confirmed that there are indeed three kinds of cones. As shown in figure 3.7, each kind of cone contains pigments that mostly absorb light of the wavelengths that correspond to red, green, and blue. Does that mean that the trichromatic theory of Young and Helmholz was correct? Yes and no. Color vision is fascinatingly complex.

Soon after Young and Helmholz stated the trichromatic theory, other scientists pointed out that it could not explain three intriguing phenomena:

1. *Complementary colors.* Artists know that yellow and blue, as well as red and green, are complementary colors. You cannot mix lights of these colors to produce a yellowish-blue or a reddish-green. If color vision is simply a matter of combinations of impulses from cones that are mostly sensitive to red, green, and blue, how could some colors be complementary in this sense?

trichromatic theory
(trī″krō-mat′ik)   The theory of color vision contending that the eye has three different kinds of cones, each of which responds to light of one range of wavelength.

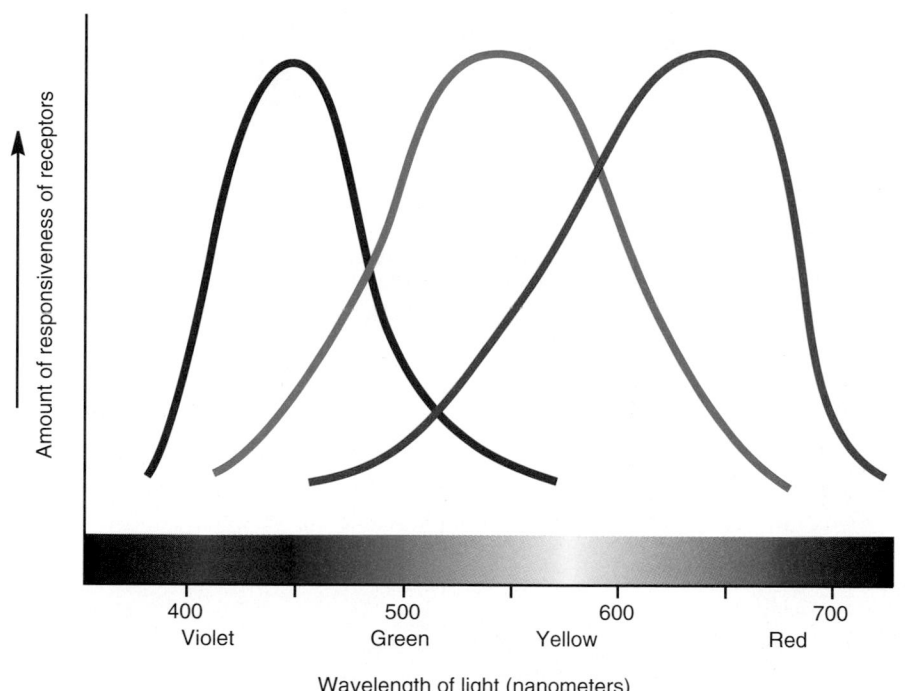

FIGURE 3.7
Our ability to see color is partly based on the fact that three kinds of cones contain pigments that respond mostly to light in the wavelengths for blue, green, and red. Note, however, that each type of cone also responds to other nearby wavelengths of light. This means, for example, that light in the yellow range stimulates both the red and the green cone receptors, but not as strongly as light in the red or green ranges, respectively.

2. *Color afterimages.* If you stare at a patch of color for a while and then shift your eyes to a white surface, you will see a ghostly "afterimage" of the patch in the color that is *complementary* to that of the original patch. For example, stare intensely for about 30 seconds at the white dot in the center of the word *red* that is printed in the color red in figure 3.8. Then stare at the blank white space above it. You will see an afterimage of the word *red,* but it will be *green.* The same thing occurs for all four of the complementary colors.

3. *Partial color blindness.* Partial color blindness affects about 8 percent of males and 1 percent of females. Most people with partial color blindness seem to see the world *almost* normally but have difficulty distinguishing between two colors. Usually, color-blind individuals cannot tell the difference between red and green, but they see yellow and blue normally (in fewer cases, they cannot distinguish yellow from blue but can see red and green normally). Note that the colors that look the same to a color-blind person are always complementary colors.

FIGURE 3.8
Stimulus used in the demonstration of afterimages.

Color blindness does not make sense in the trichromatic theory. You can explain why a person cannot distinguish between red and green by hypothesizing that something is wrong with either the red or the green receptors or both. But, according to the trichromatic theory, a person sees yellow because light of this wavelength stimulates both the red and the green receptors. If a person is color blind to red and green because there is something wrong with the red and green receptors, how can that person still see yellow? Psychologists soon realized that something more than three kinds of cones was involved in color vision.

The **opponent-process theory** was developed to explain the three phenomena that cannot be explained just by the existence of three kinds of cones. The opponent-process theory states that there are also two kinds of *color processing mechanisms,* which receive messages from the three kinds of cones (see fig. 3.9). These two color-processing mechanisms respond in *opposite* ways that correspond to the two pairs of complementary colors. For example, suppose you look at a lemon (and light in the yellow range of wavelength reflects from the lemon onto your retinas). Light of this wavelength stimulates both the red and green receptors, but not the blue receptors (see figure 3.7). The *yellow-blue (Y-B) processing mechanism* is *activated* by signals from the red and green receptors but is *slowed down* by inhibitory signals from the blue receptors. Therefore, light in the yellow wavelengths leads the Y-B mechanism to send a rapid message along the visual system to the

Opponent Process Theory

www.mhhe.com/laneye1

opponent-process theory
The theory of color vision contending that the visual system has two kinds of color processors, which respond to light in either the red-green or yellow-blue ranges of wavelength.

FIGURE 3.9

The modern theory of color vision combines the three kinds of cone color receptors of trichromatic theory with the two processing mechanisms of opponent-process theory. When light in the red wavelengths stimulates the red receptors, the receptors send a strong excitatory message to the red-green (R-G) opponent mechanism, which stimulates rapid firing of neural signals to the brain. Light in the yellow wavelengths stimulates both the red and the green receptors somewhat. They both send weak excitatory messages to the yellow-blue (Y-B) opponent mechanism, but together they are strong enough to stimulate it to send fast signals to the brain. When light is in the blue wavelengths, it stimulates the blue receptors, which send strong inhibitory messages to the Y-B opponent mechanism, leading it to fire slowly. Light in the green wavelengths leads to slow firing of the R-G opponent mechanism in a similar fashion.

Individuals with normal color vision can see the number as 8. Red-green color-blind individuals see a 3 here.

This has been reproduced from Ishihara's Tests for Colour Blindness published by KANEHARA & CO., LTD., Tokyo, Japan, but tests for color blindness cannot be conducted with this material. For accurate testing, the original plates should be used.

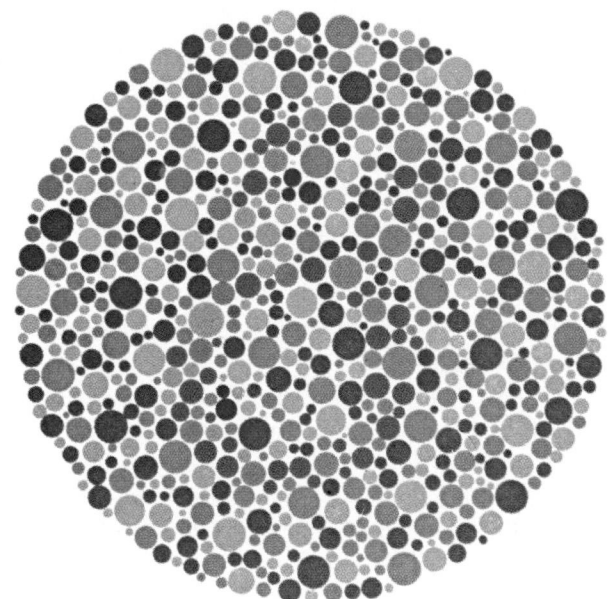

brain. This signal is the primary information used by the brain to produce the sensation of yellow on the peel of the lemon. On the other hand, the *red-green (R-G) processing mechanism* is activated by signals from the red receptors but is slowed by signals from the green receptors. When light in the green wavelengths stimulates the green receptors, the receptors send a strong inhibitory message to the red-green (R-G) opponent mechanism, which causes it to send slow neural signals to the brain. In similar ways, combinations of signals from the opponent-processing mechanisms supply the brain with the information necessary for all color sensations.

Notice that opponent-process theory explains the phenomenon of complementary colors because the R-G and Y-B mechanisms cannot signal both of their opponent colors at the same time. It also explains why afterimages are always in the opposite complementary color to the original stimulus. Staring at the red stimulus reduces the sensitivity of the red receptors (through sensory adaptation), leading the R-G system to send a signal to the brain that is interpreted as the sensation of green. The opponent-process theory also explains color blindness as an abnormality in one of the opponent-process mechanisms. Perhaps the strongest evidence for the opponent-process theory, however, is that neurons throughout the visual system and cerebral cortex respond to light in an opponent-process fashion

(Engel, 1999). For example, if a specific neuron in the retina is excited by green light, then it is inhibited from firing by red light.

Thus, the trichromatic theory accurately describes events very well at the first level of neurons in the visual system—the cones within the retina—but the opponent-process theory best describes the activities of neurons in the rest of the visual system. They are both correct, in other words, when combined (Pugh, 1988).

● **Review**

The eye is much like a human camera. The lens focuses a visual image on the retina of the eye, which contains two kinds of sensory receptor cells, the rods and cones. These transduce the wavelength, amplitude, and complexity of the light waves into neural messages. The two kinds of receptor cells perform their jobs somewhat differently. Cones work best in intense light, provide good visual acuity, and transduce information about color. Rods work well in weak light, do not provide good acuity, and do not transduce color. The eye does not function well when the intensity of light suddenly changes, but it quickly regains its sensitivity through the processes of light and dark adaptation. There are two major theoretical explanations of how the visual system transduces color. One states that three different kinds of cones are most sensitive to light of different wavelengths. The other suggests that two kinds of color-processing mechanisms in the visual system process complementary colors. Each theory is "correct" at different stages of the information processing about the wavelength of light.

● **Check Your Learning**

To be sure that you have learned the key points from the preceding section, cover the list of correct answers and try to answer each question. If you give an incorrect answer to any question, return to the page given next to the correct answer to see why your answer was not correct.

1. The _____ of the light largely determines the color that we see.

   a) intensity   c) saturation
   b) amplitude   d) wavelength

2. Light waves are transduced into neural messages by two types of receptor cells, named rods and cones, in the _____ of the eye.

   a) ciliary structure   c) retina
   b) pupil   d) iris

3. Cones are concentrated in the _____.

   a) periphery of the eye c) iris
   b) fovea   d) blind spot

4. The theory of color vision that there are three kinds of cones in the retina, which respond primarily to light in either the red, green, or blue range of wavelengths, is the _____ theory.

   a) opponent-process   c) psychophysical
   b) trichromatic   d) sensory adaptation

● **Thinking Critically About Psychology**

1. If cones give us the best visual acuity, what is the advantage of having rods as well?

2. Which theory of color vision do you think would make the most sense to an artist? Why?

Correct Answers   1. d (p. 78),   **2. c** (p. 79),   **3. b** (p. 79),   **4. b** (p. 82).

▶ HEARING: SENSING SOUND WAVES

Without hearing and vision, there probably would be no spoken or written languages, and without language most of the cultural and scientific accomplishments of human beings probably would have been impossible. The sense of hearing depends on the ear, a complex sensory instrument that transduces the physical properties of sound waves into neural messages that can be sent to the brain. Neural messages from the ears are first interpreted in the temporal lobe's auditory area and then forwarded to other parts of the brain for additional interpretation.

Sound: What Is It?

audition
(aw-dish´un)   The sense of hearing.

sound waves
Vibratory changes in the air that carry sound.

frequency of cycles
The rate of vibration of sound waves; determines pitch.

hertz (Hz)
The measurement of the frequency of sound waves in cycles per second.

intensity
The density of vibrating air molecules, which determines the loudness of sound.

pitch
The experience of sound vibrations sensed as high or low.

decibel (db)
(des´i-bel)   Measurement of the intensity of perceived sound.

Hearing, or **audition,** is the sense that detects the vibratory changes in the air known as **sound waves.** When an object, such as a tuning fork, vibrates back and forth, it sets in motion successive waves of *compression* and *rarefaction* (expansion) of the molecules of the air (see fig. 3.10). When the waves reach the ear, the reception of sound begins. As we will see, the sound waves in the air cause a chain of small structures in the ear to vibrate in a way that is eventually translated into a neural message to the brain.

Not all sound waves are alike, however, and the nature of a sound wave determines to a great extent how we will sense it. For one thing, sound waves differ in the **frequency of cycles** of compression and rarefaction of the air (see fig. 3.10). Objects that vibrate slowly create low-frequency sound waves, whereas rapidly vibrating objects produce high-frequency sound waves. The frequency of sound waves is measured in **hertz (Hz)** units, the number of vibratory cycles per second. The human ear is sensitive to sound waves in the range of 20 to 20,000 Hz. Sound waves also differ in terms of **intensity,** or how densely compacted the air molecules are in the sound wave.

The frequency of a sound wave largely determines its **pitch,** or how high or low it sounds to us. For example, striking a glass with a spoon causes a higher-frequency sound wave—which we hear as a higher pitch—than striking a bass drum. The loudness of a sound is largely determined by its intensity. Gently tapping a bass drum produces less dense compression and rarefaction, and a quieter sound, than striking it hard. Intensity is measured in **decibel (db)** units. This scale begins at zero at the absolute threshold for detecting a 1,000 Hz tone (and increases by 20 db as the intensity of the stimulus is multiplied by 10). Normal conversation averages about 60 db, whereas sounds of 120 db or more are

Graphic representation of sound wave   Rarefied air molecules   Compressed air molecules

Vibrating tuning fork

Maximum compression   Maximum rarefaction   One cycle

FIGURE 3.10
Vibrating objects, such as a tuning fork, create a sound wave of successive compression and rarefaction (expansion) in the air, which can be represented graphically as shown.

Decibels	Sounds
120	Loud thunder or rock concert
110	
100	Subway
90	City bus
85	Maximum level of industrial noise considered safe
80	Noisy automobile
70	
60	Normal conversation
50	
40	Quiet office
30	
20	Whisper
10	
0	Absolute threshold of human hearing

FIGURE 3.11

The loudness of common sounds as measured in decibel units.

Note: Prolonged exposure to sounds over 85 decibels can lead to permanent hearing loss. Even brief exposure to loudness of 150 decibels (being close to an explosion or the speakers at some rock concerts) can permanently damage hearing.

quite painful (see fig. 3.11). The **timbre** of a sound (its characteristic quality) is determined by the complexity of the sound wave—that is, the extent to which it is composed of many waves of different frequency and intensity. The voices of different people sound different to us largely because of their unique timbres.

The relationship between the physical properties of sound waves and the sensation of sound is not as simple as I have just made it seem, however. Take loudness, for example. Two tones of equal intensity may not be heard as equally loud if they are not equal in frequency. Loudness seems greatest for tones of about 3,000 to 4,000 Hz; higher- or lower-frequency sounds of the same intensity seem less loud to us.

timbre
(tim′ber, tam′br)   The characteristic quality of a sound as determined by the complexity of the sound wave.

The Ear: How Does It Work?

The ear is a sensitive sensory instrument that transduces sound waves into neural impulses to the brain. It is composed of three major sections: the outer ear, middle ear, and inner ear (see fig. 3.12).

Outer Ear

The external part of the ear, or **pinna,** which we think of as the "ear," is useful as a sound collector, and it plays an important role in locating the origins of sounds. The shape of the pinna is especially important in sound localization, as shown by the fact that temporarily smoothing the pinna with putty impairs sound localization. Connecting the outer and middle ear is the hollow **external auditory canal.** It's the part that gets waxy and the part through which sound waves reach the **eardrum,** the first structure of the middle ear.

Middle Ear

The sound wave is transduced into mechanical energy in the middle ear. Sound waves set the thin **eardrum,** which resembles the skin on a drum, into vibratory movement. The eardrum is connected to a series of three movable, interconnected bones: the **hammer,** the **anvil,** and the **stirrup,** so named because of their shapes. The vibrating eardrum sets these bones into movement, passing on the energy to the inner ear.

Inner Ear

The vibrating stirrup shakes another eardrumlike structure called the **oval window** into motion. This membrane is at the end of a long, curled structure called the **cochlea,** which is filled with fluid. The vibrating oval window creates waves in the fluid of the cochlea (see fig. 3.13). The cochlea contains two long tubes that double back on themselves and are

pinna
(pin′nah)   The external part of the ear.

external auditory canal
The tube connecting the pinna to the middle ear.

eardrum
A thin membrane that sound waves cause to vibrate; a structure of the middle ear.

hammer, anvil, stirrup
Three linked bones of the middle ear, which pass sound waves to the inner ear.

oval window
The membrane of the inner ear that vibrates, creating sound waves in the fluid of the cochlea.

cochlea
(cok′lē-ah)   A curved structure of the inner ear that is filled with fluid.

FIGURE 3.12

Major structures of the ear.

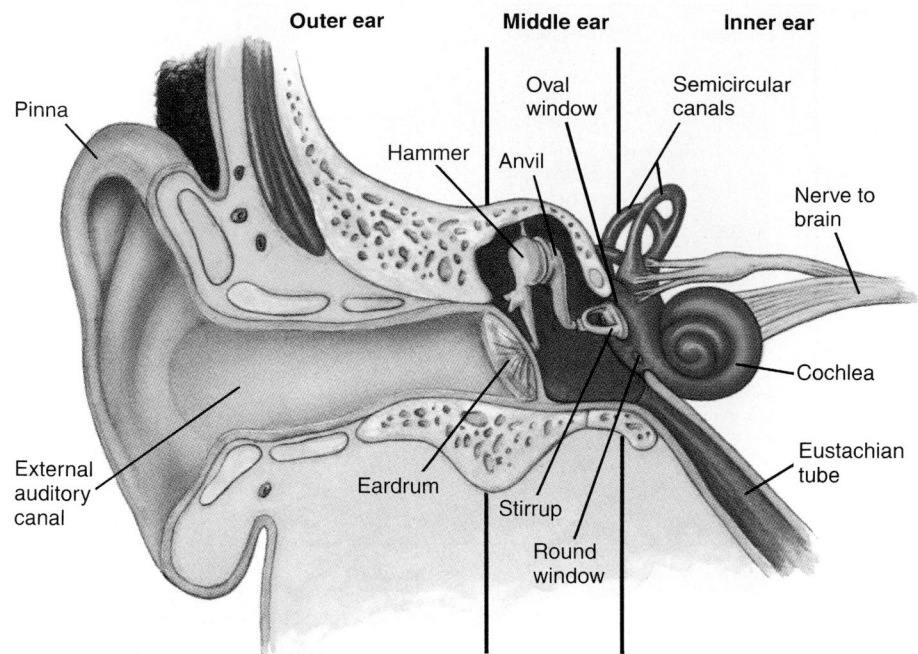

Outer ear   **Middle ear**   **Inner ear**

Pinna

Oval window

Hammer   Anvil

Semicircular canals

Nerve to brain

Cochlea

External auditory canal

Eardrum

Stirrup

Eustachian tube

Round window

round window
The membrane that relieves pressure from the vibrating waves in the cochlear fluid.

basilar membrane
(bas´ĭ-lar)   One of the membranes that separate the two tubes of the cochlea and on which the organ of Corti rests.

organ of Corti
(kor´tē)   A sensory receptor in the cochlea that transduces sound waves into coded neural impulses.

bone conduction hearing
Hearing accomplished through sounds transmitted through the bones of the head directly to the cochlear fluid.

connected only at the tip end of the spiral. The pressure of the vibrating waves is relieved by a third eardrumlike membrane at the other end of the cochlea called the **round window.** Running almost the entire length of the cochlea are several layers of membranes that separate the two tubes. The lower membrane, called the **basilar membrane,** forms a floor on which the ear's sensory receptors sit. Hairlike receptor cells are contained in the **organ of Corti.** Vibrations in the cochlear fluid set the basilar membrane in motion. This movement, in turn, moves the organ of Corti and stimulates the receptor cells it contains. These receptors transduce the sound waves in the cochlear fluid into coded neural impulses, which are sent to the brain.

How does the organ of Corti code neural messages for the brain? The *intensity* of a sound wave is coded by the number of receptors in the organ of Corti that fire. Low-intensity sounds stimulate only a few receptors; high-intensity sounds stimulate many receptors.

The *frequency* of the sound wave is apparently coded in at least two ways. First, sound waves of different frequencies stimulate firings of receptor cells at different *places* along the organ of Corti. Higher-frequency waves stimulate the organ of Corti close to the oval window; lower-frequency waves stimulate it farther along the cochlea (except for very low frequencies). Second, the frequency of the sound waves is duplicated to some extent in the *frequency* of the firings of the auditory receptors. Only at lower frequencies is each neuron able to fire at the same frequency as the sound wave. At higher frequencies, the coding of frequency is achieved by the firing of *volleys* of neural impulses by different groups of neurons, which fire in turns at the same frequency as the sound wave.

Not all sounds travel this complete route from outer ear to cochlea. Some sounds are transmitted through the bones of the head directly to the cochlear fluid. We hear ourselves speak (and eat) largely through **bone conduction hearing.** This is an important consideration in diagnosing hearing problems. People who have suffered damage to the hearing apparatus of the middle ear can hear bone-conducted sounds fairly well, but not airborne sounds. People with damage to the auditory nerve—nerve deafness—cannot hear either type of sound.

One more thing about ears deserves mentioning. Ever wonder why people have two of them? For one thing, a pair of ears gives us a spare in case something goes wrong with one, but the fact that we have two ears also serves an important function in *locating* the origin of sounds. The ears locate sounds in two ways. First, when a sound wave is coming from straight ahead or from straight behind us, the sound reaches both ears simultaneously. But, when a sound is coming from the sides or from an angle, it reaches each ear at a

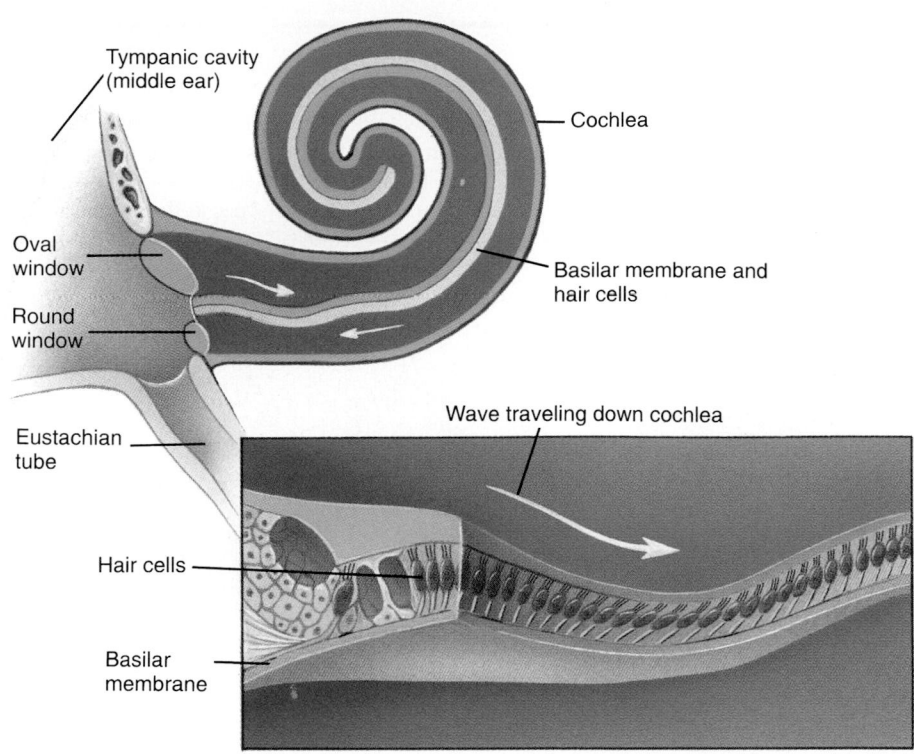

FIGURE 3.13

Vibrations from sound waves enter the cochlea through the oval window and travel the length of the cochlea, where they are transduced into neural messages by hair cell receptors in the organ of Corti.

Two factors tell the listener the location of sounds. First, a sound wave that originates from the side reaches the closer ear slightly sooner than it reaches the farther ear. Second, the head blocks some of the sound wave that reaches the farther ear, reducing the intensity of stimulation to the ear that is farther away from the source of the sound.

slightly different time. The ears are sensitive enough to this difference that they allow us to locate the direction of sounds, especially high-frequency sounds. The reason you know that the person to the left of you is blowing her nose again is because your left ear hears it before your right ear does. Second, cues for the location of high-frequency sounds are also produced by the fact that your head dampens some of the sound reaching the more distant ear, creating a difference in the intensity of the sound waves that reach each of the ears.

● Review

Sound is a physical stimulus made up of successive waves of densely and sparsely compressed air. The ear is composed of a series of structures that transmit the sound wave from the outer ear to the inner ear, where it produces vibrations in the fluid of the cochlea. The vibrations of the cochlear fluid are transduced by the ear's receptor cells in the organ of Corti. Coded neural messages are sent to the auditory sensory areas of the brain, where frequency, intensity, and complexity are interpreted as pitch, loudness, and timbre. Differences in the timing and intensity of sound waves reaching the two ears allow us to determine the location of the source of the sound.

● Check Your Learning

To be sure that you have learned the key points from the preceding section, cover the list of correct answers and try to answer each question. If you give an incorrect answer to any question, return to the page given next to the correct answer to see why your answer was not correct.

1. Objects that vibrate slowly create low-frequency sound waves, which we hear as having
   _____ .

   a) low pitch   c) simple timbre
   b) high pitch   d) complex timbre

2. The sound wave is transduced into mechanical energy (the motion of the hammer, anvil, and stirrup) in the _____ .

   a) outer ear   c) inner ear
   b) middle ear   d) pinna

3. The sound wave is transduced into neural impulses in the _____ , which is located in the cochlea in the inner ear.

   a) auditory nerve   c) organ of Corti
   b) cochlear fluid   d) pinna

4. You know that the person speaking to you is on your left because

   a) the sound reaches your left ear slightly before it reaches your right ear.
   b) the sound wave that reaches your left ear is slightly more intense than the sound wave that reaches your right ear.
   c) both of the above.
   d) neither of the above.

● Thinking Critically About Psychology

1. In terms of human adaptation and survival, what are the advantages and disadvantages of having our ears located on the sides of our heads, rather than somewhere else on the body?

2. Juan and Patrick are close friends. Juan hears normally, but Patrick is totally deaf. How might this difference in the way they experience life influence their friendship?

Correct Answers 1. a (p. 86), 2. b (p. 87), 3. c (p. 88), 4. c (p. 89).

▶ BODY SENSES: MESSAGES FROM MYSELF

The body senses tell us how the body is oriented, where it moves, what it touches, and so on. Information about orientation and movement comes from a sense organ located in the inner ear and from individual receptors spread throughout the body. Information about touch and temperature is provided by a variety of receptors located below the surface of the skin. Information about pain comes from receptors in the skin and inside the body. Although we usually are not aware that we are using this information, the body senses play an important role in keeping us standing upright, moving straight ahead, and literally out of hot water. Information from all of the body senses is sent to the somatosensory area of the parietal lobe of the cerebral cortex.

Orientation and Movement

Messages about the orientation, balance, and movement of the body come to us from two kinds of sense organs. A complicated set of sensory structures called the **vestibular organ** is located in the inner section of the ear, where it provides the cerebral cortex with information about orientation and movement. Individual sensory receptors, called **kinesthetic receptors,** located in the muscles, joints, and skin provide additional messages about movement, posture, and orientation.

Vestibular Organ

The vestibular organ is composed of two small sensory structures: the *semicircular canals* and the linked *saccule* and *utricle* (see fig. 3.14). The **saccule** and **utricle** are fluid-filled sacs in the inner ear that contain sensory receptors that keep the brain informed about the body's orientation. The part of the vestibular organ that provides the most sensitive messages to the brain about orientation, however, is the **semicircular canals.** This organ

vestibular organ
(ves-tib′ū-lar)   The sensory structures in the inner ear that provide the brain with information about orientation and movement.

kinesthetic receptors
(kin″es-thet′ik)   Receptors in the muscles, joints, and skin that provide information about movement, posture, and orientation.

saccule, utricle
(sak′ūl ū′tre-k′l)   Fluid-filled sacs of the vestibular organ that inform the brain about the body's orientation.

semicircular canals
(sem″ē-ser′kū-lar)   Three nearly circular tubes in the vestibular organ that inform the brain about tilts of the head and body.

FIGURE 3.14
Major structures of the vestibular organ.

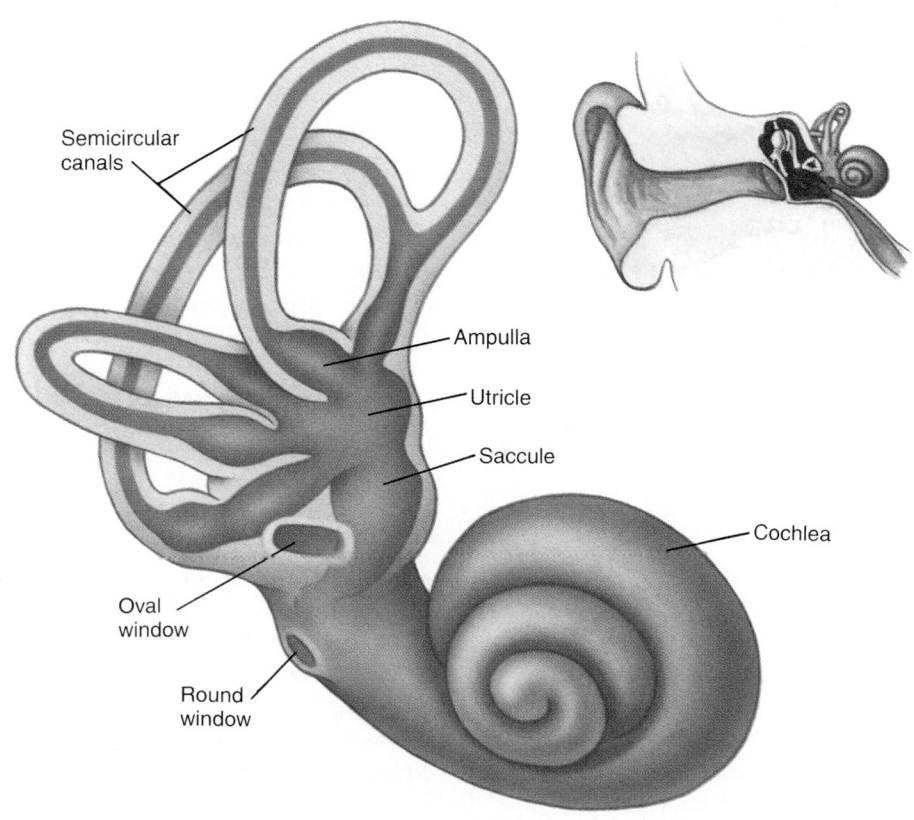

Semicircular canals

Ampulla

Utricle

Saccule

Cochlea

Oval window

Round window

The vestibular organ and kinesthic receptors help orient us, even in un-usual situations.

Robots are important to the safe handling of hazardous materials. Using what is known about the sense of touch, the inventors of the "Salisbury Hand" have given it kinesthetic sensors that simulate tension on the tendons of the hand and stimulation of the fingertips.
(Photo of Salisbury Hand at MI TAI lab courtesy of David Lampe, MIT)

cupula
(ku'-pu-lah)   A gelatin-like structure containing a tuft of hairlike sensory receptor cells in the semicircular canals.

free nerve endings
Sensory receptor cells in the skin that detect pressure, temperature, and pain.

basket cells
Sensory receptor cells at the base of hairs that detect pressure.

tactile discs
(tak'til) Sensory receptor cells that detect pressure.

specialized end bulbs
Sensory receptor cells that detect pressure and skin pleasure.

constitutes a marvelous bit of natural engineering perfectly suited to its purpose. The semicircular canals are composed of three nearly circular tubes (canals) that lie at right angles to one another, providing information on orientation of the body in three planes—left and right, up and down, and front to back. Think of the semicircular canals as the corner of a room, with one in the plane of the floor and the other two in the planes of the walls. At the base of each canal is an enlargement that holds the sensory receptors. A tuft of these hairlike cells is formed in a gelatin-like structure called the **cupula,** which sticks out into the enlargement of the canal. As the head is tilted, the fluid flows through the canal in the opposite direction. This bends the cupula and causes its receptors to fire, sending a message of "tilt" to the brain. Although the vestibular organ provides the brain with vital information about orientation and movement, it can turn from a friend to an enemy at times. When confused by rocking boats, bumping airplanes, or twisting circus rides, it can produce nausea. Why does that happen? Why would tilting the vestibular organ cause nausea and vomiting—as in "seasickness"? Experts think it is because the disorientation and dizziness of seasickness resemble the dizziness caused by poisoning. The body apparently vomits in response to dizziness regardless of the cause, just in case it is due to poisoning (Stern & Koch, 1996).

Kinesthetic Sense

Throughout the skin, muscles, joints, and tendons are kinesthetic receptors, which signal when they are moved. As the body walks, bends, writes, and so on, these receptors provide information about the location and movement of each part of the body. Close your eyes, take off your shoes, and wiggle your toes. You can tell they are wiggling because of your kinesthetic sense. Unlike the vestibular organ, the kinesthetic receptors are individual receptors that are not clumped together into sense organs. But, as reflected in the skilled movements of a musician, painter, or discus thrower, they are remarkably sensitive, allowing fine and complicated patterns of movement.

Skin Senses

We usually do not think of the skin as a sense organ, yet it's capable of picking up a number of kinds of sensory information. The skin can detect *pressure, temperature,* and *pain.* Feeling a kiss on the cheek, cold in the winter, getting hit by a rock, and all other sensations involving the skin are made up of combinations of these three skin sensations.

Although the skin can detect only three kinds of sensory information, there are at least four types of receptors in the skin: the **free nerve endings,** the **basket cells** wound around the base of hairs, the **tactile discs,** and the **specialized end bulbs.** These are shown in figure 3.15. It appears that all four play a role in the sense of touch (pressure), with the free nerve endings being the primary receptors for temperature and pain (Groves & Rebec, 1988; Hole, 1990).

Pressure

The skin is amazingly sensitive to pressure, but sensitivity differs considerably from one region of the skin to another depending on how many skin receptors are present. In the most sensitive regions—the fingertips, the lips, and the genitals—a pressure that pushes in the skin less than 0.001 mm can be felt, but sensitivity in other areas is considerably less (Schiffman, 1976). Perhaps the most striking example of the sensitivity of the skin is its ability to "read." Many blind people can read books using the Braille alphabet, patterns of small raised dots that stand for the letters of the alphabet. An experienced Braille user can read up to 300 words per minute using the sensitive skin of the fingertips (see fig. 3.16).

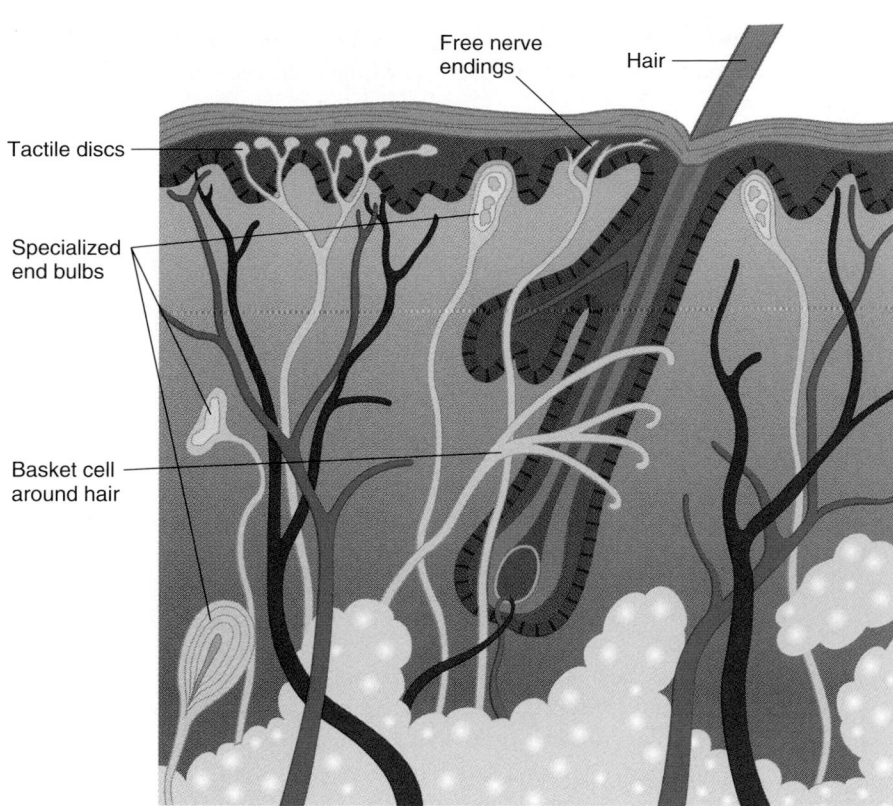

FIGURE 3.15
Diagram of the skin showing the major skin receptor cells.

Temperature

When the air outside is hot or cold, how do you sense this fact? It seems to most of us that the entire surface of the skin is able to detect temperature, but we actually sense skin temperature only through sensory receptors (free nerve endings) located in rather widely spaced "spots" on the skin. One set of spots detects warmth and one detects coldness. The information sent to the brain by these spots creates the feeling of temperature across the entire skin surface.

When the skin is warmed (for example, by air, sunlight, or water), the receptors in the warm spots send messages about warmness to the brain; when the skin is cooled, the cold spots send messages about coldness. Recall from chapter 1 (p. 8) that the sensation of intense heat is created by stimulation of *both* the warm and cold spots. Although the cold receptors are generally responsive only to cold temperatures, extreme heat also makes them fire. Therefore, high temperatures stimulate the receptors in both sets of spots to send messages simultaneously to the brain, which are interpreted as hotness.

Pain

Everyone experiences some pain. Toes get stepped on, fingers are cut, and ankles are twisted from time to time. Even though it is unpleasant, pain is the useful signal that something bad has happened to a part of the body and it needs our attention. What are the neural systems that underlie the experience of pain?

Free nerve endings throughout the body serve as **nocioceptors**—receptors for stimuli that are experienced as painful. Neural messages from the nocioceptors are transmitted to the brain along two distinct nerve pathways—*rapid* and *slow* neural pathways. This is why we often experience "first and second pain" (Melzack & Wall, 1983; Sternbach, 1978). The first pain sensation is a clear, localized feeling that does not "hurt" much, but it tells us what part of the body has been hurt and what kind of injury has occurred. The second pain is a more diffuse, long-lasting pain that hurts in the emotional sense. When you cut your finger with a knife, an initial sensation tells you that you have been cut and where

FIGURE 3.16
Raised dots used in the Braille alphabet are "read" with the fingertips.

nocioceptors
Receptors for stimuli that are experienced as painful.

the cut has occurred, followed a moment later by a more diffuse and painful sensation. The first sensation makes you drop the knife and grab your finger; the second makes you jump up and down and scream!

There are two reasons that we experience these two somewhat separate pain sensations in sequence. First, the two sensations travel on different neural pathways, which have different speeds of transmission. The rapid pathway neurons are thicker and sheathed in myelin (see p. 35), which speeds transmission. The slow pathway neurons, in contrast, are smaller and slower, unmyelinated neurons. The second reason that we experience first and second pain is that the two neural pathways travel to different parts of the brain. The rapid pathway travels through the thalamus to the somatosensory area. If you recall from chapter 2 (p. 47), this is the part of the parietal lobe of the cerebral cortex that receives and interprets sensory information from the skin and body. When the information transmitted to this area on the rapid pathway is interpreted, we know what has happened and where it has happened, but the somatosensory area does not process the emotional aspects of the experience of "pain." Information that travels on the slower pathway is routed to the limbic system (p. 45). It is here, in the brain system that mediates emotion, that the emotional "ouch" part of the experience of pain is processed.

Pain Gates

Pain involves much more than the transmission of neural messages from nocioceptors to the brain, however (Keefe & France, 1999). There is not a direct relationship between the stimulus and the amount of pain experienced. Under certain circumstances, pain messages can even be blocked out of the brain. For example, a football player whose attention is focused on a big game may not notice a painful cut until after the game is over. The pain receptors transmit the pain message during the game, but the message is not fully processed by the brain until the player is no longer concentrating on the game (Keefe & France, 1999).

Psychologist Ronald Melzack of McGill University proposed the *gate-control theory of pain* to explain such phenomena (Melzack & Wall, 1983). According to this well-supported theory, neural "gates" regulate the transmission of impulses from the nocioceptors to the brain (see fig. 3.17). All messages from nocioceptors from the body travel to the brain through the brain stem. The slow-pain neural fibers pass through neural gates in the brain stem that can be either "opened" or "closed." That is, the pain gates can make us more or less sensitive to stimulation of the nocioceptors. The pain gates can be influenced to allow more slow-pain neural transmission along the slow-pain pathways to the limbic system in two ways. First, when pain messages are received from nocioceptors—say, from a bruised toe—they sensitize the pain gates and make them transmit slow-pain impulses more readily. This is because a substance involved in slow-pain transmission—called *substance P* (for pain)—sometimes diffuses across to nearby nerves in the brain stem that ordinarily do not carry pain messages, causing them to transmit pain impulses too (Hopkins, 1997). Second, messages down from the midbrain make the pain gates more likely to allow slow-pain impulses through to the limbic system.

Fortunately, the pain gates also can be "closed" to make them less likely to transmit slow-pain impulses to the limbic system. For example, placing a sore foot in warm water helps close the gate on pain from the toe. The warm sensations block some of the pain sensations by closing the neural gates. Apparently, the rapid-pain pathways do not pass through the pain gates and cannot be blocked. The slow-pain pathways that carry the most distressing pain messages can be regulated by the pain gates under some circumstances, however (Melzack & Wall, 1983).

The pain gates appear to be operated by specialized neurons that block transmission in the neurons that carry "second pain" messages to the brain. As shown in figure 4.19, the *gate neurons* inhibit the pain neurons using substances called *endorphins*. When

Guy Gertsch, who finished the 1982 Boston Marathon in a respectable 2 hours and 47 minutes, discovered at the finish line that he had run the last 19 miles with a broken thigh bone.

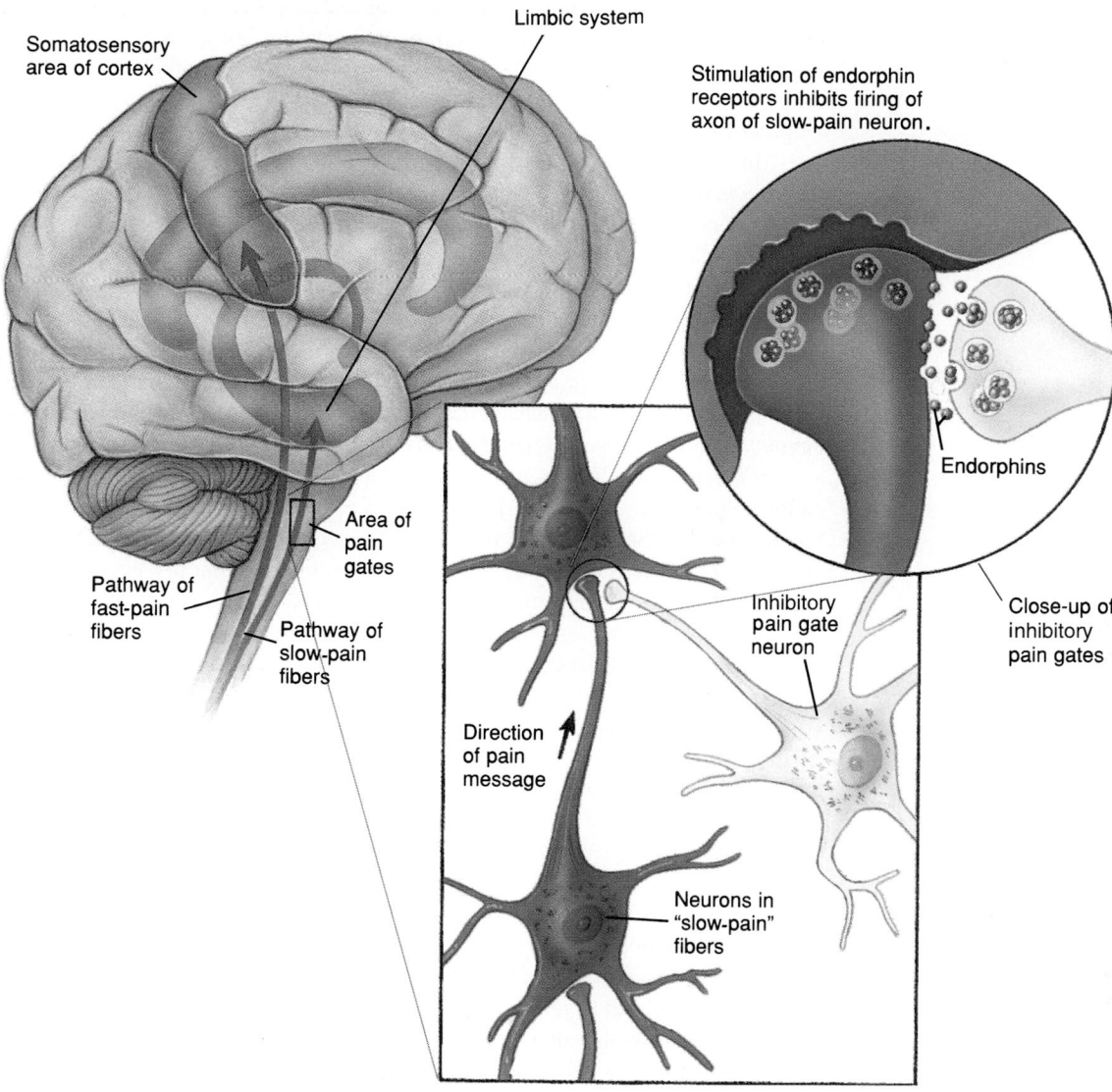

FIGURE 3.17

The operation of inhibitory pain gates. Secretion of endorphins by inhibitory gate neurons inhibits the firing of the axon of the neuron that transmits the pain message. Pain gate neurons regulate only the transmission of "slow-pain" fibers and are located primarily in the brain stem and spinal cord. Unfortunately, other pain gate neurons can make transmission of "slow-pain" messages to the limbic system more likely under some circumstances.

signaled by other sensory neurons or by neural fibers from the cortex to close the pain gate, the gate neuron inhibits the pain neuron and stops the pain message from reaching the brain.

Interestingly, women have a second pain-gate mechanism, based on the hormone estrogen, that males do not have (Mogil, Sternberg, Kest, Marek, & Liebeskind, 1993). This additional pain gate may help women deal with the pain experienced in childbirth, and its discovery may explain differences between males and females in their experience of pain and lead to more effective pain-controlling medications for women.

The discovery of a second substance that regulates the pain gates does not reduce the importance of the endorphins in both men and women, however. The discovery of the endorphins in 1973 by Candace Pert and Solomon Snyder has helped explain several mysteries about pain. First, a number of pain-killing drugs, such as the opiate morphine, clearly operate by duplicating the effects of the endorphins in inhibiting pain neurons. Indeed, the term *endorphin* means *endogenous* (produced inside the body) *morphine*. Second, the "high" that many runners feel during and right after endurance runs appears to be the result of the release of high levels of endorphins. Endorphins are released not only by specialized neurons in the spinal cord and brain stem but also by the hypothalamus and pituitary gland under times of physical or psychological stress, including the stress of endurance running. Apparently, runners are slightly high on the body's own supply of morphine.

In addition, two medical mysteries apparently can be explained by the endorphins—the effects of acupuncture and placebo medications. Pain can often be reduced by the procedure of *acupuncture*. In this procedure, needles are inserted in the skin at special points and then twirled or heated. There is little doubt that some persons receiving acupuncture experience less pain, but the question is why. One possibility is that the needles stimulate the production of endorphins, which block the pain in the pain gates. To test this hypothesis, a drug that blocks the action of the endorphins (naloxone) was administered to persons undergoing acupuncture. While the endorphin-blocking drug was active, the person receiving acupuncture experienced the normal level of pain (Price, 1988). This suggests that acupuncture may close the pain gates by stimulating the endorphins.

Placebo medications are inactive substances, such as sugar pills or injections of saline solution, that are given during studies of new medications. The effects of the actual medication are compared with those of the placebo to see whether the medication is truly effective. Physicians have long been puzzled by the fact that placebos often make patients with a wide range of discomforts feel better. It now appears that endorphins also mediate the effects of placebos. As with the acupuncture studies, giving the endorphin-blocking drug naloxone eliminates the pain-killing effects of placebos (Levine, Gordon, & Fields, 1979). Apparently, being told that you have been given a medication that will help you stimulates the release of endorphins, and you really do feel better. This raises the possibility that acupuncture is effective not because of the placement of the needles but because of the placebo effect of believing that it will work.

Phantom Limbs

Amazingly, many amputees experience their missing arm or leg as if it were still there. They feel a missing arm, for example, as if it were hanging by their side when they sit still, and swinging in coordination with their other arm and legs when they walk. This "phantom limb" is experienced not as a memory of the lost limb but as a clear and realistic sensation that the missing limb is actually there. Ronald Melzack (1992) wrote about a man who experienced his missing arm as sticking straight out to the side, so he turned sideways when he walked through doorways to avoid bumping his arm, even though he knew perfectly well that the arm was not really there.

The sadder part is that as many as 70 percent of amputees experience a disturbing pain in the phantom limb. The pain is often a burning sensation, with many persons with amputated legs reporting that their nonexistent toes feel as if they are being seared by a hot fireplace poker. Similarly, persons with amputated arms often say that they feel their phantom hand is tightly clenched, with the fingernails digging painfully into their palms. A friend of mine recently wrote to say, "My mother, who lost her left leg to polio in her early 20s, is now 73, and sometimes when I ask how her arthritis is, she often responds, 'The foot I don't have aches as much as my good one.'" Amputees are not the only persons who experience such sensations. Persons with spinal cord injuries can experience no true sensations from the parts of their body below the break in the neural pathways in the spinal cord, but they sometimes experience phantom sensations in their limbs or genitals. Similarly, persons born without arms or legs often experience phantom sensations in the missing limb (Melzack, 1992).

How is it possible to "feel" sensations from a limb that does not exist and, therefore, cannot be transmitting sensations to the brain? A team of researchers from Germany and the United States appears to have provided the answer (Flor & others, 1995). Using brain-imaging techniques, they found that, when sensory and pain neurons from one part of the body have been cut, the area of the somatosensory cortex that served that part of the body becomes sensitive to input from parts of the body that activate *nearby* portions of the somatosensory cortex. For example, in the case of a woman who has lost her left arm

Some persons who have had limbs amputated still feel "phantom limbs" in place of the missing limbs. Often, they feel pain in the phantom limbs.

HUMAN DIVERSITY

CULTURE AND PAIN

In this chapter, we examine the ways in which neural impulses from the sense organs are experienced as sensations and perceptions. Although much of this process is determined by the biological nature of the sense organs and neurons, learning experiences in our cultures apparently can influence even basic sensations such as pain.

Let's consider an example of the impact of culture on the perception of pain. Members of the Bariba society in Benin, West Africa, appear to be able to tolerate pain more easily than members of most cultures. Bariba folklore includes many examples of honored people who showed strength in the face of pain, and this calm response to pain is seen as an integral part of Bariba pride (Sargent, 1984). For example, pregnant women are expected not to let the fact that they are experiencing labor pains show to others. When labor becomes advanced, they leave the company of others to go through labor and childbirth alone, only calling for help with cutting the umbilical cord.

To the Bariba, letting other people see that they are in pain is cause for great shame. When discussing pain, many Bariba quote a Bariba proverb that translates to "Between death and shame, death has the greater beauty." According to a Bariba physician, an individual who displays pain lacks courage, and cowardice is the essence of shame. Rather than live in shame, a Bariba would rather die (Sargent, 1984). In this cultural context, one would do everything possible to avoid displaying signs of pain.

Do Bariba women who are in labor actually experience less pain than women in other cultures, or have they simply learned not to let the pain show? It is difficult to answer such questions, partly because of the difficulties involved in describing pain to another person. Because pain is a private experience, language must be used to communicate the experience to others, and language is shaped by culture. It is not surprising that there is a more limited vocabulary for describing pain in the Bariba language than in most other languages. When the Bariba discuss the experience of pain, therefore, it is difficult to know how much their description is influenced by their language.

But there is some reason to believe that the cultural emphasis on not showing reactions to pain might actually reduce the amount of pain that the Bariba experience. There is evidence that facial expressions are an important part of the experience of pain (Izard, 1977). Apparently, sensory feedback to the brain from facial muscles supplies part of the neural input for the perception of pain (along with input from the part of the body that is cramped or injured). Indeed, persons who were given electrical shocks reported less pain when they were told to make no facial reactions than when they let their emotions show in their faces (Colby, Lanzetta, & Kleck, 1977). Maybe the calm face of a Bariba woman in labor results in the experience of less pain than does the agonized grimace of women in other cultures.

According to Linda Garro (1990), it is important for medical professionals who work with people in pain to understand the impact of culture on the expression of pain. If culture is not taken into account, the physician may overestimate or underestimate the amount of pain experienced by the patient. On the other hand, it is important to remember that not all members of a culture are the same. As in all other aspects of human diversity, it is important to be aware of variation within cultures.

What did you learn about pain in your own culture? Were you taught to minimize pain because it is important to be tough? Did you learn that no one will pay attention to your pain unless you exaggerate it? How do you respond when your parent or friends are in pain? Such questions will help you think about cultural influences on perception.

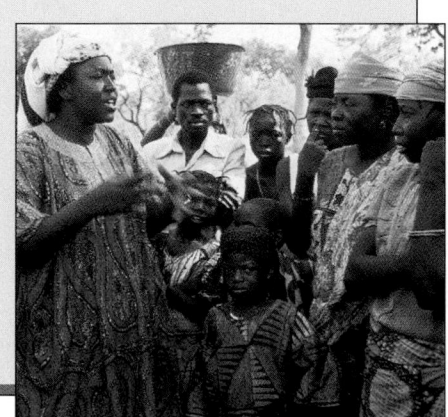

through amputation, the portion of somatosensory cortex that formerly served her left arm may begin to receive input from her face (look back to figure 2.16, p. 49 to see that the area of the somatosensory cortex that serves the face is next to the area that receives input from the arm). In addition, cutting sensory neurons from one part of the body tends to reduce the efficiency of the pain gates. This suggests that phantom pain that is perceived as being in a missing arm may come from minor irritations to the face that are allowed through the pain gate and are perceived to be pain in the missing limb because the neural message stimulates the part of the cortex that used to serve input from the arm.

The phantom limb experience is another excellent illustration of the fact that our conscious experience is not always a direct and simple representation of the sensory information that reaches the brain. Sometimes, the brain "invents" sensations and pains in limbs that do not exist.

● Review

The body contains a number of sense organs that provide vital information about the body's movement and orientation in space and about the world as it contacts our skin. Information about posture, movement, and orientation is coded and sent to the somatic sensory area of the cortex by the vestibular organ in the inner ear and by kinesthetic receptors spread throughout the body. Skin receptors send information about temperature, pressure, and pain to the same area of the brain. We experience the pain from cuts in other injuries in two steps (a first pain that tells us what has happened and where it has happened, followed by a second, more emotional pain) because these two aspects of the pain experience travel on different neural pathways to different parts of the brain. The phenomenon of pain provides a good example of the lack of direct relationship between physical stimuli and conscious sensations in that a number of factors increase or decrease the experience of pain. The phantom limb experience also provides compelling evidence that conscious experiences are constructed in the brain and do not always have a direct relationship to incoming sensations.

● Check Your Learning

To be sure that you have learned the key points from the preceding section, cover the list of correct answers and try to answer each question. If you give an incorrect answer to any question, return to the page given next to the correct answer to see why your answer was not correct.

1. Sensory receptors called _____ receptors located in the muscles, joints, and skin provide the brain with messages about movement, posture, and orientation of the body.

    a) vestibular

    b) semicircular

    c) ciliary

    d) kinesthetic

2. Which is *not* one of the four types of receptors in the skin?

    a) vestibular cells

    b) basket cells

    c) tactile discs

    d) specialized end bulbs

3. The sensation of intense heat is created by the stimulation of _____ on the skin.

    a) warm spots

    b) cold spots

    c) both warm and cold spots

    d) vestibular cells

4. According to the _____ theory of pain, placing a sore foot in warm water blocks pain signals on the slow-pain pathway by closing neural "gates" in the spinal cord and brain stem.

● Thinking Critically About Psychology

1. In what ways is the experience of pain both a psychological and a physical event?

2. Have you had experiences in your own life that would support the gate-control theory of pain?

Correct Answers 1. d (p. 91), **2. a** (p. 92), **3. c** (p. 93), **4.** gate-control.

◗ CHEMICAL SENSES: THE FLAVORS AND AROMAS OF LIFE

The senses of **gustation** (taste) and **olfaction** (smell) differ from the other senses in that they respond to chemicals rather than to energy in the environment. The chemical senses tell us about the things we eat, drink, and breathe.

Taste

We are able to taste food and other things because of the 10,000 *taste buds* on the tongue. Each taste bud contains approximately a dozen sensory receptors, called **taste cells,** grouped together much like the segments of an orange. It is the taste cells that are sensitive to chemicals in our food and drink (Bartoshuk, 1988) (fig. 3.18). The taste buds are further bunched together in bumps, called **papillae,** that can easily be seen on the tongue.

Collectively, the taste buds respond to thousands of chemicals, but all of our sensations of taste apparently result from the stimulation of different *combinations* of a small number of different types of taste receptors, which are most responsive to only one class of chemicals each. There are taste buds that respond primarily to chemicals that give rise to the sensations of *sweetness* (mostly sugars), *sourness* (mostly acids), *saltiness* (mostly salts), and *bitterness* (in response to a variety of chemicals that have no food value or are toxic). Recently, enough evidence has been accumulated to conclude that there is a fifth type of taste bud, which gives rise to the sensation of *fattiness* in response to fats (Schiffman, Graham, Sattely-Miller, & Warwick, 1998).

Interestingly, the taste buds that are most sensitive to these five classes of chemicals are not evenly distributed over the tongue. They are bunched together in different parts of the tongue, as shown in figure 3.19. This means that different parts of the tongue are sensitive to different tastes. We do not usually notice this because the differences in sensitivity are not great and because our food usually reaches all parts of the tongue during the chewing process anyway. But, if you ever have to swallow a truly bitter pill, try placing it in the exact middle of the tongue, where there are no taste receptors at all.

We lose taste buds as we age, especially over 45 years of age. Babies have the most taste buds and are very sensitive whereas older adults are less sensitive to the chemicals that give rise to taste sensations (Schiffman & others, 1998).

gustation
(gus-tā´-shun)   The sense of taste.

olfaction
(ōl-fak´-shun)   The sense of smell.

taste cells
The sensory receptor cells for gustation located in the taste buds.

papillae
(pah-pil´ē)   Clusters of taste buds on the tongue.

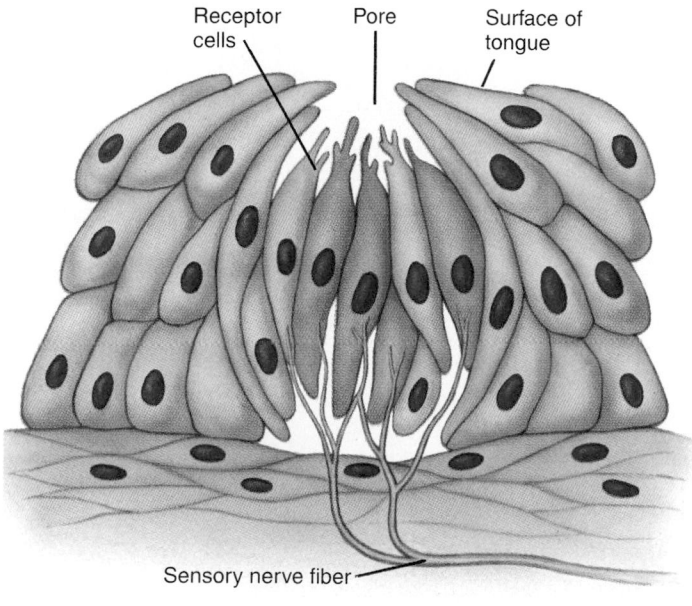

Receptor cells   Pore   Surface of tongue

Sensory nerve fiber

FIGURE 3.18

Taste buds contain clusters of taste (gustatory) receptor cells.

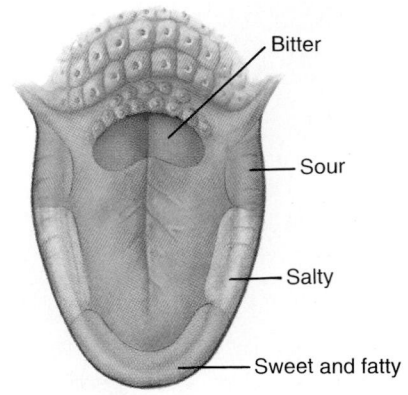

FIGURE 3.19

Areas of the tongue that are most sensitive to the five primary qualities of taste: sweet, fatty, salty, sour, and bitter.

olfactory epithelium

(ōl-fak′to-rē ep′′i-thē′lē-um)   The sheet of receptor cells at the top of the nasal cavity.

stereochemical theory

The theory that different odor receptors can be stimulated only by molecules of a specific size and shape that fit them like a "key" in a lock.

 FIGURE 3.20

Olfactory receptor cells are located in the olfactory epithelium at the top of the nasal cavity.

Our perception of food also includes sensations from the skin surfaces of the tongue and mouth: touch (food texture and thickness), temperature (cold coffee tastes very different from hot coffee), and pain (as in Jalapeño peppers). The sight and aroma of food also greatly affect our perception of food.

Smell

Chemicals in the air we breathe pass by the olfactory receptors on their way to the lungs. These receptor cells are located in a dime-sized, mucous-coated sheet at the top of the nasal cavity called the **olfactory epithelium** (see fig. 3.20). As with taste, we seem to be able to smell only a limited number of primary odors. There is less agreement among psychologists about primary odors than about primary tastes, but one widely used system of classifying odors divides all of the complex aromas and odors of life into combinations of seven primary qualities: *resinous* (camphor), *floral* (roses), *minty* (peppermint), *ethereal* (pears), *musky* (musk oil), *acrid* (vinegar), and *putrid* (rotten eggs) (Ackerman, 1991; Amoore, Johnston, & Rubin, 1964). However professionals who create perfumes and other aromas distinguish 146 distinct odors (Dravnieks, 1983).

Interestingly, nearly all of the chemicals that humans can detect as odors are organic compounds, meaning they come from living things. In contrast, we can smell very few inorganic compounds like rocks and sand. Thus, our noses are useful tools for sensing the qualities of plants and animals—necessary, among other things, to distinguish between poisonous and edible things (Cain, 1988).

Although we can smell only compounds derived from living things, chemists have long known how to create these organic compounds in test tubes. This means that any aroma can be custom-created and no longer has to be painstakingly extracted from flower petals and spices. One of the first perfumes created entirely in a laboratory was also one of the most successful fragrances ever made, Chanel No. 5. Once Marilyn Monroe boasted that she wore only Chanel No. 5 to bed, cloaking herself in a romantic blend of organic compounds created in a chemistry laboratory in 1922 (Ackerman, 1991).

How do we smell these organic molecules? According to the **stereochemical theory,** the complex molecules responsible for each of these primary odors have a specific shape that will "fit" into only one type of receptor cell, like a key into a lock. Only when

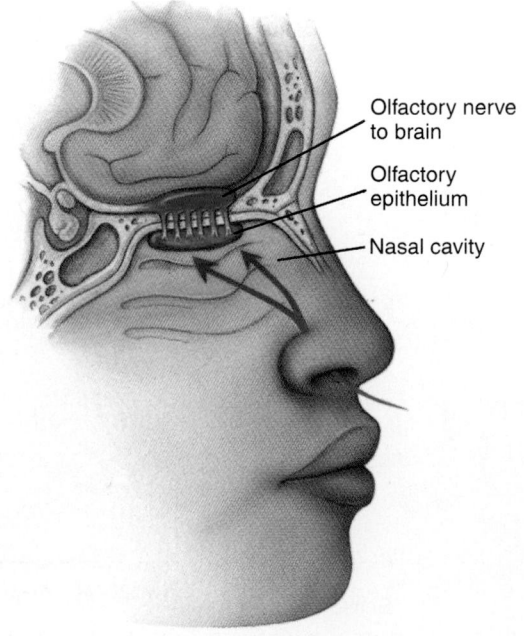

Olfactory nerve to brain

Olfactory epithelium

Nasal cavity

molecules of a particular shape are present will the corresponding olfactory receptor send its distinctive message to the brain (Cain, 1988).

The sense of smell is important in and of itself, of course, sometimes bringing joyous messages of sweet perfumes to the brain and other times warning us of dangerous and foul odors. But the sense of smell contributes to the sense of taste as well. Not only do we smell foods as they pass beneath our noses on the way to our mouths, but odors also rise into the nasal passage as we chew. We are usually unaware of the impact of smell on the sense of taste, until a head cold makes everything taste like paste. The contribution of smell to taste is important partly because of the greater sensitivity of the sense of smell. The nose can detect the molecules that we perceive as the smell of cherry pie in the air that is 1/25,000th of the amount that is required for the taste buds to identify them (Ackerman, 1991).

● Review

Chemicals in the air we breathe and in the things we eat and drink are sensed by the gustatory receptors (taste buds) on the tongue and the olfactory receptors in the nose. For both chemical senses, combinations of a relatively small number of primary sensations apparently make up the entire variety of our experiences of taste and smell.

● Check Your Learning

To be sure that you have learned the key points from the preceding section, cover the list of correct answers and try to answer each question. If you give an incorrect answer to any question, return to the page given next to the correct answer to see why your answer was not correct.

1. Each of the 10,000 _____ on the tongue contains approximately a dozen sensory receptors called taste cells.

2. All of our sensations of taste appear to result from five basic sensations of taste: sweetness, fattiness, sourness, saltiness, and _____.

3. The olfactory receptors are located in a dime-sized, mucous-coated sheet at the top of the nasal cavity called the _____.

   a) gustatory center   c) olfactory cortex
   b) olfactory epithelium   d) thalamus

4. According to the _____ theory, the molecules responsible for each of the primary odors have a specific shape that will fit into only one type of olfactory receptor cell.

   a) opponent-process   c) stereochemical
   b) trichromatic   d) camphoraceous

● Thinking Critically About Psychology

1. Why do you think some people love the smell of coffee, but other people dislike it?

2. Why do you think there is an uneven distribution of taste buds on the tongue?

Correct Answers 1. taste buds (p. 99), 2. bitterness (p. 99), 3. b (p. 100), 4. c (p. 100).

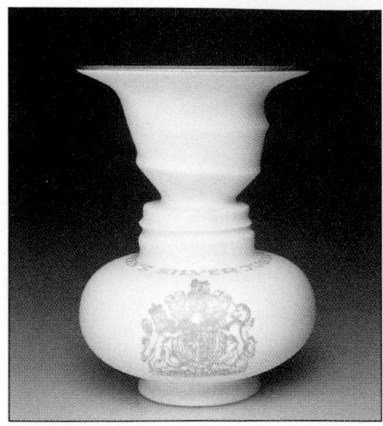

FIGURE 3.21

The distinction between figure and ground in visual perception is clearly illustrated by this vase prepared for Queen Elizabeth of England. Do you see a vase, or do you see the profiles of Queen Elizabeth and Prince Philip looking at one another? It depends on whether the dark space is the figure or the ground in your perceptual organization of the stimuli.

▶ PERCEPTION: INTERPRETING SENSORY MESSAGES

Sensations that are transmitted to the brain have little "meaning" of their own. They are in the form of raw neural energy that must be organized and interpreted in the process we call *perception.* The process is pretty much the same in all of us. If this were not the case—if each of us were to interpret sensory input in a unique way—there would be no common "reality" in the sense of a perceived world that we all share. However, some aspects of perception are unique to individuals or members of a particular culture. The specific learning experiences, memories, motives, and emotions of the individual can influence perception. For example, we all perceive the visual stimuli of a knife in pretty much the same way because of the inborn ways we organize visual information. But a knife also has unique perceptual meaning to each individual, depending on whether the person has been cut by a similar knife, has a similar favorite hunting knife, or has just been asked to carve a turkey for dinner.

In this section, we will examine the inborn organizational properties that all humans share and will briefly discuss some of the ways in which each individual's perceptions are unique. Keep in mind as we discuss perception that, although it's easy to distinguish between sensation and perception in theory, it's very difficult to do so in practice. Visual perception, for example, begins in the complex neural structures of the eye before sensory messages are transmitted to the brain (Hochberg, 1988). The distinction between sensation and perception, then, is largely an arbitrary one, but it makes our discussion of information processing by the sense organs and brain easier to understand.

Visual Perception

In the discussion that follows, we will look at the major ways in which sensory information is interpreted into meaningful perceptions, including both those that are common to us all and those that are unique to each individual. This discussion focuses on visual perception, rather than on all of the perceptual systems, for several reasons: visual perception is a highly important sensing system; scientists understand how it works better than they do other systems; and it is representative enough of other systems to tell us something about the process of perception in general.

Perceptual Organization

Raw visual sensations are like the unassembled parts of a washing machine: they must be put together in an organized way before they are useful to us. Some of the fundamental ways in which the eye and brain organize visual sensations were described about 75 years ago by Gestalt psychologists in their pioneering writings on perception (see chapter 1). These principles of perceptual organization are still worthy of our attention (Matlin, 1988; Prinzmetal, 1995). The following are five of the so-called Gestalt principles of perception:

FIGURE 3.22

This drawing can be viewed as a younger or an older woman, depending on the viewer's figure-ground organization.

1. *Figure-ground.* When we perceive a visual stimulus, part of what we see is the center of our attention, the *figure,* and the rest is indistinct background, the *ground.* The vase in figure 3.21 shows that this way of seeing can reorganize the nature of "reality." The figure and ground of this photo can be reversed to perceive either a vase or two opposing faces. In the same way, the woman in figure 3.22 could be viewed as a young woman facing away or as an older woman facing forward and downward, depending on which parts you perceive as the figure and which parts you perceive as ground. This principle of perception is very useful in showing us that what we perceive is often based more on what goes on in our brains than what is in front of our eyes. The remaining Gestalt principles amplify this point.

2. *Continuity.* We tend to perceive lines or patterns that follow a smooth contour as being part of a single unit. In figure 3.23, at which point did child B start bouncing her pogo stick? We tend to organize our perceptions of the tracks so that it appears that

girl B started at point 1, but both girls could have made sharp turns in the center and headed off at right angles. We do not naturally organize sensations in this way, however; we tend to perceive continuity in lines and patterns.

3. *Proximity.* Things that are proximal (close together) are usually perceived as belonging together. In figure 3.24, we see three vertical columns of blocks on the left side and three horizontal rows on the right side, due to proximity.

4. *Similarity.* On the left side of figure 3.25, we perceive two vertical columns of apples and two vertical columns of pears, even though they are evenly spaced. On the right side, in contrast, a different arrangement results in the perception of two horizontal rows of each fruit. Similar things are perceived as being related.

5. *Closure.* Incomplete figures, such as in figure 3.26, tend to be perceived as complete wholes. Again, we fill in missing sensory information to create complete and whole perceptions.

Our perceptions are actively organized according to these and other, similar inborn principles.

Perceptual Constancy

We perceive the world as a fairly constant and unchanging place. Tables, lamps, and people do not change in size, shape, or color from moment to moment. Yet, the sensations that tell us about these things do change considerably from moment to moment. The size of the image that falls on the retina changes as a person walks away from us, but we do not perceive the person as shrinking in size. The shape of a pot seen from different angles is different on the retina, but we do not believe that the pot is changing shape. This characteristic of perception is called **perceptual constancy.** There are several types of perceptual constancy:

1. *Brightness constancy.* A piece of white paper does not change in perceived brightness when it moves from a weakly lit room to a brightly lit room, even though the intensity of the light reaching the eye changes considerably. Fortunately for our ability to cope with the world, our perception corresponds to the unchanging physical properties of the paper, rather than to the changing sensory information about its brightness. When you stop to think about it, this is a remarkable accomplishment, but one that we take so much for granted that you may not have been aware that it was happening until you read this paragraph.

2. *Color constancy.* Colors do not appear to change much in spite of different conditions of light and surroundings that change incoming visual information.

FIGURE 3.23
At which point did girl B start jumping on her pogo stick? According to the principle of continuity, we would tend to perceive point 1 as her starting point, although either 1 or 2 would be equally possible.

perceptual constancy
The tendency for perceptions of objects to remain relatively unchanged, in spite of changes in raw sensations.

FIGURE 3.24
Do you see vertical columns or horizontal rows? The principle of proximity determines how these stimuli are organized perceptually.

FIGURE 3.25

Do you see vertical columns or horizontal rows? The principle of similarity suggests that we organize the figure on the left into vertical columns and the one on the right into horizontal rows, even though the objects are equally spaced.

FIGURE 3.26

We see a face rather than unrelated lines because of the perceptual principle of closure.

monocular cues

(mon-ok´ū-lar)   Eight visual cues that can be seen with one eye and that allow us to perceive depth.

binocular cues

(bīn-ok´ū-lar)   Two visual cues that require both eyes to allow us to perceive depth.

3. *Size constancy.* A dollar bill seen from distances of 1 foot and 10 feet casts different-sized images on the retina, but we do not perceive it as changing in size. Familiar objects do not change in perceived size at different distances.

4. *Shape constancy.* A penny seen from straight ahead casts a circular image on the retina. When seen from a slight angle, however, the image it casts is oval, yet we continue to perceive it as circular.

The process of perceptual constancy means that we automatically adjust our perceptions to correspond with what we have learned about the physical world, rather than relying solely on changing stimulus input.

Depth Perception

The retina is a two-dimensional surface. It has an up and a down, and a left and a right, but no depth. How is it, then, that we are able to perceive a three-dimensional world using a two-dimensional retina? The eye and brain accomplish this remarkable feat by using a number of two-dimensional cues to create a perceptual distance.

The 10 major cues used in depth perception are listed here. The first 8 are known as **monocular cues** because they can be seen by one eye (see fig. 3.27 on page 105); the last 2 are known as **binocular cues** because they can only be perceived using both eyes. The monocular cues are as follows:

1. *Texture gradient.* The texture of objects is larger and more visible up close and smaller when far away. On curved surfaces, the elements of texture are also more slanted when they are farther away.

2. *Linear perspective.* Objects cast smaller images on the retina when they are more distant. As a result, parallel lines, such as railroad tracks, appear to grow closer together the farther away they are from us.

3. *Superposition.* Closer objects tend to be partially in front of, or partially cover up, more distant objects.

4. *Shadowing.* The shadows cast by objects suggest their depth.

5. *Speed of movement.* Objects farther away appear to move across the field of vision more slowly than do closer objects.

6. *Aerial perspective.* Water vapor and pollution in the air scatter light waves, giving distant objects a bluish, hazy appearance compared with nearby objects.

7. *Accommodation.* As discussed earlier in the chapter, the shape of the lens of the eye must change to focus the visual image on the retina from stimuli that are different distances from the eye. This process is called accommodation. Kinesthetic receptors

Texture gradient.

Linear perspective.

Shadowing.

FIGURE 3.27

Texture gradient, linear perspective, shadowing, superposition, and aerial perspective are monocular cues used in depth perception.

Superposition.

Aerial perspective.

in the ciliary muscle, therefore, provide a source of information about the distance of different objects. This information is useful, however, only for short distances up to about 4 feet.

8. *Vertical position.* When objects are on the ground, the farther they appear to be below the horizon, the closer they appear to be to us. For objects in the air, however, the farther they appear to be above the horizon, the closer they appear to be to us.

The binocular cues are as follows:

9. *Convergence.* When both eyes are looking at an object in the center of the visual field, they must angle inward more sharply for a near object than for a distant object (see fig. 3.28). Information from the muscles that move the eyes thus provides a clue as to the distance of an object from the viewer.

10. *Retinal disparity.* Because our two eyes are a couple of inches apart, they do not see the same view of three-dimensional objects, especially when the object is close. This disparity, or difference, between the images on the two retinas is a key factor in depth perception.

Perceptual constancy helps us recognize this vase as unchanging, even though we are viewing it from different angles and from different distances.

FIGURE 3.28

The degree to which the eyes must look inward (convergence) to focus on objects at different distances provides information on the distance of that object. It's a binocular cue in depth perception because it requires the use of both eyes.

Through a combination of these monocular and binocular cues, we are able to perceive our three-dimensional world using only two-dimensional information.

Visual Illusions

Instructors of introductory psychology have long enjoyed amazing their classes with visual illusions. These illusions intentionally manipulate the cues that we use in visual perception to create an illusory perception. They are instructive, therefore, in showing us more about the process of perception and for showing us in yet *another* way that what we see is not always the same as the visual information that enters the eyes. For example, are the two horizontal lines in figure 3.29 (the Ponzo illusion) the same size? (They are, even though the upper line looks longer.) How about the two lines in figure 3.30 (the vertical-horizontal illusion)—most people see the vertical line as longer, even though they are the same length. My personal favorite is the Zoliner illusion, shown in figure 3.31. Believe it or not, the diagonal lines are parallel. Even after you cover all but two lines or measure the distance between the diagonal lines for yourself, this illusion is amazing. How do these illusions fool us? They do so by using monocular depth cues to create an illusion.

Not all visual illusions are laboratory demonstrations. They are common in everyday life. Few sights are more beautiful than a huge full moon on the horizon. Have you ever stopped to wonder why it always looks *bigger* on the horizon than overhead? It doesn't really grow, you know; it's an illusion. In fact, it's an illusion that still puzzles scientists. There is no widely accepted theory of the moon illusion (Reed, 1984; Rock & Kaufman, 1972), but it is based partly on the misperception of depth.

As shown in figure 3.32, an object that our senses tell us is *farther away* is perceived as being *larger* than an object that casts the same-size image on the retina but appears to be closer. The two triangles in this figure are the same size, but the one at the top is perceived as larger because it appears to be farther away. Ordinarily, the top triangle *would* be larger if it were farther away but could still cast as large a retinal image as a closer object.

The moon illusion is based partly on the same principle. When the moon is overhead, not only does it appear closer due to its vertical position, we have no distance cues, so depth cues do not accurately influence our perception of the moon's size. When it's near the horizon, however, it appears to be farther away because of its vertical position. In addition, we can see the moon is farther away than objects such as distant trees and buildings, which we know to be large but which cast a small image on the retina. When the size of the moon is perceived in comparison with these objects, it looks much bigger.

FIGURE 3.29

The Ponzo illusion. Are the horizontal lines the same length?

FIGURE 3.30

This figure often produces an illusory judgment of length. Which line is longer, the horizontal or the vertical line? Actually, they are the same length.

FIGURE 3.31

The Zoliner illusion. Are the diagonal lines parallel?

Individual and Cultural Influences on Perception

Up to this point, we have discussed factors that determine perception in the same way for all of us—characteristics of the inborn "wiring" of the human brain and sensory systems. But perception is strongly influenced by other factors as well. For example, a number of studies tell us that *motivation* influences perception: Hungry college students are more likely to interpret ambiguous pictures as being of food; sexually aroused males perceive females as being more physically attractive; anxious persons are more likely to interpret ambiguous sentences as being threatening; and poor children estimate the size of coins as larger than do children from higher income families (Bruner & Goodman, 1947; Eysenck, Mogg, May, Richards, & Mathews, 1991; McClelland & Atkinson, 1948; Stephan, Berscheid, & Walster, 1971).

Perception is also influenced by the different *learning* experiences of people living in different cultures. For example, persons who live in the dense rain forests of the African Congo rarely see objects at long distances. In their world, thick vegetation blocks the sight of distant objects. It is interesting, then, that, if pygmies travel to the African plains, distant buffalo are at first seen as tiny "insects" (Turnbull, 1962). Pictures they draw are flat, two-dimensional renderings without depth cues. Furthermore, when they are shown pictures like figure 3.33 and asked which animal the man is trying to spear, they answer, "The tiny rhinoceros," because they do not perceive the rhinoceros as being in the distance.

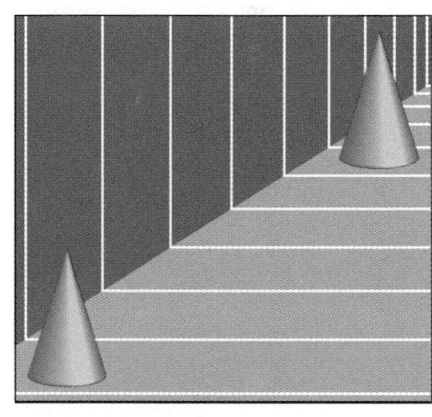

FIGURE 3.32

When two objects of the same size are perceived as being at different distances, the one that seems farther away is perceived as being larger.

FIGURE 3.33

One of the drawings used to study depth perception in different cultures. Which animal is the man about to spear?

● Review

Perception is the interpretation of sensations. It's an active process in which impressions are created that often go beyond the minimal information provided by the senses. Many of the ways in which we organize and interpret sensations are inborn and common to all humans. The Gestalt principles of perceptual organization, perceptual constancies, depth perception, and visual illusions provide examples of the active, creative nature of perception. Other factors that enter into the process of perception are unique to the individual, such as motivational states and cultural learning experiences. These factors ensure that we will perceive the world in a way that is largely universal among humans, but with a great deal of individuality due to differences in motivation, emotion, learning, and other factors.

● Check Your Learning

To be sure that you have learned the key points from the preceding section, cover the list of correct answers and try to answer each question. If you give an incorrect answer to any question, return to the page given next to the correct answer to see why your answer was not correct.

1. When we perceive a visual stimulus, the center of our attention is termed the "figure," and the indistinct background is called the "ground." Is it possible to change our perception of the same stimulus, so that the figure becomes the ground and the ground becomes the figure?

   a) yes

   b) no

2. The cues used in depth perception that require both eyes are called

   a) constant.   c) binocular.

   b) monocular.   d) dichromatics.

3. The shape of the lens of the eye must change to focus the visual image on the retina from stimuli that are different distances from the eye, providing a cue used in depth perception. This process is called

   a) superposition.   c) convergence.

   b) aerial perspective.   d) accommodation.

4. Visual perception can be influenced by

   a) motivation and emotion.   c) both a and b.

   b) learning.   d) neither a nor b.

● Thinking Critically About Psychology

1. What is the point of studying perceptual illusions? What can we learn from them?

2. What is the value of knowing that our perception is influenced by our emotions?

Correct Answers 1. a (p. 102), 2. c (p. 104), 3. d (p. 104), 4. c (p. 107).

Application *of Psychology*

VISUAL PERCEPTION, ILLUSION, AND ART

During the winter of 1993, I went to New York with my best friend to see an amazing collection of paintings, drawings, and sculpture by Henri Matisse at the Museum of Modern Art. The sheer beauty and emotional impact of these works was amazing. But, ever being the psychologist, I sometimes found myself thinking about his paintings in terms of the monocular cues to depth perception. And, as I thought about it, I found that the way Matisse used monocular cues of depth perception in his art was pretty interesting, too. Maybe looking at some paintings from this perspective will add to our appreciation of the visual arts and teach us something about depth perception.

The artist who paints a landscape, a still life, or a portrait of a person is creating a visual illusion. He or she uses what is known about the monocular cues of depth perception to create the *illusion* of a three-dimensional object (one with height, width, and depth) on a two-dimensional canvas (one with height and width only). No part of the flat canvas is farther away from the viewer than any other part, but the artist creates the illusion of depth—the impression that some parts of the painting are farther away than others—mostly by using the cues of texture gradient, linear perspective, superposition, shadowing, and aerial perspective. Cues based on the way in which the eyes focus on objects that are different distances from the eye and the binocular cues that are based on differences in the alignment of the two eyes cannot be used by the artist, but artists often achieve striking illusions of depth with the few cues at their disposal.

Look at the striking illusions of depth created in two paintings. The painting in figure 3.34 by the Spanish painter Diego Velazquez (*Las Meninas*, 1656) uses four depth perception cues to suggest depth very effectively. Notice that the man standing in the doorway is smaller than the man standing on the left (a self-portrait of the artist) and even smaller than the young blonde child who appears to be standing in the front of the painting. Note also that the wall on the right is painted on the canvas as if it is shorter at the rear of the room than in the front of the room. These are uses of the monocular cue of *linear perspective,* and they give a powerful illusion of depth to the room. Notice also that the persons that Velazquez wishes us to perceive as being in the front of the room partially cover the persons portrayed as being at the rear of the room (the cue of *superposition*). The detailed texture of the clothing of the persons in the front of the room is also clearer than that of persons at the rear of the room (the cue of *texture gradient*). Velazquez also uses shadowing effectively to create an illusion of depth, but let's study this cue in the even more effective example by Artemisia Gentileschi (fig. 3.35).

A more subtle, but wonderfully effective illusion of depth has been created in

FIGURE 3.34

Las Meninas (1656) by Diego Velazquez.
Erich Lessing/Art Resource, NY.

FIGURE 3.35

Self-portrait by Artemisia Gentileschi.
The Royal Collection © 1994 Her Majesty Queen Elizabeth II.

FIGURE 3.36

L'Atelier du Quai Saint-Michel by Henri Matisse.

Art Resource, NY © 1995 Succession H. Matisse, Paris/Artists Rights Society (ARS), New York.

FIGURE 3.37

Grand Nu Couche by Henri Matisse.

The Baltimore Museum of Art: The Cone Collection, formed by Dr. Claribel Cone and Miss Etta Cone of Baltimore, Maryland BMA 1950.258. © 1995 Succession H. Matisse, Paris/Artists Rights Society (ARS), New York.

this extraordinary self-portrait. Gentileschi gives us an amazingly three-dimensional view of herself partly by using linear perspective. Notice, for example, that her right hand appears to be farther away from us partly because it is smaller on the canvas than her left hand, which seems to be very close to us. In addition, her face partially hides the right shoulder, which seems farther away from us (superposition). But, it is Gentileschi's exceptional mastery of shadowing that brings the illusion of subtle depth to life. Her face is painted on a flat canvas, but it seems as

rounded as an apple. As a result, her left cheek seems inches closer to us than does her nose.

Sometimes, Matisse was interested in creating a sense of depth, but sometimes he intentionally ignored depth. The reclining nude in figure 3.36 (*L'Atelier du Quai Saint-Michel*), for example, is positioned in a scene painted with powerful depth cues. Notice that the building seen outside the window is shorter on the canvas than the delicate table standing in front of the window. Compare that painting with a later painting in which he has portrayed exactly

the same subject in a very different way. In *Grand Nu Couche* (fig. 3.37), Matisse has eliminated most cues of depth from the painting, including depth through shadowing. The woman is mostly a flat surface in a flat room. Matisse eliminated most depth cues intentionally to force us to see only color and form. If he had been a great chef, he might have asked us to focus on the flavors of his creations by wearing a blindfold during the meal to avoid distractions. By taking depth out of this painting, Matisse leaves us with nothing to perceive but form and color.

● Summary

Chapter 3 recognizes that we live in a physical world that we experience through our sense organs and interpret (perceive) by means of our nervous systems.

I. We are aware of the outside world because we have specialized sensory receptor cells.

   A. Sense organs transduce sensory energy into neural impulses and send neural messages to the brain for interpretation.

   B. Psychophysics is the field of psychology that studies the relationships between physical stimuli and psychological sensations and perceptions.

II. The sense organs of sight transduce light energy.

   A. The intensity of light waves largely determines brightness, whereas the wavelength (frequency) largely determines color.
   B. The eye, working much as a camera does, is the primary sense organ for seeing.
      1. Light enters the eye through the cornea (with the iris regulating the size of the pupil) and the lens into the retina.
      2. Rods and cones transduce light waves into neural impulses for transmission to the brain.
      3. The 125 million rods, located throughout the retina except for the fovea, are active in peripheral vision and vision in dim light, but they do not play a role in color vision.
      4. The 6 million cones, clustered mostly near the fovea, code information for color.
      5. Both trichromatic theory and opponent-process theory are helpful in understanding color vision.

III. The sense of hearing responds to sound waves.

   A. The frequency of sound waves determines pitch, whereas the intensity determines loudness.
   B. The ear is the primary sense organ for hearing.
      1. The outer ear functions as a sound wave collector.
      2. Sound waves vibrate the eardrum, which is connected to a series of three movable bones (hammer, anvil, stirrup) in the middle ear.
      3. The inner ear, containing the cochlea and the organ of Corti, transduces the sound wave energy into neural impulses for transmission to the brain.

IV. Chemical senses respond to chemicals rather than to energy in the environment.

   A. In the sense of taste, different classes of chemicals are experienced as sweet, sour, bitter, salty, and fatty.
   B. In the sense of smell, different classes of chemicals are experienced as different odors.

V. Internal stimuli are also received by the sensory system.

   A. The vestibular organ provides information about body orientation, whereas the kinesthetic sense reports body position and movement.
   B. The various skin senses can detect pressure, temperature, and pain.
      1. Two sensations of pain reach the brain at slightly different times because they travel on different neural pathways.
         a. The first sensation reaches the somatosensory area quickly on myelinated neurons.
         b. The more emotional type of pain reaches the limbic system more slowly on unmyelinated neurons.
      2. Many factors can block the pain gates for the emotional aspect of pain.

VI. Sensory neural impulses, when transmitted to the brain, are interpreted in a process called perception; examining visual perception demonstrates the general nature of the process.

   A. Perception is an active mental process. Gestalt principles explain many of the ways in which humans tend to organize sensory information.
   B. Individual factors, such as emotion, motivation, and previous learning, also affect our perceptions.

● Resources

1. If you think of yourself as a sensual person, and something of an intellectual, then treat yourself to the most wonderful book ever written about the senses: Ackerman, D. (1991). *A natural history of the senses.* New York: Vintage Books.

2. A readable but sophisticated examination of classical principles of perception and illusions is supplied by Sekuler, R. (1994). *Perception* (3rd ed.). Boston: McGraw-Hill.

3. If you are a serious student of visual perception or of the visual arts, you may wish to tackle an excellent in-depth analysis of this subject: Hochberg, J. (1988). Visual perception. In R. C. Atkinson, R. J. Hernstein, G. Lindzey, & R. D. Luce (Eds.), *Stevens' handbook of experimental psychology: Vol. 1. Perception and motivation.* New York: Wiley-Interscience.

4. Perhaps the ultimate sensory illusion is experienced by persons who have lost an arm or a leg. If you would like to learn about "phantom limbs," read Melzack, R. (1992). Phantom limbs. *Scientific American,* pp. 120–126.

5. A nice summary of recent concepts and techniques is provided by Keefe, F. J., & France, C. R. (1999). Pain: Biopsychosocial mechanisms and management. *Current Directions in Psychological Science, 5,* 137–141.

● Visual Review of the Sense Organs

A great deal of new information was covered in chapter 3 on the structure of the sense organs. A set of unlabeled illustrations has been prepared to help you check your learning of these structures. These reviews will be most helpful if you glance at the first one and then refer back to the illustration or illustrations on which they are based to memorize the names of the structures. Then, return to the illustration in this review section and try to write in the names of the key structures of the sense organs. Then check your labels by looking at the original figures once again. When you can label all the structures in one of the illustrations, move on to the next one.

 FIGURE 3.38

Key structures of the eye (based on fig. 3.2, p. 78).

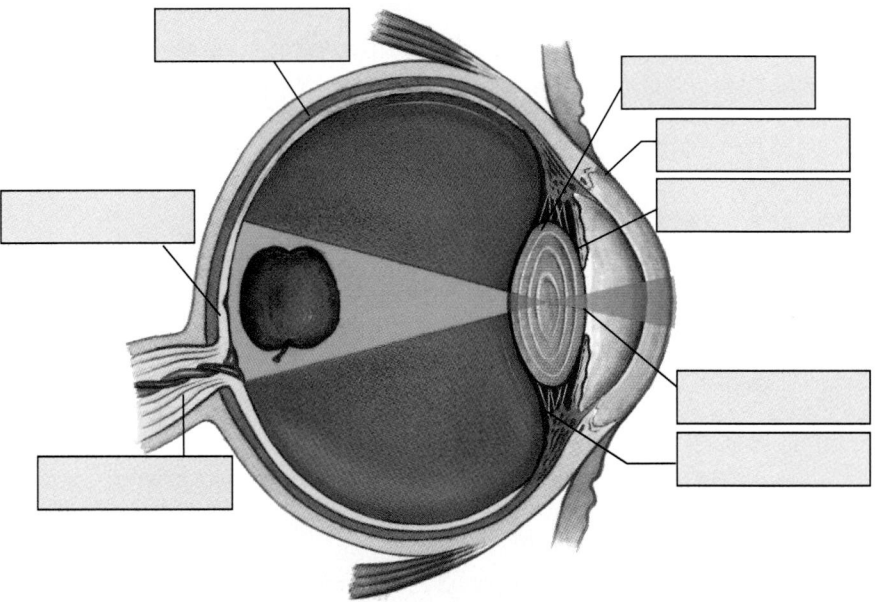

Outer ear   Middle ear   Inner ear

 FIGURE 3.39
Key structures of the ear (based on fig. 3.12, p. 88).

 FIGURE 3.40
Key structures of the cochlea (based on fig. 3.13, p. 89).

FIGURE 3.41

Key structures of the olfactory receptors (based on fig. 3.20, p. 100).

CHAPTER

4

CHAPTER OUTLINE

States of Consciousness

PROLOGUE

I t will come as no surprise to you that you are presently awake, conscious, and focusing your attention on the words of this textbook. But stop for a moment at the end of this sentence and, with your eyes closed, imagine that your book rises slowly from your lap, drifts to your face, and closes, lightly pinching your nose. Try it—seriously.

Could you see the book rise in your imagination? Did you feel a little pinch on your nose? How about when you are daydreaming—do you sometimes get lost in your thoughts and have conversations with people who are not there but who speak clearly to you, anyway?

My point is this: Life is made of many kinds of conscious awareness. Sometimes they are based on what is "out there," as when you are aware of the words in this textbook. But often you create your conscious experiences entirely in your brain—like the floating textbook that rose up and pinched your nose. You create realities in your consciousness that never were and may never be. You do so every time you imagine, daydream, or dream.

Nancy Kerr of the Georgia Mental Health Institute conducted a classic study that illustrates this point beautifully (Foulkes, 1989). Kerr studied the dreams of adult men and women who had lost their eyesight as young children. She found that, when they dreamed about friends, their dreams were very much like those of sighted adults. Indeed, when they dreamed about people they had met as blind adults—friends they had never seen—they dreamed about them in visual images. They could "see" what their friends looked like in their dreams, even though they had never seen them with their eyes. They created these visual images entirely in their brains.

In this chapter, we will define consciousness as a state of awareness—awareness of the outside world, of our own thoughts and feelings, and sometimes even of our own consciousness. Consciousness is not a single state, however. Rather, there are many different states of conscious awareness. Even during the course of a typical day our wakefulness is composed of a variety of states of consciousness: focused consciousness, loosely drifting consciousness, and daydreams.

When the waking day ends, moreover, we do not cease to be aware; rather, we experience other kinds of consciousness. As we drift off to sleep, we pass through a dreamlike "twilight" phase, and even amid the shifting stages of sleep itself we experience the strange reality of dreams. Apparently, these dreams are important to our well-being. Indeed, sleep may not rest and restore us for the next day if we do not dream sufficiently.

Other states of consciousness are experienced during hypnosis or while taking certain kinds of drugs. As you read about each form of consciousness, ask how much of the awareness comes through the sense organs that you studied in chapter 3, and how much comes from within.

consciousness
(kon'shus-nes)   A state of awareness.

CONSCIOUSNESS

What does it mean to be conscious? Clearly, it has something to do with awareness. When conscious, we are aware of the sights and sounds of the outside world, of our feelings, our thoughts, and sometimes even our own consciousness. When unconscious, we are not aware of any of these things. **Consciousness,** simply defined, is *a state of awareness.*

However, there is more than one kind of conscious state; it comes in more than the wide-awake-and-thinking variety. The qualities of conscious awareness that people experience when daydreaming, when hypnotized, when high on drugs, or when dreaming are so different from one another that we need to think of consciousness as being many different states of awareness. To understand consciousness fully, we need to explore its many varieties and the conditions under which they occur.

We spend our lives passing from one state of consciousness to another. We read a book, we daydream, we drift off to sleep, we dream, and so on. Each of these states of conscious awareness is so different from the next that the very sense of reality it imparts differs. What is logical and possible in a dream may seem absurd when considered the next day. We seldom wonder which state contains the ultimate reality, however. We assume without questioning that the waking state in which we spend most of our lives is the "real" consciousness. It's the standard by which we judge other states and find them to be "distorted" or "unreal."

Daydreams

daydreams
Relatively focused thinking about fantasies.

Daydreams are a period of thinking and feeling that is not bound by what is logical or likely to happen. Daydreams are not a sometime thing; most of us daydream many times each day. Why do we spend time in these dreamlike reveries instead of focusing all of our awareness productively on the concerns of the day?

Sigmund Freud, the Austrian founder of psychoanalysis, believed that daydreams reduced the tension left by our unfulfilled needs and wishes. What we cannot do in reality we accomplish in the fantasy world of daydreams. While daydreaming, we win the race, see our lost love return, and build a rustic home in the country with our own hands.

Was Freud right? Are daydreams a way of reducing the tension of unmet needs and unfulfilled wishes? To answer this question, researchers asked college students to jot down a summary of each of their daydreams for several days (Pope & Singer, 1978). As predicted by Freud, many daydreams involved the fulfilling of a wish. Also consistent with Freud's theory is the fact that most people feel quite relaxed during this type of daydreaming. Contrary to Freud's predictions, however, many daydreams are filled with regret, sorrow, and guilt. Other daydreams are highly sexual, such as those focusing on that gorgeous person you would love to know better. These daydreams *create* rather than release tension, casting doubt on Freud's theory of daydreaming. Instead of reducing tension, daydreams may be merely a slightly distorted reflection of our current concerns and emotions (Pope & Singer, 1978).

Divided Consciousness: Being Two Places (Mentally) at the Same Time

"I'm sorry dear, I must have lost consciousness. What were you saying?"
© The New Yorker Collection 1982 Chon Day from Cartoonbank.com. All Rights Reserved.

divided consciousness
The splitting off of two conscious activities that occur simultaneously.

Last Saturday I was asked to watch a friend record a demonstration tape of a song he had written. It was my first time in a studio and I was fascinated—they even let me record a few bars using my friend's guitar (I was less than excellent). Driving home, my thoughts raced about my own long-forgotten fantasies of making hit records. When I got home, I realized I had no recollection whatsoever of the 5-mile drive. Obviously I had negotiated several stoplights and made a couple of turns, but I was lost in my thoughts and have no recollection of the drive. Stanford University psychologist Ernest Hilgard (1975) describes such phenomena as moments of **divided consciousness.** He believes that our conscious awareness becomes "split" and we simultaneously perform two activities requiring conscious awareness (in my case, driving and thinking about recording songs).

The Concept of the Unconscious Mind

In discussing conscious experience, it's important to compare the term *conscious* with the term *unconscious.* Most people beginning to study psychology expect to learn about the **unconscious mind.** It may surprise you to know, then, that until recently the term was not even mentioned in most modern introductory psychology textbooks. Psychology is taught in most American colleges and universities from a scientific viewpoint. The term *unconscious,* in contrast, is used primarily by psychologists who take a more philosophical approach to understanding people and their problems. It would be wrong, however, to dismiss the unconscious simply as "unscientific" and not discuss it at all.

Today, most scientists agree that it's time to apply scientific thinking to the study of the unconscious. For example, when a person is in a room where more than one person is talking, most of the time we can pay attention to one voice and "tune out" the other voice. This has been called the *cocktail party phenomenon* because it happens so often at parties. However, what becomes of the other voice—the one we do not listen to? There is evidence that it reaches the brain, even though we are never *consciously* aware of it. In that sense, the voice is processed *unconsciously* by the brain. Andrew Mathews and Colin MacLeod (1986) studied this phenomenon experimentally. Participants in the study were asked to listen to two messages presented simultaneously over different earphones. They were instructed to ignore one of the messages but to repeat the other message aloud. Some of the time, the words presented to the ignored earphone were nonthreatening words, such as *friend* and *concert,* whereas threatening words, such as *assault* and *emergency,* were presented at other times. As they repeated the message, they also kept their eyes on a computer screen and pressed a key as quickly as they could after the word *press* appeared on the screen (see fig. 4.1).

unconscious mind
Mental processes that occur without conscious awareness.

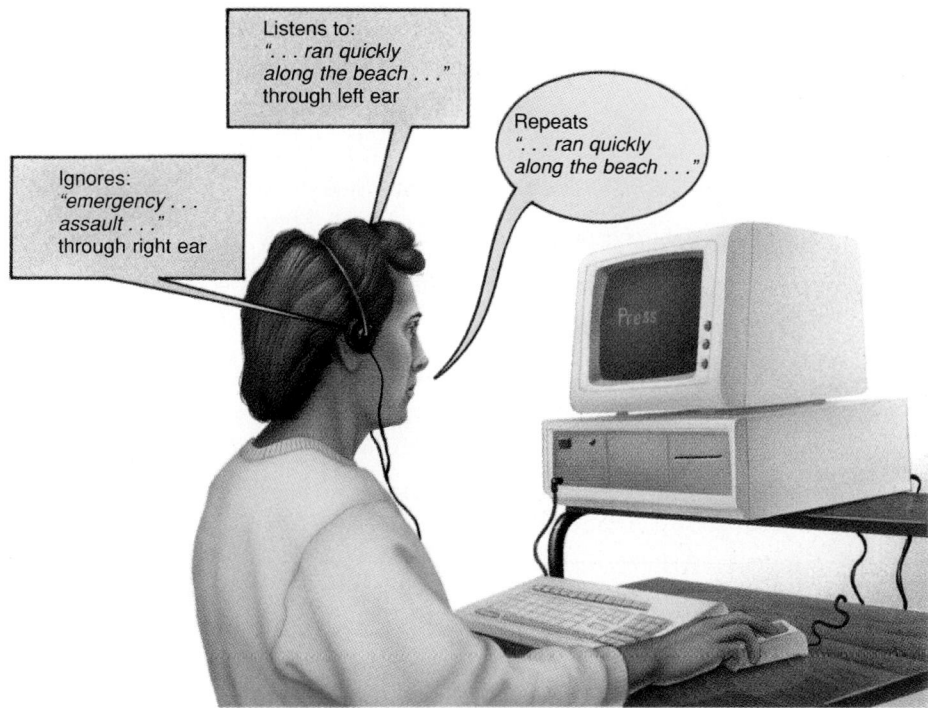

FIGURE 4.1

Participants in Mathews and MacLeod's study of unconscious information processing listened to two different messages that were presented simultaneously through different earphones. The participants were able to completely ignore one message and repeat the other one. At the same time, they pressed a key as quickly as they could when the word *press* appeared on the computer screen. Although not consciously heard, threatening words disrupted the reaction time of highly anxious individuals. This suggests that these persons had unconsciously processed the emotional meaning of the threatening words.

To be sure that the threatening words would have a great deal of emotional impact on the research participants, they were all highly anxious persons who were receiving treatment for their problems. The participants reported that they were not consciously aware of any of the ignored words because they focused all of their attention on the message they had to repeat, yet, when threatening words were being presented, the anxious individuals pressed the key significantly less quickly than when nonthreatening words were presented. Apparently, the ignored words were being processed without conscious awareness, and the emotional impact of the threatening words disrupted their performance on the reaction time task. Careful experiments of this sort may lead to a better understanding of mental processes that affect us without our being consciously aware of them.

● Review

Consciousness is composed of different states of awareness. During each day, we shift many times between normal waking consciousness and daydreams. At times, our consciousness appears to "do two things at once" in what Hilgard refers to as divided consciousness. At other times, we appear to process information in an entirely unconscious way, opening the door to the possibility of scientific studies of unconscious mental processes.

● Check Your Learning

To be sure that you have learned the key points from the preceding section, cover the list of correct answers and try to answer each question. If you give an incorrect answer to any question, return to the page given next to the correct answer to see why your answer was not correct. Remember that these questions cover only some of the important information in this section; it is important that you make up your own questions to check your learning of other facts and concepts.

Match each definition with one of the following terms:

    a) unconscious   c) divided consciousness

    b) daydreams

_____ 1. Conscious awareness when awake that is not limited to logic reality

_____ 2. Mental processes that occur without conscious awareness

_____ 3. The splitting off of two conscious activities that occur simultaneously

● Thinking Critically About Psychology

1. What is the value of daydreaming? Does it help humans survive as a species or hinder our survival?

2. Can you think of any instances when you've experienced divided consciousness?

Correct Answers 1. b (p. 118), **2. a** (p. 119), **3. c** (p. 118).

▶ SLEEP AND DREAMS: CONSCIOUS WHILE ASLEEP

Most nights, we slip gently from wakefulness into sleep, only to return from our nocturnal vacation the next morning. Is this all there is to sleeping? Is it a mere gap in awareness that consumes one-third of our lives? Sleep is not a single state; instead, it's a complex combination of states, some involving conscious awareness. We do not leave consciousness behind for the entire night when we sleep. Rather, we enter worlds of awareness with properties that are very different from those of the wide-awake world.

Stages of Sleep

Several states of conscious awareness are a part of the sleep process. As we fall asleep, we pass from waking consciousness into a semiwakeful state, into four states of progressively deeper sleep (all of which contain little or no conscious awareness), then into dream sleep, which brings a kind of conscious awareness with a reality all its own. We need to look carefully at each of these steps in the sleep cycle.

Hypnagogic State

We do not always go directly from wakefulness to sleep. Often, we daydream for a while, then pass into a "twilight" state that is neither daydreaming nor dreaming. This is the **hypnagogic state** (Mavromatis, 1987). We begin to lose voluntary control over our body movements; our sensitivity to outside stimuli diminishes; and our thoughts become more fanciful, less bound by reality. For most people, it's a highly relaxed, enjoyable state. On some occasions, however, we are rudely snapped out of the peaceful hypnagogic state—we suddenly feel as if we are falling and our body experiences a sudden jerk called a **myoclonia.**

Stages of Light and Deep Sleep

After making the transition from the hypnagogic state to sleep, we pass through four stages of progressively deeper sleep. Most sleep researchers distinguish among four levels of sleep defined on the basis of **electroencephalogram (EEG)** measures of electrical brain activity (Webb, 1968). The depth of sleep alternates upward and downward many times during the night. Indeed, young adults show an average of 34 shifts in the depth of sleep during the first 6 hours (Webb, 1968). Sleep, then, is not a single, continuous state; it is an almost constantly changing one (see fig. 4.2).

REM Sleep and Dreams

The era of the scientific study of this elusive state of consciousness was ushered in by the discovery of a relationship between dreaming and movements of the eyeballs (Kleitman, 1960). Dreams are very common during a period of sleep that is marked by rapid eye

hypnagogic state
(hip″nah-goj′ik)   A relaxed state of dreamlike awareness between wakefulness and sleep.

myoclonia
(mi″o-klō′nē-ah)   An abrupt movement that sometimes occurs during the hypnagogic state in which the sleeper often experiences a sense of falling.

electroencephalogram (EEG)
(e-lek″trō-en-sef′ah-lo-gram)   A measure of electrical brain activity.

FIGURE 4.2
Each night we pass through a complicated and irregular pattern of shifts from one stage to another.

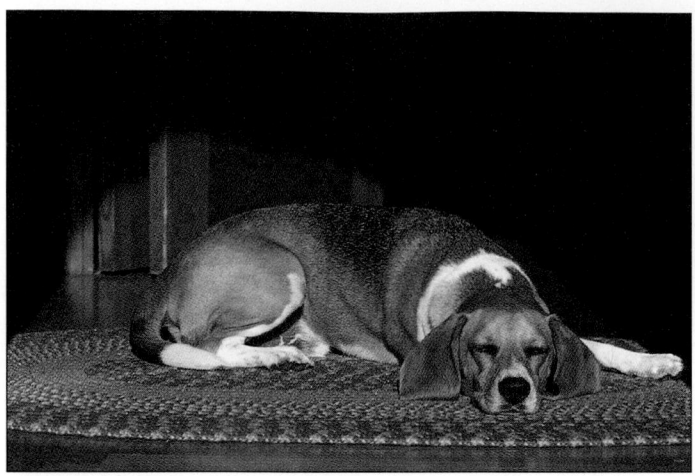

REM sleep is like an "autonomic storm," causing noticeable changes in many parts of the body—human or animal.

REM sleep
Rapid-eye-movement sleep, characterized by movement of the eyes under the lids; often accompanies dreams.

movements and brain-wave activity suggesting the presence of conscious awareness. This provided a convenient way for scientists to know when dreams were occurring so that they could study them. Because of the characteristic eye movements, this phase of sleep is referred to as *rapid-eye-movement sleep,* or **REM sleep**.

After three decades of study, it's now known that the eyeballs are not the only parts of the body that are busy during dreams. Sleep researcher Wilse Webb (1968) has likened dream sleep to an "autonomic storm." The autonomic nervous system and other parts of the peripheral nervous system (see chapter 3) are very active during dreams, causing noticeable changes in many parts of the body: Blood flow to the brain increases; the heartbeat becomes irregular; the muscles of the face and fingers twitch; and breathing becomes irregular. Interestingly, voluntary control of the large body muscles is largely lost during REM sleep, perhaps to keep us from acting out our dreams. Anyone who has watched a sleeping beagle twitch, make miniature running movements, and rasp muffled barks (at dream rabbits?) knows about these autonomic storms and knows that REM sleep is not limited to humans. This fact has been confirmed in many laboratory studies of sleeping mammals.

In addition, there is vaginal lubrication and erection of the clitoris in females and erection of the penis in males during REM sleep. Because of erections that begin during REM sleep, the penis of adult males is erect during one-fourth to one-half of an average night's sleep. This fact has led to advances in the diagnosis of conditions in which some males are unable to have an erection (known as *erectile dysfunction*). By having the patient spend a night in a sleep laboratory to see if he has erections during REM sleep, it is possible to determine if the cause of the problem is psychological (he would have erections during REM sleep) or physical (he would not have REM erections).

Time Spent Dreaming

How often do you dream? In a survey of college-aged adults, about 15 percent said that they dream every night, and another 25 percent said that they dream on most nights. On the other hand, almost a third of young adults said that they rarely or never dream (Strauch & Meier, 1996). Even if you recall a dream every night, you probably greatly underestimate the frequency of your dreams. We spend much more time in the world of dream consciousness than most of us realize.

Studies of dreaming conducted during the past 30 years show young adults have 30 to 40 REM dreams per week. We do not remember dreaming nearly this often when we are awake because we forget dreams quickly unless we awaken during or soon after the dream. But we spend about 2 hours each night in the conscious state of REM dreams. There is much more to the story of consciousness while sleeping, however. REM sleep is not the only part of the sleep cycle that contains dreams.

Non-REM Sleep and Dreams

Initially, sleep researchers believed that dreams were uncommon during the non-REM parts of the sleep cycle (Kleitman, 1960). Subsequent studies showed, however, that the number of dreams that occurs during non-REM sleep is much higher than suspected (Foulkes, 1962). Many studies have consistently shown that, when participants are awakened during non-REM phases of sleep, they report dreaming about half of the time (Horne, 1988; Strauch & Meier, 1996).

The nature of non-REM dreams is quite different from that of REM dreams, however. Non-REM dreams are more likely to consist of brief, fragmentary impressions that are less emotional and less likely to involve visual images than are REM sleep dreams. Whereas REM dreams are like watching or participating in a play, non-REM dreams resemble the ordinary process of thinking briefly about something during the daytime. In

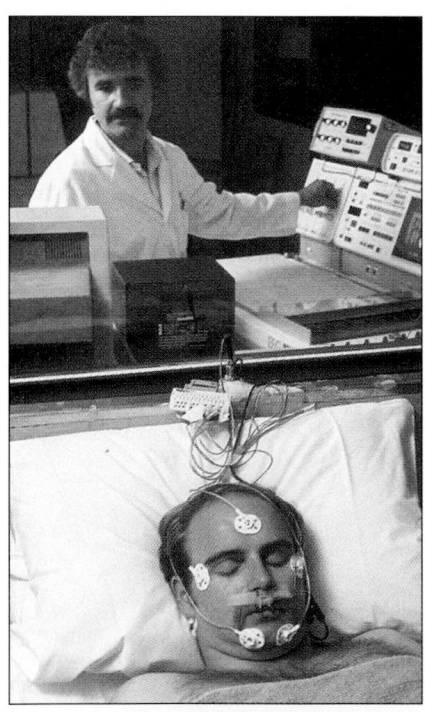

Electroencephalograms and eye muscle monitors allow psychologists to study dreams scientifically.

fact, non-REM dreams so resemble fleeting daytime thoughts that individuals awakened during a non-REM dream often deny that they had been asleep at all. Similarly, persons awakened during the non-REM phases of sleep report far more dreams if they are asked "What was going through your head before you were awakened?" instead of "Were you dreaming?" (Foulkes, 1989). Non-REM dreams are so different from REM dreams that they are often not thought of as dreams at all by participants in sleep studies. Perhaps for similar reasons, it appears that non-REM dreams are less likely to be spontaneously recalled after waking than are REM dreams (Foulkes, 1989; Hobson, 1989; Horne, 1988; Strauch & Meier, 1996).

When both REM and non-REM dreams are considered, we spend a surprising amount of time in states of consciousness during sleep. In addition to the 2 hours of REM dreaming per night, non-REM dream activity is occurring during half of the other 4 to 6 hours that we sleep each night. Unlike waking consciousness, most of the hours that we are conscious during sleep do not become part of the permanent records of our lives by being stored in memory, but modern sleep research has revealed that we are consciously aware during sleep much more than we would have ever suspected.

Content of Dreams

Dreams are one of the most fascinating aspects of human consciousness. Since at least the time of the Egyptian pharaohs, people have attempted to decipher the meaning of dreams—and psychologists are still trying. Let's begin our discussion of dreams by looking at psychological studies of what people dream about. Because dreams are private, it is interesting to compare our own dreams with those of others.

The first systematic study of dreams was conducted by Mary Whiton Calkins. You first learned Calkins' name in chapter 1, when we discussed the founders of psychology. Calkins was a pioneer in the study of memory, but she was also the founder of scientific dream research. Over a hundred years ago, Calkins and her partner wrote down a verbatim description of every dream they recalled over several months—often writing by candlelight in the middle of the night (Calkins, 1893). Since the time of Calkins, many researchers have studied thousands of dreams, both spontaneously recalled dreams and dreams that are recalled when research participants are awakened in sleep labs. Therefore, we can now confidently describe the content of human dreams.

Characters in Dreams

Who are the characters in your dreams—your friends and family? Are there strangers in your dreams? Are you a character in your own dreams? Because you are always the "author" of your dreams, it is not surprising that you often play a leading role. The dreamer has an active role in nearly three-fourths of dreams, and you are absent from your own dreams only 10 percent of the time (Strauch & Meier, 1996). About half of the other characters in your dreams are friends, acquaintances, or family members, but the other half are people you do not know or cannot recognize—or are animals 4 percent of the time. The characters in dreams are about an even mixture of men and women, with men being slightly more likely to dream about men than women are (Hall, 1951; Strauch & Meier, 1996).

Emotions in Dreams

About three-fourths of all dreams have some emotional content. Of these emotionally tinged dreams, about 60 percent have a negative tone or a mixture of negative and positive emotions (Strauch & Meier, 1996). There are gender differences in the emotional qualities of dreams, however. Overall, men are a little more likely to have positive dreams than are women. Similarly, the actions of the characters in men's dreams are somewhat more socially restrained than the characters in women's dreams. The people in men's dreams are both less likely to act in friendly ways toward other characters in the dream and less likely to act aggressively toward other dream players. When verbal or physical aggression occurs in dreams, both men and women are more likely to dream that they are the victim than the perpetrator of that aggression, but this tendency is somewhat stronger for women than men (Strauch & Meier, 1996).

Creative and Bizarre Aspects of Dreams

Dreams fascinate us largely because they can be amazingly creative and bizarre. Most of our dreams actually resemble normal, everyday life, but even our more realistic dreams often contain creative and usual elements. About three-fourths of our dreams contain at least one bizarre and unrealistic element, usually mixed into an otherwise realistic dream. On the other hand, 10 percent of our dreams involve mostly nonsensical story lines, and another 10 percent of dreams are almost completely fantastic and bizarre. Our dreams are twice as likely to be about fictional people and events than real ones, and the settings for our dreams also are more likely to be fictional than real, with sudden and unrealistic changes from one setting to another occurring in one out of four dreams (Hall, 1951; Strauch & Meier, 1996).

Meaning of Dreams

Why do we dream about the things that fill our heads during sleep? What is the meaning of dreams? A century of research suggests that some of the content of dreams is easy to understand, but the rest is still a mystery.

Day Residue and Stimulus Incorporation

day residue
Dream content that is similar to events in the person's waking life.

A large part of the content of dreams is directly related to things that are going on in our lives during the day—which Sigmund Freud called **day residue.** The majority of dreams contain at least one character or event from the preceding day—or, less often, from the preceding week or even earlier in the dreamer's life. The most important characters and events are more likely to reflect day residue than are less central parts. One clear demonstration of the importance of day residue in the content of dreams is that half of all dreams reported by research participants in sleep laboratories include the sleep researchers or parts of the laboratory in the dream (Strauch & Meier, 1996).

A naturalistic study of the impact of daytime events on the content of dreams was conducted by Wood, Bootzin, Rosenhan, Nolen-Hoeksema, and Jourdon (1992). On October 17, 1989, a major earthquake hit the San Francisco area and caused more than $5 billion in damage and killed 62 people, including 42 who were killed when a freeway collapsed on them. The researchers asked students at two universities in the San Francisco area to keep track of the number of upsetting dreams that they had during a 3-week period immediately following the earthquake. As a control group, students at the University of Arizona who had not been near the earthquake did the same thing. Not surprisingly, the students in the area of the earthquake reported more vivid, upsetting dreams than the students in Arizona. In addition, 40 percent of the students in the San Francisco area reported at least one dream about earthquakes, compared with 5 percent of the students in Arizona (Wood & others, 1992). Persons exposed to highly stressful events, such as wars, sometimes have nightmarish dreams about them for many years afterwards (Neyland & others, 1998). Clearly, events and concerns in our daily lives are among the most common things that we dream about.

Our current concerns are reflected in our dreams. After the 1989 earthquake, students in the San Francisco area reported many upsetting dreams.

Sometimes the real-world event that is included in the dream is something that is going on while we are asleep. Have you ever had a dream that somehow included the telephone or alarm clock that was ringing in your ear at the time? This phenomenon is called **stimulus incorporation**
Stimuli that occur during sleep that are incorporated into dreams either directly or in altered form.

stimulus incorporation. Sometimes the stimulus in the real environment is directly incorporated into the dream, but more often it is "transformed" somewhat. In a Swiss study, sleep participants were presented with the recorded sound of a jet plane while asleep. About one-third later reported dreaming about flying or reported hearing something that sounded like a jet plane (such as a sputtering gas stove) in their dream, but the sound was usually not heard in the dream exactly as it actually sounded (Strauch & Meier, 1996).

Dream Interpretation

We know that some of the content of dreams simply reflects the events and concerns of daily life, but what about the rest? And what is the meaning of the bizarre and fictional images in dreams? Different psychologists have very different views of the meaning of dreams, ranging from the opinion that they mean virtually nothing to the belief that they provide a rich source of information about hidden aspects of our personalities that cannot be gotten easily in other ways.

To followers of Sigmund Freud, dreams are the "royal road to the unconscious." They allow us to travel deep into the unconscious mind and view hidden conflicts and motives cloaked only by the symbols of dreams. To Freud, there are two levels of the content of dreams: manifest and latent. The events that we experience in dreams are their **manifest content.** This level held little interest for Freud; he felt that it was necessary to get beyond the surface and find out what the manifest content of the dream symbolized to discover its true meaning, or **latent content.** For example, the manifest content of a young woman's dream might involve riding on a train and becoming frightened as it enters a tunnel. On the surface, the dream is about trains and tunnels. But what does the manifest content of the dream symbolize? Freud might see the train as symbolizing a penis and the tunnel as symbolizing a vagina. Hence, the hidden, or latent, content of the dream might concern the young woman's conflicts about having sex.

Such interpretations are provocative and fascinating, but are they accurate? Psychologists simply do not agree on this issue. Because symbols can be interpreted in an infinite number of ways, we can never be sure that our interpretations are correct. Perhaps as a result, most contemporary psychologists place much less emphasis on dream interpretation than did Freud.

manifest content
According to Freud, the obvious, but superficial, meaning of dreams.

latent content
According to Freud, the true meaning of dreams that is found in the symbols of their manifest content.

 Latent Content

www.mmhe.com/laheye1

Reasons for Sleep and Dreams

Why do we sleep and dream? Do we need to sleep? What effects does a lack of sleep have on us? It is clear that we need sleep in the sense that we apparently create a "sleep debt" that needs to be made up if we miss sleep. College students at the University of Florida who participated in a sleep experiment were limited to 2 hours of sleep for one night. The next day they were irritable, fatigued, and inefficient, and the next night they fell asleep more quickly and slept longer than usual (Webb & Bonnet, 1979).

Longer periods of sleep deprivation produce more pronounced inefficiency and fatigue, but people are remarkably able to do without a lot of sleep. For example, teenager Randy Gardner set a new world record by staying awake for 264 hours as a science project with no serious ill effects, but he felt a great deal of fatigue, sleepiness, and irritability. However, when a group of volunteers gradually reduced their sleep from 8 to 4 hours a night for a period of 2 months, there were no detectable effects (Webb & Bonnet, 1979). It's when we abruptly reduce the amount of sleep, or reduce it to less than 4 hours, that we are most likely to feel ill effects and an intense need for sleep.

Sleep researchers have not yet reached an agreement as to why we sleep. There is some evidence that sleep plays a role in the restoration of the body. Long-distance runners, for example, sleep longer and show more deep sleep than usual after a race (Shapiro, Boortz, Mitchell, Bartel, & Jooste, 1982). In addition, the rate of protein synthesis is high during REM sleep (Drucker-Colin & Spanis, 1976). Sleep researcher Wilse Webb (1975) popularized a very different theory of why we sleep that suggests that sleep serves a protective rather than a restorative role. Webb was not convinced that humans have much of a physiological need for sleep. Because the eyes of animals that sleep at night are not very efficient in low light, he hypothesized that we fall asleep to keep us from moving around in the dark of night. In his view, sleep keeps us from wasting energy, falling off cliffs, and being eaten by animals that hunt at night and have better night vision.

● Review

Each night, we depart the world of waking consciousness and enter another world that we scarcely remember the next morning. Alternating among periods of sleep that contain no conscious experience, we live a life of dreams accompanied by a flurry of internal activity in the body. When studied systematically, much of the content of dreams is found to reflect daily events and concerns. Still, the meaning of dreams has long fascinated us and played a major role in Freud's attempts to understand the hidden workings of the mind.

● Check Your Learning

To be sure that you have learned the key points from the preceding section, cover the list of correct answers and try to answer each question. If you give an incorrect answer to any question, return to the page given next to the correct answer to see why your answer was not correct.

1. Research suggests that _____ may be the most important components of sleep because subjects deprived of them were irritable, inefficient, and fatigued.

   a) hypnagogic sleep   c) REM sleep and deep sleep
   b) myoclonia and REM sleep   d) naps

2. According to Freud, the _____, or true meaning of dreams, reveal(s) hidden conflicts and motives in the unconscious mind.

   a) latent content   c) events
   b) manifest content   d) colors

3. Dreaming about events that happened in the day before falling asleep is called _____.

● Thinking Critically About Psychology

1. In your opinion, why do we sleep?
2. Do dreams serve a purpose in our lives?

Correct Answers 1. c (p. 121), 2. a (p. 125), 3. day residue (p. 124).

▶ ALTERED STATES OF CONSCIOUSNESS

Thus far, we have talked about states of consciousness with which we are all familiar. We all know what it feels like to think about a problem, to dream, and to let our minds wander. Next we will turn to the so-called altered states of consciousness. We will begin by looking at the phenomenon of hypnosis and then examine the conscious altering properties of some drugs.

Hypnosis

A person who has been hypnotized can sometimes be so convinced that she is standing in a snowstorm without a coat that she shivers. Similarly, a hypnotist can tell a hypnotized person he is going back to his fourth birthday party and watch him act as if he is playing with other 4-year-olds. People who have been hypnotized like this often tell us that they actually feel the cold wind and believe that they are reexperiencing the birthday party. What is it about this state of **hypnosis** that makes it so fascinatingly different from waking consciousness?

The person becoming hypnotized focuses his or her attention firmly on the hypnotist's voice and is talked and lulled into an altered state of consciousness. This hypnotic state differs from individual to individual but typically has the following characteristics:

1. *Relaxation.* A sense of deep relaxation and peacefulness exists, often accompanied by changes in the way the body feels, such as floating or sinking.

2. *Hypnotic hallucinations.* When told to do so, the person may see, feel, or hear things in altered ways or may even experience things that are not there, such as smelling a flower that does not exist.

3. *Hypnotic analgesia.* When told to do so, the person may lose the sense of touch or pain in some region of the body. This is one of the best validated aspects of hypnosis and has led to the use of hypnosis in surgery, dentistry, and childbirth (Harmon, Hyan, & Tyre, 1990; Hilgard, 1978; Miller & Bowers, 1993; Price & Barber, 1987).

4. *Hypnotic age regression.* The person can sometimes be made to feel that he or she is passing back in time to an earlier stage of life, but most experts do not believe that hypnosis improves the recall of childhood events (Kirsch & Lynn, 1995).

5. *Hypnotic control.* The actions of hypnotized individuals sometimes seem as if they are out of their own control. When told that her arm can float, a hypnotized person's arm may seem to float up as if it were lifted by invisible balloons rather than by her own muscles (Bowers, 1976).

What is the nature of this altered state of consciousness? It took psychologists a long time to decide that it was respectable to study hypnosis, but, in the past 30 years, hypnosis has finally seen the hard light of scientific inquiry (Allen, Iacono, Laravuso, & Dunn, 1995; Barber, 1969; Bowers, 1976; Crasilneck & Hall, 1985; Miller & Bowers, 1993). Psychologists are still not in agreement on how to characterize hypnosis, however. Theodore Barber (Barber & Wilson, 1977; Kirsch & Lynn, 1995) suggested that hypnosis should not be thought of as a "trance" but as a highly relaxed state in which the person's conscious awareness is highly focused, the person's imagination is intensified, and the person is highly susceptible to the instructions of the hypnotist. Ernest Hilgard (1975), in contrast, believes that hypnosis is based on divided consciousness (see p. 118). According to Hilgard, individuals can, for example, experience a loss of pain through hypnosis because that part of consciousness can be separated from waking consciousness.

In recent years hypnosis has gained limited acceptance by the medical and dental professions for the relief of pain through hypnotic analgesia (Price & Barber, 1987). For example, patients who cannot use analgesic medications for a variety of reasons have been able to have extensive operations or undergo childbirth under hypnosis with little or no pain (Harmon & others, 1990; Hilgard & Hilgard, 1975).

Drugs and Altered Consciousness

Perhaps the most distinctly different types of altered consciousness involve taking **psychotropic drugs,** a class of drugs that alters conscious experience. These drugs exert their effects by influencing specific neurotransmitters in the brain or by

hypnosis
(hip-nō′sis)   An altered state of consciousness in which the individual is highly relaxed and susceptible to suggestions.

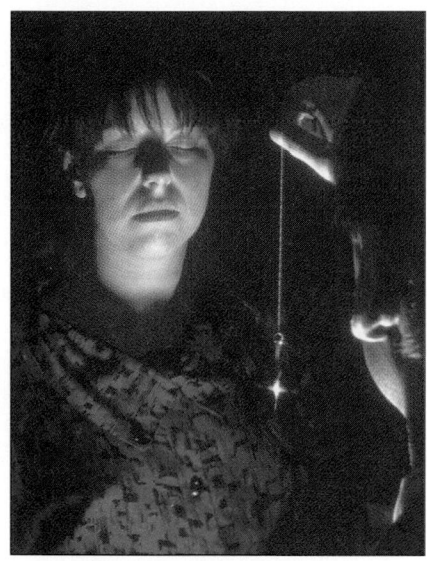

A person being hypnotized focuses attention firmly on the hypnotist's voice and is lulled into an altered state of consciousness.

These are images of the brain of a hypnotized person whose hand is immersed in a hot water bath. When the image on the right was made, the hypnotized person was told that the water was comfortable. When the image on the left was made, the person was told that the water was painfully hot. Notice the large differences in activity in the cingulate cortex—a part of the limbic system that plays a key role in the perception of the emotional aspect of pain transmitted by "slow-pain" fibers. Apparently, hypnosis reduced the emotional experience of pain in this person.

psychotropic drugs
(sī˝ko-trōp´pik)   The class of drugs that
alters conscious experience.

chemically altering the action of neurons in other ways. The range of effects of psychotropic drugs is enormous, from mild relaxation to vivid hallucinations. Perhaps even more enormous than the range of their effects, however, is the frequency of their use in contemporary society (Carroll, 2000).

Psychotropic drugs can be divided into four major categories. *Depressants* reduce the activity of inhibitory centers of the central nervous system, leading to a sense of relaxation and lowered inhibitions. *Stimulants* are drugs that increase the activity of the motivational centers and decrease action in inhibitory centers of the central nervous system, providing a sense of energy and well-being. *Hallucinogens* produce dreamlike alterations in perceptual experience. *Inhalants* are common household chemicals that are put to dangerous use by being inhaled, which produces feelings of intoxication. Not fitting easily into this classification is the drug marijuana, which induces a relaxed sense of well-being in most persons. Common members of these classes of drugs are summarized in table 4.1. Their patterns of use will be discussed in the section that follows. Although the effects of psychotropic drugs are varied, we need to consider a number of issues that are relevant to all of them. These issues include the wide variation in responses to drugs and the problems that are associated with their use.

Variable Response to Drugs

In the sections that follow, we will look at the psychological effects of a number of widely used drugs. In discussing these effects, we must keep in mind that the effects drugs have on us are far from perfectly reliable and predictable. Many factors influence the individual's response to a drug; most important among them are:

1. *Dose and purity.* Obviously, the amount of the drug taken influences its effect. Less obvious is the fact that drugs purchased on the street are often cut (mixed) with other substances, which can alter the effects of the drug.

2. *Personal characteristics.* The weight, health, age, and even the personality of the person taking a drug can influence the drug's effect.

3. *Expectations.* The effect that a person expects a drug to have, based on his or her past experiences and what the person has heard from others, partly determines the effect of the drug.

4. *Social situation.* Other people influence a person's response to the drug. The person may respond differently if the drug is taken alone versus in the midst of an upbeat party.

5. *Moods.* The mood that the person is in at the time of taking the drug can dramatically alter its effects. Alcohol, for example, can make a happy person happier or a sad person more depressed, and it can unleash violence in an angry individual.

When you consider the interplay of these factors, it's easy to see how their effects are at least partly unpredictable.

Problems Associated with Drug Use

The use of drugs to alter conscious experience carries with it certain risks. These risks differ considerably from drug to drug, but the risks associated with all drugs involve the same basic issues.

1. *Drug abuse.* A drug is being abused if taking it causes physical damage (as in liver damage caused by alcohol) or impairment of psychological or social functioning (as in frequent drinking of alcohol leading to marital conflicts).

2. *Psychological dependence.* A psychological dependence has been developed when the individual needs to use the drug regularly to maintain a comfortable psychological state, as when a person gets edgy if he or she does not smoke marijuana daily.

TABLE 4.1 — Major Psychotropic Drugs

Depressants

Tranquilizers
- Equanil (meprobamate)
- Librium (chlordiazepoxide)
- Miltown (meprobamate)
- Valium (diazepam)
- Xanax (alprazolam)

Narcotics
- Opiates (opium and its derivatives)
  - Codeine
  - Heroin
  - Morphine
  - Opium
- Synthetic narcotics
  - Demerol
  - Methadone
  - Percodan

Sedatives
- Alcohol (ethanol)
- Barbiturates
  - Nembutal (pentobarbital)
  - Quaalude (methaqualone)
  - Seconal (secobarbital)
  - Tuinal (secobarbital and amobarbital)
  - Veronal (barbital)

Stimulants

Amphetamines
- Benzedrine (amphetamine)
- Dexedrine (dextroamphetamine)
- Methedrine (methamphetamine)

Cocaine

Caffeine (in coffee, tea, and colas)

Nicotine (in tobacco)

Inhalants (Volatile Hydrocarbons)

- Cleaning fluids
- Gasoline
- Glue
- Nail polish remover (acetone)
- Paint thinner

Hallucinogens

- LSD (lysergic acid diethylamide-25)
- Mescaline (peyote)
- PCP (phencyclidine hydrochloride)
- Psilocybin (psychotogenic mushrooms)

Marijuana Family

- Marijuana
- Hashish

3. *Physiological addiction, tolerance, and withdrawal.* Many drugs quickly become involved in the chemical functioning of the body. The body adjusts to such a degree that, when the drug is not present, the body cannot function properly and the person experiences painful *withdrawal* symptoms. Addictive drugs produce progressively stronger addiction because over time the body learns to adapt more easily to the drug in its system. As *tolerance* for the drug increases, larger doses are needed to produce the same effect on consciousness. Therefore, the addicted person's body chemistry becomes progressively more tied to the drug.

4. *Direct side effects.* The direct dangers of drugs just described are not the only risks associated with their use. Psychotropic drugs rarely have effects that are limited to a single neurotransmitter or organ system. They often have powerful and potentially serious *side effects.* Some of these are merely annoyances, such as the temporary numbness in the throat caused by inhaling cocaine, whereas others are far more serious. Brain damage, heart attacks, loss of control of automobiles, violence, and suicide are only some of the common side effects of psychotropic drugs.

5. *Indirect side effects.* It has become clear that drugs are dangerous not only because of their direct psychological and medical side effects but because of their indirect effects as well. The obvious example is the greatly increased risk of infection with hepatitis or human immunodeficiency virus (HIV), which causes acquired immune deficiency syndrome (AIDS), as a result of sharing needles used for drug injection. Many drugs, however, result in slower and less immediately obvious impairment of immune system functioning that increases the risk of serious disease.

Psychotropic Drugs

Many consciousness-altering drugs are used and abused today. The drugs described in the following paragraphs are powerful in their effects, are often powerfully addictive, and are used illegally in most circumstances.

Stimulants

stimulants
Drugs that increase the activity of motivational centers and decrease activity of inhibitory centers in the central nervous system, providing a sense of energy and well-being.

amphetamines
(am-fet′ah-minz)   Powerful stimulants that produce a conscious sense of increased energy and a euphoric high.

amphetamine psychosis
(sī-kō′sis)   A prolonged reaction to the excessive use of stimulants, characterized by disordered thinking, confused and rapidly changing emotions, and intense suspiciousness.

Stimulants, often called *uppers,* are drugs that activate motivational centers and reduce activity in inhibitory centers of the central nervous system. *Caffeine,* which is found in coffee, tea, soft drinks, and some nonprescription medicines, and *nicotine,* which is found in cigarettes and other tobacco products, are by far the most widely used stimulants. As described later, these relatively mild stimulants are, nonetheless, extremely addictive and pose major health risks.

Amphetamines (trade names Dexedrine, Benzedrine, and Methedrine) are stimulant drugs that generally produce a conscious sense of increased energy, alertness, enthusiasm, and a euphoric high. They are not physically addictive but produce rapid and intense psychological dependence. Hence, the possibility for abuse is very high. The amphetamines are dangerous physically, particularly in their effects on the heart. Psychologically, the greatest risk is known as **amphetamine psychosis**—a prolonged reaction to excessive use of stimulants characterized by distorted thinking, confused and rapidly changing emotions, and intense suspiciousness.

The use of amphetamines in the United States was on the decline until the late 1980s, particularly use of the dangerous form of amphetamine known as *methamphetamine,* or *speed.* Apparently word had gotten around the street that "speed kills." But, unfortunately, when the street name for methamphetamine changed to "crystal" and "crystal meth," the bad reputation that speed had earned for serious psychological and medical side effects was lost. Today this white powder—which is usually sniffed but is also swallowed or injected—is used in virtually epidemic proportions in some areas of the country.

Cocaine is one of the more widely abused drugs in the United States. Cocaine, a stimulant much like amphetamine, is made from the leaves of the coca plant. It is taken in many forms but is most commonly inhaled as a powder, injected, or smoked in the dangerously powerful form known as crack. Cocaine produces alertness, high energy, optimism, self-confidence, happiness, exhilaration, and talkativeness. It raises body temperature, breathing, and heart rate and reduces the desire for food and sleep.

Because the cocaine high only lasts a matter of minutes, its use is often repeated each time the effect wears off. These binges of repeated cocaine use sometimes last for hours or even days, until a state of exhaustion is reached. At this point, the cocaine user *crashes,* feeling immensely tired, hungry, and in need of long periods of sleep. In the first few days following a cocaine binge, the user is absolutely miserable. Depression, agitation, confusion, paranoia, anger, and exhaustion are all part of the cocaine crash (Weddington et al., 1990).

Withdrawal from cocaine dependence differs considerably from withdrawal from heroin or nicotine addiction, especially in the absence of changes in heart rate and blood pressure, the absence of chills and sweats, and the absence of physical pain. The intense depression, agitation, and craving for cocaine during withdrawal is a mean and miserable monkey on the back of the cocaine addict, however. Although the craving diminishes as the crash wears off, it returns when the person is exposed to cocaine again, or to the people and places that are associated with cocaine use. Going straight after becoming dependent on cocaine is an enormous challenge, although it is one that can be met by genuinely motivated persons given proper treatment (Weddington & others, 1990).

Cocaine is dangerous even to the occasional user. Even small doses can lead to fatal heart attacks, and, because tolerance for

This is an image of a human brain (baseline, on left). On the right is a human brain on amphetamine. The change in color shows a marked reduction in activity in the limbic system on amphetamine.
Source: Tamminga, C. A. (1996). Images in neuroscience: Neuroimaging, XIII. *American Journal of Psychiatry, 153,* 1249.

cocaine varies considerably, it is dangerously easy for experienced occasional users to overdose accidentally. Ironically, cocaine was once a legal drug in the United States. Coca-Cola, originally marketed as a "nerve tonic," initially contained cocaine as part of its "secret formula." In 1906, the cocaine was replaced by the milder stimulant caffeine.

Cocaine was originally an ingredient of Coca-Cola at a time when use of the drug was legal. It is now an illicit stimulant, which can lead to dependence on the drug whether snorted or smoked in the form of crack.

Depressants

The **depressants** are a large class of psychotropic drugs that influence conscious experience by depressing parts of the central nervous system. Tranquilizers, sedatives, and narcotics are all depressant drugs, and, as we will see at the end of this chapter, alcohol is the most widely used depressant of all.

Sedatives and tranquilizers.   **Sedatives** are depressants that in mild doses generally produce a state of calm relaxation. They are prescribed in the United States as drugs to aid sleep and sometimes to combat anxiety. Common trade names for these drugs are Seconal, Tuinal, Nembutal, and Quaaludes (which are no longer sold in the United States but are still abused). Because they are highly addictive and dangerous to withdraw from without medical supervision and because overdoses are highly dangerous (and even small doses are dangerous when taken with alcohol), they are prescribed by physicians less frequently now than in the past. However, they are still widely abused through illegal drug markets.

Tranquilizers are milder drugs that are similar to sedatives in that they typically produce a sense of calm relaxation for a period of time. As such, they are often prescribed to reduce anxiety. Common trade names are Xanax, Valium, Librium, Ativan, Miltown, and Equanil. Like sedatives, most are dangerously addictive, often difficult to withdraw from, and are very dangerous when mixed with alcohol; they must be taken with great care. Also like sedatives, these types of downers are widely sold illegally.

Narcotics.   **Narcotics** are powerful and highly addictive depressants. The use of the narcotic drug opium, derived from the opium poppy, dates back at least 7,000 years in the Middle East. Derivatives of opium, including morphine, heroin, and codeine, are powerful narcotic drugs that dramatically alter consciousness. They generally relieve pain and induce a sudden, rushing high, followed by a relaxed, lethargic drowsiness. Narcotics create a powerful physiological addiction very rapidly. With prolonged addiction, the physical effects on the body are profoundly damaging. Compared with the use of other drugs, narcotics use in the United States is not high, but the drastic effects of opiates, including the crimes that many addicts commit to maintain their increasingly expensive habits, make it an extremely significant drug abuse problem. It became an especially difficult problem during the Vietnam War. Perhaps due to a combination of the availability of heroin and the stress of war, it was estimated that 20 percent of all Vietnam veterans tried heroin at least once (Harris, 1973).

Opium and its derivatives (the **opiates**) are not the only kinds of narcotic drugs. In recent years, synthetic narcotics have been artificially produced in drug laboratories. These synthetic narcotics include widely used painkilling drugs with trade names such as Demerol, Percodan, and Methadone.

Inhalants

Substances that when inhaled produce a sense of intoxication are called **inhalants.** To produce a "high," toxic (poisonous) substances, such as glue, cleaning fluid, and paint, are typically placed in paper bags and inhaled ("sniffed"). This type of intoxication is common

depressants
Drugs that reduce the activity of the central nervous system, leading to a sense of relaxation, drowsiness, and lowered inhibitions.

sedatives
Depressants that in mild doses produce a state of calm relaxation.

narcotics
Powerful and highly addictive depressants.

opiates
(ō′pē-ats) Narcotic drugs derived from the opium poppy.

inhalants
(in-hā′lants) Toxic substances that produce a sense of intoxication when inhaled.

HUMAN DIVERSITY

SUBSTANCE ABUSE AND HUMAN DIVERSITY

Without doubt, drug and alcohol abuse is a major problem in the United States. A large-scale study of the U.S. population (Kessler et al., 1993) found that 25 percent of adolescents and adults have had a substance abuse problem at some time in their life—that's one person out of every four! Alcohol abuse alone cost the country an estimated $10 billion in 1991 in terms of lost work time, accidents, increased medical costs, and other economic costs (Heien & Pittman, 1993), but the human cost of drug and alcohol abuse is much greater.

Who abuses drugs and alcohol in our society? Gender, ethnicity, and income level are important factors that influence the likelihood of substance abuse. Men consistently have been found to be twice as likely to abuse substances as women. The problem is very serious among women, but substance abuse is much more widespread among men.

In terms of ethnicity, African Americans have been found to be 35 percent less likely to abuse drugs and alcohol than both whites and Hispanics, but the rates of substance abuse of whites and Hispanics do not differ (Kessler et al., 1993). Apparently, there are cultural traditions in the African American community that protect against substance abuse. The lower rates of substance abuse among African Americans—which has been found in several U.S. surveys—are even more striking when findings for education and income level are considered. Persons with less education who earn less money in the United States are more likely to abuse substances than persons with more money. Thus, even though African Americans tend to earn less money, on the average, than white Americans in the United States at this time in history, their rates of substance abuse are much lower. The protective influence of ethnicity is so strong that it counters the trends associated with income and education.

It is important to understand the ways in which human diversity—gender, ethnicity, and education and income level—are linked to substance abuse. We will not fully understand the causes of substance abuse until we understand why women, African Americans, and the affluent are so much less likely to abuse drugs and alcohol.

It is equally important to remember to treat everyone as an *individual,* however. Although African American women from high-income families are at the lowest risk for substance abuse, some members of this select group have serious substance abuse problems. Similarly, most low-income white males have no difficulties with drugs and alcohol whatsoever.

Why do you think persons with low income and little education are more likely to abuse substances? What makes men more likely than women to abuse drugs and alcohol? In your opinion, why are African Americans at less risk for the abuse of these substances? Could the answers to these questions be used to reduce everyone's risk for substance abuse? Many hundreds of researchers in psychology and psychiatry are actively at work today trying to answer these important questions.

among children because the materials are relatively easy to obtain. Inhalants are highly addictive and extremely dangerous. These toxic fumes often cause permanent brain damage and other serious complications.

Hallucinogens

hallucinogens
(hah-lū′si′no-jenz) Drugs that alter perceptual experiences.

The drugs that most powerfully alter consciousness are **hallucinogens,** such as lysergic acid diethylamide (LSD), mescaline (derived from the peyote cactus), and psilocybin (derived from a kind of mushroom). These drugs typically alter perceptual experiences, but only large doses cause vivid hallucinations. In these unusual states, the drugged individual experiences imaginary visions and realities that, ironically, sometimes seem more "real" to the drug user than waking consciousness. This fact, however, may be more attributable to the drug taker's dissatisfaction with everyday life than to the drug itself.

The hallucinogens are generally not physiologically addictive, but individuals can quickly become psychologically dependent on them. In addition, although many of the drug-induced states (trips) produced by hallucinogens are experienced as pleasant, "bad trips"—frightening and dangerous drug responses—are not uncommon (McWilliams &

Tuttle, 1973). Individuals who are frightened about taking a drug but do so because of peer pressure are more likely to experience bad trips. These trips, both good and bad, can sometimes recur in flashbacks without the individual's taking the drug again. About 65 percent of flashbacks are bad trips, apparently being triggered by stress or anxiety. About 25 percent of all regular LSD users experience flashbacks, sometimes several months after the original trip (Matefy & Kroll, 1974).

One other hallucinogenic drug needs to be discussed because of its dangers. The drug phencyclidine, or PCP (angel dust), which was originally developed as an animal tranquilizer, has come into common use, especially among adolescents. The effects of PCP typically last from 4 to 6 hours. In some cases, the individual experiences auditory or visual hallucinations, but more likely the experience includes feelings of numbness, lack of muscular coordination, anxiety, and a sense of detachment from the environment. Euphoria, a sense of strength, and "dreaminess" may also be present. The individual on PCP may also engage in unconventional behavior, such as going into public places nude. Violent behavior toward others, suicide, and psychotic episodes are other possible reactions to this drug. It's generally considered one of the most dangerous drugs on the street (Petersen & Stillman, 1978).

Marijuana

Marijuana is a popular consciousness-altering drug that generally produces a sense of relaxation and well-being. In some cases, the drug alters sensory experiences and the perception of time. Not since Prohibition has any drug been so hotly debated or so widely used in spite of being illegal. It's not physically addictive; in fact, many users experience a reverse tolerance, in which smaller amounts of the drug eventually come to produce the same high. However, some psychological dependence is possible. Although the evidence as to possible physical or psychological harm is not conclusive, there is some evidence that prolonged marijuana use decreases the efficiency of cognitive processing, weakens the body's immune response, and decreases the action of male sex hormones (Wallace & Fisher, 1983). Moreover, like smoking any type of cigarette, marijuana greatly increases the risk of lung cancer. Driving an automobile or using any other form of machinery when intoxicated by marijuana (or any other substance) is also obviously dangerous.

Not since Prohibition has any drug been as hotly debated as marijuana.

Act-Alike and Designer Drugs

Until the 1980s, it was legal in most states to manufacture and sell drugs that looked and acted like illegal substances, such as amphetamines, but contained only substances that were legal to sell openly. For example, combinations of high doses of powdered caffeine and some over-the-counter decongestants produce some of the effects of amphetamines. Hence, these drugs are sometimes called *act-alike* drugs.

States have had to scramble to find ways to block the sale of act-alike drugs. These drugs are considered dangerous because of their own serious adverse effects. In addition, because the strength of drugs that act as amphetamines varies considerably, the risk of accidental overdose is very high.

Amateur chemists try to stay ahead of the law by designing new drugs that have not yet been classified as illegal—the so-called *designer drugs*. For example, the designer drugs MDA and MDMA (*ecstasy*) are derivatives of amphetamines that produce a dreamlike high lasting for up to 8 hours. Because these substances were legal until identified by law enforcement agencies as narcotics, they could be sold without penalty for a while. But the constant push to design new mind-altering drugs to stay ahead of the law means that new drugs are widely sold and used before anyone has a chance to evaluate their potential side effects. This is a major concern because any substance powerful enough to change the functioning of the brain generally carries with it serious medical and psychological risks (Carroll, 1989).

● Review

Altered states can be induced through hypnosis or by taking psychotropic drugs that alter conscious experience by influencing the action of neurons in the brain. These drugs produce changes in consciousness, ranging from mild alterations of mood to vivid hallucinations, but they also carry with them the danger of abuse, dependence, addiction, and direct physical damage in some cases. The effect of drugs on consciousness depends on a variety of factors, including dose and purity; the weight, health, age, and personality of the person taking the drug; expectations about the effects of the drug; the social situation; and the mood that the person is in at the time of taking the drug.

● Check Your Learning

To be sure that you have learned the key points from the preceding section, cover the list of correct answers and try to answer each question. If you give an incorrect answer to any question, return to the page given next to the correct answer to see why your answer was not correct.

1. The reduced experience of pain produced through hypnosis is termed:

   a) divided consciousness   c) hypnotic regression

   b) hypnotic analgesia   d) mesmerism

2. Psychologically, the greatest risk of amphetamine abuse is known as _____, which is a prolonged reaction to an excessive use of stimulants characterized by distorted thinking, confused and rapidly changing emotions, and intense suspiciousness.

   a) schizophrenia   c) overdose

   b) amphetamine psychosis   d) withdrawal

3. A long-lasting drug, originally developed as an animal tranquilizer, that typically produces numbness, a lack of muscular coordination, a sense of detachment from the environment, euphoria, and a sense of strength and that sometimes results in unconventional, psychotic, or violent behavior is _____.

   a) phencyclidine (PCP)   c) cocaine

   b) amphetamine   d) ecstasy (MDMA)

4. The drugs that most powerfully alter consciousness are _____ such as lysergic acid diethylamide (LSD), mescaline (derived from the peyote cactus), and psilocybin (derived from a kind of mushroom).

   a) inhalants   c) hallucinogens

   b) stimulants   d) depressants

● Thinking Critically About Psychology

1. How is hypnosis like dreaming? How is it different?

2. What social and personal factors induce millions of people to abuse drugs, despite the publicity regarding the negative effects of drug abuse?

Correct Answers 1. b (p. 127), **2. b** (p. 130), **3. a** (p. 133), **4. c** (p. 132).

Application *of Psychology*

THE LEGAL CONSCIOUSNESS-ALTERING DRUGS

Each day, many of us use consciousness-altering drugs, usually without even being aware that we are taking "drugs." Your coffee contains the stimulant drug caffeine, cigarettes contain the stimulant drug nicotine, and alcohol is a powerful depressant drug. Millions of individuals who would never consider using "drugs" use, abuse, or are addicted to these drugs. What are their consciousness-altering effects (and side effects)?

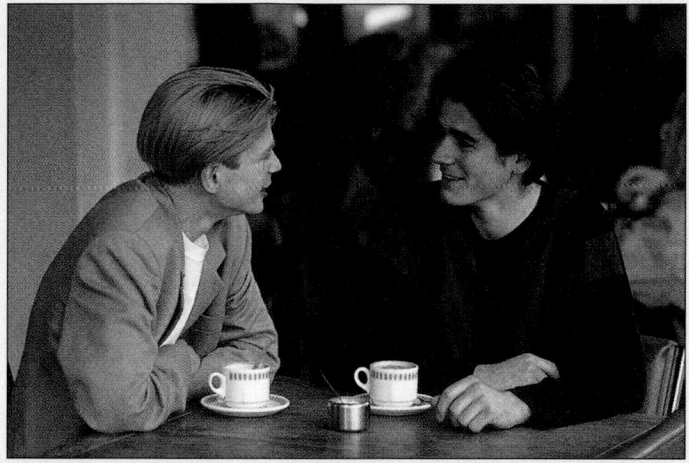

The average American drinks 36 gallons of coffee each year.

Caffeine

Eighty-five percent of Americans ingest caffeine daily (Hughes, Oliveto, Helzer, Higgins, & Bickel, 1992). Indeed, each year the average person in the United States drinks 36 gallons of coffee, 7 gallons of tea, and 30 gallons of cola and uses untold amounts of over-the-counter drugs containing caffeine (Ray, 1974). At approximately 125 milligrams (mg) per cup of coffee, that is an enormous consumption of caffeine.

You've seen the ads on television: The attractive woman, frazzled by the day's hassles, is restored to peaceful balance with a cup of coffee. Is that a good way to cope with our emotions when they have been bent and abused by life? Is caffeine good medicine for our nerves? Because caffeine is a stimulant, it does produce an increase in alertness, which helps explain the popularity of coffee, tea, colas, and other beverages that contain caffeine. But does it make you feel *better*?

Physicians and psychologists have long suspected that caffeine actually produces negative changes in emotions in many persons. David Veleber and Donald Templer (1984) conducted a study of the effects of caffeine on emotions using volunteer college students and businesspeople in the San Joaquin Valley of California. The participants completed a psychological test that measured the degree of depression, anxiety, and hostility that the individual was experiencing at the time of the test. They took the test before and 1 hour after drinking a cup of coffee.

Some of the participants drank decaffeinated coffee, whereas others received a low or high dose of caffeine in their coffee (the individuals did not know how much caffeine they were drinking, if any). The amount of caffeine was adjusted for the individual's body weight, with a 100-pound person receiving the equivalent of either one (low dose) or two cups (high dose) of strong brewed coffee.

As shown in figure 4.3, the caffeine produced small but significant changes in all three emotions. Most of us feel no ill effects from small amounts of coffee, but a large amount of caffeine is an invitation to lousy moods for all of us, and even small amounts may cause distress for sensitive individuals.

Unfortunately, serious health risks are associated with the overuse of caffeine. Although caffeine produces relatively small changes in consciousness, it has powerful effects on the body. It has long been known that consumption of eight or more cups of caffeinated coffee per day (1,000 mg) constitutes a dangerously high level of intake (Greden, 1974). Common effects of such consumption for a prolonged period of time include excessive stomach acid and ulcers, abnormal heart rhythms and accelerated heart rate, increased kidney activity, anxiety, irritability, insomnia, sensory disturbances, and definite physiological addiction with intense withdrawal symptoms when caffeine is not consumed (Greden, 1974; Hughes &

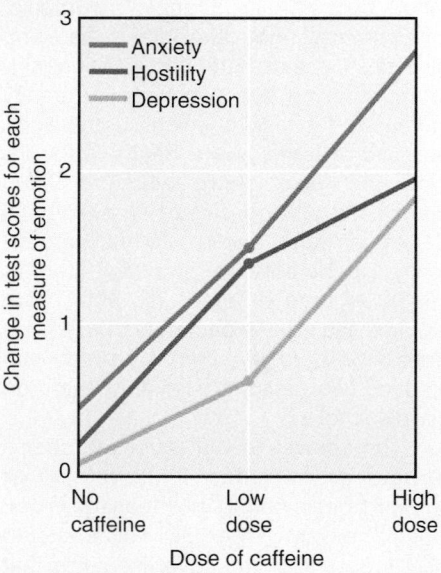

FIGURE 4.3

Change in measures of emotion after drinking either decaffeinated coffee or coffee containing small or large amounts of caffeine.

Source: Data from D. M. Veleber and D. T. Templer, "Effects of Caffeine on Anxiety and Depression," *Journal of Abnormal Psychology,* 93, 120–122, 1984. © 1984 by the American Psychological Association.

others, 1992). Prolonged use of caffeine at even moderate levels can also result in a physiological addiction to the substance.

Caffeine also produces marked increases in blood pressure, particularly during times of stress (Pincomb, Lovallo, Passey, Brackett, & Wilson, 1987). Moreover, even drinking moderately large amounts of coffee (five or more cups per day) over a period of years is associated with a two to three times greater risk of coronary heart disease, at least in men (LaCroix, Mead, Liang, Thomas, & Pearson, 1986). Drinking excessive amounts of coffee is a behavior that produces serious health risks, but even moderate amounts appear to pose some risk.

Nicotine

Nicotine found in tobacco is another widely used drug. Overall, 27 percent of adult men and 23 percent of women in the United States smoke cigarettes, with rates being highest among the least educated segment of the population and among persons with mental disorders. Although rates of smoking have dropped considerably over the past 20 years, they remain surprisingly high, given the clear evidence that cigarette smoking is highly dangerous. The life expectancy of regular smokers is reduced because smoking *greatly* increases the chances of lung and mouth cancer, heart attacks, pneumonia, emphysema, and other life-threatening diseases (Jenkins, 1988). In addition, cigarette smoking during pregnancy greatly increases the risk of lower birthweight, premature delivery, and death of the infant. Each year, approximately 135,000 people die of lung cancer in the United States; of those deaths, 101,000 are directly attributable to smoking (Jeffrey, 1988). A person aged 25 who never smokes has a life expectancy that is more than *8 years longer* than a person who smokes two packs a day. Why, then, do people smoke?

The answer to that question seems to have several parts. First, virtually all smokers begin during their teenage years, when they are especially vulnerable to peer pressure and to advertisements that portray smoking as something that strong, sexy adults do. Second, because teenagers usually know that their parents do not want them to smoke, it becomes attractive forbidden fruit and an easy way to rebel against parents. (Few teenagers are mature enough to realize that there are adults who *want* them to start smoking—the mega-rich owners of tobacco companies, who are happy to sell them an addictive drug that will kill one out of four of them.)

Third, regardless of why smokers begin to smoke, addiction soon takes over for most regular smokers (Russell, 1971; Stein & others, 1998). Nicotine is highly addictive for two primary reasons. It is a

A person who never smokes has a life expectancy of 8 years longer than a person who smokes two packs of cigarettes a day. Consequently, the cost of the smoker's life insurance averages 25 percent higher.

mild stimulant of the pleasure centers in the limbic system, and it increases alertness to a small degree by stimulating the frontal lobes of the cerebral cortex (Stein & others, 1998). More important, nicotine soothes the discomfort that it creates. Aftereffects of nicotine increase the smoker's level of irritability and discomfort after a cigarette. The next cigarette is highly reinforcing because it brings the smoker's discomfort back down to a normal level (the level before he or she began smoking), but the discomfort soon rises again after that cigarette, producing the recurrent motive to smoke (Parrott, 1999).

Alcohol

Are beer, wine, and liquor drugs? Although we do not generally think of alcohol as a "drug," it's a powerful and widely abused psychotropic drug that happens to come in liquid form. Alcohol works principally as a depressant, but it is experienced as a drug that "stimulates" sociability and exuberant activity ("partying"). This is because alcohol depresses inhibitory mechanisms in the brain. Thus, alcohol seems to stimulate the person because it makes the drinker less inhibited.

Alcohol also reduces tension and anxiety and increases self-confidence and self-esteem by erasing doubts about ourselves (Steele & Josephs, 1990). Alcohol has other effects as well. It impairs visual judgment and motor control and induces sleepiness (Matthews, Best, White, Vandergriff, & Simpson, 1996). In addition, alcohol can worsen negative moods, particularly deepening depression and mak-

ing it more likely that anger will result in verbal or physical aggression (Steele & Josephs, 1990).

Most states consider an individual legally intoxicated when .10 percent (one-tenth of 1 percent) of the volume of his or her circulating blood is alcohol. At this level, sensory and motor performance are noticeably impaired. Unfortunately, even blood-alcohol levels of .03 percent are sufficient to make driving an automobile or operating other machinery dangerous.

It is not easy to translate blood-alcohol levels into amounts of alcohol consumed because many factors influence blood-alcohol levels. Drinking on an empty stomach, drinking carbonated alcoholic beverages, drinking quickly rather than sipping, and drinking higher-proof beverages all lead to higher levels of blood alcohol, even when the same amount of alcohol is consumed under other circumstances (Chruschel, 1982). The principal complicating factor, however, is the amount of fluid in the body, which differs according to body size and sex. The liver can remove from the bloodstream the alcohol in one 12-ounce can of beer (or one glass of wine or 1 ounce of 100-proof liquor) in about 1 hour; the remainder stays in the blood. Figure 4.4 shows the average blood levels that can be expected for males and females of different sizes, but keep in mind that these are merely averages.

Except for nicotine, alcohol is the most widely abused addictive drug in the United States. Assessing the exact extent of alcohol abuse is difficult mainly for two

Males	Alcohol consumed in 1 hour	
Weight	(100 proof liquor)	Blood alcohol level
150 lbs	2 oz	.05
150 lbs	4 oz	.10*

Females	Alcohol consumed in 1 hour	
Weight	(100 proof liquor)	Blood alcohol level
100 lbs	2 oz	.09
100 lbs	4 oz	.18

*Note: Blood alcohol concentration of .03 can impair automobile driving; concentration of .10 constitutes intoxication, according to most state laws.

FIGURE 4.4

Average blood-alcohol levels as a result of drinking.

reasons. First, the amount of alcohol consumption that can lead to harmful effects varies markedly from person to person and from situation to situation. An individual who has only four drinks every New Year's Eve is an alcohol abuser if he drives himself home when intoxicated; a surgeon who has two drinks a day may be an alcohol abuser if she drinks them right before performing surgery. Second, the potential harmful effects of alcohol abuse are so varied. Heavy drinking can affect job performance, disrupt marriages, and harm one's health. It is involved in about half of all fatal fire and automobile accidents, one-third of all suicides, and two-thirds of all murders (Marlatt & Rose, 1980). Alcohol abuse frequently leads to highly stressful consequences, such as divorce and loss of employment; these stressful consequences then take a toll on health. In addition, alcohol has directly harmful effects on the liver, brain, and circulatory system.

As a result, the life span of the addicted alcoholic is 12 years shorter than average (National Institute on Alcohol Abuse and Alcoholism, 1987). Even moderately high levels of alcohol consumption create a health risk (Hennekens, Rosner, & Cole, 1978; Jenkins, 1988).

In addition, drinking during pregnancy has been linked to a form of combined physical defects and mental retardation in the infant known as *fetal alcohol syndrome* (Briggs, Freeman, & Yaffee, 1986). Although heavy drinking is most likely to lead to birth defects, no "safe" level of alcohol consumption during pregnancy has been established—and there may not be one.

In spite of the difficulties involved in defining alcohol abuse, surveys have been taken with eye-opening results. Using a broad definition of alcohol abuse, it has been found that, nearly one-third of the individuals surveyed reported at least one serious alcohol-related problem (for 21 percent of females and 41 percent of males) (Cahalan, 1970; Cahalan & Room, 1974).

Because of its powerful mood-altering qualities, alcohol can rapidly result in psychological dependence and physiological addiction (*alcoholism*).

This is not to say that alcohol is always harmful. In the survey cited (Cahalan & Room, 1974), more than half of all the drinkers reported no harmful side effects. Indeed, under some conditions, small amounts of alcohol may be beneficial to the health of some individuals. Individuals who drink an average of one drink per day or so live longer than individuals who do not drink at all (Dawson, 2000; Jenkins, 1988).

● Summary

Chapter 4 explores human awareness, normal waking consciousness, sleeping and dreaming, and altered states of consciousness.

I. Consciousness is defined as "a state of awareness" and is experienced in a variety of states.

    A. Daydreams combine the features of directed consciousness and dreamlike fantasies.

    B. At times, consciousness appears to become divided, with different conscious activities occurring simultaneously.

    C. Psychologists have conducted studies that suggest that it makes sense to say that unconscious mental processes operate in our lives.

II. Approximately one-third of our lives is spent in sleep, but not all of sleep is unconscious.

    A. Sleep begins with a semiwakeful, hypnagogic state and moves through stages of progressively deeper sleep.

    B. Dreams occur mostly during the phase of sleep known as REM sleep, but a different type of dream is common in non-REM sleep as well.

    C. Sleeping and dreaming seem important to health, but even extended periods of sleep deprivation have been shown to cause only fatigue, inefficiency, and irritability.

III. We sometimes experience more unusual altered states of consciousness.

    A. Hypnosis is sometimes used to alter consciousness and to relieve pain.

    B. Psychotropic drugs can be classified as stimulants, depressants, hallucinogens, and inhalants; the drug marijuana does not fit easily into this classification.

    C. Though risks differ from drug to drug, drug use can lead to abuse, dependence, or addiction.

    D. The more powerful drugs cause radical changes in consciousness, they can lead to serious physical and psychological problems, and many are illegal.

        1. Stimulants are not physically addictive but produce psychological dependence; they can be dangerous, particularly in their effects on the heart.

        2. Sedatives and tranquilizers are highly addictive and can be highly dangerous, particularly when taken in large doses or with alcohol.

        3. Narcotics are powerful and dangerous depressants; physiological addiction occurs rapidly, and prolonged use has profoundly damaging effects on the body.

        4. Inhalants are usually toxic and often cause permanent brain damage.

        5. Hallucinogens radically alter perception, cause hallucinations, and are often associated with bizarre or even violent behavior. Although hallucinogens are not physiologically addictive, psychological dependence is common.

        6. Marijuana is a drug that produces a sense of well-being in most people and sometimes alters perception.

    E. Even the more common legal drugs (caffeine, nicotine, alcohol) produce definite physical and psychological effects and can be quite harmful if used in excess.

● Resources

1. For a fascinating and sensible look at hypnosis, see Bowers, K. S. (1976). *Hypnosis for the seriously curious.* Monterey, CA: Brooks/Cole.

2. For more on the contents of dreams, written by Freudian psychologist, see Hall, C. S. (1951). What people dream about. *Scientific American,* 84: 60–63. For additional information on the study of sleeping and dreaming, see Webb, W. B., & Agnew, H. W. (1973). *Sleep and dreams.* Dubuque, IA: Wm. C. Brown; Horne, J. (1988). *Why we sleep.* New York: Oxford University Press; Hobson, J. A. (1989). *Sleep.* New York: Scientific

American Library; and Stauch, I., & Meier, B. (1996). *In search of dreams: Experimental dream research.* Albany: State University of New York Press.

3. A fascinating and in-depth analysis of the hypnogogic state is Mavromatis, A. (1987). *Hypnogogia.* London: Routledge.

4. For thorough summaries of mind-altering drugs, see Carroll, C. R. (2000). *Drugs in modern society* (5th ed.). Boston: McGraw-Hill; and Julien, R. M. (1992). *A primer of drug addiction* (6th ed.). San Francisco: Freeman.

5. Broad overviews of the topic of consciousness are provided by Wallace, B., & Fisher, L. E. (1991). *Consciousness and behavior,* (3rd ed.). Boston: Allyn & Bacon; Ornstein, R. (1991). *The evolution of consciousness.* New York: Prentice-Hall; and Rychlak, J. F. (1997). *In defense of human consciousness.* Washington, DC: American Psychological Association.

6. If you smoke or use smokeless tobacco and are thinking about quitting, this Web site offers useful information and links to other sites: http://unr.edu/homepage/shubinsk/smoke.html

CHAPTER

5

CHAPTER OUTLINE

Basic Principles of Learning

PROLOGUE

You behave the way you do largely because you *learned* to act that way. Take a moment and think about who you are. Now imagine that you had been adopted as an infant by a family in a distant part of the world. You would now speak a different language, eat different foods, and act in ways that are characteristic of a different culture. You would be a different person in all of these ways simply because your learning experiences were different.

In 1934, a young scientist named Ruth Benedict (pictured p. 140) published a book about remote cultures that were very different from one another. Her book tells a remarkable story about the power of learning experiences in shaping human lives. In the 1930s, the Dobu were a competitive people who generally did everything they could to acquire more possessions than anyone else. Theirs was a very violent culture, with high rates of assault and murder. In a way, they were very much like Americans—only more so. But the Zuñi people, who are native Americans who once flourished in the Southwest, were very different. The Zuñi people found greed and ambition to be repugnant. Instead, they valued generosity and modesty. They shared all wealth equally with one another and actively avoided doing anything that would bring them individual fame. Perhaps as a result, violence among the Zuñi was rare. Benedict argued that, if there were some cultures in which greed, ambition, and violence were rare, then it could not be true that these were inborn traits of all humans—they were learned traits that could be changed.

Are you still not convinced of the power of learning in shaping personalities? Benedict used courtship and marriage as another example of the great differences among cultures due to learning. In Zuñi society, male and female children were strictly separated until adolescence, allowing almost no contact before marriage. If a female and a male interacted in any way, their parents quickly arranged their marriage. Courtship often consisted of no more than the male's asking a young woman whom he had never met for a drink of water as she returned from the stream with a water jug. If she gave him a drink, they were soon married.

Courtship among the Dobu was dramatically different than among the Zuñi. In Dobu society, male and female children were not only allowed to play with each other, but sex play among children was common and approved of by adults. When children reached puberty, frequent sex was common among the unmarried males and females, with the lovemaking generally occurring openly in the one-room home of the girl's parents.

By showing scholars in the Western world that not all people were like us, Benedict helped convince many scholars that learning experiences were far more important in shaping human behavior than realized until that point. In this chapter, you will learn about three kinds of learning. In one of these types of learning, parts of the environment that you have hardly noticed before become stimuli that influence your behavior. If your water pipes were to make a groaning sound one morning while you are in the shower, you probably wouldn't pay much attention to it. But if over time the groaning always immediately preceded a sudden change in the temperature of your shower—from warm to icy cold—you would soon learn to jump at the sound of the groan. The groan would become a powerful stimulus for you.

Another kind of learning results from the *consequences* of your behavior. If you behave in a way that leads to something positive, you will probably behave that way more often in the future. If your behavior leads to something negative, on the other hand, you will be less likely to behave that way again. For example, let's say you stay up all night studying for a test. The next day, you can hardly stay awake and you can't remember half of what you learned the night before. Those are negative consequences that will lead to learning not to try that again. In contrast, if studying for a few hours each night for five nights before the test results in your first *A,* you are more likely to use that strategy again. The consequences of our behavior are a powerful source of learning.

The third type of learning comes from watching those around you. When you are in a new situation, such as your first day in a college class, you tend to notice how other students are behaving. Everybody else is taking notes—so you decide that you should, too. Instead of always having to learn from the consequences of our own actions, we can benefit from the experience of others.

As you learn about the details of the process of learning, try not to lose sight of the overall importance of the topic. Learning is one of the most important forces that made you the person you are today.

Learning is any relatively permanent change in behavior brought about through experience.

learning
Any relatively permanent change in behavior brought about through experience.

DEFINITION OF LEARNING

Life is a process of continual change. From infancy to adolescence to adulthood to death, we are changing. Many factors produce those changes, but one of the most important is the process of **learning.** Through our experiences, we learn new information, new attitudes, new fears, and new skills. We also learn to understand new concepts, to solve problems in new ways, and even to develop a personality over a lifetime. And, in the course of reading textbooks, we learn new definitions for words such as *learning:* In psychology, the term *learning* refers to any relatively permanent change in behavior brought about through experience—that is, through interactions with the environment.

As the definition states, not *all* changes in behavior are the result of learning. The term is restricted to the relatively permanent, as opposed to temporary, changes that are the result of experience, rather than changes due to biological causes such as drugs, fatigue, maturation, and injury. If a baseball pitcher throws the ball differently this season because his pitching coach has demonstrated a new way to pitch, learning has occurred—a relatively permanent change in pitching due to the experience of the coach's demonstration. But, if the pitcher's changed style is due to an injury, fatigue from throwing too much before each game, an arm strengthened by weight lifting, or biological maturation (if he is a 7-year-old Little League pitcher), we would not refer to the change in pitching as learning.

The *change in behavior* is not always immediately obvious, however. If you watch a film on the proper way to hit backhands in tennis this winter, the change will not be evident until you are on the tennis court again next spring. Notice also that the definition of learning does not restrict its usage to intentionally produced changes in behavior or even to desirable changes in behavior. For instance, if you begin to loathe fish sandwiches because you get sick after eating one, learning has occurred. The new disgust for fish sandwiches is undesirable and certainly unintentional, but it's still the result of learning.

Over the years, psychologists have isolated and studied a number of ways that learning takes place. As a result, we now understand a number of different principles of learning. In the following sections, we describe these principles of learning and indicate some of the ways that they can influence us in our daily lives.

CLASSICAL CONDITIONING: LEARNING BY ASSOCIATION

We will begin our study of specific types of learning with a simple form called *classical conditioning.* The scientific study of classical conditioning began around the turn of the

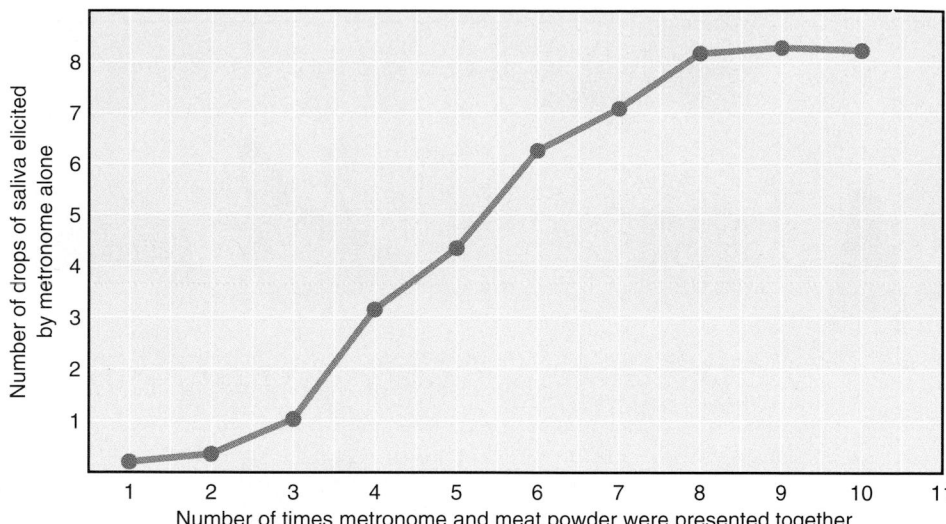

FIGURE 5.2

In Pavlov's studies, the more often the metronome was associated in time with meat powder, the more effective it was in eliciting salivation.

implications far beyond clicking metronomes and salivating dogs. Pavlov's writings became an important part of American psychology when they came to the attention of John B. Watson, who expanded upon and popularized Pavlov's views in English.

Terminology of Classical Conditioning

Before we can proceed much further in our understanding of classical conditioning, we need to learn some new terminology. Although these terms are a bit awkward at first, they will help us expand our discussion of classical conditioning to topics more relevant to your life than salivating dogs. First we use each of these four terms to refer to the specific stimuli and responses in Pavlov's experiments; then we use them with new examples. The terms are as follows:

1. *Unconditioned stimulus.* The meat powder was the **unconditioned stimulus (UCS)** in Pavlov's experiment. This is a stimulus that can elicit the response without any learning. In other words, the response to an unconditioned stimulus is inborn.
2. *Unconditioned response.* Salivation was the **unconditioned response (UCR).** It's an unlearned, inborn reaction to the unconditioned stimulus.
3. *Conditioned stimulus.* The metronome was originally unable to elicit the response of salivation, but it acquired the ability to elicit the response because it was paired with the unconditioned stimulus. It was the **conditioned stimulus (CS)** in Pavlov's studies.
4. *Conditioned response.* When the dog began salivating to the conditioned stimulus, salivation became the **conditioned response (CR).** When a response is elicited by the conditioned stimulus, it's referred to as the conditioned response.

To summarize, the meat powder was the unconditioned stimulus (UCS); the metronome was the neutral stimulus that became the conditioned stimulus (CS); salivation was the unconditioned response (UCR); and, when the salivation was elicited by the conditioned stimulus, it became the conditioned response (CR). These are difficult terms to keep straight at first; it may help to read through the diagram in figure 5.3 to review the meaning of these terms.

As a further example of classical conditioning, here's another dog story. One of my all-time best friends was a beagle named Lester. Lester had a number of fine qualities that are not always found in humans; he was affectionate, warm, and genuinely loyal. But, in all candor, Lester was also a profound coward. I will never forget the time I took him to the veterinarian for the first of a weekly series of shots. He stood perfectly still with a friendly beagle smile on his face until the needle was stuck into his hindquarter. At that point, he

unconditioned stimulus (UCS)
A stimulus that can elicit a response without any learning.

unconditioned response (UCR)
An unlearned, inborn reaction to an unconditioned stimulus.

conditioned stimulus (CS)
A stimulus that comes to elicit responses as a result of being paired with an unconditioned stimulus.

conditioned response (CR)
A response that is similar or identical to the unconditioned response that comes to be elicited by a conditioned stimulus.

FIGURE 5.3

Diagram of classical conditioning.

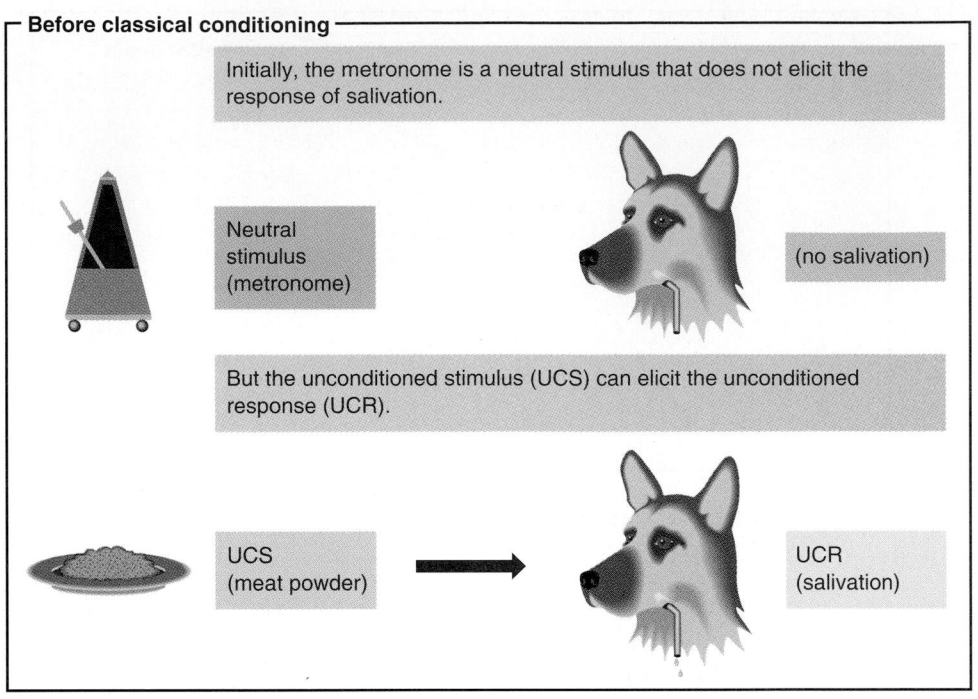

Before classical conditioning

Initially, the metronome is a neutral stimulus that does not elicit the response of salivation.

Neutral stimulus (metronome)

(no salivation)

But the unconditioned stimulus (UCS) can elicit the unconditioned response (UCR).

UCS (meat powder) → UCR (salivation)

Conditioning procedure

During the classical conditioning procedure, the neutral stimulus is presented in association with the unconditioned stimulus (UCS) to elicit the unconditioned response (UCR).

Neutral stimulus (metronome)

+

UCS (meat powder) → UCR (salivation)

Test of conditioning

After classical conditioning, the neutral stimulus becomes a conditioned stimulus (CS) that elicits the conditioned response (CR) of salivation.

CS (metronome) → CR (salivation)

produced a flinching, lurching, terrified yelp. After a few injections, Lester began yelping before the injection when he saw the vet with the needle in her hand.

Now, to be completely honest, I cannot criticize Lester too much for his cowardly behavior, because I also yelp when I see a needle coming my way. Why do you suppose that is so? Why should both of us, a grown man and a grown dog, react so strongly to the sight of a needle? After all, the sight of the needle cannot hurt you; only its stab can do that. The answer, of course, is that we have been classically conditioned to yelp at needles.

Stop for a minute and read back through the example of Lester's fear of needles and see if you can identify the CS, UCS, UCR, and CR.

The sight of the needle is the CS because it originally did not elicit the yelp; the painful stab of the needle is the UCS because it elicited the yelp; the yelp after the stab is the UCR; and, when the CS comes to elicit yelping, the yelp is the CR. I feel a little better knowing that my yelping at needles is simply a CR to a CS, but not a whole lot better; I still hate the things.

Definition of Classical Conditioning

We have finally covered enough terminology to be able to give a precise definition of classical conditioning. **Classical conditioning** is a form of learning in which a previously neutral stimulus (CS) is followed by a stimulus (UCS) that elicits an unlearned response (UCR). As a result of these pairings of the CS and UCS, the CS comes to elicit a response (CR) that, in most cases, is identical or very similar to the UCR.

For classical conditioning to take place, a CS must also serve as a reliable signal for the occurrence of the UCS (Rescorla, 1967, 1988; Woodruff-Pak, 1999). An emergency siren that goes off only in a real emergency (no routine tests or false alarms) will generate more fear responses than sirens routinely tested once a month. Similarly, if the sound of a metronome is always followed by food, salivation will be stronger than if the metronome is followed by food only some of the time.

Note that classical conditioning is considered to be a form of learning not because a new behavior has been acquired but because old behavior can be elicited by a new stimulus; behavior is "changed" only in that sense. It's important to notice also (for reasons that will be clear to you later in the chapter) that the process of classical conditioning *does not depend on the behavior of the individual* being conditioned. The metronome and the meat powder were paired whether the dog salivated or not, and the sight of the needle was followed by the stab whether Lester yelped or not. The critical elements in classical conditioning are that the CS and UCS be closely associated in time and that the CS be a reliable predictor of the UCS. Our behavior simply provides evidence that conditioning has taken place. As we will see later, if the behavior of the individual can determine whether the stimulus is presented or not, the process is not classical conditioning.

By the way, are you curious as to why it's called *classical* conditioning? This term simply refers to the fact that Pavlov performed the *classic* laboratory studies of learning. For the same reason, classical conditioning is also referred to as *Pavlovian* conditioning.

classical conditioning
A form of learning in which a previously neutral stimulus (CS) is paired with an unconditioned stimulus (UCS) to elicit a conditioned response (CR) that is identical to or very similar to the unconditioned response (UCR).

Importance of Classical Conditioning

The concept of classical conditioning would not be so widely studied by psychologists if it applied only to salivating dogs. On the contrary, classical conditioning is also helpful in understanding a number of important and puzzling issues concerning human behavior.

In 1920, behaviorist John B. Watson and his associate Rosalie Rayner published what is probably the most widely cited example of classical conditioning in psychology. Watson was convinced that many of our fears were acquired through classical conditioning and sought to test this idea by teaching a fear to an 11-month-old child, the now famous "Little Albert." Albert was first allowed to play with a white laboratory rat to find out whether he was afraid of rats: He was not at that time. Then, as he played with the white rat, an iron bar was struck loudly with a hammer behind Albert's head. As might be expected, the noise caused Albert to cry fearfully. After seven such pairings, Albert showed a strong fear response when the rat was placed near him. He had learned to fear the rat through classical conditioning.

Watson's own words provide the best description of the experiment's outcome: "The instant the rat was shown the baby began to cry. Almost instantly he turned sharply to the left, fell over on his left side, raised himself on all fours, and began to crawl away so

This photo shows behaviorist John Watson and his graduate student assistant Rosalie Rayner with Watson's most famous subject—Little Albert. In this early study on the classical conditioning of fear reactions, Watson was able to demonstrate the importance of the environment in the development of human emotions.
Courtesy of Prof. Benjamin Harris, Ph.D. Univ. of Wisconsin, Parkside.

rapidly that he was caught with difficulty before reaching the edge of the table" (Watson & Rayner, 1920, p. 3).

For understandable reasons, this experiment would not be considered ethical by today's standards. It is particularly distressing that Watson and Rayner chose not to reverse the conditioning of Albert's fear (Watson & Rayner, 1920). In a subsequent study (Jones, 1924), however, Mary Cover Jones and Watson successfully reduced fear of rabbits in another small child by gradually pairing the rabbit (CS) with cookies (UCS). This method of reversing a classically conditioned response by pairing the CS (the rabbit, in this case) with a UCS (cookies, in this case) for a response (eating the cookies) that cannot occur at the same time as the undesirable CR (crying fearfully) is called **counterconditioning.** As in the present example, the UCS for the incompatible response is typically presented first (Mary Cover Jones initially let the child start eating the cookie); then the CS (the rabbit) for the undesirable CR (fearful crying) is introduced only briefly. Over time, the CS for the undesirable response can be presented for longer periods of time, until it no longer elicits the undesirable CR.

Classical conditioning also has proved useful in explaining several questions about our health (Ader & Cohen, 1993). When the body is exposed to threats to health, such as viruses, a number of blood cells that attack the invading germs are produced. The immune system is an amazingly effective defense against disease, but it does not always operate at full capacity. Not only can fatigue and psychological stress adversely affect the functioning of the immune system (Ader, 1981), but it is now clear that immune system responses can be classically conditioned. Robert Ader (Ader & Cohen, 1981) administered a drug (the UCS) to rats that suppressed the activation of their immune system cells (the UCR). The drug was given at the same time that the rats drank saccharin-sweetened water (the CS). After several pairings of the drug and the sweetened water, the rats showed a suppression in immune cell production (the CR) just from drinking the sweetened water. The full implications of these studies have not been worked out, but it appears that classical conditioning could play a role in our resistance to disease.

counterconditioning
The process of eliminating a classically conditioned response by pairing the conditioned stimulus (CS) with an unconditioned stimulus (UCS) for a response that is stronger than the conditioned response (CR) and that cannot occur at the same time as the CR.

● Review

Your behavior is not static; it changes from day to day and from year to year as a result of your experiences. This process of behavior change is called learning. Learning is defined as any relatively permanent change in behavior brought about by experience (rather than by biological causes). The prominence of the study of learning in American psychology can be traced in part to studies of a simple but important form of learning launched around the turn of the century by Russian medical researcher Ivan Pavlov. Pavlov was studying salivary reflexes when he noticed that, after a few days in the study, his dogs began salivating before the food was placed in their mouths. He reasoned that they had learned to salivate at the sight of the attendant bringing the food because this stimulus was always associated with (immediately preceded) the food. Pavlov tested this explanation in a series of studies, in which a clicking metronome was repeatedly paired with the presentation of meat powder. As a result, the metronome soon came to elicit the response of salivation. In general, when a neutral stimulus is repeatedly paired with another stimulus that elicits an unlearned response, the previously neutral stimulus will begin to elicit the same or a very similar response. This form of learning is called classical conditioning.

● Check Your Learning

To be sure that you have learned the key points from the preceding section, cover the list of correct answers and try to answer each question. If you give an incorrect answer to any question, return to the page given next to the correct answer to see why your answer was not correct. Remember that these questions cover only some of the important information in this section; it is important that you make up your own questions to check your learning of other facts and concepts.

1. The term *learning* refers to _____.

2. The critical element in classical conditioning is that the UCS and the _____ be closely associated in time.

   a) CS   c) UCR
   b) CR   d) REM

3. A(n) _____ is a response that is similar or identical to the unconditioned response that comes to be elicited by a conditioned stimulus.

   a) unconditioned stimulus   c) conditioned stimulus
   b) unconditioned response   d) conditioned response

4. Ivan Pavlov first studied classical conditioning, but _____ popularized the idea that classical conditioning and other forms of learning were important to the development of our personalities and abilities.

   a) B. F. Skinner   c) Albert Bandura
   b) John B. Watson   d) Karen Horney

● Thinking Critically About Psychology

1. How might a student develop a classically conditioned fear response to a specific college classroom?

2. Is our ability to learn through classical conditioning generally an advantage or a disadvantage? How would Little Albert answer that question?

Correct Answers 1. any relatively permanent change in behavior brought about through experience (p. 142), **2. a** (p. 147 **3. d** (p. 145), **4. b** (p. 147).

▌ OPERANT CONDITIONING: LEARNING FROM THE CONSEQUENCES OF YOUR BEHAVIOR

If you were to start parking your car in a parking space marked "For the President Only" and your car were towed away every day as a consequence, you would probably stop parking there after a while. Similarly, if you were to move to a new seat in class and suddenly an interesting, attractive person were to start talking to you, you would probably choose to sit in that seat again. To a great extent, the frequency with which people do things increases or decreases depending on the *consequences* of their actions. Learning from the consequences of our behavior is called *operant conditioning*. The term is derived from the word *operate*. When our behavior "operates" on the outside world, it produces consequences for us, and those consequences determine whether we will continue to engage in that behavior. We can define **operant conditioning,** then, as the form of learning in which the consequences of behavior lead to changes in the probability of its occurrence (Dragoi & Staddon, 1999). In the sections that follow, we will examine three ways in which desirable and undesirable consequences influence our behavior: positive reinforcement, negative reinforcement, and punishment.

operant conditioning
(op´e-rant)   Learning in which the consequences of behavior lead to changes in the probability of its occurrence.

Positive Reinforcement

In *positive reinforcement,* the consequences of a behavior are *positive,* so the behavior is engaged in *more frequently.* Simply stated, we say that **positive reinforcement** has occurred whenever a consequence of behavior leads to an increase in the probability of its occurrence.

positive reinforcement
(re´´in-fors´ment)   Any consequence of behavior that leads to an increase in the probability of its occurrence.

FIGURE 5.4

Increasing the amount of time that a child spends playing with other children through the use of positive reinforcement.

Source: Data from K. Eileen Allen, et al., "Effects of Social Reinforcement Isolate Behavior of a Nursery School Child" in *Child Development,* 35:511–518, 1964. Copyright © 1964 The Society for Research in Child Development.

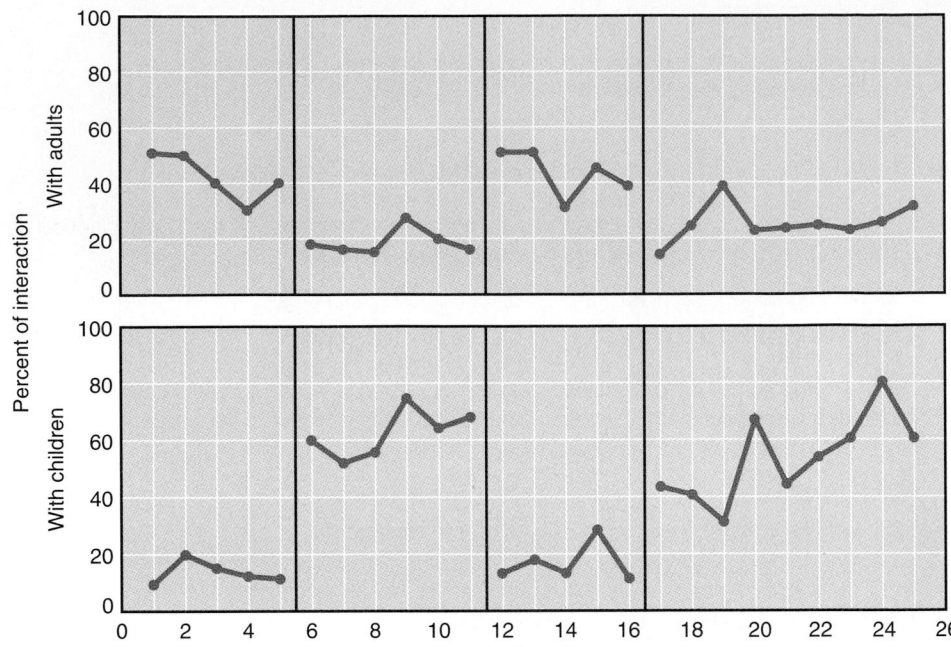

In the early 1960s, a team of preschool teachers conducted a classic study in which they helped a young girl overcome her shyness in what has become a widely cited example of the principle of positive reinforcement (Allen, Hart, Buell, Harris, & Wolf, 1964). The teachers were worried because the girl spent little time playing with the other children and too much time with her adult teachers. They decided to encourage peer play through positive reinforcement. They knew that she enjoyed receiving praise from the teachers, so they decided to praise her *only* when she was playing with another child. The results of this use of positive reinforcement are shown in figure 5.4. To be able to evaluate the results of their positive reinforcement program, the teachers first counted the frequency with which the little girl interacted with other children and with adults before anything was done to help her. Then they started to positively reinforce (praise) her for playing with other children, but otherwise they paid very little attention to her (so that she would get positive reinforcement from her teachers only for playing with peers). As can be seen in the second segment of figure 5.4, the little girl's frequency of playing with peers increased markedly when the teachers reinforced her. To be sure that the positive reinforcement and not some other factor was responsible for the changes, the teachers stopped reinforcing her for playing with peers in the third segment (the *reversal* phase) of figure 5.4 and then reinforced her again during the fourth phase. As can be seen, the frequency of peer play dropped when the positive reinforcement was discontinued but increased again when it was resumed in the fourth phase. Thus, the teachers were able to intentionally teach this child a more adaptive pattern of play by using positive reinforcement.

Many other applications have been made of this principle, ranging from teaching hospitalized schizophrenic adults more normal patterns of behavior to teaching employees to reduce the amount of damage sustained when sorting boxes for airfreight delivery. In each case, the behavior that becomes more frequent is termed the *operant response,* and the positive consequence of that response is called the *positive reinforcer.*

Two important issues in the use of positive reinforcement should be noted:

1. *Timing.* The positive reinforcer must be given within a short amount of time following the response, or learning will progress very slowly, if at all. There are some ways to get around this issue of timing (such as immediately telling an employee that she will get a bonus for making an important sale, even though the bonus will not come until the end of the month), but in general the greater the delay between the response and the reinforcer, the slower the learning. This phenomenon has been referred to as the principle of **delay of reinforcement.**

delay of reinforcement
The passage of time between the response and the positive reinforcement that leads to reduced efficiency of learning.

2. *Consistency in the delivery of reinforcement.* For learning to take place, the individual providing positive reinforcement must consistently give it after every (or nearly every) response. After some learning has taken place, it's not always necessary, or even desirable, to reinforce every response (as we will see later in the section "Schedules of Positive Reinforcement"), but consistency of reinforcement is essential in the beginning of the learning process.

I do not want to give the impression through this discussion that positive reinforcement is something that occurs only when it's intentionally arranged. The natural consequences of our behavior can be reinforcing as well. For example, we learn that some ways of interacting with our friends or supervisors just naturally lead to happier relationships, and that is positively reinforcing. We are *always* affected by the consequences of our behavior and, hence, are always in the process of learning to adjust to our world through operant conditioning.

Primary and Secondary Reinforcement

Where do positive reinforcers come from? Are they inborn or do we have to acquire them through learning? Actually, some are inborn and some are learned. There are two types of positive reinforcement, primary and secondary reinforcement. **Primary reinforcers** are ones that are innately reinforcing and do not have to be acquired through learning. Food, water, warmth, novel stimulation, physical activity, and sexual gratification are all examples of primary reinforcers.

primary reinforcers
Innate positive reinforcers that do not have to be acquired through learning.

secondary reinforcers
Learned positive reinforcers.

Secondary reinforcers (which play an important part in operant conditioning) are learned through classical conditioning. Remember that classical conditioning involves the association of two stimuli: A neutral stimulus can be turned into a secondary reinforcer by pairing it repeatedly with a primary reinforcer. Consider an example from dog training. In teaching dogs to perform complex acts, such as those required of Seeing Eye dogs, primary reinforcers such as pieces of food are used extensively. It's much more convenient, however, to reinforce the dog for good behavior simply by saying, "Good dog!" than by lugging around a pocketful of dog biscuits. Unfortunately, dogs do not know what you are saying when you praise them and would not care much if they did—that is, not until you *teach* them to care. So, how would you go about making praise into a secondary reinforcer? Actually, it's quite simple. You would only need to say, "Good dog," to the dog every time you give the dog a biscuit. After enough pairings of these two stimuli, the praise will become a secondary reinforcer and will be effective in reinforcing the dog's behavior.

Dogs are not the only creatures that learn secondary reinforcers, however. People do it, too. How many of the things that motivate us—such as school grades, prize ribbons, money, applause—were acquired through pairing with primary reinforcers? Learning undoubtedly plays a key role in turning these things into powerful reinforcers for some people.

Schedules of Positive Reinforcement

Up to this point, we have talked about positive reinforcement as if every response were always followed by a reinforcer, a situation known as *continuous reinforcement.* The world is not constructed in such a regular and simple way, however. So what happens when reinforcement follows behavior on some other schedule? In addition to continuous reinforcement, psychologists have described four types of schedules of reinforcement and have shown us the effects of each on behavior (Ferster & Skinner, 1957):

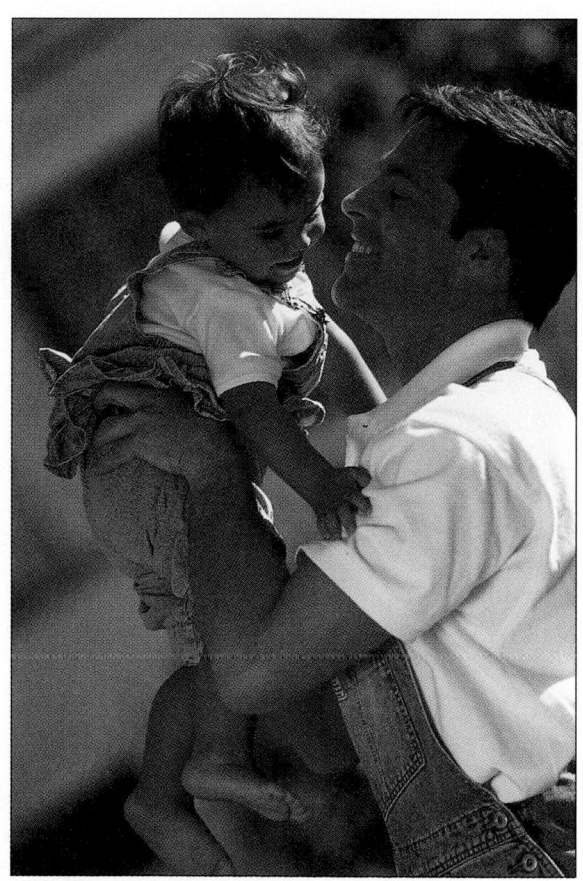

Secondary reinforcers, such as praise, are learned from primary reinforcers, such as gentle physical contact.

Gold medals are powerful secondary reinforcers.

fixed ratio schedule
A reinforcement schedule in which the reinforcer is given only after a specified number of responses.

variable ratio schedule
A reinforcement schedule in which the reinforcer is given after a varying number of responses have been made.

fixed interval schedule
A reinforcement schedule in which the reinforcer is given following the first response occurring after a predetermined period of time.

1. *Fixed ratio.* On a **fixed ratio schedule** of reinforcement, the reinforcer is given only after a specified number of responses. If sewing machine operators were given a pay slip (to be exchanged for money later) for every six dresses that were sewn, the schedule of reinforcement would be called a fixed ratio schedule. This schedule produces a fairly high rate of response because many responses need to be made to get the reinforcer, but there is typically a pause after each reinforcer is obtained (see fig. 5.5).

2. *Variable ratio.* On a **variable ratio schedule** of reinforcement, the reinforcer is obtained only after a varying number of responses have been made (see fig. 5.6). These schedules produce very high rates of responding, and the learning is rather permanent. For example, why do even successful sales representatives hustle so? They know from experience that, on the average, they will make a sale, for example, after every sixth presentation. But the fact that they cannot predict which presentation will make the sale—this one? the next one?—keeps them hopping. Another good example of reinforcement on a variable ratio is gambling. Slot machine players are reinforced for putting money into the machine and pulling the lever just often enough in an unpredictable fashion to addict many individuals to gambling.

3. *Fixed interval.* In other cases, the schedule of reinforcement is not based on the *number* of responses but on the passage of *time*. The term **fixed interval schedule** is used when the first response that occurs after a predetermined period of time is reinforced. This produces a pattern of behavior in which very few responses are made until the fixed interval of time approaches and then the rate of responding increases rapidly (see fig. 5.7). A fellow psychology professor provided this great example of a fixed interval schedule: While in graduate school, he worked as a guard at night in a steel mill. He was paid for walking around the mill each hour and punching in the time clock each time as he passed it on his rounds. He confessed that this schedule of reinforcement led to 40 minutes of sitting around each hour, followed by a brisk 20-minute walk around the mill to the time clock! Members of Congress also are on a fixed interval schedule for the response of visiting with the voters in their districts. Making a visit back home to talk to the people is of little value to the politicians until the fixed 2-year interval between elections starts to elapse. Then visits back home are reinforced by votes, so the rate of visits rises dramatically.

4. *Variable interval.* Finally, there is a schedule of reinforcement in which the first response made after a variable amount of time is reinforced. Like the variable ratio

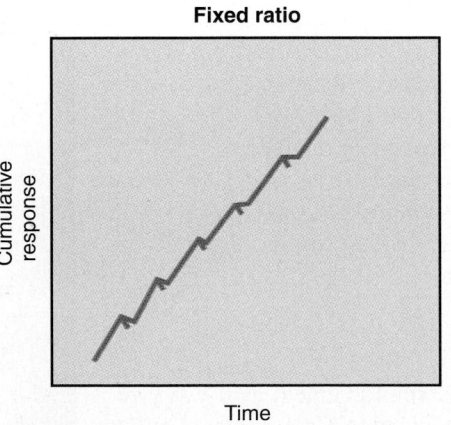

FIGURE 5.5

Pattern of behavior typically produced by a fixed ratio schedule of reinforcement. The hash marks show the delivery of reinforcement. In figures 5.5 to 5.8, steeper slopes indicate higher rates of responding.

FIGURE 5.6

Pattern of behavior typically produced by a variable ratio schedule of reinforcement.

Fixed interval

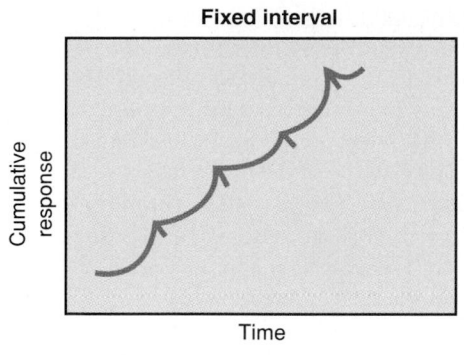

Cumulative response

Time

FIGURE 5.7

Pattern of behavior typically produced by a fixed interval schedule of reinforcement.

Variable interval

Cumulative response

Time

FIGURE 5.8

Pattern of behavior typically produced by a variable interval pattern of reinforcement.

schedule, this **variable interval schedule** produces high rates of steady response (see fig. 5.8), and, although it's not a good schedule for initial learning, it produces highly stable performance when the response has already been partially learned through continuous reinforcement. Where I grew up in Florida, there were lots of people sitting on docks and bridges with fishing poles in their hands because of variable reinforcement. You can't tell when fish are going to bite—they're unpredictable. But, for some people, catching a fish every now and then is strong enough variable interval reinforcement to keep their lines in the water as much as they can.

Thus, different schedules of positive reinforcement result in distinct patterns of behavior. It is very important for anyone responsible for managing another person's behavior, such as teachers, parents, or supervisors, to make informed choices regarding the type of reinforcement schedule to be used.

variable interval schedule
A reinforcement schedule in which the reinforcer is given following the first response occurring after a variable amount of time.

Shaping

In many situations, the response that we want to reinforce never occurs. For example, let's say you want to positively reinforce your child for cleaning her or his room. You might

Casino operators may not claim to use variable ratio schedules of reinforcement, but they know that an occasional jackpot will keep players at the slot machines.

Reinforcement of successive approximations by a violin teacher who understands shaping will help this girl become a better violinist.

shaping
A strategy of positively reinforcing behaviors that are successively more similar to desired behaviors.

Skinner box
A cage for animals, equipped with a response lever and a food tray dispenser, used in research on operant conditioning.

have to wait a long time for that behavior to occur! If left to their own devices, most children would spend little if any time cleaning their rooms. What we need to do in this case is to reinforce responses that are progressively more similar to the response that you finally want to reinforce (the "target response"). In doing so, you will gradually increase the probability of the target response and can then reinforce it when it occurs. This is called **shaping,** or the *method of successive approximations,* because we "shape" the target response out of behaviors that successively approximate it.

Before considering the practical applications of the concept of shaping, let's go back to the animal learning laboratory where so many of the principles of learning that are useful to humans were first carefully researched. Suppose you wanted to teach a rat to press a lever in the special kind of learning apparatus called the **Skinner box,** named after its creator, B. F. Skinner of Harvard University (see fig. 5.9). If you continue to take psychology courses, you may be given this assignment in a lab course: "Here's a rat and here's a Skinner box; do not come back until you have taught him to press the lever!" What do you do? If you have not read the section on shaping in your textbook, you might program the Skinner box to drop a little pellet of rat food into the food tray every time the lever is pressed and then wait—and wait and wait—for the rat to press the bar. This strategy might work in time—the rat *might* accidentally press the lever enough times to get reinforced by the food pellets enough to make this a frequent response—but I wouldn't bet on it. Rats generally do not go around pressing levers. When placed in a Skinner box, they groom themselves, bite the Plexiglas walls, urinate, defecate, and sniff a lot, but they do not press levers. How, then, do you teach the uncooperative rodent to press the lever?

You use shaping. First, whenever the rat (we'll call him "B. F." in honor of B. F. Skinner) gets up and *moves toward the lever,* give him a food pellet. After you do that a few times, the rat ought to be moving toward the lever quite a bit. Then you can wait until B. F. *touches* the lever in some way to reinforce him. Do that a few times and then wait until he *touches it with a downward pushing movement* (if at any time you have failed to reinforce him enough, you can go back a step). Then, after he is reliably touching the bar in a downward motion, B. F. should have quite a high probability of *pushing it down enough* to activate the automatic feeder, which will reinforce him for the complete response of lever pressing.

FIGURE 5.9

In this Skinner box designed for rats, the response under study is lever pressing. Food pellets, which serve as reinforcers, are delivered into the food cup on the left. The speaker and light permit manipulations of visual and auditory stimuli, and the electric grid gives the experimenter control over negative consequences (mild shock) in the box.

The principle of shaping has great importance outside of the rat lab. For example, most beginning skiers cannot be reinforced for making perfect post turns because they just are not able to do them yet. But they can be reinforced for successive approximations to good turns and thereby shaped into good skiing. In programs for children with developmental handicaps, shaping is used to teach basic skills, such as brushing teeth, performing useful jobs, and using public transportation. And how about shaping 3-year-olds to clean their rooms? At first you have to reinforce them for putting one toy away—even though the rest of the room is littered with junk. After doing that a couple of times, reinforce them for putting several toys away, and then for an "approximately" clean room, and so on until the target response occurs.

Negative Reinforcement

Reinforcers are not always positive events; sometimes the reinforcing consequence is the *removal or avoidance of a negative event.* Suppose the fellow in the apartment next door plays his stereo so loud that it has kept you awake every night this week. If you assertively ask him to turn it down and the loud music stops, that consequence will reinforce your assertive behavior. Operant learning based on negative reinforcement plays an important, but often unnoticed, role in influencing our behavior.

The concept of negative reinforcement is one that students frequently find confusing for two reasons. First, to many students, the name implies that a negative or undesirable behavior—such as a bad habit—is being reinforced. That actually does happen a lot, but the behavior that is negatively reinforced may be either desirable or undesirable. Second, even more students find the term *negative reinforcement* confusing because it sounds like a new term for punishment, which it is not. When we look at the concept of punishment later in this chapter, you will see that it is a quite different phenomenon.

What the term **negative reinforcement** *does* mean is this: A behavior is reinforced (and, therefore, becomes more likely to occur) because something negative (or unpleasant or aversive) *is removed* by the behavior or does not happen at all because of the behavior. In the previous example, the loud music was the negative thing that your assertive behavior got rid of. Your asking him to turn down the volume was reinforced through negative reinforcement (stopping the loud music), and you probably would be more likely to be assertive in the future as a result.

Two types of learning are based on negative reinforcement: escape conditioning and avoidance conditioning. As we discuss these in detail in the next two sections, the concept of negative reinforcement will become more clear.

Escape Conditioning

In **escape conditioning,** the behavior causes the negative event to *stop.* For example, if a young boy has been confined to his room for an hour, that is probably a pretty negative situation to him. If he starts to cry softly and murmur pitifully that no one loves him, and if this causes his parent to relent in a few minutes and let him out of his room, then negative reinforcement has occurred. Which behavior has been strengthened? Probably he will be much more likely to act pitifully the next time he is sent to his room because it made something negative—the confinement—stop. Escape conditioning, therefore, is a form of negative reinforcement because something negative is removed. It's called escape conditioning because the individual *escapes* from something negative (in the sense of causing it to stop).

Avoidance Conditioning

In the other form of negative reinforcement, called **avoidance conditioning,** the behavior has the consequence of causing something negative *not to happen* when it otherwise would have happened. Suppose you are terrified of pit bulldogs, but the route that you walk to campus takes you past a yard where a particularly vicious pit bull is penned up. If you find a new route to school that does not take you past a single pit bull, you will probably continue to take this route because it causes the negative event of passing the pit bull not to occur. Even if it does make you feel a bit like a coward, finding a new route is a highly

Negative Reinforcement

www.mmhe.com/laheye1

negative reinforcement
Reinforcement that comes about when the removal or avoidance of a negative event is the consequence of behavior.

escape conditioning
Operant conditioning in which the behavior is reinforced because it causes a negative event to cease (a form of negative reinforcement).

avoidance conditioning
Operant conditioning in which the behavior is reinforced because it prevents something negative from happening (a form of negative reinforcement).

reinforcing consequence. This is an example of avoidance conditioning, because the behavior of taking a new route is reinforced by avoiding something negative (the pit bull).

Negative reinforcement is a very powerful method of reinforcement, so we learn patterns of behavior quickly and easily from it. Unfortunately, what we learn are often immature ways of dealing with unpleasant situations rather than mature ways of facing them directly. The child in our first example would have been better off taking his punishment and learning how not to get into trouble next time, and the college student would have been better off getting over the fear of the penned pit bull. It's often too easy to learn a quick and easy, though inappropriate, solution through negative reinforcement.

Incidentally, when the parent let the child who was acting pitifully out of his room, the parent was probably reinforced for that lapse in discipline, too. Through what principle of operant conditioning was the parent reinforced? Because the act of letting the child out of his room caused the child's unpleasant whining to stop, the parent was reinforced through escape conditioning. Negative reinforcement of inappropriate behavior is a frequent occurrence that we need to avoid.

Punishment

Sometimes the consequence of behavior is negative, and as a result, the frequency of that behavior will decrease. In other words, the behavior has been *punished.* For example, if you buy a new set of pots and pans with metal handles and pick up a hot pan without a pot holder, a negative consequence will surely occur. And you will probably not try to pick up your new pans in that way again. **Punishment** is a negative consequence that leads to a reduction in the frequency of the behavior that produced it (Church, 1969; Tarpy & Mayer, 1978). When appropriately used, punishment can be an ethical and valuable tool for discouraging inappropriate behavior. In our society, however, *physical* punishment is still used with children by parents, teachers, and others in authority. In addition to the obvious ethical issues in using physical punishment, there are serious dangers inherent in the use of any form of punishment that must be weighed against its potential benefits.

Dangers of Punishment

The dangers inherent in punishment are as follows:

1. The use of punishment is often *reinforcing to the punisher.* For example, if a parent spanks a child who has been whining and the spanking stops the child from whining, the parent will be reinforced for spanking through negative reinforcement. This, unfortunately, may mean that the frequency of spankings, and perhaps their intensity, will increase, thereby increasing not only the amount of physical pain the child endures but also the dangers of child abuse.

2. Punishment often has a *generalized inhibiting effect* on the individual. Repeatedly spanking a child for "talking back" to you may lead the child to quit talking to you altogether.

3. We commonly react to physical punishment by *learning to dislike* the person who inflicts the pain, and perhaps by *reacting aggressively* toward that person. Sometimes an individual takes out his or her resentment on someone else if it's not possible to react directly against the person who gave the pain. Thus, punishment may solve one problem but only lead to a worse problem—namely, aggression.

4. What we think is punishment is not always effective in punishing the behavior. In particular, most teachers and parents (and many supervisors, roommates, etc.) think that *criticism* will punish the behavior at which it's aimed. However, in many settings, especially homes and classrooms filled with young children, it has been demonstrated that criticism is often a *positive reinforcer* that increases the rate of whatever behavior the criticism follows. This is because children are sometimes reinforced by the attention they receive when criticized. This has been called the **criticism trap** (Becker, Engelmann, & Thomas, 1975).

punishment
A negative consequence of a behavior, which leads to a decrease in the frequency of the behavior that produces it.

criticism trap
An increase in the frequency of a negative behavior that often follows the use of criticism, reinforcing the behavior it is intended to punish.

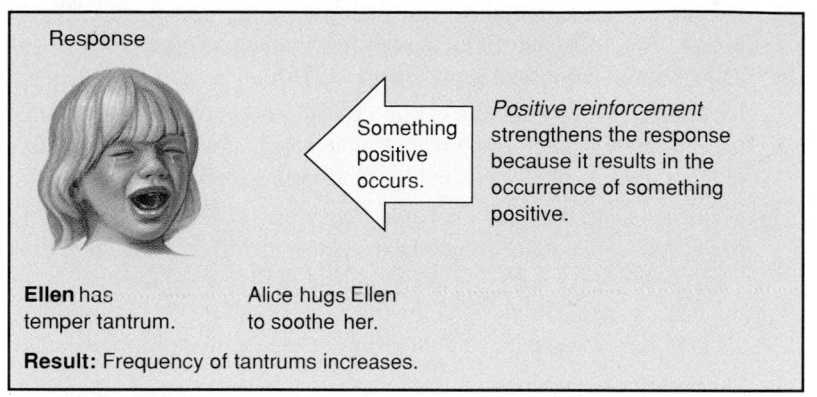

Ellen has temper tantrum.   Alice hugs Ellen to soothe her.

Result: Frequency of tantrums increases.

Positive reinforcement strengthens the response because it results in the occurrence of something positive.

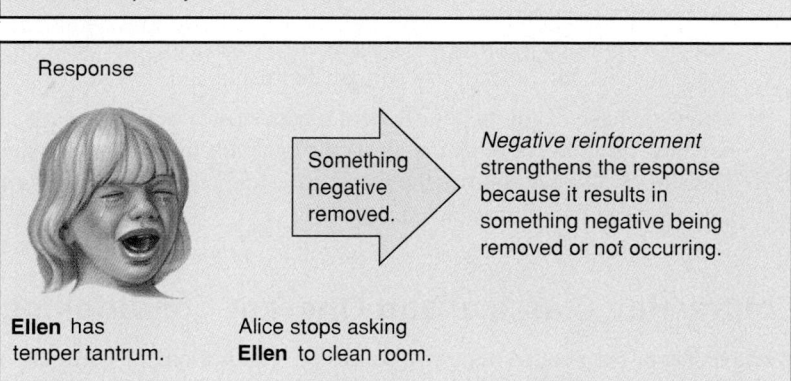

Ellen has temper tantrum.   Alice stops asking **Ellen** to clean room.

Result: Frequency of tantrums increases.

Negative reinforcement strengthens the response because it results in something negative being removed or not occurring.

In contrast, punishment *weakens* the strength of the response:

Ellen has temper tantrum.   Alice tells **Ellen** off.

Result: Frequency of tantrums decreases.

Punishment weakens the response because it results in the occurrence of something negative.

Comparison of the types of operant conditioning: positive reinforcement, negative reinforcement, and punishment. The two types of reinforcement, positive and negative, are called *reinforcement* because the response is strengthened by the consequence.

Notice that the terms *positive* and *negative reinforcement* and *punishment* have nothing to do with the nature of the response that is strengthened or weakened. This example uses a very "negative" response; however, a "positive" response could have been used to illustrate the same results in each case.

5. Even when punishment is effective in suppressing an inappropriate behavior, it does not teach the individual how to act more appropriately instead. Punishment used by itself may be self-defeating; it may suppress one inappropriate behavior only to be replaced by another one. It's not until appropriate behaviors are taught to the individual to replace the inappropriate ones that any progress can be made.

Guidelines for the Use of Punishment

The preceding list is an indictment of punishment as a method of changing behavior in childrearing, industry, education, or any other setting. It should not be considered to be a total condemnation of punishment, however. In some situations, punishment is a necessary method of changing behavior. For example, in teaching a young child not to run out into a busy street, punishment may be the only method that makes sense. In these instances, however, every effort should be made to minimize the negative side effects of punishment by following some guidelines for its use:

1. Do not use *physical* punishment. Taking away TV time from a 10-year-old or placing a 4-year-old in a chair in the corner for 3 minutes is more effective than spankings, and certainly more humane (O'Leary, 1995).

2. Make sure that you positively reinforce appropriate behavior to take the place of the inappropriate behavior you are trying to eliminate. Punishment will not be effective in the long run unless you are also reinforcing appropriate behavior.

3. Make it clear to the individual what behavior you are punishing and remove all threat of punishment as soon as that behavior stops. In other words, it might be okay to punish a certain behavior, but it does more harm than good to become generally angry at the other person for doing something inappropriate. *Do not punish people; punish specific behaviors.* And stop punishing when the inappropriate behavior ceases.

4. Do not mix punishment with rewards for the *same* behavior. For example, do not punish a child for fighting and then apologetically hug and kiss the child you have just punished. Mixtures of this sort are confusing and lead to inefficient learning.

5. Once you have begun to punish, do not back down. In other words, do not reinforce begging, pleading, or other inappropriate behavior by letting the individual out of the punishment. It both nullifies the punishment and reinforces the begging and pleading through negative reinforcement.

Contrasting Classical and Operant Conditioning

We have just talked about a number of forms of "conditioning." This blitz of new concepts can be confusing. However, if you can understand the distinction between classical and operant conditioning, the rest will be easy.

Classical and operant conditioning differ from each other in three primary ways:

1. Classical conditioning involves an association between two stimuli, such as a tone and food. In contrast, operant conditioning involves an association between a response and the resulting consequence, such as studying hard and getting an A.

2. Classical conditioning usually involves reflexive, involuntary behaviors, which are controlled by the spinal cord or autonomic nervous system. These include fear responses, salivation, and other involuntary behaviors. Operant conditioning, on the other hand, usually involves more complicated voluntary behaviors, which are mediated by the somatic nervous system.

3. The most important difference, however, concerns the way in which the stimulus that makes conditioning "happen" is presented (the unconditioned stimulus, or UCS, in classical conditioning and the reinforcing stimulus in operant conditioning). In classical conditioning, the UCS is paired with the conditioned stimulus (CS) independent of the individual's behavior. The individual does not have to do anything for either the CS or UCS to be presented. In operant conditioning, however, the reinforcing consequence occurs *only if* the response being conditioned has just been emitted; that is, the reinforcing consequence is contingent on the occurrence of the response.

Stimulus Discrimination and Generalization

Most responses do not have an equal probability of occurring in any situation. They are more likely to occur in some circumstances than in others. For example, schoolchildren are more likely to behave well when the teacher is in the room than when the teacher is not. Similarly, you are more likely to clean up your apartment when your new girlfriend or boyfriend says, "I'll be over after class," than when no one is coming. Most responses are more likely to occur in the presence of some stimuli than in the presence of others. This phenomenon is called **stimulus discrimination,** meaning that we discriminate between appropriate and inappropriate occasions for a response.

stimulus discrimination
The tendency for responses to occur more often in the presence of one stimulus than others.

Let's go back to the rat lab and see one way in which stimulus discrimination might be learned. The last time you were in the lab, you taught your rat, B. F., to press the lever through shaping and positive reinforcement for lever pressing. Let's suppose that you want him to press the bar only in the presence of a specific stimulus, such as a light; that is, you want B. F. to learn a stimulus discrimination. We start by turning on a light over the lever, letting B. F. press the lever and receive the reinforcer several times. Then we turn off the light for a little while, and we do *not* reinforce lever presses when the light is out. Then we turn the light back on and reinforce responses, turn it off and do not reinforce responses, and so on many times. The stimulus in which the response is reinforced is called S^d (short for *discriminative stimulus*), and the stimulus in which the response is never reinforced is called S^{delta}. Soon, if we follow the teaching program just outlined, B. F. will begin pressing the lever almost every time the light comes on, and almost never press it when the light is off. He will learn a stimulus discrimination.

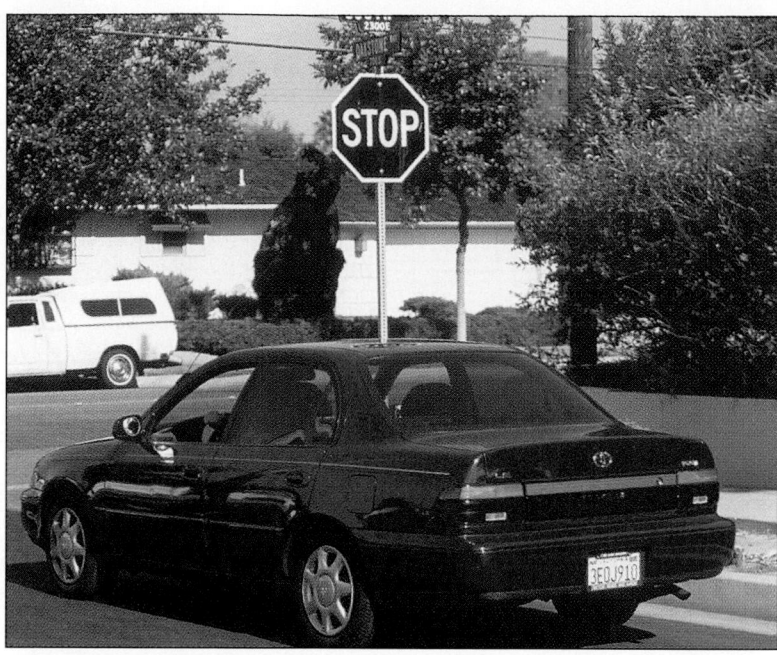

Stopping for a stop sign is one stimulus discrimination drivers must learn.

Humans have to learn stimulus discriminations, too—lots of them. We have to learn to say, "Car," only to the stimulus of a car and not to a toy wagon; we have to learn to say, "Dog," to the stimulus of the printed letters *D-O-G* and not to other letters; and so on. Many of the stimulus discriminations that we learn are much more subtle than that, however. For example, we must learn to introduce ourselves to others at a party when they are showing interest in us (rather than no interest). We have to learn to express sympathy when a sad thing has been told to us. Responses made during the presence of an S^d for that behavior will lead to favorable consequences, whereas the same behavior made during S^{delta} will often lead to unfavorable consequences. Introducing yourself to a person showing interest in you will lead to a pleasant conversation; introducing yourself to a person showing no interest can make you both feel extremely uncomfortable.

Stimulus discrimination does not occur only in operant conditioning, however. Let's say that your lab instructor wants you to use classical conditioning to teach B. F. to stop moving and to crouch in the presence of a slow-ringing bell but not a fast-ringing bell. First you need to know that rats explore freely in dim light but crouch defensively in bright light. You would start classical conditioning in the normal way, by pairing the slow ring with the UCS (bright light) for the response of crouching. After several pairings, B. F. should be crouching whenever the slow-ringing bell is sounded. If we now begin presenting the fast ring sometimes, B. F. will respond to that with the crouch response, too. But, if we continue to present both the slow and fast rings, *but pair the bright light only with the slow ring,* B. F. will respond with the fear response only to the slow ring and not the fast one; he will have learned a stimulus discrimination through classical conditioning.

The opposite of stimulus discrimination is **stimulus generalization.** This term indicates that people (as well as rats and other creatures) do not always discriminate between stimuli that are similar to one another. Stated another way, the more similar two stimuli are, the more likely the individual is to respond to them as if they were the same stimulus. A person who is afraid of Siamese cats is usually also afraid of tabby and alley cats.

stimulus generalization
The tendency for similar stimuli to elicit the same response.

As with everything else, let's go back to the lab to demonstrate stimulus generalization based on similarity in the color of the stimulus. This time, however, we will use a pigeon as our laboratory animal instead of a rat, because rats are color blind and pigeons are not. For example, we can reinforce the pigeon only for responding in the presence of a *green* light. In a while, the pigeon will emit lever presses only when the S^d of the light is present. If we begin changing the wavelength of the light stimulus, we will be able to see that, the more we change the wavelength, the less likely the pigeon will be to respond to it.

● Review

We learn from the consequences of our behavior. If our behavior leads to a positive consequence, we are more likely to engage in that behavior again, with the specific pattern of behavior depending in part on the schedule with which reinforcement is delivered. The events that serve as positive reinforcers are both inborn (primary reinforcers) and learned (secondary reinforcers). Positive reinforcement can even increase the probability of behaviors that initially never occur by reinforcing successive approximations to that behavior (shaping).

Behavior can be reinforced not only when the consequence is positive but also when the behavior removes or avoids a negative consequence (negative reinforcement). Actually, two slightly different forms of learning are based on negative reinforcement: (a) escape conditioning, in which the behavior removes a negative event, and (b) avoidance conditioning, in which behavior causes the negative event not to occur. Punishment, which is different from negative reinforcement, is a negative consequence of behavior that reduces the probability of its future occurrence.

Behavior that is reinforced only in the presence of a specific stimulus tends to occur only in the presence of that stimulus (stimulus discrimination). On the other hand, there is a strong tendency to respond to similar stimuli as if they were the same (stimulus generalization). The phenomena of stimulus generalization and discrimination also occur in classical conditioning.

● Check Your Learning

To be sure that you have learned the key points from the preceding section, cover the list of correct answers and try to answer each question. If you give an incorrect answer to any question, return to the page given next to the correct answer to see why your answer was not correct.

1. Learning from the consequences of our behavior is called _____.

   a) operant conditioning
   b) classical conditioning
   c) environmental learning
   d) cognitive learning

2. Slot machine players are on a _____ of reinforcement.

   a) variable interval schedule
   b) variable ratio schedule
   c) fixed ratio schedule
   d) fixed interval schedule

3. Negative reinforcement is another term for punishment.

   a) True
   b) False

4. The more similar two stimuli are, the more likely the individual is to respond to them as if they were the same stimulus. This is termed _____.

   a) stimulus discrimination
   b) generalized responding
   c) stimulus generalization
   d) stimulus conditioning

● Thinking Critically About Psychology

1. Do your friends ever reinforce you for behaving in ways that are not good for you? In what ways?

2. What kind of behaviors does our culture encourage for males and females? Is this done more through positive reinforcement, negative reinforcement, or punishment?

▶ EXTINCTION: LEARNING WHEN TO QUIT

The process of learning is essential to human life. Through it we learn to cope with the demands of the environment. But the world is apt to change at any time, so people have to change, too. If we were able to learn only once and never change, we would not be able to survive changes in the environment. For example, if we were Stone Age people who learned to get oranges from the tops of orange trees by shaking the trees, that learned behavior would be very useful—that is, it would be positively reinforced. But the learned behavior of shaking orange trees would no longer be useful after all the oranges had been shaken out of the tree. At that point, we would need to quit shaking orange trees! If changes in the environment did not lead to changes in our learned behavior, we would be in big trouble.

If a learned response stops occurring because the aspect of the environment that originally caused the learning changes, **extinction** has occurred. The process of extinction is similar in many respects for both classical and operant conditioning.

Removing the Source of Learning

Extinction occurs because the original source of the learning has been removed. In classical conditioning, learning takes place because two stimuli are repeatedly paired together. If Pavlov's dog were to stop receiving meat powder with the sound of the metronome, the dog would eventually stop salivating to the metronome. Or if you are hurt a couple of times when you are in the dentist's chair, the dentist's chair will come to elicit the response of fear (from the pairing of pain with the previously neutral chair). Let's suppose, however, that the clumsy dentist sells his practice to a new, truly painless dentist and you no longer get hurt in that chair. In this case, the cause of learning to fear the dentist's chair is removed. Eventually (classically conditioned fears are difficult to extinguish), the fact that the conditioned stimulus is presented alone (the dentist's chair is never again paired with pain) will lead to the extinction of the response of fear to the dentist's chair. In essence, you will have learned that the chair no longer predicts pain. Thus, using the terminology of classical conditioning, a CR will be extinguished if the CS for that response is presented repeatedly but the UCS for that stimulus is no longer paired with it.

In the case of operant conditioning, extinction results from a change in the consequences of behavior. If a response is no longer reinforced, then that response will eventually decline in frequency. If Skinner's rat were no longer given food pellets for bar presses, the bar pressing would eventually stop. Similarly, when there are no longer any oranges in the tree, the response of shaking it will no longer be reinforced and shaking will eventually stop.

There is one notable difference between extinction in classical and in operant conditioning. During the early stages of the operant extinction process, "frustration" often occurs. This may lead to a brief, rapid burst of responding before the response finally begins to disappear. When you first discover that no more oranges fall out of the tree, you might shake the tree angrily for a while.

The schedule of reinforcement and the type of reinforcement greatly influence the speed with which the extinction of operant conditioning takes place. This phenomenon is known as the **partial reinforcement effect.** Responses that have been continuously reinforced are extinguished more quickly than responses that have been reinforced on variable ratio or variable interval schedules. Perhaps this is so because it's easier to see that the reinforcement is not going to come again if it used to come after every response. It may not be a bad thing that parents, employers, teachers, and others are often too busy to reinforce every good response; a variable pattern of reinforcement makes the good response more resistant to extinction.

The most difficult responses of all to extinguish, however, are responses learned through avoidance learning. Extinction of an avoidance response should result when the negative event ceases to occur. However, if you continue to perform avoidance responses,

extinction
(eks-ting'shun)   The process of unlearning a learned response because of the removal of the original source of learning.

partial reinforcement effect
Responses that have been reinforced on variable ratio or variable interval schedules are more difficult to extinguish than responses that have been continuously reinforced.

FIGURE 5.10

The course of extinction of a classically conditioned fear of dental chairs.

Strength of fear
declines when chair is no
longer paired with pain.

Dental assistant drops
instruments and causes
"disinhibition," but
strength of fear declines
again with repeated
experiences of the
chair without pain.

Strength of fear is
finally extinguished
completely when chair
is never again paired
with pain.

Strength of fear
response increases
when chair is paired
with pain from dentist.

Passage of time without
sitting in chair leads to
"spontaneous recovery,"
but fear extinguishes again.

Another passage of
time leads to another
episode of spontaneous
recovery.

you will never see that the situation has changed. For example, if you continue to avoid the
pit bull by taking the longer route to school, you will never learn that the owner and his dog
have moved to another neighborhood.

Spontaneous Recovery and Disinhibition

The course of extinction is not always smooth. Normally, the learned response occurs many
times before extinction is complete. Consider again the fear of the dental chair: The
strength of the response gradually decreases because the CS (chair) is never again paired
with the UCS (pain). If, however, there is a long period of time between presentations of
the CS (such as a year between visits to the dentist), the fear can reappear the next time the
CS is presented (see fig. 5.10). This is termed **spontaneous recovery.** It may occur several
times during the course of extinction, but, as long as the stimulus continues to be presented
alone, the recovered response will be extinguished more quickly each time until the response no longer recovers.

In some cases, the strength of the extinguished response returns for a reason other
than spontaneous recovery. If an intense but unrelated stimulus event occurs, it may cause
the strength of the extinguished response to return temporarily. For example, if the dentist's
assistant drops a tray of dental instruments while you were sitting in the chair, your fear response might come back for a while. This phenomenon is called **disinhibition.** That term
will not seem to fit the phenomenon unless you understand that Pavlov, for theoretical reasons, believed that no response was ever really unlearned, just "inhibited" by another part
of the brain. He termed this temporary increase in the strength of the response "disinhibition" because he felt that noise temporarily reduced the inhibition of the response. Both
spontaneous recovery and disinhibition occur during the course of operant as well as classical extinction.

spontaneous recovery
A temporary increase in the strength of a
conditioned response, which is likely to occur
during extinction after the passage of time.

disinhibition
(dis″in-hi-bish′un)   A temporary increase in
the strength of an extinguished response
caused by an unrelated stimulus event.

● Review

To adapt fully to a changing world, we must be able to unlearn as well as learn. The process of
extinction begins as soon as the source of the original learning is removed. In classical conditioning, this means that no longer pairing the UCS with the CS will produce extinction of the
CR. In operant learning, no longer reinforcing the response will extinguish the response. The

course of extinction is often irregular, with the strength of the response often spontaneously recovering after long periods of time or when a strong disinhibiting stimulus occurs.

● Check Your Learning

To be sure that you have learned the key points from the preceding section, cover the list of correct answers and try to answer each question. If you give an incorrect answer to any question, return to the page given next to the correct answer to see why your answer was not correct.

1. The process of unlearning a learned response because of a change in the aspect of the environment that originally caused the learning is termed _____.

   a) repression   c) extinction
   b) forgetting   d) terminating

2. The most difficult responses of all to extinguish are responses learned through _____.

   a) avoidance learning   c) classical conditioning
   b) operant conditioning   d) experience

3. _____ is a temporary increase in the strength of an extinguished response caused by an unrelated stimulus event.

   a) Spontaneous recovery   c) Revival
   b) Disinhibition   d) Learning

● Thinking Critically About Psychology

1. What makes some behaviors more difficult to extinguish than others?
2. Have you personally tried to eliminate unwanted behaviors using extinction?

Correct Answers 1. c (p. 161), 2. a (p. 161), 3. b (p. 162).

▶ THEORETICAL INTERPRETATIONS OF LEARNING

What is learned? When an individual's behavior changes as the result of classical or operant conditioning, what exactly has happened to the individual? One view dating back at least to the time of Pavlov is that neural *connections* between brain regions associated with specific stimuli and specific responses are acquired during the learning process. For example, when a rat is reinforced for pressing a lever in the presence of a light, a connection is believed to be automatically created between brain regions associated with the light and the specific pattern of muscle movements of the lever press. The next time the light is turned on, the neural connections to the muscles will cause the lever press to occur. Research based on the connection approach emphasized readily observable changes in behavior and basically ignored internal mental processes.

Other psychologists argue that internal mental processes play a central role in the learning process and are therefore deserving of study. For these psychologists, learning involves changes in cognitions rather than specific neural connections. As noted earlier in the text, the term *cognition* refers to the intellectual processes of thinking, expecting, believing, perceiving, and so on. Adherents to this view consider that the individual (rat or human) changes cognitions about a given situation during the learning process. For example, you flinch when a light comes on that has previously been paired with an electric shock, because you *expect* it to be followed by a shock. A rat turns left in a maze because it *knows* that the food was down that way the last 10 times it ran through the maze.

Cognition or Connection?

A considerable amount of research has been conducted through the years to evaluate the connectionist and cognition theories of learning. Although most of it has been carried out using animals as subjects, what has been learned about the nature of learning is relevant to us human animals, too.

Place Learning

An ingenious experiment to test the cognitive view of learning was designed by the late Edward C. Tolman of the University of California at Berkeley (Tolman, Ritchie, & Kalish, 1946). Rats were initially trained to run down the elevated path shown in figure 5.11. They started at point A, made a series of turns (left, right, right), and ran to point B, where food was provided. In the connectionist view of learning, the rats learned to do this by learning connections between the stimuli of the alley and the particular muscle movements of running and turning. Tolman took a cognitive view, however. He believed that the rats had learned a **cognitive map** of where the food was located relative to the starting place. They did not acquire a fixed pattern of muscle movements; they acquired knowledge of the location of the food.

How can we distinguish between the cognitive and connectionist interpretations? Tolman's experimental test was ingenious. Suppose we give the rats a chance to take a shortcut directly to the food; will they take it? Or will they be unable to recognize it as a better path, because all they had learned was connections between maze stimuli and patterns of muscle movements? Tolman and his colleagues answered this question by blocking the old path (as shown in fig. 5.12) and providing a variety of new choices.

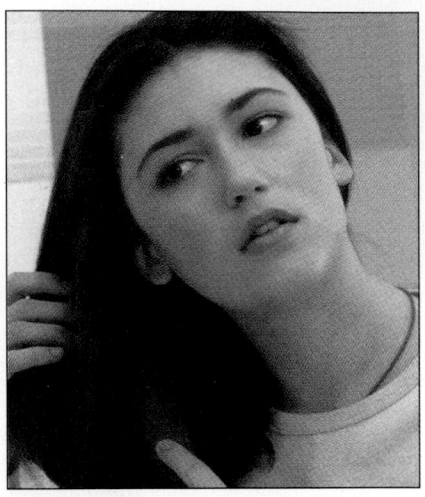

This young woman has learned that good grooming usually elicits compliments from her dates. Is this a learned behavior involving a new stimulusresponse connection or a change in cognition?

cognitive map
(kog'ni-tiv)   An inferred mental awareness of the structure of a physical space or related elements.

FIGURE 5.11

The initial part of the apparatus used in Tolman's study of cognitive aspects of learning in rats. The rat begins at point A and receives food when it has reached point B.
Source: E. C. Tolman, B. F. Ritchie, and D. Kalish, "Studies in Spatial Learning I: Orientation and the Short-Cut" in *Journal of Experimental Psychology*, 36:13–25, 1946.

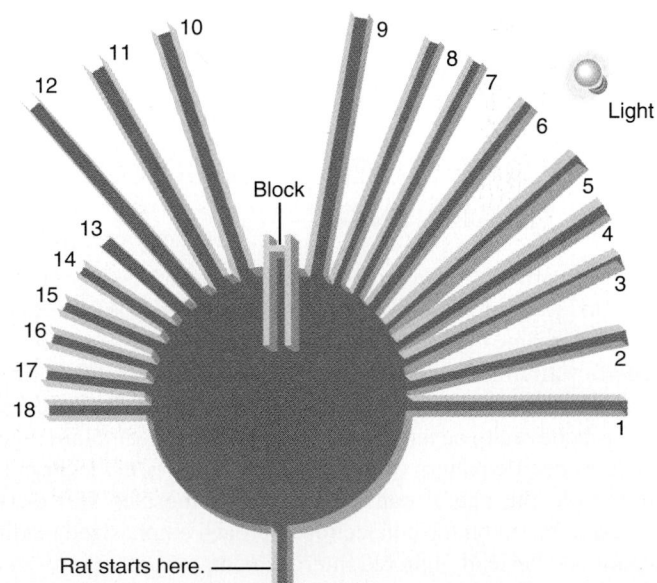

FIGURE 5.12

The modified apparatus used in the second part of Tolman's study of cognitive aspects of learning in rats.
Source: E. C. Tolman, B. F. Ritchie, and D. Kalish, "Studies in Spatial Learning I: Orientation and the Short-Cut" in *Journal of Experimental Psychology*, 36:13–25, 1946.

Interestingly, the greatest number of rats chose the path that led directly to where the food had been. Tolman interpreted this as meaning that they had learned a new cognition, knowledge of the location of the food.

Latent Learning

Tolman conducted another informative experiment that evaluated the cognitive interpretation of learning in a rather different way (Tolman & Honzik, 1930). Suppose we allow a rat to run around in a complex maze of alleys, like the one shown in figure 5.13. Would the rat learn anything? The connectionist view would say no: Learning would occur only if reinforcement were delivered at the end of the maze to "stamp in" a connection between the stimuli of the maze and a specific series of movements leading from the starting box to the box containing the food. Tolman, on the other hand, felt that the rat would learn a cognitive map of the maze, but we would not be able to see that the rat had learned it until it was given a good reason (such as food) to run to the food box.

In Tolman's experiment, three groups of hungry rats were placed in the maze and timed to see how long it took them to reach the food box. One group was reinforced each time it reached the food box, so it gradually learned to run to the food box. A second group was never reinforced, so they wandered aimlessly in the maze (never decreasing the time it took to reach the food box). The third group of rats was the interesting one, though. This group was not reinforced for going to the food box for the first 10 days but was reinforced from then on. Look at figure 5.14 to see what happened. This group showed a sudden decrease in the amount of time it took the rats to reach the goal, catching up almost immediately to the group that had been reinforced every time. Tolman interpreted these results as showing that the unreinforced rats had learned just as much about the location of the food box as the reinforced group, but they showed their learning only when given a reason to do so (the food). If learning were a matter of reinforcement strengthening connections between stimuli and responses, no learning would have been expected prior to the introduction of reinforcement.

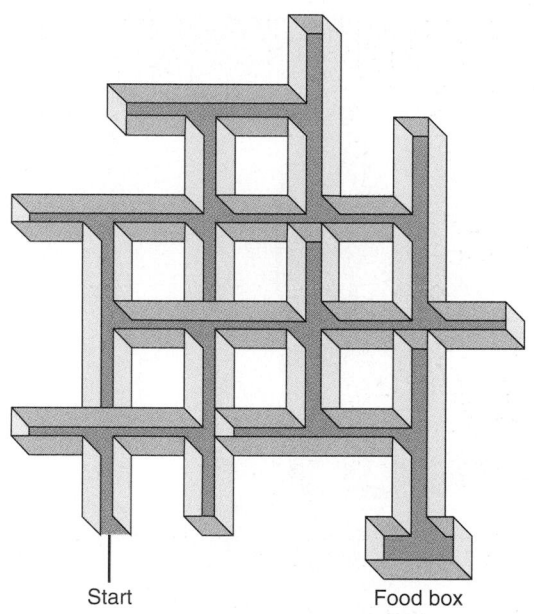

FIGURE 5.13

The maze used in Tolman's study of latent learning in rats.
Source: E. C. Tolman and C. H. Honzik, "Introduction and Removal of the Reward, and Maze Performance in Rats," *University of California Publications in Psychology,* 4:257–275, 1930.

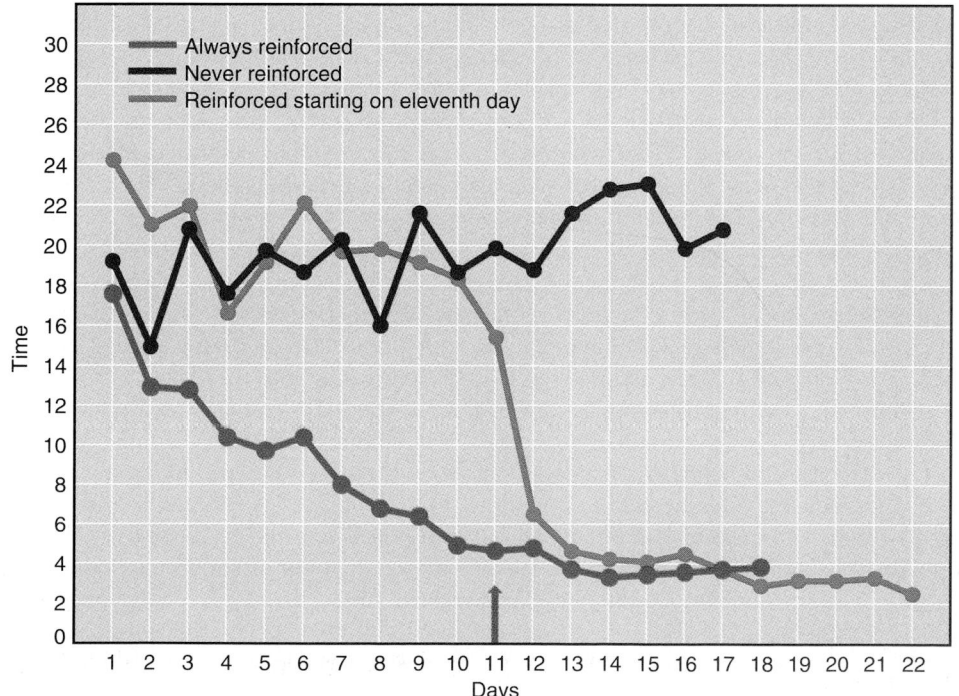

FIGURE 5.14

The results of Tolman's study of latent learning in rats. A group of rats that was never reinforced for reaching the food box did not improve in the amount of time required to reach it. But a group of rats that was reinforced each time gradually improved. A third group of rats was not reinforced for the first 10 days but was reinforced from then on. These rats' rapid improvement indicated that they had "latently" learned about the maze before they were reinforced.

Source: E. C. Tolman and C. H. Honzik, "Introduction and Removal of the Reward, and Maze Performance in Rats," *University of California Publications in Psychology,* 4:257–275, 1930.

In Köhler's view, this chimp did not learn to reach the bananas on the ceiling through a gradual learning process but, rather, through a process of sudden cognitive change involving a new understanding of the uses of the boxes.

insight
(in´sīt) A form of cognitive change that involves recognition of previously unseen relationships.

modeling
Learning based on observation of the behavior of another.

Insight Learning and Learning Sets

Perhaps the most striking evidence for the cognitive view of learning comes from a series of experiments conducted by a German Gestalt psychologist during World War I. Wolfgang Köhler was visiting the island of Tenerife (in the Canary Islands) when the war broke out and he found himself interned there for the duration of the war. He took good advantage of a poor situation, however, by conducting learning experiments with chimpanzees that were native to the island. Köhler presented the caged chimps with a number of problems to see how they learned to solve them. For example, he hung a bunch of bananas out of reach on the ceiling. At first, the chimps tried to reach the bananas by jumping. When that failed, they sat down, looking annoyed. In time, however, one of the chimps picked up the wooden boxes that were in the cage, stacked them, and climbed up to reach the bananas. From that time on, the chimps always reached bananas hung from the ceiling of the cage by stacking the boxes.

Köhler conducted many similar experiments with other chimps. For example, he placed another chimp in a cage with bananas hung from the ceiling. In this case, there were no boxes in cage, but there were two bamboo poles, which could be fitted together to make a pole long enough to reach the bananas. At first, the chimp tried to reach the bananas by jumping and then by throwing the bamboo poles at the bananas, but it soon gave up. Later, the chimp suddenly picked up the sticks, put them together, and used the new "pole" to knock down the bananas. Again, when presented with the same problem later, the chimp immediately solved it every time by putting the sticks together.

In both cases, Köhler concluded that the chimps had not learned to solve the problem by gradually strengthening neural connections between stimuli and responses but, rather, had learned through **insight**—a sudden cognitive change that solved the problem. The chimps did not gradually improve their ability to reach the bananas over time but, rather, suddenly went from being unable to reach the bananas to being able to reach them easily using their new solution. Connection theorists have a great deal of difficulty explaining this type of insightful learning.

Modeling: Learning by Watching Others

Stanford University psychologist Albert Bandura is one of the most influential contemporary proponents of the cognitive view of learning. Perhaps his most important contribution has been to emphasize that people learn not only through classical and operant conditioning but also by observing the behavior of others. Bandura calls this **modeling.** In Egypt, for example, where grasshoppers are considered to be a delicacy, people learn to eat them partly by watching other people enjoy themselves while eating grasshoppers. Similarly, patterns of speech, styles of dress, patterns of energy consumption, methods of rearing children, and myriad other patterns of behavior are taught to us through modeling.

Bandura considers modeling to be an important demonstration of the role of cognition in learning. A child who watches his older sister play baseball for several years will be able to come pretty close to playing the game properly (that is, know how to hold the bat, how to swing, where to run if he hits the ball) the very first time he is allowed to play. In Bandura's view, a great deal of cognitive learning takes place through watching, *before* there is any chance for the behavior to occur and be reinforced. But we can learn more than skills through modeling. Bandura has suggested that modeling can also remind us of appropriate behavior in a given situation, reduce our inhibitions concerning certain behaviors that we see others engaging in, or suggest to us what behaviors will lead to reinforcement.

In Bandura's ground-breaking laboratory studies of modeling, children learned to be more aggressive or less fearful as a result of simply observing the behavior of models in films. In one study (Bandura, Ross, & Ross, 1963), one group of children saw an adult kick, hit, and sit on a blow-up Bobo doll. When these children were placed in a playroom (then frustrated by having all toys except the Bobo doll taken away), they were significantly more aggressive toward the Bobo doll than was a group of children who had not seen the film—they learned to act more aggressively through modeling. In a similar study with a more uplifting conclusion, research participants who were initially strongly afraid of snakes gradually learned to be less fearful by imitating a series of actions of the model, ranging from looking at a caged snake to holding it (Bandura, Blanchard, & Ritter, 1969). Modeling can be an important and powerful form of learning.

We are not equally likely to imitate all behavior of all models, however. We are considerably more likely to imitate a model whose behavior we see reinforced **(vicarious reinforcement)** than when we see that behavior punished in the model **(vicarious punishment).** In the absence of direct knowledge of vicarious reinforcement and punishment, we are more likely to imitate the behavior of models that are high in status, attractive, likable, and successful, perhaps because we assume that their behavior often leads to reinforcement (Bandura, 1977).

In recent years, a great deal of debate has centered on the types of models that are presented to children through the medium of television. Unfortunately, there is some experimental evidence that seems to confirm these fears. It appears that television does teach children to prefer sugary foods, engage in sex-stereotyped roles, and, perhaps most disturbingly, be violent (Anderson, Lindsay, & Bushman, 1999).

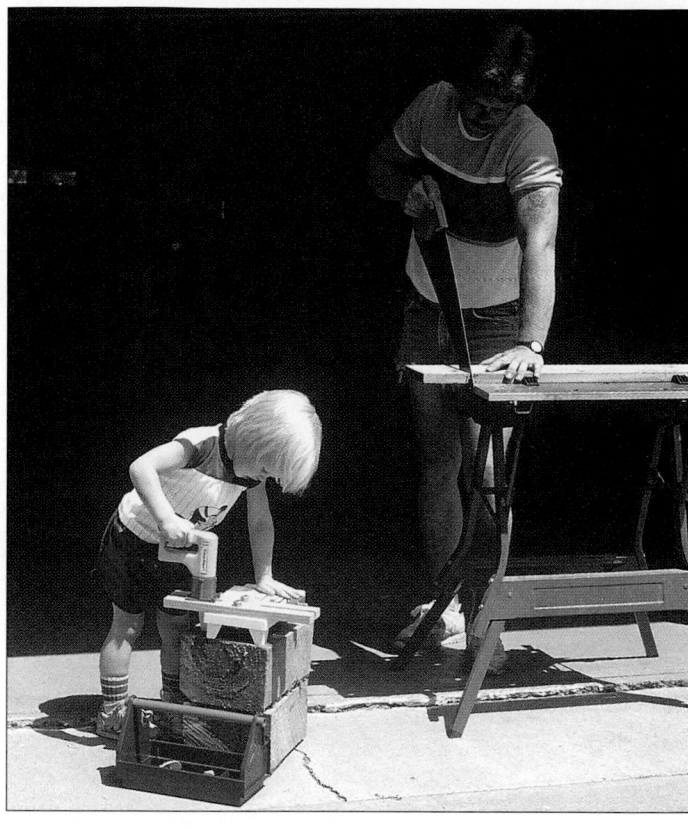

Albert Bandura's views about modeling predict that this boy will learn about carpentry from watching his father work on home projects.

Biological Factors in Learning

Learning is a powerful process that quite literally shapes our lives. But we must not overstate the importance of any psychological process, even learning. We must keep in mind that our ability to learn from experience is not limitless; it's influenced in a number of ways by biological factors. We know that it's impossible to teach goldfish to fly and owls to swim, but has it ever occurred to you that our biological nature influences what people can learn?

For example, it appears that people are biologically prepared to learn some kinds of fears more readily than others (Mineka & Sutton, 1992). It's far easier to classically condition a fear of things that have some intrinsic association with danger (snakes, heights, blood, etc.) using electric shock as the UCS than it is to condition a fear of truly neutral things (such as lunch boxes and skate keys) (Cook, Hodes, & Lang, 1986; Merckelbach, van den Hout, Jansen, & van der Molen, 1988; Ohman, Erixon, & Löfberg, 1975). Interestingly, we are prepared to learn to fear only the things that would have been frightening to our evolutionary ancestors. For example, fears cannot be easily conditioned to modern dangerous stimuli, such as electric outlets (Hugdahl & Karker, 1981).

John Garcia and his associates discussed another form of learning that exemplifies the role of biological factors in learning (Garcia, Hankins, & Rusiniak, 1974). An example of their experiments can be shown through one of my own experiences as a child. On one fateful evening, I ate eight hot dogs. Two hours later, I became more than just a little nauseated. As a result, it was many years until I ate another hot dog. This experience of learning to dislike hot dogs is an example of a **learned taste aversion.** Learned taste aversions have been the subject of much study by psychologists because they provide another good example of the role of biological factors in learning. Note that I learned to dislike the hot dogs through classical conditioning: The hot dogs were the CS and the nausea was the UCS. But think about two facts: The two stimuli were paired only *once,* but I learned a dislike that lasted for years. Moreover, there was a time interval of 2 hours between the conditioned and unconditioned stimuli. Normally a gap of more than a couple of seconds is enough to make classical conditioning impossible. For learning to take place under these conditions, we must be highly "prepared" for such learning. Indeed, this makes good sense from an evolutionary perspective; animal species that quickly learn to avoid foods that

vicarious reinforcement
(vĭ-kar′ē-us)   Observed reinforcement of the behavior of a model, which also increases the probability of the same behavior in the observer.

vicarious punishment
Observed punishment of the behavior of a model, which also decreases the probability of the same behavior in the observer.

 Learned Taste Aversions

www.mmhe.com/laheye1

learned taste aversion
(ah-ver′shun)   Negative reaction to a particular taste that has been associated with nausea or other illness.

make them sick (and hence may be poisonous) are species that are more likely to survive. A species that does not quickly learn to avoid poisonous foods is likely to perish (Kehoe & Bass, 1986).

● Review

Some psychologists believe that learning is based on the strengthening of neural connections between stimuli and specific patterns of muscle movements. Others suggest that learning involves changes in cognition (knowing what to do, where food is located, what to expect next, and so on). Research on place learning, latent learning, and insight learning provides strong support for the cognitive view of learning. Perhaps the most important learning phenomenon thought to be based on cognitive change is modeling; a great deal of our behavior is learned simply by observing the behavior of others. Although learning is a powerful force that shapes our lives, our biological characteristics place limits on it, making us better prepared to learn some things more than others.

● Check Your Learning

To be sure that you have learned the key points from the preceding section, cover the list of correct answers and try to answer each question. If you give an incorrect answer to any question, return to the page given next to the correct answer to see why your answer was not correct.

1. _____ is a sudden change in behavior that results from a recognition of previously unseen relationships.

   a) Insight   c) Operant learning

   b) Modeling   d) Conditioning

2. Learning by observing the behavior of others is termed _____ by Albert Bandura.

   a) stimulus discrimination   c) operant conditioning

   b) classical conditioning   d) modeling

3. Learned taste aversions, in which humans and nonhuman animals learn to avoid foods that make them sick, are interesting because the time interval between the CS (the taste of the food) and the UCS is much _____ than in most instances of classical conditioning.

   a) longer   b) shorter

● Thinking Critically About Psychology

1. Why are place learning, latent learning, and insight learning all considered to support cognitive theories of learning?

2. Whom do you model your behavior after? What events or personal qualities have made them your models?

Correct Answers 1. a (p. 166), 2. d (p. 166), 3. a (p. 167).

Application *of Psychology*

LEARNING THE WRONG THINGS

In this chapter, we saw that one of the good things about operant conditioning is that it helps us adapt to the realities of life. If our behavior is effective in bringing us good things, it will be positively reinforced, and we will be more likely to engage in these behaviors. On the other hand, ways of behaving that do not bring good things will be extinguished, and behaviors that bring negative consequences will be punished. We are always in the process of learning to adjust to our world through operant conditioning. But, *sometimes,* unfortunately, we learn the wrong things.

Are you superstitious? Did you ever wonder where your superstitions come from? There are probably many ways in which they are learned, but B. F. Skinner made the interesting suggestion that some of our superstitions are *learned through flukes in positive reinforcement.*

Skinner was working with pigeons that were being reinforced for pecking at a small disk when he noticed that some of them had learned superstitions. Sometimes a pigeon would engage in an unrelated behavior, such as turning around just before pecking the disk. The consequent reinforcer would reinforce the pigeon both for pecking and for the irrelevant response of turning. If the pigeon then happened to turn around again before another reinforced response, it would probably begin

turning before every peck, even though turning had nothing to do with the delivery of the food. The food would have come after the peck whether the pigeon had turned or not. In Skinner's terms, the pigeon had learned a *superstitious behavior,* a behavior that is reinforced when the reinforcing stimulus accidentally follows the response. Like all superstitions, the pigeon stubbornly kept engaging in this act, even though it served no real purpose.

You can also see superstitious behavior acquired in this way by carefully watching a discus thrower just before he or she starts to throw. Many of them go through odd little rituals. Each time the discus thrower steps in the ring, he or she engages in an identical pattern of superstitious behavior. As odd as it looks, it's probably just another form of superstitious behavior. This is how it might have been acquired: When the discus thrower is first learning to throw, the behaviors that occur before starting to throw are pretty much random. But, when the thrower uncorks a really good throw (a big reinforcer for a discus thrower), any of the random behaviors that were occurring just before the throw will be reinforced through superstitious reinforcement. This is called superstitious because the reinforcement of the good throw had nothing to do with some behavior like touching the shoulder before beginning to throw. In this way, a whole series of irrelevant behaviors may become the superstitions of the discus

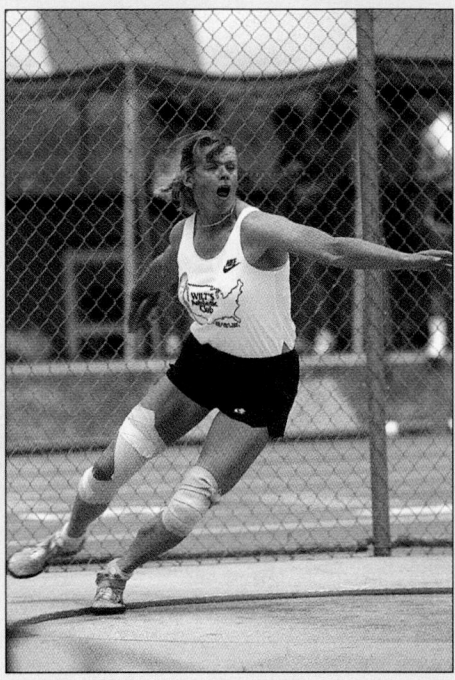

Athletes often learn superstitions from reinforcing stimuli that accidentally follow a response.

thrower without his or her ever actually noticing what has happened. Baseball players develop similar superstitious behaviors before batting or pitching. Many other everyday superstitions are probably learned in much the same way. Do you have any superstitions like this?

● Summary

Chapter 5 is about the psychological study of learning. Emphasis is on classical conditioning, operant conditioning, and extinction. The last section of the chapter explores theoretical interpretations of learning.

I. *Learning* refers to any relatively permanent change in behavior brought about through experience.

II. Classical conditioning is a form of learning in which a previously neutral stimulus (conditioned stimulus, CS) is paired with an unconditioned stimulus (UCS) that elicits an unlearned or unconditioned response (UCR). As a result, the CS comes to elicit a conditioned response (CR) that is identical or very similar to the UCR.

A. Classical conditioning occurs because of the association in time of a neutral stimulus that already elicits the response. The CS becomes a signal that predicts the occurrence of the UCS.

III. Operant conditioning is a form of learning in which the consequences of behavior lead to a change in the probability of the behavior's occurrence.

   A. In positive reinforcement, a positive consequence of behavior leads to an increase in the probability of the occurrence of the response.
      1. Primary reinforcers are innately reinforcing.
      2. Secondary reinforcers are learned through classical conditioning.
      3. Four schedules of reinforcement that result in different patterns of behavior are fixed ratio, variable ratio, fixed interval, and variable interval.
      4. Shaping is the process of positively reinforcing responses that are progressively more similar to the response that is wanted.

   B. Negative reinforcement occurs when the reinforcing consequence is the removal or avoidance of a negative event.
      1. The type of negative reinforcement in which the response causes an aversive stimulus to cease is called escape conditioning.
      2. The type of negative reinforcement in which the response prevents the occurrence of the aversive stimulus is called avoidance conditioning.

   C. Punishment is the process through which an aversive consequence of behavior reduces the frequency of a behavior.

IV. New stimuli come to influence behavior through the process of learning.

   A. A stimulus discrimination has been learned when a response is more likely to occur in the presence of a specific stimulus than in its absence.
   B. Stimulus generalization has occurred when an individual responds in the same way to a stimulus that is similar to the original stimulus.

V. The process of unlearning a learned response because of the removal of the aspect of the environment that originally caused the learning is termed extinction.

   A. During extinction, the strength of the response sometimes increases after a period of time since the last extinction trial; this is termed spontaneous recovery.
   B. An extraneous stimulus sometimes causes an extinguished response to recur; this is called external disinhibition.

VI. Psychologists disagree about whether learning results from changes in neural connections between specific stimuli and specific responses or whether learning is a change in cognition.

   A. Research that supports the cognitive view includes Tolman's studies of place learning and latent learning, Köhler's studies of insight learning, and Bandura's work on modeling.
   B. The ability of humans to learn from experience is not limitless; it is influenced in a number of ways by biological factors.

● Resources

1. Excellent summaries for the serious student of learning include: Domjan, M. (1996). *Essentials of conditioning and learning.* Monterey: Brooks-Cole; and Tarpy, R. (1997). *Contemporary learning theory and research.* Boston: McGraw-Hill.

2. For more on modeling, see: Bandura, A. (1977). *Social learning theory.* Englewood Cliffs, NJ: Prentice-Hall.

3. For B. F. Skinner's views on operant conditioning and the science of psychology in general, see: Skinner, B. F. (1974). *About behaviorism.* New York: Knopf; and Skinner, B. F. (1971). *Beyond freedom and dignity.* New York: Knopf.

4. For a firsthand account of early research on classical conditioning, see: Pavlov, I. P. (1927). *Conditioned reflexes*. Gloucester, MA: Peter Smith.

5. A still cogent and controversial novel describing the utopia that one psychologist believes could result from our using the principles of learning to design society is Skinner, B. F. (1948). *Walden two*. New York: Macmillan.

CHAPTER

6

CHAPTER OUTLINE

Memory

PROLOGUE

If we are to benefit from our experiences, we must be able to remember them. If you weren't able to remember anything tomorrow that you read in this chapter today, there would be no point in reading it. Remembering what you learn is as important as learning it in the first place.

Alexander Luria, a prominent Russian physician during the 1930s, was widely known for his research on the brain. One day, a young man (referred to as S) came to his hospital office, complaining that his memory was *too good.* He often recalled experiences in such vivid detail that he could not shake them from his consciousness. They lingered in a distracting, haunting way that impaired his ability to concentrate on his current circumstances. Because the man was clearly distraught, Luria agreed to study his problem.

Over many years, Luria tested S's memory in a number of ways. The best known of these tests involved showing S a sheet of paper containing four columns of a dozen numbers each. After viewing the numbers for a few minutes, S was able to write them out from memory without error. Moreover, without looking at the numbers again, he was able to refer to a mental image of them and tell Luria the numbers in any sequence requested. He could "read" a mental image of the numbers across the rows, down the columns, and across diagonals with apparent ease. Months later, S could still reproduce the table of numbers with few errors. In one series of experiments, he was even able to recall complex verbal material in detail after more than 15 years had elapsed.

Luria was never able to help S, but S himself found a way to make his life more comfortable. After losing many other kinds of jobs, he decided to go on stage as a "memory expert." He was able to astound audiences with his ability to recall information and was able to earn a comfortable living.

Most of us are not troubled by remembering too much—quite the opposite—most college students would like to be able to remember a lot more every time they take a test. Learning about S might help us feel a little better about our own memories, but most of us would still like to be able to remember more.

This chapter describes the ways in which the human memory works and discusses the reasons that we forget. New information that we learn can be thought of as passing through three stages in the human memory. The first stage holds information for very brief intervals—often less than a second. The next stage retains information longer, but only a little longer—up to about half a minute. The third stage seems to hold information indefinitely. These three stages of memory operate according to different rules and mostly serve different functions. But because information must pass through each stage to reach the most permanent memory store, they work together as three linked stages in the memory process.

Forgetting appears to occur for different reasons in the three stages of memory. In the first stage, information is lost because it decays quickly over time unless it moves to the next stage. Forgetting in the second stage also occurs because of the simple passage of time unless something is done to protect the information. But memory traces are frequently lost in the second stage because of interference from other memories. For example, if you look up a number in the telephone book, you may forget it if you try to remember what you planned to say.

The third stage of memory is called long-term memory. Information that reaches this stage seems to stay there permanently. Nonetheless, we are often unable to recall information from long-term memory for several reasons. Interference from similar memories is a

KEY TERMS

A postal worker needs a good memory. According to the information processing model, memory is a process involving attention, encoding, and transfer to storage from which information can be retrieved.

encode
(en´cōd)   To represent information in some form in the memory system.

stage theory of memory
A model of memory based on the idea that we store information in three separate but linked memories.

sensory register
The first stage of memory, in which an exact image of each sensory experience is held briefly until it can be processed.

common reason for being unable to recall long-term memories. In addition, long-term memories tend to change over time, making the information inaccurate. Finally, we are sometimes unable to recall some very unpleasant or threatening memories.

It's not known yet how the memory trace is stored in the brain, but several theories have been proposed. As you will see, our best clues about the biological basis of memory have come from the study of persons with a severe form of memory loss called amnesia.

THREE STAGES OF MEMORY: AN INFORMATION-PROCESSING VIEW

In recent years, psychologists have attempted to develop theories of memory using the computer as a model. These *information-processing* theories of memory are based on the apparent similarities between the operation of the human brain and that of the computer. This is not to say that psychologists believe that brains and computers operate in exactly the same way. Clearly they do not, but enough general similarity exists to make the information-processing model useful. Before looking at specific theories, let's look briefly at the general information-processing model and its terminology.

In the information-processing model, information can be followed as it moves through the following operations: input, storage, and retrieval. At each point in the process, a variety of *control mechanisms* (such as attention, storage, and retrieval) operate. Information enters the memory system through the sensory receptors. This is like your entering a term paper into your computer by typing on the keyboard. Attention operates at this level to select information for further processing. The raw sensory information that is selected is then represented—or **encoded**—in a form (sound, visual image, meaning) that can be used in the next stages of memory.

Other control mechanisms might then transfer selected information into a more permanent memory storage, like saving your term paper on a computer disk. When the stored information is needed, it is *retrieved* from memory. Before printing out your paper, you must first locate your file on the disk and retrieve it. Unfortunately, with both computers and human memory, some information may be lost or become irretrievable.

Some information needs to be stored in memory for only brief periods of time, whereas other information must be tucked away permanently. When we look at a cookbook to see how much tomato paste to add to chicken cacciatore, we need to remember that bit of information for only a few seconds. However, we must remember our social security numbers and our siblings' names for our entire lifetimes. The influential **stage theory of memory** (Atkinson & Shiffrin, 1968; Baddeley, 1999) assumes that we humans have a three-stage memory that meets our need to store information for different lengths of time. We seem to have one memory store that holds information for exceedingly brief intervals, a second memory store that holds information for no more than 30 seconds unless it's "renewed," and a third, more permanent memory store. Each of these memories operates according to a different set of rules and serves a somewhat different purpose. Because information must pass through each stage of memory to get to the next, more permanent one, these memory stores are best thought of as three closely linked "stages" of memory, rather than three separate memories. The three stages are known as the sensory register, short-term memory, and long-term memory (see fig. 6.1).

Sensory Register

The first stage of memory—the **sensory register**—is a very brief one, designed to hold an exact image of each sensory experience until it can be fully processed. We apparently retain a copy of each sensory experience in the sensory register long enough to locate and focus on relevant bits of information and transfer them into the next stage of memory. For visual information, this "snapshot" fades very quickly, probably lasting about one-quarter of a second in most cases. For auditory information, a vivid image of what we hear is

FIGURE 6.1
Stage model of memory.

retained for about the same length of time, one-quarter of a second (Cowan, 1987), but a weaker "echo" is retained for up to 4 seconds (Tarpy & Mayer, 1978). The information stored in the sensory register does not last long, but it's apparently a complete replica of the sensory experience.

Visual information in the sensory register is lost and replaced so rapidly with new information that we seldom are aware we even have such a memory store. Sometimes the longer-lasting, echolike traces of auditory information can be noticed, though. Most of us have had the experience of being absorbed in reading when a friend speaks. If we divert our attention from the book quickly enough, we can "hear again" what was said to us by referring to the echo of the auditory sensation stored in the sensory register.

Short-Term Memory

When a bit of information is selected for further processing, it's transferred from the sensory register into **short-term memory,** or **STM.** It's not necessary to intentionally transfer information to STM; generally, just paying attention to the information is enough to transfer it. You might not intentionally try to memorize the price of your dinner, but you will be able to recognize that you were given the wrong amount of change. Once information has been transferred to short-term memory, a variety of control processes may be applied. Rehearsal and chunking are two important examples of these control processes.

Rehearsal in Short-Term Memory: Overcoming STM's Limited Life Span

As the name implies, short-term memory (STM) is good for only temporary storage of information. In general, information is lost from STM in less than half a minute unless it's "renewed," and it is often lost in only a few seconds (Ellis & Hunt, 1993). Fortunately, information can be renewed in STM by mental repetition, or **rehearsal,** of the information. When a grocery list is rehearsed regularly in this way, it can be held in STM for relatively long periods of time. If the list is not rehearsed, however, it's soon lost. Rehearsing the information stored in STM has been compared to juggling eggs: The eggs stay in perfect condition as long as you keep juggling them, but, as soon as you stop juggling, they are lost.

Our first reliable estimate of the limited life span of information in STM was provided by an experiment conducted by Lloyd and Margaret Peterson (1959). The participants were shown a single combination of three consonants (such as LRP) and asked to remember it as they counted backward by threes to keep them from rehearsing the letters. The individuals counted backward for brief intervals (0 through 18 seconds) and then were asked to recall the letters. As shown in figure 6.2, the participants were able to remember the three consonants less than 20 percent of the time after only 12 seconds had passed. These findings make it clear that memories are impermanent in STM unless kept alive by rehearsal.

The information stored in STM can be of many different types of memories: the smell of a perfume, the notes of a melody, the taste of a fruit, the shape of a nose, the finger positions in a guitar chord, or a list of names. But we humans have a preference for

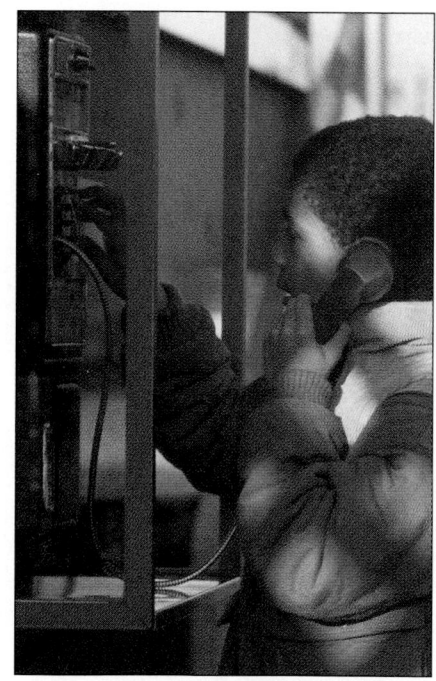

When we dial a number that we have just looked up in the telephone book, we are generally using information that has been stored only in short-term memory.

short-term memory (STM)
The second stage of memory, in which five to nine bits of information can be stored for brief periods of time.

rehearsal
Mental repetition of information for retention in short-term memory.

FIGURE 6.2

The accuracy of recall for a single group of three consonants declines rapidly when subjects are prevented from rehearsing by being asked to count backward.

Source: R. L. Peterson and M. J. Peterson, "Short Term Retention of Individual Items" in *Journal of Experimental Psychology* 58:193–198, 1959.

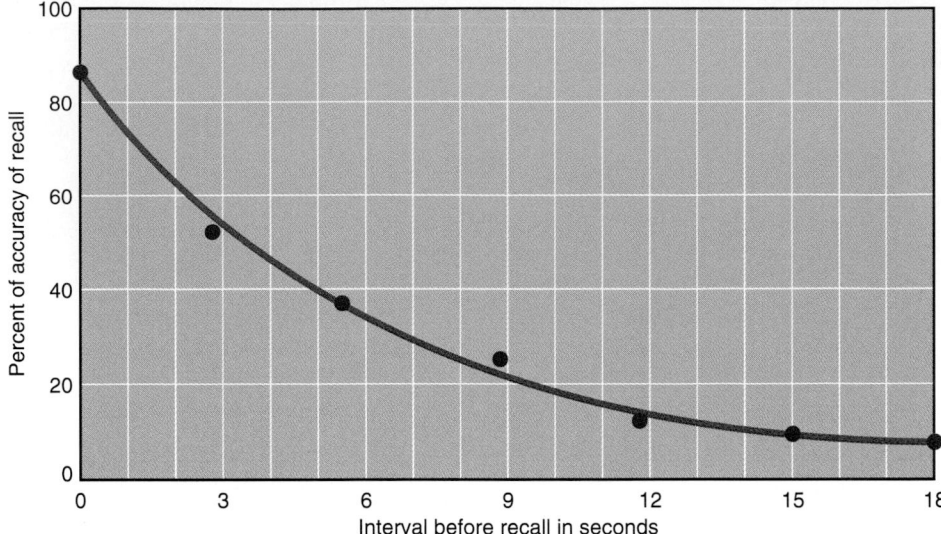

transforming information into sounds, or *acoustic codes,* whenever possible for storage in STM. If I asked you to memorize a list of letters (*B, P, V, R, M, L*), you would most likely memorize them by their "names" (bee, pee, vee, etc.) rather than by the shapes of the letters. We know this because most people say they do it this way and because the errors people make are most likely to be confusions of similar sounds (recalling *zee* instead of *bee*) rather than confusions of similar shapes (recalling *O* instead of *Q,* or *R* instead of *P*) (Reynolds & Flagg, 1983). We probably use acoustic codes in STM as much as possible because it's easier to rehearse by mentally talking to ourselves than by mentally repeating the images of sights, smells, and movements. Nonetheless, STM can store any form of information that can enter the brain through the senses.

Chunking in Short-Term Memory: Overcoming STM's Limited Capacity

Perhaps the most important thing to know about STM is that its storage capacity is quite limited. The exact capacity differs slightly for different kinds of information, but, as psychologist George Miller (1956) put it, it's constant enough to call it the *magic number seven plus or minus (±) two.* Estimates of the span of STM are obtained by asking research participants to memorize simple lists (of randomly ordered numbers, letters, and unrelated words) of different lengths. The length of the list that the participants can recall half the time is considered to represent the capacity of STM (Miller, 1956). Rarely are we able to hold more than five to nine bits of information in STM, regardless of the nature of that information. This is a very limited capacity, indeed.

In addition to temporarily storing information, STM serves another important function, which further limits its already small capacity—it serves as our *working memory* (Baddeley, 1992; 1999). This means that space in STM is used when old memories are temporarily brought out of long-term memory to be used or updated. Space in STM is also used when we think about this information (Morris, 1986). This is why you cannot remember the telephone number of the hardware store, which you just looked up, if you begin thinking about your purchase before you dial—thinking takes up space in STM and forces out the numbers. The fact that thinking uses STM also explains why it's difficult to think about problems that involve more than 7 ± 2 issues. We keep forgetting some of the aspects of complex problems because they exceed the limited capacity of STM. In such situations, writing out all the issues on paper helps keep them straight while you are thinking.

Fortunately, there are some effective ways to get around the limited capacity of STM. One way is to learn the information well enough to transfer it into long-term memory, which, as we will see shortly, has no real space limitation. Another way is to put more information into the 7 ± 2 units of STM.

STM holds 7 ± 2 bits of information. This shopper probably needs a written list.

George Miller (1956) calls the units of memory **chunks.** Although it's true that we can hold only five to nine chunks in STM, we can often put more than one bit of information into each chunk. If you were to quickly read the following list of 12 words once,

> east
> spring
> fall
> dorsal
> west
> medial
> winter
> lateral
> north
> ventral
> summer
> south

you probably would not be able to recall it perfectly 10 seconds later, because 12 chunks normally exceed the capacity of STM. But, if you reorganized the words into 3 chunks (points of a compass, seasons, and anatomical directions) and memorized those, you could remember the list quite easily. This strategy would work for you only if you were able to regroup the list into meaningful chunks, however. If you did not know the four anatomical directions, it would do you no good to memorize these terms because you could not generate the four directions when you recalled them.

Long-Term Memory

Long-term memory, or **LTM,** is the storehouse for information that must be kept for long periods of time. But LTM is not just a more durable version of STM; the stage model of memory suggests it's a different kind of memory altogether.

LTM differs from STM in four major ways: (1) the way in which information is recalled, (2) the form in which information is stored in memory, (3) the reasons that forgetting occurs, and (4) the physical location of these functions in the brain. Let's look at each of these four differences between STM and LTM separately:

long-term memory (LTM)
The third stage of memory, involving the storage of information that is kept for long periods of time.

1. Because the amount of information stored in LTM is so vast, we cannot scan the entire contents of LTM when we are looking for a bit of information, as we do in STM. Instead, LTM has to be *indexed.* We retrieve information from LTM using *cues,* much as we use a call number to locate a book in the library. This retrieval can be an intentional act (such as "What was the name of the secretary in Accounts Receivable?") or an unintentional one, as when hearing a particular song brings back memories of a lost love. In either case, only information relevant to the cue is retrieved, rather than the entire contents of LTM.

2. LTM differs from STM in the kind of information that is most easily stored. You will recall that information is usually stored in STM in terms of the physical qualities of the experience (what we saw, did, tasted, touched, or heard), with a special emphasis on acoustic codes. Although sensory memories can be stored in LTM, information is stored in LTM primarily in terms of its meaning, or *semantic codes* (Cowan, 1988).

3. LTM also differs from STM in the way forgetting occurs. Unlike STM, where information that is not rehearsed or processed appears to drop out of the system, information stored in LTM is not just durable but actually appears to be permanent. This means that "forgetting" occurs in LTM not because the memory is erased but because we are unable to retrieve it for some reason (Baddeley, 1999; Matlin, 1983).

4. Each stage of memory is handled by a different part of the brain. STM is primarily a function of the frontal lobes of the cerebral cortex (Buckner & Barch, 1999; Fuster, 1995; Williams & Goldman-Rakic, 1995), whereas information that is stored in LTM is first integrated in the hippocampus and then transferred to the areas of the cerebral cortex involved in language and perception for permanent storage (Nadel & Jacobs, 1998).

We will describe these differences in more detail in the final section of this chapter.

Types of Long-Term Memory: Procedural, Episodic, and Semantic

Tulving (1972, 1985, 1987) has proposed the existence of three kinds of long-term memory storage, each with distinctly different properties, and each probably based on different brain mechanisms. Recently, I came across a photograph taken of me on my fourteenth birthday in my home in St. Petersburg, Florida. I was holding my birthday present—my first guitar. I took guitar lessons for a while and played in several mediocre rock bands until my junior year in college. Then, I sold my guitar and concentrated on my studies. About 15 years ago, however, I bought another guitar, and playing guitar once again became a part of my life. That's the story; now for the three types of LTM:

1. When I picked up my new guitar in the music store, I found that I could still play the basic chords, even though I had not played them in years. That is a long-term **procedural memory**—memory for skills and other procedures. Memories of how to ride a bicycle, to fry an egg, or to kiss are procedural memories.

2. Although I did not stop to think about it, I also obviously remembered what a guitar was. I knew what it was when I saw it, knew what it was used for, and so on. In other words, I had not forgotten the semantic memory of the meaning of *guitar*. **Semantic memory** is memory for meaning. When you remember what a father is, what pudding is, and what the phrase "peace of mind" means, you are recalling meaning from long-term semantic memory.

3. Until my memory was jogged by finding the old photograph, however, it had been years since I had remembered when and where I had gotten my first guitar. **Episodic memory** is the kind of LTM that stores information about experiences that took place at specific times and in specific places.

The LTM mechanisms are apparently able to store procedural and semantic memories quite effectively, but LTM handles episodic information much less well. I immediately knew what a guitar was (semantic) and how to play it (procedural), but it took a photograph to recall the time and place of getting my first guitar (episodic). A great deal of research has been done to show the greater ability of LTM to store semantic than episodic memories. A clever study of the memorization of sentences by J. D. S. Sachs (1967) clearly illustrates this point. The experimenter had research participants listen to passages containing a number of different sentences. After intervals of different lengths, she asked the individuals to listen to more sentences and tell her whether they were exactly the same as one of the sentences in the passage. Some of the test sentences were the same, but some were changed either in physical form or in meaning. For example, an original sentence in the passage such as "Jenny chased Melissa" might be changed to "Melissa was chased by Jenny" (change in physical structure, but not meaning) or to "Melissa chased Jenny" (change in both physical structure and meaning). Sachs found that the participants could tell quite well if a sentence had been changed in either way, as long as the test interval was within the span of STM (about 30 seconds). However, at longer intervals, they were only accurate in detecting changes in meaning. Apparently, the meaning of the sentences (semantic memory) was held in LTM, whereas details about their physical structure (episodic memory) were forgotten when they were lost from STM.

Organization in Long-Term Memory

We noted earlier that it's possible to make more efficient use of the limited capacity of STM by organizing information into larger chunks (Miller, 1956). Organization of information is also important for LTM, but it's probably not related to a need to save capacity, because LTM has essentially unlimited capacity. Rather, organization helps to facilitate the retrieval of information from the vast amount stored in LTM. The retrieval task in LTM is vastly different from that in STM: Instead of 7 ± 2 items that can be easily searched, LTM stores such an extensive amount of information that it almost certainly must be *organized* in some fashion. For instance, it's sometimes inconvenient that the 60-odd books in my

---

procedural memory
Memory for motor movements and skills.

semantic memory
(se-man′tik)   Memory for meaning without reference to the time and place of learning.

episodic memory
(epī-sod-ik)   Memory for specific experiences that can be defined in terms of time and space.

office are not organized on my bookshelves, but I can still find what I am looking for by searching long enough. It would be impossible, on the other hand, to find the same book in the university library if the books were as unorganized and randomly placed on the shelves as mine. Like LTM, the library needs an organized way of storing and retrieving a huge amount of information.

Evidence for the organization of LTM has been available for some time. When research participants memorize new lists of items that could be categorized, they tend to recall them in related groups. For example, Weston Bousfield (1953) asked individuals to memorize a list of 60 words that could be conceptually grouped into four categories: animals, vegetables, names, and professions (*muskrat, blacksmith, panther, baker, wildcat, Howard, Jason, printer,* and so on). Even though the words were presented in random order, participants recalled them in categorical groupings significantly more often than would be expected by chance. Apparently, the words were stored in LTM according to organized categories.

In addition, there is clear evidence that recall from LTM is better when we impose more organization on the information that is stored there. Gordon Bower's Stanford University research group (Bower & Clark, 1969) asked participants to memorize 12 lists of 10 words, such as the following:

boy
boat
dog
wagon
ghost
rag
wheel
hat
house
milk

Half of the individuals were given the usual instructions to memorize the lists of words in any order, but the others were asked to "make up stories" containing all of the words in the list—to organize them into a single story. For example, the previous list could be memorized as "The boy with the hat pulled his dog and his boat in his wagon with the crooked wheel. He saw a rag hanging on a house that he thought was a ghost. It scared him so much that he spilled his milk." The group that organized the words into stories recalled an amazing 90 percent of the 12 lists of words, whereas the other group recalled only 15 percent!

The organization of memory in LTM has been characterized as an *associative network* by some theorists (Ellis & Hunt, 1993; Raaijmakers & Shiffrin, 1992). According to this view, memories are associated, or linked together, through experience. Your experience forms links between that special song and memories of your summer vacation, or between algebra and that unbearable teacher. Researchers have studied the operation of associative networks by asking research participants to answer general knowledge questions. For instance, suppose you were asked to answer the question "Is a canary a bird?" How do you access your store of information to answer correctly? An influential network model known as the *spreading activation model* (Collins & Loftus, 1975) attempts to explain this process. According to Collins and Loftus, we form links between various concepts and their characteristics based on our experience. When we are asked a question, representations of the concepts or characteristics are activated. As shown in figure 6.3, the question would activate separate memory representations of *canary* and *bird.* The model then assumes that this activation spreads out along previously formed links to other representations. In the case of *canary* and *bird,* which are very closely associated for many people, the lines of activation spreading from these representations meet quickly, and a decision can be made. If representations are not as closely associated, it takes a longer time to respond. If you were asked whether or not a penguin is a bird, your answer would probably be slower than in the canary example.

Like a library, LTM organizes information to facilitate retrieval.

FIGURE 6.3

An example of the associative links that are hypothesized to exist among bits of information stored in long-term memory in the spreading activation theory.

"Hey, good buddy!
How you doin'?"

"Can't kick, big fella.
What's shakin'?"

Serial Position Effect

www.mmhe.com/laheye1

serial position effect
Immediate recall of items listed in a fixed order is often better for items at the beginning and end of the list than for those in the middle.

levels of processing model
An alternative to the stage theory of memory stating that the distinction between short-term and long-term memory is a matter of degree rather than different kinds of memory and is based on how incoming information is processed.

Retrieval of Long-Term Memories

In some types of memory tasks, the order in which we memorize a list is as important as the items in the list. It would be useless to memorize the steps in defusing a bomb if you were not able to remember them in the right order! When psychologists have studied memory for serial lists (lists of words, numbers, and the like that must be recalled in a certain order), a surprisingly consistent finding has emerged. The recall of items in the serial lists is often better for items at the *beginning* and *end* of the list than in the middle. This is called the **serial position effect.** Many explanations have been suggested for this effect, but it's perhaps best explained in terms of the differences between short-term and long-term memory. The last items in a list are remembered well because they are still in STM, whereas the first items in a list are remembered well because they can be rehearsed enough times to transfer them firmly into LTM.

The "Tip-of-the-Tongue" Phenomenon.   We have all had the maddening experience of trying to recall a fact that we can *almost* remember—it's on the "tip of my tongue." Fortunately, there is a lesson in this on the nature of retrieval from LTM. The "tip-of-the-tongue" phenomenon was investigated by Harvard University psychologists Roger Brown and David McNeil (1966) by giving definitions of uncommon words to college students and asking them to recall the words. For example, they might be read the definition of *sampan* ("a small boat used in shallow water in Asia that is rowed from behind using a single oar"). Often, the students could recall the word *sampan.* Sometimes, though, they could not quite recall the word, and the researchers were able to create the tip-of-the-tongue sensation in these students. When this happened, the students found that they were able to recall some information about the word ("It starts with *s*" or "It sounds like *Siam*") or recall something about the thing the word referred to ("It looks a little like a junk"), even when they could not retrieve the word. Then, moments later, the word would pop into memory for some students, proving that it was there all the time but just could not be retrieved for the moment. Studies suggest that about half of the things that we can't remember, but are on the tip of our tongues, are recalled within a minute or so (Schachter, 1999), but you can drive yourself nuts for hours trying to remember the other half!

Levels of Processing: An Alternative to the Stage Model

The model suggesting that there are three separate stages of memory (sensory register, STM, and LTM) has been enormously helpful in making sense of the complex phenomenon of memory. Fergus Craik and Robert Lockhart (1972) have proposed an alternative **levels of processing model,** however, suggesting that the distinction between short-term and long-term memory is a matter of *degree* rather than separate stages. In brief, Craik and Lockhart believe that there is only one memory store beyond the sensory register. The durability of

HUMAN DIVERSITY

CULTURAL CIRCUMSTANCES AND MEMORY SKILLS

Does culture influence even basic intellectual skills, such as memory? Some psychologists believe that our cultural circumstances have a powerful impact on many fundamental aspects of intelligence. For example, psychologist Judith Kearins (1986) hypothesized that Australian aboriginal peoples possessed better visual memory skills for objects than white Australian children. She reasoned that excellent visual memory skills had allowed the aboriginal people to thrive in the challenging desert environments in which many of them live.

In Kearins' experiments, aboriginal and white adolescents were given 30 seconds to memorize the location of objects arranged on a rectangular grid. The experimenter then mixed up the objects, and each adolescent was asked to replace them in their original positions. Two of the tasks involved manufactured objects (matchbox, ring, eraser) and two involved natural objects (twig, seed pod, feather, bone, etc.). The aboriginal adolescents performed significantly better than the white Australians on all of the tasks. The white adolescents performed better when the task material was manufactured objects than they did when the objects were natural, but this distinction did not affect the performance of the aboriginal children.

Kearins found that the aboriginal and white Australian adolescents used different memory strategies to approach the task. The aboriginal adolescents sat very still, were silent, and appeared to concentrate deeply. They were slow and methodical in replacing the objects. Most of the white adolescents, on the other hand, tended to fidget and mutter and replaced the first few objects hurriedly. Kearins speculated that the white children were muttering the verbal labels of the objects in an effort to remember them, whereas the aboriginal children were more likely to memorize the arrangement of the objects in visual terms. Perhaps the different cultures emphasized verbal or visual approaches to memorization because of the importance of those skills in each culture.

Think about your own approach to memorization. How would you have approached the memory task in Kearins' experiment? Would you have memorized the placements of the objects in visual terms, or would you have memorized verbal labels for the objects ("The feather in the top-left, then, moving clockwise, the stick, the weird-looking bone . . .")? What type of information is most important for you to remember to survive in your ethnic group? What cultural differences have you noticed between your community and other ethnic communities in terms of their approach to intellectual skills? Finally, has your ethnic community influenced your approach to memorization and other intellectual skills—and, if so, how has it done so?

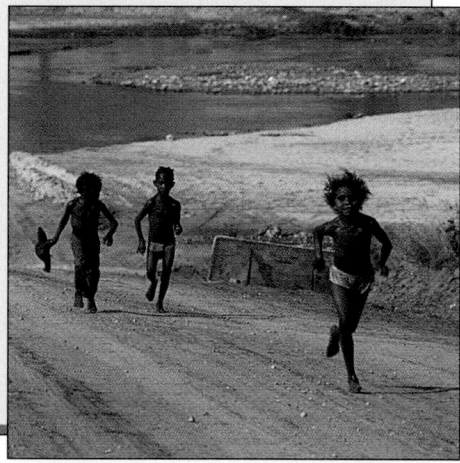

stored information depends on how well it is processed as it is being encoded for memory. Information will be kept only briefly if it's processed at a *shallow* level, but it will be kept much longer if it's processed at a *deeper* level. Thus, the differences that we have just examined between STM and LTM are not, in this view, differences between two different memory systems operating according to different principles. Rather, these differences are the results of different levels of processing during the encoding process. Furthermore, according to Craik and Lockhart, there is a continuum of levels of processing, ranging from very shallow to very deep, rather than just two types of storage (short and long).

What is the difference between deep and shallow processing? One way of putting it is to say that shallow processing involves the encoding of superficial perceptual information, whereas deep processing encodes meaning (Ellis, 1987). Consider the following list of adjectives:

soft
swift
warm
sharp
witty
bright
clean
beautiful

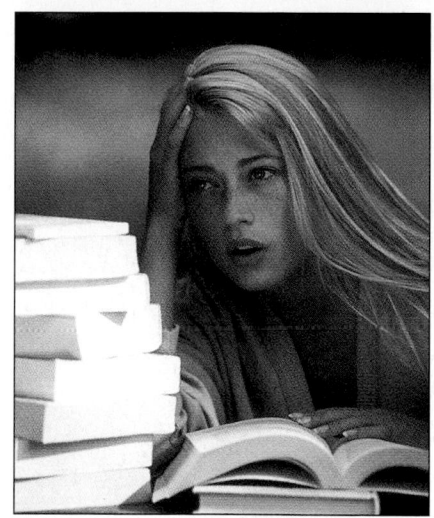

It is possible that all information stored in long-term memory is still there but cannot always be retrieved.

If you were to ask 10 acquaintances to process this list in a superficial way ("Look at each word for 5 seconds; then circle the adjectives containing the letter *i*") and ask 10 other acquaintances to process it in a deep way ("Look at each word for 5 seconds; then circle the adjectives that describe you"), which group do you think would remember more of the words if, without warning, you asked them to recall the list 10 minutes later? Craik and Lockhart's levels of processing view correctly predicts that the individuals who processed the words deeply by thinking about their meanings (the second group) will recall more of the words—not because they had stored the words in a different memory (LTM vs. STM) but because information processed more deeply is stored more permanently.

Deep processing also involves greater *elaboration* of memories during the encoding phase than does shallow processing. **Elaboration,** in this sense, means creating more associations between the new memory and existing memories (Ellis, 1987; Ellis & Hunt, 1993). For example, if you read a paragraph in a textbook and spend a few minutes relating its contents to what you had learned in the previous chapters or to your own life, you are elaborating the memory—linking it to existing memories. We have already seen how the associative network model assumes that these links are vital to your ability to use stored information. Therefore, deeply processing the new information in this way will improve your memory of the paragraph and your ability to use the information later. In contrast, simply going through the motions of rereading a paragraph several times without really thinking about it is a much less successful study technique. What is also interesting about this view of deep processing is that even superficial perceptual information can be richly elaborated, such as by relating a new telephone number to existing memories about the person you are calling. Many studies suggest that one of the best ways to promote the elaboration of new memories to improve their later recall is to relate the new information to *yourself* (Symons & Johnson, 1997). Because your perceptions of yourself are well-elaborated and accessible in memory, linking new information to yourself is an excellent way to improve memory through deep processing. The next time you read a textbook (from English literature to physics), try relating every new fact or concept to yourself in some way—it should improve your memory for that information later (Symons & Johnson, 1997).

The levels of processing view probably will not replace the STM/LTM stage model. This is not to say that the levels of processing view of memory is unimportant, however. It is a useful reminder to us that information that is learned in a shallow, rote manner will not be around in our memories very long. If you want to retain information for a long time and have the ability to retrieve it easily, you need to take the time and effort to understand and elaborate the information as you learn it.

elaboration
(e-lab″ or-rā′ shun)   The process of creating associations between a new memory and existing memories.

● Review

We can think of human memory as being composed of three different, but related, stages of memory. The sensory register holds a replica of the visual, auditory, or other sensory input for a very brief interval while relevant information is selected for further processing. Short-term memory holds information, generally as acoustic codes, for about a half minute unless it's renewed through rehearsal. The capacity of short-term memory is quite limited unless information is organized into larger chunks. Long-term memory stores information primarily in terms of its meaning, or semantic codes. Its capacity is very large, and memories stored there seem to be permanent. The store of information in LTM is so vast that it must be organized to facilitate retrieval of information. Current theories suggest that the organization is primarily in terms of categories of meaning or associative networks.

The division of memory into a distinct STM and LTM has been questioned by some theorists, however. They suggest, instead, that the duration that information can be held in memory depends on the *depth* at which it's processed, not the *stage* of memory in which it's held. Information that is processed deeply—more richly elaborated—during the encoding process is stored more permanently than information that is processed in a shallow way.

● Check Your Learning

To be sure that you have learned the key points from the preceding section, cover the list of correct answers and try to answer each question. If you give an incorrect answer to any question, return to the page given next to the correct answer to see why your answer was not correct. Remember that these questions cover only some of the important information in this section; it is important that you make up your own questions to check your learning of other facts and concepts.

1. The _____ assumes that we humans have a three-stage memory, which meets our need to store information for different lengths of time.

   a) lateral processing theory of memory

   b) stage theory of memory

   c) psychoanalytic theory of memory

   d) progression theory of memory

2. The first stage in memory is the _____, which holds an exact image of each sensory experience for a very brief time until it can be fully processed.

   a) short-term memory

   b) primary store

   c) sensory register

   d) initial memory store

3. The _____ is used to store information temporarily and to think while holding information in "working memory."

   a) short-term memory

   b) long-term memory

   c) sensory register

   d) primary store

4. Long-term memory is similar to short-term memory in terms of the way in which information is recalled, the reason forgetting occurs, and the form in which information is usually stored.

   a) True

   b) False

5. The _____ is a memory model suggesting that the distinction between short-term and long-term memory is a matter of degree rather than separate stages.

● Thinking Critically About Psychology

1. Semantic memories are more durable than episodic memories in long-term memory. This is sometimes inconvenient, but is it also advantageous in some ways?

2. Can you think of some episodic memories that have stayed especially clear through the years? What is it about those events that has caused them to be so durable?

Correct Answers 1. b (p. 174), **2. c** (p. 174), **3. a** (pp. 175–177), **4. b** (p. 177), **5.** levels of processing model (p. 180).

▌ FORGETTING AND WHY IT OCCURS

So far we have talked about remembering and forgetting in terms of the three stages of memory. We have noted that forgetting is different in STM than in LTM, but we have skirted the issue of the causes of forgetting. Why do some memories become lost or irretrievable? What causes forgetting to occur? There are four major theories of forgetting that should be discussed in some detail: *decay theory,* which states that time alone causes memory traces to fade; *interference theory,* which suggests that other memories interfere with remembering; *schema theory,* which proposes that memory traces become

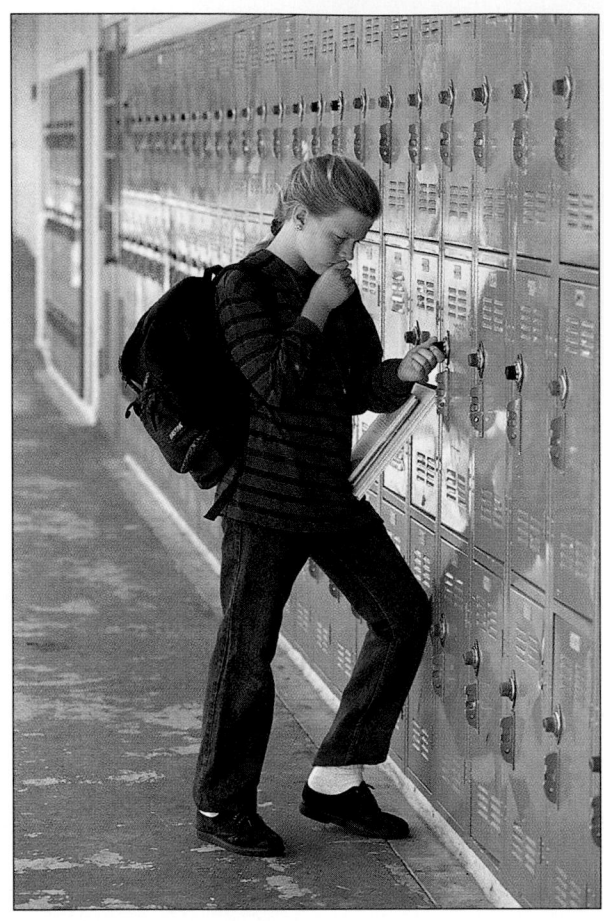

Forget the combination? According to the decay theory, forgetting occurs because time passes.

distorted with time, sometimes to the point of becoming unrecognizable; and the *theory of motivated forgetting,* which suggests that we forget information that is unpleasant or threatening.

Decay Theory

According to **decay theory,** memories that are not used fade gradually over time. This theory has been around for a long time and fits our commonsense understanding of forgetting. It had been discarded by psychologists as being wholly incorrect until recent years, however. As we will see in a moment, forgetting is more complicated than the mere fading of memory traces and involves factors other than time. The acceptance by most psychologists of some version of the three-stage conception of memory has brought the decay theory back into limited favor, however. It appears that the simple passage of time is a cause of forgetting, both in the sensory register and in STM. It does not appear that decay due to the passage of time is a cause of forgetting in LTM, however. Memory "traces" appear to be "permanent" once they make it into LTM. Forgetting does not seem to happen in LTM because of disuse over time but because other factors, particularly *interference,* make memories irretrievable.

Interference Theory

Interference theory is based on considerable evidence that forgetting in LTM does not occur because of the passage of time but, rather, because other memories interfere with the retrieval of what you are trying to recall, particularly if the other memories are similar to the one you are trying to remember. Suppose you take an interest in French impressionist painters and you read a book about the painting techniques of Degas, Monet, and Matisse. It would be no great feat to memorize each painter's techniques and keep them straight, but suppose you then learn about the techniques of three more French impressionists, and then three more. Pretty soon, recall becomes difficult, partly because the similar memories interfere with the retrieval of one another. This also happens when you try to remember a lot of telephone numbers, grocery-list items, or math formulas.

Psychologists refer to the interference built up by *prior* learning as **proactive interference** and to interference created by *later* learning as **retroactive interference.** Suppose you meet two interesting people, Rolf and Kate, on your first day of vacation at the beach. First, Rolf tells you his room number, as you listen carefully and commit it to memory. Later, Kate tells you her room number and you memorize it. Later, you try to go to Kate's room and, oops, you can't remember the number. You are the victim of *proactive interference.* The recall of Kate's number was blocked by interference from the memorization of the number that *preceded* it.

decay theory
The theory that forgetting occurs as the memory trace fades over time.

interference theory
The theory that forgetting occurs because similar memories interfere with the storage or retrieval of information.

proactive interference
(prō-ak´ tiv) Interference created by memories from prior learning.

retroactive interference
(ret˝ rō-ak´ tiv) Interference created by memories from later learning.

Proactive Interference

Rolf's number 8136

Kate's number 6213

Try to recall Kate's number 8136/6213

On the other hand, if you had tried to recall Rolf's number rather than Kate's, you might not have been able to remember it due to *retroactive interference.* The prefix *retro* means "going back." Hence, in retroactive interference, the second memorization interferes with recall of what was memorized before it.

Retroactive Interference

8136   Rolf's number

6213   Kate's number

8236   Try to recall Rolf's number

Up to this point, we have talked about interference as a cause of forgetting, or retrieval failure, in LTM. Interference is also a cause of forgetting in STM, but it may operate in a different way to disrupt memory. Whereas interference appears to confuse the process of retrieval in LTM, interfering memories seem to disrupt STM either by overloading its capacity or by weakening or completely knocking an item out of storage (Klatzky, 1980). If you look up the telephone number 689-2354 and someone says, "Maybe it's 698-5423," before you can dial, you may experience interference in STM.

Although much experimental evidence supports the interference theory of forgetting in both STM and LTM, we should not be too quick in deciding that it's the only factor involved in forgetting. For one thing, nearly all of the research evidence on interference in LTM concerns memory for isolated facts, even though LTM is better suited for storing meaning. Tulving (1972) reminds us that, in a memory experiment, it is a very different matter to forget that the list we were supposed to memorize included the word *frog* than to forget what a frog is.

Schema Theory

First presented in 1932 by Sir Fredric Bartlett, the theory that is known today as **schema theory** suggests that information stored in LTM is not forgotten in the usual sense but sometimes is recalled in a distorted, incorrect manner (Roediger & McDermott, 2000; Schachter, 1999). *Schemas* are beliefs, knowledge, and expectations. Long-term memories often become distorted because they change over time to become more consistent with our schemas. For example, imagine that you hear a story about a guy named Max, whom you believe is a rotten person. The story is favorable to him on most points but contains some negative information about him. The next day, when you tell this story to a friend, you will tend to recall the negative points about him and minimize the positive points. Because your schema for Max is negative you may unknowingly add a few fictional details that embellish the negative parts of the story or "explain away" the positive things that were said about him. Would you trust someone who doesn't like you to recall accurately a story about you?

The distortion of memories to fit our schema was demonstrated in a classic experiment (Carmichael, Hogan, & Walter, 1932). Researchers showed the participants ambiguous line drawings, as shown in the middle column of figure 6.4 (labeled "stimulus figures"). The participants were given verbal labels, telling them what each figure represented, but two groups of individuals were given different labels for each figure (shown in the figure as "word list I" and "word list II"). For example, half of the participants were told that the second figure in figure 6.4 was a "bottle," whereas the other half were told that it was a "stirrup." Later the participants were asked to draw the figures that they had seen from memory. As predicted by schema theory, the drawings were distorted to fit the labels that they had been given for the ambiguous figures.

The distortion of memories to fit our schemas does not occur gradually over time but occurs during the process of retrieval itself (Reynolds & Flagg, 1983). Indeed the distorting effect of the labels is even more dramatic when research participants are given the

schema theory
The theory that information stored in LTM sometimes changes over time to become more consistent with our beliefs, knowledge, and expectations.

FIGURE 6.4

Individuals were shown the list of stimulus figures presented in the middle column along with one of the two word lists. As can be seen in the left and right columns, the figures they drew later were reconstructed to fit the labels they had learned for them.

Source: Redrawn from L. Carmichael, H. P. Hogan, and A. A. Walter, "An Experimental Study of the Effect of Language on the Reproduction of Visually Perceived Form" in *Journal of Experimental Psychology,* 15:78–86, 1932.

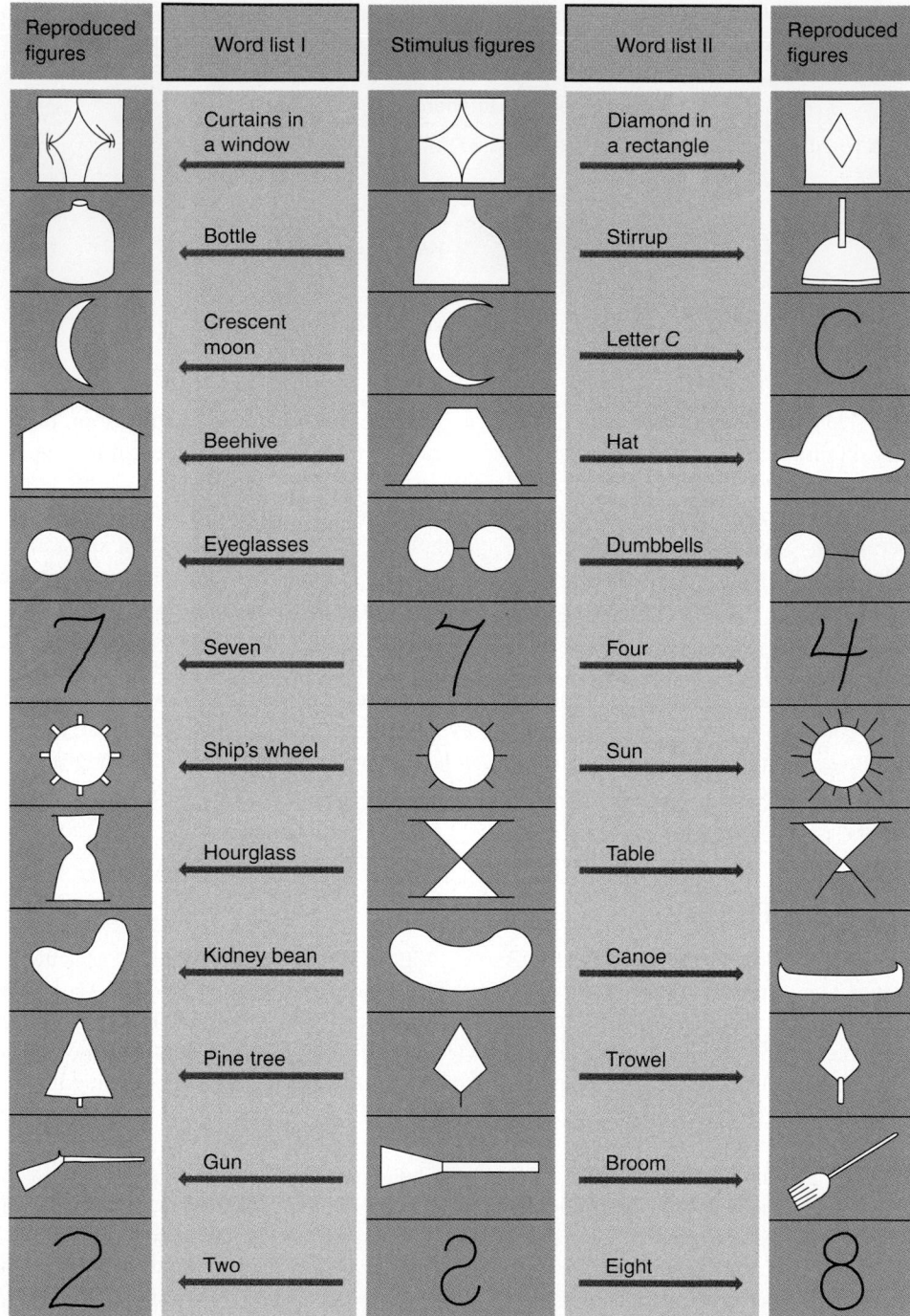

Reproduced figures	Word list I	Stimulus figures	Word list II	Reproduced figures
	Curtains in a window		Diamond in a rectangle	
	Bottle		Stirrup	
	Crescent moon		Letter *C*	
	Beehive		Hat	
	Eyeglasses		Dumbbells	
	Seven		Four	
	Ship's wheel		Sun	
	Hourglass		Table	
	Kidney bean		Canoe	
	Pine tree		Trowel	
	Gun		Broom	
	Two		Eight	

labels (*bottle, stirrup,* etc.) *just before* they are asked to draw the shapes (Hanawalt & Demarest, 1939; Ranken, 1963).

Until recent years, schema theory has had little impact on research on memory, perhaps because Bartlett (1932) originally stated this theory in rather vague terms. Over the past 20 years, however, it has become an important focus for memory researchers (Schachter, 1999). Recent versions of schema theory are based on the distinction between episodic and semantic memory. For example, John Bransford and Jeffrey Franks (1971) suggested that some information in LTM becomes distorted to fit our schemas because LTM stores *meaning* better than episodic details. When we retrieve information from LTM, we are likely to remember the gist—the general idea—of the event, but we may unknowingly distort some details, or even invent details to be consistent with the general idea.

Bransford and his associates tested this version of schema theory in the following experiment (Johnson, Bransford, & Solomon, 1973). Research participants listened to passages such as the following:

> It was late at night when the phone rang and a voice gave a frantic cry. The spy threw the secret document into the fireplace just 30 seconds before it would have been too late.

Later, the participants were asked if they had heard the following sentence.

> The spy burned the secret document 30 seconds before it would have been too late.

Notice that this is not a sentence that they had previously heard; the original sentence said nothing about actually burning the document (there might not have been a fire in the fireplace). Most participants, however, said that they had heard the second sentence. According to Bransford and colleagues, the meaning of the sentence, which strongly implies that the document was burned, was retrieved from LTM, but the details were distorted to fit the gist of the story.

We saw in chapter 3 that the human brain actively constructs complete perceptions out of the limited information provided by the senses, such as filling in the "blind spot" in visual perception. Schema theory suggests that we also sometimes construct complete memories from minimal information, or distort memories to make them more consistent. As Bartlett (1932) said, memory is partly an "imaginative reconstruction" of experience that is guided by schemas. Unfortunately, these creatively distorted memories often take on the appearance of "facts."

motivated forgetting
Forgetting that is believed to be based on the upsetting or threatening nature of the information that is forgotten.

repression
Sigmund Freud's theory that forgetting occurs because the conscious mind often deals with unpleasant information by pushing it into unconsciousness.

Theory of Motivated Forgetting

Many years ago, Sigmund Freud suggested that we forget some information because it's threatening to us in some way. We will have much more to say about the theory of **motivated forgetting** in chapter 11 on personality. Freud believed that the conscious mind often dealt with unpleasant or dangerous information by pushing it into unconsciousness, by an act of **repression.** This theory of forgetting has not been extensively tested in the laboratory, but support has come from a number of clinical case studies. There are many well-documented cases of memory loss for highly stressful events, such as auto accidents and crimes (Elliott, 1997; Squire, 1987).

This type of evidence is not strongly supportive of the theory, however, for two reasons. First, because case histories do not involve careful experimental control, other causes of memory loss are often possible, such as a blow to the head in an automobile accident. Second, as we will see in a later section, it may be that the effect of the stressful event is to disrupt the biological process of consolidating the memory trace in LTM, rather than to cause the memory to be repressed.

The Complicated Relationship Between Emotion and Memory

In recent years, it has become clear that the relationship between emotion and memory is more complex than first assumed by Freud. Emotional arousal does not always lead to poor memory—sometimes emotional arousal improves memory in some ways.

A series of well-controlled laboratory studies by psychologist Michael Bock (1986; Bock & Klinger, 1986) examined

According to Freud, motivated forgetting can occur as a result of repressing details of stressful events.

the relationship between emotional arousal and memory. When individuals were shown a list of words and asked to recall them later, they were better able to recall words with positive emotional impact (such as *kiss* and *prize*) than words with negative emotional impact (such as *disease* and *loss*). However, words with neutral emotional impact were recalled least well in Bock's studies. This suggests that, although Freud was correct in saying that negative events are recalled less well than positive events, experiences with any type of emotional impact appear to be easier to recall than neutral experiences.

Although negative emotional arousal leads to better recall than no emotional arousal, our memories of events that are associated with negative emotional arousal are often rather different from other memories, particularly when the negative emotional arousal is intense. Our memories of intensely negative events tend to be vivid but are often disorganized and confused (Nadel & Jacobs, 1998).

Vivid memories for emotional events have been termed *flashbulb memories* (Brown & Kulik, 1977). I can clearly recall some parts of the day of the assassination of President John Kennedy, and one particularly disturbing newscast describing atrocities committed by American soldiers during the Vietnam War still sticks with me. Both seem like flash photos printed on my brain, but it is likely that some of the elements of these vivid memories are confused or distorted (Nadel & Jacobs, 1998).

Where were you when you first heard about the verdict in the controversial O.J. Simpson murder trial? Were you at home? At school? Did you hear it on television or did someone tell you? Researchers at the University of California in San Diego (Schmolck, Buffalo, & Squire, 2000) asked students in a psychology class similar questions 3 days after the verdict was announced and then asked the same question 1 year and 3 years later. Three days after the verdict, virtually all of the students had a vivid, emotional "flashbulb memory" of learning the verdict. A year later, only 11 percent of the recollections of this event were highly distorted (remembering being told by your father at home instead of hearing the verdict on the radio when alone in your car), but after three years, 40 percent of the recollections were highly distorted.

● Review

There are four major causes of forgetting, each with different relevance to the three stages of memory. Forgetting in the sensory register seems to occur primarily because of simple decay of the memory over time. Forgetting in short-term memory can be attributed to decay over time, but also to interference from other similar information stored in memory. Interference from other memories explains some forgetting in long-term memory, but information also appears to be recalled inaccurately from LTM because it is distorted to be more consistent with our current schemas (beliefs, knowledge, and expectations) about that information. Recall of information about positive events appears to be better than recall of information about negative events. Therefore, Freud may have been partially correct that some memories may be less accessible because they are associated with negative emotions (motivated forgetting). Overall, however, both positive and negative emotional arousal appear to facilitate memory. Memories of intensely emotional events tend to be particularly vivid, but often became distorted over time.

● Check Your Learning

To be sure that you have learned the key points from the preceding section, cover the list of correct answers and try to answer each question. If you give an incorrect answer to any question, return to the page given next to the correct answer to see why your answer was not correct.

1. According to _____ theory, forgetting occurs simply because the memory trace fades as time passes.

   a) decay   c) diminishing

   b) disintegration   d) decline

2. _____ theory states that forgetting occurs because similar memories block the storage or retrieval of information.

   a) Disruption   c) Disturbance

   b) Interference   d) Freudian

3. _____ theory suggests that some memories become so distorted over time that they are unrecognizable.

   a) Schema   c) Retrieval

   b) Destruction   d) Distortion

4. Forgetting that occurs because the memory is upsetting or threatening is termed _____ .

● Thinking Critically About Psychology

1. Suppose you have started a company that manufactures cameras. Design an experiment to see if teaching the same employees to do two different assembly tasks produces proactive interference.

2. Based on your understanding of the four major causes of forgetting, what improvements could you make in your general study habits to improve your test performance?

Correct Answers   1. a (p. 184),   2. b (p. 184),   3. a (p. 185),   4. motivated forgetting (p. 187).

▶ BIOLOGICAL BASIS OF MEMORY

A great deal has been learned about memory in recent years through the study of the role of the brain in the storage and retrieval of information. This boom in knowledge not only gives us a better understanding of the brain, but also helps us understand memory.

Synaptic Theories of Memory: Search for the Engram

It's obvious that some physical change must take place in the nervous system when we learn something new (Baddeley, 1998; McGaugh, 1983). If some physical change did not occur, how would we be able to recall the new learning at a later time? The "something" that remains after learning—the **engram** as early memory researcher Karl Lashley called it—is the biological basis of memory. Although neuroscientists have searched for the engram for a long time, there is not yet a full consensus as to what or where it is. However, this is one of the most active areas in psychological research, and much is already known.

    A theory stated many years ago by Canadian researcher Donald Hebb (1949) is still considered to provide an accurate model of the physiological processes responsible for learning and memory (Jeffrey & Reid, 1997). According to Hebb, **synaptic facilitation** is the biological basis of learning and memory. Individual experiences result in unique patterns of neural activity, which "reverberate" through neural loops. This causes structural changes in the synapses to occur. These changes make firing in the loop more likely in the future. In other words, synapses become more efficient, or facilitated. Thus, for Hebb, changes in the synapses are the biological basis of memory.

    In a series of clever experiments conducted on sea snails (*Aplysia*), Eric Kandel and his associates (Dale & Kandel, 1990; Dash, Hochner, & Kandel, 1990; Kandel & Schwartz, 1982) have provided evidence that strongly supports Hebb's synaptic theory. Sea snails were chosen for study because they have very simple nervous systems in which it is easy to study individual neurons. In one key study (Castelluci & Kandel, 1976), the snails were classically conditioned to withdraw their gills and water siphons. First, the snails were

Engram

www.mmhe.com/laheye1

engram
(en´gram)   The as yet unidentified memory trace in the brain that is the biological basis of memory.

synaptic facilitation
The process by which neural activity causes structural changes in the synapses that facilitate more efficient learning and memory.

Aplysia, the sea snail that opened new vistas to understanding the cellular basis of learning and memory.

prepared for the study by gently touching the siphons many times. Ordinarily, sea snails retract their gills and siphons at the slightest stimulation, but they soon habituate to being touched and stop withdrawing their gills and siphons. Then, the classical conditioning began: Each snail's siphon was touched (CS); then the snail was given a mild electric shock (UCS), which caused the withdrawal of the gill and siphon (UCR). Later, when the snail was touched (CS), the gill and siphon were withdrawn (CR). (See p. 145 if you don't remember what the terms CS, UCS, UCR, and CR mean.)

The change in the synapses was studied by measuring the amount of neurotransmitter in the neuronal connections involved in the withdrawal of the gills and siphons. In the first part of the study, as each sea snail stopped withdrawing its gill and siphon when touched, the amount of neurotransmitter present at the synapse *declined;* however, after classical conditioning, the amount of neurotransmitter *increased.* Thus, Hebb appears to be correct—at least for some forms of simple learning, the learning is "remembered" at the synapse. Several groups of scientists have published evidence that suggests that the changes in the synapses are based on changes in their proteins for LTM, but not for STM (Ezell, 1994). This finding is important not only for understanding the biological basis of memory but also for indicating that STM and LTM are based on different processes in the brain.

Stages of Memory and the Brain

Some advances in our understanding of the brain's role in memory in recent years help us understand the different types of memory. I have illustrated the major brain structures involved in the three stages of memory in figure 6.5. As more is learned about the brain, this description will probably prove to be an oversimplification, but it gives you a reasonable overview of current knowledge of how the brain stores information. Consider this example: In 1990, I saw the Rocky Mountains for the first time, and I still have a clear recollection of one part of the trip. As we drove up to the mountain that the Shoshoni people named "Going to the Sun," the amazing visual stimuli from the mountain pass traveled from my eyes to the thalamus, where it was routed to the visual area of the occipital cortex (part 1 of figure 6.5). This neural activity briefly held the trace that we call the sensory register. If I had closed my eyes at that time, I would have been able to recall the visual image from the sensory register and could have kept the memory active in STM for a while in the frontal lobes of the cerebral cortex (part 2 of fig. 6.5) (Goldman-Rakic, 1992).

Because I can still recall this scene, it must have been stored temporarily and integrated in the hippocampus (Nadel & Jacobs, 1998). The hippocampus plays a key role in the transfer of information from STM to LTM (Kandel & Hawkins, 1992), but the visual image was stored permanently in the occipital lobe, where it was first processed (part 3 of figure 6.5). As I recall this memory now, my frontal lobes play the key role (part 4 of figure 6.5) (Schachter, 1999; Smith, 2000). If my experience in the Rockies had involved a negative emotion—such as my almost driving off the road as I marveled at the gorgeous view—my amygdala would also have played a role in the formation of the memory (Kandel, 1999).

Recent advances in understanding the role of brain structures may help explain why memories for events associated with intense negative emotions (flashbulb memories) tend to be vivid but disorganized (Adolphs, Tranel, & Denburg, 2000; Nadel & Jacobs, 1998). Events that create intense negative emotional arousal activate the amygdala, and its involvement tends to improve recall. On the other hand, negative emotional arousal stimulates the release of the adrenal stress hormone, cortisol, which inhibits the hippocampus (Nadel & Jacobs, 1998; Newcomer & others, 1999; Schachter, 1999). Because the hippocampus organizes the elements of complex memories that are stored in different parts of the cortex, inhibition of the hippocampus appears to result in a lack of organization in emotionally charged memories, which may make distortions more likely (Nadel & Jacobs, 1998).

1. Visual information is first routed through the thalamus to the visual area of the cerebral cortex. This neural activity is the basis for the sensory register.

2. The information is then relayed to the frontal lobes, where it can be held in short-term memory.

3. Information that is stored in long-term memory is then held in the hippocampus for weeks or months, and then transferred to the area of the cerebral cortex near where it was originally processed for long-term storage.

4. When we recall information from long-term memory, it is routed again to the frontal lobes, where it is held in short-term (or "working") memory.

FIGURE 6.5
Stages of memory and the brain.

Amnesia: Disorders of Memory

Major disorders of memory deserve our attention, both because they are important conditions in their own right and because of what they tell us about the biological basis of memory. We will begin with a clinical case history describing an individual who suffers from severe memory loss, known as *anterograde amnesia,* as a result of brain surgery. His tragic case tells us much about memory disorders and vividly shows how important an intact memory is for the normal experience of life.

Anterograde Amnesia

Anterograde amnesia, a disorder of memory characterized by an inability to consciously retrieve new information in LTM, is well exemplified in the case history of H. M. (Milner, Corkin, & Teuber, 1968). H. M. began suffering major epileptic seizures at the age of 10. The *seizures* increased in frequency to about once a week by age 27, despite the use of antiseizure medications, leading his neurosurgeon to conclude that surgery must be performed to stop them. The surgery destroyed several brain structures important in memory. The procedure dramatically reduced the incidence of the seizures but left H. M. with severe anterograde amnesia. He retained his above-average intelligence and had nearly normal memory for anything that had been stored in LTM *prior* to the surgery, but he had severe memory deficits for events that occurred *after* the surgery.

H. M.'s short-term memory was generally normal after the surgery. Like most people, he could retain verbal information in STM for about 15 seconds without rehearsal and

anterograde amnesia
(an-ter′ō-grād)   Disorder of memory characterized by an inability to store and/or retrieve new information in long-term memory.

could retain it for longer intervals if he was allowed to rehearse it. However, H. M. had serious problems in *storing new information in LTM* and then retrieving it. He had almost no knowledge of current events because he forgot the news as soon as it slipped out of STM. He could read the same magazine over and over because it was "new" to him each time. He had no idea what time of day it was unless he had just looked at a clock; and generally he could not remember that his father had died since H. M.'s operation.

The most dramatic disruption caused by his memory problems, however, was to his social life. Although he could recognize friends, tell you their names, and relate stories about them, he could do so only if he had met them before the surgery. People that H. M. met after the surgery remained, in effect, permanent strangers to him. Each time a person came to his house, he had to learn the person's name again, but he could remember it for no more than 15 seconds or so unless he continued to rehearse it. This effectively meant that H. M. was incapable of forming new social relationships—a poignant but dramatic lesson in how important a basic cognitive function such as memory is to our lives.

H. M.'s inability to make new use of LTM was not total, however. His ability to learn and retain perceptual and motor skills in LTM (procedural memory) remained good, allowing him to learn to perform employable skills under supervision. However, he had to be reminded each day what new skills he had learned to perform; if he left his job for a short while, he could not remember what kind of work it was that he did. Similarly, when other individuals with anterograde amnesia have been taught to play a simple tune on the piano, they have been able to play it the next day but are surprised by their ability to do so because they have no recollection of being taught to play the tune the day before (Hirst, 1982). Thus, the difficulties experienced by the anterograde amnesia patient in using LTM are highly selective; some kinds of long-term memories are affected, whereas others are not.

What caused H. M. to have this peculiar and sadly debilitating form of memory disorder? What happened to him during the surgery that damaged his ability to make new use of LTM? The key biological structure that was damaged in H. M.'s surgery, and is often damaged in anterograde amnesia, is the **hippocampus** (Kandel & Hawkins, 1992; Scoville & Milner, 1957). As noted earlier in the chapter, this brain structure is believed to govern the transfer of memories from STM to LTM. The case of H. M. also suggests that the hippocampus plays an important role in declarative memory, but not procedural memory (Squire, 1987; Squire, Knowlton, & Musen, 1993). Persons with anterograde amnesia like H. M. perform very badly on long-term episodic memory tasks but perform as well as normal individuals on procedural memory tasks (Graf, Squire, & Mandler, 1984; Squire & others, 1993).

Anterograde amnesia also can be caused by brain tumors, lack of oxygen to the brain, damage to blood vessels in the brain, senility, and severe nutritional deficiencies. In addition, hard blows to the head can cause anterograde amnesia, although it's often only a temporary condition (Hirst, 1982).

Retrograde Amnesia

Some individuals are unable to recall information from the past; that is, they cannot retrieve old long-term memories. **Retrograde amnesia** is just the opposite of anterograde amnesia, then, in that old rather than new long-term memories cannot be recalled. As in anterograde amnesia, however, there is typically little or no disruption of STM. Generally, the period of memory loss is not for the individual's entire lifetime. Rather, it extends back in time from the beginning of the disorder. Memory might be lost for a period of minutes, days, or even years (Kapur, 1999).

Retrograde amnesia can be caused by seizures, brain damage of various sorts, a blow to the head, or highly stressful events. When retrograde amnesia has been caused by seizures or by stress, it generally occurs alone. When it has been caused by brain damage or a blow to the head, however, it generally occurs along with anterograde amnesia. Indeed, most brain-damaged individuals with anterograde amnesia also experience retrograde amnesia for the period of a few days or weeks prior to the onset of their amnesia (Hirst, 1982).

Both anterograde and retrograde amnesia are experienced by individuals with **Korsakoff's syndrome,** a disorder caused by prolonged loss of the vitamin thiamine from

hippocampus
(hip″ o-kam′ pus)   The forebrain structure believed to play a key role in long-term memory.

retrograde amnesia
(ret′ rō-grād)   A memory disorder characterized by an inability to retrieve old long-term memories, generally for a specific period of time extending back from the beginning of the disorder.

Korsakoff's syndrome
(Kor-sak′ ofs)   A disorder involving both anterograde and retrograde amnesia caused by excessive use of alcohol.

the diet of chronic alcoholics. Because of their extreme degree of memory loss, individuals with Korsakoff's syndrome often engage in *confabulation*—when they cannot remember something that is needed to complete a statement, they make it up. Generally, they are not being knowingly dishonest but are engaging in an exaggerated version of normal reconstructive distortion.

● Review

The memory trace, or engram, must be stored in the brain in some form after learning; otherwise, recall at a later time would not be possible. Theories have been proposed about the specific nature of the engram, suggesting that it's most likely a change at the level of the neural synapse.

A group of disorders involving memory loss, known as amnesia, is instructive to study. Anterograde amnesia is characterized by a normal STM, normal memory for information that was in LTM prior to the onset of the amnesia, but with an inability to retrieve newly learned information from LTM. This condition is almost always caused by brain damage, generally involving the hippocampus. The memory disorder known as retrograde amnesia involves a loss of memory for old long-term memories, usually for a specific period of time extending back from the cause of the amnesia, such as a blow to the head, a stressful event, or a seizure. Chronic alcoholics sometimes experience such extensive brain damage due to nutritional deficiencies that they develop Korsakoff's syndrome, which is marked by both anterograde and retrograde amnesia.

● Check Your Learning

To be sure that you have learned the key points from the preceding section, cover the list of correct answers and try to answer each question. If you give an incorrect answer to any question, return to the page given next to the correct answer to see why your answer was not correct.

1. Scientists study the brain in hopes of discovering the _____, which is the change in the brain that occurs when a "memory trace" is stored.

2. The process of _____, which can produce long-lasting changes in synapses, may be the neural basis of memory formation.

   a) electroconvulsive shock   c) synaptic facilitation

   b) anterograde amnesia   d) operant conditioning

3. _____ is a disorder of memory characterized by an inability to store and/or retrieve *new* information in LTM.

4. _____ is a memory disorder characterized by an inability to retrieve *old* long-term memories.

● Thinking Critically About Psychology

1. What would life be like without your long-term memory? What role do memories play in your life?

2. Why is research on the biological basis of memory important?

EYEWITNESS TESTIMONY AND MEMORY

No evidence is more convincing to a jury than the testimony of an eyewitness to the crime. If you were a juror and you heard an intelligent, credible witness say that she *saw* Professor Plum murder the victim in the conservatory with the candlestick, wouldn't you be convinced? In many cases, of course, eyewitnesses provide accurate descriptions of crimes. But eyewitness testimony is based on *memories* of the crime, and, as we have seen in this chapter, what goes into memory is not always the same as what comes out.

The three men pictured in figure 6.6 were involved in an actual case of double mistaken identity by eyewitnesses to a crime. Lawrence Benson (left) was mistakenly arrested for rape, and George Morales (right) was erroneously arrested for robbery. Both men were arrested because they had been identified in police lineups by eyewitnesses to the crimes. Benson was cleared of the charges, however, when Richard Carbone (center) was arrested and more convincingly implicated in the rapes. After his conviction for rape, he cleared Morales by confessing to the robbery as well (Buckhout, 1974).

Consider another case of mistaken eyewitness testimony (Thomson, 1988). A woman was raped in her home. Later, she was able to give the police a detailed description of the rapist. Her description led to the arrest of Donald Thompson, who perfectly fit her description. Charges against Thompson were quickly dropped, however, as he had an airtight alibi. He was appearing live on television at the time of the rape and could not have committed the rape. In fact, the victim was watching him on television just before the rape occurred. As discussed earlier in this chapter, events that create intense negative emotional arousal—and few experiences could be more intensely negative than being raped—leave memories that are vivid but very subject to distortion. In this traumatic circumstance, the woman recalled a vivid image of the man on the television screen, but her recollection of the event was so distorted that she incorrectly recalled the man on the televi-

FIGURE 6.6

Mistakes in eyewitness testimony led to the arrest of the man on the left and the man on the right for separate crimes. Both were cleared following the conviction of the man in the middle for both crimes.

sion as being the rapist. Ironically, Donald Thompson is a respected psychologist known for his research on memory and was discussing memory distortions on television at the time.

It is frightening to think that these mistaken eyewitness identifications could have occurred, but at least these incorrectly accused individuals were not convicted. Now that DNA evidence is routinely used to investigate crimes, a considerable number of imprisoned persons—many on death row—have been found to be innocent on appeals based on DNA evidence. In one study of 40 such individuals, 90 percent of the cases of mistaken conviction involved erroneous eyewitness testimony (Wells & others, 1998).

We certainly should not conclude that eyewitness testimony is always incorrect. Still, it is both important and revealing to consider the conditions under which it is sometimes incorrect. By doing so, psychologists will be able to help law enforcement personnel obtain and use eyewitness testimony in ways that will minimize its inherent flaws (Schachter, 1999; Wells & others, 1998).

Inaccurate Recall Due to Biased Questioning

Several researchers have looked at factors that lead to inaccurate recall of information by eyewitnesses (Zaragoza & Mitchell, 1996). A number of studies sug-

gest that information contained in questions asked of the eyewitness can be a potent source of distortion. When a lawyer or police investigator asks questions about the crime, the questions may contain cues that influence retrieval to a great extent. Elizabeth Loftus has conducted several important studies that look at the effect of the questions asked of eyewitnesses (Loftus & Palmer, 1974), individuals were shown a film of an automobile accident. Later, half of the research participants were asked the first question and half were asked the second question:

1. "About how fast were the cars going when they smashed into each other?"

2. "About how fast were the cars going when they hit each other?"

The speed was estimated to be considerably faster by individuals who were asked the first version of the question ("smashed") than by those asked the second question ("hit"). One week later, all of the participants were asked the same question:

"Did you see any broken glass?"

Although the film showed no broken glass, 32 percent of the participants who had been asked how fast the cars were going when they "smashed" into each other "remembered" seeing broken glass, compared with only 14 percent of the participants who were asked the more neutral version of the question. The reconstruction theory of forgetting that we studied in this chapter would suggest that they remembered seeing broken glass when it was not there because broken glass would be consistent with two cars "smashing" together. Apparently the memory was reconstructed to include broken glass to make it more consistent.

Vicki Smith and Phoebe Ellsworth (1987) of Stanford University conducted a similar experiment, in which college students watched a videotape of a bank robbery in which the robber was not wearing gloves and did not carry a gun. Later, some of the students were asked neutral questions, such as

"Were they wearing gloves?"

"Did the other guy have a gun?"

The other students were asked misleading questions, such as

"What kind of gloves were they wearing?"

"What did the other guy's gun look like?"

As in Loftus' original studies, the misleading questions cued inaccurate recall of nonexistent gloves and guns. Interestingly, this happened only when the questioner was thought to be knowledgeable about the crime. Apparently, the memory was reconstructed to include gloves and guns only when the question implied that gloves and guns were present. Thus, the way in which an eyewitness is questioned can greatly affect the accuracy of the information recalled. This means that we must be extremely careful to allow only neutral questions in legal proceedings, particularly if the witness believes the questioner has actual knowledge of the crime—as is often the case with attorneys in trials.

A growing number of studies indicates that preschool children are particularly suggestible when they are interviewed by adults. Although their memories are often quite accurate, they sometimes provide convincing descriptions of events that never happened. This greatly complicates the investigation of allegations of sexual abuse by parents and day-care workers (Ceci & Bruck, 1995).

Eyewitnesses Who "Look but Do Not See"

We human beings are often poor eyewitnesses because we too often do not really see what we observe. In one study of this topic, research participants were shown a

"What did the other guy's gun look like?"

movie scene. Part of the way through the scene, the actor was replaced by a different actor, but only a third of the participants noticed the change (Levin & Simons, 1997). Even more strikingly, a similar study was conducted on a college campus (Simons & Levin, 1998). A person (who was one of the experimenters) walked up to another person and asked for directions. As they spoke, two men walked between them, carrying a door, blocking the person's view of the experimenter for a moment. After the door passed, the conversation about the directions was completed. Less than half of the people noticed that the experimenter changed places with a *different* experimenter behind the door.

These people who looked but did not see would have made very poor eyewitnesses if they were later called on to identify the experimenter in a police lineup. They didn't even notice that the person who began the conversation was not the same person who completed it. How could this have happened? Perhaps we often process what we observe in shallow, rather than deep ways (Schachter, 1999), and, because information that is not processed deeply is quickly forgotten, the change in people was not detected. Whatever the explanation, this phenomenon highlights the limits on the validity of eyewitness testimony.

Stereotypes and Eyewitness Testimony

Do our stereotypes and prejudices influence the accuracy of eyewitness testi-

mony? Unfortunately for the cause of justice, there is considerable reason to believe that they do.

Gordon Allport of Harvard University conducted a classic experiment some years ago that demonstrated the extent to which our memories can be distorted by our prejudices (cited in Buckhout, 1974). Allport had individuals look briefly at the picture shown in figure 6.7. Look carefully to see who is holding the straight razor. Now be prepared for a shock when you learn that an amazing 50 percent of Allport's subjects later recalled that the African American man was holding the razor. Allport's study was conducted many years ago. Does prejudice play less of a role in the United States today? Sadly, no. In a more recent series of studies, participants were shown a list of male names of famous criminals and were asked if they remembered seeing any of them mentioned in the news media. Half of the names were common names in the African American community and half were typical European names. Although none of the names were actually names of criminals, the research participants "recognized" significantly more African American names as famous criminals in several studies (Banaji & Bhaskar, 1999).

How do our prejudices influence what we remember? This probably represents distortions of memories to fit our schemas. People who believe that African Americans are more likely to be criminals will be more likely to "recall" information that is consistent with that schema. In the case of eyewitness testimony in the

FIGURE 6.7

Psychologist Gordon Allport showed individuals this picture for a very brief period of time to test the accuracy of their "eyewitness" testimony in a situation in which racial prejudice might influence their perception.

courtroom, this could lead to inaccurate testimony.

Recall of "Repressed Memories" of Sexual and Physical Abuse

The most compelling eyewitness testimony is from victims themselves. Many court cases have been in the news lately in which women and men recall that they had been abused as children, but they had not been able to remember the abuse for many years. Some psychologists believe that memories of sexual and physical abuse are often suppressed. Other psychologists who specialize in the study of memory believe that it is difficult to know when so-called repressed memories of abuse are accurate. This issue poses a serious dilemma for psychologists (Frankel, 1995). On the one hand, no psychologist wants to discourage anyone from reporting sexual abuse. The sexual abuse of children is a sadly common occurrence, and any victim with the courage to report it should be supported in every way. On the other hand, there is reason to believe that not every adult who recalls that sexual abuse occurred in childhood is recalling something that actually occurred (Pope, 1996; Spanos, 1996).

What is the evidence on the repression of upsetting memories, such as sexual abuse? One study of 590 persons who had been in automobile accidents found that 14 percent of the accident victims did not remember being in the accident one year earlier (Loftus, 1993). Similarly, in a study of adult women who reported that they were sexually abused as children, 18 percent reported that they went through a period in which they lost their memory of the sexual abuse and then recovered it later (Loftus, Polonsky, & Fullilove, 1993). These data suggest that it is possible that some people who experienced sexual abuse as a child may not remember it during parts of their adulthood.

On the other hand, it is well known that information that adults recall from childhood can be very inaccurate. The most famous example is that of Jean Piaget's "kidnapping." As you will see in chapter 9, Piaget was a well-known Swiss child psychologist. For a large part of his adult life, he remembered in some detail an incident in which someone attempted to kidnap him when he was a young child. His nanny, however, was able to chase off the would-be kidnapper and save young Jean. Many years later, however, the nanny confessed that she had made up the entire incident to gain attention. She confessed because she felt guilty

about the watch she had received as a reward. Piaget concluded that he must have heard a description during early childhood of the kidnapping attempt that never occurred and formed a memory from his visual images of what he imagined had taken place. Later those visual images seemed like a memory of a real event to Piaget.

Was Piaget's experience just a fluke, or can anyone remember experiences in childhood that never happened? Ira Hyman and his colleagues conducted a series of studies that sheds light on this question (Hyman & Billings, 1998; Hyman & Pentland, 1996). The research participants were college students whose parents had agreed to complete a questionnaire about events that had happened in the student's childhood. The researchers told the college students that they had looked over the information about childhood events provided by their parents and asked the college students to attempt to recall and describe several events. Some of the events were ones reported by the parents, but the researchers deceived the participants by asking them to describe some completely fictitious childhood events that their parents confirmed had *not* happened. For example, students were asked if they remembered running around with other kids at age 5 at a wedding reception, bumping into a table and spilling punch on the parents of the bride. In the first interview, the college students remembered almost 90 percent of the events that had actually happened in childhood, but almost no one remembered events that had never happened—not at first. Later, however, when the students were tested again, about a fourth of them "remembered" completely fictitious events from their childhood. The students were particularly likely to remember the false event if they were instructed to try to form mental images of the fictitious childhood event that the researchers led them to believe they had forgotten between testing sessions. They had constructed fictional memories of things that had never happened based on the suggestive questions asked by the researchers.

Many psychologists now believe that some memories of traumatic childhood events that some people "discover" in psychotherapy are false memories created by a combination of suggestive questioning and distortions of actual events (Hyman & Loftus, 1998). As we struggle to understand our emotional problems, we could be unintentionally influenced to recall ambiguous moments in our childhoods (such as a bath given by a babysitter or an accidental encounter with a relative who was changing clothes) as an incident of sexual abuse. A well-meaning psychotherapist might say something like, "There is a lot of evidence that people with problems like yours have been sexually abused as children but have repressed the memory. Do you have any trace of a memory from childhood that might indicate that you were abused?" (Loftus, 1997). Could being asked such a question lead a person to unknowingly construct a distorted memory of an ambiguous event—or even recall an event that never happened?

In summarizing many similar research studies, memory researcher Elizabeth Loftus put it this way:

> . . . there are hundreds of studies to support a high degree of memory distortion. People have recalled nonexistent broken glass and tape recorders, a cleanshaven man as having a mustache, straight hair as curly, and even something as large and conspicuous as a barn in a bucolic scene that contained no buildings at all. Clearly, then, inaccurate memories of traumatic childhood events are possible as well. Perhaps as psychologists learn more about memory we will be able to play a more effective role in helping others distinguish between real and imagined memories. (Loftus, 1992, p. 530)

● Summary

Chapter 6 examines how we process information and how we remember or forget that information.

I. Human memory is composed of three stages of memory.

    A. The sensory register holds an exact image of each sensory experience for a very brief interval until it can be fully processed.

    B. Short-term memory holds information for about half a minute.

        1. Information fades from short-term memory unless it is renewed by rehearsal.

        2. Short-term memory has a limited capacity of 7 ± 2 items.

        3. The capacity of STM can be increased by organizing information into larger chunks.

    C. Long-term memory stores information primarily in terms of its meaning. Information is organized in LTM primarily in categories of related meanings and according to how frequently events have been associated in our experience.

        1. Procedural memory is memory for skills and other procedures.

        2. Episodic memory is memory for specific experiences that can be defined in terms of time and space.

        3. Semantic memory is memory for meaning.

    D. The levels of processing model views the distinction between short-term and long-term memory in terms of degree, rather than separate stages.

II. There are four major causes of forgetting, each with different relevance to the three stages of memory.

    A. Decay theory states that forgetting occurs simply because time passes. This occurs in the sensory register and STM but probably does not occur in LTM.

    B. Interference theory states that forgetting occurs when other memories interfere with retrieval. Interference can occur from memories that were formed in prior learning (proactive interference) or from memories that were formed in later learning (retroactive interference).

    C. Schema theory states that memories can be distorted as they are recalled from LTM to make them more consistent with our beliefs, knowledge, and expectations.

    D. Freud believed that some unpleasant memories could not be recalled because they were repressed. Memory for positive events has been found to be better than for negative events, but memory for events associated with either positive or negative emotional arousal is usually better than for emotionally neutral events, raising questions about Freud's theory. In addition, intense negative emotional arousal can produce memories that are vivid in some ways, but distorted in other ways.

III. Much has been learned in recent years about the role of the brain in memory.
   A. The frontal lobes play a key role in STM, in encoding memories for long-term storage, and in the retrieval of information from LTM into working memory.
   B. The hippocampus is a key structure in the organization and transfer of information between STM and LTM.
   C. When events are accompanied by emotional arousal, the amygdala plays a key role in memory formation. Intense emotional arousal may suppress the organizing role of the hippocampus by releasing cortisol, however.
   D. Synaptic theories view the "engram" as a change in the pattern or strength of synaptic linkages between neurons.
   E. Amnesia is a major disorder of memory.
      1. An inability to consciously retrieve new information in LTM is anterograde amnesia. Anterograde amnesia is caused by damage in the hippocampus and other brain structures.
      2. The inability to retrieve old, rather than new, long-term memories is known as retrograde amnesia.

● Resources

1. A scholarly yet very readable analysis of cognition and memory is Ellis, H. C., & Hunt, R. R. (1996). *Fundamentals of cognitive psychology* (6th ed.). Boston: McGraw-Hill.

2. For a wonderfully well-written synopsis of what psychology has learned about human memory, see Schachter, D. L. (1999). The seven sins of memory: Insights from psychology and cognitive neuroscience. *American Psychologist, 54,* 182–203.

3. For a detailed look at the relationship between mood and memory, see Bower, G. H. (1981). Mood and memory. *American Psychologist, 36,* 129–148.

4. For more information on the biological basis of memory, see Squire, L. R. (1987). *Memory and the brain.* New York: Oxford University Press.

5. For more on the debate about false "recovered" memories and related topics, see Lynn, S. J., & McConkey, K. M. (1998). *Truth in memory.* New York: Guilford Press; and Loftus, E. F. (1997). Creating false memories. *Scientific American,* pp. 70–75.

6. For a discussion of the guidelines for collecting eyewitness testimony issued by the U.S. Department of Justice, see Wells, G.L., & others (2000). From the lab to the police station: A successful application of eyewitness research. *American Psychologist, 55,* 581–598.

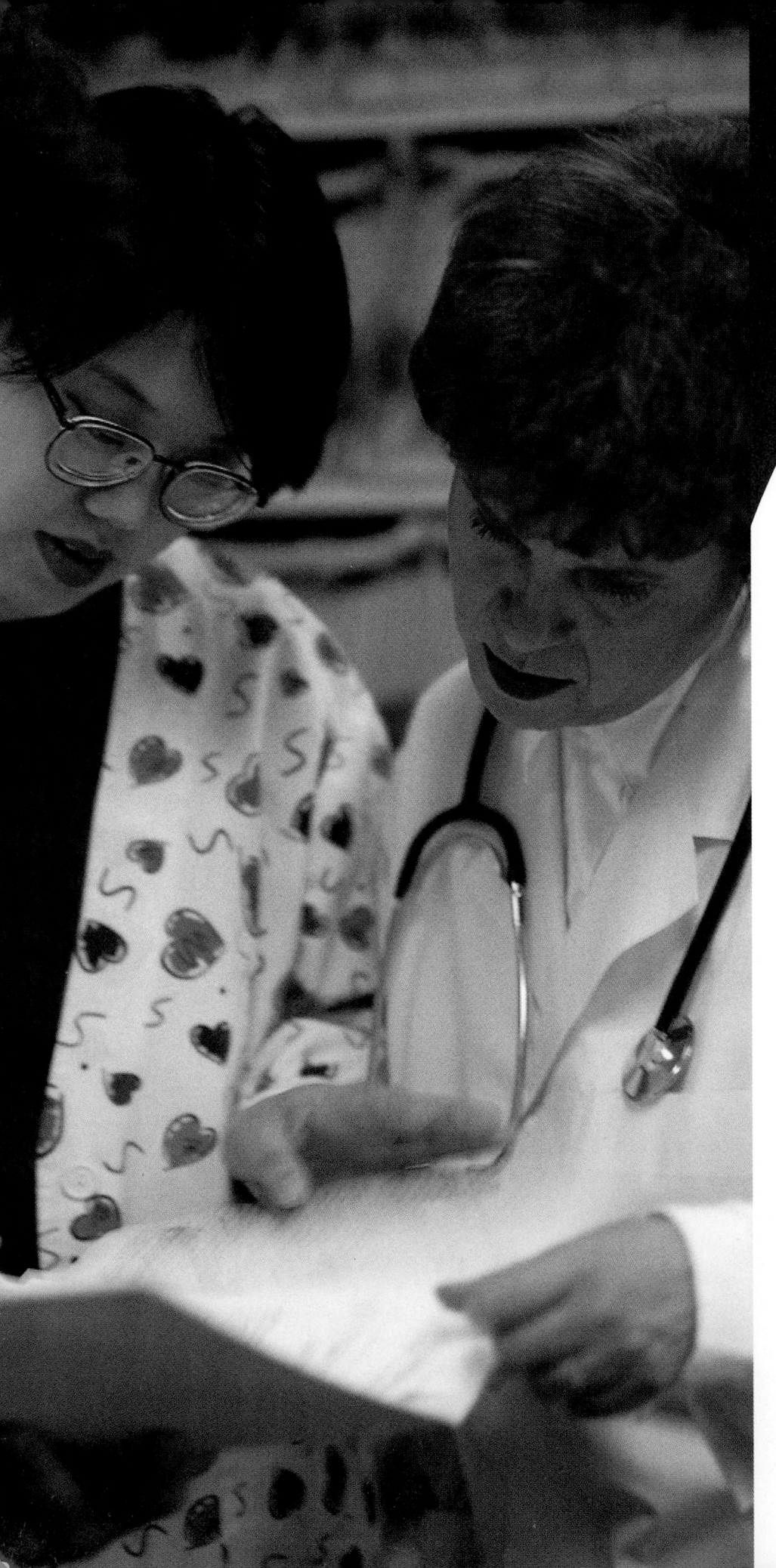

CHAPTER OUTLINE

Cognition, Language, and Intelligence

PROLOGUE

Perhaps the most important reason that the human race has survived for more than 1.5 million years is that we are intelligent. We aren't the strongest, the fastest, or the most ferocious. But, compared with other animal species, we are extremely good at solving problems. We survive cold weather by building shelters and making warm clothing; we invent wheels to move heavy objects; and we develop antibiotics when threatened by disease.

But we speak of human intelligence here not to praise it, but to marvel at its quirks, foibles, and flaws! If human intelligence is a miracle of evolution, it's an amazingly flawed miracle. When our intellectual processes are examined carefully, it's sometimes amazing that we soft-skinned and slow-moving humans have been able to survive by our wits.

To help us understand the sometimes peculiar properties of human reasoning, Daniel Kahneman and Amos Tversky conducted a fascinating series of experiments. In one study, a group of physicians was presented with the following problem:

> Imagine that the United States is preparing for the outbreak of a rare Asian disease, which is expected to kill 600 people. Two alternative programs to combat the disease have been proposed. Assume that the exact scientific estimates of the consequences of the programs are as follows: If Program A is adopted, 200 people will be saved. If Program B is adopted, there is a 1/3 probability that 600 people will be saved and a 2/3 probability that no people will be saved. Which of the two programs would you favor? (Kahneman & Tversky, 1982, p. 163)

What decision would you have made? The majority of physicians polled by Kahneman and Tversky chose Program A. The guarantee of saving 200 lives made it a better alternative than a long shot of saving all of the lives. But a fascinating thing happened when the researchers presented exactly the same problem in a different way. A second group of physicians was presented the following version of the same problem:

> If Program A is adopted, 400 people will die. If Program B is adopted, there is a 1/3 probability that nobody will die and a 2/3 probability that 600 people will die. (pp. 163–164)

Would framing the problem in this different manner have influenced your decision? It did influence the physicians. When presented in the latter way, the majority chose B. The sure death of 400 people was too difficult to accept when stated this way. There is actually no logical difference between the two ways of asking the question. Stated either way, 200 people would live and 400 people would die if Program A were adopted. But the physicians' decision making was strongly influenced by the way the question was framed. Cold logic is sometimes less important than the way in which the problem is framed.

Perhaps the best way to view human intelligence is to recognize its amazing capacity and great importance to our survival, yet to use our intelligence to understand its shortcomings and compensate for them. In this chapter, we will examine both the capacity and the limits of human reasoning.

We will use the term *cognition* in this chapter to refer to all of the intellectual processes through which we obtain information from the world, change it to meet our needs, store it for later use, and use it to solve our problems. Clearly, it's a very broad concept. Cognition is an important topic in nearly every chapter in this book. We first discussed the term in the first chapter and discussed important aspects of cognition when we studied perception, learning, and memory. In later chapters, we will discuss cognition again in other contexts. But in this chapter we will discuss several fundamental aspects of cognition—thinking, language, and intelligence.

▶ DEFINITION OF COGNITION

cognition
The intellectual processes through which information is obtained, transformed, stored, retrieved, and otherwise used.

Cognition can be defined as the intellectual processes (such as perception, memory, thinking, and language) through which information is obtained, transformed, stored, retrieved, and used. Let's analyze this complicated definition and its three primary facets:

1. *Cognition processes information.* Information is the stuff of cognition: the stuff that is obtained, transformed, kept, and used. Much of this information is dealt with in the form of categories or concepts, the subject of the next section.

2. *Cognition is active.* The information that the world gives us is actively changed, kept, and used in the process of cognition. In cognition, information is
   a) *Obtained* through the senses
   b) *Transformed* through the interpretive processes of perception and thinking
   c) *Stored and retrieved* through the processes of memory
   d) *Used* in problem solving and language

3. *Cognition is useful.* It serves a purpose. We think because there is something we do not understand. We use language when we need to communicate something to others. We create when we need something that does not exist. Humans use cognition to survive physically and to live in a social world.

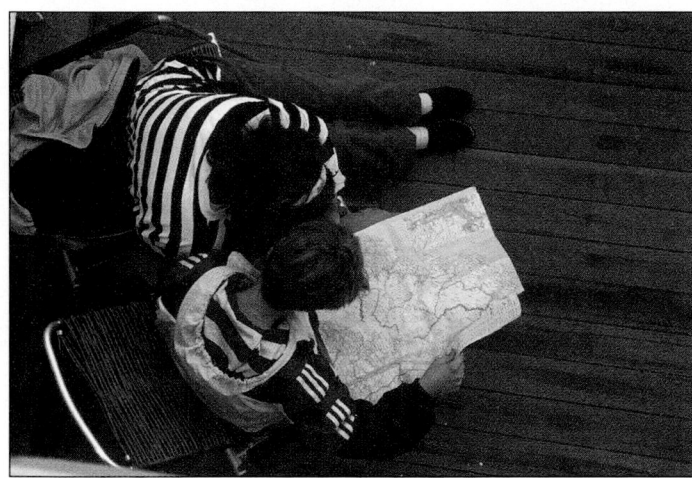

Cognition involves intellectual processes through which information is obtained, transformed, stored, retrieved, and put to use.

In this chapter, we will survey problem solving, concept formation, language, and general intelligence. Other important aspects of cognition have already been discussed in the chapters on perception, consciousness, learning, and memory. And more aspects of cognition will be mentioned in later chapters on development, emotion, personality, stress, abnormal behavior, and social psychology. Cognition is more than a topic in the science of psychology; it's a theme that cuts across many diverse topics.

▶ CONCEPTS: THE BASIC UNITS OF THINKING

concepts
(kon'septs) Categories of things, events, and qualities that are linked together by a common feature or features, in spite of their differences.

Concepts are the basic units of thinking. Concepts are general categories of things, events, and qualities that are linked by a common feature or features, in spite of their differences. About an hour ago, I went for a ride on my new bicycle. My bicycle is a specific object, but *bicycle* in general is a concept. I passed several people on bicycles as I rode—each bicycle was different in some ways from every other one, but I knew that they were all bicycles because they shared a list of characteristics (two wheels, pedals, handlebars, etc.) that all bicycles share. I also passed a lot of things that were not bicycles (cars, trucks, barbecue grills, etc.), but, being a clever fellow, I knew in a flash that they were not bicycles because they did not have the features shared by all bicycles. Keep in mind that concepts are categories of more than just concrete things—the terms *vacation, romance,* and *generosity* refer to concepts as well.

Nearly all productive thinking would be impossible were it not for concepts. Consider the following syllogism:

All human beings are mortal.
I am a human being.
Therefore, I am mortal.

When I reason in that way, I am using the general concepts of *human beings* and *mortality.* Without concepts, we would be able to think only in terms of specific things and acts. Concepts allow us to process information in more general, efficient ways. In this way, concepts are the basic units of logical thinking.

Adults take for granted that all these objects belong to the concept *bicycle.*

Natural Concepts

Eleanor Rosch (1973) has suggested that some concepts are easier for humans to learn than others; some are more *natural* than others. This idea is an important extension of the notion discussed in chapter 5 that we are biologically prepared to learn some things more readily than others. Rosch suggests that, by virtue of being born human beings, we are prepared to learn some concepts more easily than others. According to Rosch, natural concepts have two primary characteristics; they are *basic* and *prototypical.* Let's define these terms.

Natural Concepts Are Basic

A *basic concept* is one that has a medium degree of *inclusiveness.* Inclusiveness simply refers to the number of members included in a concept. Three levels of inclusiveness have been distinguished by Rosch:

1. *Superordinate concepts are very inclusive.* Therefore, they contain a great many members. For example, *vehicles* is a superordinate concept that contains all of the many cars, boats, planes, wagons, and so on that carry loads (see fig. 7.1).

2. *Basic concepts are of a medium degree of inclusiveness.* *Cars* is an example of a basic concept because it is less inclusive than the superordinate concept *vehicles,* yet this category still includes many members.

3. *Subordinate concepts are the least inclusive level of concepts.* For example, the subordinate concept *sports car* includes far fewer members than the basic concept *cars* or the superordinate concept *vehicles.*

Rosch suggests that basic concepts are more natural and, hence, easier to learn and use. She offers an observation on the way in which young children learn concepts as evidence. Children generally learn basic concepts, such as *cars,* before they learn superordinate or subordinate concepts, such as *vehicles* or *sports cars.* Why is this so? Why are basic

FIGURE 7.1

Basic concepts, which include neither the most nor the least other concepts under them, are easier to learn than superordinate or subordinate concepts.

concepts easier to learn than either superordinate or subordinate concepts? Rosch suggests that the explanation lies in several characteristics of basic concepts that "fit" the human intellect very well (Matlin, 1983; Rosch, Mervis, Gray, Johnson, & Boyes-Braem, 1976).

1. *Basic concepts share many attributes.* For example, the members of the basic concept *screwdriver* are all used to turn screws, have a metal protrusion, have a handle, are usually 4 to 10 inches long, and so on. Members of the superordinate category of *tools* have far fewer characteristics in common. Although the members of the subordinate category of chrome-plated screwdrivers have many common characteristics, only a few of them are not also common to the basic concept of screwdrivers (Jones, 1983).

2. *Members of basic concepts share similar shapes.* All screwdrivers (a basic concept) are shaped about the same, but the same cannot be said about all tools (a superordinate concept). The shapes of all chrome-plated screwdrivers (a subordinate concept) are also similar, but they are distinguishable from other screwdrivers on the basis of only one difference—the chrome plating—that has nothing to do with shape.

3. *Members of basic concepts often share motor movements.* The motor movements associated with members of basic-level concepts are similar (turning screwdrivers), but the same cannot be said for superordinate concepts (the motor movements for using different kinds of tools are very different). Members of subordinate concepts like chrome-plated screwdrivers also share motor movements, but they are generally the same or similar to the basic concept to which they belong (see fig. 7.2).

4. *Basic concepts are easily named.* If you were asked to name a half-dozen objects in your classroom, most of the words that you would use would probably refer to the basic concepts to which the objects belong. When referring to a chrome-plated screwdriver, we tend to say *screwdriver* instead of *tool* or *chrome-plated screwdriver.*

Rosch believes that these four characteristics of basic concepts make them more "natural"—easier to learn and use in the human information-processing system.

Natural Concepts Are Good Prototypes

The second defining characteristic of natural concepts is that they are good examples, or *prototypes* (Rosch, 1975). If you were asked to give the best example, or the prototype, of the superordinate concept *toy,* you might say *doll* or *toy fire truck,* but you would be unlikely to say *sandbox.* Similarly, you might think of *chair* or *sofa* as prototypes of the superordinate concept of *furniture,* but not *carpet.* Rosch suggests that natural concepts tend to be both basic and good prototypes.

FIGURE 7.2

Members of the basic concepts like *screwdrivers* often share the same motor movements in spite of other differences.

Rosch (1973) has provided intriguing evidence to support her notion that natural concepts are good prototypes in her research with the Dani tribe of New Guinea. This tribe, which possessed a very limited technology in the 1970s, has only two color concepts in its vocabulary: *mola* for light colors and *mili* for dark colors. Hence, these people were ideal individuals for research on learning new color concepts.

Rosch's Dani research participants were taught to give a label to members of a color category that corresponded to both "pure" primary colors (wavelengths that are near the middle of the range described as red or blue, for example) and intermediate colors (such as bluish-green). Both kinds of color names are basic concepts (with the superordinate concept being *color*), but the Dani learned the names of the primary colors more easily.

● Review

Concepts are the basic units of thinking. They allow us to reason because they permit us to think in general categories. Concepts are categories that have one or more features in common in spite of differences among members of that concept. All red things belong to the concept of *red* even though apples, fire trucks, and red balls differ from one another in many ways. Some concepts are defined by a single characteristic, whereas others are defined by multiple characteristics in complex ways. Not all concepts are equally easy to learn; apparently, some concepts are more "natural" than others. These natural concepts are easy to learn because they are of a medium degree of inclusiveness and are good prototypes.

● Check Your Learning

To be sure that you have learned the key points from the preceding section, cover the list of correct answers and try to answer each question. If you give an incorrect answer to any question, return to the page given next to the correct answer to see why your answer was not correct. Remember that these questions cover only some of the important information in this section; it is important that you make up your own questions to check your learning of other facts and concepts.

1. _____ are categories of things, events, or qualities that are linked by some common feature or features in spite of their differences.

2. By virtue of being born human beings, we are prepared to learn some concepts more easily than others. These concepts are termed _____.

   a) simple concepts   c) natural concepts
   b) disjunctive concepts   d) conjunctive concepts

3. Which of the following statements is *not* true?

   a) Basic concepts share many attributes.
   b) Basic concepts share similar shapes.
   c) Basic concepts often share motor movements.
   d) Basic concepts are difficult to describe in words.

● Thinking Critically About Psychology

1. What is your favorite kind of thing (think of a concept, not a specific thing)? Try to describe in words the prototype of that concept.

2. Recall what you learned about color vision earlier. Does this suggest an explanation for why primary colors are natural color concepts?

Correct Answers **1. Concepts** (p. 202), **2. c** (p. 203), **3. d** (p. 203).

PROBLEM SOLVING: USING INFORMATION TO REACH GOALS

Without concepts, sophisticated thinking would be impossible. Understanding concepts gives us insight into the *content* of thinking. Let's look now at an important example of the *process* of thinking—the question of how we use concepts to solve specific problems.

What should you do when you think you have upset your boss with the hotly political statement that you made at last night's cocktail party? Do you tell her you were just joking? Do you talk to her again tomorrow in the hope that you can agree to disagree without animosity? Do you forget about it on the assumption that she will not let politics interfere with her evaluation of your job performance? Do you wait and see if she acts as if you really did offend her—remember you only *think* you upset her—before you do anything further? What do you do?

Fortunately, no one really expects textbook writers to answer such knotty questions but merely to discuss the general process through which we solve such problems. **Problem solving** can be defined as the cognitive process through which information is used to reach a goal that is blocked by some kind of obstacle. Let's examine that process.

Cognitive Operations in Problem Solving

The focus of much current research is on the cognitive *operations* of problem solving. Operations remove obstacles to goals. What cognitive operations do we follow in trying to solve problems and reach our goals?

There are three major types of cognitive operations involved in problem solving that apparently must be performed in sequence. First, we have to perceive and formulate the problem to decide what kind of problem we face. Second, we need to evaluate the elements of the problem to decide what information and tools we have to work with. Finally, we often need to generate a list of solutions and evaluate them.

Formulating the Problem

Before we begin to solve a problem, we must be able to define it. Sometimes the problem we face is obvious. For example, I want to drive to Key West, but I don't have enough cash to buy gas; what do I do? At other times, the nature of the problem is not at all clear. For example, you may know that the goal of being promoted in your job is not being reached, but you may not know what is preventing you from being promoted. Do I need to perform my job better? Do I need to get along with my superiors better? Do I need to be more assertive in requesting a promotion? To solve a problem, *you have to know what the problem is.*

As Michael Posner (1973) has pointed out, the key to effective problem solving is often our initial formulation of the problem. Take the problem illustrated in figure 7.3, for example. If you know the radius of the circle, what is the length of line *l*?

problem solving
The cognitive process through which information is used to reach a goal that is blocked by some obstacle.

FIGURE 7.3

If you know the length of the radius of the circle (distance from the center to any side), what is the length of line *l*? This problem shows the importance of formulating a problem in the correct way.

Source: After W. Kohler, *The Task of Gestalt Psychology.* Copyright © 1969 by Princeton University Press.

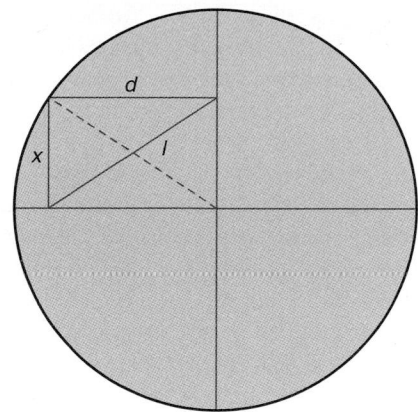

FIGURE 7.4
The problem given in figure 7.3 can be easily solved if it's viewed in the right way. Its solution requires you to think of line *l* as one of two diagonals of a rectangle rather than as part of a triangle. Line *l* is equal to the other diagonal (dotted line), which is the radius of the circle.
Source: After W. Kohler, *The Task of Gestalt Psychology.* Copyright © 1969 by Princeton University Press.

The trick is in *not* thinking of it as a problem involving the triangle *l, d, x*. Formulating the problem in *that* way blocks our being able to see what solution is called for. As can be seen in figure 7.4, the problem can be easily solved by thinking of *l* as the diagonal of the rectangle with sides *x* and *d*. The radius of the circle, then, is the other diagonal of the rectangle (dashed line in fig. 7.4), and, since our geometry teachers taught us that the two diagonals of a rectangle are equal, it's easy to determine that line *l* is the same length as the radius.

Understanding and Organizing the Elements of the Problem

After formulating the problem, we must make an inventory of the elements of the problem—the information and other resources available to us. Often, effective problem solving requires that we *flexibly* interpret the meaning and utility of these elements. Many of life's problems require an insightful reorganization of the elements of the problem: When you lock your keys in your car, a bent coat hanger becomes a door opener. One of the ways in which human problem solving is rather predictably fallible, however, is that we are often *not* flexible enough in evaluating the elements in problems. Consider the following situation. Karl Duncker (1945) has provided a problem for you to solve. See in figure 7.5 that you are given three candles, some thumbtacks, and a box of matches. Your problem is to find a way to put one of the candles on the wall in such a way that it will not drip wax on the floor or table when burning. Look at figure 7.6 when you have come up with an answer and check it out.

The limitations most of us experience in evaluating the elements of problems is that we get stuck in "mental ruts," or, in psychological terms, we get stuck in mental sets. The term **mental set** refers to a habitual way of approaching or perceiving a problem. Because problems often require a novel or flexible use of their elements, a habitual way of looking at the elements of a problem can interfere with finding a solution. If you had trouble with the Duncker candle problem, it was probably because you—like most people—thought of the box in the habitual way; the box is not immediately thought of as part of the solution because it is merely seen as an incidental item that holds the matches.

Generating and Evaluating Alternative Solutions

Very often a problem has more than one solution. Our task then is to generate a list of possible solutions, evaluate each one by attempting to foresee what effects or consequences it would produce, choose the best solution, and then develop an effective way of implementing it.

Heuristic Thinking

The cognitive strategies used to carry out the steps in the problem-solving operations just described can be of three general types: trial and error, algorithmic, or heuristic. Let's look

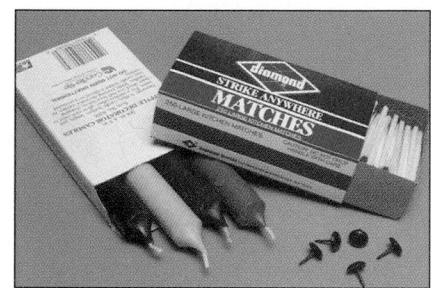

FIGURE 7.5
A Duncker candle problem. How can you mount the candle on the wall so that it will not drip wax on the table or floor when it's burning? See figure 7.6 for a good solution.

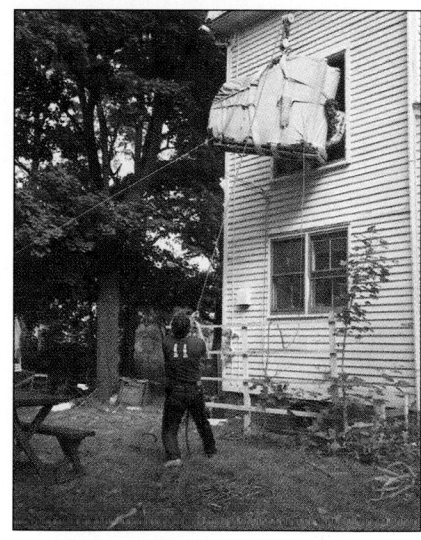

In solving a problem, we perceive and formulate the problem; we evaluate the elements; and we generate a list of possible solutions.

mental set
A habitual way of approaching or perceiving a problem.

trial and error
The random application of one possible solution after another.

algorithms
(al'go-rith'mz)   Systematic patterns of reasoning that guarantee finding a correct solution to a problem.

heuristics
Efficient problem-solving strategies that do not guarantee a correct solution.

Algorithms

www.mmhe.com/laheye1

FIGURE 7.6
One solution to the Duncker candle problem. The candle problem requires a new perception of the function of the box in which the matches came. Tacked to the wall, the box becomes a candle holder.

representativeness heuristic
The strategy of making judgments about the unknown on the assumption that it is similar to what we know.

at each of these cognitive strategies one at a time. We humans often approach problems without any cognitive strategy at all, simply trying one possible solution after another. This is usually referred to as the **trial-and-error** approach. Although common, this approach to problem solving can be very time consuming and certainly does not guarantee that a solution will be discovered.

In contrast, **algorithms** are systematic patterns of reasoning that (if followed) guarantee a correct solution. Computers generally use algorithms. Indeed, computers are especially suited for them, because they can quickly consider the many alternatives required by complex algorithms. Computers do not always use algorithms, however. For extremely complex problems, computers are sometimes programmed to use shortcuts known as **heuristics.** Heuristics are strategies that increase the probabilities of finding a correct solution. But, because they do not systematically evaluate every possible solution, heuristics do not guarantee finding the correct one. Indeed, they often lead to poor solutions.

The concept of heuristic reasoning is derived partially from research that attempts to simulate human intelligence using computers. Efforts to program computers to play the game of chess, for example, were originally frustrated by the enormous number of possible solutions that would have to be considered before making each move. To avoid such extensive algorithmic programs, heuristic programs were written. For example, the program is written to maximize protection of the queen or to control the center of the board. Moves that meet these goals are executed, but the long-range consequences of each move are not considered by the artificial intelligence program. That is why excellent chess players can generally beat computers at chess.

We need to understand the flaws inherent in heuristic reasoning because we solve problems heuristically far more often than algorithmically, largely because algorithmic reasoning takes more time and effort. Daniel Kahneman and Amos Tversky (Kahneman & others, 1982) identified two heuristics that are frequently used in human problem solving, representativeness and availability. Both are efficient, but both can result in serious logical errors. Many graduate programs in business administration devote a great deal of time to helping future managers avoid such heuristic decision making. For example, we tend to make judgments about the unknown on the assumption that it is similar to what we know (Tversky & Kahneman, 1974). This strategy is known as the **representativeness heuristic.** For example, if I describe "Lou" as shy and withdrawn, neat and tidy, and passionate about detail, what job would you guess he holds? Did an occupation come to mind—librarian, accountant, or some other occupation that you associate with those characteristics? We tend to make judgments in such situations on the basis of similarity to our stereotypes about people in different occupations. Reasoning on the basis of similarity is valid to some extent—people in different occupations do tend to differ in personality characteristics *on the average*—but it can lead to false conclusions. Not many people are librarians or accountants; that means that the vast majority of people with personalities like Lou's do something else.

Now, consider "Louise": She is in her forties. She uses no makeup and wears sandals and tie-dyed clothes decorated with designs of marijuana leaves to work; has very long hair that is braided down her back; and wears round, iridescent sunglasses every day. Is she more likely to be

a) a bank teller
b) a bank teller who is a "Dead Head"

Did you choose alternative *B,* even for a moment? The representativeness heuristic might lead you to guess that she is still a dedicated fan of the Grateful Dead (even though Jerry Garcia is now dead) and ignore other logical considerations. This would be a mistake in this case. Because all bank tellers who are Dead Heads are members of the larger class of bank tellers, alternative *A* would have been the more logical choice. Even if only a few bank tellers who aren't hooked on the Grateful Dead dress like Louise, the number of people like Louise in *A* would be greater than in *B*. On the other hand, the number of people in *B* like Louise could never be greater than the number of people like Louise in *A,* so it would be an illogical choice (Kahneman & Tversky, 1996).

Framing and Emotional Factors in Decision Making

Do you always reason logically or do your emotions influence your decision making? This chapter began with a demonstration of the powerful effects on decision making of different ways of **framing** the same question. In the Prologue, we found that physicians were more likely to adopt a medical strategy that would save 200 out of 600 people than a medical procedure that would result in 400 deaths out of 600 people (Kahneman & Tversky, 1982). Although there was no logical difference between the benefits of the two strategies, the emotional pull of the strategy that was framed as saving lives was stronger than the strategy that was framed in terms of deaths. Framing questions in positive versus negative terms can have dramatic effects on the decision making of even highly intelligent persons (Guyatt & others, 1999). Emotion and logic are intimately intertwined and not independent.

Suppose you are a stock market analyst working for a mutual fund. One morning, your boss gives you a pep talk on the opportunities to earn money for your clients, citing several examples of fortunes made. On another morning, your boss gives a sincere talk on your obligation to protect the hard-earned savings of your clients, providing examples of investors whose retirement nest eggs were wiped out. Would your investment decisions be different on those two days? Studies have shown that brief talks that change our moods can influence risk-taking behavior (Vikas & Ross, 1998). Moreover, persons in negative moods were more influenced by differences in the way that decisions were framed (as opportunities or threats) than persons in positive moods (Vikas & Ross, 1998).

In other situations, cognitive and emotional factors work together to determine our perceptions of risk. Do you feel safer driving in an automobile or flying on a commercial airplane? If you are like most people, the flight feels riskier than the drive to the airport, but, statistically speaking, you are *much* safer in the air. The website of the U.S. National Transportation Safety Board reported that U.S. commercial airlines flew 10.7 million flights in 1998, with only one accident that involved fatalities. These statistics are similar to those for other years, indicating that, each time you fly on a U.S. commercial aircraft, your chances of arriving without a fatal accident are better than 10 million to 1. This means that, if you were to fly from one city to another on U.S. commercial aircraft once every day, on the average, you would have to fly for 29,348 years before being involved in a fatal accident! According to the National Safety Council (1998), air travel is many times safer than automobile travel—1 out of every 5,000 automobiles in the United States is involved in a fatal accident every year.

Why do many of us misjudge the safety of air travel? In part, it is because airline accidents are given far more publicity than auto accidents because more people die when an aircraft crashes. In addition, images of falling from the sky into a flaming crash have a great deal of salience. This makes images of unsafe air travel easily available in memory. In addition, however, many people understand cognitively that air travel is safer than auto travel, but the idea of an automobile crash is inherently less frightening to most people, even if airline crashes are far less common. These factors add up to biased, emotional perceptions of risk.

framing
The way in which a problem or question is presented.

Creative Problem Solving: Convergent and Divergent Thinking

Creativity is highly valued in our culture but is a difficult concept to define. No specific scientific definition has been widely accepted among researchers, and a wide gulf exists between the ways in which scientists define creativity and the way it's thought of by those in the arts. We can define **creativity** in general terms, however, as the ability to produce "products" (such as plays, solutions to social problems, poems, sources of energy, symphonies) that are both novel and socially valued (useful, aesthetically beautiful, informative, and so on).

We typically view creativity as an individual ability or attribute, similar to intelligence. What, then, determines whether a particular individual is creative? Guilford (1950, 1967) has used the concepts of convergent and divergent thinking to evaluate creative

creativity
The ability to make human products and ideas (such as symphonies or solutions to social problems) that are both novel and valued by others.

convergent thinking
Thinking that is logical and conventional and that focuses on a problem.

divergent thinking
Thinking that is loosely organized, only partially directed, and unconventional.

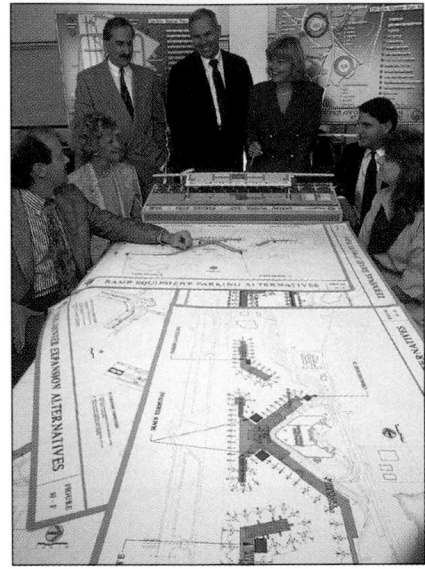

Architects need to use divergent thinking when creating the design and convergent thinking to be sure the building is structurally sound.

ability. **Convergent thinking** is logical, factual, conventional, and focused on a problem until a solution is found. When you are asked to solve an algebra problem, you use your convergent thinking skills to provide the answer. If this type of thinking sounds familiar, it should. Most formal education emphasizes the teaching and assessment of convergent thinking. Students are encouraged to discover the "right" answers. In contrast, **divergent thinking** is loosely organized, only partially directed, and unconventional. Unlike convergent thinking, divergent thinking produces answers that must be evaluated subjectively. If we were asked to list many possible uses for a brick, it is likely that some of our answers would be unique, and the "correctness" of our answers would sometimes be less unclear. In this example, individuals who list the most novel uses for common objects, whether they are "sensible" uses or not, are considered to be the most divergent thinkers. Divergent thinkers, in other words, more easily break out of mental sets that limit our thinking. In our culture, people who are good divergent thinkers tend to be thought of as creative (Butcher, 1968).

An individual's creativity might also be a result of intelligence. Most of the individuals that we think of as being highly creative are also highly intelligent (Butcher, 1968). However, most researchers in the area of creativity believe that creative thinking is to some extent separate from general intelligence. Raaheim and Kaufmann (1972) provide evidence that people who successfully solve novel problems are different from unsuccessful problem solvers in the amount of effort they make, rather than their basic intelligence. Successful problem solvers attempt more solutions to the problem before giving up. Anne Roe (1946, 1953) found that a group of creative scientists and artists shared only one common characteristic—the willingness to work really hard. It is possible to be highly creative without being highly intelligent, and vice versa.

● Review

Problem solving is the process of using information to reach a goal that has been blocked by some obstacle. We use cognitive operations to solve problems. Key steps in this process are the initial formulation of the problem, the understanding of the elements of the problem (the information and resources available for problem solving), and the generation and evaluation of alternative strategies. Problem solving can fail at any of these levels. We can be unsuccessful because we define the problem incorrectly, because we reason heuristically, because we get stuck in mental sets in perceiving the elements of the problem, or because we fail to fully evaluate the consequences of alternative solutions. In some cases, emotional factors and question framing influence logical problem solving. Creative problem solving requires the ability to think in flexible and unusual ways (divergent thinking), but the most useful creative solutions are ones that have also been thought out logically (convergent thinking). Fortunately, some intelligent people excel in both divergent and convergent thinking.

● Check Your Learning

To be sure that you have learned the key points from the preceding section, cover the list of correct answers and try to answer each question. If you give an incorrect answer to any question, return to the page given next to the correct answer to see why your answer was not correct.

1. _____ can be defined as the cognitive process through which information is used to reach a goal that is blocked by some kind of obstacle.

   a) Concept formation   c) Inductive reasoning

   b) Problem solving   d) Natural logic

2. The limitation most of us experience in evaluating the elements of problems is that we get stuck in "mental ruts," or _____, which refers to a habitual way of approaching or perceiving a problem.

   a) sets   c) algorithms

   b) convergent thinking patterns d) divergent thinking patterns

3. _____ are efficient cognitive strategies, but ones that do not guarantee finding a correct solution and often lead to incorrect solutions.

    a) Algorithms   c) Concepts

    b) Problem-solving strategies   d) Heuristics

4. _____ thinking is unconventional, loosely organized, and only partially directed.

    a) Algorithmic   c) Divergent

    b) Semantic   d) Convergent

● Thinking Critically About Psychology

1. Could a computer be programmed to solve problems like a human? What kinds of programs would be needed?

2. In solving problems, do you consider yourself to be more a convergent thinker or a divergent thinker? How does this affect the way you formulate and solve problems?

Correct Answers **1. b** (p. 206), **2. a** (p. 207), **3. d** (p. 208), **4. c** (p. 210).

▶ LANGUAGE: SYMBOLIC COMMUNICATION

Language is one of the most significant cognitive achievements of the human species. Without language, human beings and human civilization would be a pale shadow of what they are. **Language** is a symbolic code used in communication. Without an efficient means of communication, it would not be possible to coordinate the efforts of many people in a division of labor, to regulate their behavior for the common good through laws, or to amass the wisdom learned through experience by previous generations and pass it on through education. And perhaps the most keenly felt loss of all is that psychology textbooks could be neither written nor read!

Semantics: The Meaning of What Is Said

The function of language is to say something to someone. The "something" is the meaning (the **semantic content**) that is communicated through language. Suppose you want to communicate to your child that *the bananas are on the top shelf.* That idea must be translated into the language code and expressed to your child, who must receive and comprehend it by translating it back into the same idea. Thus, meaningful ideas are sent from person to person via the system of symbols that we call language.

    The fact that *semantic content* and language codes are not the same thing can easily be seen in a number of ways. For example, it is possible to express the same meaning in more than one way. *The bananas are on the top shelf* and *it's on the top shelf that the bananas are located* are physically very different patterns of sounds, but they express exactly the same meaning. Furthermore, it would be possible to express the same proposition in Chinese, Latin, French, or sign language. This distinction was made by linguist Noam Chomsky (1957), who called the superficial spoken or written structure of a statement its **surface structure** and the underlying structure that holds the statement's meaning its **deep structure.**

Generative Property of Language: Elements and Rules

Human language is a highly *efficient* system. It's particularly efficient in accomplishing so much while putting so little demand on our memories. Stop for a second and think about the sheer magnitude of language. Consider how many different things you have said in

THE FAR SIDE   By GARY LARSON

"Matthews . . . we're getting another one of those strange 'aw blah es span yol' sounds."

language
A symbolic code used in communication.

semantic content
The meaning in symbols, such as language.

surface structure
The superficial spoken or written structure of a statement.

deep structure
The underlying structure of a statement that holds its meaning.

generative
(jen′e-ra″tiv)   The ability to create an infinite set of utterances using a finite set of elements and rules.

phonemes
(fō′nēm)   The smallest units of sound in a language.

morphemes
(mor′fēm)   The smallest units of meaning in a language.

syntax
(sin′taks)   The grammatical rules of a language.

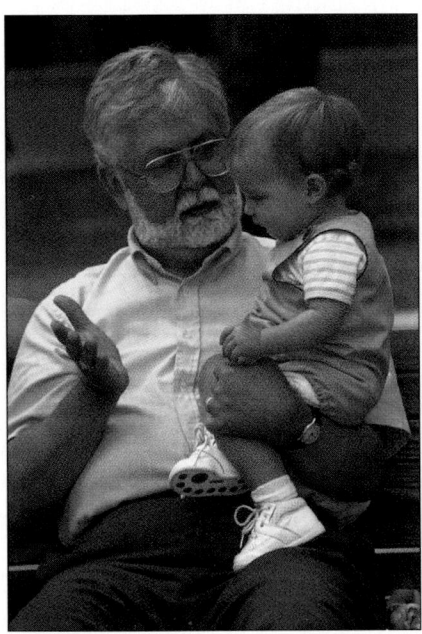

We learn language by first learning phonemes, then morphemes, followed by syntax.

"I understood each and every word you said but not the order in which they appeared."

your lifetime. If we could accurately estimate the number, it would be staggering. Now let's imagine that human language were not an efficient system. Imagine that we had to learn and remember a different utterance for everything we wanted to say. Although it would be theoretically possible to store that many utterances in long-term memory, we would have to spend every waking hour of our lives doing nothing but memorizing utterances. Obviously, we do not spend anywhere near that amount of time learning language. More important, humans do not speak using a fixed stock of utterances. We could get by in a crude and uninteresting way if we talked like that, but fortunately we do not. Every day you say utterances that no one has ever said before.

If we do not memorize our utterances, where do they come from? We make them up as we go along. In more precise terms, we "generate" language from a set of elements and a set of rules for combining them into speech. When we say that language is **generative,** we mean that an infinite set of utterances can be made using a finite set of elements and rules (Chomsky, 1957). What are these elements and rules?

Phonemes

One way of looking at the elements of language is to consider its individual sounds. **Phonemes** are the smallest units of sound in a language. In English, everything we say, and everything that we will ever say, is made up of only 44 phonemes (there are more phonemes than letters of the alphabet in English, because some letter combinations such as *ch* and *th* stand for separate phonemes). Different languages have different numbers of phonemes, but the principle is the same in every language: Every utterance is generated from a surprisingly small number of sounds.

Morphemes

When most people think about the individual building blocks of language, they have in mind something like morphemes. The **morphemes** are the smallest units of meaning in a language. Morphemes are closely related to but are not the same as words. Some morphemes stand alone as words. *Word, stand,* and *fast* are each single freestanding morphemes. Other morphemes can exist only if they are bound to other morphemes. Examples are the morpheme for past tense in push*ed,* the plural morpheme in car*s,* and the prefix morpheme *anti* meaning "against" in the word *antibiotic.* The average person knows thousands of morphemes but can speak an infinite number of utterances using a finite set of morphemes and rules for combining them.

Syntax

The rules of a language that allow an infinite number of understandable utterances to be generated are called **syntax.** There are rules for the ways in which phonemic sounds can be combined in morphemes and rules for how morphemes can be combined in utterances. For instance, in English, we learn that the suffix *-ed* communicates past tense and that the *-s* suffix denotes a plural. We learn the importance of word order. For example, we wouldn't say "this an interesting class is." These rules of syntax are the heart of generative language, for, without them, only a finite number of things could be said with the finite set of morphemes. These rules allow us to make new sentences that will immediately and effortlessly be understood by all speakers who speak normally in the same language.

We will discuss the way that language develops in the next chapter on child development, but it's interesting to note that children develop language by learning phonemes first, then morphemes, and then syntax. Children first learn to babble in the speech sounds of their language, then they use some freestanding morphemes by themselves (*mamma, milk, bye-bye*), and then they begin to acquire syntactic rules for combining morphemes into longer and more complex utterances.

Language and Thought: The Whorfian Hypothesis

Language and thinking are closely related phenomena. Although we often think in visual images, sounds, and images of movements—and some thought may involve no conscious images at all—much of our thinking takes place in the form of silent conversations with ourselves. If this is true, does language exert any influence on our thinking? If so, it is possible that people who speak different languages might think somewhat differently.

This hypothesis was stated by Benjamin Whorf (1956) and is known as the *Whorfian* hypothesis, or **linguistic relativity hypothesis.** Although Whorf was most concerned with the impact of different languages on the thinking of people from different cultures, his concrete examples of how this might happen generally concerned the relationship between language and perception. For example, Eskimos have several words for *snow* and can discriminate among different kinds of snow better than, say, lifelong residents of Florida. Does the fact that Eskimos have more words to describe different kinds of snow—and can notice small differences among different kinds of snow—mean that their additional words improve their perception of snow? Whorf proposed that the presence of these words in the Eskimo vocabulary improved visual perception. It seems at least as plausible to assume that the Eskimos first learned to perceive slight differences among different kinds of snow and *then* invented a vocabulary for talking about them to others.

A test of the Whorfian, or linguistic relativity, hypothesis was performed by researchers at the University of Alberta (Hoffman, Lau, & Johnson, 1986). Their experiment was based on the fact that each language contains terms referring to "personality types" that are important in each culture. For example, most of us understand that the "artistic type" is a person who is interested in the arts, imaginative, intense, moody, and unconventional. Each language contains such terms, but not every language has terms to describe the same personality types. For example, the Chinese language does not have a term for the artistic type, but it contains labels for other personality types that are not found in the English language. For example, the "shēn cáng bū lòu" type is recognized by speakers of Chinese to be a very knowledgeable person but one so shy that he or she is reluctant to reveal knowledge and skills unless it is absolutely necessary.

The Whorfian hypothesis suggests that these labels for personality types influence how we think about people. Do they? Fluent speakers of English were compared in their memories for, and reasoning about, hypothetical persons whose personality types were described by the experimenters. Individuals whose language contained a label for the particular personality type described by the experimenter were able to recall the hypothetical people more easily and thought about them in ways that were more consistent with the personality type. For example, English-speaking research participants recalled the characteristics of the hypothetical person described as artistic more often and reasoned about the artistic type in ways that reflected the description of his or her personality more accurately than Chinese-speaking participants. The opposite was true of the shēn cáng bū lòu type. In this sense, the words in our language do seem to influence our cognition.

Linguistic relativity has led us to reexamine some of our common language usage. Persons concerned about gender equity have lobbied for the substitution of gender-neutral terms for unnecessarily masculine terms, as in the case of changing *chairman* to *chairperson*. If Whorf is correct, using *chairman* might subtly affect the way we think about the capabilities of females to serve in leadership roles. Although some of the changes seem initially odd to some people (*server* instead of *waiter* or *waitress*), they seem to be rapidly taking over common usage. Producers of *Star Trek, the Next Generation* took this trend one step further when the original "where no *man* has gone before" was changed to "where no *one* has gone before."

Linguistic Relativity Hypothesis
www.mmhe.com/laheye1

linguistic relativity hypothesis
The idea that the structure of a language may influence the way individuals think.

Animal Languages: Can We Talk to the Animals?

Although humans have the most flexible and symbolic language for communicating propositions, we are not the only species that can communicate. Bees, for example, use a simple but elegant system to communicate messages such as *flowers containing a nectar supply are about 200 meters away on a line that is 20 degrees south of the angle of the sun.* The bee who discovers the nectar tells the other bees about it not through speech or written memos but through a symbolic dance.

If the nectar is within 100 meters of the hive, the bee does a *round dance* (see fig. 7.7), first turning a tight circle in one direction and then reversing and circling in the opposite direction. This dance does not communicate the direction of the nectar find, so it sends swarms of bees flying out in all directions within 100 meters of the hive looking for the nectar. If the nectar is 200 to 300 meters from the hive, the "speaker" bee gives better directions to his attentive audience. The bee does a *tail-wagging dance.* This dance is in the form of a tight figure eight. The direction of the nectar is communicated through the angle of the middle part of the dance relative to the sun. The distance is communicated by the rate of turning, the rate of tail wagging, and the sound made by the vibration of the wings. Distances between 100 and 200 meters are communicated through much looser figure-eight patterns in the tail-wagging dance (von Frisch, 1953).

Using these dances, bees are able to communicate rather complex messages very efficiently. Unlike humans, however, they have a limited vocabulary and can only communicate in a way that is firmly limited by inheritance. Human language, in contrast, must be learned through interactions with fluent speakers. In addition, human languages are more flexible. Animal communication can be varied little, whereas humans can generate an infinite number of unique and novel utterances.

These differences between human and animal languages have led some psychologists to assume that only humans can ever acquire a human language because we alone have the mental abilities needed for a generative language (Lenneberg, 1967). Until recently, this was an assumption that was difficult to challenge. A few attempts had been made to teach human language to animals, but they had failed. Two husband-and-wife teams of psychologists had even taken infant chimpanzees into their homes and raised them like their own children, tutoring them intensively in language. However, the better of the two chimps

FIGURE 7.7

The language dances of honeybees. The round dance indicates that nectar is within 100 meters of the hive. The tail-wagging dance points in the direction of the nectar when it's over 200 meters away. Distances between 100 and 200 meters are signaled by a third dance.

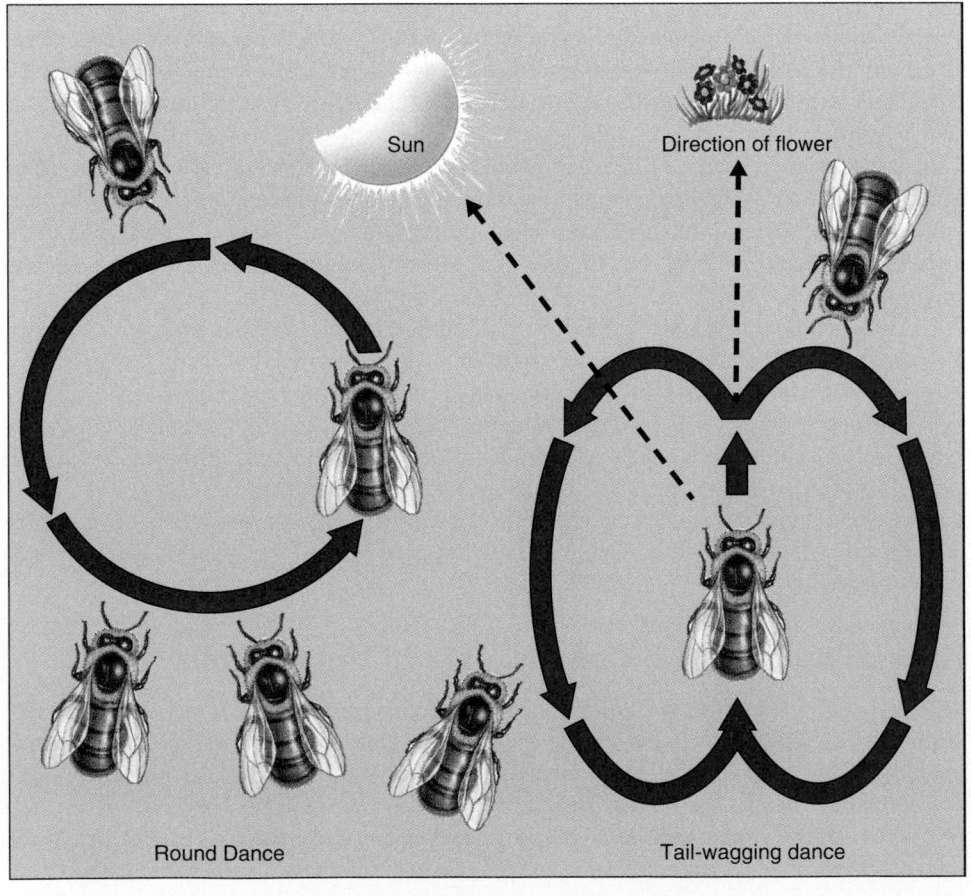

Round Dance   Tail-wagging dance

learned to speak only four words crudely (Hayes & Hayes, 1951; Kellogg & Kellogg, 1933). If humankind's nearest cousins, the apes, could not learn to speak human language, then it seemed a safe bet to assume that human abilities were required to learn a human language.

However, another wife-and-husband team of psychologists, Beatrix and Allen Gardner (1971), dramatically reopened the question. They reasoned that chimpanzees have not been able to learn to speak English simply because they possess a mouth and throat that is not well suited for spoken language, rather than because they lack adequate mental abilities. To prove their point, the Gardners raised a young chimp, Washoe, to whom they taught American Sign Language (ASL), a language made up of hand signals used by the deaf. Washoe has acquired a limited but real command of the ASL version of English. She uses more than 150 signs and uses them in such combinations as GIMME SWEET DRINK.

Washoe is not the only ape to learn a human language. Penny Patterson (1977) has taught more than 600 signs to Koko, a gorilla who may be showing even more spontaneous and generative use of language than Washoe. Koko signs THAT KOKO when she sees herself in the mirror; she once called a ring, a sign she had not been taught, a FINGER BRACELET; and she once replied to the question "How are you feeling?" by signing I WAS SAD AND CRIED THIS MORNING.

Washoe uses more than 150 ASL signs, many in combinations. Here Washoe signs SWEET in response to the lollipop.

The linguistic accomplishments of even the most advanced adult chimpanzees and apes is limited compared with that of human 3-year-olds, however. Chimpanzees use language mostly to ask for something (food, tickling games, etc.). They rarely comment on their world or ask questions to gain information (Rumbaugh & Gill, 1976; Slobin, 1979). More important to scientists, their use of signs does not appear to show syntax. For example, Washoe is as likely to request a tickling game by signing ROGER TICKLE as TICKLE ROGER. To a human, these orders of signs have different meanings, but they appear to be interchangeable to Washoe (Reynolds & Flagg, 1983). This has led some researchers to conclude that they have not mastered true human language (Terrace, 1980).

Although it may be technically accurate to conclude that Washoe and other primates have not fully mastered human syntax, this criticism misses an important point. Washoe clearly has learned to communicate with people and other chimpanzees using a form of human language. Even if her grammar is lousy, some of her statements speak volumes about the cognitive and emotional lives of our primate next-of-kin (Fouts, 1997).

● Review

Language is the efficient symbolic code used in human communication. It utilizes a finite set of sounds, units of meaning, and rules for combining them to convey a limitless set of meanings. The question of whether our language influences our cognition has not been satisfactorily answered, but current evidence suggests that it does in some ways. Although no animals have learned to use human language in the same ways as humans, surprisingly complex two-way conversations can occur between humans and apes who have been taught sign language—we can talk to some of the animals.

● Check Your Learning

To be sure that you have learned the key points from the preceding section, cover the list of correct answers and try to answer each question. If you give an incorrect answer to any question, return to the page given next to the correct answer to see why your answer was not correct.

1. While *language* is the term used to describe the symbolic code used in communication, the meaning of the code is termed _____.

   a) surface structure   c) semantics

   b) heuristics   d) syntax

2. Human language can be referred to as _____ in that an infinite set of utterances can be made using a finite set of elements and rules.

   a) divergent   c) semantic

   b) conceptual   d) generative

3. _____ refers to the rules of a language for the ways in which morphemes can be combined in that language to allow an infinite number of understandable utterances to be generated.

   a) Semantics   c) Phonemics

   b) Syntax   d) Morphemics

4. According to the _____ hypothesis, the vocabulary and structure of a language can influence the way speakers of that language think.

● Thinking Critically About Psychology

1. Does it make sense to you to say that apes are not capable of using language in a human way?

2. The Greek language has three different words for love. Would that influence the way Greeks think about and understand love?

Correct Answers 1. c (p. 211), **2. d** (p. 212), **3. b** (p. 212), **4.** linguistic relativity (or Whorfian) (p. 212).

▶ INTELLIGENCE: THE SUM TOTAL OF COGNITION

intelligence
(in-tel'i-jens)   The cognitive abilities of an individual to learn from experience, to reason well, and to cope with the demands of daily living.

In the sense used in this book, **intelligence** refers to the cognitive abilities of an individual to learn from experience, to reason well, and to cope effectively with the demands of daily living. In short, intelligence has to do with how well a person is able to use cognition in coping with the world.

The term *intelligence* was not in widespread use until it was popularized in the late 1800s by the writings of Sir Francis Galton. Galton was a cousin of Charles Darwin, the scientist credited for developing the theory of evolution based on natural selection of inherited characteristics. Galton believed that intellectual ability was inherited, and he tried unsuccessfully to develop an intelligence test to use in his research. Although he was unsuccessful in his own research, Galton gave psychology the concept of intelligence.

Differing Views of Intelligence

Since Galton's time, intelligence has been the subject of intensive research, theoretical pronouncements, and often heated debate. After nearly 100 years of scrutiny, however, psychologists still cannot agree on several basic issues. For example, opinions differ on how many kinds or dimensions of intellectual ability exist. Other psychologists believe that, instead of trying to answer that question, we should work to identify the basic cognitive components of intelligence.

Intelligence: General or Specific Abilities?

In Galton's view, intelligence is a single *general factor* that provides the basis for the more specific abilities that each of us possesses. According to this conception, if we are generally intelligent, we are more likely to develop strong mechanical, musical, artistic, and other kinds of abilities. This view that a general factor of intelligence underlies each of our more specific abilities has been advocated in more modern times by psychologist Charles Spearman (Spearman & Wynn-Jones, 1950), who used the term **g** to refer to the general factor of intelligence. Spearman based his opinion on complex mathematical analyses of intelligence test scores that support, but do not prove, his theory of general intelligence. The concept of a *g* factor of intelligence is also held by David Wechsler, who is the author of the most widely used intelligence tests for children and adults in the United States today (Wechsler, 1955).

Other psychologists have argued that intelligence is not a single general factor but a collection of many separate specific abilities. These psychologists make a great deal of the fact that most of us are much better in some cognitive skills than others, rather than being generally good at everything. Louis Thurstone (1938), for example, developed an alternative to tests of general intelligence, called the *Primary Mental Abilities Test,* that measures seven intellectual abilities. J. P. Guilford (1982), taking an even more extreme position than Thurstone, suggested that some 150 different abilities make up what we call intelligence.

Howard Gardner (1983) also has argued that there are multiple types of intelligence. Gardner became convinced that there are many separate kinds of intelligence partly by studying patients who had suffered brain damage to only some parts of the cerebral cortex. He found that these individuals lost some kinds of intellectual abilities while other kinds of intelligence were left intact. This suggested to him that different types of intelligence are mediated by different parts of the brain. Gardner also studied the fascinating abilities of rare individuals with *savant syndromes*. These individuals have low general intelligence but show extraordinary splinter skills in art, music, or arithmetic computation. As a result of his investigations, Gardner has suggested that there are *seven independent types of intelligence:*

1. Linguistic (verbal)
2. Logical-mathematical
3. Musical
4. Spatial (artistic)
5. Kinesthetic (athletic)
6. Interpersonal (social skills)
7. Intrapersonal (personal adjustment)

Gardner's definition of intelligence is much broader than the traditional one, as Gardner believes that great skill in music and good emotional adjustment should be said to reflect intelligence just as much as skill in mathematics. Most tests of intelligence focus on just verbal and logical-mathematical areas of intelligence.

The issue of one versus many types of intelligence remains unsettled today, but most authorities believe that there is truth to both approaches. That is, it is probably correct that a general factor underlies all intelligence, but people can be strong in one specific area of intelligence and weak in another. Interestingly, people with higher than average intelligence show more peaks and valleys in specific facets of their intelligence than people with below average intelligence (Hunt, 1995). Because both overall intelligence and specific strengths and weaknesses are important, it's common practice when measuring the intelligence of individuals to provide estimates of both general and more specific facets of intelligence.

Sir Francis Galton (1822–1911).

g
A broad general factor of intelligence, a concept endorsed by some investigators of intelligence.

Howard Gardner's definition of intelligence is much broader than the traditional one. He believes great skill in music or sports reflects intelligence as much as great skill in mathematics.

Fluid and Crystallized Intelligence

It is important to distinguish between *fluid intelligence* and *crystallized intelligence* (Hunt, 1995). **Fluid intelligence** is the ability to learn or invent new strategies for dealing with new kinds of problems. **Crystallized intelligence** is the ability to use previously learned skills to solve familiar problems.

It is important to note that the distinction between fluid and crystallized intelligence is not just a logical one. It is well supported by research on how intelligence changes with age. Crystallized intelligence—the ability to use familiar skills—improves throughout the years that adults work. That is one reason that most leadership jobs are held by persons over 40 (Hunt, 1995). In contrast, fluid intelligence—the ability to learn new skills for new problems—declines from middle age on (Hunt, 1995). To some extent, it really is harder to teach an old dog new tricks, but we old dogs do okay with our still-growing crystallized intelligence!

fluid intelligence
The ability to learn or invent new strategies to deal with new problems.

crystallized intelligence
The ability to use previously learned skills to solve familiar problems.

Measures of Intelligence: The IQ Test

Intelligence would be too vague a concept to be of much use to psychologists if it were not for the reasonably accurate and meaningful tests that have been developed to measure it. A measure of intelligence makes it possible to use the concept of intelligence in both research and clinical practice. As noted in chapter 1, the first person to develop a useful measure of intelligence was Alfred Binet. In 1903, he began working on developing a test that he hoped would distinguish intellectually normal from subnormal Parisian schoolchildren. In the United States, Binet's test was refined by Lewis Terman of Stanford University, as the still widely used *Stanford-Binet Intelligence Scale.* Similar tests were also developed by David Wechsler, known as the *Wechsler Intelligence Scale for Children* (3rd ed.), or *WISC-III,* and the *Wechsler Adult Intelligence Scale, Revised,* or *WAIS-R.* Items similar to those on the WISC-III are as follows:

Subject	*Examples of Items*
Information	"Which president signed the Emancipation Proclamation?"
Similarities	"How are a bell and a violin alike?"
Arithmetic	"If you buy five pieces of gum for 18 cents each, how much change would you get back from a dollar?"
Vocabulary	"What does *dissipate* mean?"

Subject	*Examples of Items*
Comprehension	"What should you do if you see another child bitten by a dog?"
Picture completion	"Show me the part that is missing in this picture." (wheel of a car)
Picture arrangement	"Arrange the pictures on these cards so they tell a story that makes sense."
Block design	"Arrange these blocks so they look like the design in this picture."
Object assembly	"Put this puzzle together as quickly as you can." (jigsaw puzzle of a dog)
Coding	"Use this key that matches numbers with geometric shapes to write the shape that goes with each number in the block below it."

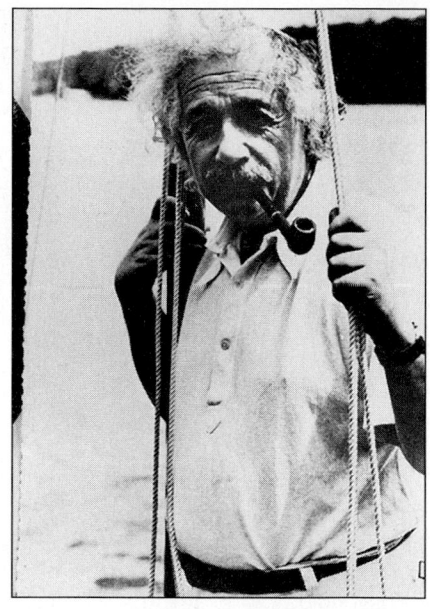

Albert Einstein had uncommon intelligence. Only about 2 percent of the general population have IQs above 130.

How is it possible to develop a test that measures intelligence when psychologists cannot decide what intelligence is? Intelligence tests are no more than a small sample of *some* of the cognitive abilities that constitute intelligence. These tests are considered useful not because we are sure they measure the right things but because they do a fairly good job of *predicting* how people will perform in situations that seem to require intelligence, such as in school or on the job. This state of affairs has led some psychologists to say—only slightly in jest—that intelligence should be defined as whatever intelligence tests measure. We cannot be very confident that intelligence tests are very good at measuring "intelligence," whatever that turns out to be. But intelligence tests are fairly good at picking out those individuals who perform well on tasks that seem to require intelligence.

Construction of Intelligence Tests

We can perhaps better understand the nature of intelligence tests and the meaning of the related term *IQ* by taking a brief look at how intelligence tests were originally constructed. Binet constructed his test by looking for a large number of items related to cognitive efficiency that differentiated children of different ages. That is, he looked for items that he thought about half the children of one age could answer but that nearly all older children could answer and very few younger children could answer. He did this based on the assumption that intellectual abilities improve with age during childhood.

Once Binet had compiled a list of items, he gave them to a large number of children of different ages to determine exactly how many children at each age level could answer each question. Then he arranged the order of the questions in the test from the least to the most difficult.

In simplified terms, the score obtained on Binet's intelligence test is equal to the number of questions answered correctly, but it's expressed in terms of the age of the children for which that score is the *average*. For example, if a child correctly answers 18 items, and the average number of items answered by children 8 years and 6 months in age is 18, then the score on the test would be expressed as "8 years 6 months." Binet called this score the *mental age (MA)*. If your mental age is higher than your actual age *(chronological age, CA),* then you are considered bright because you answered the average number of items for older children. If your mental age is lower than your chronological age, then you are considered below average in intelligence because you could answer only the average number of questions answered by younger children. This is all that an intelligence test is: a measure that compares your performance with the performance of individuals of different ages on items believed to reflect intelligence.

Is a child with a mental age of 9 years 4 months and a chronological age of 7 years 2 months brighter than a child with a chronological age of 8 years 5 months and a mental age of 10 years 3 months? Because it's difficult to compare the mental ages of children of different chronological ages, a more easily used score than the mental age was later developed

HUMAN DIVERSITY

UNDERSTANDING INTELLIGENCE FROM THE CREE PERSPECTIVE

Each culture defines intelligence differently, and children in each culture are encouraged to be intelligent in those ways. It is difficult for us to understand that different cultures have different definitions of intelligence, however, because our own view seems to be the only correct one. By definition, any view of intelligence that is different from our own seems to be "unintelligent." But, in the multicultural world in which we live, it is essential that we develop a greater understanding of different views of intelligence.

An ingenious study of differing definitions of intelligence by John Berry and his colleagues (Berry & Bennett, 1992) creatively combined research techniques from anthropology and psychology to examine the definitions of intelligence among the Cree, a tribe of Native Americans and Native Canadians in Ontario. Berry and Bennett first asked Cree adults who spoke both English and Cree to give them Cree words that had to do with intelligence, thinking, being smart, or being wise.

Twenty words obtained through this technique were written in Cree script on cards. The cards were given in random order to 60 Cree people. The individuals were asked to sort the words into piles of words with similar meaning. In this way, they were able to see which words tended to be placed in the same piles because they had similar meaning to the Cree.

The first group of similar words included the Cree words for wisdom, thinking hard, and thinking carefully. These terms were often the first Cree words given as the translation of the English word *smart* or *intelligent.*

A second group included the Cree words for respect and respectfulness. To the Cree, *respect* refers to an appreciation for people, animals, the Creator, and the land. Respectfulness involves an active and positive involvement with these things and is seen as the opposite of laziness. Respect and respectfulness from the Cree point of view involve caretaking—looking after something that is highly valued.

A third group of Cree words referred to paying attention, self-discipline, and self-control. It involved thinking before taking action and listening to what others say. Other concepts that are extremely important to Cree conceptions of intelligence include patience and perseverance, being able to look

after yourself and survive without being a drain on others, and being open to new experiences. Thus, the Cree view of intelligence is much broader than that of the European American view, including an emphasis on independence, self-reliance, self-discipline, respect for others, and respect for nature.

To instill these values in their children and raise intelligent adults, Cree parents and elders use child-rearing techniques that are sometimes quite different from those seen in many homes in the United States. For example, Cree children are encouraged to act independently without interference from adults. Adults rarely interfere with what an older child is doing, even if it is potentially dangerous, feeling that direct experience is the best teacher. In Cree culture, a high value is placed on not interfering in other people's affairs—and this courtesy is extended to children. Berry and Bennett note that some label this parenting style as neglectful, but they point out that Cree parents are often quite anxious when, for example, a child is playing with a sharp object, and they are noticeably relieved when the child puts the object down. Using such parenting methods, the Cree socialize children to be self-sufficient and independent. They learn that "one's destiny need rest in no hands but one's own" (p. 80).

How do these notions of intelligence and competence compare with those in your own culture? Give some thought to the ways in which the values that were taught in your neighborhood as you were growing up differ from those on the college campus you are attending. Keep in mind as you consider these things that the varying notions of intelligence and competence in different cultures are not superior or inferior to one another, simply different.

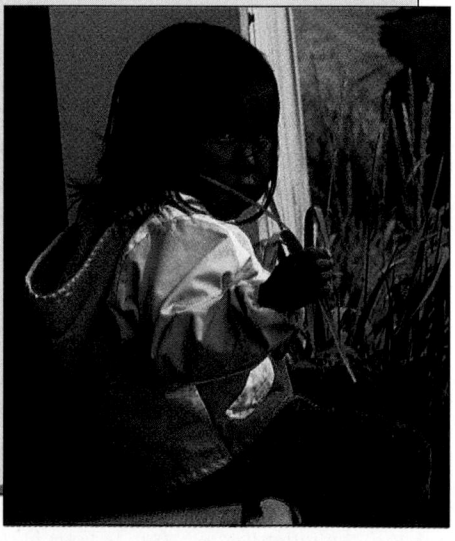

---

intelligence quotient (IQ)
A numerical value of intelligence derived from the results of an intelligence test.

for intelligence tests called the **intelligence quotient,** or **IQ.** The intelligence quotient is obtained by dividing the mental age (MA) by the chronological age (CA) so that children of different chronological ages can be directly compared. To remove the decimal point, the result is multiplied by 100. Thus, IQ = MA/CA × 100. For example, if a child's MA is 6 years 6 months and his chronological age is also 6 years 6 months, then his IQ is 100.

IQs that are over 100 indicate that the person is more intelligent than average (the MA is greater than the CA). For example, if a child obtains an MA of 10 years, but her CA

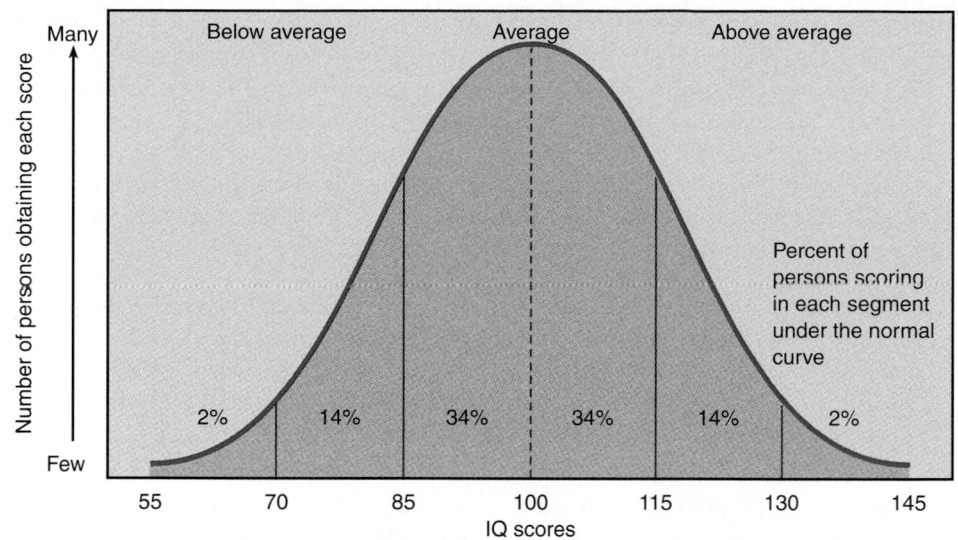

FIGURE 7.8
The normal distribution of scores on a test of intellectual ability.

is only 8 years, then her IQ is 10/8 × 100 = 125. Conversely, IQs less than 100 indicate that the individual is less intelligent than average. A child who is 10 years in CA but obtains an MA of only 7 years has an IQ of 7/10 × 100 = 70.

Actually, Binet's approach to calculating the intelligence quotient from the ratio between the child's mental age and chronological age—called the **ratio IQ**—is no longer used in contemporary intelligence tests. There are several technical reasons that the ratio IQ is no longer used, but the most important reason to understand is that there are some significant limitations to the concept of mental age. For example, a very bright 4-year-old with an IQ of 150 has the mental age of the average 6-year-old but would not handle many situations demanding intellectual ability as well as the 6-year-old. Conversely, a child with low intelligence will often seem less competent than an average younger child with the same mental age.

For these reasons, a new approach to the measurement of intellectual ability, termed the **deviation IQ,** was developed. The deviation IQ is based on an intriguing mathematical property of measurements of many phenomena, including intellectual ability. As shown in figure 7.8, the scores of large numbers of persons on tests of intelligence fall in a **normal distribution.** This means that most people will obtain the *average* score, or scores that are close to the average, on the test. As scores *deviate* from the average in either direction (either higher or lower than average), the scores become progressively less common. Thus, scores a few points above or below average are common, but scores that are many points above or below average are very uncommon.

Instead of defining an average IQ as one in which the mental age and chronological age are the same (IQ of 100), the average score on the intelligence test (the midpoint of the normal distribution) is assigned an IQ score of 100, and, based on the shape of the curve, scores above the average are assigned IQ scores above 100 and below average scores are assigned IQ scores below 100. The exact IQ score is based on how much the score deviates from the average. Look carefully again at figure 7.8 to see how this works.

Deviation IQ scores work very well for adults. They also work well for children, but children's scores have to be compared with different normal distributions for each age group because their scores increase as children grow older. The same concept of deviation from the midpoint of the normal distribution is also used in many other tests of human characteristics. Scores on the tests of academic achievement that you took in school, some of the tests of specific job skills that you will take when you apply for employment, and some tests of personality are based on the same concept as the deviation IQ.

ratio IQ
The intelligence quotient based on the ratio between the person's mental age and chronological age.

deviation IQ
The intelligence quotient based on the degree of deviation from average of the person's score on an intelligence test.

normal distribution
The symmetrical pattern of scores on a scale in which a majority of the scores are clustered near the center and a minority are at either extreme.

Characteristics of Good Intelligence Tests

When you measure the size of a window with a yardstick before buying drapes, you don't have to ask how good yardsticks are for measuring length. For the purpose you are using it, yardsticks are good measuring instruments. However for something as important, yet difficult to define, as intelligence, it makes sense for us to ask how accurate the measuring instrument is. The following is a list of criteria that an intelligence test must meet before we accept it as an adequate measuring instrument. In chapter 11, in the section on personality tests, you will see how these criteria apply equally to all psychological tests.

standardization
Administering a test in the same way to all individuals.

norms
Standards (created by the scores of a large group of individuals) used as the basis of comparison for scores on a test.

objectivity
Lack of subjectivity in a test question so that the same score is produced regardless of who does the scoring.

reliability
A test's ability to produce similar scores if the test is administered on different occasions or by different examiners.

validity
The extent to which a test measures what it's supposed to measure.

1. **Standardization.** Because intelligence tests are designed to compare the performance of one person with others, the test must be given in the same way to every person. If this were not so, differences in performance might be due to differences in the way the test is administered rather than to true differences in ability. For this reason, properly designed psychological tests contain detailed instructions telling the examiner how to administer the test to each person in the same *standardized* way.

2. **Norms.** To compare the individual's score with that of others, the developer of the test must give the test to a large sample of people who represent the general population. For example, you could not develop an intelligence test for adults by giving the test only to college students, because they are brighter than the general population. The sample used in evaluating the performance of individuals given the test is called the *normative sample*. It must be large enough to validly represent the general population and must contain approximately the same proportion of each subgroup in the general population to be a valid standard of comparison for anyone taking the test. For example, a normative sample that contained no Hispanic children would not have the same validity when used to evaluate young Hispanics.

3. **Objectivity.** An intelligence test must be constructed so that there is little or no ambiguity as to what constitutes a correct answer to each item. If there is ambiguity, and the scoring is subjective rather than *objective,* then factors other than the individual's performance might influence the scoring, such as the examiner's mood or prejudices.

4. **Reliability.** To be useful, an intelligence test must be *reliable.* This means that the scores obtained would be approximately the same if administered on two different occasions or by two different examiners. If the scores change a great deal from one testing to the next, no faith can be put in the scores.

5. **Validity.** Most important, an intelligence scale must be *valid;* that is, it must measure what it's supposed to measure. Validity can be evaluated in a number of different ways, but, for intelligence tests, the most important issue is the degree to which the test *predicts* performance on other tasks that most people agree require intelligence. This is referred to as *predictive validity.* For example, the Wechsler and Stanford-Binet intelligence tests are considered valid in part because they are fairly good predictors of performance in school. About 25 percent of the differences in school performance among a group of students can be predicted from IQ scores. This is not a high level of predictability. As you are well aware, many factors besides intelligence, such as motivation and personality, contribute to school performance. But intelligence test scores are better predictors of school performance than any other measure that psychologists or educators now possess. So, in this sense, intelligence tests are valid.

Tacit Intelligence

We have said that intelligence tests are considered to be useful because they allow psychologists to predict how well individuals will perform in situations that require intelligence. The predictions are not very precise, but they are accurate in extreme cases. That is, children with an IQ of 120 will almost always perform better in school than children with an IQ of 80, but we could not predict with much confidence that children with an IQ of 105 will perform better than children with an IQ of 95. Still, in spite of their lack of precision, intelligence tests are useful predictors.

It is important to understand that general intelligence tests like the Stanford-Binet or the Wechsler scales are limited in what they predict. They are most useful in predicting success in school and complex occupations. General intelligence tests are not useful in predicting competence in specific areas that are generally not taught in school. For example, if a general intelligence test were given to all of the adults who live in your city, the scores would not be very useful in predicting who would be the best at fishing, growing vegetables, maintaining their cars, taking photographs, picking horses at the race track, painting with water colors, or shopping for food within a budget. Some researchers have referred to these competencies as "everyday intelligence," or **tacit intelligence,** and have developed tests to measure tacit intelligence (Galotti, 1990; Schmidt & Hunter, 1993; Sternberg & Wagner, 1993).

tacit intelligence
The practical knowledge and skills needed to deal with everyday problems that are usually not taught in school.

According to Kathleen Galotti (1990) of Carleton College, a useful test of tacit intelligence must assess practical knowledge and skills in getting things done. Sternberg and Wagner (1993) developed a measure of tacit intelligence consisting of scenarios describing work-related situations in particular areas of employment. Persons taking the test are asked to rate the quality of a number of different solutions to the problems. Because different areas of employment—from plumbing to selling insurance—pose different kinds of problems, tests of tacit intelligence that are specific to a given area are most useful in predicting who will perform well in that domain (Sternberg & Wagner, 1993).

Although tacit intelligence is rather distinct from the cognitive competencies measured by general tests of intelligence, there are three ways in which tacit intelligence is related to general intelligence. First, at very low levels of general intelligence, it is rare to find individuals with highly developed tacit intelligence. Second, it is unlikely that persons of limited general intelligence will succeed in highly complex areas of tacit knowledge, such as amateur astronomy. Third, although persons with higher general intelligence are not more likely to have highly developed knowledge and skills in any particular area of everyday functioning, persons with higher general intelligence are more likely to have good practical knowledge across *many* different areas (Lubinski & Humphreys, 1997).

Individual Differences in Intelligence: Contributing Factors

Why is one person more intelligent than another person? After many years of research, it is now clear that both our heredity and our experiences combine to determine our level of intelligence (Plomin & Petrill, 1997). In chapter 2, we described how studies of twins and persons adopted at birth point to clear genetic influences on intelligence. The IQ scores of genetically identical monozygotic (identical) twins are considerably more similar than the scores of dizygotic twins, even though both kinds of twins are reared in essentially the same intellectual environment. Dizygotic twins, who are no more alike genetically than siblings born at different times, are no more similar in IQ than any other siblings. Furthermore, it makes little difference whether monozygotic twins grew up in the same home or were adopted and raised in *separate* homes. In both cases, their IQs are very similar (Erlenmeyer-Kimling & Jarvik, 1963; Hunt, 1995; Lewontin, 1982).

Adoption studies have similarly indicated that heredity is one of the more important factors determining IQ. A large number of studies have shown that the IQs of adopted children are more similar to the IQs of their biological parents with whom they never lived than those of their adoptive parents who raised them. Taken together, the twin and adoption studies make a strong case that heredity is one of the determinants of IQ.

The intellectual environment in which a child is reared is also an important factor in intelligence, however. The exposure that children have to the world of adult intelligence through interactions with their caregivers seems essential to normal intellectual

The amount of cognitive stimulation provided to infants is one factor in determining level of intelligence.

development. Children who have been so severely neglected by their parents as to be deprived of this stimulation show very slow intellectual development but usually develop more rapidly when placed in good foster homes (Clarke & Clarke, 1976). Schiff and Lewontin (1986) studied a group of children of poorly educated mothers who put one of their children up for adoption but raised their other children themselves. The children were adopted shortly after birth by much better educated families. Years later, the IQs of the adopted children averaged 109, whereas those of their non-adopted siblings averaged 95.

Recent evidence suggests that it is possible to intentionally increase intelligence scores by enriching young children's intellectual environments. In a well-designed formal experiment, infants from low-income families were randomly assigned to either environmental enrichment or a control group that received no intervention (Burchinal, Campbell, Bryant, Wasik, & Ramey, 1997). The environmental enrichment program consisted of a free early educational preschool, access to a lending library of educational toys, and home visits from child development experts who taught parents how to provide responsive and stimulating child care at home. The enrichment program produced consistently higher intelligence scores from 2 years of age to 12 years of age. At age 12, 42 percent of the control group had Wechsler intelligence scores of 85 or below, compared with only 13 percent of the early enrichment group (Campbell & Ramey, 1994). At age 15, the youths who had received early intellectual enrichment scored higher on measures of reading and mathematics achievement, had failed fewer grades, and were less likely to have been assigned to special education classes (Campbell & Ramey, 1995).

The beneficial influences of the environment on intelligence test scores is not limited to early childhood, however. Well-designed studies show that increased amounts of education result in improved scores on tests of both crystallized and fluid intelligence. Both attending more years of schooling and participating in extended year-round educational programs produce increased scores on measures of intellectual ability and academic achievement (Frazier & Morrison, 1998; Williams, 1998). Thus, there is considerable evidence that both heredity and experience influence intelligence. From a practical perspective, it seems very likely that investments in improving the level of intellectual stimulation of children from low-income families by providing free educational day care and assistance in parenting and by extending schooling throughout childhood and adolescence would pay off in terms of significant improvements in both intellectual ability and school achievement.

The Importance of Intelligence Scores in Modern Society

Intelligent test scores are important because they predict to some extent how well we will do in life. Persons with higher intelligence tend to learn more in school, get better grades, and complete more years of education (Brody, 1997; Hunt, 1995). In addition, more intelligent individuals tend to hold more complex and highly paid jobs (Brody, 1997; Hunt, 1995). The average IQ of truck drivers is a little under 100, whereas the average IQ of doctors and lawyers is 125 or higher (Hunt, 1995). At the other end of the IQ spectrum, persons with IQs below 85 (about 15 percent of the population) are very likely to have dropped out of high school, to live below the poverty line, to be unemployed for long periods, to be divorced, to receive aid for dependent children, to have health problems, and to have a criminal record. Indeed, the correlation between IQ and success in education and occupations is about as high as the correlation between people's heights and weights (Hunt, 1995).

Why does intelligence predict how well we will do in our jobs? There appear to be three major reasons:

1. Many occupations are available only to persons with college or graduate degrees, and persons with higher intelligence are more likely to qualify for advanced education (partly because admission tests largely measure intelligence) and are more likely to complete advanced degree programs once they are admitted (Brody, 1997).

2. It takes less time to train persons with higher intelligence to a high level of job knowledge and skill than persons with lower levels of intelligence (Gottfredson, 1998; Hunt, 1995). If the job skills are relatively well specified and not complex, however, level of intelligence does not influence job success very much after those skills have been learned (Hunt, 1995).

3. Persons with higher intelligence tend to perform better in complex jobs, particularly if they involve making judgments in changing situations and require constant updating of job skills (physicians, lawyers, scientists, engineers, computer programmers, etc.) (Gotfredson, 1997). Even in nonprofessional occupations, persons with higher levels of intelligence are more likely to be promoted into more complex jobs than persons with lower levels of intelligence (Wilk, Desmarais, & Sackett, 1995).

Are People Becoming More Intelligent?

James Flynn (1998) of the University of Otago in New Zealand published provocative data on changes in average intelligence test scores over successive generations—known as the "Flynn effect." In many countries around the world, there is strong evidence that intelligence scores have risen dramatically over the past few generations. When tested at the same age using the same test, people born in earlier years answered fewer questions correctly than persons born more recently. Therefore, when the raw scores of persons born in different years are converted to deviation IQ scores using the norms for the group born in the earliest years, persons born more recently have higher average IQs than persons born earlier on the average (Flynn, 1998).

The rate of increase in scores on tests of general adult intelligence (that measure both fluid and crystallized intelligence) like the Stanford-Binet and Wechsler intelligence scales are shown in figure 7.9 (Neisser, 1998). These increases are surprisingly large, but data on tests that measure only fluid intelligence show even larger gains of about 20 points per generation (every 30 years) (Neisser, 1998; Williams, 1998). The strongest evidence of changes in fluid intelligence comes from the Raven Progressive Matrices Test (Carpenter, Just, & Shell, 1990). The Raven test has been administered to representative samples of young adults each year in some countries over many years, with the best data coming from Holland. James Flynn (1999) asked us to imagine a Dutch woman with a score of 110 at age 25 years on the Raven test who taught teenagers in school from the time she was 25 until she was 55 years old. Her raw score (the number of questions answered correctly) on the Raven test did not change over that part of her life span, but her score's standing relative to her pupils' scores changed dramatically. In 1952, her score on the Raven was higher than those of 75 percent of her students. By 1967, however, her score was equal to the average score of her students, and, by 1982, 75 percent of her students had higher Raven scores than she! Her raw score did not change over time, but the raw scores of her students increased markedly over time.

Is it really possible that the students of our hypothetical Dutch teacher surpassed her in fluid intelligence to such a great degree over a span of only 30 years? On the average, are we really that much smarter than our parents? Few psychologists doubt that large

FIGURE 7.9

Intelligence scores of individuals born in different years (who were tested in different years when they reached the same age) when their scores are converted to intelligence scores based on 1932 norms.

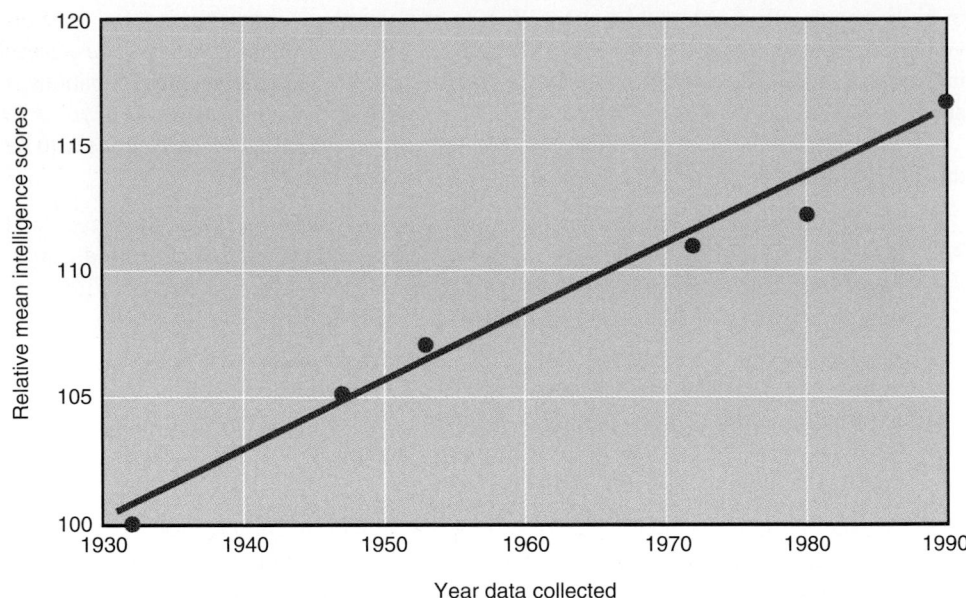

changes in intelligence test scores have occurred since the early 1900s (Hunt, 1995; Neisser, 1998; Williams, 1998), but we are all frankly shocked by these data. What do they mean? Has each generation really surpassed the previous generation so much in the wide range of competencies and cognitive skills that we call intelligence? In many ways, my grandparents seemed to be as intelligent as my children seem to be. My grandparents were very successful, but they succeeded in a much less complex world than the present world. It is simply not possible to know if they could have not been successful in coping with today's computerized, mathematics-based world.

Why are intelligence scores going up and what do the increases mean? There are at least five plausible explanations for why intelligence may have actually risen over successive generations:

1. During the same era that intelligence scores have risen, nutrition and health have improved dramatically in many parts of the world. Indeed, in the same countries that show increases in intelligence, the rates of increase in average height, weight, and life expectancy scores have been almost identical to the rate of increase in intelligence scores shown in figure 7.9 (Martorell, 1998). Women in these countries also have become more likely to receive adequate prenatal and obstetric care and are increasingly less likely to smoke and drink during pregnancy. Because nutrition and body size are positively correlated with intelligence (Sigman & Whaley, 1998), it is possible that much of the increase in intelligence scores is due to improvements in nutrition and health. Indeed, in several studies, when families of children in very poor parts of the world have been randomly assigned to an experimental group that received nutritional supplements or to a control group that did not receive supplements, the children who received nutritional supplements were found to have higher intelligence scores (Sigman & Whaley, 1998). Similarly, children with intestinal parasites are robbed of nutrition by the parasites. In economically deprived parts of the world, treating intestinal parasites (at a cost of 15 cents per child) has produced dramatic improvements in school and test performance (Williams, 1998). It seems unlikely that nutritional supplementation beyond the U.S. recommended daily allowances of nutrients improves intellectual or academic growth, however (Martorell, 1998). Vitamins are not "smart pills" for adequately nourished persons.

2. Increases in levels of education may have produced increases in intelligence test scores. This could work in two ways—indirect effects through the parents of each generation and direct effects on each generation of children. Since the beginning of

the twentieth century, each successive generation has had better educated parents. Indeed, in the United States, there has been a 10-fold increase in parental education levels during this century (Greenfield, 1998). This is important because the level of education of parents is correlated with the intelligence scores of their children (Flynn, 1998). It is possible that better educated parents provide a more intellectually stimulating home environment, which increases the intelligence test scores of their children (Greenfield, 1998). At the same time, each successive generation of children has received more education than the last. In the 1930s, the mean number of years of education in the United States was 9 years; by the 1990s, the mean had risen above 14 years (Williams, 1998). It is possible these increases in education over the years are responsible for some of the increase in intelligence test scores. In particular, schools place more emphasis on teaching skills associated with fluid intelligence today than in the days of our grandparents, when memorization of facts was the focus of education (Williams, 1998). Thus, it may make sense that scores on measures of fluid intelligence have increased more than scores on tests of crystallized intelligence over time.

3. During the twentieth century, the number of children per family decreased considerably in many countries (Lynn, 1998). This is important because some studies show a negative correlation between number of children in the family and their average intelligence (Lynn, 1998). In particular, later-born children in larger families are likely to score lower than their older siblings on measures of intellectual ability, perhaps because their parents have less time to interact with them individually (Zajonc & Mullally, 1997).

4. Children born in the latter part of the twentieth century are stimulated and challenged by a degree of environmental complexity that was unknown in 1930s (Neisser, 1998). Educational television, computers, learning toys, preschools, and other innovations may have increased intelligence by increasing children's levels of intellectual stimulation (Williams, 1998).

5. Large increases in intelligence test scores occurred during a period of time during which big changes occurred in the lives of persons of color in the United States. We will have much more to say about the apparently beneficial effects of the end of official segregation and other changes in the next section. Although this is probably a factor in the overall increase in intelligence and academic achievement in the United States, it could not explain the large increases in intelligence test scores found in countries such as Holland, where relatively few persons of color live and institutionalized segregation was never practiced.

Some psychologists who wonder if the increase in intelligence scores actually means that people have become "smarter" have pointed to the widely publicized decline in scores on the Scholastic Assessment Test (SAT). Could intelligence really be increasing when SAT scores were decreasing (Neisser, 1998)? It appears, however, the decline in SAT scores was temporary, as SAT scores have been rising again since 1960 (Zajonc & Mullally, 1997). It is difficult to interpret changes in SAT scores, in any case, as they can be due to changes in who takes the test. The SAT is normed on people who take this test each year, and only persons applying to college take the test. In contrast, the Preliminary Scholastic Assessment Test (PSAT) covers similar material and is administered to a representative sample of U.S. high school juniors each year. Although they have not risen as fast as scores on intelligence tests, average scores on the PSAT have been steadily rising since it was first administered in 1961 (Williams & Ceci, 1997).

Race-Ethnic Differences in Intelligence and Achievement: The Narrowing Gap

Data gathered since the 1930s have consistently shown that the average intelligence and academic achievement scores of African Americans are about 15 points lower than those of

FIGURE 7.10

Changes in scores on a measure of verbal intelligence among adults in the United States of African American (dots) and non-Hispanic white heritage (open circles) who were born during different years during the 1900s.

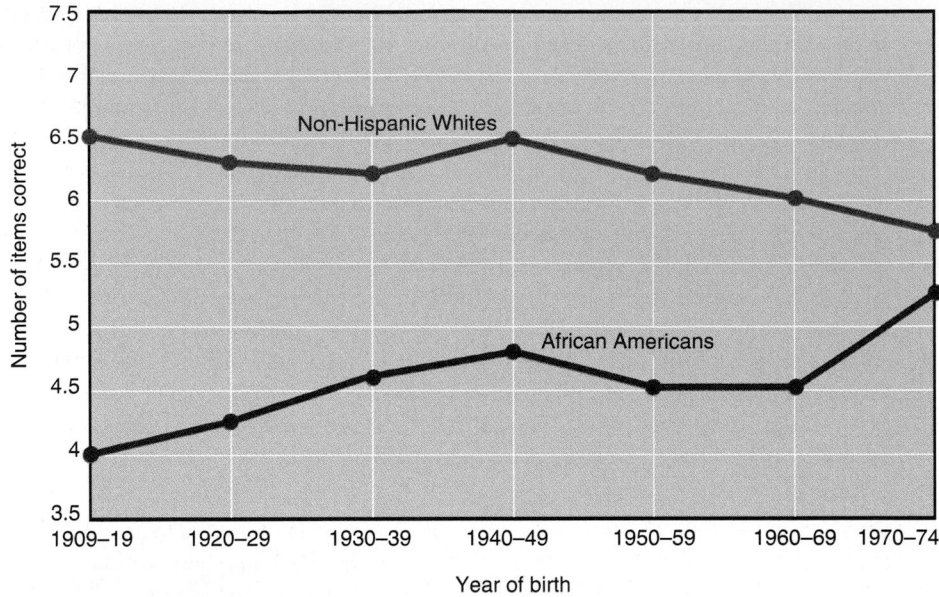

white Americans, with children of Hispanic/Latino heritage having average scores that fall between those of whites and African Americans. Asian Americans, on the other hand, have average intelligence scores that are about 5 points higher than those of whites (Williams & Ceci, 1997). If people in general have become more intelligent over successive generations, what has happened to the difference between groups that differ in race and ethnicity?

Between 1970 and 1990, more than half of the gap in reading and mathematics achievement scores between African American and non-Hispanic white 17-year-olds has closed, as measured by the National Assessment of Educational Progress (Hauser, 1998). This extremely important trend reflects greater improvements in academic achievement scores among African American than white youths (Grissmer, Williamson, Kirby, & Berends, 1998). Not as much data are available on changes in race-ethnic differences on tests of general intelligence, but there is some evidence that African Americans have shown greater gains on tests of general intelligence over the past 50 years than whites (Flynn, 1999). In addition, the results of a strong study of a measure of verbal ability are encouraging. Since the early 1970s, the General Social Survey administered a measure of verbal ability to representative samples of adults across the United States. As shown in figure 7.10, there was a large difference in scores between African American and white adults in the United States among adults born between 1909 and 1929. There has been steady improvement in the verbal ability scores of African Americans over time (and a slight decline in the scores for whites), however, which has nearly erased the race-ethnic gap among adults born between 1970 and 1974 (Huang & Hauser, 1998).

Why have such greater increases in average scores on intellectual and academic tests occurred among African Americans? No one knows for sure, but marked changes in the environment seem to be the most plausible answer. Since the end of official segregation in the United States, the educational experiences of African Americans have changed dramatically. The timing of changes in schooling related to desegregation in different regions of the country closely parallel gains in academic achievement made by African Americans in those regions (Grissmer & others, 1998). From 1973 to 1990, the mean educational level of adults increased among white families by 70 percent, but the mean educational level of adults in African American families increased by 350 percent during the same period (Williams, 1998). Because amount of schooling is related to scores on measures of both intellectual ability and academic achievement, the closing gap in ability and achievement may be due, in part, to the closing gap in educational opportunity.

Other factors probably also play a role in the narrowing gap between race-ethnic groups in the United States. For example, the average number of children in white families decreased from 4.7 to 2.4 from early 1970s to the mid-1990s, whereas the average number

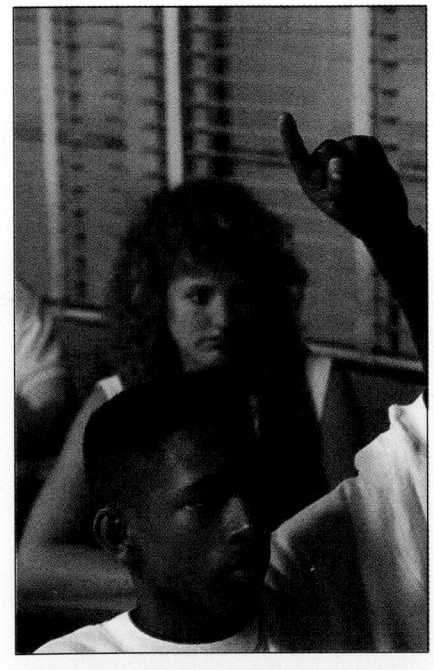

Group differences on intelligence tests, such as college entrance exams, between African Americans and white Americans appear to be dwindling as prejudice and economic barriers weaken.

of children in African American families decreased from 6.0 to 4.2 (Huang & Hauser, 1998). Because the adverse effects of larger family size on intelligence and achievement are greatest on later-born children in larger families (Zajonc & Mullally, 1997), the marked decline in the number of larger African American families may be another factor associated with improved scores. Although the average number of children in white families declined slightly more, they had smaller families to begin with and may have benefited less from the decline in family size. Changes in health and nutrition and other factors also may have contributed to the greater increase in test scores among African Americans than among whites. Unfortunately, much less information is available on trends in ability and achievement among Hispanic/Latino children and other groups.

"The Bell Curve": Policy Implications of Differences in Intelligence

In 1994, psychologist Richard Herrnstein and sociologist Charles Murray published a controversial book entitled *The Bell Curve*. They reviewed many findings from studies of intelligence and occupational success and discussed their implications for public policy. They argued that North American society is moving toward a "meritocracy," in which opportunities for advanced education and favorable kinds of employment are determined solely by each person's ability. Although individual merit is certainly not the only factor that determines success today, it is probably true that it is more important than ever before. In the past, some occupations were open only to persons from wealthy families and from certain race-ethnic groups. Although such privileges endure today, laws regarding equal opportunity in education and employment have reduced their influence.

Although life in a meritocracy is more fair in many ways than life in other social systems, Herrnstein and Murray argue that it poses new ethical problems as well. If we create a society in which the environmental contributions to intellectual ability are completely equalized (everyone has adequate nutrition, favorable intellectual environments, equal access to education, etc.), they believe that the influence of genetics on intelligence will increase. That is, heredity would be the only cause of differences among people in intelligence if everyone's environment were essentially the same. Because intelligence in its various forms (fluid, crystallized, and tacit) plays an important role in determining occupational success, Herrnstein and Murray believe that the genes that influence intelligence will play an increasingly important role in determining each person's level of occupational success. Thus, if our society eliminates all barriers to equal opportunities to succeed, Herrnstein and Murray believe that the aspects of occupational success that are linked to intelligence will be determined by our genes from the moment of conception. This would be as unfair as an aristocracy that determined that only persons of royal families be educated or own property.

In addition, Herrnstein and Murray argue in *The Bell Curve* that society is headed toward genetic decline. Because families with the lowest incomes (which Herrnstein and Murray believe mostly have genes for inferior intelligence) have more children each year than wealthier families (which they believe mostly have genes for superior intelligence), then the overall intelligence of people in the population will decline (because more of the population will have genes for inferior intelligence). This is a highly controversial hypothesis, to say the least (Neisser, 1998), but an even more controversial hypothesis concerns differences between race-ethnic groups in intelligence. Herrnstein and Murray posit that whites have higher average intelligence scores than African Americans and Hispanics partly because of genetic factors. Therefore, they predict that differences in average intelligence levels between whites and persons of color will increase because of the lower rates of reproduction among whites.

The good news is that *The Bell Curve* has provoked more thought, research, and scientific writing than any book on a psychological topic in the last 20 years. Many psychologists have argued that Herrnstein and Murray ignored important evidence in their analysis, stated hypotheses that have little scientific support, and were simply mistaken in other ways (Neisser, 1998). For example, geneticist Samuel Preston (1998) has shown that the genes for intelligence in a population would change only if people consistently had children with people of their same level of intelligence and if the genes exerted a strong influence on intelligence. His findings show that we do not mate with people of our own intelligence nearly often enough to change the genes in the population, even if the influence of genes on intelligence were very strong. Recent findings on the large increases in intelligence since the 1930s (which Herrnstein and Murray knew about but dismissed) certainly argue against their hypothesis that intelligence is going down as "inferior" genes become relatively more common. If anything, the average level of intelligence appears to be rising in the population (Flynn, 1998). Finally, there simply is no convincing evidence that differences between race-ethnic groups are rooted in genetics. Indeed, the little evidence on this issue that is available suggests that race-ethnic differences in intelligence probably do not have a genetic basis (Loehlin, Lindzey, & Spuhler, 1975). Perhaps the differences among race-ethnic groups will continue to decline, and the hypothesis that one race is genetically inferior to another will die a natural death.

Even if we believe that Herrnstein and Murray are wrong about the genetic basis of race-ethnic differences and about the harmful effects of different rates of reproduction among the rich and poor, they raise an important ethical question about the role of intellectual merit in a fair society. Is it fair for more intelligent persons to have a greater likelihood of occupational success than less intelligent persons? In the United States, the average income of persons in the top 10 percent of intelligence scores is 50 percent higher than that of persons with average intelligence scores (Ceci & Williams, 1997). Is that fair? Many people believe that allowing the most competent people to become wealthy is the engine that drives our successful economic system (to the benefit of everyone). What do you think?

If we as a society were to decide that we should minimize the effect of differences in intellectual ability on chances for occupational success, could we do so? Because intelligence is most strongly related to performance of complex jobs, and because complex managerial and professional jobs are the best paid, it seems unlikely that we could eliminate the impact of intelligence on occupational success. The amount of influence, however, depends on how our society chooses to respond to differences in intelligence. If we were to make greater efforts to match each person's unique profile of intellectual strengths to her or his job, specify the requirements of each job as well as the military does, and provide each person with the amount of training needed to reach a high level of job performance, then we could reduce the impact of intelligence on occupational success (Brody, 1997). Society could even take the step of enriching the environments of children with lower intelligence to help level the intellectual playing field (Brody, 1997). Do any of these programs seem reasonable and appropriate to you?

It should also be said that differences in intelligence are only one of the factors that create inequalities in occupational success and income in North America. The difference between persons in the top 10 percent of incomes and persons earning average incomes is four times greater than would be expected on the basis of differences in intelligence scores alone (Ceci & Williams, 1997). Many factors contribute to the huge disparity in incomes in North America today. If equality is your goal, you will have to look at more than intelligence for solutions.

● Review

The term *intelligence* refers to our ability to use cognitive processes to cope with the demands of daily life. This concept has found an important place in contemporary psychology because tests have been developed that predict with reasonable accuracy performance on tasks that require intelligence, particularly school performance. Scores on these intelligence (IQ) tests indicate whether an individual has correctly answered as many questions as the average person of his or her own age. Higher IQs indicate that the person has scored the same number of points as the average person of an older age; lower IQs indicate the opposite. Useful IQ tests must be standardized, evaluated against proper norms, objective, reliable, and valid.

Most psychologists think of intelligence both as a single general factor and as many independent facets of intellectual ability. Consequently, the most widely used IQ tests report both a general score and several more specific scores. Some facets of intelligence, however, particularly tacit intelligence, are not measured well by general tests of intelligence. It is probable that both heredity and environmental factors help determine all aspects of an individual's level of intelligence. There is encouraging evidence that intelligence is rising around the world and that the gaps between different race-ethnic groups in North America are closing.

● Check Your Learning

To be sure that you have learned the key points from the preceding section, cover the list of correct answers and try to answer each question. If you give an incorrect answer to any question, return to the page given next to the correct answer to see why your answer was not correct.

1. The term _____ refers to the cognitive abilities of an individual to learn from experience, to reason well, and to cope effectively with the demands of daily living.

2. Although the "deviation IQ" is now used in most modern intelligence tests, the original "ratio IQ" stated that IQ was equal to

   a) mental age divided by chronological age.

   b) chronological age divided by mental age.

   c) mental age divided by chronological age × 100.

   d) chronological age divided by mental age × 100.

3. Heredity is the only factor that determines a person's intelligence.

   a) True

   b) False

4. The size of differences in intelligence scores among ethnic groups in the United States is

   a) decreasing.

   b) increasing.

   c) remaining the same.

● Thinking Critically About Psychology

1. If psychologists do not agree about the nature of intelligence, how is it possible for them to agree on a test of intelligence?

2. Do you think the "Flynn effect" really means that your generation is more intelligent than your parents' generation? How do you think your parents would answer this question? Why?

Correct Answers 1. intelligence (p. 215), **2. c** (p. 221), **3. b** (p. 223), **4. a** (p. 227).

IMPROVING CRITICAL THINKING

It could be said that a successful person is not a person who has no problems—because all of us have problems—but a person who is able to solve most of his or her problems. As I have discussed in this chapter, however, we human beings are not particularly good at using cognitive skills to solve problems. Our abilities to reason—as impressive as they may be compared with those of every other creature on earth—are not always equal to the problems that face us.

There is a great deal of evidence, however, that shows that we can improve our ability to cope with the demands of life by sharpening our *critical thinking skills* (Halpern, 1998). This section provides a brief overview of a number of ways to improve critical thinking. It is not a solution by itself, however. If you are going to improve your critical thinking skills, reading this section must be only the first step in a long process it's our choice.

Increase Mental Effort

The first step in improving critical thinking skills is motivational, not cognitive. Critical thinking requires a willingness to engage in cognitive work (Halpern, 1998). It simply takes more time and effort to think carefully and critically about a problem than to make the first decision that pops into your head. On the other hand, the amount of effort needed to dig your way out of the consequences of some poor decisions is much greater. So, we either work hard to make good decisions or we work hard to clean up the messes caused by our poor decisions—it's our choice.

Improve Problem Formulation

Most of life's problems are not simple math problems that need no formulation. They are complex situations that must be stated in the form of specific problems. Experts on critical thinking recommend that we attempt to formulate all problems in at least two different ways (Halpern, 1998). This forces us into the realization that there is more than one way to think about the problem—and some of those ways lead to better problem solving than

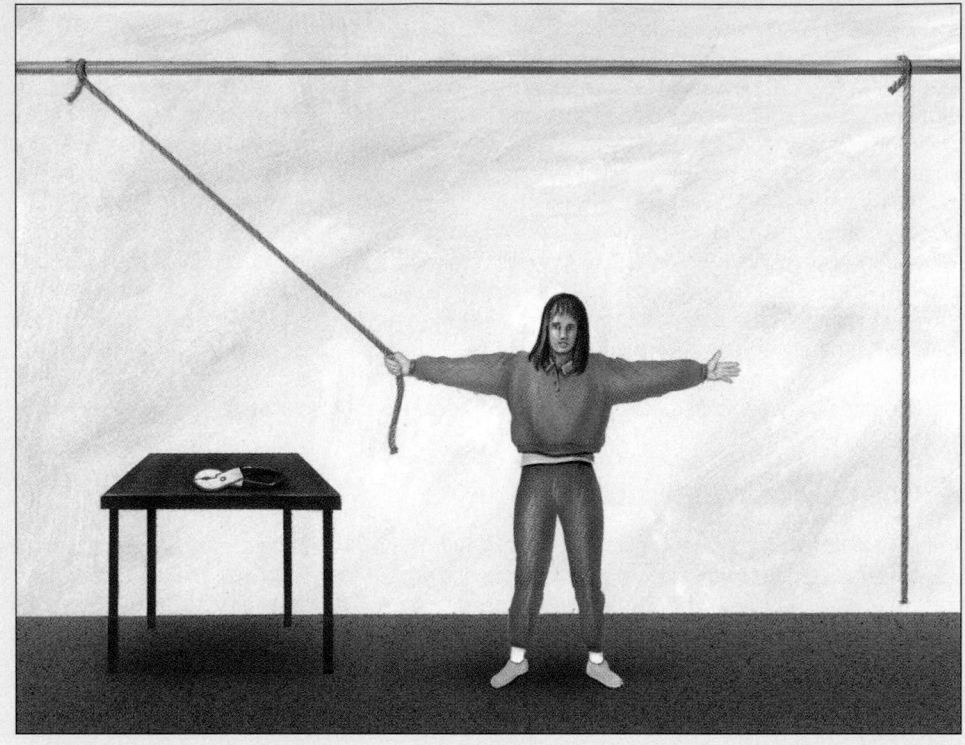

FIGURE 7.11

The Maier string problem. How do you tie the two strings together if you cannot reach them both at the same time? See figure 7.12 for the solution.

other ways. As you work to formulate the problems that face you in the best way, think about the way in which each problem has been framed (or you have framed the problem yourself). Framing the problem in different terms can lead to different decisions. The way in which a problem is formulated and framed is sometimes as important as the problem itself.

Break Out of Unproductive Mental Sets

As discussed in this chapter, mental sets are one of the most common barriers to effective problem solving. Sometimes we must break out of our habitual ways of viewing the elements of the problem to discover a solution. One of the most troublesome of these sets has been referred to as *functional fixedness.* Before we define this term, let's look at a problem where it's encountered. Consider the Maier (1931) string problem. Figure 7.11

shows that you are in a room where two strings are hanging from the ceiling. Your job is to tie the strings together. The problem is that, when holding onto one string, you cannot reach the other. The only other thing in the room with you is a pair of pliers, but, even holding onto one string with the pliers, you cannot reach the other string. What do you do? Look at figure 7.12 for the solution. The difficulty that most people have in solving this problem is similar to the one in Duncker's candle problem. We are simply not accustomed to using pliers as a pendulum to move a string, just as we wouldn't ordinarily use a matchbox as a candle holder. Karl Duncker (1945) referred to the difficulty we have in seeing new uses for objects as functional fixedness. It's a kind of mental set that interferes with problem solving by focusing our thinking about the elements in a problem on their habitual uses. Often the key to effective problem solving is being able to break out of

FIGURE 7.12
The solution to the Maier string problem is to use the pliers as a pendulum to bring the second string closer.

functional fixedness and other interfering mental sets when appropriate.

Let's look at another famous problem that was developed to illustrate the interference of mental set. Psychologist Karl Luchins (1942) asked college students to imagine that they had three jars of different sizes. They then were asked how they would measure an amount of water that was different from that held by any single jar. For example, they might be asked to measure 5 quarts when the three jars held the quantities as shown here.

How would you solve this problem? Five quarts can be measured by filling jar B, then pouring water from it until jar A is filled, leaving 25 quarts in jar B. Then jar C is filled twice from jar B, leaving 5 quarts in jar B. It's simple when you catch on to the method. In algebraic terms, the solution can be expressed as $B - A - 2C$.

After solving five more problems using jars of different sizes, all of which could be solved using the equation $B - A - 2C$, the subjects were given a problem like this: Measure 20 quarts when jar A contains 24 quarts; jar B contains 52 quarts, and jar C contains 4 quarts. This problem could also be solved using the equation $B - A - 2C$, but did you solve it that way? Or did you see that it could be solved more simply by subtracting one jar C from

Jar A	Jar B	Jar C
18 qt	43 qt	10 qt

jar A ($A - C$)? In Luchins' study, more than three-fourths of his students solved the problem the long way.

Why did Luchins' students make a difficult problem out of a simple one? Do people just have a tendency to do everything the hard way? Luchins ruled out that unlikely possibility in his experiment by having another group of students skip the first six $B - A - 2C$ problems and solve the seventh problem *first*. These students *all* used the simple $A - C$ solution. The students who took the long solution to the seventh problem after solving six $B - A - 2C$ problems simply had fallen into a "mental rut" or set.

As we look for ways to improve problem solving in everyday life, we must be

careful to examine our way of understanding the elements of the problem to avoid functional fixedness, prejudice, or other forms of mental set that may be interfering with optimal problem solving. The problem may be solvable if you look at it the right way.

Monitor Your Critical Thinking

People who are effective in critical thinking are aware that they are engaging in critical thinking (Halpern, 1998). That is, they are conscious of being critical thinkers and they monitor how well they are doing. When they catch themselves formulating problems in the first way that comes to mind, getting stuck in mental ruts, or using unproductive heuristic thinking, they pull themselves back into a critical thinking mode.

A General Strategy for Critical Thinking

This section integrates the suggestions presented above with recommendations for generating and evaluating possible solutions to problems. These suggestions are presented in the form of a general strategy for critical thinking and problem solving (Goldfried & Davison, 1976; Halpern, 1998; Turkat & Calhoun, 1980). Even following this strategy will not solve all of life's problems, but it will give you a fighting chance.

You might try going through a hypothetical problem using this strategy just to see how it works. Suppose you run out of money for school—what would the best solution to this problem be for you? A loan? A part-time job? By trying this general outline for problem solving and the other ideas presented in this section, you may be better prepared to deal with the next curve ball that life throws at you.

Here is the general strategy:

1. What is the problem?
   a. Define the problem in clear, specific terms.
   b. Define the problem in at least one other way to find the best formulation.
   c. Be aware of the potential influence of framing.
   d. Think flexibly about the elements of the problem and avoid mental sets.
   e. Draw a diagram of the problem to see how the elements relate to one another.
   f. Make a list of the additional information you need to solve the problem and get it.

2. Generate all possible solutions.
   a. At first, do not judge any solution—just keep thinking of alternative solutions.
   b. Wild ideas are welcome.
   c. See if some of your possible solutions can be combined to make a better possible solution.
3. Now, eliminate any possible solutions that are clearly poor choices.
   a. Alternatives with no chance of success should be dropped.
   b. Intuitive solutions based on heuristic reasoning should be eliminated in situations where logical (algorithmic) reasoning is possible.
4. Examine the likely consequences of the remaining possible solutions one at a time.
   a. List all possible negative consequences of this option.
   b. List all possible positive consequences of this option.
   c. Eliminate the option if it is more likely to produce negative than positive consequences.
   d. Go on to the next option (and repeat steps a–c).
   e. Compare all remaining options in terms of likely consequences.
   f. Select the solution with the greatest likelihood of more positive consequences than negative consequences.
5. Generate all possible ways to implement the solution you have chosen How can you best do this? Use steps 2–4 to select the best way to implement the solution.
6. Implement the solution.

● Summary

Chapter 7 discusses cognition, language, the meaning of intelligence, and the measurement of intelligence.

I. In the process of cognition, information is obtained through the senses, transformed through the interpretive processes of perception and thinking, stored and retrieved through the processes of memory, and used in the processes of problem solving and language.

II. Concepts, the basic units of thinking, are categories of things, events, or qualities linked together by some common feature or features.
   A. Not all concepts are equally easy for us to learn; some are more natural and easily learned than others.

III. In problem solving, information is used to reach a goal that is blocked by an obstacle.
   A. Cognitive operations are used to solve problems. After we decide what kind of problem we face, we evaluate the elements of the problem and decide what information and tools we have to work with. Then we generate a list of solutions and evaluate them.
   B. Algorithmic and heuristic operations are two types of cognitive strategies used in solving problems.
      1. Algorithmic thinking is systematic and logical.
      2. Heuristic thinking is efficient but is not guaranteed to lead to a correct solution and often causes logic and relevant information to be ignored.
   C. Emotional factors and the way in which questions are framed can influence our decisions in ways that are unrelated to the facts or the logic of the problem.
   D. Creative problem solving requires the ability to think in flexible and unusual ways (divergent thinking); the most useful creative solutions are also thought out logically and realistically (convergent thinking).

IV. Language is a symbolic code used in human communication.
   A. Semantic content is the meaning communicated through language.
   B. We generate language from a set of elements and a set of rules for combining them into speech.
      1. The phoneme is the smallest unit of sound in a language. The English language has only 44 phonemes.
      2. Morphemes are the smallest units of meaning in a language.
      3. Syntax is the rules of a language through which an infinite number of understandable utterances are generated.

C. Much of our thinking is in the form of language: The Whorfian, or linguistic relativity, hypothesis states that the structure of language influences how people think.

V. Intelligence refers to the cognitive abilities of an individual to learn from experience, to reason well, and to cope effectively with the demands of daily living.

    A. Intelligence is viewed as a single general factor by some psychologists and as many independent kinds of intellectual ability by others.

    B. Intelligence tests measure a small sample of the cognitive abilities that constitute intelligence.

        1. Useful IQ tests must be standardized, objective, reliable, valid, and evaluated against proper norms.

        2. In some cases, measures of tacit intelligence (knowledge and skills specific to a task that are usually not taught in schools) predict success better in specific everyday tasks than measures of general intelligence.

    C. Intelligence test scores are important in predicting occupational success because persons with higher scores are more likely to qualify for advanced education, take less time to train to perform job skills, and perform complex jobs better.

    D. Intelligence is influenced by both genetic and environmental factors working in combination.

    E. Scores on tests of intelligence and academic achievement have risen considerably in many countries (possibly due to improvements in health and education), and the gap between race-ethnic groups has declined in recent years.

● Resources

1. For a clear statement of the psychology of language, see Scovel, T. (1998). *Psycholinguistics.* New York: Oxford University Press.

2. A scholarly and readable overview of cognition is Hunt, R. R., & Ellis, H. C. (1999). *Fundamentals of cognitive psychology* (6th ed.). Boston: McGraw-Hill.

3. For a firsthand account of Francine (Penny) Patterson's attempt to teach language to a gorilla and of Herbert Terrace's experiences with the chimpanzee Nim Chimpsky, see Patterson, F., & Linden, E. (1981). *The education of Koko.* New York: Henry Holt; and Terrace, H. S. (1980). *Nim.* New York: Knopf.

4. For differing views on the topic of ethnic differences in intelligence, see Jensen, A. R. (1980). *Bias in mental testing.* New York: Free Press; Mackenzie, B. (1984). Explaining race differences in IQ: The logic, the methodology, and the evidence. American *Psychologist, 39,* 1207–1213; Herrnstein, R. J., & Murray, C. (1994). *The bell curve: Intelligence and class structure in American life.* New York: Free Press; and Hunt, E. (1995). The role of intelligence in modern society. *American Scientist, 83,* 356–368.

5. For an excellent discussion of the fair interpretation of ability test scores in business and government for persons of different levels of socioeconomic status and persons with sensory and physical impairments, see Sandoval, J., Frisby, C. L., Geisinger, K. F., Ramos-Grenier, J., & Scheuneman, J. D. (1998). *Test interpretation and diversity: Achieving equity in assessment.* Washington, DC: American Psychological Association.

6. For good statements on intelligence, see Frederiksen, N. (1986). Toward a broader conception of human intelligence. *American Psychologist, 41,* 445–452; and Neisser, U., & others. (1996). Intelligence: Knowns and unknowns. *American Psychologist, 51,* 77–101.

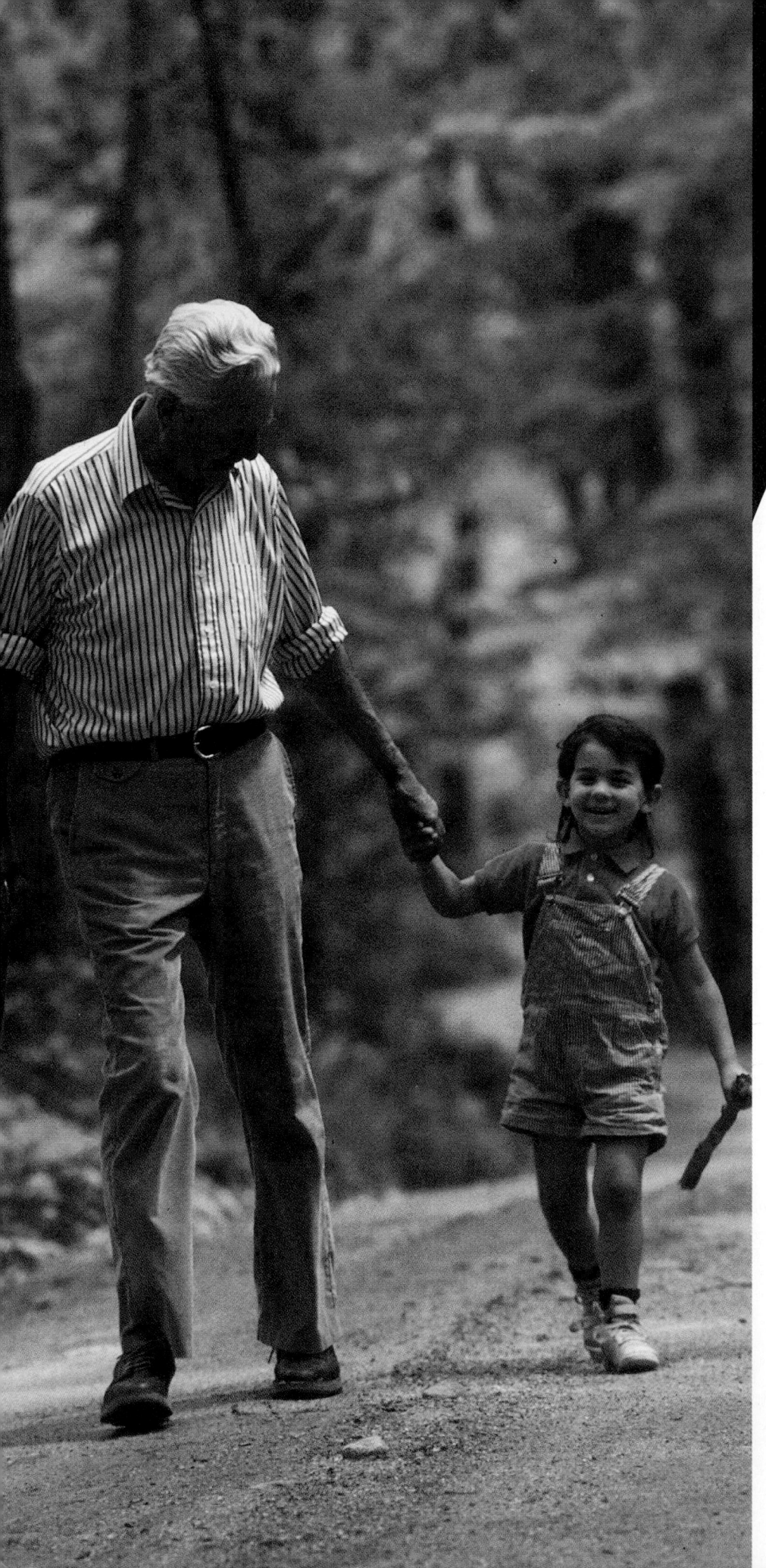

CHAPTER

8

Developmental Psychology

PROLOGUE

Jean Piaget was a notable Swiss scientist who studied the development of cognition in children until his death in 1980. His most important contribution was to show us that children of different ages understand the world in ways that are often very different from the way adults understand it. Indeed, young children understand their worlds in ways that are so different from adults that it is sometimes like trying to communicate with a creature from another galaxy!

A classic experiment by Piaget and his frequent collaborator Barbel Inhelder (1963) makes this point very well. Children of different ages were shown three small three-dimensional replicas of "mountains" arranged on a table top. On the other side of the table, a doll was seated. The children were asked to look at the mountains and then were asked to indicate which picture from several showed the mountains as the doll would see them. Six-year-olds could not do it at all, some 7- and 8-year-olds could, and children 9 to 11 years of age had no more trouble with the task than an adult would.

What does the doll see?

Life doesn't stand still. We are in a state of constant change throughout our lives. When we ask ourselves who we are, we think of ourselves in terms of who we are *now*. But we have been and will be many different people in our lifetime: an infant, a child, a teenager, a young adult, a mature person, and an aged person. The thread of continuity that runs through our lives is very real, but we change more than we realize. To understand ourselves fully, we must understand the process of **development,** the more-or-less predictable changes in behavior associated with increasing age.

development
The more-or-less predictable changes in behavior associated with increasing age.

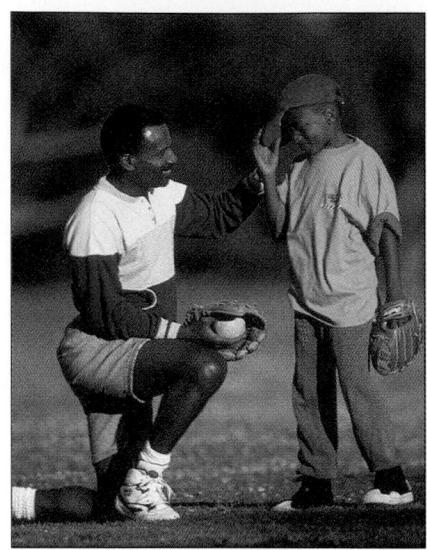

Both nature and nurture work together in development. Without seeing others play (nurture) a child won't use a baseball glove correctly. But the child must be physically developed enough to use the glove (nature).

maturation
(mach´u-rā´shun)   Systematic physical growth of the body, including the nervous system that is relatively independent of experience.

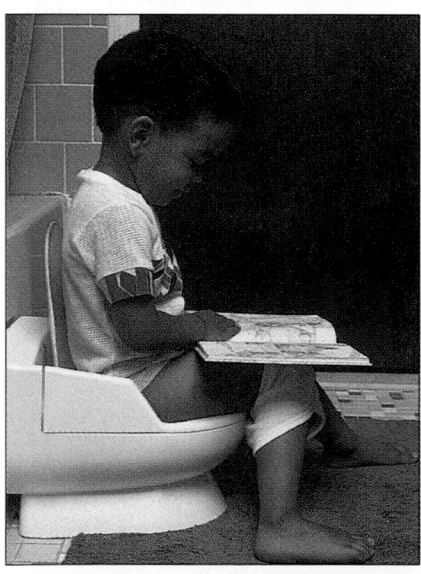

Toilet training, typical of many human behaviors, is learned more quickly when the child is maturationally ready.

BASIC PROCESSES OF DEVELOPMENT

What forces cause us to change as we pass through life? What factors determine whether we grow up to be baseball players or umpires, musicians or opticians? In this section, we will look at the factors that play key roles in the process of development. As you have probably already learned to expect, not all psychologists agree about these factors, so a variety of viewpoints are presented in this chapter.

Nature or Nurture?

Some psychological theorists believe that nearly all important developmental changes are controlled by biological factors (nature): Our behavior "unfolds" over time, like a plant growing from seed to flower. Other theorists assert that the psychological environment (nurture) is the master of our development: Our behavior is "molded" by experiences, like clay in the hands of a sculptor. The vast majority of contemporary psychologists believe, however, that both nature and nurture combine to influence our actions, thoughts, and feelings.

Language provides a good example of the rich interplay of nature and nurture in our lives. There can be no question that experience is important in language development. Children will learn to use language only if they are exposed to language, and they will learn to speak the language to which they are exposed. For example, a French child adopted by a Chinese-speaking family will grow up speaking Chinese, not French. But neither goldfish nor marmosets will learn to speak a human language when given the same amount of experience required by a human child to learn language. One must have a human brain (or, as discussed in chapter 7, an ape brain might be sufficient) to learn a human language. In the absence of the right nature, nurture can accomplish nothing.

Maturation

In the study of development, the most important aspect of nature (biological factors) is **maturation.** This term refers to systematic physical growth of the nervous system and other bodily structures. A primary question for the psychologist specializing in the study of development is "How much of the change that we see occurring with age is the result of physical maturation?"

Although both experience and maturation are important in most developmental changes, maturation is surprisingly important in many specific contexts. For example, experience obviously plays an important role in toilet training—children must be taught to use the toilet—but maturation also plays a key role. Successful toilet training is difficult for most children before the age of 24 months. They are simply not *maturationally ready* to learn that task. After 24 months of age, however, most children learn to use the toilet fairly rapidly.

An experiment using identical twin boys illustrates the idea of maturational readiness beautifully. Toilet training was begun for one boy, Hugh, when he was only 50 days old. Training for Hilton, the other twin, did not begin until 700 days of age (almost 2 years). As shown in figure 8.1, Hugh made no real progress until about 20 months of age, whereas Hilton's progress was rapid from the beginning. Both children learned, but only when they reached the proper level of maturation (McGraw, 1940).

Maturation seems to function in much the same way in intellectual, social, and other areas of development. For example, children perform cognitive tasks more quickly and accurately as they grow older, largely because the myelin coating that speeds neural transmission in the cerebral cortex (see p. 35 to refresh your knowledge about myelin) continues to grow throughout childhood (Bjorklund & Green, 1992). Perhaps partly as a result, cognition changes dramatically with age. It's unlikely that we could teach an 18-month-old to play cooperatively with other children, teach a 4-year-old the concept of physical mass, or teach the concept of justice to a 6-year-old. These behaviors and concepts generally cannot

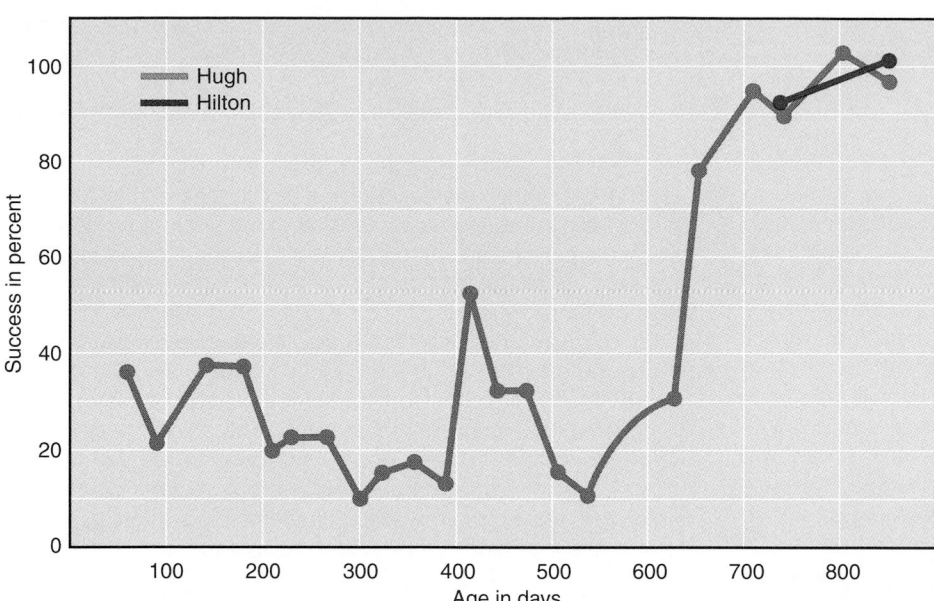

FIGURE 8.1

The importance of maturational readiness is shown in McGraw's (1940) study of toilet training twin boys named Hugh and Hilton. Although Hugh's training was begun at 50 days of age, no progress was achieved until he was about 650 days of age. In contrast, Hilton's progress was rapid because training was begun when he was maturationally ready.

Source: Data from M. B. McGraw, "Neural Maturation as Exemplified in Achievement of Bladder Control," *Journal of Pediatrics,* 16:580–590, 1940.

be learned until later ages, suggesting that maturation of the brain is one of the factors involved in the development of cognition.

Early Experience and Critical Periods

When the Puritans came to America in the 1600s, they brought with them a belief about children that most of us still hold today—namely, that early childhood is the "formative period" for our personalities. We believe that the experiences that we have as a young child powerfully and permanently shape our adult behavior. This is not just a belief held by laypeople; many psychologists hold it, too. But is it true that early experiences irreversibly form our personalities?

Imprinting

Supporting the view that our early experiences are of prime importance is a large body of research on nonhuman animals. German biologist Konrad Lorenz (1937), for example, has extensively studied the behavior and development of the graylag goose. During one phase of his investigations, he wanted to know why young goslings followed their mothers in the little, single-file parades that are the joy of farmers and park-visiting children everywhere. Do they follow the mother goose because of an inborn tendency or instinct (nature), or do they learn to follow (nurture) their mother? Lorenz found that goslings do have an inborn tendency to follow but that they will follow any moving, noisy object that they are exposed to after hatching, not just mother geese. Furthermore, once they begin following something, they generally will not follow anything else but that object. If their mother is out to lunch when they hatch and a rooster should happen to strut by, they will follow him until they are mature geese—presumably much to the rooster's embarrassment.

Lorenz called this special kind of early learning **imprinting.** He thought of it as a kind of learning that was highly constrained by maturation. The maturational control is seen clearly in the fact that imprinting can occur only during a brief, sensitive period of the bird's life called the **critical period.** If imprinting does not occur during the critical period, it probably will never occur. Still, the fact that imprinting is a kind of learning—part of nurture—is obvious because the birds will learn to follow anything that meets the

Konrad Lorenz followed by some of his goslings.

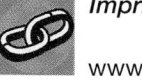

Imprinting

www.mmhe.com/laheye1

imprinting
(im′print-ing)   A form of early learning that occurs in some animals during a critical period.

critical period
A biologically determined period in the life of some animals during which certain forms of learning can take place most easily.

HUMAN DIVERSITY

RAISING A CHILD WHO CANNOT HEAR

All parents must make important decisions about raising children that can have a major impact on their child's emotional and intellectual development. The parents of children who are challenged by physical or sensory limitations, however, face a number of additional decisions. In the case of children with little or no hearing, for example, parents must first decide if the child will learn to speak orally (called "voice") or will learn sign language. The parents of Montreal Expos team member Curtis Pride felt that he would always be an outsider if he did not learn to voice (Gildea, 1993). Other parents disagree, however. They feel that the child will not be able to enter the *deaf culture* (Rutherford, 1988) if sign language is not learned. Many deaf people consider themselves as part of a distinct cultural group rather than having a physical disability. They feel that a deaf child who does not learn sign language will not fully join the only culture that will truly accept the child.

Another choice parents must make is whether to send their child to a residential school for deaf children or to send her or him to a neighborhood school with hearing children. Some parents of deaf children feel that it is best for them to learn to be part of the mainstream culture. Many deaf persons, however, feel that residential schools are better because they allow deaf children to be part of an accepting community, to communicate freely with others, and to develop more fully. Unlike some other groups who are different from the majority of the population, many deaf persons object to being "integrated" into the hearing world. No matter how hard they might try to be part of the mainstream culture, they feel that they will remain separate because few hearing people know sign language.

Jan Hafer and Ellen Richmond (1988) encourage hearing parents of deaf children to learn sign language and to learn about deaf culture and history by interacting with successful deaf persons. But many deaf children live in families where no one has learned sign language. Sign language is a complex language, and it can take parents months or years to learn it. Often, financial and time constraints make it difficult for parents to attend sign language classes, but some experts believe that not doing so can lead to isolation of the child and slow his or her language development (Dolnick, 1993, p. 48).

Technology is progressing in ways that will soon create new options for parents—and new difficult decisions to make. The television program *60 Minutes* ran a story about a deaf girl who had a device implanted in the cochlea of her ears that improved her hearing. The parents of the girl described the operation as "a miracle of biblical proportions" (Dolnick, 1993, p. 43). But some deaf persons wrote letters asserting that the surgery amounts to genocide or child abuse. For example, Roslyn Rosen, president of the National Association of the Deaf, stated that she would not prefer to be able to hear. "I'm happy with who I am, and I don't want to be 'fixed'. Would an Italian American rather be a WASP? In our society everyone agrees that whites have an easier time than blacks. But do you think a black person would undergo operations to become white?" (Dolnick, 1993, p. 38).

Do you have any characteristic that sets you apart from other persons or has created barriers for you? Are you in the minority because of your height, weight, ethnicity, sexual orientation, religion, intelligence, attractiveness, or any other feature? Some of the ways in which human beings differ from one another are more challenging or lead to greater discrimination than others, but most of us are in the minority in some way. How has this influenced you? How do you think you would be different if you had a more challenging physical characteristic?

Parents of deaf children often decide to use sign language with their children.

biological requirements. Goslings have been imprinted on quacking duck decoys and footballs pulled by squeaking pulleys. A famous photo even shows Konrad Lorenz being followed by a flock of goslings that had imprinted on him. It's not clear, however, that anything comparable to imprinting occurs in humans, although we do form attachments to our caregivers through prolonged experience with them.

Early Social Deprivation

Studies conducted with monkeys, which are closer to humans on the evolutionary ladder than geese, also show the long-lasting effects of early experience in a way that seems more relevant than imprinting to the human condition. Harry and Margaret Harlow (Harlow & Harlow, 1965; Harlow & Novak, 1973) carried out a number of studies of the role of early social experiences in development. Are our earliest social experiences especially important to the development of social behavior in childhood and adulthood? Sigmund Freud would have us believe that these **early experiences** are of the greatest significance, but until the Harlows, few researchers had experimentally tested Freud's claims.

The Harlows raised a group of infant monkeys in complete isolation for the first few months of life. Later they returned the monkeys, which had never lived with a mother, to regular group cages with other monkeys. When the monkeys reached adulthood (about 3 years of age), they were placed in breeding cages with another monkey of the other sex. It was then that the Harlows noticed that the social, sexual, and emotional behavior of these monkeys was distinctly abnormal. Females raised without early experience with a real mother appeared fearful and viciously attacked the male when a sexual advance was made. The males, on the other hand, alternated between fearfulness and overenthusiastic, clumsy sexual advances.

Although they had normal social experiences for 2 1/2 years, these monkeys' abnormal experiences during the first 6 months of life had a continuing detrimental effect on their social behavior. Moreover, when a few of the females finally became pregnant and had offspring, the lasting effects of the early social deprivation were made more clear. When the mother-deprived monkeys became mothers themselves, they rejected and even attacked their own infants. Some of the mother-deprived mothers even killed their own infants, and the rest had to be removed from the cage to prevent their deaths.

Much less is known about the effects on humans of abnormal early experiences, however. As a result, opinion is deeply divided among psychologists about this issue. Some believe that abnormal experiences produce irreversible damage (e.g., Bruner, 1974), whereas others believe that, under favorable conditions, the early effects may not be permanent (Kagan, 1984; Paris, 2000). Humans may be more open to the effects of experience throughout the life span. Still, this tentative conclusion is based on only a handful of studies of children with abnormal early experiences who were placed in good homes at an early age and showed marked improvement. Children with abnormal early experiences who live in marginally stable families might be less able to recover.

Variations in Development: Getting There at Different Times

Anyone who deals with children as a parent, a teacher, or another professional must understand that it's normal for development to be highly variable. This is true in two senses: (a) there are differences between children in their development and (b) children vary in the rate of their own development from one period to the next.

Different children develop at different rates. It's normal for one child to walk or talk several months before another child. When we look at charts of the normal age at which children sit, walk, speak in sentences, and so on, we must remember that variations from those norms may mean nothing at all. Deviations from the average are not unusual. Variation is the rule, not the exception, in child development. Any large variation in development should be discussed with a pediatrician or child psychologist, but small variations should not be a cause for concern.

It's also normal for children to be variable in their own development. Children who are shorter than their age-mates often shoot

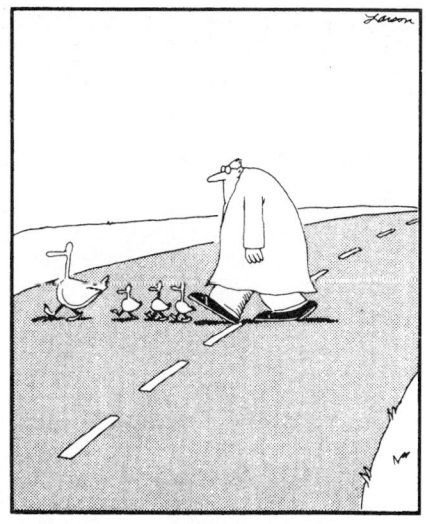

When imprinting studies go awry.

early experiences
Experiences occurring very early in development, believed by some to have lasting effects.

Harry Harlow (1905–1981).

Margaret Harlow (1918–1971).

The Harlow studies of early social deprivation in monkeys revealed that abnormal experiences during the first 6 months of life have a detrimental effect on the social behavior of adult monkeys.

Studies suggest that the effects of abnormal early experiences can be reversed by positive, appropriate experiences at later ages. Sometimes these positive experiences are with adoptive parents.

up suddenly to become taller than most. A fussy baby can become a calm, happy child. And it's not unusual for a child who was above average on an IQ test at age 4 to be just average at age 9 or vice versa. Discontinuities in development, again, are the rule rather than the exception.

● Review

Children change dramatically from birth to adulthood. This fact has led some theorists in the past to assert that developmental changes in behavior are biologically programmed to "unfold" with increasing age. Other theorists have argued that changes in behavior occur because the learning environment "molds" our development. Today it's generally believed, however, that development results from a blend of both biological and environmental influences. Maturation provides an important example of this interaction between biology and environment: Some forms of learning (which clearly depend on the environment) can occur efficiently only when the child has reached a certain level of readiness through physical maturation.

Experiences during critical periods of early development can have lifelong effects on animal behavior. The Harlows' experiments with social deprivation during the infancy of monkeys also show long-lasting effects of abnormal early experiences. Studies of human infants who had abnormal early experiences, but who were adopted by normal families during childhood, however, suggest that humans may be less permanently influenced by early experience than other animals and may be more open to environmental influences throughout the entire life span.

● Check Your Learning

To be sure that you have learned the key points from the preceding section, cover the list of correct answers and try to answer each question. If you give an incorrect answer to any question, return to the page given next to the correct answer to see why your answer was not correct. Remember that these questions cover only some of the important information in this section; it is important that you make up your own questions to check your learning of other facts and concepts.

1. In developmental psychology, the term *nurture* refers to _____ factors that influence development.

   a) biological   c) both of the above

   b) environmental   d) none of the above

2. In the study of development, the most important biological factor is _____, the systematic physical growth of the body, including the nervous system.

   a) maturation   c) growth factors

   b) hormones   d) environment

3. A biologically determined period in the life of some animals during which certain forms of learning can take place most easily is called a _____.

   a) stage   c) critical period

   b) milestone   d) landmark

4. It is normal for the development of children to be _____.

● Thinking Critically About Psychology

1. Is there any practical difference in the implications of the "molding" and "unfolding" views of development for parents?

2. Do you think there are critical periods in human development?

Correct Answers 1. b (p. 238), **2. a** (p. 238), **3. c** (p. 239), **4.** Variable (p. 241).

▶ STAGE THEORIES OF DEVELOPMENT

Although all psychologists agree that people change over time, they disagree considerably over how to conceptualize those changes. One group sees us as changing gradually with age; the other school of thought sees people as going through a series of abrupt changes from one stage to the next. To relate this difference in opinion to our previous discussion, those who see gradual changes generally lean more toward a "molding" view by which they interpret behavior as gradually changing, mostly due to increasing experience. Those who see **stages** in development typically lean toward a view in which behavior "unfolds" over time, largely due to biological maturation.

    Stage theorists believe that the changes occurring from one stage to the next make children qualitatively different (different in "kind") rather than quantitatively different (different in amount) from how they were at a previous stage. When a child learns to use simple words to express herself, for example, she has changed qualitatively; that is, she has become different from the kind of child she was when she could not use language. This qualitative change opens up new experiences and possibilities. Although stage theorists believe that changes between stages are qualitative, they believe that children also change quantitatively during each stage. For example, once the child has mastered some simple words, she will progress for a while by learning more simple words before the next qualitative change takes place (combining words syntactically).

    Stage theorists also believe that all children must pass through the same qualitatively different stages in the same order. Stages are believed to be biologically programmed to unfold in a fixed sequence in all normal persons. In addition, they believe that a child cannot progress to the next stage until the current one has been mastered. A close examination of the writings of even the staunchest stage theorists, however, shows that they recognize that the transition from one stage to the next is a gradual blending. In other words, a child may master one part of a new stage while still struggling with part of a previous stage. One gifted professor of psychology suggested to me that the stages of child development are like a rainbow: We can see that there are different colors in a rainbow, but it's not possible to see exactly where one color stops and the next one begins. Stages of development, like the colors in a rainbow, blend together.

    In the sections that follow, we will discuss several major stage theories of cognitive development, moral development, and personality development. By taking a close look at

stage
One of several time periods in development that is qualitatively distinct from the periods that come before and after.

Jean Piaget (1896–1980).

Lawrence Kohlberg (1927–1987).

"Not guilty, because puppies do these things."

each of these theories, we will better appreciate stage theories in general and will learn a little about the development of children in each of these three important areas.

Piaget's Stage Theory of Cognitive Development

Perhaps the best-known stage theory in psychology is that of Jean Piaget. Piaget was a Swiss scholar who wrote extensively about the development of cognition in children. Piaget distinguished four major stages of cognitive development. These four stages are summarized in figure 8.2. Note that the child's cognitive capacities develop rapidly until about the time of puberty but change little after that. Note, also, the magnitude of the changes in cognition that occur during the childhood stages. On the average, children progress from human beings who cannot reason in mental symbols to persons fully capable of adult reasoning in 11 short years, with many dramatic changes along the way.

We will look closely at each of these stages of cognitive development as we follow the course of normal development in detail later in the chapter.

Stage Theories of Moral Development

Two theorists have provided us with stage theories that are related to Piaget's theory of cognitive development but that focus on the development of moral reasoning.

Kohlberg's Theory of Moral Development

Lawrence Kohlberg (1969) collected data for his stage theory of moral development by presenting boys with moral dilemmas and asking for evaluations of the people and actions involved. The following is an example of the type of dilemma used by Kohlberg in his research:

> In Europe, a lady was dying because she was very sick. There was one drug that the doctors said might save her. This medicine was discovered by a man living in the same town. It cost him $200 to make it, but he charged $2,000 for just a little of it. The sick lady's husband, Heinz, tried to borrow enough money to buy the drug. He went to everyone he knew to borrow the money. He told the man who made the drug that his wife was dying and asked him to sell the medicine cheaper or let him pay later. But the man said, "No, I made the drug and I'm going to make money from it." So Heinz broke into the store and stole the drug.

Did Heinz do the right thing? Kohlberg was interested in the logical process through which people arrived at their answers to moral dilemmas. He concluded that we pass through the three major levels of the development of moral reasoning shown in table 8.1. Nearly all children use only premoral reasoning at age 7, but conventional moral reasoning predominates after age 11. Thus, Kohlberg sees the first two major shifts in moral reasoning as occurring at the same times as the beginnings of the preoperational and concrete operational stages in Piaget's theory of cognitive development. According to Kohlberg, we engage in little principled moral reasoning until age 13, and very few of us ever make it to a stage in which we reason mostly in principled ways. He gives Mahatma Gandhi, Martin Luther King, and Eleanor Roosevelt as examples of persons at the principled stage of moral reasoning (Kohlberg, 1964).

Look carefully at the description of each of Kohlberg's stages of moral development and decide if Heinz did the right thing. At the premoral level, he did the wrong thing because it would get him into trouble. At the conventional stage of moral development, Heinz would be judged to be wrong because he clearly broke the law (the conventions of right and wrong). However, from the perspective of principled reasoning, it could be argued that Heinz did the right thing. After trying to obtain the drug legally, he ignored the consequences of his action (imprisonment), disregarded the community's conventions (the laws against theft), and followed what he thought was the higher moral principle of saving his wife's life. Does that evaluation bother you? Not everyone would agree that this use of

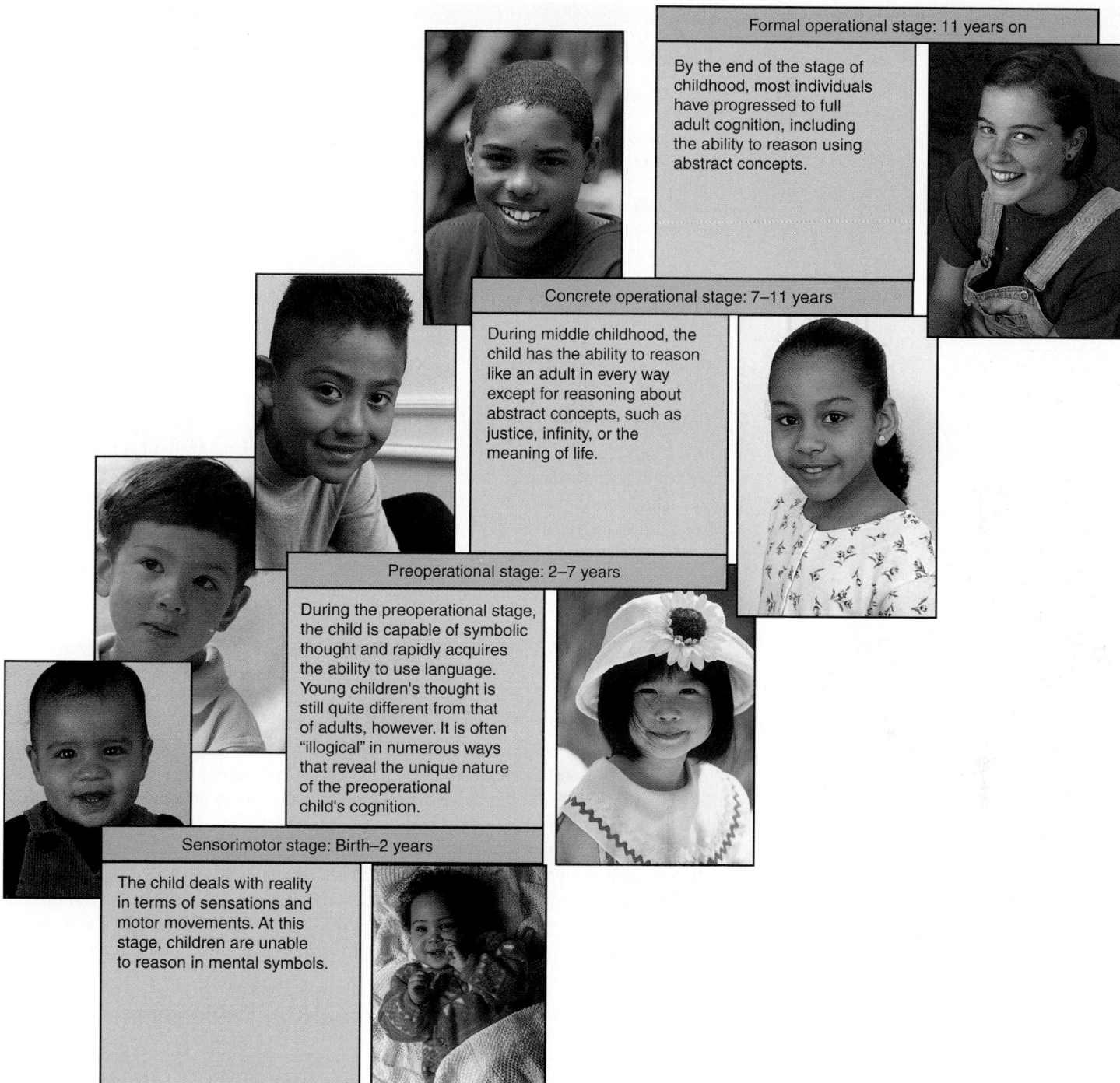

Formal operational stage: 11 years on

By the end of the stage of childhood, most individuals have progressed to full adult cognition, including the ability to reason using abstract concepts.

Concrete operational stage: 7–11 years

During middle childhood, the child has the ability to reason like an adult in every way except for reasoning about abstract concepts, such as justice, infinity, or the meaning of life.

Preoperational stage: 2–7 years

During the preoperational stage, the child is capable of symbolic thought and rapidly acquires the ability to use language. Young children's thought is still quite different from that of adults, however. It is often "illogical" in numerous ways that reveal the unique nature of the preoperational child's cognition.

Sensorimotor stage: Birth–2 years

The child deals with reality in terms of sensations and motor movements. At this stage, children are unable to reason in mental symbols.

FIGURE 8.2

Piaget's stages of cognitive development.

principled reasoning is correct because it tends to place the individual above the law. Indeed, an individual could also explain why Heinz was wrong in terms of the principled stage of moral development. For example, an individual's personal principles might say that it is better for society as a whole to always respect the property rights of others and allow Heinz's wife to die. It is not the particular decision that differs at the different levels of moral development but the nature of moral reasoning involved.

TABLE 8.1	Kohlberg's Levels of Moral Development

Premoral Level	Conventional Level	Principled Level
Young children have no sense of morality as adults understand it. They make moral judgments to obtain rewards and avoid punishment.	At this stage, children make moral decisions on the basis of what they think others will think of them, particularly parents and other persons of authority. Because society's rules, or conventions, state what is expected of them, persons at the conventional level of moral development make moral decisions based on rules.	At this stage, we judge actions on the basis of ethical principles rather than the consequences to us (as in the first two stages). The most advanced moral reasoning within this stage, according to Kohlberg, is based on one's principles of morality, even if they differ from the rules of the larger community.

Carol Gilligan.

Erik H. Erikson (1902–1994).

Gilligan's Theory of Moral Development

Because Kohlberg and others used mostly boys in the initial studies that led to Kohlberg's theory of moral development, Carol Gilligan (1982) has suggested that Kohlberg's theory does not always accurately describe moral development in girls. She argues that female children pass through somewhat different stages. Whereas male development begins with selfish self-interest and moves toward greater reliance on abstract principles of justice, females progress from self-interest toward a balanced concern for the welfare of self and others. Female moral reasoning, in other words, centers on the needs of people, rather than on abstractions.

Specifically, Gilligan (1982) suggests that females progress through the three stages of moral development shown in table 8.2. How would the morality of Heinz's actions be judged at each of these stages of moral development? As in Kohlberg's premoral stage, the kind of immature moral reasoning that Gilligan terms the morality as individual survival stage would judge Heinz to be wrong simply because he would be punished. At the morality as self-sacrifice stage, Heinz might be judged to be correct in sacrificing his own welfare to save his wife. At the morality as equality stage, one would have to equally balance the benefits to everyone in making a moral judgment.

Gilligan's contribution to our understanding of moral development has been acknowledged by Kohlberg and others (Levine, Kohlberg, & Hewer, 1985). Kohlberg argues that Gilligan has overemphasized gender differences in moral reasoning, however. Indeed, reviews of research on the subject (Jaffee & Hyde, 2000; Walker, 1986) have shown that males and females are far more similar in moral reasoning than they are different.

Erikson's Stage Theory of Personality Development

Erik Erikson provides us with a very different example of a stage theory of development. Erikson's stages are turning points, or *crises,* the outcome of which will partly determine the course of future personality development. In using the term crises, Erikson was not suggesting that these turning points are always experienced as emotionally difficult periods, although they certainly can be for some individuals. Rather, Erikson chose this term to emphasize that they can be turning points with far-reaching implications.

The eight stages of Erikson's theory of personality development, which contain the crises, are presented in table 8.3. The name given to each stage by Erikson reflects the two possible outcomes of the stage. To a great extent, particularly in infancy and childhood, the outcome is influenced by the actions of children's parents and other significant people. For example, if infants' parents provide consistent, warm, and adequate care during their child's first year (stage of basic trust vs. mistrust), they will learn to trust the world as a basically safe place. If infants are cared for inconsistently or are physically or emotionally abused, they will consider the world an unsafe place that cannot be trusted. Erikson

---

TABLE 8.2   Gilligan's Stage Theory of Moral Development

Morality as Individual Survival	Morality as Self-Sacrifice	Morality as Equality
The young child's first sense of what is "right" is what is good for him or her. Young children follow rules to obtain rewards for themselves and to avoid punishment.	The next stage of moral reasoning is attained after becoming aware of the needs of others. In this stage, the person believes that, to be good and to be approved of by others, they must sacrifice their own needs and meet the needs of others.	In the most advanced stage of moral development, the person views his or her own needs as equal to those of others. Persons as this stage of moral development have progressed from believing that they must always please others at the expense of their own wishes to a belief that everyone's needs should be met when possible and that sacrifices should be shared equally when the needs of different persons cannot all be met. This is a stage of advocacy of nonviolence—it is not right for anyone to be intentionally hurt, including the person himself or herself.

---

believed that this basic sense of trust or mistrust is usually carried with the individual throughout life.

To take another example, the challenge of the fourth stage (industry vs. inferiority) is learning to meet the demands placed on the child by parents (to clean his or her room in a way that pleases the parents), by teachers (to read, write, and calculate), and by peers (to ride a bike, to take turns). If children master these demands, they develop a belief that effort (industry) leads to success. If they fail to meet the demands of this stage, Erikson believed that a lifelong feeling of inferiority develops.

TABLE 8.3   Erik Erikson's Stages of Personality Development

Age	Name of Stage	Developmental Accomplishments or Failures
0–1 year	Basic trust vs. mistrust	Learns to feel comfortable and trust parents' care; or develops a deep distrust of a world that is perceived to be unsafe
1–3 years	Autonomy vs. shame and doubt	Learns sense of competence by learning to feed self, use toilet, play alone; or feels ashamed and doubts own abilities
3–5 years	Initiative vs. guilt	Gains ability to use own initiative in planning and carrying out plans; or, if cannot live within parents' limits, develops a sense of guilt over misbehavior
5–11 years	Industry vs. inferiority	Learns to meet the demands imposed by school and home responsibilities; or comes to believe that he or she is inferior to others
11–18 years	Identity vs. role confusion	Acquires sense of own identity; or is confused about role in life
18–40 years	Intimacy vs. isolation	Develops couple relationship and joint identity with partner; or becomes isolated from meaningful relationships with others
40–65 years	Generativity vs. stagnation	Develops a concern with helping others and leaving children, products, and ideas to future generations; or becomes self-centered and stagnant
65–years on	Integrity vs. despair	Reaps benefits of earlier stages and understands and accepts meaning of a temporary life; or despairs over ever being able to find meaning in life

● Review

Psychologists who lean toward a view that developmental changes "unfold" largely through maturation also see those developmental changes as occurring in distinct steps, or "stages," through which all children pass in the same order. Those psychologists who lean toward a view of developmental changes as being "molded" by learning experiences tend to perceive these changes as being more gradual in nature and not marked by clear-cut stages. It's useful to think of development as occurring in something like stages, but ones that are not clearly separable from one another. Stage theorists view many aspects of human existence as unfolding in stages: cognition (Piaget), moral reasoning (Kohlberg and Gilligan), and personality (Erikson). Although stage theories tend to give us the impression that all children develop at the same rate, variation in development is normal within broad limits.

● Check Your Learning

To be sure that you have learned the key points from the preceding section, cover the list of correct answers and try to answer each question. If you give an incorrect answer to any question, return to the page given next to the correct answer to see why your answer was not correct.

1. _____ distinguished four major stages of cognitive development, the sensorimotor stage, the preoperational stage, the concrete operational stage, and the formal operational stage.

   a) Jean Piaget   c) Sigmund Freud

   b) John Bowlby   d) Harry Harlow

2. Kohlberg's theory of moral development was criticized by Gilligan primarily because _____.

   a) the data did not support his conclusions   c) it was done so long ago

   b) it was based on a study of boys only   d) his subjects consisted of urban children only

3. Gilligan suggests that moral reasoning in _____ centers on the needs of people rather than on abstractions.

   a) males   c) both males and females

   b) females

4. In Erikson's stage theory of personality development, the stages are turning points, or _____, the outcome of which will partly determine the course of future personality development.

● Thinking Critically About Psychology

1. What are the similarities between the most advanced stages of moral reasoning described by Kohlberg and Gilligan?

2. What are the advantages of theories like Erikson's for understanding life-span development? What are its disadvantages?

Correct Answers **1. a** (p. 244), **2. b** (p. 244), **3. b** (p. 246), **4.** crises (p. 246).

▶ THE CONCEPT OF DEVELOPMENT ACROSS THE LIFE SPAN

We now turn our attention to the normal course of development across the human life span. Our topic will be the typical physical and psychological changes that occur in people from birth to old age. Why is this important? This section is of *fundamental* importance to understanding human condition. Although we tend to think of ourselves as the persons we are right now, human lives are in a constant state of change. The person you are today is different in some ways from the person you were 10 years ago and from the person you will be 10 years from now.

Do you have any photographs that were taken of you as an infant? How about photos of you when you were in the first grade or just starting high school? If so, you can create an amazing learning experience by laying these photos out in a time line. My, how you have grown!

I thought it would help me write this chapter if I did the same thing. The six photos below show me from 5 months to my fifties. Look at the changes! The person in all the photos is me—the thread of continuity in my life is very clear—but the changes are certainly obvious, too. Look at that bewildered infant! It's amazing to me that I was ever that small—as an infant, I weighed less than 5 percent of what I weigh now—or that there was a time when I could neither walk nor talk. By the time I was 5 and was going off to kindergarten in that dashing sailor suit, I was walking, talking, and tying my shoes. But I could not yet read a book, let alone imagine that I would ever write one.

In high school, I played football and took the advice of my coach that the only proper way to cut hair was *off*. I learned how to play guitar about the same year that this photo was taken and played in some really bad high school rock bands. Later, in the sixties, I grew more hair and sang and played a lot of folk songs (very badly, but it was cool then to sound as bad as Bob Dylan). By the seventies, I was a young professor and clinical child psychologist, working hard to establish a career. I worked long hours and spent a great deal of time with my children. I was so busy that I did not even own a guitar for most of the seventies. Is that a bit of gray creeping into my shaggy head of hair?

In the eighties, my hair was still long, but no longer brown. During this decade, I found time to play the guitar again. In fact, a friend of mine owned a recording studio and he let me live out a childhood fantasy of recording a song. That's me in the studio, listening intently to the advice of my bass player, who happens also to be my son. Many changes had taken place in my life by midlife, but when I listened to the recording I found that I still played the guitar badly and sang even worse! The last photo is me in my fifties—back to short hair and showing more than a few wrinkles. Once again, there is little time for the guitar now, but, considering my lack of talent, that's for the best.

Now, consider this question: Which picture best represents me—the real me? The answer: all of them. And that is exactly the point of this section on the life span. We are all in a constant state of change—called development—throughout our lives. If you are going to understand human lives, you must understand that fundamental point.

We will now begin to tell the story of development across the life span. We will follow the child from infancy through the stages of childhood, through adolescence, and finally through the stages of adult life.

▶ DEVELOPMENT IN INFANCY AND CHILDHOOD

A neonate will reflexively grasp anything that is placed in its hand.

neonatal period
(ne″ō-nā′tal)   The first two weeks of life following birth.

rooting reflex
An automatic response in which an infant turns its head toward stimulation on the cheek.

Neonatal Period: The Newborn

The first two weeks of life are termed the **neonatal period** and mark the transition from the womb to independent life. What is the world of the neonate like?

Physically, the neonate is weak and dependent on adults. It cannot raise its head or roll over by itself. It does have a repertoire of a few useful reflexive behaviors, however. When stimulated on one side of the mouth, for example, the neonate turns its head toward the stimulation and begins searching and sucking until something is in its mouth. This **rooting reflex** enables the baby to take its mother's nipple in its mouth and nurse.

The sensory abilities of neonates are surprisingly well developed. Their hearing is fairly good, and they react differently to different odors and tastes (Santrock, 1998). However, they are distinctly nearsighted little people. They can see fairly well (but probably fuzzily) up to about 12 inches from their eyes, but the world farther away is probably a blur to them (Salapatek, 1977). It was previously believed that the skin senses of neonates were poorly developed, but it is now clear that they are quite sensitive to touch (Santrock, 1998) and that male neonates definitely react to circumcision of the penis without anesthesia as if it were painful (Gunnar, Malone, & Fisch, 1988). Few cognitive abilities are developed during the neonatal period, but neonates respond to faces in a way that suggests that they recognize that they are a conceptual class distinct from other concepts of objects (Santrock, 1998). In most ways, however, the process of cognitive development is just beginning.

The emotions of the neonate are quite diffuse. Sleep is very common in this stage, occupying about 16 hours a day (Roffwarg, Muzio, & Dement, 1966). The neonate engages in little of what could be called social behavior, except the intimate contact between neonate and parent in cuddling and nursing. At first, the neonate is a passive participant, but, as we will see in a moment, it soon becomes an active partner in social interactions.

Although we think of infancy as a single stage of development, a tremendous amount of change occurs from birth to 2 years. This photo illustrates the physical differences in infants of 2, 3, 6, 12, 15, and 18 months. Notice the differences in how they sit—the 2-month-old can only lie there, whereas the 18-month-old can lounge casually on the arm of the couch.

Infancy: 2 Weeks to 2 Years

Physical Development

At 2 weeks of age, the baby acquires the official title of infant. Much is going on developmentally during this period of rapid change. Physical development and growth are more rapid during the first year than at any other time in life. By 2 months, many infants can raise their head and chest on their arms and can grasp an object that is held directly in front of their head and shoulders. By 6 months, many can roll over from back to front, sit, and soon begin to crawl. By 1 year, many can walk alone and grasp small objects with their fingers and thumbs. By 2 years, they are "getting into everything" and walking well, but with the peculiar gait that earns them the nickname of "toddlers."

From 2 weeks to 2 months, rapid change takes place in all senses. Clear vision increases to 12 feet during this period. By 6 months of age, their vision is 20/20 (normal). Young infants amuse themselves, and their families, by staring at interesting visual stimuli. They prefer to look at patterned stimuli with sharp contours (Banks & Salapatek, 1981). Fortunately for parents, human faces fall into this category.

Cognitive Development (Sensorimotor Stage)

Infancy is the **sensorimotor stage,** according to Jean Piaget. During the early part of this stage, the infant moves from pure reflexive actions to the ability to coordinate sensations and motor movements, such as voluntarily taking a nipple into the mouth and sucking. From about 2 months on, the infant begins to interact actively with its environment. It no longer passively stares at objects but takes great pleasure in pushing, pulling, and mouthing them. This kind of experience, in which the infant actively changes the sensations it receives by using its hands and feet to alter the environment (sensorimotor experience), is believed to be important in the development of motor behaviors such as crawling (Held & Hein, 1963). By 4 1/2 months, most infants respond positively to the sound of their names (Mandel, Jusczyk, & Pisoni, 1995).

During infancy, children develop the ability to form cognitive representations of the world. For example, by 6 to 9 months of age, the child begins to understand that objects exist even when they are out of sight. This is called **object permanence.** Before that time, if an object at which the infant is looking is hidden from sight by a card, the infant will not push the card aside to look for it. It's as if the infant does not know that the object is still there—a variation of "out of sight, out of mind." After 6 to 9 months of age, however, the infant will search for the object behind the cloth, suggesting that the infant knows that it's back there somewhere. This is both a happy and a sad development for parents. Now that the 9-month-old knows that spoons still exist when thrown on the floor, the infant quickly masters the game of "dropsies" (McCall, 1979). They joyously fill their mealtimes with the game of throwing their spoons on the floor while Dad or Mom picks them up. But, although the child can represent parts of the world in mental images, she cannot yet use those images to reason.

By 9 months, too, infants begin to understand some nouns, such as *ball* and *cookie,* and can respond to *bye-bye* and other gestures. These changes mark the beginning of a far

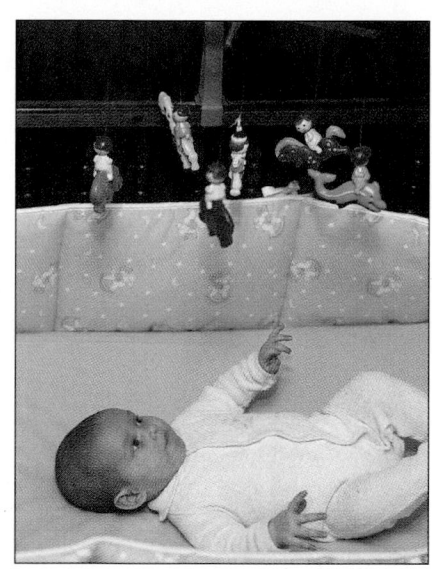

During the sensorimotor stage, infants stare at interesting visual stimuli, including human faces.

sensorimotor stage
In Piaget's theory, the period of cognitive development from birth to 2 years.

object permanence
The understanding that objects continue to exist when they are not in view.

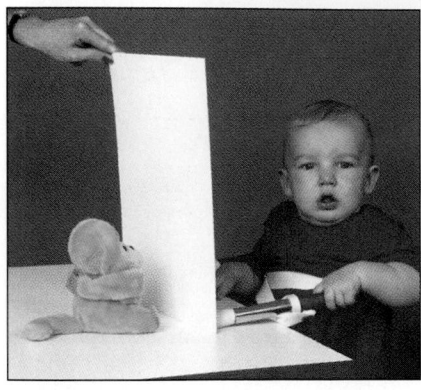

Awareness that objects still exist after they are removed from view (object permanence) emerges between the ages of 6 and 9 months.

telegraphic speech
The abbreviated speech of 2-year-olds.

attachments
The psychological bonds between infants and caregivers.

separation anxiety
The distress experienced by infants when they are separated from their caregivers.

more complex level of cognitive functioning. By 12 months, most infants can say some words, and by 18 months the infant has a speaking vocabulary of 20 words. By 18 months, the average infant can also understand prohibitions ("No, no . . . don't touch") and can respond correctly to "Show me your nose (ear, toe, mouth, etc.)." By age 2, the infant has a speaking vocabulary of 250 words and speaks in word combinations that fascinate adults in accomplishing so much by saying so little. It has often been referred to as **telegraphic speech** because it leaves out the same words that would be left out of a brief telegram. Sentences like "Milk all gone" and "Daddy silly" say all that needs to be said.

Emotional and Social Development

Infants enter the world with a restricted range of emotions that grows more complex as they mature. Neonates are capable of only three emotional expressions: surprise, pleasure, and distress (National Advisory Mental Health Council, 1995a). By about 2 months, they show their first true social behavior—they smile at the faces of their caregivers. By 4 months, they have added a fourth emotion to their repertoire—anger. The infant's repertoire of emotions expands again between 6 and 9 months, when shyness around strangers and fear of being separated from their caregivers emerge for the first time. Before 6 to 9 months, infants are generally comfortable with any adult who will take care of them, but after that time they are often fearful of anyone but their mother, father, or other caregiver (National Advisory Mental Health Council, 1995a). Infants also first learn to fear the sight of a hypodermic needle at about 6 to 9 months (Izard, 1978; Sroufe, 1978). The emergence of social smiling at 2 months is a nice reward for parents, who change diapers and walk the floor at night, but the appearance of anger and fear between 4 and 9 months is not always welcome. Both are signs of normal, healthy development of the infant's emotions, however.

Cornell University psychologist Eleanor Gibson developed an interesting method of studying the development of the fear of heights (Gibson & Walk, 1960). When 6- to 9-month-old infants are placed on the "visual cliff" (see fig. 8.3), they show fear and avoidance of the "deep" side. The visual cliff is made using a clear sheet of Plexiglas. Under one side, a patterned floor is right under the glass. On the other side, the pattern is several feet below the glass. When lighted properly, it appears to be a cliff from which the infant could fall. It's interesting to note that infants can *perceive* the depth of the visual cliff several months before they show any fear of it. They look puzzled when placed on the deep side of the visual cliff at 4 months but do not show fear until after they can crawl and have experienced stumbling and falling firsthand (Lewis & Rosenblum, 1978; Scarr & Salapatek, 1970).

By 2 years, emotions grow even more complex. By this time, many infants act guilty after misbehavior and seem to feel ashamed after failure. Two-year-old infants are richly social creatures who have formed strong **attachments** to their parents or other caregivers (Lewis & Rosenblum, 1978). The strength of this attachment can be seen in three ways. First, infants often cling, grasp, grab, and do whatever else they can to stay close to their parents. Nothing short of the parents' physical closeness and undivided attention will suffice at times. Second, when infants 6 to 9 months or older are separated from their parents, they often show intense **separation anxiety**—the crying and fussing that baby-sitters know so well. Third, infants of this age sometimes also exhibit fear of strangers; no one but the adults to whom they are attached (parents, day-care workers, grandparents) have the same soothing effect.

Early Childhood: 2 to 7 Years

According to Piaget, a qualitative change occurs as the child reaches the preoperational stage at about 2 years of age. Notice as you read this section how different the young child is from the infant. Early childhood is still a period of rapid growth, but growth is far less explosive than in infancy and declines in rate annually. Great

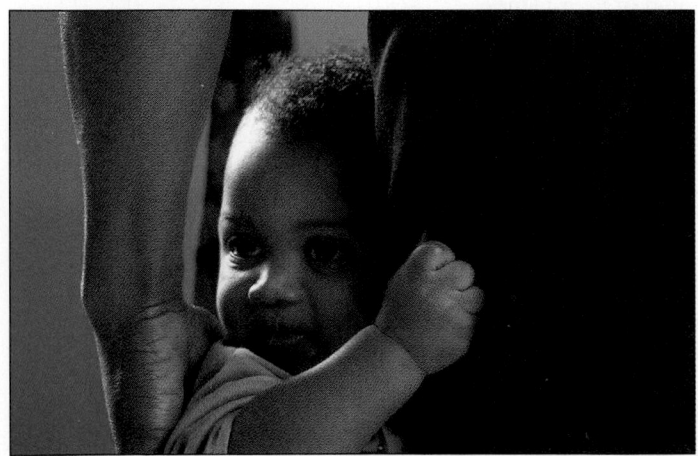

Strong attachments are formed between infants and caregivers during the first two years of life.

FIGURE 8.3
Eleanor Gibson and Richard Walk (1960) developed the visual cliff to test infant depth perception. The visual cliff consists of a thick sheet of glass placed on a table. The "shallow" end of the visual cliff has a checkerboard surface an inch or so below the glass. The "deep" end of the visual cliff has a checkerboard surface several feet below the glass. An infant who has reached the crawling stage will crawl from the center of the table across the shallow end, but not across the deep end, to reach his or her mother. This indicates that by at least the age of 6 months infants can perceive depth.

improvements in the coordination of small and large muscle groups take place during this period, which sees the emergence of hopping, skipping, throwing, and the other motor behaviors that are so much a part of early childhood.

Cognitive Development (Preoperational Stage)

The **preoperational stage** begins at 2 years of age and is a time of dramatic change in cognition. By about 2 years of age, most children are first capable of thinking in mental images. The young child's ability to think is quite different from that of adults, however.

The preoperational child's thinking is often quite illogical by adult standards. Indeed, the name of this stage comes from the fact that the child still cannot perform logical mental operations. There are a variety of other ways in which the cognition of the preoperational child is wonderfully distinct. For example, the young child's thought is **egocentric,** or self-centered. Piaget does not mean by this term that the child is selfish, but that the child is simply not able to see things from another person's perspective. Egocentrism also leads young children to believe that inanimate objects are alive, just as they are (known as **animism**). It's common for children of this age to believe that the moon is alive and actually follows them around when they are walking or riding in a car at night.

The child's imagination is often very active at this stage, and, because of her egocentrism, it's difficult at times for the child to distinguish real from imaginary. That's why imaginary friends that seem very real to the child are relatively common during this stage. Other errors of logic are quite common, too, giving young children a special kind of logic demonstrated in comments such as "Grandma, he's not your son; he's my dad!"

Transductive reasoning—errors in inferring cause-and-effect relationships—is also common in the preoperational child. For example, a preoperational child might conclude that spiders cause the basement to be cold. Indeed, the basement *is* cold and there *are* spiders in it, but young children often confuse the cause-and-effect relationships among such facts.

Children in the preoperational stage show egocentric thought. They may believe, for example, that the moon is following them as they walk or ride in a car.

preoperational stage
In Piaget's theory, the period of cognitive development from ages 2 to 7.

egocentric
(e″gō-sen′trik) The self-oriented quality in the thinking of preoperational children.

animism
(an′ĭ-mizm) The egocentric belief of preoperational children that inanimate objects are alive, as children are.

transductive reasoning
(trans-duk′tiv) Errors in understanding cause-and-effect relationships that are commonly made by preoperational children.

The most notable social changes in the preoperational period are in peer relationships. Between the ages of about 2 and about 7, children go from mostly solitary play, through parallel play, and finally on to cooperative play.

solitary play
Playing alone.

parallel play
Playing near but not with another child.

cooperative play
Play that involves cooperation between two or more children.

By the end of this period, the preoperational child begins to grasp logical operations and makes fewer cause-and-effect errors. At age 5, the child may be able to pick out all the blue marbles from a jar or all the big marbles, but thinking about two concepts at one time is still difficult. For example, picking out all the big blue marbles may still be too much.

Perhaps the most impressive developmental change during the preoperational stage is the growth in language. From a speaking vocabulary of 250 words at age 2, the child reaches a vocabulary of more than 14,000 words by age 6, learning a phenomenal average of almost 9 new words per day (Carey, 1977; Santrock, 1998). From simple 2- or 3-word combinations at age 2, the child masters much of adult syntax during the same period. Seemingly, the child has finally achieved the maturational capacity to learn language and proceeds to do so without hesitation.

Emotional and Social Development

Both positive and negative emotions are fairly well developed by age 2, but they become considerably richer and more intricate during the preoperational stage. Most of this elaboration of emotion seems to be linked to cognitive development. For example, children do not develop fears of unexperienced things—such as fires, drowning, and traffic accidents—until well into the preoperational period, when they are capable of understanding the concepts behind the fears.

The most notable social changes during this period occur in relationships with peers. At age 2, most children engage in **solitary play.** That is, they play by themselves, even if other children are present. This type of play rapidly decreases in frequency from ages 2 to 5. At first, solitary play is replaced by **parallel play,** in which children play *near* one another in similar activities, but not *with* one another. By the end of the preoperational stage, **cooperative play,** which involves a cooperative give-and-take, has become the predominant type of play (Barnes, 1971).

The shifting pattern of play seems to parallel cognitive development. In the early part of the preoperational stage, when thinking is highly "egocentric," it's not surprising that "selfishness" and lack of cooperation should prevail. Young children may not be able to understand any other type of play. As they reach the end of the stage, however, egocentric thinking declines and cooperative play increases.

A similar shift occurs in emotional outbursts from the beginning to the end of the preoperational stage. Two- and 3-year-olds typically engage in temper tantrums that are directed at no one, whereas 4- to 7-year-olds direct their aggression at others (Sheppard & Willoughby, 1975). Although this kind of behavior is hardly "sociable," it's a more social, less egocentric form of emotion than temper tantrums.

By age 2, most boys and girls have begun to act in sex-typed ways. Males tend to play with trucks, airplanes, and blocks; girls play mostly with dolls, stuffed animals, and dress-up clothes (Fagot, 1974). At this early age, they seem to have a conscious awareness of their own sex (McConaghy, 1979) and understand the sex stereotypes of the culture concerning clothing, occupations, and recreation (Ruble & Ruble, 1980).

Middle Childhood: 7 to 11 Years

These are the elementary school years. It's no accident that formal education begins in earnest during this period, because most children are then intellectually and socially ready for the demands of school. Physical growth proceeds at a fairly slow pace in middle childhood, but it's a healthy period in which most children experience little illness. Continued improvements in strength and coordination are the only notable advances.

Cognitive Development (Concrete Operational Stage)

concrete operational stage
In Piaget's theory, the period of cognitive development from ages 7 to 11.

The opening of the **concrete operational stage** is marked by important cognitive changes. Children emerge as capable thinkers who use most adult concepts except those that are abstract. They can order objects (seriation) according to size, weight, and other dimensions. They understand the **reversibility** of logical operations; having added together $7 + 2 = 9$, they have little trouble reversing the operation to see that $9 - 2 = 7$.

   One of the most fascinating acquisitions of the concrete operational child is the concept of **conservation.** When children younger than 7 are shown two wide beakers containing equal amounts of water, they have no trouble seeing that they contain the "same amount" of water. But, when the water from one beaker is poured into a tall, narrow beaker right in front of their eyes, they usually think the tall beaker contains "more" water because it's higher. Children over the age of 7 who are in the concrete operational period are not fooled by appearances in this way. According to Piaget, the concrete operational children are able to deal with conservation problems because their thought is more **decentered,** which means that they can think of more than one thing at a time. Consequently, the concrete operational child no longer has trouble picking out the big blue marbles from a jar; he or she can deal with both concepts at the same time. The rapid growth in cognitive ability during middle childhood is based on rapid increases in children's speed of processing information and expansions in the capacity of short-term memory (Fry & Hale, 1996).

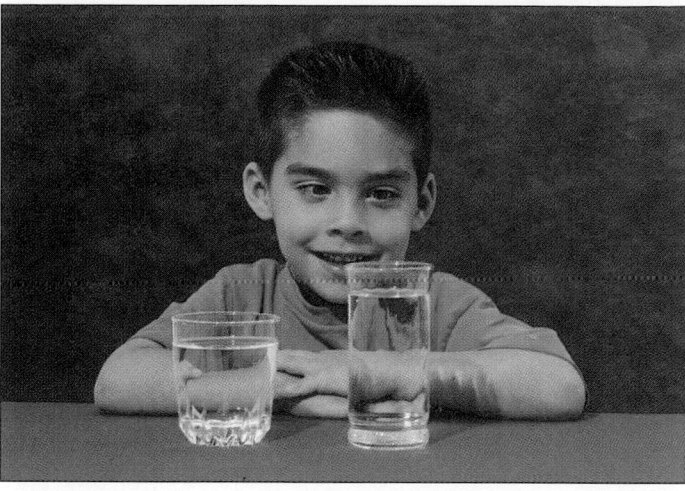

In the concrete operational stage, children learn to recognize that the volume of a liquid does not change when it is poured into a glass of a different shape.

Emotional and Social Development

Few changes of note occur in the expression of emotions during the concrete operational stage, but social relationships are markedly different than before. Children enter this period with close ties to their parents. Although these continue to be important, relationships with peers become increasingly significant during this period. Before age 7, children have friendships, but they generally are not enduring and typically are not close. After 7, peer friendships become more important to children and tend to last longer. Friendship groups, or *cliques,* also emerge during the concrete operational stage. Most friendships are with members of the same sex, and those cross-sex friendships that do exist are generally "just friends." Although the terms *boyfriend* and *girlfriend* are freely used, they have little meaning in the adult sense.

reversibility
(re-ver′sĭbil-ĭ-tē)   The concept understood by concrete operational children that logical propositions can be reversed (if $2 + 3 = 5$, then $5 - 3 = 2$).

conservation
The concept understood by concrete operational children that quantity (number, mass, etc.) does not change just because shape or other superficial features have changed.

decenter
(dē-sen′ter)   To think about more than one characteristic of a thing at a time; a capacity of concrete operational children.

● Review

When we look back over the explosive growth of the neonate into a child, it appears that there may be some utility in discussing development in terms of "stages." Interrelated changes in several behavioral systems do occur that may be dramatic enough to justify the phrase "qualitatively different stage." However, the entrance to a new stage is not marked by abrupt changes. Developmental changes are gradual and inconsistent, and they take place both within and between stages. There is value, then, in thinking of human development in terms of stages, but there are limits on that value. The detailed picture of infant and child development presented in this section shows that human growth is both a series of landmark steps and a continuous, flowing process. There are no shortcuts to describing the marvelous complexities of human development.

● Check Your Learning

To be sure that you have learned the key points from the preceding section, cover the list of correct answers and try to answer each question. If you give an incorrect answer to any question, return to the page given next to the correct answer to see why your answer was not correct.

1. Although an infant during the _____ (first two weeks of life) is weak and dependent on adults, it does have useful reflexive behaviors and has already begun to learn.

   a) trimester
   c) toddler period
   b) neonatal period
   d) prenatal period

2. By 6 to 9 months of age, a child begins to understand that objects exist even when they are out of sight. This is called _____.

   a) object permanence
   c) constancy theory
   b) continuation
   d) conservation

3. According to Piaget, the _____ stage (ages 2 to 7 years) is marked by a phenomenal growth in language.

   a) operational
   c) infancy
   b) concrete operational
   d) preoperational

4. _____ describes the concept understood by concrete operational children (ages 7 to 11 years) that quantity does not change just because shape or other superficial features have changed.

   a) Object permanence
   c) Quantity maintenance
   b) Conservation
   d) Continuity

● Thinking Critically About Psychology

1. If you were a teacher of kindergarten children, how would knowledge of the preoperational stage of cognitive development influence the way you teach?

2. If you were forced to choose, would you describe development in infancy and childhood as a series of stages or as a continuous process? How would you support your choice?

Correct Answers   1. b (p. 250),   **2. a** (p. 251),   **3. d** (p. 253),   **4. b** (p. 255).

▶ ADOLESCENT DEVELOPMENT

adolescence
The period from the onset of puberty until the beginning of adulthood.

puberty
(pū′ber-tē)   The point in development at which the individual is first physically capable of sexual reproduction.

Adolescence is ushered in by the monumental physical changes of **puberty** through which the person who was a child only yesterday becomes sexually capable of being the parent of a child. The adolescent period is marked by rapid physical growth and change and by a heightening of sexual and romantic interest in others. And it's a time in which peers are often more important than parents in terms of attachment and influence. The adolescent is capable of reasoning in abstractions for the first time. Partly for this reason, he or she may spend a great deal of time contemplating abstract issues such as justice and equality. There is no clear-cut demarcation of the end of adolescence in our society. Rather than at any specific age, individuals pass from adolescence to adulthood when they establish adult social relationships and adult patterns of work.

Physical Development

A number of psychologically important physical changes occur during adolescence, particularly during puberty, which is the onset of adolescence. These changes alter physical appearance so much that—in what seems like a moment—girls come to look like women and boys like men. Height and weight increase sharply, pushing adolescents quickly to adult size. A look in the mirror changes forever the adolescent's image of himself or herself.

Puberty begins with the production of sex hormones by the ovaries in females and the testes in males. These hormones trigger a series of physiological changes that lead to ovulation and menstruation in females and the production of sperm cells in males. These are the **primary sex characteristics** that indicate that the adolescent has the ability to reproduce. These physical changes are accompanied by activation of sexual desire and corresponding increases in dating, kissing, petting, masturbation, and other sexual activities.

Menarche, or the first menstrual period, occurs on the average at about 12 years 6 months in American females, and the production of sperm begins about two years later in males (Tanner, 1970). The age of menarche is younger today than in the past and younger here than in many foreign countries. In 1900, the average age of menarche in the United States was about 14 years, and, even today, the average age in one New Zealand tribe is over 17 years (Tanner, 1970). Researchers believe that these differences are due to improved nutrition and health care in the United States over the years, but that menarche will not begin much younger in the future as the natural limit appears to have been about reached (Petersen, 1979).

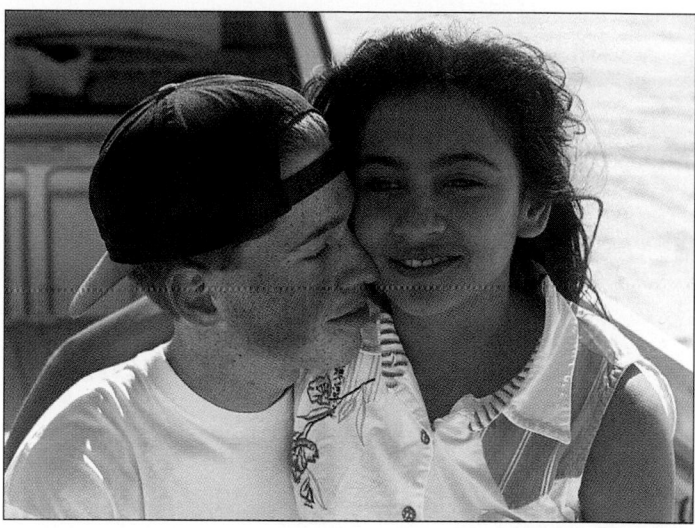
Activation of sexual desire occurs during adolescence.

The more obvious changes occurring during puberty are the development of the **secondary sex characteristics.** In females, the first change is an accumulation of fat in the breasts, which results in a slight "budding," followed by a gradual enlargement of the breasts over a period of several years. There is also a growing accumulation of fat around the hips, resulting in a broadening that further gives the appearance of the adult female body shape. Finally, about the time of menarche, pubic hair begins to grow.

In males, the first secondary sexual change is the growth of the testes, followed by a broadening of the shoulders, lowering of the voice, and growth of the penis. Soon, pubic and facial hair grow, thus creating the physical image of an adult male.

Another outwardly obvious sign of puberty is the rapid increase in weight and height known as the **adolescent growth spurt.** Just before puberty, rapid weight gain is common, mostly in the form of fat. This can be a source of concern to both the adolescent and her or his parents, but soon most of this weight is redistributed or shed. At about the onset of puberty, the adolescent suddenly shoots up in height. During the year of most rapid growth, many boys gain as much as 4 inches and 26 pounds, and many girls add as much as 3 1/2 inches and 20 pounds.

primary sex characteristics
Ovulation and menstruation in females and production of sperm in males.

menarche
(mĕ-nar´kē) The first menstrual period.

secondary sex characteristics
Development of the breasts and hips in females; growth of the testes, broadening of the shoulders, lowered voice, and growth of the penis and facial hair in males; and growth of pubic and other body hair in both sexes.

adolescent growth spurt
The rapid increase in weight and height that occurs around the onset of puberty.

Cognitive Development (Formal Operational Stage)

At about age 11, the shift from concrete operational to formal operational thought begins in some adolescents. Other individuals do not begin the shift as early or reach this advanced level of thinking until early adulthood, and some never reach it at all (Piaget, 1972; Santrock, 1998). The **formal operational stage** is characterized by an ability to use abstract concepts. The logic of formal operational thinking goes beyond the concrete details of each incident or problem to the underlying abstract principles involved.

In a classic experiment conducted by Swiss developmental psychologists Barbel Inhelder and Jean Piaget (1958), children and adolescents of different ages were given two weights that could be hooked at different places on the arms of a scale; their job was to make the scale balance. Seven-year-olds—who were at the beginning of the concrete operational stage—were generally unable to balance the scale at all. They could understand that the two weights must be placed on opposite arms of the scale, but they did not seem to understand the importance of where the weights were hooked on the arms. By the end of the concrete operational stage, age 10, most children were able to balance the scale through trial and error, but they were not able to explain in words how it worked.

By about age 14, many of the subjects had reached the stage of formal operational thinking and were able to explain that, the farther a weight is placed from the center

formal operational stage
In Piaget's theory, the period of intellectual development usually reached by about age 11 and characterized by the ability to use abstract concepts.

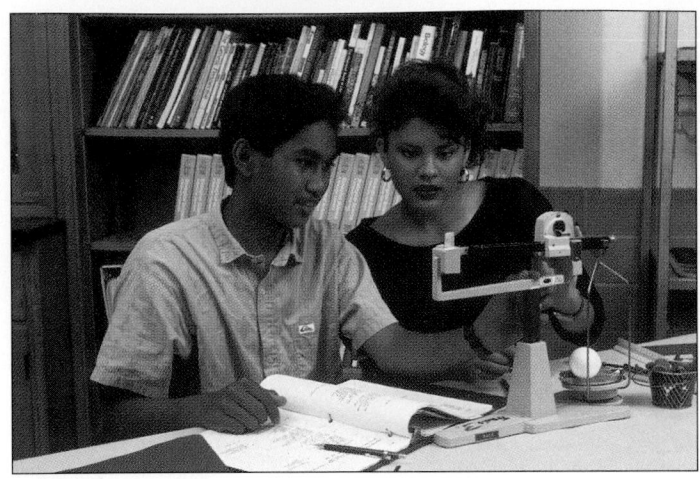

The ability to understand abstract concepts is a characteristic of formal operational thought.

Adolescent Egocentrism

www.mmhe.com/laheye1

adolescent egocentrism
The quality of thinking that leads some adolescents to believe that they are the focus of attention in social situations, to believe that their problems are unique, to be unusually hypocritical, and to be "pseudostupid."

(fulcrum) of the scale, the more downward force it exerts. These children were able, without trial and error, to place a 5-kilogram weight twice as far from the fulcrum as a 10-kilogram weight on the other side. They could also easily deduce from this principle that weights of 3 and 6 or 2 and 4 kilograms would balance on the same hooks used by the 5- and 10-kilogram weights. They understood, in other words, the *abstract* principle that it's the *ratio* of weights and distances that matters, not the specific weights involved in any one example. They were able to think in abstract logical terms.

Individuals who have achieved formal operational thinking are able to use it in many areas of their lives. Piaget suggests, for example, that adolescents often seem preoccupied by concepts such as truth, justice, and the meaning of life partly because the capacity to think in such abstract terms is new to them.

Although most adolescents have reached the level of formal operational reasoning, their cognition at times often retains an immature quality. This is not really surprising; they have recently developed the ability to reason abstractly but have little experience on which to base their abstract thoughts. In particular, David Elkind (1967, 1981; Elkind & Bowen, 1979) has pointed out that adolescents often possess a form of egocentrism that, although different from the egocentrism of young children, similarly distorts their perception of reality. There are four primary features of **adolescent egocentrism.** As you will readily notice, the thinking of fully mature adults is not always free of these characteristics. However, the four reality-distorting qualities described by Elkind are more characteristic of the adolescent stage than any other stage and they help explain why conversations between adolescents and adults are sometimes so frustrating to both parties.

The primary characteristic of adolescent egocentrism has been termed the *imaginary audience*—an audience that adolescents believe is watching everything they do. If they stumble, stammer, or wear the wrong clothes, *everyone* will notice and talk about it. The adolescent also often lives what seems to be a *personal fable*—he or she believes that no one has similar problems or could possibly understand what he or she is going through. Adolescent egocentrism is also characterized by excessive *hypocrisy*—it's okay for them to copy someone else's homework, but a teacher who leaves class to take a short personal telephone call is irresponsible in the adolescent's eyes. Finally, adolescent egocentrism involves what Elkind (1981) calls *pseudostupidity*—oversimplified logic. For example, when adolescents say, "If alcoholics know they are going to die of cirrhosis of the liver, why don't they just stop?" they fail to consider the many factors that contribute to an addiction to alcohol. Thus, their thinking is sometimes distorted a bit by their egocentrism, making their relationships with each other and with adults more difficult at times.

Emotional and Social Development

The shift from childhood to adolescence and from adolescence to adulthood is marked by changes in the emotional and social spheres of our lives. Until relatively recently, however, these changes have been more the subject of speculation than of research.

Adolescent Social Development

Adolescents also show marked changes in their social relationships. Adolescence is a time of drifting away, and sometimes of breaking away, from the family. Although relationships with peers become increasingly important through late childhood, by adolescence peers often become the most important people in the individual's life. The onset of puberty particularly brings a distancing from parents (Arnett, 1999; Galambos, 1992). The shift in orientation from parents to peers can be seen in the dramatic increase in conformity to the ideas and judgments of the peer group that occurs at the beginning of puberty (ages 11 to 13) but declines from age 15 on. In addition, young adolescents spend much more time with their peers than parents, even on weekends (Santrock, 1998).

Adolescent Emotions

Since 1904, when the first American text on adolescent psychology was published by G. Stanley Hall, a debate has continued unabated about the nature of adolescent emotions. Is it a carefree period of happiness or, as Hall would have it, a time of "storm and stress"? Like many philosophical debates that are eventually settled by scientific evidence, the truth lies somewhere between the extreme viewpoints.

Contrary to popular views of adolescence, current research suggests that about 80 percent of adolescents are relatively happy and well adjusted (Arnett, 1999; Offer & Schonert-Reichl, 1992). In most areas, adolescents are as well adjusted as children and adults, but there are three areas in which adolescents have greater problems than both younger and older individuals:

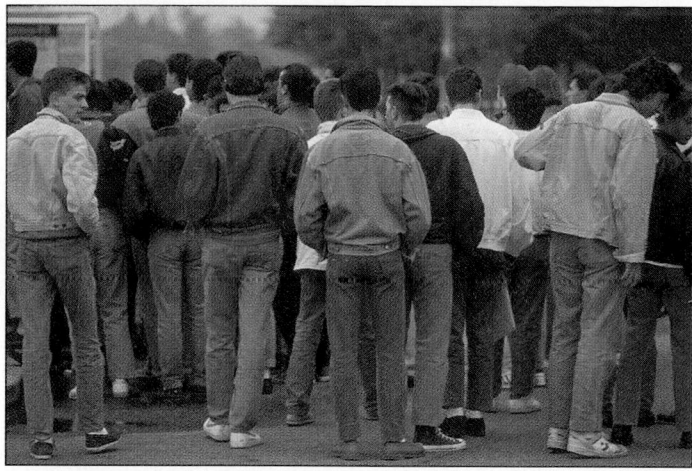

By adolescence, peers have become very important. The onset of puberty usually signals a dramatic increase in conformity to the ideas and judgments of the adolescent's peer group.

1. *Parent-child conflicts.* Conflicts between parents and children increase during early adolescence and remain common until they decline in late adolescence (Arnett, 1999). These conflicts typically focus on dating, how long teenagers should be away from home, where they can go, and who they can be with (which often reflect differences in parent and adolescent views on sex, alcohol, drugs, delinquency, and safety).

2. *Mood changes.* Many studies now show that, compared with childhood and adulthood, adolescents experience more shifts of mood (Arnett, 1999). Adolescents also are much more likely to feel self-conscious, embarrassed, awkward, lonely, nervous, and ignored.

3. *Risky behavior.* During adolescence, there is a sharp increase in the amount of behavior that exposes the child to danger. There is a marked increase in drinking to become drunk, use of drugs, reckless driving (and automobile accidents and fatalities), unprotected sex, aggression, and delinquent behavior, which does not decline until early adulthood (Arnett, 1999). Rates of suicide also increase dramatically during adolescence (but are still lower than in adulthood). Approximately 18 males per 100,000 persons aged 15 through 19 years and 4 females per 100,000 in the same age range commit suicide (Holinger & Offer, 1993).

Contrary to popular views of adolescence, current research suggests that about 80 percent of adolescents experience a relatively happy youth. However, risky behavior is common, and some adolescents do experience serious emotional and behavioral problems.

Why do these unfortunate changes take place during adolescence? No one knows for sure, but it appears that adolescence is a tough time for many youths for a combination of reasons. Changes in abstract cognition, surges in sex hormones, increases in social stress, and conflicts over autonomy during this natural period of transition all seem to be involved (Arnett, 1999).

● Review

In the span of about a decade, each individual passes from childhood to adulthood. This adolescent period of transition begins with the adolescent growth spurt and the emergence of primary and secondary sex characteristics (puberty) and ends with the assumption of adult patterns of work, living, and relationships. It's a period of dramatic physical changes. Considerable gains are made in height, weight, and strength; body fat is redistributed; and boys and girls come to look like men and women. These physical changes are often of considerable concern to self-conscious adolescents, particularly when irregularities and sex differences in physical development are obvious. Cognitively, most adolescents develop formal operational thinking, which gives them the ability to reason abstractly, but they experience an adolescent form of egocentrism. Socially, they complete the shift from a focus on their families to a focus on peers. The great majority of adolescents are well adjusted, but adolescents are moodier and engage in more parent-child conflict and risky behavior than at any other period of their lives.

● Check Your Learning

To be sure that you have learned the key points from the preceding section, cover the list of correct answers and try to answer each question. If you give an incorrect answer to any question, return to the page given next to the correct answer to see why your answer was not correct.

1. _____ is the period from the onset of puberty until the beginning of adulthood and is marked by rapid physical growth and change, as well as by a heightening of sexual and romantic interest in others.

2. The rapid increase in weight and height that occurs around the onset of puberty is known as the _____.

   a) maturation stage   c) physical development stage
   b) adolescent growth spurt   d) menarche

3. The _____ stage is characterized by an ability to use abstract concepts.

   a) concrete operational   c) preoperational
   b) formal operational   d) operational

4. We are more likely to experience which of the following during adolescence than at any other time in our lives?

   a) moodiness   c) risky behavior
   b) parent-child conflicts   d) all of the above

● Thinking Critically About Psychology

1. Although adolescence is a time when peer influence often outweighs parental influence, most adolescents continue to hold values and attitudes that are similar to those of their parents. What factors might account for this?

2. What psychological changes mark the period called adolescence? Do they seem significant enough to be treated as a separate developmental period?

Correct Answers 1. Adolescence (p. 256), 2. b (p. 257), 3. b (p. 257), 4. d (p. 259).

▶ ADULTHOOD: YOUNG ADULTHOOD THROUGH OLDER ADULTHOOD

Adulthood is the time of taking on adult responsibilities in work and social relationships. Adulthood is not a single phase of life. The challenges of adult love, work, and play change considerably during adulthood. The demands of maintaining a marriage are very different for newlyweds, parents of infants, parents of teenagers, or a couple in their 70s. Similar changes occur in the demands of work and play. In other words, adulthood is not the end of the process of development. Developmental changes *continue* throughout adulthood.

Physical Development

The life span is a continuous process of physical change. We continue to strengthen and grow well into early adulthood, but the body begins a slow process of physical decline after early adulthood. Physical speed and endurance decline gradually from early adulthood on. More and more of us need reading glasses for near vision with increasing age and have difficulty seeing in weak light and in the periphery of vision due to a loss of rod cells in the retina after middle age. Our ability to hear high-pitched tones declines after age 20, with loss of ability to hear low-pitched sounds beginning in the 60s. Our sense of taste remains pretty much intact into later life, but many older adults report that food tastes more bland. This is due to marked declines in the sense of smell with aging, which plays an important role in our appreciation of foods. Overall, men are likely to suffer these declines in hearing and smell earlier than women (Steinberg, 1995). A substantial number of older adults show marked declines due to cerebral arteriosclerosis (hardening of the arteries), which results in serious loss of intellectual ability. The rate and extent of these declines differ markedly from individual to individual, depending in part on the level of healthy exercise and activity that the individual maintains during adulthood.

Cognitive Development

It may surprise you to learn that cognitive development continues to take place during adulthood. Most of us think that cognition develops to its full potential in childhood and adolescence, then remains unchanged during adulthood. Actually, some cognitive abilities improve, some remain unchanged, and some decline during adulthood. Small but steady improvements occur from the 20s to the 70s in the components of crystallized intelligence, such as knowledge of facts and word meanings (Cornelius & Caspi, 1987; Kaufman & others, 1996; Steinberg, 1995). No declines occur before about age 75 in such fundamental aspects of intelligence as the ability to reason about everyday problems, and understand mathematical concepts, or to learn and remember meaningful information (Schulz & Ewen, 1988). Indeed, there are small increases during the adult years in our ability to solve problems of life in ways that are judged to be "wise" (Baltes & Staudinger, 1993).

On the other hand, declines do occur in fluid intelligence and short-term memory during later adulthood (Kaufman & others, 1996; Radvansky, 1999). Older adults tend to perform slightly less well than younger adults in abstract problem solving, divergent thinking, cognitive tasks that must be performed quickly, and some aspects of short-term memory (Bashore & others, 1997; Grady & others, 1995; McCrae, Arenberg, & Costa, 1987; Shimamura, Berry, Mangels, Rusting, & Jurica, 1995). Therefore, older adults perform as well as younger adults on some tasks (learning and reasoning about everyday concepts), do better than younger adults on some tasks (e.g., word meaning and decision making), but perform less well than younger adults in other ways (abstract reasoning, divergent thinking, and short-term memory). The cognitive performance of older adults is also slower than younger adults.

Sometimes the declines in specific aspects of cognitive functioning that occur in old age have important consequences. For example, adults in their 70s are more likely than adults in their 20s to forget to take their medication, particularly when they have other cognitive demands placed on them (Einstein, McDaniel, Smith, & Shaw, 1998). In many cases, however, older adults learn to make the best use of their cognitive abilities and compensate for any small declines. In evaluating the importance of cognitive declines during old age, it is important to understand that not all adults age at the same rate. There are large differences among older individuals in their cognitive abilities. In one study of adults, 50 percent of adults in their mid eighties had scores on a verbal recall task that fell within the range of scores of 20-year-olds (Rapp & Amaral, 1992).

Emotional and Social Development

What about changes in our emotions, social relationships, and personalities? Do we go through developmental changes in these areas, too? The answer is a very interesting "yes and no." Imagine that a group of 1,000 20-year-old women and men took a test that measures their typical ways of responding emotionally and socially (their personalities, in other words) and then took the same test every 10 years until they were 90. How consistent

Although personality traits remain stable throughout adulthood, most adults can expect some personality changes in their middle and later years. Most of these are positive; for example, middle-age men often become more aware of their need for affection. Middle-age women often become more self-confident.

would their personalities be across their adult lives? In one sense, their personalities would be very consistent over time, and would become increasingly consistent as they grew older. For example, people who scored higher than most other people at age 20 on a measure of emotionality would still score higher than most others at ages 30, 40, and so on. In this sense, the major dimensions of adult personality are very stable (McCrae & Costa, 1994; Moscowitz, Brown, & Cote, 1997; Roberts & DelVecchio, 2000).

In another sense, however, predictable *changes* in personality occur during the adult part of the life span (McCrae & Costa, 1999). On average, adults become less anxious and emotional, less socially outgoing, and less creative as they grow older, but become more dependable, agreeable, and accepting of life's hardships (Carstensen, Issacowitz, & Charles, 1999; McCrae & Costa, 1999). In addition, gender differences in personality become muted over time: Women become more assertive, confident, and independent, and men become more aware of their aesthetic needs and their need for affection (Stewart & Ostrove, 1998).

How can our personalities be both stable and changing over time? Although the average score of adults on, say, emotionality declines, people who are higher than others on emotionality at one age tend to stay higher than others at later ages, even though their emotionality declines along with the rest of the adult population. At 60, they are considerably less emotional than they were at 20 in adsolute terms, but they are still more emotional than most other 60-year-olds (who have become less emotional in absolute terms, too). So, the key dimensions of our personalities change with increasing age, often in ways that make life more enjoyable, but people tend to stay in their same positions on each trait relative to other people.

It should be obvious to anyone who knows the life histories of even a few individuals, however, that most human lives are not "stable" in the strictest sense. Most of us experience periods of happiness and stability in alternation with periods of discontent and change. The woman who grows unhappy with her career in retailing after 20 years and returns to college to become a minister and the man who happily remarries after an unhappy 15-year marriage are but two examples.

There is much disagreement as to the way in which to think about such changes, however. Some psychologists believe that adulthood consists of a series of "stages of development," rather like the stages of child development proposed by Piaget and others. Erik Erikson (1963) and Daniel Levinson (1978, 1986) have each proposed a set of stages of adult life. These stages are different from the stages of infant and child development in that (a) not every adult is believed to go through every stage; (b) the order of the stages can vary for some individuals; and (c) the timing of the stages is not controlled by biological maturation. Although Erikson proposes three stages of adulthood and Levinson proposes nine stages, Levinson's theory can be thought of as an elaboration of Erikson's views. For this reason, we will discuss both stage theories together. Notice that both theorists see adulthood as a series of *alternating* periods of stability and transition.

Early Adulthood: Intimacy vs. Isolation (17 to 45 Years)

Erikson (1963) discussed his proposed stages of adult life in terms of the challenges faced at each stage and the consequences of successfully or unsuccessfully meeting those challenges. These adult stages are the continuation of the stages of child and adolescent development hypothesized by Erikson. He referred to early adulthood as the stage of *intimacy versus isolation*. The challenge of this stage is to enter into committed, loving relationships with others that partially replace the bonds with parents. If we are successful in this task, we will have the intimacy needed to progress in adult life; if not, we will become isolated and less capable of full emotional development, according to Erikson.

Levinson (1986) sees the transition to early adulthood as beginning sometime between the ages of 17 and 22 for most individuals (see fig. 8.4). Early adulthood itself consists of three briefer stages. The *entry to early adulthood* lasts until approximately age 28. This is a time of creating an adult manner of working and living independently and often a time of marriage and young children. The *age 30 transition* (28 to 33) is a time of reevaluating one's start into adult life. Is this the right job for me? The right city? The right spouse? A sense of

Era of late adulthood: 60–?

Late adult transition: Age 60–65

Culminating life structure for middle adulthood: 55–60

Age 50 transition: 50–55

Entry life structure for middle adulthood: 45–50

Midlife transition: Age 40–45

Culminating life structure for early adulthood: 33–40

Age 30 transition: 28–33

Entry life structure for early adulthood: 22–28

Early adult transition: Age 17–22

Era of preadulthood: 0–22

FIGURE 8.4

Daniel Levinson's periods of adult development.

pressure often accompanies these decisions—they must be made "before it's too late." Sometimes major changes are made and sometimes the individual decides that his or her initial choices were the right ones, but either way the process of reevaluation can often be uncomfortable.

The *culmination of early adulthood* is a time of working hard toward one's goals. It extends roughly from the early thirties to about age 40. During this phase, adults sometimes join the PTA Executive Board to improve the quality of their children's school, plant trees in the yard, and work long hours for promotion to a senior position at work. The individual is often aware of feeling like a full member of the adult generation at this time.

Erikson believed that, to successfully navigate middle adulthood, people must develop a sense of generativity, or a devotion to endeavors that will last beyond their own life span.

In general, the stage of early adulthood is a demanding one. The young adult often takes on the challenges of a career, a marriage, and parenthood during the same period. Frequently, large debts are incurred in buying homes and automobiles in anticipation of greater income, which has not yet arrived. As Levinson (1986) points out, crucially important decisions must be made concerning family and occupation before one has the maturity and life experience to make them comfortably. It is, at the same time, a period of vigorous health and sexuality, rich family rewards, and the potential for occupational advancement. For most of us, it is a time when the rewards exceed the costs.

Middle Adulthood: Generativity vs. Stagnation (40 to 65 Years)

During the transition to this phase of life, we often take stock of whom we have become. This represents a marked shift from focusing on who we are *becoming* in our twenties and thirties to thinking about who we *are* during middle age (Carstensen & others, 1999). For some people, this is a positive experience—they are happy with their adult selves at the transition to midlife. For many others, this is a time of at least some disappointment. Too many promotions have been missed, too many investments have gone bad, and too many elections have been lost to believe that we can still be the unqualified success that we once dreamed of being. As a result of this appraisal of whom we have become, many people either redefine their goals (to fit their more modest accomplishments) or change directions during the transition to midlife. For example, one study of women in the "baby-boom" generation who attended a selective liberal arts college found that two-thirds made major changes in the educational or occupational work lives around the age of 40 (Stewart & Vandewater, 1998). Often this involved pursuing studies or careers that had been set aside earlier in life when traditional conceptions of female roles were more dominant. In general, the women who made such changes were more content later than the women who had wanted to make changes but did not. Both men and women often make career changes, move geographically, adopt new fitness programs, divorce, or change course in other ways during the transition to middle adulthood. In many cases, this leads to an increased sense of identity, self-direction, and competence (Stewart & Ostrove, 1998).

Erikson refers to middle adulthood as the stage of *generativity versus stagnation.* The challenge is to find meaning in our "generative" activities (work, family life, community activities, religion). In part, this requires a shift away from ourselves to focus on others. The person who successfully navigates middle adulthood develops a devotion to endeavors that live beyond their own life spans. This might take the form of building a family business, guiding one's children or grandchildren, or taking younger coworkers under one's wing as a mentor. Generativity is a matter of "reaching out" rather than being self-centered. A person who merely works hard may only be meeting his or her own selfish needs. According to Erikson, a person who is self-absorbed will stagnate and find that life loses much of its meaning during middle adulthood.

Levinson describes four brief stages of middle adulthood. Middle adulthood opens with the *midlife transition.* This transitional stage reaches a peak in the early forties. For some individuals, this transition is quite easy, but for others it's a period of anguish and turmoil. The majority of a sample of 40 men studied by Levinson—10 executives, 10 biologists, 10 factory workers, and 10 novelists—experienced at least some turmoil during their early forties. Erikson described this stage as the early peak of the struggle between generativity and stagnation—can I find meaning in my life the way it's turning out? It's also a time to face growing evidence of biological aging and to accept or agonize over one's wrinkles and gray hair.

The *entry to middle adulthood stage,* from about 45 to 50, is a period of calm and stability for most people who have emerged from the midlife transition. Individuals who are

"Nothing serious, Bob—
just a case of the forties."

happy with themselves following the midlife transition often find this period to be one of the most productive and creative times of their lives. The illusory ambitions that were shattered during the midlife transition have often been replaced with more attainable goals that are pursued with vigor. Individuals often feel that the painful process of reassessment during their early forties led to changes that left them a better person.

The *age 50 transition* is a stage that is similar to the age 30 transition. For many adults, this is a time to reassess the goals and lifestyle chosen during midlife and the entering middle adulthood stages. Another stable period from about age 55 to 65 follows the age 50 transition. Levinson refers to this stage as the *culmination of middle adulthood.*

Climacteric

Although most psychologists believe that the changes that characterize adult development are timed more by the "social clock" than by biological aging, one biological event that has an impact for many persons is the **climacteric.** The climacteric is a period beginning at about age 45 when a loss of the capacity to sexually reproduce in women and a decline in the reproductive capacity of men occurs.

In women, the decrease in the level of sex hormones during this period eventually leads to the end of menstruation, or **menopause.** This event, which takes place at 46 to 48 years of age on the average (but can normally take place between the ages of 36 and 60) is sometimes an uncomfortable time for women. It's sometimes accompanied by "hot flashes," anxiety, and depression, but most women do not find it as difficult as they were led to expect (Stewart & Ostrove, 1998).

The changes that accompany the male climacteric are generally less notable than in women. There is a decline in the number of sperm cells produced, and slight changes in the pattern of sexual arousal, but the decrease in sex hormones that occurs during the climacteric appears to have few psychological or sexual effects.

climacteric
(klī-mak′ter-ik) The period between about ages 45 and 60 in which there is a loss of capacity to sexually reproduce in women and a decline in the reproductive capacity of men.

menopause
(men′o-pawz) The cessation of menstruation and the capacity to reproduce in women.

Later Adulthood: Integrity vs. Despair (65 Years On)

Erikson refers to the late sixties and beyond as the stage of *integrity versus despair.* Levinson devotes little of his theory to the later adult years and adds little to Erikson's ideas. The older adult who sees meaning in her or his life when considered as a whole continues to live a satisfying existence instead of merely staying alive. The person who sees life as a collection of unmet goals and unanswered riddles may despair of ever achieving a meaningful life and will often withdraw and live out the remaining years like a prison sentence.

Far more older Americans find meaning rather than despair in their lives. This may come as a surprise to you. Just as most of us once thought that the process of development ended in childhood, most of us *still* think that there is little real life after age 65. Too often we think of older adults as leading colorless, joyless, passionless lives. It's surprising to some of us to learn that real *living* usually continues until death (Baltes & Staudinger, 1993).

During this century, the average life expectancy of North Americans has increased dramatically. Persons born in 1900 had a life expectancy of less than 50 years, whereas persons born in 1955 can expect to live to be 70. A child born in 1999 can expect to live to be almost 80. As life expectancy has increased, our conceptions of old age have changed dramatically, too. Today, most people can expect to have many healthy years after the traditional retirement age of 65. As a result, many plan second careers, active political involvement, writing, or other engaging activities in their sixties, seventies, and eighties. Even so, older persons increasingly have a sense that time is running out on their lives. For some older people, this is a frightening realization, but, in general, it is accompanied by

In the stage of integrity versus despair, older adults who see meaning in their lives when considered as a whole will continue to find life satisfying.

a positive focusing on the meaningful emotional priorities of life (Carstensen & others, 1999).

Evaluation of Stage Theories of Adulthood

Although they are thought-provoking and appealing in some ways, stage theories of adult development can be criticized on a number of grounds:

1. *Gender differences.* The theories of adult development offered by Erikson and Levinson clearly had men more in mind than women. Indeed, for many years, all of the participants in studies of adult development were men. It was as if women did not develop, or, if they did, it did not matter! In recent years, however, a number of studies of adult development have been conducted that suggest that there are broad similarities between the patterns of adult development in women and men (Roberts & Newton, 1987; Stewart & Ostrove, 1998).

2. *Cultural differences and historical change.* Early theories of adult development implied that they applied universally to all people born in all times. Very few studies have been conducted, however, to determine if the same patterns of adult development are found in different cultures. Indeed, we have data on only a very limited range of kinds of peoples—mostly white, college-educated, English-speaking adults. Much remains to be learned about the rest of the human race. Even within a given culture, it appears that historical change alters the course of adult development (Stewart & Ostrove, 1998). Consider the North American "baby-boom" generation born in the late 1940s and early 1950s after the end of World War II. They were born into a world of traditional gender roles but were young adults during the age of feminism and rapidly changing gender roles. As children and teenagers, they experienced the civil rights movement, the assassinations of Martin Luther King, John Kennedy, and Robert Kennedy. Later, they took sides for or against the Viet Nam War. As middle-aged adults, they lived through both the age of international terrorism and the most protracted period of economic prosperity in North American history. How have these events influenced the course of their adult development? How will the course of adult development be different for persons born in 1980 or 2000, who will have very different experiences? Until these fundamental questions are answered, we will not fully understand adult development (Stewart & Ostrove, 1998).

3. *Questions about stage theories.* Finally, it is important to note that not all developmental psychologists believe that adulthood can be thought of as a series of crises or stages. Stewart and Ostrove (1998), for example, believe that far more middle-aged adults experience positive "mid-course corrections" than "mid-life crises." Laura Carstensen believes that the processes that govern developmental change during adulthood are changeable and not tied to specific ages. Rossi (1980) similarly argues that the inevitability and negative impact of the midlife transition have been dangerously exaggerated. Indeed, theorists who oppose the idea of "stages" of adulthood have conducted studies of their own, suggesting that predictable changes do not take place at the times indicated by the stage theorists. For example, two studies found no evidence that "midlife crises" are common during the early forties (Farrell & Rosenberg, 1981).

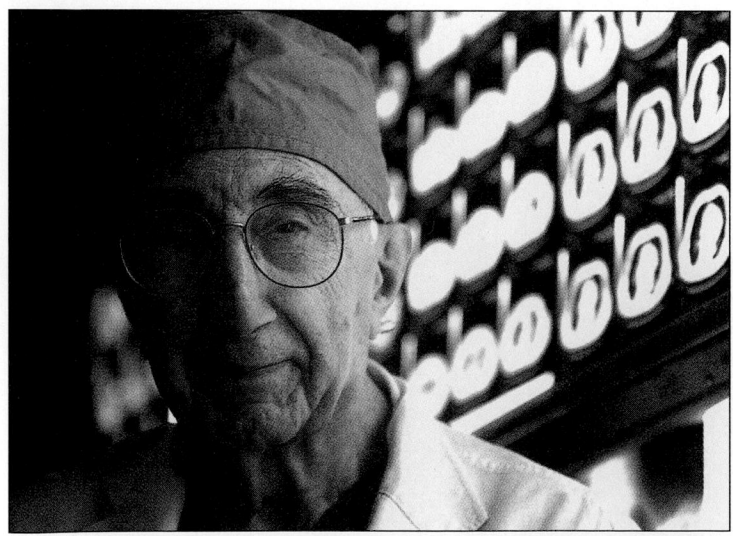

Michael DeBakey is a pioneer in heart surgery who, among other things, performed the first heart transplant surgery. Remarkably, this gifted surgeon, who was born in 1908, was still performing heart surgery in his nineties.

Causes of Aging and Predictors of Longevity

Aging is partly a biological process. Over the years, the body deteriorates—skin sags and wrinkles, artery walls become less flexible, muscular strength is lost, cardiac and respiratory efficiency declines. And there are changes in the brain as well. On the average, the total brain weight of persons in their eighties is

"I was grinding out barnyards and farmhouses and cows in the
meadow, and then, suddenly, I figured to hell with it."

about 8 percent less than that of a middle-aged person. For older persons with senile dementia, however, the brain weighs 20 percent less than in middle age (Emery & Oxmans,
1992).

Aging is not only a biological process; it involves many psychological aspects as
well. Older people are different from younger people because they have experienced more.
They have lived through eras that younger individuals have not, they have often retired
from their jobs, they no longer have living parents, they often have children who are adults,
and they have a host of other factors. Just as people experience biological aging at different rates, the psychological experience of aging also differs from person to person.

The key psychological variables that seem to be associated with happy aging are (a)
whether one stays "engaged" in life's activities and (b) whether one believes the myths
about old age. Considerable research suggests that older individuals who continue to be actively engaged in meaningful activities are the happiest as older adults (Maddox, 1964;
Neugarten & Hagestad, 1976). These activities can involve family, hobbies, sports, politics,
or employment. All that matters is that they be activities that are meaningful to the
individual.

The other key to a satisfactory older adulthood seems to be in ignoring the restrictive
myths and stereotypes of old age so prevalent in our society. Many older adults are active
in sports and creative in the arts and sciences. They sometimes attend college or throw exciting parties. In general, they do not behave like the passive, irritable "old people" of the
stereotype. Philosopher Bertrand Russell, artists Marc Chagall and Pablo Picasso, political
leaders Golda Meir and Mao Tse-tung, and psychologists Jean Piaget and B. F. Skinner
continued to be creative and productive well into their eighties.

● Review

Intelligence and personality remain relatively constant throughout the adult years in most healthy adults, but some change does take place. Some aspects of intellectual ability improve throughout adulthood, whereas other aspects do not change. Still, minor declines in some aspects of intelligence occur in most of us, particularly after age 70. Similarly, a few positive changes in personality seem to take place. Psychologists disagree as to whether the changes in adulthood can be thought of as a series of stages. Erikson and Levinson have outlined a series of stages of adult life, but we still have much to learn about adult development.

Although some older adults despair of ever achieving a meaningful pattern of living, many others achieve a sense of integrity and continue to find life meaningful and joyful until death. Aging is partly a biological process of physical deterioration, but aging is also a psychological process that can be slowed to some degree by staying engaged in meaningful activities and by not believing the many negative myths about old age that are so prevalent in our society.

● Check Your Learning

To be sure that you have learned the key points from the preceding section, cover the list of correct answers and try to answer each question. If you give an incorrect answer to any question, return to the page given next to the correct answer to see why your answer was not correct.

1. The challenge of the _____ stage is to enter into committed, loving relationships with others that partially replace bonds with parents.

   a) early adulthood   c) later adulthood
   b) middle adulthood   d) midlife

2. According to Erikson, a person in middle adulthood must be _____ (or productive) to find meaning in life.

   a) stagnant   c) generative
   b) creative   d) flexible

3. Two keys to a satisfactory older adulthood seem to be ignoring the restrictive myths and stereotypes of old age and remaining actively engaged in life.

   a) True
   b) False

● Thinking Critically About Psychology

1. How might the course of your adult development differ from that of your grandparents? How will your culture influence your development during adulthood?

2. Do you think that your personality has changed in the past 10 years? Do you expect it to change in the future?

Correct Answers   1. a (p. 262),   2. c (p. 264),   3. a (p. 267).

Application *of Psychology*

PARENTING

During the important early stages of development—infancy, childhood, and most of adolescence—we typically live with our parents. They give us food and shelter, protect us from danger, and provide many of our early learning experiences. Parents play a key role in giving children a healthy start in life. But, although parenting is important, we as a society provide parents with no training in how to raise their children. Our schools teach reading, writing, and arithmetic, but not parenting. For this reason, we will look carefully at the topic of parenting, with an emphasis on the styles of parenting that are best for children.

Parenting and Discipline Style

Discipline style is one of the most important parts of parenting. As soon as the infant can move, the adult must attempt to regulate the child's behavior to protect the child and point the child in healthy directions. In other words, the parent must provide guidance and discipline. What discipline style is the best for children? Psychologist Diana Baumrind (1983) has extensively studied the discipline styles used by parents and has divided them into three types: authoritarian, permissive, and authoritative.

The *authoritarian* parent gives strict rules to the child or adolescent with little discussion of the reasons for the rules. It is the "because I say so" approach to rules. Authoritarian parents are openly critical of their children and frequently give them instructions on how to behave. Rules are enforced by punishing a child who does not obey, sometimes quite harshly.

In contrast, the *permissive* parent gives the child or adolescent few rules and rarely punishes misbehavior. The child is given great respect and autonomy but often too much independence at too early an age.

The *authoritative* parent (notice the difference in spelling between *authoritative* and *authoritarian*) is an authority figure to the child but provides good explanations for all rules and freely discusses them with the child. In allowing their children to freely state their opinions about

Our parents care for us from infancy through adolescence and provide us with many of our most important learning experiences.

rules, and sometimes being persuaded to alter the rules by a logical argument from them, authoritative parents give children a greater sense of involvement in their own rules. Authoritative parents emphasize reinforcement of appropriate behavior and affectionate warmth over punishment and often do not use any physical punishment at all. They encourage independence, but within clearly defined limits to take the child's level of development into consideration. In short, authoritative parents show their children that they are loved and respected but provide the amount of authority that the child needs.

Which of these approaches to discipline works best? Baumrind's research clearly indicates that children whose parents adopt an authoritative style are better behaved, more successful, and happier than the children of parents who use other styles of discipline, and their families are more harmonious (Baumrind, 1983, 1991).

Direction of Effect in Child Rearing: The Two-Way Street

University of Virginia professor Richard Bell (1968) pointed out some time ago that we must be very careful in our interpretations of studies of parenting. I just said that children whose parents are authoritative are generally better behaved and

happier than children whose parents use other styles of discipline. Does this necessarily mean that authoritative parenting causes good behavior in children? Most developmental psychologists think so, but it is very likely that something else is going on as well. It is probable that children who are happy and easy to get along with make it easier for their parents to adopt an authoritative style of discipline. A happy, reasonable child can be given a great deal of independence and needs little strict discipline. But would the same parent adopt a different style of discipline if the child were irritable, defiant, and aggressive? Several studies suggest that this might be the case—that children affect their parents as much as parents affect their children.

Hugh Lytton of the University of Calgary (Anderson, Lytton, & Romney, 1986) has compared parents of normal, well-behaved children to parents with children who were so disobedient and aggressive that they had been referred to psychologists for help. He observed these two groups of parents interacting with their children in a playroom in his laboratory. As in previous studies, Lytton found that the parents of the badly behaved children were less affectionate, less likely to reward positive behavior, more critical,

A child's temperament may have as much effect on disciplinary style as the parent's choice. Lytton found that parents who usually used the authoritative style tended to become more authoritarian when faced with an unruly child.

and gave many more instructions to their children on how to behave than did the parents of the well-behaved children.

Generally, psychologists have concluded that it is exactly this pattern of authoritarian parenting that causes the children to behave badly (e.g., Baumrind, 1983). But Lytton provided a clever twist to his study. He exchanged parents and children—so that the parents of well-behaved children were matched with badly behaved children and vice versa—and observed their interactions again. When the parents of well-behaved children were faced with an aggressive, disobedient child, the formerly model parents behaved just like the parents of the badly behaved children. Quickly, they also resorted to the unpleasant, critical, authoritarian style of discipline.

So who influences whom in the family? Does the parent's discipline affect the child's behavior, or does the child's behavior influence the parent's discipline? Clearly, a great deal of both is going on. This is a very important point. Effective parenting is a very important influence on the child, but even the best parents know that different children will evoke different parenting responses from them. The parents of temperamental, difficult children will have to resist the natural tendency to make authoritarian responses to their children's provocative behavior if they are going to help their children develop optimally.

Common Discipline Mistakes

Psychologist Susan O'Leary (1995) has made a comprehensive study of the most common discipline mistakes made by ineffective parents. Parents of poorly behaved children often make the following mistakes:

1. *Lax parenting.* Ineffective parents often fail to enforce their rules for the children and give in to their children's demands to bend the rules or avoid punishment. Effective parents are consistent in the enforcement of rules.

2. *Reinforcement of inappropriate behavior.* Parents of poorly behaved children often provide positive reinforcement for inappropriate behavior. This is sometimes unintentional—such as only paying attention to their children when they misbehave—but is sometimes intentional—as in praising their child for giving another child a black eye. Effective parents provide positive reinforcement for good behavior, but not for inappropriate behavior.

3. *Verbosity.* Ineffective parents engage in lengthy arguments with their children about their misbehavior instead of simply enforcing the rules. Effective parents know that a brief explanation of why the rule is being enforced is much more effective than a lengthy debate. "I'm sorry, but you can't watch television tonight because you did not do your homework" says all that needs to be said in most cases.

4. *Overreactivity.* Ineffective parents become angry, harsh, critical, and mean when their children misbehave. Effective parents stay cool and in control as they calmly enforce the rules.

Sociocultural Factors in Parenting

Parents from all cultures want their children to be "well behaved," but they often define appropriate behavior differently and believe in different methods of child rearing. For this reason, we must understand cultural differences in parenting (Rubin, 1998). Consider one major difference among cultures: In collectivistic cultures, such as the Chinese, Japanese, and Indian cultures, the emphasis is on the well-being of the family and the larger culture, not on the well-being of each individual. In individualistic cultures, such as the mainstream culture in the United States, the emphasis is on the individual rather than the group.

The kinds of behavior that help a person succeed in collectivistic and individualistic cultures are different in some cases and, therefore, parents raise their children differently in some ways. For example, in the United States, most parents believe that being shy and inhibited places children at a disadvantage—they would prefer for their children to be outgoing and assertive instead. This is because the individuals who assert themselves most confidently will be most likely to succeed as individuals. In Chinese families, however, shyness and inhibition are viewed as advantages, as it helps the child fit into the group and yield to its wishes. It is not surprising, then, that Chinese parents praise their shy children, whereas American parents disapprove of shy behavior and sometimes seek mental health treatment for their shy children (Rubin, 1998).

Another difference between Chinese and mainstream U.S. cultures reflects the relative emphasis on academic achievement in the two cultures and differences in how it is encouraged. In the United States, Chinese immigrant parents teach mathematics skills to their young children in more formal ways and structure their children's use of time more than European American parents (Huntsinger, Jose, & Larson, 1998). Controlling for other factors, such as parental income and education, the parenting practices of Chinese American parents appear to lead to higher mathematics achievement among their children (Huntsinger & others, 1998). Importantly, the two groups of children do not differ in terms of personal adjustment, suggesting that the greater emphasis on academic achievement is not personally harmful to the Chinese American children. In these and many other ways, parenting reflects the varying goals and beliefs of people living in different cultures.

Myth of the Perfect Parent

Loving and effective parenting is the greatest gift that a parent can give a child. But it is important to point out that *perfect* parenting is not as important as some of us seem to think. Many parents act as if their children are as delicate as spun glass. They are paralyzed in their attempts to be good parents by their fear that they will do the wrong thing and scar their children for life.

Actually, children are pretty resilient creatures. Within broad limits, they will grow up very well in spite of the fact that none of them have perfect parents. They will not be miserable forever if their parents sometimes lose their tempers and speak in harsh tones, and they will learn to play with other children without being coached in every step.

That is not to say that parents cannot harm their children. Unfortunately, children are hurt badly every day by neglectful and abusive parents. But most of the minor imperfections of parenting that are characteristic of every child's upbringing are of relatively little consequence.

Day Care, Divorce, and Parenting

Until relatively recently, most children in the United States were cared for by one of their parents—almost always the mother—who stayed at home full-time to raise the children and care for the home while the other parent worked outside the home. And most of us felt that this way of raising children was the "natural" way of things. Indeed, the image of the "caretaker mother and breadwinner father" is so deeply embedded in our view of child rearing that many of us are shocked to learn that very few children are raised in that manner today. In actuality, only 7 percent of all children in the United States are raised by two married parents through their entire childhood, with the mother not working outside the home (Braverman, 1989; Silverstein, 1991).

In many families, both married parents have chosen—or have felt compelled by economic necessity—to be employed full-time outside the home. Indeed, the percentage of women with school-age children who work outside the home has risen from 40 percent in the 1970s to 75 percent in the 1990s (Silverstein, 1991). In many other cases, divorce results in the custodial parent's (usually the mother) being more likely to work outside the home. About 50 percent of all marriages now end in divorce, and divorced women are 50 percent more likely to work outside the home than married women (Scarr, Phillips, & McCartney, 1990). In addition, more

children are raised now by single parents who have never married than ever before (up over 350 percent since the 1970s) (Silverstein, 1991).

All of these changes in the nature of the American family over the past quarter century have resulted in mothers' spending less time raising their children. Who cares for the children, then? It is distressing to learn that the increased entry of mothers into the labor force has not led fathers to spend more time with their children. On the average, fathers still spend 26 minutes a day with their children under age 6, with that time decreasing to 16 minutes a day as the children grow older. Some of the job of child rearing has fallen to other family members, but many children now spend a great deal of time in day care. As psychologist Sandra Scarr put it, "Child care is now as essential to family life as the automobile and the refrigerator" (Scarr & others, 1990, p. 26).

Have these changes in how our children are raised had a harmful effect on the children? In spite of the great anguish of parents and psychologists alike, extensive research suggests that, in general, children who are in day care do not differ from children who are raised by parents in their own homes in terms of physical health, emotional or intellectual development, or attachment (Erel, Oberman, & Yirmiya, 2000; Hoffman, 1989). The key elements in the successful adaptation of children to day care appear to be the quality of the day-care environment and the quality and quantity of time spent with parents in the evenings and on weekends. The available research supports the commonsense conclusion that a poor day-care environment is harmful to children, whereas a positive day-care environment is good for children (Hoffman, 1989; NICHD Early Child Care Research Network, 1997; Scarr & Eisenberg, 1993).

The other common situation that reduces the amount of parenting is divorce. Is divorce harmful to children? There is

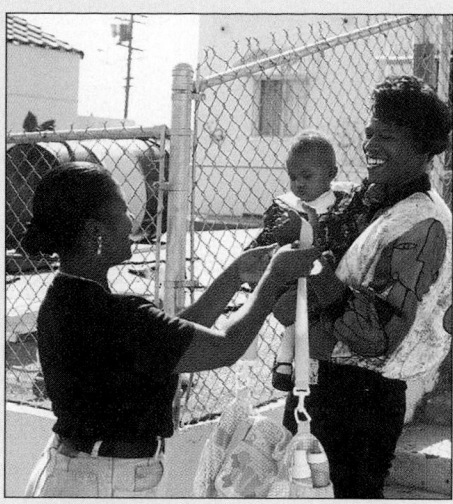

In the words of one researcher, "Child care is now as essential to family life as the automobile and the refrigerator" (Scarr, 1990). A key element in children's successful adaptation to day care is the quality of care provided.

little doubt that divorce is stressful and upsetting to all of the adults and children involved. Few children make it through the time of divorce without some emotional turmoil, which results in misbehavior and problems at school, but usually the disruption is for a relatively brief period of time (Hetherington, 1979). The children who are affected the longest by divorce are the ones whose parents were openly conflictual before the divorce and continue to have conflict in front of the children after the divorce (Atkeson, Forehand, & Rickard, 1982; Hetherington, Bridges, & Insabella, 1998) or whose parents have serious psychological difficulties (Lahey & others, 1988). Most children adapt well to divorce when their parents work out their differences after the divorce well enough to cease arguing in front of the children and cooperate in allowing each other to share in the duties and pleasures of parenting (Silverstein & Auerbach, 1999).

● Summary

Chapter 8 summarizes key concepts in developmental psychology and the major theories that explain the process of development. It describes the normal course of development from infancy and childhood, adolescence, adulthood, and later adulthood, to the time of death.

I. Some psychologists believe that developmental changes in behavior are biologically programmed to "unfold" with increasing age, whereas others believe that changes in behavior are "molded" by the environment that we experience.

   A. Today, most psychologists believe that nature (biological factors) and nurture (environment) work together to influence our actions, thoughts, and feelings.

   B. Maturation, the systematic physical growth of the nervous system and other parts of the body, is a key concept to "unfolding" theorists; learning is the key concept to "molding" theorists.

II. Some theorists believe that early childhood is the "formative period" for our personalities.

   A. Research on imprinting in animals shows that experiences during critical periods of early development can have long-lasting effects on animal behavior, but there may not be such clear-cut critical periods in human development.

   B. Margaret and Harry Harlow's experiments with social deprivation during the infancy of monkeys show long-lasting effects of abnormal early experiences, but human infants seem capable of recovering to a great extent from early abnormal experience.

   C. Parents play a key role in fostering the development of their children, but the emotions and behavior of the child also influence the parents' choice of parenting styles.

III. Stage theorists believe that all children must pass through the same qualitatively different stages in the same order.

   A. Piaget identified four stages of cognitive development from infancy to adulthood.

      1. During the sensorimotor stage (birth to 2 years), an infant experiences the world in terms of sensory information and motor activities.

      2. In the preoperational stage (2 to 7 years), children can think in mental images, but they sometimes think in ways that are illogical by adult standards.

      3. The concrete operational stage (7 to 11 years) is marked by increased ability to reason logically, except for abstract reasoning.

      4. In the formal operational stage (11 years on), an individual uses full adult logic and understands abstract concepts.

   B. Kohlberg's theory of moral development is concerned with the logical process of arriving at answers to moral dilemmas.

      1. At the premoral level, a child has no sense of morality as adults understand that term.

      2. A child's moral view is based on what others will think of him or her as stated in laws and rules at the conventional level.

      3. At the principled level, individuals judge right and wrong according to ethical principles rather than by rules or expected reward or punishment.

   C. Carol Gilligan has provided a theory that she believes more accurately describes moral development in females than does Kohlberg's.

      1. The young girl follows rules to obtain rewards and avoid punishment in the earliest stage, "morality as individual survival."

      2. Later, in the "morality as self-sacrifice" stage, the girl believes that to be good she must sacrifice her needs at times to meet the needs of others.

      3. In the most mature stage of "morality as equality," she believes that everyone's needs should be met when possible and that sacrifices should be shared equally when they are necessary.

   D. Erik Erikson's theory of development focuses on the person's developing relationships with others in the social world.

IV. Average ages at which changes in development take place are used to portray the pattern of age-related changes.

    A. The neonatal period is the first two weeks of life and marks the transition from the womb to independent life.

    B. Infancy (2 weeks to 2 years) is a time of rapid physical, perceptual, cognitive, linguistic, social, and emotional development.

    C. During early childhood (2 to 7 years), growth is less explosive and rapid than during infancy.

    D. Middle childhood (7 to 11 years) is characterized by slow physical growth, but important cognitive changes occur, such as the emergence of conservation.

V. Adolescence is the developmental period from the onset of puberty until the beginning of adulthood.

    A. The production of sex hormones in puberty triggers biological changes known as the primary sex characteristics.

        1. Menarche, the first menstrual period, occurs at about 12 years 6 months in North American females.

        2. Production of sperm begins about two years later in males.

    B. Secondary sex characteristics appear in both sexes during puberty.

    C. The adolescent growth spurt lasts for a little over a year in early adolescence.

    D. Girls tend to experience puberty about two years earlier than boys.

        1. For both sexes, different parts of the body grow at different rates, and weight and physique change in irregular ways.

        2. Within each sex, there is wide variation in the age at which puberty begins.

    E. Piaget's formal operational stage—the ability to use abstract concepts—occurs in some individuals by about age 11.

    F. Peers replace the family as the most important influence on the adolescent.

    G. Most adolescents are well adjusted, but adolescents are more likely to be moody and to engage in parent-child conflict and risky behavior than at any other time in their lives.

VI. Adulthood is not a single phase of life. Some changes involving love, work, and play continue throughout adulthood.

    A. Intelligence appears relatively stable throughout adulthood in healthy adults, with small declines beginning between ages 50 and 60, especially in the speed of intellectual processing. Some larger declines occur after age 70 in some aspects of intelligence, particularly in individuals with arteriosclerosis and other brain impairment.

    B. Some relatively predictable personality changes that occur for many people during adulthood include becoming more insightful, dependable, controlled, and content. Most aspects of personality remain relatively constant across adulthood, however.

    C. Some psychologists believe that we pass through "stages" of development during adulthood.

        1. Developmental stages of adulthood appear to differ from those of childhood in that not every adult goes through each stage, the order of the stages can vary, and the timing of the stages is not controlled by biological maturation.

        2. Erikson calls early adulthood the stage of intimacy versus isolation, during which many individuals enter committed, loving relationships.

        3. Erikson calls middle adulthood the stage of generativity versus stagnation, during which many individuals find meaning in work and family lives.

        4. Erikson calls the period from the late sixties on the stage of integrity versus despair; older adults who see meaning in their lives when considered as a whole continue to live a satisfying existence.

        5. Although the stage theories of adult development are thought-provoking, many developmental psychologists are not convinced that we pass through predictable stages or a series of crises. Stage theories can be particularly criticized for their lack of attention to possible cultural, gender, and historical differences.

VII. Psychological variables associated with happy aging are whether one stays engaged in life's activities and whether one believes the myths about old age.

● Resources

1. To read Erikson's own words about his theory of personality development, see Erikson, E. (1950). *Childhood and society*. New York: Norton.

2. To learn more about theories of moral development, see Gilligan, C. (1982). *In a different voice*. Cambridge: Harvard University Press; and Kohlberg, L. (1981). *The philosophy of moral development: Moral stages and the idea of justice.* New York: Harper & Row.

3. For a view of adolescence by adolescents themselves, see Offer, D., Ostrov, E., & Howard, K. I. (1981). *The adolescent: A psychological self-portrait.* New York: Basic Books.

4. For differing perspectives on stages of adult life, see Costa, P., & McRae, R. (1990). *Personality in adulthood.* New York: Guilford Press; Levinson, D. J. (1978). *The seasons of a man's life.* New York: Knopf; Lowenthal, M. F., Thurnher, M., & Chiriboga, D. (1975). *Four stages of life: A comparative study of women and men facing transitions.* San Francisco: Jossey-Bass; Schulz, R., & Ewen, R. B. (1988). *Adult development and aging: Emerging realities.* New York: Macmillan; McCrae, R. R., & Costa, P. T. (1994). The stability of personality: Observations and evaluations. *Current Directions in Psychological Science, 3,* 173–175; and Stewart, A. J., & Ostrove, J. M. (1998). Women's personality in middle age: Gender, history, and midcourse corrections. *American Psychologist, 54,* 165–181.

5. Behaviorist B. F. Skinner, writing in his early eighties, discusses ways to rearrange one's life circumstances to enjoy old age to its fullest in Skinner, B. F., & Vaughn, M. E. (1983). *Enjoy old age.* New York: Norton.

6. A call for new directions in psychological and medical research on aging that is fascinating and written in nontechnical language is Science Directorate, *Vitality for Life: Psychological Research for Productive Aging.* Washington, DC: American Psychological Association.

7. For great overviews of the life span, see Santrock, J. W. (2000). *Children* (6th ed.). Boston: McGraw-Hill; Santrock, J. W. (1998). *Adolescence* (7th ed.). Boston: McGraw-Hill; and Hoyer, W. J., Rybash, J. M., & Roodin, P. A. (1999). *Adult development and aging* (4th ed.). Boston: McGraw-Hill.

8. The National Parent Information Network, managed by the University of Illinois, provides excellent information to parents at www.npin.org. They can also be reched at 800-583-4135 (voice/TTY).

9. Materials designed to help prevent juvenile delinquency can be found at the Web site of the U.S. Department of Justice's Office of Juvenile Justice and Delinquency Prevention at www.ojdp.ncjrs.org.

● Visual Review of Stage Theories of Development

The following visual reviews may help you consolidate your learning of some of the information presented in this chapter in a visual for-mat. Be sure not to limit your review to these diagrams, but, be-cause they are key to understanding some of the important con-cepts of the chapter, mastering them should help you master the entire chapter.

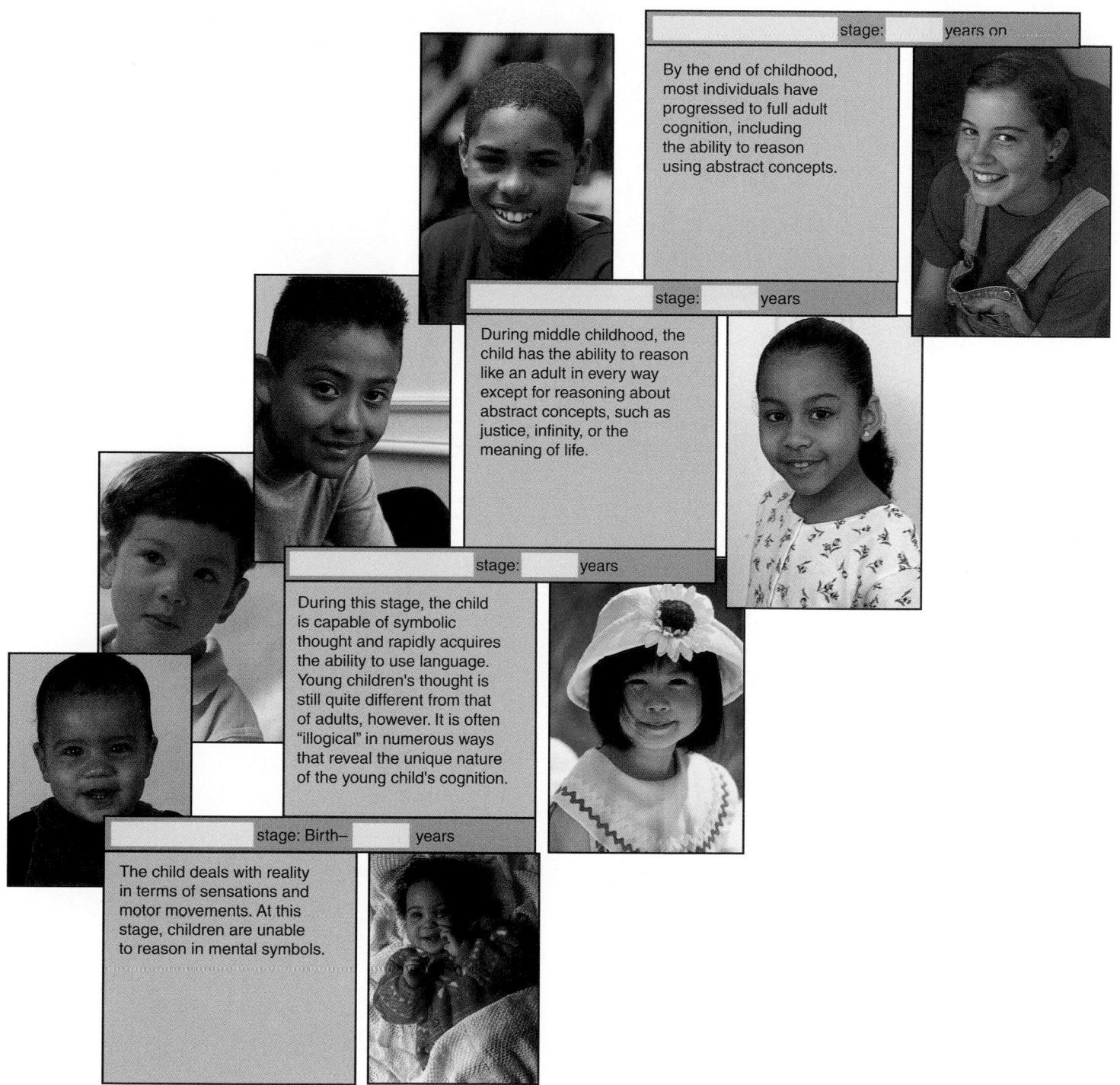

stage:　　　　years on

By the end of childhood, most individuals have progressed to full adult cognition, including the ability to reason using abstract concepts.

stage:　　　years

During middle childhood, the child has the ability to reason like an adult in every way except for reasoning about abstract concepts, such as justice, infinity, or the meaning of life.

stage:　　　years

During this stage, the child is capable of symbolic thought and rapidly acquires the ability to use language. Young children's thought is still quite different from that of adults, however. It is often "illogical" in numerous ways that reveal the unique nature of the young child's cognition.

stage: Birth–　　　years

The child deals with reality in terms of sensations and motor movements. At this stage, children are unable to reason in mental symbols.

FIGURE 8.5

This is a diagram of Piaget's stage theory of child development. Fill in the missing labels for the names of the stages and the average age ranges for the stages and check them for accuracy by referring back to figure 8.2 on p. 245.

FIGURE 8.6

This is a diagram of the stage theory of adult development proposed by Daniel Levinson. Fill in the missing labels for the names of three major adult transitions and check them for accuracy by referring back to Figure 8.4, page 263.

CHAPTER

9

Motivation and Emotion

PROLOGUE

Conducting research is one of the most consistently enjoyable parts of my career. Even if I never contribute anything really important to psychology through research, each study is an intriguing puzzle and I love finding each clue to a mystery that puts any spy novel to shame. Still, for all my love of research, I wonder if great researcher Walter Cannon could have talked me into doing for science what he persuaded his colleague A. L. Washburn to do to understand the motive of hunger.

Cannon and Washburn (1912) were trying to isolate the biological mechanism of hunger. They believed that the feeling of hunger was caused by contractions of the stomach wall. To determine whether this idea was correct, Cannon convinced Washburn to swallow a balloon that was attached to a long tube connected to an air pump. The balloon was then inflated to fill Washburn's stomach. In this way, stomach contractions could be mechanically detected because they squeezed the balloon and increased the air pressure in the tube (see fig. 9.1). While the intermittent contractions were being measured, Washburn, who could not talk because of the tube gagging his mouth and throat, indicated when he felt a conscious sensation of hunger by pressing a key connected to a recording instrument. (History does not tell us, however, whether Washburn used his other hand to signal more negative feelings to Cannon during this unpleasant experiment.)

As Cannon predicted, Washburn did feel hungry when his stomach contracted, leading them to conclude that hunger was no more than the rumbling contractions of an empty stomach. As we will see later in the chapter, such contractions are still believed to be part of the feeling of hunger for many people, but, sadly, considering Washburn's selfless contribution to science, stomach contractions are only one factor in hunger, and one of the least important factors at that.

This chapter is about our motives and our emotions. Motives are states that make us active rather than inactive and lead us to do one thing rather than another. If I have just eaten, I may take a nap or quietly read the newspaper; but, if I am hungry, I will get up and fix food. The motive of hunger activates and directs my behavior. Some motives are based on the survival needs of the body for food, water, and warmth. These biological motives are regulated by intricate and sensitive mechanisms under the control of the hypothalamus that detect the body's needs.

Other motives—the so-called psychological motives—are not directly related to the survival needs of the body. The motive to maintain a moderate level of novel stimulation and activity, the motive to achieve and be successful, and the motive to have friendly relationships with others are examples of psychological motives. These motives are often strongly influenced by learning experiences and therefore differ from individual to individual and culture to culture.

Emotions are special states that often motivate us. Emotions are a complex mixture of three different but intimately related psychological processes. First, emotions involve a positive or negative conscious experience. That simply means that all emotions feel good or bad; if they were neutral, we wouldn't call them emotions. Second, emotions are accompanied by physiological arousal of the autonomic nervous system, some endocrine glands, and other physiological systems. And, third, they usually involve some kind of related behavior. When you see a car driving toward you, you feel a negative conscious

FIGURE 9.1

Diagram of the device used in the experiment by Cannon and Washburn (1912) to find out if stomach contractions caused a conscious feeling of hunger. Note the balloon swallowed by Washburn to measure the contractions.

experience, your autonomic nervous system churns you up, and you run. As we will see, some aspects of emotions appear to be inborn, whereas other aspects are shaped by our learning experiences.

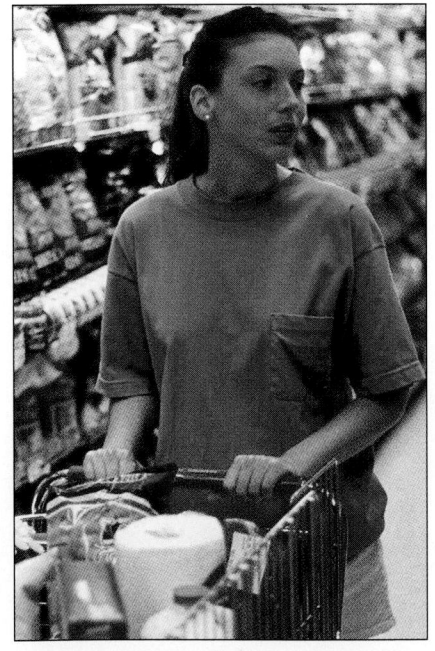

Hungry grocery shoppers are motivated shoppers who are likely to buy more food than nonhungry shoppers.

motivation
The internal state or condition that activates and gives direction to our thoughts, feelings, and actions.

DEFINITIONS OF MOTIVATION AND EMOTION

To people who are interested in human behavior, the key question is *why?* Carol wants to know why she continues to have sex with Michael when she knows she does not love him and is afraid of getting pregnant. The manager of the packing plant wants to know why two of her employees do not seem to care about doing a good job. A father wants to know why his son is not willing to work hard for good grades in school. Answers to questions like these often involve the concept of motivation—if they lead us to look *inside* the person.

The term **motivation** refers to an *internal* state that activates and gives direction to our thoughts. Meg was starting to feel a little hungry when an ad on television for tacos made her feel famished, reminded her that she had food in the refrigerator, and sent her scrambling to the kitchen. If her motive for hunger had not been activated, perhaps her motive to succeed in school might have led her in a different direction—maybe to read her psychology textbook. If no motives at all were activated, she would be doing nothing—just sitting around or maybe taking a nap. Motives are at the center of our lives—they arouse and direct what we think, feel, and do.

Some motives, such as hunger, are clearly based on internal physiological states. As we will see, several internal factors, such as the level of sugar in the blood, are important in regulating hunger. But other motives, such as the motive to succeed, are not based on simple internal physiological states. For all motives, however, *external cues* play an important role. Seeing the ad for tacos on television was an external cue that stimulated Meg's hunger motive; hearing her roommate worry aloud about passing her next psychology test would be an external cue that could have stimulated her motive to succeed.

Motivation is closely related to the topic of emotions. The term **emotion** refers to positive or negative feelings—generally reactions to stimuli—that are accompanied by physiological arousal and characteristic behavior. When we are afraid, for example, we experience an acutely unpleasant feeling: The sympathetic division of our autonomic nervous system is aroused and the fear generally shows in our behavior. The emotion of passion, on the other hand, is a conglomeration of very different feelings, biological changes, and behavior.

Motivation and emotions are closely linked concepts for three reasons: (a) The arousal of emotions activates behavior as motives do; (b) motives are often accompanied by emotions, (for example, the motive to perform well on a test is often accompanied by anxiety; sexual motivation is generally blended with the emotions of passion and love); and (c) emotions typically have motivational properties of their own—because you are in love, you are motivated to be with your special person; because you are angry, you want to strike out at the object of your anger. We will begin this chapter with a discussion of basic motives necessary for biological survival, then will move to a discussion of more "psychological" motives, and will end with a discussion of human emotions.

> ## PRIMARY MOTIVES: BIOLOGICAL NEEDS

Many human motives stem from the *need* for things that keep an organism alive: food, water, warmth, sleep, avoidance of pain, and so on. We consider these to be **primary motives** because we must meet these biological needs or die. The sexual motive is also considered to be a primary motive, not because we would die if it were not fulfilled, but because the species could not reproduce and survive if the sexual motive were not satisfied.

This chapter focuses on the biological motives of hunger and thirst, partly because they are the best understood of the primary motives. Elsewhere in the book, information is provided on the primary motives of avoidance of pain in chapter 3 and the need for sleep in chapter 4.

Homeostasis: Biological Thermostats

Most of the primary motives are based on the body's need to maintain a certain level of essential life elements: adequate sugar in the blood to nourish cells, sufficient water in the body, and so on. These critical levels are regulated by **homeostatic mechanisms.** These mechanisms sense imbalances in the body and stimulate actions that restore the proper balance. The homeostatic mechanisms of the body are often compared to the thermostats of home heating systems. When the temperature of the house falls below a preset level, the thermostat senses that fact and signals the heater to produce heat until the proper temperature has been restored; then it signals the heater to turn off. The body's responses to imbalances include both internal reactions and overt behavior. For instance, when the water level in body cells falls below a safe level, a signal is sent to the kidneys to reabsorb additional water from the urine. At the same time, a signal is sent to the brain that leads the animal—human or otherwise—to seek out and drink liquids. Similar homeostatic mechanisms are involved in hunger and the maintenance of body temperature.

Hunger: The Regulation of Food Intake

The biological control center of hunger is not the rumbling stomach. It does play a minor part in the control of hunger, but a much less important one than most of us think. Instead, the **hypothalamus** plays the controlling role in the motivation of hunger (Mook, 1986; Petri, 1986; Seeley & Schwartz, 1997). This small but extremely important forebrain structure that we first discussed in chapter 2 is involved in the regulation of many motives and emotions (see fig. 9.2).

Recent advances in our understanding of the brain have revealed that hunger is regulated by three centers in the hypothalamus. Two of these hypothalamic control centers

emotion
Positive or negative feelings generally in reaction to stimuli that are accompanied by physiological arousal and related behavior.

primary motives
Human motives for things that are necessary for survival, such as food, water, and warmth.

homeostatic mechanisms
(hō″mē-ō-stat′ik) Internal body mechanisms that sense biological imbalances and stimulate actions to restore the proper balance.

hypothalamus
(hī″pō-thal′ah-mus) The part of the forebrain involved with motives, emotions, and the functions of the autonomic nervous system.

FIGURE 9.2

Three parts of the hypothalamus play a key role in the control of hunger: the lateral feeding center, the ventromedial satiety center, and the paraventricular nucleus. The lateral feeding center directly stimulates hunger and eating. The paraventricular nucleus controls hunger through the control of blood sugar. The ventromedial satiety center operates in a feedback loop with the body's adipose cells. Secretions of leptin lead to the ventromedial satiety center to directly inhibit eating, stimulate the paraventricular nucleus, and increase the metabolism of fat cells through activation of the sympathetic nervous system (Ezell, 1995; Seeley & Schwartz, 1997).

Cerebral cortex

Hypothalamus

Pituitary gland

Sympathetic neuron

Adipose (fat) cell magnified

To sympathetic neurons

Close-up of hypothalamus

Paraventricular nucleus

Lateral hypothalamus

Ventromedial hypothalamus

Adipose cell secretes leptin

Leptin stimulates satiety center in ventromedial hypothalamus, which directly inhibits hunger, and sends message to adipose cells through sympathetic neurons and sends message to paraventricular nucleus, which controls blood-sugar levels.

lateral hypothalamus
A portion of the hypothalamus involved in feeling hungry and starting to eat (the feeding center).

ventromedial hypothalamus
A part of the hypothalamus involved in inhibiting eating when sufficient food has been consumed (the satiety center).

hyperphagia
(hī″per-fā′jē-ah) Excessive overeating that results from the destruction of the satiety center of the hypothalamus.

paraventricular nucleus
A part of the hypothalamus that plays a role in the motive of hunger by regulating the level of blood sugar.

operate in opposing ways. A *feeding system,* which initiates eating when food is needed, is located in the **lateral hypothalamus,** and a *satiety system,* which stops eating when enough food has been consumed, is located in the **ventromedial hypothalamus.**

Studies of laboratory rats have shown that, when the lateral hypothalamus (the feeding system) is electrically stimulated, rats that are too satiated (full) to eat will begin eating again. If this part of the hypothalamus is destroyed, on the other hand, rats will stop eating altogether and will starve to death if not artificially fed. Conversely, if the ventromedial hypothalamus (the satiety system) is surgically destroyed, the rats will overeat into a startling state of obesity (excessive fat). Figure 9.3 shows a normal rat and a rat with **hyperphagia** whose body weight tripled after surgical destruction of the ventromedial satiety center. These rats do not eat more times each day than normal rats but continue eating much longer each time they eat. Apparently, the destruction of part of the satiety system eliminates the homeostatic signal to stop eating when enough food has been consumed.

Alexander Reeves and Fred Plumb (1969) reported a clinical case study of a woman with tragic damage to the satiety center in the hypothalamus that bears a striking resemblance to hyperphagic laboratory animals. A 20-year-old bookkeeper sought medical help for her suddenly abnormal appetite and weight gain. X rays identified a tumor in the hypothalamus, but it could not be surgically removed. Prior to her death three years later, she regularly consumed 10,000 calories per day in an endless attempt to satisfy her hunger.

The third part of the hypothalamus that plays a role in the regulation of hunger is the **paraventricular nucleus.** This center both increases and decreases appetite by controlling the level of sugar in the blood (Martin, White, & Hulsey, 1991).

What information do the three centers of the hypothalamus use in regulating hunger? Apparently, two cues are used to regulate hunger on a daily basis, and a third cue is used to regulate body weight on a long-term basis:

1. *Stomach contractions.* Cannon and Washburn, whom we discussed at the beginning of the chapter, were partly right about the role of stomach contractions. The most immediate cue in the regulation of hunger really does come from the stomach. Contractions signal the lateral hypothalamic feeding system, whereas a full stomach activates the ventromedial satiety system.

2. *Blood-sugar levels.* Eating is also regulated on a short-term basis by the amount of sugar (glucose) in the blood. The hypothalamus contains specialized neurons that can directly detect the level of glucose in the bloodstream, but two other organs provide most of the information to the hypothalamus. The liver, which is a storehouse for sugar, detects blood glucose levels, and the upper small intestine, or *duodenum,* detects sugar in food that has just been eaten. Both organs send chemical messages to the paraventricular nucleus of the hypothalamus, which plays a role in initiating or stopping eating (Ezell, 1995; Petri, 1986).

   The role of blood glucose in the regulation of hunger has been clearly demonstrated. Two of the experimental methods involve the two hormones secreted by the islets of Langerhans (chapter 2, p. 56). When **insulin** is injected into the bloodstream of a satiated person, it causes a drop in the level of glucose, and the person feels hungry. Conversely, when the hormone **glucagon** is injected into the bloodstream of a hungry person, it produces an increase in blood glucose, and the individual no longer feels hungry.

   Blood glucose levels are a key mechanism in the short-term control of hunger, so it is important to understand a simple fact about blood glucose and hunger. When you eat, it takes a few minutes for food to be digested and enter the bloodstream in the form of glucose. If you eat slowly, therefore, your brain will have enough time to detect the increase in blood glucose and make you feel "full" before you eat more than you need. In other words, the faster you eat, the more you will eat before you feel full.

3. *Body fat levels.* The long-term maintenance of body weight is managed by the ability of the hypothalamus to detect the level of fat in the body (Mook, 1986; Petri, 1986; Seeley & Schwartz, 1997). Recent research has revealed that the adipose (fat) cells that live on your waist, hips, and elsewhere secrete **leptin** into the bloodstream. The more full of fat that the adipose cells are, the more leptin they secrete. When the circulating leptin reaches the hypothalamus, structures in and around the ventromedial hypothalamus detect it. This causes the hypothalamus to react in three ways to control body weight. First, the ventromedial satiety center sends a direct message to inhibit eating. Second, it signals the paraventricular nucleus to control hunger by regulating the level of blood sugar.

   A third action taken by the ventromedial satiety center to control body weight in response to leptin also has been discovered. It provides a new and absolutely fascinating chapter on the sublime complexity of the human body. When leptin levels are high, the ventromedial hypothalamus activates the sympathetic nervous system. Tiny branches of this nervous system actually end on the adipose cells. Stimulation of the adipose cells by the sympathetic neurons causes their metabolism to increase to burn off fat in the form of heat (Ezell, 1995).

Psychological Factors in Hunger

Although hunger is clearly a motive that is tied to biological needs, psychological factors are also involved in the regulation of food intake. Through maturation and learning, we go from an infant who only drinks milk to an adult with distinct food preferences that play an important role in our lives (Rozin, 1996). If you grew up in the American South, you might adore chittlins (deep-fried pig intestines) and stewed okra. If you grew up in another part of the world, however, the very idea of these foods might be disgusting. A Catholic woman might enjoy beef, pork, and shellfish, but eating these foods might violate deeply held religious beliefs of some of her Hindu and Jewish neighbors. Learning plays a powerful role in determining *what* we eat, *when* we eat (we are often ready to eat at our customary times

FIGURE 9.3
Destruction of the part of the hypothalamus that is involved in the satiety system causes rats to eat themselves into a state of extreme obesity called hyperphagia. A normal rat is shown on the left.

insulin
(in′su-lin)   A hormone produced by the islets of Langerhans that reduces the amount of sugar in the bloodstream.

glucagon
(gloo′kah-gon)   A hormone produced by the islets of Langerhans that causes the liver to release sugar into the bloodstream.

leptin
(lep′tin)   An enzyme produced by adipose cells that is involved in hunger.

Learning plays a role in eating habits. Many families encourage and model overeating.

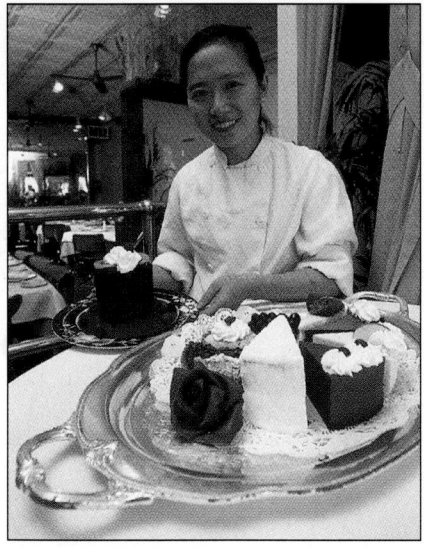

External incentives, such as the look or smell of a food, can increase our motivation to eat.

incentives
External cues that activate motives.

for eating, even if we have just had a snack), and even *how much* we eat (many families encourage and model overeating). Studies of nonhuman animals show that even rats and chimpanzees learn what to eat by watching older animals (National Advisory Mental Health Council, 1995b).

Emotions also play a role in eating. People who are anxious often eat more than usual, and people who are depressed may lose their appetite for long periods of time. Ironically, though, individuals who get depressed after starting a new regime of healthy eating and exercise often lose the will to continue. If you are temporarily depressed enough to believe that nobody cares if you live or die—even you—why would you bother to eat healthfully?

Perhaps the most troublesome psychological factors to those who are trying to control their eating, however, are **incentives.** How many times have you finished dinner at a restaurant or family gathering, feeling a bit overstuffed, only to be tempted into eating a seductive dessert? Incentives are external cues that activate motives. The smell of freshly baked bread makes you hungry; passing a fast-food joint on your way home from school creates a craving for french fries; and the sight of the dessert creates a desire to eat even when you are way past the point of biological hunger. Incentives have their effect through the same brain mechanisms that regulate the biological aspects of hunger. The sight of food causes neurons in your hypothalamus to fire, particularly if it's a favorite food, and the smell of food triggers the release of insulin, which stimulates hunger by causing your blood sugar to drop (Rolls, Burton, & Mora, 1976). Laboratory research with animals has shown that incentives can be powerful enough under some circumstances to push weight above the natural set point. All rats will overeat to the point of obesity if they have easy access to large quantities of a variety of tasty high-calorie foods (National Advisory Mental Health Council, 1995b). Unless you are trying to gain weight, therefore, it is not a good idea to keep large quantities of a variety of tasty high-calorie foods in your kitchen.

Thirst: The Regulation of Water Intake

Just as we must control the intake of food to survive, we must also regulate the intake of water. What is the homeostatic mechanism involved in thirst? Actually, there are several mechanisms as in the case of hunger; like hunger also, the key regulatory centers are in the hypothalamus.

Biological Regulation of Thirst

A *drink system* and a *stop drinking system* are regulated by different sections of the hypothalamus. Surgical destruction of the drink system causes the animal to refuse water; destruction of the stop drinking system results in excessive drinking. Although the control centers for thirst occupy much of the same areas as the centers for hunger, they operate separately by using different neurotransmitters (Grossman, 1960; Schulkin, 1999).

The hypothalamus uses three principal cues in regulating drinking: mouth dryness, loss of water by cells, and reductions in blood volume.

1. *Mouth dryness.* Dryness of the mouth is the thirst cue of which we are most consciously aware. In the 1920s, biologist Walter Cannon studied the role of mouth dryness in thirst, this time using himself as the subject. After drinking large amounts of water to be sure he was not thirsty, he injected himself with a drug that stops the flow of saliva. Very soon, he felt thirsty. Next, he injected his mouth with a local anesthetic that blocked all sensations from his mouth. This quickly eliminated the sensation of being thirsty. Cannon concluded that mouth dryness was the cue that led to the sensation of thirst, but he was only partially correct again. We know today that other factors play more important roles.

2. *Cell fluid levels.* When the total amount of water in the body decreases, the concentration of salts in the fluids of the body increases. Of particular importance to the regulation of thirst are *sodium salts* that exist primarily in the fluids outside the body's cells (because salts cannot pass through the semipermeable membranes of the cells). Decreases in the total body fluids of even 1 to 2 percent produce increases in the sodium concentration that are large enough to draw water out of the cells and *dehydrate* them (Hole, 1990; Petri, 1986). This happens to cells throughout the body, but, when certain specialized cells in the drink center of the hypothalamus dehydrate and shrivel, they send multiple messages to correct the situation. In particular, they chemically signal the **pituitary gland,** which is located just below the hypothalamic drink center, to secrete the **antidiuretic hormone (ADH)** into the bloodstream. When ADH reaches the kidneys, it causes them to conserve water in the body by reabsorbing it from the urine. In addition, the hypothalamic center simultaneously sends a message of thirst to the cerebral cortex, which initiates searching for and drinking liquids (Schulkin, 1999).

3. *Total blood volume.* The third cue used by the hypothalamus to regulate thirst is total blood volume. As the volume of water in the body decreases, the volume of blood—which is composed mostly of water—decreases as well. A decreased volume of blood is first sensed by the kidneys. The kidneys react in two ways. First, they cause blood vessels to contract to compensate for the lowered amount of blood. Second, in a series of chemical steps, they cause the creation of the substance **angiotensin** in the blood. When angiotensin reaches the hypothalamus, the drink center sends a thirst message to the cerebral cortex, which eventually leads to drinking (Schulkin, 1999).

Psychological Factors in Thirst

Psychological factors also play a role in the regulation of drinking, although overall this role does not appear to be as large as in hunger. Learning influences *which* beverages we drink (the average citizen of Nepal prefers yak's milk to cow's milk) as well as *when* we drink them (an advertising campaign has been mounted in recent years to convince us to drink colas for breakfast). Incentives, such as the sight of a glass of beer, may activate thirst in a person who is otherwise not thirsty. Stress and emotions seem to have little effect on drinking compared with eating, except in the case of beverages that contain alcohol or stimulants (coffee, tea, colas, and so on), which alter our moods.

Learning influences which beverages we drink, as well as when we drink them. For example, drinking cola at breakfast is a fairly recent idea.

pituitary gland
(pĭ-tu´ĭ-tār˝ē)   The body's master gland, located near the bottom of the brain, whose hormones help regulate the activity of the other glands in the endocrine system.

antidiuretic hormone (ADH)
(an˝tī-dī˝ū-ret´ĭk)   A hormone produced by the pituitary that causes the kidneys to conserve water in the body by reabsorbing it from the urine.

angiotensin
(an˝jē-ō-ten´sĭn)   A substance in the blood that signals the hypothalamus that the body needs water.

● Review

The term *primary motivation* refers to states based on biological needs that activate and guide behavior. Examples of primary motives include hunger, thirst, maintaining warmth, and avoiding pain. These motives must be satisfied if the organism is to survive. Primary motives are generally based on a complex number of biological factors. For example, the control centers for eating and drinking are located in the hypothalamus. The hypothalamus responds directly or indirectly to a number of body signals that food or water is needed. In the case of hunger, stomach contractions, levels of blood glucose, and levels of body fat are all involved in the regulation of eating. Thirst is similarly regulated by a combination of mouth dryness, level of fluids in the body cells, and the total volume of blood in the body.

Although the primary motives are based on biological survival needs, psychological factors are involved in these motives as well. External stimuli, such as the sight of a highly preferred food or beverage, can act as an incentive that activates eating or drinking, even when the individual is satiated. Learning also influences what, when, and how much we eat and drink.

● Check Your Learning

To be sure that you have learned the key points from the preceding section, cover the list of correct answers and try to answer each question. If you give an incorrect answer to any question, return to the page given next to the correct answer to see why your answer was not correct. Remember that these questions cover only some of the important information in this section; it is important that you make up your own questions to check your learning of other facts and concepts.

1. The term _____ refers to an internal state or condition that activates and gives direction to our thoughts, feelings, and actions.

   a) cognition   c) motivation
   b) incentive   d) physiology

2. A _____ is an internal mechanism that senses biological imbalances and stimulates actions to restore the proper balance.

3. The hunger and thirst motives are controlled by excitatory and inhibitory brain systems, with centers in the _____ playing key roles.

   a) cerebellum   c) thalamus
   b) hypothalamus   d) hippocampus

4. _____ refers to an external cue that activates primarily hunger motivation.

   a) Incentive   c) Catalyst
   b) Efferent   d) Stimulus

● Thinking Critically About Psychology

1. If you were trying to help someone control her or his food intake, how would your advice be different after reading this section?

2. How have your personal experiences influenced the expression of your hunger and thirst motives?

Correct Answers **1. c** (p. 280),   **2.** homeostatic mechanism (p. 281),   **3. b** (p. 281),   **4. a** (p. 284).

▶ PSYCHOLOGICAL MOTIVES

psychological motives
Motives related to the individual's happiness and well-being, but not to survival.

Psychological motives are motives that are not directly related to the biological survival of the individual or the species. They are "needs" in the sense that the individual's happiness and well-being depend on these motives. Even more than primary motives, psychological motives vary considerably in the degree to which they are influenced by experience. Some psychological motives are found in every normal member of a species and seem to be innate, whereas others seem to be entirely learned. In this section, we will look at three psychological motives: the need for novel stimulation, the need for affiliation with others, and the need for achievement.

Stimulus Motivation: Seeking Novel Stimulation

Did you ever come home to an empty house and flip on the radio or television just to kill the silence? Have you ever spent all day Saturday writing a term paper and then felt you *had* to get up and take a walk or talk to someone just for sheer diversion? Most people get bored easily if there is little overall stimulation or if the stimulation is unchanging. We, and other animals, have an apparently inborn motive to seek **novel stimulation.**

novel stimulation
New or changed experiences.

If you put a rat in a T-maze (see fig. 9.4) in which it must choose between turning right into an alley painted gray or turning left into one painted with complex stripes, the rat will explore the more complex, more "interesting" alley first. But the next time it will be more likely to turn into the gray alley, which it has not seen yet, apparently because it is "curious" about it (Dember, 1965).

Monkeys that are kept in boring cages will similarly work hard pressing a lever to earn a chance to look at other monkeys or even to watch a model train run (Butler, 1953). Monkeys will also work manual puzzles for hours without any reward except finally getting them apart (Harlow, Harlow, & Meyer, 1950) (see fig. 9.5). Watch a human infant play with her crib toys for a few minutes and you will see that humans, too, are motivated to manipulate, investigate, and generally shake up their environments. If you go without physical activity for a while, you will see that you have a need for activity, too.

Optimal Arousal Theory

Although no known homeostatic mechanism accounts for our need for novel stimulation, we clearly must have a certain amount of it to feel comfortable. But, just as too little stimulation is unpleasant and will motivate us to increase stimulation, *too much* stimulation is unpleasant and will motivate us to find ways to decrease it. Too many people talking at once, too much noise, or a room that contains too many clashing colors and patterns will send a person off in search of a few minutes of peace, quiet, and reduced stimulation. Apparently, an optimal level of stimulation exists, and we feel uncomfortable going either above or below this level (Korman, 1974).

Our apparent "need" for an optimal level of stimulation has led psychologists to suggest that each individual strives to maintain an **optimal level of arousal** in the nervous system. Optimal arousal theory does not suggest, however, that there is a biological need for a moderate or an optimal level of arousal. The individual can survive at high or low levels of arousal, but he or she is motivated to achieve a comfortable, optimal level of arousal by acting in ways that increase or decrease stimulation.

Not only is arousal an important motivational concept, but it's also linked to the efficiency of our performance in various situations. If arousal is too low, performance will be inadequate; if it's too high, performance may become disrupted and disorganized. This simple notion is often referred to as the **Yerkes-Dodson law,** but it's somewhat more complicated than it looks at first. The ideal level of arousal for different kinds of performance varies considerably. Football players "warm up" and "psych up" physically and emotionally to reach high levels of arousal for the game. It would be difficult to exceed the ideal level of arousal needed for highly physical contact sports. On the other hand, the performance of a skilled artisan applying pottery glazes by hand would be most efficient at much lower levels of arousal. Too much arousal, as in the form of high levels of anxiety, would tend to disrupt the delicate, skilled performance of the potter.

FIGURE 9.4
T-maze like those used to study stimulus motivation in rats.

optimal level of arousal
The apparent human need for a comfortable level of stimulation, achieved by acting in ways that increase or decrease it.

Yerkes-Dodson law
A law stating that effective performance is more likely if the level of arousal is suitable for the activity.

motive for affiliation
The need to be with other people and to have personal relationships.

  Yerkes-Dodson law

www.mmhe.com/laheye1

Affiliation Motivation

Do you usually enjoy being with friends? Do you feel lonely during periods when you do not have many friends? Human beings are social creatures. Given the opportunity, we generally prefer to have regular contact with other people. In this sense, it can be said that people have a **motive for affiliation** (Houston, 1985).

The need for affiliation is present in all normal humans, but most research on this topic concerns differences between individuals who have different levels of this motive. Individuals who are high in the need for affiliation, for example, tend to prefer being with others rather than satisfying other motives. When asked to perform a clerical task with a partner, individuals who are high in the need for affiliation, but low in the need for achievement, choose to

FIGURE 9.5
A monkey disassembling mechanical lock puzzles for no reward other than the activity and novel stimulation involved in the process.

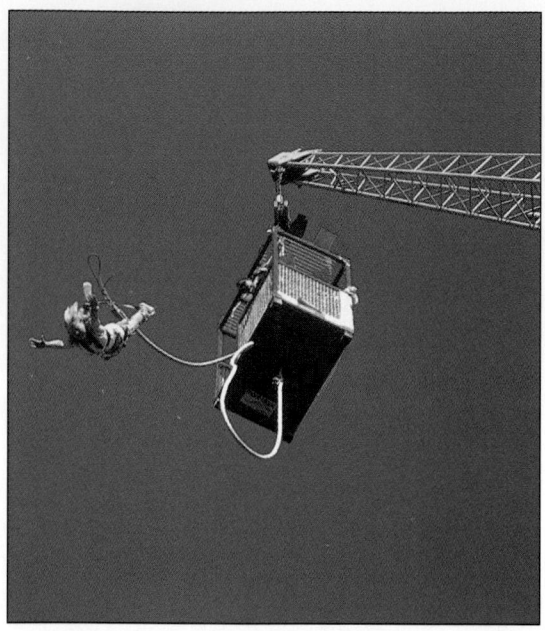

Some people always seem to need high levels of sensation. The optimal arousal theory would suggest that they are usually below their optimal level of arousal.

The motive for affiliation is present in everyone to some extent, but people differ in the strength of their need to be with others.

achievement motivation
The psychological need in humans for success.

work with a friend, regardless of how competent the friend is. In contrast, individuals who are low in the need for affiliation, but high in the need for achievement, choose the partner who they believe is most competent (French, 1956).

Two theories have been proposed to explain our apparent need for affiliation (Houston, 1985). Some believe that affiliation motivation is an inborn need that is based on natural selection. A stone-age human who chose to hunt alone would have been less able to kill large animals for food and to avoid being the prey of other animals, and thus to survive, than a human who felt a need to live and hunt with others. Thus, the forces of nature may have selected those humans with a need for affiliation—because they were the ones who survived. Other psychologists, however, believe that each human learns the motive to affiliate through his or her own learning experiences. Because infants experience being fed, cleaned, tickled, kept warm, and other positive forms of nurturing in the presence of another human being, other human beings may become "positive stimuli" through classical conditioning. Similarly, because our actions that lead us to be in the presence of others—smiling, stretching out our baby arms for a hug, and the like—often lead to pleasant outcomes, then affiliative behaviors are likely to be positively reinforced (Houston, 1985).

That motive for affiliation may be related in some way to the greater chance that humans who affiliate—flock together—will survive receives some support from the fact that affiliation motivation appears to be stronger when we are frightened about our well-being. Studies have shown that painful experiences—such as failing college tests—increase our motive to affiliate with others (Van Duuren & DiGiacomo, 1997). As the saying goes, "misery loves company." On the other hand, some people tend to have more affiliation motivation than others under most circumstances, and, when the chips are down—such as when they are fighting cancer—they are more likely to seek emotional support from family members (Manne, Alfieri, Taylor, & Dougherty, 1999). There is considerable evidence that higher levels of affiliation motivation predict better psychological adjustment throughout life, perhaps in part because the motive for affiliation promotes social support when times are tough (McAdams & Vaillant, 1982).

Achievement Motivation

Most high school senior classes vote on the female and male who are "mostly likely to succeed." Who was it in your high school class? Were they real "go-getters" who were willing to work hard to succeed? If so, they were probably high in achievement motivation. **Achievement motivation** is the psychological need to succeed in school, work, and other areas of life. Although the concept of achievement motivation has been around for a long time, a great deal of research in recent years has revitalized the topic by demonstrating that achievement motivation is more complex than originally suspected. The first scholarly works on achievement motivation portrayed it as a uniformly positive psychological force—the motivation that allowed many people to achieve the American dream of occupational and financial success. More recently, it has become clear that different people have different definitions of "success" and different motives for wanting to achieve their version of success.

We will focus our discussion of achievement motivation on a topic that is very relevant to you at this stage of your life—achievement in college—but the same ideas apply to achievement throughout life. Would you say that you are highly motivated to succeed in college? If so, how would you define success in college? Do you want to make good grades or do you want to learn a lot of new and interesting information (or both)? Andrew Elliot and Marcy Church (1997) of the University of Rochester have conducted fascinating and important studies of achievement motivation among college students. Remember that motivation activates and directs behavior. Elliot and Church distinguished three key elements in the motivation to get out of bed, go to class, pay attention, take notes, ask questions, and set aside other activities to study for tests:

1. *Mastery goals.* Persons with high mastery goals are intrinsically motivated to learn interesting and important new information. They enjoy challenging courses if they help them master new information and are disappointed by easy courses in which they get good grades but learn very little.

2. *Performance-approach goals.* Persons with high performance-approach goals are motivated to work hard to get better grades than other students to gain the respect of others.

3. *Performance-avoidance goals.* Persons with high performance-avoidance goals are motivated to work hard to avoid getting bad grades and looking unintelligent to others.

How would you rank the importance of these three sources of achievement motivation for yourself and your friends? Each of these three types of motivational goals will activate and direct work that will help you succeed, but Elliot and Church (1997) believe that they lead to rather different consequences. At the beginning of a college course on the psychology of personality, the students answered questions about their level of each of these three types of achievement motivation. At the end of the course, the students completed measures of how much they enjoyed and valued the course, and the researchers used their course grades to see how well they had performed on tests.

The different types of achievement motivation were associated with different outcomes at the end of the course. Not surprisingly, students with higher mastery goals reported enjoying the course more at the end. This was especially true if they were also low in performance-approach goals—being motivated to make good grades to impress other people interferes with enjoyment of the course. Students with higher performance-approach goals made better grades, especially if they had low mastery goals. The desire to impress other people by making good grades does lead to better grades, but sadly, wanting to learn the material for its own sake sometimes gets in the way of making good grades. The students who made the lowest grades had either low performance-approach and low mastery goals (they had little positive motivation of either type to learn the material) or they had high performance-avoidance goals (they had only negative motivation to learn the material). Students with high performance-avoidance goals at the start of the course also reported that they enjoyed the course content less than other students. Working just to avoid failure rarely makes for a positive or fruitful experience.

Thus, in order to understand one's achievement motivation for success in college, we need to understand both *what* people want and *why* they want it. Both our goals and our motives for attaining them have consequences for our success in college and enjoyment of the process. The same is true for success in other areas of life.

As if achievement motivation were not complicated enough by itself, we must also consider **fear of success** in order to understand a person's motivation to achieve. Although outperforming others often brings private feelings of satisfaction, it can invite envy that may strain social relationships (Exline & Lobel, 1999). Although this is not a concern of some people, it creates fear of success in others than can motivate them to achieve below their potential. Fear of success is more common among women than men in North America (Fried-Buchalter, 1997; Kumari, 1996), but college women with feminist, nontraditional sex-role attitudes have less fear of success than women with more traditional sex-role attitudes (Kumari, 1996). Apparently, women who adhere to traditional sex roles fear criticism and rejection if they deviate from expected passive feminine roles. Sadly, women with the highest self-esteem are most likely to have high levels of fear of success, perhaps because they feel that they could succeed if they were to try (Kumari, 1996).

Intrinsic and Extrinsic Motivation

It is important to distinguish between intrinsic and extrinsic motivation. We speak of **intrinsic motivation** when people are motivated by the inherent nature of the activity, their pleasure of mastering something new, or the natural consequences of the activity. For example, the monkeys that we mentioned earlier who will take apart mechanical puzzles for

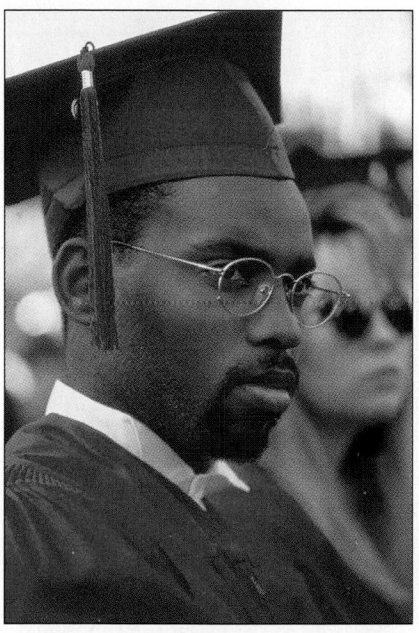

Achievement motivation is a complex psychological process. People differ both in their definitions of success and their reasons for being motivated to seek it.

fear of success
The fear of the consequences of success, particularly the envy of others.

intrinsic motivation
(in-trin´sik)   Human motives stimulated by the inherent nature of the activity or its natural consequences.

HUMAN DIVERSITY

CONFLICT AND THE FIRST-GENERATION COLLEGE STUDENT

Are you the first member of your family to attend college? If so, this fact may lead to conflicting emotions in you. Let's look at the college experiences of a man named John who now works as a psychologist. He is from a poor white family and was the first of 4 siblings and 16 cousins to finish college. He knew that his family was proud of him, but he sometimes felt that he had left his family and old friends behind in his quest for higher education. Sometimes these feelings interfered with his motivation to complete school.

Many first-generation college students struggle with similar feelings (Piorkowski, 1983; Whitten, 1992). They often perceive themselves, and are perceived by their families, as moving into a new social class. This can be anxiety provoking for both the student and the family. Issues related to group loyalty arise as the student's interests, vocabulary, and worldview become different from those of his family and neighborhood friends. Family members sometimes accuse first-generation college students of "changing" or "thinking they are better" than the family. These issues are particularly challenging for members of ethnic groups that traditionally attended college infrequently. Not only do they face strained relationships with their family and friends, but they often do not fit into the college community if they attend a majority-culture institution.

Many first-generation college students handle these conflicts very successfully. They recognize that they are part of both their college and home communities and develop strategies for moving comfortably from one to the other. They speak standard English on the college campus and speak the language of their home community, which might be Spanish, Creole, or Black English, when they are among friends. They reassure their family members by word and deed that they still feel a part of their home, even though they are changing in some ways. This is important because students who are able to integrate their old and new lifestyles more successfully make higher grades than students who experience a high degree of conflict (Whitten, 1993b).

But first-generation college students are not the only ones who experience conflicts based on their backgrounds at college. Consider Roslyn, a 38-year-old African American woman who is a third-generation college graduate. Her grandparents were college-educated teachers, and her parents both have graduate training. As a college student, she usually hid this background from her African American peers. She often had a sense of isolation because she was one of the few African American students in her dormitory whose education was being paid for entirely by her parents. She also felt guilty about having more material goods than her peers and other African Americans in her neighborhood.

What is the climate like at your institution for first-generation college students and students who do not fit the mold in other ways? How effective is your college when it comes to addressing diversity issues? How do your family and friends feel about your decision to enter college? Thinking about these questions may help you identify sources of potential conflict in yourself or understand the experience of other students better.

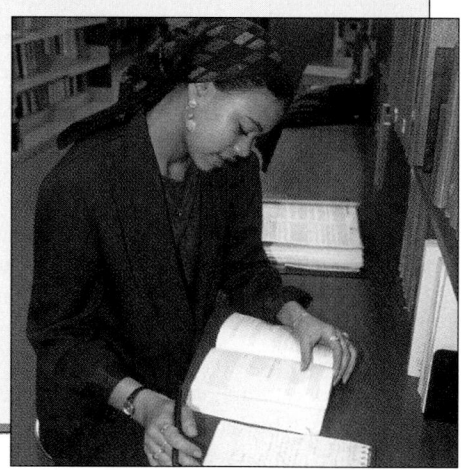

extrinsic motivation
(eks-trin'sik) Human motives activated by external rewards.

no reward other than getting them apart are intrinsically motivated to solve puzzles. People who read nonfiction books that are unrelated to their work just because it is fun to learn new things are intrinsically motivated. Similarly, people who donate anonymously to charity because they wish to help people without being recognized are intrinsically motivated. **Extrinsic motivation,** on the other hand, is motivation that is external to the activity and not an inherent part of it. If a child who hates to do arithmetic homework is encouraged to do so by payment of a nickel for every correct answer, he is extrinsically motivated. That is, he works for the external payment rather than because of an intrinsic interest in math. Similarly, a person who works hard to be a good employee because she wants to be admired by others—rather than because of a genuine interest in the work—is extrinsically motivated. People who are intrinsically motivated tend to work harder and respond to challenges by working even harder. They enjoy their work more and often perform more creatively and effectively than people who are extrinsically motivated (National Advisory Mental Health Council, 1995b). Intrinsic motivation is shaped by our learning experiences. For example, children from families who emphasize the joys and importance of learning have more intrinsic motivation to learn in school (Gottfried, Fleming, & Gottfried, 1998).

Perhaps the most significant issue concerning the distinction between intrinsic and extrinsic motivation is the question of when extrinsic rewards should be supplied by parents, teachers, and employers in an effort to increase motivation. When is it wise to use extrinsic motivation in the form of positive reinforcement to increase the frequency of some behavior (such as completing homework, delivering packages on time, and so on)? Considerable evidence suggests that, if a behavior occurs infrequently—and its intrinsic motivation can be assumed low for that individual—then extrinsic motivation can be successful in increasing the frequency of occurrence of the behavior. Children who hate to do their math homework often will do it diligently if rewarded with additional allowance money. On the other hand, if the individual is already intrinsically motivated to perform an activity, adding extrinsic motivation may detract from the intrinsic motivation. For example, when young children who like to draw pictures in school were given certificates for good drawing, they drew pictures less often than children who had not received certificates (Lepper, Greene, & Nisbett, 1973). This study, and many subsequent studies (Ryan & Deci, 2000; Tang & Hall, 1995), suggest that we must be careful to avoid squelching intrinsic motivation by providing unnecessary extrinsic rewards.

For many years, it was assumed that the best way to increase intrinsic motivation was to give people choices. When people have options, they will choose activities that they are intrinsically motivated to perform, and performing them will further enhance their intrinsic motivation. Recent findings suggest that this is true, but only in individualistic Western societies (Iyengar & Lepper, 1999). American children of European ancestry show more intrinsic motivation for school tasks and other activities that they choose themselves. In contrast, Asian American children from collectivistic cultures that place greater emphasis on the well-being of the group than on the well-being of the individual have more intrinsic motivation for activities that were selected for them by trusted authority figures or friends (Iyengar & Lepper, 1999). As in many aspects of psychological life, sociocultural factors are important in motivation.

Maslow's Hierarchy of Motives

We have touched on only a few of the human motives, but it's already obvious that we are creatures of many and varied needs. Abraham Maslow (1970) put forward an interesting theory about our many motives. According to Maslow, we are not a crazy-quilt confusion of motives; rather, our motives are organized in a hierarchy arranged from the most basic to the most personal and advanced.

Maslow's hierarchy of motives (needs) is shown in figure 9.6. If lower needs in the hierarchy are not met for the most part, then higher motives will not operate. Higher needs lie dormant until the individual has a chance to satisfy immediately pressing lower needs, such as hunger, thirst, and safety. When the lower needs have been met, then motives to develop relationships with others, to achieve a positive self-esteem, and to realize one's full potential ethically, artistically, and philosophically (**self-actualization**) become important to the individual.

Maslow's hierarchy of motives
The concept that more basic needs must be met before higher-level motives become active.

self-actualization
According to Maslow, the seldomly reached full result of the inner-directed drive of humans to grow, improve, and use their potential to the fullest.

Maslow's hierarchy of motives helps explain such things as why starving peasant farmers are not particularly interested in the political philosophies of rival governments and why, throughout history, science, art, and philosophy have mostly been produced when a nation could afford to have a privileged class who did not have to work to eat. The concept of the hierarchy of motives also helps us understand why a person would give up a prestigious, but time-consuming, career to try to save a marriage with a much-loved spouse. Higher motives become unimportant when lower motives are unmet.

But, as helpful as Maslow's hierarchy of motives is, there are some obvious exceptions to it. The hierarchy does not explain why an individual would risk her or his life to rescue a friend from a burning building. Nor does it explain why imprisoned members of the Irish Republican Army intentionally starved themselves to death in 1981 to gain what might be seen by outsiders as minor changes in how prisoners were treated. Similarly, the hierarchy fails to shed light on the common occurrence of an individual's ignoring spouse and children to pursue self-esteem in a career. Obviously, humans are sometimes willing to

FIGURE 9.6

Maslow's hierarchy of motives.

Source: Diagram based on data from *Hierarchy of Needs from Motivation and Personality,* Third Edition, by Abraham H. Maslow. Revised by Robert Frager, et al., Harper & Row, Publishers, Inc., 1954, 1987.

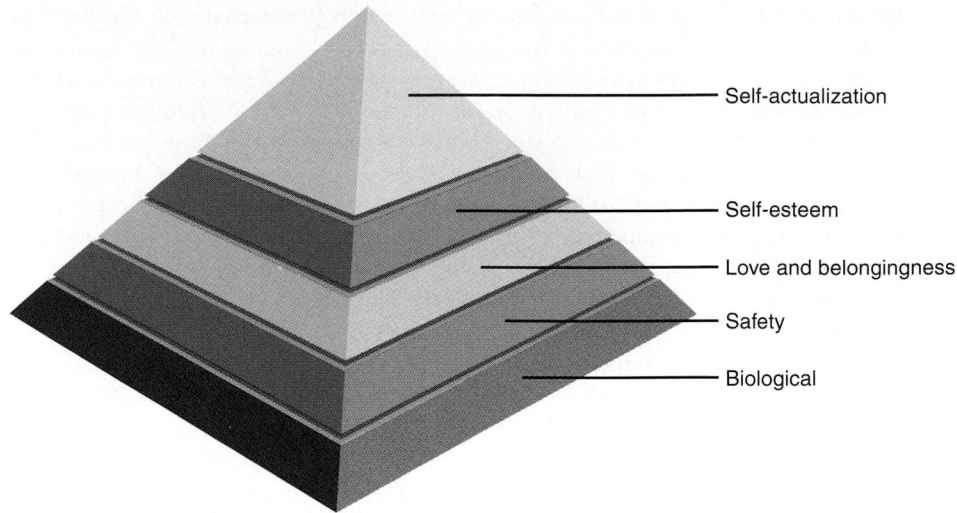

— Self-actualization

— Self-esteem

— Love and belongingness

— Safety

— Biological

endure unmet lower motives to pursue higher ones. Still, Maslow's hierarchy appears to explain more facets of motivation than it fails to explain.

Self-Actualization and the "American Dream"

Maslow believed that the highest need was for self-actualization. Because most people are unable to fully satisfy lower-level motives, he believed that few of us achieved full self-actualization. Self-actualization is defined in terms of the following characteristics (based on Jones & Crandall, 1986):

- Being dedicated to a mission in life that transcends your selfish interests
- Believing that people are essentially good and trustworthy
- Loving others even when you do not like their behavior
- Feeling adequate to deal with life
- Being able to accept your own weaknesses
- Not being dependent on the approval of others (preferring to be yourself than popular)
- Being able to express your feelings even when they are unpopular
- Being unashamed of all of your emotions, even negative emotions
- Being unafraid of failure

To what extent would you say that you are self-actualized in Maslow's terms? How common is self-actualization in contemporary American society? In 1993, Tim Kasser and Richard Ryan wrote an influential paper entitled *A Dark Side of the American Dream,* which portrayed the American dream of financial success as antithetical to self-actualization. They showed that persons who are highly motivated to achieve financial success are typically less actualized and less well adjusted. Although they presented only correlational evidence, which cannot tell us if maladjustment leads to high achievement motivation for financial success or vice versa, they theorized that motivation leads to lack of self-actualization, anxiety, depression, and health problems (Kasser & Ryan, 1993). Similarly, Charles Carver and Eryn Baird (1998) of the University of Miami found that college students' levels of motivation for financial success and status were negatively correlated with their levels of self-actualization. In contrast, the students who were motivated to achieve a different kind of success (helping others, teaching them important information and skills, and participating in social and political movements) were more self-actualized. Thus, what you want in the future is associated with different levels of well-being and self-actualization.

Importantly, however, Carver and Baird (1998) showed that our *reasons* for wanting to achieve success are almost as important as our definition of success itself. College students who were motivated to help others because helping is inherently enjoyable and important were more self-actualized than other students. Being motivated to help others was not always associated with self-actualization, however. Students who were motivated to help others because they thought it would look good on their resumes or because other people would like them better were less self-actualized than others. Students who aspired to wealth and power were less self-actualized regardless of why they wanted that kind of success, but, if they wanted financial success and power because it would provide independence and happiness, they were somewhat more actualized than students who wanted it to impress other people. Again, both your goals and your reasons for wanting them are of great psychological importance.

● Review

Psychological motives help define and shape our lives, but, unlike biological motives, they are not directly linked to the survival of the individual or the species. Some psychological motives are common to all normal members of a species and seem to be innate, whereas others appear to be primarily, if not entirely, learned. The stimulus motive—the need to maintain a moderate level of novel stimulation and activity—is an example of an apparently inborn psychological motive. The stimulus motive has led psychologists to speculate that individuals seek to maintain an optimal level of arousal in the nervous system by regulating stimulus input and activity levels. Other psychological motives appear to be influenced by social learning to a greater extent.

Most people have some need to affiliate with others, people differ in the degree of their affiliation motivation. This motive appears to be strongest when times are tough—misery loves company, as they say. This is perhaps because people who affiliate with others during those tough times reap the benefits of social support.

Achievement motivation is the drive to be successful. This is a complex phenomenon, partly because it is a combination of desires to learn and succeed, fear of failure, and fear of the problems associated with success. In addition, people differ in both their definitions of success and their reasons for seeking success. In general, people who strongly aspire to success defined in terms of wealth and power are less well adjusted and self-actualized than people who aspire to help and teach others. Regardless of an individual's definition of success, however, people who are motivated to achieve success to impress and please others tend to be less well adjusted than people who are motivated to succeed by their own values.

Some motives are intrinsic—inherent in the activity—whereas others are extrinsic to the activity. Both kinds of motives play a constructive role in our lives, but the unnecessary use of extrinsic rewards for an activity can backfire by reducing a person's intrinsic motivation for that activity. Giving persons a choice of activities improves intrinsic motivation in individualistic societies, but guidance from trusted persons improves intrinsic motivation in collectivistic societies.

● Check Your Learning

To be sure that you have learned the key points from the preceding section, cover the list of correct answers and try to answer each question. If you give an incorrect answer to any question, return to the page given next to the correct answer to see why your answer was not correct.

1. _____ motives are related to the individual's happiness and well-being, but not to survival.

   a) Primary   c) Psychological

   b) Hunger   d) Tertiary

2. The _____ law states that efficient performance is more likely if the level of arousal is suitable for the activity (neither too high nor too low).

    a) tort

    b) opponent

    c) Weber-Fechner

    d) Yerkes-Dodson

3. Threats to our well-being generally increase our _____ (or need to be with other people).

    a) achievement motivation

    b) power motivation

    c) affiliation motivation

    d) intimacy motivation

4. _____ motivation is the psychological need for success in school, occupation, and other situations.

    a) Affiliation

    b) Aggression

    c) Acceptance

    d) Achievement

5. According to Maslow's _____, an individual moves from one level of motivation to the next after fulfilling the basic needs on the lower level.

● Thinking Critically About Psychology

1. Do you think our need for affiliation is an inborn need or a learned motive? Why?

2. What is your definition of success and what are your reasons for desiring it? Are your goals related in a positive way to your well-being and self-actualization?

Correct Answers **1. c** (p. 286), **2. d** (p. 287), **3. c** (p. 287), **4. d** (p. 288), **5.** hierarchy of motives (p. 291).

▶ EMOTIONS

What do poets write about? Of all the facets of human existence, which do they choose for their themes? It's not depth perception, neural transmission, or cognitive development; it's not classical conditioning or intelligence. They write mostly about *emotions,* the experiences that give color, meaning, and intensity to our lives. One obvious reason poets focus on emotions is that emotions are interesting. People love to mull over their feelings and passions and to learn about the real or imagined emotions of others. If we did not enjoy our emotions so much, poems, plays, novels, and soap operas might not exist.

What exactly is emotion? Most psychological definitions of emotion distinguish the same basic elements of the experience of emotion: (a) There is a *stimulus situation* that provokes the reaction; (b) there is a positively and/or negatively toned *conscious experience*—the "emotion" that we feel; (c) there is a bodily state of *physiological arousal* produced by the autonomic nervous system and endocrine glands; and (d) there is related *behavior* that generally accompanies emotions—the animal that is afraid cringes, trembles, then runs (Lang, 1995).

How many different emotions are there? In one sense, the list is almost endless. A truly complete listing of emotions would have to deal with many subtle distinctions among our feelings. David Watson and Auke Tellegen (1985; Tellegen, Watson, & Clark, 1999) have proposed a model of how different emotions are related to one another that simplifies the description of the many varieties of human emotions. They suggest that most emotions can be described in terms of their placement on the "map" of emotions presented in figure 9.7. The map is created using two bipolar dimensions of emotion, much like the north-south and east-west dimensions on geographic maps. One dimension has high negative emotion at one pole and low negative emotion at the other pole. The second dimension has high positive emotion on one pole and low positive emotion on the other pole. They have used

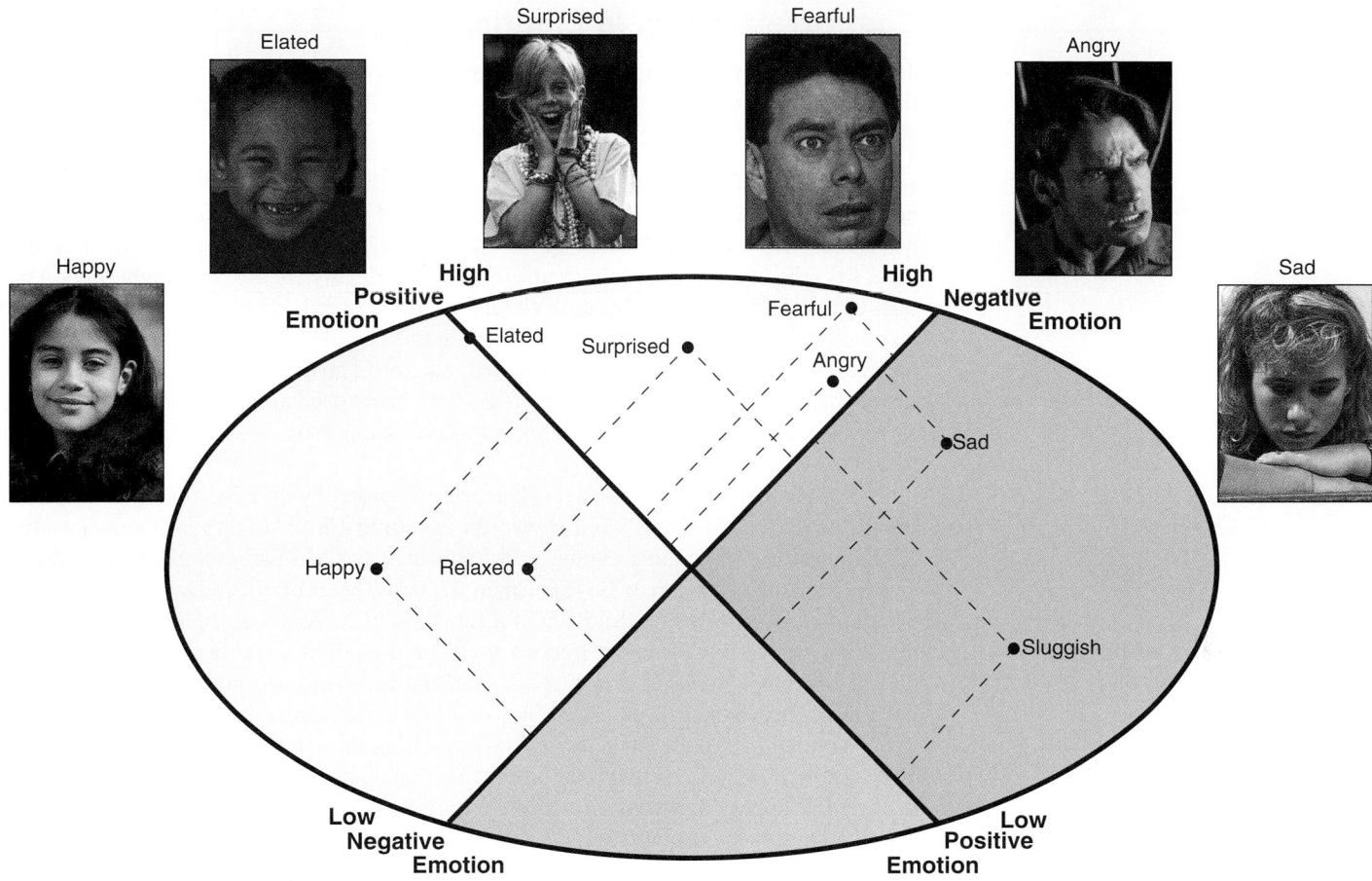

FIGURE 9.7

Watson and Tellegen's "map" of the structure and relationships among different emotions.

extensive research on how each much emotion is correlated with each other emotion (and whether the correlation is positive or negative) to place the various emotions on this map.

Watson and Tellegen's emotional map is more than just a good way to organize our description of emotions. The implication is that all of the varied human emotions can be thought of as different combinations of only two basic elements—positive and negative emotions. For example, elation is viewed as a high level of positive emotion in combination with a neutral level of negative emotion. Surprise is a combination of moderately high positive and negative emotions, and sadness is a combination of high negative emotion and moderately low positive emotion. Where on this emotional map would you place the way you felt during the most emotional part of the past week? What word(s) would you use to describe that emotion?

Notice that anger and fear are very close together on the emotional map. There are many reasons to believe that fear and anger are, in many ways, variants of the same emotion. This idea dates back to the "flight or fight" syndrome described in William James' first psychology textbook published in 1890. Intense negative emotion (which involves arousal of the sympathetic nervous system and the secretion of epinephrine and other endocrine hormones) prepares the individual to either run away in fear or to fight in anger. The two emotions are essentially identical, but situational factors (How big is the scary person in front of me? Is that a gun? Do I remember my karate?) determine whether the emotion will be experienced as fear or anger. Third, did you notice that love is not on the emotional map? Many experts consider love to be distinct from the other emotions shown in figure 9.7 (National Advisory Mental Health Council, 1995a), but the experience of romantic love often involves many emotions that are all over the emotional map!

Cognitive Factors in Emotion

The dominant contemporary theory of emotion views the *cognitive interpretation* of emotional stimuli—from both outside and inside the body—to be the key event in emotions. We will look at each of these steps individually.

Interpretation of Incoming Stimuli.   The Greek philosopher Epictetus said, "People are not affected by events, but by their interpretations of them." For example, if you receive a box in the mail that makes a ticking sound, will you be happy or afraid? If the return address says the box is from Violet, and Violet is your deadly enemy, you might think it contains a time bomb and feel afraid. If Violet is a loving friend, however, you would open the box feeling happy, expecting to find a clock. In this case, the interpretation of the stimulus, not the stimulus itself, causes the emotional reaction. Thus, information from the stimulus travels first to the cerebral cortex, where it is both interpreted and experienced. Then a message is sent down to the limbic system and autonomic nervous system that results in physiological arousal.

Evidence supporting this view has been provided by an experiment in which four groups of college students were shown an upsetting film showing a number of crude, circumcision-like operations conducted without anesthesia as part of the puberty ceremony of an Australian aborigine tribe (Speisman, Lazarus, Mordokoff, & Davison, 1964). One group of students saw the film without a soundtrack. A second group heard a soundtrack that emphasized the agony experienced by the boys. A third group heard a soundtrack that described the operations in a detached intellectual way. And a fourth group heard a soundtrack that ignored the painful operation by talking about irrelevant details.

Although all of the students saw the same film, the soundtracks apparently had a big effect on their cognitive interpretation of what they saw. The group who heard the soundtrack emphasizing the agony of the operations showed much greater autonomic arousal than the group with no soundtrack. The soundtrack that emphasized the agony led to an interpretation of the film as a more upsetting stimulus. The groups who heard soundtracks that deemphasized the emotional nature of the events, either by intellectualizing or ignoring it, showed less autonomic arousal. Apparently, the cognitive interpretation (encouraged by the soundtrack) altered the emotional meaning of the film considerably.

Interpretation of Body Stimuli.   The second step is the interpretation of stimuli from within the body that results from emotional behavior and autonomic arousal. Indeed, cognitive theory states that cognitive *interpretation* of these internal stimuli is more important than the internal stimuli themselves. This aspect of the cognitive theory of emotion was suggested by Stanley Schachter and Jerome Singer (1962). They believe that emotional arousal is diffuse and not specific to the different emotions. That is, the autonomic nervous system and endocrine glands are activated in the same global way, regardless of which emotion is being experienced. The internal stimuli from the emotional arousal of the body play an important role in the experience of the emotion, but only through a cognitive interpretation of the *source* of the arousal. For example, if you are all churned up inside after hearing gunshots in your neighborhood, you will interpret the feelings from your body as fear. But, if you feel all churned up after a kiss, you will interpret the feelings as love.

Schachter and Singer's addition to cognitive theory helps explain such things as why sexual attraction is often mistaken for love and why frightened hostages often develop friendly feelings toward their captors if they are treated with even a slight amount of respect. Because the autonomic sensations produced in emotional situations are not distinctive, it's easy to misinterpret their meaning. Sexual arousal can be mistaken for love, and fear for friendship, if we interpret the arousal incorrectly.

Schachter and Singer (1962) tested this facet of cognitive theory in an important experiment. People were taken to a laboratory for what they thought would be a study of the effects of a vitamin on vision. They were given an injection of the supposed vitamin and asked to wait with another research participant for the experiment to begin. The other person was actually an actor who worked for the experimenters. The injection contained the hormone epinephrine, a substance that causes arousal of the heart and other organs.

"David, you're denying your feelings again, aren't you?"

Schachter and Singer were interested in how the subjects would cognitively *interpret* this arousal under a number of different circumstances.

The actor behaved in a happy, silly manner with half of the participants; with the other half, he acted angry and walked out of the experiment. As predicted by Schachter and Singer, the behavior of the actor influenced the participants' cognitive interpretations of their own arousal. When they were with a happy actor, they rated themselves as happy; when they were with an angry actor, they interpreted their arousal as anger. Importantly, this effect was found only when the participants were not accurately informed about the true effects of the injection. When they were informed, the behavior of the actor did not influence their emotions—they simply attributed the arousal to the drug.

A much more interesting test of Schachter and Singer's hypothesis about the interpretation of internal arousal in emotions was conducted by Donald Dutton and Arthur Aron (1974). The research participants were unsuspecting males between the ages of 18 and 35 who were visiting the Capilano Canyon in British Columbia, Canada, without a female companion. An attractive female experimenter approached the men and asked them to answer questions as part of a survey that she was supposedly conducting on reactions to scenic attractions. The key item in the study required them to make up a brief story about an ambiguous picture of a woman. Their stories were later scored for the amount of sexual content, which was considered a measure of the amount of sexual attraction that the male participants felt toward the attractive interviewer. To provide a second measure of interpersonal attraction, the interviewer tore off a piece of paper from the survey and gave her name and phone number to a participant, inviting him to call her if he wanted to talk further.

Have I mentioned where the interviews took place? Half of the interviews were conducted in such a way as to create a high level of arousal (fear) in the male, and the other half were conducted to create a low level of arousal. The high-fear interviews were conducted while the males were *on* a 450-foot-long cable and wood suspension bridge with low handrails that stretched across the Capilano Canyon some 230 feet above rocks and shallow rapids. The authors reported that the bridge had "a tendency to tilt, sway, and wobble, creating the impression that one is about to fall over the side" (p. 511). I visited Capilano Canyon a few years ago and walked the suspension bridge, and I can personally attest to the fact that it wobbles, sways, and is generally fearsome! The low-fear interviews were conducted upstream on a solid wooden bridge that is not fear arousing.

The results strongly supported Schachter and Singer's (1962) theory that the autonomic arousal that accompanies all emotions is similar and that it's our cognitive interpretation of the cause of that arousal that is important. The participants who were highly aroused (confirmed by their own later reports) while on the high-fear, swaying suspension bridge made up stories that contained significantly more sexual imagery than the low-fear participants. The high-fear group was also more than four times as likely to call the female interviewer later. Apparently, the high-fear group interpreted their autonomic arousal as a greater degree of attraction to the interviewer.

Similar enhancement of attraction presumably occurs in other highly arousing situations, such as football games, emergency landings of airplanes, and the like. So, be careful to separate all the possible sources of arousal when you are trying to decide if you are in love. On the other hand, if you really want a blind date to be attracted to you, you might arrange to meet him or her on the Capilano Canyon suspension bridge. Of course, there's

The swaying bridge over Capilano Canyon.

The solid bridge over Capilano Canyon.

Culture influences the way we show emotions. For example, the Japanese culture tends to discourage the expression of negative emotions.

always the possibility that your date will interpret the arousal as anger toward you for getting him or her up there!

Recent advances in our ability to measure autonomic arousal suggest that slightly different patterns of arousal may be associated with somewhat different emotions, but these differences are quite subtle (Ekman, Levenson, & Friesen, 1983; Lang, 1995). The basic premise of Schachter and Singer's hypothesis, that the physiological arousal associated with different emotions is pretty much the same, is probably still reasonable in spite of these subtle differences. The interpretation of the arousal is apparently the critical variable in emotions.

Role of Learning and Culture in Emotions

Most psychologists who specialize in the study of emotions believe that at least the most basic emotions are inborn and do not have to be learned. Cats do not have to be taught how to hiss and arch their backs in rage; dogs do not have to be trained to wag their tails; and people probably do not have to learn their basic emotions, either (Izard and others, 1997). Even children who are deprived of most normal learning experiences because of being born both deaf and blind show normal emotional reactions (Eibl-Eibesfeldt, 1973).

Comparisons of different cultures, however, suggest that learning does play an important role in emotions in two ways. First, cultural learning influences the *expression* of emotions more than what is experienced. For example, some cultures encourage free emotional expression, whereas other cultures teach people, through modeling and reinforcement, to reveal little of their emotions in public. Paul Ekman (1992) of the University of California at San Francisco and his colleague conducted a clever study of the influence of cultural learning on emotional expression. They showed Japanese and American participants films of unpleasant scenes involving pain and injury and videotaped their facial expressions. When the persons from the two cultures were alone, there were no differences in their facial expressions of emotion, but, when an authority figure was also present in the room, the "Japanese more than the Americans masked negative expressions with the semblance of a smile" (Ekman, 1992, p. 34). It seems likely that the Japanese cultural prohibition against the expression of negative emotions made the difference.

Second, there is accumulating evidence that people in different cultures tend to *interpret* situations that create emotional reactions differently (Scherer, 1997). This makes perfect sense from the perspective of the cognitive theory of emotion. Recall that the same stimulus situation can elicit very different emotional reactions in two different people if they interpret the situation differently. It seems likely that these differences in our subjective interpretations are the result of different social learning experiences (Bandura, 1977, 1999). Therefore, it makes sense that people raised in different cultures might learn to interpret emotional stimuli differently.

● Review

Emotions are fascinating psychological states that are difficult to describe and define. Most definitions of emotion, however, contain four elements: (a) the stimulus that provokes the emotion; (b) the positively or negatively toned conscious experience; (c) the state of arousal of the body produced by the autonomic nervous system and endocrine glands; and (d) the behavior that characteristically accompanies emotions. The cognitive theory of emotion emphasizes the cognitive interpretation of both incoming stimuli and bodily arousal. Many elements of emotions are apparently inborn in all humans, but learning seems to play a role in determining how much emotion will be displayed, how it will be displayed, and how the stimuli that evoke emotional reactions will be interpreted.

● Check Your Learning

To be sure that you have learned the key points from the preceding section, cover the list of correct answers and try to answer each question. If you give an incorrect answer to any question, return to the page given next to the correct answer to see why your answer was not correct.

1. Emotions are defined by three elements: (a) stimulus situation, (b) conscious experience, and (c) _____ .

2. Contemporary cognitive theory states that cognitive interpretation of _____ plays a key role in the experience of arousal.

   a) incoming stimuli   c) both a and b

   b) body stimuli   d) neither a nor b

3. Cultural learning appears to play a role in both the interpretation of emotion-causing stimuli and in the expression of emotions.

   a) True   b) False

● Thinking Critically About Psychology

1. Think of an intense emotion you have recently experienced and explain the sequence of events according to each of the three theories discussed in the text.

2. How has your culture influenced your emotions?

Correct Answers   1. Physiological arousal (p. 294),   2. c (p. 296),   3. a (p. 298).

▌ AGGRESSION: EMOTIONAL AND MOTIVATIONAL ASPECTS

Aggression is a topic of paramount importance to the human race. We pride ourselves on being humane creatures who have left the brutal jungle to establish "civilized" societies. But the sad reality is that no other animal species even comes remotely close to our record of violent and harmful acts against members of our own species. Although fights to the death do sometimes occur over mates and territory in lower mammals, and apes do apparently "intentionally murder" other apes on rare occasions, no species rivals the frequency of human aggression. In my lifetime alone, hundreds of millions of humans have been killed by other humans in wars, revolutions, and acts of terrorism.

Violent crimes and murder have always been a part of human societies, but in recent years their frequency has reached unprecedented levels in many parts of the world. In spite of recent small declines, in the United States, violence has become the second most common cause of death among 15- to 24-year-olds after accidents, and it is the leading cause of death among African American males (Lore & Schultz, 1993). Perhaps most incomprehensible is the frequency of aggression toward members of one's own family. More than a third of the murders investigated by the FBI have been committed by one family member against another and some 3 percent involve the murder of a child by a parent. Each year in the United States, 4 million husbands and wives violently attack each other, resulting in severe injuries in a quarter million of the cases. Each year, too, 2 million children are kicked, beaten, or punched by their parents.

Why are human beings so aggressive? Can we do anything to curb violence in our society? Aggression is a complex phenomenon with both motivational and emotional aspects that we should carefully examine. Like most important topics in psychology, aggression has been the focus of a great deal of research and theoretical speculation. One view holds that aggression is a natural instinct; another suggests that it's a natural reaction to adverse events such as frustration and pain; and a third viewpoint considers aggression as learned behavior. We will look at these theoretical positions one at a time.

Freud's Instinct Theory: The Release of Aggressive Energy

Sigmund Freud suggested that all animals, humans included, are born with potent aggressive instincts. These instincts create a drive to commit aggressive acts that must be satisfied. In other words, they create an uncomfortable pressure that must be released in some way. Often, the aggressive instinct is released in an overt act of aggression. But the key to curbing violence, according to **Freud's instinct theory,** lies in finding nonviolent ways to release aggressive energy, such as competing in business or sports, watching aggressive sports, or reading about violent crimes. Freud's central point that aggression is instinctual has been echoed in modern times by a number of biologists who suggested that violence is necessary for the "survival of the fittest" (Lorenz, 1967).

The most controversial aspect of Freud's theory is his belief that instinctual aggressive energy must be released in some way. He calls the process of releasing instinctual energy **catharsis.** Freud's suggestion that societies should encourage the nonviolent catharsis of aggressive energy has been much debated. In particular, some psychologists believe that the ways that Freud and his followers have suggested as safe means of catharsis actually have the effect of increasing aggressions.

Freud's instinct theory
The theory that aggression is caused by an inborn aggressive instinct.

catharsis
The process of releasing instinctual energy.

Frustration-Aggression Theory
www.mmhe.com/laheye1

frustration-aggression theory
The theory that aggression is a natural reaction to the frustration of important motives.

Frustration-Aggression Theory

Other psychologists believe, like Freud, that aggression is an inborn part of human nature, but they do not agree that it stems from an ever present instinctual need to aggress. Instead, they believe that aggression is a natural reaction to the frustration (blocking) of important motives. This **frustration-aggression theory** (Berkowitz, 1993; Dollard, Doob, Miller, Mowrer, & Sears, 1939) suggests, for example, that a child who takes a toy from another child may very well get a sock in the nose, or that a nation that frustrates another nation's desire for oil or for a seaport might become a target of war. People and nations who are frustrated react with anger and aggression. It is not surprising, therefore, that violence is more common among people who live in poverty, as they are chronically frustrated in their attempts to meet even the most basic human needs (Staub, 1996).

Social Learning Theory

To Freud, people have a need to aggress that must be relieved. According to the frustration-aggression hypothesis, people aggress only in response to frustrating or other adverse circumstances. In contrast, Albert Bandura (1973) and other social learning theorists believe that people are aggressive only if they have *learned* that it's to their benefit to be aggressive. Social learning theorists do not deny that frustration can make us more likely to be angry and aggressive, but they state that we will act aggressively in reaction to frustration only if we have learned to do so. We must see others be successful by being aggressive, or we must win victories of our own through aggression (make someone stop bothering us or take away someone else's possession) before we will become aggressive people.

Social learning theorists directly conflict with Freud on the topic of catharsis. Freudian psychologists believe that we must find cathartic outlets for our aggressive energy to keep it from emerging as actual aggression. They recommend such things as yelling when angry, hitting a punching bag, and vicariously experiencing aggression by reading violent books or watching violence on television. Social learning theorists argue that these activities will not decrease violence but instead will *increase* it by teaching violence to the person (Bandura, 1973). The evidence on the practice of yelling or hitting a punching bag instead of hitting the person with whom you are angry is inconsistent, but sometimes, at least, these activities increase violent behavior (Geen & Quanty, 1977).

The evidence against the idea of vicarious catharsis through watching violence on television is quite clear, however. Televised violence does not decrease violence in those who watch it; it *increases* it. The evidence is particularly clear for children. As discussed

Freudian psychologists believe releasing aggressive feelings in a nonharmful way, like games, reduces the chance of violent behavior. However, social learning theorists believe that watching or practicing aggressive behavior, even in nonharmful ways, can actually increase the chances for violence.

more completely in chapter 5, evidence indicates that watching televised violence increases violent play, increases actual violence, and makes children less likely to intervene in the violent acts of other children (Bandura, 1973; Liebert & others, 1983; Thomas & Drabman, 1975). Because 75 percent of the television programs in the United States contain violence (compared, for example, with 10 percent in Sweden), the issue of televised violence is understandably one of national concern (Wood, Wong, & Chachere, 1991).

● Review

Aggression is a topic of concern to everyone. Three major theories have been proposed to explain human aggression. Sigmund Freud proposed that aggression is the result of an inborn motive to aggress that needs to be released. The frustration-aggression theory suggests that aggression is a natural reaction to frustration and pain. Social learning theory suggests that aggression is not an inborn behavior but that people will aggress only if they have learned to do so. The most interesting conflict between these theories concerns Freud's prescription for reducing violence in society. Freudian psychologists suggest that an outlet—catharsis—must be found for the aggressive motive but that this can be a nonviolent outlet, such as hitting a punching bag or watching violence on television. Much research on this topic suggests that Freud was wrong and supports the social learning theory view that such supposed outlets merely teach people to be more violent.

● Check Your Learning

To be sure that you have learned the key points from the preceding section, cover the list of correct answers and try to answer each question. If you give an incorrect answer to any question, return to the page given next to the correct answer to see why your answer was not correct.

Match each definition with one of the following terms:

Terms:

    a) social learning theory

    b) Freud's instinct theory

    c) frustration-aggression theory

1. According to _____, aggression is caused by an inborn aggressive instinct.

2. According to _____, aggression is a natural reaction to aversive events, such as frustration, pain, and heat.

3. According to _____, people act aggressively only if they have learned to do so.

● Thinking Critically About Psychology

1. In your opinion, which theory of aggression offers the best ideas for reducing gang violence?

2. Does the correlation between aggression and violence in television prove that social learning theorists are correct? Why or why not?

Correct Answers **1. b** (p. 300), **2. c** (p. 300), **3. a** (p. 300).

Application *of Psychology*

SHOULD YOU TRY TO LOSE WEIGHT? IF SO, HOW?

We live in a society that values thinness. Women are told in countless subtle—and sometimes blatant—ways that you must be thin to find love, to be successful, and to be happy. And men are told that fat is the equivalent of softness, weakness, and unattractiveness. Watch television one evening this week: You will see sleek and slender women and men working as attorneys, physicians, and executives. The mechanics and secretaries are much more likely to be heavy (except for the secretary for whom the husband leaves his shrill and plump wife). Who falls in love on television or in the movies? With few exceptions, it is the slender men who fall in love with slender women, and vice versa. The chubbier ones are the humorous friends who rarely find romance and never receive the big promotion at work. Drew Carey is a welcome exception but even his television character is played for laughs.

When these shows break for a commercial, we are offered countless ways to deal with the fact that we aren't the fortunate skinny ones. Advertisements for liquid diets, artificial sweeteners, and weight-loss plans are shown many times each day.

How many of us are actually "overweight" to the extent that it poses at least a minor health risk? In the United States, 31 percent of men and 24 percent of women are overweight (about half of whom are severely overweight in medical terms). Now, how many of us think we are overweight? In the United States, 37 percent of men and 52 percent of women feel that they are overweight (Brownell & Rodin, 1994). That means that a few more men think that they are overweight than actually are overweight, but more than *twice* as many women think they are overweight than is actually the case. As a result, 24 percent of men and a whopping 40 percent of women are on a diet at any one time. We Americans are very likely to decide we are too fat and try to do something about it through dieting—even if we are not actually overweight—especially American women.

We are so bombarded by the message that thin is desirable that it seems to be an unquestionable truth. It is not; it is a belief that happens to have been part of American culture since the 1960s, but not all peoples during all times have considered thin to be beautiful. Take a trip to an art museum and look at the beautiful nude women painted by artists during the seventeenth and eighteenth centuries. By current U.S. standards, these women are overweight. Even looking back to the 1950s in the United States, the women that men found to be ideal sex symbols (Marilyn Monroe, Jane Russell, and Jayne Mansfield) probably would be on diets today. Furthermore, there are considerable differences among different ethnic groups in the United States today concerning ideal body weight, with whites having stricter standards than most other groups. In addition, in many contemporary non-Western cultures, much higher amounts of body fat are considered to be beautiful. For example, the Anay tribe of Nigeria encourage weight gain in women, with the ideal body weight being in excess of 400 pounds.

People in our society, however, are unquestionably prejudiced against persons who are overweight. If you are considerably heavier than is desirable in our culture, you may be less likely to land the job, get the promotion, or attract the person you wish to attract. That is certainly not to say that you will necessarily be a less successful or happy person, but you may find that you have one strike against you.

Should you try to lose weight, then, to avoid the prejudice? It is important to keep in mind that our heredity and history of eating and exercise determine how thin we can be to a great extent. Some people can eat whatever they wish and remain thin through long periods of their lives. Others will never be able to reach the cultural ideal no matter how much they diet and exercise and would have great difficulty staying there if they were to reach it (Brownell, 1991; Devlin & others, 2000).

The most important issue to consider in thinking about dieting is that it can be dangerous. The constant pressure that women, in particular, receive to be thin leads many to dangerous patterns of eating. Some starve themselves until they reach an unhealthy body weight, sometimes to the point that they are considered to exhibit *anorexia nervosa.* Others find themselves purging (inducing vomiting)

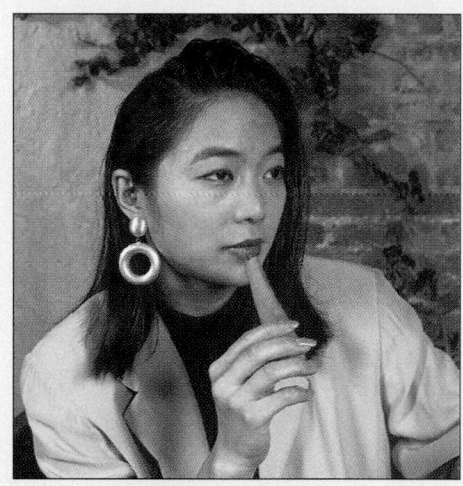

The pressure to be thin leads to unhealthy eating patterns for many people. If this carrot is not part of a balanced diet, this woman's desire to be thin may harm her health.

after eating large amounts of calories, sometimes to the extent of being considered to exhibit *bulimia.* Although the most serious cases of these disorders involve much more than a simple desire to be thin (distorted body image, compulsively rigid eating patterns, etc.) (Ruderman & Besbeas, 1992), the pressure to be thin undoubtedly leads to unhealthy patterns of eating in many Americans.

The most common threat to health, however, is so-called *yo-yo dieting.* Many dieters lose quite a few pounds, gain it back, then diet again. At first, their weight goes down and up with their eating habits like a yo-yo, but soon dieting stops working. What has happened? The body's internal *set point* mechanism for regulating body fat does not like to allow the body to lose fat. The body seems to think that fat is necessary for survival in case a famine strikes. When you diet and lose weight once, the body thinks that a famine has struck, and it learns from the experience. The next time that you diet, the body rapidly compensates for the lost calories by slowing down the rate at which you use energy *(metabolism).* So, instead of losing weight on your next diet, your reduced intake of food causes your metabolism to slow down enough to offset the reduced calories (Steen, Oppliger, & Brownell, 1988; Thompson, Jarvie, Lahey, & Cureton, 1982). Thus, yo-yo dieting is

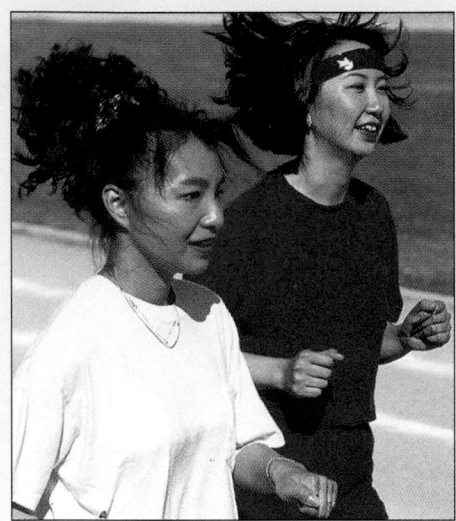

Regular moderate aerobic exercise keeps your metabolism up and provides important cardiovascular conditioning.

eventually self-defeating. More important, it is dangerous. Repeated yo-yo dieting has been found to be associated with increased heart disease in the Framingham health study, probably because it leads to fluctuations in fat levels in the bloodstream (Lissner & others, 1991). Thus, dieting can be dangerous to your health.

So, all things considered, should you diet? If you do not consider yourself to be overweight, you are probably convinced beyond a doubt that dieting is ridiculous. However, if you consider yourself to be overweight and were planning on losing a few pounds, you might be much less convinced. In fact, you may be quite confused and concerned at this point.

Fortunately, the alternatives are not simply to diet or not to diet. Instead of dieting, we have the alternative of making permanent lifestyle changes in eating and exercise. These changes will probably improve your health and will result in the loss of some weight. If you top off these changes in eating and exercise by giving up the wish to look like a star of *Friends,* you will really be ahead of the game.

Consider the following suggestions:

1. *Don't "diet."* Do not try to regulate your weight by eating less for a brief period of time than is comfortable or healthy for you. In other words, do not go on diets. Weight that is lost in that way will almost always be regained when you return to a more natural pattern of eating (Brownell, 1991). You may recall the experience with dieting of television personality Oprah Winfrey in 1990. She dieted and her weight fell from 190 to 123, but, when she stopped the diet, she regained all of the lost weight and some additional weight. In 1993, Oprah lost 60 pounds again, but regained it. Her story is not at all unusual, as the great majority of persons who lose weight through dieting regain the weight after stopping the diet, often leading to a pattern of yo-yo dieting.

2. *Eat differently.* Instead of dieting, commit yourself to a lifelong pattern of eating *differently* that you can live with. You do not have to starve yourself; you just need to choose your calories carefully. Reducing the amount of saturated fat that you eat in the form of meat and dairy products makes terrific sense, and it also reduces your chance of cardiovascular disease and some forms of cancer.

   Second, reducing the amount of processed sugar you eat makes sense because sugar gives you calories with very little nutrition and only briefly satisfies your hunger. When you eat sugar, you feel an immediate drop in hunger, but the sugar causes a sudden increase in insulin levels that typically purges the blood of more sugar than you ate, making you feel more hungry in an hour or two (Rodin, 1985).

3. *Emphasize exercise.* Increased exercise is beneficial in many ways. We are told that a pound of body fat is the equivalent of 3,500 calories, so, if you cut down by 500 calories a day, you should lose a pound every week (7 days × 500 calories = 3,500 calories in a week). Right? That arithmetic works only if your metabolism does not *slow down* by 500 calories a day to offset the loss of calories taken in.

   As I said, *the body does not like to lose fat.* As a result, you must *increase* your metabolism by increasing your activity level (Thompson & others, 1982). If you burn calories through regular and moderate aerobic exercise, you stand a much better chance of losing weight than by restricting calories alone.

4. *Do not give up because of lapses in your healthy lifestyle.* We're only human; it's easy to commit to a lifestyle change in eating, but many things can knock you off your healthy course. A week spent with your family, a vacation trip, exams, and other things can disrupt your plans to exercise and eat right. This is inevitable, but it need not mean that your plans to eat better and exercise more are impossible dreams. Just start exercising and eating right again.

● Summary

Chapter 9 defines motivation and emotion, discusses primary motives and psychological motives, and explores three theories of emotions. The topic of aggression is included in the chapter because of its close link to both emotion and motivation.

  I. *Motivation* refers to those factors that activate behavior and give it direction. Emotions are positive or negative feelings usually accompanied by behavior and physiological arousal that are generally reactions to stimulus situations.

 II. Primary motives are human motives that stem from the need for those things that keep a person alive.

  A. Homeostatic mechanisms in the body sense imbalances of essential life elements and stimulate actions that will restore the proper balance.

  B. Hunger is biologically regulated by three centers in the hypothalamus.

   1. Rats will not eat if their lateral feeding center is destroyed.

   2. Rats become hyperphagic (obese because of overeating) if the ventromedial satiety center is destroyed.

3. The paraventricular nucleus of the hypothalamus regulates blood sugar levels.

C. Cues for regulating hunger on a daily basis are stomach contractions and blood-sugar levels; body fat is apparently involved in the long-term regulation of hunger.

D. Learning influences when we eat, what we eat, and how much we eat. Hunger, as well as other motives, is affected by incentives—external cues that activate motives.

E. The hypothalamus also controls thirst. Cues used to regulate drinking are mouth dryness, loss of water by cells, and reductions in blood volume.

F. Learning influences drinking behavior and incentives can activate thirst.

III. Psychological motives are "needs" in the sense that the individual's happiness and well-being, but not survival, depend on these motives.

A. Humans and other animals have an inborn motive to seek an optimal level of arousal. The Yerkes-Dodson law states that, if arousal is too low, performance will be poor, but, if it is too high, performance may become disrupted and disorganized.

B. Individuals high in affiliation motivation tend to prefer being with others.

C. Achievement motivation is the psychological need for success. People are motivated to achieve by different combinations of:
   1. Desire to learn and master new topics and skills.
   2. Desire to do better than others.
   3. Fear of failure.

D. Motivation to achieve is reduced by fear of success in some individuals.

E. Intrinsic motivation refers to motives stimulated by the inherent nature of the activity. External motivation is motivation stimulated by external rewards.

F. According to Maslow, motives are organized in a hierarchy arranged from the most basic to the most personal and advanced.

IV. Emotions are the experiences that give color, meaning, and intensity to our lives. They are states that involve a stimulus situation, a positively and/or negatively toned conscious experience, and physiological arousal.

A. The cognitive theory of emotion emphasizes the role of cognitive interpretation of both stimuli and physiological arousal.

B. Most psychologists believe that many basic emotions are primarily inborn but that learning also plays an important role in emotions.

V. Aggression is a complex phenomenon that is not yet fully understood.

A. Freud suggested that all people are born with potent aggressive instincts that are released through catharsis.

B. Other psychologists say aggression is a reaction to the frustration (blocking) of important motives or other aversive events (the frustration-aggression hypothesis).

C. Social learning theorists explain aggression as learned behavior.

● Resources

1. For an overview of human motivation, see Franken, R. E. (1998). *Human motivation* (4th ed.). Monterey, CA: Wadsworth.

2. For a more advanced discussion of the psychology of emotion, see Ekman, P., & Davidson, R. J. (1994). *The nature of emotion: Fundamental questions.* New York: Oxford University Press.

3. For a more advanced overview of the psychology of hunger and eating, see Capaldi, E. D. (1996). *Why we eat what we eat: The psychology of eating.* Washington, DC: American Psychological Association, and Devlin, M. J., Yanovski, S. Z., & Wilson, G. T. (2000). Obesity: What mental health professionals should know. *American Journal of Psychiatry, 157,* 854–866.

4. For a wonderful book on biological and psychological aspects of emotion, see Ledoux, R. (1998). *The emotional brain.* New York: Touchstone.

5. For psychological perspectives on human aggression, see Bandura, A. (1973). *Aggression: A social learning analysis.* Englewood Cliffs, NJ: Prentice-Hall; Lore, R. K., & Schultz, L. A. (1993). Control of human aggression: A comparative perspective. *American Psychologist, 48,* 16–25; and Hamburg, D. A., George, A., & Ballentine, K. (1999). Preventing deadly conflict: The critical role of leadership. *Archives of General Psychiatry, 56,* 971–977.

CHAPTER

10

CHAPTER OUTLINE

Gender

PROLOGUE

What are women like? What are men like? Based on what you have observed, what psychological characteristics do you think distinguish women from men? In general, are women strong, caring, and wise? Are women less aggressive and independent than men? How about emotional and fearful—are those characteristic traits of women or men? Let me tell you how the great anthropologist Margaret Mead (pictured on page 307) answered these questions about women and men—she said the answers depend on their culture.

Mead studied many remote cultures during the 1920s to learn how cultures shape people through social learning. The topic of one of her most famous books was the differences between women and men in different cultures (Mead, 1935). She said that, among the Arapesh people of New Guinea, neither men nor women were likely to be aggressive or hostile. They showed very little competitiveness but worked together on joint projects, such as farming, that benefited everyone in the tribe equally. Mead described both men and women as maternal, gentle, and actively involved in raising their children. Jealousy, envy, and conflict, even between parents and adolescents, were almost nonexistent.

The Mundugamor people were quite different from the Arapesh, however. For example, both men and women were highly competitive and physically aggressive, and both found childrearing to be an unrewarding burden. Gentleness and caring were rare in dealing with children, who were required to be independent from an early age.

Among the Arapesh, therefore, both men and women displayed traits that would have been considered "feminine" in American culture, whereas both women and men displayed stereotypically "masculine" traits among the Mundugamor. Mead also described the Tchambuli people. Marked differences existed between men and women among these people, but they were the opposite of American culture. Women held the power in the village and were preoccupied with farming, fishing, and manufacturing, whereas the men played a passive, secondary role. What are women and men like, then? According to Margaret Mead, it depends on the ways they have been shaped by their culture. Not everyone shares this view, however.

Much of who you are and what you do is related to your gender. Your experiences as a young boy or girl, and the expectations of what it means to be a woman or a man are central to your total being. The ways in which we view our gender are a product of both biological and psychological factors. These factors result in some differences between men and women, but we will find that women and men are more similar in psychological terms than they are different.

▶ GENDER

We will begin our discussion of gender with a detailed look at the psychological aspects of being a male or female. We will look at the development of the identity and behaviors associated with gender and will look at similarities and differences between women and men. We will also look at the related topic of sexual orientation—the gender to whom a person is drawn romantically and sexually.

sex
The distinction between male and female based on biological characteristics.

gender
The psychological experience of being male or female.

gender identity
One's view of oneself as male or female.

gender role
The behaviors consistent with being male or female in a given culture.

sexual orientation
The tendency to prefer romantic and sexual partners of the same or different sex.

A person's **sex** is defined by his or her male or female genitals. **Gender,** in contrast, is the psychological experience of one's sex (Gentile, 1993). In most cases, a person's sex and gender are the same, but not always. It is possible for persons with male genitals to feel that their gender is female and vice versa.

It will help advance our discussion to distinguish between two important aspects of gender, gender identity and gender roles. **Gender identity** is the subjective experience of being a male or a female. As is true for all aspects of personal identity, gender identity is a part of our personalities and a central component of our self-concepts. **Gender role,** on the other hand, refers to all of the behaviors that communicate to others the degree to which we are "masculine" or "feminine" in the terms defined by our culture (Money, 1987, 1988). Thus, your gender role is the outward behavioral expression of your gender identity. Gender roles vary from culture to culture and provide a set of expectations for persons on the basis of their sex.

The term *sexuality* refers to the behaviors in which we engage to obtain sexual pleasure and to all of the feelings and beliefs that are interwoven with sexual behavior. One aspect of our psychological selves that is very much a part of both our sexuality and gender identity is **sexual orientation**—our tendency to prefer romantic and sexual partners of the same or different sex.

Gender Identity and Gender Roles

Gender identity develops early in infancy. Immediately after the infant is born (and sometimes well before birth through ultrasound imaging) the newborn is identified as either male or female based on her or his genitals. The parents select a name appropriate to the baby's gender and greet the newborn infant with cultural expectations for the behavior of boys or girls. Children quickly learn the gender behaviors that are expected of them. Parents, other family members, peers, teachers, and others communicate their behavioral expectations for girls and boys in mostly subtle, but very effective, ways.

Gender roles are the behaviors and characteristics that a culture expects of males and females based on their biological sex. Members of a culture classify behaviors as to whether they are appropriate and expected of males and females. *Feminine* behaviors are expected of females, and *masculine* behaviors are expected of males.

Early in the study of gender roles, masculinity and femininity were thought of as discrete categories (you were either masculine or feminine) that matched exactly with a person's biological sex. More recent views, however, have conceived of gender roles as being a graded continuum, with people displaying varying degrees of *both* masculinity and femininity (Bem, 1974; Spence & Helmreich, 1978). There are two reasons for this change in thinking about gender roles. First, masculinity and femininity are not opposites of each other but, rather, are two separate dimensions. And, second, both women and men can be both masculine and feminine. A person who has both masculine and feminine characteristics is referred to as **androgynous.** For example, in the United States today, a woman or man who is sensitive to others, nurturing, and emotionally expressive (traditionally feminine traits) and strong, independent, and competitive (masculine traits) would be considered to be androgynous.

Androgynous

www.mmhe.com/laheye1

androgynous
Having both typical feminine and masculine characteristics.

There is considerable evidence that people who are androgynous are more likely to adapt well to a variety of situations because they are more flexible in their approach to life's demands (Garcia, 1982; Taylor & Hall, 1982). Let's consider a simple example: A friend of mine named Kate was driving her 7-year-old friend, Kevin, to the library one afternoon when she had a sudden blowout in her car. The tire ruptured with a loud bang, and the car skidded and wobbled for a few frightening moments until Kate brought it under control. Kate heaved a sigh of relief, then spent a few minutes calming her young friend (a traditionally feminine behavior). Soon they were both belly-laughing at their inelegant halt on the side of the road. Then, she efficiently changed the tire (a traditionally masculine behavior) and drove Kevin to the library. Kate's behavior was wonderfully androgynous in that it contained the most adaptive elements of both masculine and feminine genders. Today, a growing number of men and women easily cross traditional lines of gender roles.

Androgynous men and women combine the best characteristics of the stereotypical masculine and feminine roles.

Gender Similarities and Gender Differences

Are there important psychological differences between women and men? This is not an easy question to answer for many reasons, some of which are scientific and some of which are not. Alice Eagly (1995) of Northwestern University has written, "When psychologists publish research that compares the behavior of women and men, they face political as well as scientific issues" (p. 145). The political issue is that some people—women and men alike—welcome studies that indicate that women and men are different, whereas others believe that it encourages a sexist view of women. Moreover, from a purely scientific perspective, it may be premature to reach any firm questions about psychological differences between the sexes at this point. Research is progressing at such a rapid pace that opinions are still changing.

In this section, we will summarize hundreds of well-designed studies of gender differences. Only differences that have been replicated in multiple studies are presented. After describing these gender differences, we will discuss contemporary theories of their origins. As you read this section, please note that *average* differences are described in this section. It is important, therefore, to remember that many women and men differ considerably from the "average" for their genders. For that reason, we must be careful not to let scientific evidence about average differences reinforce prejudicial gender stereotypes. The only fair way to deal with people is to evaluate them one at a time. Still, the study of gender differences is of great importance if kept in context.

Gender Differences in Physical Strength and Skills

Before we consider psychological differences, it is important to note some physical differences that will be important in our discussion of theories of the origins of gender differences. It is clear that, on the average, men have greater upper-body strength than women. There is also clear evidence that men typically can throw objects farther and throw them with greater accuracy (Buss, 1995). Although these are advantages that are of little importance in contemporary life, many psychologists believe that they tell us something about the origins of gender differences (Buss, 1995; Eagly & Wood, 1999).

Gender Differences in Cognitive Ability and Achievement

Overall, women and men are more similar in terms of cognitive ability and academic achievement than they are different. There are no gender differences in achievement in many school subjects, from English literature to psychology, but there are some areas in which women excel and some in which men excel (Table 10.1). On average, women

TABLE 10.1	Consistently Identified Gender Differences in Cognitive Ability and Achievement
On the average, women score higher than men on tests of:	**On the average, men score higher than women on tests of:**
Language skills	Spatial and mechanical reasoning
Reading comprehension	Mathematics achievement
Spelling	Science achievement
Verbal and spatial memory	Computer science
Perceptual speed	Social studies achievement
Fine motor skills	Electronics, automotive, and shop skills

Sources: Buss, 1995; Eagly, 1995; Eagly & Wood, 1999; Halpern, 1997; Hedges & Nowell, 1995; Hyde & Plant, 1995; Keenan & Shaw, 1997; Seidlitz & Diener, 1998; Steele, 1997; Stumpf & Stanley, 1998.

perform better than men in a range of language skills, verbal and spatial memory, perceptual speed, and fine motor skills, whereas men perform better than women in mathematics, science, and social studies (Stumpf & Stanley, 1998). Most of these gender differences are quite small, however. Only one difference in cognitive performance is moderately large: On the average, men tend to receive higher scores on tests of spatial and mechanical reasoning (Stumpf & Stanley, 1998).

Even when gender differences in average cognitive performance are small, however, the implications of that difference can be considerable. Consider the data on mathematical ability presented in figure 10.1. This figure presents the scores of many women and men arranged from the lowest to the highest score from left to right. The vertical height of the curves represents the number of women or men who received each score. Although the mean score of men is slightly higher than the mean score of women, the size of this difference is quite small compared with the range of differences *within* each gender. For example, the highest-scoring males differ from the lowest-scoring males *far more* than the average female and male differ from one another. Thus, even though the mean score for men is higher than the mean score for women, many women exceed the mean score for males. Why, then, is the implication of this small difference important enough to discuss?

Note in figure 10.1 that the scores of women are also bunched more tightly around the mean score than are the scores of men (Hedges & Nowell, 1995). That is, the scores of men are spread out more in both directions from the average score. When both the small gender difference in mean scores and the small gender difference in the degree of spread of scores around the mean are considered together, the implication is important. Although scores at the highest end of the scale are uncommon for both men and women, they are much more common for men than women. Indeed, seven times as many males as females place in the top 1 percent on tests of mathematical ability used in college applications (Hedges & Nowell, 1995). This helps explain why a small difference in average performance on such tests could result in many fewer women being admitted to top science and engineering programs—they are less likely to receive the highest scores on entrance exams. On the other hand, males also receive the lowest scores.

Persons with very high mathematics scores represent only a small portion of the workforce, even in scientific and engineering fields. A more powerful reason for the greater success of men in scientific and technological fields may be prejudicial barriers erected against women, and barriers in the minds of women themselves. It is very important to note that women receive *higher* school grades in mathematics courses at all grade levels, even though their average scores on tests that measure mathematical ability are slightly lower. This suggests that women are actually *better* prepared for careers in scientific and

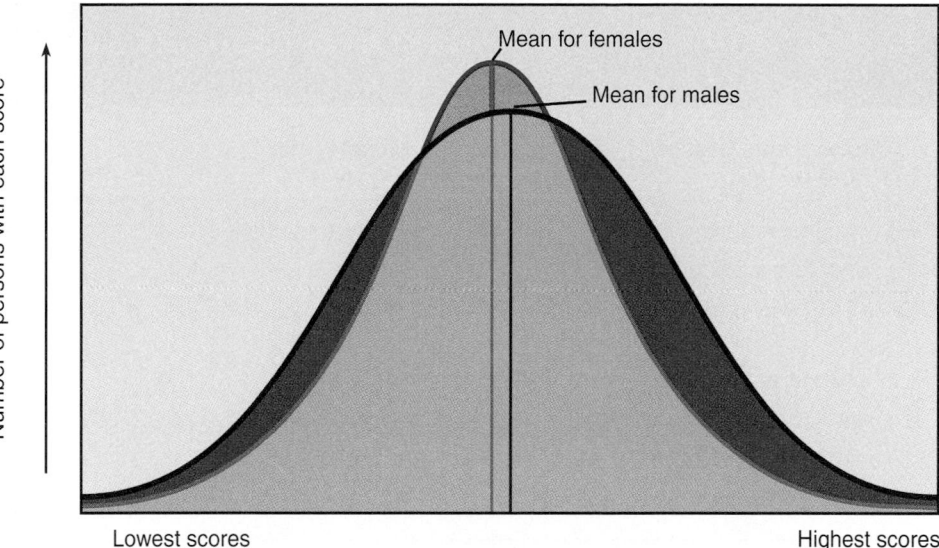

Number of persons with each score

Mean for females

Mean for males

Lowest scores   Highest scores

Test of mathematical ability

FIGURE 10.1

The number of persons receiving each score (from the highest to the lowest) on a test of mathematical ability. The mean is somewhat higher for males than females, but the vast majority of males received scores in the same range as females. Because the mean is a little higher for males, and because the spread of scores around the mean is greater for males, a higher proportion of males than females received the highest scores. In addition, however, more males than females received the lowest scores.

technological fields. Women, however, tend to attribute their success in mathematics courses to hard work, whereas men are more likely to attribute their success to their intellectual ability (Kimball, 1989). This difference in the way women and men think about their success in mathematics courses may play an important role in how they approach careers that involve mathematics.

Susan Chapman and her associates (Chapman, Krantz, & Silver, 1992) conducted a study of the career interests of women among freshmen entering Barnard College, a highly selective women's college of Columbia University. Chapman found that women's interest in careers involving mathematics was not related at all to their scores on tests of mathematics ability and achievement. On the other hand, women who reported more anxiety about their skills in mathematics were less interested in careers in science, regardless of their mathematical ability. This suggests that lack of confidence in mathematics may be a significant barrier for women.

It would be misleading to conclude our discussion of gender differences in cognitive ability and academic achievement without discussing the implications of differences in which women have the advantage. Although men score only slightly lower on tests of reading and spelling on the average, men are twice as likely to fall in the lowest 10 percent of reading scores. These essentially illiterate males have enormous difficulty finding employment in our information-based economy (Hedges & Nowell, 1995).

Gender Differences in Emotion and Social Behavior

Most gender differences in social and emotional functioning tend to be greater than gender differences in cognitive performance (Bjorklund & Kipp, 1999; Eagly & Wood, 1999; Keenan & Shaw, 1997). Many studies suggest that women are more likely than men to be nurturing, friendly, helpful, open, trusting, cooperative, and able to conceal their emotions. In contrast, men are more likely to be competitive, dominant, and assertive. Women are also more likely to be anxious, to be depressed, to have slightly lower self esteem, and to engage in indirect verbal aggression (e.g., spreading false rumors). Men, on the other hand, are more likely to engage in physical aggression and risky behavior and are more likely to commit most kinds of crimes (Bjorklund & Kipp, 1999; Eagly & Wood, 1999; Keenan & Shaw, 1997). Even though most of these gender differences are well-documented and moderately large, there are many exceptions to the rule. Even if *most* women and men have the characteristics listed in table 10.2, there are many nurturing and cooperative men and many highly competitive and aggressive women. Knowing a person's gender is not a reliable indication of his or her personality.

TABLE 10.2	Consistently Identified Gender Differences in Emotion and Social Behavior
On the average, women are more likely to	**On the average, men are more likely to**
Be nurturing and sympathetic	Be competitive and dominant
Be sociable and friendly	Be assertive
Be trusting and open	Commit most kinds of crimes (especially sex crimes)
Be cooperative and conciliatory	Be unafraid of risks
Engage in indirect verbal aggression	Engage in unprovoked physical aggression
Be anxious or depressed	Have high self-esteem
Be better able to hide their emotions	

Sources: Bettencourt & Miller, 1996; Bjorklund & Kipp, 1996; Byrnes, Miller, & Schafer, 1999; Dindia & Allen, 1992; Eagly, 1995; Eagly & Wood, 1999; Feingold, 1994; Hyde & Plant, 1995; Keenan & Shaw, 1997; Kling & others, 1999; Knight, Fabes, & Higgins, 1996.

Gender Differences in Mating and Sexual Behavior

As shown in table 10.3, many studies conducted in many cultures indicate that women and men also differ in ways related to sexual behavior and the selection of a mate (Bjorklund & Shackleford, 1999; Buss, 1995, 1999; Eagly & Wood, 1999). Men tend to prefer a mate who is younger and physically attractive but who has good housekeeping skills. On the average, they are sexually jealous and controlling of their partners but are more likely to feel comfortable with the idea of casual sex for themselves. Women, in contrast, tend to prefer mates who are somewhat older and who have good character and high earning potential. On the average, women are more threatened by the idea of their partner's emotional infidelity (caring about someone else) than their sexual infidelity, and they are more likely to be sexually intimate only with potential long-term partners (Bjorklund & Shackleford, 1999; Buss, 1995; Eagly & Wood, 1999). All of this raises a question: If men tend to have the characteristics listed in tables 10.2 and 10.3 (competitive criminal types who value superficial physical beauty and good housekeeping skills in women), how are women going find men with good character? The phrase "men of good character" seems like an oxymoron after reading this section! Fortunately for both women and men, we are not all like the people described in tables 10.2 and 10.3. The research findings summarized here do *not* mean that all men are aggressive and unfaithful brutes and that all women are caring people completely uninterested in casual sex and are not troubled by their partner's sexual infidelity. It would be a grave mistake to take the differences listed in table 10.3 too literally. These findings simply mean that many studies suggest that these characteristics are *relatively* more common among women than men and vice versa. In all of these ways, women and men are more alike than different, in spite of the differences.

One of the gender differences reported in table 10.3 is quite large, however. A revealing naturalistic study was conducted to test the notion that men are more comfortable with the idea of casual sex than women (Clark & Hatfield, 1989). On a college campus, females and males of average attractiveness who worked for the researchers walked up to college students (who did not know that they were part of a study) and asked, "Would you go to bed with me?" In two different samples, 75 percent of the men agreed to have sex, but none of the women agreed. Although there are many reasons why the women may have said no (fear for their safety seems like an obvious reason), the results of this study are consistent with those of other studies. Many studies indicate large differences between women and men in willingness to have casual sex (Oliver & Hyde, 1993). For example, college-

TABLE 10.3	Consistently Identified Gender Differences in Mating and Sexual Behavior
On the average, women are more likely to	**On the average, men are more likely to**
Prefer an older mate	Prefer a younger mate
Prefer a mate who has high earning potential	Prefer a mate who is physically attractive
Prefer a partner of good character	Prefer a mate with good housekeeping skills
Be threatened more by emotional infidelity	Be threatened more by sexual infidelity
Restrict sex to potential long-term partners	Feel comfortable with the idea of casual sex for themselves
	Be sexually jealous and controlling of their partner

Sources: Bjorklund & Kipp, 1999; Bjorklund & Shackleford, 1999; Buss, 1995; Eagly & Wood, 1999; Oliver & Hyde, 1993.

age men would ideally like to have three times as many sex partners in their lifetimes (average of 18) than would women (average of fewer than 5) (Buss, 1995), and adult men in the general population are three times more likely to have had 10 or more sex partners in their lifetimes than women (Michael & others, 1994). It is perhaps reassuring, therefore, to learn that the overwhelming majority of both married men and women in the United States (over 95 percent) are monogamous when married or in committed relationships (Michael & others, 1994).

● Review

The term *sex* refers to the biological characteristics of being male or female, whereas the term *gender* refers to the identity and behaviors associated with being a male or female in a given culture. Gender identity, the internalized sense of being either male or female, is a central aspect of the personality. It gives rise to behaviors that society expects of males and females, referred to as gender roles. Gender roles are classified as masculine or feminine, but a person may express high levels of both masculinity and femininity, a pattern referred to as androgyny. Males and females are far more similar than different in all psychological domains, but there is consistent evidence of gender differences in some aspects of cognitive performance, social and emotional behavior, sexuality, and mate selection.

● Check Your Learning

To be sure that you have learned the key points from the preceding section, cover the list of correct answers and try to answer each question. If you give an incorrect answer to any question, return to the page given next to the correct answer to see why your answer was not correct. Remember that these questions cover only some of the important information in this section; it is important that you make up your own questions to check your learning of other facts and concepts.

1. The set of behaviors that communicates to others the degree to which we are masculine or feminine is referred to as our

   a) sex.   c) gender role.

   b) sexual orientation.   d) culture.

2. A person who has both feminine and masculine gender characteristics is referred to as

   a) androgynous.   c) bisexual.

   b) polygamous.   d) heterosexual.

3. Persons with a more masculine gender identity tend to score slightly higher on tests of spatial ability than persons with a more feminine gender identity.

   a) True   b) False

● Thinking Critically About Psychology

1. What do you think has been more important in your choice of a major and in your plans for a career—your sex or your gender identity?
2. Are your abilities, emotions, and sexuality typical of your gender? Do you think these patterns of behavior are the product of evolution, of learned gender roles, or both?

Correct Answers   **1. c** (p. 308),   **2. a** (p. 308),   **3. a** (p. 310).

ORIGINS OF GENDER DIFFERENCES

Why are women and men different in the ways previously described? Current thinking is dominated by two very different theories of gender differences. One view holds that inherited biological differences between women and men have evolved over thousands of years that are responsible for gender differences in behavior. A rival theory suggests that gender differences in behavior are the result of differences in social learning experiences associated with gender roles. We will first summarize current data on gender differences in the structure of the brain and then will turn our attention to the two major theories of gender differences.

Gender Differences in the Brain

There is now consistent evidence from many brain-imaging studies demonstrating that the brain structures of men and women differ in a number of ways, in addition to the gender differences that are related to reproduction (Schulkin, 1999). In addition, there is considerable evidence from studies of both humans and nonhuman animals that differences in levels of estrogen, testosterone, and other sex hormones during gestation (when the fetus is in the womb) play an important role in the creation of gender differences in the brain that are evident during adulthood (Wisniewski, 1998). On the average, the cerebral cortex of men is about 10 percent larger than that of women from childhood through late adulthood (Collaer & Hines, 1995; Giedd & others, 1997; Hopkin, 1995; Reiss & others, 1996). This difference is due to a greater volume of white matter (myelinated axons) in men, with no gender difference in the amount of "little gray cells" (the gray matter composed of the cell bodies of neurons) (Passe & others, 1997). The right cerebral hemisphere is slightly larger than the left hemisphere to the same degree in both sexes during childhood (Reiss & others, 1996), but by adulthood the relative size of the right hemisphere is larger in men (Wisniewski, 1998). This is interesting, as most spatial abilities are mediated more by the right than the left hemisphere. Thus, the greater relative size of the right hemisphere in men is consistent with their better spatial abilities.

In addition, there are gender differences in the corpus callosum. This band of 200 million neurons connecting the two cerebral hemispheres grows in size during childhood as its neurons become fully encased in the myelin sheaths that speed neural impulses. By adulthood, the corpus callosum reaches a larger size in women than men (Collaer & Hines, 1995), possibly indicating greater integration of the two hemispheres in women (Banich, 1998). Consistent with this possibility, a fascinating gender difference has been found in cortical activity during the performance of verbal tasks (Shaywitz & others, 1995). As shown in figure 10.2, when adult women and men performed a rhyming task, there was activation only in the verbal areas of the left hemisphere in men (note that left and right are reversed in the images shown in figure 10.2). In contrast, women showed activation in both cerebral hemispheres when they performed the same task. This suggests that the cerebral hemispheres function in a more integrated manner in women during some language tasks, perhaps because of the greater connectedness of their hemispheres through the corpus callosum. This difference is consistent with the superior language skills of women.

There are also interesting gender differences in subcortical areas of the brain. As children grow older, the amygdala increases in size more rapidly in males than females (Giedd & others, 1997) and is larger in adult men (Collaer & Hines, 1995). In contrast, the hippocampus increases in size more rapidly in female children (Giedd & others, 1997) and is larger in adult women (Collaer & Hines, 1995). These differences in the amygdala and hippocampus are tantalizingly consistent with some of the gender differences previously described. Although both the amygdala and hippocampus play roles in both memory and emotion, the amygdala is more associated with the expression of aggression, whereas the hippocampus plays a key role in everyday memory and in the inhibition of previously punished behavior (Gray, 1988). Thus, the better memory performance of women and their greater inhibition and lower levels of aggression are consistent with gender differences in these key elements of the limbic system. There are also structural differences in the hypothalamus (Swaab & Hofman, 1995) that may be relevant to gender differences in emotion.

Although the similarities between gender differences in the brain and gender differences in behavior are provocative, we should not make too much of them. Both the human brain and human behavior are profoundly complex, and we are far from fully understanding the relationships between them. Even if the correlations between brain and behavior that are noted in this section prove to be meaningful, moreover, it is not clear what they mean. On the one hand, biological differences in the anatomy and physiology of the brain certainly could be the *cause* of gender differences in cognition and emotion. On the other hand, gender differences in the brain could be the *result* of gender differences in behavior and experience. The structure of the brain is not fixed at birth but is plastic and changing throughout the life span, and it is well established that variations in experience can create changes in brain anatomy and physiology (Greenough, Black, & Wallace, 1987). The fact that most of the differences between the brains of males and females are not evident until

Right   Left   Right   Left

FIGURE 10.2

These composite magnetic resonance images show the distribution of active areas in the brains of males (left) and females (right) during a "rhyming task." In males, activation is lateralized (confined) to the left interior frontal regions, but in females the same region is active bilaterally (on the right as well as on the left).

adulthood is consistent with the possibility that gender differences in behavior and experience produce gender differences in the brain. It is far too early to choose between these two possibilities—particularly because both could be correct to some extent. As will become obvious in the next sections, opinions about the origins of gender differences in behavior are quite divided at present.

Evolutionary Psychology and Gender Differences

Charles Darwin (1871) proposed that males and females in many species differ in physical appearance and behavior because past evolutionary pressures on the two sexes were different. That is, the natural forces that determine that some genes will survive (because the animal with those genes will live long enough to reproduce successfully), whereas other genes will perish, are sometimes different for females and males in Darwin's view. For example, some male hummingbirds may have long and symmetrical tails because they are sexually attractive to females (which increases the likelihood that his genes will be passed on to the next generation). Female hummingbirds that find long feathers attractive may have become common over countless generations because long feathers are associated with genes that confer resistance to parasites (which increase the likelihood that her genes will be passed on) (Geary, 1999).

Darwin's idea of different forces of natural selection on females and males has become the basis of one theory of the origin of human gender differences (Bjorklund & Kipp, 1999; Bjorklund & Shackleford, 1999; Buss, 1995, 1999; Geary, 1998, 1999). According to the **evolutionary theory of gender differences,** gender differences arise from deep within—from genes that were selected by evolutionary pressures long ago (Geary, 1998). The principle hypothesis of evolutionary theory is that gender differences emerged because ancestral *women and men faced different evolutionary pressures* during the Pleistocene era when humans eked out a living by hunting animals and gathering wild plant foods. These different pressures ultimately result from the fact that mammalian reproduction is based on the insemination of the female by the male, followed by a long period of gestation (pregnancy) and nurturing of the immature young. According to this theory, this pattern of reproduction had several implications that led to the evolution of the gender differences previously described:

1. *Evolutionary pressures associated with hunting.* Because women were slowed by pregnancy and had to stay with the young during nursing, the work of hunting large animals fell to men. Evolutionary theorists believe that this meant that strong, fearless males who could throw weapons accurately were more likely to survive. Because throwing weapons at moving animals requires good spatial abilities, males with this attribute were also more likely to survive, and men eventually came to excel in this area. There is also some evidence that spatial ability is the basis of modern men's somewhat better performance on tests of mathematical ability (Casey & others, 1995, 1997), suggesting that the natural selection of the best hunters also led to men's somewhat stronger math skills. Thus, over many generations, men's need to excel as hunters led to several gender differences according to this theory.

2. *Evolutionary selection of dominance and aggression.* Men could reproduce only if they could gain access to fertile women. One factor that increased the likelihood of mating with females during hunter-gatherer times was being stronger, more dominant, and more aggressive than male competitors (Buss, 1995). Thus, the evolutionary pressure to fend off male competitors selected these features in males. In contrast, no such pressures existed in our past that selected for aggression and dominance in females. That is, dominance and aggressiveness did not help females pass on their genes.

3. *Evolutionary pressures created by child care.* The care of young children had to fall to women during these ancestral times because nursing was the only way to nourish infants and toddlers. Evolutionary theorists suggest that the raising of young children

evolutionary theory of gender differences
The theory that gender differences are based on sex-linked genes that resulted from different evolutionary pressures on ancestral women and men.

was more successful when women banded together in groups that were large enough to scare off predators that might kill their young (Bjorklund & Kipp, 1999; Buss, 1995; Geary, 1998). Because women who were nurturing to their infants were most likely to be successful parents and because women who were sociable, cooperative, verbal, and lacking in physical aggression were most likely to be accepted in the group, women with these traits were more likely to survive and pass these genes on to future generations of females. Thus, women's need to raise children in groups created evolutionary pressures that shaped their social, emotional, and cognitive functioning.

4. *Evolutionary pressures created by gender differences in parental investment.* Because ancestral women were pregnant and nursing for long periods with each child, their level of investment in each child was very high in evolutionary terms. Because women could give birth to only a relatively small number of children, it was important that each offspring survive if their genes were to be passed on (Bjorklund & Kipp, 1999; Buss, 1995; Geary, 1998). In contrast, because the only contribution to reproduction that males were required to make was copulation, they could maximize the chances that their genes would be passed on by having sex with as many fertile females as possible. According to evolutionary theory, men tend to prefer younger, attractive women because youthfulness and the facial, hip, and breast characteristics that men find attractive are associated with reproductive health and fertility (Geary, 1999). The fact that fertilization is hidden inside the female body also contributes to the different evolutionary pressures for the two sexes. Although females always know that they are the mother of the children they give birth to, males cannot be certain that they are the father (the female could have had sex with another male without his knowledge). These facts of reproductive life meant that the level of parental investment of males in each offspring was much lower than for females, according to evolutionary theorists (Bjorklund & Kipp, 1999; Buss, 1995; Geary, 1998). Evolutionary theorists believe that this is why modern men evolved to be sexually jealous and controlling of women (to reduce the chances that they would bear the child of another man), but to be comfortable with the idea of promiscuity for themselves (because this could increase the number of children with their genes). In addition, these theorists suggest that men spend less time caring for children in all cultures that have been studied to date because of their different levels of parental investment in children (Geary, 1998).

5. *Evolutionary pressures in mate selection.* Because women are limited in their ability to gather food during some parts of their pregnancy and child rearing, they and their offspring are most likely to survive if their mate helps support them. Thus, according to evolutionary theorists (Bjorklund & Kipp, 1999; Buss, 1995; Geary, 1998), whereas men compete for mates, women *select* mates. Women have evolved to prefer mates who have the social status and skills that come with age, who have financial resources, and who have good character (which will presumably lead them to help their mate and offspring survive). Because women depended on the help of men during ancestral times, evolutionary theory suggests that this is why they are more likely to be upset by emotional infidelity (which could mean that the male would help another female survive) than sexual infidelity.

Critique of Evolutionary Psychology

What do you think of the evolutionary theory of gender differences? It isn't very romantic, and some find it to be dehumanizing. Others feel that it is a self-serving attempt by men to justify their competitiveness, promiscuity, and shirking of child care. In addition, it is concerning to many that evolutionary theory implies that women and men are locked into gender differences by their genes. Evolutionary theory can be criticized on a number of scientific grounds as well. First, by their very nature, evolutionary theories differ from most other psychological theories because they can never be directly tested. We can say whatever we want about things that happened during the Pleistocene era, but we cannot conduct formal experiments to put our hypotheses to the test. Data can be gathered to see if an evolutionary theory makes sense, but such theories are better thought of as intellectual frameworks for thinking about human behavior than testable theories per se. In addition, some of the specific arguments advanced by evolutionary theorists can be argued. For example, if women's need to group together for protection led to their greater sociability and cooperativeness, why did men's need to group together to hunt large animals not lead to the same prosocial qualities? Since greater perceptual speed is an advantage in hunting, why do women outperform men in this area? If gender differences in sexuality are inherited, why are there large differences among hunter-gatherer societies that exist today in the extent to which men control women's sexual behavior (Eagly & Wood, 1999)? Many such specific questions are left unanswered by evolutionary theory.

Social-Role Theory of Gender Differences

social-role theory of gender differences
The theory that the opportunities and restrictions inherent in women's and men's different social roles create psychological gender differences.

The major alternative to evolutionary theory is the **social-role theory of gender differences** (Bussey & Bandura, 1999; Eagly & Wood, 1999; Steele, 1997). Its primary hypothesis is that each society's division of labor, and the different social roles that it creates for women and men, are the forces that create psychological gender differences. That is, gender differences in behavior result from the different opportunities, challenges, experiences, and restrictions that social roles create for men and women.

In one important way, the two theories of gender differences are in agreement. Like evolutionary theory, social-role theory agrees that some biological gender differences led to a division of labor between the genders. Thousands of years ago, the biological realities of reproduction for women and the advantages of men's greater physical strength led most human societies to create social structures in which men had greater power and status. In turn, this difference in social status and roles—which still exists to varying degrees in virtually all human societies—led to social learning experiences that taught men to be dominant, assertive, and aggressive and taught women to be submissive, cooperative, and sociable. The division of labor encouraged women to acquire domestic skills and encouraged men to learn the skills of resource gathering (hunting in the past, wage earning today). Similarly, the childbearing and nursing role fostered the learning of helpful and nurturing behavior among women. As a result, women and men came to prefer mates than fit the stereotyped requirements of their respective social roles.

As each successive generation of children is socialized into gender-based social roles, these roles become internalized in the individual as the qualities that women and men expect and value in themselves (Eagly & Wood, 1999; Steele, 1997). Once gender-specific social roles are internalized, women and men evaluate themselves in terms of how well they fit the role assigned by society on the basis of their biological sex. Thus, gender roles create a powerful internalized force to maintain themselves.

Although social-role theory suggests that biological sex differences created the initial push for a gender-based division of labor in the past, gender roles are maintained today by current socialization practices, not by our genes. Now that hunting animals is no longer necessary and societies governed by laws have rendered physical aggression less advantageous (it mostly gets you put in jail), social-role theory posits that many gender differences are maintained today only by social pressures that are useless vestiges of past needs. Furthermore, as gender roles change in contemporary societies, psychological differences between women and men will also change (Eagly & Wood, 1999). Men may knowingly or unknowingly oppose social changes that threaten their position of power, and women may find patterns of behavior that are inconsistent with their internalized gender roles to be uncomfortable at first, however. Thus, although changes in outdated gender roles are to be expected, they may proceed slowly and bumpily at times.

"Jason, I'd like to let you play, but soccer is a girls' game."

Claude Steele (1997) of Stanford University has addressed the influence of internalized gender roles on cognitive performance. He suggests that people succeed in school subjects only when achievement is part of the person's self-definition. For example, if a woman does not believe that "I am a person who can excel in mechanical engineering courses," it is very unlikely that she will surprise herself by making good grades. Steele (1997) believes that few North American women are socialized to view themselves as competent in math and engineering, but many men are. It is these differences in socialization, rather than biological differences, that he believes create differences in performance.

Empirical support for Steele's (1997) view comes from experiments in which expectations about performance were manipulated. In one study, women and men were asked to take a difficult test of mathematics skills and concepts. Half of the participants were told that it was a test on which males outperform females, whereas the remaining participants were told that it was a test that showed no gender differences. When the participants were led to expect gender differences in performance, men correctly answered three times as many questions as women. When they were led to believe that there would be no gender differences, however, there were none—the women and men performed equally well (Steele, 1997). Thus, expectations of gender differences apparently can *create* gender differences in cognitive performance.

Additional support for social-role theory comes from studies that have asked whether differences in cognitive performance are more closely related to a person's biological sex or gender identity. Kalichman (1989) found that performance on a spatial reasoning task (on which males tend to do better) was predicted better by each participant's degree of identification with the stereotypical masculine gender role than with being a member of the male sex. That is, both males and females who were more "masculine" performed better on this task than did less masculine participants. Similarly, a number of studies show that both men and women who are characterized by androgynous gender roles (high in both masculinity and femininity) perform more accurately on a wide range of cognitive tasks (Halpern, 1992; Nash, 1975; Signorella & Jamison, 1986).

Some social-role theorists have examined gender differences in mate selection to test their hypothesis that gender differences in behavior will change as social roles for women and men change (Eagly & Wood, 1999). Among 37 cultures around the world, the degree of equality between the genders (defined in terms of the percentage of women holding high status jobs and political office and equity in incomes) varies widely. Among the cultures with the greatest degree of gender equality, the typical pattern of males preferring younger women with good domestic skills and females preferring older men with good earning potential is weakest (Eagly & Wood, 1999). Similarly, a study of 93 cultures found that girls are less likely to be socialized to be obedient and more likely to be socialized to be achievement-oriented in societies in which women can inherit property and hold political office (Low, 1989). The same study found that boys are most likely to be socialized to be competitive in societies that allow males to have multiple wives (Low, 1989). This suggests that changing social roles could produce changes in gender differences as hypothesized by social-role theory.

Critique of Social-Role Theory

What do you think about the social-role theory of gender differences? Is it consistent with your intuitions about women and men? Because it has been proposed more recently, social-role theory is less well articulated than evolutionary theory at this point. For that reason, it may be premature to evaluate it in scientific terms. It is important to note, however, that it has not yet fully addressed the significance of biological differences between women and men. Social-role theorists believe that biological differences in physical strength and reproduction helped create gender differences in the division of labor long ago but downplay the influence of contemporary biological influences on current gender differences (Eagly & Wood, 1999). Social-role theory has not yet addressed the considerable amount of data indicating that there are at least some differences in the brains of women and men. It is possible that such differences could be integrated into social-role theory, however. As discussed in the section on gender differences in the brain, the differences in brain structure could be the result of differences in the behavior and experiences of women and men. That is, it is possible that gender differences in the brain are actually the result of different social roles rather than vice versa. These and other issues have not yet been fully addressed by social-role theorists, however.

● Review

Two major theories attempt to explain gender differences. Evolutionary theory posits that gender differences evolved over many generations due to different evolutionary pressures on women and men. Social-role theory suggests that psychological gender differences arise from the different opportunities, experiences, and limitations associated with the female and male gender roles.

● Check Your Learning

To be sure that you have learned the key points from the preceding section, cover the list of correct answers and try to answer each question. If you give an incorrect answer to any question, return to the page given next to the correct answer to see why your answer was not correct. Remember that these questions cover only some of the important information in this section; it is important that you make up your own questions to check your learning of other facts and concepts.

1. Which theory of the origins of gender differences places the greatest emphasis on learning patterns of behavior from others?

   a) evolutionary theory.   b) social-role theory.

2. The theory of the origin of sex differences that views psychological gender differences as more likely to change in the near future is

   a) evolutionary theory.   b) social-role theory.

● Thinking Critically About Psychology

1. Which theory of gender differences makes the most sense to you?
2. Does evolutionary psychology encourage sexism?

Correct Answers 1. b (p. 318), 2. b (p. 316).

Application *of Psychology*

SEXUAL ORIENTATION

Close your eyes and imagine the perfect partner for you for a romantic and sexual relationship. The gender of the person that you imagine reveals a great deal about your sexual orientation. Persons who are sexually attracted to members of the other sex are termed **heterosexual.** In contrast, persons who are attracted to members of the same sex have a **homosexual** orientation. Most homosexual men use the term *gay*, whereas most homosexual women prefer the term *lesbian*. Other people are attracted to varying extents to both members of their same sex and members of the other sex. When this is the case, the sexual orientation is termed *bisexuality*.

A national survey of more than 3,000 adults conducted by the University of Chicago (Michael, Gagnon, Laumann, & Kolata, 1994) provided the first reliable figures on sexual orientation and same-sex sexual behavior among Americans. As shown in figure 10.3, 9 percent of adult males report that they have had sex with another male since puberty. About half of these males who had an early same-sex experience continue to have homosexual experiences after age 18 (4 percent of all adult males), and 2.8 percent of males identify themselves as either gay or bisexual.

Among women, 4 percent have had sex with another woman since puberty, with these experiences almost always occurring after age 18. About 1.4 percent of all adult women in the United States identify themselves as lesbian or bisexual. Thus, fewer women have same-sex experiences than men (and women tend to have these experiences at later ages), and fewer women than men identify themselves as homosexual or bisexual. In contrast, considerably more women than men report feeling sexually attracted to persons of both sexes (Laumann, Gagnon, Michael, & Michaels, 1994).

Homosexual experiences and gay and lesbian orientations were found in the University of Chicago survey to be somewhat less common than suggested by Kinsey and others, (1948) and other early researchers who were not able to interview

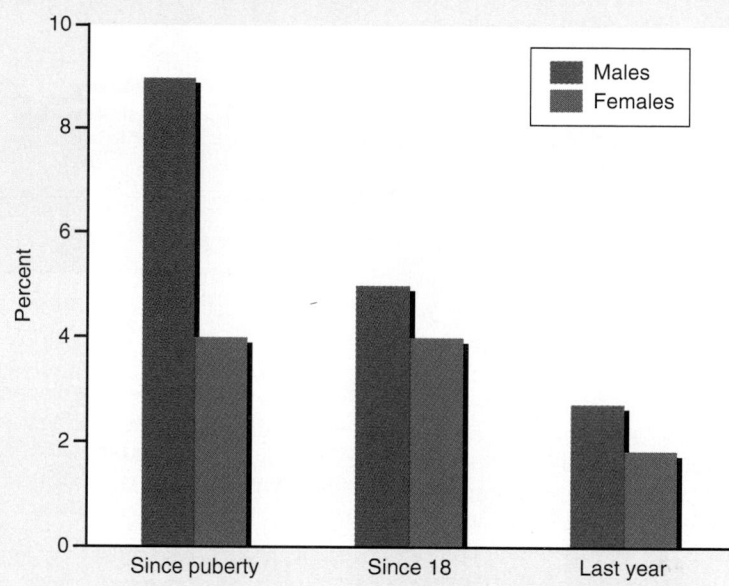

FIGURE 10.3

The percentage of males and females in the United States who have had a sexual experience with a person of the same sex since puberty, since age 18, or in the past 12 months. The percentage of persons who identify themselves as homosexual or bisexual is equal to the percentage who report having sex with a person of the same sex in the past 12 months. (Based on figure 13, page 175, Michael, Gagnon, Laumann, & Kolata, 1994.)

samples of persons that were representative of the United States. If you live in a large city, the percentages of homosexual and bisexual orientations reported by the University of Chicago study may seem low to you. That is because gays and lesbians tend to live in larger cities, rather than in suburban or rural areas. In the 12 largest U.S. cities, over 9 percent of males consider themselves to be gay or bisexual— over three times as many as in the U.S. population as a whole. Among women who live in large cities, nearly 3 percent identify themselves as lesbian or bisexual, more than twice as many as in the general population. In rural areas of the United States, only 1.3 percent of males and virtually no females identify themselves as gay or bisexual, often making life a lonely experience for the gay and lesbian men and women who live in rural areas (Michael & others, 1994).

Many myths surround homosexuality and bisexuality. For example, it is commonly believed that homosexual persons

take on the gender roles of the other sex— that gay men act feminine and lesbian women are masculine. In fact, homosexual persons, like heterosexuals, exhibit a wide range of gender roles. Another myth is that gays and lesbians try to seduce heterosexuals into becoming homosexual. Again, no evidence supports this belief.

But, as is true of myths and stereotypes about any group of people, they tend to be used to justify discrimination against members of the group. Persecution of gays and lesbians is common and has a long history. For example, homosexuals were one of the groups singled out to be killed in Nazi Germany. Still today, persecution of gays and lesbians often reaches extreme forms of violence. Acts of aggression perpetrated against gays and lesbians simply on the basis of their sexual orientation is referred to as *gay bashing*. Thousands of gays and lesbians are victimized in this way every year in the United States, making violence against homosexuals a major social problem.

Origins of Sexual Orientation

Why do some persons develop a homosexual orientation? I should acknowledge that I am reluctant to tackle this question for three reasons. First, I am not sure that I can accurately discuss—or even should discuss—deeply personal matters about which I have no direct knowledge. Second, the very act of discussing the factors that lead to homosexuality may falsely imply that I disapprove of homosexuality. Third, although advances have been made in the past decade, the scientific evidence on this topic is still quite incomplete. I ultimately decided to include this section because the question of the origins of homosexuality is so charged by religious and political beliefs and so inflamed by misunderstanding and fear that I believe that an open discussion of even incomplete facts and tentative theories may be helpful.

Do some of us *learn* to be homosexual? Many people believe that a person's first sexual experiences are so reinforcing that they shape our sexual orientation. If our first sexual experience is with a person of the same sex, will we be more likely to develop a homosexual orientation? Anthropologist Gil Herdt (1984) of the University of Chicago has argued strongly against this idea by describing the sexual practices of the Sambian people of New Guinea. Sambian men believe that boys will become men only if they ingest the sperm of older males. Therefore, at 7 years of age, boys leave their family home and live in the men's lodge, where they are initiated into ritualized homosexuality. They regularly perform oral sex on older males for several years, and then receive oral sex from younger males when they reach sexual maturity. During this time, they have no sexual contact with females. Although Sambian males report enjoyment of their youthful homosexual activities, when they are old enough to marry, almost all Sambian males prefer to have sexual relationships exclusively with females. The experience of Sambian males suggests that one does not learn to be homosexual just by having homosexual experiences as a youth. Consistent with this view, only a minority of persons in the United States who have youthful sexual experiences with a person of the same sex develop a homosexual identity in adulthood (Michael & others, 1994).

Psychologist John Money (1987, 1988) has hypothesized that social learning does play a role in the development of homosexuality, but in combination with

Heterosexual persons hold myths and stereotypes about gay men and lesbian women.

biological factors that predispose some persons to homosexuality. Several kinds of studies have provided evidence that is consistent with (but does not prove) this hypothesis:

1. Twin studies suggest that genetic factors may predispose some individuals to homosexuality (Eckert, Bouchard, Bohlen, Bohlen, & Heston, 1986). If one twin is homosexual, the other is more likely to also be homosexual if the twins are identical (who share same genetic makeup) than if the twins are fraternal (who share half of their genes on average).

2. There is substantial evidence that atypical levels of some sex hormones during prenatal development increase the likelihood of homosexuality (Meyer-Blauberg & others, 1995).

3. Many studies indicate that gay males are more likely to have more than one older male sibling (e.g., Blanchard & others, 1995, 1996; Bogaert, 1998). Because later-born males are exposed to lower levels of prenatal testosterone (Blanchard & others, 1995), this could reflect a hormonal influence on male homosexuality. Interestingly, however, birth order and the percentage of male or female siblings is apparently not related to the likelihood of female homosexuality (Bogaert, 1998).

4. There is consistent evidence that homosexuals differ from heterosexuals in the same areas of the hypothalamus and other brain structures that are different among men and women (Allen & Gorski, 1992; LeVay, 1991; Swaab & Hofman, 1990, 1995). Thus,

it seems likely that, in a few limited respects, the brains of homosexuals resemble the brains of heterosexual persons of the other sex more than heterosexual persons of their own sex.

Thus, it is possible that genetic factors and prenatal hormones organize the brains of some persons in a way that increases the likelihood that they will be homosexual. Since the differences in brain structure are not evident until early puberty (Swaab & Hofman, 1995), however, it is also possible that differences in brain structure could be the result of differences in experiences.

John Money (1987, 1988) does not believe that biological factors work alone, however, as many individuals who have these biological characteristics do not become homosexual. Rather, he believes that only some predisposed persons who have specific kinds of experiences will develop a homosexual orientation. What might those experiences be? Psychologist Daryl Bem (1996) of Cornell University has proposed a controversial theory of the interaction of predisposition and learning. Bem (1996) believes that predisposing factors lead some children to exhibit behavior more typical of the other sex and prefer to play with children of the other sex. About half of adult gay males report such atypical sex-typed behavior as children, compared to less than 15 percent of adult heterosexual males. The difference for gay women is in the same direction, but not as strong. When boys with atypical sex-typed behavior were followed into adulthood in a half-dozen studies reviewed by Bem (1996), about two-thirds identified themselves as gay as adults, compared with about 5 percent of adult males who had shown typical sex-typed behavior as children.

Bem (1996) believes that engaging in atypical sex-typed behavior creates an opportunity for two kinds of learning experiences that lead to homosexuality. First, there is substantial evidence that people rarely develop sexual or romantic feelings for the persons they spend the most time with during childhood. For example, adults who grow up on Israeli kibbutzim, where children are raised in large communal groups, almost never marry a person from their group. Similarly, adopted siblings who grew up together almost never marry, in spite of being biologically unrelated. Familiarity breeds friendships, but not sexual attraction (Bem, 1996). Bem believes that homosexuals who preferred to play with children of the other sex when they were children became too familiar with the other sex to develop sexual attraction to them.

Second, Bem (1996) believes that children who engage in atypical sex-typed behavior find children of their own sex to be upsetting. Effeminate boys and masculine girls often dislike children of their own sex who engage in typical sex-typed behavior and find them to be emotionally arousing—frightening, threatening, or disgusting. When gender-atypical children reach the period of sexual awakening in puberty, however, Ben believes that the emotional arousal created by persons of the same sex enhances sexual attraction. Recall that the cognitive theory of emotion described in the previous chapter states that any kind of emotional arousal can be misinterpreted as romantic and sexual attraction. Thus, Bem (1996) believes that we are most likely to be sexually attracted to the class of people that we find to be unfamiliar and emotionally arousing (persons of the same sex for persons who had shown atypical sex-typed behavior as children). In Bem's (1996) terms, "the exotic becomes erotic."

Does Bem's (1996) theory seem reasonable to you? It is consistent with some evidence, but it is speculative and will be difficult to test directly. Moreover, it ignores the fact that half of gay men (and an even larger proportion of lesbian women) did not show atypical sex-typed behavior as children. If his speculative theory is valid, it is likely to be valid only for some individuals.

● Summary

Chapter 10 describes the biological bases of sex, the psychological dimensions of gender and gender identity, gender differences, and the psychological and social issues related to sex and gender.

I. The terms *sex, gender identity*, and *gender role* refer to important aspects of the human experience.

   A. A person's *sex* is defined by his or her male or female genitals. Gender identity is the personal experience of being a male or a female. *Gender role* refers to the patterns of behavior that communicate to others the degree to which we are masculine or feminine in the terms defined by our culture.

   B. Gender identity and gender roles are important aspects of our self-concepts and personalities.

      1. Gender roles are described based on how feminine or masculine the person's behavior is in terms of the expectations of his or her culture.

      2. Persons who show a healthy combination of masculine and feminine characteristics (androgyny) may be better able to cope with the complex demands of life than persons who are exclusively feminine or masculine.

II. Although women and men are far more similar than different, some psychological differences between women and men have been consistently found in many studies.

   A. On the average, women perform slightly better than men in verbal skills, memory, perceptual speed, and fine motor skills, whereas men perform slightly better than women in mathematics, science, and social studies.

      1. Only one gender difference in cognitive functioning is even moderately large, however: On the average, men score considerably higher on tests of spatial and mechanical reasoning.

      2. These gender differences are more strongly related to gender identity (masculinity, femininity) than to biological sex.

   B. On the average, women are more likely than men to be nurturing, friendly, helpful, open, trusting, cooperative, able to conceal their emotions, anxious, or depressed; to have low self-esteem; and to engage in indirect verbal aggression. In contrast, men are more likely to be competitive, dominant, assertive, physically aggressive, and risk taking and the perpetrator of most kinds of crimes.

C. On the average, men prefer younger mates who are physically attractive and have good housekeeping skills. Men tend to be sexually jealous and controlling of their partners but feel comfortable with the idea of casual sex for themselves. On the average, women prefer mates who are older and have good character and high earning potential. Women tend to be more threatened by their partner's emotional infidelity than their sexual infidelity and are more likely to be sexually intimate only with potential long-term partners.

D. In spite of these differences, there is much more variation *within* each gender than *between* the genders, and many persons of each gender do not resemble the average.

III. Two theories dominate current thinking about the origins of psychological gender differences.

A. The principle hypothesis of evolutionary theory is that gender differences became coded in our genes in the distant past because ancestral women and men faced different evolutionary pressures as a result of their different roles in reproduction and hunting.

B. The principle hypothesis of social-role theory is that gender differences in reproduction led each society to create a division of labor. The different social roles that this created for women and men—and the different opportunities, experiences, and restrictions associated with these roles—are the forces that create psychological gender differences.

● Resources

1. For a summary of what is known about gender differences in cognitive abilities, see Halpern, D. F. (1997). Sex differences in intelligence: Implications for education. *American Psychologist, 52,* 1091–1102.

2. For a summary of what is known about the development of gender differences in emotion and aggression, see Keenan, K., & Shaw, D. (1997). Developmental and social influences on young girls' early problem behavior. *Psychological Bulletin, 121,* 95–113.

3. For very different views on the origins of gender differences, see Buss, D. M. (1995). Psychological sex differences: Origins through sexual selection. *American Psychologist, 50,* 164–168; Buss, D. M. (1999). Human nature and individual differences: The evolution of human personality. In L. A. Pervin & O. P. John (Eds.), *Handbook of personality: Theory and research* (2nd ed.). (pp. 31–56). New York: Guilford Press, Eagly, A. H., & Wood, W. (1999). The origins of sex differences in human behavior: Evolved dispositions versus social roles. *American Psychologist, 54,* 408–423.

4. For more information on homosexuality, see Money, J. (1988). *Gay, straight, and in-between.* New York: Oxford University Press; and Mackey, R. A., O'Brien, B. A., & Mackey, E. F. (1997). *Gay and lesbian couples: Voices from lasting relationships.* Westport, CT: Praeger Publishers/Greenwood.

5. For more on the issue of gays and lesbians in the military, see Shawver, L. (1995). *And the flag was still there: Straight people, gay people, and sexuality in the U.S. military.* New York: Harrington Park/Haworth Press.

6. For cogent discussions of feminist psychology, see Worell, J., & Johnson, N. G. (1997). *Shaping the future of feminist psychology: Education, research, and practice.* Washington, DC: American Psychological Association; and Crawford, M., & Unger, R. (2000). *Women and gender: A feminist psychology* (3rd ed.). Boston: McGraw-Hill.

7. Visit the McGraw-Hill Human Sexuality Drop In Center at http://www.mhhe.com/socscience/sex/index.htm

CHAPTER

11

CHAPTER OUTLINE

Personality Theories and Assessment

PROLOGUE

How would you describe your personality? There are thousands of words in the English language that we could use to describe our personalities, but many psychologists believe that an individual's personality can be summed up pretty well using just five basic concepts. How would you rate yourself on the following five dimensions of personality? On the first dimension, if you tend to be very relaxed and secure, give yourself a "1"—but, if you tend to be very tense and insecure, give yourself a "3." If you are neither very tense nor very relaxed, give yourself a "2" on this dimension. You could even give yourself 1.5 if you think that you are somewhere between a 1 and a 2. Now, rate yourself on the other four dimensions in the same way.

1	2	3
Relaxed and secure		.Tense and insecure
Quiet and not social		.Talkative and sociable
Down-to-earth and unadventurous		.Imaginative and daring
Irritable and ruthless		.Good-natured and kind
Careless and unreliable		.Careful and reliable

Some psychologists believe that the enormous range of variation in human personalities can be thought of as different combinations of high or low scores on these five basic dimensions of personality. How well do these five dimensions capture your personality?

In this chapter, we will discuss four approaches to the description and understanding of personality. These are trait theory, psychoanalytic theory, humanistic theory, and social learning theory. The last section summarizes several approaches to the measurement of personality.

Trait theory focuses on the best ways to describe the consistencies and organization of personality. In contrast, the other three theories are more concerned with *why* we behave as we do. Psychoanalytic theory was first stated by Sigmund Freud. Freud believed that your personality results from the struggle among opposing forces within your mind. We are born with selfish instincts, but our ability to think realistically and our values and ideals tend to hold those selfish impulses in check. The particular way in which each of us balances these forces gives us our unique personality.

Humanistic psychologists view the development of personality in an almost completely opposite way. Humanists believe that, rather than entering the world plagued with selfish instincts, we are born with a healthy, positive drive to realize our full potential. To humanists, the most important aspect of personality is the person's view of his or her self. An accurate self-concept is essential to healthy personality functioning, but humanists believe that society often sets such unrealistically high standards for what is "good" that make it difficult to see ourselves accurately. The social learning theory of personality takes a simpler view of personality development. From this perspective, personality is something that is learned through our interactions with other members of society. People are not born with powerful negative or positive drives that collide with society. We simply learn our personalities from our interactions with others.

KEY TERMS

personality 328

traits 328

psychoanalytic theory 331

unconscious mind 332

repression 332

id 333

pleasure principle 333

primary process thinking 333

ego 333

reality principle 333

superego 334

ego ideal 334

displacement 334

sublimation 334

identification 334

feelings of inferiority 335

social learning theory 337

reciprocal determination 338

self-efficacy 338

self-regulation 339

situationism 339

person × situation interactionism 339

humanistic theory 341

inner-directedness 341

subjective reality 341

self-concept 342

symbolization 342

conditions of worth 342

projective test 348

DEFINITION OF PERSONALITY

personality
The sum total of the typical ways of acting, thinking, and feeling that makes each person unique.

What do we mean when we use the term personality? It's no accident that the word *person* is in the word personality. Your personality defines you as a person, rather than just a biological conglomeration of organs. One's **personality** is the sum total of all of the ways of acting, thinking, and feeling that are *typical* for that person and make that person *different* from all other individuals.

Notice that the two emphases in this definition are on the terms *typical* and *different*. An individual's personality is composed of all the relatively unchanging psychological characteristics that are *typical* for that person. Some people are typically generous; others are typically impulsive; others are typically shy. If people did not have at least some relatively unchanging qualities, we would never know what to expect from them. Each time we encountered a friend, it would be like dealing with a stranger. We know what to expect from our friends because of the relatively unchanging psychological characteristics that make up each person's personality.

The second emphasis in the definition of personality is on the term *different*. Each person's unique pattern of typical ways of acting, thinking, and feeling sets him or her apart from each other person. Each of us is a unique person because no one else has exactly our combination of typical psychological qualities. Even if every person were exactly identical in every physical characteristic—eye color, height, weight, tone of voice—we would be able to distinguish one person from another because of their typical ways of acting, thinking, and feeling.

TRAIT THEORY: DESCRIBING THE CONSISTENCIES OF PERSONALITY

traits
Relatively enduring patterns of behavior (thinking, acting, and feeling) that are relatively consistent across situations.

What is the best way to *describe* an individual's personality? How can your entire personality best be reduced to a few words? Typically, we use terms like *friendly, aggressive, flirtatious,* and *fearful.* We are so fond of describing people in such terms, in fact, that there are more than 17,000 words for them in the English language (Allport & Odbert, 1936). In psychological terms, these words refer to **traits.** Traits are defined as relatively enduring patterns of behavior that are relatively consistent across situations. When we say that a person has the trait of friendliness, for example, we mean that she is friendly to most people and that her friendliness does not change much as time goes by.

Some psychologists have developed their ideas about traits to the extent that they are considered to be theories of personality. Unlike the other theories that we will discuss in this chapter, trait theories are more concerned with *describing* traits than *explaining* their origins. Although there are many important trait theories of personality, the best known are classic theory of Gordon Allport and contemporary "five-factor" theory.

Allport's Trait Theory

Allport (1937, 1961) believed that the most important traits were those motivational traits related to our *values.* Allport tells us that the best way to understand people and predict how they will behave in the future is to find out what they value—the things that they will strive to attain. A person who values money more than family life, for example, can be expected to accept a promotion that would mean greater pay but would require spending more time away from home. A person who values family life over money, in contrast, could be predicted to make the opposite decision.

Dennis Rodman's tendency to be flamboyant is a well-known aspect of his personality.

An important topic to all trait theorists is the ways that traits are related to one another and are organized. Because humans distinguish so many different traits in one another, each trait theorist has tried to reduce this confusing complexity by showing that some traits are more important than others. Allport (1961) believed that traits could be ranked in terms of their importance as *cardinal, central,* or *secondary.* Cardinal traits are those that dominate a person's life. The quest for knowledge could be said to be one of the cardinal traits that dominated Albert Einstein's life, whereas the desire for social justice dominated Mahatma Gandhi's behavior. Allport felt that relatively few people possessed such cardinal traits. Much more common, however, are the central traits. These are important traits that influence and organize much of our behavior. For example, one person's behavior might mostly be aimed at obtaining intimacy and sexual gratification. Another person, on the other hand, may be relatively uninterested in intimacy or sex but may strongly desire power and prestige. Secondary traits are much more specific (such as being rude to door-to-door salespeople) and much less important to a comprehensive description of a person's personality.

Gordon Allport (1897–1967).

The Five-Factor Model of Personality

Over the years, many trait models like those of Allport have been proposed, each stating that a different set of traits best describes our personalities. None of these models of personality was widely accepted in psychology, however, until recent years. Thanks in part to improvements in statistical methods and experimental strategies used to study personality traits, there is now considerable consensus among trait theorists that five basic traits provide a complete description of our personalities (Goldberg, 1993; McCrae & Costa, 1987, 1999; Wiggins & Pincus, 1992).

The so-called "big five" personality traits are described in table 11.1. These descriptions elaborate on the five dimensions of personality discussed in the prologue to this

TABLE 11.1   Brief Description of the "Big Five" Personality Traits

1. Neuroticism

Calm	versus	Worrying
At-ease	versus	Nervous
Relaxed	versus	High-strung
Secure	versus	Insecure
Comfortable	versus	Self-conscious

2. Extroversion

Retiring	versus	Sociable
Sober	versus	Fun loving
Reserved	versus	Affectionate
Quiet	versus	Talkative
Loner	versus	Joiner

3. Openness

Conventional	versus	Original
Down-to-earth	versus	Imaginative
Uncreative	versus	Creative
Narrow interests	versus	Broad interests
Unadventurous	versus	Daring

4. Agreeableness

Irritable	versus	Good-natured
Ruthless	versus	Soft-hearted
Selfish	versus	Selfless
Callous	versus	Sympathetic
Vengeful	versus	Forgiving

5. Conscientiousness

Negligent	versus	Conscientious
Careless	versus	Careful
Undependable	versus	Reliable
Lazy	versus	Hardworking
Disorganized	versus	Well organized

chapter. The most important adjectives that describe each trait are listed under the overall label of the trait. Notice that the adjectives are listed as opposites. Personality tests have been developed to measure these five traits. The goal is to use information that the person taking the test gives to determine whether the person is, for example, more "calm or worrying" or more "at ease or high-strung." Then an overall score is generated from these items to yield a description of the person on that trait and the other traits. For example, a person who revealed himself or herself as worrying, nervous, high-strung, insecure, and self-conscious would be considered to be high on neuroticism. A person who answered questions on the personality test indicating that she or he was calm, at ease, relaxed, secure, and comfortable would be considered to be very low in neuroticism. Most people, of course, would be somewhere in between. As discussed in chapter 9, these five basic traits are thought to be relatively stable across the span and to be influenced by both inheritance and experiences (McRae & Costa, 1994, 1999; Zuckerman, 1995).

By the way, are people the only animal with personalities? Does your dog or cat have a personality that makes it different from other animals? Since the time of Pavlov, there has been clear evidence that mammals have personality traits like humans, and there is recent evidence that the five-factor model describes the personalities of nonhuman mammals pretty well (Gosling & John, 1999).

● Review

Psychologists often describe the consistencies in personality in terms of traits. Traits are relatively enduring patterns of thinking, acting, and feeling that are relatively consistent across situations. Today, many psychologists believe that five basic dimensions of personality can be used to explain most of the variations among human—and even nonhuman mammal animal—personalities. Gordon Allport and other psychologists have developed their ideas about traits to the extent that they can be considered theories of personality. These theories are designed to describe personality more than explain it.

● Check Your Learning

To be sure that you have learned the key points from the preceding section, cover the list of correct answers and try to answer each question. If you give an incorrect answer to any question, return to the page given next to the correct answer to see why your answer was not correct.

1. One's _____ is the sum total of all of the ways of acting, thinking, and feeling that are *typical* for that person and make that person *different* from all other individuals.

2. _____ are defined as relatively enduring and consistent ways of behaving.

   a) States   c) Characteristics
   b) Traits   d) Conditions

3. Trait theories are more concerned with describing the nature and operation of traits than explaining their origins.

   a) True   b) False

4. Allport believed that the most important traits were those motivational traits related to our _____.

● Thinking Critically About Psychology

1. Does the five-factor model of personality leave out any important aspects of what makes you unique?

2. How would a police detective who was a proponent of trait theory attempt to catch a serial killer?

PSYCHOANALYTIC THEORY: SIGMUND FREUD

Sigmund Freud was a young physician building a medical practice in Vienna in the late 1800s. He was particularly interested in treating patients with emotional problems but felt frustrated by the lack of knowledge that existed at that time. Although he had devoted many years of study in Austria and France to the disorders of the brain and nerves, Freud found that what he had learned was of little help to his patients. Thus, being a person of considerable confidence and intelligence, Sigmund Freud set out to develop his own methods of treatment. In the course of his development of treatment methods, Freud also developed a general theory of personality, an explanation for why people develop their unique patterns of typical behavior. His view is known today as **psychoanalytic theory.**

Freud's theory of personality began with a very limited question. He wanted to understand the condition known today as *conversion disorder.* In this condition, the individual appears to have a serious medical problem, such as paralysis or deafness, for which there is no medical cause. To understand Freud's theory—which some of you will find quite shocking—we should begin with a description of one of Freud's first case studies. I think you will see the origins of his unusual ideas about what shapes our personalities in this amazing description. The young woman was not treated by Freud, but he helped her physician publish a description of her—one that had a lasting impact on his theories.

Bertha Pappenheim's unusual problems began at age 21. After 6 months of caring for her dying father each night, the formerly healthy young woman suddenly became paralyzed in her legs, arms, and neck and lost the ability to talk, except in a meaningless garble. Surprisingly, her physician could find nothing physically wrong with her. In time, her speech and muscular coordination returned, only to be followed by other strange symptoms. She was plagued by hallucinations of writhing snakes and grinning skulls; she was deaf for a time; she experienced blurred vision; and she had difficulty swallowing water for 6 weeks. But, after 18 months of frequent therapy sessions with her physician, Joseph Breuer, she was free of these bizarre maladies.

Dr. Breuer terminated his relationship with Ms. Pappenheim partly because of her improvement, but partly because he had developed strong emotional feelings for her, and he suspected that she had similar feelings for him. On the evening after his last session with Ms. Pappenheim, the young physician sat eating supper with his family when he was summoned back to Bertha's home by her maid. When Breuer arrived, he found Bertha writhing in bed, complaining of painful cramps in her lower abdomen. Suddenly, she shocked Breuer with the words, "Now Dr. Breuer's baby is coming! It is coming!" She was giving birth to a completely imaginary baby. Because of his complicated emotional feelings toward Ms. Pappenheim, Dr. Breuer transferred her to the care of another physician.

In 1895, Breuer and Freud jointly published an account of Bertha Pappenheim's problems, giving different interpretations of her symptoms. To protect her identity, she was given the pseudonym of "Anna O." Freud's theory was shocking: Freud believed that six months of being alone with her father while he was sick in bed heightened unconscious sexual desires for her father to the point that they threatened to become conscious. The paralysis and other symptoms, according to Freud, served the purpose of making it impossible for her to express her sexual longings; they held in check her nearly uncontrollable and wholly unacceptable desires. Later, Freud believed that these sexual feelings were transferred to Dr. Breuer, by whom she unconsciously wished to become pregnant.

psychoanalytic theory
Freud's theory that the origin of personality lies in the balance among the id, the ego, and the superego.

Bertha Pappenheim (1861–1936).

Freud's Mind: Three Levels of Consciousness

Freud distinguished three levels of conscious awareness—the *conscious mind,* the *preconscious mind,* and the *unconscious mind.* We are presently aware of the contents of the first level of the mind, temporarily unaware of the contents of the second level, and more permanently unaware of the contents of the third.

To Freud, the mind is like an iceberg; the **conscious mind** is merely the tip visible above the surface, whereas the bulk of the important workings of the mind lurks mysteriously beneath the surface (see fig. 11.1). Just below the surface is what Freud called the **preconscious mind.** It consists of memories that are not presently conscious but can be easily brought into consciousness. You are not thinking right now about your last meal, the name of your psychology instructor, or the taste of your favorite drink, but you could quickly bring those items into conscious awareness if you wanted to. The preconscious mind is the vast storehouse of easily accessible memories. The contents of the preconscious were once conscious and can be returned to consciousness when needed.

Further down from consciousness lies the **unconscious mind.** It stores primitive instinctual motives plus memories and emotions that are so threatening to the conscious mind that they have been unconsciously pushed into the unconscious mind through the process of **repression.** The contents of the unconscious mind, unlike the preconscious mind, are not normally accessible to consciousness. They can rarely be made fully conscious, and then only with great difficulty.

Freud's Mind: Id, Ego, and Superego

Freud also divided the mind into three parts in a different, but related, way. The best-known aspect of Freud's theory of personality is his view that the mind is composed of three parts, each with a different function: the *id,* the *ego,* and the *superego* (see fig. 11.1).

conscious mind
That portion of the mind of which one is presently aware.

preconscious mind
That portion of the mind containing information that is not presently conscious but can be easily brought into consciousness.

unconscious mind
The part of the mind of which we can never be directly aware; the storehouse of primitive instinctual motives and of memories and emotions that have been repressed.

repression
Sigmund Freud's theory that unpleasant information is often pushed into unconsciousness without our being aware of it.

FIGURE 11.1

Freud's model of personality structure. Freud theorized that we have three levels of awareness—the conscious, the preconscious, and the unconscious. To dramatize the enormous size of the unconscious, he compared it to the portion of an iceberg that lies beneath the water's surface. Freud also divided personality structure into three components—id, ego, and superego—which operate according to different principles and exhibit different modes of thinking. In Freud's model, the id is entirely unconscious, but the ego and superego operate at all three levels of awareness.

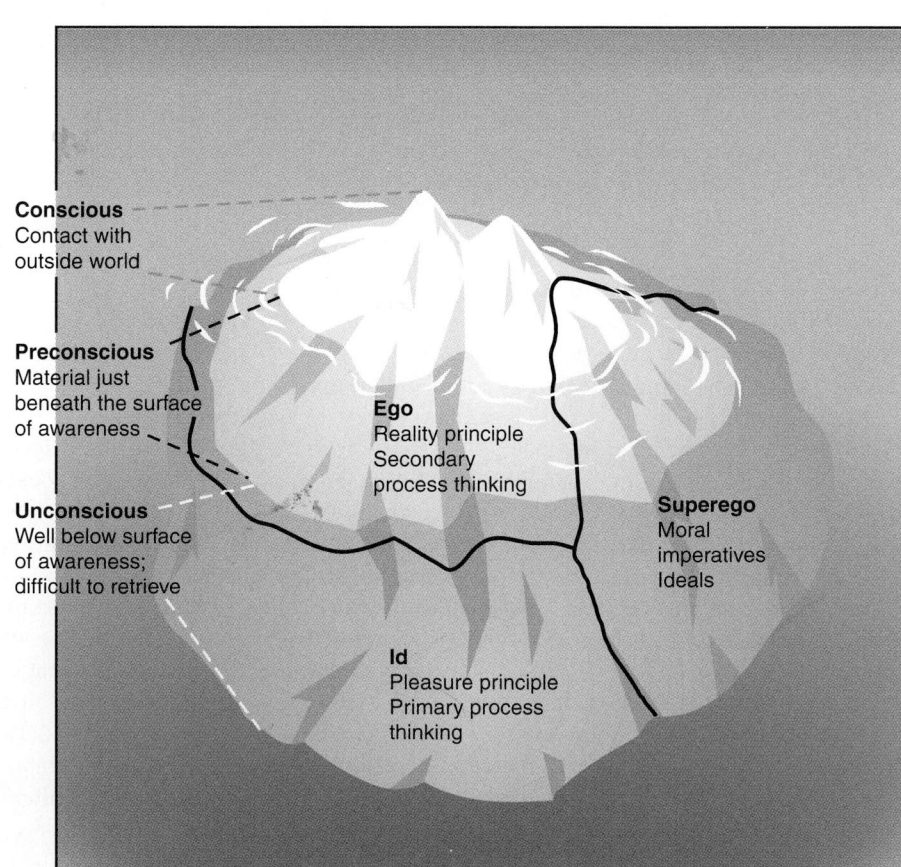

Id: The Selfish Beast

When the infant is born, the mind has only one part, the **id**. The id is composed primarily of two sets of instincts, *life instincts* and *death instincts*. Freud wrote relatively little about the death instincts, but he believed that aggression and even suicidal urges arose from these instincts. The life instincts, termed **libido** by Freud, give rise to motives that sustain and promote life, such as hunger, self-protection, and sexual desire. To Freud, the sexual and aggressive urges are by far the most important of these motives. As strange as it may seem, sex and aggression are used by Freud to explain a vast range of personality characteristics, from kindness to shyness to cruelty. Freud believed that, from birth on, every person's life is dominated by these two motives—the desire to experience sexual pleasure and the desire to harm others. Because the id operates entirely at the unconscious level of the mind, however, we are generally not aware of these motives. Only safe, watered-down versions of our true sexual and aggressive urges ever reach conscious awareness.

"Good morning, beheaded—uh, I mean beloved."

Freud's view of the dark side of the human mind is not an easy one for most of us to accept. Freud tells us that there lives within each of us a selfish, cruel beast. The beast—the id—operates according to the **pleasure principle.** The id wants to obtain immediate pleasure and avoid pain, regardless of how harmful it might be to others. But the id's selfishness is not its most alien characteristic to most of us. According to Freud, the id seeks to satisfy its desires in ways that are totally out of touch with reality. The id, in fact, has no conception whatsoever of reality. The id attempts to satisfy its needs using what Freud calls **primary process thinking**—by simply forming a wish-fulfilling *mental image* of the desired object. We use the primary process when we daydream about having sex, think about eating chocolate fudge cake, or angrily plan how to get revenge on the person who embarrassed us yesterday. Dreams are also a primary process means of fulfilling motives. The primary process satisfies motives through imagination rather than in reality.

But a person could not actually survive for long living by the pleasure principle (eventually you would get hurt if you fulfilled every selfish desire without regard for the feelings of others) or using only the primary process of wish fulfillment (forming a mental image of food will not meet the biological needs of the body for nutrition). Fortunately, during infancy, the period of time when we have only an id, we have adults around who see to it that our needs are realistically and safely met. As we grow up, our interactions with our parents and other parts of the real world lead us to convert part of the id into two other parts of the mind—the ego and the superego—that help us cope more effectively with the world. To borrow a phrase told to me by a skilled teacher, the ego and superego help us "keep a lid on the id."

id
According to Freud, the inborn part of the unconscious mind that uses the primary process to satisfy its needs and that acts according to the pleasure principle.

libido
The energy of the life instincts of sex, hunger, and thirst.

pleasure principle
According to Freud, the attempt of the id to seek immediate pleasure and avoid pain, regardless of how harmful it might be to others.

primary process thinking
According to Freud, the attempt by the id to satisfy its needs by forming a wish-fulfilling mental image of the desired object.

ego
(ē′go)   According to Freud, that part of the mind that uses the reality principle to satisfy the id.

reality principle
According to Freud, the attempt by the ego to find safe, realistic ways of meeting the needs of the id.

Ego: The Executive of Personality

The **ego** is formed because the id has to find realistic ways of meeting its needs and avoiding trouble caused by selfish and aggressive behavior. The ego operates according to the **reality principle.** This means that it holds the id in check until a safe and realistic way has been found to satisfy its motives. The ego's goal is to help the id fulfill its needs. It opposes the id's wishes only long enough to find a realistic way to satisfy them. The ego can be thought of as the *executive of the personality* because it uses its cognitive abilities to manage and control the id and balance its desires against the restrictions of reality and the superego.

Superego: The Conscience and Ego Ideal

The id and ego have no morals. They seek to satisfy the id's selfish motives without regard for the good of others. The ego tries to be realistic about how those motives are satisfied. But, as long as the needs are *safely* met, it does not care if rules are broken, lies are told, or other people are wronged. Although each of us wants our desires to be satisfied

"Fifty is plenty," "Hundred and fifty."

immediately, if everyone acted in this manner simultaneously, society would fall into chaos.

Restrictions are placed on the actions of the id and ego when the **superego** develops, the part of the mind that opposes the desires of the id by enforcing moral restrictions and by striving to attain a goal of "ideal" perfection. Parents are the main agents of society in creating the superego. They teach moral principles to their children by punishing transgressions and rewarding proper behavior. These experiences become incorporated into the child's mind as the two parts of the superego. According to Freud, parental punishment creates the set of moral inhibitions known as the **conscience,** whereas their rewards set up a standard of perfect conduct in the superego called the **ego ideal.** These two parts of the superego work together by punishing behavior that breaks the moral code through guilt and rewarding good behavior through pride. As the superego develops strength, children are able to control themselves and behave in ways that allow society to function smoothly. According to Freud's view, most of us do not steal, murder, and rape not because we do not want to or because our egos could not find relatively safe ways to do so but because our superegos hold these desires in check.

Displacement and Identification: Becoming a Member of Society

The ego is not always able to find ways to satisfy id motives that avoid trouble and stay within the moral boundaries of the superego. Sometimes the ego must settle for a *substitute* for the goal of the id. A child who would really like to kick his father may have to settle for slugging his little brother instead. Or, if his superego prohibits hurting his brother, he may have to kick his teddy bear. The process of substituting a more acceptable goal is called **displacement.**

In terms of the interests of society, the best kind of displacement is called **sublimation.** In this form of displacement, a socially desirable goal is substituted for a socially harmful goal. Competing in school is a sublimation of aggressive motives, painting nude portraits is a sublimation of sexual motives, and so on. Indeed, Freud believed that all of the cultural and economic achievements of society were the result of sublimation. Thus, the individual who sublimates id energy not only is able to fit into society but contributes to its advancement as well.

Another process that allows individuals to learn to operate in society without friction is **identification.** This term refers to the fact that we tend to base the way we think, act, and feel on other individuals who are successful in gaining satisfaction from life. According to Freud, this is more than just a superficial act of imitation; we incorporate the other person's goals, actions, and values into our personalities. Thus, children come to behave more like the adults they identify with. In this way, identification serves an important role in socializing children. Indeed, according to Freud, identification is the key step in the development of the superego. We do not fully incorporate the morals and goals of society until we identify with the parent and internalize his or her values and ideals.

Theories Derived from Psychoanalysis

Psychoanalytic thinking continues to be important in clinical and counseling psychology, but mostly through revised versions of Freud's theory of personality. Some modern psychologists adhere to an orthodox version of psychoanalysis, but far more endorse somewhat newer versions that grew out of Freudian thinking but differ on several major points. These revisions of psychoanalysis each differ from one another in some ways, but they share the view that Freud placed too much emphasis on unconscious sexual motivation and

superego
According to Freud, that part of the mind that opposes the desires of the id by enforcing moral restrictions and by striving to attain perfection.

conscience
According to Freud, the moral inhibitions of the superego.

ego ideal
According to Freud, the standard of perfect conduct of the superego.

displacement
(dis-plās´ment)   A defense mechanism in which the individual directs aggressive or sexual feelings away from the primary object to someone or something safe.

sublimation
(sub˝li-mā´shun)   According to Freud, a form of displacement in which a socially desirable goal is substituted for a socially harmful goal; the best form of displacement for society as a whole.

identification
The tendency to base one's identity and actions on individuals who are successful in gaining satisfaction from life.

Competition in sports is one way of sublimating unacceptable aggressive impulses, according to Freud.

aggression, gave too little importance to positive aspects of personality, underemphasized the importance of adequate social relationships, and was highly prejudicial toward women (Westen & Gabbard, 1999).

Carl Jung

Carl Jung was a Swiss physician who published a number of works that used Freud's ideas to explain aspects of severe mental illness, but gradually Jung came to question Freud's emphasis on sexual motivation. Jung felt that Freud took a one-sided negative view of the human condition. Although Jung thought that the unconscious mind did contain selfish and hostile forces, he believed that it also contained positive, even spiritual, motives. In fact, a fundamental characteristic of the human mind to Jung was that all important elements came in the form of *opposites*. We possess the potential to be both good and evil, feminine and masculine, mother and father. The question is simply how much of each we manifest in our personalities.

Among Jung's most original and lasting contributions to the understanding of personality are the concepts of *extroversion* and *introversion*. Each of us possesses a desire to be friendly, open to the things happening in the world, and concerned about others (**extroversion**), but each of us also possesses a tendency to focus our attention on ourselves, to be shy, and to meet our own needs (**introversion**). As with all of the polar opposites, Jung felt that it was important to allow a balance of these two opposing tendencies. We should not be too much of an introvert or too much of an extrovert.

Jung also modified Freud's view of the unconscious. He felt that we possess both a *personal unconscious* and a *collective unconscious*. The **personal unconscious** contains those motives, conflicts, and information that we have repressed into unconsciousness because they are threatening to us. The **collective unconscious** is the unconscious mind with which all humans are born. He used the term *collective* to emphasize that its contents are the same for all humans. Jung assembled a variety of evidence to suggest that every culture expresses the same sorts of unconscious motives in very much the same symbolic ways. For example, in Jung's view the sexual symbol of the phallus (the penis) has appeared in many cultures throughout history in the form of totem poles, scepters held by kings to symbolize authority, and structures such as the Washington Monument.

Alfred Adler

Alfred Adler agreed with Freud that the struggle to come to grips with one's sexual and hostile impulses was important to the development of personality, but he did not feel it was the most important factor. In his early career, Adler felt that the primary struggle in personality development was the effort to overcome **feelings of inferiority** in social relationships and to develop feelings of superiority. At first, he limited this view to individuals who were born with physical defects, as was Adler himself, but later he expanded this view to include physically normal individuals as well. Because we are all small and dependent on the protection of adults as children, we all begin life with feelings of inferiority. The task of personality development, according to Adler, is to outgrow the inferiority of childhood and to see ourselves as competent adults. Adler felt that the role of parents and other caretakers was so important in this crucial process that he devoted much of his time to the development of a preschool program that he thought fostered proper personality development. Even today, "Adlerian" preschools are popular in many parts of Europe and North America.

Later in his career, Adler deemphasized the importance of struggling to outgrow childhood feelings of inferiority. In fact, he felt that the effort to achieve feelings of superiority over other individuals was an essentially unhealthy motive. Instead, Adler felt that all human beings are born with a positive motive, *social interest,* to establish loving, helpful relationships with other people. The full development of a healthy personality requires that the individual learn to express this motive fully in his or her relationships with others. This contrasted with Freud's belief that only selfish motives are inborn.

Carl Jung (1875–1961).

extroversion
(eks″tro-ver´zhun)   According to Jung, the tendency of some individuals to be friendly and open to the world.

introversion
(in-tro-ver´zhun)   According to Jung, the tendency of some individuals to be shy and to focus their attention on themselves.

personal unconscious
According to Jung, the motives, conflicts, and information that are repressed by a person because they are threatening to that individual.

collective unconscious
According to Jung, the content of the unconscious mind with which all humans are born.

feelings of inferiority
According to Adler, the feelings that result from children being less powerful than adults that must be overcome during the development of the healthy personality.

Each of us, according to Jung, is a blend of extrovert and introvert. Jung felt that a balance of these two opposing tendencies is desirable.

Alfred Adler (1870–1937).

Karen Horney (1885–1952).

Karen Horney

German-born physician Karen Horney became a leader in the revisions of psychoanalysis some 20 years after the first contributions of Jung and Adler. But, perhaps in part because she continued to write into the 1950s, she remains the most influential of the three. Readers today generally find her ideas more contemporary than those of Freud, Jung, or Adler. Horney considered herself to be a "Freudian" throughout her career because she agreed that unconscious conflicts were the source of most human misery and maladjustment. Like Jung and Adler, however, Horney felt that Freud placed too much importance on sexual conflicts. Moreover, she believed that conflict was not the inevitable result of inborn motives in the id. She believed instead that conflicts developed only as the result of inadequate child-rearing experiences. If the child feels loved and secure, no conflicts will develop, and positive aspects of the personality will dominate. If, however, the child loses confidence in parental love—because of the parent's indifference, harshness, or overprotection or for other reasons—the child becomes anxiously insecure. And this anxious insecurity is the source of all conflicts. For example, an insecure individual may develop a need to be "perfect" and feel tormented by all revelations that he is not. Another individual may aggressively push away the affection of others out of fear that they, too, will not consistently love her, but pushing away others is in conflict with the underlying need to be loved.

● Review

Sigmund Freud's theory of personality grew out of his early interest in the cause of the unusual symptoms of some of his patients. He decided that, since they had no conscious reason to have such symptoms, the cause must be unconscious, specifically repressed sexual or aggressive desires. Through the course of many years of treating patients with a variety of psychological problems, Freud came to believe that unconscious motives, particularly sexual and aggressive ones, were the source of most aspects of our personalities. Freud divided the mind into three levels of consciousness (conscious, preconscious, and unconscious) and into three parts with different functions (id, ego, and superego). The id is the storehouse of the unconscious sexual and aggressive instincts and the inborn, selfish part of the mind that operates according to the pleasure principle. The id seeks immediate satisfaction of its needs without concern for the welfare of others. The ego is the executive of the personality, which controls the id through adherence to the reality principle; it seeks to satisfy the needs of the id in ways that are both realistic and safe. The superego represents society's rules of right and wrong that often hold the id in check, not on the basis of what is realistic but on what is moral.

The process of becoming an acceptable member of society is aided by the psychological processes of displacement and identification. When it's too dangerous to directly satisfy an id motive, the motive is displaced on a safer, substitute goal. The most desirable form of displacement from society's perspective is sublimation, in which dangerous motives are transformed into socially desirable motives. The process of identification with social models further aids the individual's acceptance as a member of society by leading to the full development of the superego.

Following the lead of Jung, Adler, and Horney, who broke away from orthodox psychoanalytic views during Freud's lifetime, contemporary psychoanalysts generally deemphasize the importance of sexual and aggressive motives. They have revised Freud's view of the inferiority of women, have emphasized the importance of social relationships in personality formation, and have stated that Freud overlooked important positive aspects of our personalities.

● Check Your Learning

To be sure that you have learned the key points from the preceding section, cover the list of correct answers and try to answer each question. If you give an incorrect answer to any question, return to the page given next to the correct answer to see why your answer was not correct. Remember that these questions cover only some of the important information in this section; it is important that you make up your own questions to check your learning of other facts and concepts.

1. The _____ mind is the part of the mind containing information that is not presently conscious but can be easily brought into consciousness.

   a) conscious   c) unconscious

   b) preconscious   d) suppressed

2. According to Freud, the _____ is the inborn part of the unconscious mind that uses the primary process to satisfy its needs and that acts according to the pleasure principle.

   a) id   c) superego

   b) ego   d) reality principle

3. Carl Jung disagreed with Freud's one-sided negative view of the human condition and proposed that all important elements came in the form of _____ such as introversion and extroversion.

   a) positive conditions   c) opposites

   b) synonyms   d) matches

● Thinking Critically About Psychology

1. Does Freud's theory describe human behavior only for Europeans and Americans of his era, or does it apply to people of any generation or culture?

2. Why do you think Karen Horney and Sigmund Freud had such different views of women?

Correct Answers   **1. b** (p. 332),   **2. a** (p. 333),   **3. c** (p. 335).

▶ SOCIAL LEARNING THEORY: ALBERT BANDURA

The social learning view of personality is vastly different from that of the psychoanalysts. Little or no attention is paid to topics such as instincts, the unconscious mind, or the developmental stages that are of primary importance to psychoanalysis. To the social learning theorist, personality is simply something that is learned; it's the sum total of all the ways we have learned to act, think, and feel. Because personality is learned from other people in society, the term *social learning* is used.

Social learning theory had its origins in the behavioral writings of Ivan Pavlov, John B. Watson, and B. F. Skinner. Each of these theorists argued that personality is no more than learned behavior and that the way to understand personality is simply to understand the processes of learning. To social learning theorists, the key concepts in the study of personality are not id, ego, and superego, but classical conditioning, operant conditioning, and modeling, which were discussed in chapter 5. We will not repeat our discussion of these principles here, but it may be helpful for you to glance back over this material.

Albert Bandura (1925–).

Role of Learning in Personality

In the social learning theory view, a person will develop an adequate personality only if he or she is exposed to good models and is reinforced for appropriate behavior. An inadequate learning environment, on the other hand, will result in inadequate personality development.

social learning theory
The viewpoint that the most important parts of our behavior are learned from other persons in society—family, friends, and culture.

The leading figure in social learning theory today and the person who gave the theory its name is Stanford University psychologist Albert Bandura (1977, 1989, 1999). In one sense, Bandura is very much a behaviorist. He agrees with the view that personality is the sum total of learned behavior. But he broke with traditional behaviorism in two main ways: (a) He sees people as playing an active role in determining their own actions, rather than being passively acted upon by the learning environment, and (b) he emphasizes the importance of cognition in personality.

Bandura (1977) portrays us as playing an active role in our own lives by stating that social learning is an example of **reciprocal determination:** Not only is a person's behavior learned, but the social learning environment is altered by the person's behavior (see fig. 11.2). The environment that we learn from, after all, is made up of people. If we behave toward them in a timid way, or a friendly way, or a hostile way, those people will react in very different ways to us—and will hence be teaching us very different things about social relationships. The aggressive, overconfident person will learn that the world is a cold, rejecting place; the friendly person will learn that the world is warm and loving. Personality is learned behavior, but it is also behavior that influences future learning experiences.

Role of Cognition in Personality

According to Bandura, our learned cognitions are the prime determinant of our behavior. A person who believes that helping others makes them less self-reliant will be stingy; a person who thinks that other people find her boring will act quiet and shy. Bandura (1982, 1999) places particular emphasis on our cognitions about our ability to handle the demands of life. In his theory, **self-efficacy** is the perception that one is capable of doing what is necessary to reach one's goals—both in the sense of knowing what to do and being emotionally able to do it. People who perceive themselves as self-efficacious accept greater challenges, expend more effort, and may be more successful in reaching their goals as a result. A person with a poor sense of self-efficacy about social poise may not accept a

reciprocal determination
(re-sip″ro-kal)   Bandura's observation that the individual's behavior and the social learning environment continually influence one another.

Self-Efficacy

www.mmhe.com/laheye1

self-efficacy
According to Bandura, the perception of being capable of achieving one's goals.

FIGURE 11.2

Social learning theorists believe in reciprocal determination; we learn our behavior from interactions with other persons, but our behavior influences how other persons interact with us.

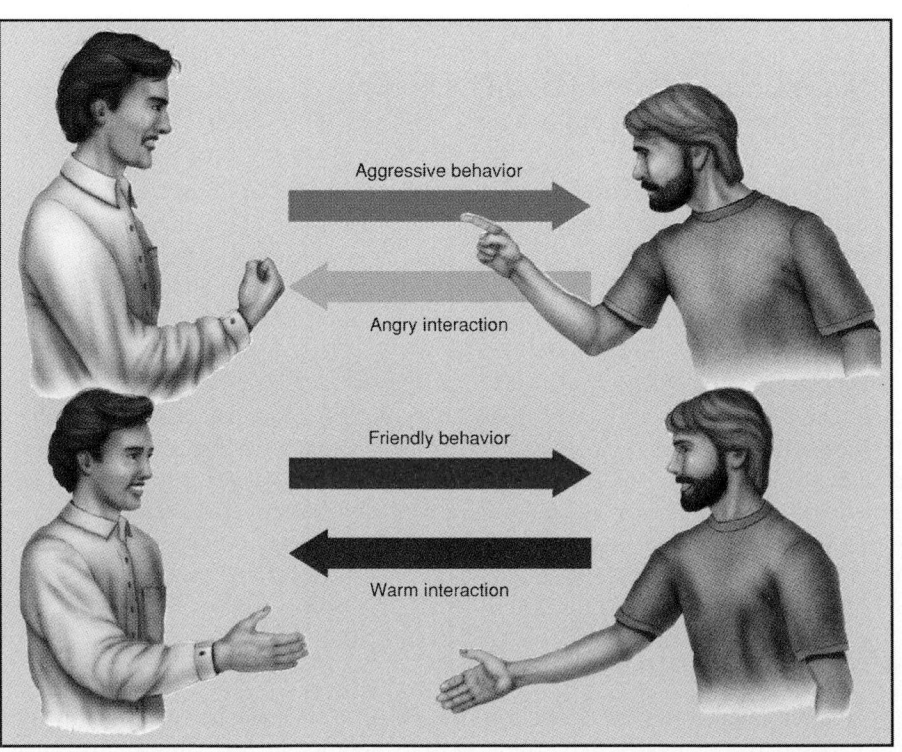

promotion at work because it would involve giving many speeches and having to negotiate with dignitaries. Although our perceptions of self-efficacy are learned from what others say about us, from our direct experiences of success and failure, and from other sources, these cognitions continue to influence our behavior "from the inside out."

Bandura (1977, 1989) also emphasizes the learning of personal standards of reward and punishment by which we judge our own behavior. We learn our personal standards from observing the personal standards that other people model and from the standards that others use when rewarding or punishing us. But, although we are the passive recipients of these standards in a sense, we then actively use them to govern our own behavior in the process that Bandura calls **self-regulation.** When we behave in ways that meet our personal standards, we cognitively pat ourselves on the back—we reinforce ourselves. We generally do not actually say to ourselves, "Good going; you did okay!" Rather, we feel a self-reinforcing sense of pride or happiness when we have met our standards (like Freud's ego ideal). Conversely, we punish ourselves (feel guilty, disappointed) when we fail to meet our personal standards (like Freud's conscience). In these ways, the process of self-regulation serves much the same purpose as Freud's superego.

Situationism and Interactionism

Are you cheerful or are you gloomy? It may well depend on the situation you are in. Some situations make us cheery and some make us gloomy. Behaviorist B. F. Skinner (1953) argued strongly against the concept of traits. He suggested, instead, that behavior is determined by the situations people find themselves in, not traits inside the person. This viewpoint, known as **situationism,** suggests that our behavior is consistent only as long as our situations remain consistent. A woman might be friendly most of the time when she is with her family, but cold and distant when she is with her gossipy coworkers, and stiff and formal with her boss. According to Skinner, people behave in ways that suit their situations, and—because situations are apt to change—behavior cannot be consistent enough to be adequately described in terms of traits.

Social learning theorists have suggested a constructive compromise between the trait and situationism positions (Bandura, 1977, 1999; Mischel & Shoda, 1999). This compromise is so important to social learning theory that is impossible to fully understand it without understanding its solution to the problem of situational influences. The solution, known as **person × situation interactionism,** suggests that our behavior is influenced by a combination of characteristics of the person *and* the situation. For example, you might know somebody who is friendly and even fairly dominant when alone with you but painfully shy at parties. Or you might know somebody who is fairly quiet and dull in one-to-one conversations with you but a witty, vibrant conversationalist at parties. These two people tell us two important things about personality: First, each person's behavior is different in the two different situations (being alone with you versus being at a party). Second, the two situations influence their behavior in *different* ways. People are influenced by situations, it's true, but different individuals are influenced by the same situations in different ways.

This is the essential point of interactionism: The only way to fully describe a person's personality is in terms of "if . . . then" statements (Mischel & Shoda, 1999). "If he feels liked by others, then he is cheerful and kind. If he thinks other people don't like him, then he is gloomy and sarcastic." Such if . . . then statements provide a description of our personalities that allows a prediction of future behavior in a variety of situations. In order to understand *why* persons behave in different situations in the various ways that they do, however, requires a deeper level of analysis. To social learning theorists, the "person variables" in the person × situation interaction are the cognitive (beliefs, etc.), motivational (goals, etc.), and emotional tendencies that we have acquired through social learning and that determine how we respond to different situations (Mischel & Shoda, 1999).

The person × situation interaction is more complicated than it first appears for two reasons. First, people play a role through selective determination in selecting and even creating the situations in which they live. For example, a very shy person may avoid social situations, whereas an aggressive person would tend to seek out challenging situations and

self-regulation
According to Bandura, the process of cognitively reinforcing and punishing our own behavior, depending on whether it meets our personal standards.

situationism
(sit″ū-ā′shun-izm)   The view that behavior is not consistent but is strongly influenced by different situations.

person × situation interactionism
(in″ter-ak′shun-izm)   The view that behavior is influenced by a combination of the characteristics of both the person and the situation.

may even provoke hostile encounters with others. If we select and create our own situations based on our personal characteristics, this means that situational factors tend to play less of a day-to-day role in influencing our behavior than they otherwise might (Emmons & Diener, 1986).

Second, Darryl Bem (Bem & Allen, 1974) has added another interesting and important footnote to the concept of interactionism. He reminds us that one of the important ways in which individuals differ from one another is that some people are influenced more by situations than others. Some people are grumpy with everybody all the time, whereas other people are friendly with some people, grumpy with others, and in-between with the rest. With this in mind, a complete description of personality must also indicate the degree to which the person is influenced by different situations.

● Review

Albert Bandura is the leading proponent of social learning theory. Although this approach to personality theory grew out of the behaviorism of Pavlov, Watson, and Skinner, Bandura expanded behavioral thinking by emphasizing the importance of cognition in personality and the active role played by individuals in the social learning process (reciprocal determinism). To the social learning theorist, the process of learning is of central importance to personality development. Social learning theorists believe that people are influenced by the situations they are in too much for simple trait descriptions to be sufficient. They emphasize person × situation interactions, however, to highlight the fact that different people are influenced by situations in different ways. Thus, personality can best be conceptualized in terms of multiple if . . . then descriptions that capture both characteristics of the person (patterns of cognition, motivation, and affect) and the influence of situations on that person.

● Check Your Learning

To be sure that you have learned the key points from the preceding section, cover the list of correct answers and try to answer each question. If you give an incorrect answer to any question, return to the page given next to the correct answer to see why your answer was not correct.

1. _____ is the theory that our personalities are formed primarily through learning from other members of society where the key concepts are classical conditioning, operant conditioning, and modeling.

2. Albert Bandura suggests that social learning is _____ : Not only is a person's behavior learned from others, but the social learning environment is altered by the person's behavior.

   a) bilateral   c) bipolar

   b) reciprocally determined   d) interactive

3. According to Bandura, _____ is the perception that one is capable of doing what is necessary to reach one's goals.

   a) cognition   c) confidence

   b) self-regulation   d) self-efficacy

4. _____ suggests that our behavior is influenced by a combination of characteristics of the person (traits) and the situation.

   a) Situationism   c) Trait theory

   b) Learning theory   d) Person × situation interactionism

● Thinking Critically About Psychology

1. How might you use Bandura's theory of personality to help you better understand your own personality?

2. How would a police detective who understood person × situation interactionism attempt to catch a serial killer?

Correct Answers **1.** Social learning theory (p. 337), **2. b** (p. 338), **3. d** (p. 338), **4. d** (p. 339).

▶ HUMANISTIC THEORY

The **humanistic theory** of psychology is often referred to as the *third force* in psychology. Although it has deep historical roots in philosophy, it has only been since the 1950s that humanism has become an influential movement in psychology. This approach to personality is the least unified and well defined of the three major viewpoints. This lack of unity is probably due less to the newness of humanistic psychology than to its origins. Each of the other two schools of thought began with the ideas of a single person. Although the views of the original leaders were subsequently revised by later followers, the original writings of Pavlov and Freud gave a certain unity to the theories that followed. Humanistic theory, on the other hand, emerged from the writings of a number of figures who only shared a few basic concepts.

The founders of humanistic psychology include Carl Rogers, Abraham Maslow, Victor Frankl, Virginia Satir, Fritz Perls, and Rollo May, to name only a few. It's impossible, therefore, to write a single statement that adequately summarizes the humanistic approach to personality. For this reason, we will focus primarily on the views of Carl Rogers, emphasizing the parts of his theory that are consistent with the views of humanists in general.

Carl Rogers (1902–1987).

Inner-Directedness and Subjectivity

Humanists believe that humans possess an internal force, an **inner-directedness,** that pushes them to grow, to improve, and to become the best individuals they are capable of being. People have the freedom to make choices, and they are generally pretty good at making intelligent choices that further their personal growth. This inner-directedness is the primary force behind the development of personality.

Obviously, humanists have a positive view of the human species, but they are not blind to the fact that life is a struggle for everyone at some point and that many people consistently make a mess of their lives. We lose our ability to grow and to make good choices when we live with critical, rejecting people or when society tries to force us to be something that we are not. And, as Maslow has pointed out, the transition to higher motives is stunted when more basic motives are unsatisfied.

The personality that develops through the positive push of inner-directedness can only be understood "from the inside out," that is, from the perspective of the individual. To the humanist, the only reality is a **subjective reality.** Everyone views life in somewhat different, highly personal terms. What is real for you may not be real for me. You may see people as basically immoral, whereas I see them as basically moral. Each person's personality is a direct reflection of the individual's subjective view of reality. Our consistent ways of acting, thinking, and feeling reflect our unique perceptions of what life is all about. And, as we will see in the next section, no subjective view of reality is more important to humanistic theorists than our subjective view of ourselves.

humanistic theory
The psychological view that human beings possess an innate tendency to improve and to determine their lives through the decisions they make.

inner-directedness
A force that humanists believe all people possess that internally leads them to grow and improve.

subjective reality
Each person's unique perception of reality that, according to humanists, plays a key role in organizing our personalities.

self-concept
Our subjective perception of who we are and what we are like.

self
According to humanists, the person one thinks one is.

ideal self
According to humanists, the person one wishes one were.

symbolization
In Rogers' theory, the process of representing experience, thoughts, or feelings in mental symbols of which we are aware.

conditions of worth
The standards used by others or ourselves in judging our worth.

The Self-Concept

The concept of the "self" is central to the personality theory of Carl Rogers and other humanists. Our **self-concept** is our subjective perception of who we are and what we are like. Of all of our subjective views of life, our view of ourselves is most important to our personalities. The concept of self is learned from our interactions with others: You might learn that you are a good athlete by seeing that you run faster than most other people or by your parents' and friends' telling you that you are a good athlete.

Rogers distinguishes between two self-concepts. There is the **self**—the person I think I am—and the **ideal self**—the person I wish I were. For example, I am pretty sure I can never be better than a "C" class racquetball player (self), but I would *love* to win tournaments in the "A" class (ideal self). On a higher plane, I see myself as a fairly nice person, but I wish I could learn to be less selfish at times. Rogers' concept of the ideal self is very similar to Freud's ego ideal.

Psychological problems can arise from three kinds of difficulties with the self and ideal self. First, excessive discrepancies between the self and the ideal self can be uncomfortable. It's okay for the ideal self to be slightly out of reach—that can stimulate us to improve ourselves. But, if the ideal self is so unrealistically perfect that we know it can never be reached, then we feel like failures.

A study by Timothy Strauman (1992) at the University of Wisconsin tested this notion. Students in introductory psychology classes were interviewed and tested to determine whether there were discrepancies between the way they view themselves (their concept of self) and the way that they think they would like to be or ought to be (two aspects of the ideal self). Students who saw themselves as different from the way that they would *like* to be were more likely to experience sadness over time, and students who saw themselves as different from the way they *ought* to be were more likely to be anxious.

Second, an inaccurate self-concept can also cause problems. If our view of our "selves" is not reasonably *congruent* (similar to the way we actually act, think, and feel), then we will develop an obscured view of ourselves. For example, if I see myself as totally free from prejudice, but I feel a twinge of resentment when someone from a minority group gets preference over me in a job promotion, then my feelings of resentment would not "fit" my self-concept. According to Rogers, I might deny those feelings that are incongruent with my self-concept by not admitting them to awareness. In Rogers' terms, we are aware of feelings and information only when they are mentally **symbolized.** The failure to symbolize parts of our experience is harmful not only because it leads to inaccurate concepts of self, but also because feelings can continue to influence us, often in conflicting or anxiety-provoking ways, even when we are not aware of them.

Third, we also deny awareness to some of our feelings and experiences as a result of our parents' and society's reactions to our behavior. By reacting with warmth and praise to some of our actions (sharing a toy with little sister), but with coldness and punishment to others (hitting little sister with the toy), our parents create **conditions of worth.** They let us know that they find us "worthy" under some conditions and "unworthy" under other conditions. We internalize many of these and perceive ourselves as worthwhile only when we act and feel in accordance with those conditions. Furthermore, we often deny feelings that are inconsistent with the internalized conditions of worth. The child, for example, may not symbolize her hostile feelings toward her sister, robbing herself of a valuable bit of self-awareness. Some psychologists believe that society's views of the ideal female and ideal male often create problems (Wood & others, 1997). When girls and boys internalize expectations for how they should ideally behave based on stereotypes of what females and males are like, conflict is created for those individuals whose actual behavior is different from their gender stereotype. Dominant females and gentle males, for example, could have difficulties accurately symbolizing these characteristics that are inconsistent with gender stereotypes in their self-concept.

Rogers' concept of unsymbolized feelings is similar in some ways to Freud's view of repressed feelings. Both can continue to influence the person, often in a harmful manner. But Freud views some repression as a necessary part of life, whereas Rogers believes that lack of awareness is always harmful. If we are to allow full expression to our inner-directed tendency to grow, we must be fully aware of (symbolize) all of our feelings and experiences. Only in this way can we accurately understand and accept ourselves for exactly what we are (while always striving to do better).

Humanism Compared with Classic Psychoanalysis and Social Learning Theory

Humanism, psychoanalysis, and social learning theory differ from one another in their views of the basic nature of human beings and of society. In classic psychoanalytic theory, people are seen as selfish and hostile at birth; they are nothing but id. Society is seen as a good force that instills the ego and superego into children, thus enabling them to behave realistically and morally enough to live in the social world.

To the humanist, the psychoanalytic view is exactly wrong. People possess a positive inborn drive to grow and improve. Instead of being born evil, the human is born basically good. Society, on the other hand, is seen by the humanist as a frequently destructive force that leads people to deny their true feelings (of jealousy, insecurity, passion) and creates unattainable ideal self-concepts (for example, American society tells us that we should all be attractive, athletic, sexy, famous, and rich).

Social learning theorists differ from psychoanalytic and humanistic theorists in their evaluation of the basic nature of humans and society. Social learning theorists see humans as neutral at birth, having the potential to learn to be either good or bad. Similarly, society can be either destructive or constructive. A part of society that teaches inappropriate behavior to its children is destructive, whereas a part of society that teaches appropriate behavior is constructive.

All three theories, however, believe that we internalize society's standards of what is desirable and moral and guide our behavior accordingly. Freud spoke of the conscience and ego ideal of the superego, Bandura used the concept of self-regulation, and Rogers spoke in terms of the ideal self. Although they differ in important ways, these are highly similar ideas about why we tend to obey the rules and standards of society. For a comparison of all three theories, see table 11.2.

TABLE 11.2   Comparison of Classic Psychoanalytic, Social Learning, and Humanistic Theories of Personality

	Classic Psychoanalytic	Social Learning	Humanistic
An "unconscious" or "unsymbolized" mind exerts a powerful influence on us.	Yes	No	Yes
We learn what is "good" and "bad" from our families and cultures.	Yes	Yes	Yes
Our internalized knowledge of what is "good" and "bad" is an important part of our personalities.	Yes (superego and ego ideal)	Yes (self-regulation)	Yes (ideal self)
People are inherently . . .	Selfish and evil	Neither good nor bad	Good
Society . . .	Usually teaches us to convert our selfish nature into positive behavior	Can influence us in either positive or negative ways	Often harms or destroys our inherent tendency to be healthy and good

Contemporary Merging of the Major Theories of Personality

For many years, the three major theories of personality have shared a few ideas, even though they have disagreed in most ways. Recently, however, exponents of the three major theories of personality have made theoretical statements that sound remarkably like one another (Bandura, 1999; Mischel & Shoda, 1999; Westen & Gabbard, 1999). It is surprising but gratifying to see groups of psychologists who once bitterly criticized each another adopt the best ideas of one another. For example, both modern psychoanalysts and social learning theorists now speak of the humanists' concept of self as the core feature of personality (Bandura, 1999; Westen & Gabbard, 1999), and the positive drive to self-actualization has been incorporated into both classic psychoanalytic (Westen & Gabbard, 1999) and social learning (Mischel & Shoda, 1999) theories. Social learning theorists are speaking about unconscious processes (Mischel & Shoda, 1999), and psychoanalysts (Westen & Gabbard, 1999) are discussing person × situation interactionism in ways that closely parallel social learning theory. If these trends continue, the three major theories of personality may eventually become a single unified theory. At present, however, the three theories still remain far apart on some core issues (see table 11.2).

Personality and Culture

Your introduction to psychology is occurring at an exciting time in the history of the field. Increasingly, psychologists are accepting the idea that sociocultural factors such as ethnicity, race, gender, sexual preference, and physical challenges are important in understanding human personality (Betancourt & Lopez, 1993; Cross & Markus, 1999). One new focus of cross-cultural research has been on the validity of North American concepts of personality in other cultures. For example, a number of studies have confirmed the five-factor model of personality in many Western and non-Western cultures (McCrae & Costa, 1997). When correlations among items were examined using translated instruments, the same pattern of inter-correlated traits emerged in many cultures. Does this mean that these five personality traits are a human universal and equally meaningful in all cultures? There are two reasons to believe that the five-factor model and other trait approaches to personality may not be as valid in non-Western cultures as they are in North America.

First, some studies show that dimensions of personality that are specific to each culture emerge along with the five factors found in Western cultures. For example, a trait referred to as Chinese traditionalism has been found in Chinese participants along with the traits usually identified in the five-factor model. This additional trait is positively correlated with life satisfaction and negatively correlated with antisocial behavior (Zhang & Bond, 1998). Thus, personality may vary across cultures in the sense that traits that are specific to each culture may help us understand a person's personality, adjustment, and well-being.

Second, and more important, the concept of personality simply may have less meaning in some cultures than in North America. In individualistic cultures such as mainstream U.S. culture, we look for explanations for a person's behavior *within* that individual. Consider the focus of personality theories that have arisen in European and North American cultures. Trait theories focus on attributes of the individual (the traits). Psychoanalytic theories focus on conflicts within the individual. Social learning and humanistic theories highlight concepts such as self-concept, self-efficacy, and self-regulation. These theories of personality consider groups outside the individual only as positive or negative social influences on the individual. It makes perfect sense to focus on the individual in individualistic cultures, but less sense in collectivistic cultures (Cross & Markus, 1999). In Japan, China, India, and other Asian cultures, the behavior of the individual is understood more in terms of the expectations, rights, and duties of being a member of a *group* (family, caste, country). Psychological explanations that focus on the individual ignore much of Asian thinking about the nature of people.

Susan Cross of Iowa State University and Hazel Markus (1999) of Stanford University offer the following concrete example of the vast difference between individual-

HUMAN DIVERSITY

ETHNICITY AND PSYCHOLOGISTS

Are you a member of an ethnic group that the majority culture often views with prejudice? A number of psychology organizations welcome student members with an interest in ethnic minority issues. In some cases, they will help you locate a psychologist who can serve as a mentor, particularly if you are considering psychology as a profession. Mentoring can be particularly helpful for students who are members of groups that have been underrepresented in psychology in the past. In addition, the American Psychological Association and other organizations can provide information on financial aid available to support graduate study.

American Psychological Association
Minority Affairs
750 West First Street, N.E.
Washington, DC 20002-4242
Telephone: (202) 336-5500
www.apa.org/mfp/homepage.html

American Psychological Society
Student Caucus/Ethnic Minority Concerns
Suite 1100
1010 Vermont Avenue, N.W.
Washington, DC 20005-4907
http://psych.hanover.edu/APS/APSSC/EMCC.html

Asian American Psychological Association
Suite 103-198
3003 N. Central Avenue
Phoenix, AZ 85012
Telephone: (602) 230-4257
www.west.asu.edu/aapa/services.htm

Association of Black Psychologists
P.O. Box 55999
Washington, DC 20040-5999
Telephone: (202) 722-0808
www.oaktreeweb.com/abpsi/membership-options.htm

National Hispanic Psychologists Association
Dr. Maryann Santos de Barona
Division of Psychology in Education
Arizona State University
P.O. Box 870611
Tempe, AZ 85287-0611
Telephone: (480) 965-1066

Association of Indian Psychologists
Dr. Carolyn Barcus
Department of Psychology
Utah State University
Logan, UT 84322
Telephone: (435) 797-1465

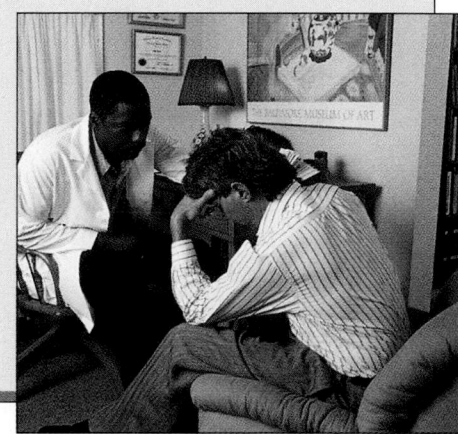

istic and collectivistic cultures views of the person. These four "personal ads" were published on the same day in two California newspapers (a general readership paper and a paper that has a readership of mostly immigrant families from India):

From the *San Francisco Chronicle*:

28 SWM, 6'1", 160 lbs. Handsome, artistic, ambitious, seeks attractive WF, 24–29, for friendship, romance, and permanent partnership.

Very attractive, independent SWF, 29, 5'6" 110 lbs., loves fine dining, the theater, gardening and quiet evenings at home. In search of handsome SWM 28–34 with similar interests.

From the *India Tribune*:

Gujarati Vaishnav parents invite correspondence from never married Gujarati well settled, preferably green card holder from respectable family for green card holder daughter 29 years, 5'4", good looking, doing CPA.

Gujarati Brahmin family invites correspondence from a well cultured, beautiful Gujarati girl for 29 years, 5'8", 145 lbs. handsome looking, well settled boy.

Notice that these four ads are similar in some ways (all refer to physical appearance and age) but very different in other ways. The ads in the general readership newspaper reflect the individualistic U.S. culture. They describe only the individual's characteristics and preferences. In contrast, the ads in the *India Tribune* reflect the collectivistic Indian culture by focusing on the individual's membership in *groups*. They were placed in the name of the families rather than the individual, and they refer to both the state in India from which the families came (Gujarati) and to the caste of the family (Vaishnav and Brahmin). It is this strong emphasis on the embeddedness of the individual in groups that have more importance than the individual that lies at the heart of collectivistic culture. In the context of collectivistic cultures, a theory of personality that focused only on forces within the individual would seem incomplete at best and misleading at worst (Cross & Markus, 1999).

But a successful personality theory must always consider the culture of any group to which it is applied. Too often, theories of personality have been developed by white psychologists based only on white North Americans and then have been applied to other ethnic and racial groups. This may create more confusion than clarification. Consider as an example the dramatically different experiences of persons of European and African heritage in the United States. The ancestors of most African Americans came to the United States in slavery, but no European entered America in forced slavery. Moreover, African Americans still live in a racist society that often treats them with anger, suspicion, and disdain. Similarly, Native Americans were once considered to be savages who could be killed without remorse to allow Europeans to settle their land, and today many Americans would prefer that they be "invisible" citizens who stay on their reservations. The prejudice experienced by Americans of Latin descent can also be intense, especially given the recent pressures to reduce immigration from Mexico and other Latin countries.

We must understand the personalities of North American ethnic minorities in the context of their culture, and their culture includes racism and economic barriers. If we do not, we run the risk of misunderstanding some characteristics of ethnic minorities that reflect their efforts to adapt to racism, chronic lack of employment, and lack of educational opportunities.

● Review

Humanism is the least unified of the three movements, but several basic concepts about personality are shared by nearly all humanists. The most significant factor in the development of personality is the positive inner-directed drive to grow and improve. Unless our experiences with society interfere with this drive, it can be counted on to direct personal growth in positive directions. The personality that develops from this growth can be understood only from the point of view of the individual. Personality is seen as reflecting each person's subjective view of reality. We act, think, and feel in accordance with how we view reality. And the most important aspect of that view of reality is our subjective concept of self. The ways I view both the self that I think I am and the self I would like to be are powerful determinants of my personality. If my ideal self is unattainably perfect, I will always fall painfully short of my standards. If my self-concept is inaccurate, I will not be able to deal with information about myself that is incongruent with my self-concept. Incongruent information is not admitted to consciousness, a state of affairs that humanists view as unhealthy for the personality.

Humanists, psychoanalysts, and social learning theorists take very different views of the basic nature of people and society. Psychoanalysts view humans as wholly selfish and hostile ids at birth. Society, in contrast, is seen as a positive force providing experiences that create the ego and superego that allow humans to function effectively in society. Humanists view people as essentially good but see society as a negative force that often interferes with the individual's inner-directed growth. Social learning theorists see people as having the potential to develop in either positive or negative ways, depending on whether their personalities were learned from positive or negative aspects of society. Although there are signs that the proponents of the major theories of personality are growing more similar over time, they remain far apart on such key issues. There is growing awareness that personality can only be understood in the context of the individual's culture.

● Check Your Learning

To be sure that you have learned the key points from the preceding section, cover the list of correct answers and try to answer each question. If you give an incorrect answer to any question, return to the page given next to the correct answer to see why your answer was not correct.

1. According to _____ theory, human beings possess an innate tendency to improve and to determine their lives by the decisions they make.

   a) social learning   c) humanistic

   b) psychoanalytic   d) conditioning

2. According to the humanists, the _____ is the person one wishes he or she were.

   a) real self   c) new self

   b) ideal self   d) self

3. Our _____ is our subjective perception of who we are and what we are like.

   a) self-concept   c) self efficacy

   b) ideal self   d) actualized self

4. Humanists believe that humans are born neither good nor evil.

   a) True   b) False

● Thinking Critically About Psychology

1. If, as the humanistic perspective suggests, reality is subjective, how can individuals ever hope to agree on anything?

2. What are the best new ideas that you learned from this summary of the three theories of personality? What are the least helpful ideas to you?

Correct Answers   1. c (p. 341),   **2. b** (p. 342),   **3. a** (p. 342),   **4. b** (p. 343).

▶ PERSONALITY ASSESSMENT: TAKING A MEASURE OF THE PERSON

Psychologists who work in business, schools, prisons, and clinics are frequently called on to make important decisions about people. Which employee should be promoted to sales manager? Should this person receive a parole from prison? What should be done to help this person out of a state of depression? Such questions can be answered only when the psychologist knows what the person is like—that is, how the person typically behaves in ways that distinguish him or her from other individuals. In other words, the psychologist must know a great deal about the person's personality.

You could probably describe the personality of your best friend, your sister or brother, or your parent fairly well. You have seen them in a variety of situations and know how they typically behave. But psychologists usually do not have the luxury of getting to know their clients over long periods of time. They must come up with a picture of their client's personality in short order. To do this, a number of ways of quickly assessing personality have been developed. These include interviews, structured observations of behavior, psychoanalytically inspired projective tests, and personality tests.

Interviews and Observational Methods

The most widely used method of personality assessment is the **interview.** Although few psychologists use it by itself, nearly every psychologist interviews the client by asking questions designed to reveal his or her personality. These interviews can range from the highly structured and formal to very unstructured.

Interviews are an essential part of getting to know the client, but they have serious limitations. For one thing, they are inherently subjective; different psychologists may evaluate the same behavior of the client during the interview in different ways. Second, interviews are artificial situations that bring into question the validity of the information obtained from them. Interviews are stressful events that may bring out atypical behavior. A person may feel very anxious when interviewing for a job but might ordinarily be a calm person when at work. In this way, interviews can be misleading. As a result, they are often supplemented by other methods to ensure a more complete and accurate view of the person's personality.

One alternative to interviewing is *observing* the person's actual behavior in a natural or simulated situation. **Observational methods** are particularly popular in business. For example, psychologists who consult with businesses on employee promotion often observe the employees being considered for promotion in situations that simulate actual managerial situations. Several employees might be given the problem of dividing up a limited budget for an employee health plan and then be observed as they negotiate a solution to the simulated problem.

Projective Personality Tests

Another method of personality assessment is the **projective test.** These tests are based on the belief of psychoanalysts that it's the unconscious mind that contains the important roots of personality. But, because the ego works fervently to keep the contents of the unconscious mind out of awareness, a way must be found to slip past the censor of the ego. Psychoanalysts believe that the motives and conflicts of the unconscious mind can be revealed by projective tests.

Projective tests ask the individual to interpret ambiguous stimuli so that the contents of the unconscious mind can be "projected" into the interpretation, much as a slide projector projects an image on a blank screen. For example, the *Thematic Apperception Test (TAT)* (Murray, 1938, 1951) asks the individual to make up a story about ambiguous pictures like the one in figure 11.3. What do you see in this picture? Is it an old woman happily remembering her youth? Is it a picture of the evil side of a young woman who is plotting the murder of her father? Psychoanalysts believe that, because the stimuli are ambiguous, the ego is not able to fully censor the unconscious thoughts and motives that are projected into the story made up about the picture.

Even more ambiguous stimuli are used in the *Rorschach inkblot test* (Rorschach, 1953). The test consists of 10 symmetrical inkblots like the ones in figure 11.4. The individuals tell what the inkblots look like and what parts of the inkblots they are focusing on. Do you see a vagina surrounded by a menacing spider? Are you projecting a fear of sex? Complex scoring systems are often used with the Rorschach inkblots (Exner, 1986), but many users interpret the responses subjectively.

Objective Personality Tests

A more recent development in personality assessment is the objective personality test. These tests have been widely used since World War II in an attempt to move away from the subjectivity of interviews and projective tests. The objective personality test consists of a number of written questions about the person. For example, the *Minnesota Multiphasic Personality Inventory* (MMPI) (now available in a revised form called the MMPI-2) consists of 567 true/false questions such as the following:

interview
A subjective method of personality assessment that involves questioning techniques designed to reveal the personality of the client.

observational methods
Methods of personality assessment that involve watching a person's actual behavior in a natural or simulated situation.

Projective Test

www.mmhe.com/laheye1

projective test
A test that uses ambiguous stimuli designed to reveal the contents of the client's unconscious mind.

FIGURE 11.3

The Thematic Apperception Test uses pictures like this to evaluate personality. The person is asked to make up a story based on such ambiguous pictures to allow the contents of the unconscious mind to be projected into the story.

1. I get along well with others.
2. Sometimes I hear voices telling me to do bad things.
3. At times I am full of energy.
4. I am afraid of losing my mind.
5. Everyone hates me.

FIGURE 11.4

In the Rorschach inkblot test, the individual is asked to explain what he or she sees in ambiguous stimuli such as these.

The MMPI-2 is an objective test in the sense that no attempt is made to subjectively understand what the person meant by the answer to each question. Rather, the person's answers are compared with the answers of other individuals with known personality characteristics who have taken the test.

The items on the MMPI-2 are divided into 10 "scales," each designed to measure a different aspect of personality. The items were selected for each scale on the basis of the responses of individuals known to have that characteristic in extreme form. For example, one scale is designed to measure the extent to which a person is prone to experience depression. The scale was developed by administering a large number of questions to a group of people who were seeking treatment for depression and a group of individuals who were not depressed. The items that were selected for the depression scale were those that the depressed people consistently answered in one way and others answered in the *opposite* way. For example, the depressed group tended to answer "true" to a question such as "Life often doesn't seem worth living," whereas the other group tended to answer "false."

This method of test construction allows for the objective interpretation of scores. A person's score on the depression scale is simply determined by the number of questions answered in the same way as the depressed group, not a selective interpretation of the person's answers. Many other objective personality tests have been developed in the same or similar ways.

"It looks as if someone spilled ink on a piece of paper and then folded it in half."

Reprinted with permission of Tom Cheney.

Evaluation of Personality Tests

It's obviously helpful for psychologists to be able to assess the personalities of the individuals with whom they are working. Not all psychologists agree, however, that personality tests are accurate enough to use for that purpose. A great deal of research has been done (but often with disappointing results) to determine whether personality tests are good at measuring what they are supposed to measure.

Research on the Rorschach, TAT, and other projective techniques suggests that these tests generally are not successful in predicting behavior (Garb, Florio, & Grove, 1998; Mischel, 1968). The objective personality tests fare better but still leave much to be desired. In spite of the fact that they were developed using groups with different personality characteristics, many studies have shown that the tests are unable to distinguish between groups that differ on these same characteristics (Mischel, 1968). Even in the most successful demonstrations, the tests are not always accurate. For example, chronic marijuana users can be distinguished from nonusers with 80 percent accuracy using objective personality tests (Hogan, Mankin, Conway, & Fox, 1970). Even so, the test is inaccurate 20 percent of the time.

Review

Because psychologists usually do not have an opportunity to assess each client's personality by getting to know the person over a long period of time, they have had to develop methods of quickly learning about a person's personality. The most widely used method of personality assessment is the interview, in which questions are asked that probe the nature of the individual's personality. Personality is often assessed by directly observing the individual in natural or simulated settings or by having people such as teachers or employers who have observed the person's behavior over a long period of time fill out checklists describing the pattern of behavior that they have observed. Psychoanalytically oriented psychologists often rely on projective tests to learn about the unconscious roots of personality. These tests ask the person to respond to ambiguous stimuli in the hope that the person will project important features of his or her unconscious mind into the interpretation of the stimuli. Psychologists who prefer less subjective methods of personality assessment often use objective tests. These utilize items that were objectively selected for the test by comparing the answers of groups of individuals who do or do not possess the personality characteristics in question. In general, objective personality tests have been shown to be somewhat effective in distinguishing among groups with various personality traits, but some psychologists question whether even these tests are accurate enough to use in making decisions that affect people's lives.

Check Your Learning

To be sure that you have learned the key points from the preceding section, cover the list of correct answers and try to answer each question. If you give an incorrect answer to any question, return to the page given next to the correct answer to see why your answer was not correct.

1. An _____ is a widely used method of personality assessment that involves questioning techniques designed to reveal the personality of the client.

   a) observational method   c) objective personality test

   b) interview   d) essay test

2. A(n) _____ such as the TAT uses ambiguous stimuli designed to reveal the contents of the client's unconscious mind.

   a) objective test   c) subjective test

   b) interview   d) projective test

3. The items on the _____, an objective test, are divided into 10 "scales," each designed to measure a different aspect of personality.

   a) Minnesota Multiphasic   c) Thematic Apperception Test
      Personality Inventory

   b) Rorschach inkblot test   d) Beck Depression Inventory

Thinking Critically About Psychology

1. How do personality tests such as the MMPI-2 differ from the tests that appear in popular magazines?

2. Could someone else really understand your personality based on your answers to a list of questions? Why or why not?

Correct Answers 1. b (p. 348), 2. d (p. 348), 3. a (p. 348).

Application *of Psychology*

SITUATIONAL INFLUENCES ON PERSONALITY IN EVERYDAY LIFE

The school of thought referred to in this textbook as *situationism* suggests that it's impossible to describe people solely in terms of traits because situations influence behavior so strongly. Take the trait of helpfulness. Are you a helpful person? Do you know people whom you would describe as being very helpful or not at all helpful? Most of us think of helpfulness as a characteristic that some people have and some people do not have—that is, we think of it as a trait. Like other traits, we generally think of helpfulness as something that comes from within our personality rather than something that is determined by the situations we are in. But let's see if that commonsense understanding of helpfulness stands up under experimental scrutiny.

One classic study (Isen & Levin, 1972) that sheds light on the effects of even subtle aspects of situations on traits went like this: A male experimenter went to a pay telephone in a covered shopping mall and attempted to make a call. He acted as if there was no answer, hung up, and left. Sometimes he left the dime in the coin return and sometimes he took it. A female experimenter was window-shopping nearby, waiting for the next person to use the phone. The person could be male or female but was a research participant in the experiment only if he or she was alone and not carrying anything.

As the person—who had no idea that he or she was a participant in a psychology experiment—left the telephone booth, the female experimenter walked in front of her or his path and dropped a folder full of papers. Was the research participant helpful? Did the person stop and help the experimenter pick up her scattered papers? More to the point of this experiment, would a subtle situational event such as finding a coin in the telephone influence a person's tendency to be helpful?

Figure 11.5 shows the surprising results of this study. One hundred percent of the female research participants and 75 percent of the male participants who had found a coin were helpful, but almost

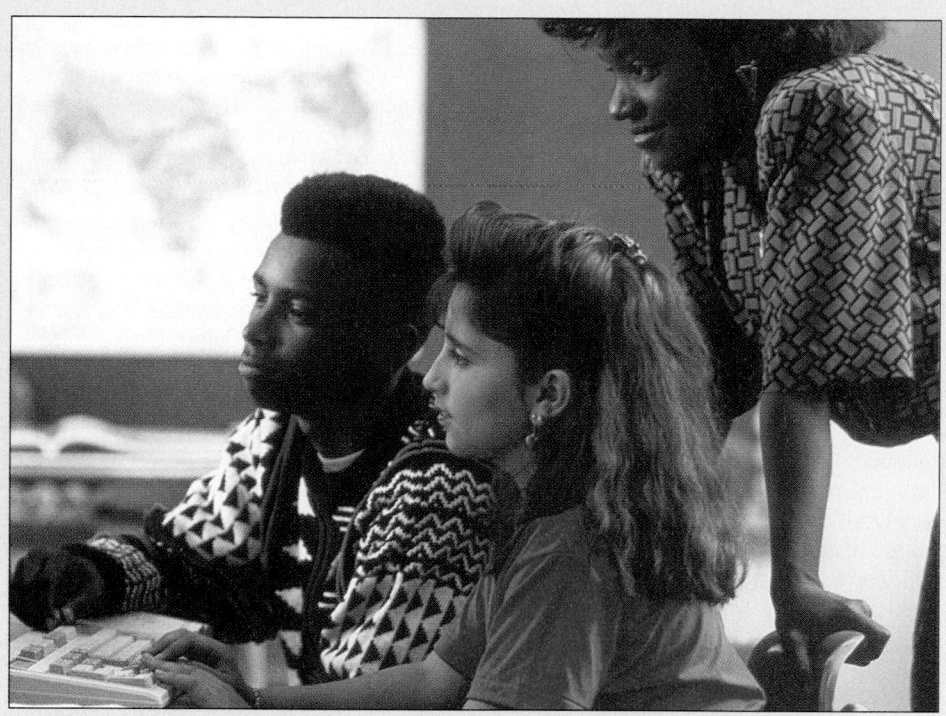

Most of us think of helpfulness as a fixed personality trait—either you tend to be helpful or not. But research suggests that our willingness to help can vary in different situations.

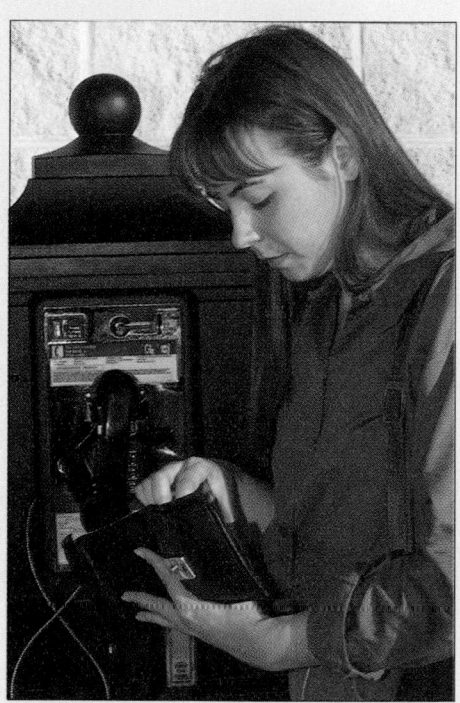

FIGURE 11.5

The percentage of subjects who stopped to help a person pick up scattered papers after finding or not finding a dime in a pay telephone coin return.

Source: Data from A. M. Isen and P. F. Levin, "The Effect of Feeling Good on Helping: Cookies and Kindness," *Journal of Personality and Social Psychology,* 21:384–388, 1972.

none of the people who had not found a coin stopped to help pick up papers.

Now what do you think about helpfulness: Is it a trait within the person or simply behavior that is determined by the situation? Even the small situational influences of finding a coin influenced helpfulness to an amazing extent. As stated in the text, few psychologists presently believe that it's sufficient to think of personality as being influenced only by situations—different people react to the same situations differently—but these experiments may help you understand why many psychologists feel that describing personality only in terms of fixed traits is inadequate as well. Both a description of characteristics of the person and how these personal characteristics interact with changing situations is needed for a full description of personality.

What about happiness and general satisfaction with life? How much is that influenced by situational influences? Many survey studies have been done in recent years in almost 100 different countries that show that some situations have a powerful influence on happiness (Myers & Diener, 1995). People who live in countries with stable democracies and people who are in stable relationships are considerably more likely to be happy than people who are not. People who live in poverty are less happy than average, but, above the poverty line, people with more money are only slightly more likely to be happy.

Situational factors can have a marked impact on our behavior. Need more convincing? Think back to chapter 9 to the discussion of "falling in love on a swaying suspension bridge" (page 297). In that section, I described a study that showed that young males were more attracted to a female interviewer when they met her on a wobbly suspension bridge high above a gorge (probably because they attributed the arousal from the bridge to the young woman). Situations also play a role in whether or not you fall in love!

Why is this point important enough for me to devote this entire section to it? We often find ourselves in the position of predicting how other people will behave. In doing so, it's important to keep the powerful influence of situations in mind. For example, think about someone you know who is in high school now (a sibling, cousin, or neighbor). Now let me ask you to use your imagination for a moment. First, imagine that you have graduated and that you were offered a wonderful job, but you have to move across country tomorrow to start the new job. As a result of the new job, you finally are able to buy a really nice car, but it won't be ready until after you have left for the new job. Do you think the high school student is mature enough to drive your car across country alone for you? As you think about this question, you will find that it is important to keep in mind the high school student's traits but also the unusual situation that she or he will be in. The same kind of reasoning should go into predicting how you will do in the new city and in the new job. You are usually a happy, outgoing person, but will you find yourself a little moody and shy in a new city where you know no one? Situations are important influences on us all.

● Summary

Chapter 11 defines personality, explores four major perspectives on personality—trait theory, psychoanalytic theory, social learning theory, and humanistic theory—and discusses several approaches to personality assessment.

I. Personality is the sum total of all of the ways of acting, thinking, and feeling that are typical for that person and make that person unique.

II. Some psychologists believe that one's personality can be described in terms of traits.

    A. Traits are defined as relatively enduring ways of behaving that are relatively consistent across different situations.

    B. The five-factor model is a widely endorsed description of the basic personality traits.

III. Psychoanalytic theory was developed by Sigmund Freud in the early twentieth century.

    A. Freud distinguished three levels of conscious awareness—the conscious mind, the preconscious mind, and the unconscious mind. In his view, the mind is composed of three parts—id, ego, and superego.

        1. The id operates on the pleasure principle. It seeks to obtain immediate pleasure and avoid pain.

        2. The ego operates on the reality principle. It seeks safe and realistic ways to satisfy the id.

        3. The superego opposes the id by imposing moral restrictions and by striving for perfection.

    B. When the ego cannot find ways to satisfy the id, it seeks a substitute.
       1. The substitution of a more acceptable goal is displacement, and displacement of a socially desirable goal is called sublimation.
       2. Identification is the tendency to sublimate by modeling our actions on individuals who are successful in life.
    C. Alfred Adler, Carl Jung, and Karen Horney broke away from Freud primarily over the issues of sexual motivation, the presence of positive aspects of personality, and the importance of adequate social relationships.

IV. To social learning theorists, the key concepts in the study of personality are learning and cognition.
    A. Our personalities are learned, but Albert Bandura says that social learning is reciprocally determined by the actions of behavior on the environment, and vice versa.
    B. Behavior is self-regulated by our internalized cognitive standards for self-reward and limited by our perception of our own self-efficacy.
    C. Behaviorist B. F. Skinner believed that people were influenced by their situations too much for trait theories to be correct. This view is known as situationism.
    D. Social learning theorists have adopted the position of person × situation interactionism. This suggests that the behavior of different people is influenced by situations in different ways because our behavior reflects both situational influences and our personal characteristics.

V. Humanistic theory is based on a belief that humans possess an inner-directedness that pushes them to grow. To the humanist, reality is subjective.
    A. Self-concept is our subjective perception of who we are and what we are like. Carl Rogers distinguishes between the self (the person I think I am) and the ideal self (the person I wish I were).
    B. Problems result when the ideal self is unrealistic or when feelings and information that are incongruent with a person's self-concept are denied conscious awareness.

VI. Personality assessment is the use of psychological methods to learn about a person's personality.
    A. The most widely used method is the interview.
    B. Personality is also assessed by observing the person's behavior in a natural or simulated situation. Rating scales help make observational methods more objective.
    C. Another widely used method of personality assessment is the projective test, which psychoanalysts believe reveals the motives and conflicts of the unconscious mind.
    D. Objective personality tests, such as the MMPI-2, consist of questions that measure different aspects of personality. Objective personality tests are generally better at assessing personality than projective techniques, but all personality tests are only partly accurate.

● Resources

1. For in-depth discussions of the major theories of personality, see Feist, J., & Feist, G. J. (1998). *Theories of personality* (4th ed.). Boston: McGraw-Hill; Hall, C. S., Lindzey, G., & Campbell, J. B. (1998). *Theories of personality* (4th ed.). New York: John Wiley.

2. For a readable, detailed summary of Sigmund Freud's basic concepts, see Hall, C. S. (1954, 1999). *A primer of Freudian psychology.* New York: Meridian Books.

3. For a summary of recent books that criticize the scientific basis of Freud's theory of personality, see Crews, F. (1996). The verdict on Freud. *Psychological Science, 1,* 63–68.

4. A readable summary of Carl Jung's theory of personality is presented in Hall, C. S., & Nordby, V. J. (1973). *A primer of Jungian psychology.* New York: Taplinger.

5. Interviews with leading humanists Carl Rogers and Abraham Maslow in the prime of their careers appear in Frick, W. B. (1971). *Humanistic psychology.* Columbus, OH: Merrill.

6. For summaries of the evolving social learning view of personality, see Bandura, A. (1977). *Social learning theory.* Englewood Cliffs, NJ: Prentice-Hall; and Bandura, A. (1999). Social cognitive theory of personality. In L. A. Pervin & O. P. John (Eds.), *Handbook of personality: Theory and research* (2nd ed., pp. 154–196). New York: Guilford.

7. No one presents Carl Rogers' views on successful and happy lives like Carl Rogers does: Rogers, C. R. (1980). *A way of being.* Boston: Houghton Mifflin.

8. For the African American perspective in psychology, see Jones, R. (Ed.). (1992). *Black psychology* (3rd ed.). Berkeley, CA: Cobb & Henry.

9. For the Hispanic/Latino perspective in psychology, see Padilla, A. M. (1995). *Hispanic psychology: Critical issues in theory and research.* Thousand Oaks, CA: Sage.

10. For powerful discussions of the role of culture in personality, see Markus, H. R., & Kitayama, S. (1991). Culture and the self: Implications for cognition, emotion and motivation. *American Psychologist, 93,* 2, 224–253; and Cross, S. E., & Markus, H. R. (1999). The cultural constitution of personality. In L. A. Pervin & O. P. John (Eds.), *Handbook of personality: Theory and research* (2nd ed., pp. 378–396). New York: Guilford.

● Visual Review of Personality Theory Figure 11.6

Reviewing the figure below may help you consolidate your learning of some of the information presented in this chapter in a visual format. Be sure not to limit your review to these diagrams, but, because they are key to understanding some of the important concepts in this chapter, mastering them should help you master the entire chapter.

An iceberg is often used to illustrate Sigmund Freud's theoretical structure of the mind. Fill in the labels for the three levels of consciousness (along the left) and the three parts of the mind (on the iceberg).

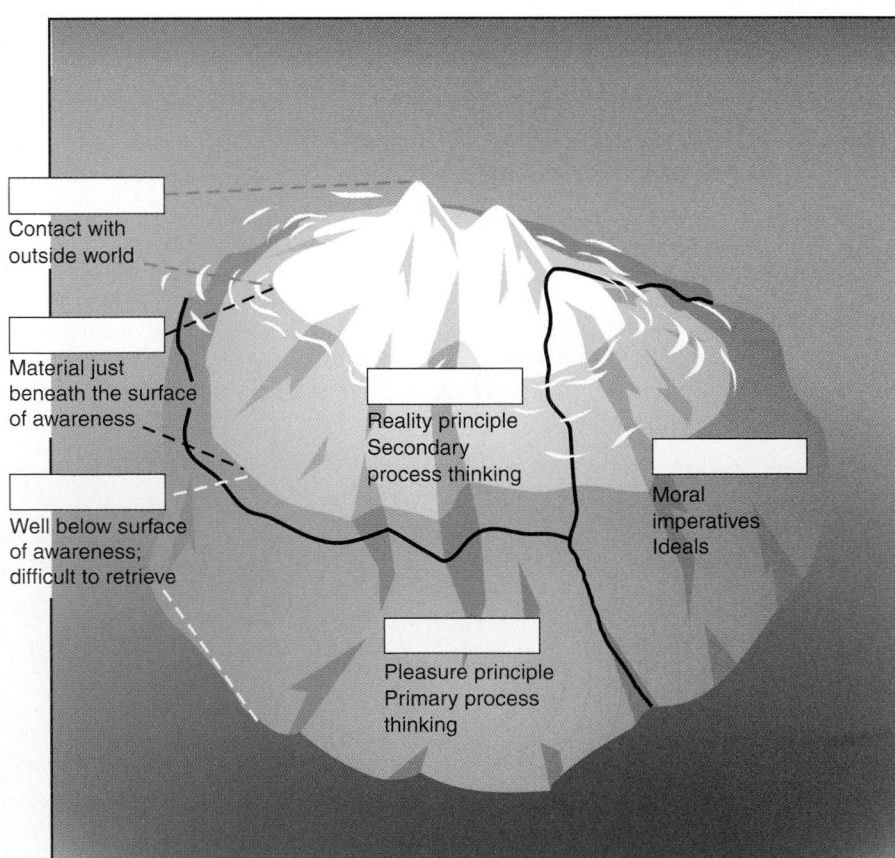

Contact with outside world

Material just beneath the surface of awareness

Well below surface of awareness; difficult to retrieve

Reality principle
Secondary process thinking

Moral imperatives
Ideals

Pleasure principle
Primary process thinking

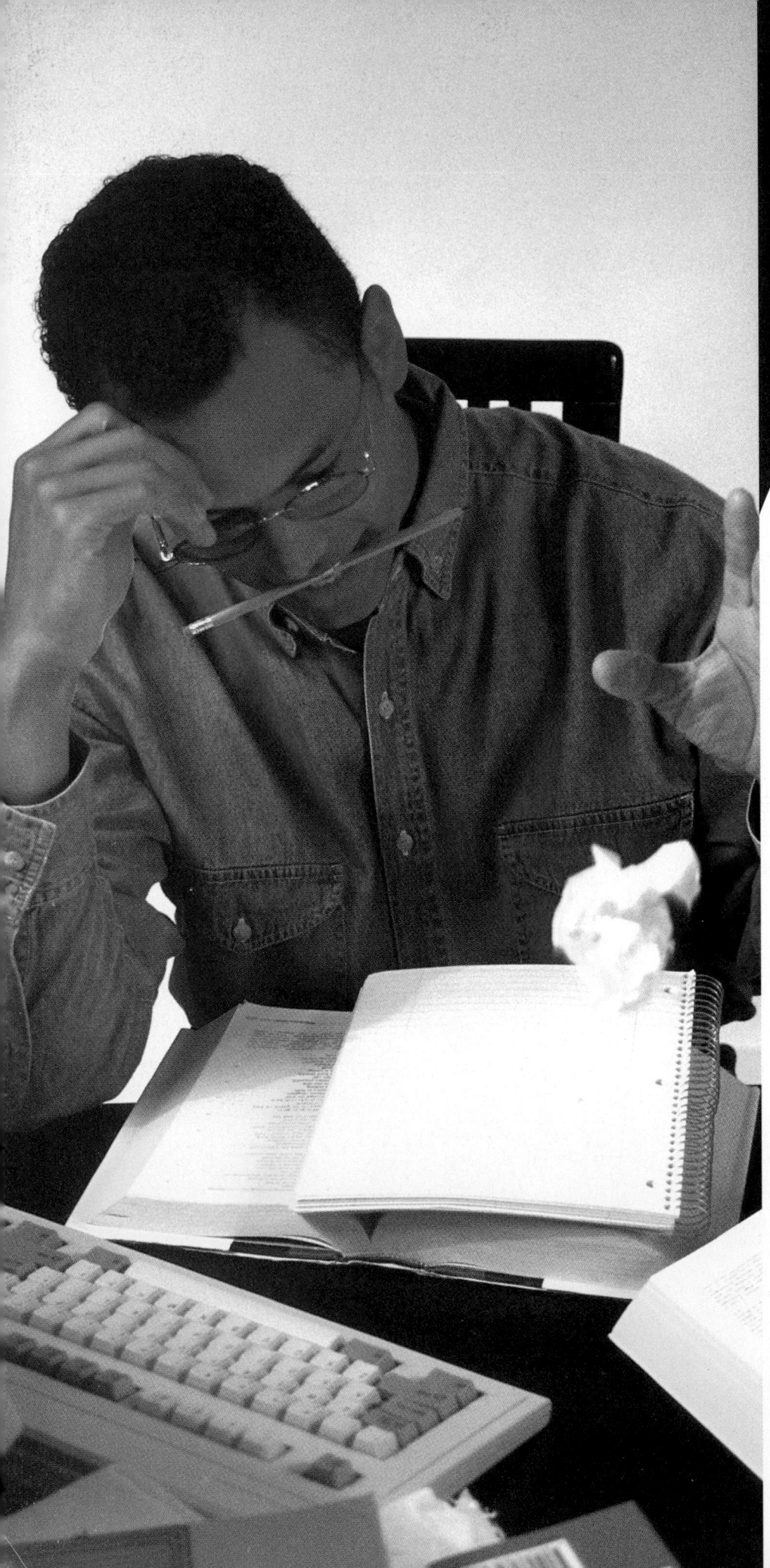

CHAPTER

12

CHAPTER OUTLINE

Stress and Health

PROLOGUE

N o one's life is free of stress. Regardless of how sensible, intelligent, or privileged you are, you will be challenged at times by frustrations, losses, changes, and conflicts. Stress comes from negative events, such as failing a college course, but stress is part of many positive events, too, such as starting a new job or having a baby. Stress is as inescapable as death and taxes.

A certain amount of stress is probably healthy—it energizes us and challenges us to grow. But stress is generally experienced as an uncomfortable, unhealthy force that most of us would be happier without. If you have experienced the death of a loved one or a divorce, you have firsthand knowledge of the emotions that such stress can bring. But don't forget that the psychological part of you exists in the biological part of you, and that what affects your "mind" also affects your body (McEwen, 1998). Consider the following landmark studies.

Bengt Arnetz of Harvard University (Arnetz & others, 1987) conducted a study of the effects of psychological stress on the body's ability to fight disease. Arnetz studied a large group of Swedish women who had lost their jobs and had remained unemployed for nine months. Compared with women with secure jobs, women who had lost their jobs had white blood cells that were less reactive to infections. Similarly, Janice Kiecolt-Glaser and colleagues (1987) of Ohio State University compared the immune system functioning of married and divorced women. The immune systems of recently divorced women functioned less well than married women, but with gradual improvements occurring over the first year after divorce. Within the group of married women, furthermore, immune functioning was poorest for those women with the unhappiest marriages. These findings may explain why disease and death rates are higher for recently divorced and unhappily married persons than for happily married persons (Kiecolt-Glaser & others, 1987).

In the few years since these remarkable studies were conducted, many other studies have confirmed their basic findings (summarized by Cohen, 1996, and Weisse, 1992). These studies offer strong evidence for the intimate relationship between our psychological lives and our physical health. It now seems clear that psychological stressors can diminish the body's ability to fight disease.

If stress is inevitable, and if too much stress is a threat to our psychological and physical well-being, then *coping* well with stress is of paramount importance. A healthy and happy person is someone who can enjoy the good times and cope with the bad. Sometimes we can cope with stress by removing it—by changing jobs or filing a complaint against a sexually harassing boss. But we cannot remove all the stress from our lives and will have to cope with some of it. Generally, we are better able to cope with the kinds of stress that we have had previous experience with and that we can control somewhat. Good social support also improves our ability to cope with stress. Simply disclosing our feelings to friends (or to a psychotherapist) has been shown to improve immune system functioning and reduce need for medical care (Pennebaker, Colder, & Sharp, 1990; Richards, Beal, Seagal, & Pennebaker, 2000). But there will be times when we cope ineffectively with stress. The trick, of course, is to cope as effectively as possible and not worry too much about the rest.

KEY TERMS

◗ STRESS: CHALLENGES TO COPING

As we noted in chapter 1, one of the goals of psychology is to *influence* your psychological functioning in beneficial ways. The specialty field of **health psychology** seeks to improve the well-being of your body as well. In this section, we will address perhaps the key factor that must be understood if psychology is to improve our health and happiness—stress. **Stress** can be thought of as any event that strains or exceeds an individual's ability to cope (Lazarus, 1999). The goal of this discussion of stress is to provide you with a new perspective on both stress and your health.

health psychology
The field of psychology that uses psychological principles to encourage healthy lifestyles and to minimize the impact of physical illness.

stress
Any event or circumstance that strains or exceeds an individual's ability to cope.

Sources of Stress

We need to begin our discussion of stress by looking at its causes. Most sources of stress are obvious to us all—they rip and tear at our lives—but other sources of stress are quite surprising. Knowing what causes stress is the first step in understanding and coping with it. The major sources of stress include the following factors.

Frustration

When we are not able to satisfy a motive, **frustration** results. You see frustration in the face of a child who cannot reach the toy he's dropped or in the exasperation of the college senior who finds that she cannot register for the one class that she needs to graduate. When frustrations are serious, as in the case of the woman who has been denied a deserved and hoped for promotion, or when they are prolonged, as when individuals living in poverty cannot obtain proper food or medical care, they can be a major source of stress.

Frustration results when we are unable to satisfy a motive.

Conflict

Conflict is closely related to the concept of frustration. **Conflict** occurs when two or more motives cannot be satisfied because they interfere with one another. Suppose you have been invited to spend a week skiing with friends, and then your car breaks down. You check your budget and find that you can afford to either fix your car *or* go skiing—that is a conflict. Psychologists use the terms *approach* and *avoidance* in discussing conflicts. In this sense, we "approach"

frustration
The result of being unable to satisfy a motive.

conflict
The state in which two or more motives cannot be satisfied because they interfere with one another.

approach-approach conflict
Conflict in which the individual must choose between two positive goals of approximately equal value.

avoidance-avoidance conflict
Conflict in which the individual must choose between two negative outcomes of approximately equal value.

approach-avoidance conflict
Conflict in which achieving a positive goal will produce a negative outcome as well.

things that we want and "avoid" things that we do not want. There are four major kinds of conflicts involving approach and avoidance (Lewin, 1931; Miller, 1944):

1. *Approach-approach conflict.* In **approach-approach conflict,** the individual must choose between two positive goals of approximately equal value. Suppose that when you finish school you are fortunate enough to be offered two attractive jobs. Both seem to offer good working conditions, good prestige, and reasonable salary. If both jobs are so good, why do you feel so anxious? Why are you having stomachaches and trouble sleeping? Even though both goals are positive—you would be happy with either job—the choice between these two goals can be very stressful. This is an example of a hidden source of stress. Because everything looks so positive, it's often difficult to see that you are in a serious conflict. The choice between two colleges, two roommates, or two ways of spending the summer can be similarly stressful.

2. *Avoidance-avoidance conflict.* This type of conflict involves more obvious sources of stress. In **avoidance-avoidance conflict,** the individual must choose between two or more negative outcomes. The person with a toothache must choose between the pain of the tooth and the anticipated discomfort of going to the dentist.

3. *Approach-avoidance conflict.* **Approach-avoidance conflict** arises when obtaining a positive goal necessitates a negative outcome as well. A student who is accepted to college in another state will be in a stressful conflict if she knows that it will mean

Approach-Avoidance Conflict
www.mmhe.com/laheye1

being separated from her serious boyfriend, who works in his family's business in her hometown. Attending the college will have both positive and negative consequences, so she may experience considerable stress, especially as the time grows nearer for beginning school.

Notice that I said the student would especially experience stress *as the time grows nearer* for her to attend college. There is an important and interesting fact about approach-avoidance conflict behind that statement. As the positive and negative outcomes grow nearer (attending college and leaving the boyfriend, respectively), either in distance or time, the relative strength of the motives to approach and avoid them changes. This change has been described graphically in terms of the gradients of approach and avoidance. Notice in figure 12.1 that the strength of the motive to avoid the negative consequence of losing the boyfriend increases quickly (has a steep gradient) as distance (or time) from the goal decreases. The strength of the motive to approach the positive goal of attending college, on the other hand, increases slowly (has a gradual gradient). At any particular distance from the goal, the effective amount of motive to approach or avoid is the remainder when the motive to avoid is subtracted from the motive to approach.

At greater distances, there is a stronger motive to approach than avoid, so the net motive is to approach. At shorter distances, the motive to avoid is stronger than the motive to approach, so there is a net motive to avoid. Let's look at what this means in terms of our example.

The student who had been accepted to college began to experience a high level of stress about the time that the strength of the approach and avoidance motives were about equal. If the motives to approach and avoid were actually about equal in strength as diagrammed in figure 12.1, she might have even changed her mind and given up her admission to college as the time to attend came nearer and the net motive switched strongly in favor of avoidance. After turning down her admission, however, she would have again been at a great "distance" from college. She might again feel a motive to approach and wish she had not decided against going.

Have you ever found yourself in such a conflict? Did you find yourself going back and forth on a decision? If so, you have had a very common human experience. The actual outcome of such a conflict depends on many factors, particularly the relative strength of the two motives.

Researcher Seymour Epstein has vividly demonstrated the stressfulness of approach-avoidance conflicts in his studies of parachute jumpers (Epstein, 1982). Epstein views parachute jumping as an approach-avoidance conflict because the jump entails both dangerous risks and exhilarating thrills. In his research, inexperienced jumpers were rigged with devices to measure the amount of sympathetic autonomic arousal by monitoring changes in skin sweat. As shown in figure 12.2, the

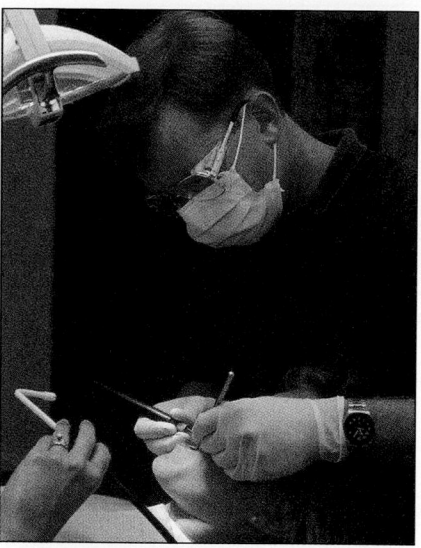

In an avoidance-avoidance conflict, the individual must choose between two or more negative outcomes, such as the pain of the tooth or the expected discomfort of going to the dentist.

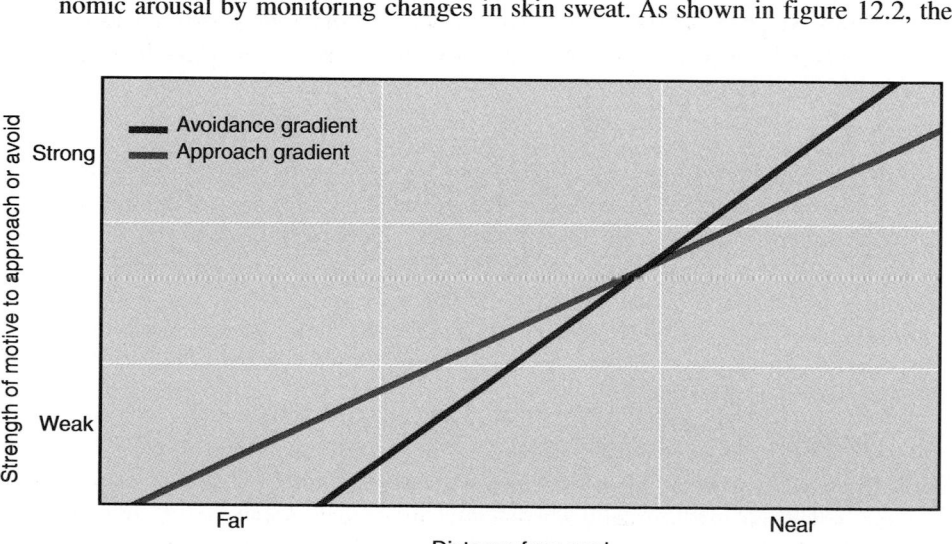

FIGURE 12.1

Gradients of approach and avoidance in an approach-avoidance conflict.

FIGURE 12.2

The amount of sympathetic autonomic arousal (as measured by changes in the electrical conductance of the skin caused by changes in skin sweat) in inexperienced parachutists at different "distances" from the approach-avoidance goal of jumping.

Source: Data from S. Epstein and W. D. Fenz, "Steepness of Approach and Avoidance Gradients in Humans as a Function of Experience: Theory and Experiment," *Journal of Experimental Psychology,* 70:1–12, 1965. Copyright 1965 by the American Psychological Association.

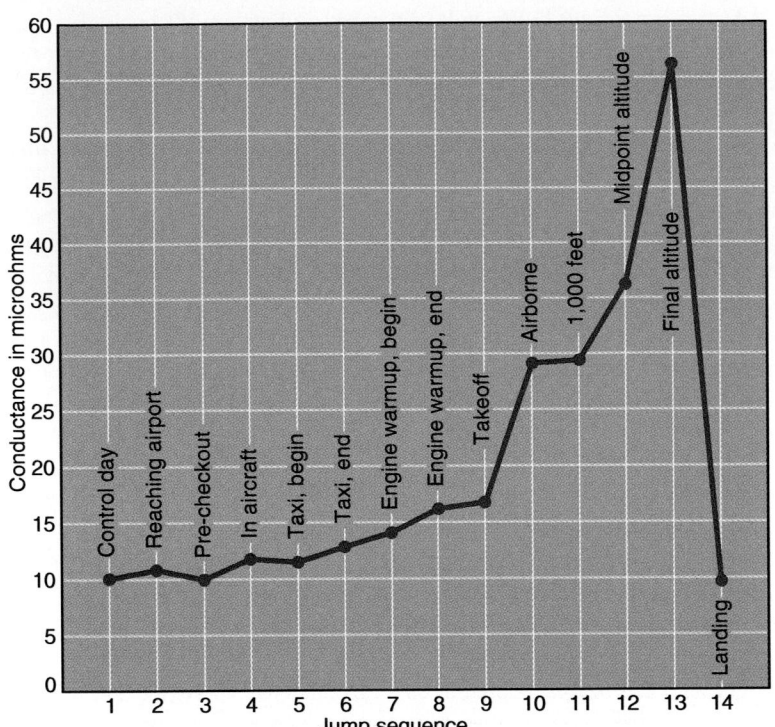

multiple approach-avoidance conflict
Conflict that requires the individual to choose between two alternatives, each of which contains both positive and negative consequences.

pressure
Stress that arises from the threat of negative events.

life events
Psychologically significant events that occur in a person's life, such as divorce, childbirth, or change in employment.

autonomic reaction of the jumpers mounted dramatically to a peak at the moment of the jump, then returned to normal levels immediately after they landed. Although few of us face such obvious approach-avoidance conflicts, the more subtle conflicts in our lives affect us in similar ways.

4. *Multiple approach-avoidance conflict.* Sometimes the conflicts that we face are complex combinations of approach and avoidance conflicts. A **multiple approach-avoidance conflict** requires the individual to choose between alternatives that contain both positive and negative consequences. Imagine that you are a promising high school athlete and you have been offered athletic scholarships to two colleges. One is from a strong school that won its conference championship in basketball last season, but you strongly dislike the coach and several of the players on the team. The other is from a weaker school that has had an embarrassing record of performance in recent years, but you like the coach and players. What do you do? Do you go to the stronger college, where there are people you do not like, or do you go to the weaker school, where you like the people with whom you would be playing? This is a multiple approach-avoidance conflict because both choices involve both positive and negative outcomes.

Pressure

Does the pressure of working for good grades ever get to you? If you have been employed, was it a high-pressure job? The term **pressure** is used to describe the stress that arises from threats of negative events. In school, there is always the possibility that you will not perform well and you will fail. Some jobs are loaded with possibilities for making a mess of things and getting fired. Some unhappy marriages are sources of pressure because one spouse always seems to displease the other, no matter how hard he or she tries to avoid it. The pressure of trying to avoid these negative events can sometimes be more stressful than the negative events themselves.

Life Events

Major **life events** create stress because they require adjustment and coping. Interestingly, the major events are often stressful whether they are negative changes, such as divorce, or positive changes, such as marriage.

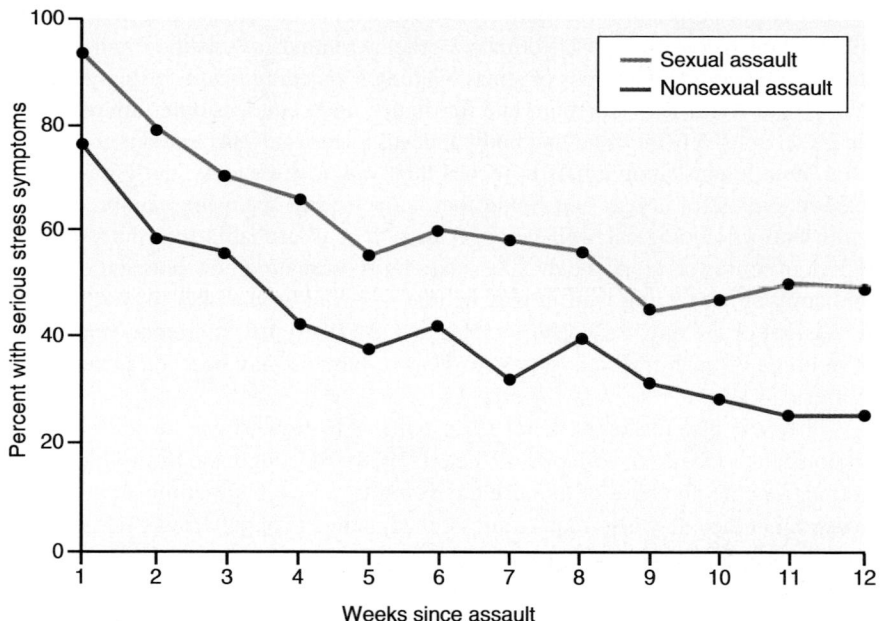

FIGURE 12.3
The percentage of women who experience serious levels of stress symptoms following the traumatic stress of assault is very high one month after the assault but declines gradually over the first year. Many women still show serious levels of stress symptoms a year after being assaulted, particularly if the assault was sexual (Foa & Riggs, 1995).

It is not surprising that negative life events can be an important source of stress: The death of a family member, learning that one has a life-threatening illness, being physically assaulted, the loss of a job, and other similar negative events are potent sources of stress (Zisook & Shucter, 1991). Consider the tragic example of the bombing of the Federal Building in Oklahoma City in 1995. The bombing killed 148 adults and 19 children. Seven weeks after the bombing, the children and teenagers in the city's public school still reported very high levels of anxiety and worries about their safety and the safety of family members. Not surprisingly, the children who had lost a parent or relative reported the highest levels of worry and anxiety (Pfefferbaum & others, 1999).

The major life events that are most common in contemporary life are such events as the loss of a job, being in an automobile accident, being the victim of a crime, being sexually assaulted, and witnessing violence. Many studies document that these events are highly stressful (Brewin, Andrews, Rose, & Kirk, 1999; Kendall-Tackett, Williams, & Finkelhor, 1993; Koren, Arnon, & Klein, 1999). For example, Edna Foa and David Riggs (1995) of the Medical College of Pennsylvania interviewed a group of women who were the victims of assault. They asked the women if they were experiencing high levels of irritability and anxiety, upsetting memories or dreams about the assault, and distressing flashbacks in which they had the illusion of being assaulted again. As shown in figure 12.3, the great majority of women experienced high levels of such stress symptoms one month after the assault, with the percentage declining gradually over the course of the first year. Overall, it is clear that being a victim of sexual assault results in more severe stress reactions than other kinds of physical assault. Over 40 percent of the women in this study who had been sexually assaulted still experienced serious levels of post-traumatic stress symptoms a year after the sexual assault.

Natural disasters also can be potently stressful negative life events. Paul and Gerald Adams (1984) showed that the 1980 Mount Saint Helens volcanic eruption was extremely stressful to the residents of nearby Othello, Washington. Compared with the preceding year, the residents of Othello made 90 percent more emergency room visits and were diagnosed by the town's physicians and mental health workers as having 200 percent more stress-related physical illnesses and psychological disorders, and the town police responded to 45 percent more reports of family violence. The number of deaths in Othello increased by 19 percent. Similar effects have been reported for persons who were in the direct path of hurricanes, earthquakes, and other life-threatening natural disasters (Asarnow & others, 1999; Escobar, Canino, Rubio-Stipec, & Bravo, 1992; La Greca, Silverman, & Wasserstein, 1998).

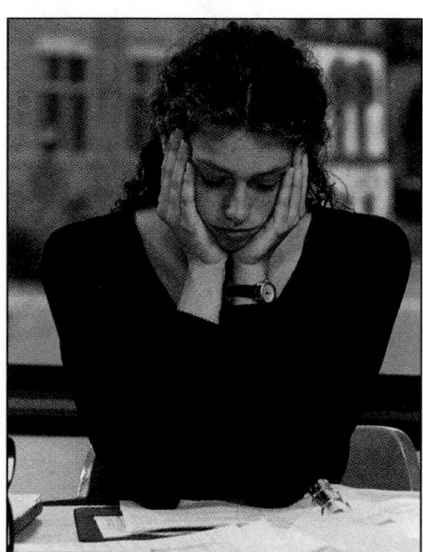

The term *pressure* is used to describe the stress that arises from threats, such as the possibility of poor performance on an exam.

It is not surprising that major negative events are stressful, but Richard Lazarus (1982) of the University of California at Berkeley reminds us that the small *hassles* of daily life are also important sources of stress. Getting a speeding ticket, losing your sunglasses, having your friend arrive an hour late for dinner, and countless other microscopic irritants can grate abrasively on mind and body. Indeed, Lazarus (1984) asked a group of 100 educated, middle-class individuals to record their major life events, daily hassles, and daily positive events for a year and found that daily hassles were the best predictors of both health and psychological well-being. Although it is probable that daily hassles are an important source of stress, we must be cautious in estimating how potent they are. If we are not happy or not feeling well, it may be that we would remember to write down more of the hassles of the day, or indeed, would be more likely to experience events like a slow drive home through traffic as a hassle. That is, hassles may be *both* a cause and a result of stress.

There is also reason to believe that *positive life events* can be stressful under some circumstances (Sarason, Johnson, & Siegel, 1978). Marriage, the birth of a child, job promotion, and the purchase of a house are examples of events that most people think of as positive, but they may also require stressful adjustments in patterns of living. Hence, positive life changes can be another source of stress of which we are typically unaware.

One lesson from these studies of life events is to space out your life changes when you can (Lloyd, Alexander, Rice, & Greenfield, 1980). Try not to graduate from college, move to a new city, take a new job, buy a new house, get married, and have a baby all in one year. If you do, don't be surprised if you are moody, have stomachaches, and have more colds.

Stress Reactions

Now that we have looked at the causes of stress, let's examine our reactions to it. When we are under stress, we feel it—we *react* to it. To fully benefit from the lessons that recent psychological and medical research has taught us about stress reactions, we must understand two important insights about stress:

1. First, we react to stress *as a whole*. That is, stress usually produces *both* psychological and physiological reactions—not one or the other, but both. If we remember from chapter 2 that several key aspects of the nervous system—the hypothalamus and the autonomic nervous system—control key aspects of both psychological functioning (emotions and motives) *and* body functioning, including the endocrine glands, this concept is easier to understand. It is through these joint systems that stress affects both our physical and psychological selves.

2. Second, our psychological and bodily reactions to stress are highly similar, whether the stress is physical or psychological. Although each source of stress evokes coping reactions that are specific to it, a *general* reaction to all types of stress also occurs, based largely on the interlinked responses of the hypothalamus, the sympathetic division of the autonomic nervous system, and the adrenal glands. This rather astonishing fact is a key to the modern field of health psychology, which we will discuss throughout this chapter.

The General Adaptation Syndrome

Let's look more closely at this general reaction to stress. Canadian medical researcher Hans Selye first gave us the insight more than 50 years ago that the body reacts in much the same general way to any threat, whether the threat is in the form of an infection, an injury, or a psychological stress. Regardless of the source of the stress, the body mobilizes its defenses to ward off the threat in a pattern referred to by Selye as the **general adaptation syndrome (GAS).** Three stages can be distinguished in this syndrome (see fig. 12.4):

1. *Alarm reaction.* As shown in figure 12.5, the body's initial response to threat or other stress is to mobilize its stored resources. The sympathetic division of the autonomic

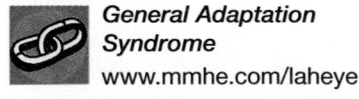

General Adaptation Syndrome
www.mmhe.com/laheye1

general adaptation syndrome (GAS)
According to Selye, the mobilization of the body to ward off threats, characterized by a three-stage pattern of the alarm reaction, the resistance stage, and the exhaustion stage.

FIGURE 12.4

Changes in resistance to stress during the three stages of the general adaptation syndrome. Note that a second stress produces a more rapid dissipation of resistance.
Source: Data from H. Selye, *The Stress of Life.* Copyright © 1976 McGraw-Hill Book Company.

nervous system increases heart rate and blood pressure, diverts blood away from digestion and into the skeletal muscles, increases perspiration, and in other ways prepares the body for a physical struggle. The endocrine glands pump epinephrine and other hormones into the bloodstream that aid the actions of the autonomic nervous system and increase levels of blood sugar. This is sometimes referred to as the *fight-or-flight* reaction, as it prepares the body to either fight with the source of stress or run away from it.

When the stress is intense or prolonged, these body changes give rise to conscious feelings of general muscle tension, stomachaches, headaches, and other feelings of "sickness" (Maier & Watkins, 1998). In the early stages of the general adaptation syndrome, it's often difficult to distinguish between the feelings associated with catching a cold, being under psychological stress, or even falling in love. Because anything that causes an alarm reaction produces essentially the same response from the body, the differences are often relatively subtle.

During the alarm reaction stage, the rapid mobilization of resources leaves the individual temporarily less resistant to the stress than originally. This state of affairs is quickly changed as the next stage is entered.

2. *Resistance stage.* During the second stage of the GAS, the body's resources have been fully mobilized, and resistance to the stress is high. This resistance is costly in terms of resources, however. If new stress (psychological or physical) is encountered, the body is less able to deal with it. In this way, psychological stress can leave the person more vulnerable to physical stress (disease), and vice versa. Moreover, if the stress continues, the individual's resources will eventually become depleted, leading to the third stage of the GAS.

3. *Exhaustion stage.* If the stress continues, the individual's resources may become exhausted, and resistance to the stress is lowered. In cases of prolonged exposure to severe physical stress (such as intense cold), death can occur during the exhaustion stage. Psychological stress is rarely able to precipitate death, but it can severely disrupt body functioning (Selye, 1976).

Notice in figure 12.4 that, if a second stressor is encountered when the individual has already entered the GAS, the progress toward exhaustion is much more rapid. Keep in mind two additional points as you think about the GAS. First, not all stressors overwhelm and exhaust the body; obviously, we cope effectively with most stress. Second, emotional and other psychological reactions to stress follow roughly the same GAS pattern, sometimes resulting in "emotional exhaustion" when coping fails.

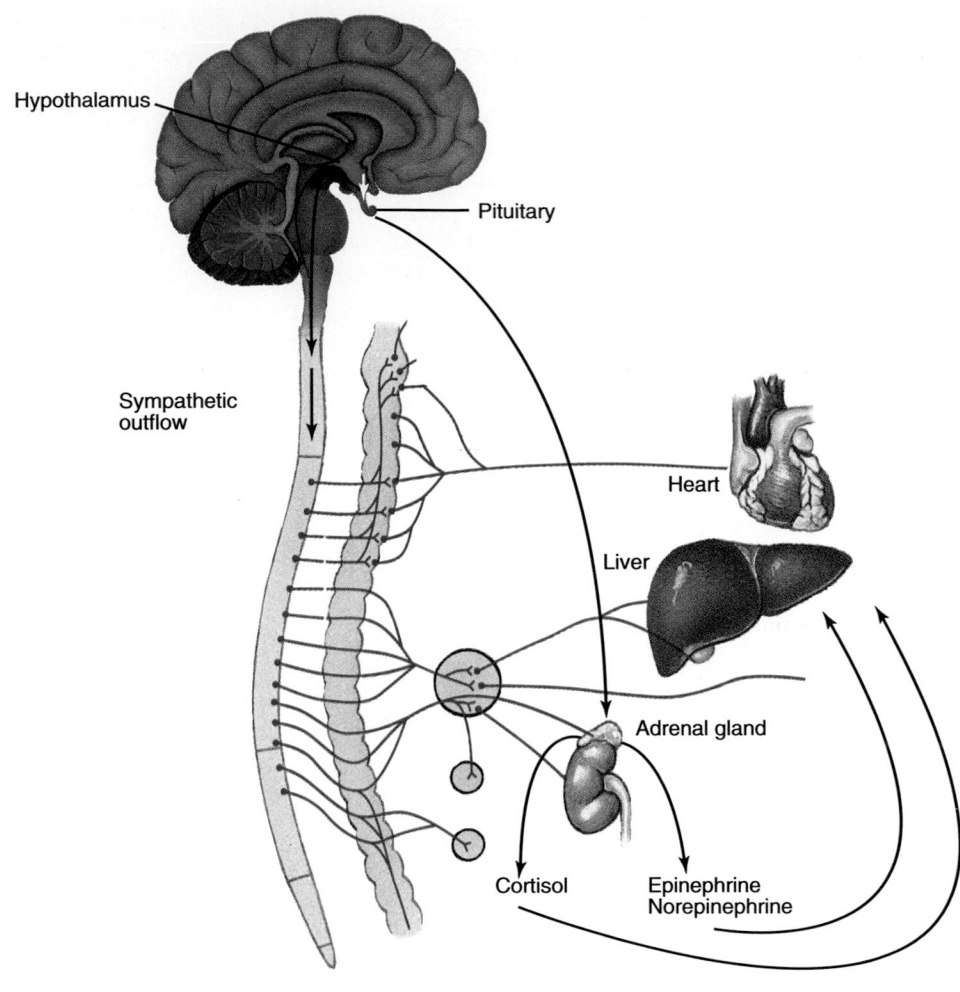

FIGURE 12.5

The body mobilizes its resources for "fight-or-flight" in the general adaptation syndrome in response to stress.

Hypothalamus

Pituitary

Sympathetic outflow

Heart

Liver

Adrenal gland

Cortisol

Epinephrine
Norepinephrine

Modern-day stressors, such as preparing forms for tax deadlines, call for all of the body's reactions of the general adaptation syndrome. Although the GAS is a lifesaver in emergencies, it can be life-threatening if stress is prolonged.

Healthy and Unhealthy Aspects of the GAS.   As Selye (1976) helped us see, the general adaptation syndrome is the body's protective response to dangers. Without the GAS, we humans would be very frail creatures, indeed. Then the body's complex reaction to stress—the GAS—is a blessing, right? Unquestionably, but it is a very mixed blessing. The GAS can be our best defense at times but our own worst enemy at other times.

The GAS does its best work during emergencies. Whether suddenly exposed to a deadly virus or being lost on a freezing ski trail, we need our bodies to respond with an alarm reaction to such emergencies. Our physical ability to endure such threats is enhanced for a while by the GAS.

Even our ability to cope behaviorally is helped by the GAS at times. I once nearly stepped on a water moccasin, and my body responded with a full-blown GAS alarm reaction. My autonomic nervous system went into screaming sympathetic arousal and produced a multitude of changes in my body that prepared me to respond behaviorally to the snake. For purposes of simplicity let's look only at changes in my cardiac system during the moments that followed. As we know from our discussion of these topics in chapter 2, sympathetic arousal caused my adrenal glands to pump epinephrine, norepinephrine, and other stress hormones into my bloodstream. These, in turn, increased my blood pressure and caused my blood to create substances that make the blood clot faster. My heart beat faster, rushing oxygen to my muscles, and blood flow was diverted from my liver and digestive organs to the muscles in my legs and arms. Those physiological changes that we call the alarm phase of the GAS were very welcome indeed as I jumped, turned tail, and ran from the water moccasin. My legs were supplied with the necessary oxygen to run to the next county, and I didn't mind one bit that my lunch was never digested properly. Because blood flow to my liver was diminished during the GAS, it was not filtered as usual and my cholesterol levels probably rose, but I didn't mind that, either. And, if I had fallen and cut my knee, I would have been glad that hormones had prepared my blood to clot quickly.

Most of the stressors that we face in contemporary society, however, are not snakes, bears, or avalanches. More often, they are the day-to-day stresses of school, work, and families. Remember, however, that the body's reaction is much the same regardless of the source of stress. As a result, the GAS is not only unnecessary for some stressors; it can be dangerous if it is prolonged.

Take the example of preparing your income taxes—an annoying stress, but not one requiring speedy legs, high blood pressure, or fast-clotting blood. Nonetheless, a group of accountants was given repeated blood tests for several months and found to have normal levels of blood-clotting factors and cholesterol, until the April 15 deadline for filing tax returns grew near; then their cholesterol and clotting factors shot up (Friedman & Rosenman, 1974). Unfortunately, elevated levels of blood pressure, cholesterol, and blood-clotting factors are a potentially deadly combination because they cause the formation of the "clots" of cholesterol inside arteries, called *plaque,* that clog and harden blood vessels. When the affected blood vessels are those that supply the heart muscles with oxygen, a heart attack can result. Since the time of this original study, many other studies have been conducted that suggest that many kinds of stressful life events affect blood clotting, blood pressure, and other aspects of the functioning of the heart that increase the risk of heart attack (Benschop & others, 1998; Kamarck & Jennings, 1991). Thus, although the GAS is a lifesaver in the face of emergencies, the GAS can paradoxically affect the cardiac system in ways that can be quite dangerous to our hearts.

Stress, the GAS, and the Immune System.   As we saw in the prologue to this chapter, another negative aspect of stress is that it decreases the effectiveness of the body's natural disease-fighting system, the **immune system.** Many studies now show that stress reduces the effectiveness of the immune system (Maier & Watkins, 1998). For example, Sheldon Cohen (Cohen, 1996) conducted an experiment on the effects of stress on immunity to the common cold virus. Volunteers completed questionnaires that measured stressful life events and were interviewed about a variety of health practices. Then they were exposed to live cold viruses and watched to see who developed a cold. Even after the effects of poor health practices (smoking, drinking, poor eating, poor exercising, and poor sleeping) were considered, life events were associated with less immunity to the cold virus. As shown in figure 12.6, more volunteers with above-average numbers of life events developed upper respiratory infections than volunteers with below-average numbers of life events. I am sorry to tell you that even the stress of studying for college examinations temporarily suppresses the immune system (Glaser & others, 1990).

Fortunately, something positive can be done about the relationship between stress and health. At the University of California at Los Angeles, researchers found that persons with medically treated cancer showed significant increases in immune system functioning as the result of a program that taught the patients to relax and cope with stress more effectively (Fawzi & others, 1990). Thus, it works both ways: Psychological factors such as stress can harm the functioning of the immune system, but psychological treatments such as stress management can restore immune system functioning in some cases.

Psychological Reactions to Stress

The physiological reactions to stress are usually accompanied by psychological reactions. These changes primarily involve emotions, motivations, and cognitions. Under stress, we feel anxious, depressed, and irritable. We experience changes in our appetite for food and may gain or lose large amounts of weight. Our interest in sex often decreases, but it may increase. Cognitive changes occur as well: We have difficulty concentrating, lose our ability to think clearly, and find that our thoughts keep returning to the source of the stress. We will have more to say on this topic in the next chapter, on abnormal behavior.

immune system
The complex body system of defenses to illness, such as white cells and natural killer cells of the blood.

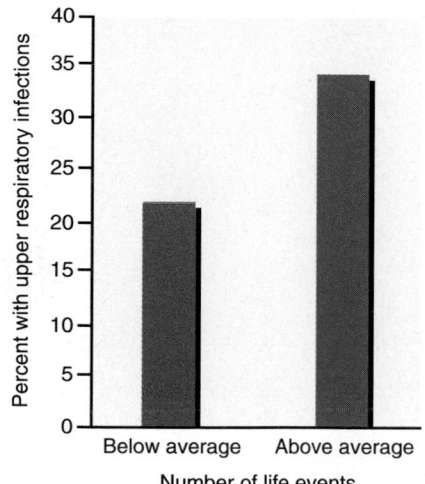

FIGURE 12.6

Volunteers with above-average numbers of stressful life events were more likely than volunteers with below-average numbers of life events to develop upper respiratory infections ("colds") after being experimentally exposed to live cold viruses.

● Review

A human life that was completely free of stress would be pretty dull, but excess stress can take a toll. Stress comes from a variety of sources in our lives. Frustration over not being able to satisfy a motive, conflicts arising from mutually incompatible motives, pressure, and unpleasant environmental conditions are all sources of stress. Similarly, life events, both negative ones such as the loss of employment and positive ones such as marriage, can be potent sources of stress. These sources of stress lead to stress reactions. People react to stress in both psychological and physical ways. Stress brings anxiety, anger, and depression but also body changes such as increased appetite, headaches, and difficulty sleeping. Under some circumstances, stress even leads to high blood pressure, increased blood cholesterol, and decreased efficiency of the body's immune system. The body tends to react to all stressors, psychological and physical ones, in much the same way. This nonspecific response to stress has been called the general adaptation syndrome.

● Check Your Learning

To be sure that you have learned the key points from the preceding section, cover the list of correct answers and try to answer each question. If you give an incorrect answer to any question, return to the page given next to the correct answer to see why your answer was not correct. Remember that these questions cover only some of the important information in this section; it is important that you make up your own questions to check your learning of other facts and concepts.

1. _____ can be thought of as any event that strains or exceeds an individual's ability to cope.

2. In _____, the individual must choose between two or more negative outcomes. For example, a person with a toothache must choose between the pain of the tooth and the expected discomfort of going to the dentist.

   a) approach-approach conflict   c) approach-avoidance conflict
   b) avoidance-avoidance conflict   d) simple conflict

3. A _____ is a psychologically significant event that occurs in a person's life; it can be positive, such as marriage, or negative, such as divorce.

   a) pressure   c) life event
   b) repression   d) milestone

4. When the body encounters a stress, such as the threat of injury, it mobilizes its defenses in a pattern referred to by Selye as the _____.

   a) alarm reaction   c) generalized stress response
   b) stress reaction   d) general adaptation syndrome

● Thinking Critically About Psychology

1. Using your knowledge of the stages of the general adaptation syndrome, what advice would you give someone who is experiencing a traumatic divorce or the breakup of a long-term relationship?

2. What are the major sources of stress in your life? Are they caused by things that you have much control over?

▶ FACTORS THAT INFLUENCE REACTIONS TO STRESS

More is involved in our reactions to stress than the stress itself. Much remains to be learned about these factors, but enough is currently known to outline some of the reasons for individual differences in reactions to stress. In addition to the sheer amount of stress, what determines how we will react to stress?

Prior Experience with the Stress

Stress reactions are generally less severe when the individual has had some prior experience with the stress event. For example, a soldier who is going into combat for the fourth time will usually be less stressed by it than a soldier facing combat for the first time. In a sense, prior exposure to a kind of stress often "inoculates" us to that stressor.

Predictability and Control

In general, stress events are less stressful when they are predictable than when they are not, and they are less stressful when the individual perceives that he or she can exert some degree of control over the stress. Let's look at several experiments that address the related issues of *predictability and control.*

Mild electric shocks are unpleasant stressful events that are often used in laboratory studies of stress. In one study, three groups of participants listened to a voice counting. At the count of 10, one group received an electric shock 95 percent of the time, the second group received a shock 50 percent of the time, and the third group received a shock only 5 percent of the time. A measure of sympathetic autonomic arousal (the amount of skin sweat) was taken during the counting. Which group do you think showed the strongest reaction? The shocks were least predictable for the group that received shocks only 5 percent of the time. Even though they received the fewest shocks, the higher degree of uncertainty resulted in greater sympathetic autonomic arousal than for the other two groups (Epstein & Roupenian, 1970). However, when the stress continues over long periods of time, predictable stress appears to become more stressful than unpredictable stress (Abbott, Schoen, & Badia, 1984).

A second line of research focuses on personal control over stress. In one study, two groups of participants participated in a difficult cognitive task in which errors were punished by electric shocks. One group could control this stressful situation by taking breaks whenever they wished, but the other group could take breaks only when told to do so. The amount of increase in blood pressure was significantly greater for the group that had no control over the stress (Hokanson, DeGood, Forrest, & Brittain, 1963).

The results of these studies are extremely important in the lesson they provide for personal stress management. Stress events in our daily lives that are not predictable or controllable are all the more stressful. It is highly important, therefore, that we seek ways to exert control over our stressors or to leave situations that result in uncontrollable stress. For example, working under a supervisor who often lashes out at you in unpredictable and uncontrollable ways may need to be dealt with by talking to your supervisor, by asking for assistance from your supervisor's boss, or by finding another job.

Social Support

The magnitude of reactions to stress is considerably less for individuals with good social support from close friends and family members than for individuals with inadequate social support. It's not yet completely clear how **social support** functions to buffer us against stress, but having someone to talk to, receive advice from, and be cheered and reassured by is an important factor determining our reactions to stress (Heller, Swindle, & Dusenbury,

Unpredictable events over which we have little control, such as when the fire alarm will call this firefighter into action, can be unpleasantly stressful.

social support
The role played by friends and relatives in providing advice, assistance, and someone in whom to confide private feelings.

1986; Kaniasty & Norris, 1995; Sutker, Uddo, Davis, & Ditta, 1995; Uchino, Cacioppo, & Kiecolt-Glaser, 1996).

Individuals with good social support are less likely to react to negative life events with depression, anxiety, and health problems. For example, persons who learn that they are infected with the human immunodeficiency virus, the virus that causes AIDS, react with less anxiety, despair, and depression if they have good social support (Dew, Ragni, & Nimorwicz, 1990). Similarly, children who have been sexually abused are less likely to experience anxiety, depression, and other symptoms of stress if they have good social support from their mothers (Kendall-Tackett & others, 1993). Likewise, a large study of elderly adults showed that men who experienced the death of a family member (who was not their spouse) were more likely to show an increase in depression if they did not have the social support of a wife or did not belong to a church or temple. Interestingly, a gender difference was found in this study. Elderly women were much less likely to become depressed than men after the death of a family member (other than a spouse), perhaps because women tend to have greater social support from friends than men (Siegel & Kuykendall, 1990).

One aspect of social support that has been studied experimentally is the opportunity to "get it off your chest." The common belief in our culture that the simple act of telling someone else about your troubles is good for you probably is correct (Kelly, 1999). A clever experiment conducted by James Pennebaker and Sandra Beall (1986) shows us the surprising extent to which this appears to be true. College student subjects participated in a study in which they spent 15 minutes on each of four consecutive nights writing to the experimenter about a traumatic event in their lives—both a description of the event itself and their feelings about it. For purposes of comparison, another group of students wrote about unimportant topics assigned by the experimenter. Writing about the traumatic events, such as the death of a family member, understandably caused the students to feel sad and to have brief elevations in blood pressure immediately after venting their feelings. However, over the next six months, the students who "got it off their chest" reported being ill less often and making fewer visits to the university health center. Apparently, it is good for your health to share your negative feelings with someone else. Therefore, having someone to confide in seems to be one of the important benefits of social support. There are risks associated with getting things off your chest, however. Sometimes revealing personal information has the effect of making us or other people look bad. It is wise to be selective in what and to whom you disclose (Kelly, 1999).

Under some circumstances, the best "social support" comes from a trained psychotherapist. We will have much more to say about this process in chapter 14, but it is important to note here that receiving psychotherapy is associated with improvements in physical as well as emotional health (Mumford, Schlesinger, & Glass, 1981).

The social support of friends and family helps buffer the effects of stress.

Person Variables in Reactions to Stress

We have seen that our reactions to stress are influenced by a number of factors: our prior experience with the stressor, the degree to which we can predict and control the stressor, and the availability of social support. But our personal characteristics—the so-called **person variables**—are also important in determining our responses to stress (Asarnow & others, 1999; Cui & Vaillant, 1996).

As we saw in chapter 11, many personality theorists believe that the best way to understand behavior is to acknowledge that we are influenced by both the situations in which we find ourselves *and* some key characteristics we have as individuals. This view, referred to as *person × situation interactionism,* was described on p. 339. In terms of stress, it means that our reactions are partly determined by the situation (the stressor, our social support, etc.) and partly determined by some of our personal characteristics (how we think about the stressor, how "reactive" our bodies are to stress, etc.).

person variables
All characteristics of an individual that are relatively enduring, such as ways of thinking, beliefs, or physiological reactivity to stress.

Cognitive Factors in Stress Reactions

An important reason that different people react differently to the same stressor is that people *think* about these events differently (Beck, 1976; Joiner & others, 1999; Lazarus, 1999; Tomaka & others, 1997). Some individuals appear more likely than others to interpret events in stress-provoking ways. For example, suppose you are a graduate student in clinical psychology and your supervisor suggests a better way to help a client. She says, "You're doing very well with this client, but a better way to help him with his fear of automobiles might be to . . ." and she proceeds to spell out her recommendations. Some individuals would be likely to interpret her statement as a combination of a nice compliment and a helpful bit of advice from a master therapist. Other individuals would interpret the same statement as a criticism of how they are doing as a student of therapy and expect to be dismissed from the program. As we have noted before, the interpretation of the event determines its stressfulness.

Emotional and Personality Characteristics in Stress Reactions

In addition to cognitive factors, differences among individuals in their characteristic emotions and personalities prior to stress influence their reactions to stress. For example, children and teenagers who tend to be more anxious prior to earthquakes, hurricanes, and other stressful events are more likely to react to the stressor with increased fears and worries (Asarnow & others, 1999; LaGreca & others, 1998). Similarly, military recruits who were more insecure and often sought reassurance from others before the stressor of basic training were more likely to be depressed afterwards (Joiner & Schmidt, 1998). Thus, the effects of stress can only be understood in terms of a person $\times$ situation interaction. Stress (a situation variable) influences people with different cognitive and emotional characteristics before the stressor (person variables) in different ways.

A personality characteristic that appears to be important in influencing the health consequences of stress has been termed the **Type A personality.** Some people simply react better than others to the stress of our pressured, competitive world. Have you ever watched a group of people play video games? For some people, it is a pleasant diversion, whereas for others it is a matter of life-or-death competition. A group of health psychologists watched subjects play a video game and took measures of the activity of their cardiovascular systems. Some subjects reacted to the game with large increases in heart rate, blood pressure, and cholesterol (Jorgensen, Nash, Lasser, Hymowitz, & Langer, 1988). What is going on here? What kind of personality reacts even to trivial competitive stress with health-threatening sympathetic arousal?

Type A personality
The pattern of behavior characterized most by intense competitiveness, hostility, overwork, and a sense of time urgency.

The classic work on Type A personality was done by Meyer Friedman and Ray Rosenman (1974), two physicians who specialize in heart disease. They were observant enough to look beyond their medical tests to see that many of their heart disease patients, particularly younger men aged 30 to 60, were often of the "same type" behaviorally. They were hard-driving, impatient, hostile individuals who rarely slowed down to smell the roses. This pattern of behavior they identified as *Type A personality.* The following characteristics more specifically describe the Type A personality (Diamond, 1982; Friedman & Rosenman, 1974; Matthews, 1982):

1. Highly competitive, hard-driving, and ambitious in work, sports, and games
2. Works hurriedly, always rushing, has a sense of "time urgency," and often does two things at once
3. Workaholic, takes little time off for relaxation or vacation
4. Speaks loudly or "explosively"
5. Perfectionistic and demanding
6. Hostile, aggressive, and frequently angry with others.

Highly motivated achievers who compete in an aggressive, hostile manner may have Type A personality, which can lead to heart disease.

If this description sounds like you, keep in mind that there is a little Type A behavior in most of us, and you should be concerned only if it's excessive.

Of all the components of the Type A behavior pattern, the most important one appears to be a *particular kind of hostility*. Individuals who are hostile in the sense of reacting to frustration with verbal aggression (yelling, criticizing, insulting) or even physical aggression seem to be at slightly higher risk for coronary heart disease, but individuals who are hostile in the sense of being chronically suspicious and resentful are not (Friedman & Booth-Kewley, 1987; Miller & others, 1996; Siegman, Dembroski, & Ringel, 1987; Weidner, Sexton, McLellarn, Connor, & Matarazzo, 1987).

Why is Type A behavior associated with increased risk of coronary heart disease? Type A behavior appears to be indirectly linked to heart disease through two major risk factors: high blood pressure and cholesterol (Matthews, 1982; Weidner & others, 1987). One theory suggests that this is because Type A individuals react physiologically more to stress than other individuals. Researchers at Duke University Medical Center (Williams & others, 1982) classified a group of undergraduate males as Type A or normal. Both groups were asked to subtract 13 from 7,683, then subtract 13 from the answer, and so on, with a prize being given to the person with the fastest subtraction rate. In this competitive situation, the Type A individuals showed greater increases in blood flow to the skeletal muscles and in the amount of epinephrine and norepinephrine in the blood. Because these changes are associated with the formation of cholesterol plaques, as we have already seen in discussing the GAS, the greater responsiveness of the Type A individuals may indirectly lead to hardening of the arteries of the heart. Similarly, Type A individuals also have been shown to respond to stress with greater increases in blood pressure—another key risk factor for coronary disease (Haynes, Feinleib, & Kannel, 1980; Matthews, 1982; Williams & others, 1982).

● Review

The magnitude of the emotional, cognitive, and physical toll that stress takes on us varies from individual to individual and from time to time for the same individual. The factors that seem to be related to the magnitude of stress reactions are prior experience with the stress, age, predictability and control over the stress, and social support.

The degree to which we react to stress also varies according to our personal characteristics. Different people react differently to stress partly because of cognitive factors. In addition, some individuals seem to react calmly to the pressures of competitive life, but the so-called Type A personality finds competitive situations to be highly stressful. The hostility that often accompanies Type A behavior seems to be a factor in the degree of wear and tear on the body, particularly cardiovascular disease.

● Check Your Learning

To be sure that you have learned the key points from the preceding section, cover the list of correct answers and try to answer each question. If you give an incorrect answer to any question, return to the page given next to the correct answer to see why your answer was not correct.

1. In general, stress events are _____ when they are predictable or controllable than when they are not.

   a) more stressful   b) less stressful

2. Having _____, or someone to talk to, receive advice from, and be cheered and reassured by, is an important factor determining our reactions to stress.

3. _____ refers to all characteristics of an individual that are relatively enduring, such as ways of thinking, beliefs, or physiological reactivity to stress.

   a) Identity   c) Individuality
   b) Person variables   d) Superego

4. A person who exhibits a pattern of behavior characterized by intense competitiveness,
   hostility, overwork, and a sense of time urgency would be identified as _____.

   a) abnormal   c) Type A personality
   b) Type B personality   d) high strung

● Thinking Critically About Psychology

1. Is there a negative aspect of your college life that could be eased by better social
   support?

2. How does our society's emphasis on monetary success and power influence the
   Type A personality?

◗ COPING WITH STRESS

An issue of utmost importance to psychologists who work to promote both mental and
physical health is that we are not all equally effective at coping with stress. What are the
best ways to cope?

Effective Coping

Effective methods of **coping** either remove the source of stress or control our reactions to it:

1. *Removing stress.* One effective way of dealing with stress is to remove the source of
   stress from our lives. If an employee holds a job that is stressful, discussions could
   be held with the employer that might lead to a reduction in the pressures of the job,
   or the employee could simply resign. If the stress stems from an unhappy marriage,
   either marriage counseling could be sought or the marriage could be ended. In a variety of ways, coping with stress can take the form of locating its source and eliminating it. Unfortunately, this is not always possible. It's not always feasible or
   appropriate to quit a job or leave a marriage, and some sources of stress, such as the
   death of a spouse, just cannot be removed.

2. *Cognitive* coping. Our cognitions are intimately linked to our reactions to stressful
   events. One effective method of coping, then, might be to change how we think
   about—or interpret—the events that push and shove our lives. For example, I know
   a musician who had a successful first record, but his second album was a flop—the
   critics panned it and the public didn't buy it. At first, he saw this as a sign that
   the first record was a fluke and that he had no real talent. As a result, the failure of the
   second album was a huge stress. However, a veteran musician convinced him that
   having an unsuccessful second album is a common "sophomore slump" among musicians who go on to be very successful. This conversation changed his interpretation
   of his unsuccessful album and allowed him to view it as a challenge to do better next
   time. Finding an interpretation that is realistic and minimizes the stress of the events
   of our lives is a key part of coping with stress (Taylor, 1999).

coping
Attempts by individuals to deal with the
source of stress and/or control their reactions
to it.

Psychologist Shelley Taylor and her colleagues (1998) have recently evaluated two cognitive strategies for coping. They evaluated a method that is widely endorsed in self-help books (imagining a positive outcome) and compared it with the cognitive strategy of imagining the steps involved in successful coping. Two groups of college students were randomly assigned to two groups at the beginning of the term. One group was asked to imagine themselves beaming with success when they received high marks in the class. The second group was asked to imagine all of the practical steps involved in getting a good grade (getting the book, reading assignments, studying in advance, etc.). The group that imagined the practical steps toward success studied more, felt less anxiety, and actually received higher grades (Taylor 1998). This suggests that practical planning is a useful strategy in some situations.

3. *Managing stress reactions.* When the source of stress cannot realistically be removed or changed, another effective option is to manage our psychological and physiological reactions to the stress. For example, an individual may decide to start a new business, knowing full well that the first year or two will be hectic. She would be unwilling, then, to remove the source of the stress (the new business) but could learn to control the reactions to the stress. One strategy might be to schedule as much time as possible for relaxing activities, such as aerobic exercise, hobbies, or time with friends. Another would be to seek special training from a psychologist in controlling the body reactions to stress by learning to deeply relax the large body muscles (relaxation training is discussed more fully in a later section of this chapter).

Happily, psychological counseling that encourages all three methods of effective coping has even been successful in changing the Type A behavior pattern. Some 20 studies have demonstrated marked improvement in the behavior pattern; more important, two of the studies followed the individuals for three years after treatment to determine whether there were actual improvements in cardiac health. It is encouraging that the treated patients showed a 50 percent reduction in heart attacks and deaths compared with Type A individuals who did not receive treatment (Nunes, Frank, & Kornfeld, 1987). We will look at some of the specific treatment procedures used to modify Type A behavior later in this chapter and at others in chapter 14.

Ineffective Coping

Unfortunately, many of our efforts to cope with stress are ineffective. They may provide temporary relief from the discomfort produced by stress but do little to provide a long-term solution and may even make matters worse. Three common, but ineffective, coping strategies are as follows:

1. *Withdrawal.* Sometimes we deal with stress by withdrawing from it. Many students encounter courses in college that are far more difficult than anything they had experienced in high school. Attempting to study difficult material can be highly stressful, and that stress can lead to a withdrawal from studying—by playing electronic games, talking on the telephone, partying, and the like. Similarly, a husband may ineffectively cope with the stress of an unhappy marriage by withdrawing to the refuge of a bar every day after work.

Notice that it is not *what* you do, but *how* and *why* you do it, that makes a coping strategy effective or ineffective. Spending your time playing electronic video games actually may be an effective coping strategy *if* you only do it for reasonable periods of time to relax. It becomes withdrawal if you use it excessively as a way to avoid the necessity for more effective coping (studying).

In this context, it is also important to recognize that there is a big difference between actually removing a source of stress and withdrawing from it. If you find that you have signed up for an extremely difficult course for which you are not prepared, dropping that class until you are ready to take it would be an effective way to *remove* the stress. However, simply not studying for the tests in that course because you have *withdrawn* to the refuge of long philosophical discussions with friends would obviously be an ineffective solution.

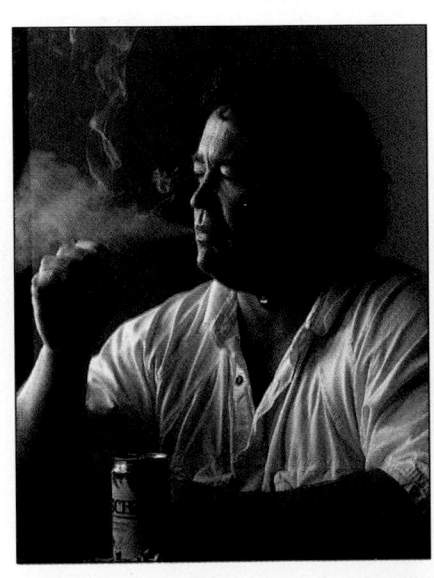

An ineffective method of coping with stress from an unhappy marriage is to withdraw to the refuge of a bar.

2. *Aggression.* As we discussed in chapter 9, a common reaction to frustration and other stressful situations is aggression. The woman who has tried unsuccessfully to create romantic interest in a man may suddenly become hostile toward him. The man who cannot get a screw to fit into a curtain rod may throw a temper tantrum and hurl the rod to the floor in disgust.

3. *Defense mechanisms.* According to Freud, one of the key functions of the ego is to "defend" the person from a buildup of uncomfortable tension. When something stressful occurs (such as frustration or embarrassment) or when conflict arises because the superego blocks an id desire, tension is created that must be discharged somehow. Freud believed that the ego possesses a small arsenal of **defense mechanisms** that are unconsciously used to discharge tension. When they are not overused, defense mechanisms can be a relatively harmless crutch to a healthy personality—all of us use them to some extent. Unfortunately, many individuals rely too heavily on defense mechanisms. The major defense mechanisms are as follows:

Displacement: When it's unsafe or inappropriate to express aggressive or sexual feelings toward the person who is creating stress (such as a boss who pressures you), that feeling can be directed toward someone safe (such as yelling at your friend when you are really angry with your boss).

Sublimation: Stressful conflicts over dangerous feelings or motives are reduced by converting the impulses into socially approved activities, such as schoolwork, literature, and sports.

Projection: One's own dangerous or unacceptable desires or emotions are seen not as one's own but as the desires or feelings of others. A person who has stressful conflicts about sex might perceive himself as having little sexual desire but might view other people as being "obsessed" with sex.

Reaction formation: Conflicts over dangerous motives or feelings are avoided by unconsciously transforming them into the opposite desire. A married man with strong desires for extramarital sex might start a campaign to rid his city of massage parlors and prostitutes. A woman who wishes her hateful mother would die might devote herself to finding ways to protect her mother's health.

Regression: Stress may be reduced by returning to an earlier pattern of behavior, such as a business executive who has a stomping, screaming temper tantrum when her company suffers a major setback.

Rationalization: Stress is reduced by "explaining it away" in ways that sound logical and socially acceptable. A man who is rejected by his lover may decide that he is glad because she had so many faults or because he really did not want to give up the single life.

Repression: Potentially stressful, unacceptable desires are kept out of consciousness without the person being consciously aware that the repression is occurring.

Denial: Upsetting or threatening thoughts and emotions related to stressful events are not allowed into conscious awareness. For example, a person who finds that she has high blood pressure during a routine medical checkup may never again think about that upsetting fact, even though her physician has urged her to change her habits of diet and exercise and take medication.

Intellectualization: The emotional nature of stressful events is lessened at times by reducing it to cold, intellectual logic. For example, the person who learns that he has lost a large sum of money in an overly risky investment may think about it in a detached way as a temporary debit in a successful lifelong program of investment, rather than as a painful financial mistake that should be avoided in the future through more careful planning.

Defense mechanisms can be effective in the short run in helping us feel better, but they inhibit long-term solutions to stress if they *distort reality* to a great extent. For example, suppose that a woman copes reasonably well with the stress of failing

Defense Mechanisms

www.mmhe.com/laheye1

defense mechanisms
According to Freud, the unrealistic strategies used by the ego to discharge tension.

"You keep insisting that this isn't happening, Edwards, but in my opinion you're mistaken. I really believe myself to be firing you."

a course in college by deciding that her instructor graded her test papers unfairly because she asks too many questions in class. If her instructor is actually fair and competent, she would be distorting reality by using the defense mechanism of rationalization. A simple change in study habits or test-taking strategies might make a big difference in her grades, but she will never see the need for change if she distorts reality through rationalization. The other defense mechanisms can be harmful in similar, reality-distorting ways.

● Review

Although some of us are exposed to more stress than others, we all face stressful events that require some form of coping. The most common sources of stress are frustration, the many forms of conflicts, pressure, and positive and negative life events. At times, we cope effectively with stress either by finding ways to remove the source of stress or by managing the stress reaction. At other times, however, we cope ineffectively through withdrawal, aggression, and defense mechanisms.

● Check Your Learning

To be sure that you have learned the key points from the preceding section, cover the list of correct answers and try to answer each question. If you give an incorrect answer to any question, return to the page given next to the correct answer to see why your answer was not correct.

1. The term _____ refers to attempts to deal with the source of the stress or control our reactions to it, or both.

   a) endurance
   b) strategize
   c) restructuring
   d) coping

2. Doing aerobic exercise to relax could be an effective coping strategy.

   a) True
   b) False

3. Spending most of your time playing video games as a way to avoid the stress of studying would be considered to be _____.

   a. cognitive coping
   b. stress management
   c) withdrawal
   d) removal

4. According to Freud, _____ are unrealistic strategies used by the ego to discharge tension, such as repression and denial.

   a) cognitive coping strategies
   b) withdrawal
   c) rationalizations
   d) defense mechanisms

● Thinking Critically About Psychology

1. What would you say are the main differences between effective and ineffective coping?
2. What kinds of help would you suggest to someone interested in finding more effective methods for coping with stress?

Correct Answers 1. d (p. 371), 2. a (p. 372), 3. c (p. 372), 4. d (p. 373).

HUMAN DIVERSITY

PSYCHOLOGY AND WOMEN'S HEALTH

Much still remains to be learned about the psychological factors that have an impact on women's health, but the National Institutes of Health has launched a large-scale effort to increase research on the health of women in 2000.

Many important health issues are unique to women (Clifford-Walton, 1998). Breast, ovarian, and cervical cancer; hysterectomy (surgical removal of the uterus); and menstrual dysfunction are concerns only of women, and osteoporosis (thinning of the bones), eating disorders, lupus, and rheumatoid arthritis are far more common in women than men. In addition, two-thirds of all surgery in the United States is performed on women, mostly because of the high rates of cesarean deliveries and hysterectomies. Women are less likely to have medical insurance than men and, when they are insured, their policies often do not cover essential preventive procedures such as Pap smears for early detection of cervical cancer (Taylor, 1999).

Women also have unique health concerns because they are often prescribed the hormone estrogen. Estrogen is contained in birth control pills and is prescribed for women who have reached menopause to replace the natural supply that has diminished. Birth control pills and estrogen replacement may increase the risk for some forms of cancer. In addition, although estrogen replacement appears to decrease the rate of heart disease, birth control pills may increase the risk for heart disease under some circumstances (Rodin & Ickovics, 1990).

In spite of these clear differences in the health concerns of women, women have been excluded from health research to a great extent in the past. This means that much of what has been learned in medical research may not apply to women. A decade ago, the National Institutes of Health mandated that women could no longer be excluded from research unless there is a strong reason. Although it took time for the new policy to affect research, there is now a greatly accelerated rate of research on the health and mental health of women.

The second reason that a focus on women's health is needed is that women are behaving more like men in recent years. The last century saw marked increases in women in risky behaviors that greatly increase the chance of illness, such as cigarette smoking, drug use, and excessive alcohol use. As a result, the death rates for men and women are growing more similar. Over the past 30 years, death due to lung cancer increased 85 percent in men but over 400 percent in women (Taylor, 1999).

Third, the equation relating health-related behaviors and illness is somewhat different for women than for men. For example, behaviors that create health risks for both women and men, such as cigarette smoking, excessive alcohol consumption, obesity, and high-fat diets are particularly dangerous for women who take birth control pills.

Another way in which the health behavior equation is different for women can be seen in the example of AIDS. Men can and do acquire the HIV virus that leads to AIDS—HIV—from intercourse with women, but it is more common for women to acquire the virus through either vaginal or anal intercourse. Whereas only 2 percent of men with AIDS acquired HIV through heterosexual intercourse, 31 percent of women with AIDS acquired HIV in this way. Thus, the risks for contracting HIV (and AIDS) from essentially the same behaviors are quite different for women and men (Rodin & Ickovics, 1990).

A third way in which the health behavior equation is different for women concerns the effects of employment. Women who are employed are generally healthier than women who are not, but women who are employed in demeaning, low-paying, and pressured jobs have much poorer health. Interestingly, women who have satisfying jobs, are married, and have children are the healthiest of all, in spite of the pressures involved in handling all of these roles (Waldron, 1991).

Gender is not the only sociocultural factor that plays a role in the health of women, of course. To understand the health behavior of women, we must also understand their ethnicity, sexual orientation, and other aspects of their sociocultural makeup (Gruskin, 1999). For example, African American women have lower rates of breast cancer than non-Hispanic white women, but, when African American women contract breast cancer, their survival rates are lower. Psychologist Beth Meyerowitz and her colleagues (1998) believe that ethnicity is related to survival from breast cancer because African American women tend to have fewer financial resources and have less access to quality health care and information about cancer. Sexual orientation also plays a role in women's health. Although lesbian women are at greatly reduced risk of contracting AIDS, they are more likely to have breast cancer. Having children reduces the risk of breast cancer and, although artificial insemination is on the rise, lesbian women are still less likely to become pregnant. In addition, lesbian women are less likely to have regular obstetric examinations and less likely to find cervical cancer early when it is most treatable. Each factor must be considered in attempting to find ways to improve the health behavior of women.

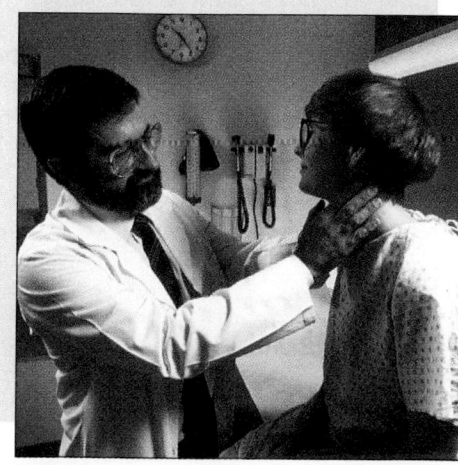

Women have different health concerns than men, but the medical profession is still dominated by men who are not properly trained to meet the needs of women.

◗ CHANGING HEALTH-RELATED BEHAVIOR PATTERNS

A major goal of health psychology is to *prevent* health problems by helping individuals modify behaviors that create health risks through strategies such as learning to relax, not smoking or abusing other substances, and exercising and eating properly (Winett, 1995).

Learning to Relax

progressive relaxation training
A method of learning to deeply relax the muscles of the body.

Is it easy for you to relax—really relax in a way that results in decreased sympathetic arousal? Relaxation is very difficult for a great many people. **Progressive relaxation training** teaches individuals to deeply relax their large body muscles. Although the method was first developed by a physician in the 1930s (Jacobsen, 1938), the use of a simplified version has been popularized primarily by psychologists (Rimm & Masters, 1979).

In progressive relaxation training, the individual is first taught to sense the difference between tense and relaxed muscles. Stop reading for a few seconds and tense the muscles in your right hand and arm as tightly as you can. Focus your attention on the tension, carefully noticing how it feels. Then release the tension, letting your hand and arm relax limply. Notice how your relaxed muscles feel. Now try tensing the muscles in your neck while leaving the muscles in your shoulders relaxed. Now relax your neck. Can you do it? Many people cannot at first, but progressive relaxation training teaches you how.

The therapist slowly takes the individual through all of the muscle groups, so that he or she becomes aware of how tension and relaxation feel. Over many sessions of practice, the individual becomes more able to achieve a very deep state of relaxation. As a result, progressive relaxation training has been found to be effective in the treatment of insomnia (sleep problems), tension headaches, migraine headaches, ulcers, general anxiety, asthma, and high blood pressure (Smyth, Soefer, Hurewitz, & Stone, 1999; Spiegler & Guevremont, 1998).

Eating Well and Exercising

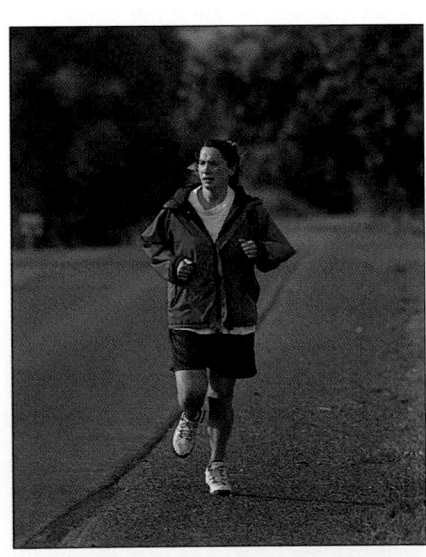

A routine of moderate exercise helps to promote good health.

Health psychologists are very much involved in encouraging a variety of other patterns of behavior that promote good health (Taylor, 1999). Marked reductions in heart attacks for vulnerable individuals result from weight reduction in overweight individuals, decreased salt intake for some individuals with high blood pressure, and moderate levels of regular exercise (Farquhar, 1979; Jenkins, 1988a, 1988b; Taylor, 1999). It is not easy to change one's pattern of eating and exercising; bad habits are difficult to break. Therefore, psychologists are often involved in the design and implementation of programs to change and maintain changes in eating and exercising.

Healthy Eating Habits

It is increasingly clear that diet plays an important role in our health. Eating excessive amounts of fatty red meats, eggs, and high-fat dairy products, for example, can lead to high levels of blood cholesterol in many individuals and contribute to hardening of the arteries and increased risk for heart attack and stroke. On the other hand, reducing blood cholesterol through diet and medication has been shown in a variety of studies to reduce the incidence and severity of coronary heart disease (Jeffrey, 1988; Taylor, 1986). Similarly, reducing the amount of salt that is ingested and controlling one's weight can have very beneficial effects on high blood pressure and coronary heart disease, and diet has been linked to some forms of cancer (Jeffrey, 1988; Taylor, 1986). In addition, many of us use enormous quantities of consciousness-altering drugs, usually without even being aware that we are taking "drugs." Our coffee contains the stimulant caffeine, cigarettes contain the stimulant nicotine, and alcohol is a powerful depressant drug. Millions of individuals who would never consider using "drugs" use, abuse, or are addicted to these drugs. Unfortunately, serious health risks are associated with the use of each of these substances.

What can be done to improve our eating patterns? One successful program blitzed the citizens of three California communities with ads advocating lower-fat diets through television, radio, newspapers, bus displays, billboards, and direct mailings in addition to one-on-one counseling in behavioral self-management skills (Meyer, Nash, McAlister, Maccoby, & Farquhar, 1980). A similar in-school program in Los Angeles found that teaching children who were at risk for chronic health problems the importance of low-fat diets produced significant changes in eating behavior (Marcus, Wheeler, Cullen, & Crane, 1987). It is difficult to change unhealthy eating behavior, but it is not impossible (Jeffrey, 1988).

Regular Aerobic Exercise

We all know that exercise is good for our health. But most of us would be surprised to see the large amount of evidence that links regular moderate aerobic exercise to good health (Jenkins, 1988a, 1988b). By moderate aerobic exercise, I mean at least 30 minutes of continuous exercise that raises the heart rate to 70 to 85 percent of maximum capacity at least four times each week (Taylor, 1986). Unless the individual has a preexisting medical problem that prohibits exercise, regular aerobic exercise has been shown to reduce high blood pressure, blood cholesterol levels, and the risk of coronary heart disease (Leon, 1983; Roy & Steptoe, 1991). Then why is it that so few of us exercise regularly? You know from my confessions in chapter 10 that my history of exercise is an irregular one. I have worked out three times this week, but last week I was "too busy" to exercise at all. Why do I—a person who values good health and decries hypocrisy—often fail to practice what I preach? The unfortunate fact is that I am not the exception but the rule. It has been estimated that only 21 percent of adults in the United States engage in regular aerobic exercise (White, Powell, Hogelin, Gentry, & Forman, 1987).

Part of the answer seems to be a lack of information. The number of Americans who exercise regularly increased by 50 percent between 1975 and 1980 (American Running and Fitness Association, 1981), probably mostly because of publicity concerning the health benefits. But the number of us who know about the health benefits of exercise and still don't exercise regularly is very high. The real problem is *adherence*. Far more of us begin exercise programs than stick with them. On the average, only half the individuals who begin a regular program of exercise are still at it only six months later (Dishman, 1982).

What, then, can a person do to help keep his or her commitment to a program of regular exercise? Psychologists are still actively working on this problem, but so far, it seems that social support from a friend who exercises with you, setting clear personal goals and providing reinforcement to yourself, and avoiding excessively strenuous exercise all help long-term adherence (Taylor, 1986). A clearer belief that regular exercise really will benefit *you* also seems to help, as individuals who believe that they should take charge of their own health and those who know they are at risk for coronary heart disease for other reasons are more likely to exercise regularly (Dishman, 1982). We all need to find a reason and a way to keep exercising.

● Review

Psychological methods have been successfully used in the prevention and treatment of medical problems. Methods have been developed to help people drink less alcohol, exercise regularly, stop smoking, lose excess weight, and make other behavioral changes that reduce the risk of heart attack and other serious diseases. Progressive relaxation training and other treatment techniques have also been successful in treating problems such as high blood pressure, headaches, epilepsy, and diabetes. The more that we are willing to apply the advances in understanding of illness from the field of health psychology to our lives, the more we will be able to prevent unnecessary disease and control the cost of health care.

● Check Your Learning

To be sure that you have learned the key points from the preceding section, cover the list of correct answers and try to answer each question. If you give an incorrect answer to any question, return to the page given next to the correct answer to see why your answer was not correct.

1. _____ refers to a method of learning to deeply relax the muscles of your body.

   a) Psychoanalysis   c) Aerobics
   b) Cognitive therapy   d) Progressive relaxation training

2. Good health is strongly related to:

   a) regular aerobic exercise   c) both a) and b)
   b) healthy eating habits   d) neither a) and b)

● Thinking Critically About Psychology

1. Do the members of your family exercise enough? If not, do you think there is any way that you could convince them to change?

2. Why do many people continue to eat foods that are high in saturated fats and simple carbohydrates when they know these foods are bad for their health?

Correct Answers 1. d (p. 375), 2. c (p. 376).

Application *of Psychology*

PREVENTION AND MANAGEMENT OF AIDS

Nine years ago, the brother of one of my colleagues died of **acquired immune deficiency syndrome,** or AIDS. This tragedy brought the spectre of AIDS very much closer to home for me, as he was a decent and talented man who died unnecessarily in his twenties.

As we are all well aware, our planet is in the midst of a truly horrible fatal epidemic of AIDS. This disease, which is caused by the *human immunodeficiency virus (HIV),* has already killed over 12 million men, women, and children worldwide, and twice that number are infected with HIV (World Health Organization, 1999). Although drugs are now available that prolong the life of persons with HIV, it is still a fatal disease.

Obviously, an epidemic of this magnitude demands our attention, but why bring up a medical disease in a psychology textbook? The answer is that, like most other physical diseases, there are important *psychological* aspects to the transmission and treatment of AIDS. It is extremely important that you, as an educated person, understand this point: Each individual's behavior determines his or her risk for AIDS.

To explain the role of psychological factors in AIDS, we will look first at the physical nature of the disease. AIDS is a disease that impairs the ability of the body's immune system to fight bacteria, viruses, and cancer. HIV has many effects on the immune system, but, most important, the virus results in mass destruction of the immune cells known as *lymphocytes* and, indirectly, leaves the important *B-cells* of the immune system useless. HIV disables the B-cells by invading the nucleus of another type of immune cell known as *T-4 Helper cells.* The T-4 Helper cells help the B-cells identify hostile bacteria and viruses and signal the B-cells to destroy them. Unfortunately, HIV either destroys the T-4 cells or deactivates them, making the B-cells useless and leaving the body vulnerable to disease. The person with AIDS does not actually die from the AIDS but from the other diseases, such as pneumonia and cancer, that flourish because of the weakened immune system.

AIDS is much more common in some sociocultural groups than others. In the United States, males are five times more likely to have AIDS than women (Centers for Disease Control and Prevention, 1999). As shown in figure 12.7, AIDS can be found in every part of the world, but it is far less common in some countries than others (World Health Organization, 1999). AIDS is relatively uncommon in Arabic countries and in Australia and New Zealand, but it is very common in Africa south of the Sahara desert, where HIV was first transmitted from monkeys to humans. In the United States, AIDS is found in all ethnic groups, but rates are higher among African Americans and Hispanics (Centers for Disease Control and Prevention, 1999).

Prevention of AIDS Through Behavior Change

Sadly, we have known how to prevent AIDS for many years, but far too many people have ignored the realities of AIDS for themselves and have not taken preventive steps. Very simply, AIDS can be prevented when people understand how HIV is transmitted and take sensible steps to avoid acquiring HIV. HIV is spread through bodily fluids, especially blood and semen. The most common means of transmission is sexual contact. The next most common modes of transmission are sharing needles during drug use and an infected mother to her infant during birth.

What is your own level of risk for contracting AIDS? Overall, men are more likely than women to become infected with HIV. As shown in figure 12.8, the most common routes of infection are different for women and men. Women are most likely to be infected with AIDS by having heterosexual sex (vaginal, oral, or anal) with an infected male or by sharing a needle with an infected person when injecting drugs. There have been very few cases of HIV infection from homosexual sex among women, but it can happen. In contrast, men are most frequently infected with HIV through sex (oral or anal) with another man or by sharing needles. Both women

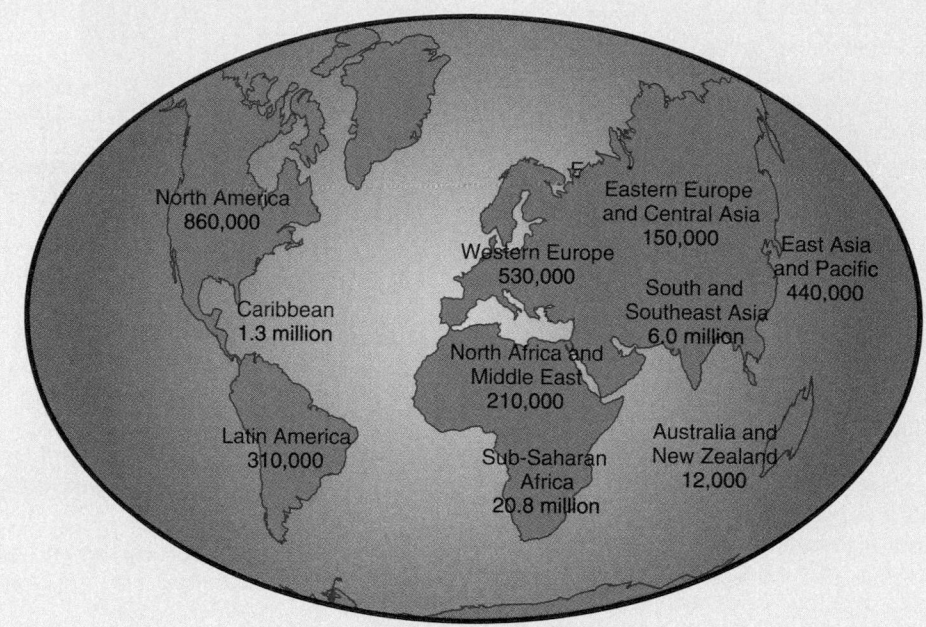

Total: 30.6 million

FIGURE 12.7

The numbers of persons living with the HIV virus or AIDS at the end of 1997 (World Health Organization, 1999).

and men have been infected from blood transfusions and tissue transplants, but better screening methods have reduced this risk.

The much smaller percentage of men than women with HIV who contracted it through heterosexual contact shown in figure 12.8 is misleading. Because men are more likely to be HIV-positive than women, the difference in the actual numbers of men and women who contracted HIV through heterosexual contact is not large. For both women and men, heterosexual contact without a condom outside of an exclusive relationship is very dangerous.

It is possible to lower your risk of infection to essentially zero by abstaining from sex (except for self-masturbation) or by having an exclusive sexual relationship with someone who is also free of HIV. All other types of sexual activity carry some level of risk of HIV infection from low to very high (see figure 12.9). Note, however, that the consistent use of condoms substantially lowers risk of HIV infection.

It is very difficult to convince people to change their behavior—especially their sexual behavior, however. College students currently have low rates of HIV infection, but, because they have been slow to adopt safe sex practices, they are at risk. Needle drug users continue to share needles because it is difficult to obtain new needles, and because some women who know they have HIV infection become pregnant in spite of the high risk of transmission to their own infants (Ironson & Schneiderman, 1991).

What can health psychologists do to help prevent AIDS? A now classic paper by Jeffrey Kelly and his colleagues (1989) provides a great example of the ways in which psychologists can help. Describing Kelly's study will involve the discussion of sexual practices that some of you may not wish to read about. But discussing these matters openly may save human lives.

Kelly's research group recruited a group of 51 gay men who did not have the AIDS virus but frequently engaged in anal intercourse and anal finger stimulation and did not consistently use condoms prior to the start of counseling. The men attended weekly group counseling sessions led by clinical psychologists that provided information on AIDS that explained why high-risk behaviors should be avoided, discussed factors that led to abandoning precautions in the past (being in a depressed mood, excessive drinking, etc.), and suggested ways to better cope with

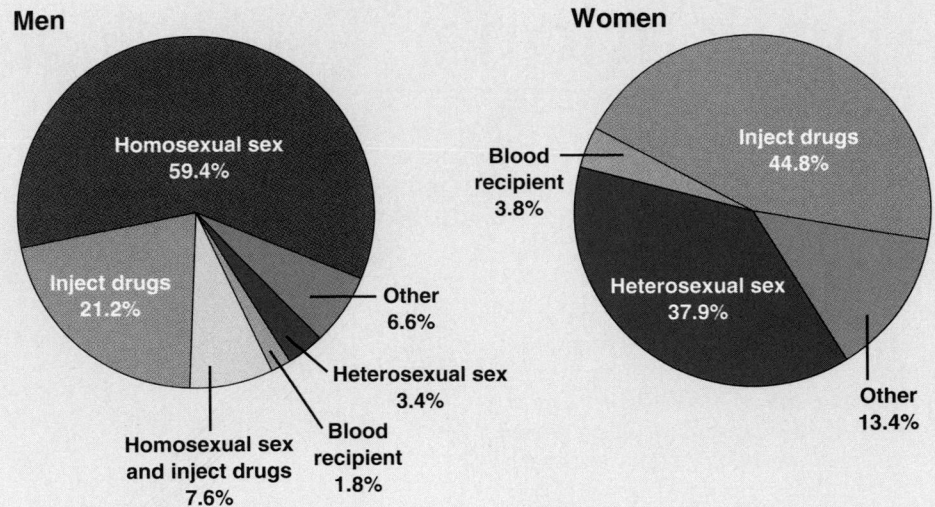

FIGURE 12.8

The percentage of cases of AIDS acquired through different routes is different for men and women.
Source: Centers for Disease Control and Prevention, 1998.

FIGURE 12.9

HIV risk and reduced-risk behaviors.

these factors in the future. The sessions helped the men learn to assertively insist that their partners follow safe sex practices and counseled the men on establishing lasting monogamous relationships.

The counseling sessions led to a steady decrease in the frequency of both forms of unprotected anal sex and an increase in the use of condoms. Eight months after the counseling sessions ended, the changes in sexual behavior were still evident. Thus, such counseling offers hope in the fight against AIDS. Recently, a number of similar counseling programs have been found to be successful, even among low-income urban populations (Kalichman, Rompa, & Coley, 1996; Weinhardt, Carey, Carey, & Verdecias, 1998). Unfortunately, not enough psycholo-

gists are trained in such counseling methods, and there is too little available funding for all types of preventive programs. Partly as a result, even persons who know they have HIV often continue to engage in high-risk sexual behavior that will spread their disease (Kalichman, 2000).

Psychological Factors in the Management of AIDS

AIDS is currently a disease with no cure. New medical treatments can slow the progress of the HIV infection, but they do not cure AIDS. Slowing the progress of the infection is an extremely worthwhile goal, both because every day of human life is precious and because it may prolong life until a medical cure is found, but AIDS is currently incurable.

A great deal of research is currently underway to find ways in which psychological interventions might be useful in helping persons with HIV adjust emotionally to their disease and even slow the progression of HIV infection. As has been stated often in this chapter, stress and other psychological variables affect the immune system. Therefore, it may be possible to develop psychological interventions that help strengthen the immune system and slow the progression of AIDS by changing health-related behavior and managing stress. Some very promising progress has been made in this area. For example, both regular aerobic exercise and stress-reduction therapy have been shown to buffer the detrimental effects of HIV on key aspects of immune functioning (Antoni & others, 1990; Antoni & others, 2000). Unfortunately, the beneficial effects of aerobic exercise are only modest, and it is not known if it actually slows progress of the HIV infection itself.

Promising results also have been reported by Shelley Taylor's research group at UCLA (Bower & others, 1998). They found that some men with HIV actively confront the reality of their impending death when they learn of their infection. For many, this is a very adaptive response. About half of the men who actively thought about their disease experienced positive shifts in their values and came to believe that the remaining years of their lives have real meaning. Importantly, the men who discovered meaning in their lives showed less rapid declines in immune functioning and had lower rates of death over three years than men who did not find meaning. This suggests that counseling methods that focus on finding meaning in life could help persons with HIV not only live richer lives but live longer lives as well. Much remains to be learned in these areas, but, fortunately, some of psychology's brightest minds have turned to this problem.

● Summary

Chapter 12 describes ways in which psychological concepts are used to improve physical health.

I. Health psychology attempts to prevent health problems by helping individuals cope with stress and change health-related behavior.

II. There are many sources of stress in our lives, some obvious and some hidden.

    A. Frustration is the result of failure to satisfy a motive.

    B. Conflict is the result of two or more incompatible motives. The four major types of conflict are

        1. Approach-approach conflict

        2. Avoidance-avoidance conflict

        3. Approach-avoidance conflict

        4. Multiple approach-avoidance conflict

    C. Pressure is the stress that arises from the threat of negative events.

    D. Both positive and negative life events can lead to stressful changes and the need for readjustment.

III. We react to stress in relatively predictable ways.

    A. Reactions to stress involve both psychological and physiological reactions.

    B. Some important general aspects of stress reactions are the same regardless of the source of stress.

        1. The fact that the body reacts to stress with an alarm reaction, a phase of resistance to the stress, and a stage of exhaustion if coping is not successful has been termed the general adaptation syndrome.

        2. Stress mobilizes the body's resources to fight or flee but suppresses the immune system and increases risk factors for heart disease (blood pressure, cholesterol, and blood-clotting factors).

        3. Common psychological reactions to stress are anxiety; depression; decreased ability to think, concentrate, and make decisions; and changes in motives, such as increased hunger and decreased interest in sex.

IV. We do not just react passively to stress; we actively attempt to cope with it.

    A. Effective coping strategies involve either removing the source of the stress or managing the degree of the stress reactions.

    B. Ineffective coping strategies do not help in the long run, either because they create more stress (such as aggression) or because they distort reality (defense mechanisms).

V. Stress requires greater control under some circumstances than others.

    A. Sources of stress are more stressful when we have no prior experience with them.

    B. Sources of stress are more stressful when they are unpredictable and when we have no control over them.

    C. Stress creates more severe reactions when we have little social support.

VI. Characteristics of the person also influence the magnitude of stress reactions in a "person × situation interaction"; these characteristics include

    A. Differences in cognitive appraisal of potential stress events influence stress reactions.

    B. Persons who tend to be anxious tend to respond to stress.

    C. The Type A behavior pattern, including hostile reaction to competitive pressure, is a risk factor for heart disease.

VII. Several aspects of our behavior are related to our health.

    A. Learning to relax deeply can reduce health risks.

    B. Abuse of substances such as alcohol and caffeine and the use of tobacco products are behaviors that create serious health risks.

    C. Health psychologists also seek to reduce health risks by helping individuals exercise properly, control their weight, and follow medical treatments properly.

● Resources

1. A sophisticated but readable discussion of stress by the father of the concept that is still very timely is Selye, H. (1976). *The stress of life.* New York: Knopf.

2. For a discussion of the role of cognitive factors in stress by the pioneer in the field, see Lazarus, R. S. (1999). *Stress and emotion: A new synthesis.* New York: Springer.

3. Excellent overviews of the field of health psychology appear in Taylor, S. E. (1999). *Health psychology.* (4th ed.). Boston: McGraw-Hill; and Wilson, D. K., Rodrigue, J. R., & Taylor, W. C. (1997). *Health-promoting and health-compromising behaviors among* minority *adolescents.* Washington, DC: American Psychological Association.

4. An excellent description of effective methods of treating victims of rape that has not gone out of date is Calhoun, K. C., & Atkeson, B. M. (1989). *Treatment of rape victims.* New York: Pergamon Press.

5. The classic, readable description of Type A personality can be found in Wright, L. (1988). The Type A behavior problem and coronary artery disease. *American Psychologist, 43,* 2–14.

6. For a Web site with a great deal of useful information about HIV and AIDS, see www.cdc.gov/nchstp/hiv_aids/pubs/facts.htm

Abnormal Behavior

PROLOGUE

Does making a speech make you nervous? How about meeting people? If these situations make you nervous, you're not alone; anxiety is quite common in these and other social situations where other people are scrutinizing you. But, for some people, the level of anxiety is so intense that it disrupts their ability to function in important social situations. Let's consider the experience of a woman whom we will call Carol. Carol is an intelligent and attractive woman who is successful in her professional career. She went to a university psychological clinic specializing in anxiety disorders to learn more about her intense anxiety in social situations.

The psychologists observed Carol in three different anxiety-provoking social situations. In the first situation, a stranger played the role of a man on a first date with Carol at a restaurant. In the second scene, a woman pretended to be a new neighbor of Carol's. In the third situation, Carol delivered a brief impromptu speech to two psychologists. During these three tests, Carol wore sensors that monitored her heart rate and blood pressure, and immediately after each test she was asked to choose statements that accurately reflected her thoughts and feelings about her performance during the tests, what she thought that other people thought about her, and her ability to cope.

Carol acted very nervously in each situation. She rarely made eye contact, spoke very little, and frequently shifted her posture. Her blood pressure and her heart rate rose dramatically, particularly during the speech, but was almost as high during the first date. She felt subjectively nervous in all situations and thought that she behaved in ways that no one would like.

Carol's anxiety was intense enough that it caused serious problems in her life. It led her to turn down dates and other social invitations, and even led her to change her major to avoid taking a course in which she would have to give speeches. Because her anxiety was serious enough to cause a problem, she was considered to have a social phobia by the psychologists—one of the forms of abnormal behavior that we will study in this chapter.

Does it surprise you to learn that something as understandable as exaggerated social anxiety would be considered to be "abnormal" by psychologists and psychiatrists? Actually, most forms of abnormal behavior aren't very different from what we would consider to be normal. Abnormal behavior is simply a pattern of acting, thinking, or feeling that is harmful in some way to the individual or to others. That may involve behavior that is quite unusual, but it also encompasses behavior that seems like only an exaggeration of normal behavior.

Abnormal behavior takes many forms. Excessive anxiety and depression are the most common types of abnormal behavior. Other types include alterations of perception and sudden changes in personality and identity. Other psychological disorders involve false beliefs and hallucinations that result in the individual's being "out of touch with reality." Other forms involve symptoms of health problems that have no known physical cause.

What causes abnormal behavior? Many answers have been given to this question throughout history. The earliest answer was that evil spirits caused it, but other views are more common today. Some theorists believe that abnormal behavior results from disturbances of the brain; others believe that it has psychological causes, such as excessive stress or faulty cognitions about ourselves or others. Currently, there is a movement toward explanations for abnormal behavior that combine both biological and psychological factors.

abnormal behavior
Actions, thoughts, and feelings that are harmful to the person or to others.

DEFINITION OF ABNORMAL BEHAVIOR

The term *abnormal* is one of the most elusive terms in psychology. It's not a difficult term to define in words, but it's a very difficult concept for most people to grasp. **Abnormal behavior** is defined as actions, thoughts, and feelings that are harmful to the person or to others. This harm may take many forms, including experiencing discomfort (as in feeling anxious or depressed), not being able to function in a job, not being able to relate to people well enough to have enduring friendships or family relationships, and having physical health problems that result from abnormal behavior (as when a person is too frightened of dental procedures to have needed oral surgery).

Part of the difficulty in understanding this concept is that most of us think of behavior as being abnormal only if it is very strange and unusual. That is not how psychologists and psychiatrists use the term *abnormal.* Mental health experts define the term *abnormal* broadly to include far more problems in living than most persons think of as "abnormal." As the term is defined by the mental health community today, approximately 20 percent of all persons in the United States have exhibited actions, thoughts, or feelings that are harmful enough to be considered to be abnormal during the past 12 months (Kessler & others, 1993; Regier & others, 1988). More strikingly, about 40 percent have had at least a mild mental health problem at some time in their lives (Kessler & others, 1993). Thus, the term *abnormal behavior* does not refer only to rare and strange problems but also to the problems in negotiating life that are experienced by many people.

Notice that abnormality is defined in terms of *harm* to the individual or others. Even if a pattern of behavior is very unusual (statistically uncommon for that group of people), it is not necessarily considered to be abnormal. Extreme intelligence and total honesty are unusual, but they hardly are considered abnormal. On the other hand, some patterns of behavior that are quite common are clearly abnormal because they are harmful. For example, the intense prejudice against Jews that was so prevalent during the days of Hitler's Germany was both common and harmful. Similarly, psychologists consider cigarette smoking, which is still fairly common in our culture today, to be abnormal behavior because of the serious health problems that it causes.

Historical Views of Abnormal Behavior

Before we discuss contemporary views of the causes of abnormal behavior, it's instructive to look back through history at beliefs about its cause. This historical perspective will make the important point that our ideas about the causes of abnormal behavior determine what we do to help those who experience it.

Supernatural Theories

The oldest writings about behavior, including those of Plato, the Bible, and the tablets of Babylonian King Hammurabi (1750 B.C.), indicate that, in our earliest belief, abnormal behavior was thought to be caused by evil spirits. Although some people disagreed with this notion during every period in history, the idea that people with psychological problems are possessed by evil spirits was the most influential view during the entire 3,500-year period of history stretching from Hammurabi to shortly before the American Revolution.

During most of the time that the supernatural theory held sway, the consequences for those with psychological problems were not too severe. Treatment mostly took the form of prayer, with the most unpleasant treatment being purgatives—foul liquids that were supposed to help the person vomit out the evil spirit. During the Middle Ages (500–1500), however, these supernatural beliefs were translated into far more harmful forms of "treatment."

In medieval Europe, the Catholic Church published an official document called the *Malleus Maleficarum,* or the *Witches' Hammer.* It gave detailed descriptions of the methods of treatment, or *exorcism,* for those people acting in abnormal ways that "revealed" possession by the devil. Treatment began with a stiff regimen of prayer, fasting, and the drinking of foul concoctions that caused vomiting, but, for those whose behavior did not

Peculiar behavior was once explained as demon possession. Here St. Catherine exorcises a demon from a woman.

improve, the *Malleus* recommended stronger methods. People who could not stop acting in deviant ways after exorcism were considered to be witches or warlocks (male witches). It was believed that the only way to save their souls was to destroy their bodies to drive out Satan. As a result, half a million so-called witches, mostly women, were put to death in Europe alone (Loftus, 1993). Even as late as 1692, 20 individuals were put to death as witches in Salem, Massachusetts. Nineteen were hanged for "witchcraft," whereas the twentieth victim died as a result of heavy rocks being placed on him in an effort to force him to confess (Phillips, 1933). Supernatural theories have less influence today than in the past, but pastoral counseling is a common form of therapy.

Biological Theories

An ancient voice that argued against the supernatural theory of abnormal behavior was fifth-century B.C. Greek physician Hippocrates. He believed that biological disorders of the body caused abnormal behavior. According to Hippocrates' view, the body contains four important fluids, or *humors:* blood, phlegm, black bile, and yellow bile. If these fluids get out of balance, illness and abnormal behavior is the result. An excess of black bile, for example, leads to depression; an excess of yellow bile causes irritability.

Hippocrates' theory was inaccurate, of course, and so he was not able to punch much of a hole in the supernatural approach. But he set the stage for later developments by suggesting that abnormal behavior might have *natural* rather than supernatural causes. During the 2,000 years after Hippocrates, a number of scientists who had been influenced by Hippocrates' idea searched in vain for a biological cause of abnormal behavior. Finally, in the 1800s, medical researchers such as German physician Richard von Krafft-Ebing made discoveries that led to a resurgence of biological theory and the eventual birth of psychiatry as a discipline.

Krafft-Ebing was working with a now rare form of severe psychological disturbance called *paresis*. He and a number of independent researchers discovered that paresis was actually an advanced stage of the venereal disease *syphilis*. Syphilis is a bacterial infection that begins with a sore, or chancre, on the genitals or on another point of entry, which is later followed by a copper-colored skin rash. The untreated disease then goes through a long "invisible" period, which eventually leads to the destruction of important body organs. If the bacteria destroy brain cells, paresis is the result. Because of the long period of time between the original infection and the later paresis, it was not known that the two conditions were related until Krafft-Ebing demonstrated through inoculation tests that all individuals with paresis also had syphilis.

The discovery that paresis had a biological cause sent shock waves through the medical community. Soon physicians—who up to this time had little to do with people with abnormal behavior—were placed in charge of mental institutions, and the medical specialty of psychiatry was formed. There were high expectations that the biological causes for all the other forms of abnormal behavior would soon be discovered. But, although the discovery of penicillin and its use in the treatment of syphilis almost totally eradicated paresis, few other biological causes of abnormal behavior were discovered. In recent years, however, major advances in the medical treatment of some severe forms of abnormal behavior have been made possible by the development of effective drug therapies.

Richard von Krafft-Ebing (1840–1902).

Psychological Theories

Hippocrates was not the only ancient Greek suggesting a *natural* explanation for abnormal behavior. Pythagoras, who also gave us geometry, was very active in the treatment of psychological problems. He held the then-radical belief that psychological problems are caused by *psychological* factors such as stress. He placed individuals with problems in "temples," where they received rest, exercise, a good diet, an understanding person to talk to, and practical advice on how to straighten out their lives. Records from his temples suggest that Pythagoras' methods were highly successful. Unfortunately, the psychological ideas of Pythagoras were not able to compete with those of the supernaturalists until modern times.

HUMAN DIVERSITY

ETHNICITY AND PSYCHOLOGICAL DIAGNOSIS

When we meet someone, our gender, our age, race, and ethnicity are factors that influence their opinion of us. But, when a person goes to a psychologist or psychiatrist because of a problem, do these sociocultural factors influence an expert's diagnosis of our problems? Unfortunately, a number of studies provide evidence that ethnicity and race can have an impact on how clinicians evaluate the problems of their clients (Trierweiler & others, 2000). Jenkins-Hall and Sacco (1991) assert that "studies suggest that therapy is not a culture-free activity and that cultural variables enter into treatment in ways that parallel their operation in society" (pp. 322–323). For example, two African American and two white female actors portrayed clients in videotaped interviews. White male and female counselors with at least three years of experience each viewed one of the videotapes and rated the psychological well-being of the person depicted in the taped interview. Did the ethnicity of the actor playing the role of the client bias the evaluation of the counselor? Sadly, the African American women who portrayed a depressed person were rated as more disturbed than the white women who portrayed a depressed person, even though they said exactly the same things on videotape and were matched on attractiveness, educational background, employment experience, and age.

Other researchers have arrived at similar conclusions. Bagley and Binitie (1970) found that psychiatrists in England were more likely to give Irish males a diagnosis of alcoholism regardless of the symptoms that they described. The authors felt that stereotypes about the drinking problems of Irish men led the psychiatrists to misinterpret the symptoms that were described to them.

The findings of more recent studies are more mixed, however. One study found no ethnic bias in diagnosis. Littlewood (1992) distributed a description of a hypothetical client to 339 mental health professionals in London, varying only the description of the patient as "born locally" or "born to Jamaican parents." There were no differences between the diagnosis for the two ethnic groups. Psychologist Gregory Irving (1999) asked 26 African American and 55 white psychologists to read descriptions of hypothetical patients. In some cases, the hypothetical person met diagnostic criteria for antisocial personality disorder (p. 559) and in some cases the person did not meet criteria for any mental health diagnosis. The psychologists were told that the hypothetical persons were either African American or white an equal number of times on a random basis. The

good news is that both the African American and white psychologists rated the problems of the hypothetical person who met criteria for antisocial personality disorder as the same regardless of whether the hypothetical person was labeled as African American or white. The troubling news is that the African American psychologists were less likely to conclude that the hypothetical person with problems needed therapy if they thought the person was African American than if they thought the hypothetical person was white. Conversely, the white psychologists rated the hypothetical person who did not meet criteria for antisocial personality disorder as less conforming to social norms and more irresponsible if the hypothetical person was labeled African American rather than white.

An international team of Japanese and European psychiatrists found that there appear to be cultural differences in the use of the diagnostic criteria for the subtypes of schizophrenia (p. 000) (Tateyama & others, 1999). When psychiatrists from the two countries read 10 summaries of persons thought to have schizophrenia, the Japanese and European psychiatrists disagreed considerably on the subtypes of schizophrenia that best fit these persons.

Although these kinds of studies have helped mental health professionals become more aware of the role that sociocultural factors can play in psychological diagnosis, we appear to have a way to go before diagnosis is practiced in a culture-free way. Prejudice is a powerful force in the lives of all humans, and psychologists and psychiatrists are only human, after all. A great deal still needs to be done at all levels of the education of mental health professionals to reduce the dangerous effects of ethnic prejudice in diagnosis (Herrera and others, 1999; Whitten, 1993a).

Have you ever been misunderstood by others because of your gender, ethnicity, race, or age? If you were a psychologist treating a person who was different from you in some way, do you think you could keep your stereotypes about others from influencing your evaluation of that person? What do you think could be done to reduce the impact of cultural stereotypes in mental health settings?

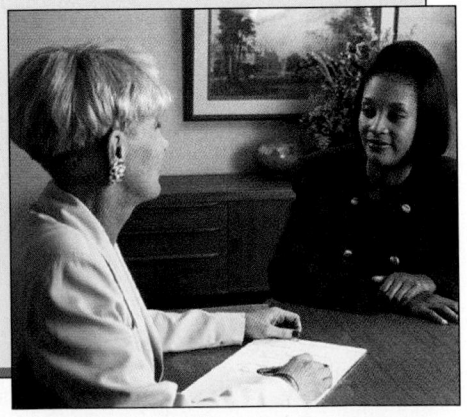

Although there were many important advocates of psychological theory, it was not until Sigmund Freud published his influential views that psychological theory was able to compete with the supernatural and biological approaches. Although Freud's model of unconscious conflicts was quite different from the ideas of Pythagoras, until recent times Freud was the leading champion of the view that psychological problems had psychological causes.

Contemporary Views of Abnormal Behavior

Today, abnormal behavior is believed to be a natural phenomenon with natural causes. As research evidence has accumulated, it has become increasingly clear that both biological and psychological factors are involved in the origins of many psychological disorders. Some disorders are solely biological in origin (such as those caused by brain injuries), and some are solely psychological in origin (such as acute grief reactions to the death of a loved one in normal individuals). But many other disorders appear to involve both kinds of causes. Inherited predispositions to certain kinds of problems, abnormal amounts of specific neurotransmitter substances in the brain, and tendencies to react autonomically to stress in an abnormal way are some of the biological factors believed to be partially responsible for a variety of psychological disorders. The psychological factors involved in these same disorders include stress, abnormal social learning histories, ineffective coping strategies, and inadequate social support. Apparently, biological and psychological factors work together to determine whether a person will experience psychological problems. For example, individuals whose autonomic nervous systems tend to react excessively to stress will have problems only if their lives are filled with considerable stress and if they cope poorly with stress. If present trends continue, we will probably see a fusion of the biological and psychological approaches into a single, naturalistic viewpoint.

The Concept of Insanity

Now that we have closely examined the term *abnormal behavior,* let's turn to the concept of **insanity.** What does it mean to be insane? Actually, *insanity* is not a psychological or psychiatric term but a legal term. And, to make matters more complex, insanity has not one but three different legal meanings, depending on whether it's used as a criminal defense, in a hearing on competency to stand trial, or in a hearing on involuntary commitment to a mental institution:

insanity
A legal definition concerning a person's inability to tell right from wrong, ability to understand the trial proceedings, or whether the person is a direct danger to self or others.

1. *Not guilty by reason of insanity.* In some states, individuals cannot be convicted of a crime if they were legally "insane" at the time the crime was committed. There are many definitions of the term *insane* in this context, but perhaps the most influential formula was proposed by the American Law Institute and adopted by many state and federal courts in the 1970s. It states, "A person is not responsible for criminal conduct if at the time of such conduct, as a result of mental disease or defect, he lacks substantial capacity either to appreciate the wrongfulness of his conduct or to conform his conduct to the requirements of the law." This definition means that people committing crimes are considered "not guilty by reason of insanity" if they had little ability to tell right from wrong or had little ability to control their actions at the time of the crime because of serious psychological problems. Generally, juries will consider only severely psychotic or severely mentally retarded persons to be insane according to this rule, and, because individuals with these problems rarely commit crimes, it's rarely a successful defense. Juries in a number of states can now find defendants "guilty but mentally ill." In this case, the person receives a prison sentence but is also given psychiatric treatment.

2. *Competence to stand trial.* The term *insanity* is also used in hearings to determine whether the individuals are competent to stand trial. In this sense, the question of insanity is whether the people are able to understand the proceedings of the trial sufficiently to aid in their own defense. Again, it's primarily severely psychotic and mentally retarded individuals who are considered incompetent according to this definition.

3. *Involuntary commitment.* A third meaning of the term *insanity* arises in hearings on the involuntary commitment of individuals to mental institutions. It's legal in most states to commit people to an institution against their will if a court finds them to be insane. The courts generally interpret this as meaning that the individuals are a direct danger—usually meaning a physical danger—to themselves or to others. Behaving

in strange ways is not enough to justify involuntary commitment. There must be an element of danger.

● Review

Actions, thoughts, and feelings that are harmful to the individual or to others are considered to be abnormal. Differing views of abnormal behavior have been taken throughout history. Abnormal behavior has been thought to result from supernatural causes or from biological abnormalities, as well as from psychological causes. The supernatural theory is of little importance in today's psychology, but both biological and psychological factors are currently thought to be involved in the origins of abnormal behavior.

In legal terms, persons are considered to be insane if they lack the capacity to deal with the demands of life in significant ways, either to avoid danger to themselves or others, to understand the difference between right and wrong and to behave accordingly, or to safeguard themselves or others. Legal decisions concerning insanity are made in the context of trials (Is a person not guilty by reason of insanity? Is a person competent to stand trial?) and in hearings concerning involuntary commitment to mental institutions.

● Check Your Learning

To be sure that you have learned the key points from the preceding section, cover the list of correct answers and try to answer each question. If you give an incorrect answer to any question, return to the page given next to the correct answer to see why your answer was not correct. Remember that these questions cover only some of the important information in this section; it is important that you make up your own questions to check your learning of other facts and concepts.

1. _____ is defined as those actions, thoughts, and feelings that are harmful to the person or to others.

2. The discovery that paresis developed from syphilis gave support to the _____ theories of abnormal behavior.

   a) supernatural   c) psychological
   b) biological   d) cognitive

3. The writings by Sigmund Freud gave the _____ theories enough credibility to compete with the other popular theories of the time.

   a) supernatural   c) psychological
   b) biological   d) cognitive

4. Research supports the view that both biological factors and psychological factors are involved in the origins of many psychological disorders.

   a) True
   b) False

● Thinking Critically About Psychology

1. Could biological and psychological theories of abnormal behavior both be correct?

2. Do you think smoking cigarettes should be considered to be abnormal? How might psychologists who hold either the continuity hypothesis or discontinuity hypothesis differ on this question?

Correct Answers 1. Abnormal behavior (p. 386), **2. b** (p. 387), **3. c** (p. 387), **4. a** (p. 389).

ANXIETY DISORDERS

Every life is a mixture of positive and negative emotions for everyone. But many people experience excessive levels of the kinds of negative emotions that we identify as being *nervous, tense, worried, scared,* and *anxious.* These terms all refer to anxiety. Ten to 15 million Americans experience such uncomfortable and disruptive levels of anxiety that they are said to have **anxiety disorders.** Women are more affected by anxiety disorders than men (Kessler & others, 1995). The kinds of anxiety disorders vary considerably, but all share heightened reactivity to anxiety-provoking events and increased vigilance (scanning and monitoring) for those events (Rosen & Schulkin, 1998).

anxiety disorders
Psychological disorders that involve excessive levels of negative emotions, such as nervousness, tension, worry, fright, and anxiety.

Phobias

A **phobia** is an intense, unrealistic fear. In this case, the anxiety is focused so intensely on some object or situation that the individual is acutely uncomfortable around it and will often go to great pains to avoid it. There are three types of phobias: (a) *specific phobia,* (b) *social phobia,* and (c) *agoraphobia.*

Specific phobia is the most specific and least disruptive of the phobias. Examples include intense fear of heights, dogs, blood, hypodermic injections, and closed spaces (Ost, 1992). Individuals with specific phobias generally have no other psychological problems, and their lives are disrupted only if the phobia creates a direct problem in daily living. For example, a fear of elevators would be highly disruptive for a person who works in a skyscraper, but it probably would not be for a vegetable farmer.

Other forms of phobia, by their very nature, frequently cause problems for the individual. The term **social phobia** is used to describe extreme anxiety about social interactions, particularly those with strangers and those in which the person might be evaluated negatively. Job interviews, public speaking, and first dates are extremely uncomfortable for individuals with social phobia. Persons with social phobia usually have unrealistically negative views of their social skills and attempt to avoid evaluation (Wallace & Alden, 1997). Because this kind of phobia hampers and limits social interactions, it can seriously disrupt the individual's social and occupational life.

Agoraphobia is the most impairing of all of the phobias. Literally meaning "fear of open spaces," agoraphobia involves an intense fear of leaving one's home or other familiar places. In extreme cases, the agoraphobic individual is totally bound to his or her home, finding a trip to the mailbox an almost intolerable experience. Other agoraphobic individuals are able to travel freely in their neighborhood but cannot venture beyond it. A 30-year-old German man recounts his experience with agoraphobia in the following passage.

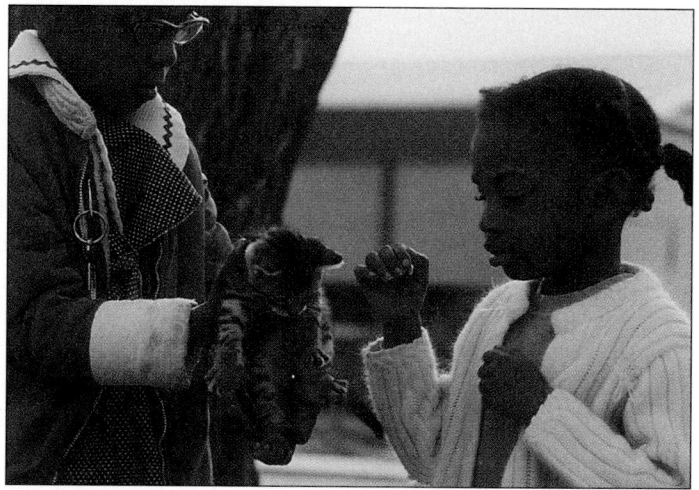
This child's fear of animals may be serious enough to be considered to be a specific phobia.

phobia
An intense, irrational fear.

specific phobia
A phobic fear of one relatively specific thing.

social phobia
A phobic fear of social interactions, particularly those with strangers and those in which the person might be viewed negatively.

agoraphobia
(ag″o-rah-fō′bē-ah)   An intense fear of leaving one's home or other familiar places.

> The brief trips to Bonn filled me with a surging sense of the impossible and the far . . . a feeling, especially as to distance, that could convert a half mile, or even five blocks from home, in terms of subjective need and cowardice, into an infinity of remoteness. . . . I start a little walk down the street about a hundred feet from the house, I am compelled to rush back, in horror of being so far away . . . a hundred feet away . . . from home and security. I have never walked or ridden, alone or with others, as a normal man, since that day. . . .

Generalized and Panic Anxiety Disorders

Whereas phobias are linked to specific stimulus situations, the other anxiety disorders involve a kind of anxiety that is independent of environmental triggers. Individuals with

generalized anxiety disorder
An uneasy sense of general tension and apprehension that makes the individual highly uncomfortable because of its prolonged presence.

panic anxiety disorder
A pattern of anxiety in which long periods of calm are broken by an intensely uncomfortable attack of anxiety.

generalized anxiety disorder experience a vague, uneasy sense of tension and apprehension, sometimes referred to as *free-floating anxiety.* Generalized anxiety makes the individual highly uncomfortable, not because it's an intense kind of anxiety—it's generally relatively mild—but because of its relentless, almost unending presence. The person with generalized anxiety disorder does experience periods of calm, but they are often few and far between.

The individual with **panic anxiety disorder** experiences a pattern of anxiety that is almost the exact opposite of generalized anxiety. There may be long periods without anxiety, but that calm is suddenly broken without warning and without obvious cause. The individual is seized by a sharp, intensely uncomfortable attack of anxiety. Respiration increases and suddenly rapid heartbeats can be felt pounding with such intensity that the individual often feels that he or she is having a heart attack, or at the very least is going crazy.

Recent research has suggested that persons with panic anxiety disorders are extremely sensitive to small changes in their anxiety (Schmidt, Lerew, & Jackson, 1997), small changes in the functioning of their autonomic nervous system, especially their heart rate (Ehlers & Breuer, 1992; Schmidt, Lerew, & Trakowski, 1997), and small changes in the level of carbon dioxide in their blood (Bellodi & others, 1998; Rapee & others, 1992). More important, they interpret these minor normal fluctuations in "catastrophic" ways. That is, their attacks of anxiety are exaggerated reactions to normal body stimuli that most persons ignore.

A relatively small percentage of the population (about 5 percent of women and 2 percent of men) experience panic attacks that are frequent and severe enough to be said to have panic disorder at some point in their lifetimes (Kessler & others, 1995), but a surprisingly high percentage of adults experience occasional attacks of panic. In one survey study of 2,375 college students, 12 percent had experienced at least one panic attack at some time during their lifetimes (Telch, Lucas, & Nelson, 1989). It is important to know that such uncomfortable events are relatively common and that they should not be a source of serious concern unless they are severe or frequent enough to disrupt the individual's functioning or well-being.

The case of Richard Benson illustrates the experience of panic anxiety disorder.

> Richard Benson, age 38, applied to a psychiatrist for therapy because he was suffering from severe and overwhelming anxiety which sometimes escalated to a panic attack. He had been treated for this problem in a private psychiatric hospital, but several weeks after his release, the severe anxiety symptoms recurred and he decided to seek outpatient therapy. During the times when he was experiencing intense anxiety, it often seemed as if he were having a heart seizure. He experienced chest pains and heart palpitations, numbness, shortness of breath, and he felt a strong need to breathe in air. He reported that in the midst of the anxiety attack, he developed a feeling of tightness over his eyes and he could only see objects directly in front of him (tunnel vision). He further stated that he feared that he would not be able to swallow.
>
> Mr. Benson indicated that he had been anxious most of his life, but it was only since his promotion at work six months ago that the feelings of anxiety became a severe problem. The intensity of the anxiety symptoms was frightening to him and on two occasions his wife had rushed him to a local hospital because he was in a state of panic, sure that his heart was going to stop beating and he would die. (Leon, 1977, p. 113)

Post-Traumatic Stress Disorder

Once begun, wars are never over for those who fight them. World War II ended more than 50 years ago, the last soldiers returned from Vietnam more than 25 years ago, and Operation Desert Storm war ended over a decade ago, yet hundreds of thousands of former soldiers continue to "fight" those wars in their minds. The men and women who served in those wars returned to safety long ago, but they are still haunted by terrible recollections of combat that intrude into their waking consciousness and fill their dreams with horror. They often feel numbed to the ordinary emotions and pleasures of life. They often feel guilt that they survived, whereas others did not, and they often feel a pervasive sense of anger and unrest. Their continuing agony has been given the unwieldy name of **post-traumatic stress disorder (PTSD).** In simple terms, they are still suffering severe stress reactions years after the traumatic stress of combat ended. Many persons who experience PTSD recover from it, but for many others it is chronic (Engdahl & others, 1997).

The Vietnam War appears to have produced an unprecedented 500,000 veterans with at least mild problems of PTSD (Barrett & others, 1996; Egendorf & others, 1981; Southwick & others, 1995). But many survivors of World War II still experience PTSD at a time in their lives when they should be enjoying peaceful grandparenthood (Lee, Vaillant, Torrey, & Elder, 1995). Indeed, nearly one-third of the men who had been prisoners of war of the Japanese during World War II still meet criteria for PTSD in their seventies (Engdahl & others, 1997). Similarly, many Jewish survivors of Nazi concentration camps in World War II still suffer from PTSD (Kuch & Cox, 1992; Yehuda & others, 1995).

Not all military personnel exposed to war develop PTSD. Understandably, those Vietnam soldiers who were more directly exposed to combat or atrocities are more likely to experience PTSD (Macklin & others, 1998; Yehuda, Southwick, & Giller, 1992). The same has been found for both World War II and Gulf War veterans (Lee & others, 1995; Southwick & others, 1995). The individual's personal characteristics and social situation may also influence susceptibility to PTSD. When the level of exposure to combat is controlled statistically, soldiers with lower scores on intelligence tests upon admission to the military are more likely to experience PTSD (Macklin & others, 1998). In addition, veterans with greater social support after the war are less likely to experience PTSD (King & others, 1998).

Our awareness of PTSD grew out of efforts to assist veterans coping with the emotional aftermath of war. Psychologists soon realized, however, that PTSD is not limited to persons who have been exposed to war. A large national study of 8,000 adults living in the United States found that 5 percent of all adult males and 10 percent of all adult females have experienced PTSD for at least a month during their lifetimes (Kessler, Sonnega, Bromet, Hughes, & Nelson, 1995).

Among men, combat-related stress is the most common single cause of PTSD (accounting for nearly 30 percent of PTSD in males), but, even for men, PTSD is often the result of other kinds of traumatic stress, such as experiencing the sudden and unexpected death of a loved one, being physically assaulted, causing automobile accidents, and witnessing violence, and disasters (Andrews & others, 2000; Breslau & others, 1998; Delahanty & others, 1997; Epstein, Fullerton, & Ursano, 1998). Among women, physical assault, rape and sexual molestation, and the witnessing of violence are the leading causes of PTSD (Breslau & others, 1997; Kessler & others, 1995). The type and amount of stress encountered in everyday life depends in part on our living circumstances. Residences along the Atlantic Coast are more likely to experience hurricanes, residents of California are more likely to experience earthquakes, and residents of inner cities are more likely to be assaulted, to be raped, or to witness violence (Breslau & others, 1997).

Most persons who experience traumatic stress in civilian life do not develop PTSD. The percentage of traumatized persons who develop PTSD depends in part on the type of stress. For example, about 15 percent of persons who experience the sudden loss of a loved one develop PTSD, and about 20 percent of victims of violent assault experience PTSD (Breslau & others, 1998). In contrast, 75 percent of women who have been raped experience PTSD for at least six months (Kessler & others, 1995).

post-traumatic stress disorder (PTSD)
The condition caused by extremely stressful experiences in which the person later experiences anxiety and irritability; has upsetting memories, dreams, and realistic flashbacks of the experience; and tries to avoid anything that reminds him or her of the experience.

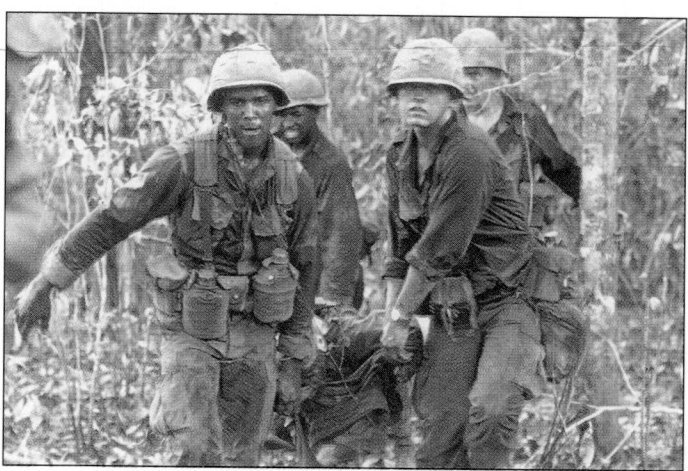

Researchers estimate that half a million Vietnam War veterans suffered some symptoms of post-traumatic stress disorder.

Obsessive-Compulsive Disorders

obsessive-compulsive disorders
Disorders that involve obsessions (anxiety-provoking thoughts that will not go away) and/or compulsions (irresistible urges to engage in specific irrational behaviors).

Also classified with anxiety disorders are the **obsessive-compulsive disorders.** Obsessions and compulsions are two separate problems, but they often occur together in the same individuals. *Obsessions* are anxiety-provoking thoughts that will not go away. They seem uncontrollable and even alien, as if they do not belong to the individual's mind. Thoughts such as a recurrent fear of losing control and killing someone or of having an incestuous sexual relationship can cause extreme anxiety.

Compulsions are irresistible urges to engage in behaviors such as repeatedly touching a spot on one's shoulder, washing one's hands, or checking the locks on doors. If the individual tries to stop engaging in the behavior, he or she experiences an urgent anxiety until the behavior is resumed. Obsessions and compulsions are often found in the same person, such as the person who compulsively washes his hands because he is obsessed with thoughts about germs. About 70 percent of all people with obsessive-compulsive disorders have both obsessions and compulsions, 25 percent have only obsessions, and 5 percent have only compulsions (Wilner, Reich, Robins, Fishman, & van Doren, 1976).

▶ SOMATOFORM DISORDERS

somatoform disorders
(sō″mah′to-form)   Disorders in which the individual experiences the symptoms of physical health problems that have psychological rather than physical causes.

Somatoform disorders are conditions in which the individual experiences the symptoms of physical health problems that have psychological rather than physical causes. *Soma* is the Latin word for body—hence, somatoform disorders are thought to be disorders in which psychological problems "take the form" of physical problems. Although these symptoms of health problems are not physically caused, they are very real and uncomfortable to the individual. In other words, they are not faked.

Somatization Disorders

somatization disorders
(sō″mah-ti-zā′shun)   Intensely and chronically uncomfortable psychological conditions that involve numerous symptoms of somatic (body) illnesses without physical cause.

Somatization Disorders

www.mmhe.com/laheye1

Somatization disorders are intensely and chronically uncomfortable conditions that indirectly create a high risk of medical complications. They are far more common in women than in men (Golding, Smith, & Kashner, 1991). They take the form of chronic and recurrent aches, pains, tiredness, and other symptoms of somatic (body) illness. In addition, individuals with these disorders frequently experience memory difficulties, problems with walking, numbness, blackout spells, nausea, menstrual problems, and a lack of pleasure from sex. These complaints are often expressed in dramatic ways that increase the probability of sympathy and special treatment from others.

Individuals with somatization problems also typically experience other psychological difficulties, particularly anxiety and depression. They frequently have problems with their jobs, schoolwork, or household responsibilities. The most dangerous aspect of somatization disorders, however, concerns the measures the affected individuals take to find relief from their discomfort. Many become addicted to alcohol or tranquilizers and often take medications prescribed by many different physicians, whom they are seeing simultaneously (without telling the other physicians), thus increasing the risk of dangerous chemical interactions among the drugs. Worse still, because of their frequent complaints to physicians, many are eventually the recipients of unnecessary surgery, especially unnecessary hysterectomies (removal of the uterus in women).

Conversion Disorders and Somatoform Pain Disorders

conversion disorders
Somatoform disorders in which individuals experience serious somatic symptoms such as functional blindness, deafness, and paralysis.

Conversion disorders are the most dramatic of the somatoform disorders. The name comes from the Freudian theory that anxiety has been "converted" into serious somatic symptoms in this condition rather than being directly experienced as anxiety. Individuals with this problem experience functional blindness, deafness, paralysis, fainting, seizures, inability to speak, or other serious impairments in the absence of any physical cause. In addition, these individuals appear to be generally ineffective and dependent upon others. These symptoms understandably impair the individuals' lives, particularly their ability to work. Conversion disorders can usually be distinguished from medical problems without great difficulty. In most cases, the symptoms are not medically possible. For example, people with conversion paralysis of the legs can be observed to move their legs normally when sleeping. Consider the following case:

> A 22-year-old man . . . was referred with complaints of night blindness and failing vision. His visual acuity had deteriorated rapidly and he was found to have tubular fields of vision and a gross abnormality of dark adaptation. . . .
>
> The onset of his symptoms seemed closely related to his difficulties with a girl-friend who lived some miles away from his home. In order to visit her he would have to drive at night which was made impossible by his night blindness. Soon after the relationship was broken and the girl became engaged to another man the symptoms cleared up. Visual acuity improved . . . and the visual fields showed only slight contraction. (Behrman & Levy, 1970, p. 193)

Conversion disorders usually begin during stress and provide some kind of benefit (i.e., reinforcement) to the individual. In the case of the 22-year-old man just described, the benefit may have been not having to admit that he did not want to visit his girlfriend.

Somatoform pain disorders are very similar to conversion disorders, except that the primary symptom is *pain* that has no physical cause. Sometimes somatoform pain can be distinguished from physically caused pain because it does not follow nerve pathways. But, in the case of low back pain, joint pains, and chest pains, a diagnosis of somatoform pain disorder can be made only after all possible physical causes have been carefully ruled out. Like conversion disorders, somatoform pain usually occurs at times of high stress and is generally beneficial to the individual in some way, as in getting the person out of a dull job and onto disability payments.

somatoform pain disorders
(sō-maʹto-form)   Somatoform disorders in which the individual experiences a relatively specific and chronic pain that has a psychological rather than physical cause.

▶ DISSOCIATIVE DISORDERS

Dissociative disorders cover a broad category of loosely related rare conditions involving sudden alterations in cognition. The various types of dissociative disorders are characterized by a change in memory, perception, or "identity." There are four kinds of dissociative disorders: *depersonalization, dissociative amnesia, dissociative fugue,* and *dissociative identity disorder.*

dissociative disorders
(dis-sōʹsē-a-tiv)   A category of conditions involving sudden cognitive changes, such as a change in memory, perception, or identity.

Depersonalization

The term **depersonalization** refers to experiences in which the individual feels that he or she has become distorted or "unreal," or that distortions have occurred in one's surroundings. The individual might feel that his hands have become enlarged or out of control. Or the individual might feel like a robot—even though she knows she is a real person—or that her parents are not real people. The individual knows that these feelings are not accurate, although they have an eerie reality to them. One of the more common experiences of depersonalization is the sense of leaving one's body and being able to look back at it from the ceiling. Experiences of depersonalization are rather common, especially in young adults. Unless they are accompanied by other problems or become recurrent to the point of being uncomfortable, these experiences are not considered abnormal. Generally, they are nothing more than an unsettling experience.

depersonalization
(de-perʹsun-al-i-zāʹshun)   The perceptual experience of one's body or surroundings becoming distorted or unreal in some way.

Dissociative Amnesia and Fugue

As described in chapter 6, amnesia is a loss of memory that can have either a physical or psychological cause. **Dissociative amnesia** is psychologically caused. It most often occurs

dissociative amnesia
A dissociative disorder that involves a loss of memory and that has a psychological rather than a physical cause.

after a period of intense stress and involves loss of memory for all or part of the stressful experience itself, such as loss of memory for an automobile accident in which the individual was responsible for the death of another person. Individuals who suffer amnesia as a result of stress generally have no other psychological problems and typically recover their memories in time.

dissociative fugue
(füg)   A period of "wandering" that involves a loss of memory and a change in identity.

Dissociative fugue states resemble amnesia in that there is a loss of memory, but the loss is so complete that the individual cannot remember his or her identity or previous life. The fugue episode is also typified by a period of semiconscious "wandering" that may take the individual around the corner or across the continent. In many instances, the individual takes on a new "personality" during the fugue episode, usually one that is more sociable, more fun-loving, and less conventional than the previous one. Generally these changes are transient. Consider the following case:

> When Mrs. Y. was brought to the hospital by her husband, she was dazed, confused, and weeping. Apparently aware of her surroundings and able to answer brief questions in filling out the admitting form, she could not, at the time, discuss any of her problems with the admitting physician. Her husband reported that she had left their home two weeks previously while he was at work. All the efforts of her husband and the police to trace her had failed until approximately 24 hours prior to her admission to the hospital when Mr. Y. received a report that a woman of her description had been arrested in a nearby city. When he arrived and identified her, she did not at first recognize him, did not know her own name, and could not remember what had happened to her or anything about her past. The police informed Mr. Y. that she had been arrested for "resorting" after a motel owner had called the police to complain that several different men had visited the motel room she had rented three days before in the company of a sailor. Mrs. Y. seemed unable to remember any of these alleged events. Gradually she came to recognize her husband as he talked anxiously with her whereupon she began to weep and requested to be brought home. . . . (Goldstein & Palmer, 1963, pp. 71–72)*

---

*From *The Experience of Anxiety: A Casebook,* Expanded Edition by Michael J. Goldstein and James O. Palmer. Copyright © 1975 by Michael J. Goldstein and James O. Palmer. Reprinted by permission of Oxford University Press, Inc.

As will be obvious in the next section, dissociative fugue is quite similar to dissociative identity disorder. For that reason, all of the controversy surrounding that diagnosis applies to dissociative fugue.

Dissociative Identity Disorder (Multiple Personality)

dissociative identity disorder
A dissociative disorder in which the individual appears to shift abruptly and repeatedly from one "personality" to another.

Individuals who exhibit **dissociative identity disorder** (formerly known as *multiple personality*) appear to shift abruptly from one "personality" to another—as if more than one person were inhabiting the same body. Generally, the two or more personalities are quite different from one another. The individual's original personality is often conventional, moralistic, and unhappy, whereas the alternative personalities tend to be quite the opposite. At least one other personality is usually sensual, uninhibited, and rebellious. In most cases, the individual reports that he or she is not aware of the other personalities when they are "in" their original personality but say that the alternative personalities "know about" their rival personalities and are often antagonistic toward the original one.

In 1977, Chris Sizemore published an autobiography revealing that she was the case of dissociative identity disorder made famous in the 1950s movie *The Three Faces of Eve.* Initially, she appeared to manifest two distinctly different personalities, referred to in the movie as Eve White and Eve Black. Eve White was depressive, anxious, conventional, and inhibited, whereas Eve Black was seductive, uninhibited, and wild. In her autobiography, Chris Sizemore reveals that she eventually went through 22 separate personalities but that in recent years she feels she has a single, well-adjusted personality. A similar pattern was reported for the case of "Sybil," a woman who believed that she had developed 16 personalities during the course of 42 years (Schreiber, 1973).

Dissociative identity disorder is a very controversial disorder today. Although there is little doubt that some people behave as if they have multiple personalities, there is great deal of debate about why they behave this way. Some mental health experts believe that dissociative identity disorder is the result of physical or sexual abuse during childhood. In this view, alternative "personalities" that do not "know" about the abuse are believed to split off from the original personality in an effort to cope with painful memories (Gleaves, 1996).

Other psychologists believe that dissociative identity disorder is the direct result of social learning (Lilienfeld & others, 1999). Sometimes, highly suggestible persons are exposed, through books or movies, to persons who are models of "multiple personalities." If they imitate these models and begin to act as if they have more than one personality, they may behave in previously unacceptable ways that are reinforced (brash, rule-breaking, or promiscuous behavior), but attribute the new behavior to "another personality," rather than accepting responsibility for the actions. Thus, in the social learning view, multiple personalities are no more than unconscious enactments of roles.

Chris Sizemore, the woman who was the subject of the book and film, *The Three Faces of Eve*. Ms. Sizemore reported that she exhibited a total of 22 distinct personalities before achieving her final, permanent personality.

In most cases, social learning theorists believe that so-called multiple personalities are taught to patients by their psychotherapists, however, rather than by books or movies (Lilienfeld & others, 1999). This surprising assertion may seem far-fetched at first, but it simply means that, when some well-intentioned therapists begin to suspect that a patient has been abused as a child or notice that they sometimes act in ways that are inconsistent with their usual behavior, they may suggest to the patient that they have one or more "hidden personalities." If the patient is highly suggestible, they may accept this idea and begin to act more and more as if they have multiple personalities. Lilienfeld and colleagues (1999) cite evidence that most cases of dissociative identity did not believe that they had multiple personalities until they began seeing a therapist who raised this possibility. Thus, therapists who look for hints of dissociative identity disorder in their patients may unwittingly teach their patients to have dissociative identity disorder. Indeed, it has been alleged that therapist influences created the multiple personalities of the person known as Sybil (Borch-Jacobsen, 1997; Rieber, 1999).

● Review

Anxiety disorders are common problems characterized by anxiety that may be experienced as low and relatively constant levels of generalized anxiety, as sharp and intense attacks of anxiety, as focalized phobias of various sorts, or linked to obsessive thoughts or compulsive actions.

In somatoform disorders, the individual experiences the symptoms of medical conditions that have psychological rather than physical causes. In some types of somatoform disorders the symptoms are dramatic and clear-cut, such as blindness, paralysis, or chronic pain. In other cases, the individual experiences multiple aches, pains, and maladies.

Dissociative disorders are psychological problems involving sudden alterations in cognition. These may take the form of memory loss, changes of identity, or feelings of unreality. In rare cases, the alteration of identity is so dramatic that the individual appears to possess more than a single personality. Social learning theorists have raised concerns that dissociative disorders may often be created by the actions of well-intentioned therapists with their highly suggestible patients.

● Check Your Learning

To be sure that you have learned the key points from the preceding section, cover the list of correct answers and try to answer each question. If you give an incorrect answer to any question, return to the page given next to the correct answer to see why your answer was not correct.

1. Psychological disorders that involve excessive levels of nervousness, tension, worry, fright, and anxiety are termed _____ disorders.

   a) depressive   c) behavior

   b) somatoform   d) anxiety

2. Individuals with _____ experience a vague, uneasy sense of tension and apprehension, sometimes referred to as free-floating anxiety, that makes the individual uncomfortable because of its prolonged presence.

   a) panic disorder   c) generalized anxiety disorder

   b.) dissociative identity disorder   d) agoraphobia

3. _____ are conditions in which the individual experiences the symptoms of physical health problems that have psychological rather than physical causes.

   a) Anxiety disorders   c) Somatoform disorders

   b) Dissociative disorders   d) Social phobias

4. _____ disorders are a category of conditions involving sudden cognitive changes, such as a change in memory, perception, or identity.

   a) Panic   c) Obsessive-compulsive

   b) Conversion   d) Dissociative

● Thinking Critically About Psychology

1. How would a social learning theorist account for a phobic fear of snakes? How might a psychoanalyst account for the same phobia?

2. Our news media seem to highlight cases of dissociative identity disorder, even though they are very rare. What role do you think the media play in our society's understanding of abnormal behavior?

Correct Answers **1. d** (p. 391), **2. c** (p. 391), **3. c** (p. 394), **4. d** (p. 395).

▶ MOOD DISORDERS

mood disorders
Psychological disorders involving depression and/or abnormal elation.

There are two primary forms of **mood disorders,** depression and mania. Depression can occur alone (a condition known as *major depression*), but mania seems to always alternate with periods of depression *(bipolar affective disorder).* Both conditions produce great misery for the individual.

Major Depression

major depression
An affective disorder characterized by episodes of deep unhappiness, loss of interest in life, and other symptoms.

The individual experiencing **major depression** is deeply unhappy and finds little pleasure in life. But major depression is more than merely intense sadness. The person with major depression believes that the future is bleak, holds a negative opinion of self and others, and often sees no reason to live. This state is accompanied by at least some of the following: increased or decreased sleep, increased or decreased appetite, loss of interest in sex, loss of energy or excessive energy, difficulties concentrating and making decisions, and sometimes suicidal thinking or actual attempts.

Fortunately, major depression is an *episodic* disorder. This means that, in 90 percent of cases, the individual experiences the symptoms for a period of time and then recovers,

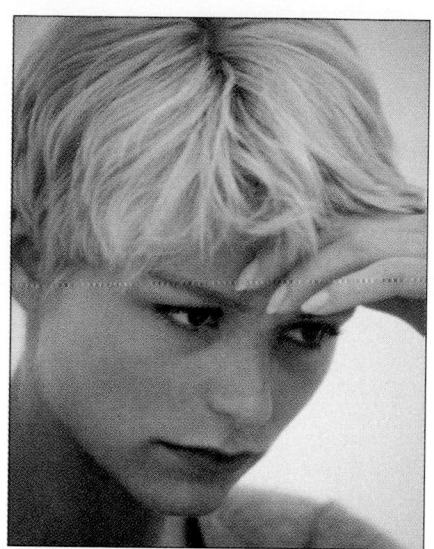

often returning to his or her normal self. The duration of episodes varies widely, but half of all persons with major depression recover in 12 to 20 weeks from the beginning of the depressive episode (Eaton & others, 1997; Solomon & others, 1997). About one-third of all individuals who experience an episode of major depression will experience only one episode, but others will be depressed only once—sometimes repeatedly—during their lifetimes if not properly treated (Eaton & others, 1997; Solomon & others, 1997, 2000). In these cases, the depression comes in recurrent episodes, which last from several weeks to many months, followed by periods of normal moods.

Major depression is quite common, affecting 10 million or more Americans. Worldwide, as many as 100 million persons experience major depression (Gotlib, 1992). The probability that an individual will develop major depression for the first time is very low until puberty, rises until a peak is reached between 45 and 55 years of age, then declines again. Overall, the risk for major depression is twice as high for women than men, particularly during middle age (Eaton & others, 1997; Lewinsohn, Duncan, Stanton, & Hautzinger, 1986).

Major depression, despite its name, is often relatively mild. People with mild depression are very uncomfortable, but they often can cope with the demands of daily living. Severe major depression is less common but far more disabling. This is often accompanied by bizarre beliefs and perceptions that represent a psychotic distortion of reality. The following excerpt describes a case of severe (psychotic) depression that required the individual to be hospitalized during treatment because of his suicidal tendencies and distortions of reality (e.g., he believed that his stomach was rotting away).

> At 51 the patient suffered from a depression and was obliged to resign his position. This depression continued for about 9 months, after which he apparently fully recovered. He resumed his work but after 2 years suffered from a second depression. Again he recovered after several months and returned to a similar position and held it until 2 months before his admission. At this time he began to worry lest he was not doing his work well, talked much of his lack of fitness for his duties, and finally resigned. He spent Thanksgiving Day at his son's in a neighboring city, but while there he was sure that the water pipes in his own house would freeze during his absence and that he and his family would be "turned out into the street." A few days later he was found standing by a pond, evidently contemplating suicide. He soon began to remain in bed and sometimes wrapped his head in the bed clothing to shut out the external world. (Kolb, 1977, p. 455)*

*From L. C. Kolb, *Modern Clinical Psychiatry*, 9th ed. Copyright © 1977 W.B. Saunders Co., Philadelphia, PA. Reprinted by permission.

The risk for major depression is significantly elevated in persons experiencing high levels of stress (Lewinsohn, Hoberman, & Rosenbaum, 1988; Mazure, 1998; Shrout & others, 1989). On the other hand, there is also clear evidence that some people are more vulnerable than others to depression for genetic reasons (Kendler & Prescott, 1999).

Cognitive Factors in Depression

Aaron T. Beck (1976) and others believe that our *cognitions* are an important factor in emotional problems. For example, Beck has suggested that negative views of oneself, the world in which we live, and the future lead some persons to experience life in such negative terms that they develop depression. Much evidence is consistent with this view, particularly Beck's theory that negative views of oneself are a critical component of depression. Recent studies (Alloy, Abramson, & Francis, 1999; Brown, Hammen, Craske, & Wickens, 1995) showed that people who believe that they fall far short of being the persons they would like to be are more likely to experience depression. One reason that depressed persons often fall short of their ideal is that their beliefs are *perfectionistic* (Hewitt, Flett, & Ediger, 1996). Paul Hewitt and Gordon Flett (1993) found that people who believe that they should be perfect in their work are likely to develop depression if they fail even slightly at work. Similarly, people who hold out perfectionistic expectations for themselves in social relationships are often depressed if their personal relationships are not going well. In contrast, people who do not expect perfection of themselves do not become depressed when things do not go well. These findings support the basic premise of the cognitive view: It is not bad things happening to us that is upsetting; it is our *interpretation* of them that makes all the difference (Gotlib, 1992; Joiner and others, 1999).

Other studies have suggested that having a positive opinion of yourself makes depression less likely following stressful life events (Hammen, Marks, Mayol, & deMayo, 1985; Holahan & Moos, 1987; Lewinsohn & others, 1988; Robinson, Garber, & Hilsman, 1995; Zuroff & Mongrain, 1987). In addition, individuals who believe that they can be happy only when they are in a close relationship are understandably more likely to respond to the loss of a relationship with depression than individuals who do not hold this dependent belief (Hammen, Elliott, Gitlin, & Jamison, 1989; Hammen & others, 1985; Zuroff & Mongrain, 1987).

It seems clear that our beliefs about ourselves and our relationships with others make us more or less vulnerable to depression when buffeted by life's inevitable stress. However, the relationship between cognition and depression is a two-way street. When persons become depressed, their cognitions change. They become more pessimistic, more critical of themselves, more likely to blame themselves for everything bad that happens, and so on. When the depression lifts, fortunately, these cognitions return to a more positive state (Dohr, Rush, & Bernstein, 1989). Thus, although negative cognitions appear to predispose us to depression, we never think more negatively than when we are depressed.

Interestingly, the research of Peter Lewinsohn and his associates (1980) suggests that at least some aspects of the "distorted" cognitions that are characteristic of depressed individuals are not distortions at all. Lewinsohn asked individuals who were experiencing major depression to participate in a group discussion for approximately 20 minutes. During this time, they were rated by a group of judges on their friendliness, assertiveness, warmth, and other social qualities. After the group discussion, each participant also rated himself or herself on the same dimensions. Another group of people who were not depressed went through exactly the same procedure.

When asked to rate their participation after a group discussion, people with major depression give more accurate ratings than do people who aren't depressed. It seems some positive "distortion" of our self-perception can be healthy.

As would have been predicted by Beck, the depressed group rated their social skills as being less adequate than did the nondepressed participants. Is this evidence that depressed individuals distort their view of themselves? Actually, it turns out that the self-ratings of the depressed group were *quite accurate* when compared with the ratings of the judges. It was the normal participants whose view of themselves was distorted! The nondepressed persons rated themselves as being significantly more socially skilled than the judges did. Furthermore, when the depressed individuals were given treatment and became less depressed, their self-perceptions became more like the normal group: They, too, began to rate themselves in unrealistically positive terms. Perhaps having this kind of "distorted" perception of ourselves is a good thing. Maybe we would all be depressed if we saw ourselves in the realistic terms in which others see us!

Bipolar Affective Disorder

bipolar affective disorder
(bī-pō′lar)　A condition in which the individual experiences periods of mania that alternate irregularly with periods of severe depression.

mania
(mā′nē-ah)　A disturbance of mood in which the individual experiences a euphoria characterized by unrealistic optimism and heightened sensory pleasures.

In the condition known as **bipolar affective disorder,** periods of mania alternate irregularly with periods of severe depression. **Mania** is a disturbance of mood that can be quite enjoyable to the individual in the short run but is usually damaging both to the person and to others in the long run. During the manic episode, the individual experiences a remarkable "high"—an intense euphoria in which sensory pleasures are heightened, one's self-esteem is very high, thoughts race, little sleep is needed, and unrealistic optimism prevails. Grandiose and financially damaging schemes and buying sprees are common during these periods, as are quitting jobs, getting a divorce, and engaging in sexual promiscuity. Psychotic distortions of reality are also common during manic periods. When well-meaning friends and family members try to control the manic individual, they are often rebuffed in sharp anger. Although an intensely pleasurable state, mania can be quite harmful to the person's finances and personal relationships. This harm can be clearly seen in the case of "Mrs. M.":

> At 17 she suffered from a depression . . . for several months, although she was not hospitalized. At 33, shortly before the birth of her first child, the patient was greatly depressed. For a period of four days she appeared in a coma. About a month after the birth of the baby she "became excited" and was entered as a patient in an institution for neurotic and mildly psychotic patients. As she began to improve, she was sent to a shore hotel for a brief vacation. The patient remained at the hotel for one night and on the following day signed a year's lease on an apartment, bought furniture, and became heavily involved in debt. Shortly thereafter Mrs. M. became depressed and returned to the hospital. . . . After several months she recovered and, except for relatively mild fluctuations of mood, remained well for approximately 2 years.
>
> She then became overactive and exuberant in spirits and visited her friends, to whom she outlined her plans for reestablishing different forms of lucrative business. She purchased many clothes, bought furniture, pawned her rings, and wrote checks without funds. She was returned to a hospital. Gradually her manic symptoms subsided, and after four months she was discharged. For a period thereafter she was mildly depressed. In a little less than a year Mrs. M. again became overactive, played her radio until late in the night, smoked excessively, and took out insurance on a car that she had not yet bought. Contrary to her usual habits, she swore frequently and loudly . . . and instituted divorce proceedings. On the day prior to her second admission to the hospital, she purchased 57 hats. (Kolb, 1977, pp. 455–456)*

*From L. C. Kolb, *Modern Clinical Psychiatry,* 9th ed. Copyright © 1977 W.B. Saunders Co., Philadelphia, PA. Reprinted by permission.

Mania may occur only once, but it usually returns in multiple episodes (Halgin & Whitbourne, 2000). When mania is recurrent, it alternates irregularly with episodes of severe depression. This alternating disorder was formerly known as *manic-depressive psychosis* and is now known as bipolar affective disorder. Bipolar affective disorders is a relatively uncommon problem; only 15 percent of individuals with affective disorder show this alternating pattern of intense highs and lows. Bipolar affective disorder is equally common among women and men (Kessler & others, 1995). Fortunately, bipolar affective disorder generally can be treated effectively with medication.

▶ SCHIZOPHRENIA

Psychologist: "Why do you think people believe in God?"

Patient: Uh, let's, I don't know why, let's see, balloon travel. He holds it up for you, the balloon. He don't let you fall out, your little legs sticking out down through the clouds. He's down to the smokestack, looking through the smoke trying to get the balloon gassed up you know. Way they're flying on top that way, legs sticking out, I don't know, looking down on the ground, heck, that'd make you so dizzy you just stay and sleep you know, hold down and sleep there. The balloon's His home you know up there. I used to sleep outdoors, you know, sleep outdoors instead of going home. He's had a home but His not tell where it's at you know. (Chapman & Chapman, 1973, p. 3)

The person giving this confused and confusing answer has a serious problem known as **schizophrenia.** Schizophrenia is an uncommon disorder that affects about 1 percent of the

Schizophrenia

www.mmhe.com/laheye1

schizophrenia
(skiz″o-fren′-ē-ah)   A psychological disorder involving cognitive disturbance (delusions and hallucinations), disorganization, and reduced enjoyment and interests.

general population. Approximately equal numbers of men and women are affected by schizophrenia (Kessler & others, 1995). However, it's a dramatic form of abnormality that, unless successfully treated, often renders normal patterns of living impossible.

Schizophrenia is characterized by three types of serious problems (Andreasen, Arndt, Alliger, Miller, & Flaum, 1995; Halgin & Whitbourne, 2000):

delusions
False beliefs that distort reality.

hallucinations
False perceptual experiences that distort reality.

1. *Delusions and hallucinations.* The central feature of schizophrenia is distortions of cognition that put the individual "out of touch with reality." Persons with schizophrenia often hold strange false beliefs (**delusions**) and have distorted and bizarre false perceptual experiences (**hallucinations**). We will discuss these distortions of cognition in greater detail in discussing the subtypes of schizophrenia.

2. *Disorganized thinking, emotions, and behavior.* As is clear in the preceding example, persons with schizophrenia often think in fragmented and disorganized ways. Their emotions and behavior are similarly disorganized and illogical at times. A person with schizophrenia might laugh when told sad news or shift rapidly from happiness to sadness and back again for no apparent reason. As a result, most of us find it very difficult to have conversations with persons with schizophrenia.

3. *Reduced enjoyment and interests.* Persons with schizophrenia often show what is called "blunted affect." They find less pleasure in life than most persons and have fewer interests and goals that are important to them. Although their emotions change in unpredictable ways, both their positive and negative emotions lack normal intensity. In many ways, they just do not care about things as much as other people. Often, this includes not being as interested in having close friendships.

Long-term studies of persons with schizophrenia show that their reduced enjoyment and interests is usually chronic and does not improve, but their delusions, hallucinations, and disorganization may improve for a while between episodes of worsened symptoms (Arndt & others, 1995; Breier, Schreiber, Dyer, & Pickar, 1991; Loebel & others, 1992). Schizophrenia is a broad class of psychotic disorders that is broken down into three major subtypes in the 1994 edition of the American Psychiatric Association's *Diagnostic and Statistical Manual of Mental Disorders (DSM-IV): paranoid, disorganized,* and *catatonic schizophrenia.* A fourth category, *undifferentiated schizophrenia,* is used to classify individuals who do not fit into the other three categories.

paranoid schizophrenia
(par'-ah-noid)   A subtype of schizophrenia in which the individual holds delusions of persecution and grandeur that seriously distort reality.

German psychiatrist Hans Prinzhorn has collected the most extensive collection of artwork by mental patients available. This painting from the collection, by August Neter, illustrates the hallucinations and the paranoid fantasies from which many schizophrenic patients suffer. In reviewing a showing of artwork by schizophrenic patients, such as the painting shown here, poet John Ashby wrote: "The lure of the work is strong, but so is the terror of the unanswerable riddles it proposes."

Paranoid Schizophrenia

A person with **paranoid schizophrenia** holds *false beliefs,* or *delusions,* that seriously distort reality. Most often, these are beliefs in the exceptional importance of oneself, so-called *delusions of grandeur*—such as being Jesus Christ, a CIA agent, or the inventor of a cure for war. These are often accompanied by delusions that, because one is so important, others are "out to get me" in attempts to thwart the individual's important mission. These are known as *delusions of persecution,* or *paranoia.*

If I were schizophrenic and believed that I were an agent of the CIA who alone had the ability to save the president from assassination by terrorists, I might also believe that my students were terrorists also who were trying to confuse and poison me. Think for a moment how bizarre I would seem to others who learned of my paranoid delusions. Think, too, about the terrifying, bewildering existence I would live if I believed those things. It would be small wonder that my emotions would seem unpredictable and strange and that I would withdraw from social contact.

Unfortunately, the cognitive disturbances of the paranoid schizophrenic do not stop with delusions. Many individuals with this disorder also experience false perceptual experiences, or *hallucinations.*

Their perceptions are either strangely distorted, or they may hear, see, or feel things that are not there. These bizarre experiences further add to the terrifying, perplexing unreality of the paranoid schizophrenic's existence.

Disorganized Schizophrenia

Disorganized schizophrenia resembles paranoid schizophrenia in that delusions and hallucinations are present, but the cognitive processes of the disorganized schizophrenic, as the name implies, are so disorganized and fragmented that the delusions and hallucinations have little recognizable meaning. The central features of this type of schizophrenia are extreme withdrawal from normal human contact and a shallow "silliness" of emotion. The disorganized schizophrenic acts in childlike ways, reacts inappropriately to both happy and sad events, and generally presents a highly bizarre picture to others.

Catatonic Schizophrenia

Catatonic schizophrenia is quite different in appearance from other forms of schizophrenia. Although catatonics sometimes experience delusions and hallucinations, their most obvious abnormalities are in social interaction, posture, and body movement. There are long periods of catatonic stupor, an inactive, statuelike state in which the individuals seem locked into a posture. Catatonic schizophrenics are often said to exhibit "waxy flexibility" during these stupors—they passively let themselves be placed into any posture and maintain it. Often the individual ceases to talk, appears not to hear what is spoken to him or her, and may no longer eat without being fed.

Frequently, however, the stupor is abruptly broken by periods of agitation. The person may pace and fidget nervously or may angrily attack others. Both of these patterns may alternate with periods of relative normality.

▶ PERSONALITY DISORDERS

To this point, we have been talking about psychological problems that develop in individuals who were once considered to be normal. To oversimplify the case, schizophrenia and the other disorders that we have considered are "breakdowns" in relatively normal persons. In contrast, the **personality disorders** discussed in this section are believed to result from personalities that developed improperly in the first place.

A number of personality disorders differ widely from one another but share several characteristics: (a) All personality disorders begin early in life; (b) they are disturbing to the person or to others; and (c) they are very difficult to treat. We will first look at two very different personality disorders to provide examples of this type of problem, then will provide brief descriptions of the other personality disorders.

Schizoid Personality Disorder

The suffix *-oid* means "like"—hence, *schizoid personality disorder* is like schizophrenia, in that blunted emotions and social withdrawal are exhibited. Unlike schizophrenia, however, this condition is not characterized by serious cognitive disturbances.

Individuals with **schizoid personality disorder** have little or no desire to have friends and indeed are not interested in even casual social contact. They are classic "loners." Usually, they are very shy as children but are not abnormally withdrawn until later childhood or adolescence. Gradually, they seem to lose interest in friends, family, and social activities and retreat more and more into a solitary existence.

They display little emotion and appear cold and aloof. Later in life, people with schizoid personality disorder often lose interest in personal appearance, hygiene, and other polite social conventions. Often they do not work and may even fall into homelessness or work as a streetwalking prostitute.

disorganized schizophrenia
A subtype of schizophrenia characterized by shallow silliness, extreme social withdrawal, and fragmented delusions and hallucinations.

catatonic schizophrenia
(kat″ah-ton′ik)   A subtype of schizophrenia in which the individual spends long periods in an inactive, statuelike state.

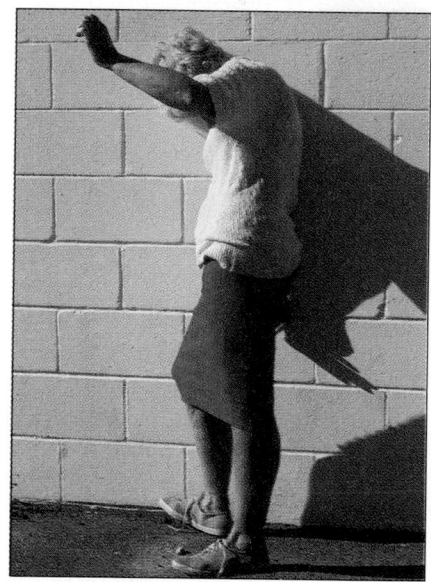

Catatonic individuals sometimes exhibit a state of catatonic stupor, during which they may maintain a single posture for several hours.

personality disorders
Psychological disorders that are believed to result from personalities that developed improperly during childhood.

schizoid personality disorder
(skiz′oid)   A personality disorder characterized by blunted emotions, lack of interest in social relationships, and withdrawal into a solitary existence.

antisocial personality disorder
A personality disorder characterized by smooth social skills and a lack of guilt about violating social rules and laws and taking advantage of others.

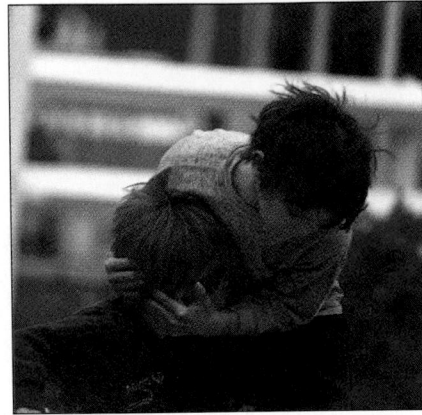

People with antisocial personality disorder frequently violate social laws and rules, while feeling little guilt about it. The disorder begins in childhood, when the person is usually highly aggressive.

Antisocial Personality Disorder

Individuals with **antisocial personality disorder** have a personality disorder quite different from the schizoid group. They frequently violate social rules and laws, take advantage of others, and feel little guilt about it. These individuals often have smooth social skills: They are sweet-talking con artists who are very likable at first. But they experience great difficulties in maintaining close personal relationships. They enter into marriages and other intimate relationships easily, but they tend to break up quickly.

Antisocial personalities have a low tolerance for frustration. They act on impulse, lose their tempers quickly, and lie easily and skillfully. They are often hardened criminals. In childhood, antisocial personalities are very difficult children. They are often bullies who fight, lie, cheat, steal, and are truant from school. They blame others for their misdeeds, feel picked on by their parents and teachers, and never seem to learn from their mistakes.

Individuals with antisocial personality disorder are often unemotional and guiltless—they are calm, cool characters. They are highly uncomfortable, however, when they are kept from excitement. They have an abnormal need for stimulation, novelty, and thrills. Because many turn to alcohol and drugs for excitement, they frequently become addicts. The primary harmfulness of the antisocial personality disorder is in the damage that is done to others. They often leave a trail of victims—victims of their lies, their crimes, their violent outbursts, and their broken intimate relationships.

The following case of antisocial personality disorder illustrates these problems well:

Donald's misbehavior as a child took many forms including lying, cheating, petty theft, and the bullying of smaller children. As he grew older he became more and more interested in sex, gambling, and alcohol. When he was 14 he made crude sexual advances toward a younger girl, and when she threatened to tell her parents he locked her in a shed. It was about 16 hours before she was found. Donald at first denied knowledge of the incident, later stating that she had seduced him and that the door must have locked itself. He expressed no concern for the anguish experienced by the girl and her parents, nor did he give any indication that he felt morally culpable for what he had done.

When he was 17, Donald left the boarding school, forged his father's name to a large check, and spent about a year traveling around the world. He apparently lived well, using a combination of charm, physical attractiveness, and false pretenses to finance his way. During subsequent years he held a succession of jobs, never staying at any one for more than a few months. Throughout this period he was charged with a variety of crimes, including theft, drunkenness in a public place, assault, and many traffic violations. In most cases he was either fined or given a light sentence.

His sexual experiences were frequent, casual, and callous. When he was 22 he married a 41-year-old woman whom he had met in a bar. Several other marriages followed, all bigamous. In each case the pattern was the same: he would marry someone on impulse, let her support him for several months, and then leave. . . . (Lahey & Ciminero, 1980, pp. 326–327)

Other Personality Disorders

The following are brief descriptions of the other eight types of personality disorders listed in *DSM-IV.* Be careful not to diagnose yourself or your friends while reading this list. The pattern must be extreme and consistent to qualify for a diagnosis.

1. *Schizotypal personality disorder:* few friendships, suspiciousness, strange ideas, such as belief that his or her mind can be read by others and that messages are being received in strange ways

2. *Paranoid personality disorder:* high degree of suspiciousness and mistrust of others, extreme irritability and sensitivity, coldness and lack of tender feelings

3. *Histrionic personality disorder:* self-centered, frequently seeking to be the center of attention, manipulating others through exaggerated expression of emotions and

difficulties, superficially charming and seductive but lacking genuine concern for others, frequent angry outbursts

4. *Narcissistic personality disorder:* unrealistic sense of self-importance, preoccupied with fantasies of future success, requires constant attention and praise, reacts very negatively to criticism or is indifferent to criticism, exploits others, feels entitled to special consideration, lack of genuine concern for others

5. *Borderline personality disorder:* impulsive and unpredictable, unstable personal relationships, angry, almost constantly needs to be with others, lack of clear identity, feelings of emptiness

6. *Avoidant personality disorder:* extreme shyness or social withdrawal in spite of a desire for friendships, extremely sensitive to rejection, very low self-esteem

7. *Dependent personality disorder:* passive dependence on others for support and decisions; has low self-esteem, and puts needs of others before self

8. *Obsessive-compulsive personality disorder:* perfectionistic, dominating, poor ability to express affection, excessive devotion to work, indecisive when faced with major decisions

● Review

Major depression involves one or more episodes of this negative mood state. These episodes range from mild to severe, with severe episodes sometimes being accompanied by bizarre perceptions and beliefs that distort reality. In bipolar affective disorder, the episodes of depression alternate irregularly with periods of the mood disturbance known as mania. Although this is an intensely pleasurable state, it's harmful in that it can lead to financial difficulties, can destroy personal relationships, and can often be accompanied by reality-distorting perceptions and beliefs.

Schizophrenia is a broad range of psychotic disorders characterized by disturbances of cognition that grossly distort reality, by distortions of emotions, and by withdrawal from social relationships. There are three major subtypes of schizophrenia. Paranoid schizophrenia is characterized by delusions of grandeur and persecution, often accompanied by hallucinations. Disorganized schizophrenia resembles paranoid schizophrenia but is typified by even more fragmented cognition and by shallow, silly emotions. Catatonic schizophrenia is quite different from the other types, being marked by stupors in which the individual may maintain postures for long periods of time. Biological factors—genetics, cortical deterioration, and abnormal prenatal development—are believed to be important in the origins of schizophrenia, but stress may be the immediate cause that triggers episodes.

Whereas other kinds of psychological disorders are thought to result from the "breakdown" of a normal personality, personality disorders are thought to result from faulty personality development during childhood. These disorders begin early in life, are disturbing to the individual or to others, and are difficult to treat. For example, individuals with schizoid personality disorder are very shy children who increasingly lose interest in social relationships as they grow older. Eventually, they lose interest in proper dress and social conditions, display little emotion, and rarely hold regular jobs. Antisocial personality disorder is characterized by rule-violating behavior as a child that develops into irresponsibility, dishonesty, and violence as adults. Such individuals are often con artists who are smooth and likable at first but who have great difficulties maintaining normal relationships. They also have an abnormal need for stimulation, and do not seem to learn from punishment.

● Check Your Learning

To be sure that you have learned the key points from the preceding section, cover the list of correct answers and try to answer each question. If you give an incorrect answer to any question, return to the page given next to the correct answer to see why your answer was not correct.

1. The individual experiencing _____ is deeply unhappy, finds little pleasure in life, and experiences other symptoms such as sleeping and eating problems and loss of energy.

   a) anxiety disorder

   b) major depression

   c) delusional disorder

   d) somatoform pain disorders

2. In the condition known as _____, periods of mania alternate irregularly with periods of severe depression.

   a) major depression

   b) mania disorder

   c) unipolar depression

   d) bipolar affective disorder

3. The three major areas of abnormality in schizophrenia are (a) _____; (b) _____; and (c) _____.

4. Strange and false perceptual experiences are termed

   a) delusions.

   b) paranoia.

   c) hallucinations.

   d) social withdrawal.

5. The type of schizophrenia characterized by stupor and "waxy flexibility" is called

   a) catatonic.

   b) paranoid.

   c) disorganized.

   d) stuporous.

6. _____ personality disorder is similar to schizophrenia, particularly in that blunted emotions and social withdrawal are exhibited, but, unlike schizophrenia, this condition is not characterized by serious cognitive disturbances.

   a) Antisocial

   b) Schizoid

   c) Dependent

   d) Histrionic

● Thinking Critically About Psychology

1. What are some possible explanations for the higher incidence of major depression in women?

2. Why do you think personality disorders are generally difficult to treat?

Application *of Psychology*

ABNORMAL PSYCHOLOGY AND CIVIL LIBERTIES

The goal of clinical psychology, psychiatry, and the other mental health professions is to help persons with mental disorders. In most cases, this means offering services to persons who come to the office or hospital and request professional services. In other cases, mental health professionals play more of an activist role. I am never more proud to be a psychologist than when I see members of my profession attempting to prevent abnormal behavior in the community, offering services to the indigent, and attempting to bring a scientific perspective to debates about important social issues. No mental health profession does enough in these areas, but these efforts are often significant.

In some cases, these outreach efforts are relatively uncomplicated matters. If enough psychologists and psychiatrists volunteer their time, and if funding can be obtained from public or private sources to rent space and pay the heating bill, it is a simple matter to set up a free clinic in an area where homeless persons live. As long as the persons who receive services voluntarily seek them, there is no conflict with the laws that protect civil liberties. In other cases, the attempt to provide assistance raises difficult legal and ethical issues.

In this section, we will discuss two important social issues to which psychology and psychiatry have recently turned their attention: homelessness and physician-assisted suicide. We will see that psychological concepts lie at the heart of these complicated issues. We will also see that important questions concerning civil liberties must be resolved before psychology will be able to play an effective role.

Abnormal Psychology and Homelessness

It has become commonplace in large cities in the United States to see homeless people sleeping on heating vents next to their bags of belongings. Who are these unfortunate persons? How have they fallen between the cracks in the world's most affluent society?

Although opinions vary, the primary factors associated with the increases in homelessness are government policies that have greatly reduced the amount of low-cost housing available to the poor, old-fashioned prejudice against ethnic minorities, and changes in vagrancy laws that, in many cases, give people the legal right to be homeless (to sleep on the street, to panhandle, etc.). Another reason for the increase in homeless persons is the inability of psychiatric hospitals and mental health centers to provide adequate services due to massive cuts in funding.

Most homeless persons—but certainly not all—have serious psychological disorders. As funding for mental health service programs is cut, the number of the homeless rises. A study of homeless individuals in inner-city Los Angeles (Koegel, Burnam, & Farr, 1988) found 62.2 percent to have a serious chronic mental disorder and/or alcohol or drug dependence. In the same city, very high rates of symptoms of schizophrenia were found among homeless adolescents (Mundy, Robertson, Robertson, & Greenblatt, 1990). A similar study in New York (Susser, Struening, & Conner, 1989) found serious mental and substance abuse disorders in 71 percent of homeless men.

We can see the role played by mental disorders in the true stories of Karen and Kevin, two homeless persons in New York City (Brosnahan & Giffen, 1993). In the words of 38-year-old Karen, "I was one of those people you see on street corners screaming at imaginary people, completely out of my mind." She was homeless for 13 years, periodically being treated in mental hospitals. But she was lucky and found her way into a program that provided consistent medication and therapy and found her affordable housing. As a result, Karen has been employed almost continuously for the past 3 years and has regained custody of her 14-year-old son.

Contrast her story to that of Kevin McKiever, the homeless man who was charged in 1991 with murdering a former Radio City Rockette with a knife. He had gone to Bellevue Psychiatric Hospital a few weeks before the stabbing, seeking treatment, but he was turned away

Many homeless people want psychiatric or psychological help. However, some mental health professionals argue that the right of some homeless people to refuse treatment must be respected as well.

because the hospital had no openings in its underfunded community-care program. Between 1975 and 1991, 52 persons were pushed in front of subway trains in New York by strangers, mostly by psychotic homeless persons (Martell & Dietz, 1992). Would these truly terrifying tragedies have happened if mental health services for the homeless were better funded and more effective?

Even if adequate funding were to be made available, however, it would not be a simple matter to provide services to all the homeless with mental disorders. Not all persons with mental disorders want treatment, especially those with substance abuse disorders and psychotic conditions. This fact has spurred tremendous debate in the mental health professions. Well-meaning professionals on both sides of this issue cannot agree on the best course of action. Some favor strong outreach programs that will search for mentally disordered homeless persons and provide them with mental hospitalization and medication, whether they want it or not. Some even favor "conservatorships," in which private individuals or public agencies are given the legal right to control the finances, medication, and hospitalization of persons with mental disorders who are judged to be incompetent to make their own decisions (Lamb & Weinberger, 1992). Other mental health professionals, however, argue that we must protect the civil rights of the homeless and provide treatment only to those who seek it voluntarily (Mossman & Perlin, 1992). Meanwhile, the public is just as deeply divided on this social issue that is, in equal measures, sad and frightening.

Physician-Assisted Suicide

Another emotionally laden issue is physician-assisted suicide. Like homelessness, this matter involves a complex interplay of civil rights and concepts from abnormal psychology.

Much of the publicity surrounding this issue has come from the outspoken efforts of Dr. Jack Kevorkian to convince lawmakers that it should be legal for Michigan physicians to assist terminally ill

Much of the controversy concerning physician-assisted suicide was created by the actions of the "suicide doctor," Dr. Jack Kevorkian.

patients in committing suicide painlessly, as by taking an overdose of sleeping pills or inhaling carbon monoxide. Dr. Kevorkian, who is a retired pathologist in Michigan, has helped many patients commit suicide. For example, he told the story of assisting the suicide of a 30-year-old man with a terminal disease commonly known as Lou Gehrig's disease. Dr. Kevorkian said that his patient wished to die because he had completely lost all motor control and knew that he would probably die by choking on his own saliva.

Dr. Kevorkian and other advocates of the right to commit suicide painlessly have argued forcefully that they are only attempting to prevent needless suffering and preserve human dignity. However, psychiatrists Herbert Hendin and Gerald Klerman (1993) and Harvey Chochinov (Chochinov & others, 1995) have written moving and cogent articles, pointing out what they believe to be the dangers involved in legalized physician-assisted suicide. They noted that studies have consistently shown that 95 percent of persons who commit suicide have mental disorders at the time of the suicide, usually depression. This is particularly true of elderly persons who take their lives during the kind of depressive episodes that are highly treatable. They state that persons who are prevented from committing suicide during an episode of depression are almost invariably grateful to be alive when they recover from the depression.

In the case of persons with terminal illnesses who seek assistance from a physician in committing suicide, Hendin and Klerman (1993) offer these sobering observations. Learning that one has a terminal illness is an extremely stressful event, but autopsy studies have shown that more elderly people commit suicide because they *mistakenly* thought they had a fatal illness than actually had such an illness. Furthermore, the first reaction of many persons who learn that they actually

have a terminal illness is depression and anxiety, but most recover from this phase and live meaningful lives until the end. Should patients with terminal illnesses be allowed to commit suicide during the initial depressed phase, when most of them would have later chosen to live? Should elderly patients who are depressed because they mistakenly believe that their relatives wish they were gone be provided with psychotherapy or assistance in suicide?

Hendin and Klerman (1993) also provide chilling evidence that suicide pacts between spouses or lovers, which are often romanticized in the press, often involve pressured decisions for one of the partners. Detailed studies of such cases reveal that suicide pacts often involve a man who wishes to die who coerces his wife into joining him to prove her love. They even report evidence from the videotaped suicide note and writings of a woman who committed suicide, perhaps partly over guilt that she had helped her 92-year-old father and 78-year-old mother commit suicide, even though she suspected that her mother had been pressured and was not ready to die. Ironically, the woman was the co-founder of the Hemlock Society, a society that advocates the right to commit suicide. Cases of double suicides must be the cause of particular concern.

Hendin and Klerman (1993) argue strongly that, if physician-assisted suicide is legalized, physicians without training in psychiatry will make decisions regarding the patient's wish to die without understanding the role that depression and other mental disorders can play in suicidal wishes. Furthermore, such laws might encourage unscrupulous physicians and nonphysicians to offer assistance in suicide without regard for the best interest of the person.

What are your thoughts about these serious and complicated issues?

● Summary

Chapter 13 introduces us to the wide range of abnormal thoughts, feelings, and actions that humans experience.

 I. Abnormal behavior includes those actions, thoughts, and feelings that are harmful to the person and/or others.

 A. Our ideas about the causes of abnormal behavior determine what we do to help those who experience it.

 B. Abnormal behavior is viewed today as a natural, rather than a supernatural, phenomenon. Both biological and psychological factors are thought to play a role in the origins of abnormal behavior.

 II. Anxiety disorders are characterized by excessive anxiety.

 A. Intense, unrealistic fears are called phobias.

 B. Generalized anxiety disorder is characterized by free-floating anxiety.

 C. Panic anxiety disorder involves attacks of intense anxiety.

 D. Obsessions are anxiety-provoking thoughts that will not go away; compulsions are urges to repeatedly engage in a behavior.

 III. Somatoform disorders are conditions in which an individual experiences symptoms of health problems that are psychological rather than physical in origin.

 A. Somatization disorders are a type of somatoform disorder that involves multiple symptoms of illness that indirectly create a high risk of medical complications.

 B. Conversion disorders are a type of somatoform disorder that involves serious specific somatic symptoms in the absence of any physical cause. Somatoform pain disorders involve pain without physical cause.

 IV. In the various types of dissociative disorders, there is a change in memory, perception, or identity.

 A. Dissociative amnesia and fugue states involve memory loss that has psychological rather than physical causes.

 B. In depersonalization, individuals feel that they or their surroundings have become distorted or unreal.

 C. Individuals who exhibit dissociative identity disorder act as if they possess more than one personality in the same body.

 V. Mood disorders are disturbances of positive or negative moods.

 A. The individual experiencing major depression is deeply unhappy and shows other characteristic symptoms.

 B. In the condition known as bipolar affective disorder, periods of mania alternate irregularly with periods of severe depression.

 VI. Schizophrenia involves three major areas of abnormality: (a) delusions and hallucinations; (b) disorganized thinking, emotions, and behavior; and (c) reduced enjoyment and interests.

 A. The paranoid schizophrenic holds false beliefs, or delusions—usually of grandeur and persecution—that seriously distort reality.

 B. Disorganized schizophrenia is characterized by extreme withdrawal from normal human contact, fragmented delusions and hallucinations, and a shallow "silliness" of emotion.

 C. Catatonic schizophrenia is marked by stupors in which the individual may maintain postures for long periods of time.

VII. Personality disorders are thought to result from personalities that developed improperly during childhood, rather than from breakdowns under stress.

    A. Schizoid personality disorders are characterized by a loss of interest in proper dress and social contact, a lack of emotion, and an inability to hold regular jobs.

    B. The antisocial personality frequently violates social rules and laws, is often violent, takes advantage of others, and feels little guilt about it.

● Resources

1. Excellent overviews of the psychology of psychological disorders appear in Davison, G. C., & Neale, J. M. (1996). *Abnormal psychology: An experimental clinical approach* (7th ed.). New York: John Wiley; and Halgin, R. P., & Whitbourne, S. K. (2000). *Abnormal psychology* (3rd ed.). Boston: McGraw-Hill.

2. For more on abnormal psychology and individual rights, see Winick, B. J. (1996). *The right to refuse mental health treatment.* Washington, DC: American Psychological Association.

3. A moving personal account of the experience of schizophrenia is found in the classic book Sechehaye, M. (1951). *Reality lost and regained: Autobiography of a schizophrenic girl.* New York: Grune & Stratton.

4. For a social learning view of dissociative identity disorder, see Spanos, N. P. (1997). *Multiple identities and false memories.* Washington, DC: American Psychological Association.

5. For an excellent discussion of depression that tends to recur during the winter months (seasonal affective disorder), see Lee, T. M. C., & others (1998). Seasonal affective disorder. *Clinical Psychology: Science and Practice, 5,* 275–290.

6. An excellent source of accurate information about psychological disorders is http://www.mentalhealth.com.

7. The web site of the American Psychological Association is an excellent resource for information about mental health. www.apa.org

CHAPTER

14

CHAPTER OUTLINE

Therapies

PROLOGUE

David had always been a neat and orderly person. During his first session with the therapist, he described with a half-hearted smile an incident in which he slipped and fell in mud on the way to his elementary school and returned home sobbing. But David's cleanliness caused only minor problems until his daughter was diagnosed with pinworms. David became intensely anxious when he heard the doctor describe how pinworms are spread through their eggs and recommend that the clothes of everyone in the family be boiled to prevent contagion.

David immediately went home and boiled the family's clothes and sheets. After he finished, he washed his hands. But as soon as he did, he thought that there might still be pinworm eggs on them and he washed them again. Soon David began worrying about germs, dirt, and feces that might be on his hands. Within days, he was washing his hands 200 times a day.

David's worst times were at night: He would lie in bed after washing his hands and try to resist the urge to get up and wash them again, only to fail over and over. When his wife became worried about his sanity, and his hands began to crack and bleed because of the constant washing, he decided to contact a therapist (based on Prochaska, 1984, pp. 268–271).

David had developed a form of abnormal behavior called obsessive-compulsive disorder. We will see in this chapter that, fortunately, several forms of treatment are effective for this and other psychological problems. One remedy for obsessive-compulsive disorder that often helps is medication, but a simple form of psychological therapy is also effective. In this therapy, the person agrees to be prevented from washing and to endure the anxiety that being unable to wash produces. In time, the anxiety usually drops to normal levels if the individual does not give in to the urge to wash (Baxter & others, 1992; Piacentini, 1999).

Psychotherapy is a process of people helping people. In psychotherapy, a trained professional seeks to help a person with a psychological problem by using methods based on psychological theories of the nature of the problem. These therapy methods include everyday activities such as asking questions, making suggestions, and demonstrating alternative ways of behaving, but psychotherapy differs from commonsense attempts to help because of the theories that determine what is asked and what is suggested. Several different forms of psychotherapy are based on the theories of personality that we studied in chapter 11.

Psychoanalysts feel that abnormal behavior is the result of unconscious conflicts among the id, ego, and superego. These conflicts remain hidden from consciousness because the ego and superego see them as dangerous and block them out. The process of psychoanalysis, then, is a process of relaxing the censorship exerted by the conscious mind and bringing unconscious conflicts into awareness, where they can be intelligently resolved. Because the contents of the unconscious are revealed only in disguised, symbolic ways, however, the psychoanalyst must help the individual interpret glimpses of the hidden side of the mind.

Humanistic psychologists also believe that the goal of psychotherapy is to help the person achieve greater self-awareness, but in ways that differ from those of psychoanalysts. Humanists believe that feelings that conflict with a person's self-concept are often denied conscious awareness. The humanistic psychotherapist seeks to help the person allow this information into his or her consciousness and thus achieve fuller self-awareness.

413

Behavior therapy is an approach to psychotherapy that is associated with the social learning view of personality. Because psychological problems are believed to be the result of unfortunate learning experiences, the behavior therapist plays the role of a teacher helping the person *unlearn* abnormal ways of behavior. Cognitive therapy is a related approach to therapy that is also based on social learning theory. Cognitive therapists believe that we have learned illogical ways of thinking that cause abnormal behavior. They attempt to change these faulty cognitions primarily by pointing out their irrationality.

Help for abnormal behavior is not delivered only in one-to-one psychotherapy, however. It's sometimes provided in the form of group or family therapy, and it often takes the form of medication and other kinds of medical treatment.

▶ DEFINITION OF PSYCHOTHERAPY

People with the serious kinds of psychological problems described in chapter 13 generally need professional help. Many forms of help are available for psychological disorders from psychologists, psychiatrists, clinical social workers, and counselors. In this chapter, the major forms of therapy are described and related to the differing theories of personality (chapter 11) and differing views of abnormal behavior (chapter 13).

psychotherapy
(sī-kō-ther'ah-pē)   A form of therapy in which a trained professional uses methods based on psychological theories to help a person with psychological problems.

In general terms, **psychotherapy** can be defined as a specialized process in which a trained professional uses psychological methods to help a person with psychological problems. The term *psychological methods* can refer to almost any kind of human interaction (such as talking or demonstrating) that is based on a psychological theory of the problem, but it does *not* include medical treatment methods such as medication.

Different forms of psychotherapy associated with psychoanalytic, humanistic, and social learning theories of personality involve very different psychological methods. The approach to psychotherapy associated with social learning theory, known as behavior therapy, views the process of helping as a form of teaching. The therapist helps the person learn not to engage in harmful behaviors and to learn adaptive behaviors to take their place. The approaches to psychotherapy associated with psychoanalytic and humanistic views of personality see their goal as providing insight—that is, bringing feelings (or conflicts of information) of which the person is unaware into conscious awareness. Although the methods of psychoanalysis and humanistic therapy differ greatly, they both view the therapist not as a teacher but as a catalyst, an agent who makes change possible but does not actually cause or enter into the change. Therapies that strive for increased awareness view the person with problems as the agent of his or her own improvement.

▶ ETHICAL STANDARDS FOR PSYCHOTHERAPY

The relationship between client and psychotherapist is a unique one. The patient divulges large amounts of personal information in an emotion-laden setting and places her or his future in the hands of the psychotherapist. Because this places the therapist in a position of power relative to the client, it's essential that the highest ethical standards be followed in the practice of psychotherapy. The following discussion of ethical principles is based on the policies developed by the American Psychological Association (1990, 1993) and the Association for Advancement of Behavior Therapy (1978).

Psychotherapy is considered to be ethical only under the following circumstances:

1. The goals of treatment must be carefully considered with the client. These goals should be in the best interest of the client and society and they must be fully understood by the client.

2. The choices for alternative treatment methods should be carefully considered. For example, after reading this chapter, you may know whether you would prefer a therapist who takes a psychoanalytic, cognitive, behavioral, or other approach.

3. The therapist must only treat problems that she or he is qualified to treat. No therapist is trained to use all forms of therapy or to handle all types of problems (adults, children, marital problems, etc.). Therefore, the therapist must refer cases that fall outside his or her expertise to qualified therapists.

4. The effectiveness of treatment must be evaluated in some way. The best way of doing this is to use meaningful measures of the problem and progress in treating it.

5. The rules and laws regarding the confidentiality of all information obtained about the client during treatment must be fully explained to the client. Under most circumstances it is unethical and illegal for the therapist to reveal any information about the person (even the fact that a person is a client in therapy) to anyone without the written permission of the client.

6. The therapist must not use the power of the intense relationship with the client to exploit the client in sexual or other ways. Sexual or romantic intimacies with clients have long been strictly forbidden, but, in contrast to novels and movies in which therapists and current or former clients fall in love and marry, ethical regulations even forbid romantic or sexual relationships with former clients under virtually all circumstances. Sexual harassment of clients is similarly strictly forbidden.

7. The therapist must treat human beings with dignity and understand and respect differences based on gender, ethnicity, sexual orientation, and other sociocultural factors. To the greatest extent possible, therapists must understand and respect human differences and not try to sway clients to their own beliefs and ways. For example, this means that a traditional male therapist must not try to influence a woman who identifies with the feminist philosophy to adopt a more subservient feminine role. Similarly, a therapist who believes that homosexuality is immoral must not attempt to convince a homosexual who is comfortable with her or his sexual orientation to change. If the therapist cannot respect the beliefs and ways of the client, the therapist must refer that person to another therapist.

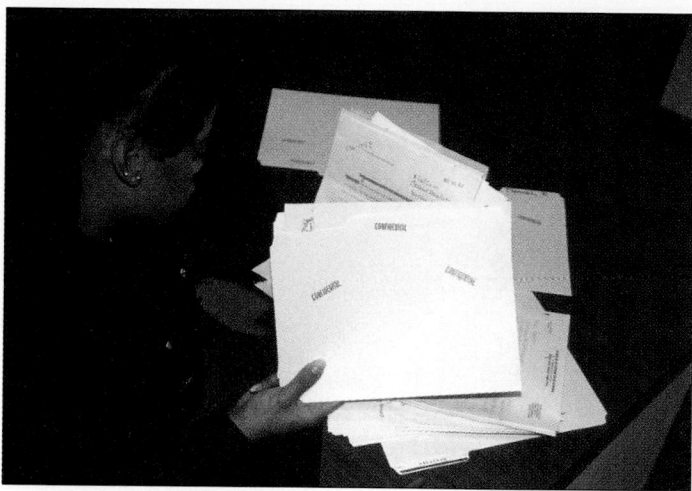

Psychotherapists must respect the rules and laws regarding the confidentiality of information about their clients.

▶ PSYCHOANALYSIS

Psychoanalysis is the approach to psychotherapy founded by Sigmund Freud. It's based on Freud's belief that the root of all psychological problems is unconscious conflicts among the id, ego, and superego. Conflicts inevitably exist among these three competing forces, but they can cause problems if they get out of hand. If too much of the energy of the superego and ego is devoted to holding the selfish desires of the id in check, or, if these prohibitions are weak and the id threatens to break free, psychological disturbances result. According to Freud, these conflicts must be brought into consciousness if they are to be solved.

Bringing unconscious conflicts into consciousness is not an easy matter, though. Recall from chapter 11 that the id is completely unconscious. Even the sexual and aggressive motives that we consciously experience have been transformed by the ego into safe and socially acceptable versions of the id's true desires. According to Freud, the ego operates as if the raw, selfish desires of the id were too dangerous to allow into consciousness, so it works diligently to dam up the id in the recesses of our unconscious mind. Special therapy methods must be used, therefore, to allow information about unconscious id conflicts to slip past the censorship of the ego.

It's generally possible to bring information out of the unconscious only when the ego's guard is temporarily relaxed, and even then, the id is able to reveal itself only in disguised, symbolic forms. Thus, the job of the psychoanalyst is to (a) create conditions in which the censorship of the ego is relaxed and (b) to interpret the disguised, symbolic revelations of the unconscious mind to the patient.

psychoanalysis
(sī'kō-ah-nal'i-sis)   A method of psychotherapy developed by Freud based on his belief that the root of all psychological problems is unconscious conflicts among the id, the ego, and the superego.

A patient and therapist in a session of orthodox psychoanalysis.

free association
A tool used by Freud in which the patient is encouraged to talk about whatever comes to mind, allowing the contents of the unconscious mind to slip past the censorship of the ego.

Techniques of Psychoanalytic Psychotherapy

Most contemporary psychoanalysts do not practice an orthodox version of psychoanalysis but, rather, practice versions based on the revisions of Jung, Adler, Horney, and more contemporary psychoanalysts. Still, many of the specific techniques of therapy used by Freud are still in use today. These include free association, dream interpretation, interpretation of resistance, and interpretation of transference.

Free Association

Freud's primary tool of therapy was the method of **free association.** In this method, the individual talks in a loose and undirected way about whatever comes to mind. No thought or feeling is to be withheld, no matter how illogical, trivial, unpleasant, or silly it might seem. Freud hoped that this technique would lead to a "turning off" of the intellectual control of the ego and allow for glimpses of the unconscious. Occasionally, as the mind wanders, the id slips out. To make this more likely to happen, Freud had his patients lie on a couch, facing the ceiling. He sat out of sight, behind them, so they would feel like they were talking to themselves rather than revealing forbidden information to another.

The "glimpses of the unconscious" revealed during free association have hidden, symbolic meaning that must be translated or interpreted to the patient by the psychoanalyst. For example, the patient might mention during the course of free association that he wanted to go hunting with his father but that he never asked him to go hunting because he was afraid that his father was too old and might get hurt. To the psychoanalyst, this statement might be about phallic symbols (guns) and the son's unresolved Oedipus conflict (see chapter 11) that has left him with an unacceptable desire to shoot his father. When interpreted to the patient, Freud believed, this information about the unconscious would help the person consciously solve his or her problems.

Dream Interpretation

dream interpretation
A method developed by Freud in which the symbols of the manifest content of dreams that are recalled by the patient are interpreted to reveal their latent content.

Dream interpretation was used by Freud in much the same manner as free association. As we mentioned in chapter 4, the obvious or manifest content of dreams is believed by psychoanalysts to symbolically mask the true or latent content of dreams. By asking patients to recall dreams, Freud believed he had obtained another "window" on the unconscious.

For example, a recurrent dream of an adolescent boy in which he was drifting through a slimy swamp on a raft, reaching down repeatedly into the dirty water and pulling up shoes might have no meaning at all to the adolescent. The psychoanalyst might translate it to mean that the boy was experiencing conflicts over his heterosexual desires. Shoes are commonly taken to symbolize vaginas in psychoanalytic thinking, and the dirty, forbidding water from which he was attempting to possess these vaginas might represent his guilt feelings about sex.

Interpretation of Resistance

resistance
Any form of patient opposition to the process of psychoanalysis.

Freud also placed heavy emphasis on the interpretation of what he called resistance in therapy. **Resistance** is any form of opposition of the patient to the process of psychoanalysis. Resistance can occur in two ways. It might take vague forms, such as missing appointments with the therapist or questioning the value of psychoanalysis. Or it might be a specific resistance to the interpretations of the therapist. In either case, resistance meant to Freud that he had located a conflict in the patient that was so laden with anxiety that the patient wanted to avoid talking about it. This avoidance of a topic made Freud all the more interested in pursuing it.

Angrily telling a psychoanalyst that he or she is wrong for suggesting that you ever wanted to have casual sex with a person you did not love may convince your therapist that this is something that you actually want to do but that you consider morally unacceptable. To give you better insight into your own motives, your psychoanalyst might interpret this resistance to you. The analyst would believe that, if you erroneously continue to think you do not want casual sex, you will not be able to understand and deal with the anxiety that you experience. If, on the other hand, you become aware that you do want casual sex, but that you feel that it would be immoral to do so, you can make more rational, informed choices about your behavior.

Interpretation of Transference

The relationship that forms between patient and therapist can also be a source of information about the unconscious to the psychoanalyst. Because the patient comes to the therapist in need of help, reveals a great deal of private information, and receives acceptance and support, it's not surprising that a rather intense relationship often develops. This relationship is not like the one you have with your dentist, but more like a close parent-child relationship.

Because of the intensity of the relationship in therapy, psychoanalysts believe that the kind of relationship the patient has with the therapist reveals a great deal about the way the patient relates to his or her parents and other significant authority figures. Psychoanalysts call this phenomenon **transference.** When patients repeatedly ask for reassurance that they will not be dropped as clients, argue about fees, or make sexual advances, they are believed to be transferring to the therapist feelings that they have for other significant adults in their lives. That is, they are feeling and acting toward the therapist in the same basic ways that they feel and act toward their parents, employers, and so on. When interpreted to the patients, psychoanalysts believe that transference can serve as another valuable source of insight.

transference
(trans-fer'ens)   The phenomenon in psychoanalysis in which the patient comes to feel and act toward the therapist in ways that resemble how he or she feels and acts toward other significant adults.

Catharsis

In addition to the interpretation of symbolic revelations of unconscious conflicts, psychoanalysis allows the patient to release some of the emotion that is pent up with unconscious conflicts. All forms of psychotherapy can be very emotional experiences that at times involve talking about highly upsetting topics. Letting these emotions out—a process psychoanalysts call **catharsis**—provides a temporary relief from discomfort. Catharsis is not a technique of psychoanalysis; rather, it is one of its benefits.

This relief does not solve problems in and of itself, but it does make the patient feel better. Catharsis may facilitate the process of psychoanalysis, however, because a patient who feels better will generally be better able to make more intelligent decisions about discoveries from the unconscious.

Catharsis

www.mmhe.com/laheye1

catharsis
The release of emotional energy related to unconscious conflicts.

Excerpt from Psychoanalytic Psychotherapy

In the following excerpt from a session of psychoanalytic psychotherapy, the therapist attempts to get the client to reinterpret his anxiety:

Client: We had a salesmen's meeting, and a large group of us were cramped together in a small room and they turned out the lights to show some slides, and I got so jumpy and anxious I couldn't stand it.

Therapist: So what happened?

C: I just couldn't stand it. I was sweating and shaking, so I got up and left, and I know I'll be called on the carpet for walking out.

T: You became so anxious and upset that you couldn't stand being in the room even though you knew that walking out would get you into trouble.

C: Yeah. . . . What could have bothered me so much to make me do a dumb thing like that?

T: You know, we've talked about other times in your life when you've become upset in close quarters with other men, once when you were in the army and again in your dormitory at college.

"Mr. Prentice is *not* your father. Alex Binster is *not* your brother. The anxiety you feel is *not* genuine. Dr. Froelich will return from vacation September 15th. Hang on."

C: That's right, and it was the same kind of thing again.

T: And, if I'm correct, this has never happened to you in a group of men and women together, no matter how closely you've been cramped together.

C: Uh. . . . Yes, that's right.

T: So it appears that something especially about being physically close to other men, and especially in the dark, makes you anxious, as if you're afraid bad things might happen in that kind of situation.

C: (Pause) I think you're right about that . . . and I know I'm not physically afraid of other men. Do you think I might get worried about something homosexual taking place?*

---

*Source: I. B. Weiner, *Principles of Psychotherapy.* Copyright © 1975 John Wiley & Sons, Inc.

Interpersonal Psychotherapy for Depression

interpersonal psychotherapy
A form of psychological therapy, based on the theories of neo-Freudian Harry Stack Sullivan, that focuses on the accurate identification and communication of feelings and the improvement of current social relationships.

In recent years, a new form of psychotherapy, known as **interpersonal psychotherapy,** has emerged from the psychoanalytic tradition, particularly the theories of neo-Freudian Harry Stack Sullivan (Klerman & Weissman, 1993; Weissman, 1999). As discussed in chapter 11, contemporary neo-Freudian theories emphasize the importance of interpersonal relationships in our lives more than unconscious sexual motivation. Therefore, interpersonal therapy is quite different from classical Freudian psychoanalysis. Interpersonal psychotherapy ignores unconscious motivation, minimizes discussion of the past, and does not involve interpretation of the individual's relationship with the therapist (transference). Instead, interpersonal psychotherapy focuses on the "here and now." Interpersonal psychotherapy is a brief form of psychotherapy that is usually completed in 12 to 16 weeks. Unlike other forms of Freudian therapies, interpersonal therapy is highly focused and structured, with therapists following detailed treatment manuals.

To date, interpersonal therapy has been developed only to treat depression. In general, interpersonal therapists believe that depression can be treated by improving our understanding of our feelings and improving how we relate and communicate to the important people in our lives. Interpersonal therapists believe that there are *four kinds of problems that cause depression:*

1. Grief over the loss of an important relationship through the break-up of a relationship, a divorce, or the death of a loved one

2. Conflicts with people who are significant to us

3. Life events that are stressful or that create threats to our self-esteem

4. Lack of social skills for establishing healthy interpersonal relationships

How does interpersonal therapy attempt to deal with depression created by these four causes? In interpersonal psychotherapy, therapists attempt to reach *seven goals* to treat depression:

1. Help the individual feel that the therapist understands his or her feelings and considers them to be important

2. Help the individual understand how his or her feelings are related to what is going on in his or her life, particularly to his or her current social relationships. The interpersonal therapist allows discussion of past social relationships (e.g., relationships with parents, former romantic partners, etc.) only to reach an understanding of how "emotional baggage" from past relationships can influence current relationships

3. Help the individual learn to express his or her feelings to other persons in constructive ways

4. Identify relationships that are too unhealthy to fix, to end them appropriately, and to move on to healthier relationships with others

5. Help the individual develop a sense of mastery of the new roles that are created by life events, such as dating again after divorce or entering a new occupation

6. Improve the individual's skills for creating healthy new relationships and maintaining them

7. Help the individual develop an optimistic focus on current opportunities for change instead of on the past

To reach these goals, the therapist keeps every session focused on the individual's feelings, his or her current life circumstances, and current options for change. For example, Charles has felt very depressed for the past few months. He has a stable job as a waiter, and he has many friends and a long-term relationship with a woman whom he hopes to marry. For the past few months, he has been having many fights with his girlfriend, who recently entered college. The interpersonal psychotherapy sessions may reveal that Charles feels unimportant to his girlfriend, now that she studies during most evenings and weekends and has less time for him than in the past. When they do have time to spend together, they often fight because Charles treats her with anger and sarcasm. The therapist would first help Charles see that his feelings involve worry that he is no longer important to her, rather than anger that she has entered college. Then the therapist would help Charles learn to calmly express his feelings of worry to his girlfriend without anger or sarcasm. This would make it easier for her to respond with nurturing and reassurance. These changes, in turn, could be expected to help reduce his feelings of depression.

The most important thing about interpersonal therapy is that it is *effective* in treating depression. A number of large and well-controlled studies have shown that it is at least as effective as the most effective forms of psychotherapy (and more effective than some types of psychotherapy) and is often as effective as antidepressant medication, with far fewer side effects (Klerman & others, 1995; Mufson, Weissman, Moreau, & Garfinkel, 1999; Rosello & Bernal, 1999; Swartz, 1999). Relatively few therapists have been trained to use this new method of psychotherapy, but, because it is effective and detailed treatment manuals are available, its availability is increasing rapidly. Because it is effective in a short period of time, the use of interpersonal therapy is advocated by many managed care organizations as an economical way of effectively treating depression (Weissman, 1999).

● Review

Psychoanalysis is the method of psychotherapy based on Freud's theory of personality. The therapist attempts to help the patient by bringing unconscious conflicts into consciousness so they can be intelligently resolved. Because the ego works to block from consciousness the contents of the unconscious mind (including conflicts among the id, ego, and superego), the psychoanalyst must create conditions to relax the censorship of the ego. Even when the unconscious mind reveals itself at these times, however, it does so in disguised, symbolic ways. This means that a second function of the psychoanalyst is to interpret the disguised information revealed during psychoanalysis to the patient. The method most commonly used by the psychoanalyst to relax the ego's censorship is free association. Comments made by the patient during these wandering, unguided conversations are believed to symbolically reveal hidden conflicts. In addition, the psychoanalyst interprets information from dreams, resistance to the process of therapy, and the way the patient acts toward the psychoanalyst (transference) to reveal further the unconscious mind to the patient. Psychoanalysis is believed to provide temporary relief by allowing the patient to vent some of the emotion tied up in unconscious conflicts (catharsis). A new form of psychodynamic psychotherapy, called interpersonal therapy, has been found to be effective in the treatment of depression. Unlike classical psychoanalysis, this form of psychotherapy focuses on the "here and now" and helps the individual accurately identify feelings, communicate feelings constructively, and improve social relationships.

● Check Your Learning

To be sure that you have learned the key points from the preceding section, cover the list of correct answers and try to answer each question. If you give an incorrect answer to any question, return to the page given next to the correct answer to see why your answer was not correct. Remember that these questions cover only some of the important information in this section; it is important that you make up your own questions to check your learning of other facts and concepts.

1. In general terms, _____ can be defined as a specialized process in which a trained professional uses psychological methods to help a person with psychological problems.

2. _____ is based on Freud's belief that the root of all psychological problems is unconscious conflicts among the id, ego, and superego that must be brought into conscious awareness.

   a) Behavior therapy   c) Psychoanalysis
   b) Client-centered therapy   d) Cognitive therapy

3. Freud's primary tool of therapy was the method of _____, in which the individual talks in a loose and undirected way about whatever comes to mind.

   a) free association   c) dream interpretation
   b) transference   d) resistance

4. _____ describes the release of emotional energy related to unconscious conflicts.

   a) Emotional cleansing   c) Liberation
   b) Catharsis   d) Outletting

5. The new form of psychotherapy based on neo-Freudian theories that avoids focus on the past and emphasizes the accurate identification of feelings, constructive communication, and improvement of social relationships is called _____.

● Thinking Critically About Psychology

1. Give a brief personality description of the type of patients who you believe would benefit most from psychoanalysis. Would you include women? How about members of ethnic groups different from Freud's?

2. What would you consider to be the strengths of psychoanalysis? What might be its weaknesses?

Correct Answers 1. psychotherapy (p. 414), **2.** c (p. 415), **3.** a (p. 416), **4.** b (p. 417), **5.** interpersonal psychotherapy (p. 418).

▶ HUMANISTIC PSYCHOTHERAPY

The humanistic and psychoanalytic schools of thought both believe that the primary goal of therapy is to bring forth feelings of which the individual is unaware into conscious awareness. Recall from chapter 11 that Carl Rogers gives us an alternative way of thinking about feelings and information of which we are not consciously aware. Unlike Freud, Rogers does not believe that we are born with an unconscious mind. Rather, we deny awareness to information and feelings that differ too much from our concepts of self and ideal self (by not symbolizing them).

Using the same example that we used to illustrate Freud's concept of the unconscious, suppose you were a person who wanted casual sex. If your ideal self (the one you think you should ideally be) were the kind of person who would never have casual sex, you might deny conscious awareness to that desire. The desire for casual sex did not arise from an unconscious id, according to Rogers, but the end result is the same: When a feeling is denied awareness, it can create anxiety until it's brought into the open. That is, it creates trouble until the individual achieves full awareness of his or her feelings. Because humanists view full self-awareness as necessary for the complete realization of our inner-directed potential, they speak of the process of therapy in terms of "growth in awareness" rather than insight.

Carl Rogers refers to his humanistic approach as **client-centered psychotherapy** (he prefers the term *client* to the more medically oriented term *patient*) because the client, not the therapist, is at the center of the process of psychotherapy (Rogers, 1951). More recently, the term *person-centered psychotherapy* has come into vogue. The emphasis is on the ability of clients to help themselves, rather than on the ability of the therapist to help the clients. The job of the therapist in client-centered therapy is not to employ specific therapy techniques or to interpret the client's behavior, but to create an atmosphere that is so emotionally safe for the clients that they will feel free to express to the therapist (and to themselves) the feelings they have denied awareness. Growth in awareness comes not from interpretations but from the client's feeling safe enough to explore hidden emotions in the therapy sessions. Rogers believes that the creation of this safe atmosphere requires three elements from the therapist. The therapist (a) must be warm; (b) must genuinely be able to like the clients and unconditionally accept everything they think, feel, or do without criticism; and (c) must have empathy—an accurate understanding and sharing of the emotions of the client. A number of studies have shown that the degree of warmth and empathy of the therapist is an important determinant of the effectiveness of psychotherapy, even when the method of psychotherapy is not client-centered therapy (Brent & Kolko, 1998; Rounsaville & others, 1987).

The closest thing to a specific "technique" in client-centered therapy is the process of **reflection.** The therapist helps the clients clarify the feelings expressed in their statements by reflecting back the emotions of the client. Sometimes the therapists ask questions, but, other than reflections, client-centered therapists say relatively little in therapy. In particular, they strictly avoid giving advice to clients. They feel that clients can easily learn to solve their own problems after they have gained awareness, but that they will remain dependent on the therapist if the therapist solves their problems for them.

Carl Rogers (top right) facilitating the discussion during a group therapy session.

client-centered psychotherapy
Carl Rogers' approach to humanistic psychotherapy, in which the therapist creates an atmosphere that encourages clients to discover feelings of which they are unaware.

reflection
(re-flek´shun)   A technique in humanistic psychotherapy in which the therapist reflects the emotions of the client to help clients clarify their feelings.

Excerpt from Client-Centered Psychotherapy

The following is an excerpt from a conversation between humanistic psychologist Carl Rogers and a client, a depressed young man. Notice the complete, nonjudgmental acceptance of the client's feelings.

Rogers: Everything's lousy, huh? You feel lousy? (Silence of 39 seconds)

Rogers: Want to come in Friday at 12 at the usual time?

Client: [Yawns and mutters something unintelligible.] (Silence of 48 seconds)

Rogers: Just kind of feel sunk way down deep in these lousy, lousy feelings, hm? Is that something like it?

Client: No.

Rogers: No? (Silence of 20 seconds)

Client: No. I just ain't no good to nobody, never was, and never will be.

Rogers: Feeling that now, hm? That you're just no good to yourself, no good to anybody. Just that you're completely worthless, huh? Those really are lousy feelings. Just feel that you're no good at all, hm?

[From a session three days later]

Client: I just want to run away and die.

Rogers: M-hm, m-hm, m-hm. It isn't even that you want to get away from here to something. You just want to leave here and go away and die in a corner, hm? (Silence of 30 seconds)

Rogers: I guess as I let that soak in I really do sense how, how deep that feeling sounds, that you—I guess the image that comes to my mind is sort of a—wounded animal that wants to crawl away and die. It sounds as though that's kind of the way you feel that you just want to get away from here and vanish. Perish. Not exist. (Silence of 1 minute)

Client: [almost inaudibly] All day yesterday and all morning I wished I were dead. I even prayed last night that I could die.

Rogers: I think I caught all of that, that for a couple of days now you've just wished you could be dead and you've even prayed for that, I guess that. One way this strikes me is that to live is such an awful thing to you, you just wish you could die, and not live. (Silence of 1 minute, 12 seconds)

Rogers: So that you've been just wishing and wishing that you were not living. You wish that life would pass away from you. (Silence of 30 seconds)

Client: I wish it more'n anything else I've ever wished around here.

Rogers: M-hm, m-hm, m-hm. I guess you've wished for lots of things but boy! It seems as though this wish to not live is deeper and stronger than anything you ever wished before. (Silence of 1 minute, 36 seconds)

Reproduced by permission of the publisher, F. E. Peacock Publishers, Inc., Itasca, Illinois. From Raymond J. Corsini & Contributors, *Current Psychotherapies,* 2nd edition. Copyright © 1979, pp. 155–159.

● Review

Humanists believe that information about individuals that differs too much from their concept of self—both the selves they think they are and the selves they think they should be—is denied awareness. This lack of awareness is harmful both because it keeps the individual from having an accurate view of self to use in making decisions and because the unsymbolized information threatens the person's inaccurate self-image and creates anxiety. Client-centered psychotherapists create a safe emotional environment in therapy that they believe will allow clients to grow in self-awareness. This is accomplished through the therapist's warmth, empathy, and unconditional acceptance. In addition, the therapist uses the technique of reflection; the humanistic therapist repeats the message that she hears in the client's statements to help the client clarify what he is feeling.

● Check Your Learning

To be sure that you have learned the key points from the preceding section, cover the list of correct answers and try to answer each question. If you give an incorrect answer to any question, return to the page given next to the correct answer to see why your answer was not correct.

1. Humanists view full *self-awareness* as necessary for the complete realization of our inner-directed potential.

   a) True   b) False

2. Rogers refers to his humanistic approach to psychotherapy as _____ because the emphasis is on the ability of the clients to help themselves rather than on the ability of therapists to help clients.

3. The process of _____ describes a technique used in client-centered psychotherapy in which the therapist restates the clients' emotions to help clients clarify their feelings.

   a) mimicking   c) repetition
   b) reflection   d) recapitulation

● Thinking Critically About Psychology

1. What would you describe as the key difference between humanistic psychotherapy and psychoanalysis? How significant is this difference?
2. Do you think the technique of reflection would help you if you sought psychotherapy?

▶ BEHAVIOR THERAPY

Behavior therapy is the approach to psychotherapy that is associated with the social learning theory of personality. Recall from chapter 11 that abnormal behavior is viewed by social learning theorists as *learned* behavior. Rather than the product of unconscious conflicts, abnormal behavior simply is learned from inappropriate experiences of classical conditioning, operant conditioning, and modeling. In other words, individuals are abnormal because their environment taught them to be. For example, a young man who was frightened by social encounters might be reinforced for social withdrawal by the reduction in anxiety (negative reinforcement) that it produced. If so, social learning theorists would predict that this individual would learn to withdraw more and more.

Because of this view of the origins of abnormal behavior, it's natural that behavior therapists would see the process of learning as central to the process of therapy as well. As mentioned earlier in the chapter, the behavior therapist plays the role of a teacher, a person who helps the client *unlearn* abnormal ways of behaving and *learn* more adaptive ways to take their place. The behavior therapist would attempt to help the socially withdrawn young man we just talked about to unlearn his fear of social interaction and then teach him appropriate ways of interacting socially.

A number of different therapy methods have been derived from the basic principles of learning for use in behavior therapy. We will survey a few of the major techniques used to reduce abnormal fears and teach new skills. As you read about each of them, notice how they teach adaptive behavior.

Fear Reduction Methods

Several behavior therapy methods are used to treat the abnormal fears that we call phobias. In different ways, each attempts to extinguish the fear response to the phobic stimulus and replace it with relaxation. The most widely used methods are systematic desensitization and graded exposure.

Developed by psychiatrist Joseph Wolpe (1958), **systematic desensitization** is a complex procedure that involves two steps—progressive relaxation training and graded exposure. The first step in systematic desensitization is **progressive relaxation training,** a method of deeply relaxing the muscles of the body. The purpose is to put the client into a deep state of relaxation that can be conditioned to the phobic stimulus in place of the fear response.

behavior therapy
Psychotherapy based on social learning theory in which the therapist helps the client unlearn abnormal ways of behaving and learn more adaptive ways to take their place.

 Systematic desensitization

www.mmhe.com/laheye1

systematic desensitization
A behavior therapy method in which the client is taught not to fear phobic stimuli by learning to stay relaxed in the presence of successively more threatening stimuli.

progressive relaxation training
A method of learning to deeply relax the muscles of the body.

graded exposure
A behavior therapy technique in which a person with a phobia is first exposed to a stimulus that is mildly fear provoking. Once the client has mastered his or her anxiety in that situation, he or she is exposed to a graded series of more fearful situations.

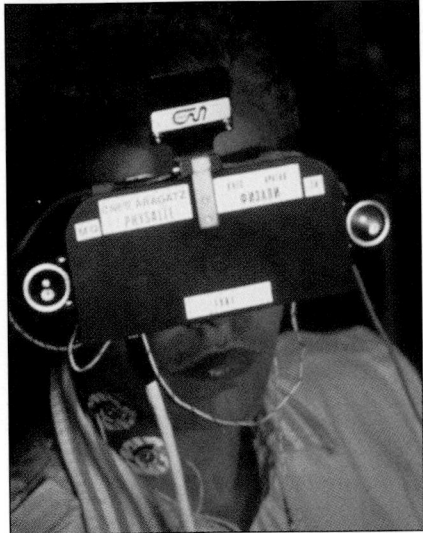

The technology of virtual reality can be used in graded exposure techniques to give the client the experience of being in a graded series of fearful situations in the therapist's office.

social skills training
The use of techniques of operant conditioning to teach social skills to persons who lack them.

role playing
A therapeutic technique in which the therapist and client act as if they were people in problematic situations.

Once the client has mastered deep muscle relaxation, the **graded exposure** part of the systematic desensitization procedure is begun. The therapist and the client rank all aspects of the phobic stimulus from least feared to most feared. For example, a medical student who is phobic of blood might react with a slight amount of fear to watching a patient's finger being pricked but with intense fear to watching open-heart surgery. A number of such fear-provoking stimuli are arranged in a graded list of phobic stimuli. The client is placed in a state of deep relaxation and asked to vividly imagine the weakest phobic stimulus on the hierarchy (in our example of the medical student, the weakest stimulus is watching a finger being pricked). If imagining that scene causes any fear at all, the individual is asked to raise a finger as a signal and stop imagining the scene. If the client can imagine the scene without fear, however, the therapist asks her to imagine the next scene. If that is too fear provoking, the client returns to the first scene for a while and later attempts to imagine the more intense scene without fear. When this can be done, she moves up the hierarchy. Over a number of sessions, the client is often able to imagine even the most feared scene without disturbing her relaxed state.

Often the graded exposure procedure is conducted in real-life settings without putting the client in a state of deep relaxation (called "in vivo graded exposure"). Typically, the therapist accompanies the patient through a series of increasingly more fearful situations, beginning with mildly fearful ones. For a person with an intense phobia of heights, the therapist might accompany the client as he or she first walks to the edge of a second-story balcony. After the client has mastered that first situation and feels calm, he or she would walk to the railing of a third-story balcony, then a fourth-story balcony, and so on, until he or she can be in high places with little anxiety. A substantial literature attests to the effectiveness of these behavior therapies for fears (Barlow, 1996; Barlow & Lehman, 1996; Kilic & others, 1997; Murphy & others, 1998). Modern technology has made graded exposure more convenient for both clients and therapists by safely exposing the client to a graded series of highly realistic frightening situations in the therapist's office using computer-generated virtual reality techniques (Rothbaum & others, 1995).

Social Skills Training

A major emphasis of behavior therapy is on the teaching of adaptive skills using methods derived from operant conditioning. People with severe anxiety disorders, affective disorders, and schizophrenia frequently have difficulties interacting with other people. They tend to appear shy, awkward, and "odd" and have difficulties expressing their feelings. Most of us experience similar difficulties in interacting with others in some situations (such as first dates and job interviews), but for some people this is a pervasive experience coloring nearly all of their social encounters and requiring a form of therapy.

In **social skills training,** *shaping* and *positive reinforcement* are used to teach persons with these social deficiencies to speak more often in social situations, to speak in a voice that is loud enough to be heard, to make appropriate eye contact, and to make fewer odd comments. This is usually accomplished by **role playing,** whereby the therapist and clients act as if they were people in problematic social situations. For example, if the client has great difficulties on job interviews and will soon be seeking a job, the therapist might role-play hypothetical job interviews. The therapist might first take the role of the client and model appropriate social behavior. Then, the client would play the role of herself in the next hypothetical job interview. The therapist would then provide positive reinforcement in the form of praise for the good aspects of the client's social behavior and suggest ways of improving the inappropriate aspects. Over a number of role-play sessions, enough improvement is usually obtained to allow the client to try role-played job interviews with other people and eventually to take a crack at the real thing.

Let's focus for a moment on a study that evaluated the effectiveness of social skills training. Robin Cappe and Lynne Alden (1986) of the University of British Columbia evaluated a combination of social skills training and systematic desensitization for persons with *social phobias* (see p. 391). Their ages ranged from 20 to 50 years, with all of them having been shy most of their lives. Most were not married and had either never dated or had not dated in years due to their shyness. Several had dropped out of college, and others held jobs that were below their capabilities due to their social anxiety.

The subjects were divided into two groups, which received different therapies. The first group was given a modified version of *systematic desensitization* (see p. 423). Each person was first trained in progressive relaxation. When this was mastered, each individual constructed a list of social situations that were arranged in order from the least anxiety provoking (e.g., "saying good morning to a waitress in a restaurant") to the most anxiety provoking (e.g., "asking a person for a date"). The person then practiced these social situations with the therapist, beginning with the least anxiety-provoking scenes and working up to the most difficult ones until he or she could perform these role-play scenes with little or no anxiety.

The second group received not only systematic desensitization but also a form of *social skills training* (see the beginning of this section) in which they were taught social skills to make them better conversationalists.

The third group did not receive any treatment during the same period in which the first two treatments were evaluated. Rather, this group, known as the *wait list control group,* was given treatment *after* the experiment was over. This group was used to rule out the unlikely possibility that simply meeting with the therapist about their shyness would be enough to make it go away. In doing so, the researchers could be more confident that it was their treatment that actually made the individuals get better.

Both treatments resulted in significant improvement in the frequency of social interactions in which the persons engaged, the comfort level (lack of anxiety) that they experienced during social interactions, and the degree of satisfaction that they derived from these social interactions. The group that received both systematic desensitization and social skills training improved the most on all three measures, however.

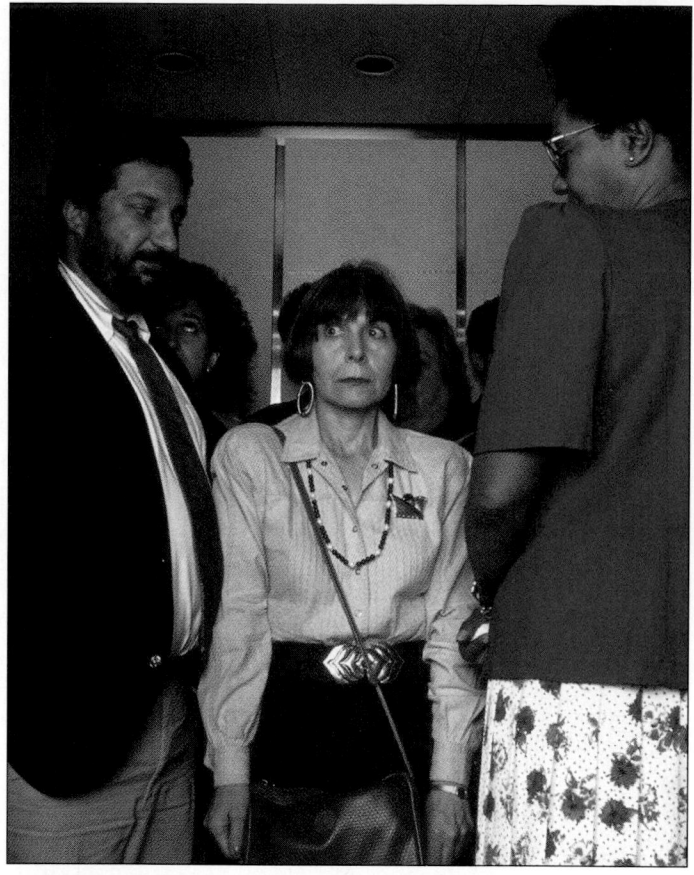

A person with a fear of elevators might be treated by asking him or her to ride in elevators all day—perhaps for several days in a row—until the anxiety was reduced. This is an example of the behavior therapy technique of flooding.

Excerpt from Behavior Therapy

In the following excerpt from a session of behavior therapy, the therapist is persuading the client to practice behaving in more effective ways in a role-playing session in the therapist's office, so that the therapist can shape and reinforce the more effective behavior. The statements in brackets are comments of the therapist that were not stated during the therapy session.

Client: The basic problem is that I have the tendency to let people step all over me. I don't know why, but I just have difficulty in speaking my mind.

Therapist: [My immediate tendency here is to reflect and clarify what the client said, adding a behavioral twist. In paraphrasing what she has already said, I can cast it within a behavioral framework by introducing such terms as *situation, respond,* and *learn.*] So you find yourself in a number of different situations where you don't re spond the way you would really like to. And if I understand correctly, you would like to learn how to behave differently.

Client: Yes. But you know, I have tried to handle certain situations differently, but I just don't seem to be able to do so.

Therapist: [Not a complete acceptance of my conceptualization, seemingly because she has tried to behave differently in the past and nothing has happened. What I should do, then, is somehow provide some explanation of why previous attempts may have failed, and use this to draw a contrast with a potentially more effective treatment strategy that we'll be using in our sessions.] It's almost as if there is a big gap between the way you react and the way you would like to react.

Client: It seems that way, and I don't know how to overcome it.

Therapist: Well, maybe you've tried to do too much too fast in the past, and consequently weren't very successful. Maybe a good way to look at the situation is to imagine yourself at the bottom of a staircase, wanting to get to the top. It's probably too much to ask to get there in one gigantic leap. Perhaps a better way to go about changing your reaction in these situations is to take it one step at a time.

Client: That would seem to make sense, but I'm not sure if I see how that could be done.

Therapist: Well, there are probably certain situations in which it would be less difficult for you to assert yourself such as telling your boss that he forgot to pay you for the past four weeks.

Client: (Laughing.) I guess in that situation, I would say something. Although I must admit, I would feel uneasy about it.

Therapist: But not as uneasy as if you went in and asked him for a raise.

Client: No. Certainly not.

Therapist: So, the first situation would be low on the staircase, whereas the second would be higher up. If you can learn to handle easier situations, then the more difficult ones would present less of a problem. And the only way you can really learn to change your reactions is through practice.

Client: In other words, I really have to go out and actually force myself to speak up more, but taking it a little bit at a time?

Therapist: [This seems like an appropriate time to introduce the function of behavior rehearsal. I won't say anything about the specific procedure yet, but instead will talk about it in general terms and maybe increase its appeal by explaining that any failures will not really "count." If the client goes along with the general description of the treatment strategy, she should be more likely to accept the details as I spell them out.] Exactly. And as a way of helping you carry it off in the real-life situation, I think it would be helpful if we reviewed some of these situations and your reactions to them beforehand. In a sense, going through a dry run. It's safer to run through some of these situations here, in that it really doesn't "count" if you don't handle them exactly as you would like to. Also, it can provide you an excellent opportunity to practice different ways of reacting to these situations, until you finally hit on one which you think would be best.

Client: That seems to make sense.

Therapist: In fact, we could arrange things so that you can actually rehearse exactly what you would say, and how you would say it.

Client: That sounds like a good idea.

● Review

The approach to psychotherapy associated with the social learning theory of personality is known as behavior therapy. Abnormal behavior is viewed as learned behavior. It's simply behavior that results from inappropriate learning experiences. The role of the behavior therapist is to serve as a teacher who helps the client unlearn abnormal behavior and learn adaptive ways of behaving to take its place. In systematic desensitization, for example, the behavior therapist teaches clients no longer to fear phobic stimuli by first teaching them to relax deeply and then exposing them to graduated versions of the phobic stimulus in their imagination until the full stimulus does not disturb the state of relaxation. In this way, relaxation, rather than fear, becomes the response to the formerly phobic stimulus. Other behavior therapy methods use principles of operant conditioning to teach specific skills.

● Check Your Learning

To be sure that you have learned the key points from the preceding section, cover the list of correct answers and try to answer each question. If you give an incorrect answer to any question, return to the page given next to the correct answer to see why your answer was not correct.

1. A _____ plays the role of teacher, a person who helps the client unlearn abnormal ways of behaving and learn more adaptive ways to take their place.

   a) psychoanalyst
   b) behavior therapist

   c) humanistic therapist
   d) group therapist

2. _____ is a behavior therapy method in which the client is taught not to fear phobic stimuli by learning to relax deeply in the presence of successively more threatening stimuli.

   a) Progressive relaxation training
   b) Meditation

   c) Reflection
   d) Systematic desensitization

3. In _____, people with social deficiencies are taught social skills through operant conditioning.

● Thinking Critically About Psychology

1. How could both social skills training and systematic desensitization be effective in treating problems such as the fear of meeting new people? What do they have in common?

2. If you needed it, do you think you would prefer graded exposure or systematic desensitization to overcome a fear of heights? Which do you think would be more successful?

Correct Answers   1. b (p. 423),   **2. d** (p. 423),   **3.** social skills training (p. 424).

▶ COGNITIVE THERAPY

Cognitive therapy is an important approach to therapy that rests on the assumption that faulty cognitions—maladaptive beliefs, expectations, and ways of thinking—are the cause of abnormal behavior. Cognitive therapy originated in Albert Ellis' (1962) *Rational-Emotive Therapy,* and in the cognitive emphasis of contemporary social learning theorists (Bandura, 1977) and contemporary psychoanalysts (Kelly, 1955). Because a great deal of carefully designed research has supported the effectiveness of cognitive therapy for anxiety and depression it has become one of the most widely used therapy approaches.

cognitive therapy
An approach to therapy that teaches individuals new cognitions—adaptive beliefs, expectations, and ways of thinking—to eliminate abnormal emotions and behavior.

Relationship Between Cognition and Behavior

Early in the development of behavior therapy, it was assumed that cognitions were relatively unimportant in the origins and treatment of abnormal behavior. For example, if a client were to go to a behavior therapist because she was unassertive, the conversations with the therapist might reveal that she believed (a cognition) that her friends would stop liking her if she expressed her true feelings to them. The behavior therapist would feel

Aaron T. Beck.

Albert Ellis.

that it would be unnecessary to change this faulty belief directly, however. The behavior therapist would assume that, if the client were taught assertive ways of expressing feelings, then she would see for herself that her friends still like her and, therefore, would change her faulty cognition herself. The cognitive therapy movement, on the other hand, suggests that behavior therapists can be more effective if they directly teach both more adaptive behavior and cognition.

Moreover, cognitive therapists believe that problems do not always stem from inappropriate overt actions. For example, some socially anxious people behave in appropriate, even charming ways in social situations, but they still experience anxiety because they inaccurately think of themselves as dull, awkward, and unlikable. Trying to modify their already appropriate overt actions would be fruitless in such cases. Instead, it's necessary to modify their maladaptive cognitions.

Maladaptive Cognitions

Psychologist Albert Ellis (1962; 1999) and psychiatrist Aaron T. Beck (Beck, 1976, 1999; Beck, Rush, Shaw, & Emery, 1979) have described a number of patterns of cognition that they believe contribute greatly to abnormal behavior and emotions.

To better understand the cognitive therapy approach, we should look more closely at one of the most widely used versions, Aaron Beck's cognitive therapy program for depression. Beck believes that depression is caused primarily by the following erroneous patterns of thinking (do not be upset if you see some of your own ways of thinking here—we all think in these erroneous ways to some extent):

1. *Selective abstraction.* Let's say you ask the woman with whom you have had a committed relationship for three years if she has kissed another man since she started dating you. She answers, "Never, not once. I've never even flirted with another man. I'm not blind and I can still tell that a guy is cute, but I'm not romantically interested in anybody but you." Most persons would be reassured by the message of commitment in that statement, but would you go into a raging fit because she said she notices that some other men are attractive? If so, that is selective abstraction—basing your thinking on a small detail taken out of context and given an incorrect meaning.

2. *Overgeneralization.* This is the process of reaching a general conclusion based on a few specific bits of evidence. The young scientist who gets a harsh rejection of the first article she submits to a scientific journal is overgeneralizing if she concludes that no journal will ever publish her research.

3. *Arbitrary inference.* This is the error of reaching a conclusion based on little or no logical evidence—as the name says, the conclusion is arbitrary. For example, if you were to receive an invitation to have lunch with your boss, would you conclude that the boss was going to gently break the news to you that you will be fired? Some people reason in this arbitrary way, concluding that everything means something bad.

4. *Magnification/minimization.* When the guy sitting next to you says that your ears have an interesting point at the top, do you magnify this statement out of proportion? ("No wonder everybody hates me—I have grotesque Mr. Spock ears!") Or, if you receive a heartfelt compliment from a friend, do you minimize it to nothing? ("Lynne just says nice things to me because she feels sorry for me.") These examples illustrate the process of magnification/minimization.

5. *Personalization.* Suppose you drove to the beach with your friends and it rained all weekend. Did you become gloomy and really mean it when you complained to your friends, "Nothing ever works out for me—every time I try to have fun it turns into a nightmare!" Some people would falsely conclude that it rained just because they were at the beach. Personalization is the erroneous pattern of reasoning in which external events are seen as being related to you when there is no logical reason for doing so.

6. *Absolutistic thinking.* The person who did not have good enough grades to get into medical school, but who has made an excellent living as a highly respected hospital

administrator tells a former classmate at his 25-year high school reunion, "Ever since college, my life has been a total failure." Although it might be realistic to say that he failed in an important arena, he certainly has not been a total failure. His absolutistic thinking in all-or-nothing terms—either everything is absolutely wonderful or everything is absolutely terrible—is erroneous and maladaptive.

It should come as no surprise that many people who think in these maladaptive ways are miserable because of it. In cognitive therapy, the therapist uses a variety of techniques of persuasion to help the client change her or his faulty patterns of thinking.

Cognitive therapy has been shown to be quite effective with a variety of anxiety disorders (Barlow, 1996; Borkovec & Costello, 1993; Bruce, Spiegel, Gregg, & Nuzzarello, 1995; Chambless & Gillis, 1993; Heimberg & others, 1998), eating disorders (Garner & others, 1993; Thackwray, Smith, Bodfish, & Meyers, 1993), and major depression (Ackerson & others, 1998; Clarkin, Pilkonis, & Magruder, 1996; Ravindran & others, 1999; Simons, Gordon, Thase, & Monroe, 1995). Indeed, in many studies, cognitive therapy has been found to be more effective than more traditional psychodynamic or humanistic therapies. Comparisons with psychiatric medication have yielded slightly more complicated findings. In the case of depression, there is evidence that cognitive therapy is equally effective as antidepressant medications in the treatment of depression (DeRubeis & others, 1999). But cognitive therapy has been shown to be more than twice as effective as medication in preventing *future* episodes of depression (Evans & others, 1992; Hollon & others, 1993).

Excerpt from Cognitive Therapy

In the following excerpt from a session of cognitive therapy, see how the therapist uses a series of probing questions to get the client to contradict her own absolutistic thinking and arbitrary inference.

Therapist: Why do you want to end your life?

Patient: Without Raymond, I am nothing . . . I can't be happy without Raymond. . . . But I can't save our marriage.

T: What has your marriage been like?

P: It has been miserable from the very beginning . . . Raymond has always been unfaithful . . . I have hardly seen him in the past five years.

T: You say that you can't be happy without Raymond. . . . Have you found yourself happy when you are with Raymond?

P: No, we fight all the time and I feel worse.

T: Then why do you feel that Raymond is essential for your living?

P: I guess it's because without Raymond I am nothing.

T: Would you please repeat that?

P: Without Raymond I am nothing.

T: What do you think of that idea?

P: . . . Well, now that I think about it, I guess it's not completely true.

T: You said you are "nothing" without Raymond. Before you met Raymond, did you feel you were "nothing"?

P: No, I felt I was somebody.

T: Are you saying then that it's possible to be something without Raymond?

P: I guess that's true. I *can* be something without Raymond.

T: If you were somebody before you knew Raymond, why do you need him to be somebody now?

P: (puzzled) Hmmm . . .

T: You seemed to imply that you couldn't go on living without Raymond.

P: Well, I just don't think that I can find anybody else like him.

T: Did you have male friends before you knew Raymond?

P: I was pretty popular then.

T: If I understand you correctly then, you were able to fall in love before with other men and other men have fallen in love with you.

P: Uh huh.

T: Why do you think you will be unpopular without Raymond now?

P: Because I will not be able to attract any other man.

T: Have any men shown an interest in you since you have been married?

P: A lot of men have made passes at me but I ignore them.

T: If you were free of the marriage, do you think that men might be interested in you—knowing that you were available?

P: I guess that maybe they would be.

T: Is it possible that you might find a man who would be more constant than Raymond?

P: I don't know, . . . I guess it's possible.

T: Do you think there are other men as good as Raymond around?

P: I guess there are men who are better than Raymond because Raymond doesn't love me.

From A. T. Beck, & others, *Cognitive Theory of Depression.* Copyright 1979 The Guilford Press, New York, NY. Reprinted by permission of the authors.

● Review

Cognitive therapy is a therapeutic approach that has grown out of both contemporary psychoanalytic theories of personality and social learning theory, but it has become subsumed by, and has contributed to the expansion of, behavior therapy. Whereas behavior therapists originally believed that the irrational beliefs and ways of thinking (cognitions) that generally accompany abnormal behavior and emotions would simply change when the behavior and emotions changed, cognitive therapists have emphasized the value in sometimes changing cognitions first. They believe that behavior and emotional problems will improve when maladaptive cognitions are changed. Consequently, cognitive therapists conduct psychotherapy in an attempt to change cognitions by demonstrating their irrationality to clients.

● Check Your Learning

To be sure that you have learned the key points from the preceding section, cover the list of correct answers and try to answer each question. If you give an incorrect answer to any question, return to the page given next to the correct answer to see why your answer was not correct.

1. _____ is an important approach to therapy that rests on the assumption that faulty cognitions—maladaptive beliefs, expectations, and ways of thinking—are the cause of abnormal behavior.

   a) Cognitive therapy   c) Anticipation therapy

   b) Psychoanalysis   d) Reflection

2. _____ refers to the cognitive distortion of basing your thinking on a small detail taken out of context and given an incorrect meaning.

   a) Selective abstraction   c) Personalization

   b) Overgeneralization   d) Absolutistic thinking

3. If a person loses her job because the company has laid off a thousand workers and then gets depressed because "I knew they thought I was awful at my job," she is engaging in

   a) selective abstraction.   c) personalization.
   b) overgeneralization.   d) absolutistic thinking.

4. In the excerpt from cognitive therapy in the preceding section, the suicidal client says, "Without Raymond, I am nothing. . . ." This person is engaging in

   a) selective abstraction.   c) personalization.
   b) overgeneralization.   d) absolutistic thinking.

● Thinking Critically About Psychology

1. We have seen that cognitive therapy is effective in treating several kinds of disorders. Can you think of other human ailments for which cognitive therapy might be effective?

2. Reexamine each of Aaron Beck's list of erroneous thinking patterns associated with depression. Can you think of any characters in novels or on television who think in these ways?

Correct Answers 1. a (p. 427), 2. a (p. 428), 3. c (p. 428), 4. d (p. 428).

▶ MEDICAL THERAPIES

In addition to psychotherapy, medical therapies are commonly used in the treatment of abnormal behavior. **Medical therapies** are generally designed to correct a physical condition that is believed to be the cause of the psychological disorder. There are three general types of medical therapy: drug therapy, in which medication is used; electroconvulsive therapy, in which seizures are electrically induced in the brain; and psychosurgery, in which brain tissue is surgically destroyed.

medical therapies
Those therapies—including drug therapy, electroconvulsive therapy, and psychosurgery—generally designed to correct a physical condition that is believed to be the cause of a psychological disorder.

Drug Therapy

By far, the most widely used medical treatment is **drug therapy,** in which medications are used to treat abnormal behavior. The idea that chemicals can be used to treat abnormal behavior dates back at least to the special diets used by Pythagoras around 490 B.C. But the widespread use of effective psychiatric drugs has come about only in the past 40 years. The era of modern drug therapy began in 1954 with the introduction of the phenothiazine drugs, such as Thorazine for the treatment of schizophrenia. Thorazine gave physicians a tool that for the first time in history substantially improved the lives of schizophrenic persons. So effective is this drug that it's given partial credit for reversing the growth in the number of patients in mental institutions during the 1960s. Other drugs were also introduced during the 1960s to help in the treatment of depression (antidepressants) and anxiety (tranquilizers).

Some examples of the most commonly used psychiatric drugs are given in table 14.1. How do medications help persons with psychological problems? Recall from chapter 2 that our biology and our psychological lives are intimately related. Modern psychiatric medications are designed to improve psychological functioning by influencing a specific neurotransmitter in the brain. For example, Prozac causes axons that secrete serotonin to reabsorb the serotonin more slowly. This keeps the serotonin active in the synapse longer, giving it more time to stimulate the dendrite of the next neuron. Because neural transmission using serotonin is believed not to operate optimally in individuals with high levels of anxiety, depression, and other problems, this medication often helps "normalize" serotonin transmission in the brain. Although many people view psychiatric medications as a way of "drugging" people with psychological problems to keep them quiet, the goal is to help their

drug therapy
A medical therapy that uses medications to treat abnormal behavior.

TABLE 14.1	Some Commonly Used Psychiatric Drugs

Physicians have a variety of medications at their disposal for use in the treatment of temporary stress reactions and psychological disorders. Some examples of these medications and their benefits are given here. Some of these medications have several uses and may be prescribed by a physician for reasons other than psychological problems.

Trade Name	Generic Name	For Relief Of
Tofranil	Imipramine	Depression
Elavil	Amitriptyline	Depression
Prozac	Fluoxetine	Depression
Xanax	Alprazolam	Anxiety
Mellaril	Thioridazine	Psychotic symptoms
Stelazine	Trifluoperazine	Psychotic symptoms
Haldol	Haloperidol	Psychotic symptoms
Navane	Thiothixene	Psychotic symptoms
Eskalith	Lithium	Bipolar affective disorder

brains operate more *normally.* Because most medications do not influence only one neurotransmitter, however, and because most neurotransmitters play other roles in the brain unrelated to emotional problems, psychiatric medications often have "side effects" that result from their impact on other neural systems. For example, prolonged use of some antipsychotic medications can result in impaired control of the body's muscles if not carefully monitored. Similarly, some antidepressant medications cause the individual to have a dry mouth and gain weight.

electroconvulsive therapy (ECT)
(e-lek″tro-con-vul′siv)   A medical therapy that uses electrical current to induce controlled convulsive seizures that alleviate some types of mental disorders.

Electroconvulsive Therapy

The idea that people can be "shocked" out of their psychological problems has been around in one form or another for 2,400 years. Hippocrates recommended the use of the herb hellebore to induce seizures that supposedly restored balance to the body's four humors. Several different kinds of "shock" treatment were popular in mental institutions during the 1800s: patients were thrown in tubs full of eels, spun in giant centrifuges, and nearly drowned by dropping them into lakes through trapdoors in bridges known as "surprise baths" (Altschule, 1965).

Other forms of shock therapy have also been used, particularly ones in which seizures are intentionally induced. In the 1930s, it was noticed that people with epilepsy rarely developed schizophrenia. Several psychiatrists experimented with chemicals that caused seizures to see if they would cure schizophrenia, but camphor, insulin, and other chemicals were found to be of little use with schizophrenics. Italian physicians first used the method of passing an electric current through two metal plates held to the sides of the head to induce convulsive brain seizures. This method, known as **electroconvulsive therapy (ECT),** continues in widespread use

Although electroconvulsive therapy, which was introduced in the 1930s, continues to be used with some severely depressed individuals, it's not endorsed universally by the mental health profession.

today. Although ineffective with most disorders, it's believed by many psychiatrists to be useful with severely depressed individuals. ECT is believed to alter the same neurotransmitters as those affected by antidepressants, but to this day no one knows for sure how ECT works.

Although ECT has been used successfully for 50 years, the procedure is surrounded by considerable controversy. In large part, this controversy is a holdover from the primitive methods that were used when the procedure was first introduced. The shocks were given without anesthesia, and the seizures were so violent that broken bones were not uncommon. Today, the use of anesthesia and muscle relaxants makes ECT a far less unpleasant experience, but some memory loss (mostly for unimportant information) is a relatively common side effect (Campbell, 1961; Lisanby & others, 2000). The use of ECT is also controversial because, even after extended use, little adequate research has been conducted to evaluate its effectiveness. Many well-designed studies have been carried out, however, that suggest it's at least somewhat effective in treating depression (Barton, 1977; McCall & others, 2000).

Psychosurgery

Undoubtedly the most controversial medical treatment for abnormal behavior is **psychosurgery,** a therapy in which the brain is operated on to try to alleviate the behavior. As with the other medical therapies, there is a historical precedent for the idea that people with psychological disorders can be helped by operating on their brains. In fact, the precedent for psychosurgery is perhaps the oldest of all. Archaeologists have found Stone Age skulls in which holes called *trephines* had been "surgically" cut with crude stone knives. These trephining operations—signs of healing indicate that some of these poor souls actually survived the procedure—were apparently performed in an attempt to treat abnormal behavior.

Surgical operations on the brain to treat psychological disorders came into vogue in the 1940s and 1950s. In the most common version, the prefrontal lobotomy, a double-edged, butter knife–shaped instrument is inserted through holes drilled in the temple region of the skull. Neural fibers that connect the frontal region of the cerebral cortex with the limbic system are cut. The theory is that the operation will prevent disturbing thoughts and perceptions from reaching the subcortical brain structures, where they would be translated into emotional outbursts. Lobotomies are not successful in most cases, however, and loss of intellectual functioning and seizures are common side effects (Barahal, 1958). Because of their ineffectiveness and because of the success of drug therapies with schizophrenics, the use of lobotomies and other forms of psychosurgery has declined considerably (Swayze, 1995). However, as late as 1973, some 500 prefrontal lobotomies were performed in the United States each year (Holden, 1973).

More recently, the development of more precise methods of operating on the brain with needle-thin electrical instruments has revived interest in psychosurgery (Martuza, Chiocca, Jenike, Giriunas, & Ballantine, 1990). These instruments are used to operate directly on the parts of the brain associated with emotional control. For example, a type of precise psychosurgery called **cingulotomy** is sometimes performed on persons with severe obsessive-compulsive disorder who have not responded to repeated attempts to treat the disorder with behavior therapy and medication. In cingulotomy, the part of the limbic system called the *cingulate cortex* (chapter 2) is partially destroyed by electrical probes. A team of researchers at Harvard Medical School (Baer & others, 1995) evaluated 18 individuals with obsessive-compulsive disorder two years after their cingulotomies to see whether they had been helpful. They found significant improvement in about one-fourth of the patients, but most cases did not benefit from the surgery. Such operations are performed infrequently and are used only as a last resort. Even in such cases, psychosurgery is still a hotly debated procedure.

Trephining operations were apparently performed in the Middle Ages to treat abnormal behavior.

 Psychosurgery

www.mmhe.com/laheye1

psychosurgery
(sī″kō-ser′jer-ē)   A medical therapy that involves operating on the brain in an attempt to alleviate some types of mental disorders.

cingulotomy
A type of psychosurgery for severe and otherwise untreatable obsessive-compulsive disorder; it involves surgical destruction of part of the cingulate cortex.

● Review

In addition to psychological treatments for psychological problems, physicians often use biological methods. The most widely used medical treatments are drugs. Drugs introduced since the 1950s have been partially responsible for the progress in treating psychological problems, which has resulted in a decrease in the number of institutionalized mental patients in the United States. Electroconvulsive therapy—in which an electric current produces controlled brain seizures—is sometimes used in the treatment of severe depression. The controversial method of psychosurgery in which parts of the brain are destroyed to prevent excessive emotional reactions is no longer widely used in the United States, but newer, more precise methods are still used in some cases as a last resort.

● Check Your Learning

To be sure that you have learned the key points from the preceding section, cover the list of correct answers and try to answer each question. If you give an incorrect answer to any question, return to the page given next to the correct answer to see why your answer was not correct.

1. The medical therapy most commonly used today is:

   a) drug therapy   b) electroconvulsive therapy

2. The infrequently used medical therapy in which the physician attempts to control abnormal behavior through surgery is called:

   a) electroconvulsive therapy   b) psychosurgery

● Thinking Critically About Psychology

1. Does drug therapy seem like an appropriate way to normalize behavior to you?
2. Would psychosurgery ever be justifiable?

Correct Answers **1. a** (p. 431), **2. b** (p. 433).

Application *of Psychology*

WHAT TO DO IF YOU THINK YOU NEED HELP

All of us face difficult and painful times in our lives. Sometimes we choose to struggle through these stressful periods on our own; sometimes we ask for the support and advice of friends; and, at times, we may seek professional help. If you, or someone close to you, are among the many millions of Americans who will use professional mental health services this year, please consider these thoughts.

First, you must face the issue of *stigma*—the implication that seeking professional help means that you are not a normal or even fully competent person. If you believe that myth, then it will be very difficult indeed for you to lift the telephone and make the first appointment. You should know, however, that mental health professionals do *not* believe there is something fundamentally wrong with people who ask for help. They know that a large portion of their clients are completely normal people who are simply asking for assistance in the tricky business of avoiding—or crawling out of—life's pitfalls. So do not be afraid to ask for help if you think you need it.

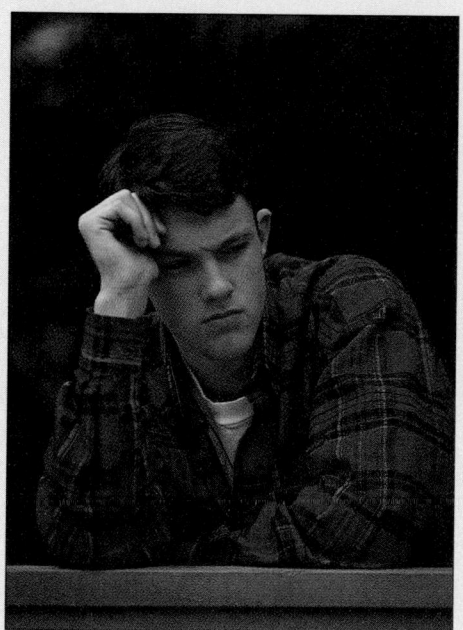

There are many ways to find help with psychological problems if you feel that you need it.

Once you have decided to seek help, where do you look for it? As we first mentioned in chapter 1, there are many different mental health professions that operate through a number of different kinds of mental health facilities. The trick is in deciding which kind of professional or facility would be best for you. For college students, this decision is often an easy one: Most colleges and universities have a student counseling or mental health center that provides high-quality services at little or no cost. The professionals who work in these centers are experienced in meeting the mental health needs of students.

In addition, most psychology departments in larger universities operate their own psychology clinics that provide services both to students and to people in the general community. And most cities have a community mental health center that provides a wide range of services. Both university psychology clinics and community mental health centers often charge fees that are based on your ability to pay. Many of these centers operate 24 hours a day, providing suicide prevention telephone lines that are listed under such titles as "help line" or "crisis line" or that can be reached through the telephone operator.

Services are also provided by professionals in private practice. Like a physician or an attorney, these individuals provide services for a fee. Psychiatrists, psychologists, and other professionals in private practice are listed in the telephone book under titles such as "Physicians—Psychiatrists" and "Psychologists." In most states, only licensed individuals can list their names in the telephone directory as a psychiatrist, psychologist, psychotherapist, counselor, or marriage counselor. In some states, however, some of these titles (except for psychologist and psychiatrist) are not regulated by law. This means that anyone—qualified or not—can set up a private practice in many states under one of these titles. You should be careful, therefore, to ask for a referral to one of these professionals from a qualified physician or psychologist if you choose their services.

Referrals are the best guide to choosing the services of a licensed psychologist or psychiatrist. Like other professions, some are better than others—or are better in dealing with certain kinds of cases—and the advice of someone who knows both you and the professionals in the community could be very helpful. If you do not have access to someone to refer you, it would be wise to ask the psychologist or psychiatrist about "board certification." It's legal in most states for a physician to practice psychiatry without having had specific training in that field, but a board-certified psychiatrist has met the criteria of a national board for competence in psychiatry. In psychology, board certification means something different. Only a small proportion of experienced psychologists take and pass a special examination of their skills. They are awarded a diploma by the American Board of Professional Psychology, which is designated in their listing in the telephone directory as "Diplomate in Clinical (or Counseling) Psychology, ABPP." Board-certified psychiatrists and psychologists are not necessarily more competent than those who are not, but it's another way of reducing the uncertainty in choosing a therapist.

Ethnic and Gender Issues in Seeking a Psychotherapist

Does your ethnicity matter in seeking psychological help? Sadly, it does. The United States has one of the most advanced mental health systems in the world, but it cannot be said to fully meet the needs of all of our citizens. As a professional who deals with persons in need of psychological help, I often see the frustration and tragedy of persons who cannot receive assistance due to lack of money or other barriers. Much has been written about inequities in the receipt of psychological services in the United States. For example, a large-scale survey conducted in Los Angeles showed that, among persons with mental disorders, only *half* as many Hispanics with psychological disorders were receiving outpatient mental health treatment as non-Hispanic whites (Hough & others, 1987). In contrast, other researchers have raised concern about the fact that African Americans are more likely than whites to be committed to psychiatric hospitals, often involuntarily, when they have a mental disorder (Lindsey & Paul, 1989; Snowden & Cheung, 1990). Thus, much remains to be done to ensure that we have not only an effective mental health system but a fair one as well.

How about gender? Are men and women provided psychological services in the same way? Nancy Felipe Russo (1990) has pointed out probable inequities in mental health services provided to women. Although national surveys have shown that women are more likely than men to exhibit the most common forms of mental disorder (anxiety and depressive disorders), fewer women receive mental health services than men. It appears that our society is more willing to provide services for the disorders that are more common in males (substance abuse, antisocial personality disorder, and schizophrenia) than the difficulties that are more likely for women. It is encouraging to note, however, that the gender of the therapist does not appear to influence the effectiveness of psychotherapy for either female or male clients (Zlotnik, Elkin, & Shea, 1998).

● Summary

Chapter 14 outlines the major forms of therapy through which individuals are helped with psychological problems.

I. Psychotherapy is the use of methods, such as talking, demonstrating, and reinforcing, that are based on a theory of psychological disorders to solve human problems.

    A. Freud is the founder of the form of psychotherapy known as psychoanalysis, which helps the patient bring unconscious conflict into consciousness. The principal techniques of psychoanalysis are

        1. Free association is used to relax the censorship of the ego.

        2. Dream interpretation allows the therapist to obtain another "window" on the unconscious.

        3. Resistance is any form of opposition of the patient to the process of psychoanalysis.

        4. Transference occurs when there is a relatively intense relationship between patient and therapist during therapy; this can be interpreted to give insights to the patient.

    B. Catharsis is the release of some of the emotion that is pent up with unconscious conflicts in psychoanalysis.

    C. A new form of psychotherapy based on neo-Freudian theories, called interpersonal psychotherapy, has been found to be effective in treating depression.

II. Client-centered psychotherapy helps the client achieve self-awareness by exploring unsymbolized feelings and information by providing a safe emotional climate. Self-awareness, in turn, is thought to lead to growth.

III. Behavior therapists use a form of psychotherapy in which they help the client unlearn abnormal behavior and learn adaptive ways of thinking, feeling, and acting.

    A. Systematic desensitization and graded exposure are widely used methods of fear reduction.

    B. Social skills training is an example of teaching new adaptive skills using methods derived from operant conditioning.

    C. Cognitive therapy rests on the assumption that the faulty cognitions that cause abnormal emotions and actions can be changed in therapy.

IV. Medical therapies are designed to correct a physical condition believed to be the cause of a psychological disorder.

● Resources

1. Descriptions of the major methods of psychotherapy are presented in Nietzel, M. T., Bernstein, D. A., & Milich, R. (1998). *Introduction to clinical psychology* (5th ed.). Englewood Cliffs, NJ: Prentice-Hall; Dryden, W., & Mytton, J. (1999). *Four approaches to counselling and psychotherapy.* New York: Routledge.

2. Group psychotherapy is discussed in depth in Yalom, I. D. (1995). *The theory and practice of group psychotherapy.* New York: Basic Books.

3. More on interpersonal psychotherapy can be found in Markowitz, J. C. (1999). Developments in interpersonal psychotherapy. *Canadian Journal of Psychiatry, 44,* 556–561.

4. Two excellent applications of the cognitive theory of emotion can be found in Beck, A. T. (1999). *Prisoners of hate: The cognitive basis of anger, hostility, and violence.* New York: HarperCollins; Ellis, A. (1999). *How to make yourself happy and remarkably less disturbable.* Atascadero, CA: Impact.

5. Four helpful booklets on depression are available from the Superintendent of Documents, Government Printing Office, Washington, DC 20402-9325:
   Depressive illness: Treatments bring new hope (017-024-01370-6).
   Bipolar disorder (017-024-01368-4).
   Plain talk about . . . depression (017-024-01382-0).
   What do you do when a friend is depressed? (017-024-01376-5).

6. If you would like help in finding affordable mental health services in your area or need to speak with a counselor in confidence about any mental health problem, call the National Mental Health Hotline of Boy's Town. Although the name of the organization is Boy's Town, it provides help to males and females of all ages. It has an extensive computerized national database that can help you find help for yourself or someone else. Its toll-free, 24-hour hot line numbers are 1-800-448-3000; TDD (hearing impaired): 1-800-448-1833.

7. An excellent source of accurate information about the psychological and treatment of mental disorders is http://www.mentalhealth.com.

8. The web site of the American Psychological Association is an excellent resource for information about getting help for mental health problems. www.apa.org

CHAPTER OUTLINE

Social Psychology

PROLOGUE

Human beings are social animals: We enjoy people, need people, and are profoundly influenced by them. Indeed, we often behave a bit like sheep in a flock. We are likely to dress and act like other people even when we are not asked to conform, and we are often influenced by persuasive arguments—even illogical ones.

Social psychologists focus on attitudes because they play a key role in our social interactions; they are a large part of what determines our behavior toward others. Most of our attitudes are learned from others and can be changed through persuasion. But other people are not the only cause of attitude change. Surprisingly, when circumstances cause our behavior to be inconsistent with our attitudes, our attitudes will often change to become consistent again with our behavior.

For most of us, our most important interactions are with the people we like and love. We like to walk with them, talk with them, and snuggle with them. Whom do you like and why? Other things being equal, we are attracted to people who are similar to us (or whose opposite characteristics are good for us), who are reasonably competent (but not perfect), who are physically attractive, and who like us, too. Once mutual attraction leads to a relationship, our likelihood of staying in that relationship is determined by (a) how well our expectations of what the person is like are met and (b) how fairly balanced the relationship is.

The process of liking or disliking others is based on a complex combination of the positive and negative qualities that we see in them. Some of our reasons for liking a person have little to do with the other person at all, however. Let's look at one extraneous factor that influences the process of liking by looking at a well-known experiment (Curtis & Miller, 1987). You walk to the psychology department to take part in a study. You are introduced to another student whom you have never met and spend five minutes in a "get to know one another" conversation. Then you are separated and taken to separate cubicles. The experimenter talks with the other student for a while, then comes to your cubicle. She tells you that the study is about the ways in which people get to know one another. She also tells you that the other student has been misled into thinking that you are not a very likable person (by showing the other student a bogus "personality test" that made you look bad). To prove it, the experimenter shows you what the other student's initial ratings of you are, and they are not very positive.

The experimenter explains that she wants to know how the other student will act toward you after being given this initial negative opinion. You and the other research participant are brought together for a 10-minute conversation. Then you and the other student rate each other on likability, warmth, and a number of other similar dimensions.

Half of the students who participated in the study were told that the other person was given positive information about them and half were told that the other person was given negative information about them. Actually, the experimenters didn't give either positive or negative information to the other students. The social psychologists who conducted this study wanted to know if we act differently toward people who we *think* like or dislike us. The experimenters observed the students through a one-way mirror and rated their behavior. You and the other research participants who thought the other students did not like them were rated as less warm and less open. In addition, the other person rated you and the

KEY TERMS

439

other individuals in your group as less likable at the end of the study, too. The other person who you *thought* did not like you actually *didn't* like you very much in the end because of how you behaved toward them. Human relationships are maddeningly complex.

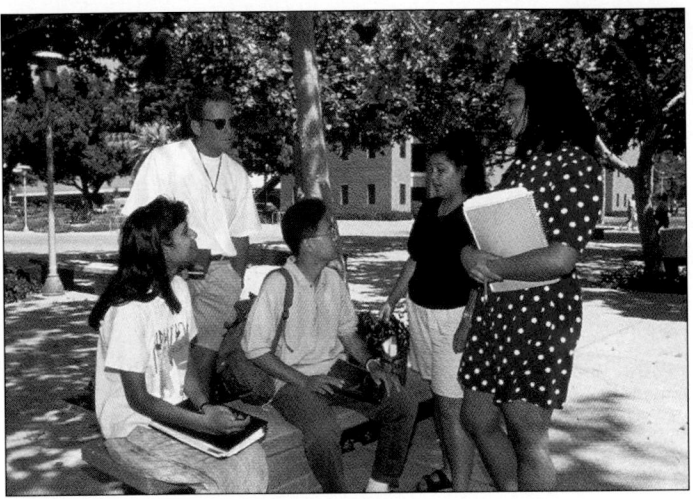

Social psychology is the branch of psychology that studies individuals as they interact with others.

social psychology
The branch of psychology that studies individuals as they interact with others.

deindividuation
State in which people in a group can feel anonymous and unidentifiable and therefore feel less concerned with what others think of their behavior.

People who are unidentifiable, or deindividuated, because they are in a large group are more likely to behave aggressively or in other unacceptable ways.

DEFINITION OF SOCIAL PSYCHOLOGY

Social psychology is a branch of psychology that studies individuals as they interact with others. Up to this point in this course, we have studied people as individuals removed from the social context in which they live. But people live with other people. Their most important learning comes from others, their most important motives are social motives, and so on.

People are almost always with others. It's part of human nature to be social. Social psychologist Elliot Aronson (1995) reminds us that this insight is among the oldest in psychology. In 328 B.C., Aristotle wrote, "Man is by nature a social animal. . . . Anyone who either cannot lead the common life or is so self-sufficient as not to need to, and therefore does not partake of society, is either a beast or a god." People need, like, and are profoundly influenced by people. Social psychologists study these attractions, needs, and influences.

It is not sufficient to study human beings in isolation; we must examine the psychology of the individual in the context of the social situations in which they live. To fully understand people, we must see how they are influenced by their social context.

GROUPS AND SOCIAL INFLUENCE

Let's begin our study of social influence with a look at the effects of being a member of a group. Although some of what you will learn will make you embarrassed to be a member of the human race, you can understand the power of social influence only by looking at both its negative and positive faces.

Lynch Mobs

Near the start of the twentieth century, an African American man named William Carr was arrested and charged with killing the cow of a white family in southern Louisiana. A mob of solid citizens took him from the sheriff, who did not resist them, and hanged him without a trial. During the era in which this hanging took place, an average of two African Americans were lynched each week in the United States. These lynchings say much about racial prejudice—a topic we will turn to later in the chapter—but they also say a great deal about the effects of groups on the behavior of individuals. The members of lynch mobs were almost never men who had murdered before when alone or who would murder alone afterward. Something about being in a group transformed individual men who were incapable of murder into a mob that was very capable of murder (Postmes & Spears, 1998).

In some situations, being in a group can make a person feel anonymous and unidentifiable. This feeling can lead to a process known as **deindividuation** (Zimbardo, 1969). In this state, people are less aware of their own behavior and less concerned with what others think of their behavior. The result can be an increased likelihood of performing actions that you typically wouldn't do. Think about your own behavior at a crowded ball game or at a large rock concert. You might have screamed vulgar insults at the opposing team or behaved less than prim and proper. The weakened restraints that result from deindividuation can have more serious effects as well. When people are unidentifiable, they are more aggressive (Zimbardo, 1969). Similarly, an analysis of lynchings occurring over a 47-year period found that the worst atrocities occurred in larger groups, where, presumably, people felt more anonymous (Mullen, 1986).

Uninvolved Bystanders

Let's look at another negative outcome of being in groups. I vividly remember reading in a magazine about the death of Kitty Genovese some years ago. I was more than a little disappointed in the human race when I read that she had been beaten and stabbed to death in a residential area of New York City over the course of 30 minutes while 38 of her neighbors came to their windows and watched. Incredibly, no one went out to help her; no one even called the police.

How could such a thing have happened? Did Kitty just happen to live in a neighborhood of uncaring cowards? Social psychologists don't think that is the answer. For example, Bibb Latané, John Darley, and Judith Rodin carried out a series of experiments in an attempt to understand the lack of action by bystanders like these. In one experiment (Latané & Rodin, 1969), a female experimenter asked college students to fill out a questionnaire, and, while they worked, she went behind a curtain, where she staged a fake accident. The students heard her climbing and then falling from a chair. She moaned as if in great pain and begged for someone to help her get her foot out from under a heavy object. When students were alone in the other part of the room, 70 percent went to help her. But, when they were paired with one other student who did not respond to the woman's pleas, only 7 percent tried to help.

In a similar experiment (Darley & Latané, 1968), college students "overheard" a staged epileptic seizure through an intercom. Eighty-five percent of the students tried to find help for the seizure victim when they thought they alone had heard it, but, when they thought that others were also listening, only 30 percent sought help. Social psychologists do not think that bystanders who fail to help in an emergency are lacking in some personal quality; rather, they are influenced by being in a group. Many studies have shown that, the larger the group, the less likely any particular person is to offer to help a person in distress (Latané & Nida, 1981).

To understand why people fail to help in such situations, we must understand that the decision to help or not help is complex (Latané & Darley, 1970). First, a person must *notice* that something is out of the ordinary. A drowning victim who is screaming for help might not be noticed because everyone else at the beach is screaming and yelling in fun. If the victim is noticed, though, the person still might not help unless the situation is *interpreted* as an emergency. The bystander might think that the drowning victim is yelling and thrashing in the water for fun. A man slumped over in the street could just be drunk and not have had a heart attack. If the situation is not interpreted as an emergency, the victim will not receive help from that bystander.

Once the event is interpreted as an emergency, the bystander must decide whether she or he should *assume responsibility* for helping. If a lifeguard is present, or if others are around to help, a bystander might not assume the responsibility for helping. Even if the bystander assumes responsibility for helping, the bystander might not help if he or she does *not know how to help*. Finally, the bystander still might *decide not to help* for some reason. For example, you might notice a commotion in the water, interpret that situation as one in which a person is drowning, assume responsibility to help the victim, and know how to swim out and rescue the person, but, if you are afraid that the person is so heavy that you would be drowned trying to help, you still might decide not to help. As you can see, the decision to help is only the last step in a complex process.

What social factors influence these decisions? Latané and Darley have suggested that being in the presence of other people primarily affects the second and third stage of the decision process—interpreting the event as an emergency and assuming responsibility for helping. When we notice an event and try to interpret it, we look to others for information.

If nobody else is making an effort to help, then it's less likely that we will help, because it looks as if there is no reason to help: "No one looks worried, so there must not be a problem." As mentioned, in the Latané and Rodin "woman in distress" experiment, 70 percent of the individuals who were alone went to find help for the person who had fallen, but that number was reduced to 7 percent when they were paired with another person (actually a confederate of the experimenter) who made no effort at all to offer help. In other bystander experiments in which the confederate tried to find a way to help, the research participants were more likely to help, too.

The second stage that the presence of other bystanders is most likely to affect is assuming responsibility for helping. Groups create a **diffusion of responsibility.** If everyone in the group is responsible for a lynching, then no one person is individually responsible: "I didn't do it; we all just got worked up and did it." In emergencies, a person who is alone is clearly responsible for helping the person in need; however, in a group of bystanders, the reasoning is that I do not need to help because someone else will.

diffusion of responsibility
The effect of being in a group that apparently reduces the sense of personal responsibility of each group member to act appropriately.

Working and Solving Problems in Groups

We humans often gather together to perform work in groups. We sometimes study together, raise barns together, and hold meetings to discuss solutions to problems in our colleges, businesses, and cities. Is this a good thing? Does working together in groups bring out the best in us? Sometimes yes, and sometimes no.

Let's first look at group efforts—all of the members are trying to reach the same goal together. Suppose you convince your instructor to use the next class period to have a tug-of-war among members of your class. Do you think that you would pull harder on the rope if you were tugging alone against one classmate, or if you were part of a team of four persons tugging against four classmates? As the number of people involved in a tug-of-war increases, the average amount of force exerted by each person *declines* (Kravitz & Martin, 1986). The diminished effort of each individual in a group of tug-of-war is partly the result of lack of coordination among members of the group—some rest while others pull, resulting in less average effort.

Working as part of a group can affect how hard we work and how well we get the job done.

But even persons who are blindfolded and led to believe that others are pulling with them exert less effort than when they think they are pulling alone (Ingham, Levinger, Graves, & Peckham, 1974). Similarly, if you are asked to clap as loudly as you can, you will make more noise if you think your clap is being measured individually than if you think the loudness of a group of clappers is being measured together (Latané, Williams, & Harkins, 1979). Social psychologist Bibb Latané of Florida Atlantic University calls this phenomenon **social loafing.**

Sometimes groups can influence our *individual* performance even when we are not working on a group project; just working in the *presence* of other people can affect our behavior. Sometimes being in a group improves our performance on individual projects. When this is the case, **social facilitation** is said to occur (Levine, Resnick, & Higgins, 1993). In one of the earliest experiments in social psychology, Triplett (1898) found that teenagers wound fishing reels faster in the presence of other teenagers doing the same thing than when they were alone. Sometimes, however, working in the presence of others impairs our individual performance, causing what is termed **social impairment.** When do other people help or hurt our performance? It depends on how difficult and unfamiliar the task is. For example, Markus (1978) asked research participants to dress in preparation for a later phase in an experiment. This task of dressing was either easy, putting on everyday shoes and socks, or difficult, involving dressing in strange, unfamiliar clothes. Participants performed this dressing task alone, with a confederate who observed them, or with a confederate who was busy repairing equipment on the other side of the room. When individuals performed the easy dressing task, they dressed faster when there was another person present in the room, compared with when they dressed alone. When the research participants

social loafing
The tendency of members of groups to work less hard when group performance is measured than when individual performance is measured.

social facilitation
An effect in which working in a group improves one's performance on individual projects.

social impairment
An effect in which working in a group impairs individual performance.

had to perform the difficult dressing task, they dressed more slowly in the presence of others than they did when they were alone.

Why does the presence of other people improve performance on easy tasks and impair performance on difficult ones? Nearly all theorists agree with Zajonc (1965) that the presence of other people is arousing. If you will recall the discussion of *optimal levels of arousal* in chapter 9, easy tasks are easier to do when people are aroused, but difficult tasks are more difficult when people are aroused. The same is true for social facilitation and social impairment. High levels of arousal, such as that produced by performing in front of an audience, may promote social facilitation for easy or skilled tasks and social impairment for difficult or unfamiliar tasks. Professional athletes, musicians, and other performers often do their best work in the presence of an audience, because they are performing skills that have been practiced over and over again. In contrast, amateur performers who lack practice and skill are likely to perform more poorly when an audience is present.

What about more intellectual tasks such as problem solving? Is it better or worse to work together in groups when trying to solve problems? Suppose a friend asks you for advice about the following dilemma:

> I want to go to graduate school in filmmaking, but to get in I have to make an impressive grade in undergraduate scriptwriting. I could take the course from a famous instructor who is respected by the graduate school, but the famous instructor is so hard that hardly anyone gets an *A* or a *B*. Or I could take the course from an easier, less famous instructor that the graduate school might not be impressed by. What should I do?

What would you recommend? Would you tell your friend to go for broke and take the course from the famous but tough instructor, even though the chances of getting a good grade are very low? Studies have shown that most of us do *not* recommend such risky options *when we are alone with the person asking for advice*. However, when *groups* of persons discuss such dilemmas, they are much more likely to take extreme positions and recommend risky options (Stoner, 1961). The discussion of issues in groups often leads to the **polarization** of thinking by pushing our opinions toward one extreme "pole" of the issue.

polarization
The tendency for group discussion to make beliefs and attitudes more extreme.

For example, suppose you are a person with mildly prejudiced views about other ethnic groups. You are with a group of people and someone makes a *very* prejudicial remark about an ethnic group. You may find yourself taking a more extreme position against prejudice than you typically would—and meaning what you say. You have been pushed toward the nonprejudiced pole of the argument, and your statements have probably driven the other person to an even more prejudiced position. A classic study of polarization of attitudes occurring in group discussions found exactly these results during a discussion of ethnic attitudes among high school students (Myers & Bishop, 1970).

Conformity, Social Roles, and Obedience

I hope that you are beginning to have a new appreciation for the powerful influence of social situations on the behavior of the individual. Clearly, social situations influence us every day in important ways. But there is still a great deal more to the story of social influence. Next, we will consider our tendency to conform to the expectations of our peer groups and our cultures, the influence of socially prescribed roles and norms on our behavior, and our tendency to obediently follow the instructions of authority figures.

Conformity

When we are members of a group, we tend to behave as others do in the group—we tend to conform. **Conformity** is yielding to group pressure to act as everyone else does, even when no direct request has been made. A most informative and now classic study of conformity was conducted by Solomon Asch (1956). He asked college students to serve as research participants in an experiment that he said concerned visual perception. Each student participated in a group with other "research participants" all of whom were actually confederates of the experimenter. The group was shown four straight lines, depicted in

conformity
Yielding to group pressure even when no direct request to comply has been made.

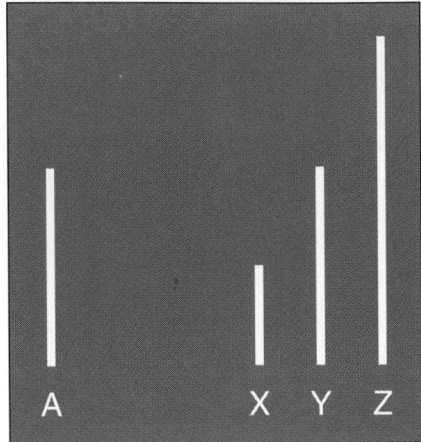

FIGURE 15.1

Stimuli like those used in Asch's study of conformity.

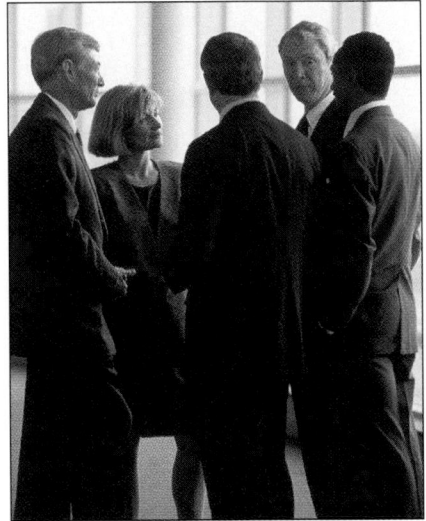

In terms of outward behavior, we tend to conform to group norms.

"All those in favor say 'Aye.'"
"Aye." "Aye." "Aye."
"Aye." "Aye."

figure 15.1. The task was to tell which of the three lines on the right side of the figure was the same length as line *A*.

The task was intentionally made easy, with line *Y* being the obvious correct choice. But the real participant was the last one in line as each student was asked to state his or her choice out loud. One by one, the confederates playing the part of real research participants chose line *X*. The distress of the real participant was immediately apparent. He seemed to be asking, "Am I crazy or are they?" But, in an amazing 74 percent of the cases, the participants conformed to the pressure of the group and gave the wrong answer at least part of the time.

How "deep" was this conformity? Did the research participants know that they were just going along with the group's opinion, or did the group actually change their judgment? People may conform for two reasons: to gain rewards and avoid punishments (such as social approval or disapproval) or to gain information. In the Asch situation, people seemed to conform for the former reason, to seek approval and avoid disapproval. How do we know? When the same line-judging experiment was conducted in a slightly different way that allowed the research participants to make their judgments privately, almost no conformity to the erroneous judgments of other individuals occurred. Apparently, we are able to make up our minds privately even in the face of pressure from others but often go along with the crowd in terms of outward behavior.

Sometimes, however, we conform to the behavior of others at a much deeper level. This happens when the "correct" judgment is less clear than in Asch's line-judging experiment. Sherif (1936) conducted a study that took advantage of a perceptual phenomenon called the *autokinetic effect*. When a person is placed in a completely darkened room with no reference points, a fixed point of light on a wall will appear to move. Because the movement of light is not real, and the distance that it seems to move differs from person to person, this is an extremely ambiguous situation (as compared with Asch's line-judging task, which was very clear-cut). Sherif placed individuals in a room with confederates and asked them to estimate the distance that a fixed light had moved. The confederates gave either extremely low or extremely high estimates of movement, and the research participants tended to agree with the confederates. In this ambiguous situation, however, they still tended to agree with the confederates even when they could report their estimates of the movement of the light in private. When the appropriate response in a situation is not clear, we look to others for information and will not only go along with them, but we may actually change our judgments.

Several factors increase the likelihood of conformity to the group:

1. *Size of the group.* Up to a point, the more people there are in a group, the more likely we are to go along. When the group gets too large, however, conformity drops off.

2. *Unanimous groups.* Conformity is highest when we face a group who all feel the same way about a topic—the group is unanimous. But, conformity is greatly reduced when even one other person in the group feels as we do.

3. *Culture and conformity.* An article by British psychologists Rod Bond and Peter Smith (1996) shows us that culture is an important factor that influences conformity. The experiment showing conformity in the judgment of the length of lines originally conducted by Solomon Asch in 1956 has now been conducted 133 times in 17 different cultures. Conformity occurs in all cultures, but persons from individualistic cultures, which place an emphasis on the welfare of the individual—as in North America—are less conforming on the Asch task than persons from collectivistic cultures, which emphasize the welfare of society as a whole, rather than the individual.

4. *Gender and conformity?* What about gender? According to our stereotypes, males are more independent and less likely to conform than females. Research conducted before the mid-1950s suggested that females were more likely to conform than males at that time. More recent research, however, has shown that this is no longer the case (Eagly, 1978; Eagly & Johnson, 1990). Maybe our stereotypes will eventually catch up with the changing realities of gender.

Social Roles and Social Norms

When people work together in groups, the efforts of each individual need to be coordinated with those of others to avoid chaos. In response to this need, every culture has evolved many **social roles** and **social norms** to give guidelines as to what is expected of us (Levine & others, 1993). Just like actors in a play who have scripts for their roles, social roles tell us how we are expected to behave. In this course, you play the role of the student, and the nice person who tells you interesting things about psychology plays the role of the instructor. Each social role gives the person a different set of expectations for appropriate behavior. You are not surprised when the person in the role of instructor stands in the front of the classroom and lectures, but you would be surprised if the student sitting next to you were to stand up and deliver a 45-minute lecture on the importance of classical conditioning to our understanding of romantic love. Social roles have a powerful impact on the behavior of individuals. When we are placed in a new role, our behavior often changes to fit the role.

We play numerous roles in our lives and each role influences us whether we are aware of it or not. I play the roles of man, spouse, father, middle-aged person, person of Irish ancestry, heterosexual, brother, son, and psychology professor, to name only the most obvious ones. Each role is a source of social influence on my behavior whether I like it or not. I can work hard at not being the typical male or the typical father, but these roles inevitably influence me. How about you? What roles do you play and how do they make you different from me?

In addition to conforming to our social roles, we also behave according to the spoken and unspoken rules known as *social norms*. The social norms of our culture tell us how we should behave in particular situations. We avoid making eye contact with other people in an elevator and cover our mouths when we cough because these are widely held social norms for Americans. Most people conform to the social norms of their culture most of the time.

The influence of roles and norms is not all bad. I have emphasized the extent to which social roles can be harmful because I want to alert you to the fact that they can detract from your individuality, but it is important to recognize that social roles and norms play an essential positive function in society. Without social roles and norms, you would not know what to expect of your psychology instructor, to take but one example. Being a student would be much more difficult if you did not know that the person who plays the role of the instructor will give lectures on which you are supposed to take notes, and that she or he will give tests and will give you a grade at the end of the term. Understanding the roles of others—and those of ourselves—greatly facilitates our ability to work together in society for the common good. But they are potent sources of influence that must be understood.

social roles
Culturally determined guidelines that tell people what behavior is expected of them.

social norms
Guidelines provided by every culture for judging acceptable and unacceptable behavior.

Obedience: Direct Influence by Authority Figures

One of the most fascinating, and often frightening, lines of inquiry in social psychology has been research on **obedience,** doing what we are told to do by people in authority. This research was prompted in part by the behavior of soldiers in World War II, and other wars, who committed unthinkable atrocities when ordered to do so. What kind of person would help abuse and murder 6 million Jews during the Holocaust? What kind of person would not refuse to obey such an order? The disturbing answer from research is that most of us are that kind of person.

Stanley Milgram (1963, 1965) conducted a series of studies that cast a glaring light on the subject of obedience. To get the full impact of his findings, try to imagine that you are a research participant in one of his experiments. You have volunteered for a study of memory. When you arrive at the appointed time, you and another person, a middle-aged man, meet a somewhat stern, authoritarian experimenter wearing a white lab coat. The experimenter chooses you to be the "teacher" in the experiment and the other participant to be the "learner." The learner will have to memorize a list of word pairs, but you have to test him and operate the equipment. The "equipment" is a console labeled "SHOCK GENERATOR" with a bank of switches marked from 15 to 450 volts.

You help strap the learner into something that looks like an electric chair, and you attach electrodes to him that are connected to the shock generator in the other room. The

obedience
Doing what one is told to do by people in authority.

In Milgram's classic obedience experiments, the "learner" was strapped to a chair while participants were instructed to use what they believed was an electric shock generator to shock him after errors in learning.

learner asks whether the experiment could be dangerous to his heart condition, but the experimenter assures him that, although the shocks could be extremely painful, they should cause no physical harm. You return to the next room, take your seat at the console, and are told how you should use the shocks to "help" the learner memorize the list.

You are to listen to him attempt to recite the list over the intercom and shock him by throwing one of the switches after each error. You are to begin with the weakest shock and increase the intensity each time he makes a mistake. You are even given a 45-volt shock so you can see what it feels like (it's unpleasant) and the experiment begins. The learner recalls the list fairly accurately but makes a few mistakes, and you shock him as you have been instructed to do.

What you do not know is that the learner is not really getting shocked. He is a confederate of the experimenter who is acting a role. He is not even talking over the intercom; you are hearing a tape recording instead. But the important thing is that you *believe* that a man with a heart condition is strapped into an electric chair in the next room and that you are giving him shocks every time he makes a mistake.

The learner groans after an intensity of 75 volts has been reached. At 150 volts, he says that his heart is bothering him and asks to be let out of the experiment. The experimenter denies the request and tells you to give him the shock when he makes a mistake. When the learner has been given the 180-volt shock, the learner screams that he cannot stand the pain, and, as you are told to turn the shock apparatus to 300 volts—the level marked "Danger: Extreme Shock"—he refuses to recite the list of word pairs any more. When you look toward the experimenter, expecting him to stop the proceedings, he firmly tells you to administer the next shock.

What would you do? Would you give the extremely dangerous shock, even though the learner was begging you to stop? Or would you refuse to continue? Milgram asked a panel of psychiatrists how many research participants they thought would continue giving shocks at this point, and they predicted that less than 5 percent would continue. What percentage would you predict? Milgram found that an incredible 65 percent not only gave the next shock but also continued participating until they had given the highest shock (450 volts).

Milgram's findings were astonishing, even to other social psychologists who understood the power of social situations. Could his results have been a fluke? Did Milgram just happen to recruit a group of sadistic individuals? To find out, Milgram repeated his study and found the same results with men and women from many different walks of life: students, blue-collar workers, white-collar workers, and professionals. He conducted his study in laboratories at prestigious Yale University and in an office space in downtown Bridgeport, Connecticut. This study has been replicated in other countries as well. The results of these studies are a painful reminder of the power of social situations and a warning of the ease with which misguided authorities can use ordinary people like you and me to obediently carry out their wishes.

It is somewhat comforting that later studies found that individuals were less likely to obey the instruction to give the high-voltage shocks when their victim was in the same room with them, acting distressed by the shocks. In addition, when the prestige of the experimenter was reduced, the percentage of obedient persons fell to about 50 percent. When the experimenter gave instructions by telephone rather than in person, the percentage fell to about 25 percent. Furthermore, when the research participant was in the presence of two other participants who refused to give the high-intensity shocks, only 10 percent obeyed the experimenter's instructions to the end. Obedience is also reduced when individuals are led to feel more personal responsibility for their actions and when it is obvious that authorities have self-serving goals. These last facts are somewhat encouraging, but they do not lessen the impact of Milgram's findings: The power of social situations over human behavior can be terrifying and must be guarded against.

A final comment is in order about Milgram's study of obedience. Although this study was of great value in exploring an important aspect of human nature, this study would not be considered ethical by today's standards. At a minimum, the experimenter would not be allowed to command the research participant to continue against her or his will—participants may leave an experiment at any time.

● Review

Because we are social animals, we are almost always in the company of others. This is a fundamentally important observation because people can be fully understood only if our social nature is understood. Other people influence our behavior and we must understand that process of influence. We all need to be more aware of the power of social situations in influencing behavior. Ironically, ignoring the power of social situations only makes us more vulnerable to their influence.

The very fact of being with others can influence behavior; people often behave differently when they are in groups than when they are alone. Mobs commit crimes that the individuals alone would not commit, and groups of bystanders fail to help people in distress even though most members of that group would have done so if alone.

Groups influence individual behavior through our strong tendency to conform with the group even when not asked to do so. We may conform in terms of outward behavior and, in some instances, may change our inner judgments and attitudes as well. Groups also influence us through the expectations for our behavior that are inherent in social roles and social norms. Frighteningly, we are likely to be persuaded to obey even inappropriate requests from a prestigious authority figure, especially when we face the authority figure alone. When working in groups, individual effort declines under some circumstances and group problem solving can become distorted.

● Check Your Learning

To be sure that you have learned the key points from the preceding section, cover the list of correct answers and try to answer each question. If you give an incorrect answer to any question, return to the page given next to the correct answer to see why your answer was not correct. Remember that these questions cover only some of the important information in this section; it is important that you make up your own questions to check your learning of other facts and concepts.

1. Social psychology is the branch of psychology that studies _____.

2. People may behave as they do in lynch mobs and at ball games because of a process called _____.

3. In problem-solving situations where the correct solution is not obvious, we are most likely to conform

   a) publicly in terms of outward behaviors.

   b) privately in terms of judgments and attitudes.

   c) neither a nor b.

   d) both a and b.

4. When workers exert less effort in a group than they would when working alone, the result is called

   a) social loafing.   c) groupthink.

   b) group polarization.   d) social facilitation.

● Thinking Critically About Psychology

1. Can you think of a situation in your life in which you blamed a person's behavior on his or her personality even though the social situation might have strongly influenced the person's behavior?

2. What do you think is the significance of Stanley Milgram's studies? What does it say about individual responsibility to behave ethically in a society?

Correct Answers 1. individuals as they interact with others (p. 440),   **2.** deindividuation (p. 440), **3. d** (p. 444),   **4. a** (p. 442).

▶ ATTITUDES AND PERSUASION

Attitudes are a pivotal concept in social psychology. They are of special interest because other people attempt to influence our attitudes through persuasion, and our attitudes are often reflected in our behavior toward others. If I give a speech to parents that changes their attitudes toward discipline practices (such as it's more important to praise children for their good behavior than to punish them for their bad behavior), they may tend to change the way they actually rear their children, too. As we will see, however, attitudes and social behavior are not perfectly correlated by any means. But there is enough relationship between the two to make attitudes a favorite topic of study of social psychologists, especially attitudes related to important aspects of social behavior such as prejudice based on a person's gender, ethnicity, age, sexual preference, or other factors.

attitudes
Beliefs that predispose one to act and feel in certain ways.

Social psychologists define **attitudes** as beliefs that predispose us to act and feel in certain ways. Note that this definition has three components: (a) *beliefs,* such as the belief that door-to-door salespeople are generally dishonest; (b) *feelings,* such as a strong dislike for door-to-door salespeople; and (c) *dispositions to behave,* such as a readiness to be rude to them when they come to the door. Where do our attitudes come from, and what causes them to change?

Origins of Attitudes

The origins of most of our attitudes are fairly obvious: We learn them directly from our experiences, and we learn them from others (Olson & Zanna, 1993). Some of our attitudes are learned from firsthand experience. Children who are bitten by dogs often carry negative attitudes toward dogs for the rest of their lives, especially toward the kind of dog that bit them. In contrast, the sweet crunch of chocolate chip cookies generally leads to a favorable attitude toward them. In other words, some attitudes appear to be *classically conditioned.* If a stimulus (dogs or cookies) is paired with a positive or negative experience, the attitude will be similarly positive or negative.

Attitudes are also commonly learned from others. Parents who model positive attitudes toward their Hispanic neighbors are likely to have children who have positive attitudes toward Hispanics. Children whose best friends think baseball is awful may pick up this attitude through modeling. Similarly, children who are reinforced by their parents and friends for prejudicial attitudes are likely to have these attitudes strengthened. In sum, other people instill attitudes in us through their modeling and reinforcement.

Persuasion and Attitude Change

persuasion
The process of changing another person's attitudes through arguments and other related means.

Attitudes are not chiseled in granite; they can change after they have been formed. Indeed, the earliest known writings on social psychology were about changing people's attitudes through **persuasion.** Aristotle's *Rhetoric* was an essay on factors that make for persuasive arguments when orators debate. You probably do not listen to many orators debate, but you are on the receiving end of other kinds of persuasive communications nearly every day. Commercials on the radio and television and advertisements in newspapers and magazines are designed to change your attitude about the sponsors' products. Political speeches and billboards are intended to persuade you how to vote. Your friend who wants to borrow your car tries to persuade you. And, when you ask your professor to let you take an exam early, you try to persuade him or her. Persuasion is a natural and necessary part of our interactions with other members of society. But, because of the potentially important consequences of persuasive communications (your friend might actually talk you into lending her your car!), it's important to know something about their nature. The persuasiveness of a communication is not determined merely by the logical quality of the argument. Logic may, in fact, be one of the *least important* factors. That's a scary thought, because we would like to believe that we live in a world where logic and truth win out. But, if you know what makes an argument persuasive, you can at least be on your guard. Notice that the qualities of persuasive communication fall into three general categories: characteristics of the *speaker,* of the *communication* itself, and of the *people who hear it.*

Characteristics of the Speaker

Several characteristics of the speaker are important in determining how persuasive a communication will be:

1. *Credibility.* If you were to listen to a speech on the value of arithmetic, do you think you would be more persuaded if the speech were given by a noted engineer or a dishwasher? Elliot Aronson and Burton Golden (1962) conducted exactly this experiment and found that the engineer swayed opinions considerably more than the dishwasher, even though they gave exactly the same speech. In fact, the same person gave the same speech each time, just the introduction identifying his job differed. Many other studies have reached the same conclusion (Aronson, 1995). Our perception of the credibility of the speaker has a great deal to do with the persuasiveness of the communication.

   But credibility should not be confused in the previous example with being highly educated, intelligent, high in status, or even nice. The key is whether the speaker is a credible source of information *about the specific argument being presented.* Elaine Walster and her colleagues performed a clever experiment that forcefully makes this point (Walster, Aronson, & Abrahams, 1966). Individuals were given newspaper clippings of interviews with either a mobster or a politician. Half of the research participants read clippings that argued for more lenient treatment of criminals by the courts, and half read arguments for stricter treatment. When the mobster argued for more lenient treatment, he was completely ineffective and, in fact, slightly swayed attitudes in the opposite direction. When the mobster argued for *stricter* treatment, however, he was as persuasive as the politician. Apparently, the reasoning was that, if a criminal (who knows about crime and would not personally benefit from stricter enforcement) thinks we need stricter enforcement of the laws, then it must be so.

   In general, the more credible the speaker, the more persuasive the message. But Carl Hovland has qualified this conclusion with the identification of what he called **sleeper effects** (Hovland & Weiss, 1951). Although attempts at persuasion by speakers who are low in credibility are ineffective at first, their messages may have an effect later. This is because people tend to forget what speaker presented what message. If you forget that a low-credibility speaker presented a certain message, then later that message will not seem so unbelievable.

2. *Attractiveness.* Other things being equal, a speaker who is attractive, popular, famous, and likable will be more effective in changing our opinions than an unattractive speaker. That is why Cindy Crawford is paid enormous sums to endorse products in commercials and I am not. Fortunately, the persuasiveness of attractive speakers seems to be limited to relatively unimportant issues—but that includes almost everything that advertisers want us to buy (Aronson, 1995; Chaiken & Eagly, 1983).

sleeper effects
According to Hovland, the potential for low-credibility speakers to influence opinion after a period of time.

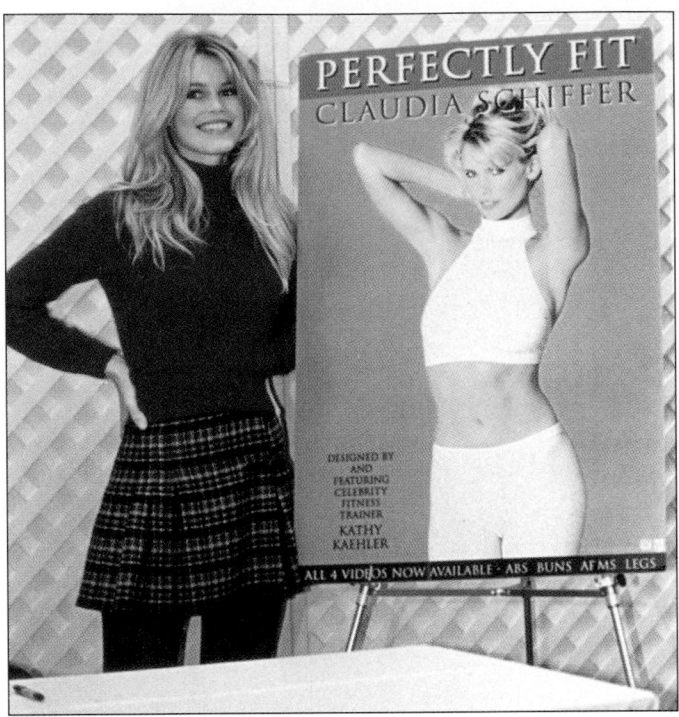

Attractive, popular, or famous speakers tend to be more persuasive than unattractive speakers. But their persuasiveness seems to be limited to relatively unimportant issues.

3. *Intent.* Speakers are generally less persuasive if they obviously intend to change your opinion, particularly if the speaker has something to gain by changing your opinion (Aronson, 1995). If a real estate agent tells you that a lot she wants you to buy is going to rise dramatically in value, you might not believe her. On the other hand, if you overhear two realtors at a cocktail party say the same thing, the message would probably be more persuasive because no one is trying to convince you or stands to make a commission from the sale.

Characteristics of the Message

In addition to the qualities of the speaker, the characteristics of the message are also important determinants of persuasiveness:

1. *Fear appeals.* Are messages that arouse fear more persuasive than unemotional ones? Adolf Hitler appealed strongly to the fears and frustrations of the German people in the speeches he gave to rally support behind his Nazi party. Were the emotions he aroused part of the reason for his success? The American Cancer Society uses scare tactics in some of their ads to convince people to stop smoking. Are they going about it in the right way?

Considerable evidence suggests that communications that arouse fear—such as graphic pictures of rotten teeth and gums in messages urging proper dental care—are more effective than the same messages without the fear-provoking images. Fear can enhance the persuasiveness of a communication, but only under certain circumstances (Mewborn & Rogers, 1979; Rogers, 1975). Listeners will respond favorably to a fear-inducing persuasive communication only if (a) the emotional appeal is a relatively strong one (but not too strong), (b) the listeners think that the fearful outcome (such as rotten teeth or lung cancer) is likely to happen to them, and (c) the message offers an effective way of avoiding the fearful outcome (such as an easy way to stop smoking). If all of these elements are present, emotional appeals can be highly persuasive.

2. *Two-sided arguments.* There are two sides to most arguments. If, for example, we use more coal in generating electric power, we will reduce our dependence on foreign oil and may be able to keep oil prices from rising. That is good. But, if we burn more coal, we will also increase pollution of the atmosphere, which will hurt people's health, damage land and water in the process of strip mining, and lose lives during the mining process. That is obviously bad. If you were trying to convince Congress to support the use of less coal, would it be more effective to state just the positive side of the argument, or both sides?

There is no simple answer to this question. In part, it depends on how favorable the audience is to your position before you start talking. If the audience is leaning in your favor or has information only about your position, your message will be more persuasive if you just tell them about the benefits of not burning coal. Telling them about the negative side to the argument may lose you some supporters. But if audience members are initially unfavorable to your position or are knowledgeable about both sides of the issue, it's generally better to give them both sides of the argument. That will make you seem more credible and less biased (Baron & Byrne, 1982), so the next time somebody does an admirable job of presenting both sides of an issue, you may be dealing with a strong believer in honesty and the democratic process, but you may just be listening to a shrewd operator who is trying to change your mind.

3. *Message framing.* If you will recall from chapter 7 on cognition, the way in which problems are presented to us in words—or *framed*—strongly influences how we

solve those problems (Rothman & Salovey, 1997). Humans are so influenced by the wording of problems that we often reach very different solutions to exactly the same problem if it is framed differently. New research suggests that the same appears to be true of persuasive communications—framing the same message in different ways can sometimes make all the difference.

An excellent and inherently important example has been provided by psychologists Beth Meyerowitz and Shelly Chaiken (1987). They compared the persuasiveness of two messages designed to encourage college-age women to conduct breast self-examinations. Two groups of women read a three-page pamphlet on breast cancer and self-examinations. Their pamphlets were identical, except for several statements. One group read statements framed to emphasize the *gains* of breast self-examination:

By doing breast self-examination now, you can learn what your normal healthy breasts feel like so that you will be better prepared to notice any small, abnormal changes that might occur as you get older. Research shows that women who do breast self-examination have an increased chance of finding a tumor in the early, more treatable stage of the disease. (p. 504)

The other group read statements framed to emphasize the *loss* involved in not conducting breast self-examination:

By not doing breast self-examination you will not learn what your normal, healthy breasts feel like so that you will be ill-prepared to notice any small, abnormal changes that might occur as you get older. Research shows that women who do not do breast self-examination have a decreased chance of finding a tumor in the early, more treatable stage of the disease. (p. 504)

Four months later, the women were interviewed to determine if the messages had had any positive effects. The results showed that the second message, framed in terms of potential loss, was more effective than the first version. Women reading the loss-framed message had much more positive attitudes toward breast self-examination and were almost twice as likely to have practiced it. Women reading the pamphlet framed in terms of potential gains were no more likely to engage in breast self-examination than a group that had not read either pamphlet. Interestingly, the two pamphlets did not arouse different amounts of fear, so we cannot conclude that this is just another example of the greater effects of fear-arousing communications. Although a great deal has been learned about the best ways to frame messages to encourage breast self-examination in recent years, health professionals infrequently frame appeals in the most effective ways (Kline & Mattson, 2000). Understanding framing helps us make the point that effective persuasion is not just the result of *what* you say, but also *how* you say it.

Characteristics of the Listeners

In addition to qualities of the speaker and the message, certain characteristics of the listeners help determine how persuasive an argument will be:

1. *Intelligence.* Less intelligent people are generally easier to persuade. The exception is when the message is complex and difficult to understand; under this condition, more intelligent listeners are easier to persuade (Rhodes & Wood, 1992).

2. *Need for social approval.* Some people have a greater need for social approval (a need to be approved of or liked by others) than other people do. People with a high need for social approval are generally easier to persuade than people who are low in this need (Baron & Byrne, 1982).

3. *Self-esteem.* Individuals whose self-esteem is moderate (have opinions of themselves that are about as positive as most people's) are generally easier to convince than peo-

ple with either high self-esteem or low self-esteem (Rhodes & Wood, 1992; Zellner, 1970). Persons with high self-esteem are generally very confident of their opinions and difficult to influence. Persons with low self-esteem, in contrast, tend not to pay attention to the communication enough to be swayed. For example, a person with a very low opinion of himself might hear a speech on financing public schools and become lost in his own thoughts about his own poor educational performance (Rhodes & Wood, 1992).

4. *Audience size.* People are generally easier to persuade when they are listening to the message in a group rather than alone. And bigger crowds lead to greater persuasion than smaller ones (Newton & Mann, 1980).

5. *Gender.* Early studies on persuasion suggested that women are more persuadable than men. However, these studies were biased, using messages that were of greater interest to men. Later studies controlling for this interest variable show that there are no differences in persuadability between men and women (Eagly, 1978).

Techniques of Persuasion

Some people are better at persuasion than other people are. This is partly because they have the characteristics of persuasive speakers, and partly because they understand the characteristics of the message and the audience just described—they know how to pitch the most persuasive argument to their audience. But many persuasive people—from politicians to salespeople—also know and use some simple *techniques of persuasion.* As you read, try to recall if these techniques have been used on you by salespeople.

A classic technique of persuasion is the *foot-in-the-door technique.* The person first makes a small, reasonable request. After you agree to that request, however, he or she follows up with a larger request. If someone were to call you at home and say that she was a researcher at another university who would like to come over and inspect your home, would you agree to let her in? Most people would be reluctant to agree, but people who first agree to answer a few questions over the telephone are more likely to allow researchers to inspect their homes. Agreeing to one small request makes us more likely to agree to a second, larger request.

The *low-ball technique* is similar to the foot-in-the-door. First, you are offered a very reasonable deal. When you accept it, the deal is changed—for the worse. This is a favorite of some auto salespeople. First, they get you to commit to a particular car for a fair price. While you're dreaming of driving this wonderful car, you get the bad news that the salesperson forgot to figure in the delivery charge and the undercoating. Now the car costs more than you thought—do you still buy it? This technique of persuasion works more often than not—most people don't walk away from the deal (Burger, 1986).

Cognitive Dissonance

www.mmhe.com/laheye1

Behavior and Attitude Change: Cognitive Dissonance Theory

As we have seen, persuasion is an important source of attitude change, but the discrepancy that often exists between our attitudes and behavior is another key cause of changed attitudes. Even though attitudes are partially defined in terms of a disposition to behave, there is sometimes a great difference between our attitudes and our behavior. For example, during the Vietnam War, many men who held attitudes that were strongly opposed to the war nevertheless obeyed their draft orders and became a part of the war. Similarly, opinion pollsters know that not everyone who has a favorable attitude toward a product will actually buy it.

An interesting point is that, when behavior and attitudes are inconsistent, the attitudes often change to match the behavior *rather than the other way around.* Leon Festinger (1957) proposed the theory of **cognitive dissonance** to explain the tendency of attitudes to sometimes shift to be consistent with behavior. This theory, which has sparked some of

cognitive dissonance
(dis′so-nans)   The discomfort that results from inconsistencies between attitudes and behavior.

the greatest controversy and most interesting research in social psychology, states that inconsistencies between attitudes and behavior are uncomfortable. This discomfort motivates people to do what they can to reduce the discomfort, or *dissonance.*

For example, if you smoke cigarettes (behavior), and you know that cigarette smoking is the leading cause of lung cancer and other serious diseases (attitude), your behavior and attitude is inconsistent, which produces dissonance. Dissonance theory predicts that either your attitude or your behavior will change to reduce the dissonance (Gibbons, Eggleston, & Benthin, 1997) (see figure 15.2). You could change the behavior and quit smoking, but that is often very difficult for many smokers. Unfortunately, human beings usually reduce dissonance in the easiest way possible. In this case, it might be easier to change your attitude toward smoking. How many smokers do you know who say that the research linking cancer and smoking is faulty or who say, "So what if smoking causes cancer; I'll die of something, anyway?" These are irrational and self-defeating arguments, but they are effective ways of reducing dissonance.

Festinger and other social psychologists have tested the theory of cognitive dissonance in a large number of experiments. One of the best known (Festinger & Carlsmith, 1959) involved asking research participants to perform a boring spool-stacking and peg-turning task for an hour. Afterward, the participants were each asked to tell the next participant that the task was an interesting one. Half of the individuals were offered $20 to say that the task was interesting, and half were offered $1. A third group of individuals stacked spools but were not asked to say anything to the next research participant. Later, all of the participants were asked how interesting they really thought the task was.

Which group do you think reported the most favorable attitude toward the task? Perhaps surprisingly—but just as predicted by cognitive dissonance theory—the most positive attitudes were expressed by the group offered only $1. The group offered $20 was not placed in a state of dissonance: "The task was really boring, but I'll lie to the next person to get the $20." The group offered $1 was placed in a state of dissonance, however; there was no good explanation for their stating an opinion about the task that was inconsistent with their attitudes, so their attitudes improved to be more consistent with their behavior.

It's a little scary, isn't it? You probably thought your attitudes were always thoughtfully arrived at and based on reality. If Festinger is right, they may sometimes reflect nothing more than an escape from cognitive dissonance.

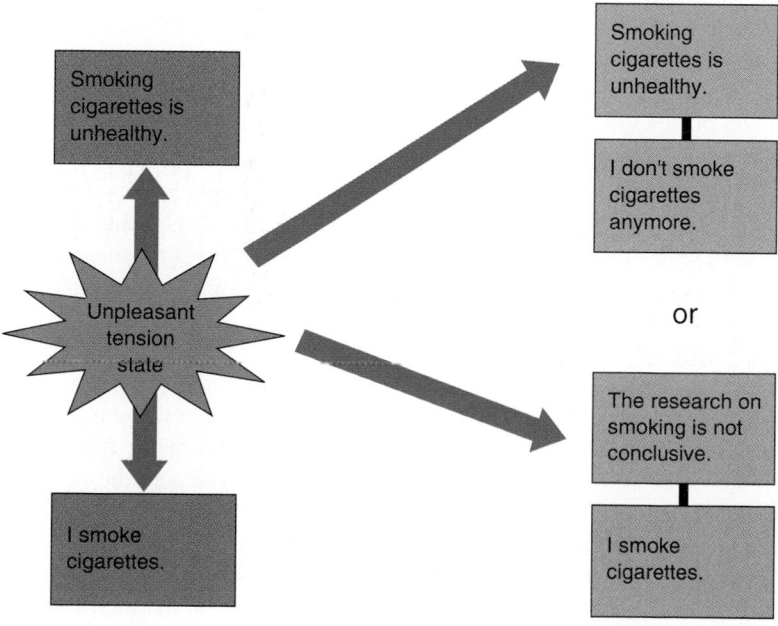

FIGURE 15.2

If attitudes and behavior are inconsistent, cognitive dissonance is created. To reduce this unpleasant state, either attitudes or behaviors change to be consistent with one another.

Prejudice

www.mmhe.com/laheye1

prejudice
A harmful attitude based on inaccurate generalizations about a group of people.

stereotype
An inaccurate generalization on which a prejudice is based.

Stereotyping people, such as the "typical" salesperson, detracts from our ability to treat members of a group as individuals and leads to faulty attributions.

attribution theory
(ah-tri-bu´shun)   The theory that people tend to look for explanations for their own behavior and that of others.

Prejudice and Stereotypes

Of all the attitudes that we hold about other people, the kind that is most worthy of improved understanding is prejudice. **Prejudice** is a harmful attitude based on inaccurate generalizations about a group of people based on their skin color, religion, sex, age, or any other noticeable difference. In some way, however, the difference is believed by the prejudiced person to imply something negative about the entire group. They're all lazy, or hysterical, or pushy.

The inaccurate generalization on which the prejudice is based is called a **stereotype.** We all hold stereotypes of other groups of people. How does a "rock star" look and act? If you were producing a movie, would you cast Bob Dole or Barbara Walters in the role of a rock star? You wouldn't because neither of them fits the stereotyped image of rock stars. What are Russians like? Do you have a stereotyped view of them? Think about it for a second. Would you cast the Spice Girls as Russian army officers in a serious dramatic film? Do you hold stereotypes of women, men, Cambodians, African Americans, old people, Cubans?

Stereotypes can be either negative or positive (you might believe that all psychology textbook authors are charming, witty, and attractive), but all stereotypes, positive or negative, are inherently harmful for three reasons:

1. *Stereotypes take away our ability to treat each member of a group as an individual.* When we hold a stereotyped view of a group, we tend to treat each member of that group as if the person has the exact characteristics of the stereotype, whether or not he or she really has those characteristics. Even when the stereotype is partially based on fact, many members of the group will differ from the stereotype in significant ways. Take the view that many of us have of Chinese Americans: One aspect of the stereotype is that they are highly intelligent. Although it's true that *on the average* Chinese Americans score slightly higher than whites on some specific measures of intelligence, not all Chinese are highly intelligent. If a teacher's expectations for a Chinese child of below-average intelligence were based on this stereotype, the child might be criticized for not living up to his or her supposed high intelligence when the child is, in fact, performing up to his or her ability. Stereotyped beliefs that an ethnic group is low in intelligence can have even more serious consequences in limiting the educational and occupational opportunities of members of that group.

2. *Stereotypes lead to narrow expectations for behavior.* Our stereotypes lead us to expect the members of the stereotyped group to behave in certain ways. For example, we expect women to be gentle, nurturing, caring, and cooperative, but we expect men to be competitive, ambitious, aggressive, and strong. Individuals of either sex who do not conform to these expectations are viewed as abnormal and are often the objects of anger or ridicule. Thus, stereotypes can be a limiting force for persons who do not conform to the narrow expectations for their group (gender, ethnicity, age, etc.).

3. *Stereotypes lead to faulty attributions.* **Attribution theory** is based on the idea that humans tend to try to explain why things happen—that is, attribute them to a cause. One of the things that we are most fond of doing is explaining behavior, both others and our own. One of your friends has just invited herself over for dinner for the third time this month. Why? Is she broke? Is she a moocher? Does she just like your company? According to attribution theory, we tend to attribute all behavior to a cause.

   Our stereotypes influence the attributions that we make about other people's behavior. As Elliot Aronson (1995) points out, if a prejudiced white man sees an overturned trash can and garbage strewn around the yard of a white family, he is apt to attribute the mess to a stray dog looking for food. But, if he sees the same thing in the yard of an African American family, he would more likely attribute it to their supposed lazy, slovenly ways.

   These faulty attributions have the effect of deepening and strengthening our prejudices as we keep "seeing" evidence that "supports" our stereotypes and rejecting evidence that is contrary to them. For more on the harmful effects of stereotypes, see

Application of Psychology: "Stereotypes and Discrimination in the Workplace" at the end of this chapter.

Causes of Stereotypes and Prejudice

If we are to have any hope of reducing prejudice, it is essential to understand the causes of these harmful attitudes. Social psychologists have proposed four explanations for why prejudice arises:

1. *Realistic conflict.* The *realistic conflict theory* suggests that people who are competing for scarce resources, such as jobs, food, and territory, come to view others in increasingly negative ways (White, 1977). Although this theory may explain some instances of prejudice, prejudice often exists when there is no conflict over resources.

2. *Us versus them.* Another source of prejudice is the tendency people have to divide the world into two groups—*us versus them* (Turner & others, 1987). Our group becomes the "in-group," and those who are excluded become the "out-group." In a classic study, Sherif & Sherif (1953) randomly divided middle-class 11- and 12-year-old boys of the same race into two groups: the Rattlers and the Eagles. After a series of activities designed to promote in-group solidarity and between-group competition, the rival groups began to engage in fighting and name calling—they developed prejudices about one another, even though the groups had been created randomly.

   Social psychologists believe that "us versus them" prejudice is common partly because it strengthens the prejudiced individuals' self-esteem. Consider the following illustrative studies (Fein & Spencer, 1997): Introductory psychology students were asked to participate in two experiments in sequence. In the first experiment, the students were asked to choose one term from a list of values (honesty, thriftiness, etc.) and write a few paragraphs saying why that value is important. Half of the students (randomly determined) were asked to choose the value that is most important to them personally and half were asked to choose the value that is least important to them. Previous studies have shown that writing about a value that is important to the individual is an effective way of strengthening his or her self-image, but writing about an unimportant value is not.

   Therefore, as the second experiment began, half of the group had just gone through an exercise that strengthened their self-image. The second experiment was presented as a study of the evaluation of job applicants. The students all read the résumé and watched the same videotape of a young female job applicant's interview for a management position. Half of the students (randomly determined) were given information indicating that the applicant was Jewish and half of the students were given information that the applicant was not Jewish. The students then rated the applicant in terms of her personality and job qualifications. The personality and qualifications of the woman was rated more negatively by non-Jewish students when she was presented as Jewish. Because the résumé and the videotape were of the same woman, these differences in ratings clearly reflect anti-Jewish prejudice. There was significantly less prejudice, however, in the ratings of students whose self-image had just been strengthened in the preceding experiment. Other follow-up studies by the same investigators showed that college students become more prejudiced in their evaluations of others when their self-images are threatened, but that having a chance to say negative things about a member of another ethnic group increases their self-esteem (Fein & Spencer, 1997). Thus, "us versus them" prejudice appears to be perpetuated partly because it bolsters the self-esteem of persons with weak self-images.

3. *Social learning.* Like any other kind of attitude, it is clear that prejudice can be learned from others. When we observe the stereotypes and prejudices expressed by parents, friends, teachers, and the media, we are likely to adopt the same prejudices.

Combating Prejudice

Prejudice is harmful to the human race. But is there anything that can be done about it? There are some effective antidotes:

1. *Recognize prejudice.* Most people believe that they are not prejudiced. We tend to view any negative attitudes we hold as true and justifiable. The first and most important step in reducing prejudice is to become aware of our own prejudices and their harmful consequences (Aronson, 1995).

2. *Control automatic responses.* It is not easy to rid yourself of prejudices that took a lifetime to acquire, even if you sincerely want to. It is possible to control our automatic prejudicial reactions, however (Devine, 1996). Imagine that a classmate asks you if she can borrow your notes from the last class. She says that she missed the class because she was sick. If she were a member of an ethnic group that your parents always said was lazy, you might immediately think, "I'll bet she was just too lazy to come to class." People who are genuinely trying to reject prejudice, however, control those immediate prejudice reactions and deal with others on their own merits—not on the basis of automatic prejudice.

3. *Increase contact among prejudiced groups.* Prejudice can sometimes be reduced by increasing direct contact with people from other groups (Dovidio & Gaertner, 1999; Stephan, 1987). As most people who attended multiethnic schools can tell you, however, simple direct contact with other ethnic groups is not enough to reduce prejudice. For the direct contact to work, it must occur under certain conditions.

   First, the two groups must be approximately *equal in status.* For example, if two groups of accountants from two different ethnic groups spend time together, their prejudice may decrease, but, if accountants from one ethnic group spend time with unskilled laborers from another ethnic group, there is little likelihood that the prejudice will diminish. Similarly, the environment in which the two groups interact should be one that encourages group equality. The interactions that occur between managers of one race and employees of another race will not decrease prejudice.

   Second, prejudice between groups will decline only if the group members *view each other as typical of their respective groups*—not as exceptions to the rule. There will be no improvement in relations if the members of one group think "This person is pretty darn smart—not like the others."

   Third, when two groups who are prejudiced against one another interact, their prejudice will decrease if they are engaged in *cooperative rather than competitive tasks.* If a city is trying to decrease prejudice among teenagers of two different ethnic groups by bringing them together in a basketball league, the ethnic groups should be mixed on the same teams, not put on opposing teams. Cooperation builds respect; competition maintains prejudice.

   Finally, *the contact should be informal,* so that one-on-one interactions can occur. Formal interactions among employees of different ethnic groups are not as beneficial as the informal time spent together on breaks or after work.

Although prejudice can sometimes be reduced through increasing contact among ethnic groups, simple direct contact, such as attending a multiethnic school, is not enough.

● Review

Attitudes are a focus of research for social psychologists because they play a key role in the interactions among people: People influence our attitudes, and those attitudes, in turn, are reflected to some extent in the way that we interact with others. Attitudes are defined in terms of three components: beliefs, feelings, and dispositions to behave. Attitudes appear to be learned, sometimes through direct experience with the object of our attitude and sometimes from others.

Attitudes are subject to change after they have been formed. One common form of attitude change is through direct persuasion by others. Nearly every day someone tries to persuade us to change our attitudes or behavior. The effectiveness of these attempts to influence depends on qualities of the speaker, the message, and the listener. Speakers are more influential when they appear credible, are attractive, and do not appear to be trying to influence us for their own personal gain. We are most likely to be influenced by fear-inducing messages if the fear appeal is moderately strong, if the listener thinks the fearful outcome is likely, and if reasonable ways of avoiding the fearful outcome are presented. Messages that present some information favoring both sides of the argument are more persuasive to listeners who are knowledgeable about both sides of an issue and are initially opposed to the message. The way that a message is framed can affect persuasion. And listeners tend to be more easily persuaded when they are less intelligent, have a high need for social approval, are somewhat low in self-esteem, and are in large groups. In most situations, gender is not related to persuadability, however.

Discrepancies between our behavior and attitudes provide another potent source of attitudes. Sometimes there is a big difference between the attitudes that we express and the way we behave. Under some circumstances, changes in behavior that create a discrepancy between behavior and attitudes are followed by a change in attitudes that makes the attitudes consistent with behavior again. This is most likely to occur when there is no obvious external cause of the change in behavior. Cognitive dissonance theory explains this change in attitude by stating that the discrepancy between behavior and attitudes creates an uncomfortable state. This discomfort is reduced when the attitudes change to fit the behavior.

Prejudice is a negative attitude based on inaccurate generalizations about a group of people. These inaccurate generalizations, called stereotypes, are inherently harmful because they make it difficult to evaluate members of that group on an individual basis and lead to faulty generalizations about their behavior. At times prejudice can be reduced if people become aware of their prejudices, control automatic prejudicial reactions, and interact more under positive conditions with members of groups against whom they are prejudiced. Increased interaction will decrease prejudice only when the interactions are among persons of equal status, when those involved in the interactions view each other as typical of their respective groups, when the interactions are cooperative rather than competitive, and when the interactions are informal.

● Check Your Learning

To be sure that you have learned the key points from the preceding section, cover the list of correct answers and try to answer each question. If you give an incorrect answer to any question, return to the page given next to the correct answer to see why your answer was not correct.

1. Attitudes consist of three components: _____, _____, and _____.

2. Which of the following speakers would be the least persuasive?

   a) a speaker who intends to persuade you, and you know it

   b) a credible speaker

   c) an attractive speaker

   d) all of the above

3. Two-sided arguments are most persuasive when

   a) the audience knows only one side of the argument.

   b) the audience knows both sides of the argument.

   c) the audience is unfavorable to your side of the argument.

   d) both b and c.

4. Prejudices are harmful attitudes based on inaccurate generalizations known as

   a) attributions.   c) negativities.

   b) stereotypes.   d) all of the above.

● Thinking Critically About Psychology

1. If you were trying to convince others to donate money to your favorite cause, how would you use the information contained in this section?

2. Design a program that might reduce racial prejudice in the high school you attended.

Correct Answers **1.** beliefs, feelings, dispositions to behave (p. 448), **2. a** (p. 450), **3. d** (p. 450), **4. b** (p. 454).

▶ INTERPERSONAL ATTRACTION: FRIENDSHIP AND LOVE

Who are your friends? Why do you suppose you became friends with them rather than with other people you know? Are you in love with someone, or have you ever been in love? What attracted you to him or her and made you experience such intense feelings? Friendship and love are powerful social phenomena that touch all of our lives in one way or another. As such, they have been of special interest to social psychologists. In this section, we will look at variables that influence our perception of others, the role played by attribution processes in person perception, the qualities of others that make them attractive to us, and the factors involved in maintaining personal relationships.

Person Perception

person perception
The process of forming impressions of others.

The first step toward understanding why we are attracted to one person rather than another is to understand something about the process of **person perception.** What factors are important in the way we perceive others? We seem to go through a complex process of "cognitive algebra" to reach an average of all the many factors that enter into our perceptions of others—with some factors contributing more to the average than others (Fiske, 1993; Kaplan, 1975). We sum up a person as if we assign a weight to each person's positive and negative characteristics in accordance with how important that characteristic is to us, and then we add them all together to arrive at a total perception of the person. But, as the following sections show, the process of person perception is complicated further by the ways we gather and use information about others.

Negative Information: The Bad Outweighs the Good

Other things being equal, we tend to assign higher weights to negative than to positive information (Hamilton & Zanna, 1972). Put yourself in this situation: You are a person who values warmth, physical attractiveness, and honesty in others. You meet a person in class whom you find extremely warm and attractive; you have an enjoyable conversation with him after class, but during the course of the conversation he asks you to help him think of a lie to tell his girlfriend explaining where he has been. Your opinion of him will probably become quite negative if honesty is really important to you. The fact that he is being dishonest with his girlfriend will overshadow all his positive characteristics. Most of us will pass up a delicious-looking cake if we know it contains even a small amount of rat poison.

Primacy Effects: The Importance of First Impressions

Our first impressions are usually very important in the person perception process. When you pause for a moment and think about this, it's quite disturbing. A factor that is irrelevant to the nature of the person we are perceiving—the order in which we learn information about that person—can greatly influence our perception of that person. All of us have our good days and bad days, and it's a shame that the perception that others form of us is influenced so much by whether they form their first impression of us on a good or a bad day.

The first information that we are exposed to about a person tends to be given greater weight than later information (Asch, 1946; Belmore, 1987; Hovland, 1957). This is called the **primacy effect.** If you were introduced to Barbara right after you heard her deliver a polished and interesting talk to your sales group on the importance of ethics in business, your impression would probably be quite positive. Later, if you were to run into her in a bar, sitting alone, looking forlorn, disheveled, and half-drunk, you would be seeing a very different side of Barbara. But, because your initial impression of her was favorable, there would be a strong tendency for you to ignore or "explain away" this new information ("Something awful must have happened to Barbara to make her act this way").

Suppose, however, that seeing Barbara in the bar was your *first* exposure to her. In that case, your first impression of her would be negative and would tend to dominate your perception of her, even after you were exposed to more positive information about her later. If your second meeting with her was hearing her lecture on business ethics, you would tend to discount the positive impression she was giving in that encounter ("She's holding herself together pretty well today—I bet most people here don't know she's really a drunken slob.").

First impressions (primacy effects) are not always of overriding importance, however. Their impact is greatly reduced under three conditions:

1. *Prolonged exposure.* Prolonged exposure to a person tends to reduce the importance of your first impression of that person. Although it's important to try to make a favorable first impression on the first day of your new job, do not worry too much about it if you do not. Eventually, your fellow employees will get to know the real you. Information about you gathered over a long period of time will erase first

primacy effect
The tendency for first impressions to heavily influence opinions about other people.

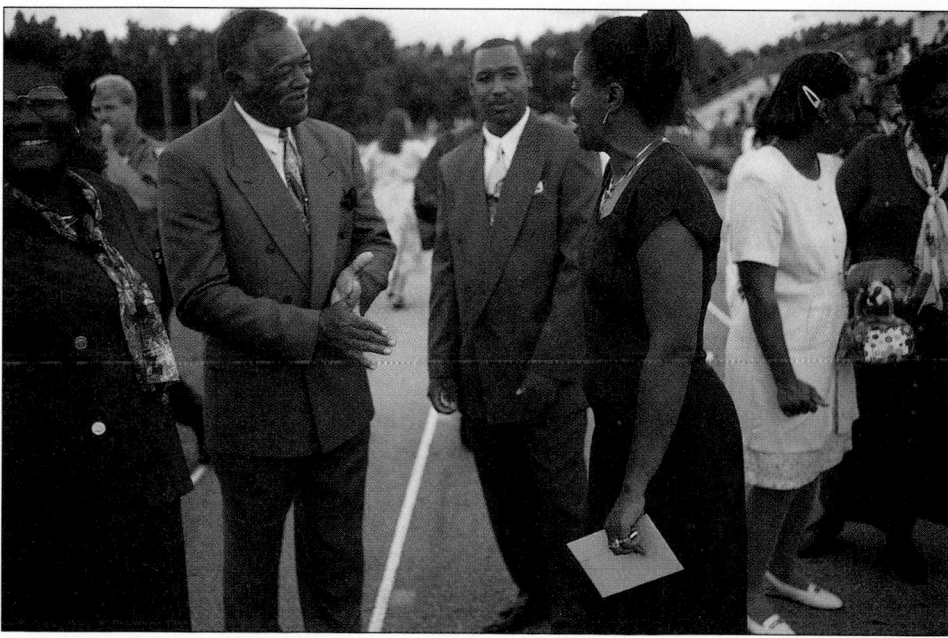

First impressions are often given greater weight than later information in the person perception process.

impressions. Working in favor of prolonged exposure's correcting any inaccuracies in our first impressions is the fact that we are more likely to notice and remember information that is inconsistent with our first impression of a person (Belmore, 1987; Belmore & Hubbard, 1987).

2. *Passage of time.* Like anything else, first impressions tend to be forgotten over time. If a substantial period of time passes between first and subsequent impressions, the more recent impression will be of greater importance. Thus, if you flubbed your first attempt to favorably impress that gorgeous person, wait awhile and try again later.

3. *Knowledge of primacy effects.* When people are warned to avoid being influenced by first impressions, the primacy effect can be reduced (Hovland, 1957). Personnel managers and others to whom accurate person perception is important are educated to the dangers of primacy effects and may be able to reduce the importance of primacy in their perceptions.

Emotions and Person Perception

Another important factor in person perception that can be irrelevant to the nature of the person about whom we are forming an impression is our emotions. The emotional state that we are in when we meet a person has a great deal to do with our liking that person (Foster & others, 1998). Positive emotional states lead to greater attraction to others than negative emotions do. William Griffith and Russell Veitch (1971) had a radio news broadcast turned on as individuals waited for an experiment in interpersonal attraction to begin. The broadcast was actually taped beforehand, so that half of the participants heard a depressing broadcast and half heard happy news. Afterward, the participants hearing the sad news did not like the strangers they had met in the experiment as well as did the persons who had heard the good news.

Attribution Processes in Person Perception

We have a strong tendency to evaluate other people both on the basis of *what* they do and *why* we think they do it. Unfortunately, when we judge the reasons that other people behave as they do, we typically *underestimate* the effects of the social situation and *overestimate* the importance of their personal characteristics (Aronson, 1995; Ross, 1977). If you meet a man at a party who is acting sullen and depressed, you are more likely to assume that he is an unhappy person in general than to assume that he is usually happy but that something happened recently to make him feel lousy.

In contrast, we are more likely to see the influence of social situations on our *own* behavior. For example, a few years ago I was invited to a large party hosted by an association of African American woman attorneys in Los Angeles. Although I usually do not think of myself as shy, I found myself quite shy in the company of these women, nearly all of whom seemed more intelligent, self-secure, and stylish than I. It was easy for me to see the effect of this social situation on my own behavior, but, if I had seen another male behaving shyly at the same party, I probably would have just assumed he was an inherently shy person without thinking about it.

Social psychologist Fritz Heider (1958) has termed this the **fundamental attribution error,** meaning our tendency to underestimate the impact of situations on others, while more readily seeing its impact on ourselves. In simple terms, **attribution** is the process of making judgments about what causes people to behave the way they do. The most important aspect of the attribution process is deciding whether a person is behaving in a particular way because of some external cause (**situational attribution**) or because of an internal motive or trait (**dispositional attribution**). Unless we can see that someone's behavior *consistently* changes in a situation, we tend to attribute that person's behavior to dispositional causes (Kelley, 1973). Because we often lack information on the extent to which another person's behavior is consistently influenced by situations, we make dispositional attributions too often.

People in all cultures make the fundamental attribution error, but people living in East Asian collectivistic cultures are less likely to do so than people living in individualistic

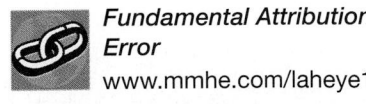

Fundamental Attribution Error
www.mmhe.com/laheye1

fundamental attribution error
The tendency to underestimate the impact of situations on others while overestimating the impact on oneself.

attribution
The process of trying to explain why things happen—that is, attribute them to some cause.

situational attribution
An explanation for behavior that is based on an external cause.

dispositional attribution
(dis″po-zish′un-al) An explanation for behavior that is based on a personal characteristic of the individual.

HUMAN DIVERSITY

STEREOTYPES ABOUT COLLEGE STUDENTS WITH PHYSICAL CHALLENGES

Most Americans are "able-bodied" persons with no serious limitations on their ability to see, hear, speak, or move about. Many of us, however, are challenged by physical conditions that make these everyday activities more difficult or impossible. Like any group that is *different* from most of the people in society, persons with physical challenges are the subject of stereotypes, prejudices, limitations, and stigma. These factors can profoundly influence their lives.

An important study by Catherine Fichten and her colleagues at Dawson College found that able-bodied students' perceptions of peers with disabilities are quite different from these students' perceptions of themselves (Fichten, Robillard, Judd, & Amsel, 1989). Three groups of students participated in the study: wheelchair users, students with a visual impairment, and able-bodied students. They completed several questionnaires that measured self-concept, dating behavior, and anxiety in social situations. First, they completed these questionnaires about themselves and then completed the same measures in the way that they thought the other groups would respond.

Fichten and her colleagues found that able-bodied students and students with physical challenges viewed each other in stereotyped ways. For example, the able-bodied students believed that the students with physical challenges were more anxious about dating and dated less frequently than able-bodied students. In addition, the able-bodied students viewed the students who had physical challenges as nervous, unaggressive, insecure, dependent, and unhappy. The stereotyping was not all negative, however. Able-bodied students also viewed students with physical challenges as quiet, honest, soft-hearted, nonegotistical, and undemanding. The students with physical challenges held stereotypes about able-bodied students, too. They viewed the able-bodied students as demanding, argumentative, overconfident, phony, and complaining.

In most instances, however, the stereotyped perceptions were based on myths. For example, Fichten and her colleagues found no differences in either the number of dates or anxiety about dating reported by students with physical challenges and able-bodied students, even though the able-bodied students thought that students with physical challenges were less satisfied with their dating. Similarly, although able-bodied students believed that the self-esteem scores of students with physical challenges were lower than their own, there were no actual differences in the self-esteem of able-bodied students, students who were visually impaired, or students who used wheelchairs. It is striking that even the students with physical challenges themselves sometimes believed the same myths about students with other physical challenges. Both able-bodied students and students with physical challenges attributed more "handicapped" stereotypes to students with physical challenges than to able-bodied students in the Fichten study.

The Americans with Disabilities Act of 1990 brought the needs of persons with physical challenges into the consciousness of people in the United States. It was designed to enable persons with physical challenges to gain access to public facilities and to the workplace. As is the case with other civil rights legislation, societal changes require more than just the passage of laws, however. If the stereotypes are to be reduced, able-bodied persons and persons with physical challenges must learn more about each other through extended contact under conditions of equal status. It is hoped, however, the laws that guarantee the rights of persons with physical challenges to education, employment, and recreation will create conditions under which persons with and without physical challenges can get to know each other as individuals. In time, such interactions may improve the degree to which people with disabilities will be able to participate fully in society without stereotypes and discrimination.

If you are not physically challenged yourself, what kinds of exposure have you had to persons who are? As you walk around your campus and your community today, notice how you react when you see a person with physical challenges. Do you react in the same way as to able-bodied persons? Can you see the influence of stereotypes in these reactions? How could you make it easier for persons with physical challenges at your school to interact with able-bodied students on an equal basis?

It is important to note that use of the term "physical disability" has been discouraged to emphasize the fact that the physical condition often does not disable the person in any absolute sense. Many persons prefer the more neutral term of "physically challenged." But some persons reject the newer term "physically challenged" as well, stating that they alone should decide whether or not their physical condition is "challenging" (Bregante, Martinez, & O'Toole, 1993).

Western cultures (Choi, Nisbett, & Norenzayan, 1999). The Chinese and Japanese, for example, are less likely than North Americans to attribute the behavior of other people to dispositional causes (to their personal characteristics) and more likely to perceive situational influences on their behavior. This makes sense, as collectivistic cultures emphasize the importance of the social context and deemphasize the importance of the individual. This encourages people to think in terms of social influences rather than personal characteristics as causes of actions. The East Asian view of the importance of situational influences on human behavior is often quite correct. As we saw in chapter 11, social situations can exert powerful influences on our behavior.

General Determinants of Interpersonal Attraction

Through the complicated process of person perception, a unique impression of each person is formed. But, although person perception is a highly personal process, some *general* factors influence whether one person will be attracted to another. These include proximity, similar and complementary characteristics, competence, physical attractiveness, and mutual liking.

Proximity

An important, but not very romantic, cause of attraction is proximity, or geographical closeness. It's difficult to fall in love with someone you hardly ever spend time with. Physical closeness and the resulting interpersonal contact are essential to the development of attraction. You are more friendly with people who live next door to you than with people who live farther away. Why does this happen? Physical proximity increases interactions, and repeated exposure to people tends to increase liking (Zajonc, 1968). Perhaps you can remember a song you didn't like at first but learned to like after hearing it played on the radio many times—it's the same with people.

Similar and Complementary Characteristics

In terms of interpersonal attraction, do "birds of a feather flock together" or do "opposites attract"? Are you more likely to be attracted to someone as a friend or lover who is similar to you in many ways or quite different from you? The answer is *both,* in different ways (Bem, 1996).

Jennifer probably values people who have an interest in exercise, nutrition, and philosophy because she is also interested in those things. It's enjoyable to have a friend who jogs with you, who pats you on the back for the healthy way you eat, and who shares long, delicious philosophical discussions with you. In general, similarity is highly important in attractiveness. We tend to be most attracted to those people who have similar values, interests, and attitudes (Caspi & Herbener, 1990; Feingold, 1988).

Opposites can also attract, however. Sometimes the attractiveness of persons unlike us is purely erotic (Bem, 1996). But, opposites also attract when the opposite characteristic *complements,* or advantageously "fits" with, one of our own characteristics. Jennifer might also be attracted to the fellow at the party tonight in part because he has an outgoing personality, whereas she is more reserved. She may feel that she is a good listener who gets along better with talkative people than with those who are quiet like herself. And she may feel that, when she is with an outgoing person at social gatherings, he makes it easier for her to interact with other couples than a quiet man does. Similarly, a dominant person might prefer a submissive person, and a person who likes to "take care of" others might prefer someone who likes to be taken care of (Winch, 1958).

Another condition under which opposites attract is when people who are different from you *like* you (Aronson, 1995). It's often more flattering and attractive to be liked by someone who holds opposite values and opinions than by someone who holds similar ones (Jones, Bell, & Aronson, 1971). But take note that opposites usually do not attract; instead, opposites usually repel in personal relationships. A person who intensely advocates liberal causes probably would not like a person who vocally supports conservative causes. And a highly religious person probably would not find a disdain for religion attractive in another person.

Competence

We tend to be more attracted to competent than to incompetent people. Intelligence, strength, social skill, education, and athletic prowess are generally thought of as attractive qualities. But people who are seen as *too* competent may suffer a loss in attractiveness, perhaps because it makes us uncomfortable to compare ourselves unfavorably with them. Elliot Aronson and associates conducted a clever experiment that demonstrates that it's best to be a *little* less than perfect (Aronson, Willerman, & Floyd, 1966). Participants listened to one of four audiotapes of people who were supposedly trying out to be members of their university's College Bowl quiz team. Two of the people scored over 90 percent correct on difficult questions and were portrayed as being honor students, athletes, and people active in student activities. The other two answered 30 percent of the questions and were portrayed as average, unathletic students. Near the end of the tape, one of the superior students and one of the average students blundered—each spilled a cup of coffee on himself. Whom from this group do you think the participants rated as most attractive? The two superior students were rated higher than the two average students, but the superior student who committed the blunder was rated as most attractive of all. Apparently, the slightly clumsy pratfall made him more endearing to others. However, the blunder did not have the same positive effect for the average student: The average student who blundered was rated least attractive of all.

Physical Attractiveness

Other things equal, people tend to be more attracted to physically beautiful people. In the absence of other information, we tend to like beautiful people more and think of them as nicer, better adjusted, more sexual, and more intelligent (Eagly, Ashmore, Makhijani, & Longo, 1991; Feingold, 1992b). Not only is physical attractiveness important, but it also seems to be the *most* important factor in the early stages of attraction (Myers, 1999).

Elaine Walster and colleagues randomly paired male and female college students for blind dates. They rated each student's physical attractiveness and gave them tests to measure attitudes, intelligence, and personality characteristics. After the blind dates, the students were asked how much they liked each other and whether they intended to go out on other dates with one another. The overwhelmingly important variable in determining attraction was physical attractiveness—more so than intelligence, personality, and attitudes. The couples who were most likely to like each other well enough to continue dating were the ones in which both the male and female rated each other as attractive (Walster, Aronson, Abrahams, & Rottman, 1966).

Physical attractiveness seems to be the most important factor in the early stages of attraction between people.

But don't despair; there is hope for the rest of us! Although we might all prefer to be dating someone who looks like Antonio Banderas or Cameron Diaz, people actually tend to choose dates and mates who closely match themselves in degree of physical attractiveness (Berscheid, Dion, Walster, & Walster, 1971). What is more, physical beauty is a highly subjective quality. Thus, even if you do not think your next-door neighbor is much to look at, chances are that someone else will come along who thinks he or she is just beautiful.

Perhaps the nicest thing about physical attractiveness and liking, though, is that the relationship goes both ways. Not only is it true that we tend to like people better when we think they are beautiful, but, as we get to like people better, we begin to think they are more beautiful (Langlois & Stephan, 1981). Thus, to a certain extent, love *is* blind and beauty *is* in the eye of the beholder—and nothing could be nicer.

Mutual Liking

Let's end this discussion of factors involved in interpersonal attractiveness on an upbeat note. Liking often leads to liking in return. If Vicki likes Neal, she has made herself more attractive to Neal simply by liking him. Neal, if he is like almost everyone else, will be more attracted to people who like him than to people who do not like him. Liking someone will not turn you into an irresistible beauty, but it will help.

One reason this seems to be so is that liking someone actually makes you seem more *physically* attractive, especially if a little lust is thrown in. You have heard people say that a person is more beautiful when in love, and it's true. Your eyes are more attractive when you are in love. Your pupils tend to be more dilated (opened) when you look at someone you find sexually attractive, and others find large pupils more attractive sexually (Hess, 1975). And your posture and movements are often more attractive and seductive. In subtle ways, you are more physically alluring when you are attracted to another person.

Another reason that liking tends to lead to liking is that you are nicer to the people whom you like, and being nicer makes you more attractive to them. A number of studies show, for example, that we tend to like people more when they praise us or when they have done favors for us. Favors and praise feel nice, and we like the giver better for having given them to us. Thus, send him flowers or give her a compact disc—it might just tip the balance of love in your favor. As you might expect, there are limits on the impact of praise and favors. If they are excessive, and especially if the other person thinks you are insincere and have selfish motives for giving them, praise and gifts will not lead to increased liking and may even lessen the liking (Aronson, 1995).

Gender Differences in Interpersonal Attraction

It's a commonly held belief in our culture that men are not very interested in romantic love but, rather, enter into long-term relationships for the sex and the domestic help (cooking, cleaning, and mending). Women, in contrast, are viewed in our society as approaching relationships in a more emotional, romantic way. The results of surveys conducted during the 1960s, however, suggested that this popular stereotype not only was incorrect but had reality reversed. Men rated falling in love as being a more important reason for beginning a relationship than did women. Women saw other qualities of the relationship, such as respect and support, as being more important. In one survey, two-thirds of male unmarried college students said they would not marry unless they felt romantic love for their prospective wife, whereas less than one-fourth of college women felt that romantic love was a prerequisite for marriage (Hill, Rubin, & Peplau, 1976; Kephart, 1967).

However, more recent surveys suggest that things have changed in the United States concerning gender differences in valuing romantic love (Simpson, Campbell, & Berscheid, 1986). Today, the great majority of both women and men feel that being in love is necessary for marriage. Perhaps as women have come to feel less dependent on marriage for financial support they have felt able to enter into marriage only when they are in love with their future partner.

This does not mean that men and women fall in love for all the same reasons, however. The evidence is clear that women place more emphasis on their romantic partner's intelligence, character, education, occupational status, ambition, and income than do men (Feingold, 1990, 1992a; Myers, 1999). These qualities are not unimportant to men, but they are comparatively more important to women. In contrast, there are no gender differences in how much sense of humor and a pleasant personality are valued in romantic relationships, but men place greater emphasis on physical attractiveness than do women. Again, it is not that physical attractiveness does not play a role in romantic attraction for women (it does), but women place considerably less emphasis on physical attractiveness than do men. Interestingly, these same results have been found in different generations in the United States and across a number of cultures (Feingold, 1992a).

It is important to keep in mind, however, that there are large differences among the members of both genders. Perhaps the most striking thing about the cognitive algebra of person perception is that different people often seem to be using different equations!

Whether a characteristic is considered positive or negative and how much weight it will carry in person perception differ markedly from individual to individual. Jennifer may feel that an interest in exercise, nutrition, and philosophy and an outgoing personality are all highly positive characteristics. Angela may feel that these characteristics are not very important one way or another. And Lydia might find them all to be highly negative characteristics. If Jennifer, Angela, and Lydia were to meet a man with these characteristics at a party, they would each form a very different perception of him. It's like that for everyone. Because different people evaluate the same characteristics in different ways, some people are going to love you, some are going to dislike you, and the rest will find you so-so.

Maintaining Relationships

We have talked about some of the factors that determine whether you will be attracted to another person. But how about the factors that are involved in maintaining relationships? Assuming that one of the people whom you are attracted to becomes your friend, lover, or spouse, what things determine whether you and your partner will stay in the relationship? So many relationships that begin in joy end in a long cry. Why? Two of the major factors are (1) the difference between what you expect to find in a relationship and what you actually find and (2) the degree to which the relationship is fairly balanced or equitable.

Expectations vs. Reality in Relationships

When you begin a relationship with someone you do not know very well, part of what you fall in love with is what you *expect* the person to be like. Some of these expectations may be based on good evidence. One of his friends has told you that he is an especially nice and fair person, so it's reasonable to expect him to be fair and nice to you. You know that he is in the same profession as you, so you can expect to be able to share your workday experiences easily with him. Other expectations are based on less evidence. He has behaved in a strong, self-assured way so far, so you assume that he will always be this way, even though the biggest challenge you have seen him handle is the waiter's mistake of bringing tomato soup instead of minestrone. You *know* that he is a wonderful lover, even though he has only just kissed you goodnight once. He dresses like an outdoorsman, so you expect him to love backpacking as much as you do. And he is well educated, so you feel sure he will share your love of serious literature.

The point is that, even when your expectations are fairly well grounded, some of them will turn out to be incorrect. He will not be exactly as you expect him to be before the relationship begins. This is one primary reason relationships end. If the other person turns out to be significantly different from the person you expected, you may be unwilling to stay in the relationship. This disappointment may not lead directly to an end of the relationship; it may affect the relationship indirectly. Disappointment can lead you to be an unenthusiastic or irritable partner, which can lead to discord and an unhappy ending of the relationship (Graziano & Musser, 1982).

Even when you know a person well before beginning a serious relationship, differences between expectations and reality can be a problem. One common source of unfulfilled expectations is the predictable shift from **passionate love** to greater **companionate love** (Hatfield, 1988; Myers, 1999). When two people first fall in love, they often feel intense passions that are a heady and magnificent mixture of romantic, sexual, and other feelings. Even in the most healthy and enduring relationships, however, passionate love gradually becomes companionate love—a less intense but wonderful blend of friendship, intimacy, commitment, and security. Although romantic and sexual emotions often continue to be an important part of companionate love, these feelings almost inevitably become less intense over time.

If one or both of the partners does not expect passionate love to change, or if the change takes place before expected, the reality of passionate love's blending into companionate love can be difficult. On the other hand, if both partners truly want a long-term relationship (many people stay in relationships only as long as the passionate love remains, then leave feeling unfulfilled or hurt), and if the disappointment that often surrounds the lessening of romantic love is handled with compassion on both sides, the transition usually can be managed.

passionate love
The mixture of romantic, sexual, and other feelings of love.

companionate love
The blend of friendship, intimacy, commitment, and security that often develops after passionate love.

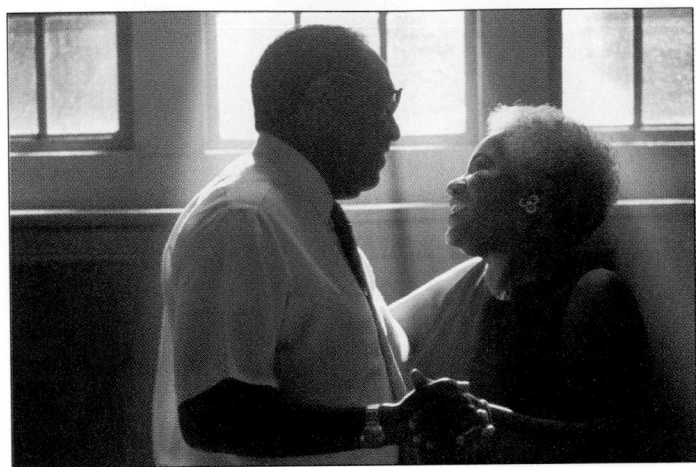

Relationships that last tend to be based on realistic expectations and on the perception of equity in the relationship.

equity theory
The theory that partners will be comfortable in their relationship only when the ratio between their perceived contributions and benefits is equal.

Finally, expectations about a love relationship can fail to match its reality because partners change over time. Sometimes, the outdoor person becomes a happy couch potato, and the party animal becomes a health-conscious, jogging vegetarian. If children arrive, and if promotions are received (or not received), these and other changes can alter the reality of the relationship as well. If these changes in one's partner are not welcome, the reality of the changed relationship can be upsetting. Sometimes, however, a change in a partner can make a good relationship even better.

Equity in Relationships

Relationships are more likely to endure when the good things that we give to our partner are about equal to what our partner gives us. These good "things" that partners give to one another are many and varied. They include compliments, back rubs, help with homework, a day off without the kids, flowers, jokes, love making, a willingness to listen about a bad day, interesting meals, kisses, and interesting conversations. They also include things like physical attractiveness (a nice-looking person is enjoyable to look at), honesty, faithfulness, and integrity.

The commonsense idea that enduring relationships are ones in which the partners give and receive in equal proportion has been formalized and improved by social psychologists (Adams, 1965; Myers, 1999; Walster & Walster, 1978) under the name of **equity theory.** Equity theory states that partners will be comfortable in their relationship only when the ratio between their perceived contributions and benefits is equal. Equity theory is often summarized by the following equation:

$$\frac{\text{Perceived benefits of person X}}{\text{Perceived contributions of person X}} = \frac{\text{Perceived benefits of person Y}}{\text{Perceived contributions of person Y}}$$

These benefits and contributions cannot be easily translated into numerical terms, but suppose for a moment that person X perceives that she "gives" 10 things to the relationship, whereas person Y perceives that he gives only 5 things. Is this an equitable relationship? It is if person X perceives 10 benefits from the relationship, whereas person Y perceives 5 benefits, because the equation is in balance:

$$\frac{10}{10} = \frac{5}{5}$$

There are two important points to notice in the equity theory equation: First, the benefits that the two people receive from one another do not have to be equal, but the *ratio* between their benefits and contributions must be equal. A person who both gives and receives a lot can be in an equitable relationship with a person who gives and receives much less.

Second, notice that the equation is written in terms of *perceived* benefits and contributions. The only person who can judge how much he or she is giving and receiving is that person. An outside observer might see a relationship as being highly inequitable when the partners themselves are very happy with it. Tender love making might be highly important to one person but much less important than good cooking to someone else. Unfortunately, people tend to believe that the amount of "good things" that we ourselves should fairly receive is higher than the amount that we think that others should fairly receive (Messick & Sentis, 1979). If we are not careful to compensate for this natural perceptual distortion, it can lead us to perceive an inequity in our relationships when there is none at all.

If either member of a relationship perceives the relationship to be inequitable, that partner will either take steps to restore equity or will leave the relationship. Interestingly, we become uncomfortable in relationships either when we feel that we receive *too little* compared with what we give *or* when we receive *too much* compared with what we give. In either case, we will be motivated to restore equity by giving more or less or by asking (or in some other way inducing) the other person to give more or less.

● Review

What determines which people we will like or love? Our perceptions of others can be thought of as being based on a complex cognitive algebra in which we reach a weighted average of all of the positive and negative characteristics we see in others. Person perception is complicated by several factors, however: Different people evaluate the same characteristics in a person in different ways, and our emotional state influences person perception; negative information about a person carries more weight than positive information; and first impressions usually are more important than later impressions.

Attribution plays an important role in our perceptions of others (particularly in individualistic cultures). We want to know what a person's enduring traits and motives are. We attribute the behavior of others to external causes (situational attributions) when it consistently occurs in only one kind of situation and they consistently react in the same way. Otherwise, we tend to attribute the behavior of others to their supposed traits and motives (dispositional attributions). We also tend to attribute our own behavior to dispositional causes, but mostly our desirable behavior. We tend to attribute our undesirable behavior to situational causes.

Although person perception is a highly complex and personal process, some general factors determine whether one person will be attracted to another. Other things being equal, you are more likely to be attracted to a person who has characteristics similar to yours or who has opposite characteristics that complement your own. Other factors in attractiveness include the other person's being competent (but not excessively competent), looking physically attractive, and liking and being nice to you.

Once two people are attracted to each other, a number of other factors are involved in whether the relationship will endure. We enter into relationships partly because of our expectations as to what the other person will be like. Because those expectations are generally based on partial information, they are sometimes not met and the relationship fails. Relationships generally fail, too, when they are not equitable. In happy relationships, each person perceives a balance between what each person puts into the relationship and what each person gets out of it.

● Check Your Learning

To be sure that you have learned the key points from the preceding section, cover the list of correct answers and try to answer each question. If you give an incorrect answer to any question, return to the page given next to the correct answer to see why your answer was not correct.

1. The process of forming impressions of others is known as

    a) person perception.   c) attribution theory.

    b) the primacy effect.   d) the fundamental attribution error.

2. The impact of the primacy effect can be reduced under three conditions: _____, _____, and _____.

3. The fundamental attribution error refers partly to our tendency to give greater weight to _____ causes of behavior in others and to neglect _____ causes when forming perceptions of others.

    a) positive; negative   c) dispositional; situational

    b) negative; positive   d) situational; dispositional

● Thinking Critically About Psychology

1. To what extent has it been true that "first impressions are lasting impressions" in your life?
2. What are the most important relationships in your life? Have you learned anything in this chapter that could help you enhance and prolong them?

Correct Answers **1. a** (p. 458), **2.** prolonged exposure, passage of time, knowledge of primacy effects (p. 459), **3. c** (p. 460).

Application *of Psychology*

STEREOTYPES AND DISCRIMINATION IN THE WORKPLACE

In 1982, Ann Hopkins was a successful consultant working for Price Waterhouse, one of the nation's "big eight" accounting firms, and she was up for possible promotion to a partnership in the firm. She had brought in $25 million dollars in business and had billed for more hours than the other 87 accountants who had been proposed for partner that year, all of whom were males. She had the praise of her clients and recommendations of supporters within the company, who described her as hardworking, demanding, exacting, independent, self-confident, outspoken, assertive, and courageous. The decision regarding her partnership was postponed for a year, and the following year she was told that she would not be considered further for partnership.

Ms. Hopkins' detractors at Price Waterhouse portrayed her as being overbearing, arrogant, self-centered, and abrasive. In more specific terms, those who voted against her criticized her for being "macho" and suggested that she needed a "course at charm school." Indeed, one partner who favored her promotion suggested that her chances would improve if she would "walk more femininely, talk more femininely, dress more femininely, wear make-up, have her hair

With the help of psychological research as evidence, Ann Hopkins successfully sued her employer for gender discrimination.

styled, and wear jewelry" (*Hopkins* v. *Price Waterhouse,* 1985, p. 1117).

In 1984, Ann Hopkins sued Price Waterhouse for violation of her civil rights under Title VII of the 1964 Civil Rights Act, which prohibits sex discrimination. Her former firm countered that she had not been denied a partnership because of her gender, but because she had problems in interpersonal skills. Nevertheless, she won her suit in federal court, and the decision was confirmed in both the Federal Court of Appeals and the U.S. Supreme Court. Federal Judge Gerhard Gesell stated in his 1990 opinion, "The firm of Price Waterhouse refused to make Ann Hopkins a partner. Gender-based stereotyping played a role in this decision" (*Hopkins* v. *Price Waterhouse,* 1990, p. 1).

Psychologist Susan T. Fiske testified on behalf of Ann Hopkins in this case, and because it was the first sex discrimination case in which psychological evidence on gender stereotyping had been introduced as evidence, the American Psychological Association filed a "friend of the court" brief that summarized what is known about gender discrimination. A full description of the court case and the brief have been published and make fascinating reading for anyone interested in the application of social psychology to real-world problems (Fiske, Bersoff, Borgida, Deaux, & Heilman, 1991).

If you recall from this chapter (pp. 454–455), stereotypes are harmful because they lead us to treat all members in the groups as the same, lead to narrow expectations for the behavior of members of the group, and lead to inaccurate attributions. The courts found that these aspects of gender stereotyping led to discrimination in the partnership decision of Ann Hopkins.

The evidence presented by Susan Fiske as an expert witness pointed to the following three sources of gender-based job discrimination. First, in studies that simulated hiring and promotion decisions in the workplace, job performances tended to be influenced by the stereotyped beliefs that we hold about the two genders. Males were viewed as more confident, influential, and deserving of respect than females, *even when the behavior of the females was exactly the same as that of the*

Psychologist Susan T. Fiske testified as an expert on gender discrimination issues in the U.S. Supreme Court case involving Ann Hopkins and Price Waterhouse Accounting Firm.

males (Fiske & others, 1991). People see what they expect to see based on gender stereotypes in the workplace.

Second, the narrow expectations for appropriate behavior that gender stereotypes encourage can play a role in discrimination in the workplace. In other job simulation studies, women in leadership roles were given lower marks than males if their leadership was carried out in ways that fit the stereotype for males—directive or authoritarian leadership. In addition, the ratings of women were lower when they were in roles that are more typically held by men than women. Thus, violating the expectations for your gender can be dangerous in the workplace (Eagly, Makhijani, & Klonsky, 1992).

Third, a number of studies have shown that faulty attributions based on gender stereotypes operate in the workplace. The supervisors of male employees tend to attribute their successes to competence and ability, but they are more likely to attribute the successes of females to good luck, to their physical attractiveness, or, at best, to hard work (Fiske & others, 1991).

Dr. Fiske also presented evidence that the kind of gender discrimination that was alleged in Ms. Hopkins' suit is more likely to occur when the number of women is few, the criteria for evaluation are ambiguous, and the amount of factual information on the employee is small. The attorney for Ann Hopkins was able to argue successfully that all three of these conditions were true for Ann Hopkins.

The courts found that these negative aspects of gender stereotyping played at least some part in Ann Hopkins being denied a partnership. The evidence suggested to the court that her detractors gave her low marks because her behavior violated the expectations for women and that these same traits would not have been grounds for denying a partnership to a male. The decision of the Supreme Court put it this way:

> An employer who objects to aggressiveness in women but whose positions require this trait places women in an intolerable Catch-22: out of a job if they behave aggressively and out of a job if they don't. Title VII [of the Civil Rights Act] lifts women out of this bind. (*Price Waterhouse* v. *Hopkins,* 1989, pp. 1790–1791) It takes no special training to discern sex stereotyping in a description of an aggressive female employee as requiring "a course at charm school." Nor . . . does it require expertise in psychology to know that,

if an employee's flawed "interpersonal skills" can be corrected by a soft-hued suit or a new shade of lipstick, perhaps it is the employee's sex and not her interpersonal skills that has drawn the criticism. (p. 1793)

The decision of the court and its affirmation by the Supreme Court should be encouraging for everyone, men and women alike, as everyone benefits when the best employees are hired and promoted. Perhaps the most encouraging aspect of the decision was that it held Price Waterhouse accountable for its failure to prevent gender discrimination from playing a role in Ann Hopkins' partnership decision. The courts concluded that the firm should have had a clearly stated and vigorously enforced partnership policy that prohibited discrimination on the basis of gender (its policy prohibited discrimination on the basis of age or health but did not mention gender or ethnicity). The firm should have investigated the criticisms against Ann Hopkins to see if they were based on gender bias, and the firm should have encouraged interactions within the firm that would decrease gender stereotyping, such as having men and women work together on mutually beneficial projects. These three points would be a good starting point for any firm that wishes to discourage discrimination on the basis of gender, ethnicity, age, disability, sexual orientation, or any other characteristic.

And the *Hopkins* v. *Price Waterhouse* decision is a warning that firms will be held accountable if they fail to deal with discrimination based on gender and other stereotypes in the workplace.

More recent studies (Biernat & Kobrynowicz, 1997) have suggested that prejudicial stereotypes can have paradoxical effects in the workplace—they usually make life more difficult for persons experiencing prejudice but sometimes help them. In the United States, negative stereotypes about both women and African Americans are common—both are often believed by employers to be less competent in managerial positions. When female and African American managers are evaluated for raises or promotions on the basis of relatively little hard evidence, they tend to be rated in a way that is consistent with the rater's prejudice. On the other hand, when there is clear evidence that a woman or an African American manager is doing a good job, they tend to be rated as even more competent than they actually are. Perhaps that glowing evaluation is largely deserved, because they have had to overcome prejudice to get where they are. The real moral of this story, however, is this: If you are in a job that is unusual for your gender or ethnic group and are doing a good job, help your employer accumulate a great deal of *objective* evidence of your competence to avoid being judged more by stereotypes about your group than by your actual performance.

● Summary

Chapter 15 defines social psychology and explores the influence people have on other people, the nature of attitudes and persuasion, and interpersonal attraction.

I. Social psychology is the branch of psychology that studies individuals as they interact with others.

II. Behavior is often influenced powerfully by its social context.
   A. Deindividuation may be responsible for some behavior in mob situations.
   B. The failure to help when in a group is a complex process. The presence of others affects the interpretation of an event as an emergency and creates a diffusion of responsibility.
   C. Individual effort may decline when people work in groups, group problem solving may lead to bad decisions when opinions become polarized, and even groups of sophisticated decision makers may be susceptible to the effects of "groupthink."
   D. Conformity is yielding to group pressure even when no direct request to comply has been made. Conformity can be seen in outward behavior only or can be seen in actual changes in beliefs.

E. Social roles and social norms are important ways in which social factors can influence the behavior of individuals.

F. Research by Stanley Milgram indicates that authority figures can command substantial obedience from individuals.

   1. Obedience is greatest when we are instructed to do something by a person who is high in status and who is physically present.

   2. Obedience is less likely to occur when we are in the presence of other disobedient individuals.

G. Although groups can have a harmful effect, it is important to remember that groups can sometimes accomplish what no single person can and that social support can soften the impact of stress.

III. Attitudes are beliefs that predispose us to act and feel in certain ways.

A. Attitudes are learned from direct experience and from others.

B. Attitude change through persuasion is determined by the characteristics of the speaker, the communication itself, and the people who hear it.

   1. Three characteristics of the speaker are important: credibility, attractiveness, and intent.

   2. Characteristics of the message that are important determinants of persuasiveness are fear appeals and message framing. Sometimes it helps to present both sides of the argument.

   3. Characteristics of the listener that help determine how persuasive an argument will be include their intelligence, their need for social approval, their self-esteem, and the size of the audience.

   4. Techniques of persuasion, such as the "foot-in-the-door" and "low-balling," are often used by persuasive individuals.

C. Attitudes sometimes change to become more consistent with our behavior, according to Leon Festinger's cognitive dissonance theory.

D. Prejudice is a harmful attitude based on inaccurate generalizations about a group of people. These generalizations are called stereotypes.

E. Stereotypes are harmful because they take away our ability to treat each member of a group as an individual and because they lead to faulty attributions.

IV. Friendship and love are social phenomena based on the process of person perception.

A. The process of person perception can be said to involve a "complex algebra" in which we combine and evaluate information about others to form an impression.

   1. Negative information is generally weighted more than positive information in person perception.

   2. First impressions (the primacy effect) generally influence person perception more than information learned later. The primacy effect is lessened under three conditions.

      a. The person has prolonged exposure to the individual about whom the first impression was formed.

      b. Time has passed since the first impression was formed, even if there has been no further exposure.

      c. The person who formed the first impression understands the primacy effect and tries to minimize it.

   3. Person perception is influenced by the emotional state of the perceiver.

B. People living in individualistic cultures (like the mainstream U.S. culture) often underestimate the power of social situations in influencing the behavior of other people and overemphasize a person's internal attributes when explaining their behavior. This bias is termed the fundamental attribution error.

C. Although many factors ensure that each individual's perception of another individual will be unique, some general factors partly determine to whom we will be attracted.

   1. In general, we tend to be attracted to persons who

      a. Have characteristics that are similar or complementary to our own

      b. Are competent but not perfect

    c. Are physically attractive

    d. Also like us

  2. Women are more likely to be attracted to a person's intelligence, character, education, occupational status, ambition, and income than are men.

  3. Men are more likely to be attracted by physical attractiveness than are women.

  4. Within each gender, however, different people perceive the same individual differently because of differences in the weight assigned to the same characteristics and even the perception of them as positive or negative.

D. Two major factors in determining if a relationship will last are the difference between what you expect to find in a relationship and what you actually find, and the degree to which the relationship is fairly balanced or equitable. The most enduring love relationships are able to make the transition from primarily passionate love to primarily companionate love.

● Resources

1. Two wonderfully readable yet scholarly overviews of social psychology are Aronson, E. (1998). *The social animal* (6th ed.). San Francisco: W. H. Freeman; and Myers, D. (1999). *Social psychology* (6th ed.). Boston: McGraw-Hill.

2. The role of cognitive factors in social interactions is described in Wyer, R. S., & Carlston, D. W. (1980). *Social cognition, inference, and attribution.* Hillsdale, NJ: Lawrence Erlbaum.

3. For a recently revised classic on the psychology of racial prejudice, see Jones, J. M. (1999). *Prejudice and racism.* Boston: McGraw-Hill.

4. Attitude change is discussed in scholarly but understandable terms in Zimbardo, P. G., & Leippe, M. R. (1991). *The psychology of attitude change and social influence* (3rd ed.). Boston: McGraw-Hill.

5. To learn more about the psychology of persuasion, see Cialdini, R. (1996). *Influence: Science and practice.* New York: Talman.

GLOSSARY

A

abnormal behavior: Actions, thoughts, and feelings that are harmful to the person or to others. (p. 386)

absolute threshold: The smallest magnitude of a stimulus that can be detected half the time. (p. 75)

acetycholine (a"suh-teel'koh"leen): A neurotransmitter used by somatic neurons that contract the body's large muscles and by neurons in the brain that apparently regulate wakefulness and dream sleep. (p. 37)

achievement motivation: The psychological need in humans for success. (p. 288)

acquired immune deficiency syndrome (AIDS): A viral disease spread by blood and other body fluids that eventually destroys the body's immune system. (p. 379)

action potential: A brief electrical signal that travels the length of the axon. (p. 34)

adolescence: The period from the onset of puberty until the beginning of adulthood. (p. 256)

adolescent egocentrism: The quality of thinking that leads some adolescents to believe that they are the focus of attention in social situations, to believe that their problems are unique, to be unusually hypocritical, and to be "pseudostupid." (p. 258)

adolescent growth spurt: The rapid increase in weight and height that occurs around the onset of puberty. (p. 257)

adrenal glands (ah-drē'nal): Two glands on the kidneys, which are involved in physical and emotional arousal. (p. 55)

afferent neurons (af'er-ent): Neurons that transmit messages from sense organs to the central nervous system. (p. 38)

agoraphobia (ag"o-rah-fō'bē-ah): An intense fear of leaving one's home or other familiar (p. 391)

algorithms (al'go-rith'mz): Systematic patterns of reasoning that guarantee finding a correct solution to a problem. (p. 208)

all-or-none principle: The law that states that, once a neural action potential is produced, its magnitude is always the same. (p. 34)

amphetamine psychosis (sī-kō'sis): A prolonged reaction to the excessive use of stimulants, characterized by disordered thinking, confused and rapidly changing emotions, and intense suspiciousness. (p. 130)

amphetamines (am-fet'ah-mīnz): Powerful stimulants that produce a conscious sense of increased energy and a euphoric high. (p. 130)

amygdala (ah-mig'dah-lah): The part of the limbic system that plays a role in emotional arousal. (p. 45)

androgynous: Having both typical feminine and masculine characteristics. (p. 308)

angiotensin (an"jē-ō-ten'sin): A substance in the blood that signals the hypothalamus that the body needs water. (p. 285)

animism (an'i-mizm): The egocentric belief of preoperational children that inanimate objects are alive, as children are. (p. 253)

anterograde amnesia (an'ter-ō-grād): A memory disorder characterized by an inability to store and/or retrieve new information in long-term memory. (p. 191)

antidiuretic hormone (ADH) (an"tī-dī"ū-ret'ik): A hormone produced by the pituitary that causes the kidneys to conserve water in the body by reabsorbing it from the urine. (p. 285)

antisocial personality disorder: A personality disorder characterized by smooth social skills and a lack of guilt about violating social rules and laws and taking advantage of others. (p. 404)

anxiety disorders: Psychological disorders that involve excessive levels of negative emotions, such as nervousness, tension, worry, fright, and anxiety. (p. 391)

aphasia (ah-fā'zē-ah): An impairment of the ability to understand or use language. (p. 46)

applied psychologists: Psychologists who use knowledge of psychology to solve and prevent human problems. (p. 15)

approach-approach conflict: Conflict in which the individual must choose between two positive goals of approximately equal value. (p. 358)

approach-avoidance conflict: Conflict in which achieving a positive goal will produce a negative outcome as well. (p. 358)

association areas: Areas within each lobe of the cerebral cortex believed to play general rather than specific roles. (p. 49)

attachments: The psychological bonds between infants and caregivers. (p. 252)

attitudes: Beliefs that predispose one to act and feel in certain ways. (p. 448)

attribution: The process of trying to explain why things happen—that is, attribute them to some cause. (p. 460)

attribution theory (ah-tri-bu'shun): The theory that people tend to look for explanations for their own behavior and that of others. (p. 454)

audition (aw-dish'un): The sense of hearing. (p. 86)

autonomic nervous system (aw"to-nom'ik): The division of the peripheral nervous system that controls the involuntary actions of internal body organs, such as heartbeat and breathing, and is important in the experience of emotion. (p. 40)

avoidance-avoidance conflict: Conflict in which the individual must choose between two negative outcomes of approximately equal value. (p. 358)

avoidance conditioning: Operant conditioning in which the behavior is reinforced because it prevents something negative from happening (a form of negative reinforcement). (p. 155)

axons (ak'sonz): Neuron branches that transmit messages to other neurons. (p. 32)

B

basilar membrane (bas'ĭ-lar): One of the membranes that separates the two tubes of the cochlea and on which the organ of Corti rests. (p. 88)

basket cells: Sensory receptor cells at the base of hairs that detect pressure. (p. 92)

behavior: Directly observable and measurable human actions. (p. 5)

behavior therapy: Psychotherapy based on social learning theory in which the therapist helps the client unlearn abnormal ways of behaving and learn more adaptive ways to take their place. (p. 423)

behaviorism (be-hāv′yor-izm): The school of psychology that emphasizes the process of learning and the measurement of overt behavior. (p. 11)

binocular cues (bīn-ok′ū-lar): Two visual cues that require both eyes to allow us to perceive depth. (p. 104)

bipolar affective disorder (bī-pō′lar): A condition in which the individual experiences periods of mania that alternate irregularly with periods of severe depression. (p. 400)

blind spot: The spot where the optic nerve attaches to the retina; it contains no rods or cones. (p. 80)

bone conduction hearing: Hearing accomplished through sounds transmitted through the bones of the head directly to the cochlear fluid. (p. 88)

brain: The complex mass of neural cells and related cells encased in the skull. (p. 32)

Broca's area: An area of the frontal lobe of the left cerebral hemisphere that plays a role in speaking language. (p. 46)

C

catatonic schizophrenia (kat″ah-ton′ik): A subtype of schizophrenia in which the individual spends long periods in an inactive, statuelike state. (p. 403)

catharsis (kah-thar′sis): The release of emotional energy related to unconscious conflicts. (pp. 300, 417)

cell body: The central part of the neuron that includes the nucleus. (p. 32)

cell membrane: The covering of a neuron or another cell. (p. 34)

central nervous system: The brain and the nerve fibers that make up the spinal cord. (p. 38)

cerebellum (ser″ē-bel′um): Two rounded structures behind the pons involved in the coordination of muscle movements, learning, and memory. (p. 44)

cerebral cortex (ser′ē-bral): The largest structure in the forebrain, controlling conscious experience and intelligence and being involved with the somatic nervous system. (p. 46)

cerebral hemispheres: The two main parts of the cerebral cortex, divided into left and right hemispheres. (p. 49)

chromosomes (krō′mo-sōmz): The strips in cell nuclei that contain genes. (p. 58)

chunks: Units of memory. (p. 177)

ciliary muscle (sil′ē-ar″e): The muscle in the eye that controls the shape of the lens. (p. 79)

cingulate cortex: The part of the limbic system that processes cognitive information in emotion. (p. 46)

cingulotomy: A type of psychosurgery for severe and otherwise untreatable obsessive-compulsive disorder; it involves surgical destruction of part of the cingulate cortex. (p. 433)

classical conditioning: A form of learning in which a previously neutral stimulus (CS) is paired with an unconditioned stimulus (UCS) to elicit a conditioned response (CR) that is identical to or very similar to the unconditioned response (UCR). (p. 147)

client-centered psychotherapy: Carl Rogers' approach to humanistic psychotherapy, in which the therapist creates an atmosphere that encourages clients to discover feelings of which they are unaware. (p. 421)

climacteric (klī-mak′ter-ik): The period between about ages 45 and 60 in which there is a loss of capacity to sexually reproduce in women and a decline in the reproductive capacity of men. (p. 265)

cochlea (cok′lē-ah): A curved structure of the inner ear that is filled with fluid. (p. 87)

cognition (kog-nish′un): The intellectual processes through which information is obtained, transformed, stored, retrieved, and otherwise used. (pp. 9, 202)

cognitive dissonance (dis′so-nans): The discomfort that results from inconsistencies between attitudes and behavior. (p. 453)

cognitive map (kog′ni-tiv): An inferred mental awareness of the structure of a physical space or related elements. (p. 164)

cognitive psychology: The viewpoint in psychology that emphasizes the importance of cognitive processes, such as perception, memory, and thinking. (p. 9)

cognitive therapy: An approach to therapy that teaches individuals new cognitions— adaptive beliefs, expectations, and ways of thinking—to eliminate abnormal emotions and behavior. (p. 427)

collective unconscious: According to Jung, the content of the unconscious mind with which all humans are born. (p. 335)

companionate love: The blend of friendship, intimacy, commitment, and security that generally develops after passionate love. (p. 465)

concepts: Categories of things, events, and qualities that are linked together by a common feature or features, in spite of their differences. (p. 202)

concrete operational stage: In Piaget's theory, the period of cognitive

development from ages 7 to 11. (p. 255)

conditioned response (CR): A response that is similar or identical to the unconditioned response that comes to be elicited by a conditioned stimulus. (p. 145)

conditioned stimulus (CS): A stimulus that comes to elicit responses as a result of being paired with an unconditioned stimulus. (p. 145)

conditions of worth: The standards used by others or ourselves in judging our worth. (p. 342)

cones: The 6 million receptor cells located mostly in the center of the retina that transduce light waves into neural impulses, thereby coding information about light, dark, and color. (p. 79)

conflict: The state in which two or more motives cannot be satisfied because they interfere with one another. (p. 358)

conformity: Yielding to group pressure even when no direct request to comply has been made. (p. 443)

conscience: According to Freud, the moral inhibitions of the superego. (p. 334)

conscious mind: That portion of the mind of which one is presently aware. (p. 332)

consciousness (kon′shus-nes): A state of awareness. (p. 118)

conservation: The concept understood by concrete operational children that quantity (number, mass, etc.) does not change just because shape or other superficial features have changed. (p. 255)

convergent thinking: Thinking that is logical and conventional and that focuses on a problem. (p. 210)

conversion disorders: Somatoform disorders in which individuals experience serious somatic symptoms such as functional blindness, deafness, and paralysis. (p. 394)

cooperative play: Play that involves cooperation between two or more children. (p. 254)

coping: Attempts by individuals to deal with the source of stress and/or control their reactions to it. (p. 371)

cornea (kor′nē-ah): The protective coating on the surface of the eye through which light passes. (p. 79)

corpus callosum (kor′pus kah-lo′sum): The link between the cerebral hemispheres. (p. 50)

cortisol: A hormone produced by the adrenal glands. (p. 55)

counterconditioning: The process of eliminating a classically conditioned response by pairing the conditioned stimulus (CS) with an unconditioned stimulus (UCS) for a response that is stronger than the conditioned response (CR) and that cannot occur at the same time as the CR. (p. 148)

creativity: The ability to make human products and ideas (such as symphonies or solutions to social problems) that are both novel and valued by others. (p. 200)

cretinism (krē′tin-izm): A type of mental retardation in children caused by a deficiency of thyroxin. (p. 56)

critical period: A biologically determined period in the life of some animals during which certain forms of learning can take place most easily. (p. 239)

criticism trap: An increase in the frequency of a negative behavior that often follows the use of criticism, reinforcing the behavior it is intended to punish. (p. 156)

crystallized intelligence: The ability to use previously learned skills to solve familiar problems. (p. 218)

cultural relativity: The perspective that promotes thinking of different cultures in relative terms rather than judgmental terms. (p. 14)

culture: The patterns of behavior, beliefs, and values shared by a group of people. (p. 13)

cupula (ku′pu-lah): A gelatin-like structure containing a tuft of hairlike sensory receptor cells in the semicircular canals. (p. 92)

D

dark adaptation: Increased sensitivity of the eye in semidarkness following an abrupt reduction in overall illumination. (p. 80)

day residue: Day content that is similar to events in the person's waking life. (p. 124)

daydreams: Relatively focused thinking about fantasies. (p. 118)

decay theory: The theory that forgetting occurs as the memory trace fades over time. (p. 184)

decenter (dē-sen′ter): To think about more than one characteristic of a thing at a time; a capacity of concrete operational children. (p. 255)

decibel (db) (des′i-bel): Measurement of the intensity of perceived sound. (p. 86)

deep structure: The underlying structure of a statement that holds its meaning. (p. 211)

defense mechanisms: According to Freud, the unrealistic strategies used by the ego to discharge tension. (p. 373)

deindividuation: State in which people in a group can feel anonymous and unidentifiable and therefore feel less concerned with what others think of their behavior. (p. 440)

delay of reinforcement: The passage of time between the response and the positive reinforcement that leads to reduced efficiency of learning. (p. 150)

delusions: False beliefs that distort reality. (p. 402)

dendrites (den′drīts): Extensions of the cell body that receive messages from other neurons. (p. 32)

deoxyribonucleic acid (DNA) (dē-ok″sē-rī″bō-nu-klā′ik): The complex molecule containing the genetic code. (p. 58)

depersonalization (dē-per″sun-al-i-zā′shun): The perceptual experience of one's body or surroundings becoming distorted or unreal. (p. 395)

depolarization: The process during which positively charged ions flow into the axon, making it less negatively charged inside. (p. 34)

depressants: Drugs that reduce the activity of the central nervous system, leading to a sense of relaxation, drowsiness, and lowered inhibitions. (p. 131)

development: The more-or-less predictable changes in behavior associated with increasing age. (p. 237)

developmental psychology: The field of psychology that focuses on the development across the life span. (p. 16)

deviation IQ: The intelligence quotient based on the degree of deviation from average of the person's score on an intelligence test. (p. 221)

difference threshold: The smallest difference between two stimuli that can be detected half the time. (p. 75)

diffusion of responsibility: The effect of being in a group that apparently reduces the sense of personal responsibility of each group member to act appropriately. (p. 442)

disinhibition (dis″in-hi-bish′un): A temporary increase in the strength of an extinguished response caused by an unrelated stimulus event. (p. 162)

disorganized schizophrenia: A subtype of schizophrenia characterized by shallow silliness, extreme social withdrawal, and fragmented delusions and hallucinations. (p. 403)

displacement (dis-plās′ment): A defense mechanism in which the individual directs aggressive or sexual feelings away from the primary object to someone or something safe. (p. 334)

dispositional attribution (dis″po-zish′un-al): An explanation for behavior that is based on a personal characteristic of the individual. (p. 460)

dissociative amnesia: A dissociative disorder that involves a loss of memory and that has a psychological rather than a physical cause. (p. 395)

dissociative disorders (dis-sō″sē-a-tiv): A category of conditions involving sudden abnormal cognitive changes, such as a change in memory, perception, or identity. (p. 395)

dissociative fugue (fūg): A period of "wandering" that involves a loss of memory and a change in identity. (p. 396)

dissociative identity disorder: A dissociative disorder in which the individual appears to shift abruptly and repeatedly from one "personality" to another. (p. 396)

divergent thinking: Thinking that is loosely organized, only partially directed, and unconventional. (p. 210)

divided consciousness: The splitting off of two conscious activities that occur simultaneously. (p. 118)

dizygotic twins (dī″zī-got′ik): Twins formed from the fertilization of two ova by two sperm. (p. 60)

dominant gene: The gene that produces a trait in an individual even when paired with a recessive gene. (p. 59)

dopamine (do″pàh′meen): A neurotransmitter substance used by neurons in the brain that control large muscle movements and by neurons in pleasure and reward systems in the brain. (p. 37)

dream interpretation: A method developed by Freud in which the symbols of the manifest content of dreams that are recalled by the patient are interpreted to reveal their latent content. (p. 416)

drug therapy: A medical therapy that uses medications to treat abnormal behavior. (p. 431)

E

eardrum: The thin membrane that sound waves cause to vibrate; a structure of the middle ear. (p. 87)

early experiences: Experiences occurring very early in development, believed by some to have lasting effects. (p. 241)

efferent neurons (ef′er-ent): Neurons that transmit messages from the central nervous system to organs and muscles. (p. 38)

ego (ē′go): According to Freud, that part of the mind that uses the reality principle to satisfy the id. (p. 333)

ego ideal: According to Freud, the standard of perfect conduct of the superego. (p. 334)

egocentric (e″gō-sen′trik): The self-oriented quality in the thinking of preoperational children. (p. 253)

elaboration (e-lab″o-rā′shun): The process of creating associations between a new memory and existing memories. (p. 182)

electroconvulsive therapy (ECT) (e-lek″trō-con-vul′siv): A medical therapy that uses electrical current to induce controlled convulsive seizures that alleviate some types of mental disorders. (p. 432)

electroencephalogram (EEG) (e-lek″trō-en-sef′ah-lo-gram): A recording of the electrical activity of the brain obtained through electrodes placed on the scalp. (pp. 43, 121)

electromagnetic radiation (e-lek″trō-mag-net′ik): A form of energy, including electricity, radio waves, and X rays, of which visible light is a part. (p. 78)

emotion Positive or negative feelings generally in reaction to stimuli that are accompanied by physiological arousal and related behavior. (p. 281)

encode (en′cōd): To represent information in some form in the memory system. (p. 174)

endocrine system (en′dō-krin): The system of glands that secretes hormones. (p. 54)

engram (en′gram): The as yet unidentified memory trace in the brain that is the biological basis of memory. (p. 189)

epinephrine (ep″i-nef′rin): A hormone produced by the adrenal glands. (p. 55)

episodic memory (epĭ-sod-ik): Memory for specific experiences that can be defined in terms of time and space. (p. 178)

equity theory: The theory that partners will be comfortable in their relationship only when the ratio between their perceived contributions and benefits is equal. (p. 466)

erectile dysfunction: A condition in which the penis does not become erect enough for intercourse under sexually arousing circumstances. (p. 445)

escape conditioning: Operant conditioning in which the behavior is reinforced because it causes a negative event to cease (a form of negative reinforcement). (p. 155)

estrogen (es′tro-jen): A female sex hormone. (p. 56)

ethnic group: A group of persons who are descendants of a common group of ancestors. (p. 13)

ethnic identity: Each person's sense of belonging to a particular ethnic group. (p. 13)

evolutionary theory of gender differences: The theory that gender differences are based on genes that resulted from different evolutionary pressures on ancestral women and men. (p. 316)

external auditory canal: The tube connecting the pinna to the middle ear. (p. 87)

extinction (eks-ting′shun): The process of unlearning a learned response because of the removal of the original source of learning. (p. 161)

extrinsic motivation (eks-trin′sik): Human motives stimulated by external rewards. (p. 290)

extroversion (eks″tro-ver′zhun): According to Jung, the tendency of some individuals to be friendly and open to the world. (p. 335)

fear of success: The fear of the consequences of success, particularly the envy of others. (p. 289)

feelings of inferiority: According to Adler, the feelings that result from children being less powerful than adults that must be overcome during the development of the healthy personality. (p. 335)

fertilization (fer′tĭ-li-zā′shun): The uniting of sperm and ovum, which produces a zygote. (p. 58)

fixed interval schedule: A reinforcement schedule in which the reinforcer is given following the first response occurring after a predetermined period of time. (p. 152)

fixed ratio schedule: A reinforcement schedule in which the reinforcer is given only after a specified number of responses. (p. 152)

fluid intelligence: The ability to learn or invent new strategies to deal with new problems. (p. 217)

forebrain: The parts of the brain, including the thalamus, hypothalamus, and cerebral cortex, that cover the hindbrain and midbrain and fill much of the skull. (p. 44)

formal operational stage: In Piaget's theory, the period of intellectual development usually reached by about age 11 and characterized by the ability to use abstract concepts. (p. 257)

fovea (fō′vē-ah): The central spot of the retina, which contains the greatest concentration of cones. (p. 79)

framing: The way in which a problem or question is presented. (p. 209)

free association: A tool used by Freud in which the patient is encouraged to talk about whatever comes to mind, allowing the contents of the unconscious mind to slip past the censorship of the ego. (p. 416)

free nerve endings: Sensory receptor cells in the skin that detect pressure, temperature, and pain. (p. 92)

frequency of cycles: The rate of vibration of sound waves; determines pitch. (p. 86)

Freud's instinct theory: The theory that aggression is caused by an inborn aggressive instinct. (p. 300)

frontal lobes: The part of the cerebral cortex in the front of the skull involved in planning, organization, voluntary motor movements, and speech. (p. 46)

frustration: The result of being unable to satisfy a motive. (p. 358)

frustration-aggression theory: The theory that aggression is a natural reaction to frustration of important motives. (p. 300)

functional MRI: A type of MRI that measures the activity of parts of the brain by measuring the use of oxygen by groups of neurons. (p. 43)

functionalism (funk′shun-al-izm): The nineteenth-century school of psychology that emphasized the useful functions of consciousness. (p. 9)

fundamental attribution error: The tendency to underestimate the impact of situations on others while overestimating the impact on oneself. (p. 460)

g: A broad general factor of intelligence, a concept endorsed by some investigators of intelligence. (p. 217)

gamete (gam′ēt): A sex cell, which contains 23 chromosomes instead of the normal 46. (p. 58)

ganglia (gang′glē-ah): Clusters of cell bodies of neurons outside of the central nervous system. (p. 41)

gender: The psychological experience of being male or female. (p. 308)

gender identity: One's view of oneself as male or female. (pp. 14, 308)

gender role: The behaviors consistent with being male or female in a given culture. (p. 308)

general adaptation syndrome (GAS): According to Selye, the mobilization of the body to ward off threats, characterized by a three-stage pattern of the alarm reaction, the resistance stage, and the exhaustion stage. (p. 362)

generalized anxiety disorder: An uneasy sense of general tension and apprehension that makes the individual highly uncomfortable because of its prolonged presence. (p. 392)

generative (jen′e-ra″tiv): The ability to create an infinite set of utterances using a finite set of elements and rules. (p. 212)

genes (jenz): The hereditary units made up of deoxyribonucleic acid. (p. 58)

gestalt (ges-tawlt′): An organized or unified whole. (p. 8)

glands: Structures in the body that secrete substances. (p. 54)

glucagon (gloo′kah-gon): A hormone produced by the islets of Langerhans that causes the liver to release sugar into the bloodstream. (pp. 56, 283)

gonads (gō′nadz): The glands that produce sex cells and hormones important in sexual arousal and that contribute to the development of secondary sex characteristics. (p. 56)

graded exposure: A behavior therapy technique in which a person with a phobia is first exposed to a stimulus that is mildly fear provoking. Once the client has mastered his or her anxiety in that situation, he or she is exposed to a graded series of more fearful situations. (p. 424)

gustation (gus-tā′shun): The sense of taste. (p. 99)

hallucinations: False perceptual experiences that distort reality. (p. 402)

hallucinogens (hah-lū′si″no-jenz): Drugs that alter perceptual experiences. (p. 132)

hammer, anvil, stirrup: Three linked bones of the middle ear, which help pass sound waves to the inner ear. (p. 87)

health psychology: The field of psychology that uses psychological principles to encourage healthy lifestyles and to minimize the impact of physical illness. (p. 358)

hertz (Hz): The measurement of the frequency of sound waves in cycles per second. (p. 86)

heuristics: Efficient problem-solving strategies that do not guarantee a correct solution. (p. 208)

hindbrain: The lowest part of the brain, located at the rear base of the skull. (p. 44)

hippocampus (hip″o-kam′pus): The part of the limbic system that plays a role in emotional arousal and memory. (pp. 45, 192)

homeostatic mechanisms (hō″mē-ō-stat′ik): Internal body mechanisms that sense biological imbalances and stimulate actions to restore the proper balance. (p. 281)

hormones (hor′mōnz): Chemical substances, produced by endocrine glands, that influence internal organs. (p. 54)

humanistic psychology: The psychological view that human beings possess an innate tendency to improve and determine their lives by the decisions they make. (p. 11)

humanistic theory: The psychological view that human beings possess an innate tendency to improve and to determine their lives by the decisions they make. (p. 341)

hyperphagia (hī″per-fā′jē-ah): Excessive overeating that results from the destruction of the satiety center of the hypothalamus. (p. 282)

hypnagogic state (hip″nah-goj′ik): A relaxed state of dreamlike awareness between wakefulness and sleep. (p. 121)

hypnosis (hip-nō′sis): An altered state of consciousness in which the individual is highly relaxed and susceptible to suggestions. (p. 127)

hypothalamus (hī″pō-thal′ah-mus): The small part of the forebrain involved with motives, emotions, and the functions of the autonomic nervous system. (p. 45, 281)

id: According to Freud, the inborn part of the unconscious mind that uses the primary process to satisfy its needs and that acts according to the pleasure principle. (p. 333)

ideal self: According to humanists, the person one wishes one were. (p. 342)

identification: The tendency to base one's identity and actions on individuals who are successful in gaining satisfaction from life. (p. 334)

immune system: The complex body system of defenses to illness, such as white cells and natural killer cells of the blood. (p. 365)

imprinting (im′print-ing): A form of early learning that occurs in some animals during a critical period. (p. 239)

incentives: External cues that activate motives. (p. 284)

inhalants (in-hā′lants): Toxic substances that produce a sense of intoxication when inhaled. (p. 132)

inner-directedness: A force that humanists believe all people possess that internally leads them to grow and improve. (p. 341)

insanity: A legal definition concerning a person's inability to tell right from wrong, ability to understand legal proceedings, or whether the person is a direct danger to self or others. (p. 389)

insight (in′sīt): A form of cognitive change that involves recognition of previously unseen relationships. (p. 166)

insulin (in′su-lin): A hormone produced by the islets of Langerhans that reduces the amount of sugar in the bloodstream. (pp. 56, 283)

intelligence (in-tel′i-jens): The cognitive abilities of an individual to learn from experience, to reason well, and to cope with the demands of daily living. (p. 216)

intelligence quotient (IQ): A numerical value of intelligence derived from the results of an intelligence test. (p. 219)

intensity: The density of vibrating air molecules; determines the loudness of sound. (p. 86)

interference theory: The theory that forgetting occurs because similar memories interfere with the storage or retrieval of information. (p. 184)

interneuron: Neurons in the central nervous system that connect other neurons. (p. 39)

interpersonal psychotherapy: A form of psychological therapy, based on the theories of neo-Freudian Harry Stack Sullivan, that focuses on the accurate identification and communication of feelings and the improvement of current social relationships. (p. 418)

interview: A subjective method of personality assessment that involves questioning techniques designed to reveal the personality of the client. (p. 348)

intrinsic motivation (in-trin′sik): Human motives stimulated by the inherent nature of the activity or its natural consequences. (p. 289)

introspection (in″tro-spek′shun): The process of looking inward at one's own consciousness. (p. 7)

introversion (in-tro-ver′zhun): According to Jung, the tendency of some individuals to be shy and to focus their attention on themselves. (p. 335)

ions (i′ons): Electrically charged particles. (p. 33)

iris (ī′ris): The colored part of the eye behind the cornea that regulates the amount of light that enters. (p. 79)

islets of Langerhans (i′lets of lahng′er-hanz): Endocrine cells in the pancreas that regulate the level of sugar in the blood. (p. 56)

kinesthetic receptors (kin″es-thet′ik): Receptors in the muscles, joints, and skin that provide information about movement, posture, and orientation. (p. 91)

Korsakoff's syndrome (Kor-sak′ofs): A disorder involving both anterograde and retrograde amnesia caused by excessive use of alcohol. (p. 192)

labia majora: The larger, outer lips of the vulva. (p. 430)

labia minora: The smaller, inner lips of the vulva. (p. 431)

language: A symbolic code used in communication. (p. 211)

latent content: According to Freud, the true meaning of dreams that is found in the symbols in their manifest content. (p. 125)

lateral hypothalamus: A portion of the hypothalamus involved in feeling hungry and starting to eat (the feeding center). (p. 282)

learned taste aversion (ah-ver′shun): Negative reaction to a particular taste that has been associated with nausea or other illness. (p. 167)

learning: Any relatively permanent change in behavior brought about through experience. (p. 142)

learning set: Improvement in the rate of learning to solve new problems through practice solving similar problems. (p. 166)

lens: The transparent portion of the eye that focuses light on the retina. (p. 99)

levels of processing model: An alternative to the stage theory of memory stating that the distinction between short-term and long-term memory is a matter of degree rather than different kinds of memory and is based on how incoming information is processed. (p. 180)

libido: The energy of the life instincts of sex, hunger, and thirst. (p. 333)

life events: Psychologically significant events that occur in a person's life, such as divorce, childbirth, and change in employment. (p. 360)

light adaptation: Regaining sensitivity of the eye to bright light following an abrupt increase in overall illumination. (p. 81)

limbic system: A complex brain system, composed of the amygdala, hippocampus, septal area, and cingulate cortex, that works with the hypothalamus in emotional arousal. (p. 45)

linguistic relativity hypothesis: The idea that the structure of a language may influence the way individuals think. (p. 213)

long-term memory (LTM): The third stage of memory, involving the storage of information that is kept for long periods of time. (p. 177)

magnetic resonance imaging (MRI): An imaging technique using magnetic resonance to obtain detailed views of brain structure and function. (p. 43)

major depression: An affective disorder characterized by episodes of deep unhappiness, loss of interest in life, and other symptoms. (p. 398)

mania (mā′nē-ah): A disturbance of mood in which the individual experiences a euphoria characterized by unrealistic optimism and heightened sensory pleasures. (p. 400)

manifest content: According to Freud, the obvious, but superficial, meaning of dreams. (p. 125)

Maslow's hierarchy of motives: The concept that more basic needs must be met before higher-level motives become active. (p. 291)

maturation (mach″u-rā′shun): Systematic physical growth of the body, including the nervous system. (p. 238)

medical therapies: Those therapies—including drug therapy, electroconvulsive therapy, and psychosurgery—generally designed to correct a physical condition that is believed to be the cause of a psychological disorder. (p. 431)

medulla (mĕ-dul′ah): The swelling at the top of the spinal cord responsible for controlling breathing and a variety of reflexes. (p. 44)

menarche (me-nar′kē): The first menstrual period. (p. 257)

menopause (mĕn′o-pawz): The cessation of menstruation and the capacity to reproduce in women. (p. 265)

mental processes: Private psychological activities that include thinking, perceiving, and feeling. (p. 5)

mental set: A habitual way of approaching or perceiving a problem. (p. 207)

metabolism (me-tab′o-lizm): The process through which the body uses energy. (p. 56)

midbrain: The small area at the top of the hindbrain that serves primarily as a reflex center for orienting the eyes and ears. (p. 44)

modeling: Learning based on observation of the behavior of another. (p. 166)

monocular cues (mon-ok′ū-lar): Eight visual cues that can be seen with one eye and that allow us to perceive distance. (p. 104)

monozygotic twins (mon″ō-zī-got′ik): Twins formed from a single ovum; they are identical in appearance because they have the same genetic structure. (p. 60)

mood disorders: Psychological disorders involving depression and/or abnormal elation. (p. 398)

morphemes (mor′fēm): The smallest units of meaning in a language. (p. 212)

motivated forgetting: Forgetting that is believed to be based on the upsetting or threatening nature of the information that is forgotten. (p. 187)

motivation: The internal state or condition that activates and gives direction to our thoughts, feelings, and actions. (p. 280)

motive for affiliation: The need to be with other people and to have personal relationships. (p. 287)

motives: Internal states or conditions that activate behavior and give it direction. (p. 11)

multiple approach-avoidance conflict: Conflict that requires the individual to choose between two alternatives, each of which contains both positive and negative consequences. (p. 360)

myelin sheath (mī′e-lin): The insulating fatty covering wrapped around part of the neuron. (p. 35)

myoclonia (mi″o-klō′nē-ah): An abrupt movement that sometimes occurs during the hypnagogic state in which the sleeper often experiences a sense of falling. (p. 121)

narcotics: Powerful and highly addictive depressants. (p. 131)

negative reinforcement: Reinforcement that comes about from the removal or avoidance of a negative event as the consequence of behavior. (p. 155)

neonatal period (ne″ō-nā′tal): The first two weeks of life following birth. (p. 250)

nerve: A bundle of long neurons outside the brain and spinal cord. (p. 33)

neuron (nu′ron): An individual nerve cell. (p. 32)

neuroscience perspective: The viewpoint in psychology that focuses on the nervous system in explaining behavior and mental processes. (p. 13)

neurotransmitters (nu″rō-tranz′-mit-erz): Chemical substances, produced by axons, that transmit messages across the synapse. (p. 35)

nocioceptors: Receptors for stimuli that are experienced as painful. (p. 93)

norepinephrine (nor′ep-i-nef′rin): A hormone produced by the adrenal glands. (pp. 37, 55)

normal distribution: The symmetrical pattern of scores on a scale in which a majority of the scores are clustered near the center and a minority are at either extreme. (p. 221)

norms: Standards (created by the scores of a large group of individuals) used as the basis of comparison for scores on a test. (p. 222)

novel stimulation: New or changed experiences. (p. 286)

obedience: Doing what one is told to do by people in authority. (p. 445)

object permanence: The understanding that objects continue to exist when they are not in view. (p. 251)

objectivity: Lack of subjectivity in a test question so that the same score is produced regardless of who does the scoring. (p. 222)

observational methods: Methods of personality assessment that involve watching a person's actual behavior in a natural or simulated situation. (p. 348)

obsessive-compulsive disorders: Disorders that involve obsessions (anxiety-provoking thoughts that will not go away) and/or compulsions (irresistible urges to engage in specific irrational behaviors). (p. 394)

occipital lobes (ok-sip′ĭ-tal): The part of the cerebral cortex, located at the base of the back of the head, that plays an essential role in the processing of sensory information from the eyes. (p. 48)

olfaction (ol-fak′shun): The sense of smell. (p. 99)

olfactory epithelium (ōl-fak′to-rē ep″i-thē′lē-um): The sheet of receptor cells at the top of the nasal cavity. (p. 100)

operant conditioning (op′e-rant): Learning in which the consequences of behavior lead to changes in the probability of its occurrence. (p. 149)

opiates (ō′pē-ats): Narcotic drugs derived from the opium poppy. (p. 131)

opponent-process theory of color vision: The theory of color vision contending that the visual system has two kinds of color processors, which respond to light in either the red-green or yellow-blue ranges of wavelength. (p. 83)

optic chiasm: The area in the brain where the optic nerves cross. (p. 80)

optic nerve: The nerve that carries neural messages about vision to the brain. (p. 80)

optimal level of arousal: The apparent human need for a comfortable level of stimulation, achieved by acting in ways that increase or decrease it. (p. 287)

organ of corti (kor′tē): A sensory receptor in the cochlea that transduces sound waves into coded neural impulses. (p. 88)

oval window: The membrane of the inner ear that vibrates, creating sound waves in the fluid of the cochlea. (p. 87)

ovaries (o′vah-rēz): Female endocrine glands that secrete sex-related hormones and produce ova, or eggs. (p. 56)

pancreas (pan′krē-as): The organ near the stomach that contains the islets of Langerhans. (p. 56)

panic anxiety disorder: A pattern of anxiety in which long periods of calm are broken by an intensely uncomfortable attack of anxiety. (p. 392)

papillae (pah-pil′ē): Clusters of taste buds on the tongue. (p. 99)

parallel play: Playing near but not with another child. (p. 254)

paranoid schizophrenia (par′ah-noid): A subtype of schizophrenia in which the individual holds delusions of persecution and grandeur that seriously distort reality. (p. 402)

parasympathetic division (par″ah-sim″pah-thet′ik): The division of the autonomic nervous system that generally "calms" internal organs. (p. 40)

parathormone (par″ah-thor′mōn): A hormone that regulates ion levels in neurons and controls excitability of the nervous system. (p. 56)

parathyroid glands (par″ah-thī′roid): Four glands embedded in the thyroid that produce parathormone. (p. 56)

paraventricular nucleus: A part of the hypothalamus that plays a role in the motive of hunger by regulating the level of blood sugar. (p. 282)

parietal lobes (pah-rī′e-tal): The part of the cerebral cortex located behind the frontal lobes at the top of the skull containing the somatosensory area. (p. 48)

partial reinforcement effect: Responses that have been reinforced on variable ratio or variable interval schedules are more difficult to extinguish than responses that have been continuously reinforced. (p. 161)

passionate love: The mixture of romantic, sexual, and other feelings of love. (p. 465)

perception (per-sep′-shun): The process of organizing and interpreting information received from the outside world. (p. 74)

perceptual constancy: The tendency for perceptions of objects to remain relatively unchanged, in spite of changes in raw sensations. (p. 103)

peripheral nervous system (pĕ-rif′er-al): The network of nerves that branches from the brain and spinal cord to all parts of the body. (p. 38)

person perception: The process of forming impressions of others. (p. 458)

person × situation interactionism (in″ter-ak′shun-izm): The view that behavior is influenced by a combination of the characteristics of both the person and the situation. (p. 339)

person variables: All characteristics of an individual that are relatively enduring, such as ways of thinking, beliefs, or physiological reactivity to stress. (p. 368)

personal unconscious: According to Jung, the motives, conflicts, and information that are repressed by a person because they are threatening to that individual. (p. 335)

personality: The sum total of the typical ways of acting, thinking, and feeling that makes each person unique. (p. 328)

personality disorders: Psychological disorders that are believed to result from personalities that developed improperly during childhood. (p. 403)

persuasion: The process of changing another person's attitudes through arguments and other related means. (p. 449)

phi phenomenon (fī fe-nom′ĕ-non): The perception of apparent movement between two stationary stimuli. (p. 8)

phobia: An intense, irrational fear. (p. 391)

phonemes (fō′nēm): The smallest units of sound in a language. (p. 212)

pineal gland (pin′ē-al): The endocrine gland that is largely responsible for the regulation of biological rhythms. (p. 56)

pinna (pin′nah): The external part of the ear. (p. 87)

pitch: The experience of sound vibrations sensed as high or low. (p. 86)

pituitary gland (pĭ-tu′i-tār″ē): The body's master gland, located near the bottom of the brain, whose secretions help regulate the activity of the other glands in the endocrine system. (p. 54, 285)

pleasure principle: According to Freud, the attempt of the id to seek immediate pleasure and avoid pain, regardless of how harmful it might be to others. (p. 333)

polarization: The tendency for group discussion to make beliefs and attitudes more extreme. (p. 443)

polarized (pō′lar-īz′d): The resting state of a neuron, when mostly negative ions are inside and mostly positive ions are outside the cell membrane. (p. 34)

pons (ponz): The part of the hindbrain that is involved in balance, hearing, and some parasympathetic functions. (p. 44)

positive reinforcement (rē″in-fors′ment): Any consequence of behavior that leads to an increase in the probability of its occurrence. (p. 149)

post-traumatic stress disorder (PTSD): The condition caused by extremely stressful experiences in which the person later experiences anxiety and irritability; has upsetting memories, dreams, and realistic flashbacks of the experience; and tries to avoid anything that reminds him or her of the experience. (p. 393)

preconscious mind: That portion of the mind containing information that is not presently conscious but can be easily brought into consciousness. (p. 332)

prejudice: A harmful attitude based on inaccurate generalizations about a group of people. (p. 454)

preoperational stage: In Piaget's theory, the period of cognitive development from ages 2 to 7. (p. 253)

pressure: Stress that arises from the threat of negative events. (p. 360)

primacy effect: The tendency for first impressions to heavily influence opinions about other people. (p. 459)

primary motives: Human motives for things that are necessary for survival, such as food, water, and warmth. (p. 281)

primary process thinking: According to Freud, the attempt by the id to satisfy its needs by forming a wish-fulfilling mental image of the desired object. (p. 333)

primary reinforcers: Innate positive reinforcers that do not have to be acquired through learning. (p. 151)

primary sex characteristics: Ovulation and menstruation in females and production of sperm in males. (p. 257)

proactive interference (prō-ak′tiv): Interference created by memories from prior learning. (p. 184)

problem solving: The cognitive process through which information is used to reach a goal that is blocked by some obstacle. (p. 206)

procedural memory: Memory for motor movements and skills. (p. 178)

progressive relaxation training: A method of learning to deeply relax the muscles of the body. (pp. 375, 423)

projective test: A test that uses ambiguous stimuli designed to reveal the contents of the client's unconscious mind. (p. 348)

psychoanalysis (sī″kō-ah-nal′i-sis): A method of psychotherapy developed by Freud based on his belief that the root of all psychological problems is unconscious conflicts between the id, the ego, and the superego. (pp. 11, 415)

psychoanalytic theory: Freud's theory that the origin of personality lies in the balance among the id, the ego, and the superego. (p. 331)

psychological motives: Motives related to the individual's happiness and well-being, but not to survival. (p. 286)

psychology: The science of behavior and mental processes. (p. 4)

psychophysics (sī″kō-fiz′iks): A specialty area of psychology that studies sensory limits, sensory adaptation, and related topics. (p. 76)

psychosurgery (sī″kō-ser′jer-ē): A medical therapy that involves operating on the brain in an attempt to alleviate some types of mental disorders. (p. 433)

psychotherapy (sī-kō-ther′ah-pē): A form of therapy in which a trained professional uses methods based on psychological

theories to help a person with psychological problems. (p. 414)

psychotropic drugs (sī″ko-trōp′pik): The class of drugs that alters conscious experience. (p. 128)

puberty (pū′ber-tē): The point in development at which the individual is first physically capable of sexual reproduction. (p. 256)

punishment: A negative consequence of a behavior, which leads to a decrease in the frequency of the behavior that produces it. (p. 156)

pupil (pyoo′pil): The opening of the iris. (p. 79)

rape: The act of forcing sexual activity on an unwilling person. (p. 440)

ratio IQ: The intelligence quotient based on the ratio between the person's mental age and chronological age. (p. 221)

reality principle: According to Freud, the attempt by the ego to find safe, realistic ways of meeting the needs of the id. (p. 333)

receptor sites: Sites on the dendrite that receive the neurotransmitter substance. (p. 35)

recessive gene: The gene that produces a trait in an individual only when the same recessive gene has been inherited from both parents. (p. 89)

reciprocal determination (re-sip″ro-kal): Bandura's observation that the individual's behavior and the social learning environment continually influence one another. (p. 338)

reflection (re-flek-shun): A technique in humanistic psychotherapy in which the therapist reflects the emotions of the client to help clients clarify their feelings. (p. 421)

rehearsal: Mental repetition of information for retention in short-term memory. (p. 175)

reliability: A test's ability to produce similar scores if the test is administered on different occasions or by different examiners. (p. 222)

REM sleep: Rapid-eye-movement sleep, characterized by movement of the eyes under the lids; often accompanies dreams. (p. 122)

representativeness heuristic: The strategy of making judgments about the unknown on the assumption that it is similar to what we know. (p. 208)

repression: Sigmund Freud's theory that unpleasant information is often pushed into unconsciousness without our being aware of it. (pp. 187, 332)

resistance: Any form of patient opposition to the process of psychoanalysis. (p. 416)

retina (ret′i-nah): The area at the back of the eye on which images are formed and that contains the rods and cones. (p. 79)

retroactive interference (ret′rō-ak′tiv): Interference created by memories from later learning. (p. 184)

retrograde amnesia (ret′rō-grād): A memory disorder characterized by an inability to retrieve old long-term memories, generally for a specific period of time extending back from the beginning of the disorder. (p. 192)

reversibility (re-ver′sĭ-bil-ĭ-tē): The concept understood by concrete operational children that logical propositions can be reversed (if $2 + 3 = 5$, then $5 - 3 = 2$). (p. 255)

rods: The 125 million cells located outside the center of the retina that transduce light waves into neural impulses, thereby coding information about light and dark. (p. 79)

role playing: A therapeutic technique in which the therapist and client act as if they were people in problematic situations. (p. 424)

rooting reflex: An automatic response in which an infant turns its head toward stimulation on the cheek. (p. 250)

round window: The membrane that relieves pressure from the vibrating waves in the cochlear fluid. (p. 88)

saccule, utricle (sak′ūl ū′tre-k′l): Fluid-filled sacs of the vestibular organ that inform the brain about the body's orientation. (p. 91)

schema theory: The theory that information stored in LTM sometimes changes over time to become more consistent with our beliefs, knowledge, and expectations. (p. 185)

schizoid personality disorder (skiz′oid): A personality disorder characterized by blunted emotions, lack of interest in social relationships, and withdrawal into a solitary existence. (p. 403)

schizophrenia: A severe psychological disorder characterized by strange, false beliefs and distorted perceptions. (pp. 402)

science: Approach to knowledge based on systematic observation. (p. 5)

secondary reinforcers: Learned positive reinforcers. (p. 151)

secondary sex characteristics: Development of the breasts and hips in females; growth of the testes, broadening of the shoulders, lowered voice, and growth of the penis and facial hair in males; and growth of pubic and other body hair in both sexes. (p. 257)

sedatives: Depressants that in mild doses produce a state of calm relaxation. (p. 131)

self: According to humanists, the person one thinks one is. (p. 342)

self-actualization: According to Maslow, the seldomly reached full result of the inner-directed drive of humans to grow, improve, and use their potential to the fullest. (pp. 291)

self-concept: Our subjective perception of who we are and what we are like. (p. 342)

self-efficacy: According to Bandura, the perception of being capable of achieving one's goals. (p. 338)

self-regulation: According to Bandura, the process of cognitively reinforcing and punishing our own behavior, depending on whether it meets our personal standards. (p. 339)

semantic content: The meaning in symbols, such as language. (p. 211)

semantic memory (se-man'tik): Memory for meaning without reference to the time and place of learning. (p. 178)

semicircular canals (sem"ē-ser'kū-lar): Three nearly circular tubes in the vestibular organ that inform the brain about tilts of the head and body. (p. 91)

semipermeable (sem"e-per'mē-ah-b'l): A surface that allows some, but not all, particles to pass through. (p. 34)

sensation (sen-sā'shun): The process of receiving, translating, and transmitting messages from the outside world to the brain. (p. 74)

sense organs: Organs that receive stimuli. (p. 74)

sensorimotor stage: In Piaget's theory, the period of cognitive development from birth to 2 years. (p. 251)

sensory adaptation: Weakened magnitude of a sensation resulting from prolonged presentation of the stimulus. (p. 75)

sensory receptor cells: Cells in sense organs that translate messages into neural impulses that are sent to the brain. (p. 74)

sensory register: The first stage of memory, in which an exact image of each sensory experience is held briefly until it can be processed. (p. 174)

separation anxiety: The distress experienced by infants when they are separated from their caregivers. (p. 252)

septal area: The part of the limbic system that processes cognitive information in emotion. (p. 46)

serial position effect: Immediate recall of items listed in a fixed order is often better for items at the beginning and end of the list than for those in the middle. (p. 180)

serotonin (ser'uh-to"nin): A neurotransmitter used by systems of neurons believed to regulate sleep, dreaming, appetite, anxiety, depression, and the inhibition of violence. (p. 37)

sex: The distinction between male and female based on biological characteristics. (p. 308)

sexual orientation: The tendency to prefer romantic and sexual partners of the same or different sex. (p. 308)

shaping: A strategy of positively reinforcing behaviors that are successively more similar to desired behaviors. (p. 154)

short-term memory (STM): The second stage of memory, in which five to nine bits of information can be stored for brief periods of time. (p. 175)

situational attribution: An explanation for behavior that is based on an external cause. (p. 460)

situationism (sit"ū-ā'shun-izm): The view that behavior is not consistent but is strongly influenced by different situations. (p. 339)

Skinner box: A cage for animals, equipped with a response lever and a food tray dispenser, used in research on operant conditioning. (p. 154)

sleeper effects: According to Hovland, the potential for low-credibility speakers to influence opinion after a period of time. (p. 449)

social facilitation: An effect in which working in a group improves one's performance on individual projects. (p. 442)

social impairment: An effect in which working in a group impairs individual performance. (p. 442)

social learning theory: The viewpoint that the most important parts of our behavior are learned from other persons in society—family, friends, and culture. (pp. 11, 337)

social loafing: The tendency of members of groups to work less hard when group performance is measured than when individual performance is measured. (p. 442)

social norms: Guidelines provided by every culture for judging acceptable and unacceptable behavior. (p. 445)

social phobia: A phobic fear of social interactions, particularly those with strangers and those in which the person might be viewed negatively. (p. 391)

social psychology: The branch of psychology that studies individuals as they interact with others. (p. 440)

social roles: Culturally determined guidelines that tell people what behavior is expected of them. (p. 445)

social-role theory of gender differences: The theory that the opportunities and restrictions inherent in women's and men's different social roles create psychological gender differences. (p. 318)

social skills training: The use of techniques of operant conditioning to teach social skills to persons who lack them. (p. 424)

social support: The role played by friends and relatives in providing advice, assistance, and someone in whom to confide private feelings. (p. 367)

sociocultural perspective: The theory of psychology that states that it is necessary to understand one's culture, ethnic identity, and other sociocultural factors to fully understand a person. (p. 13)

solitary play: Playing alone. (p. 254)

somatic nervous system (sō-mat'ik): The division of the peripheral nervous system that carries messages from the sense organs, muscles, joints, and skin to the central nervous system and from the central nervous system to the skeletal muscles. (p. 39)

somatization disorders (sō"mah-ti-zā'shun): Intensely and chronically uncomfortable psychological conditions that involve numerous symptoms of somatic (body) illnesses without physical cause. (p. 394)

somatoform disorders (sō"mah'to-form): Disorders in which the individual experiences the symptoms of physical health problems that have psychological rather than physical causes. (p. 394)

somatoform pain disorders: Somatoform disorders in which the individual experiences a relatively specific and chronic pain that has a psychological rather than physical cause. (p. 395)

somatosensory area: The strip of parietal cortex running parallel to the motor area of the frontal lobes that plays a role in body senses. (p. 48)

sound waves: Vibratory changes in the air that carry sound. (p. 86)

specialized end bulbs: Sensory receptor cells that detect pressure and skin pleasure. (p. 92)

specific phobia: A phobic fear of one relatively specific thing. (p. 391)

spinal cord: The nerve fibers in the spinal column. (p. 32)

spontaneous recovery: A temporary increase in the strength of a conditioned response, which is likely to occur during extinction after the passage of time. (p. 162)

stage: One of several time periods in development that is qualitatively distinct from the periods that come before and after. (p. 243)

stage theory of memory: A model of memory based on the idea that we store information in three separate but linked memories. (p. 174)

standardization: Administering a test in the same way to all individuals. (p. 222)

stereochemical theory: The theory that different odor receptors can be stimulated only by molecules of a specific size and shape that fit them like a "key" in a lock. (p. 100)

stereotype: An inaccurate generalization on which a prejudice is based. (p. 454)

stimulants: Drugs that increase the activity of the central nervous system, providing a sense of energy and well-being. (p. 130)

stimulus (stim'ū-lus): Any aspect of the outside world that directly influences our behavior or conscious experience. (p. 74)

stimulus discrimination: The tendency for responses to occur more often in the presence of one stimulus than others. (p. 158)

stimulus generalization: The tendency for similar stimuli to elicit the same response. (p. 159)

stimulus incorporation: Stimuli that occur during sleep that are incorporated into dreams either directly or in altered form. (p. 124)

stress: Any event or circumstance that strains or exceeds an individual's ability to cope. (p. 358)

stroke: A rupture of a blood vessel in the brain that results in the destruction of a part of the brain. (p. 46)

structuralism (struk'tūr-al-izm): The nineteenth-century school of psychology that sought to determine the structure of the mind through controlled introspection. (p. 7)

subjective reality: Each person's unique perception of reality that, according to humanists, plays a key role in organizing our personalities. (p. 341)

sublimation (sub"li-mā'shun): According to Freud, a form of displacement in which a socially desirable goal is substituted for a socially harmful goal; the best form of displacement for society as a whole. (p. 334)

superego: According to Freud, that part of the mind that opposes the desires of the id by enforcing moral restrictions and by striving to attain perfection. (p. 334)

surface structure: The superficial spoken or written structure of a statement. (p. 211)

symbolization: In Rogers' theory, the process of representing experience, thoughts, or feelings in mental symbols of which we are aware. (p. 342)

sympathetic division (sim"pah-thet'ik): The division of the autonomic nervous system that generally activates internal organs during emotional arousal or when physical demands are placed on the body. (p. 40)

synapse (sin-aps'): The space between the axon of one neuron and the dendrite of another. (p. 35)

synaptic facilitation: The process by which neural activity causes structural changes in the synapses that facilitate more efficient learning and memory. (p. 189)

synaptic gap: The small space between two neurons at a synapse. (p. 35)

synaptic knobs (si-nap'tik): The knoblike tops of axons. (p. 35)

synaptic vesicles: Tiny vessels containing stored quantities of the neurotransmitter substance held in the synaptic knobs of the axon. (p. 35)

syntax (sin'taks): The grammatical rules of a language. (p. 212)

systematic desensitization: A behavior therapy method in which the client is taught not to fear phobic stimuli by learning to stay relaxed in the presence of successively more threatening stimuli. (p. 423)

tacit intelligence: The practical knowledge and skills needed to deal with everyday problems that are usually not taught in school. (p. 223)

tactile discs (tak'til): Sensory receptor cells that detect pressure. (p. 92)

taste cells: The sensory receptor cells for gustation located in the taste buds. (p. 99)

telegraphic speech: The abbreviated speech of 2-year-olds. (p. 252)

temporal lobes: The part of the cerebral cortex extending back from the area of the temples beneath the frontal and parietal lobes containing areas involved in the sense of hearing and understanding language. (p. 48)

testes (tes'tēz): Male endocrine glands that secrete sex-related hormones and produce sperm cells. (p. 56)

testosterone (tes-tos'ter-ōn): A male sex hormone. (p. 56)

thalamus (thal'ah-mus): The part of the forebrain that primarily routes sensory messages to appropriate parts of the brain. (p. 45)

theories: Tentative explanations of facts and relationships in sciences. (pp. 5)

thyroid gland (thī'roid): The gland below the voice box that regulates metabolism. (p. 56)

thyroxin (thī-rok'sin): A hormone produced by the thyroid that is necessary for proper mental development in children and helps determine weight and level of activity in adults. (p. 56)

timbre (tim'ber, tam'br): The characteristic quality of a sound as determined by the complexity of the sound wave. (p. 87)

traits: Relatively enduring patterns of behavior (thinking, acting, and feeling) that are relatively consistent across situations. (p. 328)

transduction (trans-duk'shun): The translation of energy from one form to another. (p. 74)

transductive reasoning (trans-duk'tiv): Errors in understanding cause-and-effect relationships that are commonly made by preoperational children. (p. 253)

transference (trans-fer'ens): The phenomenon in psychoanalysis in which the patient comes to feel and act toward the therapist in ways that resemble how he or she feels and acts toward other significant adults. (p. 417)

trial and error: The random application of one possible solution after another. (p. 208)

trichromatic theory (trī"krō-mat'ik): The theory of color vision contending that the eye has three different kinds of cones, each of which responds to light of one range of wavelength. (p. 82)

Type A personality: The pattern of behavior characterized most by intense competitiveness, hostility, overwork, and a sense of time urgency. (p. 369)

unconditioned response (UCR): An unlearned, inborn reaction to an unconditioned stimulus. (p. 145)

unconditioned stimulus (UCS): A stimulus that can elicit a response without any learning. (p. 145)

unconscious mind: The part of the mind of which we can never be directly aware; the storehouse of primitive instinctual motives and of memories and emotions that have been repressed. (pp. 11, 118, 332)

validity: The extent to which a test measures what it's supposed to measure. (p. 222)

variable interval schedule: A reinforcement schedule in which the reinforcer is given following the first response occurring after a variable amount of time. (p. 153)

variable ratio schedule: A reinforcement schedule in which the reinforcer is given after a varying number of responses have been made. (p. 152)

ventromedial hypothalamus: A part of the hypothalamus involved in inhibiting eating when sufficient food has been consumed (the satiety center). (p. 282)

vestibular organ (ves-tib′ū-lar): The sensory structures in the inner ear that provide the brain with information about movement. (p. 91)

vicarious punishment: Observed punishment of the behavior of a model, which also decreases the probability of the same behavior in the observer. (p. 167)

vicarious reinforcement (vī-kar′ē-us): Observed reinforcement of the behavior of a model, which also increases the probability of the same behavior in the observer. (p. 167)

visual acuity (vizh′u-al ah-ku′i-tē): Clearness and sharpness of vision. (p. 79)

wavelength: The frequency of light waves; it determines the color we see. (p. 78)

Weber's law: A law stating that the amount of change in a stimulus needed to detect a difference is in direct proportion to the intensity of the original stimulus. (p. 76)

Wernicke's aphasia: A form of aphasia in which persons can speak normally but cannot make sense out of language spoken to them by others. (p. 48)

Wernicke's area: The language area of the cortex that plays an essential role in understanding spoken language. (p. 48)

Yerkes-Dodson law: A law stating that effective performance is more likely if the level of arousal is suitable for the activity. (p. 287)

zygote (zī′gōt): The stable cell resulting from fertilization; in humans, it has 46 chromosomes—23 from the sperm and 23 from the ovum. (p. 58)

APPENDIX: Measurement and Statistics

Richard E. Mayer *University of California, Santa Barbara*

This appendix presents the basic concepts of measurement and statistics that are used in psychological research. It discusses how psychological characteristics are measured in quantitative (numerical) terms and how statistics are used to summarize quantitative findings and reach conclusions based on them. Even if you never conduct a psychological study, you need to learn about statistics and measurements in psychology for two reasons. First, the ability to read and evaluate the research that is presented in this textbook or discussed in class helps you avoid being intimidated by the research data of "experts"; it helps you assess the soundness of an experiment; and it helps you interpret the results. Second, a basic understanding of psychological statistics and measurement is rapidly becoming a "survival skill" for every educated member of our society. You need to avoid being fooled by "scientific" surveys, advertiser's evidence, and the like. You need to be able to recognize the difference between a useful study and one that is seriously flawed. Finally, you may need to be able to use basic statistics in your business or occupation. Thus, this appendix is designed to help you as a student and as an educated citizen.

For example, suppose you come across the following article in your local newspaper:

TV Viewing Linked to School Failure

Garden City—Researchers at State University have found that students who watch in excess of three hours of television per day get lower grades than other students. The study was based on a survey of students at Garden Valley School. The average student watched approximately two hours of TV per day. Efforts to discourage TV watching have been announced by the school's principal, Mr. George Elliot. "We must get our kids to stop watching TV," Mr. Elliot stated.

As you read this summary of a research study, you should ask yourself such questions as, Is this a sound study? and How should I interpret the results? After reading this appendix, you will be better able to answer questions like these concerning research studies that you read about.

▶ DESCRIPTIVE STATISTICS

One of the basic uses for statistics in psychological studies is to *describe behavior* in an understandable way. This is called *descriptive statistics*. Two common examples of descriptive statistics are as follows:

Describing behavior concerning one variable. For example, a study may report that the "average" student watches two hours of TV per day.

Describing the relation between two variables. For example, a study may report that students who watch more television tend to score lower on tests of school achievement than those who watch less.

As you can see, descriptive statistics summarize the data for a group of subjects. Figure A.1 summarizes these two uses of statistics that are discussed in the remainder of this part of the appendix.

In the Garden Valley study, the researchers obtained data on only a small number of schoolchildren from just one school; however, the researchers want to generalize their data

Use	Situation	Example	Typical statistics
Describing one variable	There is one score for each subject.	Each of 20 students in Mrs. Perkins's class tells how many hours he or she watched TV yesterday.	Frequency distribution Mean, median, or mode Standard deviation, variance, or range
Describing the relation between two variables	There are two scores for each subject—one score on variable X and one score on variable Y.	Each of 20 students in Mrs. Perkins's class tells how many hours he or she watched TV yesterday, and each student gets a score on the school achievement test.	Correlation

to all schoolchildren in the United States. Thus, it is important for you to understand the distinction between a *parameter* and a *statistic* as they are used here:

Parameter. Parameters are numbers that describe the behavior of an *entire population.* A population consists of all possible subjects, objects, or cases, such as all schoolchildren in the United States. For example, if we were to ask every schoolchild in the United States how many hours he or she watches TV each day, then we could develop parameters such as the average number of hours of TV viewing.

Statistic. Statistics are numbers that describe the behavior of only a *sample* drawn out of a larger population. A sample is a portion of an entire population, such as some of the schoolchildren at one school.

Sample statistics—such as the average number of hours of TV watching of some students at Garden Valley School—are rarely identical to population parameters, such as the average number of hours of TV viewing of all U.S. schoolchildren.

Another distinction that you need to understand is the difference between a *variable* and a *score:*

Variable. A variable is a measurable characteristic or behavior, such as age, sex, weight, height, or shoe size. In the Garden Valley study, one variable is the number of hours of TV viewing per day.

Score. A score is the value a given person has for a given variable, such as Joe's age being 27 years or his shoe size being 8 1/2. In the Garden Valley study, Mary watched three hours of TV per day, so her score is 3 on the variable "hours of TV viewing per day."

The data for a study consist of all the scores obtained for each variable that is used.

Describing Behavior Concerning One Variable

Problem

One of the major uses of statistics in psychology is to describe the behavior of a group on one variable. For example, the Garden Valley study attempted to describe the TV-viewing behavior of schoolchildren. Let's suppose that we go to Garden Valley School and ask 20 students from Mrs. Perkins's class to tell us how many hours they watched TV yesterday. Suppose that we get one answer from each student, as listed in the left panel of figure A.2.

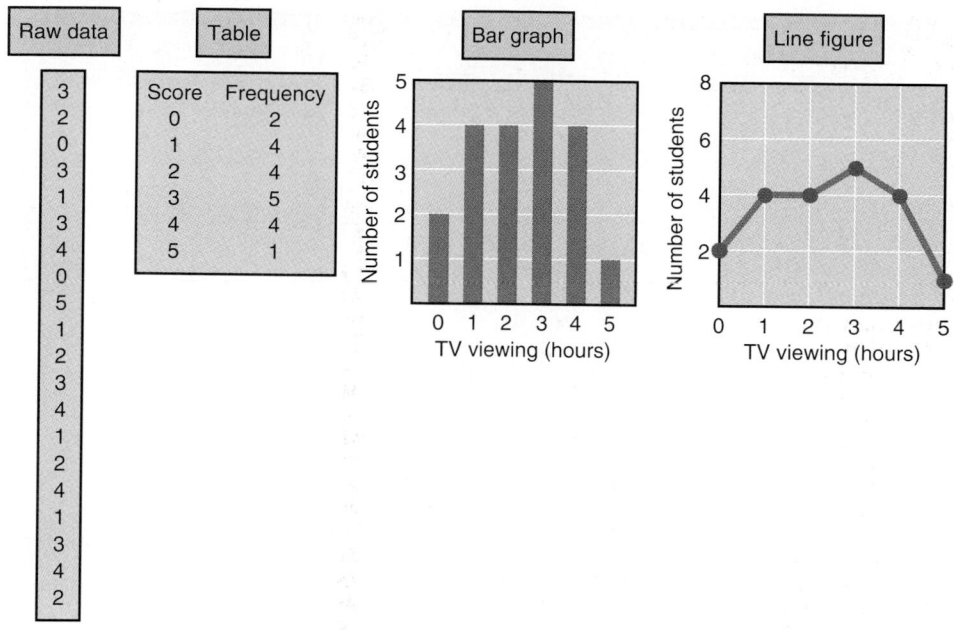

FIGURE A.2

Frequency distributions for some TV-viewing data.

Frequency Distribution

What are the TV-viewing habits of school students? One way to provide data for this question is simply to list the number of hours that each of 20 students reported watching TV. However, because it's hard to make much sense out of a long list of numbers, researchers often organize their data into a *frequency distribution*. A frequency distribution is a table or graph that shows the relationship between a score (such as number of hours of TV watching) and frequency (such as the number or percentage of students who gave each score).

Figure A.2 shows some frequency distributions for the TV-viewing data using the formats of a table, bar graph, and line figure. In the table, the first column gives the possible scores (0, 1, 2, 3, 4, or 5) for hours of TV viewing per day, and the second column gives the frequency of each score (that is, how many of the 20 students fell into that category). In the bar graph and line figure, the horizontal X-axis gives the possible scores and the vertical Y-axis gives the frequency.

Although the frequency distribution helps you organize data, you may want to summarize the description even further. You could summarize the frequency distribution by giving two numbers—a measure of *central tendency* and a measure of *dispersion*. A measure of central tendency tells where the middle of the distribution is, such as how many hours, on the average, do school students watch TV. A measure of dispersion tells you how spread out the scores are, such as how different are the school students in the number of hours they view TV? These are discussed in the next two subsections.

Central Tendency.   How many hours per day does the "average student" watch TV? There are three major measurers of central tendency: mean, median, and mode.

The *mean* is the arithmetic average of all the scores. To compute the mean, you simply add all the scores and divide the sum by the number of scores. The formula for finding the mean is $X = \Sigma X/n$, where $\overline{X}$ is the mean, ΣX is the sum or total of the scores, and n is the number of scores. The left portion of figure A.3 shows that the sum of the scores is 48, the number of scores is 20, and the mean is 2.4 hours. One problem with using mean as a measure of central tendency is that it's sensitive to extreme scores. For example, if the only student who reported watching 5 hours per day were to change his answer to 24 hours, the mean would increase considerably from 2.4 to 3.35.

The *median* is the score that divides the distribution in the middle, so that half of the frequency is greater than the median and half is less than the median. To determine the median, list the scores in ascending (or descending) order, and count down until you reach the

FIGURE A.3

Measures of central tendency for some TV-viewing data.

Mean	Median		Mode	
$\Sigma X = 3 + 2 + 0 + 3 + 1 + 3 + 4 +$ $0 + 5 + 1 + 2 + 3 + 4 + 1 +$ $2 + 4 + 1 + 3 + 4 + 2 = 48$ $n = 20$	Ranking	Scores in order	Score	Frequency
	1st	0	0	2
	2nd	0	1　Most	4
	3rd	1	2　frequent	4
	4th	1	3	5
$\overline{X} = \dfrac{\Sigma X}{n} = \dfrac{48}{20} = 2.4$	5th	1	4	4
	6th	1	5	1
	7th	2		
	8th	2	Mode = 3	
	9th　Middle of	2		
	10th　rankings	2		
	11th	3		
	12th	3		
	13th	3		
	14th	3		
	15th	3		
	16th	4		
	17th	4		
	18th	4		
	19th	4		
	20th	5		
	Median = point midway between 2 and 3 (i.e., 2.5)			

score in the middle. An example is given in the middle panel of figure A.3. As you can see, the median is not as sensitive to extreme scores. If the student who watched 5 hours were replaced by a student who watched 24 hours, the median would remain the same.

The *mode* is the score that occurs most often. For example, the mode in figure A.3 is 3 because five people watched TV for three hours while fewer than five watched TV for each other score. There can be ties among modes; for example, the scores 3, 1, 2, 1, 3, 0, 4, 1, 3, 5 have two modes—1 and 3. This called a *bimodal distribution* because there are two modes. If there is a tie among several scores, such as 1, 1, 2, 2, 3, 3, 4, 4, 0, 0, then there can be several modes—such as 5 modes in the preceding example. This is called a *multimodal distribution*. Although the mode is not often used in research studies, in some cases it may be preferred. For example, the designer of apartments will find it is *more useful* to know that the "modal" family unit is either 1 or 4 than to know that the mean family is 2.5. The builder who includes one-bedroom apartments for single adults is likely to rent the available space faster than the builder who believes that only two-bedroom apartments are needed for families with an average of 2.5 people.

Dispersion.　How different are the scores from one another? There are two major measures of dispersion from the central tendency: standard deviation and range.

The *standard deviation* is a sort of average difference between each score and the mean. It's a statistic that indicates how widely or narrowly scores are spread around the mean on the average. To compute the standard deviation, subtract the mean score from each score, square each of these differences, divide by the number of scores, and then take the square root. The formula for standard deviation is

$$s = \sqrt{\frac{\Sigma(X - \overline{X})^2}{n}}$$

where s is the standard deviation, $\Sigma(X - \overline{X})^2$ is the sum of the square of the differences, and n is the number of scores. The left panel of figure A.4 shows how to compute the standard deviation for TV-viewing scores.

FIGURE A.4

Measures of dispersion for some TV-viewing data.

Standard deviation			Range	

Raw data	Deviation $(X - \bar{X})$	Square of deviation $(X - \bar{X})^2$		
3	.6	.36	0	Lowest
2	−.4	.16	0	
0	−2.4	5.76	1	
3	.6	.36	1	
1	−1.4	1.96	1	
3	.6	.36	1	
4	1.6	2.56	2	
0	−2.4	5.76	2	
5	2.6	6.76	2	
1	−1.4	1.96	2	
2	−.4	.16	3	
3	.6	.36	3	
4	1.6	2.56	3	
1	−1.4	1.96	3	
2	−.4	.16	3	
4	1.6	2.56	4	
1	−1.4	1.96	4	
3	.6	.36	4	
4	1.6	2.56	4	
2	−.4	.16	5	Highest
		$\Sigma(X - \bar{X})^2 = 38.80$		

Range = (highest − lowest) + 1
Range = 5 − 0 + 1 = 6

$$S = \sqrt{\frac{\Sigma(X - \bar{X})^2}{n}} = \sqrt{\frac{38.8}{20}} = 1.39$$

The *range* is the distance between the highest score and the lowest score. To compute the range, simply subtract the lowest score from the highest and add 1. The right panel of figure A.4 shows that, if the lowest score is 0 and the highest score is 5, then the range is 6; that is, the distance between 0 and 5 is 6 units. The range is rarely used as a measure of dispersion because it's so sensitive to extreme scores. For example, if the student who watched 5 hours of TV were replaced by a student who watched 24 hours, the range would jump to 25.

Normal Curve. The scores for any frequency distribution can be plotted on a graph, as in the right-hand panel of figure A.2, and they can take a multitude of shapes. One important frequency distribution is the normal curve. It has fascinated scientists and statisticians because many different characteristics in nature tend to be normally distributed—such as adult height, weight, and intelligence. This does not mean they will have the same mean and standard deviation; rather, they all have the same general *shape* of frequency distribution. An example of a normal curve is given in figure A.5.

The normal curve is a frequency distribution that has the following characteristics:

Symmetrical. The right side is a mirror image of the left side.

Bell shaped. The most common scores are near the mean, with scores becoming less common as you move away from the mean in either direction.

68-95-99 density. The area on the normal curve that is within one standard deviation above the mean and one standard deviation below the mean contains 68.26 percent of the cases; within two standard deviations there are 95.42 percent of the cases; and within three standard deviations there are 99.74 percent of the cases.

To make sure that you understand the shape of the normal curve, let's try some examples. Look at the percentages of cases in each area of the normal curve in figure A.5.

FIGURE A.5

The normal curve.

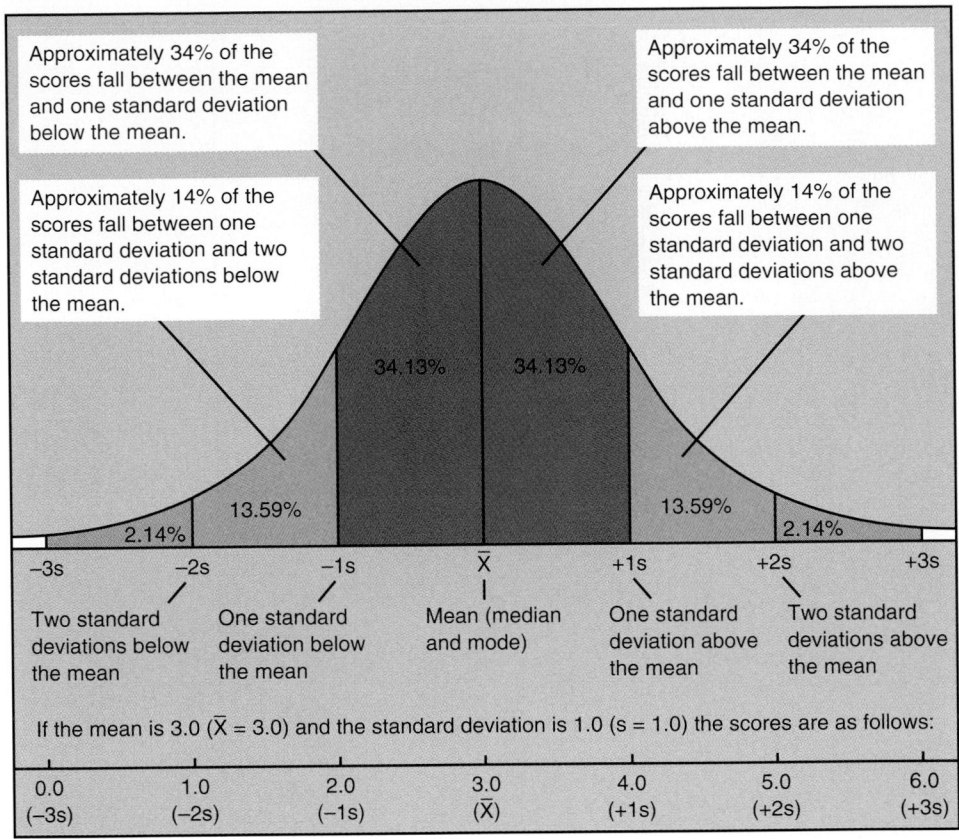

Approximately 34% of the scores fall between the mean and one standard deviation below the mean.

Approximately 14% of the scores fall between one standard deviation and two standard deviations below the mean.

Approximately 34% of the scores fall between the mean and one standard deviation above the mean.

Approximately 14% of the scores fall between one standard deviation and two standard deviations above the mean.

Suppose that Susan scores one standard deviation above the mean on a test. If the scores are normally distributed, she performed better than _____ percent of the class. Try another one: Tom scored one standard deviation below the mean, so he did better than _____ percent of the class. Finally, try this one: Mary scored better than 98 percent of the other students, so she scored _____ standard deviations (*above/below*) the mean. Look at figure A.6 for the answers.

Describing the Relation Between Two Variables

Problem

So far you have learned how to describe scores on one variable using statistics such as mean and standard deviation. However, your goal might be to describe the relation between two variables. For example, in the Garden Valley study, you might want to know whether there is any relation between the number of hours of TV viewing and the score on a school achievement test. Let's suppose we go to Garden Valley School and ask 10 students from Mrs. Perkins's class to tell us how many hours they watched TV yesterday and that we get test scores for each student's performance on a school achievement test. Thus, we will have two scores for each of 10 students, as listed in the left panel of figure A.7.

Scatter Plot

What is the relation between TV viewing and school achievement? One way to examine this question is to draw a scatter plot of the scores. A scatter plot is a graph consisting of two axes—such as hours of TV viewing on the X-axis and achievement score on the Y-axis—with one dot corresponding to each score on the two variables. An example for the Garden Valley study is shown in the right panel of figure A.7. As you can see, there seems to be a pattern in which a score on one axis is negatively, or inversely, related to a score on the other; in other words, the higher your TV-watching score, the lower your achievement score.

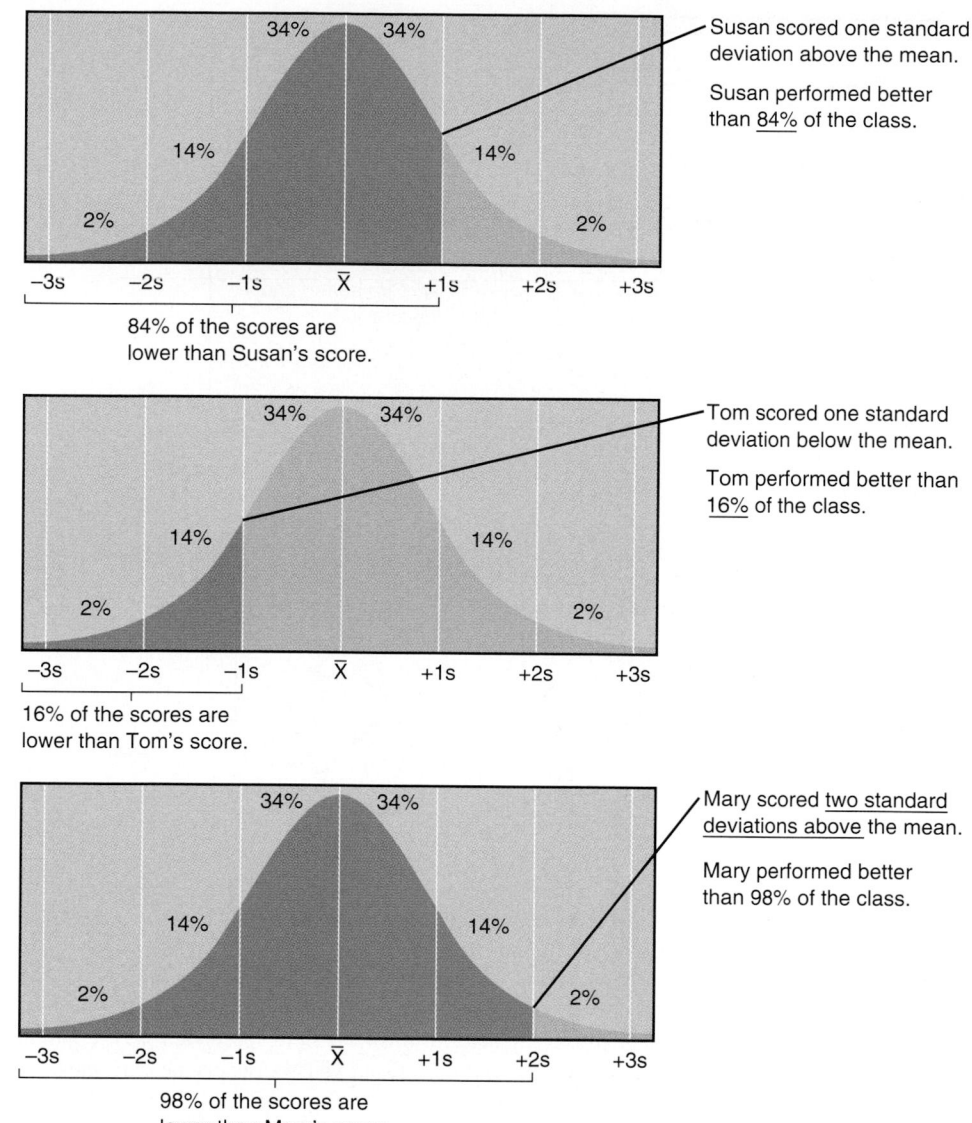

Susan scored one standard deviation above the mean.

Susan performed better than <u>84%</u> of the class.

84% of the scores are lower than Susan's score.

Tom scored one standard deviation below the mean.

Tom performed better than <u>16%</u> of the class.

16% of the scores are lower than Tom's score.

Mary scored <u>two standard deviations above</u> the mean.

Mary performed better than 98% of the class.

98% of the scores are lower than Mary's score.

FIGURE A.6

Three normal curves.

Figure A.8 shows five scatter plots, ranging from a strong positive correlation between the variables to no correlation to a strong negative correlation. Although scatter plots provide a general description of the relation between two variables, you may want to summarize the data even further. You could mathematically summarize your scatter plot by giving a quantitative measure of correlation.

Correlation

The *correlation coefficient* is a number between −1 and +1 that indicates the degree of correlation between two variables. A strong positive correlation (such as r = +.8) indicates that TV viewing is strongly related to school achievement, with more TV viewing corresponding to higher achievement. A strong negative correlation (such as r = −.8) indicates that TV viewing is strongly related to school achievement, with more TV viewing corresponding to lower achievement. A neutral correlation (coefficients close to r = .0) indicates that no relation exists between the two variables.

Figure A.8 shows the correlation coefficients for five scatter plots. You can think of correlation in the following way. First, draw a scatter plot. Then, draw a straight line through the scatter plot so that the distance between each dot and the line is minimized. The

Raw scores		
	TV-viewing score (X)	Achievement score (Y)
Student 1	2	25
Student 2	0	40
Student 3	1	40
Student 4	3	30
Student 5	5	5
Student 6	4	15
Student 7	3	20
Student 8	1	35
Student 9	2	30
Student 10	4	10

FIGURE A.7

Correlation between TV-viewing and achievement scores for 10 students.

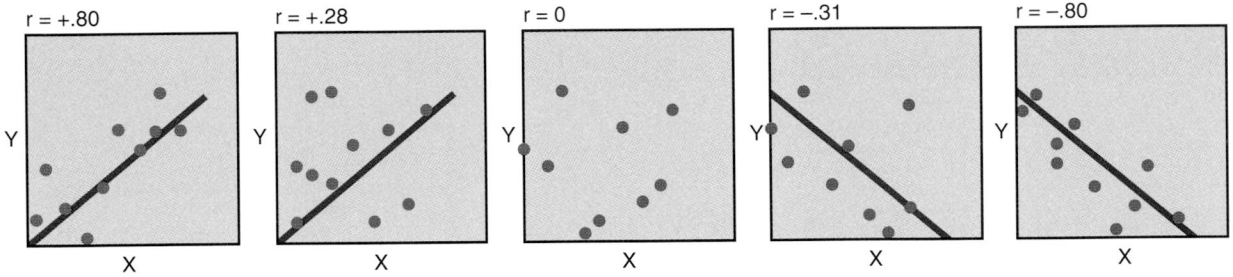

FIGURE A.8

Five scatter plots.

closer the dots are to the line, the stronger the relationship between the two variables—in either a positive correlation or a negative correlation. If the dots are spread across the whole graph, as in the middle panel of figure A.8, no correlation exists between the variables.

The formula for computing the correlation coefficient is

$$r = \frac{\Sigma xy}{\sqrt{\Sigma x^2 \cdot \Sigma y^2}}$$

where x is the difference between each X variable minus the mean; y is the difference between each Y variable and the mean; Σxy is the sum of the cross products (each x score multiplied by its corresponding y score); Σx^2 is the sum of the squares of the x scores; and Σy^2 is the sum of the squares of the y scores. Figure A.9 shows how to compute the value of r (that is, the correlation coefficient) for the Garden Valley data.

Correlation coefficients are very useful ways of summarizing the relation between variables, but they can lead to errors in interpretation. Whenever you are presented with a correlation coefficient, you should ask yourself "How should I interpret this correlation?" Some of the most common errors in interpretation follow:

Failure to recognize curvilinear trends. If you obtain a low correlation, this may be because no relation exists between the two variables, or it may be due to other factors. A correlation coefficient looks only for a straight-line relation between two variables; more of one variable is related to more (or less) of another variable. But some relationships between variables change as scores change, producing a curvilinear line that will not be reflected in the coefficient of correlation. Hence, a strong curvilinear relation may exist without producing a strong linear correlation coefficient. An example is shown in figure A.10. In this case, TV viewing up to three hours seems to

Subject	TV-viewing score (X)	Deviation $(X - \overline{X})$	Squared deviation $(X - \overline{X})^2$	Achievement score (Y)	Deviation $(Y - \overline{Y})$	Squared deviation $(Y - \overline{Y})^2$	Cross product $(X - \overline{X}) \cdot (Y - \overline{Y})$
1	2	−.5	.25	25	0	0	0
2	0	−2.5	6.25	40	15	225	−37.5
3	1	−1.5	2.25	40	15	225	−22.5
4	3	.5	.25	30	5	25	2.5
5	5	2.5	6.25	5	−20	400	−50.0
6	4	1.5	2.25	15	−10	100	−15.0
7	3	.5	.25	20	−5	25	−2.5
8	1	−1.5	2.25	35	10	100	−15.0
9	2	−.5	.25	30	5	25	−2.5
10	4	1.5	2.25	10	−15	225	−22.5
	$\overline{X} = 2.5$		$\Sigma(X - \overline{X})^2 = 22.50$	$\overline{X} = 25$		$\Sigma(Y - \overline{Y})^2 = 1350$	$\Sigma[(X - \overline{X}) \cdot (Y - \overline{Y})]$ $= -165$

$$r = \frac{\Sigma xy}{\sqrt{\Sigma x^2 \cdot \Sigma y^2}} = \frac{\Sigma[(X - \overline{X}) \cdot (Y - \overline{Y})]}{\sqrt{\Sigma(X - \overline{X})^2 \cdot \Sigma(Y - \overline{Y})^2}} = \frac{-165}{\sqrt{(22.50)(1350)}} = -.95$$

FIGURE A.9

How to compute a correlation coefficient.

FIGURE A.10

A curvilinear relation between two variables.

For 0 to 3 hours, TV-viewing and achievement scores are positively related.

For 3 to 5 hours, TV-viewing and achievement scores are negatively related.

Lack of a single linear trend produces a misleadingly low correlation.

$r = -.3$

be related positively with school achievement; thereafter, increased viewing is negatively related with school achievement.

Use of restricted range. A low correlation may also be due to using only a small range of scores along one of the variables. This is because there must be both high and low scores on each variable to see what is related to these scores. For example, if you do a separate correlation for heavy viewers (that is, three or more hours) and a separate correlation for light viewers (that is, zero to two hours), the correlation coefficients may be lowered because you included only high scores the first time and only low scores the second time. Because accurate correlations depend on the use of scores distributed across the entire range of both variables, restricting the range of one of the variables will artificially lower the correlation coefficient. Similarly, when conducting experiments using college students to see what is correlated with IQ, the experimenter may find low correlation coefficients, because most college students have high IQs and very few have lower IQs.

Inferred causation. If you obtain a high correlation (either negative or positive), you may want to make an inference concerning which variable *caused* the values of the other. For example, if TV viewing and school achievement are strongly negatively correlated, you might want to conclude that TV viewing causes poor school achievement. However, such a conclusion is not justified based on correlation coefficients.

Correlation does not mean causation. Correlation does not necessarily indicate that one variable caused the other. Although it's possible that TV viewing causes poor school achievement, it's just as logical to argue that lower school achievement causes increased TV viewing. (Students who do poorly in school are "turned off" to school, so they turn on the TV.) A third possibility is that both TV viewing and low school achievement are caused by a third variable not included in the study, such as the degree of family stability or student health.

▶ INFERENTIAL STATISTICS

Thus far you have learned how behavior can be described using statistics. In many cases, however, description of behavior is just the first step. The second basic use of statistics is to draw conclusions regarding hypotheses based on data. This is called *inferential statistics* because it involves making inferences about causes of behavior that can apply to the entire population from which the sample was taken.

Problem

In the Garden Valley study, we might want to know whether TV viewing causes poor school performance. To test this idea, we could ask 20 students from Mrs. Perkins's class to volunteer for a study of TV viewing and school achievement. We can divide our 20 students into two groups: those who are *asked* to watch two hours or less ("light group") and those who are *asked* to watch three hours or more ("heavy group"). This will provide us with two sets of achievement scores that can be analyzed with statistical tests. Figure A.11 shows the score on a school achievement test two weeks later for each of the students in the light group and each of the students in the heavy group.

Research Design

In the preceding example, we have conducted a formal experiment. To understand the nature of formal experiments, let's define some key terms:

Independent variable. The independent variable is what the experimenter tries to manipulate or to control the value of in the groups (or conditions or treatments). In the Garden Valley study, the independent variable is how much TV viewing the students were asked to do, and the two groups (or conditions or treatments) are heavy versus light.

Dependent variable. The dependent variable is the measurement that is taken as a result of the manipulations—that is, the score that each research participant gives as an outcome. In the Garden Valley study, the dependent variable is the score on the achievement test.

Hypothesis. The hypothesis is a prediction concerning the specific results of the study, in terms of the independent and dependent variables. For example, in the Garden Valley study, the hypothesis might be that heavy and light groups will not differ on school achievement scores.

Group	Achievement scores	Mean
Light	40, 35, 25, 30, 35, 40, 15, 20, 25, 35	$\bar{X}_1 = 30$
Heavy	15, 10, 20, 5, 15, 20, 25, 0, 5, 35	$\bar{X}_2 = 15$

The independent variable is amount of TV viewing.

The dependent variable is achievement score.

FIGURE A.11

Achievement scores for 10 heavy and 10 light TV viewers.

For any formal experiment that is limited to two variables, you should be able to identify the independent variable, the dependent variable, and the hypothesis.

Tests for Significance

Researchers will calculate the mean achievement score for each of the two groups and compare the results. In the Garden Valley study, the mean achievement score for the heavy TV viewers is 15, whereas the mean achievement score for the light TV viewers is 30. This does not necessarily mean that heavy TV viewers have lower scores than light viewers. Although it looks as if the heavy group scores lower than the light group, in this experiment the difference could be due to chance. For example, if you were to roll a die six times with your left hand, you might get 1, 2, 4, 3, 4, 1 for a mean of 2.5; then, if you were to roll the same die six times with your right hand, you might get 4, 6, 2, 5, 4, 3 for a mean of 4.0. This does not mean that your right hand is a better die roller than your left. The difference between 2.5 versus 4.0 is due to chance; in this case, if you had rolled the die 1,000 times with your left hand and then 1,000 times with your right, you probably would have gotten both means to average very near 3.5. Thus, in formal experiments it's possible to obtain a difference between the groups that is just due to chance. A statistical test can be performed to determine whether a difference between two means is *statistically significant*—in other words, a difference that is probably not due to chance.

A test of significance is used when each research participant has one score, and the researcher wants to determine whether the mean for one group is different from the mean for another group. The test will reveal whether the difference between the means is probably due to chance or to an actual difference between the groups. The researcher will report the results and include a *p-value,* which represents the level of significance. A p-value of .01 means that the difference in mean scores would be expected to occur by chance only 1 time out of every 100 trials, and a p-value of .05 means that the difference would be expected on the basis of chance 5 times out of 100. Usually, if a p-value is less than .05, then the differences obtained are tentatively accepted as genuine ones—that is, probably not due to chance. Such is the case with the Garden Valley data, which show the differences to exceed the .05 level of significance.

Misinterpretations

As with any statistical test, there are many ways to misinterpret the results. The following are some common mistakes:

Multiple tests. If the researcher obtains a significant result, this does not automatically guarantee that the difference is not due to chance. For example, let's suppose that we gave 20 different ability and achievement tests to our heavy and light groups and then looked for differences between the groups on each test. If we use a p-value of .05, this means that 5 percent of the time (or 1 out of 20) we would expect to find a significant difference that is due to chance. With 20 such tests, we could expect one of them to show a significant result just by chance. Thus, when an experimenter performs many statistical tests, you should be leery of the one or two tests that come out to be significant. To be on the safe side, you might like to see a replication—that is, a repeat of the same experiment with different participants.

Low sample size. If the researcher fails to obtain significant results, this does not guarantee that there is really no difference between the groups. When very low sample sizes are used (such as below 15 per group), one or two extreme scores can throw off the results. In general, small sample sizes require a larger difference between the means for the difference to be statistically significant. Thus, before you decide for sure that the difference is not significant, you should allow for a fair test—with several replications and adequate sample size.

REFERENCES

A

Abbott, B. B., Schoen, L. S., & Badia, P. (1984). Predictable and unpredictable shock: Behavioral measures of aversion and physiological measures of stress. *Psychological Bulletin, 96,* 45–71.

Ackerman, D. (1991). *A natural history of the senses.* New York: Vintage Books.

Ackerson, J., Scogin, F., McKendree-Smith, N., & Lyman, R. D. (1998). Cognitive bibliotherapy for mild and moderate adolescent depressive symptomatology. *Journal of Consulting and Clinical Psychology, 66,* 685–690.

Acocella, J. (1999). *Creating hysteria: Women and multiple personality disorder.* San Francisco: Jossey-Bass.

Adams, J. (1965). Inequity in social exchange. In L. Berkowitz (Ed.), *Advances in experimental social psychology* (Vol. 2). New York: Academic Press.

Adams, P. R., & Adams, G. R. (1984). Mount Saint Helens' ashfall: Evidence for a disaster stress reaction. *American Psychologist, 39,* 252–260.

Adelson, J. (1979, February). Adolescence and the generalization gap. *Psychology Today,* pp. 33–38.

Ader, R. (Ed.). (1981). *Psychoneuroimmunology.* New York: Academic Press.

Ader, R., & Cohen, N. (1981). Conditioned immunopharmacologic responses. In R. Ader (Ed.), *Psychoneuroimmunology.* New York: Academic Press.

Ader, R., & Cohen, N. (1993). Psychoneuroimmunology: Conditioning and stress. *Annual Review of Psychology, 44,* 53–85.

Adolphs, R., Tranel, D., & Denburg, N. (2000). Impaired emotional declarative memory following unilateral amygdala damage. *Learning and Memory, 7,* 180–186.

Allen, J. J., Iacono, W. G., Laravuso, J. J., & Dunn, L. A. (1995). An event-related potential investigation of posthypnotic recognition amnesia. *Journal of Abnormal Psychology, 104,* 421–430.

Allen, K. E., Hart, R. M., Buell, J. S., Harris, F. R., & Wolf, M. M. (1964). Effects of social reinforcement on isolate behavior of a nursery school child. *Child Development, 35,* 511–518.

Allen, L. S., & Gorski, R. A. (1992). Sexual orientation and the size of the anterior commissure in the human brain. *Proceedings of the National Academy of Sciences USA, 89,* 7199–7202.

Alloy, L. B., Abramson, L. Y., & Francis, E. L. (1999). Do negative cognitive styles confer vulnerability to depression? *Current Directions in Psychological Science 8,* 128–132.

Allport, G. W. (1937). *Personality: A psychological interpretation.* New York: Holt, Rinehart & Winston.

Allport, G. W. (1961). *Pattern and growth in personality.* New York: Holt, Rinehart & Winston.

Allport, G. W., & Odbert, H. S. (1936). Trait names: A psycholexical study. *Psychological Monographs, 47* (211), 1–171.

Altschule, M. D. (1965). *Roots of modern psychiatry* (2nd ed.). New York: Grune & Stratton.

American Psychological Association. (1982). *Ethical principles in the conduct of research with human participants.* Washington, DC: Author.

American Psychological Association. (1990). Ethical principles of psychologists. *American Psychologist, 45,* 390–395.

American Psychological Association. (1993). Guidelines for providers of psychological services to ethnic, linguistic, and culturally diverse populations. *American Psychologist, 48,* 45–48.

American Running and Physical Fitness Association. (1981). *Statistical report.* Washington, DC:

Amoore, J. E., Johnston, J. W., & Rubin, M. (1964, February). The stereo-chemical theory of odor. *Scientific American.*

Anderson, C. A. (1989). Temperature and aggression: Ubiquitous effects of heat on occurrence of human violence. *Psychological Bulletin, 106,* 74–96.

Anderson, C. A., Bushman, B. J., & Groom, R. W. (1997). Hot years and serious and deadly assault: Empirical tests of the heat hypothesis. *Journal of Personality and Social Psychology, 73,* 1213–1223.

Anderson, C. A., Lindsay, J. J., & Bushman, B. J. (1999). Research in the psychological laboratory: Truth or triviality? *Current Directions in Psychological Science, 8,* 3–9.

Anderson, K. E., Lytton, H., & Romney, D. M. (1986). Mother's interactions with normal and conduct-disordered boys: Who affects whom? *Developmental Psychology, 22,* 604–609.

Andreason, N. C. (1999). A unitary model of schizophrenia: Bleuler's "fragmented phrene" as schizoencephaly. *Archives of General Psychiatry, 56,* 781–787.

Andreasen, N. C., Arndt, S., Alliger, R., Miller, D., & Flaum, M. (1995). Symptoms of schizophrenia: Methods, meanings, and mechanisms. *Archives of General Psychiatry, 52,* 341–351.

Andrews, B., Brewin, C. R., Rose, S., & Kirk, M. (2000). Predicting PTSD symptoms in victims of violent crime: The role of shame, anger, and childhood abuse. *Journal of Abnormal Psychology, 109,* 69–73.

Angoff, W. H. (1988). The nature-nurture debate, aptitudes, and group differences. *American Psychologist, 43,* 713–720.

Antoni, M. H., & others. (1990). Psychoneuroimmunology and HIV-1. *Journal of Consulting and Clinical Psychology, 58,* 38–49.

Antoni, M. H., Cruess, D. G., Cruess, S., Lutgendorf, S., Kumar, M., Ironson, G., Klimas, N., Fletcher, M. A., & Schneiderman, N. (2000). Cogitive-behavioral stress management intervention effects on anxiety, 24-hr urinary norepinephrine output, and T-cytotoxic suppressor cells over time among symptomatic HIV-infected gay men. *Journal of Consulting and Clinical Psychology, 68,* 31–45.

Ardrey, R. (1966). *The territorial imperative.* New York: Atheneum.

Arndt, S., Andreasen, N. C., Flaum, M., Miller, D., & Nopoulos, P. (1995). A longitudinal study of symptom dimensions in schizophrenia: Prediction and patterns of change. *Archives of General Psychiatry, 52,* 352–360.

Arnett, J. J. (1999). Adolescent storm and stress, reconsidered. *American Psychologist, 54,* 317–326.

Arnetz, B., & others. (1987). Immune function in unemployed women. *Psychosomatic Medicine, 49,* 3–18.

Arnold, M. B. (1960). *Emotion and personality* (2 Vols.). New York: Columbia University Press.

Aronson, E. (1995). *The social animal* (6th ed.). San Francisco: W. H. Freeman.

Aronson, E., & Golden, B. (1962). The effect of relevant and irrelevant aspects of communicator credibility on opinion change. *Journal of Personality, 30,* 135–146.

Aronson, E., Willerman, B., & Floyd, J. (1966). The effect of a pratfall on increasing interpersonal attractiveness. *Psychonomic Science, 4,* 227–228.

Asarnow, J., Glynn, S., Pynoos, R. S., Nahum, J., Guthrie, D., Cantwell, D. P., & Franklin, B. (1999). When the earth stops shaking: Earthquake sequelae among children diagnosed for pre-earthquake psychopathology. *Journal of the American Academy of Child and Adolescent Psychiatry, 38,* 1016–1023.

Asch, S. (1946). Forming impressions of personality. *Journal of Abnormal and Social Psychology, 41,* 258–290.

Asch, S. (1956). Studies of independence and conformity. A minority of one against a unanimous majority. *Psychological Monographs, 70* (9, Whole No. 416).

Aschoff, J. (1981). *Handbook of behavioral neurobiology: Vol. 4. Biological rhythms.* New York: Plenum.

Association for Advancement of Behavior Therapy. (1978). *Ethical issues for human services* (pamphlet). New York: Author.

Atkeson, B. M., Forehand, R. L., & Rickard, K. M. (1982). The effects of divorce on children. In B. B. Lahey & A. E. Kazdin (Eds.), *Advances in clinical child psychology* (Vol. 5). New York: Plenum.

Atkinson, R. C., & Shiffrin, R. M. (1968). Human memory: A proposed system and its control processes. In K. W. Spence & J. T. Spence (Eds.), *The psychology of learning and motivation* (Vol. 2). New York: Academic Press.

Ausubel, D. P. (1960). The use of advance organizers in the learning and retention of meaningful verbal material. *Journal of Educational Psychology, 51,* 267–272.

Ayllon, T., & Haughton, E. (1964). Modification of the symptomatic verbal behaviour of mental patients. *Behaviour Research and Therapy, 2,* 87–97.

B

Baddeley, A. (1992). Working memory. *Science, 255,* 556–559.

Baddeley, A. (1998). Recent developments in working memory. *Current Opinion in Neurobiology, 8,* 234–238.

Baddeley, A. D. (1999). *Essentials of human memory.* Hove, England: Psychology Press/Taylor & Francis.

Baer, L., Rauch, S. L., Ballantine, T., Martuza, R., Cosgrove, R., Cassem, E., Giriunas, I., Manzo, P. A., Domino, C., & Jenike, M. A. (1995). Cingulotomy for intractable obsessive-compulsive disorder. *Archives of General Psychiatry, 52,* 384–392.

Bagley, C., & Binitie, A. (1970). Alcoholism and schizophrenia in Irishmen in London. *British Journal of Psychiatry, 17,* 292–304.

Bahrick, H. P. (1984). Semantic memory content in permastore: 50 years of memory for Spanish learned in school. *Journal of Experimental Psychology: General, 113,* 1–29.

Bahrick, H. P., Bahrick, L. E., Bahrick, A. S., & Bahrick, P. E. (1993). Maintenance of foreign language vocabulary and the spacing effect. *Psychological Science, 4,* 316–321.

Bahrick, H. P., Bahrick, P. O., & Wittlinger, R. P. (1975). Fifty years of memory for names and faces: A cross-sectional approach. *Journal of Experimental Psychology, 104,* 54–75.

Baltes, P. B., & Staudinger, U. M. (1993). The search for a psychology of wisdom. *Current Directions in Psychological Science, 2,* 75–80.

Banaji, M. R., & Bhaskar, R. (1999). Implicit stereotypes and memory: The bounded rationality of social beliefs. In D. L. Schachter & E. Scarry (Eds.), *Memory, brain, and belief.* Cambridge, MA: Harvard University Press.

Bandelow, B., Wedekind, D., Pauls, J., Broocks, A., Hajak, G., & Ruther, E. (2000). Salivary cortisol in panic attacks. *American Journal of Psychiatry, 157,* 454–456.

Bandura, A. (1973). *Aggression: A social learning analysis.* Englewood Cliffs, NJ: Prentice-Hall.

Bandura, A. (1977). *Social learning theory.* Englewood Cliffs, NJ: Prentice-Hall.

Bandura, A. (1982). Self-efficacy mechanism in human agency. *American Psychologist, 37,* 122–147.

Bandura, A. (1989). Human agency in social cognitive theory. *American Psychologist, 44,* 1175–1184.

Bandura, A. (1999). Social cognitive theory of personality. In D. Cervone & others (Eds.), *The coherence of personality: Social cognitive bases of consistency, variability, and organization* (pp. 185–241). New York: Guilford Press.

Bandura, A., Blanchard, E. B., & Ritter, B. (1969). The relative efficacy of desensitization and modeling approaches for inducing behavioral, affective, and attitudinal changes. *Journal of Personality and Social Psychology, 13,* 173–199.

Bandura, A., Ross, D., & Ross, S. A. (1963). Imitation of film-mediated aggressive models. *Journal of Abnormal and Social Psychology, 66,* 3–11.

Banich, M. T. (1998). Integration of information between the two cerebral hemispheres. *Current Directions in Psychological Science, 7,* 32–37.

Banich, M. T., & Heller W. (1998). Evolving perspectives on lateralization of function. *Current Directions in Psychological Science, 7,* 1–2.

Banks, M., & Salapatek, P. (1981). Infant pattern vision: A new approach based on the contrast sensitivity function. *Journal of Experimental Child Psychology, 31,* 1–45.

Barahal, H. S. (1958). 1000 prefrontal lobotomies. Five- to ten-year follow-up study. *Psychiatric Quarterly, 32,* 653–678.

Barber, T. X. (1969). *Hypnosis: A scientific approach.* New York: Van Nostrand Reinhold.

Barber, T. X., & Wilson, S. C. (1977). Hypnosis, suggestions, and altered states of consciousness. Experimental evaluation of the new cognitive behavioral theory and the traditional trance-state theory of hypnosis. In W. E. Edmundson (Ed.), *Conceptual and investigative approaches to hypnosis and hypnotic phenomena.* New York: New York Academy of Sciences.

Barger, S. D., Kircher, J. C., & Croyle, R. T. (1997). The effects of social context and defensiveness on the physiological responses of repressive copers. *Journal of Personality and Social Psychology, 73*(5), 1118–1128.

Barlow, D. H. (1996). Health care policy, psychotherapy research, and the future of psychotherapy. *American Psychologist, 51,* 1050–1058.

Barlow, D. H., & Lehman, C. L. (1996). Advances in the psychosocial treatment of anxiety disorders: Implications for national health care. *Archives of General Psychiatry, 53,* 727–735.

Barnes, K. E. (1971). Preschool play norms. A replication. *Developmental Psychology, 5,* 99–103.

Baron, J. B., & Sternberg, R. J. (Eds.). (1987). *Teaching thinking skills.* San Francisco: W. H. Freeman.

Baron, R., & Byrne, D. (1982). *Exploring social psychology* (2nd ed.). Boston: Allyn & Bacon.

Barr, C. E., Mednick, S. A., & Munk-Jorgensen, P. (1990). Exposure to influenza epidemics during gestation and adult schizophrenia. *Archives of General Psychiatry, 47,* 869–874.

Barrett, D. H., Resnick, H. S., Foy, D. W., & Dansky, B. S. (1996). Combat exposure and adult psychosocial adjustment among U.S. army veterans serving in Vietnam, 1965–1971. *Journal of Abnormal Psychology, 105*(4), 575–581.

Barsky, A. J., Fama, J. M., Bailey, E. D., & Ahern, D. K. (1998). A prospective 4- to 5-year study of DSM-III-R hypochondriasis. *Archives of General Psychiatry, 55,* 737–744.

Bartlett, F. C. (1932). *Remembering: A study in experimental and social psychology.* New York: Cambridge University Press.

Barton, J. L. (1977). ECT in depression: The evidence of controlled studies. *Biological Psychiatry, 12,* 687–695.

Bartoshuk, L. (1988). Taste. In R. C. Atkinson, R. J. Herrnstein, G. Lindzey, & R. D. Luce (Eds.), *Stevens' handbook of experimental psychology: Vol. 1. Perception and motivation.* New York: Wiley-Interscience.

Bashore, T. R., Ridderinkhof, R., & van der Molen, M. W. (1997). The decline of cognitive processing speed in old age. *Current Directions in Psychological Science, 6,* 163–169.

Baumrind, D. (1972). An exploratory study of socialization effects on Black children: Some Black-White comparisons. *Child Development, 43,* 261–267.

Baumrind, D. (1983). Rejoinder to Lewis's reinterpretation of parental firm control effects: Are authoritative families really harmonious? *Psychological Bulletin, 94,* 132–142.

Baumrind, D. (1991). Parenting styles and adolescent development. In J. Brooks-Gunn, R. Lerner, & A. Peterson (Eds.), *The encyclopedia of adolescence.* New York: Garland.

Baxter, L. R., Schwartz, J. M., Bergman, K. S., & Szuba, M. P. (1992). Caudate glucose metabolic rate changes with both drug and behavior therapy for obsessive-compulsive disorder. *Archives of General Psychiatry, 49,* 681–689.

Beatty, J. (1995). *Principles of behavioral neuroscience.* Madison, WI: Brown & Benchmark.

Beck, A. T. (1976). *Cognitive therapy and the emotional disorders.* New York: International Universities Press.

Beck, A. T. (1999). *Prisoners of hate: The cognitive basis of anger, hostility, and violence.* New York: HarperCollins.

Beck, A. T., Rush, A. J., Shaw, B. F., & Emery, G. (1979). *Cognitive therapy of depression.* New York: Guilford Press.

Beeman, M. J., & Chiarello, C. (1998). Complementary right- and left-hemisphere language comprehension. *Current Directions in Psychological Science, 7,* 2–8.

Behrman, J., & Levy, R. (1970). Neurophysiological studies on patients with hysterical disturbances of vision. *Journal of Psychosomatic Research, 14,* 187–194.

Bell, R. Q. (1968). A reinterpretation of the direction of effects in studies of socialization. *Psychological Review, 75,* 81–95.

Bellodi, L., Perna, G., Caldirola, D., Arancio, C., Bertani, A., & Di Bella, D. (1998). CO_2-induced panic attacks: A twin study. *American Journal of Psychiatry, 155*(9), 1184–1188.

Belmore, S. M. (1987). Determinants of attention during impression formation. *Journal of Experimental Psychology: Learning, Memory, and Cognition, 13,* 480–489.

Belmore, S. M., & Hubbard, M. L. (1987). The role of advance expectancies in person memory. *Journal of Personality and Social Psychology, 53,* 61–70.

Bem, D. J. (1996). Exotic becomes erotic: A developmental theory of sexual orientation. *Psychological Review, 103,* 320–335.

Bem, D. J., & Allen, A. (1974). On predicting some of the people some of the time: The search for cross-situational consistencies in behavior. *Psychological Review, 81,* 506–520.

Bem, S. (1974). The measurement of psychological androgyny. *Journal of Consulting and Clinical Psychology, 42,* 155–162.

Benedict, R. F. (1934). *Patterns of culture.* Boston: Houghton Mifflin.

Benes, F. M. (1998). Images in neuroscience: Brain development, VIII. *American Journal of Psychiatry, 155,* 1489.

Benschop, R. J., Geenen, R., Mills, P. J., Naliboff, B. D., Kiecolt-Glaser, J. K., Herbert, T. B., van der Pompe, G., Miller, G. E., Matthews, K. A., Godaert, G. L., Gilmore, S. L., Glaser, R., Heijnen, C. J., Dopp, J. M., Bijlsma, J. W. J., Solomon, G. F., & Cacioppo, J. T. (1998). Cardiovascular and immune responses to acute psychological stress in young and old women: A meta-analysis. *Psychosomatic Medicine, 60,* 289–296.

Berger, K. S. (1986). *The developing person through childhood and adolescence* (2nd ed.). New York: Worth.

Berkowitz, L. (1989). Frustration-aggression hypothesis: Examination and reformulation. *Psychological Bulletin, 106,* 59–73.

Berkowitz, L. (1993). *Aggression: Its causes, consequences, and control.* New York: McGraw-Hill.

Berlin, B., & Kay, P. (1969). *Basic color terms: Their universality and evolution.* Berkeley: University of California Press.

Bernstein, I. L., Webster, M. M., & Bernstein, P. (1982). Food aversions in children receiving chemotherapy for cancer. *Cancer, 50,* 2961–2963.

Berry, J. W., & Bennett, J. A. (1992). Cree conceptions of cognitive competence. *International Journal of Psychology, 27,* 1, 73–88.

Berscheid, E., Dion, K. K., Walster, E., & Walster, G. W. (1971). Physical attractiveness and dating choice: A test of the matching hypothesis. *Journal of Experimental Social Psychology, 7,* 173–189.

Bettencourt, B. A., & Miller, N. (1996). Gender differences in aggression as a function of provocation: A meta-analysis. *Psychological Bulletin, 119,* 422–447.

Betancourt, H., & Lopez, S. R. (1993). The study of culture, ethnicity, and race in American psychology. *American Psychologist, 48,* 6, 629.

Biernat, M., & Kobrynowicz, D. (1997). Gender- and race-based standards of competence: Lower minimum standards but higher ability standards for devalued groups. *Journal of Personality and Social Psychology, 72*, 544–557.

Bigelow, H. J. (1850). Dr. Harlow's case of recovery from the passage of an iron bar through the head. *American Journal of Medical Science, 20*, 13–22.

Birch, H. C. (1945). The relation of previous experience to insightful problem solving. *Journal of Comparative Psychology, 38*, 367–383.

Bjorklund, D. F., & Green, B. L. (1992). The adaptive nature of cognitive immaturity. *American Psychologist, 47*, 46–54.

Bjorklund, D. F., & Kipp, K. (1999). Parental investment theory and gender differences in the evolution of inhibition mechanisms. *Psychological Bulletin, 120*, 163–188.

Bjorklund, D. F., & Shackleford, T. K. (1999). Differences in parental investment contribute to differences between men and women. *Current Directions in Psychological Science, 8*, 86–89.

Blanchard, R., & others. (1995). Birth order and sibling sex ratio in homosexual male adolescents and probably pre-homosexual feminine boys. *Developmental Psychology, 31*, 22–30.

Blanchard, R., & others. (1996). Birth order and sibling sex ratio in two samples of Dutch gender-dysphoric homosexual males. *Archives of Sexual Behavior, 25*, 495–514.

Blonder, L. X., Bowers, D., & Heilman, K. M. (1991). The role of the right hemisphere in emotional communication. *Brain, 114*, 1115–1127.

Bock, M. (1986). The influence of emotional meaning on the recall of words processed for form or self-reference. *Psychological Research, 48*, 107–112.

Bock, M., & Klinger, E. (1986). Interaction of emotion and cognition in word recall. *Psychological Research, 48*, 99–100.

Bogaert, A. F. (1998). Birth order and sibling sex ratio in homosexual and heterosexual non-white men. *Archives of Sexual Behavior, 27*, 467–473.

Bond, R., & Smith, P. B. (1996). Culture and conformity: A meta-analysis of studies using Asch's (1952b, 1956) line judgment task. *Psychological Bulletin, 119*, 111–137.

Borch-Jacobsen, M. (1997). Sybil—The making and marketing of a disease: An interview with Herbert Spiegel. In T. Dufresne (Ed.), *Freud under analysis: History, theory, practice: Essays in honor of Paul Roazen*. Northvale, NJ: Jason Aronson.

Borkovec, T. D., & Costello, E. (1993). Efficacy of applied relaxation and cognitive-behavioral therapy in the treatment of generalized anxiety disorder. *Journal of Consulting and Clinical Psychology, 61*, 611–619.

Bouchard, T. J., & McGue, M. (1981). Familial studies of intelligence: A review. *Science, 212*, 1055–1059.

Bousfield, W. A. (1953). The occurrence of clustering in recall of randomly arranged associates. *Journal of General Psychology, 49*, 229–240.

Bousfield, W. A., & Sedgwick, C. H. (1944). An analysis of sequences of restricted associative responses. *Journal of General Psychology, 30*, 149–165.

Bower, G. H. (1973). Educational applications of mnemonic devices. In K. O. Doyle (Ed.), *Interaction: Readings in human psychology*. Boston: D. C. Heath.

Bower, G. H., & Clark, M. C. (1969). Narrative stories as mediators for serial learning. *Psychonomic Science, 14*, 181–182.

Bower, J. E., Kemeny, M. E., Taylor, S. E., & Fahey, J. L. (1998). Cognitive processing, discovery of meaning, CD-4 decline, and AIDS-related mortality among bereaved HIV-seropositive men. *Journal of Consulting and Clinical Psychology, 66*, 979–986.

Bower, T. G. R. (1971). The object in the world of the infant. *Scientific American*, pp. 30–38.

Bowers, K. S. (1976). *Hypnosis for the seriously curious*. Monterey, CA: Brooks/Cole.

Bracha, H. S., Torrey, E. F., Gottesman, I. I., Bigelow, L. B., & Cunniff, C. (1992). Second-trimester markers of fetal size in schizophrenia: A study of monozygotic twins. *American Journal of Psychiatry, 149*, 1355–1361.

Bransford, J. D., & Franks, J. J. (1971). The abstraction of linguistic ideas. *Cognitive Psychology, 2*, 331–350.

Braverman, L. B. (1989). Beyond the myth of motherhood. In M. McGoldrick, C. M. Anderson, & F. Walsh (Eds.), *Women and families*. New York: Free Press.

Bregante, J. L., Martinez, K., & O'Toole, C. J. (1993). *New bridges: Building community between disabled and nondisabled women*. Presentation at the Fifth International Interdisciplinary Conference on Women.

Breier, A., Schreiber, J. L., Dyer, J., & Pickar, D. (1991). National Institute of Mental Health longitudinal study of chronic schizophrenia: Prognosis and predictors of outcome. *Archives of General Psychiatry, 48*, 239–246.

Brent D. A., & Kolko, D. J. (1998). Psychotherapy: Definitions, mechanisms of action, and relationship to etiological models. *Journal of Abnormal Child Psychology, 26*, 17–25.

Breslau, N., Davis, G. C., Peterson, E. L., & Schultz, L. (1997). Psychiatric sequelae of posttraumatic stress disorder in women. *Archives of General Psychiatry, 54*, 81–87.

Breslau, N., Kessler, R. C., Chilcoat, H. D., Schultz, L. R., Davis, G. C., & Andreski, P. (1998). Trauma and posttraumatic stress disorder in the community. *Archives of General Psychiatry, 55*, 626–632.

Brewin, C. R., Andrews, B., Rose, S., & Kirk, M. (1999). Acute stress disorder and posttraumatic stress disorder in victims of violent crime. *American Journal of Psychiatry, 156*, 360–366.

Briggs, G. C., Freeman, R. K., & Yaffe, S. J. (1986). *Drugs in pregnancy and lactation*. Baltimore: Williams & Wilkins.

Brody, N. (1997). Intelligence, schooling, and society. *American Psychologist, 52*, 1046–1050.

Brooks, C. M. (1988). The history of thought concerning the hypothalamus and its functions. *Brain Research Bulletin, 20*, 657–667.

Brosnahan, M., & Giffen, D. (1993). Out of hospitals, left on the streets. *New York Times*, No. 49, 416, pp. 7–11.

Brown, G. P., Hammen, C. L., Craske, M. G., & Wickens, T. D. (1995). Dimensions of dysfunctional attitudes as vulnerabilities to depressive symptoms. *Journal of Abnormal Psychology, 104*, 431–435.

Brown, R., & Kulik, J. (1977). Flashbulb memories. *Cognition, 5*, 73–99.

Brownell, K. D., & Rodin, J. (1994). The dieting maelstrom: Is it possible and advisable to lose weight? *American Psychologist, 49*, 781–791.

Bruce, T. J., Spiegel, D. A., Gregg, S. F., & Nuzzarello, A. (1995). Predictors of alprazolam discontinuation with and without cognitive behavior therapy in panic disorder. *American Journal of Psychiatry, 152*, 1156–1160.

Bruner, J. S. (Ed.). (1974). *The growth of competence*. New York: Academic Press.

Bruner, J. S., & Goodman, C. C. (1947). Value and need as organizing factors in perception. *Journal of Abnormal and Social Psychology, 42*, 33–44.

Buchsbaum, M. (1983). The mind readers. *Psychology Today*, pp. 58–62.

Buckhout, R. (1974). Eyewitness testimony. *Scientific American*, pp. 23–33.

Buckner, R. L., & Barch, D. (1999). Memory, 1: Episodic memory retrieval. *American Journal of Psychiatry, 156*, 1311.

Buenker, J. D., & Ratner, L. (1992). *Multiculturalism in the United States: A comparative guide to acculturation and ethnicity*. Westport, CT: Greenwood.

Burchinal, M. R., Campbell, F. A., Bryant, D. M., Wasik, B. H., & Ramey, C. T. (1997). Early intervention and mediating processes in cognitive performance of children of low-income African American families. *Child Development, 68*, 935–954.

Burger, J. M. (1986). Temporal effects on attributions: Actor and observer differences. *Social Cognition, 4*, 377–387.

Burgess, A. W., & Holstrom, K. L. (1974). Rape trauma syndrome. *American Journal of Psychiatry, 131*, 981–986.

Burling, T. A., & others. (1989). Computerized smoking cessation program for the worksite: Treatment outcome and feasibility. *Journal of Consulting and Clinical Psychology, 57*, 619–622.

Buss, A. (1989). Personality as traits. *American Psychologist, 44*, 1378–1388.

Buss, D. M. (1995). Psychological sex differences: Origins through sexual selection. *American Psychologist, 50*, 164–168.

Buss, D. M. (1999). Human nature and individual differences: The evolution of human personality. In L. A. Pervin & O. P. John (Eds.), *Handbook of personality: Theory and research* (2nd ed.), (pp. 31–56). New York: Guilford.

Bussey, K., & Bandura, A. (1999). Social cognitive theory of gender development and differentiation. *Psychological Review, 106*, 676–713.

Butcher, H. J. (1968). *Human intelligence: Its nature and assessment*. New York: Harper Torchbooks.

Butler, R. A. (1953). Discrimination learning by rhesus monkey by visual-exploration motivation. *Journal of Comparative and Physiological Psychology, 46*, 95–98.

Byrnes, J. P., Miller, D. C., & Schafer, W. D. (1999). Gender differences in risk taking: A meta-analysis. *Psychological Bulletin, 125*, 367–383.

Cain, W. S. (1988). Olfaction. In R. C. Atkinson, R. J. Herrnstein, G. Lindzey, & R. D. Luce (Eds.), *Stevens' handbook of experimental psychology: Vol. 1. Perception and motivation*. New York: Wiley-Interscience.

Calahan, D. (1970). *Problem drinkers*. San Francisco: Jossey-Bass.

Calahan, D., & Room, R. (1974). *Problem drinking among American men*. New Brunswick, NJ: Rutgers Center of Alcohol Studies.

Calkins, M. W. (1893). Statistics of dreams. *American Journal of Psychology, 5*, 311–343.

Campbell, D. E. (1961). The psychological effects of cerebral electroshock. In H. J. Eysenck (Ed.), *Handbook of abnormal psychology*. New York: Basic Books.

Campbell, F. A., & Ramey, C. T. (1994). Effects of early intervention on intellectual and academic achievement: A follow-up study of children from low-income families. *Child Development, 65*, 684–698.

Campbell, F. A., & Ramey, C. T. (1995). Cognitive and school outcomes for high-risk African American students at middle adolescence: Positive effects of early intervention. *American Educational Research Journal, 32*, 743–772.

Cannon, T. D., Mednick, S. A., Parnas, J., Schulsinger, F., Praestholm, J., & Vestergaard, A. (1993). Developmental brain abnormalities in the offspring of schizophrenic mothers: I. Contributions of genetic and perinatal factors. *Archives of General Psychiatry, 50*, 551–564.

Cannon, T. D., vanErp, T. G. M., Huttunen, M., Lonnqvist, J., Salonen, O., Valanne, L., Poutanen, V. P., Standertskjold-Nordenstam, C. G., Gur, R. E., & Yan, M. (1998). Regional gray matter, white matter, and cerebrospinal fluid distributions in schizophrenic patients, their siblings, and controls. *Archives of General Psychiatry, 55,* 1084–1091.

Cannon, W. B. (1927). The James-Lange theory of emotions: A critical examination and an alternative theory. *American Journal of Psychology, 39,* 106–124.

Cannon, W. B., & Washburn, A. L. (1912). An explanation of hunger. *American Journal of Physiology, 29,* 441–454.

Cappe, R. F., & Alden, L. E. (1986). A comparison of treatment strategies for clients functionally impaired by extreme shyness and social avoidance. *Journal of Consulting and Clinical Psychology, 54,* 796–801.

Carey, S. (1977). The child as a word learner. In M. Halle, J. Bresnan, & G. A. Miller (Eds.), *Linguistic theory and psychological reality.* Cambridge, MA: MIT Press.

Carmichael, L., Hogan, H. P., & Walter, A. A. (1932). An experimental study of the effect of language on the reproduction of visually perceived form. *Journal of Experimental Psychology, 15,* 73–86.

Carpenter, P. A., Just, M. A., & Shell, P. (1990). What one intelligence test measures: A theoretical account of the processing in the Raven Progressive Matrices Test. *Psychological Review, 97,* 404–431.

Carroll, C. R. (1989). *Drugs in modern society* (2nd ed.). Dubuque, IA: Wm. C. Brown.

Carroll, C. R. (2000). *Drugs in modern society* (5th ed.). Boston: McGraw-Hill.

Carstensen, L. L., Isaacowitz, D. M., & Charles, S. T. (1999). Taking time seriously. A theory of socioemotional selectivity. *American Psychologist, 54,* 165–181.

Carver C. S., & Baird, W. (1998). The American dream revisited: Is it what you want or why you want that matters. *Psychological Science, 9,* 289–292.

Casey, M. B., Nuttall, R., Pezaris, E. (1997). Mediators of gender differences in mathematics college entrance test scores: A comparison of spatial skills with internalized beliefs and anxieties. *Developmental Psychology, 33,* 669–680.

Casey, M. B., Nuttall, R., Pezaris, E., & Benbow, C. P. (1995). The influence of spatial ability on gender differences in mathematics college entrance test scores across diverse samples. *Developmental Psychology, 31,* 697–705.

Caspi, A., & Herbener, E. S. (1990). Continuity and change: Assortative marriage and the consistency of personality in adulthood. *Journal of Personality and Social Psychology, 58,* 250–258.

Castelluci, V., & Kandel, E. R. (1976). Presynaptic facilitation as a mechanism for behavioral sensitization in *Aplysia. Science, 194,* 1176–1178.

Cattell, R. B. (1982). *The inheritance of personality and ability.* New York: Academic Press.

Cattell, R. B., Saunders, D. R., & Stice, G. F. (1950). *The 16 personality factor questionnaire.* Champaign, IL: Institute for Personality and Ability Testing.

Ceci, S. J., & Bruck, M. (1995). *Jeopardy in the courtroom.* Washington, DC: American Psychological Association.

Ceci, S. J., & Williams, W. M. (1997). Schooling, intelligence, and income. *American Psychologist, 52,* 1051–1058.

Centers for Disease Control and Prevention. (January 1999) *HIV/AIDS Surveillance.* Atlanta Author.

Chaiken, S., & Eagley, A. H. (1983). Communication modality as a determinant of persuasion: The role of communicator salience. *Journal of Personality and Social Psychology, 45,* 241–256.

Chambless, D. L., & Gillis, M. M. (1993). Cognitive therapy of anxiety disorders. *Journal of Consulting and Clinical Psychology, 61,* 248–260.

Chapman, L. J., & Chapman, J. P. (1973). *Disordered thought in schizophrenia.* New York: Appleton-Century-Crofts.

Chapman, S. F., Krantz, D. H., & Silver, R. (1992). Mathematics anxiety and science careers among able college women. *Psychological Science, 3,* 292–295.

Chase, W. G., & Simon, H. A. (1973). The mind's eye in chess. In W. G. Chase (Ed.), *Visual information processing.* New York: Academic Press.

Chochinov, H. M., Wilson, K. G., Enns, M., Mowchun, N., Lander, S., Levitt, M., & Clinch, J. J. (1995). Desire for death in the terminally ill. *American Journal of Psychiatry, 152,* 8.

Chodorow, N. J. (1989). Family structure and feminine personality. In *Feminism and psychoanalytic theory.* New Haven: Yale University Press.

Choi, I., Nisbett, R. E., & Norenzayan, A. (1999). Causal attribution across cultures: Variation and universality. *Psychological Bulletin, 125,* 47–63.

Chomsky, N. (1957). *Syntactic structures.* The Hague: Mouton.

Chruschel, T. L. (1982). General pharmacology and toxicology of alcohol. In F. Hoffmeister & G. Stille (Eds.), *Psychotropic agents. Part III: Alcohol and Psychotomimetics* (Vol. 55). New York: Springer-Verlag.

Church, R. M. (1969). Response suppression. In B. A. Campbell & R. M. Church (Eds.), *Punishment and aversive behavior.* New York: Appleton-Century-Crofts.

Clark, K. B., & Clark, M. P. (1939). The development of self and the emergence of racial identification in Negro preschool children. *Journal of Social Psychology, 10,* 591–599.

Clark, R. D., & Hatfield, E. (1989). Gender differences in receptivity to sexual offers. *Journal of Psychology & Human Sexuality, 2,* 39–55.

Clarke, A. M., & Clarke, A. B. D. (Eds.). (1976). *Early experience: Myth and science.* New York: Appleton-Century-Crofts.

Clarkin, J. F., Pilkonis, P. A., & Magruder, K. M. (1996). Psychotherapy of depression: Implications for reform of the health care system. *Archives of General Psychiatry, 53,* 717–723.

Clifford-Walton, V. A. (1998). Feminist perspectives on women's health research. In S. E. Romans & others (Eds.), *Folding back the shadows: A perspective on women's mental health.* Dunedin, New Zealand: University of Otago Press.

Clum, G. A., Clum, G. A., & Surls, R. (1993). A meta-analysis of treatments for panic disorder. *Journal of Consulting and Clinical Psychology, 61,* 317–326.

Cohen, L. G., Celnik, P., Pascual-Leone, A., Corwell, B., Falz, L., Dambroasia, J., Honda, M., Sadato, N., Gerloff, C., & Catala, M. D. (1997). Functional relevance of cross-model plasticity in blind humans. *Nature, 389,* 180–183.

Cohen, S. (1996). Psychological stress, immunity, and upper respiratory infections. *Current Directions in Psychological Science, 5,* 86–90.

Cohen, S., & Williamson, G. (1991). Stress and infectious disease in humans. *Psychological Bulletin, 109,* 5–24.

Cohn, E. G., & Rotton, J. (1997). Assault as a function of time and temperature: A moderator-variable time-series analysis. *Journal of Personality and Social Psychology, 72,* 1322–1334.

Colby, C. Z., Lanzetta, J. T., & Kleck, R. E. (1977). Effects of the expression of pain on autonomic and pain tolerance responses to subject controlled pain. *Psychophysiology, 14,* 537–540.

Collaer, M. L., & Hines, M. (1995). Human behavioral sex differences: A role for gonadal hormones during early development? *Psychological Bulletin, 118,* 55–107.

Collins, A. M., & Loftus, E. F. (1975). A spreading activation theory of semantic processing. *Psychological Review, 82,* 407–428.

Cook, E. W., Hodes, R. L., & Lang, P. (1986). Preparedness and phobia: Effects of stimulus content on human visceral learning. *Journal of Abnormal Psychology, 95,* 195–207.

Cooper, J., & Mackie, D. (1983). Cognitive dissonance in an intergroup context. *Journal of Personality and Social Psychology, 44,* 536–544.

Cooper, J. R., Bloom, F. E., & Roth, R. H. (1986). *The biochemical basis of neuropharmacology* (5th ed.). New York: Oxford University Press.

Cornelius, S. W., & Caspi, A. (1987). Everyday problem solving in adulthood and old age. *Psychology and Aging, 2,* 144–153.

Cowan, N. (1987). Auditory sensory storage in relation to the growth of sensation and acoustic information extraction. *Journal of Experimental Psychology, 13,* 204–215.

Cowan, N. (1988). Evolving conceptions of memory storage, selective attention, and their mutual constraints within the human information-processing system. *Psychological Bulletin, 104,* 163–191.

Craik, F. I. M., & Lockhart, R. S. (1972). Levels of processing. A framework for memory research. *Journal of Verbal Learning and Verbal Behavior, 11,* 671–684.

Craik, F., Moroz, T. M., Moscovitch, M., Stuss, D. T., Winocur, G., Tulving, E., & Kapur, J. (1999). In search of the self: A positron emission tomography study. *Psychological Science, 10,* 26–34.

Crasilneck, H. B., & Hall, J. A. (1985). *Clinical hypnosis: Principles and applications* (2nd ed.). Orlando: Grune & Stratton.

Cross, S. E., & Markus, H. R. (1999). The cultural constitution of personality. In L. A. Pervin & O. P. John (Eds.), *Handbook of personality: Theory and research* (2nd ed., pp. 378–396). New York: Guilford.

Cui, X., & Vaillant, G. E. (1996). Antecedents and consequences of negative life events in adulthood: A longitudinal study. *American Journal of Psychiatry, 153,* 1.

Curtis, R. C., & Miller, K. (1987). Believing another person likes or dislikes you: Behaviors making the beliefs come true. *Journal of Personality and Social Psychology, 51,* 284–290.

Dale, N., & Kandel, E. R. (1990). Facilitatory and inhibitory transmitters modulate spontaneous transmitter release at cultured Aplysia sensorimotor synapses. *Journal of Physiology, 421,* 203–222.

Dalman, C., Allebeck, P., Cullberg, J., Grunewald, C., & Köster, M. (1999). Obstetric complications and the risk of schizophrenia. *Archives of General Psychiatry, 56,* 234–240.

Darley, J., & Latané, B. (1968). Bystander intervention in emergencies. Diffusion of responsibility. *Journal of Personality and Social Psychology, 8,* 377–383.

Darling, N., & Steinberg, L. (1993). Parenting style as context: An integrative model. *Psychological Bulletin, 113,* 487–496.

Darwin, C. (1871). *The descent of man and selection in relation to sex* (Vols. 1 and 2). London: Murray.

Dash, P. K., Hochner, B., & Kandel, E. R. (1990). Injection of the cAMP-responsive element into the nucleus of Aplysia sensory neurons blocks long-term facilitation. *Nature, 345,* 718–721.

Davidson, R. J. (1992). Emotion and affective style: Hemispheric substrates. *Psychological Science,* 39–43.

Davidson, R. J., Ekman, P., Saron, C. D., Senulis, J. A., & Friesen, W. V. (1990). Approach-withdrawal and cerebral asymmetry: Emotional expression and brain physiology. *Journal of Personality and Social Psychology, 58,* 330–341.

Dawson, D. A. (2000). Alcohol consumption, alcohol dependence, and all-cause mortality. *Alcoholism: Clinical & Experimental Research, 24,* 72–81.

Deese, J., & Deese, E. K. (1979). *How to study* (3rd ed.). New York: McGraw-Hill.

Delahanty, D. L., Herberman, H. B., Craig, K. J., Hayward, M. C., Fullerton, C. S., & Ursano, R. J. (1997). Acute and chronic distress and posttraumatic stress disorder as a function of responsibility for serious motor vehicle accidents. *Journal of Consulting and Clinical Psychology, 65*(4), 560–567.

Dember, W. N. (1965). The new look in motivation. *American Scientist, 53,* 409–427.

Denmark, F. (1998). Women and psychology: An international perspective. *American Psychologist, 53,* 465–473.

DeRubeis, R. J., Gelfand, L. A., Tang, T. Z., & Simons, A. D. (1999). Medications versus cognitive behavior therapy for severely depressed outpatients: Mega-analysis of four randomized comparisons. *American Journal of Psychiatry, 156,* 1107–1013.

Devine, P. G. (1996, January/February). Breaking the prejudice habit. *Psychological Science Agenda,* pp. 10–11.

Devlin, M. J., Yanovski, S. Z., & Wilson, G. T. (2000). Obesity: What mental health professionals should know. *American Journal of Psychiatry, 157,* 854–866.

Dew, M. A., Ragni, M. V., & Nimorwicz, P. (1990). Infection with human immunodeficiency virus and vulnerability to psychological distress. *Archives of General Psychiatry, 47,* 437–445.

Diamond, E. L. (1982). The role of anger and hostility in essential hypertension and coronary heart disease. *Psychological Bulletin, 92,* 410–433.

Dindia, K., & Allen, M. (1992). Sex differences in self-disclosure: A meta-analysis. *Psychological Bulletin, 112,* 106–124.

Dishman, R. K. (1982). Compliance/adherence in health-related exercise. *Health Psychology, 1,* 237–267.

Dohr, K. B., Rush, A. J., & Bernstein, I. H. (1989). Cognitive biases and depression. *Journal of Abnormal Psychology, 98,* 263–267.

Dollard, J., Doob, L. W., Miller, N. E., Mowrer, O. H., & Sears, R. R. (1939). *Frustration and aggression.* New Haven: Yale University Press.

Dolnick, E. (1993). Deafness as culture. *Atlantic Monthly, 272,* 37–53.

Dovidio, J. F., & Gaertner, S. L. (1999). Reducing prejudice: Combating intergroup biases. *Current Directions in Psychological Science 8,* 101–105.

Dragoi, V., & Staddon, J. E. R. (1999). The dynamics of operant conditioning. *Psychological Review, 106,* 20–61.

Dravnieks, A. (1983). Odor character profiling. *Journal of the Air Pollution Control Association, 33,* 752–755.

Drucker-Colin, R. R., & Spanis, C. W. (1976). Is there a sleep transmitter? *Progress in Neurobiology, 6,* 1–22.

Duncker, K. (1945). On problem solving. *Psychological Monographs, 58*(5).

Dutton, D. G., & Aron, A. P. (1974). Some evidence for heightened sexual attraction under conditions of high anxiety. *Journal of Personality and Social Psychology, 30,* 510–517.

Eagly, A. H. (1978). Sex differences in influenceability. *Psychological Bulletin, 85,* 86–116.

Eagly, A. H. (1995). The science and politics of comparing women and men. *American Psychologist, 50,* 145–158.

Eagly, A. H., Ashmore, R. D., Makhijani, M. G., & Longo, L. C. (1991). What is beautiful is good, but . . . A meta-analytical review of research on the physical attractiveness stereotype. *Psychological Bulletin, 110,* 109–128.

Eagly, A. H., & Johnson, B. T. (1990). Gender and leadership style. *Psychological Bulletin, 108,* 233–256.

Eagly, A. H., Makhijani, M. G., & Klonsky, B. G. (1992). Gender and the evaluation of leaders: A meta-analysis. *Psychological Bulletin, 111,* 3–22.

Eagly, A. H., & Wood, W. (1999). The origins of sex differences in human behavior: Evolved dispositions versus social roles. *American Psychologist, 54,* 408–423.

Eaton, W. W., Anthony, J. C., Gallo, J., Cai, G., Tien, A., Romanoski, A., Lyketsos, C., & Chen, L. (1997). Natural history of diagnostic interview schedule/DSM-IV major depression. *Archives of General Psychiatry, 54,* 993–999.

Ebert, P. D., & Hyde, J. S. (1976). Selection for agonistic behavior in wild female *Mus musculus. Behavior Genetics, 6,* 291–304.

Eckert, E. D., Bouchard, T. J., Bohlen, J., & Heston, L. L. (1986). Homosexuality in monozygotic twins reared apart. *British Journal of Psychiatry, 148,* 421–425.

Egendorf, A., Kaduschin, C., Laufer, R. S., Rothbart, G., & Sloan, L. (1981). *Legacies of Vietnam: Comparative adjustment of veterans and their peers.* (Publication No. V101 134P-630). Washington, DC: U.S. Government Printing Office.

Ehlers, A., & Breuer, P. (1992). Increased cardiac awareness in panic disorder. *Journal of Abnormal Psychology, 101,* 371–382.

Eibl-Eibesfeldt, I. (1973). The expressive behavior of the deaf and blind-born. In M. von Cranach & I. Vine (Eds.), *Social communication and movement.* New York: Academic Press.

Einstein, G. O., McDaniel, M. A., Smith, R. E., & Shaw, P. (1998). Habitual prospective memory and aging: Remembering intentions and forgetting actions. *Psychological Science, 9,* 284–288.

Ekman, P. (1992). Facial expressions of emotion: New findings, new questions. *Psychological Science, 3,* 34–38.

Ekman, P., Levenson, R. W., & Friesen, W. V. (1983). Autonomic nervous system activity distinguishes among emotions. *Science, 221,* 1208–1210.

Elkind, D. (1967). *Children and adolescents: Interpretive essays on Jean Piaget.* New York: Oxford University Press.

Elkind, D. (1981). Understanding the young adolescent. In L. D. Steinberg (Ed.), *The life cycle: Readings in human development.* New York: Columbia University Press.

Elkind, D., & Bowen, R. (1979). Imaginary audience behavior in children and adolescents. *Developmental Psychology, 15,* 38–44.

Elliot, A. J., & Church, M. A. (1997). A hierarchical model of approach and avoidance achievement motivation. *Journal of Personality and Social Psychology, 72,* 218–232.

Elliott, D. M. (1997). Traumatic events: Prevalence and delayed recall in the general population. *Journal of Consulting and Clinical Psychology, 65,* 811–820.

Ellis, A. (1962). *Reason and emotion in psychotherapy.* New York: Lyle Stuart.

Ellis, A. (1999). *How to make yourself happy and remarkably less disturbable.* Atascadero, CA: Impact.

Ellis, H. C. (1987). Recent developments in human memory. In V. Mokosky (Ed.), *The G. Stanley Hall Series.* Washington, DC: American Psychological Association.

Ellis, H. C., & Hunt, R. R. (1993). *Fundamentals of cognitive psychology.* Madison, WI: Brown & Benchmark.

Emery, V. O., & Oxmans, T. E. (1992). Update on the dementia spectrum of depression. *American Journal of Psychiatry, 149,* 305–317.

Emmons, R. A., & Diener, E. (1986). Situation selection as a moderator of response consistency and stability. *Journal of Personality and Social Psychology, 51,* 1013–1019.

Engle, S. A. (1999). Using neuroimaging to measure mental representations: Finding color-opponent neurons in visual cortex. *Current Directions in Psychological Science, 8,* 23–27.

Epstein, R. S., Fullerton, C. S., & Ursano, R. J. (1998). Posttraumatic stress disorder following an air disaster: A prospective study. *American Journal of Psychiatry, 155*(7), 934–938.

Epstein, S. (1982). Conflict and stress. In L. Goldberger & S. Breznitz (Eds.), *Handbook of stress.* New York: Free Press.

Epstein, S., & Roupenian, A. (1970). Heart rate and skin conductance during experimentally induced anxiety. *Journal of Personality and Social Psychology, 16,* 20–28.

Erel, O., Oberman, Y., & Yirmiya, N. (2000). Maternal versus nonmaternal care and seven domains of children's development. *Psychological Bulletin, 126,* 727–747.

Erikson, E. (1963). *Childhood and society.* New York: Norton.

Erlenmeyer-Kimling, L., & Jarvik, L. F. (1963). Genetics and intelligence: A review. *Science, 142,* 1477–1479.

Escobar, J. I., Canino, G., Rubio-Stipec, M., & Bravo, M. (1992). Somatic symptoms after a natural disaster: A prospective study. *American Journal of Psychiatry, 149,* 965–967.

Evans, M. D., & others. (1992). Differential relapse following cognitive therapy and pharmacotherapy for depression. *Archives of General Psychiatry, 49,* 802–808.

Exline, J. J., & Lobel, M. (1999). The perils of outperformance: Sensitivity about being the target of a threatening upward comparison. *Psychological Bulletin, 125,* 307–337.

Exner, J. (1986). *The Rorschach: A comprehensive system: Vol. 2. Current research and advanced interpretation.* New York: Wiley.

Eysenck, M. W., Mogg, K., May, J., Richards, A., & Mathews, A. (1991). Bias in interpretation of ambiguous sentences related to threat in anxiety. *Journal of Abnormal Psychology, 100,* 144–150.

Ezell, C. (1994). The long and short of short- and long-term memory. *Journal of NIH Research, 6,* 56–61.

Ezell, C. (1995). Fat times for obesity research: Tons of new information, but how does it all fit together? *Journal of NIH Research, 7,* 39–43.

Fagot, B. I. (1974). Sex differences in toddlers' behavior and parental reaction. *Developmental Psychology, 10,* 554–558.

Farquhar, J. W. (1979). *The American way of life need not be hazardous to your health.* New York: Norton.

Farrell, M. P., & Rosenberg, S. D. (1981). *Men at midlife.* Boston: Auburn House.

Fawzi, F. I., & others. (1990). A structured psychiatric intervention for cancer patients: 2. Changes over time in immunological measures. *Archives of General Psychiatry, 47,* 729–736.

Fein, S., & Spencer, S. J. (1997). Prejudice as self-image maintenance: Affirming the self through derogating others. *Journal of Personality and Social Psychology, 73,* 31–44.

Feingold, A. (1988). Matching for attractiveness in romantic partner and same-sex friends: A meta-analysis and theoretical critique. *Psychological Bulletin, 104,* 226–235.

Feingold, A. (1990). Gender differences in effects of physical attractiveness on romantic attraction: A comparison across five research paradigms. *Journal of Personality and Social Psychology, 59,* 981–993.

Feingold, A. (1992a). Gender differences in mate selection processes: A test of the parental investment model. *Psychological Bulletin, 112,* 125–139.

Feingold, A. (1992b). Good-looking people are not what we think. *Psychological Bulletin, 111,* 304–341.

Feingold, A. (1994). Gender differences in personality: A meta-analysis. *Psychological Bulletin, 116,* 429–456.

Ferster, C. B., & Skinner, B. F. (1957). *Schedules of reinforcement.* New York: Appleton-Century-Crofts.

Festinger, L. A. (1957). *A theory of cognitive dissonance.* Evanston, IL: Harper & Row, Peterson.

Festinger, L. A., & Carlsmith, L. M. (1959). Cognitive consequences of forced compliance. *Journal of Abnormal and Social Psychology, 58,* 203–210.

Fichten, C. S., Robillard, K., Judd, D., & Amsel, R. (1989). College students with physical disabilities: Myths and realities. *Rehabilitation Psychology, 34,* 243–257.

Fisher, R. P., & Geiselman, R. E. (1988). Enhancing eyewitness memory with the cognitive interview. In M. M. Gruneberg, P. E. Morris, & R. N. Sykes (Eds.), *Practical aspects of memory: Current research and issues: Vol. 1. Memory in everyday life* (pp. 34–39). Chichester, England: Wiley.

Fiske, S. T. (1993). Social cognition and social perception. *Annual Review of Psychology, 44,* 155–194.

Fiske, S. T., Bersoff, D. N., Borgida, E., Deaux, K., & Heilman, M. E. (1991). Social science research on trial: Use of sex stereotyping research in *Price Waterhouse v. Hopkins. American Psychologist, 46,* 1049–1060.

Flor, H., Elbert, T., Knecht, S., Wienbruch, C., Pantev, C., Birbaumer, N., Larbig, W., & Taub, E. (1995). Phantom-limb pain as a perceptual correlate of cortical reorganization following arm amputation. *Nature, 375,* 482–490.

Flynn, J. R. (1998). IQ gains over time: Towards finding the causes. In U. Neisser (Ed.), *The rising curve: Long-term gains in IQ and related measures* (pp. 25–66). Washington, DC: American Psychological Association.

Flynn, J. R. (1999). Searching for justice: The discovery of IQ gains over time. *American Psychologist, 54,* 5–20.

Foa, E. B., & Riggs, D. S. (1995). Posttraumatic stress disorder following assault: Theoretical considerations and empirical findings. *Current Directions in Psychological Science, 4,* 61–65.

Folkman, S., & Lazarus, R. S. (1986). Stress processes and depressive symptomatology. *Journal of Abnormal Psychology, 95,* 107–113.

Forgas, J. P., & Bower, G. H. (1987) Mood effects on person-perception judgments. *Journal of Personality and Social Psychology, 53,* 53–60.

Foster, C. A., Witcher, B. S., Campbell, W. K., & Green, J. D. (1998). Arousal and attraction: Evidence for automatic and controlled processes. *Journal of Personality and Social Psychology, 74,* 86–101.

Foulkes, D. (1989, December). Understanding our dreams. *Natural Science,* pp. 296–301.

Foulkes, D., & Schmidt, M. (1983). Temporal sequence and unit composition in dream reports from different stages of sleep. *Sleep, 6,* 265–280.

Foulkes, W. D. (1962). Dream reports from different stages of sleep. *Journal of Abnormal and Social Psychology, 65,* 14–25.

Fouts, R. (1997). *Next of kin: What chimpanzees have taught me about who we are.* New York: William Morrow.

Fowles, D. C. (1992). Schizophrenia: Diathesis-stress revisited. *Annual Review of Psychology, 43,* 303–336.

Foxx, R., & Rubinoff, A. (1981). A behavioral treatment of caffeinism. *Journal of Applied Behavior Analysis, 14,* 21–30.

Foxx, R. M., & Brown, R. A. (1979). Nicotine fading and self-monitoring for cigarette abstinence or controlled smoking. *Journal of Applied Behavior Analysis, 12,* 111–125.

Frankel, F. H. (1995). Discovering new memories in psychotherapy—Childhood revisited, fantasy, or both? *New England Journal of Medicine,* 591–594.

Franz, E. A., Waldie, K. E., & Smith, M. J. (2000) The effect of callostomy on novel versus familiar bimanual actions: A neural dissociation between controlled and automatic processes? *Psychological Science, 11,* 82–85.

Frazier, J. A., & Morrison, F. J. (1998). The influence of extended-year schooling on growth of achievement and perceived competence in early elementary school. *Child Development, 69,* 495–517.

French, E. G. (1956). Motivation as a variable in work-partner selection. *Journal of Abnormal and Social Psychology, 53,* 96–99.

Fried-Buchalter, S. (1997). Fear of success, fear of failure, and the imposter phenomenon among male and female marketing managers. *Sex Roles, 37,* 847–859.

Friedman, H. S., & Booth-Kewley, S. (1987). The "disease-prone" personality: A meta-analytic view of the construct. *American Psychologist, 42,* 539–555.

Friedman, H. S., Tucker, J. S., Schwartz, J. E., Tomlinson-Keasey, C., Martin, L. R., Wingard, D. L., & Criqui, M. H. (1995). Psychosocial and behavioral predictors of longevity: The aging and death of the "termites." *American Psychologist, 50,* 69–78.

Friedman, M., & Rosenman, R. H. (1974). *Type A behavior and your heart.* New York: Knopf.

Fry, A. F., & Hale, S. (1996). Processing speed, working memory, and fluid intelligence: Evidence for a developmental cascade. *Psychological Science, 7,* 237–241.

Furomoto, L. (1992). Joining separate spheres—Christine Ladd-Franklin, woman-scientist (1847–1930). *American Psychologist, 47,* 174–182.

Furomoto, L., & Scarborough, E. (1986). Placing women in the history of psychology: The first women psychologists. *American Psychologist, 41,* 35–42.

Fuster, J. M. (1995). *Memory in the cerebral cortex.* Cambridge, MA: MIT Press.

Galambos, N. L. (1992). Parent-adolescent relations. *Current Directions in Psychological Science, 1,* 146–149.

Galanter, E. (1962). *New directions in psychology.* New York: Holt, Rinehart & Winston.

Galotti, K. (1990). Approaches to studying formal and everyday reasoning. *Psychological Bulletin, 105,* 331–351.

Garb, H. N., Florio, C. M., & Grove, W. M. (1998). The validty of the Rorschach and Minnesota Multiphasic Personality Inventory: Results from meta-analyses. *Psychological Science, 9,* 402–404.

Garcia, J., Hankins, W. G., & Rusiniak, K. W. (1974). Behavioral regulation of the *milieu interne* in man and rat. *Science, 185,* 824–831.

Garcia, L. T. (1982). Sex-role orientation and stereotypes about male-female sexuality. *Sex Roles, 8,* 863–876.

Garcia-Vera, M. P., Labrador, F. J., & Sanz, J. (1997). Stress-management training for essential hypertension: A controlled study. *Applied Psychophysiology and Biofeedback, 22,* 261–283.

Gardner, B. T., & Gardner, R. A. (1971). Two-way communication with an infant chimpanzee. In A. M. Schrier & F. Stollnitz (Eds.), *Behavior of nonhuman primates* (Vol. 4). New York: Academic Press.

Gardner, H. (1983). *Frames of mind: The theory of multiple intelligence.* New York: Basic Books.

Garner, D. M., Rockert, W., Davis, R., Garner, M. V., Olmsted, M. P., & Eagle, M. (1993). Comparison of cognitive-behavioral and supportive-expressive therapy for bulimia nervosa. *American Journal of Psychiatry, 150,* 37–46.

Garraghty, P. E., Churchill, J. D., & Banks, M. K. (1998). Adult neural plasticity: Similarities between two paradigms. *Current Directions in Psychological Science, 7,* 87–91.

Garro, L. C. (1990). Culture, pain and cancer. *Journal of Palliative Care, 6,* 34–44.

Gazzaniga, M. (1992). *Nature's mind: The biological roots of thinking, emotion, sexuality, language, and intelligence.* Boston: Houghton Mifflin.

Gazzaniga, M. S. (1967). The split brain in man. *Scientific American,* pp. 24–29.

Gazzaniga, M. S. (1983). Right hemisphere language following brain bisection: A 20-year perspective. *American Psychologist, 38,* 525–537.

Gazzaniga, M. S. (1998, July). The split brain revisited. *Scientific American,* pp. 50–55.

Gazzaniga, M. S. (2000). *Cognitive neuroscience: A reader.* Malden, MA: Blackwell.

Geary, D. C. (1998). *Male, female: The evolution of human sex differences.* Washington, DC: American Psychological Association.

Geary, D. C. (1999). Evolution and developmental sex differences. *Current Directions in Psychological Science, 8,* 115–120.

Geen, R. G., & Quanty, M. B. (1977). The catharsis of aggression: An evaluation of a hypothesis. In L. Berkowitz (Ed.), *Advances in experimental social psychology* (Vol. 10). New York: Academic Press.

Gentile, D. A. (1993). Just what are sex and gender, anyway? A call for a new terminological standard. *Psychological Science, 4,* 120–126.

Gershon, E. S., & Rieder, R. O. (1992, September). Major disorders of mind and brain. *Scientific American,* pp. 126–133.

Gibbons, F. X., Eggleston, T. J., & Benthin, A. C. (1997). Cognitive reactions to smoking relapse: The reciprocal relation between dissonance and self-esteem. *Journal of Personality and Social Psychology, 72,* 184–195.

Gibson, E., & Walk, R. (1960). The "visual cliff." *Scientific American,* pp. 64–71.

Giedd, J. N., Castellanos, F. X., Rajapakse, J. C., Vaituzis, A. C., & Rapoport, J. L. (1997). Sexual dimorphism of the developing human brain. *Progress in Neuro-Psychopharmacology & Biological Psychiatry, 21,* 1185–1201.

Gilbertini, M., Graham, C., & Cook, M. R. (1999). Self-report of circadian type reflects phase of the melatonin rhythm. *Biological Psychology, 50,* 19–33.

Gilligan, C. (1982). *In a different voice.* Cambridge, MA: Harvard University Press.

Glaser, R., & others. (1990). Psychological stress-induced modulation of interleukin 2 receptor gene expression and interleukin 2 production in peripheral blood leukocytes. *Archives of General Psychiatry, 47,* 707–712.

Gleaves, D. H. (1996). The sociocognitive model of dissociative identity disorder: A reexamination of the evidence. *Psychological Bulletin, 120,* 42–59.

Goldberg, L. R. (1993). The structure of phenotypic personality traits. *American Psychologist, 48,* 26–34.

Goldfried, M., & Davison, G. (1976). *Clinical behavior therapy.* New York: Holt, Rinehart & Winston.

Golding, J. M., Smith, R., & Kashner, T. M. (1991). Does somatization disorder occur in men? *Archives of General Psychiatry, 48,* 231–235.

Goldman-Rakic, P. S. (1992). Working memory and the mind. *Scientific American,* pp. 111–117.

Goldstein, M. J., & Palmer, J. O. (1963). *The experience of anxiety.* New York: Oxford University Press.

Gosling, S. D., & John, O. P. (1999). Personality dimensions in nonhuman animals: A cross-species review. *Current Directions in Psychological Science 8,* 69–75.

Gotlib, I. (1992). Interpersonal and cognitive aspects of depression. *Current Directions in Psychological Science, 1,* 149–154.

Gottfredson, L. S. (1997). Why g matters: The complexity of everyday life. *Intelligence, 24,* 79–132.

Gottfried, A. E., Fleming, J. S., & Gottfried, A. W. (1998). Role of cognitively stimulating home environment in children's academic intrinsic motivation: A longitudinal study. *Child Development, 69,* 1448–1460.

Grady, C. L., McIntosh, A. R., Horwitz, B., Maisog, J. M., Ungerleider, L. G., Mentis, M. J., Pietrini, P., Schapiro, M. B., & Haxby, J. V. (1995). Age-related reductions in human recognition memory due to impaired encoding. *Science, 269,* 218–220.

Graf, P., Squire, L. R., & Mandler, G. (1984). The information that amnesic patients do not forget. *Journal of Experimental Psychology, Learning, Memory, and Cognition, 10,* 164–178.

Gray, J. A. (1988). The neuropsychological basis of anxiety. In C. G. Last & M. Hersen (Eds.), *Handbook of anxiety disorders.* Elmsford, NY: Pergamon Press.

Graziano, W. G., & Musser, L. M. (1982). The going and parting of the ways. In S. Duck (Ed.), *Personal relationships 4: Dissolving personal relationships.* London: Academic Press.

Greden, J. F. (1974). Anxiety or caffeinism: A diagnostic dilemma. *American Journal of Psychiatry, 131,* 1089–1092.

Greenfield, P. (1998). The cultural evolution of IQ. In U. Neisser (Ed.), *The rising curve: Long-term gains in IQ and related measures* (pp. 81–124). Washington, DC: American Psychological Association.

Greenough, W. T., Black, J. E., & Wallace, C. S. (1987). Experience and brain development. *Child Development, 58,* 539–559.

Griffith, W., & Veitch, R. (1971). Influences of population density on interpersonal affective behavior. *Journal of Personality and Social Psychology, 17,* 92–98.

Grilo, C. M., Shiffman, S., & Wing, R. R. (1989). Relapse crises and coping among dieters. *Journal of Consulting and Clinical Psychology, 57,* 488–495.

Grissmer, Williamson, Kirby, & Berends. (1998). Exploring the rapid rise in Black achievement scores in the United States (1970–1990). In U. Neisser (Ed.), *The rising curve: Long-term gains in IQ and related measures* (pp. 251–286). Washington, DC: American Psychological Association.

Grossman, S. P. (1960). Eating and drinking elicited by direct adrenergic and cholinergic stimulation of hypothalamus. *Science, 132,* 301–302.

Groves, P. M., & Rebec, G. V. (1988). *Introduction to biological psychology.* (3rd ed.). Dubuque, IA: Wm. C. Brown.

Gruskin, E. P. (1999). *Treating lesbians and bisexual women: Challenges and strategies for health professionals.* Thousand Oaks, CA: Sage

Guilford, J. P. (1950). Creativity. *American Psychologist, 5,* 444–454.

Guilford, J. P. (1967). *The nature of human intelligence.* New York: McGraw-Hill.

Guilford, J. P. (1982). Cognitive psychology's ambiguities: Some suggested remedies. *Psychologist Review, 89,* 48–59.

Gunnar, M. R., Malone, S., & Fisch, R. O. (1988). The psychobiology of stress and coping in the human neonate: Studies of adrenocortical activity in response to stress in the first week of life. In T. Field, P. McCabe, & N. Schneiderman (Eds.), *Stress and coping.* Hillsdale, NJ: Lawrence Erlbaum.

Gustavson, C. R., Garcia, J., Hankins, W. G., & Rusiniak, K. W. (1974). Coyote predation control by aversive conditioning. *Science, 184,* 581–584.

Guyatt, G. H., Cook D. J., King, D., Norman, G. R., Kane, S. L., & van Ineveld, C. (1999). Effect of framing of questionnaire items regarding satisfaction with training on residents' responses. *Academic Medicine, 74,* 192–194.

Hafer, J. C., & Richmond, E. D. (1988). What hearing parents should learn about deaf culture. *Perspectives for Teachers of the Hearing Impaired, 7,* 2–5.

Halgin, R., & Whitbourne, S. K. (2000). *Abnormal psychology: Clinical perspectives on psychological disorders.* Boston: McGraw-Hill.

Hall, C. S. (1951). What people dream about. *Scientific American,* pp. 60–63.

Halpern, D. (1992). *Sex differences in cognitive abilities* (2nd ed.). Hillsdale, NJ: Erlbaum.

Halpern, D. F. (1997). Sex differences in intelligence: Implications for education. *American Psychologist, 52,* 1091–1102.

Halpern, D. F. (1998). Teaching critical thinking for transfer across domains: Dispositions, skills, structure training, and metacognitive monitoring. *American Psychologist, 53,* 449–455.

Hamilton, D. L., & Zanna, M. P. (1972). Differential weighting of favorable and unfavorable attributes in impressions of personality. *Journal of Experimental Research in Personality, 6,* 204–212.

Hammen, C., Elliott, A., Gitlin, M., & Jamison, K. R. (1989). Sociotropy/autonomy and vulnerability to specific life events in patients with unipolar depression and bipolar disorders. *Journal of Abnormal Psychology, 98,* 154–160.

Hammen, C., Marks, T., Mayol, A., & deMayo, R. (1985). Depressive self-schema, life stress, and vulnerability to depression. *Journal of Abnormal Psychology, 94,* 308–319.

Hanawalt, H. F., & Demarest, I. H. (1939). The effect of verbal suggestion in the recall period upon the reproduction of visually perceived forms. *Journal of Experimental Psychology, 25,* 159–174.

Haney, C., & Zimbardo, P. (1998). The past and future of U. S. prison policy: Twenty-five years after the Stanford prison experiment. *American Psychologist, 53,* 709–727.

Harlow, H. F. (1949). The formation of learning sets. *Psychological Review, 56,* 51–56.

Harlow, H. F., & Harlow, M. K. (1965). The affectional systems. In A. M. Schrier, H. F. Harlow, & F. Stollnitz (Eds.), *Behavior of nonhuman primates* (Vol. 2). London: Academic Press.

Harlow, H. F., Harlow, M. K., & Meyer, D. R. (1950). Learning motivated by a manipulation drive. *Journal of Experimental Psychology, 40,* 228–234.

Harlow, H. F., & Novak, M. A. (1973). Psychopathological perspectives. *Perspectives in Biology and Medicine, 16,* 461–478.

Harmon, T. M., Hyan, M. T., & Tyre, T. E. (1990). Improved obstetric outcomes using hypnotic analgesia and skill mastery combined with childbirth education.

Journal of Consulting and Clinical Psychology, 58, 525–530.

Harris, T. G. (1973, July). As far as heroin is concerned, the worst is over. *Psychology Today,* pp. 68–79.

Hatfield, E. (1988). Passionate and companionate love. In R. J. Sternberg & M. L. Barnes (Eds.), *The psychology of love.* New Haven: Yale University Press.

Hauser, R. M. (1998). Trends in Black-White test-score differentials: I. Uses and misuses of NAEP/SAT data. In U. Neisser (Ed.), *The rising curve: Long-term gains in IQ and related measures* (pp. 219 249). Washington, DC: American Psychological Association.

Hayes, K. J., & Hayes, C. (1951). Intellectual development of a home-raised chimpanzee. *Proceedings of the American Philosophical Society, 95,* 105–109.

Haynes, S. G., Feinleib, M., & Kannel, W. B. (1980). The relationship of psychosocial factors to coronary heart disease in the Framingham Study. Part III: Eight-year incidence of CHD. *American Journal of Epidemiology, 3,* 37–58.

Hazlett, E. A., & others. (1999). Three-dimensional analysis with MRI and PET of the size, shape, and function of the thalamus in the schizophrenia spectrum. *American Journal of Psychiatry, 156,* 1190–1199.

Hebb, D. O. (1949). *Organization of behavior.* New York: Wiley.

Hedges, L. V., & Nowell, A. (1995). Sex differences in mental test scores, variability, and numbers of high-scoring individuals. *Science, 269,* 41–45.

Heider, E. R., & Oliver, D. C. (1972). The structure of color space in naming and memory for two languages. *Cognitive Psychology, 3,* 337–354.

Heider, F. (1958). *The psychology of interpersonal relations.* New York: Wiley.

Heien, D. M., & Pittman, D. J. (1993). The external costs of alcohol abuse. *Journal of Studies on Alcohol, 54,* 302–307.

Heimberg, R. G., Liebowitz, M. R., Hope, D. A., Schneier, F. R., Holt, C. S., Welkowitz, L. A., Juster, H. R., Campeas, R., Bruch, M. A., Cloitre, M., Fallon, B., & Klein, D. F. (1998). Cognitive behavioral group therapy vs. phenelzine therapy for social phobia. *Archives of General Psychiatry, 55,* 1133–1141.

Held, R., & Hein, A. (1963). Movement-produced stimulation in the development of visually guided behavior. *Journal of Comparative and Physiological Psychology, 56,* 23–44.

Heller, K., Swindle, R. W., & Dusenbury, L. (1986). Components of social support processes. *Journal of Consulting and Clinical Psychology, 54,* 466–470.

Heller, W., Nitscke, J. B., & Miller, G. A. (1998). Lateralization in emotion and emotional disorders. *Current Directions in Psychological Science, 7,* 26–32.

Hendin, H., & Klerman, G. (1993). Physician-assisted suicide: The dangers of legalization. *American Journal of Psychiatry, 150,* 143–145.

Hennekens, C. H., Rosner, B., & Cole, D. S. (1978). Daily alcohol consumption and fatal coronary heart disease. *American Journal of Epidemiology, 107,* 196–200.

Herdt, G. (1984). *Ritualized homosexuality in Melanesia.* Berkeley: University of California Press.

Herek, G. M. (1990). Gay people and government security clearance. *American Psychologist, 45,* 1035–1042.

Herek, G. M. (1993). Sexual orientation and military service: A social science perspective. *American Psychologist, 48,* 538–549.

Herrera, J. M., Lawson, W. B., & Sramek, J. J. (1999). *Cross cultural psychiatry.* Chichester, England: John Wiley & Sons.

Hess, E. H. (1975, November). The role of pupil size in communication. *Scientific American,* pp. 110–119.

Hetherington, E. M., Bridges, M., & Insabella, G. M. (1998). What matters? What does not? Five perspectives on the association between marital transitions and children's adjustment. *American Psychologist, 53,* 167–184.

Hetherington, M. (1979). Divorce: A children's perspective. *American Psychologist, 34,* 851–858.

Hewitt, P. L., & Flett, G. L. (1993). Dimensions of perfectionism, daily stress, and depression: A test of the specific vulnerability hypothesis. *Journal of Abnormal Psychology, 102,* 58–65.

Hewitt, P. L., Flett, G. L., & Ediger, E. (1996). Perfectionism and depression: Longitudinal assessment of a specific vulnerability hypothesis. *Journal of Abnormal Psychology, 105,* 276–280.

Hilgard, E. R. (1975). Hypnosis. *Annual Review of Psychology, 26,* 19–44.

Hilgard, E. R. (1978). Hypnosis and pain. In R. A. Sternbach (Ed.), *The psychology of pain.* New York: Raven Press.

Hilgard, E. R., & Hilgard, J. R. (1975). *Hypnosis in the relief of pain.* Los Altos, CA: William Kaufmann.

Hill, C., Rubin, Z., & Peplau, L. (1976). Breakups before marriage: The end of 103 affairs. *Journal of Social Issues, 32,* 147–168.

Hirst, W. (1982). The amnesic syndrome: Descriptions and explanations. *Psychological Bulletin, 91,* 435–460.

Hobson, J. A. (1989). *Sleep.* New York: Scientific American Library.

Hochberg, J. (1988). Visual perception. In R. C. Atkison, R. J. Herrnstein, G. Lindzey, & R. D. Luce (Eds.), *Stevens' handbook of experimental psychology: Vol. 1. Perception and motivation.* New York: Wiley-Interscience.

Hoffman, C., Lau, L., & Johnson, D. R. (1986). The linguistic relativity of person cognition: An English-Chinese comparison. *Journal of Personality and Social Psychology, 51,* 1097–1105.

Hoffman, L. W. (1989). Effects of maternal employment in the two-parent family. *American Psychologist, 44,* 283–292.

Hogan, R., Mankin, D., Conway, J., & Fox, S. (1970). Personality correlates of undergraduate marijuana use. *Journal of Consulting and Clinical Psychology, 35,* 58–63.

Hokanson, J. E., DeGood, D. E., Forrest, M. S., & Brittain, T. M. (1963). Availability of avoidance behaviors for modulating vascular-stress responses. *Journal of Personality and Social Psychology, 67,* 60–68.

Holahan, C. J., & Moos, R. H. (1987). Risk, resistance, and psychological distress: A longitudinal analysis with adults and children. *Journal of Abnormal Psychology, 96,* 3–13.

Holden, C. (1973). Psychosurgery: Legitimate therapy or laundered lobotomy? *Science, 179,* 1109–1112.

Hole, J. W. (1990). *Human anatomy and physiology* (5th ed.). Dubuque, IA: Wm. C. Brown.

Holinger, P. C., & Offer, D. (1993). *Adolescent suicide.* New York: Guilford Press.

Hollon, S. D., Shelton, R. C., & Davis, D. D. (1993). Cognitive therapy for depression: Conceptual issues and clinical efficacy. *Journal of Consulting and Clinical Psychology, 61,* 270–275.

Hopkin, K. (1995). Sugar 'n spice vs. puppy-dog tails: Sex differences in the brain. *Journal of NIH Research, 7,* 39–43.

Hopkins, K. (1997). Show me where it hurts: Tracing the pathways of pain. *Journal of NIH Research, 9,* 37–43.

Horgan, J. (1993, June). Eugenics revisited. *Scientific American,* pp. 122–131.

Horne, D. J., Taylor, M., & Varigos, G. (1999). The effects of relaxation with and without imagery in reducing anxiety and itchy skin in patients with eczema. *Behavioural and Cognitive Psychotherapy, 27,* 143–151.

Horne, J. (1988). *Why we sleep: The functions of sleep in humans and other mammals.* New York: Oxford University Press.

Hough, R. L., & others. (1987). Utilization of health and mental health services by Los Angeles Mexican-Americans and non-Hispanic whites. *Archives of General Psychiatry, 44,* 702–709.

Houston, J. P. (1985). *Motivation.* New York: Macmillan.

Hovland, C. I. (Ed.). (1957). *The order of presentation in persuasion.* New Haven: Yale University Press.

Hovland, C. I., & Weiss, W. (1951). The influence of source credibility on communication effectiveness. *The Public Opinion Quarterly, 15,* 635–650.

Huang, M., & Hauser, R. M. (1998). Trends in Black-White test-score differentials: II. The WORDSUM Vocabulary Test. In U. Neisser (Ed.), *The rising curve: Long-term gains in IQ and related measures* (pp. 303–334). Washington, DC: American Psychological Association.

Hugdahl, K., & Karker, A. C. (1981). Biological versus experiential factors in phobic conditioning. *Behaviour Research and Therapy, 16,* 315–321.

Hughes, J. R., Oliveto, A. H., Helzer, J., Higgins, S. R., & Bickel, W. K. (1992). Should caffeine abuse, dependence, or withdrawal be added to DSM-IV and ICD-10? *American Journal of Psychiatry, 149,* 33–40.

Hunt, E. (1995). The role of intelligence in modern society. *American Scientist, 83,* 356–368.

Huntsinger, C. S., Jose, P. E., & Larson, S. L. (1998). Do parent practices to encourage academic competence influence the social adjustment of young European American and Chinese American children? *Developmental Psychology, 34,* 747–756.

Hyde, J. S., & Plant, E. A. (1995). Magnitude of psychological gender differences: Another side to the story. *American Psychologist, 50,* 159–161.

Hyman, I. E., & Billings, F. J. (1998). Individual differences in the creation of false childhood memories. *Memory, 6,* 1–20.

Hyman, I. E., & Loftus, E. F. (1998). Errors in autobiographical memory. *Clinical Psychology Review, 18,* 933–947.

Hyman, I. E., & Pentland, J. (1996). The role of mental imagery in the creation of false memories. *Journal of Memory and Language, 35,* 101–117.

Ingham, A. G., Levinger, B., Graves, J., & Peckham, V. (1974). The Ringelmann effect: Studies of group size and group performance. *Journal of Experimental Social Psychology, 10,* 371–384.

Inhelder, B., & Piaget, J. (1958). *The growth of logical thinking from childhood to adolescence.* New York: Basic Books.

Ironson, G., & Schneiderman, N. (1991). Psychoimmunology and HIV-1: Scope of the problem. In N. Schneiderman (Ed.), *Psychoimmunology and HIV-1.* Geneva: World Health Organization.

Isen, A. M., & Levin, P. F. (1972). The effect of feeling good on helping: Cookies and kindness. *Journal of Personality and Social Psychology, 21,* 384–388.

Iverson, L. L. (1979). The chemistry of the brain. *Scientific American,* pp. 134–149.

Iyengar, S. S., & Lepper, M. R. (1999). Rethinking the value of choice: A cultural perspective on intrinsic motivation. *Journal of Personality and Social Psychology, 76,* 349–366.

Izard, C. E. (1977). *Human emotions.* New York: Plenum.

Izard, C. E. (1978). Emotions as motivations: An evolutionary-developmental perspective. In H. E. Howe & R. A. Dienstbeier (Eds.), *Nebraska Symposium on Motivation* (Vol. 26). Lincoln: University of Nebraska Press.

Izard, C. E. (1991). *The psychology of emotions.* New York: Plenum Press.

Izard, C. E. & others. (1997). The ontogeny and significance of infants' facial expressions in the first 9 months of life. *Developmental Psychology, 31,* 997–1013.

Jacobson, E. (1938). *Progressive relaxation.* Chicago: University of Chicago Press.

Jaffee, S., & Hyde, J. S. (2000). Gender differences in moral orientation: A meta-analysis. *Psychological Bulletin, 126,* 703–726.

Janis, I. L. (1982). *Groupthink: Psychological studies of policy decisions and fiascoes.* Boston: Houghton Mifflin.

Jeffrey, K. J., & Reid, I. A. (1997). Modifiable neuronal connections: An overview of psychiatrists. *American Journal of Psychiatry, 154,* 156–164.

Jeffrey, R. W. (1988). Risk behaviors and health: Contrasting individual and population perspectives. *American Psychologist, 44,* 1194–1202.

Jenkins, C. D. (1988a). Dietary risk factors and their modification in cardiovascular disease. *Journal of Consulting and Clinical Psychology, 56,* 350–357.

Jenkins, R. W. (1988b). Epidemiology of cardiovascular diseases. *Journal of Consulting and Clinical Psychology, 56,* 324–332.

Jenkins-Hall, K., & Sacco, W. P. (1991). Effect of client race and depression on evaluations by white therapists. *Journal of Social and Clinical Psychology, 10*(3), 322–333.

Johnson, M. K., Bransford, J. P., & Solomon, S. (1973). Memory for tacit implications of sentences. *Journal of Experimental Psychology, 98,* 203–205.

Joiner, T. E., & Schmidt, N. B. (1998). Excessive reassurance-seeking predicts depressive but not anxious reactions to acute stress. *Journal of Abnormal Psychology, 107,* 533–537.

Joiner, T. E., Metalsky, G. I., Lew, A., & Klocek, J. (1999). Testing the causal mediation component of Beck's theory of depression: Evidence for specific mediation. *Cognitive Therapy & Research, 23,* 401–412.

Jones, A., & Crandall, R. (1986). Validation of a short index of self-actualization. *Personality and Social Psychology Bulletin, 12,* 63–73.

Jones, E., Bell, L., & Aronson, E. (1971). The reciprocation of attraction from similar and dissimilar others: A study in person perception and evaluation. In C. McClintock (Ed.), *Experimental social psychology.* New York: Holt, Rinehart & Winston.

Jones, G. V. (1983). Identifying basic categories. *Psychological Bulletin, 94,* 423–428.

Jones, M. C. (1924). A laboratory study of fear: The case of Peter. *Pedagogical Seminary, 31,* 308–315.

Jorgensen, R. S., Nash, J. K., Lasser, N. L., Hymowitz, N., & Langer, A. W. (1988). Heart rate acceleration and its relationship to total serum cholesterol, triglycerides, and blood pressure. *Psychophysiology, 25,* 39–44.

Kagan, J. (1984). *The nature of the child.* New York: Basic Books.

Kahneman, D., & Tversky, A. (1982). The psychology of preferences. *Scientific American,* pp. 160–173.

Kahneman, D., & Tversky, A. (1996). On the reality of cognitive illusions. *Psychological Review, 103,* 582–591.

Kalichman, S. C. (1989). Sex roles and sex differences in adult spatial performance. *Journal of Genetic Psychology, 150,* 93–100.

Kalichman, S. C. (2000). HIV transmission risk behaviors of men and women living with HIV-AIDS: Prevalence, predictors, and emerging clincial interventions. *Clinical Psychology: Science and Practice, 7,* 32–47.

Kalichman, S. C., Rompa, D., & Coley, B. (1996). Experimental component analysis of a behavioral HIV-AIDS prevention intervention for inner-city women. *Journal of Consulting and Clinical Psychology, 64* (4), 687–693.

Kamarck, T., & Jennings, J. R. (1991). Biobehavioral factors in sudden cardiac death. *Psychological Bulletin, 109,* 42–75.

Kandel, E. R. (1999). Biology and the future of psychoanalysis: A new intellectual framework for psychiatry revisited. *American Journal of Psychiatry, 156,* 505–524.

Kandel, E. R., & Hawkins, R. D. (1992). The biological basis of learning and individuality. *Scientific American,* pp. 79–86.

Kandel, E. R., & Schwartz, J. H. (1982). Molecular biology of learning: Modulation of transmitter release. *Science, 218,* 433–443.

Kandel, E. R., Schwartz, J. H., & Jessel, T. M. (1995). *Essentials of neural science and behavior.* East Norwalk, CT: Appleton & Lange.

Kaniasty, K., & Norris, F. H. (1995). Mobilization and deterioration of social support following natural disasters. *Current Directions in Psychological Science, 4,* 94–98.

Kaplan, M. F. (1975). Information integration in social judgment: Interaction of judge and informational components. In M. F. Kaplan & S. Schwartz (Eds.), *Human judgment and decision processes.* New York: Academic Press.

Kapur, N. (1999). Syndromes of retrograde amnesia: A conceptual and empirical synthesis. *Psychological Bulletin, 125,* 800–825.

Kasser, T., & Ryan, R. M. (1993). A dark side of the American dream: Correlates of financial success as a central life aspiration. *Journal of Personality and Social Psychology, 65,* 410–422.

Katz, J., Weiner, H., Gallagher, T., & Hellman, L. (1970). Stress, distress, and ego defenses. *Archives of General Psychiatry, 23,* 131–142.

Kaufman, A. S., Kaufman, J. C., Chen, T. H., & Kaufman, N. L. (1996). Differences on six horn abilities for 14 age groups between 15–16 and 75–94 years. *Psychological Assessment, 8,* 161–171.

Keane, T. M., & Kaloupek, D. G. (1982). Imaginal flooding in the treatment of posttraumatic stress disorder. *Journal of Consulting and Clinical Psychology, 50,* 138–140.

Kearins, J. (1986). Visual spatial memory in aboriginal and white Australian children. *Australian Journal of Psychology, 38*(3), 203–214.

Keefe, F. J., & France, C. R. (1999). Pain: Biopsychosocial mechanisms and management. *Current Directions in Psychological Science, 5,* 137–141.

Keenan, K., & Shaw, D. (1997). Developmental and social influences on young girls' early problem behavior. *Psychological Bulletin, 121,* 95–113.

Kehoe, P., & Bass, E. M. (1986). Conditioned aversions and their memories in 5-day-old rats during suckling. *Journal of Experimental Psychology: Animal Behavior Processes, 12,* 40–47.

Kelley, H. H. (1973). The processes of causal attribution. *American Psychologist, 28,* 107–128.

Kellogg, W. N., & Kellogg, L. A. (1933). *The ape and the child.* New York: McGraw-Hill.

Kelly, A. E. (1999). Revealing personal secrets. *Current Directions in Psychological Science 8,* 105–109.

Kelly, G. A. (1955). *The psychology of personal constructs.* New York: Norton.

Kelly, J. A., St. Lawrence, J. S., Hood, H. V., & Brasfield, T. L. (1989). Behavioral intervention to reduce AIDS risk activities. *Journal of Consulting and Clinical Psychology, 57,* 60–67.

Kelsoe, J. R., Cadet, J. L., Pickar, D., & Weinberger, D. R. (1988). Quantitative neuroanatomy in schizophrenia: A controlled magnetic resonance imaging study. *Archives of General Psychiatry, 45,* 533–541.

Kendall-Tackett, K. A., Williams, L. M., & Finkelhor, D. (1993). Impact of sexual abuse on children: A review and synthesis of recent empirical studies. *Psychological Bulletin, 113,* 164–180.

Kendler, K. S., & Prescott, C. A. (1999). A population-based twin study of lifetime major depression in men and women. *Archives of General Psychiatry, 56,* 39–44.

Kephart, W. (1967). Some correlates of romantic love. *Journal of Marriage and the Family, 29,* 470–474.

Kessler, R. C., McGonagle, Z. S., Nelson, C. B., Hughes, M., Eshelman, S., Wittchen, H. U., & Kendler, K. S. (1993). Lifetime and 12-month prevalence of DSM-III-R psychiatric disorders in the United States: Results from the National Comorbidity Survey. *Archives of General Psychiatry, 51,* 8–19.

Kessler, R. C., Sonnega, A., Bromet, E., Hughes, M., & Nelson, C. B. (1995). Posttraumatic stress disorder in the national comorbidity survey. *Archives of General Psychiatry, 52,* 1048–1060.

Kiecolt-Glaser, J. K., Fisher, L. D., Orgrocki, P., Stout, J. C., Speicher, C. E., & Glaser, R. (1987). Marital quality, marital disruption, and immune function. *Psychosomatic Medicine, 49,* 13–30.

Kilic, C., Noshirvani, H., Basoglu, M., & Marks, I. (1997). Agoraphobia and panic disorder: 3.5 years after alprazolam and/or exposure treatment. *Psychotherapy & Psychosomatics, 66,* 175–178.

Kilpatrick, D. G., Best, C. L., Veronen, L. J., Amick, A. E., Villeponteaux, L. A., & Ruff, G. A. (1985). Mental health correlates of criminal victimization: A random community survey. *Journal of Consulting and Clinical Psychology, 53,* 866–873.

Kimball, M. M. (1989). A new perspective on women's math achievement. *Psychological Bulletin, 105,* 198–214.

Kimberg, D. Y., Esposito, M. D., & Farah, M. J. (1998). Cognitive functions in the prefrontal cortex: Working memory and executive control. *Current Directions in Psychological Science, 6,* 185–192.

Kimmel, E. B. (1992). Women's contributions to psychology. *Contemporary Psychology, 37,* 201–202.

King, L. A., King D. W., Keane, T. M., Fairbank, J. A., & Adams, G. A. (1998). Resilience-recovery factors in post-traumatic stress disorder among female and male Vietnam veterans: Hardiness, postwar social support, and additional stressful life events. *Journal of Personality and Social Psychology, 74*(2), 420–434.

Kinney, D. K., Levy, D. L., Todd-Yurgelun, D. A., Tramer, S. J., & Holzman, P. S. (1998). Inverse relationship of perinatal complications and eye tracking dysfunction in relatives of patients with schizophrenia: Evidence of a two-factor model. *American Journal of Psychiatry, 15,* 976–978.

Kinsbourne, M. (1988). *Cerebral dysfunction in depression.* Washington, DC: American Psychiatric Association Press.

Kinsey, A. C., Pomeroy, W. B., & Martin, C. E. (1948). *Sexual behavior in the human male.* Philadelphia: W. B. Saunders.

Kirkpatrick B., Ran, R., Amador, X. F., Buchanan, R. W., McGlashan, T., Tohen, M., & Bromet, E. (1998). Summer birth and the deficit syndrome of schizophrenia. *American Journal of Psychiatry, 155,* 1221–1226.

Kirsch, I., & Lynn, S. J. (1995). The altered state of hypnosis: Changes in the theoretical landscape. *American Psychologist, 50,* 846–858.

Kitayama S., Markus, H. R., Matsumoto, H., & Norasakkunkit, V. (1997). Individual and collective processes in the construction of the self: Self-enhancement and self-criticism in Japan. *Journal of Personality and Social Psychology, 72,* 1245–1267.

Klatzky, R. L. (1980). *Human memory: Structures and processes.* San Francisco: W. H. Freeman.

Kleitman, N. (1960). The nature of dreaming. In G. E. W. Wolstenholme & M. O'Connor (Eds.), *Ciba Foundation symposium on the nature of sleep.* Boston: Little, Brown.

Klerman, G. L., & Weissman, M. M. (1993). *New applications of interpersonal psychotherapy.* Washington DC: American Psychiatric Press.

Klerman, G. L., Weissman, M. M., Rounsaville, B., & Chevron, E. S. (1995). Interpersonal psychotherapy for depression. *Journal of Psychotherapy Practice & Research, 4,* 342–351.

Kline, K. N., & Mattson, M. (2000). Breast self-examination pamphlets: A content analysis grounded in fear appeal research. *Health Communication, 12,* 1–21.

Kling, K. C., Hyde, J. S., Showers, C. J., & Buswell, B. N. (1999). Gender differences in self-esteem. *Psychological Bulletin, 125,* 470–500.

Knight, G. P., Fabes, R. A., & Higgins, D. A. (1996). Concerns about drawing causal inferences from meta-analyses: An example in the study of gender differences in aggression. *Psychological Bulletin, 119,* 410–421.

Koegel, P., Burnam, A., & Farr, R. K. (1988). The prevalence of specific psychiatric disorders among homeless individuals in the inner city of Los Angeles. *Archives of General Psychiatry, 45,* 1085–1092.

Kohlberg, L. (1964). The development of moral character. In M. L. Hoffman & L. W. Hoffman (Eds.), *Review of child development research* (Vol. I, p. 400). New York: Russell Sage Foundation.

Kohlberg, L. (1969). Stage and sequence: The cognitive-developmental approach to socialization. In D. A. Goslin (Ed.), *Handbook of socialization theory and research.* Chicago: Rand McNally.

Köhler, W. (1969). *The task of gestalt psychology.* Princeton, NJ: Princeton University Press.

Kolb, L. C. (1977). *Modern clinical psychiatry* (9th ed.). Philadelphia: W. B. Saunders.

Koren, D., Arnon, I., & Klein, E. (1999). Acute stress response and posttraumatic stress disorder in traffic accident victims: A one-year prospective follow-up study. *American Journal of Psychiatry, 156,* 367–373.

Korman, A. K. (1974). *The psychology of motivation.* Englewood Cliffs, NJ: Prentice-Hall.

Krasner, L. (1988). Mary Cover Jones: A legend in her own time. *The Behavior Therapist, 11,* 101–102.

Kravitz, D. A., & Martin, B. (1986). Ringelmann rediscovered: The original article. *Journal of Personality and Social Psychology, 50,* 936–941.

Krueger, R. W. C. F. (1929). The effect of overlearning on retention. *Journal of Experimental Psychology, 12,* 71–78.

Kruglanski, A. W. (1986, August). Freeze-think and the Challenger. *Psychology Today,* pp. 48–49.

Kübler-Ross, E. (1969). *On death and dying.* New York: Macmillan.

Kuch, K., & Cox, B. J. (1992). Symptoms of PTSD in 124 survivors of the holocaust. *American Journal of Psychiatry, 149,* 337–340.

Kumari, R. (1996). Relationship of sex role attitudes and self-esteem to fear of success among college women. *Psychological Studies, 40,* 82–86.

Kunugi, H., & others. (1995). Schizophrenia following in utero exposure to the 1957 influenza epidemics in Japan. *American Journal of Psychiatry, 152,* 450–452.

LaCroix, A. Z., Mead, L. A., Liang, K., Thomas, C. B., & Pearson, T. P. (1986). Coffee consumption and the incidence of coronary heart disease. *New England Journal of Medicine, 315,* 977–982.

Lader, M. H., & Mathews, A. (1970). Physiological changes during spontaneous panic attacks. *Journal of Psychosomatic Research, 14,* 377–382.

LaGreca, A. M., Silverman, W. K., & Wasserstein, S. B. (1998). Children's predisaster functioning as a predictor of posttraumatic stress following Hurricane Andrew. *Journal of Consulting and Clinical Psychology, 66,* 883–892.

Lahey, B. B., & Ciminero, A. R. (1980). *Maladaptive behavior.* Glenview, IL: Scott, Foresman.

Lahey, B. B., Hartdagen, S. E., Frick, P. J., McBurnett, K., Connor, R., & Hyrd, G. W. (1988). Conduct disorder: Parsing the confounded relation to parental divorce and antisocial personality. *Journal of Abnormal Psychology, 97,* 334–337.

Lamb, H. R., & Weinberger, L. E. (1992). Conservatorship for gravely disabled psychiatric patients: A four-year follow-up study. *American Journal of Psychiatry, 149,* 909–913.

Lang, P. J. (1995). The emotion probe: Studies of motivation and attention. *American Psychologist, 5,* 372–385.

Langlois, J. H., & Stephan, C. W. (1981). Beauty and the beast: The role of physical attractiveness in the development of peer relations and social behavior. In S. S. Brehm, S. M. Kassin, & F. X. Gibbons (Eds.), *Developmental social psychology.* New York: Oxford University Press.

Larson, R., & Richards, M. H. (1994). *Divergent realities: The emotional lives of mothers, fathers, and adolescents.* New York: Basic Books.

Latané, B., & Darley, J. (1970). *The unresponsive bystander: Why doesn't he help?* New York: Appleton-Century-Crofts.

Latané, B., & Nida, S. (1981). Ten years of research on group size and helping. *Psychological Bulletin, 89,* 308–324.

Latané, B., & Rodin, J. (1969). A lady in distress: Inhibiting effects of friends and strangers on bystander intervention. *Journal of Experimental Social Psychology, 5,* 189–202.

Latané, B., Williams, K., & Harkins, S. (1979). Too many hands make light the work: The causes and consequences of social loafing. *Journal of Personality and Social Psychology, 37,* 822–832.

Lauer, C., Rieman, D., Lund, D., & Berger, M. (1987). Shortened REM latency: A consequence of psychological strain? *Psychophysiology, 24,* 263–271.

Laumann, E. O., Gagnon, J. H., Michael, R. T., & Michaels, S. (1994). *The social organization of sexuality: Sexual practices in the United States.* Chicago: University of Chicago Press.

Lazarus, R. S. (1982). Thoughts on the relations between emotion and cognition. *American Psychologist, 37,* 1019–1024.

Lazarus, R. S. (1984). On the primacy of cognition. *American Psychologist, 39,* 117–123.

Lazarus, R. S. (1991). *Emotion and adaptation.* New York: Oxford University Press.

Lazarus, R. S. (1999). *Stress and emotion: A new synthesis.* New York: Springer.

Lee, K. A., Vaillant, G. E., Torrey, W. C., & Elder, G. H. (1995). A 50-year prospective study of the psychological sequelae of World War II combat. *American Journal of Psychiatry, 152,* 4.

Lenneberg, E. H. (1967). *Biological foundations of language.* New York: Wiley.

Leon, A. S. (1983). Exercise and coronary heart disease. *Hospital Medicine, 19,* 38–59.

Leon, G. R. (1977). *Case histories of deviant behavior: An interactional perspective* (2nd ed.). Boston: Holbrook Press.

Leonard, W. E. (1928). *The locomotive god.* London: Chapman & Hall.

Lepper, M. R., Greene, D., & Nisbett, R. E. (1973). Undermining children's intrinsic interest with extrinsic reward: A test of the "overjustification" hypothesis. *Journal of Personality and Social Psychology, 28,* 129–137.

LeVay, S. (1991). A difference in hypothalamic structure between heterosexual and homosexual men. *Science, 253,* 1034–1037.

Leventhal, H., & Tomarken, A. J. (1986). Emotion: Today's problem. *Annual Review of Psychology, 37,* 565–610.

Levin, D. T., & Simons, D. J. (1997). Failure to detech changes to attended objects in motion pictures. *Psychonomic Bulletin & Review, 4,* 501–506.

Levine, C., Kohlberg, L., & Hewer, A. (1985). The current formulation of Kohlberg's theory in response to critics. *Human Development, 28,* 94–100.

Levine, J., & others. (1987). The role of denial in recovery from coronary heart disease. *Psychosomatic Medicine, 49,* 109–117.

Levine, J. D., Gordon, N. C., & Fields, H. C. (1979). The role of endorphin in placebo analgesia. In J. J. Bonica, J. G. Liebeskind, & D. Albe-Fressard (Eds.), *Advances in pain research and therapy* (Vol. 3). New York: Raven Press.

Levine, J. M., Resnick, L. B., & Higgins, E. T. (1993). Social foundations of cognition. *Annual Review of Psychology, 44,* 585–612.

Levinson, D. J. (1978). *The seasons of a man's life.* New York: Knopf.

Levinson, D. J. (1986). A conception of adult development. *American Psychologist, 41,* 3–13.

Lewin, K. (1931). Environmental forces in child behavior and development. In C. Murchison (Ed.), *A handbook of child psychology.* Worcester, MA: Clark University Press.

Lewinsohn, P. M., Duncan, E. M., Stanton, A. K., & Hautzinger, M. (1986). Age at first onset for nonbipolar depression. *Journal of Abnormal Psychology, 95,* 378–383.

Lewinsohn, P. M., Hoberman, H. M., & Rosenbaum, M. (1988). A prospective study of risk factors for major depression. *Journal of Abnormal Psychology, 97,* 251–264.

Lewinsohn, P. M., Mischel, W., Chaplin, W., & Barton, R. (1980). Social competence and depression: The role of illusory self-perceptions. *Journal of Abnormal Psychology, 89,* 203–212.

Lewis, M., & Rosenblum, L. A. (Eds.). (1978). *The development of affect.* New York: Plenum.

Lewontin, R. (1982). *Human diversity.* New York: Scientific American Library.

Liebert, R. M., Neale, J. M., & Davidson, E. S. (1983). *The early window: The effects of television on children and youth.* New York: Pergamon Press.

Lilienfeld, S. O., Kirsch, I., Sarbin, T. R., Lynn, S. J., Chaves, J. F., Ganaway, G. K., & Powell, R. A. (1999). Dissociative identity disorder and the sociocognitive model: Recalling the lessons of the past. *Psychological Bulletin, 125,* 507–523.

Lindsey, K. P., & Paul, G. L. (1989). Involuntary commitment to public mental institutions: Issues involving the overrepresentation of blacks as assessment of relevant functioning. *Psychological Bulletin, 106,* 171–183.

Linton, M. (1979, July). I remember it well. *Psychology Today,* pp. 89–98.

Lisanby, S. H., Maddox, J. H., Prudic, J., Devanand, D. P., & Sackheim, H. A. (2000). The effects of electroconvulsive therapy on memory of autobiographical and public events. *Archives of General Psychiatry, 57,* 581–590.

Lissner, L., & others. (1991). Variability of body weight and health outcomes in the Framingham population. *New England Journal of Medicine, 324,* 1839–1844.

Littlewood, R. (1992). Psychiatric diagnosis and racial bias: Empirical and interpretative approaches. *Social Science and Medicine, 34*(2), 141–149.

Lloyd, C., Alexander, A. A., Rice, D. G., & Greenfield, N. S. (1980). Life change and academic performance. *Journal of Human Stress, 6,* 15–25.

Loebel, A. D., Lieberman, J. A., Alvir, J. M. J., Mayerhoff, D. I., Geisler, S. H., & Szymanski, S. R. (1992). Duration of psychosis and outcome in first-episode schizophrenia. *American Journal of Psychiatry, 149,* 1183–1188.

Loehlin, J. C., Lindzey, G., & Spuhler, J. N. (1975). *Race differences in intelligence.* San Francisco: Freeman.

Loftus, E. F. (1992). When a lie becomes memory's truth: Memory distortion after exposure to misinformation. *Current Directions in Psychological Science, 1,* 121–123.

Loftus, E. F. (1993). The reality of repressed memories. *American Psychologist, 48,* 518–537.

Loftus, E. F. (1997). Creating false memories. *Scientific American,* pp. 70–75.

Loftus, E. F., & Palmer, J. C. (1974). Reconstruction of automobile destruction: An example of the interaction between language and memory. *Journal of Verbal Learning and Verbal Behavior, 13,* 585–589.

Loftus, E. F., Polonsky, S., & Fullilove, M. T. (1993). *Memories of childhood sexual abuse: Remembering and repressing.* Unpublished manuscript and Columbia University cited in Loftus, E. F. (1993). The reality of repressed memories. *American Psychologist, 48,* 518–537.

London, E. D., & others. (1990). Morphine-induced metabolic changes in the human brain: Studies with positron emission tomography and [fluorine 18] fluorodeoxyglucose. *Archives of General Psychiatry, 47,* 73–81.

Longo, D. J., Clum, G. A., & Yeager, N. J. (1988). Psychosocial treatment for recurrent genital herpes. *Journal of Consulting and Clinical Psychology, 56,* 61–66.

Lore, R. K., & Schultz, L. A. (1993). Control of human aggression: A comparative perspective. *American Psychologist, 48,* 16–25.

Lorenz, K. (1937). The companion in the bird's world. *Auk, 54,* 245–273.

Lorenz, K. (1967). *On aggression.* New York: Bantam.

Low, B. S. (1989). Cross-cultural patterns in the training of children: An evolutionary perspective. *Journal of Comparative Psychology, 103,* 311–319.

Lubinski, D., & Humphreys, L. G. (1997). Incorporating general intelligence into epidemiology and the social sciences. *Intelligence, 24,* 159–202.

Luchins, K. S. (1942). Mechanization in problem solving: The effects of "Einstellung." *Psychometric Monographs, 54*(6).

Lynn, R. (1998). The decline in genotypic intelligence. In U. Neisser (Ed.), *The rising curve: Long-term gains in IQ and related measures* (pp. 335–364). Washington, DC: American Psychological Association.

Mack, G. I. (1999). Effects of race on the clinical assessment of antisocial personality disorder and psychopathy. *Dissertation Abstracts International: Section B: the Sciences & Engineering, 59,* 4472.

Macklin, M. L., Metzger, L. J., Litz, B. T., McNally, R. J., Lasko, N. B., Orr, S. P., & Pitman, R. K. (1998). Lower precombat intelligence is a risk factor for posttraumatic stress disorder. *Journal of Consulting and Clinical Psychology, 66*, 323–326.

Maddox, G. L. (1964). Disengagement theory: A critical evaluation. *The Gerontologist, 4*, 80–83.

Maier, N. R. F. (1931). Reasoning in humans: II. The solution of a problem and its appearance in consciousness. *Journal of Comparative and Physiological Psychology, 12*, 181–194.

Maier, S. F., & Watkins, L. R. (1998). Cytokines for psychologists: Implications of bidirectional immune-to-braincommunication for understanding behavior, mood, and cognition. *Psychological Review, 105*, 83–107.

Mandel, D. R., Jusczyk, P. W., & Pisoni, D. B. (1995). Infants' recognition of the sound patterns of their own names. *Psychological Science, 6*, 314–317.

Manne, S., Alfieri, T., Taylor, K., & Dougherty, J. (1999). Preferences for spousal support among individuals with cancer. *Journal of Applied Social Psychology, 29*, 722–749.

Marcus, A. C., Wheeler, R. C., Cullen, J. W., & Crane, L. A. (1987). Quasi-experimental evaluation of the Los Angeles Know Your Body program: Knowledge, beliefs, and self-reported behaviors. *Preventive Medicine, 16*, 803–815.

Markus, H. (1978). The effect of mere presence on social facilitation: An unobtrusive test. *Journal of Experimental Social Psychology, 14*, 389–397.

Marlatt, G. A., & Rose, F. (1980). Addictive disorders. In A. E. Kazdin, A. S. Bellack, & M. Hersen (Eds.), *New perspectives in abnormal psychology* (pp. 298–324). New York: Oxford University Press.

Martell, D. A., & Dietz, P. E. (1992). Mentally disordered offenders who push or attempt to push victims onto subway tracks in New York City. *Archives of General Psychology, 49*, 472–475.

Martin, R. J., White, B. D., & Hulsey, M. G. (1991). The regulation of body weight. *American Scientist, 79*, 528–541.

Martorell, R. (1998). Nutrition and the worldwide rise in IQ scores. In U. Neisser (Ed.), *The rising curve: Long-term gains in IQ and related measures* (pp. 183–206). Washington, DC: American Psychological Association.

Martuza, R. L., Chiocca, E. A., Jenike, M. A., Giriunas, I. E., & Ballantine, H. T. (1990). Stereotactic radiofrequency thermal cingulotomy for obsessive compulsive disorder. *Journal of Neuropsychiatry, 2*, 331–336.

Maslow, A. (1967). A theory of metamotivation: The biological rooting of the value-life. *Journal of Humanistic Psychology, 7*, 93–127.

Maslow, A. (1970). *Motivation and personality* (2nd ed.). New York: Harper & Row.

Masters, W. H., & Johnson, V. E. (1966). *Human sexual response.* Boston: Little, Brown.

Matefy, R. E., & Kroll, R. G. (1974). An initial investigation of psychedelic drug flashback phenomena. *Journal of Consulting and Clinical Psychology, 42*, 854–860.

Matlin, M. (1983). *Cognition.* New York: Holt, Rinehart & Winston.

Matlin, M. W. (1988). *Sensation and perception* (2nd ed.). Boston: Allyn & Bacon.

Mathews, K. E., & Canon, L. K. (1975). Environmental noise level as a determinant of helping behavior. *Journal of Personality and Social Psychology, 32*, 571–577.

Matthews, A., & MacLeod, C. (1986). Discrimination of threat cues without awareness in anxiety states. *Journal of Abnormal Psychology, 95*, 131–138.

Matthews, D. B., Best, P. J., White, A. M., Vandergriff, L., & Simpson, P. E. (1996). Ethanol impairs spatial cognitive processing: New behavioral and electrophysiological findings. *Current Directions in Psychological Science, 5*, 111–115.

Matthews, E. L. (1982). Psychological perspectives on the Type A behavior pattern. *Psychological Bulletin, 91*, 293–323.

Mavromatis, A. (1987). *Hypnogogia.* London: Routledge.

Mazure, C. M. (1998). Life stressors as risk factors in depression. *Clinical Psychology: Science and Practice, 5*, 291–313.

McAdams, D. P., & Vaillant, G. E. (1982). Intimacy motivation and psychosocial adjustment: A longitudinal study. *Journal of Personality Assessment, 46*, 586–593.

McCall, R. B. (1979). *Infants.* Cambridge, MA: Harvard University Press.

McCall, W. V., Reboussin, D. M., Weiner, R. D., & Sackheim, H. A. (2000). Titrated moderately suprathreshold vs. fixed high-dose right unilateral electroconvulsive therapy: Acute antidepressant and cognitive effects. *Archives of General Psychiatry, 57*, 438–444.

McCarley, R. W., & others. (1989). CT abnormalities in schizophrenia. *Archives of General Psychiatry, 46*, 698–708.

McClelland, D. C., & Atkinson, J. W. (1948). The projective expression of needs: I. The effect of different intensities of the hunger drive on perception. *Journal of Psychology, 25*, 205–222.

McConaghy, M. J. (1979). Gender permanence and the genital basis of gender: Stages in the development of constancy of gender identity. *Child Development, 50*, 1223–1226.

McCrae, R. R., Arenberg, D., & Costa, P. T. (1987). Declines in divergent thinking with age: Cross-sequential analyses. *Psychology and Aging, 2*, 130–137.

McCrae, R. R., & Costa, P. T. (1990). *Personality in adulthood.* New York: Guilford Press.

McCrae, R. R., & Costa, P. T. (1997). Personality trait structure as a human universal. *American Psychologist, 52*, 509–516.

McCrae, R. R., & Costa, P. T. (1999). A five-factor theory of personality. In L. A. Pervin & O. P. John (Eds.), *Handbook of personality: Theory and research* (2nd ed., pp. 139–153). New York: Guilford.

McCrae, R. R., & Costa, P. T., Jr. (1994). The stability of personality: Observations and evaluations. *Current Directions in Psychological Science, 3*, 173–175.

McCrae, R. R., & Costa, P. T. (1987). Validation of the five-factor model of personality across instruments and observers. *Journal of Personality and Social Psychology, 52*, 81–90.

McEwen, B. S. (1998). Protective and damaging effects of stress mediators. *The New England Journal of Medicine, 338*, 171–179.

McGaugh, J. L. (1983). Preserving the presence of the past. Hormonal influences on memory storage. *American Psychologist, 38*, 161–174.

McGraw, M. B. (1940). Neural maturation as exemplified in achievement of bladder control. *Journal of Pediatrics, 16*, 580–590.

McNeil, T. F., Cantor-Graae, E., Weinberger, D. R. (2000). Relationship of obstetric complications and differences in size of brain structures in monozygotic twin pairs discordant for schizophrenia. *American Journal of Psychiatry, 157*, 203–212.

McWilliams, S. A., & Tuttle, R. J. (1973). Long-term psychological effects of LSD. *Psychological Bulletin, 79*, 341–351.

Mead, M. (1935). *Sex and temperament in three primitive societies.* New York: Morrow.

Mednick, S. A., Machon, R. A., Huttunen, M. O., & Bonett, D. (1988). Adult schizophrenia following prenatal exposure to an influenza epidemic. *Archives of General Psychiatry, 45*, 189–192.

Melzack, R. (1973). *The puzzle of pain.* New York: Basic Books.

Melzack, R. (1992, April). Phantom limbs. *Scientific American*, pp. 120–126.

Melzack, R., & Wall, P. D. (1983). *The challenge of pain.* New York: Basic Books.

Mercklebach, H., van den Hout, M., Jansen, A., & van der Molen, G. M. (1988). Many stimuli are frightening, but some are more frightening: The contributions of preparedness, dangerousness, and unpredictability to making a stimulus fearful. *Journal of Psychopathology and Behavioral Assessment, 10*, 355–366.

Messick, D. M., & Sentis, K. P. (1979). Fairness and preference. *Journal of Experimental Social Psychology, 15*, 418–434.

Mewborn, C. R., & Rogers, R. W. (1979). Effects of threatening and reassuring components of fear appeals on physiological and verbal measures of emotion and attitudes. *Journal of Experimental Social Psychology, 15*, 242–253.

Meyer, A. J., Nash, J. D., McAlister, A. L., Maccoby, N., & Farquhar, J. W. (1980). Skills training in a cardiovascular health education campaign. *Journal of Consulting and Clinical Psychology, 48*, 129–142.

Meyer, D. E., & Schvaneveldt, R. W. (1971). Facilitation in recognizing pairs of words: Evidence of a dependence between retrieval operations. *Journal of Experimental Psychology, 90*, 227–234.

Meyer-Blauberg, H. F. L., & others. (1995). Prenatal estrogens and the development of homosexual orientation. *Developmental Psychology, 31*, 12–21.

Meyerowitz, B. E., & Chaiken, S. (1987). The effect of message framing on breast self-examination attitudes, intentions, and behavior. *Journal of Personality and Social Psychology, 52*, 500–510.

Meyerowitz, B. E., Richardson, J., Hudson, S., & Leedham, B. (1998). Ethnicity and cancer outcomes: Behavioral and psychosocial considerations. *Psychological Bulletin, 123*, 47–70.

Meyers, C. A., Berman, S. A., Scheibel, R. S. & Hayman, A. (1992). Case report: Acquired antisocial personal disorder associated with unilateral left orbital frontal lobe damage. *Journal of Psychiatry and Neuroscience, 17*, 121–125.

Michael, R. T., Gagnon, J. H., Laumann, E. O., & Kolata, G. (1994). *Sex in America: A definitive survey.* Boston: Little, Brown.

Milgram, S. (1963). Behavioral study of obedience. *Journal of Abnormal and Social Psychology, 67*, 371–378.

Milgram, S. (1965). Some conditions of obedience and disobedience to authority. *Human Relations, 18*, 57–76.

Miller, G. A. (1956). The magic number seven, plus or minus two. Some limits on our ability to process information. *Psychological Review, 63*, 81–97.

Miller, J. G. (1999). Cultural psychology: Implications for basic psychological theory. *Psychological Science, 10*, 85–91.

Miller, M. E., & Bowers, K. S. (1993). Hypnotic analgesia: Dissociated experience or dissociated control? *Journal of Abnormal Psychology, 102*, 29–38.

Miller, N. E. (1944). Experimental studies of conflict. In J. McV. Hunt (Ed.), *Personality and the behavior disorders* (Vol. 1). New York: Ronald Press.

Miller, T. Q., Smith, T. W., Turner, C. W., Guijarro, M. L., & Hallet, A. J. (1996). A meta-analytic review of research on hostility and physical health. *Psychological Bulletin, 119*, 322–348.

Milner, B. (1974). Hemispheric specialization: Scope and limits. In F. O. Schmitt & F. G. Worden (Eds.), *The neurosciences: Third study program* (pp. 75–89). Cambridge, MA: MIT Press.

Milner, B., Corkin, S., & Teuber, H. L. (1968). Further analysis of the hippocampal amnesic syndrome: 14-year follow-up study of H. M. *Neuropsychologia, 6*, 215–234.

Mineka, B., Davidson, M., Cook, M., & Keir, R. (1984). Observational conditioning of snake fears in rhesus monkeys. *Journal of Abnormal Psychology, 93,* 355–372.

Mineka, S., & Sutton, S. K. (1992). Cognitive biases and the emotional disorders. *Psychological Science, 3,* 65–69.

Mischel, W. (1968). *Personality and assessment.* New York: Wiley.

Mischel, W., & Shoda, Y. (1999). Integrating dispositions and processing dynamics within a unified theory of personality: The cognitive-affective personality system. In L. A. Pervin & O. P. John (Eds.), *Handbook of personality: Theory and research* (2nd ed., pp. 197–218). New York: Guilford.

Mogil, J. S., Sternberg, W. F., Kest, B., Marek, P., & Liebeskind, J. C. (1993). Sex differences in the antagonism of swim-stress induced analgesia: Effects of gonadectomy and estrogen replacement. *Pain, 53,* 17.

Money, J. (1987). Sin, sickness, or status: Homosexual gender identity and psychoneuroendocrinology. *American Psychologist, 42,* 384–389.

Money, J. (1988). *Gay, straight, and in-between.* New York: Oxford University Press.

Mook, D. G. (1986). *Motivation: The organization of action.* New York: W. W. Norton.

Moore-Ede, M. C., Sulzman, F. M., & Fuller, C. A. (1982). *The clocks that time us.* Cambridge: Harvard University Press.

Morell, P., & Norton, W. T. (1980, May). Myelin. *Scientific American,* pp. 88–118.

Morris, N. (1986). A working memory, 1974–1984. A review of a decade of research. *Current Psychological Research and Reviews, 5,* 281–295.

Moscovitch, M., & Olds, J. (1982). Asymmetries in emotional facial expressions and their possible relation to hemisphere specialization. *Neuropsychologia, 20,* 71–81.

Moscowitz, D. S., Brown, K. W., & Cote, S. (1997). Reconceptualizing stability: Using time as a psychological dimension. *Current Directions in Psychological Science, 6,* 127–132.

Mossman, D., & Perlin, M. L. (1992). Psychiatry and the homeless: A reply to Dr. Lamb. *American Journal of Psychiatry, 149,* 951–957.

Mufson, L., Weissman, M. M., Moreau, D., & Garfinkel, R. (1999). Efficacy of interpersonal psychotherapy for depressed adolescents. *Archives of General Psychiatry, 57,* 573–579.

Mullen, B. (1986). Atrocity as a function of lynch mob composition: A self-attention perspective. *Personality and Social Psychology Bulletin, 12,* 187–197.

Muller, E. E., & Nistico, G. (1989). *Brain messengers and the pituitary.* Orlando: Academic Press.

Mumford, E., Schlesinger, H. J., & Glass, G. V. (1981). Reducing medical cost through mental health treatment: Research problems and recommendations. In A. Broskowski, E. Marks, & S. H. Budman (Eds.), *Linking health and mental health.* Beverly Hills, CA: Sage.

Mundy, P., Robertson, M., Robertson, J., & Greenblatt, M. (1990). The prevalence of psychotic symptoms in homeless adolescents. *Journal of the American Academy of Child and Adolescent Psychiatry, 29,* 724–731.

Murphy, M. T., Michelson, L. K., Marchione, K., Marchione, N., & Testa, S. (1998). The role of self-directed in vivo exposure in combination with cognitive therapy, relaxation training, or therapist-assisted exposure in the treatment of panic disorder with agoraphobia. *Journal of Anxiety Disorders, 12,* 117–138.

Murray, H. (1938). *Exploration in personality.* New York: Oxford University Press.

Murray, H. (1951). Uses of the T. A. T. *American Journal of Psychiatry, 107,* 577–581.

Myers, D. (1999). *Social psychology* (6th ed.). Boston: McGraw-Hill.

Myers, D. G., & Bishop, G. D. (1970). Discussion effects on racial attitudes. *Science, 169,* 778–779.

Myers, D. G., & Diener, E. (1995). Who is happy? *Psychological Science, 6,* 10–18.

Nadel, L., & Jacobs, W. J. (1998). Traumatic memory is special. *Current Directions in Psychological Science, 7,* 154–157.

Nash, S. C. (1975). The relationship among sex-role stereotyping, sex-role performance, and sex differences in spatial visualization. *Sex Roles, 1,* 15–32.

National Advisory Mental Health Council. (1995a). *Basic behavioral research for mental health: A national investment.* Rockville, MD: National Institute of Mental Health.

National Advisory Mental Health Council. (1995b). Basic behavioral science research for mental health: A national investment (emotion and motivation). *American Psychologist, 50,* 838–845.

National Institute on Alcohol Abuse and Alcoholism. (1987). *Report.* Washington, DC: U.S. Government Printing Office.

National Safety Council. (1998). *Accident facts.* Itasca, IL: National Safety Council.

Neisser, U. (1998). Rising test scores and what they mean. In U. Neisser (Ed.), *The rising curve: Long-term gains in IQ and related measures* (pp. 3–24). Washington, DC: American Psychological Association.

Neugarten, B. L. (1964). *Personality in middle and late life.* New York: Atherton Press.

Neugarten, B. L., & Hagestad, G. O. (1976). Age and the life course. In R. H. Binstock & E. Shanas (Eds.), *Handbook of aging and the social sciences.* New York: Van Nostrand Reinhold.

Newcomer, J. W., Selke, G., Melson, A. K., Hershey, T., Craft, S., Richards, K., & Alderson, A. L. (1999). Decreased memory performance in healthy humans induced by stress-level cortisol treatment. *Archives of General Psychiatry, 56,* 527–533.

Newton, J. W., & Mann, L. (1980). Crowd size as a factor in the persuasion process: A study of religious crusade meetings. *Journal of Personality and Social Psychology, 39,* 874–883.

Neyland, T. C., & others. (1998). Sleep disturbances in the Viet Nam generation: Findings from a nationally representative sample of male veterans. *American Journal of Psychiatry, 155,* 929–933.

NICHD Early Child Care Research Network. (1997). The effects of child care on infant-mother security: Results of the NICHD study of early child care. *Child Development, 68,* 860–879.

Nopoulos, P., Torres, I., Flaum, M., Andreasen, N. C., Ehrhardt, J. C., & Yuh, W. T. C. (1995). Brain morphology in first-episode schizophrenia. *American Journal of Psychiatry, 152,* 1721–1723.

Nunes, E. V., Frank, K. A., & Kornfeld, D. S. (1987). Psychologic treatment for the Type A behavior pattern and for coronary heart disease: A meta-analysis of the literature. *Psychosomatic Medicine, 48,* 159–166.

Offer, D., & Schonert-Reichl, K. A. (1992). Debunking the myths of adolescence: Findings from recent research. *Journal of the American Academy of Child and Adolescent Psychiatry, 31,* 1003–1014.

Ohman, A., Erixon, G., & Löfberg, I. (1975). Phobias and preparedness: Phobic versus neutral pictures as conditioned stimuli for human autonomic responses. *Journal of Abnormal Psychology, 84,* 41–45.

O'Leary, A. (1990). Stress, emotion, and human immune function. *Psychology Bulletin, 108,* 363–382.

O'Leary, S. G. (1995). Parental discipline mistakes. *Current Directions in Psychological Science, 4,* 11–13.

Oliver, M. B., & Hyde, J. S. (1993). Gender differences in sexuality: A meta-analysis. *Psychological Bulletin, 114,* 29–51.

Olson, J. M., & Zanna, M. P. (1993). Attitudes and attitude change. *Annual Review of Psychology, 44,* 117–154.

Ost, L. G. (1992). Blood and injection phobia: Background and cognitive, physiological, and behavioral variables. *Journal of Abnormal Psychology, 101,* 68–74.

Paris, J. (2000). The primacy of early experience: A critique, an alternative, and some clinical implications. *Journal of Psychiatric Practice,* May, 147–151.

Parrott, A. C. (1999). Does cigarette smoking cause stress? *American Psychologist, 54,* 817–820.

Passe, T. J., Rajagopalan, P., Tupler, L. A., Byrum, C. E., MacFall, J. R., & Krishnan, K. R. R. (1997). Age and sex effects on brain morphology. *Progress in Neuro-Psychopharmacology & Biological Psychiatry, 21,* 1231–1237.

Patterson, F. (1977). The gestures of a gorilla: Language acquisition in another primate species. In J. Hambrug, J. Goodall, & L. McCown (Eds.), *Perspectives in human evolution* (Vol. 4). Menlo Park, CA: W. A. Benjamin.

Pearlson, G. D., & others. (1989). Ventricle-brain ratio, computed tomographic density, and brain area in 50 schizophrenics. *Archives of General Psychiatry, 46,* 690–697.

Pennebaker, J. W., & Beall, J. K. (1986). Confronting a traumatic event: Toward an understanding of inhibition and disease. *Journal of Abnormal Psychology, 95,* 274–281.

Pennebaker, J. W., Colder, M., & Sharp, L. K. (1990). Accelerating the coping process. *Journal of Personality and Social Psychology, 58,* 528–537.

Pennebaker, J. W., Kiecolt-Glaser, J. K., & Glaser, R. (1988). Disclosure of traumas and immune function: Health implications for psychotherapy. *Journal of Consulting and Clinical Psychology, 56,* 239–245.

Perls, F. S., Hefferline, R. F., & Goodman, P. (1951). *Gestalt therapy.* New York: Julian Press.

Petersen, A. C. (1979, January). Can puberty come any faster? *Psychology Today,* pp. 45–56.

Petersen, R. C., & Stillman, R. C. (1978). *Phencyclidine (PCP) abuse: An appraisal* (National Institute on Drug Abuse Monograph No. 21). Washington, DC: U.S. Government Printing Office.

Peterson, L., Brown, D., & Aronson, H. (1998). Faculty gender, status, roles, and privileges in applied doctoral programs. *The Clinical Psychologist, 51,* 11–16.

Peterson, L. R., & Peterson, M. J. (1959). Short-term retention of individual items. *Journal of Experimental Psychology, 58,* 193–198.

Petitto, J. M., Gariepy, J.- L., Gendreau, P. L., Rodriguez, R., & Lewis, M. H. (1999). Differences in NK cell function in mice bred for high and low aggression: Genetic linkage between complex behavioral and immunological traits. *Brain, Behavior, and Immunity, 13,* 175–186.

Petri, H. L. (1986). *Motivation: Theory and research* (3rd ed.). Belmont, CA: Wadsworth.

Pfefferbaum, B., Nixon, S. J., Tucker, P. M., Tivis, R. D., Moore, V. L., Gurwitch, R. H., Pynoos, R. S., & Geis, H. (1999). Posttraumatic stress responses in bereaved children after the Oklahoma City bombing. *Journal of the American Academy of Child and Adolescent Psychiatry, 38,* 1016–1023.

Phillips, J. D. (1933). *Salem in the seventeenth century.* Cambridge, MA: Riverside Press.

Phinney, J. (1996). When we talk about American ethnic groups, what do we mean? *American Psychologist, 51,* 918–927.

Piacentini, J. (1999). Cognitive behavioral therapy of childhood OCD. *Child and Adolescent Psychiatric Clinics of North America, 8,* 599–616.

Piaget, J. (1972). Intellectual development from adolescence to adulthood. *Human Development, 15,* 1–12.

Piaget, J., & Inhelder, B. (1963). *The child's conception of space.* London: Routledge and Paul.

Pincomb, G. A., Lovallo, W. R., Passey, R. B., Brackett, D. J., & Wilson, M. F. (1987). Caffeine enhances the physiological response to occupational stress in medical students. *Health Psychology, 6,* 101–112.

Piorkowski, G. (1983). Survivor guilt in the university setting. *Personnel and Guidance Journal, 61,* 620–622.

Plomin, R. (1989). Environment and genes: Determinants of behavior. *American Psychologist, 44,* 105–111.

Plomin, R. (1994). Genetics and experience: The interplay between nature and nurture. Thousand Oaks, CA: Sage.

Plomin, R. (1995). Molecular genetics and psychology. *Current Directions in Psychological Science, 4,* 114–117.

Plomin, R. (1999). Genetics of childhood disorders: III. Genetics and intelligence. *Journal of the American Academy of Child and Adolescent Psychiatry, 38,* 786–788.

Plomin, R., & Petrill, S. A. (1997). Genetics and intelligence: What's new? *Intelligence, 24,* 53–77.

Pope, K. S. (1996). Memory, abuse, and science: Questioning claims about the false memory syndrome epidemic. *American Psychologist, 51,* 957–974.

Pope, K. S., & Singer, J. L. (Eds.). (1978). *The stream of consciousness.* New York: Plenum.

Posner, M. I. (1973). *Cognition: An introduction.* Glenview, IL: Scott, Foresman.

Postmes, T., & Spears, R. (1998). Deindividuation and anti-normative behavior: A meta-analysis. *Psychological Bulletin, 123,* 238–259.

Prentice, W. C. H. (1954). Visual recognition of verbally labeled figures. *American Journal of Psychology, 67,* 315–320.

Preston, S. H., (1998). Differential fertility by IQ and the IQ distribution of a population. In U. Neisser (Ed.), *The rising curve: Long-term gains in IQ and related measures* (pp. 377–388). Washington, DC: American Psychological Association.

Price, D. D. (1988). *Psychological and neural mechanisms of pain.* New York: Raven Press.

Price, D. D., & Barber, J. (1987). An analysis of factors that contribute to the efficiency of hypnotic analgesia. *Journal of Abnormal Psychology, 96,* 46–51.

Prinzmetal, W. (1995). Visual feature integration in a world of objects. *Current Directions in Psychological Science, 4,* 90–94.

Prochaska, J. O. (1984). *Systems of psychotherapy: A transtheoretical analysis* (2nd ed.). Pacific Grove, CA: Brooks/Cole.

Pugh, E. N. (1988). Vision: Physics and retinal physiology. In R. C. Atkinson, R. J. Herrnstein, G.

Lindzey, & R. D. Luce (Eds.), *Stevens' handbook of experimental psychology: Vol. 1. Perception and Motivation.* New York: Wiley-Interscience.

Raaheim, K., & Kaufmann, G. (1972). Level of activity and success in solving an unfamiliar task. *Psychological Reports, 30,* 271–274.

Raaijmakers, J. G. W., & Shiffrin, R. M. (1992). Models for recall and recognition. *Annual Review of Psychology, 43,* 205–234.

Rachman, S. (1966). Sexual fetishism: An experimental analogue. *Psychological Record, 16,* 293–296.

Radvansky, G. A. (1999). Aging, memory, and comprehension. *Current Directions in Psychological Science, 8,* 49–53.

Ranken, H. B. (1963). Language and thinking: Positive and negative effects of naming. *Science, 141,* 48–50.

Rapee, R. M., Brown, T. A., Antony, M. M., & Barlow, D. H. (1992). Response to hyperventilation and inhalation of 5.5% carbon dioxide enriched air across the DSM-III-R anxiety disorders. *Journal of Abnormal Psychology, 101,* 538–552.

Rapp, P. R., & Amaral, D. G. (1992). Individual differences in the cognitive and neurobiological consequences of normal aging. *Trends in Neuroscience, 15,* 340–344.

Raugh, M. R., & Atkinson, R. C. (1975). A mnemonic method for learning a second-language vocabulary. *Journal of Educational Psychology, 67,* 1–16.

Ravindran, A.V., Anisman, H., Merali, Z., Charbonneau, Y., Telner, J., Bialik, R.J., Wiens, A., Ellis, J., & Griffiths, J. (1999). Treatment of primary dysthymia with group cognitive therapy and pharmacotherapy: Clinical symptoms and functional impairments. *American Journal of Psychiatry, 156,* 1608–1617.

Ray, O. S. (1974). *Drugs, society, and human behavior* (2nd ed.). St. Louis: C. V. Mosby.

Rechtschaffen, A., & Buchignami, C. (1983). Visual dimensions and correlates of dream images. *Sleep Research, 12,* 189.

Reed, C. F. (1984). Terrestrial passage theory of the moon illusion. *Journal of Experimental Psychology: General, 113,* 489–516.

Reeves, A., & Plumb, F. (1969). Hyperphagia, rage, and dementia accompanying a ventromedial hypothalamic neoplasm. *Archives of Neurology, 20,* 616–624.

Regier, D. A., & others. (1988). One-month prevalence of mental disorders in the United States: Based on five epidemiological catchment area sites. *Archives of General Psychiatry, 45,* 977–986.

Rein, S., & Spencer, S. J. (1997). Prejudice as self-image maintenance: Affirming the self through derogating others. *Journal of Personality and Social Psychology, 73,* 31–44.

Reiss, A. L., & others. (1996). Brain development, gender and IQ in children: A volumetric imaging study. *Brain, 119,* 1763–1774.

Rescorla, R. A. (1967). Pavlovian conditioning and its proper control procedures. *Psychological Review, 74,* 71–80.

Rescorla, R. A. (1988). Pavlovian conditioning: It's not what you think it is. *American Psychologist, 43,* 151–160.

Reynolds, A. G., & Flagg, P. W. (1983). *Cognitive psychology* (2nd ed.). Boston: Little, Brown.

Rhodes, N., & Wood, W. (1992). Self-esteem and intelligence affect influenceability: The mediating role of message reception. *Psychological Bulletin, 111,* 156–171.

Richards, J. M., Beal, W. E., Seagal, J. D., & Pennebaker, J. W. (2000). Effects of disclosure of traumatic events on illness behavior among psychiatric prison inmates. *Journal of Abnormal Psychology, 109,* 156–160.

Rieber, R. W. (1999). Hypnosis, false memory and multiple personality: A trinity of affinity. *History of Psychiatry, 10,* 3–11.

Rimm, D. C., & Masters, J. (1979). *Behavior therapy* (2nd ed.). New York: Academic Press.

Roberts, P., & Newton, P. M. (1987). Levinsonian studies of women's adult development. *Psychology and Aging, 2,* 154–163.

Robins, R.W., Goslin, S. D., & Clark, K. H. (1999). An empirical analysis of trends in psychology. *American Psychologist, 54,* 117–128.

Robinson, N. S., Garber, J., & Hilsman, R. (1995). Cognitions and stress: Direct and moderating effects on depressive versus externalizing symptoms during the junior high school transition. *Journal of Abnormal Psychology, 104,* 3.

Robinson, R. G., & Starkstein, S. E. (1990). Current research in affective disorders following stroke. *Journal of Neuropsychiatry and Clinical Neurosciences, 2,* 1–14.

Rock, I., & Kaufman, L. (1972). The moon illusion. In R. Held & W. Richards (Eds.), *Perception: Mechanisms and models.* San Francisco: W. H. Freeman.

Rodin, J. (1985). Insulin levels, hunger, and food intake: An example of feedback loops in body weight regulation. *Health Psychology, 4,* 1–18.

Rodin, J., & Ickovics, R. (1990). Women's health: Review and research agenda as we approach the 21st century. *American Psychologist, 45,* 1018–1034.

Roe, A. (1946). The personality of artists. *Educational Psychology Measurement, 6,* 401–408.

Roe, A. (1953). *The making of a scientist.* New York: Dodd, Mead.

Roediger, H. L., & McDermott, K. B. (2000). Tricks of memory. *Current Directions in Psychological Science, 9,* 123–127.

Roffwarg, H. P., Muzio, J. N., & Dement, W. C. (1966). Ontogenetic development of the human sleep-dream cycle. *Science, 152,* 604–619.

Rogers, C. R. (1951). *Client-centered therapy: Its current practice, implications, and theory.* Boston: Houghton Mifflin.

Rogers, R. W. (1975). A protection motivation theory of fear appeals and attitude change. *Journal of Psychology, 91,* 93–114.

Rolls, E. T., Burton, M. J., & Mora, F. (1976). Hypothalamic neuronal responses associated with the sight of food. *Brain Research, 111,* 53–66.

Romer, D., Gruder, C. L., & Lizardo, T. (1986). A person-situation approach to altruistic behavior. *Journal of Personality and Social Psychology, 51,* 1001–1012.

Rorschach, H. (1953). *Psychodiagnostics* (5th ed.). New York: Grune & Stratton.

Rosch, E. (1973). Natural categories. *Cognitive Psychology, 4,* 328–350.

Rosch, E. (1975). Cognitive representations of semantic categories. *Journal of Experimental Psychology: General, 104,* 192–233.

Rosch, E. H., Mervis, C. B., Gray, W. B., Johnson, D. M., & Boyes-Braem, P. (1976). Basic objects in natural categories. *Cognitive Psychology, 8,* 382–439.

Rosello, J., & Bernal, G. (1999). The efficacy of cognitive-behavioral and interpersonal treatments for depression in Puerto Rican adolescents. *Journal of Consulting and Clinical Psychology, 67,* 734–745.

Rosen, J. B., & Schulkin, J. (1998). From normal fear to pathological anxiety. *Psychological Review, 105*(2), 325–350.

Rosenzweig, M. R. (1984). *Cognition.* New York: Holt, Rinehart & Winston.

Ross, L. (1977). The intuitive psychologist and his shortcomings: Distortions in the attribution process. In L. Berkowitz (Ed.), *Advances in experimental social psychology* (Vol. 10, pp. 173–220). New York: Academic Press.

Rossi, A. S. (1980). Aging and parenthood in the middle years. In P. B. Balter & O. G. Brim (Eds.), *Life-span development and behavior* (Vol. 3). New York: Academic Press.

Roth, S., & Cohen, L. J. (1986). Approach, avoidance, and coping with stress. *American Psychologist, 41,* 813–819.

Rothbaum, B. O., Hodges, L. F., Kooper, R., Opdyke, D., Williford, J. S., & North, M. (1995). Effectiveness of computer-generated (virtual reality) graded exposure in the treatment of acrophobia. *American Journal of Psychiatry, 152,* 626–628.

Rothman, A. J., & Salovey, P. (1997). Shaping perceptions to motivate healthy behavior: The role of message framing. *Psychological Bulletin, 121,* 3–19.

Rounsaville, B. J., Chevron, E. S., Prusoff, B. A., Elkin, I., Imber, S., Sotsky, S., & Watkins, J. (1987). The relation between specific and general dimensions of the psychotherapy process in interpersonal psychotherapy of depression. *Journal of Consulting and Clinical Psychology, 55,* 379–384.

Rovee-Collier, C. (1999). The development of infant memory. *Current Directions in Psychological Science, 8,* 80–85.

Roy, M., & Steptoe, A. (1991). The inhibition of cardiovascular responses to mental stress following aerobic exercise. *Psychophysiology, 28,* 689–700.

Rozin, P. (1996). Towards a psychology of food and eating: From motivation to model to marker, morality, meaning, and metaphor. *Current Directions in Psychological Science, 5,* 18–24.

Rubin, K. H. (1998). Social and emotional development from a cultural perspective. *Developmental Psychology, 34,* 611–615.

Ruble, D. N., & Ruble, T. L. (1980). Sex stereotypes. In A. G. Miller (Ed.), *In the eye of the beholder: Contemporary issues in stereotyping.* New York: Holt, Rinehart & Winston.

Ruderman, A. J., & Besbeas, M. (1992). Psychological characteristics of dieters and bulimics. *Journal of Abnormal Psychology, 101,* 383–390.

Rumbaugh, D. M., & Gill, T. V. (1976). The mastery of language-type skills by the chimpanzee (*Pan*). In S. Harnad, H. Steklis, & J. Lancaster (Eds.), *Origins and evolution of language and speech.* New York: New York Academy of Sciences.

Rumelhart, D. E., & McClelland, J. L. (Eds.). (1986). *Parallel distributed processing: Explorations in the microstructure of cognition, Vol. 1: Foundations.* Cambridge, MA: MIT Press.

Russell, M. A. H. (1971). Cigarette smoking: Natural history of a dependence disorder. *British Journal of Medical Psychology, 44,* 1–16.

Russo, N. F. (1990). Overview: Forging research priorities for women's mental health. *American Psychologist, 45,* 368–373.

Rutherford, S. D. (1988). The culture of American deaf people. *Sign Language Studies, 59,* 129–147.

Ryan, R. M., & Deci, E. L. (2000). Self-determination theory and the facilitation of intrinsic motivation, social development, and well-being. *American Psychologist, 55,* 68–78.

Sachs, J. D. S. (1967). Recognition memory for syntactic and semantic aspects of connected discourse. *Perception and Psychophysics, 2,* 437–442.

Salapatek, P. (1977). Stimulus determinants of attention in infants. In B. Wolman (Ed.), *International encyclopedia of psychiatry, psychology, psychoanalysis, and neurology* (Vol. 10). New York: Aesculapis.

Santrock, J. W. (1998). *Children* (5th ed.). Boston: McGraw-Hill.

Sarason, I. G., Johnson, J. H., & Siegel, J. M. (1978). Assessing the impact of life change: Development of the life experiences survey. *Journal of Consulting and Clinical Psychology, 46,* 932–946.

Sargent, C. (1984). Between death and shame: Dimensions of pain in Bariba culture. *Social Science and Medicine, 19,* 1299–1304.

Scarr, S. (1990). Mother's proper place: Children's needs and women's rights. *Journal of Social Behavior and Personality, 15,* 507–515.

Scarr, S., & Eisenberg, M. (1993). Child care research: Issues, perspectives, and results. *Annual Review of Psychology, 44,* 613–644.

Scarr, S., Philips, D., & McCartney, K. (1990). Facts, fantasies, and the future of childcare in the United States. *Psychological Science, 1,* 26–35.

Scarr, S., & Salapatek, P. (1970). Patterns of fear development during infancy. *Merrill-Palmer Quarterly, 16,* 53–90.

Schachter, D. L. (1999). The seven sins of memory: Insights from psychology and cognitive neuroscience. *American Psychologist, 54,* 182–203.

Schachter, S., & Singer, J. E. (1962). Cognitive, social and physiological determinants of emotional state. *Psychological Review, 69,* 379–399.

Scherer, K. R. (1997). The role of culture in emotion-antecedent appraisal. *Journal of Personality Assessment, 73,* 902–922.

Schiff, M., & Lewontin, R. (1986). *Education and class: The irrelevance of IQ genetic studies.* Oxford, England: Clarendon.

Schiffman, H. R. (1976). *Sensation and perception. An integrated approach.* New York: Wiley.

Schiffman, S. S., Graham, B. G., Sattely-Miller, E. A., & Warwick, Z. S. (1998). *Current Directions in Psychological Science, 7,* 137–143.

Schmidt, F. L., & Hunter, J. E. (1993). Tacit knowledge, practical intelligence, general mental ability, and job knowledge. *Current Directions in Psychological Science, 2,* 8–9.

Schmidt, N. B., Lerew, D. R., & Jackson, R. J. (1997). The role of anxiety sensitivity in the pathogenesis of panic. Prospective evaluation of spontaneous panic attacks during acute stress. *Journal of Abnormal Psychology, 106*(3), 355–364.

Schmidt, N. B., Lerew, D. R., & Trakowski, J. H. (1997). Body vigilance in panic disorder: Evaluating attention to bodily perturbations. *Journal of Consulting and Clinical Psychology, 65*(2), 214–220.

Schmolck, H., Buffalo, E. A., & Squire, L. A. (2000). Memory distortions develop over time: Recollections of the O. J. Simpson trial verdict after 15 and 32 months. *Psychological Science, 11,* 39–45.

Schreiber, F. R. (1973). *Sybil.* New York: Henry Regnery.

Schulkin, J. (1999). *The neuroendocrine regulation of behavior.* New York: Cambridge University Press.

Schulz, R., & Ewen, R. B. (1988). *Adult development and aging: Myths and emerging realities.* New York: Macmillan.

Scoville, W. B., & Milner, B. (1957). Loss of recent memory after bilateral hippocampal lesions. *Journal of Neurology, Neurosurgery, and Psychiatry, 20,* 11–21.

Seeley, R. J., & Schwartz, M. W. (1997). The regulation of energy balance: Peripheral hormonal signals and hypothalamic neuropeptides. *Current Directions in Psychological Science, 6,* 39–44.

Segall, M. H., Campbell, D. T., & Herskovits, M. J. (1963). Cultural differences in the perception of geometric illusions. *Science, 139,* 769–771.

Seidlitz, L., & Diener, E. (1998). Sex differences in the recall of affective experiences. *Journal of Personality and Social Psychology, 74,* 262–271.

Selye, H. (1976). *The stress of life.* New York: Knopf.

Shapiro, C. M., Boortz, R., Mitchell, D., Bartel, P., & Jooste, P. (1982). Slow-wave sleep: A recovery period after exercise. *Science, 214,* 1253–1254.

Shaywitz, B. A., Shaywitz, S. E., Pugh, K. R., Constable, R. T., Skudlarski, P., Fulbright, R. K., Bronen, R. A., Fletcher, J. M., Shankweiler, D. P., Katz, L., & Gores, J. C. (1995). Sex differences in the functional organization of the brain for language. *Nature, 373,* 607–609.

Sheppard, W. C., & Willoughby, R. H. (1975). *Child behavior.* Chicago: Rand McNally.

Sherif, M. (1936). *The psychology of social norms.* NY: Harper.

Sherif, M., & Sherif, C. W. (1953). *Groups in harmony and tension: An integration of studies of intergroup relations.* NY: Harper & Brothers.

Shimamura, A. P., Berry, J. M., Mangels, J. A., Rusting, C. L., & Jurica, P. J. (1995). Memory and cognitive abilities in university professors: Evidence for successful aging. *Psychological Science, 6,* 271–277.

Shrout, P. E., Link, B. G., Dohrenwend, B. P., Skodol, A. E., Stueve, A., & Mirotznik, J. (1989). Characterizing life events as risk factors for depression: The role of fateful loss events. *Journal of Abnormal Psychology, 96,* 460–467.

Siegel, J. M., & Kuykendall, D. H. (1990). Loss, widowhood, and psychological distress among the elderly. *Journal of Consulting and Clinical Psychology, 58,* 519–524.

Siegman, A. W., Dembroski, T. M., & Ringel, N. (1987). Components of hostility and the severity of coronary heart disease. *Psychosomatic Medicine, 49,* 127–137.

Sigman, M., & Whaley, S. E. (1998). In U. Neisser (Ed.), *The rising curve: Long-term gains in IQ and related measures* (pp. 155–182). Washington, DC: American Psychological Association.

Signorella, M., & Jamison, W. (1986). Masculinity, femininity, androgyny, and cognitive performance: A meta-analysis. *Psychological Bulletin, 100,* 207–228.

Silverstein, L. B. (1991). Transforming the debate about child care and maternal employment. *American Psychologist, 46,* 1025–1032.

Silverstein, L. B., & Auerbach, C. F. (1999). Deconstructing the essential father. *American Psychologist, 54,* 397–407.

Simons, A. D., Gordon, J. S., Thase, M. E., & Monroe, S. M. (1995). Toward an integration of psychologic, social, and biological factors in depression: Effects on outcome and course of cognitive therapy. *Journal of Consulting and Clinical Psychology, 63,* 369–377.

Simons, D. J., & Levin, D. T. (1998). Failure to detect changes to people during a real-world interaction. *Psychonomic Bulletin & Review, 4,* 644–649.

Simpson, J. A., Campbell, B., & Berscheid, E. (1986). The association between romantic love and marriage: Kephart (1967) twice revisited. *Personality and Social Psychology Bulletin, 12,* 363–372.

Skinner, B. F. (1953). *Science and human behavior.* New York: Macmillan.

Slobin, D. I. (1979). *Psycholinguistics.* Glenview, IL: Scott, Foresman.

Smith, E. E. (2000). Neural bases of working memory. *Current Directions in Psychological Science, 9*, 45–49.

Smith, M. L., & Glass, G. V. (1977). Meta-analysis of psychotherapy outcome studies. *American Psychologist, 32*, 752–760.

Smith, V. L., & Ellsworth, P. C. (1987). The social psychology of eyewitness accuracy: Misleading questions and communicator expertise. *Journal of Applied Psychology, 72*, 294–300.

Smyth, J. M., Soefer, M. H., Hurewitz, A., & Stone, A. A. (1999). The effect of tape recorded relaxation training on well-being, symptoms, and peak expiratory flow rate in adult asthmatics: A pilot study, *Psychology and Health, 14*, 487–501.

Snowden, L. R., & Cheung, F. K. (1990). Use of inpatient mental health services by members of ethnic minority groups. *American Psychologist, 45*, 347–355.

Snyder, M., Tauke, E. D., & Berscheid, E. (1977). Social perception and interpersonal behavior: On the self-fulfilling nature of social stereotypes. *Journal of Personality and Social Psychology, 35*, 656–666.

Solomon, D. A., Keller, M. B., Leon, A. C., Mueller, T. I., Shea, M. T., Warshaw, M., Maser, J. D., Coryell, W., & Endicott, J. (1997). Recovery from major depression. *Archives of General Psychiatry, 54*, 1001–1006.

Solomon, D. A., Keller, M. B., Leon, A. C., Mueller, T. I., Lavori, P. W., Shea, T., Coryell, W., Warshaw, M., Turvey, C., Maser, J. D., & Endicott, J. (2000). Multiple recurrences of major depressive disorder. *American Journal of Psychiatry, 157*, 229–233.

Southwick, S. M., Morgan, C. A. III, Darnell, A., Bremner, D., Nicolaou, A. L., Nagy, L. M., & Charney, D. S. (1995). Trauma-related symptoms in veterans of Operation Desert Storm: A 2-year follow-up. *American Journal of Psychiatry, 152*, 8.

Spanos, N. P. (1996). *Multiple identities and false memories: A sociocognitive perspective.* Washington, DC: American Psychological Association Press.

Spearman, C. E., & Wynn-Jones, L. (1950). *Human ability.* London: Macmillan.

Speisman, J. C., Lazarus, R. S., Mordokoff, A. M., & Davison, L. (1964). Experimental reduction of stress based on ego-defense theory. *Journal of Abnormal and Social Psychology, 68*, 367–380.

Spence, J. T., & Helmreich, R. L. (1978). *Masculinity and femininity: Their psychological dimensions, correlates, and antecedents.* Austin: University of Texas Press.

Spiegler, M. D., & Guevremont, D. C. (1998). *Contemporary behavior therapy* (3rd ed.). Pacific Grove, CA: Brooks/Cole.

Spitzer, R. L., Terman, M., Williams, J. B. W., Terman, J. S., Malt, U. F., Singer, F., & Lewy, A. J. (1999). Jet lag: Clinical features, validation of a new syndrome-specific scale, and lack of response to melatonin in a randomized, double-blind trial. *American Journal of Psychiatry, 156*, 1392–1396.

Squire, L. R. (1987). *Memory and the brain.* New York: Oxford University Press.

Squire, L. R., Knowlton, B., & Musen, G. (1993). The structure and organization of memory. *Annual Review of Psychology, 44*, 453–495.

Sroufe, L. A. (1978). The ontogenesis of emotion. In J. Osofoslay (Ed.), *Handbook of infancy.* New York: Wiley.

Stagner, R. (1958). The gullibility of personnel managers. *Personnel Psychology, 11*, 347–352.

Stapp, J., Tucker, A. M., & VandenBos, G. R. (1985). Census of psychological personnel, 1983. *American Psychologists, 12*, 1317–1351.

Stark, E. (1984, October). To sleep, perchance to dream. *Psychology Today.*

Starkstein, S. E., & Robinson, R. G. (1988). Lateralized emotional response following stroke. In M. Kinsbourne (Ed.), *Cerebral dysfunction in depression.*

Washington, DC: American Psychiatric Association Press.

Starkstein, S. E., Robinson, R. G., & Price, T. R. (1988). Comparison of patients with and without poststroke major depression matched for size and the location of lesion. *Archives of General Psychiatry, 45*, 247–252.

Staub, E. (1996). Cultural-societal roots of violence: The examples of genocidal violence and of contemporary youth violence in the United States. *American Psychologist, 51*, 117–132.

Steele, C. M. (1997). A threat in the air: How stereotypes shape intellectual identity and performance. *American Psychologist, 52*, 613–629.

Steele, C. M., & Josephs, R. A. (1990). Alcohol myopia: Its prized and dangerous effects. *American Psychologist, 45*, 921–933.

Steen, S., Oppliger, R., & Brownell, K. D. (1988). Metabolic effects of repeated weight loss and regain in adolescent wrestlers. *Journal of the American Medical Association, 260*, 47–50.

Stein, E. A., & others. (1998). Nicotine-induced activation in the human brain: A functional MRI study. *American Journal of Psychiatry, 155*, 1009–1015.

Steinberg, J. (1995). The graying of the senses. *Journal of NIMH Research, 7*, 32–33.

Steketee, G., & Cleere, L. (1990). Obsessive-compulsive disorders. In A. S. Bellack, M. Hersen, & A. E. Kazdin (Eds.), *International handbook of behavior modification and therapy* (2nd ed., pp. 307–332). New York: Plenum.

Stephan, W. G. (1987). The contact hypothesis in intergroup relations. In C. Hendrick (Ed.), Group processes and intergroup relations. *Review of Personality and Social Psychology, 9*, 41–67.

Stephan, W., Berscheid, E., & Walster, E. (1971). Sexual arousal and heterosexual perception. *Journal of Personality and Social Psychology, 20*, 93–101.

Stern, K., & McClintock, M. K. (1998). Regulation of ovulation by human pheromones. *Nature, 392*, 177–179.

Stern, R. M., & Koch, K. L. (1996). Motion sickness and differential susceptibility. *Current Directions in Psychological Science, 4*, 115–120.

Sternbach, R. A. (Ed.). (1978). *The psychology of pain.* New York: Raven Press.

Sternberg, R. J. (1979). The nature of mental abilities. *American Psychologist, 34*, 214–230.

Sternberg, R. J. (1981). Testing and cognitive psychology. *American Psychologist, 36*, 1181–1189.

Sternberg, R. J. (1997). The concept of intelligence and its role in lifelong learning and success. *American Psychologist, 52*, 1030–1037.

Sternberg, R. J., & Gardner, M. K. (1982). A componential interpretation of the general factor in human intelligence. In J. J. Eysenck (Ed.), *A model for intelligence.* Berlin: Springer.

Sternberg, R. J., & Lubart, T. I. (1992). Buy low and sell high: An investment approach to creativity. *Current Directions in Psychological Science, 1*, 1–5.

Sternberg, R. J., & Lubart, T. I. (1993). Creative giftedness: A multivariate investment approach. *Gifted Child Quarterly, 37*, 7–15.

Sternberg, R. J., & Wagner, R. K. (1993). The egocentric view of intelligence and job performance is wrong. *Current Directions in Psychological Science, 2*, 1–5.

Stewart, A. J., & Ostrove, J. M. (1998). Women's personality in middle age: Gender, history, and midcourse corrections. *American Psychologist, 55*, 1185–1194.

Stewart, A. J., & Vandewater, E. A. (1999). "If I had it to do over again . . ." Midlife review, midcourse corrections, and women's well-being in midlife. *Journal of Personality and Social Psychology, 76*, 270–283.

Stoner, J. A. F. (1961). *A comparison of individual and group decisions involving risk.* Unpublished master's thesis, Massachusetts Institute of Technology, Cambridge.

Strauch, I., & Meier, B. (1996). *In search of dreams: Experimental dream research.* Albany: State University of New York Press.

Strauman, T. J. (1992). Self-guides, autobiographical memory, and anxiety and dysphoria: Toward a cognitive model of vulnerability to emotional distress. *Journal of Abnormal Psychology, 101*, 87–95.

Stumpf, H., & Stanley, J. C. (1998). Stability and change in gender-related differences on the College Board Advanced Placement and Achievement Tests. *Current Directions in Psychological Science, 7*, 192–196.

Suomi, S. (1988). *Genetic and environmental influences on social-emotional development in rhesus monkeys.* Presentation to the Fourth Annual Colloquium of the Center of Family Research, University of Georgia.

Susser, E., & others. (1996). Schizophrenia after prenatal famine: Further evidence. *Archives of General Psychiatry, 53*, 25–31.

Susser, E., Struening, E. L., & Conner, S. (1989). Psychiatric problems in homeless men. *Archives of General Psychiatry, 46*, 845–850.

Susser, E. S., & Lin, S. P. (1992). Schizophrenia after prenatal exposure to the Dutch hunger winter of 1944–45. *Archives of General Psychiatry, 49*, 983–988.

Sutker, P. B., Uddo, M., Davis, J. M., & Ditta, S. R. (1995). War zone stress, personal resources, and PTSD in Persian Gulf war returnees. *Journal of Abnormal Psychology, 104*, 444–452.

Swaab, D. F., & Hofman, M. A. (1995). Sexual differentiation of the human hypothalamus in relation to gender and sexual orientation. *Trends in Neurosciences, 18*, 264–270.

Swaab, D. F., & Hofman, M. A. (1990). An enlarged suprachiasmatic nucleus in homosexual men. *Brain Research, 537*, 141.

Swartz, H. A. (1999). Interpersonal psychotherapy. In M. Hersen & A. Bellack (Eds.), *Handbook of comparative interventions for adult disorders* (2nd ed., pp. 139–155). New York: John Wiley.

Swayze, V. W. (1995). Frontal leukotomy and related psychosurgical procedures in the era before antipsychotics (1935–1954): A historical overview. *American Journal of Psychiatry, 152*, 505–515.

Symons, C. S., & Johnson, B. T. (1997). The self-reference effect in memory: A meta-analysis. *Psychological Bulletin, 121*, 371–394.

Tamminga, C. A. (1996). Images in neuroscience: Neuroimaging, XIII. *American Journal of Psychiatry, 153*, 1249.

Tang, S. -H., & Hall, V. C. (1995). The overjustification effect: A meta-analysis. *Applied Cognitive Psychology, 9*, 365–404.

Tanner, J. M. (1970). Physical growth. In P. H. Mussen (Ed.), *Carmichael's manual of child psychology* (Vol. 1). New York: Wiley.

Tarpy, R. M., & Mayer, R. E. (1978). *Foundations of learning and memory.* Glenview, IL: Scott, Foresman.

Tateyama, M., Kudo, I., Hashimoto, M., Abe, Y., Kainuma, Yoshimura, K., Asai, M., Bartels, M., & Kasper, S. (1999). Is paranoid schizophrenia the most common subtype? Comparison of subtype diagnoses by Japanese and European psychiatrists, using summaries of the same patients. *Psychopathology, 32*, 98–106.

Taylor, M. L., & Hall, J. A. (1982). Psychological androgyny: Theories, methods, and conclusions. *Psychological Bulletin, 92*, 347–366.

Taylor, S. E. (1986). *Health psychology*. New York: Random House.

Taylor, S. E. (1999). *Health psychology* (4th ed.). Boston: McGraw-Hill.

Taylor, S. E., Pham, L. B., Rivkin, I. D., & Armor, D. A. (1998). Harnessing the imagination, mental simulation, self-regulation, and coping. *American Psychologist, 53,* 429–439.

Telch, M. J., Lucas, J. A., & Nelson, P. (1989). Nonclinical panic in college students: An investigation of prevalence and symptomology. *Journal of Abnormal Psychology, 98,* 300–306.

Tellegen, A., Watson, D., & Clark, L. A. (1999). On the dimensional and hierarchical structure of affect. *Psychological Science, 10,* 297–303.

ten Broeke, E., Korrelboom, K., & de Jongh, A. (1998). Is prolonged exposure to traumatic memories necessary in PTSD. *Gedragstherapie, 31,* 273–290.

Terrace, H. S. (1980). *Nim.* New York: Knopf.

Thackwray, D. E., Smith, M. C., Bodfish, J. W., & Meyers, A. W. (1993). A comparison of behavioral and cognitive-behavioral interventions for bulimia nervosa. *Journal of Consulting and Clinical Psychology, 61,* 639–645.

Thayer, R. E. (1987). Energy, tiredness, and tension effects of a sugar snack versus moderate exercise. *Journal of Personality and Social Psychology, 52,* 119–125.

Thomas, M. H., & Drabman, R. S. (1975). Toleration of real-life aggression as a function of exposure to televised violence and age of subject. *Merrill-Palmer Quarterly, 21,* 227–232.

Thompson, J. K., Jarvie, G. J., Lahey, B. B., & Cureton, K. J. (1982). Exercise and obesity: Etiology, physiology, and intervention. *Psychological Bulletin, 91,* 55–79.

Thomson, D. M. (1988). Context and false recognition. In G. M. Davies & D. M. Thomson (Eds.), *Memory in context: Context in memory* (pp. 285–304). Chichester, England: Wiley.

Thurstone, L. L. (1938). Primary mental abilities. *Psychometric Monographs* (1).

Tice, D. M., & Baumeister, R. F. (1997). Longitudinal study of procrastination, performance, stress, and health: The costs and benefits of dawdling. *Psychological Science, 8,* 454–458.

Tolman, E. C., & Honzik, C. H. (1930). Introduction and removal of reward, and maze performance in rats. *University of California Publications in Psychology, 4,* 257–276.

Tolman, E. C., Ritchie, B. F., & Kalish, D. (1946). Studies in spatial learning. I: Orientation and the shortcut. *Journal of Experimental Psychology, 36,* 13–25.

Tomaka, J., Blascovich, J., Kibler, J., & Ernst, J. M. (1997). Cognitive and physiological antecedents of threat and challenge appraisal. *Journal of Personality and Social Psychology, 73,* 63–72.

Triandis, H. (1991). *Training for diversity.* Paper presented to the annual meeting of the American Psychological Association, San Francisco.

Trierweiler, S. J., Neighbors, H. W., Munday, C., Thompson, E. E., Binion, V. J., & Gomez, J. P. (2000). Clinician attributions associated with the diagnosis of schizophrenia in African American and non-African American Patients. *Journal of Consulting and Clinical Psychology, 68,* 171–175.

Triplett, N. (1898). The dynamogenic factors in peacemaking and competition. *American Journal of Psychology, 9,* 507–533.

Tulving, E. (1972). Episodic and semantic memory. In E. Tulving & W. Donaldson (Eds.), *Organization and memory.* New York: Academic Press.

Tulving, E. (1985). How many memory systems are there? *American Psychologist, 40,* 385–398.

Tulving, E. (1987). Multiple memory systems and consciousness. *Human Neurobiology, 6,* 67–80.

Turkat, I. D., & Calhoun, J. F. (1980). The problem-solving flow chart. *The Behavior Therapist, 3,* 21.

Turnbull, C. (1962). *The forest people.* New York: Simon & Schuster.

Turner, J. C., Hogg, M. A., Oakes, P. J., Richer, S. D., & Wetherell, M. S. (1987). *Rediscovering the social group: A self-categorization theory.* Oxford, England: Blackwell.

Tversky, A., & Kahneman, D. (1974). Judgment under uncertainty: Heuristics and biases. *Science, 185,* 1124–1131.

Tversky, A., & Kahneman, D. (1983). Extensional versus intuitive reasoning: The conjunction fallacy in probability judgment. *Psychological Review, 90,* 293–315.

Uchino, B. N., Cacioppo, J. T., & Kiecolt-Glaser, J. K. (1996). The relationship between social support and physiological processes: A review with emphasis on underlying mechanisms and implications for health. *Psychological Bulletin, 119,* 488–531.

Van Duuren, F., & DiGiacomo, J. P. (1997). Degrading situations, affiliation, and social dependency. *European Journal of Social Psychology, 27,* 495–510.

Veleber, D. M., & Templer, D. I. (1984). Effects of caffeine on anxiety and depression. *Journal of Abnormal Psychology, 93,* 120–122.

Ventura, J., Neuchterlein, K. H., Lukoff, D., & Hardesty, J. P. (1989). A prospective study of stressful life events and schizophrenic relapse. *Journal of Abnormal Psychology, 98,* 407–411.

Vikas, M., & Ross, W. T. (1998). The impact of positive and negative affect and issue framing on issue interpretation and risk taking. *Organizational Behavior and Human Decision Processes, 76,* 298–324.

von Frisch, K. (1953). *The dancing bees: An account of the life and senses of the honeybee.* New York: Harcourt, Brace, & World.

Wadden, T. A., Vogt, R. A., Anderson, R. E., Bartlett, S. J., Foster, G. D., Kuehnel, R. H., Wilk, J., Weinstock, R., Buckenmeyer, Berkowitz, R. I., & Steen, S. N. (1997). Exercise in the treatment of obesity: Effect of four interventions on body composition, resting energy expenditure, appetite, and mood. *Journal of Consulting and Clinical Psychology, 65,* 269–277.

Waldron, I. (1991). Gender and health-related behavior. In D. S. Goodman (Ed.), *Health behavior: Emerging research perspectives.* New York: Plenum.

Walker, L. (1986). Cognitive processes in moral development. In G. L. Sapp (Ed.), *Handbook of moral development: Models processes, techniques, and research.* Birmingham: Religious Education Press.

Wallace, B., & Fisher, L. E. (1983). *Consciousness and behavior.* Boston: Allyn & Bacon.

Wallace, S. T., & Alden, L. E. (1997). Social phobia and positive social events: The price of success. *Journal of Abnormal Psychology, 106*(3), 416–424.

Wallas, G. (1926). *The art of thought.* New York: Harcourt Brace.

Walster, E., Aronson, V., & Abrahams, D. (1966). On increasing the persuasiveness of a low prestige communicator. *Journal of Experimental Social Psychology, 2,* 325–343.

Walster, E., Aronson, V., Abrahams, D., & Rottman, L. (1966). Importance of physical attractiveness in dating behavior. *Journal of Personality and Social Psychology, 5,* 508–516.

Walster, E. W., & Walster, G. W. (1978). *Equity: Theory and research.* Boston: Allyn & Bacon.

Wampold, B. E., Mondin, G. W., Moody, M., Stich, F., Benson, K., & Ahn, H. (1997). A meta-analysis of outcome studies comparing bona fide psychotherapies: Empirically, "all must have prizes." *Psychological Bulletin, 122,* 203–215.

Watson, D., & Tellegen, A. (1985). Toward a consensual structure of mood. *Psychological Bulletin, 98,* 219–235.

Watson, J. B., & Rayner, R. (1920). Conditioned emotional reactions. *Journal of Experimental Psychology, 3,* 1–4.

Watson, R. I. (1971). *The great psychologists* (4th ed.). Philadelphia: J. B. Lippincott.

Webb, W. B. (1968). *Sleep: An experimental approach.* New York: Macmillan.

Webb, W. B. (1975). *Sleep, the gentle tyrant.* Englewood Cliffs, NJ: Prentice-Hall.

Webb, W. B. (1982). Sleep and biological rhythms. In W. B. Webb (Ed.), *Biological rhythms, sleep, and performance* (pp. 87–110). New York: Wiley.

Webb, W. B., & Bonnet, M. H. (1979). Sleep and dreams. In M. E. Meyer (Ed.), *Foundations of contemporary psychology.* New York: Oxford University Press.

Wechsler, D. (1955). *Manual for the Wechsler Adult Intelligence Scale.* New York: Psychological Corporation.

Weddington, W. W., & others. (1990). Changes in mood, craving, and sleep during short-term abstinence reported by male cocaine addicts. *Archives of General Psychiatry, 47,* 861–868.

Weidner, G., Sexton, G., McLellarn, R. M., Connor, S. L., & Matarazzo, J. D. (1987). The role of Type A behavior and hostility in an elevation of plasma lipids in adult women and men. *Psychosomatic Medicine, 49,* 136–145.

Weinhardt, L. S., Carey, M. P., Carey, K. B., & Verdecias, R. N. (1998). Increasing assertiveness skills to reduce HIV risk among women living with a severe and persistent mental illness. *Journal of Consulting and Clinical Psychology, 66,* 680–684.

Weisse, C. S. (1992). Depression and immunocompetence: A review of the literature. *Psychological Bulletin, 111,* 475–489.

Weissman, M. M. (1999). Interpersonal psychotherapy and the health care scene. In D. S. Janowsky (Ed.), *Psychotherapy indications and outcomes* (pp. 213–231). Washington DC: American Psychiatric Press.

Wells, G. L. (1993). What do we know about eyewitness identification? *American Psychologist, 48,* 553–571.

Wells, G. L., & Bradfield, A. L. (1999). Distortions in eyewitnesses' recollections: Can the postidentification-feedback effect be moderated? *Psychological Science, 10,* 138–144.

Wells, G. L., Small, M., Penrod, S., Malpass, R. S., Fulero, S. M., & Brimacombe, C. A. E. (1998). Eyewitness identification procedures: Recommendations for lineups and photospreads. *Law and Human Behavior, 22,* 603–647.

Wender, P. H., Kety, S. S., Rosenthal, D., Schulsinger, F., Ortmann, J., & Lunde, I. (1986). Psychiatric disorders in the biological and adoptive families of adopted individuals with affective disorders. *Archives of General Psychiatry, 43,* 923–929.

Westen, D. (1998). The scientific legacy of Sigmund Freud: Toward a psychodynamically informed psychological science. *Psychological Bulletin, 124,* 333–371.

Westen, D., & Gabbard, G. O. (1999). Psychoanalytic approaches to personality. In L. A. Pervin & O. P. John (Eds.), *Handbook of personality: Theory and research* (2nd ed., pp. 57–101). New York: Guilford.

Wheeler, M. A., Stuss, D. T., & Tulving, E. (1997). Toward a theory of episodic memory: The frontal lobes and autonoetic consciousness. *Psychological Bulletin, 121,* 331–354.

White, C. C., Powell, K. E., Hogelin, G. C., Gentry, E. M., & Forman, M. R. (1987). The behavioral risk factor surveys: IV. The descriptive epidemiology of exercise. *Preventive Medicine, 3,* 304–310.

White, R. K. (1977). Misperception in the Arab-Israeli conflict. *Journal of Social Issues, 25,* 41–78.

Whitten, L. (1992). Survival guilt and survival conflict in African-American college students. In M. Lang & C. Ford (Eds.), *Strategies for retaining minority students in higher education.* Springfield, IL: Charles C Thomas.

Whitten, L. (1993a). Infusing Black psychology into the introductory psychology course. *Teaching of Psychology, 20*(1), 13–21.

Whitten, L. (1993b). Survival conflict, coping style and perception of the college classroom: Factors in the academic success of African-American college students in three colleges in the New York/New Jersey metropolitan area. *Afro-Americans in New York Life and History, 17,* 41–55.

Whorf, B. L. (1956). Science and linguistics. In J. B. Carroll (Ed.), *Language, thought and reality: Selected writings of Benjamin Lee Whorf.* Cambridge, MA: MIT Press.

Wiens, A., Ellis, J., & Griffiths, J. (1999). Treatment of primary dysthymia with group cognitive therapy and pharamacotherapy: Clinical symptoms and functional impairments. *American Journal of Psychiatry, 156,* 1608–1617.

Wiggins, J. S., & Pincus, A. L. (1992). Personality: Structure and assessment. *Annual Review of Psychology, 43,* 473–504.

Wilk, S. L., Desmarais, L. B., & Sackett, P. R. (1995). Gravitation to jobs commensurate with ability: Longitudinal and cross-sectional tests. *Journal of Applied Psychology, 80,* 79–85.

Wilkinson, R., Allison, S., Feeney, M., & Kaminska, Z. (1989). Alertness of night nurses: Two shift systems compared. *Ergonomics, 32,* 281–292.

Williams, G. V., & Goldman-Rakic, P. S. (1995). Modulation of memory fields by dopamine D1 receptors in prefrontal cortex. *Nature, 376,* 572–575.

Williams, R. B., Lane, J. D., Kunn, C. M., Melosh, W., White, A. D., & Schanberg, S. M. (1982). Type A behavior and elevated physiological and neuroendocrine responses to cognitive tasks. *Science, 218,* 483–485.

Williams, W. M. (1998). Are we raising smarter children today? School- and home-related influences on IQ. In U. Neisser (Ed.), *The rising curve: Long-term gains in IQ and related measures* (pp. 125–154). Washington, DC: American Psychological Association.

Williams, W. M., & Ceci, S. J. (1997). Are Americans becoming more or less alike? Trends in race, class, and ability differences in intelligence. *American Psychologist, 52,* 1126–1235.

Wilner, A., Reich, T., Robins, I., Fishman, R., & van Doren, T. (1976). Obsessive-compulsive neurosis. *Comprehensive Psychiatry, 17,* 527–529.

Winch, R. F. (1958). *Mate-selection.* New York: Harper & Row.

Winett, R. A. (1995). A framework for health promotion and disease prevention programs. *American Psychologist, 50,* 341–350.

Wisniewski, A. B. (1998). Sexually-dimorphic patterns of cortical asymmetry, and the role for sex steroid hormones in determining cortical patterns of lateralization. *Psychoneuroendocrinology, 23,* 519–547.

Wolpe, J. (1958). *Psychotherapy by reciprocal inhibition.* Stanford, CA: Stanford University Press.

Wood, J. M., Bootzin, R. R., Rosenhan, D., Nolen-Hoeksema, S., & Jourdon, F. (1992). Effects of the 1989 San Francisco earthquake on frequency and content of nightmares. *Journal of Abnormal Psychology, 101,* 219–224.

Wood, W., Christensen, P. N., Hebl, M. R., & Rothgerber, H. (1997). Conformity to sex-typed norms, affect, and the self-concept. *Journal of Personality and Social Psychology, 73,* 523–535.

Wood, W., Wong, F. Y., & Chachere, J. G. (1991). Effects of media violence on viewers' aggression in unconstrained social interaction. *Psychological Bulletin, 109,* 371–383.

Woodruff-Pak, D. S. (1999). New directions for a classical paradigm: Human eyeblink conditioning. *Psychological Science, 10,* 1–3.

World Health Organization. (1999). *Current and future directions of the HIV/AIDS pandemic.* Geneva.

Wyatt, R. J. (1996). Neurodevelopment abnormalities and schizophrenia: A family affair. *American Journal of Psychiatry, 53,* 11–15.

Yehuda, R., Kahana, B., Schmeidler, J., Southwick, S. M., Wilson, S., & Giller, E. L. (1995). Impact of cumulative lifetime trauma and recent stress on current posttraumatic stress disorder symptoms in holocaust survivors. *American Journal of Psychiatry, 152,* 12.

Yehuda, R., Southwick, S. M., & Giller, E. L. (1992). Exposure to atrocities and severity of chronic posttraumatic stress disorder in Vietnam veterans. *American Journal of Psychiatry, 149,* 333–336.

Zajonc, R. B. (1965). Social facilitation. *Science, 149,* 269–274.

Zajonc, R. B. (1968). Attitudinal effects of mere exposure. *Journal of Personality and Social Psychology Monograph Supplement, 9,* 1–27.

Zajonc, R. B., & Mullally, P. R. (1997). Birth order: Reconciling conflicting effects. *American Psychologist, 52,* 685–699.

Zamble, E., Mitchell, J. B., & Findlay, H. (1986). Pavlovian conditioning of sexual arousal: Parametric and background manipulations. *Journal of Experimental Psychology: Animal Behavior Processes, 12,* 403–411.

Zaragoza, M. S., & Mitchell, K. J. (1996). Repeated exposure to suggestion and the creation of false memories. *Psychological Science, 1,* 294–300.

Zellner, M. (1970). Self-esteem, reception, and influenceability. *Journal of Personality and Social Psychology, 15,* 87–93.

Zhang, J., & Bond, M. H. (1998). Personality and filial piety among college students in two Chinese societies: The added value of indigenous constructs. *Journal of Cross-Cultural Psychology, 29,* 402–417.

Zimbardo, P. G. (1972). The pathology of imprisonment. *Society, 9*(6), 4.

Zimbardo, P. (1969). The human choice: Individuation, reason, and order versus deindividuation, impulse, and chaos. In W. Arnold and D. Levine (Eds.), *Nebraska Symposium on Motivation, 17,* 237–307.

Zisook, S., & Shuchter, S. R. (1991). Depression through the first year after the death of a spouse. *American Journal of Psychiatry, 148,* 1346–1352.

Zlotnick, C., Elkin, I. & Shea, M. T. (1998). Does the gender of a patient or the gender of a therapist affect the treatment of patients with major depression? *Journal of Consulting and Clinical Psychology, 66,* 655–659.

Zuckerman, M. (1995). Good and bad humors: Biochemical bases of personality and its disorders. *Psychological Science, 6,* 325–332.

Zuroff, D. C., & Mongrain, M. (1987). Dependency and self-criticism: Vulnerability factors for depressive affective states. *Journal of Abnormal Psychology, 96,* 14–22.

CREDITS

PHOTOGRAPHS

LINE ART

Chapter 1
Fig 1.5: Based on data from J. Stapp, et al., "Census of Psychological Personnel: 1983," in *American Psychologist.* 12:1317–1351. Copyright 1985 by the American Psychological Association.

Chapter 2
Fig 2.16: Data from W. Penfield and T. Rasmussen, *The Cerebral Cortex of Man.* Copyright 1950 Macmillan Publishing Co., New York.

Chapter 4
Fig 4.3: "Data from M.C. Moore-Ede, F.M. Sulzman, and C.A. Fuller, *The Clocks That Time Us.* Copyright 1982 Harvard University Press. Fig 4.4: Data from D.M. Veleber and D. Templer, "Effects of Caffeine on Anxiety and Depression," *Journal of Abnormal Psychology*, 93, 120–122, 1984. Copyright 1984 by the American Psychological Association.

Chapter 5
Fig 5.4: Data from K. Eileen, et al., "Effects of Social Reinforcement Isolate Behavior of a Nursery School Child," in *Child Development* 35:511–518, 1974. Copyright 1964 The Society for Research in Child Development. Fig 5.12: E.C. Tolman, B.F. Ritchie, and D. Kalish, "Studies in Spatial Learning I: Orientation and the Short-Cut," in *Journal of Experimental Psychology,* 36:13–25, 1946. Fig 5.13: E.C. Tolman, B.F. Ritchie, and D. Kalish, "Studies in Spatial Learning I: Orientation and the Short-Cut," in *Journal of Experimental Psychology,* 36:13–25, 1946. Fig 5.14: E.C. Tolman and C.H. Honzik, "Introduction and Removal of the Reward, and Maze Performance in Rats," University of California Publications in *Psychology,* 4:257–275, 1930. Fig 5.15: E.C. Tolman and C.H. Honzik, "Introduction and Removal of the Reward, and Maze Performance in Rats," University of California Publications in *Psychology,* 4:257–275, 1930. Fig 5.17: H.F. Harlow, "The Formation of Learning Sets" in *Psychological Review,* 56:51–56, 1949. Fig 5.18: Reprinted from *Behaviour Research and Therapy,* Vol 2. By T. Ayllon and E. Haughton, "Modification of the Symptomatic Verbal Behavior of Mental Patients," pp. 87–97. Copyright 1964, with permission from Elsevier Science.

Chapter 6
Fig 6.3: R.L. Peterson and M.J. Peterson, "Short Term Retention of Individual Items," in *Journal of Experimental Psychology,* 58:193–198, 1959. Fig 6.5: Redrawn from L. Carmichael, H.P. Hogan, and A.A. Walter, "An Experimental Study of the Effect of Language on the Reproduction of Visually Perceived Form," in *Journal of Experimental Psychology,* 15:78–86, 1932.

Chapter 7
Fig 7.3: After W. Kohler, *The Task of Gestalt Psychology.* Copyright 1969 by Princeton University Press. Fig 7.4: After W. Kohler, *The Task of Gestalt Psychology.* Copyright 1969 by Princeton University Press. Fig 7.9: Based on Figure 2 of U. Neisser "Rising Test Scores and What They Mean." In U. Neisser (Ed.), *The Rising Curve: Long-Term Gains in IQ and Related Measures,* p. 303–334. Copyright © 1998 by the American Psychological

Association. Adapted with permission. Fig 7.10: Based on P.A. Carpenter, M.A. Just, and P. Shall "What One Intelligence Test Measures: A Theoretical Account of the Processing in the Ravens Progressive Matrices Test," *Psychological Review,* 97:404–432. Copyright © 1990 by the American Psychological Association. Adapted with permission. Fig 7.11: Based on Figure 3, M. Huang & R.M. Hauser, "Trends in Black-White Test-Score Differentials: II. The WORDSUM Vocabulary Test." In U. Neisser (Ed.) *The Rising Curve: Long-Term Gains in IQ and Related Measures,* p. 303–334. Copyright © 1998 by the American Psychological Association. Adapted with permission.

Chapter 8
Fig 8.1: Data from M.B. McGraw, "Neural Maturation as Exemplified in Achievement of Bladder Control," *Journal of Pediatrics,* 16:580–590, 1940. Fig 8.4: Print Rights Credit: From the *Seasons of a Man's Life* by Daniel J. Levinson, et al. Copyright © 1978 by Daniel J. Levinson. Reprinted by permission of Alfred A. Knopf, a Division of Random House, Inc.

Chapter 9
Fig 9.6: Diagram based on data from *Hierarchy of Needs from Motivation and Personality,* 3rd edition, by Abraham H. Maslow. Revised by Robert Frager, et al., Harper & Row Publishers, Inc., 1954, 1987. Fig 9.7: Based on Figure 2, p. 302 of A. Tellegen, D. Watson, and L.A. Clark, "On the Dimensional and Hierarchical Structure of Affect," *Psychological Science* 10:297–303, 1999.

Chapter 10
Fig 10.3: From *Sex in America: A Definitive Survey* by Robert Michael, et al., Copyright © 1994 by CSG Enterprises, Inc., Edward O. Laumann, Robert T. Michael, and Gina Kolata. By permission of Little, Brown & Company, Inc.

Chapter 11
Fig 11.5: Data from A.M. Isen and P.F. Levin, "The Effect of Feeling Good on Helping: Cookies and Kindness," *Journal of Personality and Social Psychology,* 21:384–388, 1972.

Chapter 12
Fig 12.2: Data from S. Epstein and W.D. Fenz, "Steepness of Approach and Avoidance Gradients in Humans as a Function of Experience: Theory and Experiment," *Journal of Experimental Psychology* 70:1–12, 1965. Copyright 1965 by the American Psychological Association. Fig 12.3: Based on Figure 1, p. 63 of F.G. Foa and D.S. Riggs, "Post Traumatic Stress Disorder Following Assault: Theoretical & Empirical Findings," *Current Directions in Psychological Science* 4:61–65, 1995. Fig 12.4: Data from H. Selye, *The Stress of Life.* Copyright © 1976 McGraw-Hill Book Company. Fig 12.6: Based on Figure 2, p. 88 of S. Cohen, "Psychological Stress Immunity, and Upper Respiratory Infections," *Current Directions in Psychological Science* 5:86–90, 1996.

Chapter 13
Fig 13.1: Data from M. Lader and A. Matthews, "Changes in Autonomic Arousal in a Woman Undergoing a Spontaneous Panic Attack," *Journal of Psychosomatic Research,* 14:377–382. Copyright 1970, Pergamon Press, Ltd.

Chapter 14
Table 14.2: Data from M.L. Smith and G.V. Glass, "Meta-Analysis of Psychotherapy Outcome Studies," *American Psychologist,* 32:752–760. Copyright 1977 by the American Psychological Association.

NAME INDEX

SUBJECT INDEX